LAW & SOCIETY
Readings on the Social Study of Law

LAW & SOCIETY
Readings on the Social Study of Law

EDITED BY

Stewart Macaulay
University of Wisconsisn

Lawrence M. Friedman
Stanford University

John Stookey
Arizona State University

W.W. NORTON & COMPANY
New York   London

The text of this book is composed in Times Roman
Composition by ComCom
Manufacturing by Courier, Westford
Book Design by Andy Zutis

Library of Congress Cataloging-in-Publication Data

Law & society : readings on the social study of law / Stewart Macaulay, Lawrence
    M. Friedman, John Stookey, [editors].
        p.   cm.
        1. Sociological jurisprudence.   I. Macaulay, Stewart, 1931–   .
    II. Friedman, Lawrence Meir, 1930–   . III. Stookey, John A.
    K370.L384   1995
    340'.115—dc20   94-45951
                                                                          CIP
                                                                          REV.

ISBN 0-393-96713-1

W. W. Norton & Company, Inc., 500 Fifth Avenue, New York, N.Y. 10110
W. W. Norton & Company Ltd., 10 Coptic Street, London, WC1A 1PU

1 2 3 4 5 6 7 8 9 0

To Jackie, Monica and Joe, John, Phil, and Laura

SM

To Leah, Jane, Amy, Paul, Sarah, and David

LMF

To my mother, and to the memory of my father and my wife

JS

Many Thanks

Contents

1
Introduction
1

2
The Legal System in Operation
19

vii

3

Where Does Law Come From? The Impact
of Society on Law

169

4

The Impact of Law on Society
415

5

The Legal System as a Social System: Structure, Rules, and Roles

659

Article and Book Credits

Index

Preface

Many people helped us produce this volume and we owe them thanks. Dr. Joyce Sterling, a professor at the University of Denver College of Law, taught from versions of the book. She, and her students, offered valuable criticism and suggestions. Dr. Susan Silbey, Department of Sociology, Wellesley College read a version of the manuscript and also offered valuable criticism and suggestions. Our colleagues Herbert Kritzer, Howard Erlanger, and Lauren Edelman all offered help on specific problems and a number of suggestions. Once again Dr. Jacqueline Macaulay took time from her law practice to read much of this book and debate assertions contained in various articles and our notes and questions. Our publisher asked several prominent law and society scholars to review parts of the book. They also offered excellent suggestions. The three editors claim equal credit (or blame) for the work. Mistakes are ours and not those of our colleagues who helped us.

Of course, we also must thank our colleagues, both in the United States and elsewhere, who have taught us so much about legal systems in operation. We apologize to our friends whose work we did not quote or cite. These are teaching materials and not necessarily a collection of the best articles in the law and society field. Sometimes, after all, a badly flawed article provokes much better class discussion than a masterpiece to which we can only react with applause. Also, space limitations demanded that we do without articles that all three editors admire. It is, perhaps, a sign of progress in the field that there are many more good articles than we have room for in this book.

1

Introduction

This is a book of readings about law, legal systems, and legal institutions. But it is a book with a particular slant. The readings primarily approach that system from an *outside* rather than the *inside* perspective, which focuses on legal rules and procedures as seen from inside the legal system, often in an idealized form. This introduction will try to explain what we mean by this last statement. It will also give a brief account of the history and present status of "outside" studies and approaches to law.

THE OUTSIDE POINT OF VIEW

Roughly, this point of view looks at legal phenomena from the standpoint of one or more of the social sciences: sociology, anthropology, economics, psychology, political science, and perhaps others. Of course, these are all quite different fields, and they each have their own slant, their own peculiar way of looking at human behavior and human thought. An economist might be interested, for example, in exploring the question whether it would be more effective to give a company a subsidy to keep it from dumping toxic wastes, as opposed to fines and criminal sanctions. An anthropologist might be interested in how cultures differ in the ways they handle disputes between husband and wife. A psychologist might want to find out how juries actually go about making their decisions. Each field has its own little stock of favorite questions (and answers), and its own pet methodologies.

1

But the social sciences do have certain traits in common. Perhaps the most important is a commitment to empirical observation and scientific measurement, as far as this is possible. Related to this is a commitment to objectivity and neutrality—again, as far as possible. Sophisticated social scientists are not naive about science and its limits. They know they themselves are only human. They realize they have prejudices and values like everybody else. The best of them will try very hard to keep these from contaminating their work.

There are some critics who think that objectivity and scientific neutrality are delusions; that "value-free" social science is a myth, or, worse, a fraud. There is more than a grain of truth in this accusation. Values, attitudes, viewpoints and prejudices drive a social scientist to choose particular topics and points of view, and inevitably color the way questions get asked, and even how data get analyzed. (Indeed, it is social science itself that gave us this insight into the sociology of knowledge and science). The social sciences use many methods, but all of them are flawed or limited. None can promise to produce pure, objective, uncontrovertible truth.

Besides, the subject matter (law) is particularly cantankerous. It is very hard to study law scientifically. The things we want to describe and analyze often are not tangible objects that can be measured with practical yardsticks. They involve morals, ideas, attitudes, personal privacy, economic interests, and other tangled and delicate stuff. Law involves social constructs—the real world (whatever that would mean) gets transformed and twisted as its raw material gets converted into law. It is easier, for example, to study accidents than to study torts. Judgments of judges, jurors, or lawyers transform a collision between two autos into a tort. Moreover, when the people inside the legal system manipulate the data and the ideas, they may produce a picture that does not jibe well with the perceptions of the people who actually lived through the collision or were affected by it. As a result, we cannot assume that there is some underlying reality that corresponds to the concept of a tort.

Furthermore, we can no longer ignore the fact that those who make and run the legal system in any society are not a random cross-section of the public. In our society they have been overwhelmingly white males. Women and minority group members, in recent years, have challenged a whole flock of presuppositions underlying law and legal institutions. They have forced theorists and practitioners to confront the experience of subordinated groups. Similar voices have been heard from the sexual minorities and from other disadvantaged people. A lot of this work, of course, is deeply controversial. But legal scholarship, and law-and-society scholarship, can only benefit when forced to confront their assumptions, ruling ideas, and habits. Scholarship has had to learn, the hard way, how much gender, race, class, and life-style colored the way people—including legal officials and scholars—look at the world.

Still, having said all this, we have to admit that we do not share the deepest skepticism about law and society studies. We share Felice Levine's more optimistic view. She writes:

> [O]ne learns from the various critiques and . . . these critiques are not necessarily separate and apart from science, but part of the dialogue of doing science in a better way. For those who value the process of learning and the value of understanding without any illusion of absolute certainty of what we know, such critiques are instructive and integral to the activity and integrity of science itself. We must keep in mind that science is a social process and, like all social processes, it is dynamic, even at times erratic, but capable of change. Thus, the critiques are grist for doing science in a more profound way.[1]

Despite all the doubting and the theorizing, there remains an enormous difference between honest research on law and no research at all; between trying to be fair and looking for examples to support a political or ideological position. For example, a sociologist may try, as honestly as she can, to observe how many people bring their cars to a stop at a stop sign, and how many race right on through. There may be all sorts of problems and failings in the research. However, if it is done at all properly, it is vastly different from just making up the data out of one's head, and passing it off as observation. One test of fairness is whether the researcher is willing to accept results that go against the grain—results that she does not like and did not expect. There is also, we think, an enormous difference between theory based on data, or designed to guide the collection of data; and theory concocted in pure thought, which has not been and cannot be tested. While pure thought may be pregnant with insight, sometimes (perhaps often) it is only fantasy.

In any event, the social sciences have over the years evolved many traditions, methods, and credos (they are often in conflict with each other). There are also traditions, methods, and credos relating to the social science or outside study of law. This differs, as we have said, from the way insiders tend to look at the system. The insiders include lawyers and judges. But Mr. and Ms. Public may also adopt an inside view, because they live in society, and have pretty definite ideas about at least some legal issues. The inside approach is concerned not so much with empirical, measurable reality, with what is going on in the world, as it is with what is correct, or what ought to be.

After all, most legal questions have some sort of answer. A woman

---

1. Felice J. Levine, "'His' and 'Her' Story: The Life and Future of the Law and Society Movement," 18 *Florida State University Law Review* 69, 86 (1990). See also, William C. Whitford, "Critical Empiricism," 14 *Law & Social Inquiry* 61 (1989); William C. Whitford, "Lowered Horizons: Implementation Research in a Post-CLS World," 1986 *Wisconsin Law Review* 755.

who runs a consulting business out of her home asks a tax lawyer whether she can deduct some of her heating bills as business expenses. She expects a professional answer—she wants to be told whether she can deduct, or she can't, or whether it depends on this or that. She expects the answer to come from the law, though she may not be clear on where one finds that or what it consists of. She is asking an inside question, and she demands an inside answer.

There is also a very large normative element in discussions of law—people argue and discuss what *should be* legal or illegal, and what is morally or politically or otherwise right (or wrong). Indeed, both lawyers and lay people alike often fudge or confuse legal "correctness" and ethical "rightness." Is it right to put murderers to death? Should we let school teachers in public schools offer prayers in class? These are obviously normative or ethical questions—questions about what ought to be done. But they also happen to be legal or constitutional issues in this country. It is not easy to keep the two dimensions apart—assuming they should be.

To take one example: cruel and unusual punishment is forbidden by the Bill of Rights. Many opponents of the death penalty say that it is cruel and unusual punishment, and therefore forbidden. But in some ways this is a rather odd statement. After all, a majority of the justices of the Supreme Court in a number of cases has specifically decided that the death penalty is not cruel and unusual punishment. And the Supreme Court has the last word on the official legal meaning of the Constitution.

The person who insists that, despite the Supreme Court's decisions, the death penalty is cruel and unusual is saying, "I think the death penalty is wrong and should be abolished." But she is also saying something more, something about law, the Constitution, and what the correct reading of the Constitution ought to be. She is making a point about the differences between legal and moral validity. The point may be, and often is, inchoate and confused. But that people make this point is an important social fact which itself may have consequences. The social study of law has to take into account such things as values, beliefs, ideas, and attitudes. They are basic to any legal system.

Of course, the social scientist has no way to suggest an answer to the question, is the death penalty constitutional? She can only discuss and describe why people think it is or it is not. She can only discuss and describe which people (or judges) think so, and how opinion varies from men to women, whites to blacks, young to old, and the like. She can compile and analyze data on the actual impact of the death penalty. She can show where movements for and against the death penalty come from, politically or historically speaking, and so on.

But these are not trivial contributions to the debate itself; nor are they frivolous and unimportant questions to research. Indeed, some of us think this work of social scientists goes to the very heart of the whole law enterprise. Some of us (the editors of this book very notably) think that there is no task more important than understanding the factual and social underpinnings of the legal system. The work of grasping the nature of the system, and explaining it, is crucial in a society which thinks it is committed to the rule of law, whatever that might mean.

From an instrumental point of view, it would seem easier to defend the death penalty if you could prove that it saved lives by deterring murders. Moreover, people who are in favor of the death penalty would be a lot more comfortable if they could prove that no innocent people (or at least only a tiny number of innocent people) had been or were likely to be put to death by mistake. Better yet if we could show that racial discrimination was not involved in the choice of which convicted murderers get the death sentence, and which do not.

However, not many people think we can prove or disprove any of these propositions. This raises a question: what do we do if we can not answer such questions? Is common sense good enough? Do we keep on putting people to death unless the opponents can make out a stronger case? Who has the burden of proof? Suppose we could show that the death penalty deters, but only somewhat; and we could show that there is some racial discrimination, but not an enormous amount. Who decides how much is too much? Obviously, the social sciences do not and cannot give us answers. However, without a social science perspective, it is easy to evade such issues, and to reduce the whole matter to political sloganeering.

Law, however, is not just social engineering. Law is one way of declaring what is morally right and wrong. The death penalty is an important symbol of a society's abhorrence of murder. It may be a factor in reinforcing all of the norms in the culture that keep individuals to some degree safer in their daily lives. Some people may simply feel better if they see that those who commit horrible murders pay the ultimate price. Indeed, for them, putting murderers to death may be part of what the legal system must do to gain and retain legitimacy. (In some cultures, for example, it is legitimate for a victim's family to seek revenge; and our culture certainly does not totally condemn a person who takes revenge on a rapist or killer.) Other people see the symbolism and the lesson as all wrong: the death penalty, along with violence in film and television, teaches that killing is an appropriate solution to problems. Of course, just what the death penalty symbolizes and to whom are also empirical questions.

In other words, we think it is clear that a law and society perspective can contribute a lot to clarify and improve debates about such issues as the death penalty. But if we are realistic, we have to ask, who is the audience for this kind of scholarship? The Supreme Court? The President? Legislators? The Supreme Court seems, at times, to ignore or distort social science findings to suit its preconceived policy positions. The President, and the legislators, are interested in getting elected— sometimes it seems as if the only contribution of the social sciences they care about are public opinion polls. Interest groups look for findings that they can use, that suit them, that cut their way, as they battle to get their way in the legislative marketplace. They may tend to ignore or distort data which comes out the "wrong" way.

A social science perspective is but one of many influences on the total legal culture that tells policy makers what must be done. Claims about facts do not automatically change the world. Indeed, the social study of law includes study of the process by which empirical works— or, contrariwise, colorful anecdotes, scandals, just plain lies, and conventional wisdom—affect ongoing legal systems. We should neither claim too much nor too little for our enterprise of looking at law in action or the actual or likely impact of law.

THE RIDDLE OF LEGAL AUTONOMY

It is one thing to look at a legal system from the outside. It is quite another to say that the outside viewpoint *explains* what makes a legal system tick much better than any inside explanation. Which approach gives you a better handle on how legal systems work hinges on whether or not legal systems are autonomous.

An "autonomous" legal system would be "one that is independent of other sources of power and authority in social life," according to Richard Lempert and Joseph Sanders.[2] A legal action in an autonomous system is "influenced only by the preestablished rules of the legal system." It defines events "in its own terms," and is "independent of society's other mechanisms of social control." Lempert and Sanders (p. 403) also insist that an autonomous system is "self-legitimating." Its "rules and rulings are accepted because they are legal," and not for some other reason. For example, an autonomous legal system is not legitimated by political, social, or ethical considerations. And such outside factors, in an autonomous system, do not influence what the legal system does.

We will not enter into a long discussion of legal autonomy at this point. Nobody thinks the legal system is *totally* autonomous, that is, completely independent of the society in which it is imbedded. Nobody really thinks the legal system goes entirely its own way, deciding everything according to legal criteria, with no room for political pressure, ethical considerations, economic consequences and the like. A

---

2. *An Invitation to Law and Social Science* (New York: Longman, 1986), p. 402.

totally autonomous legal system would be very undesirable; and is probably impossible, at least in any society we know about.

But is the legal system *partially* autonomous? Is there something tough, unyielding and resistant to change, something self-contained about it? Does it march to its own drummer, at least sometimes? Does it follow its own internal program when it can? Most lawyers probably think so, and so too do most lay people who have given the matter any thought. However, the important question is, how autonomous? How much of the system is self-generated, technocratic, traditional, insulated from the outside world, and how much is not?

A judge may say that he decides cases "according to the law," and he does not let any other consideration sway him. The head of an agency like the Food and Drug Administration may say that she has decided to ban a birth control pill, because the agency's rules and procedures make this the legally correct thing to do, and not because of political pressure or public opinion. These legal officials are asserting that they possess political independence, and also some sort of autonomy. It is not easy to know whether they are telling the truth; or even whether they *think* they are telling the truth.

Sometimes it is good to be cynical about statements like the ones the judge and the agency head made. But surely some actors sometimes feel (and behave?) this way. The exact situation makes a difference. Birth control pills are controversial; routine decisions about food dyes may not be. The *structure* of the legal system may also make a difference: if the director of an agency is likely to be shot at dawn if she does something that displeases the head of state, she is certainly unlikely to make herself a martyr. But if a judge has life-tenure (as our federal judges do), or if an agency head cannot be removed by the President, it may be a different story.

What does seem fairly clear is that legal systems as a whole cannot be autonomous *in the long run.* That is, sooner or later their shape gets bent in the direction of their society (more or less), regardless of any technical, traditional or historical elements. Medieval law looked, smelled, and acted medieval. The law of the Trobriand Islanders or the ancient Egyptians seemed molded to the structure and culture of those societies. The law of modern free-market states is full of rules that support or presuppose free markets. Modern legal systems contain an endless list of prescriptions and institutions that concern clean air and water, toxic waste, gene splicing, computer hacking—all of which are specific to the age we live in. These legal arrangements are awfully hard to label as autonomous, though of course they may have an autonomous trait here and there.

How could it be otherwise? Legal systems do not exist to answer abstract questions; they solve (or mis-solve) problems. But these problems are, necessarily, problems of the society in which they are embedded; and those of no other society. The problems are those that bother real people, living in real time, in real social relations with each other. And the legal solutions to these problems, too, will have to take on the coloration of the culture that supplies both question and answer.

Social scientists who study law tend to emphasize the role of the outside. In other words, they tend to explain happenings within the system in terms of social forces—political pressures, internalized values, cultural norms, economic interests, and so on. They tend to de-emphasize "internal" technical legal aspects of the system. Insiders on the other hand are bound up in their daily work life with details of law. They tend to explain what happens in the system in exactly such terms. The insiders include law professors and others who make their living expounding and explaining what the law is and how it works.

Some of the biases of the editors of this book ought to be obvious by now. They would not have edited this book if they did not believe in the external way of looking at legal systems, and if they did not distrust the internal point of view as a sufficient explanation of legal action. But it is important to remind ourselves that nobody can prove that legal systems are or are not autonomous; or prove that the outside approach is a better one; or measure the exact degree to which legal systems do or do not respond or relate to their specific societies. There is no principle which insists that every legal system is as autonomous or nonautonomous as every other one. It is *possible* that American law is more legalistic than the law of some other country or society. It is also possible that some fields of law are more autonomous than others. One who favors an outside approach still must consider the degree to which legal doctrines influence the output of a legal system. It would be foolish to assume that legal thought never made a difference. Similarly, it would be foolish to assume that legal thought explained everything about a legal system.

The issues brought up in this introduction will not be solved here, or anywhere. They will run through almost every page of the readings that follow.

COMPLEXITY AND CHANGE

Legal systems, we must remember, are incredibly complicated. They also change over time. They are also culture-bound, or at least tied to specific cultures. These are three elementary but crucial facts about our own legal system, and also about legal systems generally in the modern world.

The first point, the complexity of the system, is fairly obvious. The law is an enormous, complicated business. Nobody knows all of American law, or even all of American tax law, or even all of the American law relating to taxes on corporations. There is simply too much of it. Law is conventionally divided into fields, such as personal injury law, divorce law, food and drug law, copyright law, criminal law, tort law, and so on.

These fields, in the aggregate, cover (or at least touch on) almost every
conceivable aspect of life. This is true of every modern society. But there
is a special wrinkle to the law of the United States. This is a federal system. The country is blessed (if that is the word) with 50 legal systems,
one for each state. There is also the national (federal) system of courts
and laws, not to mention various territorial systems, and the system in the
District of Columbia. There are also thousands of cities, towns, town-
ships, counties, and special subdivisions (sewer and school districts, port
authorities, and so on), all of which have power to make laws, or at least
rules and regulations, or ordinances. In every state, in the cities, and
above all in the federal government, there are administrative agencies,
large and small. For example, on the federal level we can point to the
Securities and Exchange Commission, the Food and Drug Administration, the Social Security Administration. On the state level we can recognize medical and dental licensing boards and highway commissions. On
the local level we can see zoning commissions and school boards. These
too churn out rules and regulations, decisions and orders, almost beyond
counting.

And of course this vast body of legal material is constantly changing. Each rule and regulation, each court decision reported and published, every statute passed is at least a minor change, a footnote, in the
immense book of the laws. The pace of social change has increased
enormously in our times, and the pace of legal change has increased
along with it.

Law is also an unusually parochial discipline. Chemical engineering
or molecular biology is more or less the same subject in China, Hondu-
ras, or the United States of America. Even the social sciences tend to
transcend national borders. But a knowledge of French law does not
equip anybody to practice law in, say, Iran or Japan. Every country has
its own (official) legal system, and no two are the same, or even
approximately the same. They vary according to the differences in the
culture, tradition, economics, and politics of the particular countries.
There is, therefore, an immense body of legal systems all over the
world. A "science," even a social science, of law, perhaps ought to
have principles or generalizations that go beyond a particular legal system.[3] Are there such principles?[4] Can we say anything of value about
legal systems as a whole? Or about some subgroup: legal systems in

---

3. When we make such statements, we must be cautious and be sure that we are pointing to the same thing when we assert principles that apply to *the law* of the United States
and *the law* of France. Some things an American scholar might think of as legal might
not be seen as "law" by a French scholar.

4. Donald Black, *The Behavior of Law* (New York: Academic Press, 1976), offered
some general "laws" about legal systems. For a critical analysis of Black's propositions
about legal systems, see Gloria T. Lessan and Joseph F. Sheley, "Does Law Behave? A
Macrolevel Test of Black's Propositions on Change in Law," 70 *Social Forces* 655
(1992).

Western industrial countries, for example; or legal systems in countries of the Far East, for example?

Most of these questions have no answers. There are not many studies that try to compare systems of law, or parts of them, in an empirical, social-scientific way. It is not easy to do so. There are theoretical and practical obstacles. But in an age of global communication, an age of global economies, the legal systems of the world are becoming more and more interconnected. This trend is likely to continue. Law, and the study of law, are likely to become at least a bit less parochial. So too of the social study of law.

"PRIVATE" GOVERNMENT

We have spoken, thus far, mostly about *official,* formal legal systems. These systems are what law students (on the whole) study, and what ordinary legal scholars write about. But the formal legal system, as it exists on paper, is not the real system, the living system, the lived system of law; and the social study of law is concerned with the whole system, and all its working parts, formal and informal, official and unofficial, legitimate and illegitimate.

The real legal system differs from the official legal system in two significant ways. First, it contains informal, unofficial elements that surround, supplement, supplant, and complement the official, formal elements. In criminal law, this is the world of plea bargaining ("copping a plea") and the dozens of arrangements, shortcuts, rules of thumb, patterns of behavior that people inside the system know about, but that law school courses in criminal law or procedure mention very little if at all. It is the world in which the police sometimes beat prisoners, and in which they let other prisoners go, or even take bribes.

Second, everywhere in society we find law-like systems or institutions, side-by-side with, or acting as rivals to, the official system. There are, for example, what we might call "private governments":

> We live in a world of "legal pluralism" where rules are made and interpreted and sanctions imposed by many public and private governments which are only loosely coordinated . . . Examples of private governments range from the Mafia to the American Arbitration Association. Trade associations, sports leagues, church groups, neighborhood organizations and many other "private" units such as business corporations exercise what are, effectively, legal powers. They make rules . . . they interpret them in their day-to-day operations; they offer benefits . . . and they may suspend or expel members, associates or employees as a sanction.[5]

5. Stewart Macaulay, "Law and the Behavioral Sciences: Is There any There There?" 6 *Law and Policy* 249 (1984).

Throughout this book, we will see examples of informal patterns of legal behavior, and we will also see examples of pluralism and of "private governments." Some patterns amount to what we might even call legal subcultures. There is, of course, no single general culture in any society beyond a certain size. In the United States, for example, ideas and behaviors differ as between men and women, young and old, black and white, Protestant and Catholic, and within communities of Asian Americans, or Armenian-Americans, or auto dealers, jazz musicians, nurses, cab drivers, gang members, heroin addicts—any community or group that can be described at all has its own "dialect" of culture. The same is true of *legal* culture. There will be many not always consistent legal cultures in any society. This adds a layer of complexity to our subject; but throughout this book of readings, these subcultures will figure very prominently. The legal system cannot be understood without them.

LAW-AND-SOCIETY SCHOLARSHIP

The study of the relationship between law and society, practically speaking, goes back to the 19th century, when modern social science began to develop. Sir Henry Maine, whose book, *Ancient Law,* appeared in 1861, was one of the pioneers. Maine looked at the law in a broad historical sweep, and he aimed to relate types of social structure to types of legal systems. Karl Marx, another seminal if controversial 19th century figure, wrote little explicitly about law. He considered law basically a by-product of economic structure and an instrument of repression in the hands of social and economic elites. His general approach has, however, continued to be influential with neo-Marxists and others. Emile Durkheim (1858–1917), another of the founding figures in modern social thought, has had particular influence on the sociology of crime and deviance.[6]

Max Weber (1864–1920) probably is the most important historical figure in the development of the sociology of law. Weber himself was trained as a lawyer. Concepts developed by Weber still are extremely useful in law-and-society scholarship, and we will meet some of them later in these materials.[7]

After the death of Weber, the social study of law seemed to pause; the work done in the next 30 years hardly compares to that done during the golden age of Weber and Durkheim. There were, however, some

---

6. See Kai Erikson, *Wayward Puritans* (New York: John Wiley & Sons, 1966), pp. 6–13.

7. Another classical figure worth mentioning is Eugen Ehrlich (1862–1922), whose fame rests on the concept of "living law." Ehrlich was, perhaps, the first jurist seriously interested in rules which people actually followed in their daily lives as opposed to the rules "on the books."

signal contributions by anthropologists studying law.[8] But neither legal academia nor the world of the social sciences paid much attention to the relationship between the legal and social systems in America or in other societies.

The field came into its own in the second half of the 20th century. Social science in general had a boom period after the Second World War. In the United States, such dramatic decisions as *Brown v. Board of Education* (1954) refocused attention on the social importance of law. In addition, private foundations began to invest a certain amount of money into socio-legal research, which provided yet another stimulus.

The last 25 years have been years of steady and impressive growth in the field. In many ways, law and society studies are flourishing today. The Law and Society Association, the umbrella group for scholars in the field in the United States, is more than a quarter-century old. It was founded by a handful of social scientists, aided and abetted by an aberrant lawyer or two.[9] Much of the founding energy was generated at the University of Wisconsin, and Prof. J. Willard Hurst of the Law School was a potent influence. Hurst himself was a legal historian, but his influential works on that subject pointed the way to the social study of law in American society.[10]

Today, the Law and Society Association (LSA) has over 1,000 members, holds annual meetings, and publishes a journal, the *Law & Society Review*. There are other journals on the subject published in the United States—*Law and Social Inquiry*, for example, which is the organ of the American Bar Foundation. There are also journals on specialized subjects. For example, *Law and Human Behavior* concentrates on articles about psychology and law. The *Journal of Law and Economics* does the same for economists who look at law.

The field shows considerable vitality in many other countries as well. The Japanese counterpart to the Law and Society Association has hundreds of members (it was also established long before LSA). There are a number of national law-and-society organizations in Europe, and journals on the

8. One notable book was Bronislaw Malinowski's, *Crime and Custom in Savage Society* (London: K. Paul, Trench, Trubner & Co., 1926). Another classic of legal anthropology, *The Cheyenne Way: Conflict and Case Law in Primitive Jurisprudence* (Norman: University of Oklahoma Press, 1941), deserves special mention because it was a collaboration between an anthropologist, E. Adamson Hoebel, and a law professor, Karl Llewellyn. Llewellyn is thus one of the few scholars who bridged the world of legal education and the world of law-and-society studies.

9. For an account of the founding of the Law and Society Association, see Felice J. Levine, "Goose Bumps and 'The Search for Signs of Intelligent Life' in Sociolegal Studies: After Twenty-Five Years," 24 *Law & Society Review* 7, 10–19 (1990).

10. See, e.g., J. Willard Hurst, *The Growth of American Law: The Law Makers* (Boston: Little, Brown & Co., 1950); J. Willard Hurst, *Law and Social Process in United States History* (Ann Arbor: University of Michigan, 1960). For an appraisal of Hurst's contributions, see Harry N. Scheiber, "At the Borderland of Law and Economic History: The Contributions of Willard Hurst," 75 *American History Review* 744 (1970).

subject are published in, for example, Australia, Canada, France, Germany, the Netherlands, Italy, Japan, and the United Kingdom. Important work takes place in Belgium and Denmark as well as elsewhere. At one time there was an active law and society group in Poland, and the end of Communism has opened the door to further development in that country. There are, however, somewhat distinctive national styles. Many continental scholars who teach and write about law-and-society studies come from backgrounds in legal philosophy, and tend to be more interested in large questions of theory, than in the nitty-gritty of empirical research. (In fact, many American scholars interested in theory seem to prefer the import models).[11] To be sure, there is also a tradition of empirical research in Europe, but research on the law in action is, on the whole, more often found in America. There is likely to be more and more debate and discussion across national lines in our increasingly global field.

Law and society studies, on the whole, have not made much of a dent in legal education. Most of the members of the Law and Society Association are not lawyers and are not associated with law schools. They are social scientists, in political science, sociology, psychology, anthropology, and economics departments, with a scatterating of philosophers, historians, and other disciplinary affiliations. A fair number of colleges and universities have departments of legal studies, or offer courses and programs on criminal justice, or business law, or the like: in some of these programs, law and society studies form an important component. All in all, there are probably about a thousand or more active scholars (the number is a sheer guess), in all sorts of disciplines. These scholars generate a substantial output of essays, review articles, research projects, and monographs, every year.

Still, it is fair to ask, what has the field accomplished, after all? What do we know that we did not know before? What are the insights, the contributions to understanding? There have been a fair number of general treatments of the field, here and abroad; and a few attempts at synthesizing the field, or coming up with some sort of general theory.[12] In the vast body of work, as Stewart Macaulay has

11. See Johan Galtung, "Structure, Culture, and Intellectual Style: An Essay Comparing Saxonic, Teutonic, Gallic and Nipponic Approaches," 20 *Social Science Information* 817 (1981).

12. See, for example, Lempert and Sanders, *An Invitation to Law and Social Science;* Lawrence M. Friedman, *The Legal System: A Social Science Perspective* (New York: Russell Sage Foundation, 1975); Roger Cotterrell, *The Sociology of Law: An Introduction* 2d ed. (London: Butterworth's, 1992); Adam Podgorecki, *A Sociological Theory of Law* (Milan: Giuffrè, 1991); Donald Black, *Sociological Justice* (New York: Oxford University Press, 1989) and *The Behavior of Law* (New York: Academic Press, 1976) and, of course, many books in languages other than English. On the use of social research *in* the legal system, see two collections of sources: Wallace D. Loh, *Social Research in the Judicial Process: Cases, Readings, and Text* (New York: Russell Sage Foundation, 1984); and John Monahan and Laurens Walker, *Social Science in Law: Cases and Materials* 3d ed. (Westbury, N.Y.: Foundation Press, 1993).

put it: "social science and law has washed up a few shining nuggets."[13] He summed up the basic insights that the field has contributed, as follows:

1. *Law is not free.* There are barriers to access to the legal system. which some people can jump far more easily than others . . . . When we turn to social regulation, we find that it involves costs which some can pass along to others. It usually is fruitful to ask who benefits from and who pays for any type of legal action. Often we will find that regulation operates as a kind of regressive taxation, burdening the have-nots far more than the haves.

2. *Law is delivered by actors with limited resources and interests of their own in settings where they have discretion.* "Street-level bureaucrats" such as police, assistant prosecuting attorneys, case workers, clerks of court, those handling intake at administrative agencies and many more, have discretion although no one planned it that way. This is true for a number of reasons. Policies conflict and the rules may be unclear. As a result, those who deal with the public may have a choice of goals to pursue or rationalizations for whatever they want to do to serve the public or their own self interest. Those who do the day-to-day work of a legal agency often are hard to supervise because they control the official version of events by writing reports in the files. Resource constraints often make it impossible to "go by the book" since officials cannot do everything mandated. If those enforcing a law cannot carry out all their duties, they must choose which of them under what circumstances they will attempt to implement. Those choices of "street-level bureaucrats" are unlikely to be random or neutral in their impact. They will be affected by folk wisdom or bias, reward and punishment structures, and self-interest.

3. *Many of the functions usually thought of as legal are performed by alternative institutions, and there is a great deal of interpenetration between what we call public and private sectors . . . .*

4. *People, acting alone and in groups, cope with law and cannot be expected to comply passively.* Many people are able to ignore most legal commands, or redefine them to serve self-interest or "common sense," and live with a vague and often inaccurate sense of the nature of law and legal process—all without encountering serious problems. There is great opportunity for evasion in a society that values privacy, civil liberties, and limited investment in government. Coping with the law can become a game that offsets any sense of obligation. Many participants in social fields and networks pass along techniques of evasion, legitimate breaking the law, honor the

13. Macaulay, "Law and the Behavioral Sciences: Is There Any There There?" 6 *Law & Policy* 149, 152–55 (1984).

crafty, and even sanction those who would comply. The law is frequently uncertain and plausible arguments can be fashioned to rationalize much of what many people want to do. This means that there is great opportunity for bargaining in the shadow of the law or in the shadow of questionable assumptions about the law. Thus, people's views of the likely legal consequences of action at best affect but do not determine their behavior. Sometimes, however, the command of the law rings loud and clear and has direct impact on behavior. In short, the role of law is not something that can be assumed but must be established in every case.

5. *Lawyers play many roles other than adversary in a courtroom.* Lawyer self-interest, and their view of what is best for a client, often dictates that litigation should be avoided, and lawyers seek other ways to provide service to clients. They tend to know who makes decisions and what kinds of appeals, legal and other types, are likely to be effective. They know how to bargain and how to manipulate situations so that accommodations can be reached. Often they serve as coercive mediators, acting in settings where their profession itself is a tacit threat of trouble if people do not behave reasonably. Instead of pursuing only their client's immediate interest, lawyers often act as what Justice Brandeis called "counsel for the situation," seeking what they see as the best long term solution for all concerned. Often lawyers, with more or less success, seek to transform clients' perceptions about what is just, or at least tolerable. Often they deal with bruised egos and manage public relations far more than they vindicate clients' rights . . . . [T]he wide variety of roles played by lawyers is a factor in making the functioning of social institutions far more complex than formal descriptions assume. For example, many lawyers' stock in trade includes their contacts with officials, knowledge of acceptable rhetoric, and awareness of mutually advantageous possibilities. Thus, they are able to cut through formal channels and get things done. When this happens regularly, behavior in a corporation or a public agency no longer follows official procedures . . . .

6. *Our society deals with conflict in many ways, but avoidance and evasion are important ones* . . . . We may pass symbolic laws declaring the good, the true and the beautiful, but we leave enforcement to local option. We find social consensus at a high level of abstraction and so keep our doctrines ambiguous or contradictory. This avoids the costs of definition and of deciding that some interpretations of values are right while others are wrong. Thus, a simple means-and-ends view of law should be suspect . . . .

7. *While law matters in American society, its influence tends to be indirect, subtle and ambiguous.* It is easy to find gaps between the promise and performance of our law. Americans are selectively law abiding . . . Nonetheless, law matters in a number of ways. For example, many ideas that are part of our common normative vocab-

ulary are crystallized in law, and they both help rationalize action and affect our expectations about the social world . . . . While the ability of the legal system to prompt social change that is unwanted by a large or powerful minority may be limited, often law can add gasoline to an already burning fire. The struggle to gain legal rights can be the focus of a social movement, forcing reformers to define goals and to select means to obtain them. Even failed reform efforts may influence the behavior of both proponents and opponents. Moreover, law can restrain power in many situations. For many reasons, those with power hesitate to exercise it too crudely. The effort to cloak an exercise of power with a mantle of right or to cover up abuses are costly exercises which, at times, deter action. Law and lawyers have helped gain accommodations for some of the less powerful by using legal symbols and procedures. In this culture even the counterattacks by the powerful have to be rationalized in legal rhetoric. This effort may affect both the form and substance of the way such battles are fought and resolved.

Macaulay (one of the editors of this book) is naturally favorable to the field, and cautiously impressed with its accomplishments. There have also been some dissenting and doubting voices.[14] A number of scholars have accused the field of repetition, triviality, falling into a rut, spinning wheels.[15] Others, more recently, have raised fairly fundamental questions about the value of socio-legal research, or its approach. They espouse what they call a more "interpretive," more self-conscious style of examining legal phenomena. We will return to these issues at various points. After going through the material, readers should be able to judge for themselves whether the law and society enterprise has been worthwhile; and whether some or all of the criticisms directed at it are well-taken.

The various social sciences, too, do not agree on methods, approaches, and points of view. In many ways, the economists stand apart from the others. In the law school world, "law and economics" refers to a movement which attempts to use tools of neo-classical economics to critique law and legal rules in terms of efficiency and wealth-maximization. Many of its practitioners tend to feel that the other social sciences are weaklings, that they lack a good, solid theory

14. See, e.g., Roger B.M. Cotterrell, "Law and Sociology: Notes on the Constitution and Confrontations of Disciplines," 13 *Journal of Law and Society* 9 (1986); Austin Sarat and Susan Silbey, "The Pull of the Policy Audience," 10 *Law & Policy* 97 (1988); Roman Tomasic, "Continuity and Change in the Society of Law," 11 *Adelaide Law Review* 70 (1987); David M. Trubek, "Where the Action Is: Critical Legal Studies and Empiricism," 36 *Stanford Law Review* 575 (1984); David M. Trubek and John Esser, "'Critical Empiricism' in American Legal Studies: Paradox, Program or Pandora's Box?" 14 *Law and Social Inquiry* 3 (1989).

15. Richard Abel, "Redirecting Social Studies of Law," 14 *Law & Society Review* 805 (1980).

to give them backbone, and that they display liberal political bias or worse.[16] There will be references to this body of work as well.

WHAT LIES AHEAD?

In Chapter 2, we deal with descriptions of the legal system. The general idea is that there are different ways of describing legal systems—different methods and approaches; and these affect the way one actually sees a legal system.

Chapter 3 asks the question: where does law come from? Simple, pre-literate societies do not have formal legal systems. At what point in social evolution do such systems make their appearance, and why? This is a global, historical question. The United States, and all other modern societies, already have formal legal systems. The chapter also asks more particular questions about the emergence of laws, legal doctrines, legal institutions. How do we explain, say, why American courts began to pay attention to gender discrimination, or why Congress passed a law outlawing discrimination on the basis of sex? This chapter will deal with pressure groups, public opinion, and related subjects, among others.

Chapter 4 turns the question of Chapter 3, in a way, upside down. It asks about the impact of law: what effect does law or some particular legal rule or institution have on the way people think and behave. The impact question is actually quite a complex one, and includes a whole range of sub-questions—for example, the question (much debated) of deterrence. Does the death penalty have any effect on the murder rate? How would we go about answering this question? In this chapter, too, we ask how messages from the legal system get communicated to the public, or part of it, and what effect the legal communication system has on obedience or disobedience to law.

Chapter 5 deals with the structure of the legal system—its organizational shape. The chapter also introduces readers to the sociology of legal *roles,* that is, the main players and actors inside the system (judges and lawyers, very notably).

In some ways the model for the book is the law school casebook, where student and teacher work before, during and after class to build a structure out of raw materials. The main points are not neatly summa-

16. Robert C. Ellickson, *Order Without Law* (Cambridge: Harvard University Press, 1991), p. 147, notes "sociologists and their allies have been handicapped because they do not agree on, and often don't show much interest in developing, basic theoretical building blocks." Ellickson criticizes both law and economics and law and society work. He notes "[t]he late Arthur Leff, who read extensively in both [fields], saw law-and-economics as a desert and law-and-society as a swamp. Just as aridity requires critical exposure, so does swampiness." Ellickson conducts a splendid field study and then offers his own theory, attempting to bridge the gap between these two fields.

rized at the end of each section and chapter. The book is not a "reader" in the social science tradition. The materials are used to develop themes, and there is a strong overall structure reflecting the judgments—perhaps biases—of the authors. Opposing views are frequently paired. Those working with the book must deal with controversy and important questions without certain answers. Of course, this is a reflection of law school style. We think it leads to active class participation and discussion. The many notes and citations after each article are meant as aids to instructors and suggestions for students who wish to pursue some matters more deeply.

We have taught from these materials several times as they took shape. The book works for us. Generally, students respond favorably to the course. Law students are often wary of the social science vocabulary and techniques at first; social science students worry that they are not surefooted enough on the paths of the law. As time goes on, distinctions between lawyer and social scientist tend to drop out, as the group deals with common problems.

We are amused that some law professors ready, willing and able to master the black arts of the Internal Revenue Code, seem to turn pale when confronted with simple tables and graphs. And sociologists who think nothing of invading the world of medicine or religion sometimes treat the legal domain as a cave inhabited by fire-eating dragons.

But we have tried to avoid the more exotic methods and vocabulary of social science. Sometimes we offer explanations in notes and questions after readings. The law, too, is kept clean and simple. Our experience is that such a book can be easily taught by a law professor with little background or experience in the social sciences. Social scientists without legal training have also coped quite easily with the materials. True, the ideal teacher might be one who has completed training in both fields. We are beginning to see people with doctorates in social science fields as well as law degrees. Nonetheless, such people are and will be rare enough so that this area is likely to remain open to amateurs in one field or another for a long time to come. That indeed is part of its charm and its potency.

2
The Legal System in Operation

INTRODUCTION

A major goal of the law and social sciences movement has been to describe empirically the way the legal system works. When scholars do this, they find that reality does not fit the idealized official pictures of the legal system; nor does the way law works conform to conventional wisdom, which can be overcritical or sensationalized, or too complacent.

Common wisdom often reflects negative myths about the legal system. We hear wistful calls for a return to the "good old days," when the litigation rate was low, or when there was no plea bargaining to blight the system of criminal justice. Research often shows that these claims do not rest on facts. What people think about the legal system, as it works, is not based on solid investigation.

But then where *do* these ideas come from? We begin this chapter by asking this question. The rest of the chapter compares this common wisdom with portraits scholars draw of the way the legal system actually operates. Along the way, we raise questions about what it means to describe a legal system. Some issues of method will be discussed.

19

HOW DO PEOPLE LEARN ABOUT THE LEGAL SYSTEM?

We all have views about how the legal system works. Some of these views come from education or experience in early childhood. Others come from our experiences with the legal system as adults. Still others come from the media—TV shows about law, police, or lawyers—or what we read in novels or newspapers or see in the movies. How accurate are those views? Not very, most people would think. In the wake of the Clarence Thomas nomination hearings in 1991, President Bush lamented:

> The scenes from the Senate bore little resemblance to the tidy legislative process that we all studied in school and we describe to our children, now, maybe to our grandchildren .... And the process seemed unreal, more like a satire than like the Government in which all of you, in which I, take so much pride; more like a burlesque show than a civics class.[17]

The President was criticizing the confirmation process; but he may have unintentionally indicted lay ideas about the legal system too. What was wrong may have been what we were taught about the legal system, not what it was in fact doing. Maybe we all absorb tidy descriptions of the legal process. In fact it is anything but tidy.

It will come as no surprise to learn that what we see and hear in the news and entertainment media is pretty inaccurate:

1. *Law, Lawyers, and Popular Culture*

Lawrence M. Friedman

98 *Yale Law Journal* 1579, 1588 (1989)

☐ Popular culture is involved with law: and some of the more obvious aspects of law are exceedingly prominent in popular culture. But of course not all of law. No songs have been composed about the Robinson-Patman Act, no movies produced about capital gains tax. This is not surprising, since most people do not have a clue as to what these are all about. But there are also no songs, movies or TV programs about Medicare, dog licenses, zoning laws, or overtime parking, all of which most people certainly do know something about. On the other

---

17. 27 Weekly Compilation of Presidential Documents, Monday, October 28, 1991, Number 43, p. 1496.

hand, television would shrivel up and die without cops, detectives, crimes, judges, prisons, guns and trials.

This suggests a first, obvious point: popular culture as reflected in the media, is not, and cannot be taken as, an accurate mirror of the actual state of living law. Suppose our legal sources were all destroyed in a nuclear nightmare which wiped out the West Digest, the Federal Register, the revised statutes, federal and state, and all casebooks. Later generations digging in the ruins, discover intact only the archives of NBC Television. The diggers would certainly get a distorted picture of the legal system. They would learn little or nothing about property law, tax law, regulation of business, and very little about tort law or even family law; but they would find an enormous amount of material on police, murder, deviance, rape, and organized crime.

Quantity is not accuracy, moreover, and the products of popular culture are wildly off-key even with respect to those parts of the legal system that they deal with obsessively. Cop shows aim for entertainment, excitement; they are not documentaries. They exaggerate ludicrously, for dramatic effect. Crime shows, for example, overrepresent violent crimes; shoplifting is no great audience-holder, but murder is. □

So far we have seen an interesting contradiction in the ways people are taught about legal institutions. On the one hand the educational system provides a tidy view of the process; on the other hand, the media sensationalize the picture. Powerful interests in society have a stake in the legal system and therefore a stake in presenting the system to the public in a way that furthers those interests. Was the recent controversy over huge jury awards in civil cases to some degree created by the insurance industry, to scare the public?

2. The Question of Jury Competency and the Politics of Civil Justice Reform: Symbols, Rhetoric, and Agenda Setting

Stephen Daniels

52 *Law and Contemporary Problems* no. 4, pp. 269, 309–10 (1989)

□ The current attacks on civil juries cannot be understood and evaluated in a political vacuum. The attacks are an integral part of a concerted campaign aimed at the enactment of substantial change in the civil justice system that would benefit the insurance industry, physicians, certain manufacturers, and others. The campaign and the attacks arose in response to serious problems in the adequacy, availability, and affordability of liability insurance in the mid-1980's. Two competing and mutually exclusive characterizations of this situation emerged, and the winning characterization will determine the nature of subsequent public policy response to the situation.

One side sees the problem as a consequence of the recurring boom and bust nature of the insurance industry business cycle. They argue that the causes of this cycle lie within the industry itself, and that the solution is greater regulation of the insurance industry. The other side, primarily, though not exclusively, the insurance industry, labels this situation as a crisis and clearly blames the civil justice system. The remedy for this crisis is fundamental reform of the civil justice system. Characterizing the situation in this way also helps to divert attention away from the causal role of the insurance industry's boom and bust business cycle, and away from a solution of substantially greater industry regulation. Crisis rhetoric has been used in the effort to gain access first to the public agenda and then to the policy agenda.

The political strategy underlying the attacks on jury competence undercut the substance of such criticisms. Three kinds of evidence have been regularly used to highlight the failures of juries; horror stories, aggregate data, and opinion polls. Critically examining how each type of evidence is used in the policy debate over the crisis reveals how little the evidence actually tells about the products of jury decisionmaking. There is no indication that the widely used horror stores accurately portray typical jury cases. In fact, some stores are grossly inaccurate and distorted, and some were apparently fabricated. They are examples of the tactical use of passion and consequently are important in the policy debate not because of their accuracy but because they arouse anxiety and public support for a particular characterization of juries and the civil justice system.

Aggregate data have been used to demonstrate the excesses of juries in two principal ways: by presenting data on trends in awards for the high profile areas of medical malpractice and products liability; and by presenting data on trends in verdicts of $1 million or more. Neither, however, holds up under examination as an accurate picture of the products of jury decisionmaking. But accuracy may not be the real aim of such evidence either. These hard data serve as symbolic benchmarks around which people can shape their perceptions of the crisis. These benchmarks are used to arouse concern by evoking a belief that a crisis exists, that juries are largely to blame, and that immediate political action is required.

Finally, the opinion poll data actually tells us nothing about juries per se. They represent a different message and a different way of verifying the crisis characterization. They tell us not that juries and the civil justice system actually have run amok, but that many people so believe. In other words, the message is that a sizable proportion of the public accepts a particular characterization of the situation and its causes, one consistent with the interests of the civil justice reformers.

In this sense, the polls are an indication of successful agenda-building. In addition, the polls represent an alternative way of verifying the crisis characterization—*vox populi.* In doing so, their use represents the ultimate tactical use of passion—appealing to feeling rather than thought and giving unsound assumptions about juries and civil justice a scientific and quantitative aura, thereby cutting off the need for further systematic examination. Additionally, the results of the opinion polls act as symbolic benchmarks that help reinforce unexamined assumptions about the civil justice system while perpetuating the sense of anxiety and crisis. □

One of the major tasks that sociolegal research has set for itself is to examine empirically many of these assumptions about the legal system that have been learned from schools, parents, the media, and organized interests in society.

NOTES AND QUESTIONS

1. Live television coverage of the American legal system has grown exponentially in the last decade. When a Supreme Court Justice is nominated, the Senate Hearings on the nominee are now broadcast live. Similarly, we have C-SPAN, which broadcasts congressional sessions live. Additionally, in the early 90s a new cable network was formed to broadcast trials. Combined with this is a growing tabloid television industry that focuses often sensationalized attention on famous trials, like that of the police officers who were accused of assaulting Rodney King in Los Angeles or the rape trial of former heavy weight champion of the world, Mike Tyson. What are the consequences of such coverage? Will this mass media attention serve to give the public a more complete picture of the legal system, or is it likely to further distort our image of the system?

In the early 1990s a new type of crime program appeared. "America's Most Wanted" and "Unsolved Mysteries" present dramatizations of actual crimes. Viewers are urged to call the police with information related to the crime. Gray Cavender and Lisa Bond-Maupin, in "Fear and Loathing on Reality Television: An Analysis of 'America's Most Wanted' and 'Unsolved Mysteries,'" 63 *Social Inquiry* 305 (1993), report that the dramatizations paint a picture of an unsafe and unpredictable world. The programs do not reflect actual crime statistics or the real nature of the risks faced by most of the population. "Modern danger legitimizes public surveillance . . . [T]hese programs encourage wide dispersal of community social control" (p. 315).

2. For further discussion of law and popular culture, see: Stewart Macaulay, "Images of Law in Everyday Life: The Lessons of School, Entertainment and Spectator Sports," 21 *Law & Society Review* 185 (1987). Macaulay says that most members of the public learn about the legal system in school and from watching films and television far more than from experience. The information conveyed often is very misleading. Moreover, people learn about the obligation to obey law from school, entertainment and spectator sports. People also learn how to rationalize evasions of the rules. They learn to

redefine obligation so that they are not "really" cheating. Sometimes the norm is: do it, but "don't get caught."

Paul Joseph and Sharon Carton, in "The Law of the Federation: Images of Law, Lawyers, and the Legal System in 'Star Trek: The Next Generation,'" 24 *University of Toledo Law Review* 43 (1992), mention a vision of the future suggesting an ideal society where (in the 24th century) people have learned to live together without lawyers and formal procedures. What might this TV program suggest about the 20th century legal system to its audience?

3. What does Daniels mean by "horror stories"? Can you think of an example? See the article by Robert Hayden in Chapter 3.

4. Daniels claims that the insurance companies may be spreading propaganda about high damage awards. He also cites evidence that most people believe the propaganda. Why is this so? The air is full of all sorts of advocacy on all sides of all issues. What determines which stories get high levels of belief?

5. Some people, of course, learn about the legal system from personal experience. Some receive traffic tickets. Some, (or their family members or friends) are arrested, prosecuted, and sanctioned. Many learn about law and lawyers when they seek a divorce or cope with child custody or support. Some deal with tax audits. Others seek licenses for their businesses.

Working class and poor people often attempt to use the police and courts to solve neighborhood problems. They may call the police to deal with family fights or neighborhood problems. Barbara Yngvesson, in "Making Law at the Doorway: The Clerk, The Court, and the Construction of Community in a New England Town," 22 *Law & Society Review* 410 (1988); and in "Inventing Law in Local Settings: Rethinking Popular Legal Culture," 98 *Yale Law Journal* 1689 (1989), reports on when citizens demand that lower courts issue a criminal complaint, in situations where the police have declined to make an arrest. The cases involved such problems as disputes about noisy motorcycles, walking across another's land to gain access to one's own, neighborhood fights, and controlling teenage runaways. These cases are handled by clerks of court. Some clerks use a legal vocabulary; some take a more common sense approach. Sometimes clerks channel a problem into a legal approach, but often they try to handle what they view as "garbage cases" by lectures or forced negotiated solutions among those affected. Obviously, these clerks were teaching the public lessons about the law.

Sally Engle Merry, in "Concepts of Law and Justice Among Working Class Americans: Ideology as Culture," 9 *Legal Studies Forum* 59 (1985); and in "Everyday Understandings of the Law in Working-Class America," 13 *American Ethnologist* 253 (1986), observed citizens in a northeastern city who were using lower criminal and civil courts to deal with a wide variety of family, neighbor, romantic, and business problems. She "wanted to know how they understood the legal system and how that understanding changed as a result of their experiences in court." Working-class Americans understand legal rights as involving "control [of] who is on one's property and what happens on one's property . . . [and] rights not to be insulted, harassed, or hit by neighbors or family members without sufficient reason" (p. 67). Ordinary Americans who gain experience with these lower courts:

continue to believe in legal rights and see these rights as constitutive of their social relationships. But, the meaning of rights shifts as the understanding of legal action changes. Rights become resources, not guarantees. They become opportunities for action depending on the social context and history of the problem and the plaintiff's skill in navigating the complicated waters of the ideologically plural legal arena . . . . The ideology of formal justice exercises some control over the interpretation of events and the generation of social practices, but it is not passively received and absorbed either by the officials in the lower court or the working-class clients of the court. Definitions of legal rights in social relationships are constructed by litigants and courts officials as they deal with day-to-day problems in the court. (p. 266)

Merry also studied affluent American suburbs in her article, "Mending Walls and Building Fences: Constructing the Private Neighborhood," 33 *Journal of Legal Pluralism* 71 (1993). Here, "[i]nstead of informal social controls such as gossip, scandal, fear of ostracism, and failure of reciprocity," people "practice avoidance, tolerance, conciliatory approaches, and secret complaints . . . [but this is] coupled with extensive legal regulation . . ." (pp. 86–87). In these neighborhoods, there are regulations about zoning, dogs, quiet, and the like. Those who live in such places may regard "[a]ppeals to law in situations of conflict . . . as more civilized than fighting or backbiting and as symbolic of a more autonomous, middle- and upper-class existence" (p. 88). Nonetheless, those who live in affluent neighborhoods have little chance to learn about law from experience unless they face a problem that they cannot ignore.

    6. There are popular views of law—popular legal culture—and there is also the legal culture of lawyers, judges, and other members of the legal profession. Those who do research on legal systems and those who try to reform law also have their own viewpoints, attitudes and unexamined assumptions. We can ask how and to what extent these professional views "trickle down" to the lay public? How do these views influence what appears in newspapers, magazines, television news programs and talk shows, as well as entertainment broadcasts and films?

    Professor Marc Galanter tells us about the prevailing paradigm held by legal professionals:

3. *Notes on the Future of Social Research in Law*[18]

☐ Legal scholars and professionals, while accentuating various differences with one another, display a broad agreement about the nature of legal phenomena. I refer not to concurrence in some body of tested propositions, but adherence, usually tacit, to a set of propositions which, taken together, provide a cognitive map or paradigm of legal reality. This paradigm provides a lens through which legal phenomena are perceived and suggests how these perceptions are to be arranged. It is worthy of consideration because it influences our interpretation of

18. Unpublished paper, February 1974.

the world out there and, by suggesting what are worthwhile and important questions and what are suitable answers, it shapes our view of what are worthy scholarly endeavors and educational experiences.

The contents of the received paradigm are familiar and by no means startling. They are not so much affirmed as assumed. Not assumed to be literally true—their inapplicability in particular instances may be conceded—but to partake of a general correctness that is usually thought to require neither explanation nor investigation. They have a composite character, fusing both descriptive and normative . . . .

The common paradigm, if stated in propositional form, would include, *inter alia* something like the following:

1. *Governments* are the primary (if not the exclusive) locus of legal controls; that part of the legal process which is governmental is the determinative source of regulation and order in society.
2. The legal rules and institutions within a society form a *system* in the sense of a naturally cohering set of interrelated parts articulated to one another so that they form a coherent whole, animated by common procedures and purposes.
3. The central and distinctive element of this system is a body of normative learning (consisting, in various versions, of rules, and/or standards, principles, policies) and of procedures for discerning, devising and announcing them.
   3A. Purposiveness: rules are (should be) designed to embody principles or effectuate policies.
4. Legal systems are centered around and typified by *courts,* whose function is to announce, apply, interpret (and sometimes change) rules on the basis of or in accordance with other elements of this normative learning.
   4A. The basic, typical, decisive mode of legal action is *adjudication (i.e.,* the application of rules to particular controversies by courts or court-like institutions in adversarial proceedings).
5. The rules (authoritative normative learning) represent (reflects, expresses, embodies, refines) general (widely-shared, dominant) social preferences (values, norms, interests).
   5A. Broad participation in rule-making by adjudication (and by representative government) insures that the rules embody broad social interests.
6. Normative statements, institutions and officials are arranged in hierarchies, whose members have different levels of authority.
   6A. "Higher" elements direct (design, evaluate) activity; "lower" ones execute activity.
   6B. Higher elements control (guide) lower ones.
7. The behavior of legal actors tends to conform to rules (with some slippage and friction).
   7A. Officials are guided by rules.

    7B. The rules control the behavior of the population.

    7C. Conformity is the result of assent and the (threat of) application of governmental force.

8. If the above obtain, then:

    8A. The authoritative normative learning generated at the higher reaches of the system provides a map for understanding it; and

    8B. The function of legal scholarship is to cultivate that learning by clarification and criticism; and

    8C. Legal scholarship directs itself to remedy imperfections—to bring legal phenomena into conformity with paradigm assumptions . . . .

No one is likely to affirm these propositions, or all of them, quite so baldly. [Indeed, I am not sure they would be explicitly affirmed at all. For present purposes it is sufficient that legal scholars tend to act "as if" they affirmed them.] . . . . If we look at the legal process in America, we find that as descriptive propositions these assertions do not self-evidently fit the reality very well . . . . Within the received paradigm, with its picture of a hierarchy of agencies applying a hierarchy of rules, more or less in accordance with the picture propounded in our higher law, each instance of the gap tends to be dismissed as an exception—something atypical, peripheral and transient. That is, awareness of such discrepancies does not induce professionals (or others) to relinquish their model of the legal system. Rather it spurs them to add *ad hoc* explanations to account for these irregularities.[19] □

19. For a critique of this kind of legal centralism, see Robert C. Ellickson, *Order Without Law* (Cambridge: Harvard University Press, 1991), pp. 138–47.

THE FORMAL LEGAL SYSTEM IN OPERATION

Criminal Processes

4. *"Handling" Family Violence: Situational Determinants of Police Arrest in Domestic Disturbances*

Sarah Fenstermaker Berk

Donileen R. Loseke

15 *Law & Society Review* 317 (1981)

I. INTRODUCTION

☐ Social science has recently discovered what many Americans have known for a long time: the home can be a dangerous place. National Crime Survey results show that spousal assault is more likely to result in an injury, and more likely to require medical attention or hospitalization for its victims, than is assault by a stranger. Estimates that over one fourth of all murders in the United States are intrafamilial conjure up chilling images of American family life.

The "discovery" of violence in the family, particularly between spouses, has drawn significant attention . . . . Police intervention in domestic disputes[20] is a primary focus of these concerns, particularly of researchers concerned with "wife-battery." As front-line agents of social control in domestic disturbances, police are the proximate rep-

---

20. Police normally use a reporting category of "domestic disturbance" when responding to calls involving family members. Bard and Zacker (1974) [The reference is to Morton Bard and Joseph Zacker, "Assaultiveness and Alcohol Use in Family Disputes: Police Perceptions," 12 *Criminology* 281 (1974).] found that, according to police, as many as two-thirds of these calls are "previolent" in nature. That is, police report that they are called before situations escalate to actual physical violence. In another study, Emerson (1979)[The reference is to Charles D. Emerson, "Family Violence: A Study of the Los Angeles County Sheriff's Department," *The Police Chief* 43 (June, 1979).] found that 80 percent of police contacts in domestic situations involved no allegation of physical violence. However, this exclusive use of the term "disturbance" as a reporting category is misleading for the approximately 30 percent of contacts where violence does occur. While the term "disturbance" will be used throughout this discussion, the reader should be aware that it masks a good deal of physical violence in a significant number of incidents.

resentatives of state policy. Many alternative social services have been developed to provide refuge for battered women, and these depend in large part on police cooperation; police must inform family violence victims of the availability of shelters and sometimes escort victims to safety. Thus police practices represent the critical link, both to the prosecution process and to the provision of victim services in a community.

Perhaps the most salient critique of police practices centers on the arrest of offenders in domestic violence incidents. It is often alleged that police decisions to arrest are determined by traditional attitudes which support the right of husbands to physically sanction their wives, coupled with a reluctance to intervene in a "family" matter. As Roy (1977:138)[21] claims, "the family . . . is immune to the benefit of intervention from the law." There is widespread agreement with this view of police arrest practices; what little comparative evidence exists on police arrest rates lends some support to these general indictments.[22] For example, Black (1971)[23] found that police arrest practices vary with the relationship of victim and offender. Eighty-eight percent of *felony* assaults involving strangers resulted in arrest, compared to 77 percent of felony assaults involving friends, and 45 percent involving family members. For *misdemeanor* crimes, however, *higher* rates of arrest were found for offenders related to their victims. The offender's demeanor, and the desire of the victim to have the offender arrested, were the strongest determinants of police arrest practices. When faced with family disturbances, do police engage in other than "normal" arrest practices? Dobash and Dobash (1979:207),[24] for example, conclude that:

> Research relating to the use of discretion among police officers has revealed that officers are very unlikely to make an arrest when the offender has used violence against his wife. In other violent situations, officers typically arrest the attacker *regardless of the characteristics of the victim and offender or the circumstances surrounding the crime* [emphasis in original].

21. [The reference is to Maria Roy, "Some Thoughts Regarding the Criminal Justice System and Wife-Beating," in Maria Roy (ed.), *Battered Women: A Psychosociological Study of Domestic Violence* (New York: Van Nostrand Reinhold, 1977)].

22. Little empirical research is available directly comparing domestic and nondomestic police contacts . . . . More important, perhaps, is that some otherwise useful studies proceed from the assumption that police handling of domestic disturbances is quite different from their handling of other crimes; they fail to make the assumption itself an empirical question.

23. [The reference is to Donald J. Black, "The Social Organization of Arrest," 23 *Stanford Law Review* 1087 (1971).]

24. [The reference is to R. Emerson Dobash and Russell Dobash, *Violence Against Wives: A Case Against Patriarchy*. (New York: The Free Press, 1979).]

The message behind the criticisms of police practice in domestic disturbances is clear: police are not doing their job. Yet it is not entirely clear what that job is or should be. Social science research to date reflects little effort to integrate general understandings of the discretionary role of police with systematic evidence of the actual practices of police in domestic disputes. There appear to be two perspectives on police arrest practices. One addresses police work in general through empirical studies; the other, as yet largely nonempirical, confines itself to police intervention in domestic violence incidents in particular.

The present analysis is an initial attempt to bridge the gap between a general perspective on police discretion and a view of the immediate decisions police make when faced with domestic disturbances. Specifically, with data drawn from 262 domestic disturbance police reports forwarded to the District Attorney's Unit of the Santa Barbara Family Violence Program, we will consider what factors affect the propensity of the police to make an arrest. A variety of exogenous variables speaking to the immediate circumstances under which police must act will be considered.

Before examining the data, we will briefly review some perspectives relevant to an understanding of police decision making in domestic disturbances. Critical considerations of police "law enforcement" activities in incidents of domestic violence will be placed in a broader perspective on police work as the management of "critical situations," where arrest represents only one choice among many options.

II. POLICE DISCRETION AND DOMESTIC DISTURBANCES

Since the police often seem to be arresting everyone *but* family violence offenders, it is understandable that police attitudes toward women in general, and a specific reluctance to cast women as victims within a family setting, would be an initial target for those seeking reform of police practice. A recurring theme in the domestic violence literature is the effect of society's patriarchal attitudes as reproduced in police dealings with offenders and victims in family violence. [There are] historical precedents for the husband's legal right to "control" his wife. While formal laws have changed, . . . police practices [may] mirror traditional prejudices. Martin (1976: 96)[25] observes, "Police officers are usually male; therefore, they identify more readily with the husband than with the female victim."

25. The reference is to Del Martin, *Battered Wives* (San Francisco: Glide Publications, 1976).

It is said that such traditional police attitudes find strong reinforcement in general patterns of official response to family crisis. For example, Roy (1977:138)[26] argues that:

> Underlying the criminal justice system is the covert toleration of wife-beating, indicated in the policy and personal attitudes of police, prosecutors and judges . . . police policy of arrest avoidance, the incredible lengthy response time to calls for help, the "take a walk around the block" recommendations of police, prosecuting attorneys and judges, and the policy to "cool out" the husband and "turn off" the wife all contribute to the perpetuation of violence behind closed doors within the sanctity of the family.

Empirical studies of police intervention in domestic disturbances make it clear that the police may well be reluctant to arrest family violence offenders. The conflict between the individual "call for help" and the larger organizational mandate of police departments, the absence of occupational rewards attached to legal intervention in domestic disturbances, the lack of victim cooperation, and general occupational orientations to domestic disturbance[27] are all cited as reasons why police may view arrest as a low priority or even distasteful course of action, and one worth avoiding.

These indictments of police handling of domestic disturbances, and the empirically derived explanations for why criminal sanctions are not more frequently invoked, portray such disturbances as *unique* situations in which police fail to make arrests when they "should." They convey the image that the police response is *uniquely* subject to the forces of male prejudice, occupational socialization, organizational pressure, and chaotic police-citizen encounters. This view of police practice implies that: (1) the police officer's primary job is to invoke legal sanctions; (2) when arrest does not occur (for whatever reason) in situations of domestic disturbance, a central police mandate has been violated; and (3) such violations of expectations are especially frequent in domestic disturbance interventions, representing a systematic bias in the application of police power and prerogative.

In stark contrast to this view, studies of the general role of police in society have amply demonstrated that most of what police do on the job can only remotely be viewed as "law enforcement." Even minimal

---

26. [The reference is to Maria Roy, "Some Thoughts Regarding the Criminal Justice System and Wife-Beating," in Maria Roy (ed.), *Battered Women: A Psychosociological Study of Domestic Violence* (New York: Van Nostrand Reinhold, 1977).]

27. Traditional police folklore, however, does portray the domestic disturbance as one of the most dangerous policing situations. Some departments have a policy of pro forma back-up units for domestic calls. Recent research finds no evidence for assuming that police face particular peril on domestic disturbance calls.

familiarity with the day-to-day work of police demands a rejection of the notion that police primarily react to crime, apprehend and arrest criminals, and lead them to jail.

Few of those knowledgeable about police work argue that arrest is more than a rare occurrence. While the possibility for the "good pinch" has a great deal of symbolic value in a work life characterized by dull, repetitive tasks, police-citizen encounters which result in arrest are few and far between.[28] In short, to conceptualize police work as primarily "law enforcement" is to ignore the essential features of a police officer's work environment and to misapprehend the nature of police discretion on the job.

Wilson's (1968)[29] study of police officers was one of the first to demonstrate that the law both supplies an available resource to police and lays a constraint on their activities. The law may be invoked by a police officer in the course of his/her duties, but—perhaps more important—it also constrains the officer by proscribing choices that are not available to "maintain order." Moreover, Goldstein (1977)[30] argues that it is impossible to understand the work of police without stepping outside the framework of the law. He argues that the bulk of police work takes place prior to invocation of legal sanction, makes use of the law for purposes other than legal sanction, or occurs entirely outside the legal framework.

28. It is not necessary to burden the text with documentation of this observation about police work. Yet, for those readers unfamiliar with the literature on policing, some past studies are worth noting. Bittner (1974) [The reference is to Egon Bittner, "Florence Nightingale in Pursuit of Willie Sutton: A Theory of the Police," in Herbert Jacob (ed.), *The Potential for Reform of Criminal Justice* (Beverly Hills: Sage Publications, 1974).] estimates that, depending upon characteristics of the patrol area, the average officer can expect to make approximately 26 arrests per year, with five arrests for serious (e.g., felony) crimes. Likewise, Black (1971) [The reference is to Donald J. Black, "The Social Organization of Arrest," 23 *Stanford Law Review* 1087 (1971)] found that for over 5,000 police-citizen contacts, fewer than two percent resulted in arrest. Finally, Wilson (1968)[The reference is to James Q. Wilson, *Varieties of Police Behavior: The Management of Law and Order in Eight Communities*. (Cambridge: Harvard University Press, 1968)] estimates that fewer than one third of police contacts with the citizenry involve matters which are even remotely criminal in nature; Goldstein (1977) [The reference is to Herman Goldstein, *Policing a Free Society*. (Cambridge: Ballinger, 1977).] argues that perhaps fewer than one in ten police contacts involve law breaking.

29. [The reference is to James Q. Wilson, *Varieties of Police Behavior: The Management of Law and Order in Eight Communities*. (Cambridge: Harvard University Press, 1968).]

30. [The reference is to Herman Goldstein, *Policing a Free Society*. (Cambridge: Ballinger, 1977).]

Bittner (1967a;[31] 1967b;[32] 1970;[33] 1974)[34] provides the most instructive commentary on the discretionary nature of police work. He argues that policing in general, and the decision to arrest and charge in particular, represents only one decision point for the officer who must "handle the situation." (Wilson, 1968: 31).[35] Given the wide array of tasks in which police engage, officers must interpret each situation in light of their own orientations and prejudices and their understandings of the occupational constraints under which they work, as well as choose the most suitable method for coping with policing situations. As only one method for managing encounters with citizens, arrest may or may not be selected by the officer as the best means to solve the problem at hand. Thus, Bittner (1974: 27) speaks directly to confusions over police decision making:

> I am not aware of any descriptions of police work on the streets that support the view that patrolmen walk around, respond to service demands, or intervene in situations, with the provisions of the penal code in mind, matching what they see with some title or another, and deciding whether any particular apparent infraction is serious enough to warrant being referred for further process .... In the typical case the formal charge *justifies* the arrest a patrolman makes but is *not* the *reason* for it. The actual reason is located in the domain of considerations ... as the need to "handle the situation," and invoking the law is merely a device whereby this is sometimes accomplished [emphasis in original].

The many activities of the police are not well described simply as "law enforcement." Rather, says Bittner (1970: 39) the police have a unique mandate to distribute "situationally justified force." This differentiates the police from all other governmental or private agents who might be called upon to manage similarly conflictual situations.

If arrest is merely one of several police options to "handle the situation," the observed reluctance of the police to arrest domestic violence offenders should not be surprising. Yet, the particular features of

31. [The reference is to Egon Bittner, "The Police on Skid-Row: A Study of Peace Keeping," 32 *American Sociological Review* 699 (1967).]

32. [The reference is to Egon Bittner, "Police Discretion in Emergency Apprehension of Mentally Ill Persons," 14 *Social Problems* 278 (1967).]

33. [The reference is to Egon Bittner, *The Functions of the Police in Modern Society*, (Maryland: National Institutes of Mental Health, (1970).]

34. [The reference is to Egon Bittner, "Florence Nightingale in Pursuit of Willie Sutton: A Theory of the Police," in Herbert Jacob (ed.), *The Potential for Reform of Criminal Justice*. (Beverly Hills: Sage Publications, (1974).]

35. [The reference is to James Q. Wilson, *Varieties of Police Behavior: The Management of Law and Order in Eight Communities*. (Cambridge: Harvard University Press, 1968).]

domestic disturbances demand empirical investigation. Those concerned with more than speculation about the determinants of police arrest in domestic disturbances are directed to the site where such "remedies" are played out . . . . Our analysis will emphasize the immediate characteristics of domestic disturbances salient to police, and therefore most likely to shape their arrest decisions.

III. THE DATA

In the fall of 1978, the Law Enforcement Assistance Administration (LEAA) provided funding to the Santa Barbara County Family Violence Program (FVP) to improve public response to domestic violence incidents. While all forms of family violence were to be addressed, the FVP became involved primarily with incidents in which both offender and victim were adults. Together with Santa Barbara County funding, the LEAA funds were used to establish several FVP service components. Program components included: (a) public information, (b) training and education for police and community social service personnel, (c) mandatory counseling for offenders diverted from the prosecutory process, (d) counseling for victims and offenders on a voluntary basis, (e) two shelters for battered women and their children which offered emergency housing and telephone crisis counseling, and (f) a special unit under the auspices of the District Attorney's office with responsibility for review of domestic disturbance incidents and subsequent decisions to prosecute.

The sample of domestic disturbance incidents used in this analysis is drawn from data provided through the special unit of the District Attorney's office of Santa Barbara County. County-wide law enforcement personnel were to submit copies of all reports of domestic disturbance contacts to a Deputy District Attorney (DDA) in charge of the special unit. While the DDA was responsible for review of all incidents and decisions to prosecute, additional activities were undertaken by the unit. These included telephoning victims to ask if they were interested in program services (e.g., counseling, shelters), notifying offenders and victims by mail that services could be provided for them (e.g., voluntary counseling), or that their actions had come to the attention of the District Attorney's Office. Finally, an "offender index" was constructed to keep track of incidents which, though minor, were frequent enough that they might eventually lead to a decision to prosecute.

The total number of incident reports reaching the DA's office (May 1, 1978 through June, 1979) was 730. This number includes all cases submitted to the DA's FVP unit, regardless of the action taken on them. Some were investigated for possible prosecution; some were used for the "offender index" or mail contact; and others received no formal action. While each report submitted to the unit represented some domestic disturbance contact by the police, a subset of these incidents was chosen for the present analysis. The great variation in the amount of information provided through police reports, as well as the variation in specificity of police categorization of "domestic" and "disturbance" required that difficult methodological decisions be made about the sample of incidents to be examined and the treatment of police incident reports. A brief discussion of these issues is presented in the next section of the paper.

IV. REFINING THE SAMPLE

Police Reports: Sampling and Coding Strategies

A large number of the 730 domestic disturbance police contacts was not suitable for this analysis. The total number includes police reports ranging from rather lengthy "arrest" reports, to more modest "incident" reports, to very brief "field cards."

Information on field cards is limited to five lines for the officer to write especially pertinent information about the incident, as well as the name, race, sex, and age of involved parties. Typically, field cards are filled out by police to record minimal contact with citizenry, and serve primarily as an account for the time police spend on duty. Often the only descriptive remark on the cards is that "all was quiet" when police arrived.

Incident reports (sometimes called offense reports or case sheets) represent more lengthy police contact and contain much more information about the incident. Finally, documentation on arrest reports is usually quite extensive, and includes the most complete history of events reconstructed by police on the scene. Thus, the degree to which each type of report offered codable information varied, with the field cards providing very little usable documentation of incident characteristics.[36]

---

36. Police decisions regarding the type of report chosen to document an incident pose many empirical questions worth investigating. To date, few researchers have explored such issues. One exception is the work of Pepinsky (1976) [The reference is to Harold E. Pepinsky, "Police Patrolmen's Offense-Reporting Behavior," 13 *Journal of Research in Crime and Delinquency* 33 (1976)], which examined police reporting in all types of encounters. Most interesting for our purposes, however, are his findings concerning the critical role played by dispatchers in determining police decisions to report offenses. Arguing that, to a large extent, officers meet the expectations implied in the terms given them by dispatchers, Pepinsky (1976: 35) found that:

> To a remarkable extent, the patrolmen's decisions as to whether to report offenses were determined by the terms of the calls they had received from the dispatcher . . . In the vast majority of cases in which the dispatcher named an offense in the call the patrolmen reported offenses.

While we are currently undertaking a study of dispatchers in Santa Barbara County, for now we must be satisfied with a partial understanding of the context in which police decisions are made during the domestic disturbance.

For the present analysis, it was decided that only reports which had sufficiently detailed information to convey a picture of the immediate characteristics of the incident confronting police would be analyzed. The sample was refined to include only incident or arrest reports; police-citizen contacts documented through field cards simply had too much missing data to warrant serious consideration. With this exclusion, the number of cases analyzed dropped to 405.

It is clear that this methodological decision carries important substantive implications for the external validity of our findings. By examining only reports with more detailed documentation, we necessarily analyze only those domestic disturbance incidents which are deemed serious enough *by the police* to warrant more thorough attention, and a nontrivial amount of police time. By excluding the field cards we have effectively limited our sample to only those police-citizen contacts in which the possibility of arrest is likely to be real. Indeed, the very existence of an incident or arrest report indicates that police interpreted the situation as requiring greater police time, more detailed documentation, and as one in which a crime may have been committed. In short, we have consciously traded higher *internal* validity for lower external validity. The data that will be used are characterized by promising information about the arrest decision. Thus, internal validity is not jeopardized as long as one understands that any findings are *conditional* upon the earlier police decision to complete an incident or arrest report, and cannot be generalized to all "domestic disturbance" calls.

Operationalizing the Term "Domestic"

. . . For the present study, we classified as "domestic" only those incidents where the principals were adults involved in a heterosexual "romantic," or conjugal relationship prior to, or at the time of, the incident. We employed two criteria for selection in this dimension: (a) legal relationship (e.g., married, separated, divorced), and (b) relationship which constituted sharing of a residence (e.g., common-law marriage, past or present "live-in" relationships). This definition allows for considerably more conceptual clarity in analyzing police response to domestic disturbance; and it is also parsimonious. Moreover, our decision is fully consistent with much of the literature cited earlier which argues that there is something "special" about the ways in which police respond to violence between a man and a woman who live in such "domestic" situations. By excluding incidents involving parents and children, siblings, same sex adults, and the like, we are focusing on just those police-citizen encounters that are deemed especially problematic. This strategy resulted in a further reduction of our sample to 270 cases.

Operationalizing the Term "Disturbance"

There are divergent perceptions as to what constitutes a disturbance, when disturbances should be termed "violence," and when violence is severe enough to warrant research concern. Operational definitions of "disturbance" or "violence" have often depended upon the alleged severity of the conflict. But such definitions have generated quite different estimates of the extent of family violence in America, and they have not escaped criticism. Commenting on the "objective" measurement of violent acts, Walker (1978: 160)[37] argues:

> It is too narrow to permit real understanding of the problem. Including psychological abuse in the definition is indeed messy. But in my research with battered women, they insist that it is as powerful as physical force in perpetuating the reign of terror under which they live.

In this study we tried to avoid imposing external definitions of violence on data coded from police reports. Instead, we relied on police reports themselves for definitions of "disturbances"; we followed the lead of the police officer interpreting the events and included in the definition not only physical violence and the threat of violence, but also property damage and verbal arguments. Sometimes a police report noted offenses such as "drunk and disorderly behavior," "disturbing the peace," or "trespassing." Where such offenses were linked to an initial domestic problem, they were included. By contrast, incidents centering on such things as missing persons, immigration, or suicide attempts were dropped from consideration if there were no mention of any connection to a domestic problem.

In eight of the incidents, only a female was arrested. The details of these cases suggested quite strongly that police officers were confronted with an unusual series of events, and thus one might imagine that their handling of the cases was atypical. These eight cases were excluded, leaving a final sample of 262 police reports. Figure 1 depicts the process and results of our data refinement efforts.

V. A Methodological Note on Police Reports

Our data are limited to information about domestic disturbance incidents contained in police reports. This required us to make certain assumptions about the nature and quality of such reports. Since these assumptions are critical to the analysis, it is best to describe them more fully.

37. [The reference is to Lenore J. Walker, Testimony of Lenore Walker, in the U. S. Commission on Civil Rights, Battered Women. Issues in Public Policy. Washington, D. C.: U.S. Government Printing Office (1978).]

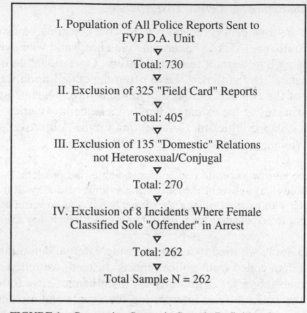

FIGURE 1   Successive Stages in Sample Definition for
Domestic Disturbance Police Incident Reports

For almost twenty years, researchers who have employed "official" statistics and reports as sources of data have understood that such data are often not what they appear to be. Official police reports may be an imperfect reflection of police behavior, just as official crime statistics may have less to do with crime and more to do with the vagaries of bureaucratic infighting, record keeping, and political survival. It has been argued that there is often little epistemic relation between "real" life and "officially reported" life.

What is the relationship between what the police actually do and what they report? First, one might argue that police reports accurately reflect not only the "actual" characteristics of the policing situation, but also all the characteristics about it that are worth noting. That is, if one were to discuss a domestic disturbance with the police and involved parties, the incident characteristics reported by police would be reliably substantiated. It is probably safe to dismiss this argument, since it makes no allowance for (a) the necessary loss of information posed by reporting of any kind, or (b) the inevitable differences of perspective among the parties.

Second, there is the argument that the occupational setting in which police must operate and their socialization to the job promote the writing of reports to justify actions already taken. We could assume, for example, that police incident reports on domestic encounters focus primarily on characteristics of the situation that would "fit" the decision made by the police. Whether reported incident characteristics would square with the "actual" situation is beside the point. With this argument, the relationship between police reports and police decisions changes. The underlying causal model, roughly put, would be that of police decisions "causing" police reports. Indeed, under this logic, a more reasonable model specification would be to reverse the independent and dependent variables such that one would investigate the determinants not of police actions, but of police reporting. Police decisions (e.g., arrest) would become exogenous predictors of reported incident characteristics.

To our knowledge, there has been no rigorous investigation of the relationship between policing and police reporting. No study compares *observed* police behavior at the scene with police reportage about events after the fact. For example, there is no analysis from which we might learn that "X percent of the time," police will fail to record that the offender is intoxicated, if an *a priori* decision has been made to avoid arrest. The difficulties of carrying out such an investigation are obvious. However, less systematic, but certainly rich, descriptions of police life do suggest that police are subject to the temptation to distort or falsify reports to cover previous action. John Van Maanen's description of police socialization practices emphasizes the depth of personal loyalty among officers and the acceptance of a "cover your ass" perspective. But the distortion or falsification of some reports does not mean that such practices are frequent or that police reports typically make little reference to "actual" incident characteristics.[38] What is clear is that under certain circumstances (e.g., when the possibility of sanction for police action exists) reporting may turn from routine interpretation to the reconstruction of events to cover questionable action. This possibility counsels caution in the use of police reports.

Our prior discussion of police decision making as a function of the situated qualities of each policing encounter suggests a third perspective on the relationship between police reports and police decisions. Our conceptualization of policing as the "handling" of situations implies that police reports will reflect critical features of a domestic disturbance intervention as perceived by the reporting officer. The situational exigencies of policing require the police to interpret events, take action appropriate to those interpretations, and then file reports which correspond to those actions. Even allowing for some puffery in reporting, it is likely—and we assume—that police reports reflect real and significant features of each encounter as interpreted by officers. These features are

38. On simply pragmatic grounds, frequent distortion or falsification of records is probably inadvisable. First, it probably takes considerably more time to do an adequate job of "covering" through the report than it does to simply fill out the report by making reference to events witnessed and reported. Second, police are not wholly unaccountable for either their actions or their version of events which justify their actions. For example, in the courtroom, witnesses (whether "outsiders" or involved parties) are routinely asked for their accounts of "what happened."

the salient "signs" of the encounter, since they serve to direct the police toward a decision, and ultimately justify that decision.

VI. Incident Characteristics as Predictors of Arrest

A wide variety of notations were made by police on domestic disturbance incident and arrest reports. These notations identified the critical dimensions of police decision making and formed the basis for an *a priori* specification of the model.[39] Table 1 displays the means for all the variables relevant to the analysis.[40]

The dependent variable of "arrest" included arrests made at the scene and those made soon afterward at some other location. The mean of .39 for the "arrest" variable indicates that arrests are made 39 percent of the time for the incidents in our sample. However, since poorly documented contacts and cases where either the female or both principals were arrested were dropped from the sample, the mean should not be interpreted as an arrest percentage for *all* police contacts with domestic disturbance.[41] California police have a number of arrest options. First, the officer may arrest an individual if there is probable cause to believe that a felony has been committed. However, conflicting accounts, and the physical evidence necessary to justify such a decision, make this a difficult option for the police to exercise. Second, while at the scene, officers may witness the commission of a wholly separate misdemeanor or felony which can be used to justify arrest and removal of the offender. In our sample, such charges included "drunk and disorderly conduct" (if in a public place), "assaulting an officer," "trespassing," and "destroying telephone company property" (i.e., ripping the phone from the wall). Finally, police may encourage a witness (usually the

39. If information were not included on the reports, we did not "guess." For example, if a male and female with identical last names were noted as involved in a disturbance, but were not listed as married, we did not assume they were. We only coded what was actually on the reports, since our interest is in those incident characteristics which police deem important enough to consciously document. Moreover, police were not instructed as to what they should write in their reports. Other research on this topic has either used special forms to document domestic disturbance, and/or has involved training officers in what to look for and note. This strategy may generate much more information, but hardly results in a reflection of what police "normally" do in the immediate context of domestic disturbance calls.

40. A number of variables were dropped from the analysis, either because they were redundant, or because there was insufficient variance to warrant further examination. In addition, the exogenous variables represent the "lowest common denominator" of police reporting. There was considerable variation in the specificity with which police officers reported important features of domestic disturbances. For example, some officers went to great lengths to describe the details of the physical environment, the claims made by principals, and their own impressions of the situation. Others provided only the "bare facts" of the incident. As a result, we found that our coding had to comply with the average report, which was typically rather brief.

41. For the full sample of all disturbance contacts (N = 730), arrest occurred in almost 14 percent of the cases.

TABLE 1   MEANS FOR SELECTED DOMESTIC DISTURBANCE INCIDENT
CHARACTERISTICS; N = 262

Variable	Mean
Arrest (dummy)	.385
Principals Married (dummy)	.477
Male White (dummy)	.454
Female Calls Police (dummy)	626
Incident on Saturday or Sunday (dummy)	.427
Both Principals Present (dummy)	.492
Female Only Alleges Violence (dummy)	.592
Male Drinking (dummy)	.179
Property Damage (dummy)	.149
Injuries (dummy)	.442
Citizen's Arrest Signed or Promised (3 ordinal levels: −1, 0, +1)	.156
Both Principals Present X Property Damage (dummy)	.050
Both Principals Present X Injuries (dummy)	.252
Both Principals Present X Male Drinking (dummy)	.118
Both Principals Present X Female Only Alleges Violence (dummy)	.305

female victim) to sign a citizen's arrest warrant. Regardless of the charge, this is a common basis of police arrest in domestic disturbance. Where a complaint is signed, police need not establish probable cause or witness the assault. Police are required to "transport" the offender from the scene, with the complainant being legally responsible for the actual arrest. From police incident reports, it was not possible to estimate the frequency of each "type" of arrest. The arrest variable thus reflects different kinds of arrest decisions.

Table 1 also reports the means for all variables employed in this analysis, including four interaction terms and their components. Discussion here, however, will center only on those variables which were actually used in the multivariate models predicting police arrest.

Two of the independent predictors listed in Table 1 represent, respectively, characteristics of the principals presumed important to police decision making, and the circumstances surrounding police intervention. First, in almost 48 percent of the incidents, principals were married (as opposed to divorced, separated, or "living together"). This dummy variable was included in the analysis to address the empirical question of whether police decision making varies by the legal relationship between principals. A number of studies have speculated that police are less likely to arrest husbands engaged in spousal violence; police, it is presumed, see marriage as legitimating the authority of husbands to "control" their wives.

Second, the dummy variable for the race of the male is categorized as "male white," and its effects can be distinguished from the dropped residual categories of Mexican (27 percent), black (16 percent), and "other" (12 percent). The vast majority of the disturbances occurred between principals of the same race; consequently, a race variable for the female was dropped from the analysis to avoid collinearity. *A priori*, we suspected that the probability of arrest would be reduced if the male were white. That is, police might be inclined to choose less drastic intervention strategies for white males, and be less inclined to treat nonwhite offenders leniently.

The next three variables, "female calls police," "incident on Saturday or Sunday," and "injuries," describe characteristics of the incident itself, rather than attributes of principals. In 63 percent of the incidents, the female principal called the police. In most of the other instances, neighbors made the initial police contact. In only a few instances did other family members (e.g., male, children) call the police. Occasionally, other social service agents (e.g., shelter personnel) alerted police to the disturbance. We speculated that if the woman involved in a domestic disturbance (i.e., the likely victim) were *able* to call the police, and the disturbance had consequently not reached the attention of "outsiders" (e.g., neighbors), this might lead police away from resolving the situation through arrest. Thus, this variable might, at least in part, be a surrogate for both severity of conflict and the degree to which the disturbance is a "private" trouble—two dimensions of the situation which may be critical to police decision making.

Forty-three percent of the domestic disturbance calls were received on weekends. A dummy variable ("incident on Saturday or Sunday") was included to distinguish the effect of this time period from all others in the week. In part, the inclusion of this variable speaks to anecdotal data received from police themselves. Their comments suggest that outcomes may be somewhat different when demands on police time are great.[42] Decisions to initiate the lengthy process of arrest may be less likely when, as on weekends, there are multiple competing demands for police intervention.

Forty-four percent of the incidents were accompanied by police notation of injuries to one or both parties, and the fifth variable included captures these effects. Inclusion of this dummy variable speaks directly to the police option of arrest for the felony of spouse abuse. Recall that in this situation, police are not dependent on victim cooperation to make an arrest, yet they do face the difficult task of collecting enough physical evidence to justify their decision. Thus, we assumed that arrest might be more likely if police were confronted with physical evidence that an assault had occurred.[43] In the coding of reports, we found that

---

42. As one officer told us: "A lot of times the dispatcher will give you more than one call . . . they will give you three at a time. You got to make them short and sweet."

43. LaFave (1965:121) [The reference is to Wayne R. LaFave, *Arrest. The Decision to Take a Suspect Into Custody* (New York: Little, Brown & Co., 1965)] quotes a Detroit Police Manual: In any case where an officer suspects that a disturbance may result in the injury of any person, it is advisable for the officer to take the person causing the disturbance into custody, at least temporarily, even though it may be against the wishes of the family involved.

police were more likely to note those injuries they could see, as opposed to those that were merely claimed by disputants.

The sixth variable is an ordinal level measure for whether police mentioned that a citizen's arrest warrant was signed (or signature promised the next day). In almost 16 percent of the incidents, the female signed an arrest warrant. Of course, police may have a good deal to do with how this option is presented to the victim, or whether it is presented at all. For example, impressionistic data suggest that if officers are eager to make an arrest, but have little evidence to justify such a choice, they may spend considerable time urging the female to sign a warrant. This can often be a lengthy battle of wills, since the warrant also exacts a promise that the complainant will cooperate with prosecution of the offender. This is a promise that many women are understandably reluctant to make. On the other hand, if police see no purpose served by arrest, they may either fail to mention the option of citizen's arrest, or spend time discouraging the woman from this course of action.[44] Nevertheless, once a warrant is signed, police will seek arrest of the offender.

The construction of this variable was intended to reflect the degree to which the citizen's arrest warrant is salient to police decision making. The ordinal variable ranges from −1 (woman flatly refuses to sign) to +1 (woman signs or promises to sign form). The "zero" level for this variable indicates that police made no notation of the procedure.

The four remaining variables in the equation are all interaction terms, with four characteristics of the incident placed in interaction with the variable "both principals present." The justification for these variables follows directly from the perspective emphasizing the discretionary judgments of police and the situated determinants of their decisions. If one assumes that police are faced with situations they must "handle," and if the offender has fled the scene (41 percent of the incidents), then the immediate situation has perhaps "handled" itself. In other words, the *immediate* circumstances of disturbance which may have required "nonnegotiably coercive" solutions have largely disappeared. In contrast, if both parties to the conflict are present when police arrive, the police must weigh alternatives and seek resolutions in a context of *ongoing* confrontation and potential for escalation. Thus,

---

44. The dependence upon the citizen's arrest warrant in domestic disturbance has been identified as a significant problem for arrest and prosecution rates. While this characteristic of domestic disturbance has been identified as unique,LaFave(1969: 198) [The reference is to Wayne R. LaFave, "Noninvocation of the Criminal Law by Police," in Donald R. Cressey and David A. Ward (eds.), *Delinquency, Crime and Social Process* (New York: Harper and Row, 1969)] argues otherwise:

> Police nonenforcement is also the rule when the victim of a minor offense does not wish to expend his own time in the interests of successful prosecution. This occurs not only with minor property crimes, when the victim is concerned primarily with restitution, but also with many other offenses arising out of family relationships or other associations, such as that between landlord and tenant or employer and employee.

we anticipated that it is under the "condition" of the presence of both principals that the effects of other incident characteristics would be of special importance in police arrest decisions.

The four characteristics of the immediate situation all center on the critical "signs" which police may use to justify both their interpretations of the situation and their resolution of it. First, our *a priori* expectation for the effect of "property damage" when both principals are present, was an increased likelihood of arrest. Evidence of property damage, particularly when the "offender" is present, might be an important cue to the officer that without arrest, the conflict might well resume. However, this variable has very little variance, with only five percent of the incidents described by this combined characteristic.

Second, an interaction term was included to combine the effects of the presence of both principals with injury to at least one of them. Twenty-five percent of the incidents are so characterized. Police notation of injury is the only variable which is included in the model for its main effects and for its interaction with the presence of both principals. We anticipated that different processes were involved depending upon whether injuries served as physical evidence for arrest under a charge of felony spouse abuse (main effect), or served as a salient clue to the certainty of past violence and the probability of later conflict were an arrest not made (interaction term). No other variable coded from police report forms can so obviously serve this dual role of providing physical evidence necessary for felony spouse abuse arrest,[45] as well as convey a high probability of further conflict between principals on the scene. Yet, in either form, the expectation was that injuries would heighten the probability of arrest.

In 12 percent of the incidents, both principals were present when police intervened, and police noted drinking by the male. The complementary categories of drinking by the female (3 percent), or drinking by both (2 percent) were dropped. "Drinking" can range from notations that the male "had been drinking" to notations that the male was "highly intoxicated." Since it is not illegal to be intoxicated in one's own home, we reasoned that police use this information to assess the efficacy of various remedies in light of likely future action by the offender. Moreover, since citizen demeanor is critical to police attitude and action, alcohol use by the male may well lead to "arrestable" offenses (e.g., "resisting an officer") unrelated to the domestic disturbance itself. Given such possibilities, we expected male drinking to increase the probability of arrest.

The final interaction term describes 30 percent of the incidents where both principals are present at the point of intervention and the female alleges that violence occurred. The complementary categories

45. All other variables depend on allegations by principals which are difficult to substantiate (e.g., "female only alleges violence"), or center on actions by principals which are perfectly legal in one's own home (e.g., "property damage," "male drinking").

where neither party alleges violence (61 percent), and the less frequent occurrences where both parties (8 percent) or only the male allege violence (1 percent) were dropped. Given that police are confronting what may be an ongoing situation, this variable was expected to accompany an increased likelihood of arrest. The allegation of violence solely by the female may provide police with a clear identification of an "offender" and may suggest a situation best resolved through arrest.

VII. Findings

. . . The independent variable exerting the strongest effect on arrest decisions is the ordinal variable "citizen's arrest." The probability of arrest increases by 30 percent in the change from refusal of the female victim to sign a warrant to no mention of the warrant by police; it increases another 30 percent from "no mention" to "signs" or "promises to sign." Impressionistic data suggest that if police see the citizen's arrest warrant as the best solution to handling the situation and the woman refuses to sign, arrest on any grounds is highly unlikely. For example, as one officer said: "If she's been putting up with it, I say sign it [citizen's arrest warrant], or forget it."

Two of the four interaction terms prove significant to police arrest decisions, and evidence far stronger effects than preliminary models run with main effects only. When both principals remain at the scene, the effects of alcohol use by the male, or an allegation of violence by the female, significantly increase the probability of arrest. Alcohol use or the male's intoxication are strong cues for an arrest disposition. Not only does intoxication suggest the continued volatility of the situation, and thus no immediate solution to the disturbance, but it may also lead to a more convenient arrest charge (e.g., resisting or assaulting an officer) as an alternative to a charge of spouse abuse.

The second of the four interaction terms that exerted significant effects was the combination of the presence of both principals and an allegation of violence by the female. Under this condition, police arrests increased by over 30 percent. The presence of two disputants who may be classified as "victim" and "offender" may provide the impetus for police to dismiss remedies other than arrest. The remaining two interaction terms ("both principals present X property damage"; "both principals present X injuries") showed nonsignificant effects on arrest. The regression coefficients are also very small, especially given the large causal effects just discussed.

The failure of the interaction variable for injuries is all the more disappointing given the null finding for the main effect of injuries. However, the t-value of 1.30 and the regression coefficient of over .08 suggest that perhaps "something" is going on. Indeed, we suspect that with a more sensitive measure reflecting the severity of injuries, important effects might well surface.

There is one negative effect that is significant. If the female alerts police to the disturbance, the probability of arrest decreases by almost 21 percent. We expected that this variable might indicate to the police that the conflict was not severe, or that the disturbance was confined to the principals themselves. If the most likely victim of domestic dispute calls the police, the disturbance has clearly not reached the point where she is physically incapable of calling for police intervention. Further, it may mean that the disturbance has not reached the point where neighbors, friends, or social service agents are alerted. If we assume that the decision to arrest is in part determined by police assessments of the severity of conflict, this finding makes some sense. One might speculate also that police response to domestic disturbances is affected by whether or not an "outsider" assumes a role in the dispute (e.g., makes a complaint, witnesses the disturbance, etc.). Once the disturbance has escalated beyond the immediate household, the police response may be correspondingly more severe. Arresting an offender, for example, not only limits the immediate conflict, but avoids further complaints from "outsiders."

The remaining three independent variables did not prove statistically significant in either equation. The race of the male, and whether or not the incident occurred on a weekend, produced only trivial effects. This suggests that the immediate characteristics of the situation, rather than ascribed characteristics of the disputants (e.g., race), or factors external to the disturbance (e.g., demands on police time) are most critical to police decision making.

Marital status was also not a significant predictor of arrest. Recall, others (e.g., Dobash and Dobash, 1979[46]; Martin, 1976[47]) have argued that police are reluctant to subject husbands to the sanction of arrest. However, it is important to stress that we are not comparing police arrest practices in situations unrelated to domestic violence (e.g., stranger assault, conflict between acquaintances, etc.) to incidents of domestic violence; nor have we included cases where the probability of arrest is very low. Consequently, the null findings may not be that surprising, and even a positive relationship may have a reasonable explanation. Since married individuals have an ongoing relationship, the police may anticipate more disturbance calls in the immediate future. An arrest may then be a particularly effective way to terminate immediate conflict. Regardless, this finding certainly argues for more systematic attention to the role of marital status in police response to domestic disturbance.

Taken together, the findings suggest that domestic disturbance incident characteristics which prove most critical to explaining police

46. [The reference is to R. Emerson Dobash and Russell Dobash *Violence Against Wives: A Case Against Patriarchy.* (New York: The Free Press, 1979).]

47. [The reference is to Del Martin, *Battered Wives* (San Francisco: Glide Publications, 1976).]

arrest center on the police encounter itself. The circumstances under which police intervention is sought, the assessments by police which arise from direct encounters with disputants, and the role of citizen's arrest procedures all converge on the situated quality of arrest decisions in domestic disturbances.

VIII. Discussion and Conclusions

In this analysis, police decisions to arrest in domestic disturbances were taken as problematic, with arrest conceptualized *a priori,* as only one resource available to police to "handle" the situation. Through a multivariate analysis of 262 police reports, recorded incident characteristics were examined for their impact on variation in police decisions to arrest. Four variables which derived from immediate characteristics of the incident proved significant to arrest decisions. Significant positive influence was exerted by whether the female victim signed a citizen's arrest warrant (+.30). When both principals were present at the point of police intervention, the female's allegation of violence (+.32), and drinking by the male (+.20) also increased the likelihood of arrest. The probability of arrest decreased (−.21), however, when the female made the initial call for help to the police.

The results presented here suggest a model of police decision making rife with situationally determined contingencies. Police assessment of the situation, and later justifications for their actions, depend in part upon the ways in which the actors themselves set the stage for police management or "handling" of the situation. Our results indicate that when police arrive at the scene of a domestic disturbance, they have to construct a "story" of what has happened from the immediate characteristics of the encounter. The officer's interpretation of salient "signs" in the context of the immediate situation leads to the construction of a "theory" of events, and prediction of the likely results of potential choices. The evidence suggests that police management of domestic disturbances and components critical to decision making do not necessarily center on the collection of evidence for "proof" that laws have been violated.

While police decision making may depend largely on situation-specific interpretations, police do not approach domestic disturbances (or any other policing task) without predilections. The discretionary options open to police to "handle the situation" require knowledge of past decisions and their outcomes, as well as normative notions as guides to actions. Yet, police management of domestic disturbance is not *wholly* determined by legal considerations, by an officer's personal or occupational prejudices, or by some unchecked free association with the events of the encounter.

An officer's interpretation of events, and the ways in which these interpretations are assessed and ultimately acted upon, constitute a far more complex process than prior research and speculation on police response to domestic violence would suggest. A close reading of the domestic violence literature and its critique of police practices conveys a false and misleading dichotomy: police arrest, or they do not arrest. This narrow understanding of actual police practice directs our attention to the possibility of police abuse of power, but directs attention away from the potentially problematic nature of the routine exercise of police discretion.

Given the limited options that police have in the handling of domestic disturbances, they obviously can and sometimes do abuse their powers. However, the more essential point, supported by our analysis, is that police interpretations of the situation, their prior experience, and the situation-specific rationales for decisions are all inherent in the policing enterprise. They do not constitute an *abuse* of discretionary powers; they are part of the *normal* exercise of duty.

The very real plight of battered women has led many observers to plead for a more liberal use of the arrest option. Swift and sure arrest may deter future violence by the offender, as well as convey societal-level disapproval of violence in the home. It may be that violent family conflicts demand unique treatment by police. Yet, can police be "re-educated" to handle such situations differently? The question must remain largely unanswered in light of our inadequate understanding of the link between police attitudes toward family violence, women as victims, and the situational exigencies posed by domestic disturbances. Recent research by the authors (Berk et al., 1979[48]; 1980[49]) suggests that educating the police about management of domestic disturbances can yield significant changes in police practice. We have found that police do respond to encouragement to enhance both the quality and the frequency of their reporting on domestic disturbances. These findings suggest that more ambitious goals in police training might result in changes in actual police practice. For example, training programs explicitly directed to the reading of situational "cues" could be developed.

Yet, an argument for changes either in police training or in police arrest practices is meaningless without commensurate attention to the larger criminal justice system in which police operate. First, whatever positive effects found as a result of past educational programs directed toward improving police practice depended primarily on the direct support and encouragement of the District Attorney's Office and police administrators. Unless police officers are made to understand that changes in practice (a) are expected of them as employees, and (b) will

48. [The reference is to Richard A. Berk, Sarah Fenstermaker Berk, and Donileen R. Loseke, *A Preliminary Evaluation of the Santa Barbara Family Violence Program*, Unpublished, University of California at Santa Barbara (1979).]

49. [The reference is to Richard A. Berk, Donileen R. Loseke, Sarah Fenstermaker Berk, and David Rauma "Bringing the Cops Back In: A Study of Efforts to Make the Criminal Justice System More Responsive to Incidents of Family Violence," 9 *Social Science Research* 193 (1980).] [Eds. note].

be accompanied by corresponding changes in other areas of the criminal justice system, little change will result. Second, arguments that police "should" frequently arrest family violence offenders come perilously close to encouraging greater jeopardy for victims unless accompanied by recommendations for massive changes in prosecutorial and judicial practices. In a judicial system which seldom tries spouse abuse offenders and rarely convicts them, women are seldom protected from violent reprisals.

Looking to the future, it is clear that more rigorous empirical study is needed comparing police responses to domestic disturbances with their responses to nondomestic conflict situations. The continued role of mysogynist [sic] ideas in shaping police attitudes and predispositions also needs additional exploration. The role of the police dispatcher in "setting the stage" for the encounter itself and the decisions which ensue is also of more than passing interest. Finally, we need to know more about the interpretive process behind police reporting practices in domestic disturbance situations. Until this kind of research is undertaken, police handling of domestic disturbances will remain obscure. □

NOTES AND QUESTIONS

1. The products of the law and society movement include a body of knowledge about (or picture of) the legal system, but an integral part of the enterprise is the study and elaboration of research methods useful for studying the law in action. We will identify and discuss various social science methods as we encounter them. The Berk and Loseke article exemplifies a very common approach to law and social science research: hypothesis testing, using statistics. We will try to clarify some of what is involved.[50]

A. *The Research Question.* Any piece of law and social science research seeks to answer a research question. An empirical research question is one that is answerable by observation or by other "facts" gathered by the researcher. While this sounds obvious, it is always useful to ask, and sometimes difficult to answer, what question motivates the research. What is the research question in the Berk and Loseke article?

B. *Hypotheses.* This form of social science analysis proceeds by evaluating what is currently known about the research question and from that information positing an answer (or various answers) to the question. These proposed answers, or conjectures, are called hypotheses.

For example, let's assume that our research question is why courts give the death penalty to some first degree murderers but not others. After an extensive review of previous studies, existing data, and our own insights, we hypothesize that because of inherent racism in the American legal system, an African-American murderer is more likely to get the death penalty than is a Caucasian

50. This approach is discussed in any standard social science research methods book. A particularly good description can be found in Earl Babbie, *The Practice of Social Research* 5th ed. (Belmont, Cal.: Wadsworth Publishing Co., 1989). See also Michael O. Finkelstein and Bruce Levin, *Statistics for Lawyers* (New York: Springer Verlag, 1990); John Monahan and Laurens Walker, *Social Science in Law: Cases and Materials* (Westbury, N.Y.: Foundation Press, 1994), pp. 31–83.

murderer. However, as with all complex socio-legal phenomena, we also realize that there are probably a large number of other factors that are also related to whether a murderer gets the death penalty. For example, age and gender may be important, and so are various aggravating and mitigating circumstances. Therefore, any serious attempt to understand a particular phenomena will consider a range of potential explanations.

C. *Variables.* In the empirical hypothesis testing tradition, a hypothesis is a statement of conjecture that typically connects two or more variables. Variables are simply things that take on different values. In our example, whether someone gets the death penalty is a variable: you either get it or you don't. Race is also a variable: defendants have different races. Similarly, the presence or absence of aggravating or mitigating circumstances are variables.

Hypothesis testing is based on the assumption that we can explain or predict one variable by finding a relationship between it and one or more other variables. Thus, in the death penalty example, we have hypothesized that we can explain or predict who will get the death penalty and who will not by looking to the race, gender, and age of the defendant and the surrounding circumstances of the offense.

Variables can be divided into two types: dependent and independent.[51] In social science language the factor we are trying to explain is referred to as the dependent variable. On the other hand the variables we use to explain the dependent variable are referred to as independent variables. (In popular speech, we often speak about cause and effect). In our example, this means that the decision whether to give the death penalty is the dependent variable and race, gender, and age, as well as circumstances, are the independent variables.

What is the dependent variable in the Berk and Loseke Study? What are the independent variables?

Notice that the nature of variables differ.[52] Some have relationships that can be expressed arithmetically—for example, consider the age of those convicted of murder: if one person is 50 years old, he is twice as old as another person who is 25. However, investigators often use variables that do not have this kind of counting relationship. Whether or not a court sentences a convicted murderer to death is such a variable. We might code "1" for yes and "0" for no (or we can think of "1" as indicating presence of the variable and "0" indicating absence), and use these values in our analysis. Often social scientists say that transforming yes/no answers into numbers involves using a *"dummy variable"* because the investigator transforms the data into a numerical form necessary for statistical analysis. Berk and Loseke use several such dummy variables.

We also might want to assess the influence of the religion of those convicted and death sentences. We could code as follows: "Roman Catholic = 1; Protestant = 2; Jewish = 3; other = 4; and no religion = 5." This would create a *nominal scale* where the numbers only served to keep what is different apart and join together what is considered equivalent. While we can use such nominal values in our analysis, we cannot use the values on our 1 to 5 scale as we would use 1 and 0 to indicate whether a court imposed a death sentence. We must remember that having no religion is not 5 times more or less of anything

---

51. There also can be intervening variables, but we need not discuss them here.

52. See Johan Galtung, *Theory and Methods of Social Research,* rev. ed. (Oslo: Universitetsforlaget, 1969), pp. 72–79.

than being Roman Catholic. Moreover, by coding two people as falling into category 1, we have treated a devout Roman Catholic man and a woman who occasionally attended Mass as if the differences in their religious practices made no difference.

Finally, we can have an *ordinal scale* which expresses the order of a number in a series. For example, we might ask judges who presided at murder trials to rank the attorneys for convicted murderers as poor, just adequate, competent, very good and outstanding. We might code these responses as −2, −1, 0, +1, and +2. Again, we must wonder whether a judge who ranked one lawyer as "very good" and another as "outstanding" was asserting that the second lawyer was twice as good as the first.

D. Operationalization and Data Collection. After a hypothesis has been formulated the author must decide how to measure the variables and how data will be collected to test the hypothesis. As we learned in Berk and Loseke, deciding how to measure a variable is called "operationalizing" the variable. For example, those coding observed data may be told to count a person with characteristics A, B, and C as falling into category #2 of the variable under study. Some of those assigned to category #2 will also have characteristic D while others will not. Social scientists might argue about whether the investigator really measured the category #2 variable if those with characteristics A, B, and C, were lumped together with characteristics A, B, C, and D. How did Berk and Loseke operationalize each of their variables? What data did they collect? Do you see any problems with their operationalizations or data collections that might bias their results?

E. Analysis. One of the primary uses of statistics in social science research is to determine the extent to which independent variables are related to dependent variables. In considering Berk and Loseke, we are interested in how well the various independent variables allow us to predict whether a particular domestic violence situation will result in an arrest. There are a large number of statistical measures that attempt to answer such a question. Different types of measures are appropriate for different types of variables. We cannot go into them fully in this course. However, the reader of social science research does need to be aware of at least three general forms of statistical analysis: (1) tests of significance, (2) measures of the *degree* of association (correlations), and (3) measures of the *nature* of association (multiple regression).

Tests of significance ask whether we can account for the relationship between variables by mere chance association. Much social research deals with a limited sample of the relevant events. For example, Berk and Loseke did not study all domestic violence situations in all locations but only those from a particular time in a particular location. Social scientists use a variety of statistical techniques to indicate whether the relationship between the variables is "statistically significant." These techniques determine the probability that the observed relationship would be found in the sample if, in fact, there was no relationship between these variables in the entire population. Suppose, for example, we studied samples of men and women law professors of the same age and with similar experience. We found that the women were paid an average of $1,000 a year less than the men. Suppose our sample consisted of five professors. Then suppose, instead, it consisted of 500. We would run in each case a statistical test of significance to determine the probability that we would find such a salary difference in our samples if there were no such difference in the entire population of men and women law professors. We very likely would find that the sample of five would *not* yield significant results, but our sample of 500 might well do so.

Conventionally, *p* (the probability that a particular result was obtained by chance) must be *less* than .05 ("*p* < .05" indicates that the probability that the observed difference would occur by chance is one in twenty) for the result to be called statistically significant. This is not a law of nature but a custom as to where a line is to be drawn. If the chances are less than one in twenty that the result was obtained by chance, the custom is that one can reason as if the results are *not* chance or random, without offending other members of the statistical guild.

But demanding significance at the .05 level may be too conservative and cause a misinterpretation of our data. Social scientists often talk of Type I and Type II errors. We make a Type I error when we accept results that actually are the product of chance. We make a Type II error when we reject results that actually would be obtained with another sample. An investigator can minimize Type I errors by lowering her test for significance to, for example, .01 (or 1 in a 100) rather than .05 (or 1 in 20). However, this move will increase the likelihood of Type II error.

But how should we treat a result that is not statistically significant by whatever test we deem appropriate under the circumstances—our study of five law professors, for example? Statistical logic does not permit us to say that the result was caused by chance. *Chance is only an explanation that we have not ruled out.* If we drew a different sample (a larger one, for example), we might find a significant result. We can illustrate the point by an analogy: Suppose a defendant is tried for first degree murder. The judge instructs the jury that it must determine whether the evidence establishes guilt beyond a reasonable doubt. The jury returns a "not guilty" verdict. We cannot say that we know that the defendant did not commit first degree murder. All we know is that the prosecution failed to prove that the defendant did.[53]

When an investigator fails to obtain significant results, the investigator may still theorize about relationships with the same freedom as a scholar or journalist who does not purport to use statistics. Moreover, the "not significant" results may still serve as scraps of evidence "suggesting" certain relationships. However, such arguments are entitled to just as much but no more weight than other theoretical or speculative work.

Which of the independent variables in Berk and Loseke are significantly related to the decision whether to arrest?

A measure of the degree of association asks how much a particular independent variable helps us to predict a dependent variable. While these measures can be expressed in different ways, the conventional way to express them is in decimal form varying between 0 and 1. 0 indicates that a particular independent variable does not help us to predict the dependent variable at all. Conversely, a 1 indicates that knowing the independent variable allows us to predict the dependent variable perfectly.

---

53. Jurors in Scotland are given three options: they can render a verdict of guilty, not guilty, or not proven. "Not statistically significant" is roughly analogous to the Scottish verdict of not proven. The Scottish verdict is controversial. Some argue that it is a second class acquittal that leaves a cloud over the accused; some argue that it allows a jury to evade the duty to decide cases; others defend it as a way accurately to reflect the jury's judgment about the case. See *The Guardian,* June 1, 1993, p. 18.

Measures of the degree of association rest on *correlations*. Correlation means that two things occur together—when one thing is found, another will be found as well. Summer and heat are positively correlated. Two things are negatively correlated when the presence of one is associated with the absence of the other. Summer and snow are negatively correlated. Lack of correlation means that whether one thing occurs or does not occur when we find the other depends on chance. Notice that a correlation does not mean necessarily that one thing *causes* the other. For example, suppose we found that longer prison sentences are positively correlated with high crime rates. The correlation itself tells us nothing about whether harsh sentences cause increasing crime, increasing crime causes harsh sentences, some unknown third factor causes both heavy sentences as well as high amounts of crime, or one or more unknown factors cause the sentences while one or several other unrelated factors cause the crime, and the correlation is but a coincidence. We must explain correlations on the basis of logic, theory, hunch or other data. Correlations do not speak for themselves.

We can illustrate correlations and make some further points by considering a simple graph. Suppose we are interested in whether the percentage of left-handed pitchers on major league baseball teams is related to the percentage of games that the teams won. Suppose, very improbably, we found that teams that had 100% left-handed pitchers won 100% of their games; those with no left-handed pitchers won none; those with 50% left-handers won 50% of their games and so on. We could represent this by the line of stars on the following table:

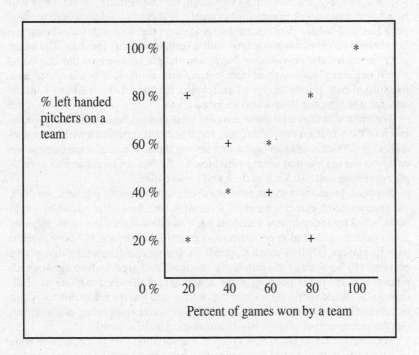

If these percentages were so neatly correlated, we would say that "r = +1.00." We would speak of the "positive slope" of the correlation because a line connecting the points on the graph would run upward to indicate the more we have of one thing, the more we have of another.

Suppose we found the absolute opposite situation. The more left-handed pitchers on a team, the less games the team won. Assume that teams with all left-handed pitchers lost all their games; those with 80% won only 20%; those with none at all won all their games. Here "r = −1.00." A line plotted on the graph would have a "negative slope," as the plus signs in the graph indicate. Of course, in neither case would our data prove whether left-handed pitchers had anything with winning or losing. The team with all left-handed pitchers, for example, could also have the best batters in the league. These batters could be the cause of the team's success.

Finally, suppose that half the teams in the major leagues had 10% left-handed pitchers on their pitching staffs and half had 90%. The same number of teams from each group won 20%, 40%, 60%, 80%, or 100% of their games. There is no correlation at all between the two factors—the percentage of left-handed pitchers seems to have nothing to do with the number of games a team wins—and so we would say that "r = 0.00." If we plotted the percentage of left-handed pictures and the percentage of victories, our marks would scatter without pattern on our chart.

Of course, we seldom find sets of data yielding such neat patterns as in our first two examples. Most sets of data, when plotted on graphs, produce a scattered array of points. One can try to draw a straight line through the array so that the line comes as close as possible to all the points. If there is no relationship between the variables being considered, the "best-fitting" straight line will be a horizontal line as in our third example. If there is a relationship, we will get a line somewhere between the horizontal and the diagonal. Calculating the "r" statistic involves assessing how well a straight line fits the data. The value of "r" is called the *correlation coefficient*. It is a measure of the degree to which one thing goes with or does not go with another. It is expressed as a measure of how far the degree of correlation is from +1.00, 0.00 or −1.00, or how far it is from the three lines described above.

We often will deal with more complex relationships, and want to know how much of the variation concerning one variable can be attributed to each of several other variables or to an interaction among them. We need a measure of *the nature of the association* among variables. To do this, we could turn to a *multiple regression analysis* such as Berk and Loseke used.

Suppose, in addition to the percentage of (A) left-handed pitchers, we think the percentage of games a baseball team wins (the dependent variable) might be affected by independent variables such as (B) whether the team plays its home games on natural grass rather than an artificial surface, (C) how much it pays its players, (D) how much it spends on finding and developing new young players, (E) how many players leave the team and sign as free agents with other teams, (F) the population of the area in which the team markets its products (such as television rights and the right to use the team logo on caps and jackets), (G) the batting averages of its regular players other than pitchers, and (H) the percentage of players whose astrological sign is Taurus.

We might want to know how much of the variation (the percentage of wins by each team in the league) is explained by some combination of these factors. First, we would create an equation that, on the basis of theory or intuition, seemed to express likely relationships. For example, we might think that all of the eight factors we suggested contributed to the percentage of games a team won, but some of them may contribute much more than others. We could express this as:

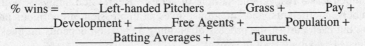

% wins = _____Left-handed Pitchers _____Grass + _____Pay + _____Development + _____Free Agents + _____Population + _____Batting Averages + _____Taurus.

Second, we would calculate a weight for each of our predictor variables—that is, *how much of the variance* can we attribute to factor A, how much to factor B and so on? We would then fill in the blanks in our equation with values which when added together predict the percentage of wins. Finally, we might try other equations that combined the factors differently. Then we would look for the best "fit" of our data to our theories—we would ask which equations seemed to express sensible relationships in light of the values which we entered.

There are a number of common problems encountered when using regression analysis. We can illustrate one by pointing out that factor (F), the population of the area in which the team markets its products is likely to be closely related to the amount of money the team has to spend. The available income, in turn, will be related to how much the team can pay its players (C) and spend on player development (D). Unless we separate the influence of such confounding factors, we are likely to over- or underestimate the impact of each of these three factors on each team's success. Finkelstein and Levin[54] explain a particularly severe version of the problem as follows:

> Suppose that in a wage regression model almost all high-paid employees were men with special training and almost all low-paid employees were women without training. Sex and special training are then highly correlated. Data exhibiting such correlations are said to be collinear; where one factor is nearly a linear function of several other factors, the data are said to be multicollinear, a not uncommon occurrence in a multiple regression equation . . . .
>
> [T]he effect [of multicollinearity] is simply to increase the standard errors of the coefficients, thus making significance tests less powerful and coefficient estimates less reliable.
>
> The reason for the unreliability is not hard to see. In the example, if sex and special training were perfectly correlated it would be impossible to distinguish their separate effects on wages because they would always move together. When explanatory factors are highly but not perfectly correlated, assessment of their separate effects depends on the few cases in which they do not move in tandem. The enlarged standard errors of the coefficients reflect the smallness of the effective sample size.

Macaulay[55] warns that regression analysis must be used intelligently; it is not a form of magic. He argues that regression analysis is "powerful but limited." As some have pointed out, it may yield highly misleading results if the data are not randomly selected from the population being studied. In law and

54. Michael O. Finkelstein and Bruce Levin, *Statistics for Lawyers* 351 (New York: Springer Verlag, 1990).

55. Stewart Macaulay, "Law and the Behavioral Sciences: Is There Any There There?" 6 *Law & Policy* 149, 159–61 (1984).

society work, unfortunately, this nonrandomness happens all too often. Scholars "are lucky to find anyone who knows what is happening who will talk to us, much less a respectable sample of actors." Regression analysis, with its numbers, coefficients, and equations, gives an impression of enormous precision, but each part of the process of building a equation depends on guesses, estimates, and matters of judgment.

This criticism, Macaulay continues, "is particularly apt when regression analysis is applied to macrodata gathered by public agencies. Too often these data are a mess." An "informed consumer" has to "approach studies relying on multiple regression cautiously because too many researchers apply the technique mechanically without concern for its limitations."

Macaulay comments:

In my experience, those who know the most about regression analysis are the most hesitant to use it inappropriately and are the most careful in spelling out assumptions and limitations . . . . [T]he major contribution of regression analysis of large sets of data often is to suggest areas for further study. For example, Unnever[56] . . . studied sentencing in drug cases tried in Miami. He contrasted defendants with privately retained attorneys and those represented by public defenders, asking which were sentenced to prison more often. He found (p. 220) that "defendants with private attorneys were significantly less likely to receive a prison sentence than those who had public defenders. The odds of incarceration were nearly halved if a defendant had a private attorney." On one hand, we could object that the category "private attorney" may involve lumping together the most competent tigers of the defense bar with the dregs of the profession. On the other hand, as Unnever says (213 n.2), "[f]uture research is needed to empirically determine what the components of successful legal representation are . . . " It seems unlikely that *all* private lawyers do better than *all* public ones. My guess is that a select few private attorneys who specialize in drug cases involving wealthy clients account for most of the difference. If so, I would be prompted to move to an in-depth study of their practices to explain this success. Whatever the appropriate questions, answers will not be found in tables of numbers. Rather, one must learn a great deal about the Miami drug scene, the nature of the defendants, narcotics officers, prosecutors, court personnel, and local politicians as well as more about defense lawyers . . . . For example, one would have to rule out the possibility that the difference found by Unnever reflected the willingness of some private lawyers to bribe some judges, a practice in which public defenders do not engage. Regression analysis, alone, is unlikely to suggest or rule out this explanation.

2. Berk and Loseke want to study family violence. Why do you think they are interested in this particular problem? Note that they exclude from their study violence between members of gay and lesbian couples, and cases in

---

56. James Unnever, "Direct and Organizational Discrimination in the Sentencing of Drug Offenders," 30 *Social Problems* 212 (1982).'

which the woman rather than the man is arrested. Are these exclusions justified? Do they suggest anything about the ideas underlying this study?

3. The dependent variable in this study is *decisions by the police to make arrests* in cases of family violence. Why did Berk and Loseke chose to measure this particular variable? What are the advantages and disadvantages of using arrests as the measure to be studied? There are other ways to study domestic violence. One can, for example, study why women do or don't call police; why they do or don't decide to prosecute. See David A. Ford, "Prosecution as a Victim Power Resource: A Note on Empowering Women in Violent Conjugal Relationships," 25 *Law & Society Review* 313 (1991).

We also might study the impact of arresting husbands who batter their wives. Do those husbands arrested change their behavior in the future? If so, do they retaliate against wives who had them arrested or do they stop beating their wives? Does the risk of arrest change the behavior of other husbands? Lawrence W. Sherman and Richard A. Berk, "The Specific Deterrent Effects of Arrest for Domestic Assault," 49 *American Sociological Review* 261 (1984), reported the results of a field experiment on domestic violence which was conducted in Minneapolis. Police responding to domestic violence complaints arrested, counseled, or ordered the suspect to leave for eight hours. Suspects were randomly assigned to the three treatments. Official recidivism measures show that arrested suspects showed less subsequent violence than those who were ordered to leave. Victim reports showed that those arrested were less likely to be violent subsequently.

This study received great publicity, and it prompted changes in the official policy of many police departments. Richard O. Lempert, "From the Editor," 18 *Law & Society Review* 505 (1984), objected to making policy based on one study conducted in one city over a short period of time. He criticized the efforts of the researchers to gain maximum publicity for the results because they should have known that this publicity was likely to prompt other cities to adopt a mandatory arrest policy. One could advocate this policy for normative reasons, but one was not justified in championing it on the ground that "science" had proved that arrest deterred recidivism. Lawrence W. Sherman and Ellen G. Cohn, "The Impact of Research on Legal Policy: The Minneapolis Domestic Violence Experiment," 23 *Law & Society Review* 117 (1989), responded to Lempert. They reported a survey showing the influence of the original Minneapolis study on the policies of police departments. They set out the many threats to the validity of the original Minneapolis study. They, nonetheless, argue that the publicity encouraged replication of research at other sites and improved the knowledge base for policy recommendations. Do you find this justification convincing?

We also might want to explain why a mandatory arrest policy had limited impact. Official policy undoubtedly influences practice, but it is not the only influence. We might want to study these other influences. For example, Kathleen J. Ferraro, "Policing Woman Battering," 36 *Social Problems* 61 (1989), reports a study of actual practices in Phoenix, a city which had a presumptive arrest policy in cases of spouse battering. Despite the policy, police officers made arrests in only 18 percent of assaults involving intimate partners. She concludes: "If officers view policies as rhetoric to quiet the 'women's libbers,' they are not likely to be concerned about the consequences of their street level decisions."

Richard A. Berk, David Rauma, Donileen R. Loseke and Sarah Fenster-

maker Berk, "Throwing the Cops Back Out: The Decline of a Local Program
to Make the Criminal Justice System More Responsive to Incidents of Domestic Violence," 11 *Social Science Research* 245, 278–79 (1982), comment:

> By and large, wife battery is seen as a "private matter" in which the
> criminal justice system should not intervene . . . . [T]here are no doubt
> significant numbers of Americans who endorse the dominant role of
> husbands within households and view wife battery as little more than an
> unfortunate excess. In this normative climate, organizational change and
> individual efforts must be truly extraordinary if the criminal justice sys-
> tem is to be made more responsive. And . . . they must remain extraordi-
> nary over time.

4. How accurate are police reports? The authors point out that the police
sometimes twist or falsify their reports. But the authors are still willing to
"assume . . . that police reports reflect real and significant features of each
encounter as interpreted by officers." Does this mean that this study tells us,
not about family violence, but about the way the police interpret and react to
family violence?

5. The findings, the authors claim, suggest a "model" of police decision
making. Are their conclusions justified by their findings? The last section talks
a lot about police strategies, and the frame of mind of the police. What evidence do the authors have of these strategies and perceptions?

6. This is a study of Santa Barbara County, California, in the late 1970s.
Are the findings and conclusions valid for other places—for example, Cook
County, Illinois; or Paris, France?

7. Are these findings valid for other periods of history? Domestic violence
has a long history, which is only just beginning to be uncovered. Two recent
studies are, Elizabeth Pleck, *Domestic Tyranny: The Making of Social Policy
against Family Violence from Colonial Times to the Present* (New York:
Oxford University Pres, 1987); and Linda Gordon, *Heroes of Their Own Lives:
The Politics and History of Family Violence. Boston 1880–1960* (New York:
Viking, 1988).

8. Berk and Loseke focus on one type of arrest situation: domestic violence. However, there is an extremely large body of research that focuses more
generally on the question of the police decision whether to arrest. A 1984 special issue on "Discretion in Law Enforcement" in *Law and Contemporary
Problems* (Vol. 47) provides a useful overview of various attempts to study
police discretion.

One way to view police discretion is in terms of the distinctions among
total, full and actual enforcement.

5. Police Discretion Not to Invoke the Criminal Process: Low-Visibility Decisions in the Administration of Justice

Joseph Goldstein

69 *Yale Law Journal* 543 (1960)

☐ Under the rule of law, the criminal law has both a fair-warning function for the public and a power-restricting function for officials. Both post- and pre-verdict sanctions, therefore, may be imposed only in accord with authorized procedures. No sanctions are to be inflicted other than those which have been prospectively prescribed by the constitution, legislation, or judicial decision for a particular crime or a particular kind of offender. These concepts, of course, do not preclude differential disposition, within the authorized limits, of persons suspected or convicted of the same or similar offenses. In an ideal system differential handling, individualized justice, would result, but only from an equal application of officially approved criteria designed to implement officially approved objectives. And finally a system which presumes innocence requires that preconviction sanctions be kept at a minimum consistent with assuring an opportunity for the process to run its course.

A regularized system of review is a requisite for insuring substantial compliance by the administrators of criminal justice with these rule-of-law principles. Implicit in the word "review" and obviously essential to the operation of any review procedure is the visibility of the decisions and conduct to be scrutinized. Pretrial hearings on motions, the trial, appeal and the writ of habeas corpus constitute a formal system for evaluating the actions of officials invoking the criminal process. The public hearing, the record of proceedings, and the publication of court opinions—all features of the formal system—preserve and increase the visibility of official enforcement activity and facilitate and encourage the development of an informal system of appraisal. These proceedings and documents are widely reported and subjected to analysis and comment by legislative, professional, and other interested groups and individuals.

But police decisions not to invoke the criminal process, except when reflected in gross failures of service, are not visible to the community. Nor are they likely to be visible to official state reviewing agencies, even those within the police department. Failure to tag illegally parked cars is an example of gross failure of service, open to public view and recognized for what it is. An officer's decision, however, not to investigate or report adequately a disturbing event which he has reason to believe constitutes a violation of the criminal law does not ordinarily carry with it consequences sufficiently visible to make the community, the legislature, the prosecutor, or the courts aware of a possible failure of service. The police officer, the suspect, the police department, and frequently even the victim, when directly concerned with a decision not to invoke, unlike the same parties when responsible for or subject to a decision to invoke, generally have neither the incentive nor the opportunity to obtain review of that decision or the police conduct associated with it. Furthermore, official police records are usually too incomplete to permit evaluations of nonenforcement decisions in the light of the purposes of the criminal law. Consequently, such decisions, unlike decisions to enforce, are generally not subject to the control which would follow from administrative, judicial, legislative, or community review and appraisal.

. . . The police have a duty not to enforce the substantive law of crimes unless invocation of the process can be achieved within bounds set by constitution, statute, court decision, and possibly official pronouncements of the prosecutor. *Total enforcement,* were it possible, is thus precluded, by generally applicable due-process restrictions on such police procedures as arrest, search, seizure, and interrogation. *Total enforcement* is further precluded by such specific procedural restrictions as prohibitions on invoking an adultery statute unless the spouse of one of the parties complains, or an unlawful-possession-of-firearms statute if the offender surrenders his dangerous weapons during a statutory period of amnesty. Such restrictions of general and specific application mark the bounds, often ambiguously, of an area of *full* enforcement in which the police are not only authorized but expected to enforce fully the law of crimes. An area of *no enforcement* lies, therefore, between the perimeter of *total enforcement* and the outer limits of *full enforcement.* In this *no enforcement* area, the police have no authority to invoke the criminal process.

Within the area of *full enforcement,* the police have not been delegated discretion not to invoke the criminal process. On the contrary, those state statutes providing for municipal police departments which define the responsibility of police provide:

It shall be the duty of the police . . . under the direction of the mayor and chief of police and in conformity with the ordinances of the city, and the laws of the state . . . . to pursue and arrest any persons fleeing from justice . . . to apprehend any and all persons in the act of committing any offense against the laws of the state . . . and to take the offender forthwith before the proper court or magistrate, to be dealt with for the offense; to make complaints to the proper officers and magistrates of any person known or believed by them to be guilty of the violation of the ordinances of the city or the penal laws of the state; and at all times diligently and faithfully to enforce all such laws . . . .*

---

* [The example is drawn from the Michigan statutes.]

Even in jurisdictions without such a specific statutory definition, declarations of the *full enforcement* mandate generally appear in municipal Charters, ordinances or police manuals. Police manuals, for example, commonly provide, in sections detailing the duties at each level of the police hierarchy, that the captain, superintendent, lieutenant, or patrolman shall be responsible, so far as is in his power, for the prevention and detection of crime and the enforcement of all criminal laws and ordinances. Illustrative of the spirit and policy of full enforcement is this protestation from the introduction to the Rules and Regulations of the Atlanta, Georgia, Police Department:

> Enforcement of all Criminal Laws and City Ordinances, is my obligation. There are no specialties under the Law. My eyes must be open to traffic problems and disorders, though I move on other assignments, to slinking vice in back streets and dives though I have been directed elsewhere, to the suspicious appearance of evil wherever it is encountered . . . . I must be impartial because the Law surrounds, protects and applies to all alike, rich and poor, low and high, black and white . . . .

Minimally, then, *full enforcement,* so far as the police are concerned, means (1) the investigation of every disturbing event which is reported to or observed by them and which they have reason to suspect may be a violation of the criminal law; (2) following a determination that some crime has been committed, an effort to discover its perpetrators; and (3) the presentation of all information collected by them to the prosecutor for his determination of the appropriateness of further invoking the criminal process.

Full enforcement, however, is not a realistic expectation. In addition to ambiguities in the definitions of both substantive offenses and due-process boundaries, countless limitations and pressures preclude the possibility of the police seeking or achieving *full enforcement.* Limitations of time, personnel, and investigative devices—all in part but not entirely functions of budget—force the development, by plan or default, of priorities of enforcement. Even if there were "enough police" adequately equipped and trained, pressures from within and without the department, which is after all a human institution, may force the police to invoke the criminal process selectively. By decisions not to invoke within the area of full enforcement, the police largely determine the outer limits of actual enforcement throughout the criminal process . . . . □

9. In a classic work on police discretion, Donald Black, "The Social Organization of Arrest," 23 *Stanford Law Review* 1087 (1971), sets out a number of propositions about the exercise of actual enforcement:

> A. Most arrest situations arise through citizen rather than police initiative. Modern police departments are geared to respond to citizen calls for service.

B. Arrest practices sharply reflect the preferences of citizen complainants, particularly when the complainant has a strong desire for leniency; less frequently when the preference is for arrest.

C. The stronger the evidence in the field situation, the more likely is an arrest. Yet even when the evidence against a suspect is very strong, the police frequently take action short of arrest.

D. The probability of arrest is higher for serious crimes than for those of a relatively minor nature.

E. The greater the relational distance between a complainant and a suspect, the greater is the likelihood of arrest. Arrest is less likely if the parties are friends, neighbors, or acquaintances, least likely if they are family members.

As Berk and Loseke point out, many commentators have argued that proposition E, which encompasses domestic violence situations, reflects police bias against the claims of women. How do Berk and Loseke deal with this charge? On what basis do they make their conclusion? Do Berk and Loseke favor greater or lesser constraints on police discretion? In your opinion would it be appropriate for a police department to mandate that an arrest occur in every domestic situation in which there is arguably sufficient evidence for that arrest? Even if desirable, would such a mandate be possible?

10. Herman Goldstein, in *Problem Oriented Policing* (Philadelphia: Temple University Press, 1990), argues for a new approach to policing. We must, he argues, put aside the idea that the police merely enforce the law. Law is but one tool among many that police use to cope with problems they face such as street-walking prostitutes, domestic violence, or gangs. Once we recognize this, we can consider how police should respond. The question should be whether the response is appropriate and effective rather than whether arrests are made as a response to violations of the criminal law. Goldstein takes a normative position based, in large part, on his empirical knowledge of what police do. Other normative positions, of course, are possible. But we must avoid demanding that police do what they cannot do in light of their resources and other structural constraints upon them.

See, also, Albert J. Meehan, "'I Don't Prevent Crime, I Prevent Calls': Policing as a Negotiated Order," 15 *Symbolic Interaction* 455 (1992). Meehan studied how police officers dealt with juveniles in two suburban towns. Usually it was doubtful whether there had been a violation of any formal rule of law when citizens called complaining about juveniles. Nonetheless, officers had to satisfy citizens who called, and good officers controlled their sectors so that citizens would have no complaints. The most frequent police activity was to move the young people from a gathering place where they might annoy neighbors to another location where this was less likely to happen—the officers called this "brooming." Obviously, the threat of arrest always was in the background. However, officers thought that the juvenile justice system was so easy on young offenders that all an arrest did was teach a young person and his or her friends that an arrest was nothing to be concerned about. Do you see any normative objections to the practice of "brooming?" If you disapprove of such practices, what would you have the police do when adults complain about gatherings of juveniles on corners, in shopping centers or fast food restaurant parking lots, or in public parks?

11. One issue that is not addressed in the articles discussed so far is police brutality. The police beating of Rodney King, the criminal trial and acquittal of the officers, the resulting large scale 1992 riots in Los Angeles, and King's lawsuit against Los Angeles certainly brought this issue to the forefront. This particular episode also points to the difficulty of studying police behavior. It was only because an unobtrusive observer happened to be in a position to video tape the incident that it was ever brought to the attention of the public. Police decisions, like decisions of many others in the legal system, are often invisible. This makes it difficult for police to be held accountable. It also makes it difficult to study the exercise of police discretion. The Rodney King incident also raises the issue of police racism. Is it possible to design a realistic study to show if the police are racist and, if so, how this trait affects police discretion?

6. The Practice of Law as Confidence Game: Organizational Cooptation of a Profession[57]

Abraham S. Blumberg

1 *Law & Society Review* No. 2, 15 (June 1967)

☐ Scant attention—apart from explorations of the legal profession itself—has been given to the sociological examination of legal institutions, or their supporting ideological assumptions. Thus, for example, very little sociological effort is expended to ascertain the validity and viability of important court decisions, which may rest on wholly erroneous assumptions about the contextual realities of social structure. A particular decision may rest upon a legally impeccable rationale; at the same time it may be rendered nugatory or self-defeating by contingencies imposed by aspects of social reality of which the lawmakers are themselves unaware.

Within this context, I wish to question the impact of three recent landmark decisions of the United States Supreme Court; each hailed as destined to effect profound changes in the future of criminal law administration and enforcement in America.

[The cases referred to are Gideon *v.* Wainwright, 372 U.S. 335 (1963), which "required states and localities henceforth to furnish counsel in the case of indigent persons charged with a felony"; Escobedo *v.* Illinois, 378 U.S. 478 (1964), in which the "court asserted that counsel must be permitted when the process of police investigative effort shifts from merely investigatory to that of accusatory"; and Miranda *v.* Arizona, 384 U.S. 436 (1966), which held that "police interrogation of any suspect in custody, without his consent, unless a

57. Reprinted from *Law and Society Review* by permission. Copyright © 1967 by the Law and Society Association.

defense attorney is present, is prohibited by the self-incrimination provision of the Fifth Amendment." Blumberg continues:]

In all three decisions, the Supreme Court reiterates the traditional legal conception of a defense lawyer based on the ideological perception of a criminal case as an *adversary, combative* proceeding, in which counsel for the defense assiduously musters all the admittedly limited resources at his command to *defend* the accused. The fundamental question remains to be answered: Does the Supreme Court's conception of the role of counsel in a criminal case square with social reality?

The task of this paper is to furnish some preliminary evidence toward the illumination of that question. Little empirical understanding of the function of defense counsel exists; only some ideologically oriented generalizations and commitments. This paper is based upon observations made by the writer during many years of legal practice in the criminal courts of a large metropolitan area. No claim is made as to its methodological rigor, although it does reflect a conscious and sustained effort for participant observation.

COURT STRUCTURE DEFINES ROLE OF DEFENSE LAWYER

The overwhelming majority of convictions in criminal cases (usually over 90 percent) are not the product of a combative, trial-by jury process at all, but instead merely involve the sentencing of the individual after a negotiated, bargained-for plea of guilty has been entered. Although more recently the overzealous role of police and prosecutors in producing pretrial confessions and admissions has achieved a good deal of notoriety, scant attention has been paid to the organizational structure and personnel of the criminal court itself. Indeed, the extremely high conviction rate produced without the features of an adversary trial in our courts would tend to suggest that the "trial" becomes a perfunctory reiteration and validation of the pretrial interrogation and investigation.

The institutional setting of the court defines a role for the defense counsel in a criminal case radically different from the one traditionally depicted. Sociologists and others have focused their attention on the deprivations and social disabilities of such variables as race, ethnicity, and social class as being the source of an accused person's defeat in a criminal court. Largely overlooked is the variable of the court organization itself, which possesses a thrust, purpose, and direction of its own. It is grounded in pragmatic values, bureaucratic priorities, and administrative instruments. These exalt maximum production and the particularistic career designs of organizational incumbents, whose occupational and career commitments tend to generate a set of priorities. These priorities exert a higher claim than the stated ideological goals of "due process of law," and are often inconsistent with them.

Organizational goals and discipline impose a set of demands and conditions of practice on the respective professions in the criminal court, to which they respond by abandoning their ideological and professional commitments to the accused client, in the service of these higher claims of the court organization. All court personnel, including the accused's own lawyer, tend to be coopted to become agent-mediators who help the accused redefine his situation and restructure his perceptions concomitant with a plea of guilty.

Of all the occupational roles in the court the only private individual who is officially recognized as having a special status and concomitant obligations is the lawyer. His legal status is that of "an officer of the court" and he is held to a standard of ethical performance and duty to his client as well as to the court. This obligation is thought to be far higher than that expected of ordinary individuals occupying the various occupational statuses in the court community. However, lawyers, whether privately retained or of the legal-aid, public defender variety, have close and continuing relations with the prosecuting office and the court itself through discreet relations with the judges via their law secretaries or "confidential" assistants. Indeed, lines of communication, influence and contact with those offices, as well as with the Office of the Clerk of the court, Probation Division, and with the press, are essential to present and prospective requirements of criminal law practice. Similarly, the subtle involvement of the press and other mass media in the court's organizational network is not readily discernible to the casual observer. Accused persons come and go in the court system schema, but the structure and its occupational incumbents remain to carry on their respective career, occupational and organizational enterprises. The individual stridencies, tensions, and conflicts a given accused person's case may present to all the participants are overcome, because the formal and informal relations of all the groups in the court setting require it. The probability of continued future relations and interaction must be preserved at all costs.

This is particularly true of the "lawyer regulars" *i.e.*, those defense lawyers, who by virtue of their continuous appearances in behalf of defendants, tend to represent the bulk of a criminal court's non-indigent case workload, and those lawyers who are not "regulars," who appear almost casually in behalf of an occasional client. Some of the "lawyer regulars" are highly visible as one moves about the major urban centers of the nation, their offices line the back streets of the courthouses, at times sharing space with bondsmen. Their political "visibility" in terms of local club house ties, reaching into the judge's chambers and prosecutor's office, are also deemed essential to successful practitioners. Previous research has indicated that the "lawyer regulars" make no effort to conceal their dependence upon police, bondsmen, jail personnel. Nor do they conceal the necessity for maintaining intimate relations with all levels of personnel in the court setting as a means of obtaining, maintaining, and building their practice. These informal relations are the sine qua non not only of retaining a practice, but also in the negotiation of pleas and sentences.

The client, then, is a secondary figure in the court system as in certain other bureaucratic settings. He becomes a means to other ends of the organization's incumbents. He may present doubts, contingencies, and pressures which challenge existing informal arrangements or disrupt them; but these tend to be resolved in favor of the continuance of the organization and its relations as before. There is a greater community of interest among all the principal organizational structures and their incumbents than exists elsewhere in other settings. The accused's lawyer has far greater professional, economic, intellectual and other ties to the various elements of the court system than he does to his own client. In short, the court is a closed community.

This is more than just the case of the usual "secrets" of bureaucracy which are fanatically defended from an outside view. Even all elements of the press are zealously determined to report on that which will not offend the board of judges, the prosecutor, probation, legal-aid, or other officials, in return for privileges and courtesies granted in the past and to be granted in the future. Rather than any view of the matter in terms of some variation of a "conspiracy" hypothesis, the simple explanation is one of an ongoing system handling delicate tensions, managing the trauma produced by law enforcement and administration, and requiring almost pathological distrust of "outsiders" bordering on group paranoia.

The hostile attitude toward "outsiders" is in large measure engendered by a defensiveness itself produced by the inherent deficiencies of assembly line justice, so characteristic of our major criminal courts. Intolerably large caseloads of defendants which must be disposed of in an organizational context of limited resources and personnel, potentially subject the participants in the court community to harsh scrutiny from appellate courts, and other public and private sources of condemnation. As a consequence, an almost irreconcilable conflict is posed in terms of intense pressures to process large numbers of cases on the one hand, and the stringent ideological and legal requirements of "due process law," on the other hand. A rather tenuous resolution of the dilemma has emerged in the shape of a large variety of bureaucratically ordained and controlled "work crimes," short cuts, deviations, and outright rule violations adopted as court practice in order to meet production norms. Fearfully anticipating criticism on ethical as well as legal grounds, all the significant participants in the court's social structure are bound into an organized system of complicity. This consists of a work arrangement in which the patterned, covert, informal breaches, and evasions of "due process" are institutionalized, but are, nevertheless, denied to exist.

These institutionalized evasions will be found to occur to some degree, in all criminal courts. Their nature, scope and complexity are largely determined by the size of the court, and the character of the community in which it is located, *e.g.,* whether it is a large, urban institution, or a relatively small rural county court. In addition, idiosyncratic, local conditions may contribute to a unique flavor in the character and quality of the criminal law's administration in a particular community. However, in most instances a variety of stratagems are employed—some subtle, some crude, in effectively disposing of what are often too large caseloads. A wide variety of coercive devices are employed against an accused-client, couched in a depersonalized, instrumental, bureaucratic version of due process of law, and which are in reality a perfunctory obeisance to the ideology of due process. These include some very explicit pressures which are exerted in some measure by all court personnel, including judges, to plead guilty and avoid trial. In many instances the sanction of a potentially harsh sentence is utilized as the visible alternative to pleading guilty, in the case of recalcitrants. Probation and psychiatric reports are "tailored" to organizational needs, or are at least responsive to the court organization's requirements for the refurbishment of a defendant's social biography, consonant with his new status. A resourceful judge can, through his subtle domination of the proceedings, impose his will on the final outcome of a trial. Stenographers and clerks, in their function as record keepers, are on occasion pressed into service in support of a judicial need to "rewrite" the record of a courtroom event. Bail practices are usually employed for purposes other than simply assuring a defendant's presence on the date of a hearing in connection with his case. Too often, the discretionary power as to bail is part of the arsenal of weapons available to collapse the resistance of an accused person. The foregoing is a most cursory examination of some of the more prominent "short cuts" available to any court organization. There are numerous other procedural strategies constituting due process deviations, which tend to become the work style artifacts of a court's personnel. Thus, only court "regulars" who are "bound in" are really accepted; others are treated routinely and in almost a coldly correct manner.

The defense attorneys, therefore, whether of the legal-aid, public defender variety, or privately retained, although operating in terms of pressures specific to their respective role and organizational obligations, ultimately are concerned with strategies which tend to lead to a plea. It is the rational, impersonal elements involving economies of time, labor, expense and a superior commitment of the defense counsel to these rationalistic values of maximum production of court organization that prevail, in his relationship with a client. The lawyer "regulars" are frequently former staff members of the prosecutor's office and utilize the prestige, know-how and contacts of their former affiliation as part of their stock in trade. Close and continuing relations between the lawyer "regular" and his former colleagues in the prosecutor's office generally overshadow the relationship between the regular and his client. The continuing colleagueship of supposedly adversary counsel rests on real professional and organizational needs of a *quid pro quo,* which goes beyond the limits of an accommodation or *modus vivendi* one might ordinarily expect under the circumstances of an otherwise seemingly adversary relationship. Indeed, the adversary features which are manifest are for the most part muted and exist even in their attenuated form largely for external consumption. The principals, lawyer and assistant district attorney, rely upon one another's cooperation for their continued professional existence, and so the bargaining between them tends usually to be "reasonable" rather than fierce.

FEE COLLECTION AND FIXING

The real key to understanding the role of defense counsel in a criminal case is to be found in the area of the fixing of the fee to be charged and its collection. The problem of fixing and collecting the fee tends to influence to a significant degree the criminal court process itself, and not just the relationship of the lawyer and his client. In essence, a lawyer-client "confidence game" is played. A true confidence game is unlike the case of the emperor's new clothes wherein that monarch's nakedness was a result of inordinate gullibility and credulity. In a genuine confidence game, the perpetrator manipulates the basic dishonesty of his partner, the victim or mark, toward his own (the confidence operator's) ends. Thus, "the victim of a con scheme must have some larceny in his heart."

Legal service lends itself particularly well to confidence games. Usually, a plumber will be able to demonstrate empirically that he has performed a service by clearing up the stuffed drain, repairing the leaky faucet or pipe—and therefore merits his fee. He has rendered, when summoned, a visible, tangible boon for his client in return for the requested fee. A physician, who has not performed some visible surgery or otherwise engaged in some readily discernible procedure in connection with a patient, may be deemed by the patient to have "done nothing" for him. As a consequence, medical practitioners may simply prescribe or administer by injection a placebo to overcome a patient's potential reluctance or dissatisfaction in paying a requested fee, "for nothing."

In the practice of law there is a special problem in this regard, no matter what the level of the practitioner or his place in the hierarchy of prestige. Much legal work is intangible either because it is simply a few words of advice, some preventive action, a telephone call, negotiation of some kind, a form filled out and filed, a hurried conference with another attorney or an official of a government agency, a letter or opinion written, or a countless variety of seemingly innocuous, and even prosaic procedures and actions. These are basic activities, apart from any possible court appearance, of almost all lawyers, at all levels of practice. Much of the activity is not in the nature of the exercise of the traditional, precise professional skills of the attorney such as library research and oral argument in connection with appellate briefs, court motions, trial work, drafting of opinions, memoranda, contracts, and other complex documents and agreements. Instead, much legal activity, whether it is at the lowest or highest "white shoe" law firm levels, is of the brokerage, agent, sales representative, lobbyist type of activity, in which the lawyer acts for someone else in pursuing the latter's interests and designs. The service is intangible.

The large scale law firm may not speak as openly of their "contacts," their "fixing" abilities, as does the lower level lawyer. They trade instead upon a facade of thick carpeting, walnut paneling, genteel low pressure, and superficialities of traditional legal professionalism. There are occasions when even the large firm is on the defensive in connection with the fees they charge because the services rendered or results obtained do not appear to merit the fee asked. Therefore, there is a recurrent problem in the legal profession in fixing the amount of fee, and in justifying the basis for the requested fee.

Although the fee at times amounts to what the traffic and the conscience of the lawyer will bear, one further observation must be made with regard to the size of the fee and its collection. The defendant in a criminal case and the material gain he may have acquired during the course of his illicit activities are soon parted. Not infrequently the ill gotten fruits of the various modes of larceny are sequestered by a defense lawyer in payment of his fee. Inexorably, the amount of the fee is a function of the dollar value of the crime committed, and is frequently set with meticulous precision at a sum which bears an uncanny relationship to that of the net proceeds of the particular offense involved. On occasion, defendants have been known to commit additional offenses while at liberty on bail, in order to secure the requisite funds with which to meet their obligations for payment of legal fees. Defense lawyers condition even the most obtuse clients to recognize that there is a firm interconnection between fee payment and the zealous exercise of professional expertise, secret knowledge, and organizational "connections" in their behalf. Lawyers, therefore, seek to keep their clients in a proper state of tension, and to arouse in them the precise edge of anxiety which is calculated to encourage prompt fee payment. Consequently, the client attitude in the relationship between defense counsel and an accused is in many instances a precarious admixture of hostility, mistrust, dependence, and sycophancy. By keeping his client's anxieties aroused to the proper pitch, and establishing a seemingly causal relationship between a requested fee and the accused's ultimate extrication from his onerous difficulties, the lawyer will have established the necessary preliminary groundwork to assure a minimum of haggling over the fee and its eventual payment.

In varying degrees, as a consequence, all law practice involves a manipulation of the client and a stage management of the lawyer-client relationship so that at least an *appearance* of help and service will be forthcoming. This is accomplished in a variety of ways, often exercised in combination with each other. At the outset, the lawyer-professional employs with suitable variation a measure of sales-puff which may range from an air of unbounding self-confidence, adequacy, and dominion over events, to that of complete arrogance. This will be supplemented by the affectation of a studied, faultless mode of personal attire. In the larger firms, the furnishings and office trappings will serve as the backdrop to help in impression management and client intimidation. In all firms, solo or large scale, an access to secret knowledge, and to the seats of power and influence is inferred, or presumed to a varying degree as the basic vendible commodity of the practitioners.

The lack of visible end product offers a special complication in the course of the professional life of the criminal court lawyer with respect to his fee and in his relations with his client. The plain fact is that an accused in a criminal case always "loses" even when he has been exonerated by an acquittal, discharge, or dismissal of his case. The hostility of an accused which follows as consequence of his arrest, incarceration, possible loss of job, expense and other traumas connected with his case is directed, by means of displacement, toward his lawyer. It is in this sense that it may be said that a criminal lawyer never really "wins" a case. The really satisfied client is rare, since in the very nature of the situation even an accused's vindication leaves him with some degree of dissatisfaction and hostility. It is this state of affairs that makes for a lawyer-client relationship in the criminal court which tends to be a somewhat exaggerated version of the usual lawyer-client confidence game.

At the outset, because there are great risks of nonpayment of the fee, due to the impecuniousness of his clients, and the fact that a man who is sentenced to jail may be a singularly unappreciative client, the criminal lawyer collects his fee in advance. Often, because the lawyer and the accused both have questionable designs of their own upon each other, the confidence game can be played. The criminal lawyer must serve three major functions, or stated another way, he must solve three problems. First, he must arrange for his fee; second, he must prepare and then, if necessary, "cool out" his client in case of defeat[58] (a highly likely contingency); third, he must satisfy the court organization that he

---

58. Talcot Parsons indicates that the soical role and function of the lawyer can be therapeutic, helping his client psychologically in giving him necessary emotional support at critical times. The lawyer is also said to be acting as an agent of social control in the counseling of his client and in the influencing of his course of conduct. See T. Parsons, *Essays in Sociological Theory* 382 et seq. (Glencoe, Ill.: Free Press, 1958); E. Goffman, "On Cooling the Mark Out: Some Aspects of Adaptation to Failure," in *Human Behavior and Social Processes*, A. Rose, ed. (Boston: Houghton Mifflin, 1962), pp. 482–505. Goffman's "cooling out" analysis is especially relevant in the lawyer-accused client relationship.

has performed adequately in the process of negotiating the plea, so as to preclude the possibility of any sort of embarrassing incident which may serve to invite "outside" scrutiny.

In assuring the attainment of one of his primary objectives, his fee, the criminal lawyer will very often enter into negotiations with the accused's kin, including collateral relatives. In many instances, the accused himself is unable to pay any sort of fee or anything more than a token fee. It then becomes important to involve as many of the accused's kin as possible in the situation. This is especially so if the attorney hopes to collect a significant part of a proposed substantial fee. It is not uncommon for several relatives to contribute toward the fee. The larger the group, the greater the possibility that the lawyer will collect a sizable fee by getting contributions from each.

A fee for a felony case which ultimately results in a plea, rather than a trial, may ordinarily range anywhere from $500 to $1,500. Should the case go to trial, the fee will be proportionately larger, depending upon the length of the trial. But the larger the fee the lawyer wishes to exact, the more impressive his performance must be, in terms of his stage managed image as a personage of great influence and power in the court organization. Court personnel are keenly aware of the extent to which a lawyer's stock in trade involves the precarious stage management of an image which goes beyond the usual professional flamboyance, and for this reason alone the lawyer is "bound in" to the authority system of the court's organizational discipline. Therefore, to some extent, court personnel will aid the lawyer in the creation and maintenance of that impression. There is a tacit commitment to the lawyer by the court organization, apart from formal etiquette, to aid him in this. Such augmentation of the lawyer's stage managed image as this affords, is the partial basis for the *quid pro quo* which exists between the lawyer and the court organization. It tends to serve as the continuing basis for the higher loyalty of the lawyer to the organization; his relationship with his client, in contrast, is transient, ephemeral and often superficial.

DEFENSE LAWYER AS DOUBLE AGENT

The lawyer has often been accused of stirring up unnecessary litigation, especially in the field of negligence. He is said to acquire a vested interest in a cause of action or claim which was initially his client's. The strong incentive of possible fee motivates the lawyer to promote litigation which would otherwise never have developed. However, the criminal lawyer develops a vested interest of an entirely different nature in his client's case: to limit its scope and duration rather than do battle. Only in this way can a case be "profitable." Thus, he enlists the aid of relatives not only to assure payment of his fee, but he will also rely on these persons to help him in his agent-mediator role of convincing the accused to plead guilty, and ultimately to help in "cooling out" the accused if necessary.

It is at this point that an accused-defendant may experience his first sense of "betrayal." While he had perhaps perceived the police and prosecutor to be adversaries, or possibly even the judge, the accused is wholly unprepared for his counsel's role performance as an agent-mediator. In the same vein, it is even less likely to occur to an accused that members of his own family or other kin may become agents, albeit at the behest and urging of other agents or mediators, acting on the principle that they are in reality helping an accused negotiate the best possible plea arrangement under the circumstances. Usually, it will be the lawyer who will activate next of kin in this role, his ostensible motive being to arrange for his fee. But soon latent and unstated motives will assert themselves, with entreaties by counsel to the accused's next of kin, to appeal to the accused to "help himself" by pleading. *Gemeinschaft* sentiments are to this extent exploited by a defense lawyer (or even at times by a district attorney) to achieve specific secular ends, that is, of concluding a particular matter with all possible dispatch . . . .

In effect, in his role as double agent, the criminal lawyer performs an extremely vital and delicate mission for the court organization and the accused. Both principals are anxious to terminate the litigation with a minimum of expense and damage to each other. There is no other personage or role incumbent in the total court structure more strategically located, who by training and in terms of his own requirements, is more ideally suited to do so than the lawyer. In recognition of this, judges will cooperate with attorneys in many important ways. For example, they will adjourn the case of an accused in jail awaiting plea or sentence if the attorney requests such action. While explicitly this may be done for some innocuous and seemingly valid reason, the tacit purpose is that pressure is being applied by the attorney for the collection of his fee, which he knows will probably not be forthcoming if the case is concluded. Judges are aware of this tactic on the part of lawyers, who, by requesting an adjournment, keep an accused incarcerated a while longer as a not too subtle method of dunning a client for payment. However, the judges will go along with this, on the ground that important ends are being served. Often, the only end served is to protect a lawyer's fee.

The judge will help an accused's lawyer in still another way. He will lend the official aura of his office and courtroom so that a lawyer can stage manage an impression of an "all out" performance for the accused in justification of his fee. The judge and other court personnel will serve as a backdrop for a scene charged with dramatic fire, in which the accused's lawyer makes a stirring appeal in his behalf. With a show of restrained passion, the lawyer will intone the virtues of the accused and recite the social deprivations which have reduced him to his present state. The speech varies somewhat, depending on whether the accused has been convicted after trial or has pleaded guilty. In the main, however, the incongruity, superficiality, and ritualistic character of the total performance is underscored by a visibly impassive, almost bored reaction on the part of the judge and other members of the court retinue.

Afterward, there is a hearty exchange of pleasantries between the lawyer and district attorney, wholly out of context in terms of the supposed adversary nature of the preceding events. The fiery passion in defense of his client is gone, and the lawyers for both sides resume their offstage relations, chatting amiably and perhaps including the judge in their restrained banter. No other aspect of their visible conduct so effectively serves to put even a casual observer on notice, that these individuals have claims upon each other. These seemingly innocuous actions are indicative of continuing organizational and informal relations, which, in their intricacy and depth, range far beyond any priorities or claims a particular defendant may have.

Criminal law practice is a unique form of private law practice since it really only appears to be private practice. Actually it is bureaucratic practice, because of the legal practitioner's enmeshment in the authority, discipline, and perspectives of the court organization. Private practice, supposedly, in a professional sense, involves the maintenance of an organized, disciplined body of knowledge and learning; the individual practitioners are imbued with a spirit of autonomy and service, the earning of a livelihood being incidental. In the sense that the lawyer in the criminal court serves as a double agent, serving higher organizational rather than professional ends, he may be deemed to be engaged in bureaucratic rather than private practice. To some extent the lawyer-client "confidence game," in addition to its other functions, serves to conceal this fact.

THE CLIENT'S PERCEPTION

The "cop-out" ceremony, in which the court process culminates, is not only invaluable for redefining the accused's perspectives of himself, but also in reiterating publicly in a formally structured ritual the accused person's guilt for the benefit of significant "others" who are observing. The accused not only is made to assert publicly his guilt of a specific crime, but also a complete recital of its details. He is further made to indicate that he is entering his plea of guilt freely, willingly, and voluntarily, and that he is not doing so because of any promises or in consideration of any commitments that may have been made to him by anyone. This last is intended as a blanket statement to shield the participants from any possible charges of "coercion" or undue influence that may have been exerted in violation of due process requirements. Its function is to preclude any later review by an appellate court on these grounds, and also to obviate any second thoughts an accused may develop in connection with his plea.

However, for the accused, the conception of self as a guilty person is in large measure a temporary role adaptation. His career socialization as an accused, if it is successful, eventuates in his acceptance and redefinition of himself as a guilty person.[59] However, the transformation is ephemeral, in that he will, in private, quickly reassert his innocence. Of importance is that he accept his defeat, publicly proclaim it, and find some measure of pacification in it.[60] Almost immediately after his plea, a defendant will generally be interviewed by a representative of the probation division in connection with a presentence report which is to be prepared. The very first question to be asked of him by the probation officer is: "Are you guilty of the crime to which you pleaded?" This is by way of double affirmation of the defendant's guilt. Should the defendant now begin to make bold assertions of his innocence, despite his plea of guilty, he will be asked to withdraw his plea and stand trial on the original charges. Such a threatened possibility is, in most instances, sufficient to cause an accused to let the plea stand and to request the probation officer to overlook his exclamations of innocence.

The table that follows is a breakdown of the categorized responses of a random sample of male defendants in Metropolitan Court[61] during

59. This does not mean that most of those who plead guilty are innocent of any crime. Indeed, in many instances those who have been able to negotiate a lesser plea, have done so willingly and even eagerly. The system of justice-by-negotiation, without trial, probably tends to better serve the interests and requirements of guilty persons, who are thereby presented with formal alternatives of "half a loaf," in terms of, at worst, possibilities of a lesser plea and a concomitant shorter sentence as compensation for their acquiescence and participation. Having observed the prescriptive etiquette in compliance with the defendant role expectancies in this setting, he is rewarded. An innocent person, on the other hand, is confronted with the same set of role prescriptions, structures and legal alternatives, and in any event, for him this mode of justice is often an ineluctable bind.

60. "Any communicative network between persons whereby the public identity of an actor is transformed into something looked on as lower in the local scheme of social types will be called a 'status degradation ceremony.'" H. Garfinkel, "Conditions of Successful Degradation Ceremonies," 61 *Am. J. Soc.* 420–24 (1956). But contrary to the conception of the "cop out" as a "status degradation ceremony," is the fact that it is in reality a charade, during the course of which an accused must project an appropriate and acceptable amount of guilt, penitence and remorse. Having adequately feigned the role of the "guilty person," his hearers will engage in the fantasy that he is contrite, and thereby merits a lesser plea. It is one of the essential functions of the criminal lawyer that he coach and direct his accused-client in that role performance. Thus, what is actually involved is not a "degradation" process at all, but is instead, a highly structured system of exchange cloaked in the rituals of legalism and public professions of guilt and repentance.

61. The name is of course fictitious. However, the actual court which served as the universe from which the data were drawn, is one of the largest criminal courts in the United States, dealing with felonies only. Female defendants in the years 1950 through 1964 constituted from 7%–10% of the totals for each year.

1962, 1963, and 1964 in connection with their statements during presentence probation interviews following their plea of guilty.

It would be well to observe at the outset, that of the 724 defendants who pleaded guilty before trial, only 43 (5.94 percent) of the total group had confessed prior to their indictment. Thus, the ultimate judicial process was predicated upon evidence independent of any confession of the accused.

As the data indicate, only a relatively small number (95) out of the total number of defendants actually will even admit their guilt following the "cop-out" ceremony. However, even though they have affirmed their guilt, many of these defendants felt that they should have been able to negotiate a more favorable plea. The largest aggregate of defendants (373) were those who reasserted their "innocence" following their public profession of guilt during the "cop-out" ceremony. These defendants employed differential degrees of fervor, solemnity and credibility, ranging from really mild, wavering assertions of innocence which were embroidered with a variety of stock explanations and ratio-

TABLE 1   Defendant Responses As To Guilt Or Innocence After Pleading Guilty*

Nature of Response		Number Of Defendants
Innocent (Manipulated)	"The lawyer or judge, police or D.A. 'conned me'" "Wanted to get it over with" "You can't beat the system"	86
Innocent (Pragmatic)	"They have you over a barrel when you have a record"	147
Innocent	"Followed my lawyer's advice" (Advice of counsel)	92
Innocent (Defiant)	"Framed"—Betrayed by "Complainant," "Police," "Squealers," "Lawyer," "Friends," "Wife," "Girlfriend"	33
Innocent (Adverse social data)	Blames probation officer or psychiatrist for "Bad Report," in cases where there was prepleading investigation	15
Guilty	"But I should have gotten a better deal" Blames lawyer, D.A., Police, Judge	74
Guilty	Won't say anything further	21
Fatalistic (Doesn't press his "Innocence," won't admit "Guilt")	"I did it for convenience" "My lawyer told me it was only thing I could do" "I did it because it was the best way out"	248
No Response		8
Total		724

*N = 724; Years—1962, 1963, 1964.

nalizations, to those of an adamant, "framed" nature. Thus, the "Innocent" group, for the most part, were largely concerned with underscor-
ing for their probation interviewer their essential "goodness" and
"worthiness," despite their formal plea of guilty. Assertion of his innocence at the post plea stage, resurrects a more respectable and acceptable self concept for the accused defendant who has pleaded guilty. A
recital of the structural exigencies which precipitated his plea of guilt,
serves to embellish a newly proffered claim of innocence, which many
defendants mistakenly feel will stand them in good stead at the time of
sentence, or ultimately with probation or parole authorities.

Relatively few (33) maintained their innocence in terms of having
been "framed" by some person or agent-mediator, although a larger
number (86) indicated that they had been manipulated or "conned" by
an agent-mediator to plead guilty, but as indicated, their assertions of
innocence were relatively mild.

A rather substantial group (147) preferred to stress the pragmatic
aspects of their plea of guilty. They would only perfunctorily assert
their innocence and would in general refer to some adverse aspect of
their situation which they believed tended to negatively affect their bargaining leverage, including in some instances a prior criminal record.

One group of defendants (92), while maintaining their innocence,
simply employed some variation of a theme of following "the advice of
counsel" as a covering response, to explain their guilty plea in the light
of their new affirmation of innocence.

The largest single group of defendants (248) were basically fatalistic.
They often verbalized weak suggestions of their innocence in rather halt-
ing terms, wholly without conviction. By the same token, they would not
admit guilt readily and were generally evasive as to guilt or innocence,
preferring to stress aspects of their stoic submission in their decision to
plead. This sizable group of defendants appeared to perceive the total
court process as being caught up in a monstrous organizational apparatus, in which the defendant role expectancies were not clearly defined.
Reluctant to offend anyone in authority, fearful that clear cut statements
on their part as to their guilt or innocence would be negatively construed,
they adopted a stance of passivity, resignation and acceptance. Interestingly, they would in most instances invoke their lawyer as being the one
who crystallized the available alternatives for them, and who was therefore the critical element in their decision-making process.

In order to determine which agent-mediator was most influential in
altering the accused's perspectives as to his decision to plead or go to
trial (regardless of the proposed basis of the plea), the same sample of
defendants were asked to indicate the person who first suggested to
them that they plead guilty. They were also asked to indicate which of
the persons or officials who made such suggestion, was most influential in affecting their final decision to plead.

The following table indicates the breakdown of the responses to the
two questions:

TABLE 2   ROLE OF AGENT-MEDIATORS IN DEFENDANT'S GUILTY PLEA

Person Or Official	First Suggested Plea Of Guilty	Influenced The Accused Most In His Final Decision To Plead
Judge	4	26
District Attorney	67	116
Defense Counsel	407	411
Probation Officer	14	3
Psychiatrist	8	1
Wife	34	120
Friends And Kin	21	14
Police	14	4
Fellow Inmates	119	14
Others	28	5
No Response	8	10
Total	724	724

It is popularly assumed that the police, through forced confessions, and the district attorney, employing still other pressures, are most instrumental in the inducement of an accused to plead guilty. As Table 2 indicates, it is actually the defendant's own counsel who is most effective in this role. Further, this phenomenon tends to reinforce the extremely rational nature of criminal law administration, for an organization could not rely upon the sort of idiosyncratic measures employed by the police to induce confessions and maintain its efficiency, high production and overall rational-legal character. The defense counsel becomes the ideal agent-mediator since, as "officer of the court" and confidant of the accused and his kin, he lives astride both worlds and can serve the ends of the two as well as his own.

While an accused's wife, for example, may be influential in making him more amenable to a plea, her agent-mediator role has, nevertheless, usually been sparked and initiated by defense counsel. Further, although a number of first suggestions of a plea came from an accused's fellow jail inmates, he tended to rely largely on his counsel as an ultimate source of influence in his final decision. The defense counsel, being a crucial figure in the total organizational scheme in constituting a new set of perspectives for the accused, the same sample of defendants were asked to indicate at which stage of their contact with the counsel was the suggestion of a plea made. There are three basic kinds of defense counsel available in Metropolitan Court: Legal-aid, privately retained counsel, and counsel assigned by the court (but may eventually be privately retained by the accused).

The overwhelming majority of accused persons, regardless of type of counsel, related a specific incident which indicated an urging or suggestion, either during the course of the first or second contact, that they

TABLE 3   STAGE AT WHICH COUNSEL SUGGESTED ACCUSED TO PLEAD (N = 724)

Contact	Counsel type							
	Privately Retained		Legal-Aid		Assigned		Total	
	N	%	N	%	N	%	N	%
First	66	35	237	49	28	60	331	46
Second	83	44	142	29	8	17	233	32
Third	29	15	63	13	4	9	96	13
Fourth Or More	12	6	31	7	5	11	48	7
No Response	0	0	14	3	2	4	16	2
Total	190	100	487	101*	47	101*	724	100

*Rounded percentage

plead guilty to a lesser charge if this could be arranged. Of all the agent-mediators, it is the lawyer who is most effective in manipulating an accused's perspectives, notwithstanding pressures that may have been previously applied by police, district attorney, judge or any of the agent-mediators that may have been activated by them. Legal-aid and assigned counsel would apparently be more likely to suggest a possible plea at the point of initial interview as response to pressures of time. In the case of the assigned counsel, the strong possibility that there is no fee involved, may be an added impetus to such a suggestion at the first contact.

In addition, there is some further evidence in Table 3 of the perfunctory, ministerial character of the system in Metropolitan Court and similar criminal courts. There is little real effort to individualize, and the lawyer's role as agent-mediator may be seen as unique in that he is in effect a double agent. Although, as "officer of the court" he mediates between the court organization and the defendant, his roles with respect to each are rent by conflicts of interest. Too often these must be resolved in favor of the organization which provides him with the means for his professional existence. Consequently, in order to reduce the strains and conflicts imposed in what is ultimately an overdemanding role obligation for him, the lawyer engages in the lawyer-client "confidence game" so as to structure more favorably an otherwise onerous role system.

CONCLUSION

Recent decisions of the Supreme Court, in the area of criminal law administration and defendant's rights, fail to take into account three crucial aspects of social structure which may tend to render the more libertarian rules as nugatory. The decisions overlook (1) the nature of courts as formal organization; (2) the relationship that the lawyer-regular *actually* has with the court organization; and (3) the character of the lawyer-client relationship in the criminal court (the routine relationships, not those unusual ones that are described in "heroic" terms in novels, movies, and TV).

Courts, like many other modern large-scale organizations possess a monstrous appetite for the cooptation of entire professional groups as well as individuals. Almost all those who come within the ambit of organizational authority, find that their definitions, perceptions and values have been refurbished, largely in terms favorable to the particular organization and its goals. As a result, recent Supreme Court decisions may have a long range effect which is radically different from that intended or anticipated. The more libertarian rules will tend to produce the rather ironic end result of augmenting the *existing* organizational arrangements, enriching court organizations with more personnel and elaborate structure, which in turn will maximize organizational goals of "efficiency" and production. Thus, many defendants will find that courts will possess an even more sophisticated apparatus for processing them toward a guilty plea! □

NOTES AND QUESTIONS

1. Most criminal cases in the United States are terminated by plea bargains. Plea bargaining—"copping a plea"—is a practice in which a defendant agrees to plead guilty or give up his right to a trial, in exchange for a promise to drop some charges, reduce some charges, or lower the sentence. For example, a United States Justice Department study showed that 52 out of every 100 felony arrests were terminated by a plea bargain in 1988. The same data also found that 75 of each 100 felony indictments were terminated by plea bargains. See Barbara Boland, Paul Mahanna, and Ronald Sones, *The Prosecution of Felony Arrests,* 1988; United States Department of Justice, Office of Justice Programs, Bureau of Justice Statistics, February, 1992. The chart on the following page is from this report:

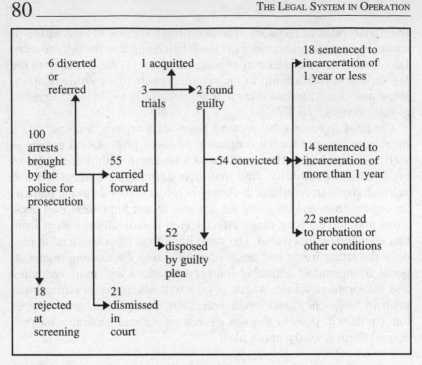

FIGURE 1   Typical outcome of 100 felony arrests brought by the police for prosecution

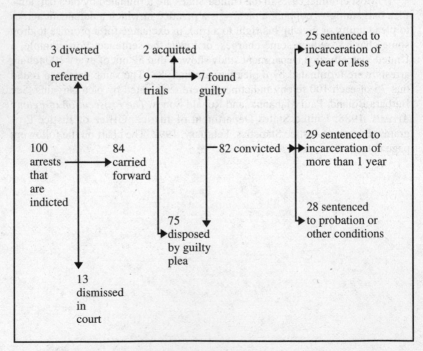

FIGURE 2   Typical outcome of 100 felony arrests that result in indictment

2. Many television shows about the police or courts now discuss or refer to the plea bargaining system. But this media awareness is a relatively recent phenomena. Plea bargaining was only discovered by the press and television in the 1970s. Studies such as that by Blumberg, as well as Donald Newman, *Conviction: The Determination of Guilt or Innocence Without Trial* (New York: Little, Brown & Co., 1966) and Dominick R. Vetri "Guilty Plea Bargaining: Compromises by Prosecutors to Secure Guilty Pleas," 112 *University of Pennsylvania Law Review* 865 (1964), may have helped make the public more aware of plea bargaining.

There is now a tremendous body of research on plea bargaining. A helpful place to begin thinking about the various aspects of plea bargaining is a special issue of 13 *Law & Society Review* (1979). Other useful studies include: Lynn Mather, *Plea Bargaining or Trial? The Process of Criminal-Case Disposition.* (Lexington, Mass: Lexington Books, 1979); Milton Heumann, *Plea Bargaining: The Experiences of Prosecutors, Judges, and Defense Attorneys* (Chicago: University of Chicago Press, 1978); James Eisenstein and Herbert Jacob, *Felony Justice: An Organizational Analysis of Criminal Courts* (Boston: Little, Brown & Co., 1977). See also John Padgett, "Plea Bargaining and Prohibition in the Federal Courts, 1908–1934," 24 *Law & Society Review* 413 (1990).

3. From the 1970s on, there has been an increasing call to reduce the amount of plea bargaining. For example, in 1975 the attorney general of Alaska ordered all of the prosecutors in his office to stop plea bargaining. Also, the Alaska Supreme Court prohibited bargaining by judges. As a result of these steps, explicit plea bargaining did in fact decrease significantly. Interestingly, however, a large proportion of the defendants continued to plead guilty. Apparently, the defendants feared that if they demanded a trial and lost, they would receive a more substantial penalty. Michael L. Rubinstein and Teresa L. White, "Alaska's Ban on Plea Bargaining," 13 *Law & Society Review* 367 (1979). There is also some indication that a prohibition on plea bargaining in El Paso, Texas was successful. See Malcolm Holmes, Howard Daudistel, and William Taggart, "Plea Bargaining Policy and State District Court Caseloads: An Interrupted Time Series Analysis," 26 *Law and Society Review* 139 (1992).

Many other efforts to abolish explicit bargaining have been less successful. A typical example was the prohibition of charge bargaining in drug sale cases by a Michigan prosecutor. Although the prosecutors in his office ceased charge bargaining, some judges began to engage in sentence bargaining with defense attorneys and judges also dismissed or diverted more cases from court. Thus the bargaining process became more complicated and less certain, but the proportion of trials increased only slightly. See Thomas W. Church, Jr. "Plea Bargains, Concessions, and the Courts: Analysis of a Quasi-Experiment," 10 *Law & Society Review* 377 (1976).

Why is plea bargaining so difficult to eliminate? Why did it arise in the first place? On the history of plea bargaining, see Lawrence M. Friedman, "Plea Bargaining in Historical Perspective," 13 *Law & Society Review* 247 (1979). Who is advantaged by plea bargaining? Who is disadvantaged? What does the difficulty in getting rid of plea bargaining tell us about how the legal system operates in general? What message does it send about the importance of informal bargaining?

4. Plea bargaining is controversial. Samuel Krislov, "Debating on Bargain-

'ing: Comments From a Synthesizer," 13 *Law & Society Review* 573, 575–76, 578–81 (1979), summarizes many of the objections to the practice:

> [There are] six families of objections to plea bargaining . . .
>
> At the simplest level the objection is to the notion of . . . haggling over the price. To some it is objectionable because it is unseemly in itself. Others feel that it is unjust because it produces differential results. And finally, there are those who argue that the accused should not participate in defining the punishment.
>
> A second family of objections argues that because plea bargaining takes place *in camera* it undermines the appearance of justice. The privacy of the proceedings not only permits collusion but, even more, suggests to outsiders the possibility of collusion . . . .
>
> A third family of objections is to confounding the question of guilt and innocence with that of the level of punishment, resolving them together instead of through some two-stage process.
>
> A fourth objection is to the coercive element in plea bargaining, that induces the accused either to plead guilty in return for a lighter sentence (as in the previous objection), or to give up other rights in return for some advantage . . . .
>
> A fifth family of objections relates to the question of who sets the punishment. It asserts that the principal problem is the appropriate authority. Should it be (1) the judge . . . ; (2) the police, who investigate; (3) a neutral prosecutor; or (4) the lawyers and parties in what is, after all, a laissez faire society . . . . ?
>
> The final argument against plea bargaining is that punishment is ad hoc rather than regular and predictable . . . .
>
> If Americans demand the imposition of extreme sentences so that they can read about them in newspapers, but then do not insist that they be executed in practice—on the contrary, compel mitigation by withholding the funds that would make it possible to carry out the sentence—then the experts not only can but must do something to subvert the system. If we mandate jail for everyone but have no places for them, the experts must develop a queue or an alternative disposition or somehow shorten the prison term . . . .
>
> Thus, we do not have an ideal of public control subverted by expert discretion but an unworkable system mandated by the legislature, which the expert must somehow make work because in fact the legislature has no other concrete expectations . . . . If our criminal system is in fact made workable only by the exercise of expert discretion, where should experts get guidance? And to what extent should they be explicit about what they are doing?

Lawyers, jurists, political figures, scholars—these are the people who either object to or defend plea bargaining. But what do defendants themselves think about the system? For an answer, see chapter three of Jonathan D. Casper, *American Criminal Justice: the Defendant's Perspective* (Englewood Cliffs, N.J.: Prentice-Hall, 1972).

5. Is plea bargaining exclusively American? On England, see John Baldwin and Michael McConville, "Plea Bargaining and Plea Negotiation in

England," 13 *Law & Society Review* 287 (1979). England is of course also a common law jurisdiction. In many legal systems, there is no such thing as a guilty plea. The state is always supposed to make out its case, whether or not the defendant claims innocence. In such a system, of course, it is less likely that there can be plea bargaining, in the literal sense.

But are there "deals" nonetheless? Consider the following, with regard to the practice in Germany, described in William L. F. Felstiner, "Plea Contracts in West Germany," 13 *Law & Society Review* 309 (1979):

> A West German penal order is a court order prepared by a prosecutor and signed by a judge. It describes the wrongful behavior of the defendant and the evidence gathered by the state and indicates the applicable provisions of the criminal code. It then specifies the punishment to be imposed upon the defendant. If the defendant does not object in writing or in person within one week, the order becomes effective and has the same status as a conviction after trial. If the defendant objects to the order, it is nullified and the case will go to trial. The prosecutor may not make a second attempt to dispose of a case by penal order. Since 1975, the penal order may not provide for imprisonment. The most common penalties are fines and suspensions of drivers' licenses.
>
> Penal orders may be used only for crimes called Vergehen, the American equivalent of which is misdemeanors involving criminal intent or criminal negligence and felonies concerned with protecting property. Vergehen do not encompass petty traffic offenses or violations of business and health regulations . . . Nevertheless, a wide range of crimes from shoplifting and speeding to car theft, embezzlement, and grand larceny may be the subject of penal orders.
>
> The penal order was designed to handle the routine, unproblematic case. It is a cursory procedure, and is not to be used if either the person or the behavior involved appears to require individualized treatment. The penal order is therefore inappropriate if the file shows any doubt about the guilt of the defendant, or a record of repeated violations, or behavior growing out of a disturbed interpersonal relationship.
>
> Penal orders are numerically important in criminal case dispositions in West Germany. In the 1960s more cases were disposed of by penal order than by trial . . . . In 1976 . . . the proportions of penal orders and trials in the lower criminal courts were roughly equal . . . .
>
> In this discussion of penal orders . . . I have skirted around the issue of bargaining in the administration of the penal order system. It is a hard subject to approach through interviews, particularly for a foreigner. Because bargaining is not supposed to take place in West German criminal practice, it is difficult to know how much answers are shaded and how much self-deception occurs. With those reservations, I offer the following observations:
>
> > 1. Whatever negotiation does take place is more apt to be initiated by defense lawyers than by defendants. Any acknowledgment that it may occur seems to crop up in the kinds of cases where lawyers are regularly involved: tax cases in which penal orders may be substantial, loss of

license in motor vehicle cases where insurance provides a lawyer, and cases related to businesses that have employed lawyers for other purposes. That negotiations may be lawyer-specific is a testament to the force of the ideology, to the need to bargain without appearing to do so, which naturally requires an insider's grasp of ritual.

2. Bargaining about criminal justice is distasteful to West Germans . . . .

3. In the United States we tend to negotiate ambiguous and difficult cases. The Germans try these cases. They want to try them because they are difficult; we want to negotiate them because they are difficult to try.

4. There is not much to be gained by bargaining. If jail is a possibility, then a penal order is out of the question. The defendant's view of a "fair" fine can be transmitted to the prosecutor, but the amount of fines is rarely open to wide prosecutorial discretion. The prosecutor may occasionally reduce the fine slightly to induce acceptance of the penal order and save some investigatory effort. But these cases are rare and the stakes are small. Traffic cases, in which loss of license is a possibility, may be a situation where bargaining could achieve important gains. But both the prosecutors and defense lawyers I interviewed stated that in drunken driving cases, at least, the penalty followed automatically from the level of alcohol detected in the defendant's blood.

5. Styles of negotiation are a construct of culture. American lawyers offer and counteroffer. German lawyers hint, suggest, and consider. There are no outright offers and the number of rounds is very limited. How close the different styles are in function is problematic. Given similar stakes, I would predict that similar tasks would be accomplished, but the stakes in Germany are much lower.

6. To Germans who understand the American terminology, bargaining implies both reciprocal concessions from prosecutor and defendant and the probability of a series of offers and counter offers. Initial positions tend to be exaggerated in anticipation of further negotiations. Such behavior does not occur in either the straightforward handling of penal orders or in dickering over a penal order. It is for this reason that I have coined the term "plea contracts" for the title of this paper. The prosecutor (and judge) make an offer . . . . If the defendant accepts it, both sides are spared a trial. The defendant may be making a concession: he does not require the state to prove his guilt in court. Although it would be possible to say that the state also has made a concession—it does not insist that the defendant be tried in open court and it tells the defendant in advance what the penalty will be, state officials do not regard these events as benefits granted to a cooperative defendant but rather as the

process to which qualifying defendants are entitled under routine practice. When a defense lawyer suggests that his client would probably accept a penal order that stipulated a fine at a certain level, he is not making an opening offer in a predictable series, nor is he threatening any dilatory or obstructionist tactics if a different order is made. He is merely signaling what his client believes would be a tolerable outcome of the proceedings.

In fact, it seems to be generally agreed by recent German scholars who study criminal process that the "deal," or informal agreement, is a common phenomenon in that country.

6. In "The Pull of the Policy Audience," 10 *Law & Policy* 97 (1988), Austin Sarat and Susan Silbey criticize many studies in the sociology of law for paying too much attention to the "policy audience." What they mean is that these studies are written in the hope that policy-makers will listen to their suggestions and make certain changes. What's wrong with that? In their opinion, this "pull of the policy audience" biases the scholars toward mere technical improvements and reforms, minor changes, band-aids instead of radical surgery. The "policy audience" consists of the people in power. Hence, the scholars themselves become servants of power, instead of people who analyze and critique the deep structural problems of our society.

Sarat and Silbey use Blumberg as an example of what they mean. They think he reads cases like *Gideon* and *Miranda* as if they were to be taken at face value; he assumes, they say:

[T]he Court's intention is to provide defendants with resources to resist pressure put upon them by court organization. Here one encounters the limits of his critique and the way it legitimates policy elites even as it tries to educate them. Legal decision makers are thus portrayed as benign in their intentions but naive in their anticipations. He writes as if the revelation of the possible unanticipated outcomes of the Court's decisions will, in itself, move judges to amend or alter those decisions to avoid what he observes correctly to be "the rather ironic end of augmenting the existing organizational arrangements."

Is this your reading of Blumberg? What sorts of descriptions of legal "reality" would not be subject to this line of criticism? How would Sarat and Silbey have conducted a study of plea bargaining in a lower New York court? In what ways would someone who took their critique seriously frame research questions and seek to answer them? Could the same kinds of criticism as Sarat and Silbey made of Blumberg be leveled at Berk and Loseke? Indeed, if one should not write for the policy audience, what audience should one write for?

7. For more material on courts, see below, chapter 5, Part D-1. On the methodology of studying courts, see Malcolm F. Feeley, *The Process Is the Punishment: Handling Cases in a Lower Criminal Court* 147–53 (New York: Russell Sage Foundation, 1979). This study perceptively discusses the limits of both qualitative and quantitative methods of describing the work of courts.

Civil Law Processes

CONTRACT LAW

7. Non-Contractual Relations in Business: A Preliminary Study[62]

Stewart Macaulay

28 *American Sociological Review* 55 (1963)

☐ What good is contract law? who uses it? when and how? Complete answers would require an investigation of almost every type of transaction between individuals and organizations. In this report, research has been confined to exchanges between businesses and primarily to manufacturers. Furthermore, this report will be limited to a presentation of the findings concerning when contract is and is not used and to a tentative explanation of these findings.

This research is only the first phase in a scientific study. The primary research technique involved interviewing 68 businessmen and lawyers representing 43 companies and six law firms . . . . All but two of the companies had plants in Wisconsin; 17 were manufacturers of machinery but none made such items as food products, scientific instruments, textiles or petroleum products. Thus the likelihood of error because of sampling bias may be considerable.[63]

. . . This study represents the effort of a law teacher to draw on sociological ideas and empirical investigation. It stresses, among other things, the functions and dysfunctions of using contract to solve exchange problems and the influence of occupational roles on how one assesses whether the benefits of using contract outweigh the costs.

To discuss when contract is and is not used, the term "contract" must be specified. This term will be used here to refer to devices for conducting exchanges. Contract is not treated as synonymous with an exchange itself, which may or may not be characterized as contractual. Nor is contract used to refer to a writing recording an agreement. Contract, as I use the term here, involves two distinct elements: (a) rational planning of the transaction with careful provision for as many future

62. Reprinted from The American Sociological Review by permission. Copyright © 1963 American Sociological Association.

63. However, the cases have not been selected because they *did* use contract. There is as much interest in, and effort to obtain, cases of nonuse as of use of contract. Thus, one variety of bias has been minimized.

contingencies as can be foreseen, and (b) the existence or use of actual or potential legal sanctions to induce performance of the exchange or to compensate for non-performance.

These devices for conducting exchanges may be used or may exist in greater or lesser degree, so that transactions can be described relatively as involving a more contractual or a less contractual manner (a) of creating an exchange relationship or (b) of solving problems arising during the course of such a relationship. For example, General Motors might agree to buy all of the Buick Division's requirements of aluminum for ten years from Reynolds Aluminum. Here the two large corporations probably would plan their relationship carefully. The plan probably would include a complex pricing formula designed to meet market fluctuations, an agreement on what would happen if either party suffered a strike or a fire, a definition of Reynolds' responsibility for quality control and for losses caused by defective quality, and many other provisions. As the term contract is used here, this is a more contractual method of creating an exchange relationship than is a home-owner's casual agreement with a real estate broker giving the broker the exclusive right to sell the owner's house which fails to include provisions for the consequences of many easily foreseeable (and perhaps even highly probable) contingencies. In both instances, legally enforceable contracts may or may not have been created, but it must be recognized that the existence of a legal sanction has no necessary relationship to the degree of rational planning by the parties, beyond certain minimal legal requirements of certainty of obligation. General Motors and Reynolds might never sue or even refer to the written record of their agreement to answer questions which come up during their ten-year relationship, while the real estate broker might sue, or at least threaten to sue, the owner of the house. The broker's method of *dispute settlement* then would be more contractual than that of General Motors and Reynolds, thus reversing the relationship that existed in regard to the "contractualness" of the *creation* of the exchange relationships.

TENTATIVE FINDINGS

It is difficult to generalize about the use and nonuse of contract by manufacturing industry. However, a number of observations can be made with reasonable accuracy at this time. The use and nonuse of contract in creating exchange relations and in dispute settling will be taken up in turn.

The creation of exchange relationships. In creating exchange relationships, businessmen may plan to a greater or lesser degree in relation to several types of issues. Before reporting the findings as to practices in creating such relationships, it is necessary to describe what one can plan about in a bargain and the degrees of planning which are possible.

People negotiating a contract can make plans concerning several types of issues: (1) They can plan what each is to do or refrain from doing; e.g., S might agree to deliver ten 1963 Studebaker four-door sedan automobiles to B on a certain date in exchange for a specified amount of money. (2) They can plan what effect certain contingencies are to have on their duties; e.g., what is to happen to S and B's obligations if S cannot deliver the cars because of a strike at the Studebaker factory? (3) They can plan what is to happen if either of them fails to perform; e.g., what is to happen if S delivers nine of the cars two weeks late? (4) They can plan their agreement so that it is a legally enforceable contract—that is, so that a legal sanction would be available to provide compensation for injury suffered by B as a result of S's failure to deliver the cars on time . . . .

Most larger companies, and many smaller ones, attempt to plan carefully and completely. Important transactions not in the ordinary course of business are handled by a detailed contract. For example, recently the Empire State Building was sold for $65 million. More than 100 attorneys, representing 34 parties, produced a 400-page contract. Another example is found in the agreement of a major rubber company in the United States to give technical assistance to a Japanese firm. Several million dollars were involved and the contract consisted of 88 provisions on 17 pages. The 12 house counsel—lawyers who work for one corporation rather than many clients—interviewed said that all but the smallest businesses carefully planned most transactions of any significance. Corporations have procedures so that particular types of exchanges will be reviewed by their legal and financial departments.

More routine transactions commonly are handled by what can be called standardized planning. A firm will have a set of terms and conditions for purchases, sales, or both printed on the business documents used in these exchanges. Thus, the things to be sold and the price may be planned particularly for each transaction, but standard provisions will further elaborate the performances and cover the other subjects of planning. Typically, these terms and conditions are lengthy and printed in small type on the back of the forms. For example, 24 paragraphs in eight-point type are printed on the back of the purchase order form used by the Allis Chalmers Manufacturing Company. The provisions: (1) describe, in part, the performance required, e.g., "DO NOT WELD CASTINGS WITHOUT OUR CONSENT"; (2) plan for the effect of contingencies, e.g., ". . . in the event the Seller suffers delay in performance due to an act of God, war, act of the Government, priorities or allocations, act of the Buyer, fire, flood, strike, sabotage, or other causes beyond Seller's control, the time of completion shall be extended a period of time equal to the period of such delay if the Seller gives the Buyer notice in writing of the cause of any such delay within a reasonable time after the beginning thereof"; (3) plan for the effect of defective performances, e.g., "The buyer, without waiving any other legal rights, reserves the right to cancel without charge or to postpone deliveries of any of the articles covered by this order which are not shipped in time reasonably to meet said agreed dates"; (4) plan for a legal sanction, e.g., the clause "without waiving any other legal rights," in the example just given.

In larger firms such "boiler plate" provisions are drafted by the house counsel or the firm's outside lawyer. In smaller firms such provisions may be drafted by the industry trade association, may be copied from a competitor, or may be found on forms purchased from a printer. In any event, salesmen and purchasing agents, the operating personnel, typically are unaware of what is said in the fine print on the back of the forms they use. Yet often the normal business patterns will give effect to this standardized planning. For example, purchasing agents may have to use a purchase order form so that all transactions receive a number under the firm's accounting system. Thus, the required accounting record will carry the necessary planning of the exchange relationship printed on its reverse side. If the seller does not object to this planning and accepts the order, the buyer's "fine print" will control. If the seller does object, differences can be settled by negotiation.

This type of standardized planning is very common. Requests for copies of the business documents used in buying and selling were sent to approximately 6,000 manufacturing firms which do business in Wisconsin. Approximately 1,200 replies were received and 850 companies used some type of standardized planning. With only a few exceptions, the firms that did not reply and the 350 that indicated they did not use standardized planning were very small manufacturers such as local bakeries, soft drink bottlers and sausage makers.

While businessmen can and often do carefully and completely plan, it is clear that not all exchanges are neatly rationalized. Although most businessmen think that a clear description of both the seller's and buyer's performances is obvious common sense, they do not always live up to this ideal. The house counsel and the purchasing agent of a medium sized manufacturer of automobile parts reported that several times their engineers had committed the company to buy expensive machines without adequate specifications. The engineers had drawn careful specifications as to the type of machine and how it was to be made but had neglected to require that the machine produce specified results. An attorney and an auditor both stated that most contract disputes arise because of ambiguity in the specifications.

Businessmen often prefer to rely on "a man's word" in a brief letter, a handshake, or "common honesty and decency"—even when the transaction involves exposure to serious risks. Seven lawyers from law firms with business practices were interviewed. Five thought that businessmen often entered contracts with only a minimal degree of advance planning. They complained that businessmen desire to "keep it simple and avoid red tape" even where large amounts of money and significant risks are involved. One stated that he was "sick of being told, 'We can trust old Max,' when the problem is not one of honesty but one of reaching an agreement that both sides understand." Another said that businessmen when bargaining often talk only in pleasant generalities, think they have a contract, but fail to reach agreement on any of the hard, unpleasant questions until forced to do so by a lawyer. Two outside lawyers had different views. One thought that large firms usually planned important exchanges, although he conceded that occasionally matters might be left in a fairly vague state. The other dissenter represents a large utility that commonly buys heavy equipment and buildings. The supplier's employees come on the utility's property to install the equipment or construct the buildings, and they may be injured while there. The utility has been sued by such employees so often that it carefully plans purchases with the assistance of a lawyer so that suppliers take this burden.

Moreover, standardized planning can break down. In the example of such planning previously given, it was assumed that the purchasing agent would use his company's form with its 24 paragraphs printed on the back and that the seller would accept this or object to any provisions he did not like. However, the seller may fail to read the buyer's 24 paragraphs of fine print and may accept the buyer's order on the seller's own acknowledgment-of-order form. Typically this form will have ten to 50 paragraphs favoring the seller, and these provisions are likely to be different from or inconsistent with the buyer's provisions. The seller's acknowledgment form may be received by the buyer and checked by a clerk. She[64] will read the face of the acknowledgment but not the fine print on the back of it because she has neither the time nor ability to analyze the small print on the 100 to 500 forms she must review each day. The face of the acknowledgment—where the goods and the price are specified—is likely to correspond with the face of the purchase order. If it does, the two forms are filed away. At this point, both buyer and seller are likely to assume they have planned an exchange and made a contract. Yet they have done neither, as they are in disagreement about all that appears on the back of their forms. This practice is common enough to have a name. Law teachers call it "the battle of the forms."

Ten of the 12 purchasing agents interviewed said that frequently the provisions on the back of their purchase order and those on the back of a supplier's acknowledgment would differ or be inconsistent. Yet they

---

64. [At the time of this study, clerks working for the firms where interviews were conducted were overwhelmingly women, holding a relatively low status job. Few, if any, had the legal training necessary to give them the ability to analyze the legal consequences of the terms and conditions on the back of the business forms which they had to process in great quantity; even a woman or a man who had such training would not have had the time to undertake this task adequately.]

would assume that the purchase was complete without further action unless one of the supplier's provisions was really objectionable. Moreover, only occasionally would they bother to read the fine print on the back of suppliers' forms . . . .

Sixteen sales managers were asked about the battle of the forms. Nine said that frequently no agreement was reached on which set of fine print was to govern, while seven said that there was no problem. Four of the seven worked for companies whose major customers are the large automobile companies or the large manufacturers of paper products. These customers demand that their terms and conditions govern any purchase, are careful generally to see that suppliers acquiesce, and have the bargaining power to have their way. The other three of the seven sales managers who have no battle of the forms problem, work for manufacturers of special industrial machines. Their firms are careful to reach complete agreement with their customers. Two of these men stressed that they could take no chances because such a large part of their firm's capital is tied up in making any one machine. The other sales manager had been influenced by a law suit against one of his competitors for over a half million dollars. The suit was brought by a customer when the competitor had been unable to deliver a machine and put it in operation on time. The sales manager interviewed said his firm could not guarantee that its machines would work perfectly by a specified time because they are designed to fit the customer's requirements, which may present difficult engineering problems. As a result, contracts are carefully negotiated.

A large manufacturer of packaging materials audited its records to determine how often it had failed to agree on terms and conditions with its customers or had failed to create legally binding contracts. Such failures cause a risk of loss to this firm since the packaging is printed with the customer's design and cannot be salvaged once this is done. The orders for five days in four different years were reviewed. The percentages of orders where no agreement on terms and conditions was reached or no contract was formed were as follows:

1953	75.0%
1954	69.4%
1955	71.5%
1956	59.5%

It is likely that businessmen pay more attention to describing the performances in an exchange than to planning for contingencies or defective performances or to obtaining legal enforceability of their contracts. Even when a purchase order and acknowledgment have conflicting provisions printed on the back, almost always the buyer and seller will be in agreement on what is to be sold and how much is to be paid for it. The lawyers who said businessmen often commit their firms to significant exchanges too casually, stated that the performances would be defined in the brief letter or telephone call; the lawyers objected that nothing else would be covered. Moreover, it is likely that businessmen are least concerned about planning their transactions so that they are legally enforceable contracts. For example, in Wisconsin [at the time of this study] requirements contracts—contracts to supply a firm's requirements of an item rather than a definite quantity—probably were not legally enforceable. Seven people interviewed reported that their firms regularly used requirements contracts in dealings in Wisconsin. None thought that the lack of legal sanction made any difference. Three of these people were house counsel who knew the Wisconsin law before being interviewed. Another example of a lack of desire for legal sanctions is found in the relationship between automobile manufacturers and their suppliers of parts. The manufacturers draft a carefully planned agreement, but one which is so designed that the supplier will have only minimal, if any, legal rights against the manufacturers. The standard contract used by manufacturers of paper to sell to magazine publishers has a pricing clause which is probably sufficiently vague to make the contract legally unenforceable. The house counsel of one of the largest paper producers said that everyone in the industry is aware of this because of a leading New York case concerning the contract, but that no one cares. Finally, it seems likely that planning for contingencies and defective performances are in-between cases—more likely to occur than planning for a legal sanction, but less likely than a description of performance.

Thus one can conclude that (1) many business exchanges reflect a high degree of planning about the four categories—description, contingencies, defective performances and legal sanction—but (2) many, if not most, exchanges reflect no planning, or only a minimal amount of it, especially concerning legal sanctions and the effect of defective performances. As a result, the opportunity for good faith disputes during the life of the exchange relationship often is present.

The adjustment of exchange relationships and the settling of disputes. While a significant amount of creating business exchanges is done on a fairly noncontractual basis, the creation of exchanges usually is far more contractual than the adjustment of such relationships and the settlement of disputes. Exchanges are adjusted when the obligations of one or both parties are modified by agreement during the life of the relationship. For example, the buyer may be allowed to cancel all or part of the goods he has ordered because he no longer needs them; the seller may be paid more than the contract price by the buyer because of unusual changed circumstances. Dispute settlement involves determining whether or not a party has performed as agreed and, if he has not, doing something about it. For example, a court may have to interpret the meaning of a contract, determine what the alleged defaulting party has done and determine what, if any, remedy the aggrieved party is entitled to. Or one party may assert that the other is in default, refuse to proceed with performing the contract and refuse to deal ever again with the alleged defaulter. If the alleged defaulter, who in fact may not be in default, takes no action, the dispute is then "settled."

Business exchanges in non-speculative areas are usually adjusted without dispute. Under the law of contracts, if B orders 1,000 widgets from S at $1.00 each, B must take all 1,000 widgets or be in breach of contract and liable to pay S his expenses up to the time of the breach plus his lost anticipated profit. Yet all ten of the purchasing agents asked about cancellation of orders once placed indicated that they expected to be able to cancel orders freely subject to only an obligation to pay for the seller's major expenses such as scrapped steel. All 17 sales personnel asked reported that they often had to accept cancellations. One said, "You can't ask a man to eat paper [the firm's product] when he has no use for it." A lawyer with many large industrial clients said,

> Often businessmen do not feel they have "a contract"—rather they have "an order." They speak of "cancelling the order" rather than "breaching our contract." When I began practice I referred to order cancellations as breaches of contract, but my clients objected since they do not think of cancellation as wrong. Most clients, in heavy industry at least, believe that there is a right to cancel as part of the buyer-seller relationship. There is a widespread attitude that one can back out of any deal within some very vague limits. Lawyers are often surprised by this attitude.

Disputes are frequently settled without reference to the contract or potential or actual legal sanctions. There is a hesitancy to speak of legal rights or to threaten to sue in these negotiations. Even where the parties have a detailed and carefully planned agreement which indicates what is to happen if, say, the seller fails to deliver on time, often they will never refer to the agreement but will negotiate a solution when the problem arises apparently as if there had never been any original contract. One purchasing agent expressed a common business attitude when he said,

> if something comes up, you get the other man on the telephone and deal with the problem. You don't read legalistic contract clauses at each other if you ever want to do business again. One doesn't run to lawyers if he wants to stay in business because one must behave decently.

Or as one businessman put it, "You can settle any dispute if you keep the lawyers and accountants out of it. They just do not understand the give-and-take needed in business." All of the house counsel interviewed indicated that they are called into the dispute settlement process only after the businessmen have failed to settle matters in their own way. Two indicated that after being called in, house counsel at first will only advise the purchasing agent, sales manager or other official involved; not even the house counsel's letterhead is used on communications with the other side until all hope for a peaceful resolution is gone.

Law suits for breach of contract appear to be rare. Only five of the 12 purchasing agents had ever been involved in even a negotiation concerning a contract dispute where both sides were represented by lawyers; only two of ten sales managers had ever gone this far. None had been involved in a case that went through trial. A law firm with more than 40 lawyers and a large commercial practice handles in a year only about six trials concerned with contract problems. Less than 10 per cent of the time of this office is devoted to any type of work related to contracts disputes. Corporations big enough to do business in more than one state tend to sue and be sued in the federal courts. Yet only 2,779 out of 58,293 civil actions filed in the United States District Courts in fiscal year 1961 involved private contracts. During the same period only 3,447 of the 61,138 civil cases filed in the principal trial courts of New York State involved private contracts. The same picture emerges from a review of appellate cases.[65] Mentschikoff has suggested that commercial cases are not brought to the courts either in periods of business prosperity (because buyers unjustifiably reject goods only when prices drop and they can get similar goods elsewhere at less than the contract price) or in periods of deep depression (because people are unable to come to court or have insufficient assets to satisfy any judgment that might be obtained). Apparently, she adds, it is necessary to have "a kind of middle-sized depression" to bring large numbers of commercial cases to the courts. However, there is little evidence that in even "a kind of middle-sized depression" today's businessmen would use the courts to settle disputes.

At times, relatively contractual methods are used to make adjustments in ongoing transactions and to settle disputes. Demands of one side which are deemed unreasonable by the other occasionally are blocked by reference to the terms of the agreement between the parties. The legal position of the parties can influence negotiations even though legal rights or litigation are never mentioned in their discussions; it makes a difference if one is demanding what both concede to be a right or begging for a favor. Now and then a firm may threaten to turn mat-

---

65. My colleague Lawrence M. Friedman has studied the work of the Supreme Court of Wisconsin in contracts cases. He has found that contracts cases reaching that court tend to involve economically-marginal-business and family-economic disputes rather than important commercial transactions. This has been the situation since about the turn of the century. Only during the Civil War period did the court deal with significant numbers of important contracts cases, but this happened against the background of a much simpler and different economic system. [This study has since been published as *Contract Law in America: A Social and Economic Case Study* (University of Wisconsin Press, 1965).]

ters over to its attorneys, threaten to sue, commence a suit or even litigate and carry an appeal to the highest court which will hear the matter. Thus, legal sanctions, while not an everyday affair, are not unknown in business.

One can conclude that while detailed planning and legal sanctions play a significant role in some exchanges between businesses, in many business exchanges their role is small.

TENTATIVE EXPLANATIONS

Two questions need to be answered: (A) How can business successfully operate exchange relationships with relatively so little attention to detailed planning or to legal sanctions, and (B) Why does business ever use contract in light of its success without it?

Why are relatively non-contractual practices so common? In most situations contract is not needed.[66] Often its functions are served by other devices. Most problems are avoided without resort to detailed planning or legal sanctions because usually there is little room for honest misunderstandings or good faith differences of opinion about the nature and quality of a seller's performance. Although the parties fail to cover all foreseeable contingencies, they will exercise care to see that both understand the primary obligation on each side. Either products are standardized with an accepted description or specifications are written calling for production to certain tolerances or results. Those who write and read specifications are experienced professionals who will know the customs of their industry and those of the industries with which they deal. Consequently, these customs can fill gaps in the express agreements of the parties. Finally, most products can be tested to see if they are what was ordered; typically in manufacturing industry we are not dealing with questions of taste or judgment where people can differ in good faith.

When defaults occur they are not likely to be disastrous because of techniques of risk avoidance or risk spreading. One can deal with firms of good reputation or he may be able to get some form of security to guarantee performance. One can insure against many breaches of contract where the risks justify the costs. Sellers set up reserves for bad debts on their books and can sell some of their accounts receivable. Buyers can place orders with two or more suppliers of the same item so that a default by one will not stop the buyer's assembly lines.

---

66. The explanation that follows emphasizes a considered choice not to plan in detail for all contingencies. However, at times it is clear that businessmen fail to plan because of a lack of sophistication; they simply do not appreciate the risk they are running or they merely follow patterns established in their firm years ago without reexamining these practices in light of current conditions.

Moreover, contract and contract law are often thought unnecessary because there are many effective non-legal sanctions. Two norms are widely accepted. (1) Commitments are to be honored in almost all situations . . . . (2) One ought to produce a good product and stand behind it. Then, too, business units are organized to perform commitments, and internal sanctions will induce performance. For example, sales personnel must face angry customers when there has been a late or defective performance. The salesmen do not enjoy this and will put pressure on the production personnel responsible for the default. If the production personnel default too often, they will be fired. At all levels of the two business units personal relationships across the boundaries of the two organizations exert pressures for conformity to expectations. Salesmen often know purchasing agents well. The same two individuals occupying these roles may have dealt with each other from five to 20 years. Each has something to give the other. Salesmen have gossip about competitors, shortages and price increases to give purchasing agents who treat them well. Salesmen take purchasing agents to dinner, and they give purchasing agents Christmas gifts hoping to improve the chances of making a sale. The buyer's engineering staff may work with the seller's engineering staff to solve problems jointly. The seller's engineers may render great assistance, and the buyer's engineers may desire to return the favor by drafting specifications which only the seller can meet. The top executives of the two firms may know each other. They may sit together on government or trade committees. They may know each other socially and even belong to the same country club. The interrelationships may be more formal. Sellers may hold stock in corporations which are important customers; buyers may hold stock in important suppliers. Both buyer and seller may share common directors on their boards. They may share a common financial institution which has financed both units.

The final type of non-legal sanction is the most obvious. Both business units involved in the exchange desire to continue successfully in business and will avoid conduct which might interfere with attaining this goal. One is concerned with both the reaction of the other party in the particular exchange and with his own general business reputation. Obviously, the buyer gains sanctions insofar as the seller wants the particular exchange to be completed. Buyers can withhold part or all of their payments until sellers have performed to their satisfaction. If a seller has a great deal of money tied up in his performance which he must recover quickly, he will go a long way to please the buyer in order to be paid. Moreover, buyers who are dissatisfied may cancel and cause sellers to lose the cost of what they have done up to cancellation. Furthermore, sellers hope for repeat orders, and one gets few of these from unhappy customers. Some industrial buyers go so far as to formalize this sanction by issuing "report cards" rating the performance of each supplier. The supplier rating goes to the top management of the seller organization, and these men can apply internal sanctions to salesmen, production supervisors or product designers if there are too many "D's" or "F's" on the report card.

While it is generally assumed that the customer is always right, the seller may have some counterbalancing sanctions against the buyer. The seller may have obtained a large downpayment from the buyer which he will want to protect. The seller may have an exclusive process which the buyer needs. The seller may be one of the few firms which has the skill to make the item to the tolerances set by the buyer's engineers and within the time available. There are costs and delays involved in turning from a supplier one has dealt with in the past to a new supplier. Then, too, market conditions can change so that a buyer is faced with shortages of critical items. The most extreme example is the post World War II gray market situation when sellers were rationing goods rather than selling them. Buyers must build up some reserve of good will with suppliers if they face the risk of such shortages and desire good treatment when they occur. Finally, there is reciprocity in buying and selling. A buyer cannot push a supplier too far if that supplier also buys significant quantities of the product made by the buyer.

Not only do the particular business units in a given exchange want to deal with each other again, they also want to deal with other business units in the future. And the way one behaves in a particular transaction, or a series of transactions, will color his general business reputation. Blacklisting can be formal or informal. Buyers who fail to pay their bills on time risk a bad report in credit rating services such as Dun and Bradstreet. Sellers who do not satisfy their customers become the subject of discussion in the gossip exchanged by purchasing agents and salesmen, at meetings of purchasing agents' associations and trade associations, or even at country clubs or social gatherings where members of top management meet. The American male's habit of debating the merits of new cars carries over to industrial items. Obviously, a poor reputation does not help a firm make sales and may force it to offer great price discounts or added services to remain in business. Furthermore, the habits of unusually demanding buyers become known, and they tend to get no more than they can coerce out of suppliers who choose to deal with them. Thus often contract is not needed as there are alternatives.

Not only are contract and contract law not needed in many situations, their use may have, or may be thought to have, undesirable consequences. Detailed negotiated contracts can get in the way of creating good exchange relationships between business units. If one side insists on a detailed plan, there will be delay while letters are exchanged as the parties try to agree on what should happen if a remote and unlikely contingency occurs. In some cases they may not be able to agree at all on such matters and as a result a sale may be lost to the seller and the buyer may have to search elsewhere for an acceptable supplier. Many businessmen would react by thinking that had no one raised the series of remote and unlikely contingencies all this wasted effort could have been avoided.

Even where agreement can be reached at the negotiation stage, carefully planned arrangements may create undesirable exchange relationships between business units. Some businessmen object that in such a carefully worked out relationship one gets performance only to the letter of the contract. Such planning indicates a lack of trust and blunts the demands of friendship, turning a cooperative venture into an antagonistic horse trade. Yet the greater danger perceived by some businessmen is that one would have to perform his side of the bargain to its letter and thus lose what is called "flexibility." Businessmen may welcome a measure of vagueness in the obligations they assume so that they may negotiate matters in light of the actual circumstances.

Adjustment of exchange relationships and dispute settlement by litigation or the threat of it also has many costs. The gain anticipated from using this form of coercion often fails to outweigh these costs, which are both monetary and non-monetary. Threatening to turn matters over to an attorney may cost no more money than postage or a telephone call; yet few are so skilled in making such a threat that it will not cost some deterioration of the relationship between the firms. One businessman said that customers had better not rely on legal rights or threaten to bring a breach of contract law suit against him since he "would not be treated like a criminal" and would fight back with every means available. Clearly, actual litigation is even more costly than making threats. Lawyers demand substantial fees from larger business units. A firm's executives often will have to be transported and maintained in another city during the proceedings if, as often is the case, the trial must be held away from the home office. Top management does not travel by Greyhound and stay at the Y.M.C.A. Moreover, there will be the cost of diverting top management, engineers, and others in the organization from their normal activities. The firm may lose many days work from several key people. The non-monetary costs may be large too. A breach of contract law suit may settle a particular dispute, but such an action often results in a "divorce" ending the "marriage" between the two businesses, since a contract action is likely to carry charges with at least overtones of bad faith. Many executives, moreover, dislike the prospect of being cross-examined in public. Some executives may dislike losing control of a situation by turning the decision-making power over to lawyers. Finally, the law of contract damages may not provide an adequate remedy even if the firm wins the suit; one may get vindication but not much money.

Why do relatively contractual practices ever exist? Although contract is not needed and actually may have negative consequences, businessmen do make some carefully planned contracts, negotiate settlements influenced by their legal rights and commence and defend some breach of contract law suits or arbitration proceedings. In view of the findings and explanation presented to this point, one may ask why. Exchanges are carefully planned when it is thought that planning and a potential legal sanction will have more advantages than disadvantages. Such a judgment may be reached when contract planning serves the internal needs of an organization involved in a business exchange. For example, a fairly detailed contract can serve as a communication device within a large corporation. While the corporation's sales manager and house counsel may work out all the provisions with the customer, its production manager will have to make the product. He must be told what to do and how to handle at least the most obvious contingencies. Moreover, the sales manager may want to remove certain issues from future negotiation by his subordinates. If he puts the matter in the written contract, he may be able to keep his salesmen from making concessions to the customer without first consulting the sales manager. Then the sales manager may be aided in his battles with his firm's financial or engineering departments if the contract calls for certain practices which the sales manager advocates but which the other departments resist. Now the corporation is obligated to a customer to do what the sales manager wants to do; how can the financial or engineering departments insist on anything else?

Also one tends to find a judgment that the gains of contract outweigh the costs where there is a likelihood that significant problems will arise.[67] One factor leading to this conclusion is complexity of the agreed performance over a long period. Another factor is whether or not the degree of injury in case of default is thought to be potentially great. This factor cuts two ways. First, a buyer may want to commit a seller to a detailed and legally binding contract, where the consequences of a default by the seller would seriously injure the buyer. For example, the airlines are subject to law suits from the survivors of passengers and to great adverse publicity as a result of crashes. One would expect the airlines to bargain for carefully defined and legally enforceable obligations on the part of the airframe manufacturers when they purchase aircraft. Second, a seller may want to limit his liability for a buyer's damages by a provision in their contract.

For example, a manufacturer of air conditioning may deal with motels in the South and Southwest. If this equipment fails in the hot summer months, a motel may lose a great deal of business. The manufacturer may wish to avoid any liability for this type of injury to his customers and may want a contract with a clear disclaimer clause.

Similarly, one uses or threatens to use legal sanctions to settle dis-

---

67. Even where there is little chance that problems will arise, some businessmen insist that their lawyer review or draft an agreement as a delaying tactic. This gives the businessman time to think about making a commitment if he has doubts about the matter or to look elsewhere for a better deal while still keeping the particular negotiations alive.

putes when other devices will not work and when the gains are thought to outweigh the costs. For example, perhaps the most common type of business contracts case fought all the way through to the appellate courts today is an action for an alleged wrongful termination of a dealer's franchise by a manufacturer. Since the franchise has been terminated, factors such as personal relationships and the desire for future business will have little effect; the cancellation of the franchise indicates they have already failed to maintain the relationship. Nor will a complaining dealer worry about creating a hostile relationship between himself and the manufacturer. Often the dealer has suffered a great financial loss both as to his investment in building and equipment and as to his anticipated future profits. A cancelled automobile dealer's lease on his showroom and shop will continue to run, and his tools for servicing, say, Plymouths cannot be used to service other makes of cars. Moreover, he will have no more new Plymouths to sell. Today there is some chance of winning a law suit for terminating a franchise in bad faith in many states and in the federal courts. Thus, often the dealer chooses to risk the cost of a lawyer's fee because of the chance that he may recover some compensation for his losses.

An "irrational" factor may exert some influence on the decision to use legal sanctions. The man who controls a firm may feel that he or his organization has been made to appear foolish or has been the victim of fraud or bad faith. The law suit may be seen as a vehicle "to get even" although the potential gains, as viewed by an objective observer, are outweighed by the potential costs.

The decision whether or not to use contract—whether the gain exceeds the costs—will be made by the person within the business unit with the power to make it, and it tends to make a difference who he is. People in a sales department oppose contract. Contractual negotiations are just one more hurdle in the way of a sale. Holding a customer to the letter of a contract is bad for "customer relations." Suing a customer who is not bankrupt and might order again is poor strategy. Purchasing agents and their buyers are less hostile to contracts but regard attention devoted to such matters as a waste of time. In contrast, the financial control department—the treasurer, controller or auditor—leans toward more contractual dealings. Contract is viewed by these people as an organizing tool to control operations in a large organization. It tends to define precisely and to minimize the risks to which the firm is exposed. Outside lawyers—those with many clients—may share this enthusiasm for a more contractual method of dealing. These lawyers are concerned with preventive law—avoiding any possible legal difficulty. They see many unstable and unsuccessful exchange transactions, and so they are aware of, and perhaps overly concerned with, all of the things which can go wrong. Moreover, their job of settling disputes with legal sanctions is much easier if their client has not been overly casual about transaction planning. The inside lawyer, or house counsel, is harder to classify. He is likely to have some sympathy with a more contractual method of dealing. He shares the outside lawyer's "craft urge" to see exchange transactions neat and tidy from a legal standpoint. Since he is more concerned with avoiding and settling disputes than selling goods, he is likely to be less willing to rely on a man's word as the sole sanction than is a salesman. Yet the house counsel is more a part of the organization and more aware of its goals and subject to its internal sanctions. If the potential risks are not too great, he may hesitate to suggest a more contractual procedure to the sales department. He must sell his services to the operating departments, and he must hoard what power he has, expending it on only what he sees as significant issues.

The power to decide that a more contractual method of creating relationships and settling disputes shall be used will be held by different people at different times in different organizations. In most firms the sales department and the purchasing department have a great deal of power to resist contractual procedures or to ignore them if they are formally adopted and to handle disputes their own way. Yet in larger organizations the treasurer and the controller have increasing power to demand both systems and compliance. Occasionally, the house counsel must arbitrate the conflicting positions of these departments; in giving "legal advice" he may make the business judgment necessary regarding the use of contract. At times he may ask for an opinion from an outside law firm to reinforce his own position with the outside firm's prestige.

Obviously, there are other significant variables which influence the degree that contract is used. One is the relative bargaining power or skill of the two business units. Even if the controller of a small supplier succeeds within the firm and creates a contractual system of dealing, there will be no contract if the firm's large customer prefers not to be bound to anything. Firms that supply General Motors deal as General Motors wants to do business, for the most part. Yet bargaining power is not size nor share of the market alone. Even a General Motors may need a particular supplier, at least temporarily. Furthermore, bargaining power may shift as an exchange relationship is first created and then continues. Even a giant firm can find itself bound to a small supplier once production of an essential item begins for there may not be time to turn to another supplier. Also, all of the factors discussed in this paper can be viewed as components of bargaining power—for example, the personal relationship between the presidents of the buyer and the seller firms may give a sales manager great power over a purchasing agent who has been instructed to give the seller "every consideration." Another variable relevant to the use of contract is the influence of third parties. The federal government, or a lender of money, may insist that a contract be made in a particular transaction or may influence the decision to assert one's legal rights under a contract.

Contract, then, often plays an important role in business, but other factors are significant. To understand the functions of contract the whole system of conducting exchanges must be explored fully. More types of business communities must be studied, contract litigation must be analyzed to see why the nonlegal sanctions fail to prevent the use of legal sanctions and all of the variables suggested in this paper must be classified more systematically. ☐

NOTES AND QUESTIONS

1. Among other things, Professor Macaulay's study is a study of the non-use of formal processes of law. But most of us in our everyday life do not use formal processes of law. In what sense, then, is a study of the nonuse of law a study of law, and how does one determine which nonuses of law are, in some sense, legally relevant or relevant to the sociology of law?

The great German sociologist Max Weber was centrally concerned with the role of law in a capitalist society. He recognized that courts see few contract cases, but in a capitalist society "economic exchange is quite overwhelmingly guaranteed by the threat of legal coercion," and a "stable private economic system of the modern type . . . [would be] . . . unthinkable without legal guarantees." Max Rheinstein (ed.), *Max Weber on Law in Economy and Society,* pp. 29–30 (Shils and Rheinstein trans., Cambridge, Mass.: Harvard University Press, 1954). Is Macaulay's study in any way inconsistent with this view? Could the system of dispute avoidance and out-of-court settlement which Macaulay describes exist without the developed rules of contract law and the judicial institutions available to fill the gap when the informal system fails? To what extent do transactions in international trade suggest that a great deal of capitalism can function without formal rules and institutions?

2. To what extent is Macaulay's study about nonuse of law, and to what extent is it about informal rules that do not coincide with the ones "in the books"? Are Macaulay's businessmen following a different code of rules? Insofar as they do follow a different code of rules, should we also call this law?

What would Macaulay find if he conducted a similar study today? How different would the business world look, and why?

In 1985 the Wisconsin Law Review published a symposium on the occasion of the 20th anniversary of Macaulay's article.[68] Macaulay considered his 1963 article in the light of twenty years' experience. He said that there was more business contract litigation than there had been in the early 1960s. In some cases major long-term continuing relationships had collapsed, and parties had turned to litigation. The energy crisis of the 1970s upset assumptions about the costs of performing contracts and provoked many appellate opinions. The decline of the American industrial economy produced controversies about how to spread the costs throughout the society. The shift to new technologies, such as computers, left a gap between expectations and what sellers were able to deliver.

However, Macaulay pointed out that many of the famous 1970s and 1980s contracts cases discussed in law reviews and contracts casebooks, which had resulted in appeals and published opinions, were resolved in the end by settle-

---

68. See "Symposium—Law, Private Governance and Continuing Relationships," 1985 *Wisconsin Law Review.*

ments or bankruptcy. He concluded: "While our court reports have registered a great deal of contracts litigation in recent years, all of these attempts to use contract law have revealed that the second part of my 1963 critique still has force. The legal system in operation simply fails to vindicate rights or offer much to those who seek redress from the courts."[69]

In 1988, the Wisconsin Business Disputes Research Group was formed to study changes in governance structures of American business and the increasing use of law since the 1970s. Galanter, Macaulay, Palay, and Rogers, "The Transformation of American Business Disputing: A Sketch of the Wisconsin Project," 12 *Oñati Proceedings: Disputes and Litigation* 153, 157 (1991) assert:

> [T]he sheer level of business consumption of legal services has dramatically increased. Firms use lawyers more, and business, as the pre-eminent consumer of legal talent, has increased its relative share of total U.S. consumption of legal services. Perhaps most striking here is the increased litigation of inter-firm commercial disputes, that is, the resort to "contractual"—as opposed to what Macaulay (1963), writing a quarter of a century ago, called "non-contractual"—mechanisms for resolving those disputes. Readier recourse to court is reflected in the fact that since 1970 contract actions, (not tort or civil rights actions, as commonly assumed) have become the largest category of civil cases in the federal courts . . . . Preliminary data, for example, suggest that the share of diversity [of citizenship jurisdiction cases in the federal courts involving] contract . . . identifiable as inter-corporate disputes enjoyed a spectacular fourfold increase from 1971 to 1986.
>
> These quantitative data are congruent with a wealth of more qualitative anecdotal observation, revealed in the business press and in our own conversations with business figures. Throughout the American business community, we hear, firms are using law more often and more aggressively in their dealings with other firms . . . .

The Business Disputes Group's study of dispute resolution in the automotive sector of the American economy, however, found little increase in litigation over the past 25 years despite great changes in the industry. The large automobile companies have been able to draft business agreements which ward off litigation by the firms with which they deal. Moreover, the legal staffs of the automobile manufacturers have taken aggressive steps to minimize the costs of dispute resolution. Standard form contracts have been redrafted to minimize disputes and give automobile manufacturers advantages in processing any disputes that do arise. These companies seek to settle disputes quickly, and they make great use of settlements, experts and arbitration to resolve disputes.

3. Is it likely that Macaulay's findings reveal something only about the United States or do they suggest something more fundamental about legal systems generally? What political and legal characteristics might be important in determining whether Macaulay's findings would be replicated in another coun-

---

69. See Macaulay, "An Empirical View of Contract," 1985 *Wisconsin Law Review* 465.

try?[70] Louis Uchitelle, "The Art of a Russian Deal: Ad-Libbing Contract Law," *New York Times,* Jan. 17, 1992, A1, cols. 3–4, discusses doing business in Russia after the collapse of the Soviet Union. Practically, there are no courts that can enforce a Western style contract law. Business turns on mutual benefit and trust. If both parties are benefiting from a deal, they will continue to perform. Parties can provide that disputes will be submitted to an arbitration panel in Stockholm, Sweden, but such panels face great difficulties making and enforcing decisions. Nonetheless, business takes place.

TORT LAW

8. Settled Out of Court: The Social Process of Insurance Claims Adjustment

H. Laurence Ross

2nd ed. (New York: Aldine Publishing Co., 1980)

☐ . . . The major thesis of this book is that legal relationships cannot be understood as a product of the formal law alone, but must be understood in terms of the interplay between the formal law and aspects of the situation in which the law is applied. The determination of legal rights is in the vast majority of cases undertaken by means of informal procedures, the character of which substantively changes the rights thus processed. Moreover, the changes are not random. Informality does not mean lack of structure. Informal procedures exhibit regularities that result from the goals and purposes of the people involved, and from sociologically comprehensible pressures and strains upon them.

The regularities induced from the observation of the day-to-day working out of legal relationships constitute the law in action. It is these regularities that have to be taken into account by the ordinary man and his attorney when the question of rights and duties becomes

70. See, Britt-Mari Blegvad, "Commercial Relations, Contract, and Litigation in Denmark: A Discussion of Macaulay's Theories," 24 *Law & Society Review* 397 (1990). See also Hugh Beale and Anthony Dugdale, "Contracts Between Businessmen," 2 *British Journal of Law & Society* 45 (1975); Terence Daintith, "The Design and Performance of Long-Term Contracts," in Terence Daintith and Gunther Teubner (eds.), *Contract and Organisation: Legal Analysis in the Light of Economic and Social Theory* 164 (Berlin, N.Y.: W. de Gruyter, 1986); Terence Daintith, "Mining Agreements as Regulatory Schemes," in Gunther Jaenicke (ed.), *International Mining Investment: Legal and Economic Perspectives,* 141 (Papers and Proceedings of the AIW Institute Conference, Bad Homburg and Frankfurt 1988); Werner Raub and Jeroen Weesie, *The Management of Matches: Decentralized Mechanisms for Cooperative Relations with Applications to Organizations and Households* (Utrecht University [Netherlands]: Institute for the Study of Cooperative Relations, 1991).

concrete. I propose that the legal critic and the social analyst ought to share this perspective . . . .

THE TORT LAW IN ACTION

In the insured claim, it is the adjuster's task to evaluate the case according to the criteria of formal law, and to negotiate a settlement that will be justified in the light of these criteria and avoid the expensive formal procedure of courtroom trial.

The formal law of torts specifies that someone injured in an automobile accident may recover from a driver if he can show, by the preponderance of evidence, that the driver violated his duty to conduct the vehicle in the manner of an ordinarily prudent person. The driver, however, need pay nothing if he in turn can show by the preponderance of evidence that the claimant also violated a similar duty. Various qualifications apply, depending on the jurisdiction. For example, a governmental or charitable organization may be excused from paying claims, or a husband may not be able to recover from his wife, or a guest from his host. In some exceptional states payment may be reduced rather than eliminated where the claimant's negligent behavior has contributed to the accident. The formal law prescribes a recovery sufficient to make the claimant "whole," repaying in cash for everything he has lost in the accident (regardless of whether or not some other source such as health insurance or sick leave has also compensated for the accident-related losses), and for pain, suffering and inconvenience in addition to more tangible losses.

The formal criteria might lead to the expectation that relatively few people injured in an automobile accident would receive reparation. Most drivers may be thought to be ordinarily prudent people, and even where one is not, formal law embodies the difficulty of affirmative proof of unreasonable behavior. Moreover, to the extent that numbers of negligent drivers are on the highway, an equivalent number of negligent claimants might be expected, who ought to recover nothing. On these assumptions one would expect most claimants to be denied completely, the balance recovering something more than their economic losses. In contrast, the actual picture of recoveries shows that most people injured in traffic accidents are paid, and those who are seriously injured are paid in the large majority of cases. The amount of recoveries fits the formal model only for small claims; where injuries are serious, most claimants fail to recover even their out-of-pocket losses.

The reason the distribution predicted by knowledge of the formal law does not fit the observed distribution of claims settlements is that other factors influence the settlement process. Some of these have been described in this book. Among them are the attitudes and values of the involved personnel, organizational pressures, and negotiation pressures. They exert a direct effect on the enormous majority of bodily claims . . . .

The personalities—attitudes and opinions—of the personnel are perhaps the least significant of the factors mentioned. Generally speaking, adjusters approach their work with conventional business values. Other things equal, they will seek low, conservative settlements, although a sense of fairness makes them disinclined to settle for less than net out-of-pocket losses in a case that is deemed to warrant any settlement at all. The goal of paying no more and no less than these tangible losses is often achieved in routine cases settled directly with the claimant. This is a settlement that many adjusters would characterize as ideal. However, many settlements are made for amounts quite different from the ideal, reflecting pressures and constraints of the employee role and the negotiating situation. Personal dispositions may affect the style with which an adjuster responds to external demands, but they seem to be relatively unimportant in determining the outcome of claims.

Organizational pressure would seem to be a more important factor than personality in affecting the outcome of claims. Pressures from the supervisory structure can even lead adjusters to violate some of the most important company rules, such as those forbidding nuisance payments. Perhaps unexpectedly, the most insistent of organizational pressures is not to keep payments low, but to close files quickly. The closing of files represents for adjusters something of the same kind of central goal as the attainment of good grades represents for the college student, or number of placements for an employment counselor, or a high clearance rate for policemen . . . . [T]he chief effect of this pressure on the behavior of claims men is to increase the number and raise the level of payments. This effect is unexpected and unrecognized by many claims department executives, who are insulated from the front lines by organizational distance, but it is understandable as a means to alleviate specific and recurring pressures experienced by adjusters from their supervisors. The pressure to close files quickly also causes adjusters to simplify their procedures of investigation, as well as their thinking in evaluation. Although the textbooks and manuals propose elaborate and time-consuming routines, the case load prescribes short cuts and approximations . . . .

Another important factor affecting settlement outcomes, particularly with represented claimants, is the medium of negotiation. Negotiation is a social process with a strong implicit rule structure and a repertory of tactics different from those available in litigation. In the case at hand, the most effective tactics threaten recourse to the expense of formal trial, and these threats can be nailed down with commitments. Bodily injury claims negotiators are in roughly the same position as negotiators for two nations disputing a border city, where all involved know that each party can obliterate a major interior city of the other. In such a situation there is strong pressure for compromise, as opposed to an all-or-none disposition. It does not matter much that the formal law prescribes the latter.

As a consequence of these and other pressures, the tort law in action is differentiated from the formal law by its greater simplicity, liberality, and inequity. The concepts of the formal tort law are quite complex: definitions of both damages and negligence suggest the need for case-by-case consideration. The rule of contributory negligence as a bar to recovery makes the formal law appear close-fisted, though it may be lavish in the recovery that it grants a "blameless" victim of a "negligent" driver. Above all, the formal tort law—like the bulk of Anglo-American law—is equitable in its insistence that cases similar in facts be treated in a similar fashion. The law in action departs from the formal law on these three main dimensions.

In order to process successfully vast numbers of cases, organizations tend to take on the characteristics of "bureaucracy" in the sociological sense of the term: operation on the basis of rules, government by a clear hierarchy, the maintenance of files, etc. Such an organizational form produces competence and efficiency in applying general rules to particular cases, but it is not well suited to making complex and individualized decisions. One form of response of bureaucracies to such demands involves a type of breakdown. There will be long delays, hewing to complicated and minute procedures, and a confusion of means with ends. A common and perhaps more constructive response is to simplify the task. This was the tack taken by the claims men I studied. Phone calls and letters replaced personal visits; only a few witnesses, rather than all possible, would be interviewed; and the law of negligence was made to lean heavily on the much simpler traffic law.

Traffic laws are simple rules, deliberately so because their purpose is to provide a universal and comprehensible set of guidelines for safe and efficient transportation. Negligence law is complex, its purpose being to decide after the fact whether a driver was unreasonably careless. However, all levels of the insurance company claims department will accept the former rules as generally adequate for the latter purpose. The underlying reason for this is the difficulty if not impossibility of investigating and defending a more complex decision concerning negligence in the context of a mass operation. In the routine case, the stakes are not high enough to warrant the effort, and the effort is not made. The information that a given insured violated a specific traffic law and was subsequently involved in an accident will suffice to allocate fault. No attempt is made to analyze why this took place or how. The legal concepts of negligence and fault in action contain no more substance than the simple and mechanical procedures noted here provide.

The law of damages is also simplified in action. Although the measurement of special damages appears rather straightforward even in formal doctrine, some further simplification occurs in action when, for instance, life table calculations are used to compute future earnings. More important, the measurement of pain, suffering, and inconvenience is thoroughly routinized in the ordinary claim. The adjuster generally pays little attention to the claimant's privately experienced discomforts and agonies; I do not recall ever having read recitals of these matters in the statements, which are the key documents in the settlement process and in which all matters considered relevant to the disposition of a claim are recorded. The calculation of general damages is for the most part a matter of multiplying the medical bills by a tacitly but generally accepted arbitrary constant. This practice is justified by claims men on the theory that pain and suffering are very likely to be a function of the amount of medical treatment experienced. There is of course a grain of truth in this theory, but it also contains several sources of error. Types of injury vary considerably in the degree of pain and suffering, the necessity for treatment, and the fees charged for treatment; and the correlations between these elements are low. I believe that the more important reason for the use of the formula is again that all levels of the claims department find it acceptable in justifying payment over and beyond special damages. The formula provides a conventional measurement for phenomena that are so difficult to evaluate as to be almost unmeasurable. It provides a rule by which a rule-oriented organization can proceed, though the rule is never formalized. This simplification also meets the comparable needs of plaintiffs' attorneys and is acceptable to them as well. Because of the mutual acceptability of the formula, attorneys will try to capitalize on it by adding to the use and cost of medical treatment, a procedure known as "building" the file, and adjusters will argue concerning the reasonableness of many items that purport to be medical expenses and thus part of the base to which the formula is applied. The procedure is still far less complicated—and less sensitive—than that envisaged in the formal law. Thus again it appears that, relative to the formal law, the law in action is simple and mechanical. Although more individual consideration occurs in larger cases, the principle of simplification governs to a great degree the entire range of settled claims.

The tort law in action is more liberal than the formal law. The formal law of negligence appears to be very stingy from the victim's point of view . . . . The doctrine of contributory negligence is of course the main block to recovery in the formal tort law, and it is this doctrine that is most strongly attenuated in action.

The principal evidence of this attenuation is in the large number of claims on which some payment is made. Insurance company procedures create a file for nearly every accident victim involved with an insured car. Any reasonable estimate of the number of cases in which the insured is not negligent plus the number in which the claimant is contributorily negligent suggests that well under half of all claims deserve payment by formal standards . . . . [C]ontrary to formal expectations the majority of claims are paid, and where serious injuries are involved virtually all claimants recover something from someone else's liability insurance . . . . It is true that in larger claims particularly, the payments may not equal the economic loss experienced, but they may still exceed the level of payment required by the formal law with its rule of contributory negligence.

In small claims, a fair number of denials are successfully made. The adjuster rationalizes his actions on the basis of formal law and the company is shielded from reprisals by high processing costs for the claimant relative to the amount at stake. The adjuster closes his files by denial when he feels the formal law warrants this and also that the claimant will take his case no farther. When he believes that the formal law favors the claimant, and thus finds himself ethically obliged, or when he believes the claimant is determined to press the claim, a payment can be made of considerable magnitude relative to the economic loss involved, although collateral sources—e.g., Blue Cross and sick pay—are usually deducted from negotiated settlements.

In claims based on large losses, the claimant's threat to litigate becomes more credible, and denial thus becomes more difficult. However, the adjuster uses the uncertainty of the formal process as a tool to secure a discount from the full formal value of the claim. Although processing costs may be disregarded, most claimants seem to prefer a definite settlement for a lower amount of money to the gamble of trial for a higher amount of money. The company—like a casino, which is able to translate a large number of gambles into mathematical certainty—is indifferent between these outcomes and can demand a concession for the definite settlement . . . .

The tort law in action may also be termed inequitable. It is responsive to a wide variety of influences that are not defined as legitimate by common standards of equity. The interviews and observations I conducted convinced me that the negotiated settlement rewards the sophisticated claimant and penalizes the inexperienced, the naive, the simple, and the indifferent. Translating these terms into social statuses, I believe that the settlement produces relatively more for the affluent, the educated, the white, and the city-dweller. It penalizes the poor, the uneducated, the Negro, and the countryman. It is also responsive to such matters as the appearances and personalities of the parties and witnesses to the accident. Above all, it rewards the man with an attorney, despite the adjuster's honestly held belief that the unrepresented claimant will fare as well. Apart from the discrimination embodied in allowing recovery of different levels of lost income, these differences are unjustified in formal law, yet their effect on negotiated settlements is considerable.

Although this research was based for the most part on experience in a single, narrow, area of the law, I believe that the distinctions noted here between the formal law and the law in action may be more generally applicable. Wherever law or any other body of rules is applied on a day-to-day basis by a bureaucracy, pressures similar to those observed here may be expected to be present and to produce similar results. Simplification is the essence of mass procedures, and one would expect to find a deemphasis upon sensitivity, individualization, and subtlety in such situations, regardless of the complexity of the philosophy underlying the procedure. Where every man has his day in court, where each is judged according to his ability, where the whole man is being treated, an examination of the machinery in action can be predicted to yield evidence of routinization, categorization, and regimentation. Liberality or something akin to it may also be expected when rules are applied by a bureaucracy, depending on the extent to which sheer volume is emphasized by the processor. The bureaucratic employee under these circumstances seeks a trouble-free and expeditious resolution of disputes, and this may lead more frequently than previously thought to a liberal treatment of the case. Finally, inequity in the sense of applying formally inapplicable criteria is also likely to mark a wide variety of situations in which bureaucracies apply rules. Cases that are alike according to the formal rules may be for many reasons dissimilar when regarded as material to be processed. Factors ranging from the bureaucrat's idiosyncratic whim to strong and systematic organizational pressures may be expected to affect both the process and the outcome wherever the formal law or other rule is put into action. □

NOTES AND QUESTIONS

1. Ross turns up the rather surprising result that insurance companies often pay claims which the law would probably not require them to pay if they defended the claims in court. Why is this so? What does it tell us about the role of legal rules in the insurance settlement process?

2. Ross paints a picture of a process that resolves disputes informally, rather than through the formal use of law. However, he suggests that formal law does play an important role in this informal process. What is this role? How does that role compare to the role played by law in criminal cases and contract disputes? How would Blumberg (with regard to criminal plea bargaining), Macaulay (with regard to commercial disputes), and Ross (with regard to automobile accident disputes) react to the following statement:

Formal law is usually irrelevant; individual goals and private bargaining explain the outcomes in most disputes.

3. According to Ross, informal bargaining often results in inequitable outcomes. A similar judgment could be made about arrests and plea bargaining. How do we guarantee fairness in an informal setting, where formal rules do not explicitly limit and control options?

4. The research method used by Ross follows to some degree the hypothesis testing tradition seen in the Berk and Loseke article. However, like many law and social science research projects, Ross used a two stage process, com-

bining an initial inductive phase and a later deductive phase. The initial inductive phase involved conducting in-depth interviews with insurance adjusters and their supervisors. These interviews were supplemented with direct observations of adjusters at work. He also interviewed plaintiff's attorneys. From these interviews and observations, Ross inductively developed a series of general propositions about the resolution of automobile accident disputes. From these propositions he deduced a series of expectations (or hypotheses) that were then tested with regard to over 2,200 insurance files on bodily injury claims.

5. Are claims adjusters deliberately ignoring the law? Do they actually know what "the law" is supposed to be? Bear in mind that most claims adjusters are not lawyers and have never taken a course in tort law (or any other branch of law). To what extent does this help explain Ross' findings, and the generalization he makes in the last paragraph?

6. For an account of English practices in personal injury cases, see Hazel Genn, *Hard Bargaining: Out of Court Settlement in Personal Injury Actions* (Oxford: Oxford University Press, 1987).

DOMESTIC RELATIONS

9. Bargaining in the Shadow of the Law: The Case of Divorce

Robert Mnookin
and Lewis Kornhauser

88 Yale Law Journal 950 (1979)

2. HOW LEGAL RULES CREATE BARGAINING ENDOWMENTS

☐ Divorcing parents do not bargain over the division of family wealth and custodial prerogatives in a vacuum; they bargain in the shadow of the law. The legal rules governing alimony, child support, marital property, and custody give each parent certain claims based on what each would get if the case went to trial. In other words, the outcome that the law will impose if no agreement is reached gives each parent certain bargaining chips—an endowment of sorts.

A simplified example may be illustrative. Assume that in disputed custody cases the law flatly provided that all mothers had the right to custody of minor children and that all fathers only had the right to visitation two weekends a month. Absent some contrary agreement acceptable to both parents, a court would order this arrangement. Assume further that the legal rules relating to marital property, alimony, and child support gave the mother some determinate share of the family's economic resources. In negotiations under this regime, neither spouse would ever consent to a division that left him or her worse off than if he or she insisted on going to court. The range of negotiated outcomes would be limited to those that leave both parents as well off as they would be in the absence of a bargain.

If private ordering were allowed, we would not necessarily expect parties to split custody and money the way a judge would if they failed to agree. The father might well negotiate for more child-time and the mother for less. This result might occur either because the father made the mother better off by giving her additional money to compensate her for accepting less child-time, or because the mother found custody burdensome and considered herself better off with less custody. Indeed, she might agree to accept less money, or even to pay the father, if he agreed to relieve her of some child-rearing responsibilities. In all events, because the parents' tastes with regard to the trade-offs between money and child-time may differ, it will often be possible for the parties to negotiate some outcome that makes both better off than they would be if they simply accepted the result a court would impose.

3. PRIVATE ORDERING AGAINST A BACKDROP OF UNCERTAINTY

Legal rules are generally not as simple or straight forward as is suggested by the last example. Often, the outcome in court is far from certain, with any number of outcomes possible. Indeed, existing legal standards governing custody, alimony, child support, and marital property are all striking for their lack of precision and thus provide a bargaining backdrop clouded by uncertainly. The almost universal judicial standard for resolving custody disputes is the "best interests of the child." Except in situations when one parent poses a substantial threat to the child's well-being, predicting who will get custody under this standard is difficult indeed, especially given the increasing pressure to reject any presumption in favor of maternal custody. Similarly, standards governing alimony and child support are also extraordinarily vague and allow courts broad discretion in disputed cases.

Analyzing the effects of uncertainty on bargaining is an extremely complicated task. It is apparent, however, that the effects in any particular case will depend in part on the attitudes of the two spouses toward risk—what economists call "risk preferences." . . .

4. TRANSACTION COSTS

Costs are involved in resolving the distributional consequences of separation or divorce, and in securing the divorce itself. The transaction costs that the parties must bear may take many forms, some financial and some emotional. The most obvious and tangible involve the expenditure of money. Professional fees—particularly for lawyers—must be paid by one or both parties. In addition, there are filing fees and court costs. More difficult to measure, but also important, are the emotional and psychological costs involved in the dispute-settlement process. Lawsuits generally are emotionally burdensome; the psychological costs imposed by bargaining (and still more by litigation) are particularly acute in divorce.

The magnitude of these transaction costs, both actual and expected, can influence negotiations and the outcome of bargaining. In the dissolution process, one spouse, and that spouse's attorney, can substantially affect the magnitude of the transaction costs that must be borne by the other spouse. As is generally the case, the party better able to bear the transaction costs, whether financial or emotional, will have an advantage in divorce bargaining. .

In divorce, transaction costs will generally tend to be (1) higher if there are minor children involved, because of the additional and intensely emotional allocational issues to be determined; (2) an increasing function of the amount of property and income the spouses have, since it is rational to spend more on negotiation when the possible rewards are higher; and (3) higher when there is a broad range of possible outcomes in court.

5. STRATEGIC BEHAVIOR

The actual bargain that is struck through negotiations—indeed, whether a bargain is struck at all—depends on the negotiation process. During this process, each party transmits information about his or her own preferences to the other. This information may be accurate or intentionally inaccurate; each party may promise, threaten, or bluff. Parties may intentionally exaggerate their chances of winning in court in the hope of persuading the other side to accept less. Or they may threaten to impose substantial transaction costs—economic or psychological—on the other side. In short, there are a variety of ways in which the parties may engage in strategic behavior during the bargaining process.

Opportunities for strategic behavior exist because the parties often will not know with certainty (1) the other side's true preferences with regard to the allocational outcomes; (2) the other spouse's preferences or attitudes towards risk; and (3) what the outcome in court will be, or even what the actual odds in court are. Although parents may know a great deal about each other's preferences for money and children, complete knowledge of the other spouse's attitudes is unlikely.

How do parties and their representatives actually behave during the process? Two alternative models are suggested by the literature: (1) a *Strategic Model,* which would characterize the process as "a relatively norm-free process centered on the transmutation of underlying bargaining strength into agreement by the exercise of power, horse-trading, threat, and bluff"; and (2) a *Norm-Centered Model,* which would characterize the process by elements normally associated with adjudication—the parties and their representatives would invoke rules, cite precedents, and engage in reasoned elaboration. Anecdotal observation suggests that each model captures part of the flavor of the process. The parties and their representatives do make appeals to legal and social norms in negotiation, but they frequently threaten and bluff as well.

C. THE TASK FACING THE SPOUSES AND THE PROCESS OF NEGOTIATION

The task facing divorcing spouses can be summarized, based on the preceding analysis, as one of attempting through bargaining to divide money and child-rearing responsibilities to reflect personal preferences. Even though the interests of the two parents may substantially conflict, opportunities for making both parents better off through a negotiated agreement will exist to the extent that parental preferences differ.

This analysis suggests why most divorcing couples never require adjudication for dispute settlement. The parties gain substantial advantages when they can reach an agreement concerning the distributional consequences of divorce. They can minimize the transaction costs involved in adjudication. They can avoid its risks and uncertainties, and negotiate an agreement that may better reflect their individual preferences.

Furthermore, divorcing spouses usually have no incentive to take cases to court for their precedential value. Unlike insurance companies, public-interest organizations, and other "repeat players," a divorcing spouse will generally have no expectation that an adjudicated case will create precedent, or that any precedent created will be of personal benefit in future litigation.

Given the advantages of negotiated settlements, why do divorcing spouses ever require courtroom adjudication of their dispute? There are a variety of reasons why some divorce cases will be litigated:

1. *Spite.* One or both parties may be motivated in substantial measure by a desire to punish the other spouse, rather than simply to increase their own net worth.

2. *Distaste for Negotiation.* Even though it costs more, one or both parties may prefer the adjudicative process (with third-party decision) to any process that requires a voluntary agreement with the other spouse. Face-to-face contact may be extremely distasteful, and the parties may not be able to negotiate—even with lawyers acting as intermediaries—because of distrust or distaste.

3. *Calling the Bluff—The Breakdown of Negotiations.* If the parties

get heavily engaged in strategic behavior and get carried away with making threats, a court-room battle may result, despite both parties' preference for a settlement. Negotiations may resemble a game of "chicken" in which two teenagers set their cars on a collision course to see who turns first. Some crack-ups may result.

4. *Uncertainty and Risk Preferences.* The exact odds for any given outcome in court are unknown, and it has been suggested that litigants typically overestimate their chances of winning. To the extent that one or both of the parties typically overestimate their chances of winning, more cases will be litigated than in a world in which the outcome is uncertain but the odds are known. In any event, when the outcome is uncertain, settlement prospects depend on the risk preferences of the two spouses.

5. *No Middle Ground.* If the object of dispute cannot be divided into small enough increments—whether because of the law, the practical circumstances, or the nature of the subject at issue—there may be no middle ground on which to strike a feasible compromise. Optimal bargaining occurs when, in economic terminology, nothing is indivisible.

These points can be illustrated through a simple example. Assume a divorcing couple has no children and the only issue is how they will divide 100 shares of stock worth $10,000. Let us further assume that it would cost each spouse $1,000 to have a court decide this issue, and that each spouse must pay his own litigation costs.

If the outcome in court were entirely certain, would the parties ever litigate? Suppose it were clear that a court would inevitably award one-half of the stock to each spouse because it would be characterized as community property. If the issue were litigated, each spouse would end up with only $4,000. One might expect that the parties would normally simply settle for $5,000, and save the costs of litigation. Taking the issue to court would substitute an expensive mode of dispute resolution—adjudication—for a cheaper mode—negotiation.

Even when the outcome in court is certain, litigation is still possible. A spouse might engage in strategic behavior and threaten to litigate in order to get more than half. Suppose the husband threatened to litigate unless the wife agreed to accept a settlement of $4,500. The wife might accept $4,500 but only if she believed the threat. She would know with proper legal advice that her husband would only end up with $4,000 if he litigated. Therefore the threat ordinarily would not be credible. She might call his bluff and tell him to sue. If the wife were convinced, however, that her husband was motivated by spite and in fact preferred to litigate rather than accept less than $5,500, she might accept $4,500. If the outcome in court is certain, absent spite, strategic behavior, or a distaste for negotiations, adjudication should not generally occur; litigation would impose an expensive mode of dispute settlement when a less expensive alternative could achieve the same result.

What about cases in which the result in court is uncertain? Assume, for example, that there is a fifty percent chance that the husband will get all $10,000, and a fifty percent chance that the wife will get all $10,000. A settlement in these circumstances obviously depends on the risk preferences of the two spouses. If both are risk neutral, then both will negotiate the same way as they would if they knew for certain that a court would award each of them $5,000—the "expected" value of the litigation in this case.

To the extent that the parties are both risk averse—each is prepared to accept less than $5,000 to avoid the risks of litigation—the parties have a broader range of possible settlements that both would prefer to the risks of litigation. This might facilitate agreement.

Conversely, if both parties are risk preferers—each prefer the gamble to an offer of the expected value of $5,000—all cases are likely to be litigated. When one party is a risk preferer and the other is risk-averse, it is difficult to predict the effect on the rate of litigation. In any negotiated outcome, a risk preferer will have an advantage over the party who is risk-averse. □

NOTES AND QUESTIONS

1. Mnookin and Kornhauser talk about "bargaining in the shadow of the law." How does their view of the role of law in divorce and custody negotiations compare with the role of law in criminal cases, and in contract and tort disputes? Why might the "shadow" of the law play a more important role in some types of disputes than others?

2. There are many areas of law and life where bargaining and mediation go on, but do they really always take place in the "shadow" of the law? In "Internal Dispute Resolution: The Transformation of Civil Rights in the Workplace," 27 *Law & Society Review* 497 (1993), Lauren B. Edelman, Howard S. Erlanger, and John Lande studied how employers deal internally with complaints about discrimination based on race, gender, and similar factors. The authors conducted interviews with personnel who handled such complaints in ten large organizations. They concluded "law plays a very peripheral role in complaint handlers' orientations toward discrimination complaints . . . . [The management representatives] tend to subsume legal goals under managerial goals." The "overriding objective" of the complaint-handlers was to "maintain the smooth functioning of the organization" (p. 511). Nor did any of the complaint-handlers adopt "formal legal standards in their internal dispute handling." The law does not cast much of a shadow in these companies. "Rather than adopting the calculus of the courts and EEO [Equal Employment Opportunity] agencies, complaint-handlers simply construe law as a requirement of fair treatment" (p. 513).

What these managers do, in short, is try to resolve the problem to the satisfaction of everybody. This means that they will handle *any* kind of complaint that presents a managerial problem. Hence, although "organizational concerns tend to eclipse the shadow of the law," at the same time, these people "also resolve cases that do not actually involve discrimination. In this sense, law casts a broad shadow; it encourages the resolution of many complaints that would find no remedy under law" (p. 518).

The picture painted by Edelman and her associates might be taken as rather benign, but the authors feel that the managerial techniques have the potential to "undermine legal rights by failing to define and articulate the boundaries of those rights and by indicating to employees that problems are interpersonal, psychological, or managerial in nature rather than legal" (p. 528). Is this a fair criticism? How would you remedy the situation if you thought it needed change?

3. Over the last century there has been a shift in the civil (noncriminal) docket of American courts. Domestic relations and tort issues make up a higher percentage of the case-load than before. See Lawrence Friedman and Robert Percival, "A Tale of Two Courts: Litigation in Alameda and San Benito Counties," 10 *Law & Society Review* 267 (1976); Wayne McIntosh, *The Appeal of Civil Law: A Political-Economic Analysis of Litigation* (Urbana, Ill.: University of Illinois Press, 1990). Such cases are usually resolved pretty informally. This means that what we traditionally think of as the work of courts—dispute resolution—has been in part replaced by administrative processing, default divorces, and ratification of out of court settlements. Taking this into consideration, along with the prevalence of plea bargaining in criminal cases, how would you describe the role or function of trial courts in American society? How does this "in-action" picture of courts differ from the conventional image?

4. Mnookin and Kornhauser identify some reasons why couples may go to court instead of negotiating, even though negotiation is generally cheaper and easier. Are these reasons the same as the reasons which might lead a defendant to turn down a chance to plea-bargain? Or which might lead an accident victim to bring a tort action instead of settling out of court? Are there some general principles which determine when people use the formal legal system, and when they prefer informal bargaining and negotiation?

5. Herbert M. Kritzer, in *Let's Make a Deal: Understanding the Negotiation Process in Ordinary Litigation* (Madison, Wis.: University of Wisconsin Press, 1991), pp. 73–5, 103–04, 132–33. argues that we must be careful with the "bargaining in the shadow of the law" metaphor. What do we mean by "bargaining" and by the "shadow of *the law?*" Kritzer asserts that there are two different "shadows" of law, which might give one party a measure of bargaining power. In tort cases appellate decisions provide *"relatively* little basis for prediction," especially about the money damages that might be gained through litigation. But there is another "shadow" of law: "the ability to impose costs on the opponent and the capability of absorbing costs."

Kritzer does not think that these factors are critical to settlements in ordinary civil cases. In tort cases, lawyers use the contingent fee system. This offsets the ability of corporations and insurance companies to absorb the costs of litigation. But defendants who face many similar claims have a certain amount of incentive to litigate so that contingent fee plaintiff's lawyers get the message that frivolous suits will not pay.

Kritzer's data[71] show that it is not in the contingent fee lawyer's own financial interest to engage in tactical bargaining (i.e., making demands that are sub-

---

71. Kritzer analyzed data collected by the Civil Litigation Research Project during 1979–80 at the University of Wisconsin-Madison. David Trubek, William L.F. Felstiner, Joel Grossman, and Austin Sarat collaborated in thinking through the design of the research, planning the data collection, and the early analyses. See David M. Trubek, Austin Sarat, William L.F. Felstiner, Herbert M. Kritzer, Joel B. Grossman, "The Costs of Ordinary Litigation," 31 *UCLA Law Review* 72 (1983).

stantially different from the acceptable outcome) in ordinary litigation. Such a lawyer profits from rapid turnover of cases, with relatively little effort devoted to each one. Moreover, a contingent fee lawyer gains by establishing a reputation with defense lawyers as one who makes reasonable demands.

Kritzer's study further shows that we should interpret the term "bargaining" carefully. He found:

—Most [tort] cases are settled with one or two exchanges of offers and/ or demands.

—Most lawyers devote relatively small amounts of time to actual negotiation.

—A large portion of initial offers and demands are very close to the acceptable settlement.

—Relatively few cases involve substantial shifts in offers and demands in the course of the bargaining.

—Plaintiffs are less likely to engage in tactical bargaining . . . than are defendants.

—Contingent-fee lawyers do not obtain higher effective hourly rates by engaging in tactical bargaining.

A lawyer who handles personal injury claims has suggested that in the late 1980s and early 1990s, about ten years after Kritzer's data was gathered, there may be more bargaining in the shadow of the law. In many states there is now a well-established right to recover against insurance companies that refuse in bad faith, to settle where there is little question of liability or the amount due. Plaintiffs' lawyers bargaining with insurance companies routinely mention this doctrine when they meet resistance from insurers. To what extent, if at all, does this undercut Kritzer's point?

Kritzer concedes that the picture may be different in divorce where the stakes (the couple's assets) are fixed and known and the problem is one of division. He notes that Eleanor E. Maccoby, Charlene D. Depner, and Robert H. Mnookin, in "Custody of Children Following Divorce," in E. Mavis Hetherington and Josephine D. Arasten (eds) *Impact of Divorce, Single Parenting and Step-Parenting on Children* (Hillsdale, N.J.: Lawrence Erlbaum Associates, 1988), p. 91, suggest that the shadow of what might happen in litigation affects child custody arrangements in California. However, Judith A. Seltzer and Irwin Garfinkel, in "Inequality in Divorce Settlements: An Investigation of Property Settlements and Child Support Awards," 19 *Social Science Research* 82 (1990), found no impact of a legal shadow on property and support settlements in Wisconsin.

Herbert Jacob, "The Elusive Shadow of the Law," 26 *Law & Society Review* 565, 586 (1992), reports:

The expectation that bargaining occurs in the shadow of the law is not a general rule but one that is contingent on many conditions. My research suggests that the language in which a claim is initially framed combined with the manner in which attorneys are used and the success of consultation with personal networks are perhaps the key variables in determining the strength of the shadow of the law.

6. What evidence, if any, is there that Mnookin and Kornhauser are right in the statements they make about bargaining? How do they know what motivates couples? Consider the following excerpt:

10. Participation and Flexibility in Informal Processes: Cautions from the Divorce Context

Howard S. Erlanger,

Elizabeth Chambliss,

and Marygold S. Melli

21 *Law & Society Review* 585 (1987)

I. INTRODUCTION

☐ . . . Our analysis is based on in-depth interviews with the parties and lawyers in twenty-five stipulated (i.e., informally settled) divorce cases as well as the court records pertaining to each settlement. All twenty-five cases involve minor children, and all were closed in Dane County (Madison), Wisconsin, in June or July of 1982. They were selected from all such cases closed during this period on the basis of participants' accessibility. Altogether the data include forty-three party interviews and thirty lawyer interviews. In addition to the respondents from these cases, we interviewed four family court judges who handled divorces in the county at the time of the study . . . .

II. ASSUMPTIONS ABOUT INFORMAL DIVORCE SETTLEMENT

Proponents of the informal process assume that two characteristics operate to the benefit of divorcing parties. One is the potential for flexibility: The informal setting can offer divorcing couples the opportunity to create personalized settlements—compromises that reflect the interests of each party . . . Of course, this flexibility is not unrestrained, since the court, representing the public, has significant interests in divorce outcomes as well, particularly with respect to child support. Although flexible, informal settlement is said to occur "in the shadow of the law,"* that is, within legal limits provided by judicial review. Thus, the

---

*[The reference is to Mnookin and Kornhauser, Reading No. 9, supra.]

informal settlement process has in part a "best-of-both-worlds" reputation, potentially combining the consistency of legal standards with the opportunity for flexibility and case-by-case decision making.

The second characteristic of the informal process is that it allows parties to participate in decision making. This is related to the benefit of flexibility, in that participation is the method by which flexibility is achieved. But participation is also considered meaningful in its own right, for when the parties have more control over decisions, they are more likely to take responsibility for them; furthermore, they will be more satisfied with a self-imposed result than with one that is court imposed . . . . This is considered crucial in cases involving child support orders because child support non-compliance is a problem of major economic proportions . . . .

III. INFORMAL SETTLEMENT: CHOICE OR CONSTRAINT?

B. Pressures to Settle Informally

The factors that induce settlement in other legal settings are amply present in divorce cases. For instance, in most families divorce severely disrupts the financial status quo, and financial divisions and obligations typically remain unresolved as the case is pending. There may also be a cash flow problem; many parties cannot afford to go to court or to continue paying attorneys as disputes wage on. A lack of financial resources prevented many respondents from even considering a formal trial:

> My attorney told me that if I had gone to court—I had already paid him $175—gone in there and started arguing with her about this and that, the judge would have thrown us out, and it would have cost us $75 to go back in. Every time he entered the court with me . . . it would cost me $75 [and] cost her $75 (H).[72]

Financial pressures sometimes prompted a settlement even against an attorney's strong objections:

> My attorney was upset with me, he even wrote me a letter saying he was upset that I had agreed [to pay] $400 a month child support because he thought that was a high figure and we could do much better. At that time I was not interested as much in myself as I was in getting the damn thing over. I didn't want to go on and keep fighting—I think my attorney fees were already up to $1,700 . . . . [The divorce proceedings] put me in such a financial bind . . . (H).

---

72. [The authors indicate that their quotations are from a husband (H), a wife (W), a wife's lawyer (WL), a husband's lawyer (HL), or a judge (J).]

Within the settlement process, parties often exercised financial leverage against each other. One woman reports that she settled only because her husband withheld temporary support payments:

> I had to say that I was signing this freely, which of course was a lie because at this point my mortgage payment was six days past due, and [his] lawyer was standing there with the check in his pocket saying, "Sign or you don't get the money" (W).

In addition to financial pressures, parties and lawyers also refer to a kind of social pressure to resolve divorce disputes without trial. The lawyers in particular describe a widespread professional belief that divorce litigation is traumatic and that good lawyers keep their clients out of court, especially in cases involving children. Most of the lawyers we interviewed say they feel responsible for encouraging informal settlement and will pressure parties to accept settlements that they, as attorneys, find reasonable:

> I personally feel that if a case does go to trial I have failed in some way. I have not found the right compromise. I have not been creative enough. And I have not been persuasive enough to get the thing resolved short of litigation (WL).

Some attorneys also say that if they cannot persuade their client to accept a certain settlement, they arrange for a four-way meeting between clients and lawyers or a pretrial conference before the family court commissioner. As one lawyer explains:

> Then they are faced with the other person and it makes them all of a sudden see the reality of the situation and it is not a game anymore. It is also so uncomfortable that they want to get it over with (HL).

External pressure to settle may become more direct as a hearing date approaches. One judge says that if parties are supposed to have a stipulation but don't, he threatens them with significant delay in finalizing their divorce:

> I'll say, "Look folks, you've got three-quarters of an hour left before I go on to something else. If you can settle, we'll go on to court and get this thing over with today. Otherwise, you can have a date [far in the future]" (J).

Our interviews with the parties indicate that pressures from lawyers and judges can be quite effective, for it is difficult to continue to press demands without procedural support. One woman's comments are particularly illustrative:

> I said to [my lawyer], "You cannot make me sign those papers . . . you're talking about 14 years of my life . . . . I'm still carrying on the

responsibility for two kids . . . and if I stay [in the house] till the kids are out of school I'll owe [my husband] $26,000." And [my lawyer] said to me, "It's already been typed up. If you want to stop it now, fine. Go get yourself another lawyer, see how soon you get in court. If you want to stick around and fool around with that jerk, do it . . . . I won't have anything to do with it." Well, I was worn down . . . . I cried through the whole thing, I could hardly say yes, I could hardly sign it. I walked out of there and cried for probably two weeks straight (W).

Besides financial and procedural pressures, which are well documented in most informal settings, the divorce process provides other, context-specific pressures as well. Ending a marital relationship is a consuming enterprise, and perhaps more than any other legal context, divorce is infused with extreme personal emotion. In some cases, parties may want nothing more than to terminate their marriage as soon as possible. A number of respondents report settling strictly out of impatience to end the process; others were involved in new relationships and wanted a quick settlement so they could remarry; some were simply eager to return to some semblance of a stable life style. Not only does divorce typically result in the total upheaval of both parties' personal lives but it also affects children and may strain parent-child relationships. For some a prolonged dispute is simply intolerable for this reason, and they settle because they have reached, as one respondent calls it, a "folding point":

> You know, after you go on with a divorce for two years, there is a folding point. I guess this is where I folded—and it ended up it was $13,000 I owed him . . . (W).

> Yes, I was very disappointed. I don't think [the settlement] was right . . . but at that point I really wanted to get out of the divorce. I wanted to quit paying the attorney and get this thing finaled out. It gets pretty heavy, you lose your sense of being . . . . You're really put down (H).

C. The Emotional Intensity of Nonmutual Divorce

Although disputes in other informal settings are subject to financial, procedural, and emotional pressures, the informal divorce process is arguably unique in its vulnerability to the idiosyncrasies of interpersonal conflict. Nearly every lawyer we interviewed distinguished divorce from other types of cases, observing that divorce was by far the most emotionally draining area of their practice. As one lawyer quipped, "Divorce is 99 percent psychotherapy, 1 percent law." The very intimacy that supposedly makes divorce well-suited to informal resolution may instead hamper rational negotiation of terms. As one practitioner observes:

Your client in a personal injury action, they generally don't know the person who ran them over. Their only contact with them was for that brief fleeting moment when they were hit by the car. And they probably haven't seen them since, and maybe will never see them again. They therefore don't have much of an opportunity to generate strong emotional feelings toward them. They may be very dissatisfied with what happened, the fact that they ended up being injured, and went through pain and suffering and all of this and it was that person's fault. But generally speaking, a large dose of money is going to cure a lot of [that]. I have never had a personal injury case where the client has said at any time during the proceedings, you know "that person is a real son-of-a-gun and I don't care about the money, I don't care about anything. I just want you to get him. I want to go to trial and stand up and tell the whole world what a rotten driver he or she may be." . . . If you switch over to a divorce action, obviously the parties know each other . . . . In the vast majority of cases, they have strong feelings (HL).

Even in other legal actions involving long-term relationships, such as contract disputes in business, the negotiation context may be qualitatively different than it is in divorce. One lawyer points out that

in business and such, the major tool is your ability to walk out, but in divorce, you are going to have to have a resolution someday . . . . And in divorce the concept of fairness arises whereas in business it doesn't make any difference, because it just doesn't apply. I mean if you want to buy some real estate you don't have to give them a fair price, you can just offer them half of what you think it is worth . . . . If he agrees, fine; and if he doesn't, fine (HL).

The emotional intensity of divorce is particularly evident when the decision to end the marriage is not mutual. Like financial and procedural pressures, emotional pressures can affect parties differently; one party may be eager to settle while the other is reluctant to proceed. The ground for divorce in Wisconsin is an "irretrievable breakdown" of the marriage. Clearly, if one party wants out of the marriage, this requirement is met; thus, there is no guarantee that divorce is a mutual decision. In a number of our cases, while one party was extremely impatient to finalize the divorce, the other party wanted nothing less than a "day in court"—a chance to vilify the initiating spouse. These emotional conflicts can color the whole settlement process:

[The time frame of a divorce] . . . depends upon the emotional states of the parties . . . . One of the things that becomes apparent often is that when proposals are submitted to one of the parties and there's a great deal of discussion about whether it should be this way or that way and eventually there's an agreement to most things but then the proposal is rejected on some minor point. Just offhand, rejected. If that happens a couple of times with the same party, I become curious as to whether or not that person's agenda is really to get a divorce . . . . It's coming too close to having the divorce completed and the real agenda is NOT to get a divorce. But you can't always pick up on that, and [so you don't want] to advance a case too quickly, when one of the parties is not yet accepting (WL).

Similar observations have led Griffiths (1986: 155)[73] to observe that "lawyers and clients are in effect largely occupied with two different divorces: lawyers with a legal divorce, clients with a social and emotional divorce."

D. Implications for Informal Processes

The existence of these pressures in divorce is difficult to reconcile with the widely held notion that contested divorces are confined to the courtroom whereas informal settlement is reserved for parties who "agree." Instead it seems that informal settlement in divorce, as in other legal settings, is often subject to substantial constraint. It may be perceived by the parties as a matter of necessity rather than choice. Direct negotiation may not even occur, and when it does it may be contentious, superficial, and adversarial. Some informal settlements may be no less imposed than judgments at trial. Cooperative negotiation of the dispute to a mutually satisfactory outcome, based on offer and compromise, is the exception rather than the rule. As a result, the positive consequences of informal settlement must be considered variable rather than certain. It is in this context that we wish to reexamine the role of flexibility and participation in the settlement process.

IV. REEXAMINING FLEXIBILITY

. . . In divorce, the same flexibility that allows generosity and creative arrangements also allows emotional intimidation, asset-hiding, and the exertion of financial leverage. For example, a number of women report that they accepted poor settlement terms because their husbands were threatening custody battles:

> [My husband] . . . was threatening that if I went for half [the property] he would go for custody, . . . assuming that he would not get it, but he would drag it out as long as possible and have as nasty a battle as possible. I really didn't want to have the kids to have to go through that . . . didn't want to go through that prolonged fight. So, I decided to go ahead with what we had come up with . . . even though I knew it was not a fifty-fifty split (W).

73. [The reference is to John Griffiths, "What Do Dutch Lawyers Actually Do in Divorce Cases?" 20 *Law & Society Review* 135 (1986).]

Even in the absence of outright threats, the "flexibility" of the informal setting invites the intrusion of nonlegal considerations into what are ostensibly legal decisions. In our interviews, settlement decisions regarding matters such as support were typically attributed to the parties' emotional attitudes and relative eagerness to end the process. Parties who were impatient to settle sacrificed property and support rights to satisfy a more immediate desire to end the process; a reluctance to settle, on the other hand, worked to the party's benefit in terms of settlement outcome . . . .

A. *The Limits of Procedural and Substantive Safeguards*

In divorce, the problems of the informal process are theoretically counteracted by the requirement of judicial review. The "shadow of the law" argument implies that while flexibility and cooperation may not occur in every case, at least all cases will be subject to legal constraints, first, because parties will negotiate with legal expectations in mind, and second, because of the review process itself, when judges will presumably refuse to ratify one-sided or unworkable arrangements . . . .

Yet there are some problems with this argument, as to both the efficacy of review and the existence of endowments that review requirements are said to create. First, as Mnookin and Kornhauser[*] acknowledge, the existing review process is widely considered to be a "rubber stamp," with harried judges eager to finalize any arrangements made by the parties. In our interviews, the need for court ratification was typically dismissed as an insignificant concern, as one client commented: "I'd heard that if things are settled when you go to the judge, then it's a relatively pro forma appearance. And that's exactly what it turned out to be" (H). Thus, the general view is that as long as issues are settled, the judge will accept whatever decisions the parties present. As one of the judges remarked: "If they know what they're doing, even if it's out of line, then it's not my job to change their decision . . . . I don't know if I have ever changed an amount [for support] set by a couple" (J).

The hypothesis that endowments will structure the bargaining process because parties will bargain with judicial review in mind is also problematic. First, it assumes parties have access to legal information, or at least to information about their judge's expectations regarding child support and property division. The parties we interviewed received most of their legal information from their attorneys. Thus, to the extent that formal endowments exist, they are subject to attorneys' interpretations, which potentially alters the entitlements created by the law. At the very least, then, we would argue that the shadow of the law is being cast by the lawyers, who declare their expectations of judicial behavior . . . .

---

*[The reference is to Reading no. 9, supra.]

Perhaps more fundamentally, the existence of consistent formal criteria for decision making is itself debatable. Several of the lawyers we interviewed report that they have difficulty discerning court standards and that they cannot predict the outcomes of court processes. Some lawyers also indicate they feel uncomfortable trying to advise clients about what is fair or what to aim for in a given divorce case. One lawyer remarks: "So much of it is judgmental . . . . [Clients] ask questions like 'Is it fair?' and I just want to say—forgive my language 'Well, shit, I don't know, I'm just guessing like you'" (WL).

Even the lawyers in our sample who do think there are set standards and who do say they can predict outcomes differ in their opinion of the content of those court standards; obviously, they cannot all be correct. Some lawyers attempt to "divide hardship," that is, to make each parent absorb equal deficiencies of income. Others measure the adequacy of support by looking at the custodial parent's budget, trying to make sure the custodian can make ends meet, or by looking at the supporting parent's ability to pay. Still others focus on a flat amount of support per child. Many lawyers also stress that their settlement strategy in any given case depends heavily on who is representing the other spouse. Thus, it is doubtful that parties receive consistent legal information and advice.

Over 90% of divorce cases, according to most estimates, are settled through stipulation, and it is the rare case that is completely litigated. This fact opens the possibility that the shadow of the law, which presumably constrains negotiating parties, is instead cast by them. In other words, in litigation, judges may be following the patterns they see in informal settlements rather than the other way around; thus instead of "bargaining in the shadow of the law," one should refer to "litigating in the shadow of informal settlement." Even one who accepts the logic of this argument might still defend the endowments assumption. One could say that what matters is not some abstract analysis about who sets the patterns but rather the participants' *perceptions* of that process. Parties who feel constrained will act as if they are, whether or not they in fact are.

To our respondents, however, legal constraints are decidedly less important than the other pressures we have discussed; many parties even disregarded the advice of their attorneys. For instance, in some cases in which the client was impatient to settle, the lawyer's dissatisfaction with the terms was ignored:

My lawyer . . . wanted to wait until fall to make sure, to try to get a better handle on if [my husband's] business was successful. He thought my name should remain on it as part-owner . . . . I really wanted to get out of it, and didn't want to just mess around. I mean [he may have been] right—[but] I didn't care who was right at that point, and I still don't. It was more important to get out of the marriage (W).

While lawyers are often accused of stirring up trouble in divorce cases, it is clear that in some cases, they are unable to do so even when they think it is necessary to protect their client's interests. Against custody threats and other tactics, a lawyer's reassurances and support may be insufficient to keep clients from folding, as one lawyer explains:

> Her husband was using the threat of a custody issue to keep his payments down and she was insisting that I follow that approach. In other words, I take it very easy on him and as I recall, even from the beginning, no support [was] ordered . . . . She wanted me to forget about the father's responsibility to the children as far as money goes . . . . She was such a basket case . . . . He had just frightened her to death (WL).

Thus, even if the "shadow of the law" is a factor in informal settlement decisions, it is not the only factor, and its impact should not be overestimated. □

NOTES AND QUESTIONS

1. How do negotiation and mediation affect women as opposed to men? In "Killing Us Softly: Divorce Mediation and the Politics of Power," 40 *Buffalo Law Review* 441 (1992), Penelope E. Bryan argues that the "seductive marketing rhetoric" of divorce mediation hides the reality, which is that mediation favors men over women. The negotiation process is tilted, she claims, in favor of the party with more money and power—almost always the man. There are also psychological factors; for example, women tend to have lower self-esteem, are more crushed by the divorce process, are more easily influenced, and have a tendency to conform rather than to dominate and fight. See also Trina Grillo, "The Mediation Alternative: Process Dangers for Women," 100 *Yale Law Journal* 1545 (1991).

Bryan concludes that "mediation exploits wives by denigrating their legal entitlements, stripping them of authority, encouraging unwarranted compromise, isolating them from needed support, and placing them across the table from their more powerful husbands and demanding that they fend for themselves." How does this conclusion square with Erlanger, Chambliss, and Melli? with Mnookin and Kornhauser?

2. Plea bargaining is, arguably, rather special to American law. Divorce and divorce negotiations are not. The process in other countries does not seem much different from the process described in studies of divorce in the United States, at least not in contemporary times. See, for example, John Griffiths, "What do Dutch Lawyers Actually do in Divorce Cases?" 20 *Law and Society Review* 135 (1986).

3. Erlanger, Chambliss, and Melli used "in-depth interviews." Other scholars have used "ethnographic" methods to study lawyer-client interactions. Ethnographic research has a rich tradition in the study of law and the legal system. See, for example, Karl N. Llewellyn and E. Adamson Hoebel, *The Cheyenne Way* (Norman: University of Oklahoma Press, 1941). Ethnography and other interpretive methodologies have been more recently put forward as alternatives to the hypothesis testing tradition (and its variants). See Christine Harrington and Barbara Yngvesson, "Interpretative Sociolegal Research," 15 *Law & Social Inquiry* 135 (1990).

Ethnography was originally an anthropological method used to study different cultures. It seeks to position the researcher within the research setting, thereby permitting close and intensive observation of the subject. See June Starr, *Dispute and Settlement in Rural Turkey: An Ethnography of Law* (Leiden: Brill, 1978). The researcher's goal is to understand the behavior in question from the perspective of those being observed. As a critique of hypothesis testing, ethnography attempts to minimize preconceived notions about the observed behavior and to avoid questions that simply squeeze the actions of others into categories provided by the researcher, and formed by her a priori. For accounts of how researchers cope with many of the difficulties in this approach, see Robert J. Thomas, "Interviewing Important People in Big Companies," 22 *Journal of Contemporary Ethnography* 80 (1993); Richard Wright, Scott H. Decker, Allison K. Redfern, Dietrich L. Smith, "A Snowball's Chance in Hell: Doing Fieldwork with Active Residential Burglars," 29 *Journal of Research in Crime and Delinquency* 148 (1992).

Unlike hypothesis testing which may be done from "afar," ethnography requires the researcher to immerse herself in the situation. This approach usually does not employ quantification and often uses extensive quotations— allowing those being studied, rather than the researcher, to construct the meaning of the observed events.

What are the advantages and disadvantages of an ethnographic approach as compared to the hypothesis testing approach? What are its limits? John Van Maanen, in "The Fact of Fiction in Organizational Ethnography," 24 *Administrative Science Quarterly* 539, 549 (1979), raises many of the problems with ethnographic approaches. He points out:

> The results of ethnographic study are . . . mediated several times over— first, by the fieldworker's own standards of relevance as to what is and what is not worthy of observation; second, by the historically situated questions that are put to the people in the setting; third, by the self-reflection demanded of an informant; and fourth, by the intentional and unintentional ways the produced data are misleading.

Does the hypothesis testing approach always avoid these sources of error?

Are there potential ethical problems with an ethnographic approach? Is the ethnographer a researcher, a spy or, sometimes, a little of both? Melville Dalton, "Preconceptions and Methods in *Men Who Manage*," in Phillip E. Hammond (ed.) *Sociologists at Work* 50, 66–67 (New York: Basic Books, 1964), discusses both ethnographic methods and ethical issues. Dalton studied practices in several businesses. He served as an employee of one and was a former employee of another. He drew on his contacts and friendships to gain information or to prompt others to talk about the topics on which he was conducting research. He gained information about the salaries of managers through his friendship with secretaries. One secretary supplied this information in exchange for his continuing comments about one of his friends whom the secretary was dating. Whatever the ethics of deceiving friends and associates or gaining information that Dalton would not have been given had he asked for it, how can readers know whether Dalton's account is accurate and how can they appraise his interpretations of his data? In the language of social science, could another researcher replicate his study?

Legislative Process

11. *The Calculus of Consent*[74]

James Buchanan and
Gordon Tullock

☐ . . . [W]e propose to examine the operation of a single collective decision-making rule, that of simple majority, under certain highly restricted assumptions. Theorists of the democratic process have, traditionally, paid little attention to the actual operation of voting rules, and they seem, by and large, to have been uninterested in making generalized predictions regarding the results of actual political decision-making. This relative neglect is explained, at least in part, by the implicit assumption that participants in collective choice seek to further the "public interest," although . . . this concept is never defined . . . .

[O]ur purpose . . . is that of analyzing the operation of voting rules as one stage in the individual's constitutional-choice problem, that of choosing the voting rules themselves. The working of a voting rule can be analyzed only as it produces results over a series of issues.

MAJORITY VOTING WITHOUT LOGROLLING

Once it is recognized that the political process embodies a continuing stream of separate decisions, the most general model must include the possibility of vote-trading, or, to use the commonly employed American term, *logrolling*. The existence of a logrolling process is central to our general analysis of simple majority voting, but it will be helpful, by way of comparison, to consider briefly a model in which logrolling is not permitted to take place, either by legal institutions or by certain widely acknowledged moral precepts. There are certain relatively rare institutional situations in which logrolling will not be likely to occur, and in such situations the contrasting analytical model may be explanatory. The best example is the standard referendum on a simple issue. Here the individual voter cannot easily trade his own vote on the one issue for reciprocal favors on other issues because, first, he is uncertain as to when other issues will be voted on in this way, and, second, he and his immediate acquaintances represent such a small part of the total electorate that such trading effort may not be worth while. Further-

74. *The Calculus of Consent*, (Ann Arbor: University of Michigan Press, 1962), pp. 131–45, reprinted by permission.

more, the secret ballot, normally employed in such cases, makes it impossible for any external observer to tell whether voting commitments are honored or not. Under circumstances such as these, the individual voter will make his voting decision in accordance with his own preferences on the single question posed.

In this model each voter indicates his preference, and the preference of the majority of the whole group is decisive. The defect in this procedure, a serious one, . . . is that it ignores the varying intensities of preference among the separate voters. A man who is passionately opposed to a given measure and a man who is slightly favorable but does not care greatly about it are given equal weight in the process of making final decisions. It seems obvious that both of these individuals could be made better off, in terms of their own expressed preferences, if the man strongly opposed should be permitted in some way to "trade" or exchange something with the relatively indifferent supporter of the proposed measure. Applying the strict Pareto rules[75] for determining whether one social situation represents an improvement over another, almost any system of voting that allows some such exchange to take place would be superior to that system which weights all preferences equally on *each issue* . . . .

Permitting those citizens who feel strongly about an issue to compensate in some way those whose opinion is only feebly held can result in a great increase in the well-being of both groups, and the prohibition of such transactions will serve to prevent movement toward the conceptual "social optimality" surface, under almost any definition of this term.

Note that the results under logrolling and under nonlogrolling differ only if the minority feels more intensely about an issue than the majority. If the majority is equal or more intense in its preferences, its will must prevail in either model. It is only when the intensity of preferences of the minority is sufficiently greater than that of the majority to make the minority willing to sacrifice enough votes on other issues to detach marginal voters from the majority (intense members of the majority group may, of course, make counteroffers) that the logrolling process will change the outcome . . . .

The above discussion suggests that a reasonably strong ethical case can be made for a certain amount of vote-trading under majority-rule institutions. We emphasize, however, that our model, which incorporates the logrolling model as the general case, is not chosen because of the ethical desirability of the institutions analyzed. Positive theory must

---

75. [The reference is to concepts developed by the Italian economist and social thinker, Vilfredo Pareto. A situation represents an improvement if every individual affected by it is, in his view, better off; or if one or more individuals are better off, and none are, in their view, worse off. A situation is "optimal" when it is no longer possible to make a change which satisfies these conditions. See Buchanan & Tullock, ch. 13.]

always analyze those institutions that are, in fact, general (the test of generality being the validity of the predictions made), quite independently of ethical or moral considerations. Therefore, even if vote-trading should be viewed as morally reprehensible behavior, it might still be necessary to analyze the phenomenon carefully if it were observed in the operation of real-world political processes.

TWO TYPES OF LOGROLLING

Logrolling seems to occur in many of the institutions of political choice-making in Western democracies. It may occur in two separate and distinct ways. In all of those cases where a reasonably small number of individuals vote openly on each measure in a continuing sequence of measures, the phenomenon seems pervasive. This is normally characteristic of representative assemblies, and it may also be present in very small governmental units employing "direct democracy." The applicability of our models to representative assemblies has already been mentioned. Under the rules within which such assemblies operate, exchanges of votes are easy to arrange and to observe. Such exchanges significantly affect the results of the political process. It seems probable that this fact provides one of the major reasons for the widespread use of representative democracy.

Logrolling may occur in a second way, which we shall call *implicit logrolling*. Large bodies of voters may be called on to decide on complex issues, such as which party will rule or which set of issues will be approved in a referendum vote. Here there is *no* formal trading of votes, but an analogous process takes place. The political "entrepreneurs" who offer candidates or programs to the voters make up a complex mixture of policies designed to attract support. In so doing, they keep firmly in mind the fact that a single voter may be so interested in the outcome of a particular issue that he will vote for the one party that supports this issue, although he may be opposed to the party stand on all other issues. Institutions described by this implicit logrolling are characteristic of much of the modern democratic procedure. Since the analysis is somewhat more incisive in the first type of logrolling, we shall not discuss the second type at this point.

A SIMPLE LOGROLLING MODEL

Let us consider a simple model. A township inhabited by one hundred farmers who own similar farms is cut by a number of main highways maintained by the state. However, these are limited-access highways, and the farmers are permitted to enter this primary network only at the appropriate intersections with local roads. All local roads are built and maintained by the township. Maintenance is simple. Any farmer who desires to have a specific road repaired is allowed to present the issue to the whole group for a vote. If the repairing proposal is approved by a simple majority, the cost is assessed against all of the farmers as a part of the real property tax, the rate of which is automatically adjusted upward or downward so as to make revenues always equal to expenditures. The principal use of the local roads by the farmers is getting to and from the major state highways. Since these major highways cut through the whole district, there are four or five farmers dependent on each particular piece of local road, and each farmer requires at least one local road to provide him with access to the main network.

In this model the simple referendum system would result in no local road being repaired because an overwhelming majority of the farmers would vote against the repairing of any given road, considered separately. A logrolling system, however, permits the local roads to be kept in repair through the emergence of bargains among voters. The actual bargaining may take a number of forms, but most of the "solutions" will tend to be unstable. In any case, "equilibrium" involves some overinvestment of resources.

One form that an implicit bargain might take is the following: Each individual might determine, in his own mind, the general standard of maintenance that should be set for all local roads. That is to say, he would balance, according to his own scale of preferences, the costs of maintaining his own road at various levels of repair with the benefits expected, and try to reach a decision at the point where expected marginal costs equal marginal benefits. Generalizing this, he could then vote on each separate project to repair a given road in the same way that he would vote for repairs on his own road. If all voters would follow this rule of reaching decisions, we would find a schedule of voting behavior such as that shown below in Figure 12. Each mark or dot on the horizontal line represents the "idealized" standard of maintenance on all roads for a single voter. If a proposal for repairing a given road falls to the left of his own position on this scale, the individual will support it; if a proposal falls to the right of his own position, he will vote against it. If each road has at least one farmer living along it whose preference for general road repairs falls to the right of the median (A in Figure 12), then a proposal for road repair will be advanced as soon as any given road falls below this farmer's standard of maintenance. Successive further proposals would be made as the road deteriorated further. When the deterioration of any road reached the median level, a repair project would secure approval by simple majority vote. Hence, all local roads would, in this model, tend to be maintained up to the standard indicated by the median preference.

This result will not represent a fully "efficient" solution in any Pareto sense, but it is possible to support this procedure on ethical grounds. In fact, this solution seems to be the one that most of the proponents of majoritarian democracy have in mind when they discuss democratic process. In any event, we propose to use this solution, which we shall call the "Kantian," as a more or less "correct" solution against which we shall contrast our more realistic result.

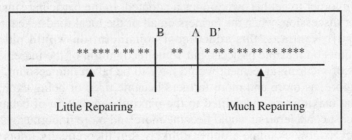

FIGURE 1

If the farmers of the township generally follow such a policy in voting, then *any* single farmer could benefit himself simply by voting against all proposals to repair roads other than his own and by voting to repair his own road at each opportunity. This single departure from the general pattern of behavior would shift the median of the schedules slightly so that the taxes on the farmer concerned would be reduced or his road kept in better-than-average repair. If the other farmers living along this road should follow the first farmer's example (we shall call such farmers "maximizers"), they would be able to shift the standards of repair so that the road on which they live would be repaired at level B´ while reducing the standard on all other roads to B in Figure 12. Since the largest share of the costs of keeping their own road in repair would fall on other taxpayers, while the largest share of their own taxes would go to the repair of other roads, this change in behavior would be greatly to the advantage of the maximizers and greatly to the disadvantage of the "Kantians," although in the initial stages the disadvantages would not be concentrated to the same degree as the advantages.

If the farmers located on a second local road should also switch to a maximizing pattern of behavior, this action would have the effect of bringing the level of road-repairing on the two roads particularly affected down toward that which would prevail under the generalized Kantian system, while still further lowering the standards on the remaining "Kantian" roads. However, it seems probable that, finding themselves in this situation, the two groups of maximizers could benefit by forming a coalition designed to raise the standards of maintenance on the two roads. Let us consider the situation that would be confronted by an individual maximizer when he tries to decide whether or not to enter into such a coalition with other maximizers. Since he will pay only about 1/100 of the cost, almost any proposal to repair his own road will be supported by him. If, however, in order to obtain support for some repair project for his own road, he must also vote for the repair of another road, the individual must also count the cost to him of other repair projects. In weighing costs and benefits, he must consider not only the tax cost to himself from a proposal to repair his own road but also the tax cost to him of the other repair jobs which he must support in order to get his own proposal adopted. In the particular situation under discussion, when the farmers on all of the local roads except two are still Kantians, this added cost consideration would put few restraints on feasible projects, but some recognition of the incremental costs of securing agreement would have to be taken into account. Furthermore, as more and more farmers became tired of being exploited by the maximizers and shifted to the maximizing pattern of behavior, this cost consideration would become more and more important.

Let us now examine a rather unlikely, but theoretically important, special case. Suppose that exactly 51 of the 100 farmers follow a maximizing policy, while 49 are pure "Kantians." Let us further suppose that all of the maximizers live on some local roads, while all of the Kantians live on other roads. Under these circumstances, the Kantians clearly would never be able to get their roads repaired at all, but the level of repairs on the maximizers' roads is more difficult to determine. In order to simplify the issue somewhat, let us assume (plausibly) that these roads are maintained on such a high level that all of the Kantian farmers would vote against all further repair proposals. In this case, it would be necessary to attain the approval of all of the maximizers to carry any single repair project. A maximizing farmer, considering the repair of his own road, would necessarily be forced to take into account his share in the costs of repairing the roads of all maximizers. He would have to consider the incremental taxes that he must pay in order to repair the roads of all other parties to the bargain. His calculus requires, however, only that he compare his own marginal benefits against his own marginal costs. No knowledge of anyone else's utility function is required. The individual need only decide whether the total bargain is or is not to his advantage.

For the Kantians, note that, while no roads leading to their own farms will be repaired, they will be required to contribute toward the repair of the roads leading to the farms of the maximizers. Thus, a part of the total repair costs in the township will be paid by persons who are not parties to the decisive bargain, and, since the maximizers count only the costs to themselves when they make voting decisions, the general standard of road maintenance on the roads of the maximizers will tend to be higher than it would be if the Kantians were also included in the calculus. Under such conditions as these, where "virtue" so conspicuously would not pay, it seems likely that at least some of the Kantians would decide to switch to a maximizing policy. For simplicity, let us assume that they all do so at the same time. Since these reluctant maximizers would still be in a minority, their changes of heart would not immediately redound to their private benefit. However, it might be relatively easy for this minority, acting as a coalition, to find two of the original maximizers who would, in return for a promise of very good maintenance on their own roads, desert their former colleagues. It is again obvious, however, that the new majority would now be equally susceptible to similar desertions. A permanent coalition of 51 farmers formed for the purpose of exploiting the remaining 49 could not be considered to be stable in the usual sense of this term. In the terminology of game theory, . . . any combination of 51 voters dominates any combination of less than this number, but no combination of 51 dominates all other combinations of 51.

The outcome is clearly indicated. Each farmer would enter into bilateral agreements with enough other farmers on other roads to insure that his own road is repaired. The individual farmer would then be forced to include as a part of the cost of getting his own road repaired the cost (to him) of repairing the roads of 50 other farmers. These bilateral agreements would overlap, however. Farmer A (more precisely, the group of farmers living on Road A) would bargain with Farmers B, C, . . . , M. Farmer M, on the other hand, might make up a majority bargain from an agreement with Farmer A and Farmers N, O, . . . , Z.

In counting the costs to himself involved in the repair of other roads necessary to secure the repair of his own road, each farmer would consider only the repair of those roads which he agrees to support. In this way his expenditure pattern would include as a free gift the tax payments of 49 voters. The fiscal institutions postulated insure that all 100 voters share in the costs of each repair project approved, but a minimum participation of only 51 voters in the net benefits is required by simple majority voting. The natural result would be that each road in the township would be maintained at a level considerably higher and at a greater expense than is rational from the individual standpoint of the farmers living along it. Each individual in the group would be behaving quite rationally, but the outcome would be irrational. This apparent paradox may be explained as follows: Each voter pays enough in support for the repair of other roads to attain a position of equivalence between estimated individual marginal costs and individual marginal benefits, but the payments included in his private calculus make up only a part of the costs of total road repair that he must, as a taxpayer in the community, support. There are other roads which will be repaired because of successful bargains to which he is not a party. Taken as a group, the road repair projects for which he votes represent a good bargain for the individual; but other *ad hoc* bargains will also take place. The individual will, of course, vote against all projects included in these outside bargains, but he will be in the minority. Therefore, he will have to bear a part of the costs.

Any individual farmer who followed another course of action would be worse off, however, than the individual whose behavior is considered here. For example, a Kantian farmer would never have his own road repaired, but he would have to pay taxes for the support of other local roads. In any practical situation the whole decision-making process would tend to become one of elaborate negotiations, open and concealed, taking place at several levels of discourse. The man who is the most effective bargainer would have a considerable advantage. However, the general pattern of results may be less than optimal for all parties (optimal being defined here in terms of either the Kantian or the Paretian solution).

POSSIBLE OBJECTIONS

We may now consider certain possible objections that may be raised against the reasoning implicit in our simple logrolling model. It may be argued that those individuals whom we have called maximizers would be behaving wickedly and that ethical considerations will prevent a majority of the population in the real world from following such a course of action. Ethical and moral systems vary greatly from culture to culture, and the strength of moral restraints on private action is not readily predictable. We do not want to preclude the possible existence somewhere of a system of human behavior which could effectively restrain logrolling, but surely the American behavior pattern contains no such restraints. Under our system open logrolling is normally publicly characterized as "bad," but no real stigma attaches to those who participate in it. The press describes open logrolling arrangements without apparent disapproval, and, in fact, all of our political organizations operate on a logrolling basis. Moreover, no stigma at all attaches to implicit as opposed to open logrolling.

A second argument asserts that each farmer in our model community would soon realize that if he adopted a maximizing pattern of behavior, this would lead all other farmers to do the same thing. Since the "maximizing equilibrium" is worse for almost all farmers than the "Kantian median," each farmer would, on the basis of his own cold and selfish calculation, follow the Kantian system. This argument is familiar, and it is precisely analogous to the one which holds that no single labor union will force wage rates up for its own members because it will realize that such action will lead other unions to do the same and that the eventual outcome will simply be higher prices and wages without any increase in real incomes. There seems to be overwhelming empirical evidence that men do not act in this way. The argument overlooks the fact that there will, of course, be shortrun gains to the individuals or groups who initiate action first. In addition, the argument seems to contain a logical flaw. It is based on the observation that, in any series of actions by a number of men, there must be a first step. If this can be prevented, then the whole series can be prevented. This observation is, in itself, correct; but there must also be a second, a third, and a fourth step, etc., in each series. If any one action in the series is prevented, then the whole series cannot be completed. If all of our maximizing farmers should refrain from following a maximizing course of action because each one felt that his own personal adoption of such behavior would lead to a switch to a position of "maximizing equilibrium," then, if only one of them had done so, we could construct an exactly similar argument "proving" that none of the remaining ninety-nine would follow his example. However, if the second argument is true, the first is false; hence, the chain of reasoning contains an inconsistency.

Note that our refutation of this argument does not preclude an individual's taking the attitude: "If *no one* else acts, I shall not act." However, not only must *all* members of the group assume this attitude if the argument is to be valid, but *each* member of the group must also believe that *all* other members will take this attitude. This combination of attitudes, which would amount to complete mutual trust, seems highly improbable in any real-world situation. The argument that all individuals in the group will be worse off than if they all adopted Kantian norms of behavior does have some relevance for the support of *constitutional* changes in the decision-making rules or institutions for choice. While it may never be to the interest of the individual to refrain from adopting a maximizing attitude, given the rules as laid down, it may well be to his long-range interest to support a change in these rules themselves, which, by definition, will be *generally applicable.*

ALTERNATIVES

One means through which the separate farmers in our model might enter into a bargain so as to insure results somewhat closer to the Kantian median would be the development of a specific formula that would determine when a road should be repaired. Yet another means would be the delegation of decision-making authority to a single individual or small group. These become practicable institutions, however, only within the confines of a set of closely related issues that may be expected to arise: in our model, separate proposals for road repair. In the more general and realistic case where governmental units must consider a continuing stream of radically different projects, neither an agreed-on formula nor a single expert or group of experts would seem feasible. A formula that would permit the weighing of the costs and the benefits of such diverse programs as building irrigation projects in the West to increase agricultural production, paying farmers in the Midwest to decrease agricultural production, giving increased aid to Israel, and dredging Baltimore's harbor, is inconceivable. There could not, therefore, be any real agreement on any automatic or quasi-automatic system of allocating collective resources, and the delegation of authority to make such decisions would mean the abandonment of the legislative process as such. We are reduced to the reaching of separate decisions by logrolling processes, given the constitutional rules as laid down in advance.

MAJORITY RULE AND EXTERNAL COSTS

This is by no means so much a tragedy as our simple model may have appeared to suggest. Implicit in the comparison of the logrolling solution with the Kantian solution has been the idea that the external costs imposed on the individual by the "maximizing equilibrium" exceed those resulting from the Kantian "equilibrium." This will be true if individual farmers are primarily interested in the repair of their own roads, as our model postulates. If, by contrast, some or all of the farmers should be genuinely and intensely interested in the standards of general road repair over the whole township, the Kantian solution might be worse than the maximizing one. This is because the Kantian solution under simple majority rule can take no account of varying intensities in individual standards. For example, if there should exist a minority of farmers who feel very intensely that much more should be spent on road repairs than the majority of other voters, whose standards are somewhat indifferently held, the maximizing solution, which does result in a standard of general repair above the Kantian median, may be more "desirable" on certain commonly acknowledged welfare grounds than the Kantian solution. In this case the introduction of logrolling into the Kantian model could be beneficial to all parties.

A central feature of our analysis is the demonstration that the operation of simple majority rule, quite independently of any assumption about individual motivation, will almost always impose external costs on the individual. If more than a simple majority is required for decision, fewer resources will be devoted to road-building in our model, and the individual comparison of marginal benefits and marginal costs would tend to approach more closely the calculus required by the economists' standard criteria for attaining a Pareto optimality surface . . . . [H]owever, when any consideration of more inclusive voting rules is made, the incremental costs of negotiating bargains must also be taken into account.

GENERALIZATIONS

. . . We shall now inquire as to what extent our simple logrolling model can be generalized. It would appear that any governmental activity which benefits specific individuals or groups in a discriminatory fashion and which is financed from general taxation would fit our model well. It is not, of course, necessary that the revenues employed in paying for the projects be collected equally from all voters, either in terms of tax rates or tax collections. The minimum necessary condition is that the benefits from public activity be significantly more concentrated or localized than the costs. This is a very weak condition, and many budgetary patterns seem to meet it. If the taxes are collected by indirect methods so that individuals cannot really tell how much they individually pay for each specific public-service project, this accentuates the distortions described by our analytical model. In the marginal case the individual may be indifferent about projects benefiting others, the costs of which seem slight to him and also difficult to measure. Under these circumstances he would be particularly likely to trade his support for such projects, which may appear costless or nearly so, for reciprocal support for his own pet proposals.

Additional types of governmental activity may also be fitted into the analysis. Other forms of taxation-expenditure problems are most easily incorporated. First, we may suppose that there is some governmental activity that provides general benefit to all voters, e.g., police protection, which is financed out of general taxation. In this case the maximizing solution and the Kantian solution will tend to be identical to the extent that the benefits and the taxes are truly general. However, as soon as general taxation is departed from, parallel reasoning to that above demonstrates that special tax exemptions and favors to individuals and groups will be introduced . . . .

If our analysis is to be applied even more generally to all public activity it must be radically generalized. For any individual voter all possible measures can be arrayed according to his intensity of interest. His welfare can be improved if he accepts a decision contrary to his desire in an area where his preferences are weak in exchange for a decision in his favor in an area where his feelings are stronger. Bargains among voters can, therefore, be mutually beneficial. Potentially, the voter should enter into such bargains until the marginal "cost" of voting for something of which he disapproves but about which his feelings are weak exactly matches the expected marginal benefits of the vote or votes secured in return support for issues in which he is more interested. Thus, he will expect to benefit from the total complex of issues which enter into his set of bargains with his fellows. In making such bargains, however, the individual must try to gain the assent of only a bare majority of other voters, not of all of them. On any given issue he can simply ignore 49 per cent of the individual decision-makers. This means that he can afford to "pay" more for other support because a part of the inconvenience caused by the measure will fall on parties who are not members of the decisive bargaining coalition.

Unfortunately, from the point of view of the individual voter, the converse also holds true. Bargains will certainly be concluded in which the single voter does not participate. Yet he will have to bear a part of the costs of action taken. As a result, the whole effect of the measures which result from his bargains and on which he votes on the winning side will be beneficial to him; but this will tend, normally, to be only slightly more than one half of all "bargained" measures passed, and the remainder will be carried out adverse to his interest. The same result would hold true for the *average* voter under a pure referendum system. The whole problem analyzed here can be eliminated by changing the rule which compels the minority to accept the decisions of the majority without compensation. So long as this rule is employed to make collective decisions, the individual voter must expect to incur external costs as a result of public or collective action. ☐

NOTES AND QUESTIONS

1. What is the social value of logrolling according to Buchanan and Tullock? How does it permit legislators to express the intensity of their feelings (or those of their constituents)?

In 1911, Wisconsin Statute Sec. 13.05 was passed. Entitled "Logrolling prohibited," it provided that:

> Any member of the legislature who gives, offers or promises to give his vote or influence in favor of or against any measure or proposition pending or proposed to be introduced, in the legislature in consideration or upon condition that any other person elected to the same legislature will give or will promise or agree to give his vote or influence in favor of or against any other measure or proposition pending or proposed to be introduced in such legislature, or who gives, offers or promises to give his vote or influence for or against any measure on condition that any other member will give his vote or influence in favor of any change in any other bill pending or proposed to be introduced in the legislature may be fined not less than $500 nor more than $1000 or imprisoned not less than one year nor more than 3 years.

What would Buchanan and Tullock think about this statute as a matter of policy? How likely would it be, according to them, that the statute would be carried out in fact?

2. Is there an ethical argument against the Buchanan and Tullock conclusion? Can you also construct an argument against the authors, using their own approach? For example, they admit that logrolling will result in "over-investment." What do they mean by over-investment? Why is it an argument against allowing logrolling?

3. Buchanan and Tullock are an example of yet another approach used in law and social science: a microeconomic model. This approach is significantly different from the others we have seen because it is not empirical. Think about the article; what data did the authors present to support their analysis? The answer is none. Rather, their approach is based on the positing of simplifying

assumptions and deducing from those assumptions, in a formal, nonempirical way, conclusions about a particular situation.[76]

The key assumption of economic analysis is that individuals are rational actors who seek to maximize their goal attainment. In traditional economic analysis the goal to be maximized is profits. What is the analog to profits in the Buchanan and Tullock article? What other assumptions do the authors make in reaching their conclusions?

4. What are the strengths and weaknesses of the approach used by Buchanan and Tullock—that is, economic model building? How could an empirical, hypothesis-testing or ethnographic approach contribute to understanding of logrolling and other forms of bargaining in legislatures? There is a body of literature that looks empirically at logrolling and finds it to be a rather common, though implicit, phenomena. For example one congressman described the process as follows:

> There isn't any definite exchange of favors. Like — may come up to me and say that this thing means a lot to him and to his district and ask for my support, but when I need him, I'm not going to go back and remind him that I voted with him and now I want him to vote with me. And if I were to say something like, "Remember that when I need you," it would be like questioning his integrity. But I do think that if I ask him for something in the future, he might remember. And if I would have fought him on this, then he'd say, "Where was — when I needed him?"[77]

5. As we have noted, Buchanan and Tullock is not a study of the operations of an actual legislature. Thomas Stratmann, "The Effects of Logrolling on Congressional Voting," 82 *American Economic Review* 1162 (1992), looks at the *actual votes* of members of Congress on subsidies involved in proposed amendments to the farm bill of 1985. His research supports Buchanan and Tullock: "Evidence is found that legislators trade votes and that legislators with intense preferences are most likely to trade votes."

In the United States we have a weak party system. Legislators are much more independent of their party than legislators are in European parliamentary systems. In those systems the governing party makes policy and expects members to vote as a bloc to support it. Parties tend to be far more programmatic than in the United States; voters usually are less concerned with the candidate than with the position of the party. Insofar as there is bargaining about votes, it is more likely to involve party officials and particular legislators. In most of these systems, dissatisfied legislators can call for a vote of no confidence. If enough legislators vote for it, the governing party must call for a new election. Often in parliamentary systems there are many parties and no one party succeeds in gaining an absolute majority of the members. Various leaders will attempt to assemble a coalition of parties so that they can assume power. This opens another opportunity for bargaining about positions.

---

76. For an interesting account of economic analysis of the legal system, see A. Mitchell Polinsky, *An Introduction to Law and Economics,* 2d ed. (Boston: Little, Brown & Co., 1989).

77. John W. Kingdon, *Congressmen's Voting Decisions* 101, 3rd ed. (Ann Arbor: University of Michigan Press, 1989).

Members of the American Congress often bargain with the President. A vote on a key bill may gain the Representative or Senator some tangible benefit for his or her district or state. Of course, some votes are what Buchanan and Tullock call Kantian. Occasionally some legislators ignore the wishes of their party, other legislators offering vote trades, lobbyists and even the majority in their district and vote for what they think is right. When would you expect to find logrolling? When would you expect to find Kantian votes on principle?

Members of legislatures do not just vote on legislation. They participate in the work of various committees. Carl E. Van Horn, "Congressional Policymaking: Cloakroom Politics and Policy," in Christopher J. Deering, ed., *Congressional Politics* (Chicago, Ill.: Dorsey Press, 1989), argues that the activity of committees and subcommittees are at the core of congressional lawmaking. Most of this activity takes place far from the public eye. Representatives can act in this arena without too much concern for the wishes of their constituents. Here interest groups seek influence by offering campaign contributions, workers who will participate in the next election, and votes from those in the district whom they purport to influence. Bargaining and compromise are the central features of committee politics. Vague laws are preferred; problems are delegated to administrative agencies or the courts; and often we see gridlock because it is easier to block action than to act. Van Horn concludes: "From the perspective of most members of Congress, cloakroom politics works rather well. By serving up short term fixes that satisfy constituents, current political problems are solved and others are avoided."

Ostensibly, committee hearings serve to gather information which may serve as a basis for legislation. However, occasionally a hearing may provoke publicity and affect public attitudes. A number of American legislators have risen to national prominence as a result of mass media coverage of such hearings. Legislators may engage in symbolic action. They work to gain the attention of the national media: For example, they seek to appear on television programs such as "Meet the Press" or "Face the Nation." Often this involves gaining identification as an expert in certain areas.

Legislators usually have staffs who assist them in performing the tasks of representatives. See, e.g., Barry A. Kinsey, "Congressional Staff: The Cultivation and Maintenance of Personal Networks in an Insecure Work Environment," 13 *Urban Life* 395 (1985). One important task is constituent service. A constituent who is involved in a dispute with, for example, the Veterans Administration may call his or her United States Senator. A member of the Senator's staff will call the Veterans Administration and investigate the situation. At the minimum, such a call usually prompts a detailed explanation of the agency's decision in the constituent's case. Sometimes the legislator's interest in the case actually may prompt administrators to reverse an earlier denial of benefits in the guise of an explanation. Sometimes those working in an agency find it easier to grant a constituent's request than explain the reasons for denying it to a legislator interested in the matter. This may make the difference in close cases.

Finally, no discussion of legislation can avoid the subject of lobbyists and special interest groups. Such groups may do no more than offer information to legislators. Some may offer campaign contributions to legislators likely to support the lobby's interests. Others can mobilize voters in the legislator's district at election time. These explicit and tacit bargains too are part of the process. Janet M. Grenzke, "PACs and the Congressional Supermarket: The Currency is Complex," 33 *American Journal of Political Science* 1 (1989), finds little evidence that campaign contributions buy the roll-call votes of members of Congress. Rather contributions, at best, may help a political action committee gain access to the legislator. She concludes that the influence, if any, is indirect and subtle.

Eric M. Uslaner, "Legislative Behavior: The Study of Representation," in Samuel Long (ed.), *Annual Review of Political Science* (Norwood, N.J.: Ablex Publishing Corp., 1986), suggests that legislators anticipate the reactions of their constituents because legislators fear that constituents might be mobilized and vote against them. However, legislators lack good information about their constituents' views concerning many matters, particularly those which are not salient at the moment. Lobbyists, Uslaner suggests, seek to persuade legislators that their views are those of the entire electorate.

Administrative Process

12. *Going By the Book: The Problem of Regulatory Unreasonableness*

Eugene Bardach
and Robert Kagan

(Philadelphia: Temple University Press, 1982)

THE GOOD INSPECTOR

☐ Regulatory agencies need powerful tools of legal coercion because there are bad apples, eager to exploit vague rules and the cumbersome mechanisms of due process. Moreover, the threat of effective enforcement also is needed to keep good apples good. Thus the legal reforms of the 1960s and 1970s, designed to increase the regularity of detection and punishment, can be viewed as a natural evolution of regulatory enforcement, "selected" by a political environment that sought more security from social harms. But the tools of coercive enforcement easily can be used for legalistic, indiscriminate, and unresponsive enforcement. The newly evolved, tougher breed of inspector too often seems to take unreasonably costly bites from good apples along with justifiable bites from bad apples, thus provoking resistance and ending needed cooperation. If the political environment sought to select the fittest enforcement strategy, therefore, it might favor the evolution of a still more sophisticated type of enforcement official, one who would retain strong, modern enforcement tools but would use them more flexibly and selectively, what we would call the "good inspector."

. . . The inspector who walks through a factory and faithfully enforces each regulation may not detect or do anything about more serious sources of risk that happen to lie outside the rulebook; at the same time, he alienates the regulated enterprise and encourages noncooperative attitudes. In light of these developments, one might expect regulatory agencies to evolve enforcement strategies designed to persuade the regulated enterprise to do more than is strictly required by law. An agency's goal would not be merely to secure compliance with rules per se, but to mobilize available resources to solve particular social problems in the most efficient and least disruptive way . . . . Enforcement officials would use their powers to induce management to invest in the training of middle- and lower-level personnel so that they would devise appropriate preventive measures and implement them alertly.

Agency personnel, in attempting to adapt more closely to their environment, might take on another and perhaps more difficult task—making regulation more reasonable . . . . Regulations would not be enforced in situations where they do not make sense. And if, for whatever reasons, inspectors were denied discretion to suspend rule enforcement themselves, the good inspector would draw upon his experience in the field and inform top regulatory policymakers about overinclusive or ineffective rules. In the same vein, agency officials would attempt to educate legislators and elected chief executives about the causes of and correctives for unreasonable overregulation that originated in statutes and in broadly conceived policies.

But the good inspector still would be tough when toughness was required. His effort to seek cooperation would not blind him to the possibility that personnel in the regulated enterprise may seek to evade even reasonable regulatory requirements, provide him with misleading information, or exaggerate the costs or technical difficulties of compliance. Thus the inspector would attempt to distinguish violations due to narrowly profit-motivated calculations from those that stemmed from mistakes, poor management, or legitimate disagreement with the rules, and he would be willing and able to use coercive enforcement techniques when necessary.

All this is, of course, somewhat utopian. Not every regulatory official can be a perfect judge of what is or is not reasonable or an expert in eliciting cooperation. Yet the ideal of "the good inspector" serves as a model toward which enforcement might evolve and, as the examples to be presented will suggest, one that is not entirely unattainable.

THE "GOOD COP" AND THE "GOOD INSPECTOR"

. . . The good inspector . . . has the knack of gaining compliance without stimulating legal contestation. In agencies not imbued with a legalistic ethos, persuasiveness becomes the supreme virtue . . . . A supervisor of inspectors in the California State Fire Marshal's Office said,

"Going to court is an admission that you've failed." In the Consumer Protection Division of the Massachusetts Attorney General's Office, "The investigator who . . . manages to extract large refunds and manages to do so in a friendly, congenial manner without apparently brandishing his authority is considered to be a very good investigator."

A friendly, congenial manner, however, is only one aspect of being effective and persuasive. One critical ingredient is the capacity to be reasonable, to distinguish serious from nonserious violations, and to invest effort in the former. This capacity seems closely related to technical competence—an ability to provide technically persuasive explanations for regulatory requirements and to understand how the regulations affect production or managerial functions. Lack of technical competence is a likely corollary of legalistic enforcement. Without reasonably developed knowledge of the degree of risk raised by a particular practice or process, an inspector cannot judge with any confidence whether a violation is serious or whether "giving more time" to comply is too risky. Without a sense of the technical and economic problems of compliance, the inspector cannot evaluate the businessman's excuses or complaints with any confidence. According to FDA and air pollution control agency supervisors, poorly educated or inexperienced inspectors have no self confidence when confronting company engineers because they cannot tell whether they are "being snowed" or presented with valid arguments. Their most likely response, the supervisors agreed, is not to give in but to try to gain some control over the situation by retreating to the rule book, insisting on literal adherence to the regulations . . . .

Because such judgments are sometimes difficult, the good inspector must have not only technical competence but also the tough-mindedness to probe the businessman's explanations and excuses in a polite but critical manner. He must be willing and able to exercise authority. Experienced enforcement officials we interviewed often referred to inspectors who simply could not come down hard when regulated businesses were unjustifiably stalling them. This problem recurs, according to some enforcement officials, because the field attracts idealists, young people who want to do good but who are not prepared to deal with conflict. Technical training is "only one of many necessary qualities," a nursing home regulator said. "For instance, you need presence. You have to look and act like you know what you're doing. Schools of social work train practitioners, not inspectors."

A corollary of the ability to be tough when need be is the ability to be patient and persistent in the face of resistance, to sort through heated charges of unreasonableness for those that are valid, while calmly rejecting those that are not. A nursing home regulator said:

> We want people that can accept a stressful situation . . . . It is important that they be able to deal with the situation by being creative and by not becoming upset. When push comes to shove, the inspector has to be able to handle abuse—take charges of harassment.

The good inspector, in short, tries to keep disagreements with business from degenerating into a hopelessly adversarial relationship.

RECIPROCITY

An enforcement official's ability to win cooperation is rooted in the relationship of reciprocity or exchange that he manages to establish . . . .

It is easiest to visualize the elements of such a reciprocal relationship at the level of face-to-face encounters between inspectors and regulated businessmen. The inspector has three major things he can trade for greater efforts toward responsible social behavior. First, at a bare minimum, he can give the regulated businessman a fair hearing; he can treat him with respect and take his arguments and problems seriously. When he must insist on strict compliance, he gives reasons. In other words, he exhibits *responsiveness*. Second, the inspector can selectively negate, modify, or delay the enforcement of regulations when their literal application to a particular violation would be unreasonable or of secondary importance. In short, he can give *forbearance*. Third, he can provide *information* to the regulated enterprise that reduces the difficulty or cost of compliance, or at least makes the required compliance measures seem understandable and justifiable. The same elements of exchange—responsiveness, forbearance, and information—can also be offered on a more systematic basis by higher enforcement officials or explicitly embodied in the regulations themselves.

The inspector's ability to initiate an exchange relationship derives in large measure from his power of threat and coercion. He gains a hearing by virtue of his power to cause trouble for the regulated enterprise—by issuing citations, threatening legal penalties, and creating the risk of adverse publicity . . . .

Those sanctioning powers, however, must be used judiciously. Indeed, the inspector's ability to obtain information and evidence that would support the use of legal sanctions depends, at least in part, on the implied promise that the information supplied will be interpreted fairly and that those legal powers will not be employed indiscriminately and unreasonably. A federal official in charge of enforcing quality-of-care regulations in nursing homes observed, "Unless you have some way of eliciting information, you don't know whether your rules fit the situation or not." A reputation for reasonableness brings the enforcement official more complete access and better information. More information increases his legal power. And more legal power gives him more to trade for cooperation.

RESPONSIVENESS: THE INSPECTOR AS POLITICIAN

One premise of the concept of responsiveness is the old assumption that power can be abused: the government might be wrong; the regulations might be overinclusive; governmental officials entrusted with a single altruistic mission might be unduly self-righteous or narrow-minded. The concept of responsiveness also rests on the premise that regulated enterprises by and large are involved in providing valued goods and services to the community, that their managers have at least some concern about the same social problems that preoccupy the regulators, and that those managers typically have a good deal more knowledge than the regulators about how those problems might be solved most efficiently . . . . The reasonable regulatory order, therefore, often might be better determined through a dialogue between inspector and regulated firm than by governmental fiat or unilateral judgments by enforcement officials. From this standpoint, it seems desirable to treat regulated enterprises and their managers not only as objects of regulation but also as participants in regulation, as thoughtful citizens entitled to some say about the implementation of public policy—especially as it affects their particular enterprise.

If regulated entities are citizens whose participation is valued, the individual inspector, in some sense, can serve as a politician who represents them (among other constituents) in their interactions with the government. Like a democratic politician, the inspector can be a messenger through whom the government is educated by those it seeks to govern, a receptor of information about unanticipated costs of the laws as written and of information about how the regulations could be modified. That does not mean, of course, that the regulatory official should be the unthinking mouthpiece of the enterprises he regulates. The politician must mediate between conflicting elements in his constituency and in the polity as a whole. The inspector-as-politician represents those to be protected by the regulatory program as well as the regulated enterprise and indeed ought ordinarily to give the former element in his constituency the heavier weighting.

Resistance to regulatory requirements is sometimes based on misunderstanding of their purpose and necessity. Sometimes the popular understanding of regulations exaggerates the stringency of actual legal obligations or neglects exceptions built into the rules that counter ostensible unreasonableness. Sometimes regulated businessmen fail to recognize the pervasiveness or seriousness of the problems the regulations were enacted to solve. Like a good politician, the inspector can attempt to elicit compliance in such cases by providing substantive reasons for particular regulatory requirements or by giving his constituent some understanding of collective problems that may extend beyond the individual constituent's perspective. Hawkins observed that British water pollution inspectors, in their encounters with operating officials in enterprises that create pollution, will sometimes explain the various uses to which the water containing the effluent will be put downstream . . . or sometimes they will impose a moral burden on the polluter by describing the treatment which the water has already received upstream to render it suitable for his own use . . . saying, "How would you like it if you had this sort of discharge coming into your intake?"*

. . . The inspector must often point out to good apple firms that the regulatory program or the law in question is socially necessary because many other firms do not act as well as they do. Thus, Silbey points out, the antifraud investigators constantly remind the businessmen about the big cases the office has prosecuted in the past, as if to show the respondent "that there are bad guys out there, worse than they are, and that the Attorney General is trying to get them."* Such efforts toward consciousness raising, in fact, are perhaps the most important contribution regulatory agencies can make. An inspector who begins his site-visit with a discussion of the persistence of industrial accidents, or poor nursing care, or discrimination, and who asks the regulated enterprise what it is doing to reduce such problems (and how successful it is), might do much more good than an inspector who begins by leafing through his rule book and recording violations.

FORBEARANCE

Forbearance entails: (1) overlooking violations that pose no serious risk under the circumstances; (2) not enforcing regulatory requirements that would be especially costly or disruptive in relation to the additional degree of protection they would provide; (3) granting reasonable time to come into compliance and accepting measures that would provide substantial if not literal compliance; and (4) making allowance for good faith efforts on the part of the regulated enterprise. If the inspector explicitly communicates these acts of forbearance to managers of the regulated enterprises, he is actually giving them something—and at little cost to those the program is designed to protect. In a world dominated by legalism and mistrust, simply refraining from treating someone as if he were a criminal gives the inspector a reputation for reasonableness—something he can use in asking the regulated firm for significant and perhaps costly changes in procedures or facilities.

Many agencies make some formal efforts to distinguish serious from

---

*[The reference is to Keith Hawkins, *Environment and Enforcement* (Oxford: Clarendon Press, 1984).]

*[The reference is to Susan Silbey, "Consumer Justice: The Massachusetts Attorney General's Office of Consumer Protection," (Ph.D. diss., University of Chicago, 1978).]

nonserious violations and willful from nonwillful ones. The Occupational Safety and Health Act mandates stiffer fines for serious and willful violations than for nonserious first-time violations and provides stipulated discounts from the fine for factors such as employer good faith. The FDA sends an "adverse findings letter" to food processors and drug manufacturers for violations of "good manufacturing practice" regulations that supervisors judge to be nonserious, and stronger "regulatory letters," requiring a response, for defects thought to raise great hazards for consumers . . . .

The strategy of not penalizing violations automatically does seem to help in eliciting cooperation. Both trucking association and government enforcement officials observed that many truckers encourage MCSU [Motor Carrier Safety Unit, California Highway Patrol] inspectors to list problems on compliance reports because it alerts them to potentially dangerous problems. An enforcement official said, "Companies call up and ask us to come in and inspect them." Yet independent and knowledgeable observers, such as inspectors from companies that insure trucking firms, are strongly of the view that the MCSU's cooperative posture does not lead to undue softness or capture by the industry . . . .

. . . For the strategy of forbearance to have its greatest effectiveness, however, inspectorial responses should probably emerge from an interactive process, as in the practices of the [MCSU] . . . .

Inspectors have the legal power and obligation to order a truck "out of service" if it "would pose an imminent hazard." The inspectors' operations manual, however, emphasizes that this sanction is not to be used automatically for any set class of regulatory violations they notice, but should be used as a matter of "professional judgment." Nor does a violation, or any set number of them, automatically result in a penalty action. Rather, the inspector is instructed to consult with the terminal manager after the inspection, to point out hazards and evaluate them jointly, and to obtain his written commitment to make repairs in some agreed upon order. The inspectors, accordingly, are quite open about their priorities. "The main objective is to keep the roads safe," said one, "so if the fleet is good but the records are bad, then I might let it slide for a while." Discussing violations of safety regulations, an MCSU inspector told us, "I try to remain flexible. If he can't take care of [a certain violation] today—say his truck has got to go to Fresno— I'll say, 'O.K., as long as you do X, Y, and Z before you go,' and he promises to fix it after the run." . . .

In some U.S. agencies, the concept of forbearance has been embodied in official policies that accept substantial compliance or even partial compliance—rather than insisting on literal compliance—with respect to smaller enterprises confronted with large expenditures for new and more stringent regulations . . . .

Even without explicit legal authorization, some enforcement officials build good will and obtain added cooperation by quietly extending deadlines for especially costly abatement measures. The Food and Drug Division of the California Department of Health seems to follow this practice systematically. Its inspectors check food and drug manufacturers' compliance against immensely detailed "good manufacturing practice" regulations that are said to be more strict than federal standards. Although inspectors are obligated to cite each deviation, the agency does not automatically initiate any penalty action, civil or criminal, or order an embargo. Rather, the inspectors' supervisors or regional office directors negotiate time limits and conditions for correcting each violation and then order a reinspection. The agency is willing to consider extenuating circumstances, such as the difficulty in getting a new part or the seasonal production deadlines for perishable fruits, if it concludes the hazards are tolerable and the company is acting in good faith. Where disputes (or violations) persist, the division usually holds an informal conference before initiating prosecution or a civil suit. No records are kept of these conferences. The firm usually sends a quality control engineer and a line manager; only occasionally does an attorney appear. Rarely, according to industry executives, does the agency relent on substantive requirements, but it often will grant more time and will accept temporary, less expensive solutions if the plant offers a convincing permanent corrective plan and has a reputation for reliability . . . .

One of the few areas of discretion OSHA enforcement officials have under the law concerns the establishment of compliance deadlines. Substantively, OSHA rules insist on "engineering out" health hazards, such as violations of noise standards, rather than abatement by use of personal protective equipment. Exceptions on the basis of economic feasibility are defined so stringently that formal variances are virtually impossible to obtain. Many regional enforcement officials seem to deal with this rigidity, however, by granting long abatement times when high compliance costs are involved. For example, of 23 OSHA enforcement files involving noise violation selected randomly in a study by John Mendeloff*—the average abatement period granted by regional officials was two years, usually followed by further extensions. One underlying value that can justify such extensions was expressed by a state air pollution control official. A manufacturing company in his district has a huge "coke calcining" oven that for some time had been in violation of the state's relatively new, and more stringent, standards on particulate emissions, even though the oven was equipped with a first-generation emission control device. The enforcement official recognized that there were technical problems involved and that no ready-made emission control device was available; the

*[The reference is to John Mendeloff, *Regulating Safety* (Cambridge, Mass.: MIT Press, 1979).]

oven had to be redesigned. What was important to him was that the company had designed a new burner and had begun installation—a complex job involving building a whole new physical support structure: "As long as they're willing to spend money on the problem and they are spending money, they're showing a good-faith effort, and I don't think any penalty is appropriate." . . .

One other area in which forbearance can often win an agency goodwill concerns reporting requirements. Presumably, the more information that flows to an agency, the more easily it can monitor compliance and build a data base for use in policy analysis. Carried along by this logic, however, the tendency of reporting systems to become oppressively costly and time consuming is by now almost legendary. The detailed records and reports are required of the good apples and the bad apples alike. They often generate more information than agency officials can hope to comb through. The Bay Area Air Pollution Control District, for example, recently repealed a regulation requiring manufacturing firms to report to the agency by telephone every breakdown in production or abatement equipment that might cause the firm to exceed legal emission levels. A district enforcement official estimated, however, that only 200 of the 10,000 or so reports received had involved significant pollution problems. Now, he said, the number of calls is greatly reduced, saving agency officials the labor of recording and responding to each call (as they had to under the repealed regulation). Yet the serious problems, he felt, were still being reported—reports were reduced, but not important information. This result, he acknowledged, was contrary to the expectation of agency enforcement staff, which had opposed the repeal (an industry sponsored measure), fearing it would impair effectiveness.

BARGAINING: TRADING FORBEARANCE FOR MEANINGFUL COMPLIANCE

Enforcement officials, of course, often can justifiably demand an explicit price for withholding legalistic enforcement and penalties—a commitment by the regulated enterprise to undertake serious reforms. A familiar model is the criminal prosecutor who strikes some counts from an indictment and recommends a suspended sentence and probation in return for (1) a guilty plea with respect to the central offense and (2) a legal obligation to act in designated socially responsible ways during the probationary period. The threat behind the bargain is that a breach of the terms of probation by the defendant, a second offense, will result in a heavier penalty. The plea bargain saves everyone the costs and tensions of full-scale litigation and, when it results in probation, establishes at least some possibility of rehabilitation rather than exacerbating the defendant's resentment against the system . . . .

A more far-reaching—and potentially more dangerous—practice is for the agency to exact, as a quid pro quo for nonenforcement, actions not specifically required by the regulations, such as changes in operating procedures that would help prevent serious violations in the future. By analogy, a judge sometimes attaches certain conditions to suspension of a sentence of incarceration—such as regular reporting of activities to a probation officer, or participation in a drug therapy or safe-driving program, or specified community service even though such remedial actions are not the normal legal obligations of citizens. Most examples of this kind of bargaining in the regulatory process that we have heard of did not occur in on-site encounters between inspectors and regulated enterprises. More often, bargains were struck at the courthouse door, after prosecution had begun. Some statutes, however, explicitly try to establish an earlier forum for plea bargaining; before initiating prosecution or before issuing a recall order, the agency is instructed to provide the regulated enterprise with an opportunity for an informal hearing.

There seems to be a tendency for such lawyer-conducted hearings, however, to take on a legalistic cast—to focus on whether the agency has a good legal case rather than on whether enforcement should be suspended on policy grounds. Such a hearing does not provide the same flexibility and opportunity for building cooperation as plea bargaining conducted by front-line inspectors or investigators. Still, agency-level informal hearings do provide the opportunity for bargaining over what kind of *remedy* will be effective yet reasonable. Sometimes they can be quite creative, as when they focus on improving organizational capabilities for future compliance, rather than on mandating specific facilities. The most far-reaching models for such bargains have been provided by the federal Securities and Exchange Commission. In return for dropping civil penalty actions, it has extracted "consent decrees" whereby defendants agreed to establish audit committees to monitor corporate procedures that had led to security law violations or to appoint a majority of "independent" directors to the corporate governing board. Some other agencies have taken smaller steps in that direction . . . .

There are risks of abuse in this plea-bargaining process. [Susan] Silbey's study of the Massachusetts Attorney General's Consumer Protection Office recounts a number of instances in which investigators threatened businesses with strict enforcement of entirely tangential regulations unless the firms gave refunds to dissatisfied customers, even when the agency had no evidence of violation of the consumer deception law in the transactions in question. Many agencies, consequently, shy away from demanding any extra effort or compliance measures not specifically mandated by law, even in return for dropping or not initiating formal enforcement. That, they say, is harassment. In any case, the regulated enterprises might well complain to legislators that it is harassment, and in truth, it is difficult to distinguish the legitimate plea bargain from the illegitimate extortionate bargain, although we would think it is not impossible to articulate criteria for doing so.

SUPPLYING INFORMATION: THE INSPECTOR AS CONSULTANT

Insofar as regulatory violations and hazards stem from employee inattentiveness, inadequate supervision, corporate misperception of risks, or ignorance of preventive measures—and according to enforcement officials in many fields, this is often the case—the regulatory agency may well have something to teach the regulated enterprise. Drawing on its cumulative experience with a variety of firms, it can provide information about risks and abatement techniques and ways of avoiding future violations. Backed by the implicit threat of enforcement, the agency, rather than compelling change by formal legal action, can "buy" it by providing information that will help the enterprise avoid expensive trouble in the future. Like a private business consultant, the inspector who finds a violation can attempt to analyze its causes, to diagnose weaknesses in the company's control system, and to point out cost-effective ways of preventing a recurrence . . . .

The most obvious information an inspector can provide, of course, is about significant hazards that have escaped the attention of company officials . . . . A blood bank inspector told us that he draws upon innovations he sees in the most modern establishments to tell smaller, less-specialized hospitals how blood-warming machines, for example, can best be maintained, monitored, and repaired. Virtually every factory safety engineer we interviewed said that OSHA inspectors could play a potentially valuable role because, as one manager put it, however hard the company tried, "An outsider can notice something dangerous in your house that you just take for granted." This is especially true with respect to smaller firms that lack specialized safety or quality control personnel. But large corporations also occasionally report helpful contributions from inspectors who consciously adopt a more consultative stance.

> Kenneth Wold, for example, is director of worker health and safety for an aluminum reduction plant in Kentucky. A state office called KOSHA has taken over enforcement of the Occupational Safety and Health Act. "The federal people who came in weren't very effective," Wold told us. "They didn't point out significant hazards and concentrated on unimportant things." But KOSHA inspectors who have visited the plant on an average of once a year "have been helpful in the closing conferences . . . ."
>
> "They might see a bench grinder with a tool that's not well adjusted . . . . The KOSHA man might find it at a time when our inspec-

tors have missed it and the man and the foreman have become a bit lackadaisical." . . .

. . . Agencies could enhance inspectors' ability to play this role if they consciously tried to serve as a data bank of abatement techniques, at least where problems are not standardized and hence where such information is not being supplied by the private market (such as pollution equipment suppliers or consulting firms). Ignorance of solutions, in fact, is surprisingly common. Although business enterprises may share information about the existence of safety or environmental problems, they are often reluctant to share information about solutions, for success in finding more cost-effective methods of complying with regulations has become an important way of gaining a competitive edge. Consequently, business managers often say they would welcome advice from regulatory officials about abatement methods. For example, maintenance of sophisticated air pollution control equipment, such as baghouses and scrubbers, is a major expense. Breakdowns are frequent. There is a constant search for ways of extending "bag life." Companies withhold that information from one another, but they must report breakdowns to agency officials, who perhaps could analyze and disseminate aggregate data . . . . Similarly, an exhaustive plant-by-plant study of occupational health problems in major copper smelters discovered considerable variation in measurement and protective engineering techniques to deal with known chemical hazards. The authors urged OSHA to establish "a widely accessible data bank" concerning health measurement and abatement technologies, rather than sending in inspectors with general checklists not geared to the specific problems of the industry. In 1979, in fact, California founded a Toxic Substance Repository at the University of California to accumulate information about occupational hazards and provide technical information, including abatement methods, to manufacturers and unions.

Diagnosis of the causes of violations is perhaps the most important kind of information an inspector can provide. To do so, the inspector's inquiry must go beyond the mere fact of a violation and extend into motivational areas . . . . To plumb motivation and to analyze the human factors in the causal pattern may require a subtle probing of a manager's knowledge and priorities . . . .

To draw out and evaluate a manager's knowledge and priorities, however, an inspector usually must establish a nonthreatening atmosphere, an interpersonal relationship that seems premised on cooperative problem solving, so that the manager is not completely defensive . . . .

[I]nspectors, at least in theory, . . . might diagnose faulty supervisory routines and managerial omissions. The safety director of a large corporation sketched this scenario when we asked him what he thought OSHA inspectors should do.

OSHA inspectors have the right to talk to employees. They'll go up to a machine operator and ask if everything is OK. What they really mean is, "Is there a violation I can write up?" If the man points out a broken electrical cord or plug, the OSHA guy will just write it up and put it on the list of citations.

What they should do is this: He should ask the employee, "How long has it been that way? Did you tell your foreman about it?" He should call over the foreman and ask why it was still that way. Maybe the foreman will say, "I've told him three times . . . you're supposed to go to Supply and get a new cord." Then why didn't he? Maybe his job is set up so he can't. Maybe the inspector will find out there's no procedure for checking cords, or that there is, but the employees don't know it well.

. . . To undertake this diagnostic and catalytic role, an inspector would have to spend proportionately more time talking with managers and professionals in the regulated enterprise and interviewing operating employees, and would have to spend proportionately less time looking at physical facilities in search of violations. To play the diagnostic role, moreover, the inspector often must study the enterprises' records to try to locate *patterns* of accidents or defects, partly in order to target his own investigation and, more important, in order to focus managerial attention on serious problem areas in the particular enterprise. For example:

> Frank McDonald is an inspector for the division of the California Department of Health responsible for enforcing safety regulations for blood and plasma centers. On site visits, he says he sharply questions employees performing transfusions about the procedures they routinely follow, and how they would deal with certain emergencies. If anyone fails his test, he informs the employee's supervisor and discusses methods of correcting the problem, such as better training or changes in supervisory procedures, but usually does not issue a citation. He says, "We're not here to put people out of business. The reason for inspection is to help them improve. You can't just kick 'em in the ass without telling them how to make things better. If you have to get tough, you do, but what we really want is for them to do a better job."
>
> Similarly, McDonald says he reviews the detailed records that must be kept for each donor not so much to find violations—failure to make or countersign an entry—but as a clue to the center's operating style. For example, he looks to see if the information taken from donors (which is essential to guard against "overbleeding" and to maintain blood quality) is recorded neatly. "This may seem picky but it's not. If it's scribbled in that might be a sign that they're asking the questions very hastily or just going through the motions. Then I get suspicious, and I try to listen in on a few interviews."

The inspector-as-consultant can also alert company management to incompetent supervisors or gaps in internal control systems. One federal

Railroad Administration inspector, checking Conrail records, noticed that there was no record of any managerial response to certain reports of rail defects filed by company track inspectors. He spelled out his findings in a citation and levied a fine against Conrail; the corporation suspended the responsible supervisor. This kind of discovery seems to elicit a more cooperative attitude from the regulated enterprise.

The good inspector would also attempt to use his legal leverage to induce enterprises to study and improve their own procedures for preventing harm. An example is a special diagnosis-oriented inspection program under which FDA officials prod each food and drug manufacturer to analyze its own production processes to locate the most common sources of contamination and key indicators of potential breakdowns in quality control processes. Inspectors are then instructed to focus their investigations on these critical points, as opposed to routinely checking compliance with the FDA's almost endless list of "good manufacturing practice" regulations. In effect, this is a program for evaluating and improving the company's own quality control system and capacity for problem detection.

THE GOOD INSPECTOR AND GOOD INSPECTION

. . . [O]ur portrait of the good inspector illuminates the nature of the enforcement task. The good inspector is really anyone who can do good inspection. But good inspection does not depend merely on the personal characteristics and skills of the inspector, however important these may be. Good inspection can flourish only in an organizational and political environment that cultivates it, or at least permits it. It is the regulatory agency, and not merely the individual enforcement official, that must foster flexible enforcement and try to foster cooperation through consultation and tough bargaining . . . . □

NOTES AND QUESTIONS

1. Unlike some of the articles that we have read so far, Bardach and Kagan take a definite normative stand: they say that not only is discretion inevitable in the regulatory process, but it is also desirable. What evidence do they provide to support this position? What role do they think "law" ought to play in the administrative process?

Political scientist Theodore Lowi, in a classic work, *The End of Liberalism* 2nd ed. (New York: W. W. Norton, 1979), argues that in fact too much administrative discretion is detrimental to a democracy—decisions are made by the unelected and the unaccountable. He therefore calls for a system in which legislation authorizing administrative regulation must be explicit and limiting. In Bardach and Kagan's terms, he calls for "legalism." Bardach and Kagan support their case in terms of efficiency. Lowi counters by focusing on equality and democracy. How would Bardach and Kagan respond?

3. According to Bardach and Kagan, what role does bargaining play in the

administrative process? Why would a regulator who had the full power of the law behind her bother to bargain with a violator of the law?

4. Bardach and Kagan are writing about the "good inspector." But the subtitle of their book is "The Problem of Regulatory Unreasonableness." There are, in other words, lots of not-so-good inspectors and regulators, who "go by the book," or behave in a way that is harsh, punitive, unyielding.

For example, OSHA had a policy of "unannounced inspections." These were bitterly resented by factory managers and safety engineers, who felt they had nothing to hide, and resented having to "drop what they are doing whenever the inspector knocks." In general, when regulatory systems "seem to act unreasonably, businessmen react defensively." A vicious circle is set up. "Enforcement officials . . . respond with enhanced mistrust and legalism. Businessmen become still more resentful and retaliate with various forms of noncooperation and resistance" (pp. 106–07).

In addition, the "good inspector" can get into trouble because he is good (that is, flexible and cooperative). It is much safer to "go by the book;" this avoids the possibility of bad publicity. The individual regulator is never going to be crucified for sticking to the rules; but a policy of discretionary "underenforcement" is vulnerable politically; and may even expose the inspector to such "predators" as journalists. Any "investigative reporter in need of a story can be sure to find one by looking deep enough into a regulatory regime" (p. 206).

How can we structure a system that is neither too lax nor too tight? Does the subject-matter of regulation make a difference? Should there be one technique for food companies, another for car-manufacturers; one technique for consumer safety, another for worker safety?

5. Stewart Macaulay, in "Business Adaptation to Regulation: What Do We Know and What Do We Need to Know?" 15 *Law & Policy* 259–62 (1993), summarizes much of the literature on the operation of administrative agencies:

> Our conventional picture of administration looks something such as this: a legislature grants power to an agency to solve an existing or avoid a potential social problem. The agency makes rules, grants licenses or conducts investigations. Almost everyone learns of the rules and complies. A few people fail to get the word or try to evade. The agency uncovers their illegal actions, holds hearings, and then it imposes sanctions upon those found to have violated the rules. Others learn of the proceedings and they are deterred from evasion. As a result, everyone lives happily ever after, and the good, the true and the beautiful is achieved.
>
> The empirical picture in most societies differs from this conventional sketch. Of course, my colleague Willard Hurst would stress that regulation often works. Effective regulation means that we can drink the water and the milk. Highways are planned, built and repaired. We can rely on systems for providing telephones, water, electricity and natural gas. Doctors, lawyers, dentists, hair stylists and automobile drivers get licenses and lose them when they injure the public. While we do not get 100% compliance, we seldom get 0% compliance. Even when we would like more effective regulation, regulation matters to business and it must cope with it. [Hazel] Genn reports, for example, that most firms which she studied carry out the orders of administrative inspectors: "Most of

the people interviewed maintain that they simply did what they were
told by the inspector because they did not believe that they had a choice
or that there was scope for negotiation."*

Nonetheless, . . . studies have shown that regulatory agencies often
do not even try to enforce the law completely against all of those who
should comply. Agencies often have selective enforcement strategies.
For example, they may attack critical problems of interest to the press,
public and legislators. They deal with atrocity stories as long as the stories continue to shock the public. Agencies may attempt to get national
corporations to change their standard practices so they comply with the
regulations. These corporations must guard their reputations, and they
seek to avoid news stories about violating regulations. If the agency can
bring these corporations into compliance, much behavior will be influenced. A corporation may respond by revising its standard procedures
and gearing its own internal reward and punishment system to get its
employees to carry out the regulatory policy. In this way a private government supplements the enforcement activities of the public one. At the
same time the agency may be putting less egregious violations aside,
perhaps until another day.

Agencies frequently are reactive rather than proactive. They often
respond to complaints in a routinized fashion. For example, in many
states an agency is charged with enforcing a variety of consumer protection laws. The agency may try to attack clearly bad people in publicized
proceedings, but most of the agency's activity involves writing letters: a
consumer sends a complaint against a business to the agency. The
agency writes the business asking about the dispute. Often the business
responds by promising to review the matter. Many agencies count this as
a successful handling of a complaint in their official statistics. In some
cases it works: a store manager, faced with a letter on official stationery,
may look at the situation and offer the customer a refund or a good deal
on another product. In other cases, however, the store manager offers no
more than a gesture, and the still unhappy consumer just gives up.

Agencies often engage in soft law enforcement. They spend their
time trying to teach people how to comply and to persuade them to do
so. They publish booklets about complying with the law, and they offer
a telephone hot line answering questions posed by those regulated. The
Internal Revenue Service even offers official interpretations of the statutes as applied to situations posed by taxpayers, or their lawyers or
accountants, in formal requests.

As a part of soft law enforcement, agencies often engage in implicit
and explicit bargaining . . . . We bargain in the shadow of the law, and
our system gives us many tools for doing so. Lawyers for businesses
which are the targets of regulation can mount constitutional challenges
to the regulatory statute or the agencies' procedures. They can offer
legal arguments, construing legislation or the agencies' own rules in
ways which block enforcement against their clients. Finally, American
legal procedure offers a skilled lawyer many opportunities for delay. If
the agency thinks fast action to protect the public is vital, then delay

---

* [The reference is to Hazel Genn, Business Responses to the Regulation of Health and
Safety in England, 15 *Law & Policy Quarterly* 219 (1993).

becomes a bargaining tool. Some large businesses can threaten to go to the legislature and get the statute that empowers the agency changed or its budget reduced.

Regulators vary widely in their enforcement behavior. Braithwaite, Walker and Grabowsky[78] studied Australian administrative agencies and found seven types. They called their categories conciliators, benign big guns, diagnostic inspectorates, detached token enforcers, detached modest enforcers, token enforcers and modest enforcers. Obviously, these terms need a great deal of explanation, but they suggest the range of behavior. Notice that they found no strict enforcers. The strictest agencies were only modest enforcers, at least as judged by Braithwaite and his colleagues. They speculate that the pattern they found might not be exclusively Australian, but an American reader can certainly recognize what they are talking about.

. . . An empirical picture of regulation suggests that business often will have room to maneuver, and many of the papers detail tactics and strategies. However, an important lesson . . . is variability . . . . [S]maller firms which attempt to hide and avoid regulation . . . do not learn exactly what the law requires, and they rationalize their noncompliance by pointing to the complexity or unreasonableness of regulation. We must remember that the number of people engaged in enforcing the law almost always is incredibly small compared to the number of people who should comply. Our police and administrative investigators are hardly occupying armies. This means there will be many chances to evade and hide.

. . . [L]arger, highly motivated, firms . . . hire their own experts to deal with regulation. Just this act may increase compliance. The need to comply reinforces the business' need for the expert, and the expert is likely to push his or her own agenda within the business. For example, over the past twenty years many American state courts have adopted rules which make it more difficult for employers to fire employees at will. Both the federal government and the states also have attempted to regulate discrimination in employment on the basis of race, religion, gender, age, physical handicaps and the like. This challenge to traditional practices has raised the status of the personnel departments. Personnel specialists stress the legal threats both to help their employers and to justify gaining power and increased budgets. Many firms have instituted elaborate internal procedures in response to the threat of regulation. It is likely that these procedures have offered employees more protection than has been achieved by law suits and administrative proceedings.

6. The styles of administrative behavior probably differ greatly depending on *what* is being regulated and *who* is subject to the regulation. Welfare mothers, for example, are likely to be treated differently from big businessmen. We may evaluate the exercise of discretion differently too. On welfare administration, see, for example, Joel Handler, *Protecting the Social Service Client: Legal and Structural Controls on Official Discretion* (New York: Academic

---

78. "An Enforcement Taxonomy of Regulatory Agencies," 9 *Law & Policy* 323 (1987).

Press, 1979); and Daniel Katz, et al., *Bureaucratic Encounters: A Pilot Study of the Evaluation of Government Services* (Ann Arbor, Mich.: Survey Research Center, Institute for Social Research, 1975).

7. Bardach and Kagan are writing about the United States. But there may be different national styles of regulation. See Steven Kelman, *Regulating America, Regulating Sweden: A Comparative Study of Occupational Safety and Health Policy* (Cambridge, Mass.: MIT Press, 1980).

THE LEGAL SYSTEM IN OPERATION: HIGHLIGHTING THE IMPORTANCE OF DISCRETION, BARGAINING, AND "THE LAW"

In this chapter we have offered a number of studies which show various legal institutions in operation. The picture drawn is somewhat different from the one which an outsider would draw, if she worked only with formal legal material, such as statutes, cases, administrative orders, or police manuals of procedures. Similarly, it is probably a different picture than we often get from the educational system, or the news, or the entertainment industry; or reports from interest groups with an axe to grind. Our picture is very complex: life influences law which influences life which influences law and so on. In that complex interaction, three factors emerge as important: discretion, bargaining and "the law" itself.

Discretion is everywhere in the legal system. This means that in order to understand the law-in-action, we must understand what motivates the exercise of discretion; and what are the constraints on this exercise. This is true whether we are talking about police, lawyers, administrative inspectors, or legislators.

"Bargaining" is also pervasive in the legal system. It is, in fact, one form that discretion takes. Most disputes ultimately get resolved informally. Formal law thus has no chance to shape outcomes totally. Police bargain with complainants; legislators bargain with each other; lawyers bargain with their clients; inspectors bargain with the companies they are regulating. We can ask questions about the consequences of bargaining. Bargaining precludes the winner-take-all results that formal law sometimes dictates; but still, as we saw, there can be definite winners and losers in a settlement. Under bargaining, winning and losing is not necessarily related to "legal" right or wrong; it may be related to the power and resources of the bargainers. See Penelope Bryan, above p. 127; Marc Galanter, "Why the Haves Come Out Ahead: Speculations on the Limits of Legal Change," 9 *Law & Society Review* 95 (1974).

While discretion and informal bargaining occur everywhere in the legal system, law is not necessarily unimportant. "Law" (in the sense of formal rules and the structures to enforce them) clearly seems to limit some forms of discretion. For example, the Constitution, and the courts' interpretations of the Constitution, seem to put a brake on some forms of police discretion. Similarly, the "law" sets boundaries within which informal bargaining will take place. As we have seen, there is considerable dispute about exactly how important "law" is, or should be, in shaping the legal system in action. Can "law" significantly limit discretion? Should it? There is a wide range of opinions. Similarly, the importance of "law" to the informal bargaining process is a bone of contention. Some feel that "law" not only sets boundaries within which bargaining takes place, but makes bargaining possible: without rules and procedures to bargain in the shadow of, bargaining would not occur. Others find a less significant role for "law" and feel that bargaining is an inevitable part of any dispute situation even where no "law" is present.

Thus we have a picture of the legal system as an area of discretion and bargaining, with "law" playing at least some role in structuring and regulating what the system does in fact. If we accept this picture as more or less accurate, what difference does it make? How might we appraise the consequences of a system based on a mixture of discretion and bargaining with formal legal processes at the margin? Stewart Macaulay, in "Business Adaptation to Regulation: What Do We Know and What Do We Need to Know?" 15 *Law & Policy* 259 (1993), indicates some of the conflicting arguments:

> Let me play law professor and tell two inconsistent stories . . .[79] Discretion and bargaining in the shadow of the law may have consequences which we like or dislike. First, some people might find a great deal wrong with the picture . . . . Discretion, bargaining and other forms of adaptation defeat rational planning and coherent regulatory programs. Selective and partial enforcement means that the legislative policy underlying the regulation will be carried out only partially and unpredictably. Instead of planned social change, enforcement practice yields evasion, coping, adaptation and some unknown degree of compliance. We may assume that problems are being solved when they are only being papered over.
>
> Moreover, many may not see the exercise of discretion and the bargains struck as legitimate. Agencies may craft a strategy, but on closer examination these strategies reveal governmental weakness and the need to accommodate private power. Agency employees may divert the goals of the organization to suit their own programs. They may wish to

---

79. See Leif Johansen, "The Bargaining Society and the Inefficiency of Bargaining," 32 *Kyklos* 497 (1979); Genevra Richardson, "Policing and Pollution: The Enforcement Process," 10 *Policy & Politics* 263 (1982); Gerd Winter, "Bartering Rationality in Regulation," 19 *Law & Society Review* 219 (1985).

enhance their status as experts and avoid the conflict inherent in enforcing the law. Discretion and bargaining always raise the possibility of bribery. Money may change hands, favors may be exchanged or a governmental official who exercises discretion reasonably may be paving the way toward a high position with the businesses he or she is now charged with regulating.

Soft law enforcement takes place back-stage and the audience is composed only of the insiders. The regulatory agency does not gain support from the larger public, and it loses the chance to put issues on the public agenda. Compromises fail to vindicate rights and reinforce their standing in the culture. You don't get a chance to hold the bad people up to public scorn. Occasionally, the mass media may spot that an agency has treated a large corporation very favorably, but the press finds it hard to discover what has happened and why. Moreover, the status quo will be the baseline from which accommodations are made. Bargains move incrementally from the existing situation. An environmental protection agency, for example, could not expect an industry to agree to close all of its plants and go out of business because this was the only way to avoid a kind of pollution. Also, inequality is preserved. Large firms can threaten more credibly to go to court with a chance of winning. Large firms more often are in a position to contribute to a political action committee and thus provoke a legislator to criticize an agency's action.

Finally, bargains and compromises may transform rather than solve problems. Redefining the situation often is part of the process of gaining agreement. This favors short-run adaptations rather than costly long-run solutions. While this may be fine in the short-run, it may only put off a problem which must be solved. Sometimes problems just go away; sometimes problems put off are harder to solve because they have been put off.

Let me leap to the other side and defend the system which we have found. Grant Gilmore said: "In Heaven there will be no law, and the lion will lie down with the lamb . . . . The worse the society, the more law there will be. In Hell there will be nothing but law, and due process will be meticulously observed."[80] We may not be able to afford to pay the price of complete application of all the laws in formal regulatory procedures. We run our society with remarkably few police, administrators and judges, and I do not detect a great willingness to pay more taxes to provide more legal officials. Furthermore, it is almost impossible to draft laws which capture all of the nuances of real life. It is hard to anticipate all of the exceptions we want to make to general rules. To a great extent, we've tried to do this with the Internal Revenue Code and the regulations drafted to interpret it. We've created an extraordinarily expensive system, which still fails to provide rules for everything. It

80. G. Gilmore, *The Ages of American Law* 110–11 (New Haven: Yale University Press, 1977). I like Martha Minow's improvisation on Gilmore's statement: "Grant Gilmore warned that the pathway to hell is paved with due process." Minow, "Interpreting Rights: An Essay for Robert Cover," 96 *Yale Law Journal* 1860, 1909 (1987).

takes bargaining and compromise to make the exceptions and tailor the punishment to fit the crime.

Cooperation usually is better than coercion. Our society honors freedom and persuasion. Many Americans react to coercion by evasion or resistance. When parties reach a negotiated result, the conventional wisdom of alternative dispute resolution is that they will be more committed to it. Maybe we honor a certain amount of deviation in our society. Americans comply with laws which they think make sense, but not those they see as foolish. If we have space for a range of deviation from the present wishes of the majority, it may help hold a multi-cultural society together. In the short-run, at least, perhaps it is better if we can get a substantial amount of compliance from the largest businesses and leave smaller firms alone. This may help infant industries survive, and when, and if, they grow, then we can bring them into line.

Some of our laws reflect our aspirations rather than the power configuration of those affected by them. Full enforcement might provoke a powerful minority with intensely held beliefs. Soft law enforcement may help us mark time until actual working assumptions come to match our aspirations crystallized in laws.

Having said all this, we should note all the opportunities for research implicated in my stories. The two arguments that I have just presented rest on many unproved factual assumptions. Both my attack and my defense sound good to me. However, I doubt whether either position would apply to all situations. Some arguments may make a lot more sense in one situation than in another. Moreover, business adaptation to regulation—creative compliance, evasion, bargaining in the shadow of the law and all the rest—may have consequences which I haven't imagined.

It should be clear that while law and social science research can help to construct a picture of the legal system in action, it cannot resolve all of the issues of interpretation and evaluation. Nonetheless, the themes presented in Chapter 2 will appear again and again in the chapters to follow. In a sense, they are building blocks of any theory about the relationship of law to society and society to law.

LEGAL CULTURE: DESCRIPTIONS OF WHOLE LEGAL SYSTEMS

As this chapter has tried to make clear, there are many ways to describe a legal system; you can approach this task from many different disciplinary angles, and with different goals in mind.

Most of the material in this chapter has been about specific *aspects* of a legal system. Legal anthropologists, in particular, have been interested in trying to describe whole systems, not literally of course, but in terms of certain crucial underlying cultural traits. Culture is a much used, much abused, term with a broad range of meanings. Here we use it simply to mean ways of life—repetitive patterns of thought and behavior that characterize some community, people or group.

Classical legal anthropology honed its skills on preliterate peoples or communities that had ways of settling disputes, to be sure, but that lacked the blessings (such as they are) of written laws, codes, and lawyers. But complex societies also have "cultures," and their legal systems have underlying traits that can be described as the essence of their legal culture.

It is much harder to try to distill the core notions of, say, Japanese legal culture than the culture of a small group of a few hundred people who live on a South Pacific island. Yet in scholarly journals and the popular press there are questions, assertions, and discussions about the *nature* of certain modern legal cultures at the national level. For example, we hear endlessly about the differences between American legal culture—said to be litigious, rights-conscious, and adversarial—and the legal cultures of Asia, said to be oriented more toward compromise, harmony, and the like.

The Korean legal scholar Dae-Kyu Yoon considers this issue in *Law and Political Authority in South Korea* (Boulder: Westview Press, 1990). Yoon distinguishes between two aspects of legal culture: "procedural legal values," which are concerned with the management of conflict, and "substantive legal values," which are "based on fundamental assumptions concerning the distribution and application of resources in society."

He then discusses Korean legal culture. The orthodox view is that "Confucian values" and a "centralized bureaucracy," over the years have "fostered an entrenched authoritarian outlook on life and society." In Korean society, the family was the central focus of the social order, and the family was strongly patriarchal. Because of its culture and tradition, Korea was unable to assimilate adopted Western laws. Such laws did not work in Korea because Korea lacked the "cultural background or matrix which produced Western law." Western law came out of a society whose culture, unlike the one found in Korea, stressed "individualism, universalism, impersonalism, egalitarianism, rationalism, [and] achievement motivation."

Yoon criticizes this account of Korean legal culture which he calls "cultural determinism." Cultural determinism ignores political and economic factors and overemphasizes history and tradition. It ignores the fact that European countries "themselves went through traditional stages." Also, some non-European countries, such as Japan, seem to have adopted and adapted Western laws and Western legal ways quite successfully.

Law, according to Yoon, "though inseparably related to culture," is not "subordinated to it." The tie between law and culture is variable and problematic. "Introduction of a foreign law can be in itself a means of cultural modification." As society changes, so do its values. This means that the "traditional culture of a society" cannot really be "in full accord with contemporary values . . . . Values in today's Korean society are in a state of flux, for social change has been sudden and drastic." In other words, as Korea modernizes, as it moves into the world economy and becomes part of global culture, its "traditional" legal culture inevitably alters and loses whatever potency it was assumed to possess.

NOTES AND QUESTIONS

1. What Yoon describes as the conventional picture of Western law is particularly relevant to the United States. In general, American legal culture has been labeled as individualistic, legalistic, rights-conscious—not merely in comparison with Japan or Korea but also in comparison with European societies. On these aspects of American legal culture, see Robert L. Kagan, "Do Lawyers Cause Adversarial Legalism? A Preliminary Inquiry," 19 *Law and Social Inquiry* 1 (1994). There are, of course, many who think that the rather unflattering portrait of American legal behavior is overdrawn—compare the discussions by Engel and Greenhouse, below, p. 249.

Of course, even if American culture is not as individualistic, legalistic and rights-conscious as it is sometimes described, it may be more so than most other societies. But we have very little systematic information about differences in legal culture. There have been some attempts at comparison. On Australia, see Jeffrey Fitzgerald, "Grievance, Disputes and Outcomes: A Comparison of Australia and the United States," 15 *Law in Context* 1 (1983); on France versus the United States, see Laurent Cohen-Tanugi, *Le Droit sans l'état: Sur la Democratie en France et en Amerique* (Paris: Presses Universitaires de France, 1985). Cohen-Tanugi praises the law-orientation of the United States, and regrets the fact that French law gives less play to individual rights-consciousness.

Erhard Blankenburg has carried out research on "comparative legal culture." He compared the Netherlands with the German province of Nordrhein-Westfalen, which lies just across the border, and whose population is culturally quite similar to that of the Netherlands. The official law of the two jurisdictions is also quite similar. But there are great differences in the *use* of law and litigation. Blankenburg ascribes these differences to a cluster of factors, many of which are structural and institutional—for example, the Dutch provide much more generously for free legal advice to people at the lower end of the economic scale. See Blankenburg, "The Infrastructure for Avoiding Civil Litigation: Comparing Cultures of Legal Behavior in the Netherlands and West Germany," 28 *Law & Society Review* 789 (1994). A short essay, in English, which also gives the main themes of Blankenburg's research, is "Legal Cultures Compared," in Vincenzo Ferrari, ed., *Laws and Rights: Proceedings of the International Congress of Sociology of Law for the Ninth Centenary of the University of Bologna* (Milan: Giuffrè, 1991), p. 93.

2. The Japanese case has attracted particular attention in recent years, because Japan has been such an enormous success economically. It is also a society with relatively few people entitled to call themselves "lawyers," and

not much litigation. This tempts some people to suggest that the secret of Japanese success lies, in part at least, in the Japanese avoidance of law, and their use of mediation, compromise, bureaucratic "guidance," and the like. For a comprehensive discussion of Japanese legal culture, see Frank K. Upham, *Law and Social Change in Postwar Japan* (Cambridge: Harvard University Press, 1987). See also Michael Young, "Judicial Review of Administrative Guidance," 84 *Columbia Law Review* 923 (1984); J. Mark Ramseyer, "The Costs of the Consensual Myth: Antitrust Enforcement and Institutional Barriers to Litigation in Japan," 94 *Yale Law Journal* 604 (1985). While Japan has fewer lawyers than most industrialized countries, we should remember that many activities normally handled by lawyers in the United States are handled in Japan by those not entitled to call themselves lawyers there. Adam Meyerson, in "Why There Are So Few Lawyers in Japan," *Wall Street Journal,* Feb. 9, 1981, p. 14, cols. 3–6 points out:

> Notaries, for example, handle Japanese real estate transactions that you would need a lawyer for in the U.S. Family disputes and divorce cases are handled by special mediators rather than lawyers. Specialists can draft wills, litigate small claims, provide tax advice or write contracts without being admitted to the bar. Many Japanese companies have legal staffs of 60 or 70 professionals, doing work similar to that of U.S. business attorneys, but not officially registered as lawyers . . . .
>
> Japanese companies . . . almost never take lawyers with them in their dealings with government ministries, as American companies do in Washington and state capitals. And though they often protest government decisions politically, Japanese companies almost never sue government ministries . . . .
>
> Japanese companies seldom make either acquisitions or diverstitures, preferring to start new ventures directly. There is therefore little need for takeover litigation or for much of the corporate and securities work so important to U.S. law firms.

Professors Kahei Rokumoto and Shozo Ota of the University of Tokyo, in "The Issues of Lawyer Population in Japan," in Kahei Rokumoto (ed.) *The Social Role of the Legal Profession* 193 (Proceedings of the International Colloquium of the International Association of Legal Science 1993), consider the argument that Japan is served by the functional equivalent of lawyers. They discuss what they call "quasi-lawyers." These include tax attorneys, patent attorneys, judicial scriveners, administrative scriveners, public accountants, notaries, and staff members of corporate legal sections. While Rokumoto and Ota accept that such people must be taken into account when we compare a western society with Japan, they also argue that Japan needs far more lawyers than it has, to meet the demands of a modern society. Rokumoto and Ota point out:

> The main political goal in transplanting the Western legal system [to Japan after the Meiji Restoration in 1867] was to abolish the extra-territorial jurisdiction accorded to Western powers in the treaties that Japan was forced to enter. Law was generally regarded as a technique for state officials to control and guide the people who depended on them, but not

as a means that citizens can use to regulate their own affairs, sometimes against the will of the state. (p. 194)

Is Japanese legal culture really as anti-litigation and pro-compromise as advertised? Not everyone thinks so. For example, *The New York Times,* Sept. 1, 1987, p. 4, cols. 1–6, reported:

Japan has become known as a land where people do not sue, obeying a cultural taboo against resorting to the courts. But many here suggest that if Japanese do not sue as much as Americans, it is more because doing so is such an ordeal than out of a cultural embrace of harmony. Trials are long, court fees can be high and judges often exert pressure to settle.

Such a system, critics charge, can also hurt less powerful groups in Japanese society—those who do not have enough money to pay for expensive court cases or those without enough political influence to press for changes in Japan's legislature.

"Japanese like this image of themselves as a harmonious, nonlitigious society, but it's more a myth than anything else," said Isaac Shapiro, a partner at Skadden, Arps, Slate, Meagher & Flom who grew up in Japan and whose practice includes Japan . . . .

Professor [Nobuyoshi] Toshitani [University of Tokyo] argued that many elements in the Japanese legal system discourage lawsuits and promote settlements. "In one word, the Japanese legal system is bankrupt."

Hiroshi Wagatsuma and Arthur Rosett, in "Cultural Attitudes Towards Contract Law: Japan and the United States Compared," 2 *Pacific Basin Law Journal* 76, 96–97 (1983), assert:

[t]he Japanese live by the illusion of harmony, while Americans live by the illusion of autonomy and self-sufficiency . . . . [T]he attitudes of the Japanese toward business transactions and contract which are regarded as uniquely Japanese . . . are also found in American society, although the significance of that behavior may be defined differently by each culture . . . . [C]ultural and legal systems are not given much choice regarding the harsh realities of the world within which they must operate, but there do appear to be genuine choices of our illusions in this world. Such choices seem to have important consequences for the society that makes them . . . . [These choices] influence perceptions in important ways and thereby ultimately change the reality of the situation.

Do most Americans "live by the illusion of autonomy and self-sufficiency" rather than that of harmony? Do Americans, in fact, honor and support those who stand up and assert their rights? For another view of the nature of Japanese legal culture and Japanese law and lawyers, see John O. Haley, *Authority without Power: Law and the Japanese Paradox* (New York: Oxford University Press, 1991). See, also, Yoshiharu Matsuura, "Law and Bureaucracy in Modern Japan," 41 *Stanford Law Review* 1627 (1989), a critical review of Frank Upham's book on Japan, n. 2 supra.

Most of the large literature on Japanese law and lawyers has concerned business and economic law. But see Daniel H. Foote, "The Benevolent Paternalism of Japanese Criminal Justice," 80 *California Law Review* 317 (1992); Nobuyoshi Araki, "The Flow of Criminal Cases in the Japanese Criminal Justice System," 31 *Crime & Delinquency* 601 (1985).

   3. Pyong-Choon Hahm, in *The Korean Political Tradition and Law* 190 (Seoul: Hollym Corp., 1967), states that for a Korean, it is "not decent or 'nice' to insist on one's legal right. When a person hauls another person into court, he is in fact declaring war on him . . . . Thus, a Korean cannot think of law as anything other than oppressive." Would Yoon agree? Would most Americans think "when a person hauls another person into court, he is in fact declaring war on him . . . ."?

3

Where Does Law
Come From?
The Impact of
Society on Law

INTRODUCTION

This chapter asks how law is generated. What forces in society influence or create particular kinds of law? In most Western democratic
capitalist or welfare states, theory asserts that a major, if not the primary, source of law is the will of the people. Political parties which
advocate programs that fail to gain or lose favor can be driven from
office at elections. Citizens, or at least organized groups of some citizens, have many ways to convey their wishes to political leaders. We
must remember that many other governmental systems, both past and
present, offer different theories to justify their laws. Some claim that
their laws reflect the will of God. Some claim the right of a ruler, or of
a leadership group, to make the laws without public consent: the right
of kings, chiefs, or elders to rule.

American theory is complex. On one hand, we claim that our laws
reflect popular will. On the other hand, we cannot simply state "our
law is what the people want." The idea of the "rule of law" is both an
expression of the ideal of popular sovereignty and a denial of popular
sovereignty as absolute. Federal and state constitutions limit popular
will. These constitutions allocate powers among the branches of government, and among local, state and federal governments. The federal
and state constitutions also contain bills of rights, which purport to
defend minorities against the will of the majority. But even the American Constitution, which is drenched with natural law ideology, suf-
fused with the notion of fundamental rights beyond the power of tem-

169

porary majorities to interfere with, and which is itself difficult to amend, claims to be an expression of the popular will. Originally, of course, it was adopted by means of a vote.

Social scientists are interested in human behavior as well as in professed ideals, although they recognize that professed ideals profoundly influence behavior. Hence the emphasis in this Chapter will be on the *actual* sources of law; who, what, and how? For example, to what extent does law reflect "custom" or "public opinion?" Both of these are difficult concepts. In some very simple societies, the distinction between "public opinion," "custom" and "law" lacks clarity and focus. In these societies there may be no written language, no legal profession as such, and breaches of expected right behavior are handled, along with disputes between individuals, by leaders in a more-or-less informal setting. In these societies, social control is a reflection of custom. We can call the process "law" or we can reserve this term for more complex social processes. But we must be cautious not to attach labels without thought. People still make judgments in simple societies when they give meanings to custom in particular situations. Customs often are ambiguous; or the demands of one custom may be at least partially offset by another pointing in a different direction.

Moreover, we can ask about the *source* of a custom and its applications. How much of the content of the norms can be explained by the fact that the tribe is nomadic? lives on fish and game? is warlike? lives in a desert? is surrounded by fierce enemies? has a high infant mortality rate? What is the precise role of economic and social forces in forming custom? To what extent do the group's norms influence or control behavior? To what extent do they only serve to legitimate, or attempt to legitimate, behavior which the material conditions of life have shaped or caused?

In more complex societies all of these questions about customs remain. In addition, there are problems of defining and measuring "public opinion." Some topics are matters of intense concern; as to others, most people are indifferent. And what do we mean by the "public?" Some members of society can make their views known easily; others are almost invisible. Does public opinion come welling up as some sort of mysterious force or is it, to a large extent, manufactured by those in a position to do so? Then, too, the structure of the legal system itself—the way in which "custom" and "public opinion" are translated into "law"—may affect the degree to which law reflects custom and public opinion.

The first section of this chapter deals with the origin of legal systems. Under what conditions do groups add a legal system to an informal system of social control? In the second section we discuss how social changes in the United States have resulted in a fundamental change in our legal culture—our expectations about and demands from the legal system. Section three provides an explicit exploration of the impact of public opinion on law. How is public opinion measured? How is public opinion "made?" How is public opinion "fed into the legal system?" Our fourth section examines sources of law other than the general public, including interest groups, elites, and social classes. To what extent is the American legal system democratic? Who, if anyone, controls the legal system? Finally, we discuss case studies of the relationship between social change and legal change in the United States.

LAW AS PART OF A COMPLEX SYSTEM OF SOCIAL CONTROL: WHEN DO WE FIND A LEGAL SYSTEM?

13. *Social Factors in the Development of Legal Control: A Case Study of Two Israeli Settlements*[81]

Richard D. Schwartz

63 *Yale Law Journal* 471 (1954)

☐ Legal control is not exercised against all disturbing behavior. Sometimes, such behavior never reaches the courts. At other times, it is not sanctioned by the courts because, we are told, it should be left to the *interior* forum, as the tribunal of conscience has been aptly called. The effects of non-legal or informal control, whether or not adequately described in terms of "conscience," seem to be an important factor in a court's decision to withhold sanction.

The relationship between legal and informal controls can be theoretically stated and empirically described. The cultures of two Israeli communities were compared in an effort to determine the social effects of economic collectivism. One of the differences noted was that the collective community, or *kvutza*, had no distinctly legal institution, whereas the *moshav*, a semi-private property settlement, did . . . .

In the interactive aggregates of individuals which we call *social groups*, two main forms of control may be distinguished: that which is carried out by specialized functionaries who are socially delegated the task of intra-group control, and that which is not so delegated. These

---

81. Reprinted by permission of the Yale Law Journal Company and Fred B. Rothman & Company from *The Yale Law Journal,* Vol. 63, p. 471. The numbers inserted in brackets are related to the third note and question.

will be respectively designated *legal* and *informal* controls. When, as is often the case, these two forms of control are in competition, the likelihood of legal control arising at all in a given sphere is a decreasing function of the effectiveness of informal controls. It is the thesis of this article that the presence of legal controls in the moshav, the semi-private property settlement, but not in the kvutza, the collective settlement, is to be understood primarily in terms of the fact that informal controls did not operate as effectively in the moshav as in the kvutza.

CONTROL SYSTEMS IN THE KVUTZA AND MOSHAV

In most of their superficial characteristics, the two settlements are essentially similar. Both were founded at the same time, 1921, by young settlers who had come from Eastern Europe "to build a new life." Though the kvutza was smaller at first, it has grown to a population (just under 500 persons) which is almost identical in size with that of the moshav. Both are located on a slope of the Jezreel Valley where they have to deal with the same climate and similar topography. Both have about two thousand acres of land, which supports a mixed farming economy. Both populations have rejected many of the East-European Jewish customs, including traditional religious practices. Though many other Israeli collectives are left-wing socialist, the members of the kvutza under consideration resemble those of the moshav in adhering to the social-democratic political philosophy represented by the *Mapai* party.

Despite these similarities, the two communities have differed from the outset in their members' ideas about economic organization. In the kvutza, members felt they could implement the program, "from each according to his abilities, to each according to his need," as the way to create a "just society." Moshav members, many of whom had spent a few years in collectives, decided that the family should be the unit of production and distribution, and that thus a class of small independent farmers could be developed in the moshav which would provide a strong agricultural base for the country.

As far as could be ascertained, there were no initial differences in specific ideas concerning legal control. Legal jurisdiction over crimes and civil wrongs is recognized by all to reside in the State of Israel, but very few cases involving members of these settlements have been brought before the State's courts or, earlier, before the courts of the British Mandate. The minimal role of these courts has resulted from an absence of serious crime, the shielding of fellow members from British (and now to a lesser extent even Israeli) "outsiders"; and internal controls which effectively handle existing disturbances. In both settlements, the power to exercise these internal controls stems from the

General Assembly, a regularly held meeting of all members in which each one present casts a single vote. This form of government works effectively in both communities, perhaps because they are small enough for everyone to be heard and homogeneous enough so that there is basic agreement on means and ends. While the kvutza meetings are more frequent and cover a broader range of issues, moshav sessions are held at least bi-weekly and are generally well attended.

In both settlements, the General Assembly delegates responsibility for certain activities to committees whose membership it approves. Committees are, if anything, more active in the kvutza [the collective], which has separate permanent groups to deal with questions of economic coordination, work assignment, education, social affairs, ceremonies, housing, community planning, and health. The moshav also has its committees, but most of these deal with agricultural matters, particularly the dissemination to individual farmers of the kind of scientific information which is handled by managers in the kvutza.

The moshav's Judicial Committee, however, is a specialized agency for which no counterpart is found in the kvutza. This Committee consists of a panel of seven members elected annually by the General Assembly for the purpose of dealing with internal disputes. Complaints by members against members are brought before the Committee either directly or by referral from the General Assembly. A hearing of the complaint is then conducted by a panel of three drawn from the larger Committee. After investigating the circumstances and hearing the direct testimony of both sides, a panel decides whether and how the defendant should bear responsibility. Fines and damages, the major types of punishment, are usually paid upon imposition, but if not, they are enforceable by the secretary of the moshav. Though these panels follow simple procedures, there can be no doubt that they have acted as an agency of legal control in the moshav.

[1] An example will illustrate the operation of this moshav system of legal control. A fifteen-year-old boy took a neighbor's jeep without permission, picked up some of his friends, and went for a joyride outside the village. During the ride, he crashed into a tree and damaged the fender and door of the vehicle. The owner brought a complaint against him which was heard by the panel. When the boy admitted his actions, he was charged for the full cost of repairs. The debt was subsequently discharged by the boy's parents, and the case was considered closed.

By contrast, the kvutza has not delegated sanctioning responsibility to any special unit. Even when administrative or legislative action results in gain or loss to an individual, this is not its primary purpose. In the event of a dispute between workers, for example, the Work Assignment Committee or the Economic Council may decide that the interests of production would be better served if one or both of the workers were transferred. But the objective of such action is not punitive; rather it is to ensure the smooth functioning of the economy, and the decision is made in much the same manner as any decision relating to production. In the course of its legislative work, the General Assembly of the kvutza also makes decisions which modify the gains and losses of members. Many of these are policy decisions which apply to classes of members, but sometimes an individual's behavior provides the occasion for a policy debate in the Assembly. [2] One young member, for example, received an electric teakettle as a gift from his sister in the city. Though small gifts could be retained as personal property, the kettle represented a substantial item, and one which would draw upon the limited supply of electricity available to the entire settlement. Moreover, the kvutza had already decided against supplying each room with a kettle on the grounds that this would be expensive and would encourage socially divisive private get-togethers. By retaining the kettle, therefore, the young man was threatening the principles of material equality and social solidarity on which the kvutza is believed to rest. This at any rate was the decision of the Assembly majority following three meetings during which the issue was debated. Confronted with this decision, the owner bowed to the general will by turning his teakettle over to the infirmary where it would be used by those presumed to be in greatest need of it. No organized enforcement of the decision was threatened but had he disregarded the expressed will of the community, his life in the kvutza would have been made intolerable by the antagonism of public opinion.

As will become apparent, it is the powerful force of public opinion which is the major sanction of the entire kvutza control system. It may be focused, as in the case of the electric teakettle, by an Assembly decision, or it may, as occurs more commonly, be aroused directly by the behavior it sanctions. In either case, it is an instrument of control which is employed not by any specialized functionaries but by the community as a whole. Since public opinion is the sanction for the entire kvutza control system, that system must be considered informal rather than legal. We turn now to a more detailed consideration of the factors which have made this system of control so much more effective in the kvutza than in the moshav . . . .

The kvutza is in effect a large primary group whose members engage in continuous face-to-face interaction. Each able-bodied member works eight to ten hours a day, six days a week, at a job which is usually performed wholly or partially in the presence of others. The results of his efforts become known to his associates, the work manager, and the top officials who coordinate the economy. All three meals are eaten in a collective dining hall usually in the company of five other residents who happen to have arrived at the same time. Members of each sex share common washing and shower facilities, and these are used by most members at the same time, during the limited period when hot water is available. Housing is concentrated in one area of the kvutza and consists of rows of long houses, each partitioned to make six rooms, with a married couple or two roommates occupying each room. Because most rooms are surrounded by other dwellings, it is easily possible for neighbors to observe entrances and exits and even some behavior within. Child rearing is the primary responsibility of special nurses and teachers, but parents spend about two hours with their children on work days and usually more than this on their days of rest. Much of this relationship is subject to public view as parents and children stroll around the kvutza, eat together occasionally in the dining hall, or play in front of their rooms. Other leisure activities are also subject to public observation: participating in Assembly and Committee meetings, celebrating kvutza holidays, attending lectures and films, perusing newspapers and periodicals in the kvutza reading room, or taking a vacation tour of the country. Even sexual relations, particularly if they are illicit, can become the subject of general public knowledge, although this was the one type of activity excepted by a member when he said, "amongst us, all things except one are done together."

The same conditions of continuous interaction also make it possible to circulate information throughout the entire community. Mealtime and showering are two informal occasions when large numbers of people forgather and find opportunity for conversation. The shower in particular is a forum for the transmission of information where one can hear about anything from fractured ankles to broken hearts. Though "I heard it in the shower" is a kvutza equivalent for "take this with a grain of salt," much genuine news is disseminated there. Compared with these informal techniques, the weekly news bulletin and the Assembly meetings run slow supplementary seconds.

Moshav conditions do not permit as great a degree of public observation. Work is typically conducted alone, with other members of the family, or occasionally with the voluntary aid of a friend. As long as the moshav farmer maintains a solvent establishment and discharges such community obligations as payment of taxes and correct use of cooperative facilities, he is free to manage his farm as he sees fit. Meals consisting largely of produce from the farmstead are prepared by the housewife and eaten in a family dining room which occupies a central place in the home. Houses are small bungalows ranging from three to six rooms, separated from neighboring dwellings by a hundred yards or more, and screened by hedges and fruit trees. Many activities which are publicly performed in the kvutza can be, and usually are, carried out in the privacy of the moshav home, among them economic husbandry, care of clothing, showering, washing, child rearing, and such recreation as visiting, reading, and listening to the radio. There are, to be sure, places where members come into contact, such as the produce depots, cooperative store, Assembly and committee meetings, and cinema. Though such contacts provide some opportunities for the circulation of information, they are fewer and the information circulated is less complete than in the kvutza.

At least partially as a result of these differences, kvutza members do in fact learn more about the activities of more of their members than is known in the moshav. Less than a week of residence was necessary in the kvutza before virtually everyone knew the ostensible purpose of the writer's stay, whereas similar knowledge was not diffused as widely (or accurately) during two months in the moshav. Information thus transmitted is not confined to work performance and consumption, though these are of great interest, but range over such details as mail received, visitors contacted, time spent with children, and even style of underclothes worn. As a result, it becomes possible to control types of behavior in the kvutza which never become public knowledge in the moshav . . . .

Public opinion can be manifested often, swiftly, subtly, and with varying degrees of intensity in the kvutza. In the course of a day's continual interaction, positive or negative opinion may be communicated by the ways in which members glance at an individual, speak to him, pass him a requested work implement or dish of food, assign him work, give him instructions, sit next to him, and listen to his comments. To an experienced member, these small signs serve to predict more intense reactions of public acclaim or social isolation. They therefore acquire sanctioning power in and of themselves and become able to control the behavior in question before extremes are reached. In the moshav, by contrast, there are fewer opportunities to convey public opinion quickly and accurately because there is so much less contact between members in the course of the daily regime. This is an important limitation in the use of public opinion as a means of control in the moshav . . . . [In the kvutza] children are raised from infancy in the constant company of other children of their own age with whom they sleep, eat, bathe, dress, play, and later attend school. Though control is at first the task of the nurses, it is increasingly taken over by the children themselves. Their community is organized politically in a manner similar to the adult kvutza, with children's public opinion playing a corresponding part. [3] When one child was caught stealing bananas reserved for the babies, the Children's Assembly decided to punish the culprit by abrogating their own movie privileges. Though this was explained to the adults on the grounds that all were involved in the guilt of one, a reason of at least equal importance was the children's expectation that this reaction would provide such a loss to all the children that a potential wrongdoer would repeat the precipitating action at his peril. At any rate, the practice of stealing was greatly reduced following this reaction.

During their years of training, the kvutza children become very alert to their peers' opinions, on which they are dependent for virtually all their satisfactions. While they are growing up, this force is used to ensure conformity to the standards of the children's community. These standards may conflict with those of the adult community, resulting in behavior which seems wild and capricious to the adults. But adult members remark repeatedly on the suddenness with which, following their accession to formal membership at eighteen, children of the kvutza "mature," i.e., learn to conform to adult standards. This is in contrast to the moshav where adolescence is a period of great stress extending over several years. Moshav children, brought up in the close-knit farm family under their parents' control, never seem to develop the great respect for public opinion characteristic of the kvutza.

Supplementing migration and socialization practices are the day-to-day experiences of adult kvutza members. Quick and accurate response to public opinion enables the member to align his behavior with community standards, and thus to enhance his chances of attaining the acceptance and prestige which are needed for even small advantages. In the kvutza environment, one is rewarded for responding to the unfavorable reaction of his comrades when he talks too long in the Assembly, does not volunteer for emergency work service, wears inappropriate clothes, or debunks a kvutza celebration. Failure to respond has been known to result in serious difficulties, [4] such as that experienced by a teacher who so antagonized public opinion by declining to dig trenches during Israel's War of Independence that he was denied a requested change of job a full year later.

In the moshav, this kind of pressure is exerted less frequently and effectively, if for no other reason than that there are fewer gains for which the individual is dependent on the community. Near self-sufficiency in economic affairs makes it difficult for the moshav to exert informal control. Primary reliance is placed on sanctions such as fines or, in a few cases of economic failure, expulsion from the settlement . . . .

The effectiveness of kvutza informal controls is enhanced by a system of norms classifying all behavior with reference to desirability. This system is detailed, generally unambiguous, applicable to wide, clearly defined segments of the population, and well known to the members. As a result it provides consistent guides for the application of sanction and at the same time forewarns potential sanctionees of the consequences of their acts. Such norms, found in every sphere of kvutza life, are particularly striking in economic matters. . . .

Consumption activities in the kvutza are also controlled with the aid of explicit general norms. Objectives which these are supposed to serve include distribution according to need, frugality, solidarity, and of course adequate sustenance of the population. Since differential need is very difficult to ascertain, the kvutza tendency has been to distribute scarce items equally, on the assumption that need is generally equal. Exceptions are made in instances where this is obviously not the case, for example, when youth, age, illness, or pregnancy furnishes grounds for special diet, housing, or medical care. Aside from these, however, consumption of scarce goods is supposed to be as nearly equal as possible. Adults are expected to eat together in the common dining hall at specified times. There they are served meals which are planned by the dietician with an eye toward fitting the budget adopted by the General Assembly. Crops drawn directly from the land are usually sufficiently abundant to permit unrestricted consumption, but other foods such as margarine, fish, meat, hard cheese, and eggs are distributed in limited equal quantities. Though the norms governing such consumption may be a mystery to new arrivals, members are fully aware of them. [5] Occasionally questions arise as to the kinds of dishes for which a given serving may be exchanged, but these are authoritatively settled by the dietician. Similarly, clothes are expected to be issued equally except for differences of sex and size. Women are permitted a small degree of discretion in the selection of materials, but no one may exceed the ration and standard for a given sex, of such items as work shirts, work shoes, and sweaters. In housing, correct behavior is even less complicated: one is expected to live in the room assigned by the Housing Committee, whose discretion is limited by policies established in the General Assembly. Explicit general norms also cover such matters as participation in kvutza festivals, visiting of children by parents, and preservation of a minimal privacy in rooms . . . .

One of the greatest weaknesses of kvutza controls arises from failure to specify the identity and special privileges of the high prestige members. Managers and old-timers are distinguished in fact from the ordinary workers and "simpletons" in the deference shown them and, within narrow limits, in the preference they may receive in housing, furniture, travel, and education for their children. Deviations from the general norms by the "important" people are less disturbing than if performed by ordinary members, since kvutza public opinion recognizes their special worth and power. But difficulties sometimes arise from uncertainty as to how important a given individual is and what privileges, if any, are due him.

Such problems tend to be minimized by a denial that important people are treated differently in any way, or that there is in fact a special managerial status. That an equalitarian society should be unwilling to recognize such privileges is not surprising. Material advantages given the important people are rationalized in terms of the norms and their accepted exceptions. For example, new housing units, built by the kvutza to accommodate an increased population, were made more elaborate than earlier ones by the inclusion of shower and toilet facilities. These units were designated from the first as "old-timers' housing," and it was explained that the increased age of this group made it difficult for them to use the central facilities. On closer questioning, however, it was revealed that these rooms were not intended for other inhabitants who were also advancing in years, namely, a few recent immigrants of middle-age and several resident parents of members. Though the physical need of such persons was at least as great as that of the old-timers, no one even considered the possibility that they should be given modern accommodations as permanent quarters. Actually the reason was a feeling of injustice that so much be given to people who had done so little for the kvutza, but this was never publicly articulated and the fiction prevailed that the distribution met the requirement of "equal or according to need." Accordingly, the behavior, which was in fact a non-disturbing deviation from the general norm, was classified as acceptable behavior and was not negatively sanctioned as were other deviations from the norm.

In most areas, however, norms have been developed which clearly distinguish acceptable from disturbing behavior in a given situation for a clearly delimited category of persons. Ambiguities which arise are usually brought before the General Assembly and are conclusively resolved by its decision. Sometimes the kvutza reaches a consensus informally. The resultant norms are applied with a high degree of certainty. Though for our purposes the reasons need not be spelled out, it would appear that kvutza norms can be unambiguous and simple because behavioral alternatives and variations are sharply limited and because a homogenous population is in general agreement in distinguishing desirable from undesirable behavior among these clear and limited alternatives. Moshav norms, by contrast, are far less explicit, uniformly applied, or generally agreed upon. While it is important that a farmer manage his own holdings effectively and be a good neighbor, the exact pattern of actions by which this can be accomplished has never been authoritatively laid down. In most areas, the individual is likely to have his own ideas about the proper behavior in a given circumstance. On particular occasions involving the duty to aid one's sick neighbor, cooperation in the use of machinery, and a member's violation of State ration controls, widespread difference of opinion was discerned among moshav members. This difference was partly attributed to the influence on each member of such factors as the effect of the particular behavior on his own economic interest; his relations with the actor in question: and his conception of the responsibility owed to the moshav by its members. Such crucial questions as property relations in the family and between neighbors are still being deliberated and moshav members vary widely in their views on such matters. The problem of succession is just beginning to arise with regularity, and its importance and difficulty for a village with limited, indivisible and inalienable farmsteads may hardly be over-estimated. Perhaps a uniform set of norms will be evolved over a period of time to deal with such problems, or perhaps the problems, especially concerning property, defy informal sanctions. At any rate, for the present, there is little agreement. It is small wonder, then, that the moshav system of informal controls has been supplemented by a specialized group of deliberators able to make norms and to ensure their sanction by legal means . . . .

Tendency toward Informal Sanction

As far as could be ascertained, the conditions which promoted effective informal control existed from the first or arose early in the history of the kvutza. Since it started out as a small settlement with a homogeneous population, it was, if anything, even more of a primary group during its formative years than at present. There is sufficient evidence in reports of old-timers to indicate that pertinent behavior was readily perceived, that public opinion was an easily implemented and effective sanction, and that unambiguous norms defined the circumstances under which such sanctions should be employed. There were, to be sure, instances where these controls failed to work, as for example in regard to the use of spending money. [6] An early norm permitted each member to take as much money from a common fund as he felt he needed for personal expenses. In practice this is said to have resulted in low expenditures by the "idealistic" members and disproportionately high ones by those with a weaker sense of social responsibility. When public opinion proved incapable of controlling this socially disturbing behavior, the General Assembly modified the norm to stipulate a yearly amount for each member's personal use. Clarification of the distinction between acceptable and disturbing behavior in this area permitted the effective application of negative sanction to the latter, with the result that few members exceeded their allotted amount thereafter. The desired result was achieved by changes which increased the effectiveness of informal sanction rather than substituting legal controls for them.

Because effective informal control was achieved in the kvutza, the tendency for its subsequent use was increased. That this tendency was high is indicated not only by the many successful instances of its use, but perhaps even more by the persistence with which it was employed on the rare occasions when it failed. [7] Most striking among the illustrations of this is the case of a woman who was considered by the entire kvutza to be anti-social. Soon after her arrival she began to behave very aggressively, quarreling with all her fellow workers in the kitchen and even striking them. Though the use of violence against a fellow member was shocking to the other members, only the usual mild sanctions were at first applied. For some reason, however, social disapproval failed to deter the woman. She continued the same course of behavior through seven years, during which she was subjected to more vigorous informal controls and was at the same time denied formal membership. But she was never subjected to force, expulsion, or even to material disadvantage. Only during her eighth year in the kvutza was a different type of sanction directed against her: she was given no work assignment and was deprived of the opportunity to work for the kvutza. After a year in which her isolation was thus increased, she bowed to the pressure and left the kvutza. Whether the new sanction be designated informal or legal, it is clear that it was an alternative to the traditional informal sanctions of public opinion. That it was employed only after seven years of persistent exercise of the traditional sanctions is striking indication of the firmness with which the latter were established.

In the moshav, the tendency to exercise informal controls seems much less powerful . . . . Conditions which would minimize the effectiveness of such sanctions . . . are traceable to the economic structure of the moshav, and thus it is reasonable to assume that they also existed at the inauguration of the community. If so, they preceded the rise of legal controls which evolved gradually during the first twenty years of the settlement's history. During this period and subsequently, informal controls have regularly been tried, but have been ineffective, presumably because of inadequate information, implementation, sanction magnitude, and norms. In the course of time, members have learned that informal controls are ineffective; the resultant lowered tendency to invoke these controls, resulting in even less frequent and less vigorous attempts to use them, has further diminished their effectiveness. [8] This attitude toward informal controls was exemplified by moshav reaction to the prank of a group of adolescents who raided a melon patch and openly ate the stolen melons. Indignation ran high because the melons had been specially cultivated for the wedding feast to be given in honor of the marriage of the farmer's daughter. Failing action by the Judiciary Committee, the feeling prevailed that there was "nothing at all to do" about it. Said one member, "If you scold those fellows, they laugh at you." So on the informal level, no serious attempt was undertaken to exert effective control.

Competing Reaction Tendencies

Infrequent and nonvigorous exertion of informal sanctions in the moshav may result in part from the competition of legal controls as an effective alternative. It is, of course, impossible to explain the original occurrence of legal controls in these terms, but once they had become established, their success as a competing reaction could have been expected to reduce the impact of informal sanctions. Within the kvutza, there was no comparable history of legal controls which might have constituted a competing alternative to the prevailing system. Free from such competition, the impact of informal sanctions could have been expected to continue without abatement. □

Notes and Questions

1. In order to test the impact of particular factors, a social scientist will often "hold constant" certain other factors. This is the function of a control group. For example, if one wanted to determine whether taking a particular drug would eliminate allergic reactions, one might try to find two groups of

people who suffered from allergies. Ideally, these people would be similar in all relevant characteristics. One group would take the drug while the other would not. If the treatment group then suffered fewer allergic reactions than the control group, a scientist could ascribe the difference to the effect of the drug. However, suppose that during the experiment, most people in the treatment group also installed in their homes elaborate heating and air conditioning systems with dust and mold filters. Then the scientist could not be sure whether the drug or the climate control systems produced the observed differences in allergic reactions between the treatment and control groups.

What factors does Schwartz "hold constant" in his study of the moshav and kvutza? Do you see any possible confounding factors in his study? That is, are there differences between the two settlements other than those Schwartz points to which might have caused the resort to a judicial committee in one but not the other?

In a true experiment, subjects are randomly assigned to one or another group. But if we are dealing, as Schwartz is, with real-life groups, we have what we may call a quasi-experiment—not quite so rigorous as a true experiment, but good enough for most purposes.

2. Allan E. Shapiro, in "Law in the Kibbutz: A Reappraisal," 10 *Law & Society Review* 415 (1976), and Michael Saltman, in "Legality and Ideology in the Kibbutz Movement," 9 *International Journal of the Sociology of Law* 279 (1981), both criticize Schwartz's explanation for the presence or absence of law in settlements. Shapiro points out that over time the amount of face-to-face interaction has decreased in all of the settlements. However, this has not prompted the collectively run settlements to create judicial committees. Moreover, the existing judicial committees in the cooperatives have fallen into disuse. Saltman argues: "[t]here are few societies in the history of mankind that can rival the kibbutz for its ideological self awareness." What Schwartz calls informal sanctions are responses to ideology as applied to concrete situations. The General Assembly of a kibbutz should be viewed as a legal institution which focuses public opinion in particular situations. How would you expect Schwartz to respond to these critics? For his reply to Shapiro, see 10 *Law & Society Review* 439 (1976).

This debate reflects a long-standing controversy in social theory and social science. How far should we explain what people do by how they explain their actions? Some social theorists prefer to point to social structure, such as being rich or poor, owning a factory, or working in it; or prefer to explain in terms of culture, race, gender, or position in society. People who take this position tend to think that people *act,* and then later rationalize their actions by resorting to norms, ideology, philosophy, and the like. How people see the world and what they think is the good, the true, and the beautiful can be explained by material conditions; or these ideas themselves can be taken as basic, shaping, social facts.

3. Schwartz faces a classic definitional problem in viewing social control in smaller groups of people: what shall we classify as "legal" control and what shall we call control by custom reinforced by reputational sanctions? See Donald Black, "Crime as Social Control," 48 *American Sociological Review* 34 (1983).

We could talk about the law of elevator behavior. Most Americans understand certain norms about behavior while riding in an elevator. May I sing or play my radio very loud? May I touch you when the elevator fills and we are standing shoulder to shoulder? And so on. There are sanctions if I violate any of these norms. I may *feel* foolish. You may communicate your displeasure to me by body language or by a sarcastic remark. Insofar as I care about your opinion, this is a sanction. If the violation of the norms is sufficiently egregious, the offended party may attempt to inflict injury on the other. For example, if a man attempts to touch a woman in an elevator in a sufficiently offensive way, she may slap him in the face or spray his face with a chemical which she keeps in her purse.

Furthermore, those riding in the elevator may be influenced by what may happen after the trip is over. If the man and woman are fellow workers in an office, she may gossip about his behavior in the elevator. She may tell a relative or a close friend. That person may then beat the man who offended her.

We could sketch a similar analysis of customs about giving wedding or birthday gifts and obligations to reciprocate. Physical violence is unlikely in these situations, but former friends can refuse to speak to one another. They can force mutual friends to choose one or the other. Nonetheless, most of us probably would not see these customs reinforced by reputational or physical sanctions as legal. We may want to reserve the term "legal" for something more structured or more analogous to state action.

At the outset of the article, Schwartz says that legal control "is carried out by specialized functionaries who are socially delegated the task of intra-group control . . ." He finds little legal control in the kvutza (the collective). However, consider the eight cases that he describes: (1) the jeep joyride, (2) the electric teakettle, (3) the stolen bananas, (4) the teacher who did not volunteer to dig trenches, (5) the exchangeable dishes of food, (6) the spending money, (7) the anti-social woman, and (8) the stolen melons. Cases two through seven occurred in the kvutza, but do you accept Schwartz's argument that none are examples of legal control because sanctions were not imposed by "specialized functionaries who are socially delegated the task of intragroup control . . ."? The General Assembly decided cases 2, 6, and 7; the Children's Assembly decided case 3; the Work Committee case 4; and the Dietician case 5. Is the key to Schwartz's definition the term "specialized"? That is, because the General Assembly includes everyone, there is no specialized agent of control. Even granting this, is there not an important difference between the relatively unstructured system of rewards and punishments that exists in the daily life of the kibbutz, using such sanctions as smiles and frowns, and what is likely to take place when a formal meeting of everyone is called to consider a member's teakettle? Should this difference prompt us to call the General Assembly an agent of legal control? Furthermore, can we view the actions of the Work Committee and the Dietician as a form of administrative law?

Schwartz, at another point in his article, offers a different indicator of legality: "Since public opinion is the sanction for the entire kvutza control system, that system must be considered informal rather than legal." Could we argue that Schwartz ignores the presence of real sanctions within the kvutza—consider the threat of expulsion, either physically or psychologically. See case (7), the anti-social woman. Why is the sanction of expulsion not sufficient to make this social control system "legal?"

4. Suppose a large shopping center hires a staff of specialized social control agents. They are provided uniforms modeled on those typically worn by

police officers. They wear badges, and they carry guns and two-way radios. Those who run the shopping center call these social control agents "our police" or "our officers." In fact, they have no more formal legal authority than any other citizen. Largely, they serve to deter shoplifting, mugging, and assaults at the shopping center just by being there. If they apprehend someone who has attempted to do any of these things, they call the public police to come and make a legal arrest. Would Schwartz call this an example of legal control or informal control?

Suppose a uniformed police officer employed by a city walks a beat in a neighborhood. She has the power to arrest those whom she sees violating city ordinances or state laws. However, suppose this officer also works with youth groups in a basketball league and tries to get parents involved. As a result, she comes to know both the children and parents in her area. Instead of arresting young teenagers for minor violations of public law, she tells their mothers about their conduct. The chance that she will tell mothers itself becomes an important sanction within the neighborhood. Would Schwartz see this as an example of legal or informal control?

Is the division of social control systems into informal and legal ones a useful way to understand differences between such systems? What are its advantages and disadvantages? Even if we conclude that a sharp distinction cannot be made and risks distorting our picture of law in action, does Schwartz's study raise important questions? Remember, too, that Schwartz's two Israeli settlements and our example about the temporary society of the elevator all exist within a formal legal system. If there were a murder at the kibbutz or in the elevator, those involved would surely call the public police.

5. Donald Black, in the article cited in Note and Question 3, suggests that people create legal systems when self-help and group control are likely to be ineffective. For example, small shopping centers usually rely on self-help and group controls, backed up by the possibility of calling the police. Larger shopping centers have more people to control. They often create their own internal systems of private police. Schwartz describes the moshav's judicial committee as a poor substitute for the face-to-face controls in the kvutza. Is legal control necessarily ineffective or does it have costs which groups such as the moshav is unwilling to pay?

James Garbarino, in "The Price of Privacy in the Social Dynamics of Child Abuse," 56 *Child Welfare* 565 (1977), argues that people in American society relinquish kinship and neighborhood bonds for the benefits of privacy as they become middle class. They escape the scrutiny of relatives and neighbors. However, the cost of privacy is the reduction of observation and monitoring by interested parties with a commitment to the welfare of individuals in families. This, he argues, opens the door to spouse battering and child abuse. He advocates establishing intrusive monitoring networks and providing legal support for intrusion by concerned neighbors and professionals such as social workers. Is it likely that most Americans would accept Garbarino's position? Are spouse battering and child abuse found only in middle class neighborhoods? If not, why not?

6. Michael Saltman, in "Legality and Ideology in the Kibbutz Movement," 9 *International Journal of the Sociology of Law* 279 (1981), points out that members of Israeli settlements occasionally have gone to Israeli courts to avoid being expelled from their kibbutz. Members who want to leave a kibbutz

have sometimes sued for a share of what they have contributed to the collective. Many settlements have create procedures dealing with expulsion and payments to those who wish to leave, largely in response to the threat of legal actions. Can you think of similar examples of appeals to the formal legal system by members of family, occupational, or social groups in American society?

7. Assume that we accept Schwartz's description and explanation for what he observed. How far can he generalize, beyond these two settlements in Israel at the time when he studied them? John Hagan, John H. Simpson and A. R. Gillis, in "The Sexual Stratification of Social Control: A Gender-Based Perspective on Crime and Delinquency," 30 *British Journal of Sociology* 25 (1979), argue that women are more frequently the instruments and objects of informal social controls, while men are more frequently the instruments and objects of formal social controls. This is because women have been watched more and have been less free to act without being subject to informal sanctions. Many more men than women are arrested and imprisoned in most legal systems, and Hagan and his coauthors, somewhat like Schwartz, argue that this is a consequence of the absence of effective informal controls. (They suggest that as gender roles change, women will be freed of some of this informal control. This may mean that more women will commit more crime and be arrested and imprisoned more frequently). Can we put Schwartz's study together with studies such as that of Hagan, Simpson, and Gillis, and draw some generalizations about when we should expect to find attempts at legal control?

A NOTE ON LEGAL EVOLUTION

Do legal systems, once they are in place, evolve in some particular direction, and, if they do, why? Do "modern" social systems generate specifically "modern" legal systems with regard to their formal characteristics?

Any discussion of these issues would have to begin with the justly famous work of Max Weber.

14. *Max Weber on Law in Economy and Society**

Max Rheinstein, ed.

(Cambridge, Mass: Harvard University Press, 1954)

[Weber discusses legal thought in Germany, where, around the turn of the century, legal scholarship was highly conceptual. Jurists analyzed typical forms of business transactions—between buyers and sellers, for example—and defined them as legal relationships, that is, as relation-

*Prof. Rheinstein edited this volume of Weber's writings about law and legal systems.

ships that could be discussed in legal terms (not Mr. Schmidt and Mrs. Schiller, but "bailor" and "bailee"). These "legal relationships" could be further arranged, analyzed, and classified logically, giving rise to what Weber calls "systematization." This never appears, he says, except in "late stages of legal modes of thought. To a youthful law, it is unknown." "Systematization" represents an "integration of all analytically derived legal propositions in such a way that they constitute a logically clear, internally consistent, and, at least in theory, gapless system of rules, under which, it is implied, all conceivable fact situations must be capable of being locally subsumed . . . . Even today not every body of law (e.g., English law) claims that it possesses the features of a system."

Legal systems can differ, then, in the degree to which they are "systematized." There are other differences in the "technical apparatus of legal practice." Weber analyzes the following four "possible type situations:"]

☐ Both law-making and law-finding may be either rational or irrational. They are "formally irrational" when one applies in law-making or law-finding means which cannot be controlled by the intellect, for instance when recourse is had to oracles or substitutes therefor. Law-making and law-finding are "substantively irrational" on the other hand to the extent that decision is influenced by concrete factors of the particular case as evaluated upon an ethical, emotional, or political basis rather than by general norms. "Rational" law-making and law-finding may be of either a formal or a substantive kind. All formal law is, formally at least, relatively rational. Law, however, is "formal" to the extent that, in both substantive and procedural matters, only unambiguous general characteristics of the facts of the case are taken into account. This formalism can, again, be of two different kinds. It is possible that the legally relevant characteristics are of a tangible nature, i.e., that they are perceptible as sense data. This adherence to external characteristics of the facts, for instance, the utterance of certain words, the execution of a signature or the performance of a certain symbolic act with a fixed meaning, represents the most rigorous type of legal formalism. The other type of formalistic law is found where the legally relevant characteristics of the facts are disclosed through the logical analysis of meaning and where, accordingly, definitely fixed legal concepts in the form of highly abstract rules are formulated and applied. This process of "logical rationality" diminishes the significance of extrinsic elements and thus softens the rigidity of concrete formalism. But the contrast to "substantive rationality" is sharpened, because the latter means that the decision of legal problems is influenced by norms different from those obtained through logical generalization of abstract interpretations of meaning. The norms to which substantive rationality accords predominance include ethical imperatives, utilitarian and other expediential rules, and political maxims, all of which diverge from the formalism of the "external characteristics" variety as well as from that which uses logical abstraction. However, the peculiarly professional, legalistic, and abstract approach to law in the modern sense is possible only in the measure that the law is formal in character. In so far as the absolute formalism of classification according to "sense-data characteristics" prevails, it exhausts itself in casuistry.[82] Only that abstract method which employs the logical interpretation of meaning allows the execution of the specifically systematic task, i.e., the collection and rationalization by logical means of all the several rules recognized as legally valid into an internally consistent complex of abstract legal propositions . . . .

Present-day legal science, at least in those forms which have achieved the highest measure of methodological and logical rationality, . . . proceeds from the following five postulates: viz., first, that every concrete legal decision be the "application" of an abstract legal proposition to a concrete "fact situation"; second, that it must be possible in every concrete case to derive the decision from abstract legal propositions by means of legal logic; third, that the law must actually or virtually constitute a "gapless" system of legal propositions, or must, at least, be treated as if it were such a gapless system; fourth, that whatever cannot be "construed" legally in rational terms is also legally irrelevant; and fifth, that every social action of human beings must always be visualized as either an "application" or "execution" of legal propositions, or as an "infringement" thereof . . . .

The Anti-Formalistic Tendencies of Modern Legal Development

From a theoretical point of view, the general development of law and procedure may be viewed as passing through the following stages: first, charismatic legal revelation through "law prophets"; second, empirical creation and finding of law by legal honoratiores, i.e., law creation through cautelary jurisprudence[83] and adherence to precedent; third, imposition of law by secular or theocratic powers; fourth and finally, systematic elaboration of law and professionalized administration of justice by persons who have received their legal training in a learned and formally logical manner. From this perspective, the formal qualities of the law emerge as follows: arising in primitive legal proce-

---

82. Casuistry = a quibbling or evasive way of dealing with difficult cases of duty; sophistry.

83. In "cautelary jurisprudence," lawyers reason by analogy with almost no attempt at inductive or deductive reasoning. Concepts are extended as needed, but lawyers do not attempt to move from particular situations to general propositions which will govern future cases. This is a long way from Weber's "formal rationality."

dure from a combination of magically conditioned formalism and irrationality conditioned by revelation, they proceed to increasingly specialized juridical and logical rationality and systematization, passing through a stage of theocratically or patrimonially conditioned substantive and informal expediency. Finally, they assume, at least from an external viewpoint, an increasingly logical sublimation and deductive rigor and develop an increasingly rational technique in procedure.

Since we are here only concerned with the most general lines of development, we shall ignore the fact that in historical reality the theoretically constructed stages of rationalization have not everywhere followed in the sequence which we have just outlined, even if we ignore the world outside the Occident. We shall not be troubled either by the multiplicity of causes of the particular type and degree of rationalization that a given law has actually assumed. As our brief sketch has already shown, we shall only recall that the great differences in the line of development have been essentially influenced, first, by the diversity of political power relationships, which . . . have resulted in very different degrees of power of the imperium vis-a-vis the powers of the kinship groups, the folk community, and the estates; second, by the relations between the theocratic and the secular powers; and, third, by the differences in the structure of these legal honoratiores who were significant for the development of a given law and which, too, were largely dependent upon political factors.

Only the Occident has witnessed the fully developed administration of justice of the folk-community . . . and the status group stereotyped form of patrimonialism; and only the Occident has witnessed the rise of the rational economic system, whose agents first allied themselves with princely powers to overcome the estates and then turned against them in revolution; and only the West has known "Natural Law," and with it the complete elimination of the system of personal laws and of the ancient maxim that special law prevails over general law. Nowhere else, finally, has there occurred any phenomenon resembling Roman law and anything like its reception. All these events have to a very large extent been caused by concrete political factors, which have only the remotest analogies elsewhere in the world. For this reason, the stage of decisively shaping law by trained legal specialists has not been fully reached anywhere outside of the Occident. Economic conditions have, as we have seen, everywhere played an important role, but they have nowhere been decisive alone and by themselves. To the extent that they contributed to the formation of the specifically modern features of present-day Occidental law, the direction in which they worked has been by and large the following: To those who had interests in the commodity market, the rationalization and systematization of the law in general and, with certain reservations to be stated later, the increasing calculability of the functioning of the legal process in particular, constituted one of the most important conditions for the existence of economic enterprise intended to function with stability and, especially, of capitalistic enterprise, which cannot do without legal security. Special forms of transactions and special procedures, like the bill of exchange and the special procedure for its speedy collection, serve this need for the purely formal certainty of the guaranty of legal enforcement . . . .

[T]he expectations of parties will often be disappointed by the results of a strictly professional legal logic. Such disappointments are inevitable indeed where the facts of life are juridically "construed" in order to make them fit the abstract propositions of law and in accordance with the maxim that nothing can exist in the realm of law unless it can be "conceived" by the jurist in conformity with those "principles" which are revealed to him by juristic science. The expectations of the parties are oriented towards the economic and utilitarian meaning of a legal proposition. However, from the point of view of legal logic, this meaning is an "irrational" one. For example, the layman will never understand why it should be impossible under the traditional definition of larceny to commit a larceny of electric power. It is by no means the peculiar foolishness of modern jurisprudence which leads to such conflicts. To a large extent such conflicts rather are the inevitable consequence of the incompatibility that exists between the intrinsic necessities of logically consistent formal legal thinking and the fact that the legally relevant agreements and activities of private parties are aimed at economic results and oriented towards economically determined expectations. It is for this reason that we find the ever-recurrent protests against the professional legal method of thought . . . .

Contemporary Anglo-American Law.

The differences between continental and common law methods of legal thought have been produced mostly by factors which are respectively connected with the internal structure and the modes of existence of the legal profession as well as by factors related to differences in political development. The economic elements, however, have been determinative only in connection with these elements. What we are concerned with here is the fact that, once everything is said and done about these differences in historical developments, modern capitalism prospers equally and manifests essentially identical economic traits under legal systems containing rules and institutions which considerably differ from each other at least from the juridical point of view . . . .

Indeed, we may say that the legal systems under which modern capitalism has been prospering differ profoundly from each other even in their ultimate principles of formal structure.

Even today, and in spite of all influences by the ever more rigorous demands for academic training, English legal thought is essentially an empirical art. Precedent still fully retains its old significance, except that it is regarded as unfair to invoke a case from too remote a past, which means older than about a century. One can also still observe the charismatic character of law-finding, especially, although not exclusively, in the new countries, and quite particularly the United States. In practice, varying significance is given to a decided case not only, as happens everywhere, in accordance with the hierarchical position of the court by which it was decided but also in accordance with the very personal authority of an individual judge. This is true for the entire common-law sphere, as illustrated, for instance, by the prestige of Lord Mansfield. But in the American view, the judgment is the very personal creation of the concrete individual judge, to whom one is accustomed to refer by name, in contrast to the impersonal "District Court" of Continental-European officialese. The English judge, too, lays claim to such a position. All these circumstances are tied up with the fact that the degree of legal rationality is essentially lower than, and of a type different from, that of continental Europe. Up to the recent past, and at any rate up to the time of Austin, there was practically no English legal science which would have merited the name of "learning" in the continental sense. This fact alone would have sufficed to render any such codification as was desired by Bentham practically impossible. But it is also this feature which has been responsible for the "practical" adaptability of English law and its "practical" character from the standpoint of the public.

The legal thinking of the layman is, on the one hand, literalistic. He tends to be a definition-monger when he believes he is arguing "legally." Closely connected with this trait is the tendency to draw conclusions from individual case to individual case: the abstractionism of the "professional" lawyer is far from the layman's mind. In both respects, however, the art of empirical jurisprudence is cognate to him, although he may not like it. No country, indeed, has produced more bitter complaints and satires about the legal profession than England. The formularies of the conveyancers, too, may be quite unintelligible to the layman, as again is the case in England. Yet, he can understand the basic character of the English way of legal thinking, he can identify himself with it and, above all, he can make his peace with it by retaining once and for all a solicitor as his legal father confessor for all contingencies of life, as is indeed done by practically every English businessman. He simply neither demands nor expects of the law anything which could be frustrated by "logical" legal construction.

Safety valves are also provided against legal formalism. As a matter of fact, in the sphere of private law, both common law and equity are "formalistic" to a considerable extent in their practical treatment. It would hardly be otherwise under a system of stare decisis and the traditionalist spirit of the legal profession. But the institution of the civil jury imposes on rationality limits which are not merely accepted as inevitable but are actually prized because of the binding force of precedent and the fear that a precedent might thus create "bad law" in a sphere which one wishes to keep open for a concrete balancing of interests. We must forego the analysis of the way in which this division of the two spheres of stare decisis and concrete balancing of interests is actually functioning in practice. It does in any case represent a softening of rationality in the administration of justice. Alongside all this we find the still quite patriarchal, summary and highly irrational jurisdiction of the justices of the peace. They deal with the petty causes of everyday life and . . . they represent a kind of Khadi[84] justice which is quite unknown in Germany. All in all, the Common Law thus presents a picture of an administration of justice which in the most fundamental formal features of both substantive law and procedure differs from the structure of continental law as much as is possible within a secular system of justice, that is, a system that is free from theocratic and patrimonial powers. Quite definitely, English law-finding is not, like that of the Continent, "application" of "legal propositions" logically derived from statutory texts.

These differences have had some tangible consequences both economically and socially; but these consequences have all been isolated single phenomena rather than differences touching upon the total structure of the economic system. For the development of capitalism two features have been relevant and both have helped to support the capitalistic system. Legal training has primarily been in the hands of the lawyers from among whom also the judges are recruited, i.e., in the hands of a group which is active in the service of the propertied, and particularly capitalistic, private interests and which has to gain its livelihood from them. Furthermore and in close connection with this, the concentration of the administration of justice at the central courts in London and its extreme costliness have amounted almost to a denial of access to the courts for those with inadequate means. At any rate, the essential similarity of the capitalistic development on the Continent and in England has not been able to eliminate the sharp contrasts between the two types of legal systems. Nor is there any visible tendency towards a transformation of the English legal system in the direction of the continental under the impetus of the capitalist economy. On the contrary, wherever the two kinds of administration of justice and of legal training have had the opportunity to compete with one another, as for instance in Canada, the Common Law way has come out on top and has overcome the continental alternative rather quickly. We may thus conclude that capitalism has not been a decisive factor in the promotion of that form of rationalization of the law which has been peculiar to the

84. Khadi: the "Moslem judge who sits in the market place and, at least seemingly, renders his decisions without any reference to rules or norms but in what appears to be a completely free evaluation of the particular merits of every single case." Max Rheinstein, Preface to *Max Weber on Law in Economy and Society,* at xiviii.]

continental West ever since the rise of Romanist studies in the medieval universities . . . .

Whatever form law and legal practice may come to assume under the impact of [the] various influences [of modern society], it will be inevitable that, as a result of technical and economic developments, the legal ignorance of the layman will increase. The use of jurors and similar lay judges will not suffice to stop the continuous growth of the technical element in the law and hence of its character as a specialists' domain. Inevitably the notion must expand that the law is a rational technical apparatus, which is continually transformable in the light of expediential considerations and devoid of all sacredness of content. This fate may be obscured by the tendency of acquiescence in the existing law, which is growing in many ways for several reasons, but it cannot really be stayed. All of the modern sociological and philosophical analyses, many of which are of a high scholarly value, can only contribute to strengthen this impression, regardless of the content of their theories concerning the nature of law and the judicial process . . . .

The decisive reason for the success of bureaucratic organization has always been its purely technical superiority over every other form. A fully developed bureaucratic administration stands in the same relationship to nonbureaucratic forms as machinery to nonmechanical modes of production. Precision, speed, consistency, availability of records, continuity, possibility of secrecy, unity, rigorous coordination, and minimization of friction and of expense for materials and personnel are achieved in a strictly bureaucratized, especially in a monocratically organized, administration conducted by trained officials to an extent incomparably greater than in any collegial form of administration . . . .

The utmost possible speed, precision, definiteness, and continuity in the execution of official business are demanded of the administration particularly in the modern capitalistic economy. The great modern capitalist enterprises are themselves normally unrivaled models of thoroughgoing bureaucratic organization. Their handling of business rests entirely on increasing precision, continuity, and especially speed of operation . . . .

In the place of the old-type ruler who is moved by sympathy, favor, grace, and gratitude, modern culture requires for its sustaining external apparatus the emotionally detached, and hence rigorously "professional," expert; and the more complicated and the more specialized it is, the more it needs him. All these elements are provided by the bureaucratic structure. Bureaucracy provides the administration of justice with a foundation for the realization of a conceptually systematized rational body of law on the basis of "laws," as it was achieved for the first time to a high degree of technical perfection in the late Roman Empire. In the Middle Ages the reception of this law proceeded hand in hand with the bureaucratization of the administration of justice. Adjudication by rationally trained specialists had to take the place of the older type of adjudication on the basis of tradition or irrational presuppositions.

Rational adjudication on the basis of rigorously formal legal concepts is to be contrasted with a type of adjudication which is guided primarily by sacred traditions without finding therein a clear basis for the decision of concrete cases. It thus decides cases either as charismatic justice, i.e., by the concrete "revelations" of an oracle, a prophet's doom, or an ordeal; or as khadi justice non-formalistically and in accordance with concrete ethical or other practical value-judgments; or as empirical justice, formalistically, but not by subsumption of the case under rational concepts but by the use of "analogies" and the reference to and interpretation of "precedents." The last two cases are particularly interesting for us here. In khadi justice, there are no "rational" bases of "judgment" at all, and in the pure form of empirical justice we do not find such rational bases, at least in that sense in which we are using the term. The concrete value-judgment aspect of khadi justice can be intensified until it leads to a prophetic break with all tradition, while empirical justice can be sublimated and rationalized into a veritable technique. Since the non-bureaucratic forms of authority exhibit a peculiar juxtaposition of a sphere of rigorous subordination to tradition on the one hand and a sphere of free discretion and grace of the ruler on the other, combinations and marginal manifestations of both principles are frequent. In contemporary England, for instance, we still find a broad substratum of the legal system which is in substance khadi justice to an extent which cannot be easily visualized on the Continent . . . . The first country of modern times to reach a high level of capitalistic development, i.e., England, thus preserved a less rational and less bureaucratic legal system. That capitalism could nevertheless make its way so well in England was largely because the court system and trial procedure amounted until well in the modern age to a denial of justice to the economically weaker groups. This fact and the cost in time and money of transfers of landed property, which was also influenced by the economic interests of the lawyers, influenced the structure of agrarian England in the direction of the accumulation and immobilization of landed property . . . .

The demands for "legal equality" and of guaranties against arbitrariness require formal rational objectivity in administration in contrast to personal free choice on the basis of grace, as characterized the older type of patrimonial authority. The democratic ethos, where it pervades the masses in connection with a concrete question, based as it is on the postulate of substantive justice in concrete cases for concrete individuals, inevitably comes into conflict with the formalism and the rule-bound, detached objectivity of bureaucratic administration. For this reason it must emotionally reject what is rationally demanded. The propertyless classes in particular are not served, in the way in which bourgeois are, by formal "legal equality" and "calculable" adjudication and administration. The propertyless demand that law and administration serve the equalization of economic and social opportunities vis-a-vis the propertied classes, and judges or administrators cannot perform this function unless they assume the substantively ethical and hence nonformalistic character of the Khadi. The rational course of justice and administration is interfered with not only by every form of "popular justice," which is little concerned with rational norms and reasons, but also by every type of intensive influencing of the course of administration by "public opinion," that is, in a mass democracy, that communal activity which is born of irrational "feelings" and which is normally instigated or guided by party leaders or the press. As a matter of fact, these interferences can be as disturbing as, or, under circumstances, even more disturbing than, those of the star chamber practices of an "absolute" monarch. ☐

NOTES AND QUESTIONS

1. What are examples, in modern law, of formal rationality, substantive rationality, formal irrationality, substantive irrationality? How would you classify the following:

a. Congress passes a law requiring all buildings above a certain size to have ramps so that people in wheelchairs have access to them;

b. two couples are on their way to the movies, and cannot decide which of two to go to; they toss a coin to decide;

c. the Supreme Court, in *Roe v. Wade*, decided that restrictions on abortion in the early months of pregnancy violated a woman's right to privacy, a right not expressly stated in the Constitution;

d. in the early years of the Chinese Revolution, "tribunals" were empowered to roam about in the country and do "revolutionary justice;" they punished landlords and other "class enemies;" there was no right of appeal from the decisions of these tribunals.

e. judges in family courts are told to award custody according to the "best interests" of the children; the judge hears arguments, talks to the parents, reads the report of a social worker, and makes his decision;

f. in a criminal case, a jury may decide on guilt or innocence; the jury deliberates in secret, and does not give any reasons for its decision, which (if the jury acquits) is absolutely final;

g. an American state requires a license to hunt deer; to get a license, an applicant has to pay $10 and be over 21 years of age, and a resident; a forty-three year old woman applies, fills out a form, pays the money to a clerk, and shows her driver's license; the clerk then issues a license to hunt deer;

h. a statute forbids divorced people from marrying again within a year from the date of the decree. Mr. and Mrs. Smith get a divorce on June 1st; later, they reconcile, and two months after the divorce, they remarry in a civil ceremony. The question is, is this remarriage legally valid? A court holds that it is not, because it took place within one year, even though the

Smiths argue that the statute was not supposed to apply to the case where the divorced couple marries each other.

2. Is Weber's famous scheme really evolutionary at all? Certainly, "irrational" legal systems seem to appear earlier in history than "rational" ones. Weber says that the general development of law can be looked upon "from a theoretical point of view" as passing through certain stages. What does he mean by this? Are the movements from stage to stage always in the same direction?

Consider the following comment, by Joyce S. Sterling and Wilbert E. Moore, in "Weber's Analysis of Legal Rationalization: A Critique and Constructive Modification," 2 *Sociological Forum* 67, 75 (1987):

Although Weber denied that he was posing a unilineal process of rationalization, he did tend to view legal systems as moving from irrational to rational and from substantive to formal rationality. However, he saw a chronic tension between the formal and substantive rationalization of law . . . , a tension that revolves around the issue of autonomy or predictability. From Weber's perspective, the need to resort to outside ethical or political systems for decision-making lessens the predictability and therefore formal rationality of the legal system. The use of "discretion" in the legal system would be contrary to the movement towards an autonomous legal system . . . ; the attainment of formal-rational law would be inhibited by demands for substantive justice.

What is unique about Weber's sociology of law is that he links his typology of legal thought to his typology of political structure . . . . Distinguishing between domination and legitimacy . . . , he identified three pure forms of legitimation: traditional, charismatic, and legal "domination" (rational authority). As law becomes rationalized it becomes its own legitimizing principle . . . . In logically formal-rational law, the universal principles derived from the legal system itself create the basis for legitimate domination. Weber suggested that there was a direct correlation between the rationalization of law and evolution toward legal domination, which he described as a four-stage process. This correlation is enhanced by the growth of a modern bureaucracy.

Stage 1. Charismatic legal revelation through the use of prophets. This stage is associated with formal irrationality . . . . Law is "inspired" rather than arising through a process of consensus . . . .

Stage 2. Empirical creation and finding of law by legal honoratiores. Decision-making is arbitrary and based on individual cases; it is substantively irrational (*khadi* justice). The legal sphere is differentiated into criminal and civil law . . . .

Stage 3. Imposition of law by secular or theocratic powers. Since there is a systematic body of rules from religion, ethics, etc. this stage is associated with substantive rationality. This stage represents "deduced" law (natural) and we find the legal spheres differentiated into sacred and secular law.

Stage 4. Systematized elaboration of law and professionalized administration of justice by persons who have been trained in a formally logical manner. This stage of enacted laws (positive) is associated with formal rationality. The legal spheres are differentiated into private and public law.

3. Further, on legal evolution, see Richard D. Schwartz and James C. Miller, "Legal Evolution and Societal Complexity," 70 *American Journal of Sociology* 159 (1964); Howard Wimberley, "Legal Evolution: One Further Step," 79 American Journal of Sociology 78 (1973). Why do we care whether legal systems evolve? Evolutionary theories often are linked with ideas of progress. In what way would an evolution from substantively rational to formally rational legality be progressive?

4. Is it possible to have a modern legal system which is not "rational" in Weber's terms? Weber, as Sterling and Moore point out, was "preoccupied in much of his writing with explaining why capitalism arose in the West." But Sterling and Moore say that he denied that "European legal systems were merely the result of capitalism." Instead, he emphasized other factors. He put great stress on the "development of a profession of lawyers," and the development of legal rules "structured by legal factors (and not by religious factors or traditional values)," and on "decisions based on universal rules." Law was "crucially related to but not determined by economic forces; it is thus an autonomous force in social development."

A "logically formal rational legal system" does not *create* capitalism, but "the fit is ideal when it does occur." England, the first country to develop industrial capitalism, had a rather "irrational" legal system—it used juries, lay magistrates, precedent instead of universal rules. Weber never really solved the "England problem," but he certain did try. Weber argued, Sterling and Moore tell us, that the system, though "irrational," produced predictable results "since the courts favored the capitalists in their use of precedent and denied justice to the lower classes. He maintained that the introduction of due process rules even provided an element of formal rationality." On Weber's "England problem," see David M. Trubek, "Max Weber on Law and the Rise of Capitalism," 1972 *Wisconsin Law Review* 720; Sally Ewing, "Formal Justice and the Spirit of Capitalism: Max Weber's Sociology of Law," 21 *Law & Society Review* 487 (1987).

5. Sterling and Moore are among recent scholars who have tried to modify or adapt the Weberian scheme. They argue that Weber neglected an important formative aspect of legal systems: the "goals" of the system. For example, a "culture may place ultimate value" on "economic prosperity." This, or some other goal, would be a "precondition" to "defining the forms of legal rules." Weber looked at these goals as something "outside" the legal system; any explicit use of goals in rule-formation was an example of "substantive rationalization." This meant that there was a kind of conflict between "strict legalism" and "democratic values" or "social justice." But values are important in guiding and shaping the "legal changes that are characterized as rational." Their analysis continues as follows:

> Finally, we dichotomize rationality as formal and instrumental. Weber divided his category of "logical formal rationality" into two parts: generalization and systematization. The second part of the dichotomy, systematization, remains in the category of formal rationality in our scheme, along with his category of "legal formalism"—tidying the rules of pro-

cedures. The other aspect of Weber's logical formal rationality, generalization, becomes part of our category of instrumental rationality, seriously neglected by Weber.

The use of the concept of instrumental rationality and of the dialectical dilemmas will provide us with a potentially powerful tool for analysis of legal development. By modifying some of Weber's insights into the nature of formal and substantive rationality, we believe that we can construct a concept that will overcome some of the problems generally associated with the Weberian perspective. The most commonly referred to problems include inflexibility, conservatism, and rigidity . . . Though we want to take advantage of Weber's concerns with predictability, calculability, and universality, we need to build into our concept of instrumental rationality a learning mechanism for the system. In order to achieve this, we recognize important overlaps between the norms of the legal system and those of the wider political system. Although we recognize that the rules can be rationalized, essentially "internally" to the legal system itself, that rationalization may have little to do with maintenance of political order, resolving disputes, or accomplishing various articulated social goals.

What are the components of instrumental rationality? We have identified three major types: the rules for making rules, autonomous legal rationalization, and adaptive rationalization. The primary focus of Weber's typology of legal decision-making was "logical formal rationality." We have incorporated the "generalization" aspect of his concept into our category of autonomous legal rationalization. Although we view this as a necessary aspect of rationality, it is not by itself sufficient. Weber realized the importance of autonomous legal predictability, but he failed to distinguish the political state from the legal state: i.e., goal setting and articulation of the claims to legitimacy, as distinguished from rules of normative compliance and resolution of disputes. The failure to distinguish political and legal factors may account for the fact that Weber never directly addressed the problem of order in society—a recurring question for sociologists. He did elsewhere discuss the forms of political legitimacy, the rationale of power, and the reality of a diversity of interests. In response to these problems the politico-legal system generates the rules to deal with disputes and to preserve the integrity of the state. That is ineluctably more of a political process than a mere question of legal draftsmanship.

Both the "rules for making rules" and "autonomous legal rationalization" are derived from Weber's discussion of "formal rationality," but they become instrumentally rational by stipulation of the purposes served by the legal order. One of the problems inherent in the Weberian conception of formally rational rules is that they become constrained, mechanical, and impersonal in order to meet the criteria of universality . . . . [L]anguage is too imprecise and indeterminate, and this imprecision results in poor communication of the rules both from the point of view of the officials as well as that of the clientele. From the Weberian perspective, the central goals of the social order are efficiency, freedom, and fairness. However, while this perspective sees formal rules as contributing to the central goals, it does not recognize that the communication problem may undermine the achievement of these same goals. Thus, *if* order is to be maintained, the moral judgments of the community (or at least of the state) are to be upheld, and various social purposes of the law-giver are to be achieved, *then* the forms and types of rules must themselves comply with clear criteria of efficiency. Our definition of rules may be closer to . . . the term "standards" . . . than to the more inflexible definition used by Weber. These rules can communicate "rules of the game" if they express the structure and framework of action. For example, rules of grammar in language do not tell you what to say, but they do convey the structure of how to communicate.

As mentioned earlier, autonomous legal rationality includes the criteria of generalization. If the social goal of fairness is to be achieved, then it is necessary that the citizens be treated in an equal and uniform manner by officials. To achieve equal treatment, the system invents distinctly legal mechanisms that equalize the outside social inequality of participants in the legal system (i.e., plaintiffs and defendants). These include contingent fees, class action litigation, and the appointment of public defenders. The procedural rules generated by the legal system specify how the system is to operate, including the actors internal to the system. Autonomous legal rationality assumes specialization of the law and legal actors. The development of generalized rules separates the legal norms from the more general political and social norms existent in the society. However, we have noted earlier that values influence the initial formation of the legal rules . . . These same values at certain moments influence the courts to view cases and actors as social categories rather than legal categories. The influences of these values become limitations on the relative autonomy of the system in the form of dialectical dilemmas . . . In this way, there is an interaction effect between . . . irrationality [and] rationality . . . .

Our final type of instrumental rationality—adaptive rationalization—refers to the attempt to make legal systems congruent with other forms of structural rationalization. This criterion subsumes Weber's category of "substantive rationality." It also subsumes Teubner's (1983)[85] "reflexive rationality." . . . [H]is argument is that in a highly differentiated social system the state's legal system must not only be responsive to its social environment but also *aid* and monitor decision-making, order-maintaining, and dispute-resolution in myriad specialized organizational contexts that cannot in fact be centrally controlled. Nonet and Selznick (1978)[86] had argued for "responsive laws." To this Teubner wishes to add some perspectives from the works of German theorists [Jürgen] Habermas and [Niklas] Luhmann, who urge the importance of increasing functional differentiation and the limits this places on "total" legal control . . . .

85. [The reference is to Gunther Teubner, "Substantive and Reflexive Elements in Modern Law," 17 *Law & Society Review* 239 (1983).]

86. [The reference is to Philippe Nonet and Philip Selznick, *Law and Society in Transition: Toward Responsive Law* (New York: Octagon Books, 1978).]

Reflexive theory advocates . . . view political, economic, and legal systems as semi-autonomous spheres that develop their own separate internal forms of rational logic that do not communicate with one another. These views may be carrying the notion of autonomous systems to an extreme, for from a macro perspective, there is always some interpenetration of these systems. For this reason, we have distinguished our third type of instrumental rationality—adaptive rationalization. While the present model emphasizes the forms of rationality internal to the legal system, it also acknowledges the overlapping and potential conflict in the various systems of rationality. We are recommending a model that stresses the rationality of systems; it does not necessarily imply that all the inputs or even outputs will be rational. We may find descriptions of legal institutions that on an individual level would not fit the Weberian model of formal rationality, but do conform to the model on a societal level.

An example of an informal legal institution that actually conforms to the notion of instrumental rationality would be the use of alternative methods of dispute resolution to solve legal disputes (e.g., torts, divorce, custody cases). The mediation processes involved in these instances of legal conflict are not governed by a large number of formal, written rules. However, if an ethnographer were to describe the actual behavior of these dispute resolution sessions, we would find that there are universal and generalizable rules operating in the process. How does this differ from the Weberian perspective and in what way is it in fact compatible? Simon (1983:1240)[87] has presented an alternative vision that defines the boundaries and characteristics of a systemic view. Although his model would not fit the traditional Weberian mode of formal rationality, it would fit quite comfortably within the instrumental rationality perspective.

Simon illustrates his opposing vision by describing the transformation of welfare administration in Massachusetts. His description of welfare administration reform in the late 1960s and early 1970s is characterized by three themes: formalization of rules; bureaucratization of administration; and proletarianization of the work force. These three themes characterize the doctrine of legality under the "dominant vision" necessary to achieve the social goals of efficiency, freedom, and fairness. While the "dominant vision" is not attributable to Weber, the themes of formality and hierarchical bureaucracy do fit the Weberian analysis of formal rationality . . . . His critique of the Weberian model demonstrates that the goals become displaced in the process of transforming welfare administration to comply with a formally rational legality . . . . [W]e think that Weber was not unaware of the problems of the "iron cage" that would be created by a formally rational system. However, we want to focus on Simon's proposal for an opposing vision. He proposes that a view of society as characterized by shared value and trust or humanitarian goals is both necessary and achievable. The neces-

87. [The reference is to William Simon, "Legality, Bureaucracy, and Class in the Welfare System," 92 *Yale Law Journal* 1198 (1983).]

sity to incorporate collective values within the framework is consistent with our notion of adaptive rationalization. The three themes that are associated with the opposing view are the development of standards rather than rules, decentralization, and professionalism. This alternative vision seems compatible with our notion of instrumental rationality. The advantage of this model is that it allows for the inclusion of a more informal legal decision-making organization within the framework of instrumental rationality.

Although Weber recognized the importance of legal specialization and professionalization, he may not have recognized that these qualities allow the adoption of standards that would guide decision-making without becoming an inflexible trap . . . . The professional commands mysteries useful to the laity (and the laity includes administrators), but not shared by them. To the degree that professionals are goal-oriented and not primarily rule-oriented, they increase the chances of practical problem-solving.

Why do we assume that the rationality of law as applied by judges in a society has a great deal to do with economic development? Certainly, major corporations, particularly those in industries such as oil exploration and development, are able to deal all over the globe. In at least some nations where oil or other valuable raw materials are discovered, law is largely the will of the ruler or subject to modification through bribery. Nonetheless, major oil firms manage to invest millions of dollars and gain a large return on their money. Corruption or legal irrationality are just risks which business people can discount. Does this suggest that Weber's ideas about the evolution of the *form* of law are less relevant to economic development than they might seem?

6. In recent years, there has been a movement in the United States to make sentences in criminal cases more uniform and predictable. This is done through "guidelines," which limit severely the discretion of the judge to fix the sentence. The "guidelines" take into account certain factors (what was the crime? was the defendant convicted before of a similar crime? and so on). Once you have the factors, you can fairly well predict the sentence, within pretty narrow limits. Sentences of this kind at least look like "formal rationality" in Weber's terms. But are they? If so, are they doomed to failure because "formal rationality" cannot work in the United States? See Joachim J. Savelsberg, "Law that Does Not Fit Society: Sentencing Guidelines as a Neoclassical Reaction to the Dilemmas of Substantivized Law," 97 *American Journal of Sociology* 1346 (1992); Donald F. Anspach and S. Henry Monsen, "Determinate Sentencing, Formal Rationality, and Khadi Justice in Maine: An Application of Weber's Typology," 17 *Journal of Criminal Justice* 471 (1989). See the discussion on sentencing guidelines, in Chapter 5 p. 790.

7. There is an enormous literature on the work of Max Weber (1864–1920). An English translation of Weber's sociology of law (*Max Weber on Law in Economy and Society,* Max Rheinstein ed. Cambridge, Mass.: Harvard University Press), appeared in 1954. See also David Trubek, "Reconstructing Max Weber's Sociology of Law," 37 *Stanford Law Review* 919 (1985); David Trubek, "Max Weber's Tragic Modernism and the Study of Law in Society," 20 *Law & Society Review* 573 (1986), essay-reviews of Anthony Kronman, *Max Weber* (Stanford, Ca.: Stanford University Press, 1983).

8. Some drastic and dramatic examples of legal change in the legal systems of whole societies seem not to be the result of evolution at all. Rather, Western systems conquer and displace traditional systems of law. This happened under colonialism in Africa and Asia.

Modernizing countries often try to leapfrog into the modern world through adopting a Western legal system. This was the case in Japan, for example. See pp. 166–67. It also was the case in Turkey. In 1926, Turkey adopted the Swiss Civil Code as part of the revolutionary program of the great Turkish leader, Kemal Ataturk. From then on, the official law of Turkey was very modern and western. Villagers in rural Turkey continued, however, to use their own time-honored ways of handling disputes. See June O. Starr, *Dispute and Settlement in Rural Turkey: An Ethnography of Law* (Leiden: Brill, 1978).

9. On the general question of colonial and other forms of imported law, see Sandra B. Burman and Barbara E. Harrell-Bond, *The Imposition of Law* (New York: Academic Press, 1979). Included in this book are essays on a number of societies, including the native American tribes. In one of these essays, by Francis Svensson, "Imposed Law and the Manipulation of Identity: the American Indian Case" pp. 69, 86, the author remarks that in most colonial situations, the natives far outnumber the colonizers. However, "American Indians, like Australian Aborigines and Maoris, do not have the luxury of outnumbering the invaders." Does this fact mean that the minority group will be totally unable to resist the imposition of an alien legal system? How might the colonized group resist?

10. Sally Engle Merry, "Anthropology, Law, and Transnational Processes," 21 *Annual Review of Anthropology* 357 (1992), notes:

> Although colonizing nations' interests in political takeover were narrowly economic, they typically sought to reform family life and work habits as well. Colonial law was used to create a wage labor force available to the plantation, mine, and factory out of peasant and subsistence producers . . . . Much early legal regulation of colonized peoples forced them to become a capitalistic work force by requiring regular hours, punishing failure to work, outlawing festivals and other entertainments . . . prohibiting alcoholic beverages, controlling vagabondage, and defining criminality . . . . (pp. 363–364).

Merry's comment suggests that "traditional law" was bound to change even when it was not supplanted because the conditions of social and economic life under colonialism were different from those before. After all, modern economies have transformed the traditional legal systems of Western nations too. See Yoon, above, pp. 164–65.

The colonial powers tended to consider traditional law, tribal law, or custom as if it were something fixed, unchanging and inert. In fact, the legal codes of the peoples of Africa and Asia were subtle and supple, both before and after the coming of the Europeans. See Martin Chanock, *Law, Custom, and Social Order: The Colonial Experience in Malawi and Zambia* (Cambridge: Cambridge University Press, 1985).

A fascinating account of the transformation of a native culture is given by Mari J. Matsuda, in "Law and Culture in the District Court of Honolulu, 1844–1845: A Case Study of the Rise of Legal Consciousness," 32 *American Jour-*

nal of Legal History 16 (1988). Matsuda examined the records of the basic courts that operated during the period of the Hawaiian monarchy. She found that Hawaiians "flocked to the new courts to resolve disputes and to punish crimes," although the courts were highly "Westernized."

Before the period of Western contact, there was a rich, vital Polynesian culture on the islands. Hawaiians lived "in villages tied by kinship." The social system was strongly hierarchical, ranging from commoners to great chiefs. There was a complex agricultural system. Cooperation, obedience, and collective effort were pillars of the economy. There "was no cash economy . . . . It was considered shameful to drive a hard bargain, or to fail to share with others in need."

The arrival of Western traders and missionaries had a profound effect on the polity, on religion, and on the economy. The Hawaiian monarchy established a system of courts. The judges were lay people, and the proceedings were conducted in the Hawaiian language. These courts decided a whole range of civil and criminal cases. On the criminal side, there were many cases of theft—a crime that once had been rare in the islands. But the "introduction of Western living" brought about much social change: Hawaiians moved to the port towns, "drawn by the promises of wealth and adventure that the traders brought." When Hawaiians became urbanized, they "left their constant source of food and shelter," and entered into the world of the "cash economy." The "social and cultural restraints against theft," such as "shame" and "ostracism," had been "effective in the communal villages," but these restraints worked much less well in the harbor-towns. Also, "Westerners introduced a whole new range of coveted goods," and many Hawaiians were caught in the "trap of rising expectations."

On the civil side, many of the cases in the courts indicate a changing conception of property. Matsuda reports:

> Confusion over ownership and use is evident in the cases of theft or contract that follow this general pattern:
>
> > Party A: B has my horse and will not give it to me.
> > Party B: It is not his horse; it is my horse, A gave it to me.
> > Party A: I did not give it to him; I let him use it because he was my friend.

This paraphrased version of a story that is repeated in the Minute Books indicates the confusion that the concept of property engendered with Native Hawaiians. In pre-contact Hawaii, ownership of important goods, land, and resources was communal and was understood in terms of use rights rather than unitary absolute dominion. An individual or group may have had the right to gather thatch, for example, only from a particular section of land, and only during a particular time. Property was fragmented among various uses, various times, and various people. Families and groups of individuals could share components of property, and all were subject to the claims of others, such as the chiefs, that would take precedence. This sophisticated conception of ownership conflicted with the rather unsophisticated, unitary and physicalist conception of ownership introduced by nineteenth-century Westerners.

The Hawaiian conception of ownership was further complicated by the Hawaiian practice of giving away goods in exchange as part of the bonds of reciprocity and community. In the Hawaiian universe, the purpose of material wealth was to give it away and to thereby achieve a sense of self-worth and status, and to bind others to aid one in the future. In the Western universe, the purpose of material wealth was to hoard as much as possible so as to obtain more, to impress others, and to accumulate an abundance. The Hawaiians in Honolulu were becoming more and more attuned to the Western understanding of the purpose of property. This transition is also indicated in the many theft and contract cases that involve the pattern described above.

In the case of *Kapule and Naihe*, for example, Naihe reports how the trouble began:

> The reason for this is my wife rode to Moanalua and the horse fell down. There is a piece of property Kapule and I enjoy. He was very hospitable and gave medical attention. Kapule gave my wife and me things to make our difficulty there more bearable. Afterwards we gave Kapule money and some clothes. Kapule even gave Keaka, my wife, a horse. Then Keaka said to me "I am embarrassed by Kapule, your punalua [2 men sharing the same woman], because he gave me a horse. I am thinking of giving our canoe to your punalua." I said no. My wife returned to Ewa. After that, Keaka spoke again to me and asked to give the canoe. I agreed to give the canoe because he gave that very valuable horse. That horse which was given to my wife, Kapule and another gave [sic] to Kaanaana, their daughter in Kahuku.

The exchange of property Naihe described is not Western-style, tit-for-tat barter. Rather, it is consistent with Hawaiian use of exchange to enhance mutual obligation and to achieve self-worth. As relations between the parties deteriorated, Naihe reported an entangled dispute that takes on a more Western conception of property:

> Kapule did not agree to this saying "these gourds were sold to Naihe. I sold them for $17.00." Then Kapule called for the money. [Naihe said] "I don't have it." That is what I said. Kapule said "I want to sail on our canoe." [I] gave it as [I] was done [with it]. Later Kapule came on that canoe. When I heard, I told my punalua to keep the canoe which he did. We three fought and I got the canoe. This is why I am keeping [it] because Kapule refused to give us [Naihe and Keaka] the horse.

The dispute then became a legal one, with each party claiming an enforceable right to the exchanged properties. The judges resolved the dispute by awarding Kapule the horse and Naihe the canoe. The Western conception of property—absolute dominion, individual ownership, legally enforceable title—prevailed and, more importantly, was promoted by the Native Hawaiians in their act of bringing this dispute to court.

The court records in general, says Matsuda, "suggest three ways in which law altered Hawaiian consciousness." First, the new "state-sponsored formal mechanism for dispute resolution" displaced "existing customary mechanisms." Moreover, the adoption of the new system "carried with it implicit assumptions about power. The power to decide disputes was the power to distribute land, goods, and wealth with finality." This power had once resided in the "hierarchy of the kinship community," but now the power had passed to the courts, thus further undermining traditional authority structures.

Second, the new legal system "promoted an ideology of property that competed with native ideology." Hawaiians came gradually to "accept the legitimacy of absolute, individual dominion over property." The new-fangled courts ignored the old system of "communal ownership and generous exchange." The new concept of property proved to be a concept of "irresistible force." Indeed, "the emergence of the concept of private property in lay discourse so early in the development of the system of statutes and courts suggests that the concept was transferred in part from lay Westerner to lay Hawaiian before the full-fledged, formal reception of Western law."

Third, the "system of legal rules and judicial enforcement provided a welcome mat" for foreigners interested in economic development and the introduction of capitalism. The law "welcomed business and the new business interests brought more people, things, and ideas that were non-Hawaiian."

Matsuda concludes with this point: "The ordinary Hawaiian, sometimes viewed as the passive victim of outside forces, was in fact an active and creative participant in the changing culture of the islands. Hawaiians used the courts and the law, adjusting quickly to a radically different social order." Unfortunately, the end result was arguably "harmful to Hawaiians," because it paved the way for the destruction of their culture and for the loss of their independence.

11. Weber's discussion of "rational" and "irrational" legal systems, and the literature on "traditional" legal systems, suggest or presuppose a distinction between "modern" legal systems and all others. Can we draw up a list of characteristics of "modern" legal systems that set them off from older and more traditional systems? Marc Galanter, in "The Modernization of Law [Chapter 11 of Myron Weiner, ed., *Modernization* 153 (New York: Basic Books, 1966)], attempted to do this.

Galanter defines modernity as consisting of a "cluster of features that characterize, to a greater or lesser extent, the legal systems of the industrial societies of the last century." He lists eleven of these features:

First, modern law consists of rules that are uniform and unvarying in their application. The incidence of these rules is territorial rather than "personal;" that is, the same rules are applicable to members of all religions, tribes, classes, castes, and localities and to both sexes. The differences among persons that are recognized by the law are not differences in intrinsic kind or quality, such as differences between nobles and serfs or between Brahmans and lower castes, but differences in functional condition, and achievement in mundane pursuits.

Second, modern law is transactional. Rights and obligations are apportioned as they result from transactions (contractual, tortious, criminal, and so on) between parties rather than aggregated in unchanging clusters that attach to persons because of determinants outside the particular transactions. That is, legal rights and duties are not determined by factors such as age, class, religion, sex, which are unrelated to the particular transaction or encounter. Such status clusters of rights and obligations as do exist are based on mundane function or condition (for example, employer, a business enterprise, wife) rather than on differences in inherent worth or sacramental honor.

Third, modern legal norms are universalistic. Particular instances of regulating are devised to exemplify a valid standard of general applicability, rather than to express that which is unique and intuited. Thus the application of law is reproducible and predictable. [Khadi] justice is replaced by Kant's Categorical Imperative.

Now let us consider the kind of institutional arrangements and techniques for administering these rules.

Fourth, the system is hierarchical. There is a regular network of courts of first instance to apply this law and a regular structure of layers of appeal and review to ensure that local action conforms to national standards. This enables the system to be uniform and predictable. This kind of hierarchy, with active supervision of subordinates, is to be distinguished from hierarchic systems in which there is a delegation of functions to subordinates who enjoy complete discretion within their jurisdictions. Independent legal fiefdoms are transformed into provinces.

Fifth, the system is organized bureaucratically. In order to achieve uniformity, the system must operate impersonally, following prescribed procedures in each case and deciding each case in accordance with written rules. In order to permit review, written records in prescribed form must be kept in each case.

Sixth, the system is rational. Its procedures are ascertainable from written sources by techniques that can be learned; and transmitted without special nonrational gifts. Rules are valued for their instrumental utility in producing consciously chosen ends, rather than for their formal qualities. Theological and formalistic techniques, for example, in the field of evidence are replaced by functional ones.

Seventh, the system is run by professionals. It is staffed by persons chosen in accordance with testable mundane qualifications for this work. They are fulltime professionals, not persons who engage in it sporadically or avocationally. Their qualifications come from mastery of the techniques of the legal system itself, not from possession of special gifts or talents or from eminence in some other area of life. The lord of the manor and religious dignitaries are replaced by trained professional jurists, by police, examiners, and other enforcement specialists.

Eighth, as the system becomes more technical and complex, there appear specialized professional intermediaries between the courts and the persons who must deal with them. Lawyers replace mere general agents.

Ninth, the system is amendable. There is no sacred fixity to the system. It contains regular and avowed methods for explicitly revising rules and procedures to meet changing needs or to express changing preferences. Thus it is possible to have deliberate and measured innovation for the achievement of specific objectives. Legislation replaces the slow reworking of customary law.

Finally, let us consider the relation of law to political authority.

Tenth, the system is political. Law is so connected to the state that the state enjoys a monopoly over disputes within its cognizance. Other tribunals for settling disputes, such as ecclesiastical courts and trade associations, operate only by the state's sufferance or in its interstices and are liable to supervision by it.

Eleventh, the task of finding law and applying it to concrete cases is differentiated in personnel and technique from other governmental functions. Legislative, judicial, and executive are separate and distinct.

Galanter points out that no real legal system is "really so unified, regular, and universalistic"; all real-life systems are messy and pluralistic. The process of modernization "does not continue relentlessly until it produces a legal system that corresponds to our model in every detail—that is, completely unified, uniform, hierarchic, and so on. As society becomes modernized in all spheres, new kinds of diversity and complexity are generated."

Consider these eleven traits. Assuming Galanter has the list more or less right, exactly what is their nature? Are they functional prerequisites—something a modern legal system cannot do without? Or are they simply eleven traits that go along with modernity, but which are not organically connected to it, causally or otherwise? One point of Schwartz's study of the two Israeli settlements, of course, was to suggest that a given set of social conditions was likely to produce a particular type of legal arrangement. Can a similar argument be made with regard to Galanter's traits? Can we say that modernity in the socio-economic sense produces a legal system characterized by the eleven traits in question?

It is not always easy to spot a "functional prerequisite." For example, we could show that there is a strong correlation between literacy and a high standard of living; between urbanization and a high gross national product; between wearing neckties, suits, and dresses (rather than traditional costumes) and national wealth. However, no one would argue seriously that wearing Western clothing is a precondition for modernizing. One might make such an argument about urbanization or literacy. Why do we think one correlation is more important than the others?

For another look at the characteristics of modern law, see Lawrence M. Friedman, "Is There a Modern Legal Culture?" 7 *Ratio Juris* 117 (1994).

12. What does Galanter mean by "universalism?" The term is, to be sure, often used, and often it is contrasted with "pluralism" or "legal pluralism." Legal pluralism has many meanings, but its core reference is to the existence of more than one (formal or informal) legal system or legal order within a single jurisdiction. For example, the citizens of, say, Wisconsin are subject to one body of law, but Native Americans who live in that state, to some extent, are governed by tribal law as well as the law of Wisconsin. Citizens of Wisconsin may enter the jurisdiction of a private government as they enter a shopping center which has its own rules and police to implement them. Students at Stanford University are controlled by the laws of California but also by many university regulations and sanction systems. In theory, these multiple levels of rule-making and sanctioning can be harmonized, but reality tends to be much more messy.

Most writers suggest that modernization tends toward the reduction of legal pluralism, and most jurists seem to think that this is a good thing. Why else spend so much effort on "harmonizing" laws and on uniform and model laws? But the virtues and vices of pluralism are not easy to sum up in a single formula.

Armando Guevara-Gill and Joseph Thome, in "Notes on Legal Pluralism," 2 *Beyond Law* 75 (July 1992, ILSA, Bogota, Columbia), attack the attempt "to create national, integrated and homogeneous societies out of multicultural, multiethnic and highly differentiated human landscapes." The nation-states of Latin America pursued policies that were "ethnocidal—and, in some instances, plainly genocidal," in their passion to modernize and assimilate native peoples. Guevara-Gil and Thome appeal to the concept of legal pluralism as a way of "deconstructing the prevailing concept of the state as a monolithic entity." They also feel the concept is useful as a tool toward achieving "multi-cultural and democratic political arrangements."

13. Is a modern Western legal system necessary for economic development? Jane Kaufman Winn, in "Relational Practices and the Marginalization of Law: Informal Financial Practices of Small Businesses in Taiwan," 28 *Law & Society Review* 193 (1994), is skeptical and points to Taiwan's successful economic development. She finds that "the relational structure of traditional rural Chinese society has survived in a modified form in modern Taiwan, and this modern form selectively blends elements of the modern legal system, networks of relationships, and the enforcement services of organized crime." Taiwan's legal system indirectly supports relational practices rather than working through the kind of universal normative order often associated with the idea of a modern legal system. See also Frank K. Upham, "Speculations on Legal Informality: On Winn's 'Relational Practices and the Marginalization of Law'," 28 *Law & Society Review* 233 (1994).

SOCIAL CHANGE AS AN ENGINE OF LEGAL CHANGE

PLURALISM, CONTROL BY ELITES OR CLASS DOMINATION: WHOSE OPINION COUNTS?

The Social Context of Legal Change: Toward a General Theory Albert V. Dicey, an English legal scholar, offered what has become a classic theory of the influence of what he called public opinion on social and legal change in his lectures given at the Harvard Law School in 1898.[88] The process begins, according to Dicey, with a new idea which "presents itself to some one man of originality or genius." Dicey is thinking of people such as Adam Smith, Bentham, or Darwin; we might add Marx, and, perhaps, Keynes. Then the great man's friends adopt the idea and "preach" it to others. Gradually a whole school "accept[s] the creed." As time passes, "the preachers of truth make an impression, either directly upon the general public or upon some person of eminence, say a leading statesman, who stands in a position to impress ordinary people and thus to win the support of the nation" (p. 23). However, something must happen so that people will listen to a truly

88. See Dicey, *Lectures on the Relation Between Law and Public Opinion in England During the Nineteenth Century,* 2d ed. (London: Macmillan, 1914).

new idea and change their values. Dicey talks of "accidental conditions" which enable popular leaders to seize the opportunity—his example is the Irish famine which enabled Cobden and Bright to gain acceptance of Adam Smith's doctrine of free trade. Professor Marc Galanter has diagrammed Dicey's theory as follows:

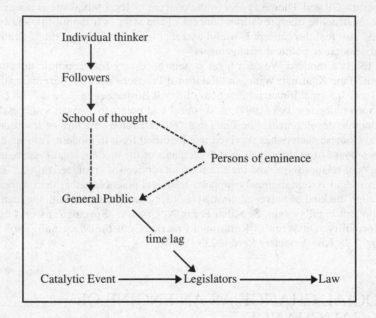

A number of points must be made about this theory. The line flowing from the great man may be too simple. At any one time, a number of schools of thought, each of which could influence persons of eminence, are in contention. A member of Parliament in Dicey's day could have converted to the ideas of Adam Smith or to those of Karl Marx. Obviously, some schools of thought will be more acceptable than others. Moreover, law can respond to a crisis and thus feed back to influence public opinion. "Laws of emergency often surreptitiously introduce or reintroduce into legislation, ideas which would not be accepted if brought before the attention of Parliament or of the nation . . . " (p. 45). Laws fashioned to cope with a crisis influence opinion just by being laws. "A principle derives prestige from its mere recognition by Parliament" (pp. 41–42).

Dicey talks of the "gradual, or slow, and continuous" (p. 27) development of tides of public opinion in England. Public opinion is that of "the majority of those citizens who have at a given moment taken an effective part in public life" (p. 10). Generally, there are few abrupt changes. While the theory seems to rest on the model of religious conversion, in the ordinary situation we may have to await the retirement or death of those who hold power and their replacement by those who have been educated to the ideas of more modern thinkers. Dicey tells us:

Legislative opinion must be the opinion of the day, because, when laws are altered, the alteration is of necessity carried into effect by legislators who act under the belief that the change is an amendment; but this law-making opinion is also the opinion of yesterday, because the beliefs which have at last gained such hold on the legislature as to produce an alteration in the law have generally been created by thinkers or writers, who exerted their influence long before the change in the law took place. Thus it may well happen that an innovation is carried through at a time when the teachers who supplied the arguments in its favour are in their graves, or even—and this is well worth noting— when in the world of speculation a movement has already set in against ideas which are exerting their full effect in the world of action and of legislation. Bentham's Defence of Usury supplied every argument which is available against laws which check freedom of trade in money-lending. It was published in 1787; he died in 1832. The usury laws were wholly repealed in 1854, that is sixty-seven years after Bentham had demonstrated their futility; but in 1854 the opponents of Benthamism were slowly gaining the ear of the public, and the Money-lenders' Act, 1900, has shown that the almost irrebuttable presumption against the usury laws which was created by the reasoning of Bentham has lost its hold over men who have never taken the pains or shown the ability to confute Bentham's arguments . . . . Law-making in England is the work of men well advanced in their life; the politicians who guide the House of Commons . . . are few of them below thirty, and most of them are above forty years of age. They have formed or picked up their convictions, and, what is of more consequence, their prepossessions, in early manhood, which is the one period of life when men are easily impressed with new ideas. Hence English legislators retain the prejudices or modes of thinking which they acquired in their youth; and when, late in life, they take a share in actual legislation, they legislate in accordance with the doctrines which were current, either generally or in the society to which the law-givers belonged, in the days of their early manhood . . . .

We need not therefore be surprised to find that a current of opinion may exert its greatest legislative influence just when its force is beginning to decline. The tide turns when at its height; a school of thought or feeling which still governs law-makers has begun to lose its authority among men of a younger generation who are not yet able to influence legislation.

Dicey sees judges as even more likely to lag behind public opinion than legislators. Judges are "guided to a considerable extent by the dominant current of public opinion" (p. 363), but "they are also guided by professional opinions and ways of thinking which are, to a certain extent, independent of and possibly opposed to the general tone of public opinion . . . . They are men advanced in life. They are for the most part persons of a conservative disposition" (p. 364). Note all the empirical and cultural assumptions (including many about age and aging) that are embedded in Dicey.

Contrast with Dicey, the views of Antonio Gramsci (1891–1937).

Gramsci was a leader of the Italian Communist Party who was imprisoned by Mussolini. Unlike many Marxists, Gramsci rejected the idea that political developments and law can be explained as an expression of economic structure or that there are objective laws of historical development. He wrote about hegemony or the cultural ascendancy of the dominant class. The moral and cultural integration of the masses into a system operating against their interests makes physical coercion unnecessary in all but extreme circumstances. The ruling class controls the ideas that people find acceptable because it controls political parties, schools, universities, the mass media, trade unions, and churches.

Except in times of acute stress, the dominant class preserves its hegemony over others because all the classes accept a world view in which the existing order is seen as natural and proper. This general consciousness underlies legal rules, literature, economic behavior, and indeed everything that people do . . . . Policies endured and became the reference points for incremental change, then, because they were interpretations of a value system which preserved existing power relationships . . . . Power explains the persistence of some interpretations of shared values; it does not . . . explain innovation . . . To use it we must explain how all people came to share a world view which advanced the interests of only some of them.

Gramsci points to the work of "traditional intellectuals" as the mechanism for achieving consensus. In the American context, the people who articulate systems of values have included lawyers, ministers and journalists. These intellectuals, often having social roots in the dominant class, translate the values and habits of that class into an ideology which becomes "common sense." Sometimes, especially in democracies, this happens in mobilizing political support . . . . One aspect of this mobilization of popular support is that intellectuals must develop new concepts of the proper world order in response to changes in the material basis of the dominant class' power. Thus, as the economic focus of the dominant class changed from land to industry, industrialism was changed in the intellectual and then popular view from a monster which would destroy the American Eden into a benevolent donor of material well-being. When power relations between different groups in society change, the ideological system which once adequately justified the relation of one group to another will have to adjust.[89]

89. Mark Tushnet, "Lumber and the Legal Process," 1972 *Wisconsin Law Review* 114, 130–31. See also Joseph V. Femia, "Gramsci's Patrimony," 13 *British Journal of Political Science* 327 (1983); Duncan Kennedy, "Antonio Gramsci and the Legal System," 6 *ALSA Forum* 32 (1982); Maureen Cain, "Optimism, Law and the State: A Plea for the Possibility of Politics," in B.–M. Blegvad, C. M. Campbell and C. J. Schuyt (eds.), *European Yearbook in Law and Sociology* (The Hague: M. Nijhoff, 1977); Leonard Salamini, "Towards a Sociology of Intellectuals: A Structural Analysis of Gramsci's Marxist Theory," 6 *Sociological Analysis & Theory* 1 (1976).

When we compare Dicey and Gramsci, we can note that Dicey seems to approve of the system that he describes while Gramsci views it as a system of exploitation. However, apart from their evaluations of what they see, is there a real difference between Dicey and Gramsci's descriptions of the process by which public opinion influences law?

Does the following article reflect the views of Dicey or Gramsci? Does it suggest still a different view about the sources of legal reform?

15. *Social Change and the Law of Industrial Accidents*[90]

Lawrence M. Friedman
and Jack Ladinsky

67 *Columbia Law Review* 50 (1967)

☐ Sociologists recognize, in a general way, the essential role of legal institutions in the social order. They concede, as well, the responsiveness of law to social change and have made important explorations of the interrelations involved. Nevertheless, the role law plays in initiating—or reflecting—social change has never been fully explicated, either in theory or through research. The evolution of American industrial accident law from tort principles to compensation systems is an appropriate subject for a case-study on this subject . . . .

II. DEVELOPMENT OF THE LAW OF INDUSTRIAL ACCIDENTS

A. Background of the Fellow-Servant Rule

At the dawn of the industrial revolution, the common law of torts afforded a remedy, as it still does, for those who had suffered injuries at the hands of others. If a man injured another by direct action—by striking him, or slandering him, or by trespassing on his property—the victim could sue for his damages. Similarly, the victim of certain kinds of negligent behavior had a remedy at law. But tort law was not highly developed. Negligence in particular did not loom large in the reports and it was not prominently discussed in books of theory or practice. Indeed, no treatise on tort law appeared in America until Francis Hilliard's in 1859; the first English treatise came out in 1860 . . . .

---

90. Reprinted by permission. Copyright © 1967 *Columbia Law Review*.

In theory, at least, recovery for industrial accidents might have been assimilated into the existing system of tort law. The fundamental principles were broad and simple. If a factory worker was injured through the negligence of another person—including his employer—an action for damages would lie. Although as a practical matter, servants did not usually sue their master nor workers their employers, in principle they had the right to do so.

In principle, too, a worker might have had an action against his employer for any injury caused by the negligence of any other employee. The doctrine of *respondeat superior* was familiar and fundamental law. A principal was liable for all negligent acts of his agent . . . . Conceivably, then, one member of an industrial work force might sue his employer for injuries caused by the negligence of a fellow worker. A definitive body of doctrine was slow to develop, however. When it did, it rejected the broad principle of *respondeat superior* and took instead the form of the so-called fellow-servant rule. Under this rule, a servant (employee) could not sue his master (employer) for injuries caused by the negligence of another employee. The consequences of this doctrine were far reaching. An employee retained the right to sue the employer for injuries, provided they were caused by the employer's personal misconduct. But the factory system and corporate ownership of industry made this right virtually meaningless. The factory owner was likely to be a "soulless" legal entity; even if the owner was an individual entrepreneur, he was unlikely to concern himself physically with factory operations. In work accidents, then, legal fault would be ascribed to fellow employees, if anyone. But fellow employees were men without wealth or insurance. The fellow-servant rule was an instrument capable of relieving employers from almost all the legal consequences of industrial injuries. Moreover, the doctrine left an injured worker without any effective recourse but an empty action against his co-worker.

When labor developed a collective voice, it was bound to decry the rule as infamous, as a deliberate instrument of oppression—a sign that law served the interests of the rich and propertied, and denied the legitimate claims of the poor and the weak . . . . Conventionally, then, the fellow-servant rule is explained as a deliberate or half-deliberate rejection of a well-settled principle of law in order to encourage enterprise by forcing workmen to bear the costs of industrial injury. And the overthrow of the rule is taken as a sign of a conquest by progressive forces . . . . [But] from the standpoint of social change, good and evil are social labels based on perceptions of conditions, not terms referring to conditions in themselves. Social change comes about when people decide that a situation is evil and must be altered, even if they were satisfied or unaware of the problem before. In order, then, to understand the legal reaction to the problem of industrial accidents, one must understand how the problem was perceived within the legal system and by that portion of society whose views influenced the law.

B. Birth and Acceptance of the Rule

The origin of the fellow-servant rule is usually ascribed to Lord Abinger's opinion in *Priestley v. Fowler*,[91] decided in 1837. Yet the case on its facts did not pose the question of the industrial accident, as later generations would understand it; rather, it concerned the employment relationships of tradesmen. The defendant, a butcher, instructed the plaintiff, his servant, to deliver goods which had been loaded on a van by another employee. The van, which had been overloaded, broke down, and plaintiff fractured his thigh in the accident. Lord Abinger, in his rather diffuse and unperceptive opinion, reached his holding that the servant had no cause of action by arguing from analogies drawn neither from industry nor from trade:

> If the master be liable to the servant in this action, the principle of that liability will . . . carry us to an alarming extent . . . . The footman . . . may have an action against his master for a defect in the carriage owing to the negligence of the coachmaker . . . . The master . . . would be liable to the servant for the negligence of the chambermaid, for putting him into a damp bed; . . . for the negligence of the cook in not properly cleaning the copper vessels used in the kitchen.

These and similar passages in the opinion suggest that Abinger was worried about the disruptive effects of a master's liability upon his household staff. These considerations were perhaps irrelevant to the case at hand, the facts of which did not deal with the household of a nobleman, great landowner, or rich merchant; *a fortiori* the decision itself did not concern relationships within an industrial establishment. Certainly the opinion made extension of the rule to the factory setting somewhat easier to enunciate and formulate technically. But it did not justify the existence of an industrial fellow-servant rule. The case might have been totally forgotten—or overruled—had not the onrush of the industrial revolution put the question again and again to courts, each time more forcefully. *Priestley v. Fowler* and the doctrine of *respondeat superior* each stood for a broad principle. Whether the one or the other (or neither) would find a place in the law relative to industrial accidents depended upon needs felt and expressed by legal institutions in response to societal demands. Had there been no *Priestley v. Fowler*, it would have been necessary—and hardly difficult—to invent one.

91. 150 Eng. R. 1030 (Ex. 1837).

In the United States, the leading case on the fellow-servant situation was *Farwell v. Boston & Worcester Railroad Corp.*,[92] decided by Massachusetts' highest court in 1842. The case arose out of a true industrial accident in a rapidly developing industrial state. Farwell was an engineer who lost a hand when his train ran off the track due to a switchman's negligence. As Chief Justice Shaw, writing for the court, saw it, the problem of Farwell was how best to apportion the risks of railroad accidents. In his view, it was superficial to analyze the problem according to the tort concepts of fault and negligence. His opinion spoke the language of contract, and employed the stern logic of nineteenth century economic thought. Some occupations are more dangerous than others. Other things being equal, a worker will choose the least dangerous occupation available. Hence, to get workers an employer will have to pay an additional wage for dangerous work. The market, therefore, has already made an adjustment in the wage rate to compensate for the possibility of accident, and a cost somewhat similar to an insurance cost has been allocated to the company. As Shaw put it, "he who engages in the employment of another for the performance of specified duties and services, for compensation, takes upon himself the natural and ordinary risks and perils incident to the performance of such services, and *in legal presumption, the compensation is adjusted accordingly.*" The worker, therefore, has assumed the risk of injury—for a price. The "implied contract of employment" between the worker and employer did not require the employer to bear any additional costs of injury (except for those caused by the employer's personal negligence) . . . . Shaw and his generation placed their hopes of salvation on rapid economic growth. Perhaps they were anxious to see that the tort system of accident compensation did not add to the problems of new industry. Few people imagined that accidents would become so numerous as to create severe economic and social dislocations. On the contrary, rash extension of certain principles of tort law to industrial accidents might upset social progress by imposing extreme costs on business in its economic infancy. The 1840's and 1850's were a period of massive economic development in New England and the Midwest . . . . Textiles, and then iron, spearheaded the industrial revolution; westward expansion and the railroads created new markets. Communities and states made a social contribution to the construction of railroads through cash subsidies, stock subscriptions, and tax exemptions. The courts, using the fellow-servant doctrine and the concepts of assumption of risk and contributory negligence, socialized the accident costs of building the roads. That these solutions represented the collective, if uneasy, consensus of those with authority and responsibility is supported by the fact that every court of the country, with but one tran-

92. 45 Mass. (4 Met.) 49 (1842).

sient exception, reached the same conclusion in the years immediately following *Farwell*. Moreover, the fellow-servant rule was not abolished by any legislature in these early years. Although legislative inaction is not a necessary sign of acquiescence, it at least indicates lack of a major feeling of revulsion.

C. Weakening the Rule

A general pattern may be discerned which is common to the judicial history of many rules of law. The courts enunciate a rule, intending to "solve" a social problem—that is, they seek to lay down a stable and clearcut principle by which men can govern their conduct, or, alternatively, by which the legal system can govern men. If the rule comports with some kind of social consensus, it will in fact work a solution— that is, it will go unchallenged, or, if challenged, will prevail. Challenges will not usually continue, since the small chance of overturning the rule is not worth the cost of litigation. If, however, the rule is weakened—if courts engraft exceptions to it, for example—then fresh challenges probing new weaknesses will be encouraged. Even if the rule retains some support, it will no longer be efficient and clearcut. Ultimately, the rule may no longer serve anybody's purposes. At this point, a fresh (perhaps wholly new) "solution" will be attempted.

The history of the fellow-servant rule rather neatly fits this scheme. Shaw wrote his *Farwell* opinion in 1842. During the latter part of the century, judges began to reject his reasoning. The "tendency in nearly all jurisdictions," said a Connecticut court in 1885, was to "limit rather than enlarge" the range of the fellow-servant rule . . . .

The rule was strong medicine, and it depended for its efficacy upon continued, relatively certain, and unswerving legal loyalty. Ideally, if the rule were strong and commanded nearly total respect from the various agencies of law, it would eliminate much of the mass of litigation that might otherwise arise. Undoubtedly, it did prevent countless thousands of lawsuits; but it did not succeed in choking off industrial accident litigation. For example, industrial accident litigation dominated the docket of the Wisconsin Supreme Court at the beginning of the age of workmen's compensation; far more cases arose under that heading than under any other single field of law. Undoubtedly, this appellate case-load was merely the visible portion of a vast iceberg of litigation. Thus, the rule did not command the respect required for efficient operation and hence, in the long run, survival.

One reason for the continued litigation may have been simply the great number of accidents that occurred. At the dawn of the industrial revolution, when Shaw wrote, the human consequences of that technological change were unforeseeable. In particular, the toll it would take of human life was unknown. But by the last quarter of the nineteenth century, the number of industrial accidents had grown enormously. After 1900, it is estimated, 35,000 deaths and 2,000,000 injuries occurred every year in the United States. One quarter of the injuries produced disabilities lasting more than one week. The railway injury rate doubled in the seventeen years between 1889 and 1906.

In addition to the sheer number of accidents, other reasons for the increasing number of challenges to the rule in the later nineteenth century are apparent. If the injury resulted in death or permanent disability, it broke off the employment relationship; the plaintiff or his family thereafter had nothing to lose except the costs of suit. The development of the contingent fee system provided the poor man with the means to hire a lawyer . . . .

The contingent fee system was no more than a mechanism, however. A losing plaintiff's lawyer receives no fee; that is the essence of the system. The fact is that plaintiffs won many of their lawsuits; in so doing, they not only weakened the fellow-servant rule, but they encouraged still more plaintiffs to try their hand, still more attorneys to make a living from personal injury work. In trial courts, the pressure of particular cases—the "hard" cases in which the plight of the plaintiff was pitiful or dramatic—tempted judges and juries to find for the little man and against the corporate defendant. In Shaw's generation, many leading appellate judges shared his view of the role of the judge; they took it as their duty to lay down grand legal principles to govern whole segments of the economic order. Thus, individual hardship cases had to be ignored for the sake of higher duty. But this was not the exclusive judicial style, even in the appellate courts. And in personal injury cases, lower court judges and juries were especially prone to tailor justice to the case at hand. For example, in Wisconsin, of 307 personal injury cases involving workers that appeared before the state supreme court up to 1907, nearly two-thirds had been decided in favor of the worker in the lower courts. In the state supreme court, however, only two-fifths were decided for the worker. Other states undoubtedly had similar experiences. Whether for reasons of sympathy with individual plaintiffs, or with the working class in general, courts and juries often circumvented the formal dictates of the doctrines of the common law.

Some weakening of the doctrine took place by means of the control exercised by trial court judge and jury over findings of fact. But sympathy for injured workers manifested itself also in changes in doctrine. On the appellate court level, a number of mitigations of the fellow-servant rule developed near the end of the nineteenth century. For example, it had always been conceded that the employer was liable if he was personally responsible (through his own negligence) for his worker's injury. Thus, in a Massachusetts case, a stable owner gave directions to his employee, who was driving a wagon, that caused an accident and injury to the driver (or so the jury found). The employer was held liable. Out of this simple proposition grew the so-called vice-principal rule, which allowed an employee to sue his employer where the negligent employee occupied a supervisory position such that he could more properly be said to be an alter ego of the principal than a mere fellow-servant. This was a substantial weakening of the fellow-servant doctrine. Yet some states never accepted the vice-principal rule; in those that did, it too spawned a bewildering multiplicity of decisions, sub-rules, and sub-sub-rules . . . .

There were scores of other "exceptions" to the fellow-servant rule, enunciated in one or more states. Some of them were of great importance. In general, an employer was said to have certain duties that were not "delegable"; these he must do or have done, and a failure to perform them laid him open to liability for personal injuries. Among these was the duty to furnish a safe place to work, safe tools, and safe appliances . . . . Had the courts been so inclined, they might have eliminated the fellow-servant rule without admitting it, simply by expanding the safe place and safe tool rules. They were never quite willing to go that far, and the safe tool doctrine was itself subject to numerous exceptions. In some jurisdictions, for example, the so-called "simple tool" rule applied:

> Tools of ordinary and everyday use, which are simple in structure and requiring no skill in handling—such as hammers and axes—not obviously defective, do not impose a liability upon employer[s] for injuries resulting from such defects.

Doctrinal complexity and vacillation in the upper courts, coupled with jury freedom in the lower courts, meant that by the end of the century the fellow-servant rule had lost much of its reason for existence: it was no longer an efficient cost-allocating doctrine. Even though the exceptions did not go the length of obliterating the rule, and even though many (perhaps most) injured workers who had a possible cause of action did not or could not recover, the instability and unpredictability of operation of the common law rule was a significant fact.

The numerous judge-made exceptions reflected a good deal of uncertainty about underlying social policy. The same uncertainty was reflected in another sphere of legal activity—the legislature. Though the rule was not formally abrogated, it was weakened by statute in a number of jurisdictions . . . . [By the 1850s] the railroads replaced the banks as popular bogeymen . . . . Some of the fear of excessive economic power was transferred to them. Disregard for safety was one more black mark against the railroads; farmers, small businessmen, and the emerging railroad unions might use the safety argument to enlist widespread support for general regulation of railroads, but the essential thrust of the movement was economic. The railroads were feared and hated because of their power over access to the market. They became "monopolistic" as the small local lines were gradually amalgamated into large groupings controlled by "robber barons." Interstate railroad nets were no longer subject to local political control—if anything, they controlled local politics, or so it plausibly appeared to much of the public. Farmers organized and fought back against what they identified as their economic enemy. It is not coincidental that the earliest derogations from the strictness of the fellow-servant rule applied only to railroads. For example, the first statutory modification, passed in Georgia in 1856, allowed railroad employees to recover for injuries caused by the acts of fellow-servants, provided they themselves were free from negligence. A similar act was passed in Iowa in 1862. Other statutes were passed in Wyoming (1869) and Kansas (1874). The chronology suggests—though direct evidence is lacking—that some of these statutes were connected with the general revolt of farmers against the power of the railroad companies, a revolt associated with the Granger movement, which achieved its maximum power in the 1870's . . . .

The Granger revolt, and similar movements, were not without lessons for the railroad companies. Despite the fall of Granger legislatures, the legal and economic position of the railroads was permanently altered. Great masses of people had come to accept the notion that the power of the railroads was a threat to farmers and a threat to the independence and stability of democratic institutions. Out of the ashes of ineffective and impermanent state regulation of railroads arose what ultimately became a stronger and more systematic program of regulation, grounded in federal power over the national economy.

The Interstate Commerce Commission was created in 1887, chiefly to outlaw discrimination in freight rates and other practices deemed harmful to railroad users. The original legislation had nothing to say about railroad accidents and safety. But this did not long remain the case . . . . In 1893, Congress required interstate railroads to equip themselves with safety appliances, and provided that any employee injured "by any locomotive, car, or train in use" without such appliances could not "be deemed . . . to have assumed the risk thereby occasioned."

The Federal Employers' Liability Act of 1908 went much further; it abolished the fellow-servant rule for railroads and greatly reduced the strength of contributory negligence and assumption of risk as defenses. Once the employers had been stripped of these potent weapons, the relative probability of recovery by injured railroad employees was high enough so that workmen's compensation never seemed as essential for the railroads as for industry generally. The highly modified FELA tort system survives (in amended form) to this day for the railroads. It is an anachronism, but one which apparently grants some modest satisfaction to both sides. Labor and management both express discontent with FELA, but neither side has been so firmly in favor of a change to workmen's compensation as to make it a major issue.

FELA shows one of many possible outcomes of the decline in efficacy of the fellow-servant rule. Under it, the rule was eliminated, and the law turned to a "pure" tort system—pure in the sense that the proclivities of juries were not interfered with by doctrines designed to limit the chances of a worker's recovery. But the railroads were a special case. Aside from the special history of regulation, the interstate character of the major railroads made them subject to national safety standards and control by a single national authority. For other industrial employers, the FELA route was not taken; instead, workmen's compensation acts were passed. In either case, however, the fellow-servant rule was abolished, or virtually so. Either course reflects, we can assume, some kind of general agreement that the costs of the rule outweighed its benefits.

D. Rising Pressures for Change

The common law doctrines were designed to preserve a certain economic balance in the community. When the courts and legislatures created numerous exceptions, the rules lost much of their efficiency as a limitation on the liability of businessmen. The rules prevented many plaintiffs from recovering, but not all; a few plaintiffs recovered large [awards of damages]. There were costs of settlements, costs of liability insurance, costs of administration, legal fees and the salaries of staff lawyers. These costs rose steadily, at the very time when American business, especially big business, was striving to rationalize and bureaucratize its operations. It was desirable to be able to predict costs and insure against fluctuating, unpredictable risks. The costs of industrial accident liability were not easily predictable, partly because legal consequences of accidents were not predictable. Insurance, though available, was expensive.

In addition, industry faced a serious problem of labor unrest. Workers and their unions were dissatisfied with many aspects of factory life. The lack of compensation for industrial accidents was one obvious weakness. Relatively few injured workers received compensation. Under primitive state employers' liability statutes, the issue of liability and the amount awarded still depended upon court rulings and jury verdicts. Furthermore, the employer and the insurance carrier might contest a claim or otherwise delay settlement in hopes of bringing the employee to terms. The New York Employers' Liability Commission, in 1910, reported that delay ran from six months to six years.

When an employee did recover, the amount was usually small. The New York Commission found that of forty-eight fatal cases studied in Manhattan, eighteen families received no compensation; only four received over $2,000; most received less than $500. The deceased workers had averaged $15.22 a week in wages; only eight families recovered as much as three times their average yearly earnings. The same inadequacies turned up in Wisconsin in 1901. Of fifty-one fatal injuries studied, thirty-four received settlements under $500; only eight received over $1,000.

Litigation costs consumed much of whatever was recovered. It was estimated that, in 1907, "of every $100 paid out by [employers in New York] on account of work accidents but $56 reached the injured workmen and their dependents." And even this figure was unrepresentative because it included voluntary payments by employers . . . . A large fraction of the disbursed payments, about one-third, went to attorneys who accepted the cases on a contingent basis.

These figures on the inadequacy of recoveries are usually cited to show how little the workers received for their pains. But what did these figures mean to employers? Assuming that employers, as rational men, were anxious to pay as little compensation as necessary to preserve industrial peace and maintain a healthy workforce, the better course might be to pay a higher net amount direct to employees. Employers had little or nothing to gain from their big payments to insurance companies, lawyers, and court officials. Perhaps at some unmeasurable point of time, the existing tort system crossed an invisible line and thereafter, purely in economic terms, represented on balance a net loss to the industrial establishment. From that point on, the success of a movement for change in the system was certain, provided that businessmen could be convinced that indeed their self-interest lay in the direction of reform and that a change in compensation systems did not drag with it other unknowable and harmful consequences . . . .

When considerations of politics were added to those of business economics and industrial peace, it was not surprising to find that businessmen gradually withdrew their veto against workmen's compensation statutes. They began to say that a reformed system was inevitable—and even desirable. A guaranteed, insurable cost—one which could be computed in advance on the basis of accident experience—would, in the long run, cost business less than the existing system. In 1910, the president of the National Association of Manufacturers (NAM) appointed a committee to study the possibility of compensating injured workmen without time-consuming and expensive litigation, and the convention that year heard a speaker tell them that no one was satisfied with the present state of the law—that the employers' liability system was "antagonistic to harmonious relations between employers and wage workers." By 1911 the NAM appeared convinced that a compensation system was inevitable and that prudence dictated that business play a positive role in shaping the design of the law—otherwise the law would be "settled for us by the demagogue, and agitator and the socialist with a vengeance." Business would benefit economically and politically from a compensation system, but only if certain conditions were present. Business, therefore, had an interest in pressing for a specific kind of program, and turned its attention to the details of the new system. For example, it was imperative that the new system be in fact as actuarially predictable as business demanded; it was important that the costs of the program be fair and equal in their impact upon particular industries, so that no competitive advantage or disadvantage flowed from the scheme. Consequently the old tort actions had to be eliminated, along with the old defenses of the company. In exchange for certainty of recovery by the worker, the companies were prepared to demand certainty and predictability of loss—that is, limitation of recovery. The jury's caprice had to be dispensed with. In short, when workmen's compensation became law, as a solution to the industrial accident problem, it did so on terms acceptable to industry. Other pressures were there to be sure, but when workmen's compensation was enacted, businessmen had come to look on it as a positive benefit rather than as a threat to their sector of the economy.

E. The Emergence of Workmen's Compensation Statutes

The change of the businessmen's, the judge's, and the general public's attitudes toward industrial injuries was accelerated by the availability of fresh information on the extent of accidents and their cost to both management and workers. By 1900, industrial accidents and the shortcomings of the fellow-servant rule were widely perceived as *problems* that had to be solved. After 1900, state legislatures began to look for a "solution" by setting up commissions to gather statistics, to investigate possible new systems, and to recommend legislation. The commissions held public hearings and called upon employers, labor, insurance companies, and lawyers to express their opinions and propose changes. A number of commissions collected statistics on industrial accidents, costs of insurance, and amounts disbursed to injured workmen. By 1916, many states and the federal government had received more-or-less extensive public reports from these investigating bodies. The reports included studies of industrial accident cases in the major industries, traced the legal history of the cases, and looked into the plight of the injured workmen and their families.

From the information collected, the commissions were able to calculate the costs of workmen's compensation systems and compare them with costs under employers' liability. Most of the commissions concluded that a compensation system would be no more expensive than the existing method, and most of them recommended adoption, in one form or another, of workmen's compensation. In spite of wide variations in the systems proposed, there was agreement on one point: workmen's compensation must fix liability upon the employer regardless of fault.

Between 1910 and 1920 the method of compensating employees injured on the job was fundamentally altered in the United States. In brief, workmen's compensation statutes eliminated (or tried to eliminate) the process of fixing civil liability for industrial accidents through litigation in common law courts. Under the statutes, compensation was based on statutory schedules, and the responsibility for initial determination of employee claims was taken from the courts and given to an administrative agency. Finally, the statutes abolished the fellow-servant rule and the defenses of assumption of risk and contributory negligence. Wisconsin's law, passed in 1911, was the first general compensation act to survive a court test. Mississippi, the last state in the Union to adopt a compensation law, did so in 1948 . . . .

In essence, then, workmen's compensation was designed to replace a highly unsatisfactory system with a rational, actuarial one. It should not be viewed as the replacement of a fault-oriented compensation system with one unconcerned with fault. It should not be viewed as a victory of employees over employers. In its initial stages, the fellow-servant rule was not concerned with fault, either, but with establishing a clear-cut, workable, and predictable rule, one which substantively placed much of the risk (if not all) on the worker. Industrial accidents were not seen as a social problem—at most as an economic problem. As value perceptions changed, the rule weakened; it developed exceptions and lost its efficiency. The exceptions and counter-exceptions can be looked at as a series of brief, ad hoc, and unstable compromises between the clashing interests of labor and management. When both sides became convinced that the game was mutually unprofitable, a compensation system became possible. But this system was itself a compromise: an attempt at a new, workable, and predictable mode of handling accident liability which neatly balanced the interests of labor and management.

III. THE LAW OF INDUSTRIAL ACCIDENTS AND SOCIAL THEORY: THREE ASPECTS OF SOCIAL CHANGE

This case study, devoted to the rise and fall of the fellow-servant rule, utilizes and supports a view of social change as a complex chain of group bargains—economic in the sense of a continuous exchange of perceived equivalents, though not economic in the sense of crude money bargains. It also provides a useful setting for evaluating three additional popular explanations of the origin or rate of social change . . . .

A. The Concept of Cultural Lag

. . . In a famous book written in 1922, the sociologist William Fielding Ogburn used the example of workmen's compensation . . . to verify his "hypothesis of cultural lag." "Where one part of culture changes first," said Ogburn, "through some discovery or invention, and occasions changes in some part of culture dependent upon it, there frequently is a delay . . . . The extent of this lag will vary . . . but may exist for . . . years, during which time there may be said to be a maladjustment." In the case of workmen's compensation, the lag period was from the time when industrial accidents became numerous until the time when workmen's compensation laws were passed, "about a half century, from 1850–70 to 1915." During this period, "the old adaptive culture, the common law of employers' liability, hung over after the material conditions had changed."

The concept of cultural lag is still widely used, . . . and the notion that law fails to adjust promptly to the call for change is commonly voiced. In popular parlance, this or that aspect of the law is often said to "lag behind the times." This idea is so pervasive that it deserves comment quite apart from its present status in sociological thought.

The lesson of industrial accident law, as here described, may be quite the opposite of the lesson that Ogburn drew. In a purely objective (nonteleological) sense, social processes—and the legal system—cannot aptly be described through use of the idea of lag. When, in the face of changed technology and new problems, a social arrangement stubbornly persists, there are social reasons why this is so; there are explanations why no change or slow change occurs. The legal system is a part of the total culture; it is not a self-operating machine. The rate of response to a call for change is slow or fast in the law depending upon who issues the call and who (if anybody) resists it. "Progress" or "catching up" is not inevitable or predictable. Legal change, like social change, is a change in behavior of individuals and groups in interaction. The rate of change depends upon the kind of interaction. To say that institutions lag is usually to say no more than that they are slow to make changes of a particular type. But why are they slow? Often the answer rests on the fact that these institutions are controlled by or respond to groups or individuals who are opposed to the specific change. This is lag only if we feel we can confidently state that these groups or individuals are wrong as to their own self-interest as well as that of society. Of course, people are often wrong about their own self-interest; they can be and are short-sighted, ignorant, maladroit. But ignorance of this kind exists among progressives as well as among conservatives—among those who want change as well as among those who oppose it. Resistance to change is "lag" only if there is only one "true" definition of a problem—and one "true" solution.

There were important reasons why fifty years elapsed before workmen's compensation became part of the law. Under the impact of industrial conditions Americans were changing their views about individual security and social welfare. Dean [Roscoe] Pound has remarked that the twentieth century accepts the idea of insuring those unable to bear economic loss, at the expense of the nearest person at hand who can bear the loss. This conception was relatively unknown and unacceptable to judges of the nineteenth century. The fellow-servant rule could not be replaced until economic affluence, business conditions, and the state of safety technology made feasible a more social solution. Labor unions of the mid-nineteenth century did not call for a compensation plan; they were concerned with more basic (and practical) issues such as wages and hours. Social insurance, as much as private insurance, requires standardization and rationalization of business, predictability of risk, and reliability and financial responsibility of economic institutions. These were present in 1909, but not in 1850.

Prior to workmen's compensation, the legal system reflected existing conflicts of value quite clearly; the manifold exceptions to the fellow-servant rule and the primitive liability statutes bear witness to this fact. These were not symptoms of "lag"; rather, they were a measure of the constant adjustments that inevitably take place within a legal system that is not insulated from the larger society but an integral part of it. To be sure, the courts frequently reflected values of the business community and so did the legislatures, but populist expressions can easily be found in the work of judges, legislatures, and juries. In the absence of a sophisticated measuring-rod of past public opinion—and sophisticated concepts of the role of public opinion in nineteenth century society—who is to say that the legal system "lagged" behind some hypothetical general will of the public or some hypothetically correct solution?

The concept of lag may also be employed in the criticism of the courts' use of judicial review to retard the efficacy of social welfare legislation. In 1911, the New York Court of Appeals declared the state's compulsory workmen's compensation act unconstitutional. As a result of this holding, the state constitution had to be amended—two years later—before workmen's compensation was legally possible in New York. Because of the New York experience, six states also amended their constitutions and others enacted voluntary plans. The issue was not finally settled until 1917, when the United States Supreme Court held both compulsory and elective plans to be constitutional. But it adds little to an understanding of social process to describe this delay in terms of the concept of cultural lag. Courts do not act on their own initiative. Each case of judicial review was instigated by a litigant who represented a group in society which was fighting for its interests as it perceived them; these were current, real interests, not interests of sentiment or inertia. This is completely apart from consideration of what social interests the courts thought they were serving in deciding these cases—interests which hindsight condemns as futile or wrong, but which were living issues and interests of the day.

Conflicts of value also arose in the legislatures when they began to consider compensation laws. The Massachusetts investigating commission of 1903 reported a workmen's compensation bill to the legislature, but the bill was killed in committee on the ground that Massachusetts could not afford to increase the production costs of commodities manufactured in the state. Once more, the emergence of compensation depended upon a perception of inevitability—which could cancel the business detriment to particular states which enacted compensation laws—and of general economic gain from the new system. It is not enough to sense that a social problem exists. Rational corrective action demands relatively precise and detailed information about the problem, and clear placement of responsibility for proposing and implementing a solution. For many years legislatures simply did not consider it their responsibility to do anything about industrial injuries. Since they did not view accidents as a major social problem, and since state legislatures were weak political structures, they were content at first to leave accidents to tort law and the courts. Moreover, state agencies were not delegated the task of collecting information on the nature and extent of industrial accidents until relatively late. The Wisconsin legislature created a Bureau of Labor and Industrial Statistics in 1883, but did not provide for the collection of data on industrial accidents until 1905. When a need for accident legislation was perceived, individual legislators, under pressure of constituencies, began to introduce work accident indemnity bills. Some were inadequately drafted; most were poorly understood. In order to appraise potential legislation, investigating commissions were created to collect information, weigh the costs and report back alternative solutions.

What appears to some as an era of "lag" was actually a period in which issues were collectively defined and alternative solutions posed, and during which interest groups bargained for favorable formulations of law. It was a period of "false starts"—unstable compromise formulations by decision makers armed with few facts, lacking organizational machinery, and facing great, often contradictory, demands from many publics. There was no easy and suitable solution, in the light of the problem and the alignment of powers. Indeed, workmen's compensation—which today appears to be a stable solution—was only a compromise, an answer acceptable to enough people and interest groups to endure over a reasonably long period of time.

Part of what is later called "lag," then, is this period of false starts—the inadequate compromises by decision makers faced with contradictory interest groups pressing inconsistent solutions. There may not *be* a "solution" in light of the alignment of interests and powers with respect to the problem at any given point in time. Perhaps only a compromise "solution" is possible. What later appears to be the final answer is in fact itself a compromise—one which is stable over some significant period of time. Sociologically, that is what a "solution" to a problem is: nothing more than a stable compromise acceptable to enough people and interest groups to maintain itself over a significant period of time.

Theoretically, of course, total victory by one competing interest and total defeat of another is possible. But in a functioning democratic society, total victories and defeats are uncommon. Total defeat would mean that a losing group was so utterly powerless that it could exert no bargaining pressure whatsoever; total victory similarly would imply unlimited power. In the struggle over industrial accident legislation, none of the interests could be so described. Different perceptions of the problem, based at least in part on different economic and social stakes, led to different views of existing and potential law. When these views collided, compromises were hammered out. Workmen's compensation took form not because it was (or is) perfect, but because it represented a solution acceptable enough to enough interests to outweigh the costs of additional struggle and bargaining. If there was "lag" in the process, it consisted of acquiescence in presently acceptable solutions which turned out not to be adequate or stable in the long run. "Lag" therefore at most means present-minded pragmatism rather than long-term rational planning.

B. Cross-Cultural Borrowing

. . . Workmen's compensation was not an American innovation; there were numerous European antecedents. Switzerland passed a workmen's compensation act in 1881; Germany followed in 1884 with a more inclusive scheme. By 1900 compensation laws had spread to most European countries. In 1891 the United States Bureau of Labor commissioned John Graham Brooks to study and appraise the German system. His report, published in 1893, was widely distributed and successfully exposed some American opinion-leaders to the existence of the European programs. Most of the state investigating commissions also inquired into the European experience, and a number of early bills were modeled after the German and British systems.

Though workmen's compensation can therefore be viewed as an example of cross-cultural borrowing, care must be exercised in employing the concept. Successful legal solutions to social problems are often borrowed across state and national lines but this borrowing must not be confused with the actual "influence" of one legal system over another. "Influence" carries with it an implication of power or, at the least, of cultural dominance. The forces that led to a demand for workmen's compensation were entirely domestic, as this study has argued. The fact that European solutions to similar problems were studied and, to an extent, adopted here shows not dominance but an attempt to economize time, skill, and effort by borrowing an appropriate model. It would be quite wrong to detect European legal "influence" in this process. The existence of the European compensation plans was not a cause of similar American statutes. Rather, the interest

shown in the foreign experiences was a response to American dissatisfaction with existing industrial accident law. Similarly, the current
drive for an American ombudsman is not an example of the "influence"
of Scandinavian law. A foreign model here sharpens discussion and
provides a ready-made plan. Yet the felt need for such an officer has
domestic origins.

C. Great Men and Social Change

Sociologists are fond of pointing out the inaccuracy of the "great-
man theory of history," which holds that particular persons play irre-
placeably decisive roles in determining the path of social change. The
influence of single individuals, they say, is hardly as critical as historians would have us believe. The role of outstanding persons in bringing
about workmen's compensation acts seems on one level quite
clear . . . . Reformers and academicians served as important middlemen
in mediating between interest groups and working out compromises.
Their arguments legitimated the act; their zeal enlisted support of middle-class neutrals. They were willing to do the spadework of research,
drafting, and propagandizing necessary for a viable law. In the passage
of many other welfare and reform laws, outstanding personalities can
be found who played dominant roles in creating and leading public
opinion—for example, Lawrence Veiller for the New York tenement
housing law of 1901, Harvey Wiley for the Federal Food and Drug
Act.

The great-man hypothesis is not susceptible of proof or disproof.
But the course of events underlying workmen's compensation at least
suggests that social scientists are properly suspicious of placing too
much reliance on a great-man view. If the view here expressed is correct, then economic, social, political and legal forces made workmen's
compensation (or some alternative such as FELA) virtually inevitable
by the end of the nineteenth century. Outstanding men may be necessary in general for the implementation of social change: someone must
take the lead in creating the intellectual basis for a change in perception. Nonetheless, when a certain pattern of demand exists in society,
more than one person may be capable of filling that role. Particular
individuals are normally not indispensable. The need is for talent—
men with extraordinary ability, perseverance, and personal influence,
men who can surmount barriers and accomplish significant results.
Obviously, the absence of outstanding persons interested in a particular
cause can delay problem solving or lead to inept, shoddy administration. The appearance of truly exceptional persons at the proper moment
in history is undoubtedly not automatic. But talent, if not genius, may
well be a constant in society; and the social order determines whether
and in what direction existing talent will be exerted.

Thus, it would be foolish to deny that specific individuals exert great influence upon the development of social events, and equally foolish to conclude that other persons could not have done the job as well (or better) if given the opportunity. "Great men," however, must be in the right place, which means that society must have properly provided for the training and initiative of outstanding persons and for their recruitment into critical offices when needed. In difficult times, great businessmen, political leaders, musicians, or physicists will emerge. "Great men" appear "when the time is ripe"—but only insofar as society has created the conditions for a pool of creative manpower dedicated to the particular line of endeavor in which their greatness lies. ☐

NOTES AND QUESTIONS

1. In his "The Economic Interpretation and the Law of Torts," 53 *Harvard Law Review* 365 (1940), Roscoe Pound wrote:

> What stands out in the history of Anglo-American law is the resistance of the taught tradition in the hands of judges drawn from any class you like, . . . against all manner of economically or politically powerful interests.

Pound then discusses *Priestley v. Fowler* and the rise of the fellow-servant rule. He argues that the rule was not the product of "a tribunal consciously expressing in legal doctrine the self interest of a dominant social or economic class." Rather, it was the result of the "conception of liability" entertained by courts and lawyers generally in the early 19th century. No court, however composed, would have decided otherwise.

> An exclusively economic interpretation of single decisions and single items of judicial action leaves out of account the tenacity of the taught tradition. It takes no account of the instinctive tendency of the lawyer to refer every case back to some general principle. It ignores the prevailing mode of thought of the time which often reflects an economic situation of the past when the taught ideal was formulated.

Is Pound consistent with Dicey? with Gramsci? Do Friedman and Ladinsky ignore "the taught tradition?" Do they leave out of their reckoning the training, habits and inherited modes of thought of the legal profession? How might they respond to Pound's critique? Is their position a materialist one that downplays the force of ideas and values in explaining major legal change?

2. In their discussion of "lag," Friedman and Ladinsky state:

> Theoretically . . . total victory by one competing interest and total defeat of another is possible. But in a functioning democratic society, total victories and defeats are uncommon. Total defeat would mean that a losing group was so utterly powerless that it could exert no bargaining pressure whatsoever; total victory similarly would imply unlimited power.

Elliott Currie, in "Sociology of Law: The Unasked Questions," 81 *Yale Law Journal* 134, 139–40 (1971), takes exception to this passage. He says:

> The implication is not only that the decline of the "fellow-servant rule" and the rise of workmen's compensation represented such a pluralistic bargaining process, but that the United States, on the basis of this and other evidence, is "a functioning democratic society."
>
> Does the empirical evidence presented by Ladinsky and Friedman support these contentions? A close reading suggests otherwise. Their own evidence, in fact, indicates quite strongly that it was in the interest of the business community to promote workmen's compensation laws, and that without the recognition of that interest on the part of business the laws would not have come into existence. This does not necessarily mean that workmen's compensation was a "total victory" for business, but neither does it suggest a process of bargaining and compromise among competing social interests. What it most clearly suggests is that in capitalist society business holds what amounts to a veto power over legal change . . . . Nowhere is it suggested that labor (or anyone else) possess a similar power over the adoption or rejection of social reform measures. Fitting this analysis into the "bargaining" model of social change seems a rather Procrustean exercise. The theory seems tacked on to the data, an article of faith more than anything else.

Is Currie's criticism well-taken? Does true bargaining, as he seems to imply, necessarily require something approximating an equality of bargaining power?

3. William Chambliss, in "The Criminalization of Conduct," in H. Laurence Ross (ed.), *Law and Deviance* (Beverly Hills: Sage Publications, 1981), says that Friedman and Ladinsky express an "eclectic radical pluralist view of the relationship between ideology and economic structures." However, the "emphasis in the end is on the importance of consensually held values rather than economic relations as the determinant of law." Is this a fair reading of Friedman and Ladinsky?

There is a long tradition in sociology which explains law as the product of some sort of social consensus. One group of theorists who lean in this direction are the so-called structural-functionalists. Social order, for them, flows from internalized values and is enforced through informal sanctions. Disputes can arise when the values are ambiguous, and legal institutions determine how values are to be applied to particular cases. Scholars writing from "a conflict perspective," however, challenge the idea that law reflects a consensus about values. Law represents, instead, power and the exercise of power, no matter how the power-holders rationalize what they are doing. Law legitimates the use of violence, or the threat of violence, against those who disagree with the dominant view. See, for example, Emilio Lamo de Espinosa, "Social and Legal Order in Sociological Functionalism," 4 *Contemporary Crisis* 43 (1980).

For conflict theorists, society is not harmonious and stable but is held together by the use or threats of force. Police officers with clubs or a SWAT team with automatic weapons attacking any group that threatens the stability of the existing order—these are the reality of law. Instead of normative consensus, conflict theorists say that those at the bottom of the distribution of wealth and status see cheating, manipulation or simple resignation as the ways to cope with an unjust system which cannot be confronted directly.

Austin Turk, in "Law as a Weapon in Social Conflict," 23 *Social Problems* 276 (1976), points out that, even when it is not corrupt, the legal system may promote conflict rather than social integration. Control of the system itself, for example, is a prize about which groups can fight; the power to appoint judges and administrators is one of the things gained by winning elections. Moreover, the chance to mobilize whatever power the courts possess can be an incentive to abandon acceptance of the status quo. The chance of victories before the courts and legislature may undercut compromise, generating more conflict rather than stabilizing the society. Unpopular statutes or court decisions may provoke great dissensus. The abortion decisions of the United States Supreme Court, for example, were not the product of consensus nor did they produce consensus about how the society should deal with abortion.

Alan Hunt, in "Dichotomy and Contradiction in the Sociology of Law," 8 *British Journal of Law & Society* 47 (1981), argues that law reflects both consent and coercion but that social theorists emphasize one or the other in accordance with their ideological position. He finds that they fail to advance "a coherent presentation of a mode of combination of the apparently opposed characteristics of law so as to produce a unitary conception not reducible to a choice between opposites or a fluctuation between them" (pp. 72–73). Do Friedman and Ladinsky present a picture of consensus, conflict or something else? Do they satisfy Hunt's goal of a "unitary conception not reducible to a choice between opposites or a fluctuation between them?"

4. One possible incentive for legal change is people's perception of a significant gap between what the law promises and what it delivers. For example, suppose a government claims support because it promotes full employment and a certain degree of upward mobility. When government fails to do this, people may support new legislative programs or new political leaders and parties. In extreme cases, people may support a dictator's rise to power. However, we know that many people expect little from government or view the legal system with cynicism and do nothing beyond complaining or making jokes.

Robin Stryker, in "Rules, Resources, and Legitimacy Processes: Some Implications for Social Conflict, Order, and Change," 99 *American Journal of Sociology* 847 (1994), attempts to cope with the difficult and disorderly concept of "legitimacy." Stryker sees at least three meanings of the term. At one extreme, legitimacy refers to deep approval of the rules—attachment, loyalty, allegiance, and a favorable view of the legal system or some of its institutions. At the other extreme, the term simply refers to a kind of consent; consent can mean active participation, passive acquiescence or even sullen obedience. All we know, however, in a consent situation is that the rules are not sufficiently *illegitimate* to provoke resistance. A third meaning is cognitive; people recognize rules as binding, although they may not consciously support them. "Valid rules are part of a meaningful and natural order defining the way things are." We get and renew drivers licenses; we drive on the right side of the road (or the left, in some countries); we expect others to do the same. Most people simply accept these rules and practices, and give little or no thought to the sanctions, formal or informal, that would be used in case of violation.

Stryker notes that principles of legitimacy may conflict. The legitimacy of law, traditionally, rests on its procedures and on the claims of legal reasoning. But in this century, science and technology also pose powerful claims to act as the source of legal legitimacy—for example, when a child psychologist offers her expert opinion in court about "the best interests of the child." Effectiveness, rather than legal logic, becomes the basis of interpreting law.

If there are multiple sources of legitimacy, people *may* come to question the authority of law—especially if the outcome does not meet their wishes or expectations. Some scholars think they see something they call a "legitimacy crisis." What follows from such a crisis, if one in fact exists? Perhaps resistance and revolution; perhaps mobilization and participation in the political process. But if the parties to social conflict simply make use of "institutionalized legal and political rules," any such "legitimacy crisis" would be "contained and . . . limited to playing itself out within the rules of representative democracy" (p. 903).

Tom R. Tyler and Gregory Mitchell, "Legitimacy and the Empowerment of Discretionary Legal Authority: The United States Supreme Court and Abortion Rights," 43 *Duke Law Journal* 703 (1994), studied why Americans are and are not willing to accept the Supreme Court as the appropriate institution to decide controversial questions such as abortion rights. In a survey of a random sample of population in the San Francisco Bay Area, they found that the public was divided over whether women should be free to have abortions if they do not have a good reason for getting them.

They found many people who thought that the Supreme Court should *not* be empowered to make policy decisions about abortion. Only 36% said that such a power should remain with the Court while 59% thought that the Court's power over abortion decisions should be reduced. However, those in their sample who regarded the institutional role of the Supreme Court as legitimate were more likely to defer to its judgments about abortion rights. Legitimacy primarily turned on perceptions of the Justices as neutral and not driven by political pressure or personal bias. Those who regarded abortion as immoral, however, were less willing to allow the Supreme Court to make abortion policy decisions. Satisfaction with the outcome of the Court's decision did exert a statistically significant influence on some respondents' willingness to leave the question to the Court. Tyler and Mitchell report:

> Interestingly, views about abortion (whether it is moral and whether it should be legal) had only a minor effect on judgments of empowerment [acknowledging an external authority's legitimacy to make a controversial decision]. Even more strikingly, agreement with past Court decisions had only a minor effect on empowerment. Together, these judgments explained only 6% of the variance in empowerment, compared to the 12% explained by decisionmaking characteristics. Thus, general views of the Court had more influence on judgments concerning empowerment in the particular case of abortion than did evaluations of past Court efforts to deal with the abortion issue. [p. 770]

To what extent are Stryker's and Tyler and Mitchell's views consistent with those of Dicey, Gramsci, or Friedman and Ladinsky? The subject of legitimacy is taken up again in Chapter 4.

5. Maureen Cain, "The Main Themes of Marx' and Engels' Sociology of Law," 1 *British Journal of Law and Society* 136 (1974); Cain and Hunt (eds.), *Marx and Engels on Law* (New York: Academic Press, 1979), point out that Marx and Engels had no coherent theory of law. Their comments on law were fragmentary. Later Marxists largely fabricated theories of law on the basis of general Marxist concepts and approaches.

In a Marxist theory, we begin with the economic base—how people produce wealth and how they divide what is produced. However, there is also a superstructure of ideology by which a society explains itself, and law is part of this ideology. Controversy swirls around the importance of such ideas. A pure materialist would treat them as little more than noise in the system. However, others who claim allegiance to Marxist thought see the *state* as relatively autonomous. This relative autonomy of state actors develops because those who run the state have their own interest in preserving their place and position. The dominant class uses the state to legitimate and defend class privileges through the exercise of power. The dominant class justifies the legal system and laws by claiming that they rest on custom, natural law and right reason, or on consensus and bargaining among interests. The individual rights approach, typical of capitalist legal systems, obscures real power relationships. All are declared equal before the law despite gross inequalities which usually make assertions of those rights by the dominated impossible. For example, the largest corporation and the poorest citizen both have the same right to due process of law. However, one is far better able to make use of that right than the other.

Some Marxists argue that you cannot reduce law to no more than what the powerful (the dominant class) want. The powerful can lose a particular battle. It may be more important to uphold values fundamental to the capitalist order than to gain a particular victory. Law, thus, can become the ground for struggle. Sometimes different factions within the dominant class engage in bargaining. The manufacturers of textiles may want a tariff while the manufacturers of jet aircraft may fear retaliation by other nations and thus advocate free trade. Sometimes law will yield social change, or at least give this appearance. The dominant class may have to buy off parts of the working class in times of economic crisis. Thus, we can get laws which appear to benefit labor. However, if such reforms ever threatened to go too far, the dominant class still retains the power to preserve its position. Its lawyers and other agents can block or delay enforcement of the rules. Marxists, of course, deny that laws produced by these bargains or military intervention can ever produce lasting stability in a capitalist system. Ultimately, the contradictions of capitalism will overturn this system.[93]

93. See, e.g. Bob Jessop, "On Recent Marxist Theories of Law, the State, and Juridico-Political Ideology," 8 *International Journal of the Sociology of Law* 339 (1980); Otwin Marenin, "Parking Tickets and Class Repression: The Concept of Policing in Critical Theories of Criminal Justice," 6 *Contemporary Crises* 241 (1982); David F. Greenberg, "On One-Dimensional Marxist Criminology," 3 *Theory and Society* 611 (1976).

SCANDALS AND CRISES—REAL AND CONSTRUCTED: MANU-
FACTURING PUBLIC OPINION

NOTE: 16. Upton Sinclair, *The Jungle,* and the Background of the First Food and Drug Act, 1906

At about the turn of the century, there was considerable agitation in the country for some form of government regulation of the quality of food products. In particular, people were shocked when they learned about the quality of meat products. During the Spanish-American war, it was alleged that American soldiers were forced to eat cans of "embalmed beef." (Theodore Roosevelt testified before the Senate that he would just as soon eat his old hat as the canned food shipped to the men in Cuba). Some states passed laws about food quality. Within the government, Dr. Harvey W. Wiley worked tirelessly to expose adulter-ation of food products and to get Congress to pass legislation that would ensure the sale of only safe and wholesome food and drugs. Wiley revealed many horrible practices of manufacturers—practices which cheated the public, and, in some cases, poisoned them. Still, Congress had not passed a food and drug law when, in 1906, Upton Sinclair published *The Jungle*, a novel about life in Chicago, centering around the stockyards.

Sinclair was an ardent Socialist. He believed that capitalism was the source of the evil that he saw about him, and he became convinced, as he wrote in his autobiography, that "the heart and center of the evil lay in leaving the social treasure, which nature had created, and which every man has to have in order to live, to become the object of a scram-ble in the marketplace, a delirium of speculation."[94] The turn of the century was a period in which socialism had considerable appeal to some American intellectuals. It was also a period in which "muckrak-ers" were educating the reading public about corruption, vice and deg-radation in American society and about the destruction of American ideals and myths. Or so it looked to Sinclair.

Sinclair's early novels came to the attention of the editor of a radical magazine, *The Appeal to Reason*. The editor offered Sinclair $500 for serial rights to a new novel. Sinclair selected the Chicago stockyards as the scene for his book. In 1904, Sinclair went to Chicago, and for seven weeks he "lived among the wage slaves of the Beef Trust."[95] Then he went home, and wrote a novel based on his experiences.

The Jungle tells the story of a Lithuanian immigrant named Jurgis Rudkus. He came to the United States, full of naive faith in America. He settled in "Packingtown," the stockyard area of Chicago. The

---

94. U. Sinclair, *American Outpost, A Book of Reminiscences* 143 (New York: Farrar & Rinehart, 1932).

95. Ibid., p. 154.

American dream turns into a nightmare for Rudkus, his family, and his friends. Every possible horror and tragedy is inflicted on Rudkus and his circle. He is exploited at work, in his rented home, and on the streets. His wife dies in childbirth. His son drowns. Women dear to him are driven into prostitution. He is injured on the job, laid off, and eventually blacklisted. He becomes a wanderer, but he also becomes a socialist, convinced that only through this means can the world be saved.

In the first half of the book, there are passages that vividly describe conditions in the packing plants. Tubercular pork was sold for human consumption. Old sausage, rejected in Europe and shipped back "mouldy and white," would be "dosed with borax and glycerine, and dumped into the hoppers, and made over again for home consumption." Meat was stored in rooms where "water from leaky roofs would drip over it, and thousands of rats would race about on it." The packers would put out poisoned bread to kill the rats; then the rats would die, and "rats, bread, and meat would go into the hoppers together." Most horrifying of all was the description of the men in the "cooking rooms." They "worked in tank-rooms full of steam," in some of which there were "open vats near the level of the floor." Sometimes they fell into the vats "and when they were fished out, there was never enough of them left to be worth exhibiting—sometimes they would be overlooked for days, till all but the bones of them had gone out to the world as Durham's Pure Leaf Lard."

The book became notorious while *The Appeal to Reason* was still printing it as a serial. George P. Brett, for Macmillan & Co., offered to publish the book if Sinclair would remove the "objectionable passages." Sinclair refused. Other publishers turned it down. Sinclair appealed to the readers of the magazine for support, and they sent in enough money to finance an edition of the novel. Then Doubleday, Page & Co. became interested in publishing the book. Worried about its accuracy, they investigated the situation in Chicago. They became convinced that Sinclair was telling the truth about conditions in "Packingtown," and they published an edition of the book, early in 1906.

The Jungle created a furor when it appeared. A copy was sent to President Theodore Roosevelt, and letters from the public poured in to the President. "Mr. Dooley," the fictional creation of Finley Peter Dunne, painted the following imaginary picture of Roosevelt's entourage confronting *The Jungle*:

Tiddy was toying with a light breakfast an' idly turnin' over th' pages iv th' new book with both hands. Suddenly he rose fr'm th' table, an' cryin': "I'm pizened," begun throwin' sausages out iv th' window. Th' ninth wan sthruck Sinitor Biv'ridge[96] on th' head an' made him a blond.

96. Senator Albert Beveridge of Indiana.

It bounced off, exploded, an' blew a leg off a secret-service agent, an' th' scatthred fragmints desthroyed a handsome row iv ol' oak-trees. Sinitor Biv'ridge rushed in, thinkin' that th' Prisidint was bein' assassynated be his devoted followers in th' Sinit, an' discovered Tiddy engaged in a hand-to-hand conflict with a potted ham. Th' Sinitor fr'm Injyanny, with a few well-directed wurruds, put out th' fuse an' rendered th' missle harmless. Since thin th' Prisidint, like th' rest iv us, has become a viggytaryan . . .

The meat-packers fought back with propaganda of their own, and they did their best to block legislation in Congress. But this time they were not successful. Roosevelt appointed two investigators, and their report confirmed Sinclair's findings. At first, Roosevelt did not release their report. Senator Albert Beveridge had "hammered out the draft of a meat-inspection law," which he attached as a rider to the agricultural appropriation bill. It called for postmortem examination of meat, inspection of meat products, control of sanitation, and exclusion of "harmful chemicals and preservatives." The packers refused to cooperate. The President then released the report.

He also applied pressure for the passage of the pure food law, which had been bottled up in Congress. In this he was greatly helped by the great public uproar over *The Jungle*. The packers and food manufacturers fought a rear-guard action. But one executive admitted that "the sale of meat and meat products has been more than cut in two." State food and drug officials and Dr. Wiley also lobbied for passage. In 1906, Congress passed and the President signed both a pure food and a meat inspection law.

What was Sinclair's reaction to all this? *The Jungle* made him famous. But to him, there was an element of disappointment—or irony—in the outcome. He said: "I aimed at the public's heart, and by accident I hit it in the stomach." Socialism was not advanced by *The Jungle*, although that was Sinclair's real purpose in writing the book.

NOTES AND QUESTIONS

1. Can you think of other examples of the influence of scandal on the formation of law? Both the press and television offer a constant diet of exposé journalism. Are there examples where it has had a major impact? Or is the impact of this kind of journalism likely to be a general distrust of government and large business organizations?

2. When will attempts to create scandal work to provoke legislation? For example, Ralph Nader, in *Unsafe at Any Speed* (New York: Grossman, 1965) attacked General Motor's Corvair automobile. The book was a major factor in prompting Congress to pass legislation regulating automobile safety. A few years later, Fred McClement, an Eastern Airlines pilot, wrote *It Doesn't Matter Where You Sit* (New York: Holt, Rinehart & Winston, 1969). This was an attack on the original Boeing 727, an aircraft on which many readers of these materials have flown. Several 727s crashed, and McClement charged that the

plane was defectively designed. As far as we can tell, McClement's book had no impact. The plane was redesigned and renamed and later became one of the best-selling passenger jet planes. Can you think of reasons why the threat of defective automobiles provoked legislation while the threat of defective passenger jet planes did not? Alternatively, is it fair to conclude that scandal has no impact on airline safety in general? Should we view the McClement book as but a small part of the total public concern about airline safety, fueled by detailed television and newspaper accounts of crashes?

17. The Cultural Logic of a Political Crisis: Common Sense, Hegemony and the Great American Liability Insurance Famine of 1986[97]

Robert M. Hayden

INTRODUCTION

☐ In ordinary discourse, political crises are urgent occasions, something has happened that threatens to disrupt normal social, political or economic life, and the threat must be met. The urgency of the matter is a reflection of its status as a departure from the normal, everyday course of events. A crisis is perceived as a unique event or sequence of events, which is threatening precisely because it is unusual. Crisis implies a breakdown of ongoing systems, or the threat of one. If the system is seen as being capable of correcting itself, then there is no crisis.

In this everyday sense, each crisis seems to be due to a unique constellation of objective factors, such as the introduction of Soviet missiles into Cuba, the repeated failure of a monsoon and thus of crops, the collapse of a dam, or an attack on American warships by North Vietnamese torpedo boats. Such a departure from normality can be corrected by temporary or one-shot measures, the removal of the missiles, the emergency distribution of food, the provision of temporary housing and loans for rebuilding, or the bombing of North Vietnam and the dispatch of American marines to the South. As a political tactic, calling attention to the crisis is a good way of marshaling support for the desired corrective measures.

Yet, . . . calling something a crisis may be an act of arbitrary labeling for a recurring situation, an attempt to divert attention from the repetitive nature of the problem and thus to avoid inquiry into possible

97. *Studies in Law, Politics, and Society,* Volume 11, pp. 95–117. (Greenwich, Conn.: JAI Press Inc., 1991).

underlying causes for the recurrences. If a kind of unfortunate event is recurrent steps may be taken to avoid it, but if it is unique, who can be blamed for failing to foresee the unforeseeable? Such a diversionary strategy seems particularly likely to be utilized in situations where some widespread injury has already taken place, in an attempt to avoid blame . . . .

The political debate in such circumstances will probably center on whether an admitted disaster can be described as unavoidable or unforeseeable, and thus not the fault of any particular political actors. Such unforeseeable disasters may be represented by specific terms or labels; an "act of God" in American English can not be blamed on men, whereas in India famine is seen as a recurring event that is caused by the unpredictable nature of the environment, particularly the monsoon. Disasters that can be covered by such terms may recur, but they can not be predicted with certainty, much less prevented, and thus can not be blamed on political or economic actors.

One implication of viewing crises as political labels rather than objective phenomena is that the labeling often may be most easily accomplished in the absence of much empirical data. If there is substantial evidence indicating that the condition does obtain, then the labeling is not arbitrary. When such data are lacking, political actors are free to argue about what people assume that they know. In the absence of data, arguments may be based on "common sense," as defined by [Clifford] Geertz, the underlying cultural assumptions of the way the world works, an unreflective form of practical knowledge. Whereas such common sense arguments may refer to some limited quantitative data, they seem more likely to be based on anecdotes, accounts of particular incidents that provide graphic illustrations of the speaker's point. This kind of rhetoric has been described . . . as the "tactical use of passion," as argument that "seeks to eliminate the mind and the critical faculties" and provoke "feeling rather than thought".

One might argue that even in such cases the presentation of reliable, representative data should be able to defeat claims based on common sense, but in fact the opposite seems more likely to be true. A well-structured common sense argument may pre-empt the consideration of data that would contradict it, because if everyone knows the way the world works, what is the point of discussing the matter? Indeed, how could anyone with any common sense deny that the world works that way? The problem may be rephrased in terms of hegemony, which has been closely linked analytically with the common sense of the dominant subculture in a given social field. Hegemony, or common sense, may serve to hinder perceptions of discrepant data or discussions of them. As Geertz says, "common sense rests its case on the assertion that it is not a case at all . . . . The world is its authority." These concepts are useful for exploring the history and implications of a recent American political crisis, which we may call the Great Liability Insurance Famine of 1986. In that year the costs of insurance for many doctors, businesses and municipalities jumped sharply, and in some cases insurance became unavailable at any price. The effects of this famine threatened to be severe. Doctors increased their charges or threatened to leave practice, businesses gave up otherwise profitable lines of products, cities canceled services, all because liability insurance was either unobtainable or unaffordable. Much of the blame for this situation was placed on the legal system, which was accused of giving outrageous, unjustified awards in many cases, causing the insurance companies to pass on their increased costs in the form of higher premiums. The political response was impressive. "Reforms" of the civil justice system as a means of combating the liability insurance famine were considered by the federal government and forty of the fifty states, of which at least thirty-three have enacted such legislation. It seemed to be common sense that the legal system was to blame.

Yet the evidence linking the increase in insurance costs to the actions of the legal system was weak. Some quantitative data from isolated parts of the country were cited repeatedly, but they were not put into any larger context and can not be considered to be representative of the country as a whole. Further, and more recently, more broadly based data run contrary to the idea that the legal system was responsible for the increase in liability insurance costs, but these data have not attracted much attention.

The lack of interest in reliable statistical data may not have had much importance because most of the political arguments were carried out primarily by reference to anecdotes rather than numbers. If true, these anecdotes were certainly graphic illustrations of flaws in the legal system. However, on investigation, most of the anecdotes have been shown to be distortions of actual legal cases, and in some instances outright fabrications. Although corrected versions have been made available they are not often cited, and the original anecdotes continue to be used in arguing that the legal system is responsible for the liability insurance crisis.

This paper attempts to explain why that argument has had such success despite the lack of empirical data to support it . . . . I will argue that the continued success of the anecdotes is due to their reflection of American common sense, everyone *knows* that the legal system is faulty, and the anecdotes are simply further confirmation of this perception. It is this common sense view that accounts for the lack of interest in either the corrected versions of the anecdotes or in data that are contrary to the view that the courts caused the liability insurance famine. It may be a truism to say that it is hard to argue against common sense, but this platitude (itself a bit of common sense) has deeper political significance. In the present case, I will show why the anecdotes are so commonsensical by pointing out their reliance on broad themes of American culture. Further, these anecdotes and their use in a political debate reveal the hegemonic use to which such cultural concepts can be put. Common sense may be shared by the common man or woman, but it is generated by elites. This last point has important implications for interpretive anthropology, which has been said frequently to ignore the distribution and uses of cultural knowledge. By explicitly raising the political implications of American common sense regarding the legal system, this essay is meant to point out the potential for applying interpretive anthropological analysis to specific current social issues.

THE LIABILITY INSURANCE FAMINE AS A CRISIS IN CIVIL JUSTICE: THE POLICY DEBATE AND EVIDENCE FROM RESEARCH

The Insurance Famine and its Repercussions

In 1986, it seemed to become common knowledge that liability insurance had suddenly become scarce and expensive. The "insurance crisis" received wide publicity, including cover stories in *Time* and *Forbes* magazines, advertisements or "public service announcements" in the press and on television and discussion by syndicated columnists, editorial writers and political figures. The U.S. Department of Justice issued a *Report on the Causes, Extent, and Policy Implications of the Current Crisis in Insurance Availability*. As mentioned earlier, forty states and the federal government considered statutes aimed at alleviating the situation.

The sudden scarcity of affordable liability insurance threatened disruption of many kinds of business and professional activities. Some businesses stopped manufacturing or selling items such as lacrosse helmets or woodworking machinery, parades and public celebrations were canceled, day care centers and midwives went out of business, and prices for some items went up, all due to either increased insurance premiums or inability to secure insurance. Even charities and human services organizations were put in jeopardy because of increased costs for liability insurance for their directors and officers. Perhaps most seriously, doctors practicing certain specialties, notably obstetrics, either stopped practicing or threatened to do so, due to huge increases in their malpractice insurance costs. Medical associations have also charged that increases in the number of medical malpractice lawsuits has forced doctors to practice "defensive medicine," ordering tests that are not medically necessary and thus running up the costs of health care.

Blaming the Civil Justice System

These threatened disruptions of everyday life made the liability insurance famine appear to be a crisis, needing urgent political action to alleviate it. In order to correct a situation, however, it is necessary to determine what caused it. In the case of the liability insurance famine, this determination was easy, most commentators and participants put the blame on the civil justice system. One strain of argument was expressed in terms of an increasingly litigious population and a "litigation explosion" in the courts. Those making this argument asserted that Americans had become "the most litigious society in the world", that "across the country, people are suing each other with abandon", and that "everybody in the USA suddenly wants to sue anybody with liability insurance coverage" . . . [T]his argument actually predates the 1986 famine, but [it] seems to have been intensified by the liability insurance crisis. The assertion that Americans are now litigious is the conceptual core of the rhetoric surrounding the liability insurance crisis.

A second cause of the insurance crisis was said to be that juries were "running amok" in giving overly generous awards to plaintiffs, and that the courts were becoming too liberal in permitting new kinds of claims to be brought. The two trains of thought were frequently joined to argue that the sudden increase in cases, coupled with the new generosity of courts and juries in making awards, had caused the insurance companies to suffer major losses and thus forced them to drive up their premium charges. The Justice Department's Report stated this position succinctly, "The increase in the number of tort lawsuits and the level of awarded damages (or settlements) in and of itself has an obvious inflating effect on insurance premiums". Showing rather less restraint, a *USA Today* editorial asserted that "greed has turned the temple of justice, long a hallowed place, into a pigsty. The time has come to clean it up." Put bluntly, the liability insurance crisis was thus blamed on a newly litigious American population that brings improper cases ("We have met the enemy and he is us," as Pogo once said), and on a legal system that encourages people to do so. These causes were, as the Justice Department said, obvious. The reforms suggested by these and other commentators were basically aimed at making cases harder to bring and harder to win, and at limiting the amounts that could be awarded if a plaintiff were still to succeed. These reforms of the legal system would serve to discourage the greedy, litigious plaintiffs, and thus to restore order to the courts and to society.

Pointing to the "obvious" responsibility of increased litigation rates and awards for the insurance liability crisis is to suggest that this analysis of the situation is common sense; anyone can see that it is so. However, research on the subject indicates that the case may not be so simple. Before discussing the research findings, it should be noted that an alternative explanation for the liability insurance famine has also been suggested, which is that the sharp increase in prices is due to the cyclical nature of the insurance business. This argument has been raised by lawyers' associations, the National Association of Attorneys General and the National Consumers' Union. In this view, the insurance business is driven by larger economic factors affecting investment markets, and the present crisis is due to the competitive activities of the insurance companies themselves. The pattern is one of boom and bust, growth, followed by sharp competition that induces dramatic price cutting and the acceptance of bad risks, followed by hard times when the bad risks must be paid off and the lower prices have led to a decline in cash flow. This sequence of events has recurred several times over approximately the last forty years.

The alternative argument is complex, and its merits cannot be evaluated here, but it is important to know that a counter to the argument blaming the legal system for the liability insurance crisis does exist. This alternative is gaining in acceptance: even pro-business journals like *Forbes* and *The Economist* accept it as part of the explanation for the insurance crisis, and at least one large insurance company (American International Group) mentions the practices of the insurance industry as partly responsible for the liability insurance famine. Further, fourteen states have passed laws regulating some aspect of the insurance business as a means of combating the liability insurance crisis. These laws were enacted as part of the legislation reforming the civil justice system, but the provisions regarding insurance were much weaker than those addressed to the legal system. The most frequent insurance regulation (passed by eleven states) was to require that the insurance industry supply data to state regulatory authorities. The insurance industry has strongly resisted any regulation, and at least one state (West Virginia), under heavy insurance industry pressure has repealed the section of its laws aimed at regulating the companies.

The existence of this alternative argument and the insurance industry's response to attempts to regulate its practices bring us back to the view of crisis—as an arbitrary label that can disguise a recurring condition as a unique unforeseeable event. If the alternative argument were to be accepted, it is likely that the legislative response would be to attempt to reform the insurance system rather than the courts. The insurance industry, however, is devoting a $6.5 million dollar public relations campaign towards the goal of obtaining reform of the civil justice system. The "public service announcements" mentioned earlier, which dwell on the faults of the courts system, are part of that campaign. Many of them suggest that readers or viewers write the Insurance Information Institute ("A non-profit action and information center") for further information; those who did so would receive a nine page pamphlet entitled *The Lawsuit Crisis*. Thus, whereas the liability insurance famine was itself undoubtedly real, the promulgation of the view that the courts were responsible for the situation may have been a diversionary tactic by the insurance industry and other business interests to direct attention away from the industry's own practices. In addition, the crisis presented an opportunity to bring about changes in the civil justice system that the insurance industry had long sought. If awards were to become harder to win and for lower amounts when won, the insurance industry would have to pay out less money. Thus blaming the legal system for the liability insurance famine would offer substantial rewards to the insurance industry.

Empirical Questions and Research Findings on Civil Justice

In view of the seriousness of the situation and the urgent need to correct it, one might have expected the various commentators and policymakers to have sought substantial reliable data on the factors that might have caused the insurance crisis. Instead, a few statistics were cited repeatedly to show that the courts were responsible for the problem, with little or no effort made to check these figures for reliability or representativeness. In the light of more recent research, the figures seem questionable on both counts. I will briefly discuss some of these questions, not to prove or disprove the issue, but rather to show that the figures can be seriously challenged and do not themselves prove the responsibility of the legal system for the liability insurance crisis.

The most basic claim is that there has been a "litigation explosion," an enormous increase in the numbers of cases filed in American courts. For example, a syndicated columnist has asserted that "massive, mushrooming litigation" is "clogging the courts" and causing "horrendous ruptures and dislocations at a flabbergasting cost to the nation". Similar sentiments have been expressed by other columnists, editorial writers, law deans and professors, judges, and then-Chief Justice Warren Burger. Available data cast doubt on these assertions, however. In the state courts, where over 98 percent of lawsuits are filed, per capita rates of cases filed declined over the period 1981–1984, though they had climbed in the period 1978–1981. In the federal courts, civil case filings did increase substantially over the decade 1975–1984, but the increases were not uniform. The aggregate figures for the federal courts can be broken down by type of case. The largest increases were actually caused by government lawsuits against individuals to recover overpayment of veterans' benefits (up 6,683%!) and by suits for reinstatement on the social security rolls by people who were stricken from them under a new government policy (up 413%). These two kinds of cases between them accounted for close to half of the total increase over the decade, and they can hardly be seen as evidence of a new litigiousness among the population.

If we break down the total figures and look at torts, which are the kinds of suits most relevant to the liability insurance crisis, and specifically at products liability, the picture is unclear. In the state courts tort filings rose by 9 percent over the six years 1978–1984 while the population grew by 8 percent over that period. More detail is available from the federal courts for the period 1975–1984: tort filings in general increased by 46%, and product liability cases by 272 percent. This last figure in particular may mean that there was an explosion of product liability cases, but [Marc] Galanter points out that many of the cases involved single products which injured many people, such as asbestos (which accounted for approximately one third of the products liability cases in 1985) and the dalkon shield intrauterine device case. In any event, in the light of available data it is by no means clear that there has been an "explosion" of litigated cases, as charged by those who would hold the legal system responsible for the liability insurance crisis.

Neither is there clear evidence for the proposition that judges and juries have been "running amok" in making generous awards and thus increasing costs to the insurance companies. Perhaps the most commonly cited figures concern the magic number of $1 million. Thus *Time* [Magazine] states that "The average verdict in product liability cases now tops $1 million; preliminary figures for 1985 indicate that the average verdict in medical malpractice cases also exceeded $1 million for the first time." The source of the figures appears to be Jury Verdict Research Inc., a firm that gathers figures on jury verdicts throughout the country and sells the data to lawyers as an aid in negotiating settlements. However, the selection criteria used by Jury Verdicts Research in compiling their data biases their figures towards higher awards, and the firm itself has stated that their figures should not be considered evidence of "skyrocketing claims". The other frequently cited source of data was a Rand Corporation study of civil jury verdicts in Cook County, Illinois, but this one jurisdiction, which includes Chicago, can not be seen as representative of the country as a whole. Further, the use of average (arithmetic mean) awards is not appropriate in this realm, as most awards are for far less than this average, which is thus driven by the relatively few very large awards. A more representative measure would be the median award, which is less affected by the outliers.

More representative and appropriate data have been gathered by researchers at the American Bar Foundation, who gathered data on jury verdicts in 43 counties in 10 states, generally for the period 1981–1985. While not claiming that their data constitute a representative sample of jury awards in the United States, they do say that their survey reflects "a combination of regional balance and available source materials". Instead of using means, they use medians, and their figures are strikingly different from those usually cited by proponents of the liability insurance crisis as being caused by the legal system.

Median jury awards in civil cases in 29 of the 43 sites are below $50,000 (and below $25,000 in 23 sites) and in the majority of cases the 75th percentile is below $100,000. The median award is over $50,000 in fourteen sites, all but one of which are in California and New York, and the California figures may be biased towards the higher end because of the structure of the available data. The only true hot spot in terms of high jury awards in the locations studied is New York City, where the awards are much higher than in the rest of the country and the rest of New York State.

. . . [P]roduct liability and medical malpractice awards are significantly higher than those in the general run of cases, but such cases make up small proportions of the total number of jury verdicts. Further, medical malpractice and product liability cases often involve catastrophic injuries, so it is hard to assert that larger awards in these kinds of cases are necessarily, or even often, unjustified or improper.

Again, these data are not mentioned to prove or disprove the argument that the legal system is to blame for the liability insurance crisis, but to show that there are data that cast doubt on that assertion. What is perhaps most interesting is that, until the publication of Galanter's first piece on the so-called litigation explosion [in 1983],[98] few had bothered to ask whether there really was a problem with the civil justice system. Instead, it seems to have been "common sense"; everyone knew there was a litigation explosion, so the evidence for it did not need to be checked.

Galanter's challenge to this received wisdom was noteworthy enough to warrant stories in *Time, Newsweek,* and the *New York Times.* Nevertheless, it does not seem to have diminished the growth of the litigation explosion literature, particularly in regard to the liability insurance crisis. Some highly respectable commentators simply dismissed the Galanter challenge without discussing it. Thus, for example, a former United States Attorney General, asked to comment on a Galanter piece in a law review, stated that "the real crisis facing the civil justice system cannot be seen as Professor Galanter suggests through the application of statistical paradigms." Similarly, a United States Circuit Court of Appeals judge (and former University of Chicago law professor) called Galanter's data "interesting but very spotty" and hence unpersuasive (Posner 1985)[99]—a position that might qualify, in view of the nature of the Galanter critique, as an academic version of the old its-all-done-with-mirrors trick. Most telling, however, is the continued growth of the litigation explosion literature and the assertion that this explosion is responsible for the liability insurance famine, repeating the claims that Galanter and others have questioned without

98. [The reference is to Marc Galanter, "Reading the Landscape of Disputes: What We Know and Don't Know (and Think We Know) About Our Allegedly Contentious and Litigious Society," 31 *UCLA Law Review* 4 (1983).].

99. [The reference is to Richard Posner, *The Federal Courts: Crisis and Reform* (Cambridge, Mass.: Harvard University Press, 1985).]

mentioning the contrary evidence. Despite the widespread publicity given the challenges, the received wisdom continues to reign, impervious to contradictory data.

ARGUING BY ANECDOTE: THE TACTICAL VALUE OF OUTRAGEOUS STORIES

One reason why contradictory data may have had little effect on discussions of the supposed litigation explosion and consequent liability insurance famine could be that numerical data have not really been central to perceptions of these phenomena. Much of the rhetoric of the litigation explosion hinges on anecdotes, presented as true stories, which portray the population as litigious and the courts as either blind or stupid in their failure to stop improper suits. These "horror stories" are promulgated by the insurance industry and some business interests, as part of a campaign to reform the civil justice system.

The use of anecdotes is an example of "the tactical uses of passion," a recourse to emotion rather than reason in argument, which may be able to forestall questioning of a speaker's statements by creating an emotional attachment to his or her positions. One such tactic is "the rhetoric of assertion," "those devices that allow one to make assertions, to close off questioning and doubt, and to exclude other peoples' assertions." [F.G.] Bailey suggests that the use of "vivid examples" may be useful aids because they render discourse more immediate and concrete. One might go further, however, and suggest that certain kinds of "vivid examples" may accomplish directly one of the main tasks of this rhetoric, the acceptance of a speaker's opinions or values as facts, something that no sensible person could deny.

. . . [O]ne way to create this acceptance is simply to present an opinion as fact . . . . I suggest that this device can also be extended: if certain facts are true, then "by the very nature of things" a larger truth also holds. Anecdotes, if believable, may in this way be used as assertions of a greater truth. The more believable the anecdote, the more credible the greater "truth" it implies—and the less likely that a counterargument will be attempted.

The trick with such a rhetorical tactic may be in constructing believable anecdotes. One way of doing so is to make the stories concrete and heavily detailed. Another way is to present an anecdote that fits the audience's common sense of the way the world operates. If we recall again Geertz's comment that common sense makes its case by not having to make it, a story that meets the local cultural logic of the nature of things seems likely to have inherent believability without need of substantiation. If such a story implies a greater truth that is also compatible with common sense the anecdote, and the greater truth, may be nearly immune from contradiction.

Much of the argument that the courts have caused the liability insurance famine has been supported by anecdotes of outrageous cases and outlandish awards. A few particularly graphic tales have been cited repeatedly, such as the following:

The Psychic and the CAT Scan: This story was carried by AP and UPI, and appeared in many newspapers; this version was recounted by *Consumer Reports:* "Judith Haimes was awarded close to $1-million by a Philadelphia jury last March after she said that a CAT scan at Temple University Hospital made her lose her psychic abilities."

The Pinto and the Horse: This story was broadcast on the CBS program *60 Minutes,* and has also appeared in *Forbes* ("The Tort Reform Quagmire," 1986) as follows:

> Ford Motor . . . lost a $1.5 million jury decision to the estate of a woman who was killed when her car hit a horse, causing it to jump through the roof of her 1980 Ford Pinto.

The Ladder in the Manure: This tale was also broadcast on *60 Minutes:* A man who was shingling a barn set his ladder up in a pile of manure. The man fell and was injured when the ladder slipped in the manure, and won $300,000 from the manufacturer of the ladder because the manufacturer had not warned the buyer about the danger of setting the ladder up in something as slippery as manure.

The Drunk Driver and the Phone Booth: This story was originally circulated as part of an ultimately successful effort to deny re-election to then Chief Justice of California Rose Bird, but was picked up by *The Wall Street Journal* and used in an editorial on the liability insurance crisis, as follows: "A man is injured when a drunk driver crashed into a telephone booth and California Chief Justice Rose Bird rules that the company that designed the booth is liable."

These anecdotes, brief as they are, have great evocative power. Their sheer outrageousness sums up the problems of the civil justice system, for any system that permits awards in these cases must be in urgent need of repair. At the same time, these stories seem to conform with some elements of American cultural logic, because they were apparently so plausible as to be accepted initially without much question. Indeed, one of the most interesting features of these stories is that most journalists fail to check the facts before running the story. Grossly inaccurate stories have appeared in such respected publications as *The Economist, The Wall Street Journal,* and the CBS news show *60 Minutes.* Even respected scholars in the field of law and social science seem to accept these stories at face value.

In their widespread acceptance without need of substantiation, these stories are similar to urban folklore. I will look more closely at why the stories are so evocative in the next section. First, however, the cases behind the stories should be examined more thoroughly. What turns out to be outrageous is not the actions of courts and juries, but rather the distorted forms in which the cases are presented. On closer examination, they look rather different:

The Psychic and the CAT Scan: Consumer Reports investigated this case, and reports that the judge told the jury to disregard the assertion of loss of psychic powers. The verdict was actually based on the jury's determination that the hospital had been negligent in administering a contrast dye to the plaintiff's brain, leading to adverse physical reactions, after the patient had informed the doctor that she was allergic to the dye. Further, the jury's verdict was thrown out by the judge, who ordered the case retried. Thus no money was ever awarded for lost psychic powers.

The Pinto and the Horse: This case was investigated by two reporters from the monthly paper *The American Lawyer,* who went to original court documents and spoke with the plaintiff's lawyer. In their account the horse did not "jump through the roof," but rather slid across it when it was struck by the car, and the roof collapsed under the horse's weight. Federal safety standards require that a car roof withstand the lesser of either 5000 pounds or one-and-a-half times its unloaded weight, in order to protect the passengers in the event of a rollover, and the Pinto's roof collapsed under much less weight. Thus the suit concerned a defective product that had led to someone's death.

The Ladder in the Manure: This matter was also investigated by the reporters from *The American Lawyer,* who again went to the court documents and also interviewed some of the jurors who made the award. They found that the matter of the manure had little or nothing to do with the case. Instead, the jurors found that the evidence showed that the ladder, which had a safety rating that indicated that it could support 1,000 pounds at midpoint, broke with less than 450 pounds on it. Thus, rather than being a case of a runaway jury rewarding a plaintiff who was injured by his own stupidity, this too concerned a defective product that had caused severe injury.

The Drunk Driver and the Phone Booth: According to the American Trial Lawyers' Association, in the case of *Bigbee v. Pacific Telephone Co.* five of six justices on the California Supreme Court, including Chief Justice Bird, ruled in 1983 that the question of liability in this case should be decided by a jury rather than dismissed out of hand, as the trial court had done. This particular phone booth had been hit by a car at least once before, so the accident was not a freak occurrence, and it had a jammed door, which prevented the plaintiff from fleeing when he saw the drunk bearing down on him. The ruling of the court was that under these circumstances a jury could find the company liable, and thus that the trial judge had erred in not letting them consider it. The Court did not itself express any view on liability. The effect of the Supreme Court's decision was to return the case to the lower court for trial, but a settlement was reached without trial.

Other such horror stories have also been debunked, but the genre continues. The tactical value of such stories is great, because by their emotional impact they obviate the lack of solid data on the issue at hand. Further, they cannot be easily countered, for only a callous politician could assert that there is not an urgent problem when confronted with such stories. Anecdotes thus seem particularly useful for characterizing a situation as a crisis, perhaps more so than quantitative data, because while data can be debated, who can counter a good anecdote?

"LITIGIOUSNESS" AS AN AMERICAN CULTURAL CATEGORY

There is a common pattern to these anecdotes. In all of them, an innocent defendant is forced to pay a large award to a plaintiff who was himself to blame for the injury, or who was simply the unfortunate victim of bad luck. The stories thus carry two negative connotations for the legal system. The first is that the courts are flawed in that they make bad decisions in the cases brought to them and give improper awards. The second is farther reaching, by rewarding these undeserving cases, the courts encourage people to bring more improper cases. Underlying the entire rhetoric is the view that the cases are litigious, improper subjects for court action. They should not even be brought to court, much less succeed. This concept is the key to the rhetoric on the litigation explosion and the associated arguments on the liability insurance crisis.

On the surface there is an apparent contradiction in saying that Americans think that something should not be brought to court. Law and legal institutions in America are generally seen as having a great deal of public support, and judges and courts generally receive high ratings in public opinion surveys. Tocqueville, of course, saw respect for the law as a basic element of American democracy, whereas [D.] Schneider viewed law as a basic cultural order of American kinship.[*]

The matter is not so simple, however. Recent ethnographic work on litigation in America indicates that while courts and law may be viewed favorably in the abstract, their invocation in certain kinds of cases is not. Specifically, there seems a marked inclination to see as improper the invocation of the legal system as a means of redressing personal wrongs or gaining compensation for injuries. Such use of the courts is viewed as litigious, or, more colloquially, "quick to sue," or "sue happy". If Schneider is right and Americans view law as an order based on reason, this kind of case, which is unreasonable, can not be legitimately legal.

---

[*] [The reference is to D. Schneider, *American Kinship: A Cultural Account* 2d ed. (Chicago: University of Chicago Press, 1980).] Thus one might expect that litigation, as the invocation of law, would be favorably viewed by Americans.

Carol Greenhouse [in an unpublished paper] draws on linguistic and ethnographic evidence to argue that individual recourse to law for compensation for one's personal physical or social injuries (for example, civil rights) is distasteful to most Americans because it violates a basic principle of American culture: equality. Americans view equality as essential to proper social relations, but the invocation of a court in a personal dispute is an attempt to transform the opposition of equal persons into a hierarchical relationship of the plaintiff and the state versus the defendant.

David Engel (1984)[100] makes a related point in his analysis of views on court use in rural Illinois. His informants held individualism as a guiding tenet, with the proper order of society being one in which individuals contracted their own obligations and were responsible for carrying them out. These people viewed personal injury litigation as an attempt to have the state impose obligations on the opposing party, who had not assumed them voluntarily. Further, personal injury cases were seen as violating the norm of personal responsibility in that they reward people who have not earned the money. Thus this kind of litigation was perforce improper.

Yet a third reason why litigation for one's own benefit may be seen as improper can be inferred from Hochschild's study (1981)[101] of American beliefs concerning distributive justice, which indicates that redistribution of wealth by government action is not favored by most Americans. Awards in personal injury suits may be seen as attempts to achieve such redistribution, and thus as improper. This theme parallels that expressed by Engel's informants concerning the impropriety of rewarding someone who has not earned the money through work.

These three themes—equality, individual responsibility, and hostility to redistribution—are mutually reinforcing. Their effect on perceptions of the propriety of litigation can be further explored by looking at what kinds of civil cases are considered proper use of the courts, primarily debt or contract. Engel's informants were very firm in seeing contract cases as the proper realm for court action. A member of the county sheriff's department in the rural county that Engel studied stated that many people thought that the police should simply go and collect overdue contractual debts, without waiting for a court order. The informant acknowledged that such an action by the police is impossible without a court order, but stated that "a lot of people" "feel that they shouldn't have to hire an attorney for something that's an agreement. It's a law, it should be acted upon."

---

100. [The reference is to David Engel, "The Ovenbird's Song: Insiders, Outsiders and Personal Injuries in an American Community," 18 *Law & Society Review* 551 (1984).]

101. [The reference is to Jennifer Hochschild, *What's Fair? American Beliefs About Distributive Justice* (Cambridge, Mass.: Harvard University Press, 1981).]

The sanctity of contract in America is a fourth theme, and one that is more than just a folk belief. Much of legal scholarship and thought has been based on a transactional view of society and law, in which individuals should be free to bargain with each other. This view is encapsulated in the provision of the United States Constitution, Article I Section 10.1 that no state shall pass any "law impairing the obligation of contracts."

The propriety of contract cases may also be inferred from their absence from the litigation explosion and liability famine horror stories, all of which are concerned with tort actions. It is striking that little reference is made to what is arguably the most run-amok jury of all time, the Texas jury that awarded close to ten billion dollars to Pennzoil against Texaco after the latter interfered with Pennzoil's alleged contract to buy a third oil company. Even when the case is mentioned, it is not seen as litigious; Pennzoil is generally granted legitimacy in its invocation of the courts in the contract-related matter. Similarly, no mention is made of the $52 million that an Illinois jury awarded an ice cream manufacturer who asserted that McDonald's had breached an oral contract with him. A deal, it seems, is a deal, to be enforced in court if necessary. Other personal matters, however, are none of the courts' business.

THE CULTURAL LOGIC OF THE CAMPAIGN AGAINST THE COURTS

There is a pronounced moral tone to the litigation explosion literature, the "flood" of litigation is seen as a sign of the atrophy of traditional bonds and the moral decline of the nation. As expressed by an attorney who specializes in defending against personal injury claims, "the fundamental cause of this [juries that have "run amok"] . . . is the basic erosion in our society of the philosophy of individual responsibility.". Individualism is basic to western culture, and self-reliance has been seen as an American "core value." In bringing an interpersonal dispute or a products liability or personal injury case a person thus violates important principles of American culture, and is unworthy of receiving benefits from his litigation.

I believe that it is for this reason that those who argue that there is a crisis in American civil justice have gotten such dramatic impact from the horror stories. The roofer and the Pinto driver in the original stories are careless or stupid, at fault themselves for their injuries, while the "psychic" is to most people probably a nut. The man injured in the phone booth was unlucky, but then he became greedy in trying to gouge the innocent phone company. Why should the courts reward stupidity, or lunacy, or greed? Indeed, how can they properly do so?

By portraying the plaintiffs in these cases as so obviously unworthy and the defendants as blameless, the cases become violations of common sense. Anyone can see that they are outrageous. The only exception seems to be judges and juries. For the real importance of these stories lies not so much in the fact that someone is perverse enough as to try to bring the cases, but rather that courts are so foolish as to accept them. Geertz's analysis of common sense is again pertinent; one who does not exercise common sense, who is not able to come to sensible conclusions on the basis of the accepted "actualities of experience" is a fool. The civil justice system must be reformed because judges and juries have become foolish. They lack the common sense that prevailed in earlier times. The evidence is the horror story, that litigious plaintiffs succeed.

Of course, to say that horror stories succeed because they play into dominant themes of American culture is not to say that "culture" or the themes themselves are deterministic in any mechanical sense. Instead, the cultural themes are seen as resources that can be drawn on by social actors as they seek to serve their own ends. The invocation of such themes in an argument concerning the interpretation of elements of the social world may lead, if the argument is accepted, to the establishment of the themes themselves as "common sense," accepted wisdom. The particular cultural themes may in this way become part of what [Pierre] Bourdieu terms the habitus, those largely unconscious principles that structure interpretation and hence social action. Political argument may thus aim at altering common sense by selectively playing on some cultural themes to the exclusion of others.

The non-mechanistic nature of this model can be seen in the present context, because there are also many folk beliefs in American culture that envision businessmen as greedy and out to take advantage of the public, and these could be cited to build the case that the insurance companies themselves are responsible for the "crisis." Why these themes have not been invoked as successfully as those that attack the courts is an important question. One reason may be that even if beliefs unfavorable to industry are widespread, the anticourt arguments succeed because those making them are better placed to make their case than their opponents. As mentioned earlier, the insurance industry has been engaged in a $6.5 million public relations campaign to blame the "crisis" on the courts. This campaign may be effective both because it draws on established themes in American culture and because it is organized and well supported, whereas those who would argue against it are less well organized and do not have comparable resources to devote to countering the insurance industry's argument. Further, by focusing the debate on the legal system, the insurance campaign has largely pre-empted other considerations, at least in the short term. "Crises" may provide some of the best opportunities for this kind of strategic argument, and elites are often best placed to sustain such a campaign. These last two points will be considered further below.

COMMON SENSE AND HEGEMONY: THE LIMITS OF REASON

Theory 1: *Common sense represents matters . . . as being what they are in the simple nature of the case . . . . They are depicted as inherent in the situation, intrinsic aspects of reality, the way things go.*

Theory 2: *Every established order tends to produce . . . the naturalization of its own arbitrariness.*

Practice: Are you not aware that conviction has never yet been produced by an appeal to reason, which only makes people uncomfortable? If you want to move them, you must address your arguments to prejudice and the political motive.

The view that most non-contract civil matters do not belong in court seems widespread. A poll commissioned by the insurance industry in 1986 indicated that 64 percent of the population thinks that too many lawsuits are being filed and that 56 percent believe that the courts are awarding too much in civil cases, and other polls have reported similar findings. Another insurance industry supported poll indicates that a majority of people would favor the reforms proposed by the insurance industry, to make cases harder to win and for less money. Even many of the people who themselves bring cases to lower courts agree that the matter does not really belong there, saying that they have only invoked the law because there was no other option as all other attempts at gaining satisfaction failed.

Even legal professionals and those who staff the legal system, who might have been expected to have favored the use of the law (and, not incidentally, of their own services) dislike many non-contract civil cases. At the lowest level of courts, interpersonal disputes are seen as "garbage cases," "not worth the court's time." At the upper reaches of the legal system, former Chief Justice Burger often spoke of the unsuitability of courts for many kinds of civil cases. In fact, the "litigation explosion" literature in legal journals has been characterized as "the product of a narrow elite of judges (mostly federal), professors and deans at eminent law schools, and practitioners who practice in large firms and deal with big clients and big cases." These few high status individuals have set the tone and terminology of the entire issue.

The liability insurance crisis thus seems to be a case where an elite discourse has become the sensibility of the common person: common sense which indicates hegemony. The process of shaping such common sense involves the utilization of the political power inherent in shared cultural themes to achieve specific goals, which at the same time restates the cultural system. It is not necessarily the case that the cultural themes being utilized fit only the course of action advocated, but once that course has been established, other possible interpretations are nearly ruled out. A hegemonic schema is one that is not only dominant, but that has also become, for most if not all members of the society, the only conceivable position. This aspect of hegemony is exemplified by the liability insurance anecdotes, in the transformation of real legal cases into anecdotes illustrating the flaws of the courts. Judging from the more full information presented by the debunkers of the anecdotes, in each case it was reasonable to see the matter as the jury did, as involving a plaintiff seriously injured by the negligent action of the defendant. Yet each anecdote instead portrays a blameless defendant and an unworthy plaintiff, and it is this second version that is transmitted, usually without question, by reputable scholars and news media.

Elites will generally be better placed than most other people to establish such hegemonic concepts. In the present context, for example, it is quite possible that the public opinion surveys indicating dissatisfaction with the courts are reflecting the insurance industry's public relations campaign. However, this is not to suggest that hegemony may be easily achieved by conscious efforts, or to imply conspiracy by any class of social actors. As Bourdieu points out, actions by a dominant or elite class that are not consciously coordinated may be harmonious because of the common interests of those making them, and may thus reinforce each other without being orchestrated. In the present case, I am asserting that the repetition of an argument by various elites is harmonious and effective because it independently draws on a body of important cultural themes, in the process restating and reinforcing the impact of those themes that may, if they are accepted, widely be viewed as "common sense." The themes themselves, and hence common sense, are not a static body of beliefs, but change as they are restated. Because elites are better positioned to publicize such restatements, they are better placed to structure the development of the conceptual framework.

Because they require urgent action, "crises," once established, may provide the best opportunities for this kind of manipulation of common sense. If it seems that the apparent crisis must be met by immediate action, it becomes possible to avoid much rigorous investigation of the situation and increases reliance on anecdotal arguments. As the American litigation horror stories show, anecdotes can be rather easily constructed to illustrate the points one wants to make. Thus the values exhibited by a set of cultural beliefs may be manipulated to justify an urgent course of action, with that justification itself then altering perceptions of the symbolic system, and thus common sense.

What provokes unease in this analysis is the limited role of reason. The rhetoric involved in this kind of manipulation draws on . . . "the tactical uses of passion" rather than the dispassionate analysis of data. Indeed, as we have seen, involving common sense may largely preclude the consideration of data. It is here, however, where interpretive anthropological analyses of culture may be most useful. If nothing else, anthropologists are experts at challenging common sense. Whereas cultural interpretations of the kind used in this paper may not decide issues such as whether the liability famine is caused by the legal system, they may serve to cast doubt on common sense answers to political questions—and establishing such doubt could well be the most important element in widening debate. Thus the role of interpretive anthropology may [not be] to resolve issues, but to raise the level of the debate. ☐

NOTES & QUESTIONS

1. The "tort crisis" described in Hayden has led to another theme: litigation is hurting America's competitiveness in a world economy. American business, it is alleged, has had to pay the costs of medical insurance and products liability unlike their foreign competitors; and this raises their prices and hurts them in world markets. Much of this case also rests on anecdotes, many of them totally fabricated. The proponents of reform have cited data trying to show that tort lawsuits and jury awards to plaintiffs have been increasing sharply. Michael J. Saks, "Do We Really Know Anything About the Behavior of the Tort Litigation System—and Why Not?," 140 *University of Pennsylvania Law Review* 1147 (1992), has analyzed the litigation explosion claims very critically. He points out that we know little, if anything, about the number of claims that could have gone to court but did not. Moreover, those arguing that we face a crisis have never established that tort and product liability trials reach the wrong result in a significant number of cases. Saks concludes:

> A comprehensive picture [of the tort litigation system], based on the best available evidence, suggests a system that behaves quite differently from what is widely assumed.
>
> A tiny fraction of accidental deaths and injuries become claims for compensation; even known actionable injuries rarely become lawsuits. In both federal and state courts, torts has not been the largest or the fastest growing area of civil litigation. The great majority of all kinds of civil suits result in negotiated settlements. On average, these settlements undercompensate the plaintiff's losses. Modest losses are fully or overcompensated, but the larger the loss suffered, the more pronounced the undercompensation. The great majority of jury verdicts reach the same result that judges would in the same cases. The degree of judge-jury agreement is all the more striking when we recognize that the clearest cases are removed from the system before trial. In the aggregate, jury awards are remarkably predictable. Over half the variation can be accounted for merely by knowing the severity of the plaintiff's injuries. Paralleling settlements, however, jury awards overcompensate small losses, undercompensate larger losses, and on average undercompensate plaintiffs. Judicial review at and after trial tends to reduce rather than increase awards, most dramatically for punitive damages.
>
> At nearly every stage, the tort litigation system operates to diminish the likelihood that injurers will have to compensate their victims. Only a small fraction of the costs created by actionable injuries will ever be paid by the injurers. Although the tort system plays only a tiny part in

the compensation of victims of accidental injury, and does so at relatively high transaction costs, it may be more efficient and effective as a deterrent. At the same time that it provides such infrequent and partial compensation, it succeeds in generating huge overestimates of its potency in the minds of potential defendants.

Although the preceding sketch is faithful to the available empirical evidence, the available evidence provides a poor basis for resting any conclusions about the behavior of the tort litigation system . . . . In short, official statistics have failed to track much of the most basic information about the performance of the system, and they continue to be deficient in many respects . . . .

Reform efforts must guess at which problems are real and which are mythical. Being the product of guesswork, some reforms will produce effects contrary to the intentions of their makers; indeed, some already have.

For a similar critical analysis of the data involved in the supposed insurance crisis, see Stephen Daniels, "The Question of Jury Competence and the Politics of Civil Justice Reform: Symbols, Rhetoric, and Agenda Setting," 52 *Law and Contemporary Problems* 269 (1989).

2. The insurance and litigation explosion cause produced reforms in many states. Milo Geyelin, "Overhaul of Civil Law in Colorado Produces Quite Mixed Results," *Wall Street Journal,* March 3, 1992, A1, col. 1, reports:

Everyone talks about legal reform, but Colorado has bet the ranch on it.

State laws here protect ski resorts and dude ranches from lawsuits over accidental injuries. Bars are virtually immune from legal blame for the acts of drunk patrons. Jury awards for pain and suffering top out at $250,000. And defendants can't be forced to ante up more in damages just because they have the deepest pockets . . . .

Shocked by soaring commercial and municipal insurance rates, Colorado began reforming its civil system six years ago. Though many states have enacted laws to limit civil suits and damage awards, none has done more than Colorado.

The idea was to make insurance more available, knock down premiums and give businesses a breather from costly litigation. More than that, reformers wanted to redress what they perceived as an injustice: the prevalence of unpredictable and often unjustified jury awards spurred on by avaricious lawyers working for contingency fees.

So what's the verdict? Insurance companies that fled Colorado in droves in the mid-1980s, blaming lawyers and high jury awards, have come back, bringing with them increased competition. Limits on damages have helped lower insurance companies' payouts, leading to some drops in insurance rates. Lawsuits of dubious merit are filed less frequently now because they are harder to prove. Defendants seem less inclined to settle out of court just to avoid the nuisance and risk of litigating.

But, to the dismay even of some reformers, that's not the entire story. Commercial insurance premiums have gone down much less than the business community anticipated. Auto insurance, the major insurance cost for consumers, is actually more expensive than it was before the legal reforms were passed.

Frivolous suits are less likely to reap big awards, but so are lawsuits that nearly anyone would consider valid. Cases involving catastrophic injury to the plaintiff and egregious wrongdoing by the defendant are highlighting the flip side of reform: The most seriously hurt are most likely to see their damages reduced the most under the new laws.

A propane gas explosion in the mountain resort of Crested Butte in March 1990 illustrates some of the unexpected problems with legal reform. Investigators found that the gas supplier, Salgas, Inc., had violated more than a dozen state safety regulations. Three people were killed, and 14 were injured. One of the injured, Roxie Lypps, a former teacher and part-time bank employee, was buried beneath bricks and debris and had severe burns over 40% of her body. After two years of painful burn therapy and skin grafts, Ms. Lypps is still unable to work full time and faces an increased risk of skin cancer.

A Denver state court jury awarded Ms. Lypps $1.5 million last November. Of that amount, $486,000 was for punitive damages intended to punish Salgas and its parent, Empire Gas Co. of Lebanon, Mo., for negligence. The rest was compensation for injuries. But in December, a judge was forced to reduce the total amount by more than half. One reason: The jury's award of $600,000 for pain and suffering was over the state limit of $250,000.

That reduced Ms. Lypps's compensatory damages to $621,642. Then another Colorado law came into play: Individual defendants in civil suits can't be forced to pay more than their share of the blame when others at fault have no money. In this case, Empire and Salgas blamed the blast on a repair two previous owners had made. The previous owners were out of business and uninsured. But the jurors weren't told this because another Colorado law prohibits lawyers from disclosing whether defendants have insurance. When the jury divided the blame equally among all four companies, the net effect was to cut Ms. Lypps's remaining compensation to $310,822.

That, in turn, knocked down the punitive damages because Colorado law prohibits juries from assessing more in damages to punish wrongdoers than they award to compensate victims. Ultimately, Ms. Lypps expects to receive a total of about $316,000 after all her legal fees and other expenses are deducted.

"I'm well beyond [concern over] the money," says Ms. Lypps, 47 year old. "But the court system should allow the jury to award what they feel is fair . . . . To me it's totally unfair. We end up being the victims again."

In cases of serious injuries such as hers, what remains may not be enough to pay for medical care and rehabilitation. Because defendants and their insurers are now insulated from huge damages, costs are transferred to state and federally funded health programs when victims' insurance limits run out . . . .

Highly publicized accidents such as the one at Crested Butte and another at Berthoud Pass, near Denver, are contributing to legislators' caution [about continued reform efforts]. In the Berthoud Pass incident, a state road worker clearing fallen rocks from the pass shoved a 6.7-ton boulder down the mountain in 1987, thinking it would roll just a few feet. The rock crashed into a tour bus 725 feet below, killing eight and injuring 25.

One tourist, Marcus Lang, who was blinded and brain-damaged, lingered in Denver General Hospital for almost a year before he went home to West Germany and died. Under Colorado's governmental immunity law, toughened in 1986 and upheld by the Colorado Supreme Court this month, the state's total liability for all the victims combined couldn't exceed $400,000. Mr. Lang's medical bills alone exceeded $328,000. (Mr. Lang's estate hasn't received anything as yet from Colorado because the case is still being litigated.)

Many Colorado residents were appalled. "I think we did need legal reform, but now the pendulum has begun to swing back, so the person who needs compensation can get it," says Republican House Majority Leader Scott McInnis, an early reform supporter who now is backing off . . . .

3. Despite articles such as those by Hayden and Saks, newspapers accounts like the *Wall Street Journal* article, and efforts by the American Bar Association, the fight against the "litigation explosion" continues. Why? Part of the explanation may be the unpopularity of lawyers. Lawyers bear the blame; they make money from lawsuits, and therefore they have a selfish reason for whipping up claims. Attacks on lawyers are an old theme in popular culture. We can point to Carl Sandburg's poem, "The Lawyers Know Too Much," in *Smoke and Steel* (New York: Harcourt, Brace & Howe), 1920, where he asks, "Why does a hearse horse snicker hauling a lawyer away?" Anti-lawyer jokes are common. The image is that lawyers create trouble among people who would otherwise be peaceful. For a discussion of the public's negative perceptions of lawyers, see Marc Galanter, "Predators and Parasites: Lawyer-Bashing and Civil Justice," 28 *Georgia Law Review* 633 (1994). Galanter points out that in the 1970s, President Carter and others criticized lawyers for not working to provide greater access to the courts for those who could not afford legal services. During the 1980s, a different group of critics argued that lawyers brought too many cases to court. See also the discussion of the legal profession in Chapter 5.

4. William T. Harris, "A Public Choice Analysis of the Evolution of Tort Law: Liabilities, Lotteries, and Redistribution," 51 *American Journal of Economics and Sociology* 101 (1992), notes that the pay out rates are very similar for tort and lotteries. About half the liability premiums paid by those insured are returned to successful plaintiffs, and about half the total ticket sales in lotteries are returned to winners. He concludes:

There is another similarity insofar as the total number of individuals who "win big" in liability cases and in lotteries is a minuscule percentage of the total population. Although, possibly, both liability insurers and promoters of state lotteries would like the public to believe large numbers of individuals are made instant millionaires from lottery games and lawsuits, the fact is that only a very few fortunate people "win big". Nevertheless, both lawsuits and lotteries allow people the (albeit extremely remote) chance to win large sums of money for a relatively small premium or payment.

Given the similarities between lotteries and current rules of personal injury liability, it can be plausibly argued that a sufficiently large number of individuals have been willing to accept an arguably inefficient system of loss shifting for the same reasons that they have enacted through their state legislatures an arguably inefficient system of wealth transfers. Rational individuals may have chosen to have available the opportunity to participate in another "lottery game," liability lawsuits.

Do you find this plausible? Does it shed any light on why there is a "liability crisis?"

It is easy to exaggerate the response to the crisis. In most states, the movement to reform tort law has not resulted in much change of liability law. No one suggests rolling liability law back to where it was, say, before the liability "explosion" of the past few decades. What does this fact do to Hayden's thesis?

At one point Hayden makes some remarks about American culture. He says that the horror cases shock people because they offend certain root notions of the culture—especially ideas of individualism and self-reliance. But is Hayden correct? In *Total Justice* (New York: Russell Sage Foundation, 1981), Lawrence Friedman tried to explain the rise of high liability in terms of American culture. Friedman's argument is that in the 19th century people did not expect "justice" in the sense of recovery of damages in compensation for injuries. Nobody had insurance, medicine was incapable of curing people, the welfare state did not exist, and plagues, calamities, and depressions occurred at random intervals. All of this made life a colossal drama of uncertainty. But the rise of insurance, the welfare state, modern medicine, and the like produced a culture in which there is a "general expectation of justice." In the event of calamity, Americans now assume *somebody* will pay.

If Friedman is right, how do his ideas square with Hayden's?

DOUBTS AND QUALIFICATIONS ABOUT LAW AS THE PRODUCT OF PUBLIC OPINION

18. *Parental Authority: The Community and the Law*[102]

Julius Cohen,

Reginald A. Robson

and Alan P. Bates

☐ [This important study, a rare example of close collaboration between legal scholars and social scientists, attempted to measure "the moral sense of the community," and compare this "moral sense" with

102. Copyright © 1958 Rutgers University Press. Reprinted from pp. 76–78, 193–95, by permission.

"legal norms". The study was conducted in Nebraska. A trained staff of interviewers administered questions to a carefully selected sample of residents of the state. The total sample population was 860.

The questions concerned various aspects of social and legal norms relating to the authority of parents over children. A sample section of the study follows. First the question is given, as administered to the subjects, then the position of the law is stated, then the "view of the community," then a comparison of the two.]

The Issue: Parental authority to disinherit the child completely. Question 23 deals with this.

QUESTION 23A: "Suppose that either the husband or wife is dead, and the survivor willed all of his or her property to persons or groups outside the family, and left nothing at all for the children. If the parent is legally allowed to do this, it could mean that the child might have to depend on some outside source for the necessities of life. On the other hand, if the parent is prevented by law from doing this, he would not be able to will his property as he sees fit. In these circumstances, do you think that the parent should legally be allowed to will all of his or her property to persons or groups outside the family and leave nothing at all for the children, or should the law prevent this?"

Position of the law: It would seem that the parent would be permitted to disinherit his offspring, except for an amount that would be required to support parentless children under 14. Beyond this exception, the privilege of testamentary disposition would not be affected by the age or economic status of the children, or by the intrinsic worth of the object of the disposition; nor would the privilege be affected if exercise of it resulted in benefit to one child and not to another.

Views of the community: In responding to the situation presented in Question 23A the members of the sample were asked to indicate whether their opinion would be affected by the fact that the child was under or over 21 years of age (23Bi and 23Bii). Following this, in Questions 23Ci and 23Cii, the factor of the economic status of the child was introduced into the picture. Next, in Questions 23Di and 23Dii, respondents were asked to take into consideration with respect to the basic issue the question of the worthiness of the recipients of the parental estate. In the final sub-question (23E), people were asked to suppose that the parent left all his assets to only one of several children, all of whom were in about the same financial circumstances. The way in which community opinion is distributed and its degree of stability in these changing contexts are recorded in Table 12.

A quick comparison of "Allow" and "Prevent" responses for all parts of this question shows that in all cases a clear majority (and in several instances a very large majority) is of the opinion that the law should not allow a parent to disinherit a child completely. We find an extremely high congruence of views where the child is under 21 years

TABLE 12   SHOULD THE LAW ALLOW PARENTS TO DISINHERIT CHILDREN? EXPRESSED IN PERCENTAGES OF TOTAL POPULATION)

Question	Allow	Prevent	Don't Know
23A (See above.)			
23Bi and Bii			
Child is under 21 years of age.	5.5	93.4	1.2
Child is over 21 years of age.	35.5	63.4	1.2
23Ci and Cii			
Child is poor.	7.0	92.0	1.0
Child is well-off financially.	40.8	57.3	1.9
23Di and Dii			
Parents leave assets to unworthy group.	5.1	93.8	1.0
Parents leave assets to worthy group.	18.6	79.2	2.2
23E Discrimination between children exists.	19.4	78.5	2.1

of age, where the child is poor and where the parent leaves his assets to some beneficiary unworthy to receive them.

If the child is over 21 years of age, more than a third of the population would agree that parents should be legally entitled to omit the child from the will. Likewise, where the child is well-off financially in his own right, 40.8% would support a parent's right to make no provision for the child. A much less notable, but still considerable effect is produced by the assumption that the parent wishes to leave all his assets to a worthy cause; 18.6% would agree that the law should support the parent with such a purpose in mind. By and large, however, there appears to be an impressively high degree of agreement in the population that parents do have an obligation to their children which extends beyond their own death.

So far as the relation between community opinion and law on this issue is concerned, it is plain that most persons in the population disagree with the law, except in the case where a parentless child under 14 would be left without support. As indicated earlier, the law in this instance would require the parent's estate to provide support for the child.

[At the end of the study, the authors summed up their findings. They found wide disharmony between social and legal norms in Nebraska. "Of the 17 issues examined, the community and the existing law would disagree as to ten, agree as to five, and perhaps evenly divide as to one . . . . The majority in the community would favor greater legal restrictions on parental authority over the child than the law presently requires" (pp. 193–94).

These findings, somewhat to the authors' surprise, reflected general community feelings and did not vary as between "social groupings." "By and large, there are no substantial differences between the views of the members of various social groupings within the community toward the issues we studied, based on such factors as sex, residential area, religion, age, income, parenthood, schooling and occupation" (p. 195).

Why the great variance between community and legal norms? The authors saw three major factors: the "built-in professional conservatism" of lawyers and judges; the lack of "pressure" from the public for change; and the "inadequacy of prevailing techniques utilized by law-makers for ascertaining the moral sense of the community" (p. 195).] □

19. *Review of Cohen, Robson & Bates*[103]

Luke Cooperrider

57 Michigan Law Review 1119 (1959)

□ A law professor and two sociologists report herein on a joint attempt to assess the degree of congruence between existing legal doctrine, in a defined area of application, and a factor which the authors call "the moral sense of the community." The justification for the study is provided by the law member of the team, and proceeds from the observation that legal scholars, groping for standards of criticism external to the law, seem to gravitate toward a "sense of justice," or of "injustice"— toward a view of morality, at least, which is shared, to some degree, by the people in the community wherein the law is applicable. The authors vigorously and repeatedly disclaim a position on whether or to what extent such a common moral sense should by the law be taken into account. They assert, however, that law-makers, both legislative and judicial, do in fact frequently refer to it, and the argument is that if the moral sense of the community is relevant at all, then it makes sense to consider how that datum may be ascertained more scientifically than by the divination or intuition of the individual judge or legislator. Their study is offered as an example of how this may be done by making use of the developed techniques of public opinion research. They do not suggest, of course, the canvassing of the community's moral sense in order to establish premises for the adjudication of individual cases. It is argued, rather, that within a given area of law it would be possible to establish community reactions to a selected battery of propositions, and that these reactions could then be used as analogical bases for prediction of community reaction to other situations in a way which, to lawyers, would be quite familiar. Their project is an experimental survey of this type in the general area of parent-child relations . . . .

It is, perhaps, unresponsive to argue the merits of the questions which were propounded to the public, for, as I have said, the authors carefully disclaim any position on the extent to which the law should seek to effectuate the community moral sense which they were investigating. They set out to establish a method, not a matrix for the remaking of the law in the area of family relations. They were, nevertheless, unable completely to conceal their feeling that their study could be used by "lawmakers whose juristic philosophy stakes out as an objective a high degree of harmony between the existing law and the moral sense of the community" as a ready-made set of specifications for law revision in the area of family law. Furthermore, as it seems to me, their failure to consider the basic question—what bearing should community moral attitudes have with reference to the specific problems propounded—has led them into a fallacy which is fundamental, and which would be very difficult to avoid in any similar project . . . .

On . . . six issues where disagreement between law and morals was found, the law, at the present time, occupies a position of laissez faire. The questions relate to parental "authority" (1) to determine whether a child may have a college education, (2) to determine the child's religious affiliation, (3) to prevent the child from entering a career of his own choosing, (4) to transfer custody of a child to another person without legal supervision, (5) to disinherit the child, and (6) to treat the child's earnings as the parent's own property. In all six cases it is assumed that the law bestows upon the parent the "authority" indicated, and in all six cases the community view, according to the survey, was that the law should "prevent" the parents from exercising such authority. It is on these six issues that an unequivocal discrepancy is found between the law and the moral standards of the community, and it must be principally in connection with these issues that we judge the authors' assertions that there is a serious lag between law and public opinion, a lag which they suggest is to be attributed to imperfections in the political process, and to the "dissenting acquiescence" of a population too inert to resist.

Considering these six issues, it will be noted that the parental "authority" referred to in the first three instances is nothing more than the de facto compulsion which the parent, by the very existence of the family relation, is enabled to exert. The extent of its legal recognition is that the state has not established procedures for supervising it, and the probability is that if an issue between parent and child were in some manner raised in court, the court would refuse to interfere unless the acts by which the compulsion was exerted were criminal, or so abusive as to place in legal jeopardy the parent's custody of the child. In assessing the reasons mentioned by the respondents for their indicated views, the authors thought that there was a noteworthy absence of feeling that the law should not intrude itself into the parent-child relationship. The percentage of those who took the "allow" position and who adverted to this point was relatively small, throughout. The authors' interpretation of this fact is exemplified by the following comment: "Although where the choice of a child's religious affiliation is concerned, there is greater expressed sentiment in the community against the role of government than when the issue relates to the availability of a college education, the predominant sentiment, nevertheless, would still recognize the need to respect the child's independent choice of religious affiliation, and, if required, to employ legal sanctions against the parent to effectuate it" (p. 171). A bit farther on the authors indicate that "Those who favored some legal control of parental authority . . . were not asked just what specific type of legal controls should be imposed: this would have been far too involved and complicated for our undertaking. It is fairly safe to assume that they favored some government-sanctioned means—the exercise of authority outside the realm of parental control for the achievement of the given ends" (p. 186, emphasis added, in part.).

I agree that it would probably have been both impracticable and useless to have raised the "how" question with the average member of the public. But is it not of the essence? I submit that these answers cannot be taken to be, in any practical sense, a true representation of community desires, for it is apparent that the respondents had not the slightest awareness of the practical implications of their answers. Some of the questions incorporated a caveat, "if the law prevented the parents from keeping the child out of college, it would reduce parental control and increase the amount of outside authority over the family to that extent." But how much meaning does this carry to one who is not familiar with the workings of the political-legal machinery of the state? If the questions had been formulated not in the denatured "should the law allow or prevent?" form, but in the terms in which they would be faced by the legislator or the judge—"Should a statute be enacted establishing a Family Liberties Commission with power to conduct investigations into invasions by parents of certain enumerated liberties of their children, to issue subpoenas and compel testimony, and to issue cease and desist orders against parents found to have committed such invasions, and to maintain actions in court to compel obedience to such orders, etc."—or—"Should a child who feels himself aggrieved by the act of his parent refusing to him his right of free religious association be permitted to maintain in the courts an action for injunctive relief, etc."—is it likely that the citizenry would have exhibited the same enthusiasm for the Big Brother approach that this survey seems to have revealed?

The other three of the six instances of disagreement between law and morals are somewhat different, involving situations (transfer of custody, disinheritance, parental ownership of child's earnings) which can, by a lawyer, be more easily conceived of as subjects of legal regulation. As the descent of property is already regulated by law, there would be no great derangement if the applicable law excluded complete disinheritance of a child. It might be doubted that the respondents have envisioned all the implications, but at least the probabilities are greater here that an implementation of their views would not produce practical consequences which would shock the majority of people affected. Administrative difficulties are certainly very substantial with reference to the custody and ownership of earnings issues, however. It is easy to pass a law—"Any person who, without prior approval of the probate court, gives his child into the custody of another person (permanently? for a period in excess of—days? with the intent to abandon custody himself?) shall be guilty of a misdemeanor." Enforcement would be another matter, family connections being as casual as, regrettably, they sometimes are. And with reference to the child's earnings, how should the law attend to their protection? It would be possible, I suppose, to require all parents to account as fiduciaries, periodically or upon the attainment by their children of majority, but I would imagine that compliance would be secured only to the accompaniment of a considerable amount of kicking and screaming.

. . . To me [the study] furnishes strong evidence of the necessity for continuing close attention to the factors which make it practicable and desirable to seek some social objectives through legal standards and sanctions, while making it equally apparent that other objectives must be left to other forms of social control. I have no doubt that the moral views indicated by the survey are effective in assuring that few parents actually exercise the full extent of the "authority" over their children which the law would probably tolerate. I am equally certain that to attempt to bring the law into alignment with these views would be rank folly. Law does not consist solely of norms of conduct. The official sanction through which the norm is enforced is an inescapable concomitant. A personal conviction as to what, in the abstract, ought to be, may serve very well as a moral standard, operating through the conscience and will of the individual, but it cannot be assumed that the same conviction would survive a marriage to official compulsion. Many of the norms which were approved by the respondents in the Nebraska survey are such that they could be brought to bear upon the community only through legal sanctions which, according to this reader's intuition, would be found, by the same persons who approved the norms, to be quite intolerable, and by the agents of the law to be incapable of administration. I would submit, therefore, that an inquiry into popular views of "what the law should be" can be most misleading if it does not raise, with the persons interviewed, the legislative question in all its complexity. If that question were raised, I would doubt the ability of the great majority of all citizens to respond to it in an informed and intelligent way. Query, then, whether the law-maker can expect as much help from the opinion surveyor as these authors suggest. □

NOTES AND QUESTIONS

1. Did Cohen, Robson, and Bates really measure the moral sense of the "community" or that of individuals in isolation? Is there a difference? Should they have separately tried to ascertain what "leaders" felt about these questions? Was it wrong to give equal weight to the opinions of educated, articulate people, and those who had never even considered the problem? See Herbert Marcuse, "Repressive Tolerance," in Robert Wolff et al., *A Critique of Pure Tolerance* 81–117 (Boston: Beacon Press, 1965).

2. To what extent, if at all, should a legislator, administrator or judge consult the moral sense of the community? Consider the following:

> Many things that are immoral are, nevertheless, not proper subjects for criminal punishment. And some things that unthinking public opinion has put in criminal codes ought now to be taken out . . . .
> Quantification of public opinion will be useful, for example, to persuade legislators that the voters are not as benighted as some suppose . . . . But, as respects law reform, precise knowledge of prevailing public attitudes can hardly do more than indicate the limit of mass tolerance for immediate changes.

from Louis B. Schwartz, "Ascertaining the Moral Sense of the Community: A Comment," 8 *Journal of Legal Education* 319, 320 (1955).[104] Is Schwartz's general viewpoint the same as Cooperrider's? What are the similarities and differences?

3. Cohen, Robson, and Bates found that the community wanted more controls than the law afforded them. Perhaps a sophisticated survey would show that the general public is considerably less willing to allow holders of unpopular views to express themselves than are leaders and elites, and these in turn show less tolerance than the courts do, in interpreting the first amendment to the Constitution. This point was made in Samuel A. Stouffer, *Communism, Conformity and Civil Liberties* (Garden City, N.Y.: Doubleday, 1955), and it continues to hold true. See Herbert McClosky and Alida Brill, *Dimensions of Tolerance: What Americans Believe about Civil Liberties* (New York: Russell Sage Foundation, 1983). This would also be the case with regard to the question of tolerance for "obscene" and "pornographic" literature. Should law reflect current community sentiments absolutely? Where should the line be drawn?

4. If the moral sense of the community should be consulted, how should it be done?
   a. What are the advantages and disadvantages of using modern survey research methods?
   b. Can one defend from a sociological point of view the use of the lawmaker's hunch or intuition about the moral sense of the community? Is the lawmaker entitled to consider herself as an adequate sample of the community's moral sense? What influences her behavior and hunches and what influences her perception of her role?

---

104. Copyright 1955. Reprinted with the permission of the *Journal of Legal Education*.

5. Is the legal model of Cohen, Robson, and Bates accurate? That is, have they really measured the law with the same care that they lavished on "public opinion"? Alan Milner, in a review of the study published in 21 *University of Pittsburgh Law Review* 147 (1959),[105] makes this remark:

> In a study which sets out to contrast the "moral sense" with the "law," the latter gets an unjustifiably static treatment. "Law" to Messrs. Cohen, Robson and Bates consists of norms "in the more traditional sense . . . law ready to be applied if and when the occasion calls". This apparently means an application of statutes and judicial precedent without insight or imagination—a condition of immobility which hardly matches up to the decisions of which we know the courts are capable. Into all the questions of their study, for instance, the authors introduced "significant factual variations" to gauge the moral sense more accurately. They naturally found the answers to their questions varying just as significantly. But nowhere is there the slightest suggestion that if a judge were faced with a similar variation, he might find a legal way to label it significant and so come up with a decision to suit his own moral sense.

6. Americans today are the targets of a large amount of public opinion polling by political candidates. How far can we trust the answers? George F. Bishop, Robert W. Oldendick, Alfred J. Tuchfarber, and Stephen E. Bennett, in "Pseudo-Opinions on Public Affairs," 44 *Public Opinion Quarterly* 198 (1980), asked people in a survey, "Do you agree or disagree with the idea that the 1975 Public Affairs Act should be repealed?" There is no such statute. However, about one third of their sample offered an opinion.

7. Is Cohen, Robson, and Bates's study, even on the authors' own terms, valid only for Nebraska? valid only for the period studied? It is, after all, more than 35 years old. If one wished to take community sentiments into account in another state, would one need a fresh survey, and in what detail? How long does the moral sense of the community last? If one decided to change the law to conform with community sentiment (assuming that were possible), at what point would one have to seek a fresh reading of the public pulse? Is there a difference between immediate public reaction to an event and a stable view held widely over a period of time? Would such a difference affect your answers to these questions?

8. Berl Kutchinsky, reporting studies from several countries in Europe, remarks:

> The fact that the general public has little knowledge about some specific laws is not very surprising. More unexpected perhaps are the findings that quite often knowledge about specific laws is rather poor in those specific groups for which the laws were made . . . . Another fact revealed by [these] studies . . . is the rather low level of knowledge about issues on which the general public might be expected to be well informed . . . . [T]he knowledge of certain laws is widespread. Many sections of criminal law are in fact common knowledge, for instance

105. Reprinted by permission.

laws prohibiting theft, murder and robbery. This does not affect the general conclusion, however, that public knowledge concerning legal topics is considerably poorer than presumed by the legal authorities and by many scholars.

Kutchinsky, "The Legal Consciousness: A Survey of Research on Knowledge and Opinion about Law," in Adam Podgorecki et al., *Knowledge and Opinion About Law* at 101, 103, 104, 105 (London: Martin Robertson, 1973).[106]

A number of studies in the United States, based on samples from various cities and groups, show that people know surprisingly little about specific provisions of the law but that the rich and better educated know more than the poor and poorly educated.[107] Kirk R. Williams, Jack P. Gibbs, and Maynard L. Erickson, in "Public Knowledge of Statutory Penalties: The Extent and Basis of Accurate Perception," 23 *Pacific Sociological Review* 105 (1980), report a study of the knowledge of adults in Tucson, Arizona. Those surveyed were aware that particular activities that the authors mentioned were crimes. However, the respondents were unaware of the statutory maximum sentences for these crimes. They tended to underestimate the potential maximum sentences, but they had a rough idea of the statutory ranking of the seriousness of crimes. The authors note that people do not have to have precisely accurate knowledge of the risks involved in crime for the law to have a deterrent effect.

The American Public, the Media & the Judicial System: A National Survey on Public Awareness and Personal Experience (New York: Hearst Corporation, 1983), reports a study of public knowledge about law. Respondents were invited to match names of prominent people with their positions in government and private organizations. Only 41 percent knew that Warren Burger and Sandra Day O'Connor then were Supreme Court Justices, and only 13 percent recognized Lewis Powell's position on the Supreme Court of the United States. Although 97 percent knew that everyone accused of a serious crime is entitled to representation by a lawyer, 50 percent thought that in a criminal trial it is up to the defendant to prove his innocence. Forty-five percent thought that a district attorney must defend a person accused of a crime who could not afford a lawyer; 39 percent incorrectly thought that if a court declares a business bank-

106. Reprinted by permission.

107. See, for example, Charles F. Cortese, "A Study in Knowledge and Attitudes Toward the Law: The Legal Knowledge Inventory," 3 *Rocky Mountain Social Science Journal* 192 (1966); LaVell E. Saunders, "Collective Ignorance: Public Knowledge of Family Law," 24 *The Family Coordinator* 69 (1975); Timothy M. Sheehan, "Why Don't Fine Artists Use Statutory Copyright?—An Empirical and Legal Survey," 22 *Bulletin of the Copyright Society of the U.S.A.* 242 (1975); Marc G. Singer, "Comprehension of Right-To-Work Laws Among Residents of the Right-To-Work States," 16 *Journal of Collective Negotiations* 311 (1987); Dennis H. Tootelian, "Potential Impact of 'Cooling-Off' Laws on Direct-to-Home Selling," 51 *Journal of Retailing* 61 (1975); Martha Williams and Jay Hall, "Knowledge of the Law in Texas: Socioeconomic and Ethnic Differences," 7 *Law & Society Review* 99 (1972); Trudie F. Smith, "Law Talk: Juveniles' Understanding of Legal Language," 13 *Journal of Criminal Justice* 339 (1985); Note, "Legal Knowledge of Michigan Citizens," 71 *Michigan Law Review* 1463 (1973). But compare Gregory Casey, "Popular Perceptions of Supreme Court Rulings," 4 *American Politics Quarterly* 3 (1976).

rupt, all personal property owned by the businessperson and his or her family must be sold to pay creditors.

What are we to make of this ignorance of the law? On one hand, Adam Podgorecki, in his study of Polish opinion on parental authority (generally, he covered the same area as Cohen, Robson, and Bates), found that people had fairly good knowledge of some legal principles—those which touch on "the nature of basic rights and obligations and broad categories of what is allowed and forbidden." However, they had "rather poor" knowledge of structures and mechanisms of law—the "available methods for the realization of the objectives enshrined in legal principles." See Podgorecki, "Public Opinion on Law," in *Knowledge and Opinion about Law* 65 (London: Martin Robertson, 1973).[108] On the other hand, Saunders, in the article cited above, found that his respondents did not know that Oregon law gave minors the right to venereal disease treatment, birth control information, and medical treatment without parental knowledge or consent. He suggests that "legislators and others do not publicize the provision of those laws for fear that if the public knew about them they would seek the repeal of such laws" (p. 72).[109] Does Podgorecki's point save the idea that law is the expression of the will of the people? Does Saunders' point undercut it?

6. Some of the many issues the public feels strongly about have an odd kind of one-sidedness. Pornography is a good illustration. It is regularly denounced by traditional conservatives. In addition, some feminists, led by Catharine MacKinnon and Andrea Dworkin, have entered the arena, trying to control or abolish pornography as a form of subjugation of women. On the other side, while it is easy to find people who defend pornography on free speech grounds, these people do not actually *praise* pornography. They simply say that it is something that has to be tolerated, perhaps as part of the price of freedom.

Yet the anti-pornography movement has had only limited success. The MacKinnon-Dworkin ordinance against pornography, enacted in Indianapolis, was declared unconstitutional. And never before has pornography been so common, so available, so accessible—so popular. This situation suggests how hard it is to measure "public opinion." Obviously, lots of men (and some women) buy or use pornographic materials, but they do not go about bragging about it. These people do not, perhaps, register their tastes in surveys.

What does the struggle over pornography suggest about the influence of "public opinion" on law? To what extent is this a question of "fact" or "science" rather than a question of morality and values, and how does this classification affect the political dynamics of the law on pornography? See Daniel Linz, Steven D. Penrod, and Edward Donnerstein, "The Attorney General's Commission on Pornography: The Gaps Between 'Findings' and Facts," 1987 *American Bar Foundation Research Journal* 713. See also Robin West, "The Feminist-Conservative Anti-Pornography Alliance and the 1986 Attorney General's Commission on Pornography Report," ibid., p. 681.

108. Reprinted by permission.

109. Copyright 1975. Reprinted by permission of the National Council on Family Relations.

LAW AS THE PRODUCT OF LEGAL CULTURE

20. *Legal Culture and the Welfare State*[110]
Lawrence M. Friedman

☐ . . . The legal system, in short, is a ship that sails the seas of social force. And the concept of *legal culture* is crucial to an understanding of legal development. By legal culture, we mean the ideas, attitudes, values, and beliefs that people hold about the legal system . . . . Not that any particular country has a single, unified legal culture. Usually there are many cultures in a country, because societies are complex, and are made up of all sorts of groups, classes and strata. One should also distinguish between *internal* legal culture (the legal culture of lawyers and judges) and *external* (the legal culture of the population at large). We can, if we wish, also speak about the legal culture of taxi drivers, or rich people, or businessmen, or black people. Presumably, no two men or women have exactly the same attitudes toward law, but there are no doubt tendencies that correlate systematically with age, sex, income, nationality, race and so on. At least this is plausible .. . .

Social scientists, approaching the legal system, begin with a master hypothesis: that social change will lead, inexorably, to legal change. This of course puts the matter far too simply. If one asks, *how* social change leads to legal change, the first answer is: by means of legal culture. That is, social change leads to changes in people's values and attitudes, and this sets up chains of demands (or withdrawals), which in turn push law and government in some particular direction . . . .

. . . [T]he increase in scope and power [of government, in the last century or so] has been in response to demands from society itself. The state did what people wanted it to do ("people" here meaning whoever had influence or power) . . . .

Technological and social changes in society, of course, lie behind rising demands . . . . All societies are interdependent, but in modern industrial society there is a new, peculiar form of interdependence. *Strangers* are in charge of important parts of our lives—people we do not know, and cannot control . . . Hence we demand norms from the state, from the collectivity, to guarantee the work of those strangers whose work is vital to our lives, which we cannot guarantee by ourselves.

Out of this cycle of demands, the modern state builds up a body of health and safety law. The rules become denser, more formal. *Informal*

---

110. In Gunther Teubner (ed.), *Dilemmas of Law in the Welfare State* (1985), pp. 13, 17, 18–19, 20, 22, 23.

norms are effective in regulating relationships, for small groups, families, people in face to face contact, in villages, in tribal life. They are not good enough for relationships among strangers, who "meet" only in the form of a product that one group makes and the other consumes; or who "meet" in an auto accident. Informal norms do not work for many problems and relationships in large, complex, mobile societies, when the villages have shattered into thousands of pieces, only to form again into the great ant-hills of our cities. For such societies, and such relationships, people demand active intervention from the generalized third party, or, in other words, the law . . . .

Yet the more the state undertakes, the more it creates a *climate* that leads to still further increases in demand. This is because of a fundamental—and very natural—change in the legal culture. State action creates *expectations*. It redefines what seems to be the possible human limits of law; it extends the boundaries. After a while, what is possible comes to be taken for granted, and then treated as if it were part of the natural order. Taxes creep forward slowly, benefit programs are added on one at a time, programs of regulation evolve step by step. Each move redefines the scope of the system. The next generation accepts what its parents argued about, as easily as it accepts sunshine and rain. Expectations, then, have been constantly rising . . . .

. . . Obviously, especially in hard times, the state has trouble keeping its promises; and population trends (too many old people on pensions) make things worse . . . .

. . . Demands on government in the 19th century were restrained by the feeling, in area after area, that there was nothing that could be done . . . . The uncertainty of life must have had a profound effect on legal culture. People *expected* misfortune, and they expected "injustice"—not necessarily human injustice, but the injustice of an unjust world, a world so arranged as to strike out in capricious and unfair ways, or at any event, mysterious, unfathomable ways . . . .

In the contemporary world, the situation has turned upside down. A great revolution in expectations has taken place, of two sorts: first, a general expectation that the state will guarantee total justice, and second (and for our purposes more important), a general expectation that the state will protect us from catastrophe. It will also make good all losses that are not our "fault." The modern state is a welfare state, which is also an insurance state—a state that knows how to spread the risks . . . □

21. *American Legal Culture: The Last Thirty-five Years*

Lawrence M. Friedman

35 *St. Louis Law Journal* 529 (1991)

□ . . . Legal institutions are reflections of social institutions; and they . . . have been thoroughly revised and revamped and remolded over the years.

In the last thirty-five years, there have been dizzying changes in every area of life . . . . And, corresponding to the dramatic changes in technology, and in social arrangements, there have been major changes too, in legal culture—by which I mean the attitudes and expectations of the public with regard to law—and through these changes, in the very fabric of the law itself . . . .

The very fact of change—constant, ceaseless change—is of prime importance in the legal culture. Change is so obvious, so palpable, that it comes to be accepted; it comes to be taken as normal. At one time, law was treated as timeless, immemorial: sacred custom, encrusted with tradition. Stasis was normal; change was exceptional, unexpected, unwanted. A more instrumental concept of law took hold roughly two centuries ago; and each time the pace of social change ratchets upward, the law itself changes, and, more significantly, the *idea* of a fixed, settled law receives a further blow. What was once inscribed on tablets, and supposed to last an eternity, now comes in looseleaf binders, with pocket-parts for instantaneous change; and new editions every year . . . . [I]n the computer age, people grow accustomed to the fact of rapid change, rapid manipulation of facts and principles, rapid storage, rapid unstorage; people are therefore less likely to accept the status quo, more apt to demand change that works in their favor. At least this is a working hypothesis.

No field of law has remained static over the last 35 years; many fields have been thoroughly transformed. Constitutional law, and the related field of civil rights, have perhaps changed most of all. (Paradoxically, the keystone text, the 14th Amendment, is exactly the same as it was in 1868; in this branch of law, of course, "interpretation" is all . . . .)

The civil rights revolution, of course, was enormously important in its own right. No problem in American law, and in American life, has been more important, more deep-seated, than the relationship between the black and the white populations; and the relationship between women and men is if anything even more fundamental and pervasive. Changes in that relationship dig very deep into the social fabric. Thirty-five years have brought about dramatic reordering. But the civil rights revolution and the feminist movement are also indicators or outcroppings of an even broader, wider transformation in law and in life. The movements are signs of the tremendous, growing strength of a radical form of *individualism,* an aspect of general and legal culture which has, more than anything else, contributed to the remaking of American life and law.*

It may seem peculiar to treat the struggle for the rights of (say) blacks and Hispanics as illustrations of radical individualism; a case could be made that the civil rights movement, and the various liberation movements that followed after it, show the power of claims for *group* rights, rather than for individual rights. But this proposition, I believe, is misleading. The essence of each liberation movement is the demand that society treat each individual *as* an individual, a unique person; and not as a member of a race, class, religion, gender, or group. "Discrimination" means throwing all blacks, or women, or gays, or handicapped people, into a single basket, making judgments on the basis of group stereotypes or prejudices. Even the arguments for affirmative action are, at bottom, individualistic: past discrimination has put *individuals* at a disadvantage, and it takes special measures to bring them to the starting line.

Individualism, especially in the form which Robert Bellah and his associates have called "expressive individualism,"[111] is, in general, a feature of character-formation in modern, Western society. But it seems particularly strong, even virulent, in the United States .... At least for white males, the United States from the outset was a country of amazing mobility—geographic, social, cultural. Compared to the United States, even the democracies of Europe seemed stagnant, hidebound, traditional.

The technological changes of the last thirty-five years have only strengthened American individualism. They have further weakened traditional authority—including the authority of the family. Indeed, the classic patriarchal family hardly exists any more in the United States. But neither does the matriarchal family. Families may be "headed" by men or (increasingly) by women; but to be "head" of a family is no longer what it used to be; it no longer means some sort of absolute authority.

In traditional societies, authority was vertical, hierarchical. The primary group—those who were in face-to-face contact—exerted the most decisive influence on members of society. The family was in con-

---

* [On this point, see, in more detail, Lawrence M. Friedman, *The Republic of Choice: Law, Authority, and Culture* (Cambridge, Mass.: Harvard University Press, 1990).]

111. R. Bellah, et al., *Habits of the Heart: Individualism and Commitment in American Life* (Berkeley, Cal.: University of California Press, 1985). Expressive individualism is the view that each person "has a unique core of feeling and intuition that should unfold or be expressed if individuality is to be realized." Id. at 334.

trol of the personality and character of the child, and the family, along with village notables—local priests, elders, chiefs, squires—transmitted values and ideas to the child. No other influences could even reach the child in its isolated hut or home. In the television age, on the other hand, authority and power have become much more horizontal. The child is no longer isolated. The parents no longer have the first and last word; their authority is no longer exclusive. From almost day one, images and messages flow in from outside—from television most notably—messages from a larger world. This is one of the major reasons for the emergence of a new kind of person: the expressive individual, oriented toward fads, and fashions, toward the values of television rather than the values of tradition, toward the authority of peers rather than the authority of parents.

The media allow information to reach "huge audiences" in an instant; they increase "opportunities for individuals to obtain information and organize it according to their needs;" the media have a vast "linking power," an ability to "locate persons with certain qualities or interests and communicate with them." This power permits and fosters the formation of horizontal interest groups—groups that are geographically distant, made up of separate individuals, bound together in a "community" formed by mail, radio, or TV. These groups—for or against handgun control; concerned with women's rights or conversely with the traditional family; for environmental protection, or preservation of rare animals; for more or better taxes; for control of poverty—these are the dynamos that turn the engine of public policy today.

Individualism, I believe, underlies the civil rights revolution and its satellites; but it also crops up in every corner of the legal system. It pervades family law, for example. The no-fault divorce, which swept the country from 1970 on, legitimized, in effect, the idea of divorce on demand. Whatever else no-fault divorce means, it represents the triumph of expressive individualism. It strips marriage of the aura of sacredness, of permanence; it denies a public or state interest in the continuation of marriage. Marriage becomes, instead, simply a matter of individual choice. The parties decide when to begin it and when to end it. When marriage fails to bring fulfillment, to either partner, that partner has the absolute right to break the marriage off—and start again, with someone else. That this conception has been so successful in the last two decades, that it spread from West to East so rapidly; that it dealt so cavalierly with traditional scruples against divorce-at-will only demonstrates how strong, how deep-seated, were the changes in legal culture that reached their climax in this period.

The decline of authority is also a decline in trust. Fewer people today seem willing to believe what authorities tell them, including authorities they themselves elected to office. Governments have always lied to their subjects; but the subjects seem less and less inclined to believe what they hear. Of course, to a large extent this skepticism is healthy; and it is a good thing to have such laws as the Freedom of Information Act on the books. But skepticism makes it much harder for leaders to lead; the followers show too much disinclination to follow. It was once possible for government to announce plans for an airport, a highway, a shopping center, and then follow through on the plans. Now there are many more steps in the process, no one accepts the plans as final, the only certainties are controversy, lawsuits, delay.

Most . . . are likely to approve of many of the developments of the last 35 years—surely they applaud most of the aims and results of the civil rights revolution. They are also likely to approve of environmental militance; certainly of laws about clean air and clean water, and preservation of wilderness. (Developments in family law are likely to be more controversial.) But not everything that has happened over the last thirty-five years wins high ratings. It seems undeniable that there has been a surge in social pathology in the last thirty-five years. The experts haggle over crime statistics; but there is little doubt that serious, violent crime has exploded in number since the second World War. The poor have always been with us; but the rockbottom welfare poor seem in a more hopeless state than the "respectable" poor of the nineteenth century. Juvenile delinquency, gang wars, the drug culture, homelessness—all of these appear to be symptoms of deep social illness. The cities are in decay. The ghettos seethe with rage.

The causes of social disorganization run deep, of course. But in one sense social illness may be only the flip side of expressive individualism—the fall-out, the detritus, the side-effects. The culture does not encourage people to submerge themselves in some larger cause or entity. The main job of life, as most people see it, is the job of crafting a meaningful self. A certain number—a fairly large number—fail at this job; and failure sometimes brings radical discontent; radical discontent can lead in turn to pathology and crime. I do not mean to suggest that these are the only or even the main explanations of what is wrong with society; there is plenty of blame to go around, and all the civil rights legislation has certainly not gotten rid of racism or sexism, for example; subordination and oppression are still facts of American life. But surely the legal culture has to bear some of the blame for the sorry state of society: the weakness of authority, the aggrandizement of the naked self.

So far I have spoken about changes in legal culture, as they relate to areas of law that affect individuals—civil rights, family law—as well as criminal law and law with regard to forms of deviance. The technological revolution has also of course affected business law in many large and small ways. Many of these effects are quite obvious. Rapid technological change creates new areas of business law; and gives fresh tasks to old areas, like the law of patents and copyrights. But the communications revolution has affected business and business law in more subtle and more profound ways.

The United States became rich and powerful within the protective walls of its oceans. It developed an enormous domestic market, and it thrived on this market. Distance and cost of transport were much more important than any tariff walls in protecting those markets from foreign competition. Exports and imports, significant as they were, never dominated economic life in the nineteenth century. This remained true well into the twentieth century. All this, of course, has now drastically altered. Business is international; no country is an island. Transport and communications here, too, are largely responsible. And as business internationalizes, the law necessarily follows along in its path. Law firms set up branches in Brussels, Singapore, Riyadh. The premises of field after field—antitrust law; immigration law; intellectual property—have to be re-examined, in the light of the demands of a world economy.

The communications revolution has helped reshape American federalism, or what is left of it. In the nineteenth century, and well into the twentieth century, the states were arguably more important in the legal life of the country than the federal government. Law meant, on the whole, local law. States' rights were taken seriously as a fact and as an ideology. The federal government raised a small army and navy, sold or gave away the public lands, and ran the post office. Almost everything else was done by the states.

What killed states' rights was not the Civil War, not the fourteenth amendment, but the railroad, the telegraph, the telephone; the automobile and the jet; and most decisively, television and the computer. A landmark in legal history was the creation of the Interstate Commerce Commission in 1887. This famous statute regulated (or tried to regulate) the great interstate railroad nets. The states were unable, legally and factually, to get a grip on railroads whose tentacles gripped the entire country. Afterwards, the power of the federal government grew slowly but definitely, always in response to the interstate nature of business. The New Deal was another watershed; the great depression almost destroyed state and local government; national calamity gave the federal government an opening, and Washington expanded its power at the expense of the exhausted and bankrupt states.

But there had been panics and depressions before. What was different was the social context. Trains, cars, and planes bound the country firmly into a single economic unit. The telephone and telegraph made it possible to communicate from coast to coast in seconds or minutes. Also, the New Deal emerged in the age of the radio; and Franklin Delano Roosevelt was a master of the art of the radio broadcast. In the days of Lincoln, or even Teddy Roosevelt, how many people in the country recognized the sound of the President's voice? But FDR could reach over the heads of governors and mayors; his "fireside chats" spoke to the whole country at once. Newsreels and newspaper photographs made him an instantly visible presence.

Roosevelt would have been a master of television too. Television is basically a creature of the last thirty-five years, and it has made the President—any and every President—a familiar figure in the home. We see him every day, on the evening news. He speaks directly to the country—indeed, to the world.

And what we see is the President as a human being as well as a leader; television shows us (or we think it shows us) the inside story, not just of the President, but of the celebrities, the lifestyles of the rich and famous, how they look, dress, act, and behave. In fact, political leadership gets converted by TV into just another kind of celebrity status. Everything is visual; everything is a matter of image, impression, manipulation. National networks blot out the local and the trivial; we see the big picture, the national picture, the Presidential picture. The scheme that the framers of the Constitution so carefully devised was a scheme based on slow motion, on localism, on grass roots democracy. It cannot survive as such, in an age of network broadcasting and satellites.

The states retain, of course, considerable legal power and importance. They run the criminal justice systems, the education systems, they manage tort law, family law, real property. Nonetheless, federalism is only a whisper, a shadow of its former self. The Supreme Court upheld the civil rights law of the 1960s on the basis of a commerce clause argument that the nineteenth century would have laughed off the stage. The most local greasy spoon in the South was within the reach of the federal government. And no doubt this is as it should be—in the late twentieth century. Indeed, today not a single branch of law—not education, crime, sex, or real estate—is immune from some form of federal intervention. Nobody seriously believes that the commerce clause, or any other text of federalism, impedes national policy, in any legal domain, in any significant way. If there is a demand for a national policy, in any field, there is a way to do it; and the borders of the states have melted or withered away.

Television and other forms of communication, moreover, have become crucial to the whole political system. They are, to begin with, fiendishly expensive. They increase enormously the corrosive power of money and money-raising on political life. Corruption and money-grubbing by politicians are of course old American habits. But the gross forms of corruption have been replaced by a more subtle and perhaps more dangerous form. Running for office now means scrambling for millions of dollars to buy time on television stations, and to reach huge audiences by any and all means.

In the last thirty-five years, it has become more and more clear that we live in a world of danger, opportunity, and (above all) change. Change in society at large means change in legal culture, in the way people look at the law, what they want and expect from it. In an open society, what they want more and more is free choice and individual rights. This silent, powerful force, of will and desire, conscious and unconscious, has shaken the tree of justice to its roots. ☐

NOTES AND QUESTIONS

1. Is Friedman's argument about legal culture consistent with Friedman and Ladinsky on law, technology, and social change? What is the relationship between his view of the effect of legal culture and the theory of pluralist bargaining? How do Dicey's and Gramsci's views bear on the concept of legal culture?

2. To what degree, if at all, does Friedman's legal culture approach support the claim that law is the will of the people? How is one to deal with the fact that some people in a society are violently opposed to some laws? Does he ignore conflict? How would he deal with Cohen, Robson, and Bates?

3. "Legal culture," as the term is used in Friedman's piece, is one of a family of concepts that includes "legal consciousness" (this term is particularly common among European law and society scholars), the "sense of justice," and the like. The terms are not always carefully defined or easily distinguished from each other.

One particularly thought-provoking use of the term "legal consciousness" can be found in Patricia Ewick and Susan S. Silbey, "Conformity, Contestation, and Resistance: An Account of Legal Consciousness," 26 *New England Law Review* 731, 739–41 (1992). Ewick and Silbey first discuss two views of legal consciousness which they then discard in favor of their own formulation. The first is "ideas and attitudes of individuals which determine the form and texture of social life." They associate this view with the "classical liberal tradition in political and legal theory." It focuses on *individuals*. Political and social life are seen as aggregations of individuals who shape the world with their interests and wishes.

Other scholars take a quite different approach. For them, consciousness is a *result*, not a cause. It is derived from "social structures." This view is held by Marxists and "structuralists," who "argue that individuals are only the bearers of social relations, and consequently, social relations, not individuals, are the proper objects of analysis." Some scholars who take this view discount the formative importance of "law and legal consciousness." In other words, whatever people may think, their ideas as well as the law itself are produced by the shape of society—capitalist, communitarian, democratic, or authoritarian.

Ewick and Silbey do not subscribe wholeheartedly to either of these conceptualizations. For them, legal consciousness refers to a way in which "ordinary people—rather than legal professionals—understand and make sense of law" (p. 731). They explain it further as follows:

> [W]e conceive of consciousness as part of a reciprocal process in which the meanings given by individuals to their world, and law and legal institutions as part of that world, become repeated, patterned and stabilized, and those institutionalized structures become part of the meaning systems employed by individuals. We understand consciousness to be formed within and changed by social action. It is, then, less a matter of disembodied mental attitude than a broader set of practices and repertoires, inventories that are available for empirical investigation.

Conceptualized in this way, consciousness is neither fixed, stable, unitary, nor consistent. Instead, we see legal consciousness as something local, contextual, pluralistic, filled with conflict and contradiction.

Which of the three views is the most similar to Friedman's concept of "legal culture?" How close is Ewick and Silbey's view to Friedman's? If we substituted this view for "legal culture," what modifications, if any, would we want to make in Friedman's explanation of how social change leads to legal change?

4. Sally Merry, in "Everyday Understandings of the Law in Working-Class America," 13 *American Ethnologist* 253 (1986), also examined ideas and attitudes about law. Her subject was "legal ideology." More precisely, she studied the way in which working class Americans, who turned to courts to resolve disputes, thought about law and how they used the legal system. But their attitudes (or ideologies) were of a peculiarly double nature. One one hand, they saw themselves as "endowed with a broad set of legal rights, loosely defined, which shade into moral rights." They believed, for example, that people have "rights to property, to privacy, and to a certain level of respect as a person."

But they also had a "second set of ideas" about the nature of legal rights and the processes for enforcing these rights. This can be described as "an ideology of situational justice."

> In this view, enforcement of laws is not automatic; it must be triggered by complaints. Furthermore, all cases with the same label—harassment, assault—are not viewed as equally serious. Seriousness, and therefore the odds that the court will do anything, such as imposing a penalty, depends on several things. First, it depends on who you are: whether or not you have a job, money, and a reputation for being in trouble with the law in the past . . . . Second, seriousness depends on the situation surrounding the specific incident, not simply the legal definition of the charge—the relationship between the parties, the mutuality of the conflict, the intent of the offender, the extent of the injury, the past history of the problem. Fights between relatives or neighbors, even when these involve serious injury or personal loss, are not considered real crimes . . . .
>
> Rights become resources, not guarantees. They become opportunities for action depending on the social context and history of the problem and the plaintiff's skill in navigating the complicated waters of the ideologically plural arena. (pp. 258, 266)

Merry does not accept wholesale Gramsci's concept of the hegemony of the dominant class. Such a hegemony would be, presumably, expressed in a particular dominant ideology. Is there a dominant ideology that controls and constrains "legal" ideologies? If there is, how powerful is it? Merry believes that the question is essentially "empirical." We should not simply assume that "hegemony" is a total fact.

What is the relationship between Merry's concept of legal ideology and the concepts of legal culture and legal consciousness?

HOW DOES PUBLIC OPINION, LEGAL CULTURE, OR POWER AFFECT
THE LEGAL SYSTEM?

22. Worker Insurgency, Radical Organization and New Deal Labor Legislation

Michael Goldfield

83 *American Political Science Review* 1257 (1989)

☐ Discussions in the social science literature about the reasons for the
passage of class legislation during the New Deal period have become
quite contentious recently. These debates raise important issues of wide
interest, including fundamental questions of U.S. politics, the nature of
the modern state, and basic problems of social science methodology.
Yet they may also be characterized by their neglect of what I will argue
is a central issue. Although the 1930s represented a high-water mark
for labor insurgency, broad social movements, and radical organization, few of the participants in the debates over the New Deal have considered these factors to be important influences in national politics.

It is not by accident, of course, that discussions of fundamental
questions of U.S. politics should focus on New Deal social legislation:
the New Deal is often regarded as the beginning of an activist state in
the United States, when class-based legislation emerged as a major
item on the political agenda; the electoral realignment represented by
the New Deal ostensibly enlarged the political arena to include workers, Afro-Americans, and the poor generally; it also was a time of great
stress and conflict, when contending forces struggled over the reshaping of policy and politics and hence, when certain aspects of politics
and social life were more exposed to view. Class legislation passed
during the New Deal period is sometimes described as "radical", even
"revolutionary". That piece of legislation to which the most extreme
adjectives have been applied is undoubtedly the 1935 National Labor
Relations Act (NLRA or Wagner Act) referred to as "innovative",
"radical," and "one of the most drastic legislative innovations of the
decade" . . . . [T]he NLRA was clearly not a routine piece of legislation. It was one in which labor organizations, corporations, and many
other groups had a keen interest and a major stake in influencing its
outcome (both passage and final content). Thus, if one wants to examine how groups, classes, parties, state capacities, organizations and
structures influence fundamental issues of public policy and especially
whether labor militancy, social movements, and radical organization
are important to consider, the passage of the NLRA is a reasonably

good place to start. Equally important, it is an important test case that all analysts of the New Deal and theorists of the state believe their approach is best able to explain.

In this article I attempt to document and argue that labor militance and radical organization did have major influence on the passage of the 1935 NLRA. Though this corrective, I would argue, is not unimportant, my real intention and hidden agenda is to open a Pandora's box of key issues for the study of U.S. politics and the study of the modern state. I want to suggest the importance of the past and potential effects of broad social movements in affecting U.S. politics. Thus, I wish to open the door to remedying a general neglect not just for the 1930s but certainly for the 1960s as well . . . Finally, I will argue that no theory or research agenda for study that ignores these factors can prove to be complete or adequate.

BACKGROUND

Prior to the 1930s, unions, whatever their legal status (and this varied by state), were de facto illegal. Employers could often threaten, intimidate, and fire their workers, who themselves had little recourse. In the case of strikes, workers could be imprisoned, and their unions could easily be served with injunctions and destroyed. In all too many cases, employers with their private police forces (or public ones that followed their directives) would arrest, beat, and murder militant workers with impunity. While certain of these employer activities were illegal (though rarely punished) many successful weapons for combating unions were quite legal. Two of the main such legal tactics were the yellow-dog contract, a hiring agreement in which a worker pledged never to join a union, and easily obtained court injunctions, making unions responsible for a whole range of nebulous damages.

A steady stream of labor legislation during the 1930s wiped out the legal basis for antiunion employer tactics. The 1932 Norris-LaGuardia Act declared the yellow-dog contract unenforceable and greatly limited the use of injunctions. The 1933 section 7(a) of the National Industrial Recovery Act (NIRA) asserted—though with no enforcement powers—the rights of workers to join organizations of their own choosing. In 1934, an amended and strengthened Railway Labor Act was rewritten with strong provisions banning company unions and protecting the rights of noncompany unions. The 1935 NLRA set up the federally administered National Labor Relations Board (NLRB) with broad powers to oversee the certification of unions and to penalize employers who did not accept the rights of employees to organize unions. In 1937, reversing its early precedents, the U.S. Supreme Court upheld the NLRA.

Whatever the substantive impact of this stream of labor legislation, its climax was the passage of a dramatic "prounion" bill opposed by a large majority of major capitalists and their organizations. Thus, the question of why it was passed at all and why it took such a seemingly prounion form cry out for an explanation.

EXPLANATIONS FOR THE NLRA

One of the most prominent attempts to explain the events that culminated in the passage of the NLRA is that of Theda Skocpol and her collaborators. Their views, which emphasize the autonomy of the state from societal forces, are particularly useful to examine, first because they are consciously framed in opposition to other competing explanations and second, because the state autonomy position is most opposed to the explanation I will argue is the best one. The views of the state autonomists may be summarized as follows:

1. On theoretical grounds, the state is most fruitfully viewed as potentially autonomous. Pluralists, elite and corporate liberal theorists, diverse types of Marxists, and others all err by wrongly viewing the state as dominated by, or the product of, various societal forces.

2. The New Deal period, or at least part of it—most especially those instances where labor legislation (particularly the NLRA) was passed—was one in which the state was actually quite autonomous from societal influences. All other theories fail (sufficiently) to take account of this autonomy.

3. The argument is sustained in good part by an admirable attempt to eliminate contending explanations. Against pluralists it is argued that labor legislation was not passed because of its being supported by a multi-interest group reform coalition. Nor was it passed because of the leading role of President Roosevelt, as suggested by Schlesinger and others, since the president's priorities did not include the strengthening of unions. Neither the NLRA nor section 7(a) were the result of agendas by liberal corporate elites, as is asserted by elite theorists and corporate liberal theorists or certain capital-intensive segments of the business community . . . . Still less was the passage of labor legislation a response to working class disruptions . . . The passage of the NLRA was also not a response by procapitalist state managers to working class pressure or growing organizational strength, a response designed to control workers . . . . Labor was too weak to play such a role . . . . In fact, in an argument that is viewed as giving the coup de grace to various structural Marxist positions, it is argued that labor legislation preceded the upsurge in union growth in the 1930s. Contrary to the claims . . . that such legislation would arise to control working class struggles, its passage stimulated and facilitated the growth of the union movement . . . .

4. Rather, the key is an understanding of the autonomous state struc-

tures, particularly the milieu in which Senator Robert Wagner operated and the political resources which he had developed. The role of Wagner and his advisers was heightened in part due to state incapacity resulting from the political and regulatory failure of the National Recovery Administration (NRA). At a reasonably fluid juncture, when societal groups were weak (i.e., labor) or isolated (i.e., business) and liberal Democrats had gathered ascendancy in Congress as a result of the 1934 midterm elections, an unusually skillful senator with a history of legislative successes; a competent full-time research staff, including assistants with legal bill-writing talents; and a long-standing association with "progressive" reform groups—lacking the support of the president or his main advisors—with great perseverance carried the day, directing the passage of the NLRA . . . . Thus, the passage of the NLRA is "very much a tale of state and party" . . . .

METHOD

. . . I will distinguish between INFLUENCE1, providing the impetus for a bill to pass even if the content is not what the influencer wanted; INFLUENCE2, where the content is more or less what the influencer wanted, that is, the influencer dominates the content; [and] INFLUENCE3, where the result of the bill, that is, the policy implementation, has the outcome that the influencer wanted. In addition, I might distinguish INFLUENCE4, the ability to block or control legislation, to force compromises that weaken the final act, or otherwise to control the agenda of decision making.

In many instances, Skocpol and the state autonomists attempt to criticize various Marxist, corporate liberal, and elite theorists by arguing against an especially strong form of INFLUENCE3, when in fact the position only requires INFLUENCE1 or INFLUENCE2, or at most a weak form of INFLUENCE3. For example, the state autonomists argue that U.S. capitalists did not "control" the state in the implementation of the NIRA because the NIRA (which all agree was designed and implemented by business) had inadvertent effects that were to their disadvantage . . . . In particular, the NIRA failed to bring about economic recovery, and through the vagaries of 7(a) stimulated large-scale labor-management disharmony and conflict, eventually leading to the greater empowerment of workers.

Let us leave aside the empirical aspect of the above argument and concentrate on its logic. The claim that recovery was beyond capitalist control because state structures were not fully developed conflates the various types of influence. It is indisputable, of course, that capitalists to some degree influenced the passage of the NIRA in the form of INFLUENCE1 or INFLUENCE2. Skocpol supposes, however, that a claim that the capitalist class is dominant in the political system implies not only that they will control the implementation of public policy (perhaps a weak form of INFLUENCE3) but that they will also achieve their intended goals (a very strong form of INFLUENCE3). This argument glosses over the forms of capitalist dominance and seems particularly off the mark in the disputes with Marxists. Part of the ABCs of Marxist analysis is that crises are endemic to capitalism. While crises may be accelerated, exacerbated, or occasionally postponed and dampened by activities of the state, they are largely a product of the nature of capitalist society, hence beyond the "management" of the capitalist state . . . . Thus, the inability of the NRA to bring about recovery is a telling point only if one already accepts the potentially autonomous and omnipotent power of the capitalist state (i.e., a totally instrumentalist view of the state over society), which no view that emphasizes the importance of societal forces would likely grant.

The critique creates other straw men as well. Skocpol and her colleagues seem to read Marxism as believing that reforms (short of the abolition of capitalism) must always disproportionately benefit only capitalists since capitalists dominate the state. The state autonomist's failure to make distinctions in types of influence leads them to miss crucial points and to ignore forms of influence that are less than absolute.

The problem also seems to arise in the state autonomists' dismissal of the claims of the historic corporate influence over various reformers. The state autonomists wish to argue that certain liberal reformers (e.g., Wagner, the Commons group in Wisconsin) and certain organizations (e.g., the American Association for Labor Legislation) had independent reform agendas that were neither controlled nor influenced nor coincident with those of major capitalists. To make this claim . . . , however, it is not enough to show that instances of INFLUENCE3 did not obtain in some or even all cases. The historical and conjectural ties between capitalists and liberal reformers . . . and corporate liberal theorists are indeed extensive and impressive. It is, of course, important not to accept "guilt by association" arguments as constituting strong causal links. But it is also important for those who deny their importance to discuss the significance of links that appear, at least on the surface, to be far more than circumstantial. Skocpol, for instance, dismisses the question entirely with a misplaced analogy. She argues that discussing the connections would be similar to claiming that Marxist theory was sponsored by capitalists, since Engels, who gave Marx money, was the nephew of a capitalist. It is not unreasonable to distinguish capitalists and their progeny (assuming Engels may legitimately be described as such), acting as socially maverick individuals who use personal monies to support liberal or radical causes from corporate leaders and their representatives, acting in concert, expressing political and organizational goals for the advancement of their interests as capitalists. And are not the linkages between activist organizations and their benefactors decidedly different in each case? All evidence suggests that we can and do make such distinctions. The proof of certain liberal reformers' independence from capitalists (i.e., lack of influence)—never really addressed by the state autonomists—is a prerequisite for the plausibility of their positions.

Similar problems arise in discussion of capitalist opposition to Roosevelt (INFLUENCE 4). Few participants in the New Deal debates seem to regard it as more than one type of phenomenon. Capitalist opposition is a loaded term, representing a whole family of activities, not the single phenomenon implied in most discussions of the New Deal. There are a variety of degrees, with huge qualitative differences between various positions on the spectrum. We might easily distinguish between mild and strong forms of opposition to particular policies, opposition to the whole thrust of the New Deal reform agenda, active campaigning against New Deal politicians and the reelection of Roosevelt himself, and finally active work for his impeachment. It should be noted in passing that FDR's political skills and willingness to compromise kept certain opponents from moving too far along this spectrum for too long a period of time.

Although FDR was in fact opposed by a large majority of big businessmen on certain issues (the NLRA being perhaps the most notable), the good will, contacts, and lines of communication he had previously established kept business from going into more extreme forms of opposition. Never did he face opposition of the type faced by the moderate quasi-socialist Upton Sinclair in the 1934 California gubernatorial campaign. No significant business groups demanded impeachment. Thus, the rhetorical descriptions of an embattled FDR facing a united, aroused capitalist opposition fail to distinguish analytically very different forms of capitalist opposition (INFLUENCE4), hardly doing justice to the actual situation.

THE NATURE OF LABOR INFLUENCES: SOME MODELS

With these distinctions in mind, I now turn to the notion of labor influence . . . itself in need of clarification. Since so little attention is paid in the New Deal debates to the possibility of labor influence, most models exist either implicitly or in undeveloped form.

One such model, disclaimed by all, involves a "powerful mass of organized workers" rising up and overwhelming "a united power elite position" . . . Such a situation has virtually never happened. The working class seizing the capitalists by the throat and taking their stolen change from out of the capitalist money bags is a powerful illusion, but an illusion nevertheless. Many who attempt to downplay the importance of working class influence implicitly attack this straw man, thus deflecting attention away from the more likely forms of labor influence.

A second model of labor influence on public policy is perhaps provided in Sweden. There, political parties (the Social Democrats and their allies) and several union federations (the Landsorganisationen and the Tjänstemannens Centralorganisation) represent the whole Swedish working class. These working class organizations formulate demands, negotiate with other peak political groups and employer organizations, and assist in implementing the final policies. In such a situation, the "influence" of labor organizations—if not workers themselves—is often easily ascertainable. Those who look for the clear imprint of labor on particular provisions of various bills implicitly advance this as their testable hypothesis. Such a model, however, rarely applies to situations of mass, newly organized worker insurgency; it clearly does not characterize the influence of labor in the Roosevelt era. Both of these latter models might conceivably represent forms of INFLUENCE2 or INFLUENCE3.

A third model of labor influence is the . . . disruption model, where capitalists respond to the spontaneous, unorganized, disruptive threats of the poor and underrepresented, clearly a form of INFLUENCE1. Criticism of [this] account plays a central role in Skocpol's analysis of the NLRA. This model, while fitting the general contours of certain aspects of the 1930s and coming closest to the view presented here, is also not without its problems. Its emphasis on spontaneity and disruptions leads one to overlook the role of highly organized radical organizations not only in organizing social protest but in tactical and strategic planning as well. Most threatening activity during the 1930s was actually highly organized and under radical leadership. In addition, it fails to understand the importance of the jockeying for position and influence between mainstream and radical groupings and its effect on public policy debates. Further, real patterns of influence during the 1930s were frequently more complicated, with the leading disrupters and their supporters sometimes vigorously opposing "their" legislation, particularly the NLRA.

If these three models were the only ones that could represent labor influence on the state, the case for labor influence on the New Deal would be difficult. There exist other models, however, where influence is less direct, but still easily discernible.

More common, in fact, are concessions granted by a government in order to stem working class militance and organized radicalism. Sometimes the results are reluctantly supported or even opposed by the ruling classes, sometimes they are only an indirect response to insurgent demands. An example of the latter are the welfare state policies instituted by Bismarck in late-nineteenth-century Prussia after a decade of antisocialist laws had failed to stem the growth of the world's largest Marxist working class party. To fail to see the agitation and struggles of the highly organized and disciplined German Social Democratic party as the moving force would be seriously to distort history. Likewise, while the Russian czar "gave" his constituents the Duma in 1906, few have failed to recognize it as a response to the massive working class and peasant insurgency and the well-organized forms of radical organization associated with the 1905 revolution.

The current process of unionization in South Africa is instructive in looking at models of working class influence, particularly with respect to the lag time between labor insurgency and its effect (INFLUENCE 1) on the public policy process. The most recent development of unions began in 1973 as economic expansion, fueled by huge rises in the price of gold (South Africa's major export), created an enormous demand for African labor. Strike waves, coupled with informal demands, spread. The strikes in 1973, which received large international publicity, were particularly embarrassing for many foreign companies. They also made profitable business difficult for the affected firms. Since open organization and leadership were illegal, formal bargaining could not occur. Workers engaged in guerillalike activities. As one manager stated, he was neither willing nor able "to negotiate with 1500 workers on a football field." Since repression would not work, certain capitalists developed a preference for orderly labor-management relations. One could search in vain for black worker input into the political negotiations that led to the 1979 enactment of the Wiehahn proposals legalizing black unions. One could cite the importance of militant intentional support by protesters and unions, the role of foreign companies ostracized in their native lands, the speaking out of South African liberals, and the centrality of the rapidly expanding economy. But a refusal to recognize the pre-eminent role of the struggles of African workers (even though their strike rates tapered off several years before 1979) would be sorely mistaken.

These remarks are meant merely to indicate the complexities involved in the notions of labor influence and have not yet addressed the specific arguments against labor as a major factor in the passage of the NLRA. This task will be the burden of the next two sections.

EVALUATING LABOR INFLUENCE ON NEW DEAL LABOR LEGISLATION

The most important arguments by the state autonomists directed against the role of labor influence in the passage of the NLRA would seem to be the following: (1) The timing of the labor upsurges did not occur at the right times to have influenced labor legislation; (2) Even if it had, labor was too weak to have influenced either 7(a) or the NLRA; and most importantly, (3) The causality goes the other way, that is, the passage of 7(a) was the main stimulator of the labor upsurge from 1933 to 1953, and the NLRB largely enabled the growth of unionism from 1935–38.

My plan in what follows will be to cast doubt on all three of these arguments. In addition, I will attempt to highlight the important effects of the interaction between labor militancy, social movements, and organized radicalism in the policy process. The last of the above three arguments will be examined first. The most decisive way to discredit a causal argument is to show that the effect actually preceded the supposed cause. Thus, the claim that union growth and activities influenced or caused the passage of labor laws may be disproved by showing that little or no activity or organization preceded the passage of the laws. Likewise, the argument that the laws caused the development of organization and activity may be easily disproved by showing that activity and organization (or its significant development) preceded the passage of the legislation. The dichotomies are rarely, however so clear-cut.

The question of the degree to which particular pieces of labor legislation may have stimulated, facilitated, or caused union growth and militancy is a complex one. A definitive proof would involve showing not merely that legislation preceded or even assisted union growth but that it would not have taken place otherwise—an extremely heavy burden. Moreover, the claim may be either weak or strong. A weak claim might assert that the law functioned symbolically to stimulate labor activity. This claim is difficult to disprove unless the law is shown to have been enacted after the development of the activity. It is similarly difficult to prove conclusively. A stronger claim is that the actual administration of the law either removed previous obstacles or facilitated and encouraged the activities in other ways. One must also leave room for the likelihood of joint causality, unless this possibility is ruled out by the temporal sequences. Whichever type of claim one makes, the examination cannot be dealt with lightly. Yet few analysts attempt to examine the question of labor influence in a rigorous manner. [Kenneth] Finegold and Skocpol, for instance, make an extremely strong claim for the causal role of the NLRA, signed into law on 22 June 1935: "This act, and the independent National Labor Relations Board established to enforce it, facilitated labor organization and recognition, so much so that union membership grew from less than 4 million in 1935 to over 8 million in 1939 and doubled again during the war."

An analysis of this claim will show a number of problems with the state autonomist argument. The best place to begin, however, is with certain questions of fact. The tremendous growth in labor union membership during World War II was hardly a doubling, going from over 10 million in 1941 to a little over 14 million in 1945. Though I do not wish to be overly picky about these figures, it is important to set the record straight. Furthermore, as virtually all commentators agree, this growth during the war was not by and large due to provisions of the

TABLE 1   UNION MEMBERSHIP, 1897–1948 (SELECTED YEARS)

	Number of Members (in thousands)			Number of Members (in thousands)	
Year	Wolman Series	BLS Series	Year	Wolman Series	BLS Series
1897	447	—	1932	3,144	3,050
1900	868	—	1933	2,973	2,689
1901	1,125	—	1934	3,609	3,088
1904	2,073	—	1935	—	3,584
1912	2,452	—	1936	—	3,989
1914	2,687	—	1937	—	7,001
1916	2,772	—	1938	—	8,034
1917	3,061	—	1939	—	8,763
1918	3,467	—	1940	—	8,717
1919	4,125	—	1941	—	10,201
1920	5,048	—	1942	—	10,380
1921	4,781	—	1943	—	13,213
1922	4,027	—	1944	—	14,146
1923	3,622	—	1945	—	14,322
1929	3,443	—	1946	—	14,395
1930	3,393	3,401	1947	—	14,787
1931	3,358	3,310	1948	—	14,319

Source: Wolman Series is taken from Leo Wolman, *Ebb and Flow in Trade Unionism* (New York: National Bureau of Economic Research, 1936). BLS Series is taken from Goldfield 1989.

TABLE 2   NLRB ELECTION RESULTS, 1935–48

Year[a]	Elections	Elections Won	Eligible Voters	Valid Voters	Union Voters
1935–36	31	18	9,512	7,734	4,569
1936–37	265	214	181,424	164,307	113,484
1937–38	1,152	945	394,558	343,587	282,470
1938–39	746	574	207,597	177,215	138,032
1939–40	1,192	921	595,075	532,355	435,832
1940–41	2,568	2,127	—	729,915	589,921
1941–42	4,212	3,636	1,296,567	1,067,037	895,254
1942–43	4,153	3,580	1,402,040	1,126,501	923,169
1943–44	4,712	3,983	1,322,225	1,072,594	828,583
1944–45	4,919	4,078	1,087,177	893,758	706,569
1945–46	5,589	4,446	846,431	698,812	529,847
1946–47	6,920	5,194	834,553	805,474	621,732
1947–48	3,222	2,337	384,565	333,900	256,935

Source: All figures are from NLRB annual reports for the appropriate fiscal year.
[a]NLRB fiscal years begin 1 July of first year and end 30 June of second year.

NLRA. Rather, the expansion of unions, the signing and maintaining of union shop agreements, and the growth in union membership, although under the auspices of the NLRB, took place according to rules established by the War Labor Board. Full union shop agreements were a condition for an employer's receiving a government contract, as long as unions honored no-strike agreements, something that some perspective [sic] observers argue ultimately weakened unions. Even more important, union growth during wartime often relies on favorable economic conditions (especially a tight labor market) and a desire for social tranquillity and labor peace, thus making claims about its relation to particular state activities exceedingly complex.

The argument for the prewar period is especially dubious. Although the NLRA was signed into law in June 1935, the NLRB settled very few cases before it was upheld by the Supreme Court in the Jones and Laughlin case in April 1937. Until this time, virtually all employers refused to cooperate with the board. As can be seen from Table Two, only several thousand workers (less than 1% of the total) were organized under NLRB auspices before 1 July 1936, the end of the first full year of functioning under the NLRA. Union membership, 3 1/2 million in 1935, grew to slightly under 4 million in 1936. In 1937, in the aftermath of the Flint strike (28 December 1936–11 February 1937), General Motors, Chrysler, and Big Steel were unionized, along with hundreds of other companies. Within one month after the end of the Flint strike, 247 other sitdown strikes had taken place, involving almost 200 thousand workers. Union membership surged to over seven million by the end of the year—the dam had been broken with little help from the NLRB.

If the NLRA (which only became truly functional at the tail end of the 1934–38 labor upsurge) and section 7(a) of the NIRA (which had no enforcement powers) were not administratively significant, it is still possible that they played an important symbolic, stimulating role. Legislation and small public policy changes have been known to have such effects on social movements. It is certain however, that one cannot take the claims of conservative, moderate, or even sometimes left-wing union officials as proof of this. The passage of the Clayton Act in 1914, an act dubbed by then AFL president Samuel Gompers to be "Labor's Magna Charta," clearly played no such role. The question of how to decide the symbolic significance of the NLRA is not an easy one. It would be foolish to argue that these pieces of labor legislation had no positive effect. My hypothesis is that they were one of a number of stimulating factors, certainly less important than successful, often highly publicized strikes.

The degree to which the state autonomists overemphasize the importance of symbolic legislative actions like the NLRA and of institutional bureaucracies, ignoring the historical context in which they exist, is suggested in what happened after the enormous labor upsurge of 1937.

By the next year, with a legally reaffirmed NLRA, union growth had begun to slow then stagnate. If one were concerned largely with correlations and temporal sequences and with attempts to always find primary causes in state activities rather than with an attempt to understand the deeper causes, one might argue that the NLRA itself was responsible for inhibiting union growth. Such an argument, however, would be perverse, attributing more instrumental causal import to public policy than is reasonable in this case. Skocpol, in her haste to find state-centered explanations, attributes this stagnation (less than a year after the NLRA actually began functioning) to the shift in political winds. It is at least as likely, however, that the causal arrows point in the other direction. The 1938 economic downturn, of course, bears some responsibility for slowing unionization. The major factor, however seems to have been the widening split between the AFL and the CIO, described by some observers as a "civil war." This split allowed the Right and corporations to regain the offensive. Without this split—and consequent AFL attacks on the NLRB, coupled with AFL political support for conservative congressmen—it is unlikely that unions or the NLRB would have been as vulnerable as they were. Thus, one must conclude that the NLRA, while it may have facilitated some union growth, was probably not a major cause of the tremendous union upsurge from 1934 to 1938.

AN ALTERNATIVE MODEL

Further objections to the notion of labor influence on the passage of the NLRA will be dealt with in the context of my discussion of an alternative model. The purpose of this model will be to explain why the NLRA was passed and the important role that labor influence played. In short, my model may be outlined as follows:

1. New Deal labor legislation was a result of interaction between labor movement growth and activity, the increasing strength and influence of radical organizations, particularly the Communist party, liberal reformers with both immediate and historical corporate ties, and government officials (or state managers) with primary concern for preserving social stability and assuring the continued electoral success of the Roosevelt-led Democratic party. Thus, the alternative theory, in contrast to the others, stresses interactions between actors on level 4.0 in Figure 1, the impact of these interactions on the public policy process, and the special importance of boxes 4.4, 4.5, and 4.6.

2. While the particular content of virtually all the New Deal legislation was a direct, though evolving, product of longstanding reform agendas, the impetus for passage, some features of the bills, and the immediate reasons why the legislation was passed (i.e., why a large number of senators and congressmen voted for it, why business did not oppose it in a more extreme manner, and why the president signed it)

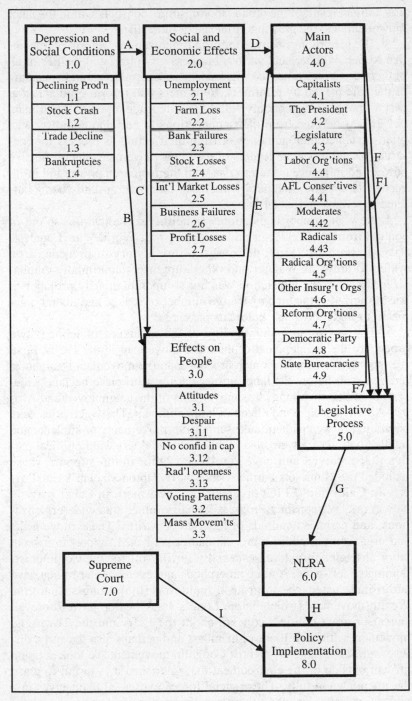

FIGURE 1   Reasons for the Passage of the NLRA

was a direct result of the broad labor upsurge, conflicts within the labor movement, and the growing influence of radicalism.

3. The historic ties between reform organizations, reform politicians like Robert Wagner, and various business groupings and the ties of all of them at various times to AFL leaders are central to an understanding of the role played by reformers. Reformers and reform groups had at best a limited semiautonomy with little independent power. Their main power was derived from their connections to certain capitalists who often sustained their activities or from their acting as brokers for conservative and moderate leaders of the labor movement. Their effective power and influence tended to rise with the increased power and influence of labor. They had narrow room for maneuver, usually being buffeted by events and social forces.

4. New Deal labor legislation was neither so radical nor so out of context from previous legislation as many post World War II analysts have portrayed it. First, there was a long history of precedents on which to draw, as Wagner and other supporters continually emphasized. Second, the legislation was not so unambiguously prolabor: it was criticized at the time by a large number of radical and liberal organizations and individuals before its passage.

5. The key to an understanding of the influence of labor is two aspects of the development of the labor movement in the 1930s. First, the labor movement was much broader than the movement to organize unions. Well before the labor upsurge at the workplace became widespread, militant working class movements of the unemployed and African-Americans were mobilized in large numbers. These activities were paralleled by sympathetic and supportive movements of students and intellectuals. There were also highly influential left-wing political parties that received and gave significant labor union support; these included the Minnesota Farmer-Labor party, Upton Sinclair's End Poverty In California (EPIC) organization, the American Labor party in New York, Wisconsin's Progressive party, other statewide organizations, and perhaps hundreds of local labor parties. These movements and organizations added a breadth and broad-based support to nascent labor struggles, providing especially fertile soil for the Communist-dominated left-wing. A more amorphous and even broader milieu gave additional sustenance to protest, including Huey Long's Share the Wealth movement (which before Long's assassination gave Roosevelt cause for great political concern about the Left) and the Townsend movement with its millions of members and perhaps also the early, diffuse, antirich, eventually rightist Coughlin movement. To look at union growth outside of the environment that nourished it is to fail to grasp the phenomenon fully. These social forces expressed themselves in a variety of ways, including their translation into electoral victories for FDR and New Deal insurgents in Congress, thus providing a more responsive legislative environment to be influenced directly. Second,

throughout the 1930s there was tremendous conflict (largely ideological) within the labor movement. There was a growing split between conservative AFL leaders (with their historic ties to reformers and liberal capitalists) and the Left, which for the first half of the decade was becoming an increasing threat to the former.

This descriptive model for the passage of the NLRA differs in fundamental ways from that of the state autonomists. It not only pays far greater attention to the influence of societal forces on the political arena, but also looks at the state-society interactions that help explain both the periods of greater influence of certain governmental figures like Robert Wagner and certain of the characteristics of the final bill.

While all five parts are important for the model, the central burden of such a theory is the demonstration of three linkages: (1) that there existed a strong and important connection between the radical labor upsurge and the broader social movements; (2) that a growing political conflict was taking place within the labor movement, whose balance of power was beginning to shift from conservative leaders and organizations to more radical groupings: and (3) that both these phenomena had a central impact on the labor reform process. I will attempt to demonstrate these linkages in a preliminary fashion by examining the factors that led to the passage of the NLRA.

HOW THE NLRA CAME TO PASS

The first task will be to show the strength of early New Deal social movements and their impact on, and support for, the more slowly emerging labor movement. In this context, I will also begin to outline the linkages mentioned above. My central caveat will be that standard modes of evaluating organizational and movement strength by membership figures, electoral impact, or legislative influence are even more problematic during times of popular insurgencies than they are during more normal times. The first most dramatic mass response to the Depression came from the unemployed.

THE UNEMPLOYED

Unemployment quickly became the dominant political focus at the beginning of the depression. Millions of people roamed the country looking for work. Large shantytowns grew inside and outside major cities. State governments approached bankruptcy with relief efforts that scarcely scratched the surface of the problem. Protests of the unemployed from 1930 to 1932 were often massive and militant. No serious commentator doubts that they were virtually all radical-led, largely by open communists. On 6 March 1930, well before the passage of any of the new labor legislation, over one million people demonstrated across the country under Communist Party (CP) leadership against unemployment. Harvey Klehr describes massive funeral rallies led by the communists in key cities around the country. In New York City, in January 1930, 50 thousand attended the funeral for a party activist killed by the police. A similar funeral in Detroit in 1932 for four party activists killed by the police at a protest march on Ford's River Rouge plant was attended by 20–40 thousand people: "Above the coffin was a large red banner with Lenin's picture". Perhaps the high point of such activity was in Chicago. In one incident in 1931, five hundred people in a Chicago southside African-American neighborhood brought back furniture to the home of a recently evicted widow. The police returned, opened fire, and three people lay dead. The coffins were viewed, again under an enormous portrait of Lenin. The funeral procession with 60 thousand participants and 50 thousand cheering onlookers was led by workers carrying communist banners: "Within days, 2,500 applications for the Unemployed Councils and 500 for the Party were filled out". From all indications, these protests, as well as the political character of their leadership, often making the front page news, did not fail to leave deep impressions on many people in positions of power, as well as on the more disadvantaged members of the citizenry.

OTHER PROTESTS

The struggles of farmers likewise developed widespread militancy, often involving as many as tens of thousands in direct actions. Activities included the withholding of produce from the market because of low prices and the stopping of banks from auctioning mortgage-defaulted properties, sometimes by armed "penny sales." Communist and radical influence here, while not nearly as extensive as among the unemployed, was far from negligible. In the early stages of the Depression, when virtually all farmers were desperate, militant farm organizations, particularly the Farmers Holiday Association, were sympathetic and supportive to union struggles.

Large-scale protests by students, often under CP influence, began in the early 1930s. At the same time, thousands of intellectuals and artists, including a number of the nation's most prominent, publicly declared their allegiance to communism. In numerous instances, these intellectuals formed support committees and publicized working class grievances widely.

Perhaps nowhere was the upsurge so militant and the rapid influence of communists as dramatic as it was in African-American communities. In 1931, the CP took initiative in a case that was to gain it major political leadership among African-Americans throughout the country. The case was that of the Scottsboro boys, nine African-American youths seized from a freight train in rural Alabama, accused of raping two white girls who had been riding with them on the same train. The Scottsboro defense laid the basis for the large-scale influence and recruitment of African-Americans of every stratum throughout the United States. Defense activities involving significant numbers of whites, as well as many blacks, were numerous, widely attended, broadly supported, and well publicized. These activities and the reputation gained by the CP as a reliable defender of black people gave it entree and influence among highly concentrated African-American industrial workers, including in such important places as the Birmingham steel mills, the Briggs automobile plants in Detroit, and the Ford River Rouge plant, then, as now, the largest plant in the United States.

This atmosphere of social protest and radicalism was nourished and gained recruits from the broader milieu of unorthodox movements, and local-and state-level labor parties. Within this environment the labor movement began to assert itself in the nation's workplaces.

THE WORKPLACE

Throughout the 1920s, groups of communists had organized themselves in industrial plants throughout the country. In many of the ununionized industries, they were the only organized forces, occasionally having the broad sympathies of their fellow workers on the basis of clandestinely published shop papers. In the fur and leather industries, centered primarily in New York City, the union was openly led by communists. In a number of other industries (including mining, textile, and some maritime sectors), they led and participated in large scale though generally unsuccessful strikes. In early 1933, however, months before the passage of NIRA, the CP, along with members of the Industrial Workers of the World and independent radicals, led a series of successful strikes at Briggs in Detroit that were to help them establish early hegemony and respect in the auto industry. It is not always clear from reading historical accounts how much to generalize from the reactions of individual capitalists and business organizations to the labor struggles of the early 1930s. It is somewhat easier to see the distress of established AFL leaders at the degree of opposition growing within their own organizations and their eclipse among newly organizing workers.

All the central aspects of the alternative model which were magnified greatly in the wake of the 1934 labor upsurge, are belittled in importance by Skocpol. The long, continuous decline in union membership from 1920 to 1933, was reversed in 1934, as union membership increased by 20%, rising by over 600 thousand members. Strike statistics took an extraordinary leap. But these are mere incidental statistics, which fail to convey the depth of the explosion. One does not even have to rely on enthusiastic radical accounts, accurate as they may be. Irving Bernstein for instance writes over three decades later of 1934:

> A handful of years bear a special quality in American labor history. There occurred at these times strikes and social upheavals of extraordinary importance, drama, and violence which ripped the cloak of civilized decorum from society, leaving exposed naked class conflict. Such a year was 1886 with the great strikes of the Knights of Labor and the Haymarket Riot. Another was 1894, with the shattering conflict of Eugene Debs' American Railway Union against the Pullman company and the government of the United States. Nineteen thirty-four must be added to this roster.
>
> In the summer of that year Eric Sevareid, who covered the great trucking strikes for the *Minneapolis Star* returned home to find his father on the screened porch. The elder, a Minneapolis businessman, was reading the headlines and his face was pale. "This," he said, "this—is revolution!"

Three labor struggles, if not revolutionary, were certainly deep social upheavals: in the 1934 conflicts in Toledo, Minneapolis and San Francisco, highly organized workers were victorious. All three struggles were led by avowed revolutionary groups and linked previously mobilized, separate constituencies. In Toledo, the working class and organizations of the unemployed formed a major alliance with tens of thousands of radical-led unemployed workers battling scabs and National Guardsmen to a standstill, rescuing a defeated strike. In San Francisco even the conservative AFL unions were drawn into the general strike. And in Minneapolis—a previous open shop, low-wage citadel—not merely the unemployed AFL unions and Farmer-Labor party organizations but militant farmers under the banner of the Farmers Holiday Association joined in the struggles of the Minneapolis working class. These great battles stimulated and encouraged workers throughout the country, both directly and indirectly, well after the successful strikes had ended. After the 1934 San Francisco general strike, the longshore and maritime industries along the whole West Coast remained aflame with militancy, largely under communist leadership. The Trotskyist-led triumph in Minneapolis laid the future basis for the successful organization of over-the-road truck drivers through the Midwest. And in auto organizing outside of Detroit by communist-led shop groups and in Detroit by the radical Mechanics Education Society of America was greatly accelerated. As happened in General Motors after the 1936–37 Flint strike, workers engaged in numerous unofficially sanctioned (and undoubtedly officially *unrecorded*) job actions, gaining working conditions that employers never would have conceded in the previous bargaining. Most likely these strikes increased the fear among the rich of revolution. In all probability they made politicians committed to capitalism somewhat apprehensive. For AFL leaders, however, these strikes must have had the appearance of the grim reaper. They signified the existence of an emerging mass-based labor movement led by radicals completely outside their control. This movement threatened to overwhelm them even inside the confines of their own organizations.

THE RESPONSE TO THE LABOR UPSURGE

The most reasonable hypothesis to account for the passage of the NLRA is that labor militancy, catapulted into national prominence by the 1934 strikes and the political response to this movement, paved the way for the passage of the act. Having talked about the insurgency, I shall dwell on the response to it.

First, the labor insurgency with its accompanying conflict and violence caused by intransigent company resistance had reached proportions truly alarming to the economic and political elites. To interpret this concern as having abated due to downward fluctuations in strike statistics in early 1935 is to miss a central aspect of political and social reality. The 1934 labor revolt, for instance, was the dramatic centerpiece of a highly effective speech given by Robert Wagner at the House Labor Committee Hearings on 13 March 1935 and on the Senate floor on 7 May 1935. During the 1934 hearings prior to the 1934 successful radical-led strikes and after, there were many who predicted increasing unrest. These included not only labor leaders such as Sidney Hillman of the Amalgamated Clothing Workers and John L. Lewis of the miners but many other public and private figures. On 29 May 1934 Senator LaFollette talked about growing labor unrest and "this impending crisis . . . which will bring about open industrial warfare in the United States". On the same date Representative Connery noted, "You have seen strikes in Toledo, you have seen Minneapolis, you have seen San Francisco and you have seen some of the southern textile strikes but . . . you have not yet seen the gates of hell opened and that is what is going to happen from now on." And contrary to the perceptions of Skocpol and other state autonomists, most observers saw only an increase of labor "strife" throughout the spring of 1935. On 13 March 1935, Wagner, for example, the state autonomists' archetypical state reformer, spoke of the "rising tide of industrial discontent". These sentiments and the fear of even greater labor struggles are echoed by virtually every commentator during the spring of 1935. No opponent in the hearings or on the floor of Congress ever rises to suggest the opposite or even that the descriptions are overdone. Even William Green the ever cautious head of the AFL attempted to use labor unrest to political advantage. On 23 May 1935 the nations' presses reported that he addressed a rally of 25 thousand workers in Madison Square Garden in New York City, with another 25 thousand standing outside. Here Green threatened (in a manner reminiscent of his performance over the 1933 Black bill) a national general strike if the NLRA was not passed. Though this may have been merely puffery and bluster on Green's part, the results of his threat were different in 1935. This time, on the next day, according to the *New York Times,* 250 thousand New York City needle trade workers quit work early in support of Green's demand.

The response to this increasing unrest was, of course, not uniform. Differing perspectives emerge quite sharply in the discussions of the NLRA. Most critics, as well as supporters, recognized that the NLRA was designed to empower AFL unions. Large numbers of employers and their organizations opposed the NLRA because they believed it would strengthen or give unfair monopolies to the AFL. This position was perhaps typified in the remarks of James A. Emery, the general counsel for the National Association of Manufacturers. On 26 March 1934, Emery argued at the Senate hearings that the bill would issue a monopoly to the AFL: "It is a deliberate step toward a Nation unionized by the act of Government". And there were, of course, more extreme opponents, whose views of the NLRA ranged from "pregnant with class antagonism" to "[based on] Karl Marx's philosophy of economics". Some other larger employers, however, although opposed to the NLRA on various grounds, seemed more sympathetic to empowering the AFL and diffusing strikes. Members of this tendency worried that the NLRA would lead to more conflict and provide greater power to communists. These views are perhaps represented in the statements of Henry I. Harriman, the president of the U.S. Chamber of Commerce on 29 March 1934. Harriman and others pushed for certain amendments, but did not oppose the NLRA in principle.

There were also large numbers of individuals and groups from the Left who opposed the bill. It was viewed by many, including the ACLU, as potentially restrictive of the right to strike and too biased toward the allegedly procompany AFL. Leftist groups in general (with the exception of the Socialist party, which supported the NLRA) were suspicious of any expansion of government authority to intervene in labor-management relations. The NAACP and the Urban League also voiced opposition, unless the bill were to include guarantees for the rights of African-American workers. These groups and individuals, while occasionally representing broad constituencies and significant popular impulses, had little direct political influence in 1934 and 1935 (i.e., they had INFLUENCE1 but not INFLUENCE2).

The dominant political response to the increasingly powerful labor upsurge between 1933 and 1935, however, was to support the NLRA. The virtually unanimous opinion among New Deal Democrats and progressive Republicans (the overwhelming majority in both Houses after the November 1934 elections) was that government regulation was necessary to constrain, limit, and control the increasingly militant labor movement. This position, a central feature of the preamble and section 1 of the bill, runs like a bright yellow thread through the hearings and the floor debates of both Houses. Representative Withrow of Wisconsin on 18 June 1935, the last day of floor debate in the House, argued "As has been said by the gentleman from Pennsylvania [Rich], strikes have been prevalent in this country during the last two years . . . . The passage of this legislation is the only cure for the labor difficulties which have been characteristic for the past few years". And as Representative Sweeney of Ohio predicted on the same date, "Unless this Wagner-Connery dispute bill is passed we are going to have an epidemic of strikes that has never before been witnessed in this country".

The question naturally arises why repression and resistance were not considered a live option by political leaders in 1934 and 1935. In other words, what was attractive about mobilizing government support for moderate unionism by reducing employer capabilities for resistance? Two factors were important in making this latter option the most compelling one. The first had to do with the general social and political unrest in the country. The second (and perhaps most immediately important) had to do with the rapidly growing strength of radicalism in the working class in the United States. As Frances Perkins notes over a decade later it is easy for even a former participant to forget the atmosphere of political crisis that existed in the first half of the 1930s. To some political and economic elites, the possibility of revolution against the capitalist system was quite real . . . . Many diverse references are available indicating that individual executives and some politicians in the United States during the 1930s feared a revolution. Adolph Berle, Donald Richberg, and others thought government reforms were immediately necessary to avoid more radical demands and activity. Perkins for instance, was urged in the spring of 1933 by Berle, her close friend, to leave Washington before "widespread violence" broke out. As Schlesinger states, "It was now not just a matter of staving off hunger . . . . It was a matter of staving off violence, even (at least some thought) revolution. Whether revolution was a real possibility or not, faith in a free enterprise system was plainly waning."

Into this social milieu, tempered by the raised, then shattered hopes of the country in the NRA in general and section 7(a) for workers, burst the 1934 strikes, led by avowed revolutionaries, magnified by the linkages to other insurgent constituencies, the aftermath of which promised continued struggles on even broader scales. The 1934 events hang like a veil over the NLRA hearings and floor debates not just in 1934 but through the spring of 1935. To deny the impact of the 1934 upsurge is to miss a central aspect of reality. Theories that lead their adherents to overlook or slight these labor struggles must be deemed deficient. References to the dip in recorded strikes during early 1935, even if they did reflect a temporarily lowered level of insurgency, would tell us little about the threat that the 1934 strikes made, both to corporate elements and to AFL leaders as well. Those who pushed for the NLRA placed many of their arguments within this context.

There was also deep concern that the rising level of conflict caused mainly by the intransigence of most employers, was in good part the reason for the growing strength of labor radicalism and the relative weakening position of the AFL. The AFL was caught in the early thirties between a rock and a hard place. On the one side they were attacked and disowned by militants whose tactics they would not support, and on the other they were beaten back by recalcitrant employers who were not amenable to persuasion and moderate pressure. The complaint that employer hostility and government complicity were helping revolutionary labor groups may be heard repeatedly from top conservative AFL leaders, including William Green and John Frey, president of the AFL Metal Trades Department. This sentiment is voiced sharply by Frank I. Dillon, the director of auto organizing, personally selected by Green; Dillon had played a major role in undermining the then-upcoming auto strike in 1934. On 28 March 1935, at the House Hearings, Dillon stated,

> It is significant to here record the fact that Communists and communistic theories are more prevalent and substantially stronger among employees within the auto industry now than 1 year ago, constituting an actual menace to the future of the industry and a challenge to our form of government. It is my humble judgment that this feeling of bitterness, hatred, and resentment now so prevalent among auto workers is the direct result of management's failure to genuinely conform to the spirit and intent of section 7(a) of the NIRA.

However self-serving these claims may appear, the analysis has the ring of truth, reflecting the AFL loss of the emerging autoworkers' movement to the Left and the future UAW-CIO leadership.

Thus, there began to emerge a growing concensus among liberal politicians that the best way to preserve order, prevent high levels of strike activity, slow the spread of communism, and diffuse serious challenges to the capitalist system was by creating a government-supported legal environment where moderate forces, particularly the AFL leadership group, were protected and not so disadvantaged as at present. Hence, certain moderate forces were in favor of the NLRA because they thought it would strengthen the hand of the AFL. As Lloyd Garrison, the chairman of the pre-NLRA National Labor Relations Board argued on 15 March 1935, "I am for it as a safety measure, because I regard organized labor in this country as our chief bulwark against communism and other revolutionary movements . . . . I think that those employers who are out to strangle organized labor, are simply playing into the hands of the extremists."

To many in 1935, it did indeed seem that a specter was haunting the United States. In a sentiment echoed by diverse people during the

NLRA debate, Representative Connery on 4 April 1935 responded to the testimony of Dr. E. R. Lederer, who represented the Petroleum Industry's opposition to the bill:

> Dr. Lederer, I believe personally that the big corporations, like the Standard Oil Company, the Shell Oil Company, and these big textile industries, and the automobile industry, are very short-sighted . . . . They regard us as enemies of the employers, as actually being inimical to the employers, when we are not. What we are trying to do, Dr. Lederer, is to save those corporations from communism and bloodshed, and, Dr. Lederer, the Government wants them to give labor of the United States a fair deal. The American Federation of Labor, to which you referred, is the bulwark that is holding back communism in the United States among the workers, by having them in organized units where they can be self-respecting American citizens and have a chance to bargain collectively for their rights. They are keeping men in line who, if they did not have that union, would say 'All right, we get no protection from the government: we are slaves to our employers. Let us go out like they did in Russia and let us turn the government upside down and take the money away from these fellows . . . . ' I am surprised that the big employers cannot see that, and do not regard the committee as their friend rather than an enemy.

And so the NLRA passed, first the Senate, then the House of Representatives—overwhelmingly. It is, of course not necessary to argue that everything turned out exactly the way it was planned in the 1930s. It certainly took a good many years before labor insurgency was tamed and the influence of radicalism was checked. A convincing argument, however, can be made that the strategy was ultimately successful.

CONCLUSION

The foregoing analysis has suggested that the state autonomy model, which searches for primary explanations of politics in "states and parties" seriously slights the importance of the influence of labor militancy and radical organization in the passage of the 1935 NLRA. An alternative model examining the state and parties in conjunction with, and in the context of, the influence of key class actors is better able to account for the bill's enactment . . . .

Labor influence was central to the structure of the political situation in 1934 and 1935, both because of the growing strength of its insurgent and disruptive activities and because of the growing strength of highly organized radicalism. Because of this latter development, repression by companies (often aided by local police and state-directed National Guardsmen) was not an unproblematic option; it was already discrediting the more collaborationist wing of the AFL and giving greater legitimacy to radicalism. Liberal politicians (many with longstanding direct and indirect ties to corporate reform groups) thus reacted with a combination of sympathy and alarm at the growing labor upsurge with all its complexities.

If labor militance, social movements, and radical organization have had a major impact on public policy and on the general politics of the 1930s, no model of the modern state or research program for studying it [that] makes it difficult for the conscientious investigator to uncover this impact is adequate. Thus, the state autonomist approach and others that slight these factors must be judged inadequate. If the politics of class and social protest have been important in the past, they may be potentially important for the future. More attention should be paid in the political science profession to the study of these factors in the 1930s and the 1960s. The periods of relative quiet as well as the crescendos may be worth explaining, since they too may prove central to understanding what is essential about U.S. politics. □

23. *Explaining New Deal Labor Policy*

Theda Skocpol
and Kenneth Finegold

84 American Political Science Review 1257 (1989).

□ On 5 July 1935 President Franklin Roosevelt signed the National Labor Relations Act (NLRA, or Wagner Act) into law. This measure, which had passed both the Senate and the House during the previous month, established a legally enforceable right for U.S. industrial workers to unionize by majority vote. The Wagner Act outlawed company-run unions and explicitly protected the prerogative of unions to engage in strikes. It also set up the National Labor Relations Board (NLRB) to manage representation elections and explicitly proscribed methods by which employers might interfere with workers rights to organize autonomously.

The Wagner Act embodied the culmination of the New Deal's break with the officially repressive, antiunion policies of the 1920s. Yet the Wagner Act also represented a turnaround from the industrial labor policies of the early New Deal. The Roosevelt administration's pre-1935 policy about labor organization was neither opposition to unions nor unequivocal backing for the union shop. Without creating means of enforcement, the early New Deal authoritatively encouraged all sorts of worker associations including company unions and plural unions in single workplaces; and it also established federal agencies to mediate labor disputes as a way to avoid or settle strikes. This initial labor strategy of New Deal, embodied in section 7a of National Industrial Recovery Act (NIRA) of March 1933, was continued in various administrative steps taken under that law, and was reiterated as late as June 1934 in Public Resolution No. 44. When it was enacted just a year later, therefore, the Wagner Act was not just a further repudiation of repression of industrial labor unions. It represented a triumph for an approach to industrial labor disputes and unions within the evolving New Deal itself—a transition from mediation to enforcement and a move away from simple acceptance of company unions and organizational pluralism to support for majority-elected unions independent of employer domination . . . .

THE INADEQUACIES OF GOLDFIELD'S ANALYSIS OF THE NLRA

With or without Goldfield's emphasis on the role of radical organizers, an interpretation of the Wagner Act as a deradicalizing response to a mobilized working class is inconsistent with the contents and origins of this crucial legislation. Anxious to see the NLRA as an effort to quell worker unrest, Goldfield misrepresents the plain intentions of the law. He never mentions that its promoters favored strengthened unions as a means to promote national economic recovery by raising wages and mass consumption, a purpose emphasized (along with furthering industrial peace) in the law's preamble (section 1). The NLRA's sponsors believed that industrial peace could come only after the rights of independent labor unions were strengthened, a process that they realized might entail bitter conflicts with business. Goldfield claims that the Wagner Act was intended to avert strikes but fails to report that a guarantee of unions' rights to strike (section 13) was deliberately written into the act to avert the possibility that it could be used to outlaw strikes. Similarly, Goldfield repeatedly asserts that the Wagner Act was meant to protect the position of the American Federation of Labor (AFL) against industrial unions yet omits to mention that Wagner and his staff turned down an AFL request to reword their bills to protect the AFL against the jurisdictional claims of emerging industrial unions.

The aftermath of the Wagner Act also belies Goldfield's account of its intentions. Senator Wagner and other key promoters and supporters of the National Labor Relations Act continued to support its approach after the strike wave of 1937 and after the NLRB became a strong promoter of the (often radical-led) industrial unions of the Congress of Industrial Organizations in competition with craft unions affiliated with the AFL. Had the Wagner Act truly been designed to avoid strikes or protect conservative AFL leaders, one would have expected the act's original drafters and supporters—not just Republicans and conservative Democrats—to have sought legislative amendments or administrative changes to rein in growing industrial unions and the NLRB. But no such thing, happened, because Wagner and other leftist liberals of the New Deal were truly seeking to expand the labor movement, not to "constrain and limit" labor to the established unions of 1935.

Goldfield's causal argument about why the Wagner Act passed in 1935 is equally defective. Introducing worthwhile conceptual distinctions between direct and indirect labor influence, Goldfield correctly suggests that social movements can create an overall context in which political leaders feel they must "do something" to deal with disorder. This exactly parallels earlier arguments of ours. But then Goldfield tries to short circuit many causally relevant factors by attributing the activities of the politicians who drafted, voted for, and signed the 1935 Wagner Act to pressure from labor and other popular insurgencies.

Quoting statements from Senator Robert Wagner and other supporters of Wagner bills about the difficulties posed by industrial strikes, Goldfield claims that during 1934 and 1935 New Dealers' worries about labor disorders meant that "they had narrow room for maneuver, usually being buffeted by events and social forces". Repression of strikes could not be contemplated, Goldfield claims, because there was so much social unrest that federal repression would inevitably have sparked further political radicalization and possible revolution. This argument is not credible. Federal troops could have been use against major strikes either in 1934 or in 1937, as they were after the end of World War 1. That such troops were not used was a political choice, congruent with the nature of the coalitions that elected an reelected Roosevelt in 1932 and 1936. Goldfield asserts that the only conceivable alternative to repression and revolution was the Wagner Act. Thus, in the model he proposes, indirect influence from ongoing labor unrest is turned into the cause of the passage of the 1935 Wagner Act: "The most reasonable hypothesis to account for the passage of the NLRA is that labor militancy, catapulted into national prominence by the 1934 strikes and the political response to this movement, paved the way for the passage of the act".

Goldfield repeatedly speculates about the supposed possibilities for greater radicalization and social revolution in the 1930s, but we do not have to speculate counterfactually to show that repression and the Wagner Act were not the only possible federal actions during the unrest of 1934–35. We know from the historical legislative record that these were not the only alternatives debated and tried by the New Deal politicians. The strike wave of 1934 accompanied Senator Robert Wagner's efforts to put through Congress a labor disputes bill that very closely paralleled the eventual Wagner Act of 1935—and one cannot say that Wagner devised his approach "in response" to the 1934 strikes, because the basic principle of his labor laws were well established by late 1933. During 1934 business leaders, Congress, and the Roosevelt administration were concerned about labor unrest; such worries did not, however, lead them to support Wagner's 1934 bill. Business leaders were vociferously opposed to the 1934 Wagner bill, as they would be to its successor a year later. Moreover, in 1934 President Roosevelt recapitulated his administration's initial approach to labor unrest by asking Charles Wyzanski, counsel to the Labor Department, and Donald Richberg, of the National Industrial Recovery Administration, to draft a new bill, Public Resolution No. 44, which he then conveyed to congressional leaders. Passed in June 1934, this law empowered the president to establish a board to investigate labor disputes: it did not give the new board any direct enforcement powers, and it did not contain the Wagner bills substantive provisions ruling out company unions or guaranteeing labor unions' majority rule and the right to strike. Leon Keyserling, Wagner's associate in drafting his labor bills, has recently said that the primary objective of No. 44 was to derail the 1934 Wagner bill. After Public Resolution No. 44, Senator Wagner continued to maneuver on behalf of his approach, standing fast in the face of much counterpressure from the president, officials of the Labor Department and the NIRA, and certain congressional leaders.

There were, in short, sharp differences between the president and most executive branch officials on the one hand and Senator Wagner on the other about how the New Deal should relate to organized labor—differences that were articulated before the strike wave of 1934. Goldfield ignores these crucial differences. Since his vague labor insurgency model cannot account for the differences among New Deal leaders or explain the turnaround from the June 1934 Public Resolution No. 44 to the July 1935 Wagner Act, it is not causally adequate.

WHY DID THE WAGNER ACT PASS?

Strike volume declined somewhat from 1934 to 1935: and in May 1935 labor secretary Frances Perkins declared that there was no reality to the much-advertised strike epidemic. But even if one regards labor unrest (or the perception of it) as a relatively constant contributing factor, one must pinpoint factors that changed between June 1934 and July 1935 to explain why the second Wagner bill passed a year after the first one had failed and been replaced by Public Resolution No. 44. One needs a temporally grounded model that spells out interactions among continuing conflicts over the role of unions, electoral outcomes, sequences of public policies, and rivalries of political actors situated at different specific locations within the federal government.

There were two critical changes between mid-1934 and mid-1935. First, breaking with the usual pattern in which an administration in power loses congressional seats in an off year, the fall 1934 elections substantially strengthened liberal Democratic ranks in Congress, while weakening Republicans and Democratic conservatives. Redistricting had created more urban seats in Congress, and working-class ethnic voters were increasingly turning out for the Democratic party. Shifts in electoral politics, not increases in workplace militancy, were thus what heightened labor influence on legislation—and liberal influence more generally—between 1934 and 1935. Wagner and his allies could be more confident in forcing their labor bill to a vote in 1935 even in the face of presidential reluctance to endorse it.

Second, the early New Deal's keystone policy for economic recovery, regulating industry, and dealing with business—the National Industrial Recovery Act—met its demise between 1934 and 1935. The NIRA was ruled unconstitutional in May 1935, and even before this legal coup de grace it had become obvious to business leaders and to the Roosevelt administration that the NIRA was not a successful economic recovery measure. Just as Roosevelt had to face strengthened, independent-minded liberal forces in Congress, after the fall of 1934, he came to a bitter impasse with business leaders and found himself without an official economic recovery strategy. The NIRA's demise also undercut Hugh Johnson and Donald Richberg, two of the most vociferous Roosevelt administration opponents of Wagner's approach to unions: and this gave Wagner and his labor board allies broader leeway to argue within Congress and executive circles in favor of their bill. In the vacuum created by the end of the NIRA, they presented the NLRA as a good way both to promote economic recovery and to put labor relations on a new footing. Congress passed Wagner's second labor bill in 1935, and President Roosevelt finally decided to accept it after it had gone through the Senate and was pending in the House.

Our model also highlights the larger institutional contexts and longer-term processes that connected the Wagner Act to earlier, unsuccessful New Deal policies (invoking variables that are not encompassed in Goldfield's Figure 1). We especially point to the playing out within society and government of the unintended effects of the National Industrial Recovery Act of 1933. The enduring administrative weaknesses of the U.S. national government, the federal executive's overdependence on trade associations and business corporations to implement economic policies, and the institutional capacities of the courts and Congress to check or get around executive policy initiatives—all of these institutional features of the state in relation to the capitalist economy ensured the failure of the NIRA as an economic recovery strategy and as a method for mediating labor disputes. The Wagner Act would not have been possible had the NIRA succeeded—embodying, as it did, a rapprochement between the Roosevelt administration and sectors of business that favored administrative price fixing and either company unions or no unions at all.

Yet even as it failed, the NIRA spurred social and political forces that led toward the Wagner Act. Section 7a of the 1935 law emboldened labor organizers without constraining opposition to unions, through feeding industrial unrest. What is more, Senator Wagner and virtually all of lawyers and economists he worked with in drafting successive versions of what became the National Labor Relations were members of, or directly concerned with the problems of, the various labor boards established under the NIRA. The specific ideas that went into Wagner labor bills can be traced to their drafter's frustrating efforts to implement NIRA labor mediation policies. The NIRA labor boards provided the precise context within which actors within the state tried to cope with labor unrest and especially with the unwillingness of most business to accept independent labor unions. Initial failures and frustrations under NIRA led these official actors to believe that more state building had to be done, that is, it led them to formulate the strong, substantive legal guarantees for independent unions and the means for federal enforcement against business resistance which made the Wagner Act an innovative departure within the New Deal as a whole. The Wagner Act was the product of administratively situated policy learning, because, as Leon Keyserling has put it, section 7(a) "stirred things up but couldn't be enforced." . . .

THEORETICAL AND METHODOLOGICAL IMPLICATIONS

Michael Goldfield accompanies his account of the Wagner Act with broader appeals that we can endorse with certain additions and qualifications. He calls for precise modeling of causal processes of politics and rightly says that hypotheses and models have to be tested against both available evidence and theoretical competitors. We can only add that good models and causal hypotheses need to be tested against concrete historical variations in outcomes. Scholars should not just present stories based on selective descriptions and counterfactual speculations but actually account for variation in specified types of outcomes. Had Goldfield held himself to this standard, he could not have put forward the argument he did. His model fails to explain not only the contrasts between New Deal labor laws in 1934 and 1935 but also, for example, the interactions of U.S. labor mobilizations with governmental policy making in the 1935, as compared to the interactions leading up to 1919, when President Wilson used federal troops against strikes in coal and steel, and the interactions of the mid-1940s, when a postwar strike wave led to passage in the following year of the Taft-Hartley Act (which attached important anti-union provisions to the NLRA).

Goldfield argues that the effects of industrial labor actions on public policy outcomes may be registered in different ways. When labor cannot directly determine state actions through measures taken by political parties that hold governmental power, labor may exert influences by other means. Strikes or broader unrest may help to bring about initiatives "by a government in order to stem working class militance and organized radicalism." Or (although Goldfield does not mention this possibility) labor may amass sufficient electoral power as a minority within established parties to encourage government to take its interests into account in some way. All possible alternative forms of labor influence do need to be explored. (They have been, for example, in the extensive cross-national literature on the development of welfare state policies.) Yet an important caveat needs to be voiced about Goldfield's notion that analysts can expect to find straightforward relationships between militant labor unrest and governmental "concessions" (as he calls them). In none of the historical examples that Goldfield cites—the welfare reforms of Bismarck's Germany in the 1880s, the recent policies toward black trade unions of the white South African regime or the labor legislation of the New Deal—were governmental authorities in a position where they "had to" respond to labor unrest with only one sort of "concessions." In all of these cases alternative responses were possible, including repression and various sorts of reforms. The policy responses actually made depended on the consequences of prior policy attempts; the capacities of administrative and political institutions to devise and implement measures: and on shifting ideas, political alliances, and balances of power among economic and political elites. Unrest from below may have pressured governments to do something. But the sheer fact of that unrest cannot explain why these governments did what they did when they did it. □

NOTES AND QUESTIONS

1. The Wagner Act has struck many scholars as an interesting puzzle in historical explanation. On one hand, it recognized unions as legitimate organizations and created a structure for organizing unions in particular plants and for collective bargaining. It is hard for people today to realize what a radical change this represented from the views of most Americans up to 1930. On the other hand, the Wagner Act did not create a system of worker control of industry; it left the structure of industry in place. Some radicals see it as selling out far too cheaply in terms of what might have been possible at the time. Contrast Richard A. Epstein, "A Common Law for Labor Relations: A Critique of the New Deal Labor Legislation," 92 *Yale Law Journal* 1357 (1983) and Richard A. Posner, "Some Economics of Labor Law," 51 *University of Chicago Law Review* 988 (1984), who see the Wagner Act as a private-regarding interest-group statute which distorts efficiency by fostering cartelization in the labor market.

The Wagner Act and New Deal labor policy were packaged to look less radical to various audiences. American labor law rests on traditional liberal capitalist notions: whether to have a union and which one, is decided by a democratic election; union-management relations are the product of collective bargaining (contract); and management action can be challenged by unions and their members by arbitration, a form of industrial due process. See, e.g., James B. Atleson, *Values and Assumptions in American Labor Law* (Amherst, Mass.: University of Massachusetts Press, 1983); William E. Forbath, *Law and the Shaping of the*

American Labor Movement (Cambridge, Mass.: Harvard University Press, 1991); Karl E. Klare, "Judicial Deradicalization of the Wagner Act and the Origins of Modern Legal Consciousness, 1937–1941," 62 *Minnesota Law Review* 265 (1978); Katherine Van Wezel Stone, "The Post-War Paradigm in American Labor Law," 90 *Yale Law Journal* 1509 (1981). See also, Kenneth M. Casebeer, "Holder of the Pen: An Interview with Leon Keyserling on Drafting the Wagner Act," 42 *University of Miami Law Review* 285 (1987).

Joel Rogers argues that American labor law, including the Wagner Act, kept the costs of union organizing very high, limited coordination, and encouraged the use of particularistic bargaining strategies. See Rogers, "Divide and Conquer: Further Reflections on the Distinctive Character of American Labor Laws," 1990 *Wisconsin Law Review* 1. See, also, Alan Hyde, "A Theory of Labor Legislation," 38 *Buffalo Law Review* 383 (1990). If these views are correct, do they fit Goldfield's argument or Skocpol-Finegold?

2. Note the structure of the arguments that Goldfield and Skocpol-Finegold make. How does each side attempt to explain what caused what? Is it possible to decide which side is right and which is wrong? Could Senator Wagner and his staff have fashioned what became the Wagner Act ten or twenty years earlier? Might another senator and his or her staff have fabricated a labor law with different features, and a different impact, than the Wagner Act?

3. What does the story of the passage of the Wagner Act teach us about social influence on law? For example, is Goldfield's account consistent with Friedman's legal culture perspective? Is Skocpol and Finegold's position more consistent with it? Is either position, or are both positions, consistent with the process described in Friedman and Ladinsky? For example, is the Skocpol and Finegold position a "great man" theory? In an earlier paper, "Political Response to Capitalist Crisis: Neo-Marxist Theories of the State and the Case of the New Deal," 10 *Politics & Society* 155, 191–92 (1980), Skocpol asserted:

> [T]he interesting thing about the reformist phase of the New Deal (1935–38) is that, although tendencies existed that might conceivably have added up to a social-democratic Keynesian breakthrough, the existing governmental and party structures so patterned political conflicts and so limited the possibilities for political transformations as to prevent any such breakthrough from actually occurring. Instead, the direct consequence of labor reforms, and of the enhanced labor and liberal power that accompanied them, was not economic recovery through social-democratic Keynesianism but increased social and political tension, leading by 1938–39 to an insecure impasse for the domestic New Deal.

What kind of argument is this? What might it say about a pluralist theory?

Mark Barenberg, in "The Political Economy of the Wagner Act: Power, Symbol, and Workplace Cooperation," 106 *Harvard Law Review* 1379 (1993), argues:

> [T]he convergence of two key elements was decisive in the immediate origins of the Wagner Act. The opportunity for such a dramatic legislative initiative was generated by "mass politics" in the form of popular electoral realignment, populist political organization, and mass labor unrest (often outside the compass of organized interest groups and propelled by radical activists and managerial belligerents with no intention

of securing legislative reform similar to the Wagner Act). That opportunity was seized by loosely interconnected networks of political-technocratic entrepreneurs driven by progressive ideological commitment and ambition. Fortuitously located at the central nodal point was Robert Wagner, the progressive "powerhouse" of the New Deal legislative program . . . . (p. 1389)

One reason for the relative importance of mass politics over interest-group deal-making in the origin of New Deal labor legislation is, of course, the very *saliency* of the political issues at stake at a moment of extraordinary social crisis . . . . Such issue-saliency and attendant mass mobilization offer one explanation for the relative down-grading of interest-group politics . . . [T]he substance of New Deal labor policy was not the intentional outcome of group deals. In respectively exacerbating and leading worker unrest, employers and radical organizations had no intent to achieve, and in fact opposed the kind of legislative response that their actions helped produce. (pp. 1400–01)

Wagner's Senate office . . . [was] the nerve-center of a network of progressive policy entrepreneurs whose ideological commitments and ambitions are not reducible to interest-group reflexes . . . . Because of Robert Wagner's early immersion in New York State reform politics, he was, by the time he took his United States Senate seat in 1927, already on "intimate terms" with many of "the hard core of Progressive social reformers" who had continued their reform efforts into the 1920s. His first legislative aide, Simon Rifkind, established a formal ongoing communication with "a nationwide network of professional and academic social scientists," numbering approximately 250, who were regularly mobilized for consultation and lobbying in the legislative battles that Wagner spearheaded. Contemporary observers recognized Wagner as the first legislator to draw so systematically on the newly consolidated social sciences of the interwar period. (pp. 1403–04)

What explains Wagner's ultimate success? Wagner had become the main bridge between the two dominant ideological blocs in the Democratic Senatorial contingent—the progressive insurgents, whose ranks were swollen by the 1934 election, and the "regulars"—especially as to the issues that became salient after the stock market crash . . . . Equally important, no other legislator had the longstanding personal and political friendship with FDR [President Roosevelt] that gave such pre-eminence to Wagner's legislative role in the New Deal. FDR's resulting dependence on Wagner's legislative leadership, in turn, gave the Senator the leverage *against* FDR to insist that his labor legislation go forward . . . . [A]fter the Supreme Court's nullification of the Recovery Act in May, 1935, the New Deal was left without a program that either addressed economic recovery directly or eased the labor unrest that threatened recovery indirectly. Robert Wagner was ready in the wings with a portion of a recovery program, which bore the stamp of progressive debate and experience.

Is Barenberg's position consistent with that of Friedman and Ladinsky? Is his a "great man" theory of history? Does he side with Goldfield, Skocpol, and Finegold or none of these authors?

4. Skocpol insists that we should treat the "state" not as some kind of bloodless abstraction, but as a concrete interest group, made up of human beings. Similarly, the "legislature" (Congress, state legislatures, various Parliamentary bodies) is made up of actual men and women. They do not automatically or magically reflect what their constituents want (assuming we know what that is). Does a Congressional representative, for example, always vote the way her constituents want her to vote, or the way powerful and articulate constituents would like her to? or as she pleases? Do representatives from "safe" districts pay less attention to constituents than those who are in marginal, contested districts? The answers *seem* obvious, but it turns out that research on these issues raises as many problems as it solves. The linkages between representatives and constituents are very obscure. See Eric M. Uslaner, "The Study of Representation," in Long (ed.), *Annual Review of Political Science* (Norwood, N.J.: Ablek Publishing Corp., 1986), for a thorough discussion of the methodological issues and the results of the studies thus far. Recall, too, Buchanan and Tullock, in Chapter 2.

CASE STUDIES OF THE PRODUCTION OF LAW

We have looked at a number of theories about how society affects law, and we have looked at the process of elections and lobbying to gain various ends. Now we turn to several case studies. Does each one fit one or another larger theory about the influence of society on law? Does the case study teach us something about the process by which classes, interests, specific groups, or various elites produce legal change? What do they teach us about the legitimating claim that law is the will of the people?

EXPERT REFORM: CHANGING AMERICA'S DIVORCE LAWS

In the following reading, Herbert Jacob begins by noting that since 1965 there have been radical changes in legal expectations about family life. States have passed laws eliminating any penalty for adultery or other marital misbehavior. We have no-fault divorce. There is no presumption that the mother gets custody of young children. A family's property is regarded as marital property belonging to both husband and wife, and it will be divided in an equitable or equal manner. Wives' rights to support from husbands are problematic. The old alimony system is gone.

These laws were not the product of social protest or lobbying by an established interest group. They were accompanied by little political conflict. The major changes in divorce law involved much activity, but most of it took place out of sight. This "silent revolution" took place as part of *the routine policy process* before one state legislature after another. The proponents advocated their reforms as narrow proposals which would produce little real change and cost little money. They relied on experts who emphasized the incremental character of their suggestions. They avoided media attention by casting their action as technical. They built a consensus through consultation with interested parties before seeking legislation. Thus, when routine policy alterations such as this "surface in the form of legislative proposals, a consensus has already been built around a preferred solution in a manner to minimize controversy" (p. 13).

The reform statutes passed because of changes in the social and economic environments of families. Fewer men and women marry. People live longer, and so their lifespan covers many years after children are grown. Women have fewer children. More women, but fewer children, are in the labor market. Women find it necessary to work if the family is to reach a middle class life style. People saw the breakup of marriage was morally possible. Movie stars and public figures got divorces, and this suggested the possibility to others.

Feminist rhetoric affected how many Americans expressed their ideal of the family. It helped change the idea that there were distinctive gender roles. Moreover, it was anathema to feminists for the law to treat ex-wives as incompetents who could not care for themselves.

24. *Silent Revolution*

Herbert Jacob

(Chicago: University of Chicago Press, 1988)

☐ The companionate marriage style has become dominant. The romantic ideal not only rules courtship, but it also governs the criteria for continuing marriages. The life span of most Americans produces a prolonged period during which marriages can persist. For most of that time, as we have already indicated, children are not present to focus affection and activity. But in addition, the life style of urban Americans throws husbands and wives together more than in earlier times. In-laws, siblings, and cousins more often live in different neighborhoods or different cities than that of the husband and wife. Neither can find refuge with a nurturing relative as easily as before. The bar, the movie theater, and even the ball park have been largely replaced by television, so that people spend more of their free time at home than before. Finally, husbands and wives have more free time. The standard work week has become five days so that many have the weekend entirely free from work. The workday is usually only eight hours, leaving evenings free from obligatory activities.

In these circumstances, marriages which are not companionate quickly become intolerable. Intolerable marriages more frequently lead to divorce and alternative life-styles appear viable.

One alternative is to seek the companionship of another man or woman. In the early part of the century, both men and women had few contacts with those of the opposite sex other than their kin. Men mostly worked with other men; women stayed at home and visited with other women. By the 1980s that had changed, so that many men came into contact with women other than their wives at their work, and most women who worked came into contact with men other than their husbands. The increased contact between men and women at their workplace undoubtedly accounts for the increased prominence of sexual harassment incidents. But in addition, the increased contact brought men and women together in situations which could lead to friendship and alternatives to companionship within an existing marriage.

Moreover, the moral imperative of lifetime marriage had become undermined. Divorce in the minds of many was transformed from an act of immorality to a symptom of social illness. The remedy was not to punish or to persist in what religion prescribed. Rather, unhappiness resulting from an unsatisfying marriage was perceived as an infirmity that could be either treated with psychotherapy or excised by divorce. The perception of marital unhappiness as a condition to be assuaged rather than one to be abhorred grew gradually in tandem with the broader redefinition of mental illness and social maladjustments. It contributed to legitimizing divorce because divorce was seen as one of several alternative effective treatments . . . .

CALIFORNIA'S BOLD STEP

It remained for California to step into the future and explicitly embrace the no-fault concept in divorce. California illustrates the potential for innovation through a routine policy-making process, for it was the first state to adopt no-fault divorce in the context of a thorough reform of its divorce procedures; yet it did so with minimal controversy.

The Social and Political Context of California's Divorce Reform

No-fault was the sort of innovation that many Americans have come to expect of California. That state has long been viewed as an incubator for novel social ideas. Its population had the reputation of adopting a relaxed life style that included not only suburban living and patio barbecues, but also loose marriages and easy divorces. It was, after all, the home of Hollywood; and while the escapades of movie stars did not typify the average Californian, they established an ambience of nonchalance and experimentation that sometimes permitted Californians to adopt novel ideas.

California in the mid-1960s differed from New York in many ways. California's population had much shallower roots than New York's. The families of most Californians had moved west from elsewhere in the United States since the Great Depression, leaving behind other relatives. They lived in rapidly growing cities which had been ranches and fruit orchards a few years earlier. California's ethnic composition was quite different from that of eastern states because more of its ethnics were Oriental and later Chicano as well as Irish, Italian, and black. Its Catholic population was smaller than New York's, and the church had not acquired as open a political role. Even in the 1960s, ethnicity played a different and smaller role in California policies than in New York; it was more important that ballot tickets be balanced along geographic lines that recognized the gulf between southern and northern California than that Irish or Italian candidates be offset with blacks or Jews.

Fluidity marked California's policies as it characterized its people. It had been possible for Earl Warren to run for governor on both the Republican and Democratic tickets. The legislature was organized along partisan lines, but it was possible for Republicans to support a Democrat for presiding officer of the assembly as late as 1980. Nonpartisanship had become much more entrenched in California than in New York, while machine polities based on patronage scarcely existed. The major political organizations centered on ideological issues in statewide elections and recruited volunteer workers to the California Republican Assembly and the California Democratic Council rather than to "regular" party organizations.

The 1960s were marked by many political crosscurrents in California. In 1958, California elected the liberal (and Catholic) Edmund Brown, Sr. to the governorship and kept him in office until the conservative Ronald Reagan defeated his third-term bid in 1966. Racial tension erupted in the Los Angeles Watts neighborhood riot in 1965 and in Oakland in 1968, together with simultaneous riots in other northern cities, causing the nation to recognize that race relations were not just a southern problem. The "free speech movement" at the University of California's Berkeley campus focused attention on the rebellious hippy style of a conspicuous minority of its youth. A sometimes raucous but always tense campaign to liberalize California's abortion law occupied the attention of many during the last years of the decade. That bill reached Governor Reagan's desk only a few months before no-fault divorce.

The intellectual climate surrounding divorce was also somewhat different in California than in New York. Traditional values of family life rooted in religion dominated discussions in New York. Californians more openly espoused the newer clinical and therapeutic conceptions which saw marital failure as a symptom of psychological incompatibility and maladjustment rather than as an indication of sin. Such ideas had won widespread acceptance among mental health professionals by the 1960s throughout the United States, but in California they were publicly articulated with stark clarity in legislative hearings . . . . The therapeutic view received unexpected support from the religious sector when in June of 1966, just after New York had passed its new divorce law, a committee appointed by the Archbishop of Canterbury of the Church of England issued its report on divorce. That report, *Putting Asunder*, advocated eliminating adultery and other marital offenses as grounds for divorce and replacing them with marital breakdown. The English commission couched its recommendations in conservative language which would permit judges the discretion to "dissolve the marriage if, and only if, having regard to the interests of society as well as of those immediately affected by its decision, it judged it wrong to maintain the legal existence of a relationship that was beyond all probability of existing again." Moreover, if the court were not convinced that the marriage "had in fact broken down irreparably, [it] would have a duty to refuse a decree despite the express agreement of the parties." However, the commission's view that divorce was justified when marriages had broken down and its support for no-fault divorce were unequivocal. The publication of this church report made advocacy of no-fault appear much less radical . . . The report arrived just in time to buttress California's no-fault proposal, which itself was published at the end of 1966.

In addition, by the mid-1960s the no-fault concept had gained considerable visibility in other contexts. Workmen's compensation, adopted in the first decades of the twentieth century, explicitly replaced a fault-based system of compensating workers for injuries incurred in industrial accidents. In the 1950s and early 1960s proposals for adopting a no-fault automobile accident insurance plan had evoked considerable discussion and controversy. Those plans, eventually adopted in many states, were intended to eliminate fault-based litigation and replace it with compensation of insured drivers from their own insurance policies. No personal connection existed between advocates of no-fault automobile insurance and no-fault divorce, but discussions of no-fault accident insurance familiarized people with the concept and made it appear less radical when it was proposed for divorce.

One further distinction differentiated California from New York. California's divorce law was in practice among the most lenient in the nation. As Herma Hill Kay, a teacher of family law at the University of California's Boalt Hall School of Law and a leader in the reform movement, put it: "It was impossible to make divorce easier in California than it already was." It was, however, a fault-grounded divorce law. To obtain a divorce, husband or wife had to demonstrate that the other spouse had committed a marital offense, such as adultery, cruelty, or desertion. In most cases, the wife was the plaintiff and her complaint usually alleged cruelty, which encompassed a host of sins ranging from disparaging remarks to spouse abuse. The testimony was often arranged and fake, disguising a mutual or negotiated decision to end the marriage. It was this element of dishonesty that provoked some of the proponents of change to seek a no-fault statute and, as in New York, it provided a technical cover for advocating a revolutionary liberalization. But unlike New York, the production of fraudulent evidence was not a visible industry, and the no-fault concept was openly discussed in California, having even been articulated in a California Supreme Court case as early as 1952 in an opinion by the renowned Chief Justice Roger Traynor.

A high divorce rate paralleled California's easy divorce law. Although California's divorce rate did not approach Nevada's and was indeed only eleventh in the nation, it was perceived as being a divorce-prone state by its natives. However, California's law had one quirk that motivated some people to migrate to Nevada for their divorce: a California divorce was not final until one year had passed. During this interlocutory period, ex-spouses were not permitted to remarry. This provision had been intended to prevent hasty divorces motivated by a passing fancy for another man or woman. In fact, it proved to be a major inconvenience, because in the 1960s extramarital cohabitation had not yet become widespread or socially accepted, but many people getting a divorce wanted to begin a new family soon after ending their first marriage . . . .

Innovation through Routine Policy Making

Innovation is usually thought to involve at least two stages. The first is the identification of a problem that involves a serious performance gap requiring a solution. The second is the formulation of a solution. Thereafter, those responsible for making policy decisions must be convinced that the solution is a viable and attractive response to the problem.

Performance gaps are usually a prerequisite for innovation because people are loath to change adequately working procedures. The character of such gaps, however, varies considerably because they are subjective phenomena. It is rare for everyone to agree that a policy is failing or to concur on the dimensions of the failure. Often the client or objects of a policy have a different perception than its administrators, as when people who must wait for months to receive a government payment complain but the administrators of the agency making the payment think all is proceeding normally. The measurement instrument is frequently at issue, with one group arguing that it indicates failure while another points to a different set of facts which suggests adequate performance from their perspective. Thus, parents may complain that their children are not learning to read well enough while school administrators point with satisfaction to rising test score levels. Even the goals of a policy may become subject to dispute, as when one group of citizens calls on the police to stop speeding drivers on their residential street while another group decries the waste of police on traffic enforcement while drug sales flourish.

Performance gaps may be the result of a gradual decay in the operation of a policy or the consequence of a sudden external shock which dramatically changes the conditions confronting administrators. In the former case, a series of small events pulls a policy's achievements increasingly away from its stated goals, creating a gradual awareness of the policy's inadequacy. The social security crisis of the late 1970s was an example of such a gradual decay, when slowly rising payments were not matched by rising revenues for the system. At other times, performance gaps occur because of a sudden change in the environment which the policy and its administrators cannot accommodate. The discovery of AIDS, for instance, suddenly created a public health crisis which pointed to the inadequacy of existing measures for the prevention of sexually transmitted diseases.

In every case the definition of the performance gap is both subjective and of central importance to the subsequent adoption of innovative solutions. Because it is subjective, it may be manipulated by those seeking to promote or block a change. Both sides, however, recognize its crucial significance for the adoption process, because the manner in which the gap is defined either excites or lulls potential opponents. Defined expansively, a performance gap invites wide group participation and public controversy; defined narrowly, it demarcates a restricted field of groups and makes it unlikely that the media will publicize the push for reform.

The formulation of solutions is often dominated by self-appointed experts. The solutions may be specifically designed to address the performance gap, or they may have been devised for other purposes and simply found available for application to the newly discovered performance gap. In the former case, decision makers embark on a rational search-and-choice process in which experts examine the dimensions of the problem, consider available alternative solutions in terms of their promised costs and benefits, and recommend the one with the greatest potential net benefits. Since many of the costs and benefits are difficult to measure, the process depends much more on informed intuition than on mechanical calculation; consequently, the conclusions drawn by the experts are often subject to conflicting interpretations. In many instances, however, the selection of an innovation may be quite different and involve less rational choice and more coincidence . . . . [S]olutions are sometimes devised for other purposes and [we look] for problems to which they may be attached. A common example is the personal computer which a businessman may purchase for status reasons and then leave to sit on his desk; he may ultimately use it to make corporate financial calculations for which he had never previously felt a need. In this instance, the computer created both the performance gap and its solution. It is likely that experts identify such a solution because of their familiarity with new ideas. Its adoption, however, very much depends on the constellation of participants who happen to be present when the decision is made. Thus, the innovation process may involve much less rational calculation than the search-and-choose model suggests.

The adoption of no-fault divorce in California illustrates these processes in the context of routine policy making. It shows how a major alteration of public policy may occur with few of the trappings of public debate and controversy. It involved the manipulation of the definition of a performance gap and the adoption of an innovative solution which was waiting to be matched to the problem of divorce.

The Reformers

A key to the distinctive development of divorce reform in California was the identity of the reformers and the manner in which they defined the performance gap and devised their no-fault solution. As other students of innovation have found, the impetus for reform came from a small band of self-appointed experts who elevated the discrepancies between black-letter law and the law-in-action to the status of a performance gap and formulated the solution.

The experts consisted of a small group of elite matrimonial lawyers in the San Francisco Bay area who had long regretted the bitterness engendered by the adversarial divorce process which they witnessed in their professional lives. They felt that much of the conflict they saw in their offices and in divorce courtrooms was the unnecessary product of statutes which required the fabrication of ugly events that would justify divorce on the grounds of extreme cruelty. Their goal was both to eliminate the perjurious evidence which tainted matrimonial lawyers in the eyes of their colleagues and to humanize the divorce process by decreasing the level of conflict. They had quietly worked for many years to win the support of mental health professionals and the organized bar for such a reform.

It is worth noting that some plausible goals which would have sparked intense opposition were not embraced by the reformers. They did not explicitly advocate making divorce easier because divorce was better than family conflict. They did not formulate their goals in terms of achieving equality for women, nor did they champion divorce reform in order to permit greater individual choice among alternate family forms. Instead, the reformers hewed to objectives which appeared politically innocuous.

At the group's core were Herma Hill Kay, a law professor at Boalt Hall (University of California, Berkeley), Richard Dinkelspiel, a San Francisco attorney who was also prominent in Catholic lay circles,

Kathryn Gehrels, a prominent San Francisco attorney who handled many upper-class divorces, and Irving Phillips, a psychiatrist associated with the University of California Medical School. These four, who enjoyed both professional and friendship bonds, were interested in no-fault reform principally because it appealed to them on intellectual grounds. They saw it as a cure for the hypocrisy which permeated divorce proceedings in California as they had in New York, and they saw such a change as worthy of the long tradition of reform leadership which characterized much California law making.

A second group of divorce reformers centered around Los Angeles and consisted of Pearce Young, a prominent assemblyman, Roger Pfaff, a vocal judge who presided over the conciliation court in Los Angeles, and several Beverly Hills matrimonial lawyers. The Los Angeles contingent did not always agree with the San Francisco Bay area proponents of divorce law reform, but they provided the necessary southern leg of interest in divorce reform so that the effort could not be dismissed as a northern California aberration.

Laying the Foundation for Reform

As early as 1962, the legislature's Assembly Interim Committee on the Judiciary considered amending the state's domestic relations law, but that committee concerned itself principally with changing the law's provisions for an interlocutory divorce that forced people to wait a year before remarrying. It never reached more fundamental issues. Two years later, domestic relations law was again targeted by the assembly's interim judiciary committee. That committee conducted a wide-ranging examination of California's marriage and divorce laws. It held hearings from January to October of 1964 in Santa Monica, Sacramento, and twice in Los Angeles. It heard numerous witnesses who ascribed divorce to a variety of causes ranging from the advent of the automobile (where out-of-wedlock pregnancies were conceived in back seats) to the changing role of women; they discussed problems of property distribution and child custody. Among the remedies mentioned were family life education courses in schools, marriage counseling, a family court, mandatory divorce counseling, and gender-neutral provisions for child custody.

Many of the members of the core group of divorce reformers testified. Herma Hill Kay addressed each of the four hearings; Judge Pfaff also appeared at each. Los Angeles attorneys Harry Fain and Stuart Walzer, later members of the governor's commission, presented their views, as did the later executive director of the governor's commission, Aiden Gough. Assemblyman Pearce Young, later co-chair of the governor's commission, also participated in the committee's work.

These hearings provided an opportunity for Kay and others to introduce the no-fault concept and some of the other innovations which later marked the 1969 law. No-fault surfaced at the very beginning, when at the committee's January, 1964 hearing Kay testified:

> ... as long as we are not going to require any detailed evidence as to the grounds for divorce and as long as we have a large number of default divorces in this State, it seems to me a good idea to permit parties to have at least one ground for divorce in which fault is not made necessary.

By October, Kay was ready to make much more specific and far-reaching proposals. She pointed to a Pennsylvania legislative proposal drafted by New York's divorce expert Henry H. Foster, Jr., which unabashedly favored divorce by mutual consent "which of course is true as a matter of practice now but it is not the way the statutes are drafted." However, not all members of the committee were ready to support her proposal. The chairman on that day, assemblyman Willson, demurred saying: "I recognize the problem that you would have in trying to get such a ground through the Legislature and through the people of the state . . . " When Kay became more explicit in her support for no-fault, Willson interrupted: "Well now, Professor Kay, I can't subscribe to that. You will have to exclude me from that. I think it is possible for a woman to be wrong or a man to be wrong and break up a marriage." That did not deter Kay from proceeding to advocate elimination of adversarial-style proceedings in divorce cases and establishment of a new family court system to hear all matters related to divorce and other family problems. Thus, two years before the Archbishop of Canterbury's report made no-fault a widely discussed concept and before New York's divorce reform law, Kay outlined the basic features of a complete reform of American divorce law.

Kay was not the only witness to make wide-ranging proposals, although she was probably the most widely respected witness to do so. Judge Pfaff urged extension of his conciliation procedures to the entire state so that more marriages would be saved. Representatives of the U.S. Divorce Reform League advocated taking divorce cases out of court and giving men more rights with respect to their children.

The committee's report, however, scarcely reflected such proposals. It made few specific recommendations and lamely suggested the need for further study and deliberation. No immediate action came from the year's work.

Formulation of the Divorce Proposals

After a hiatus of sixteen months, divorce reforms suddenly revived. Governor Edmund Brown appointed a commission on the family in May of 1966, just as he was preparing to run for a third term against the movie actor and political novice, Ronald Reagan. The idea for the commission seems to have come from the Bay area group, which had a conduit to the governor's office through a former law student of Kay. The official proclamation of the commission did not reveal its likely outcome; its title was the innocuous "Governor's Commission on the Family." It was charged to "study and suggest revision, where necessary, of the substantive laws of California relating to the family," to examine the feasibility of developing courses in family life for California's schools, to consider the possibility of developing a uniform national standard for marriage and divorce jurisdiction, and to look into the establishment of a system of family courts. In fact, the commission responded only to the first and last elements of this charge.

The commission included many of the core Bay area persons who had pressed for divorce law reform, as well as some key legislators and prominent jurists and lawyers from the Los Angeles area. The spark plugs of the commission, however, were the Bay area members, who formulated many of its recommendations. Potential opposition from some conservative members was averted by the illness of one of their key spokesmen, Judge Pfaff, who urged conciliation procedures but resisted more fundamental changes; his dissent was limited to a letter to Dinkelspiel, who was co-chair, but it was not printed in the commission's report.

Unlike the interim commission of the legislature, the governor's commission held no public hearings. Indeed, it seems to have worked entirely in the shadow of the heated gubernatorial campaign that took place during most of its life. It issued no press releases and its work did not reach the attention of the media until it was completed and its report published. Under this cloak of obscurity, the commission forged its radical proposal; but while the commission worked, Governor Brown lost the gubernatorial election. With the much more conservative Ronald Reagan in the wings, the commission rushed to complete its work before inaugural day; it managed to convey its report to Governor Brown just two weeks before he left office and its authority expired.

The governor's commission was careful to veil its proposals in as conservative a guise as possible. It first highlighted its plan to consolidate all family disputes in a newly constituted family court that would be available in every county. That court and the conciliation and counseling services connected with it were to help save families from stress and dissolution. Moreover, the commission clothed its report in pro-family vocabulary. It argued that the goal of the law should be "to further the stability of the family" and that the existing law

represents by its ineptitude an abdication of the public interest in, and responsibility toward, the family as the basic unit of our society. The direction of the law must be, as we have said, toward family stability— toward preventing divorce where it is not warranted, and toward reducing its harmful effects where it is necessary.

The commission's second thrust was its radical contribution, but it too was described with a conservative vocabulary. Claiming that it simply wished to align the law with the divorce process as it really worked, the commission proposed eliminating all fault grounds for divorce and replacing them with the requirement that irreparable breakdown of the marriage exist. Lest that this be seen as an invitation to easy divorce, the commission wrote:

> We cannot overemphasize that this standard does not permit divorce by consent, wherein marriage is treated as wholly a private contract terminable at the pleasure of the parties without an effective intervention by society. The standard we propose requires the community to assert its interest in the status of the family, and permits dissolution of the marriage only after it has been subjected to a penetrating scrutiny and the judicial process has provided the parties with all of the resources of social science in aid of conciliation.

Note that the commission invoked not only society's interest in stable families but also the therapeutic potential of science that might be harnessed by its proposal. In addition, the commission quoted at length from the Archbishop of Canterbury's report in support of its no-fault proposal.

In order to reduce the law's contribution to marital conflict, the commission also suggested abandoning the conventional vocabulary of litigation in divorce cases. Instead of styling divorce actions in the usual way, "Jones v. Jones," cases were to be referred to as "In re the marriage of Jones." Instead of a complaint, a "petition of inquiry" was to initiate the proceedings. Even the term "divorce" was to be replaced with "marital dissolution." Each of these proposals closely followed the suggestions made by Herma Hill Kay two years earlier to the interim study committee of the California legislature. Kay, of course, was a key member of the governor's commission and played a central role in drafting its recommendations.

A third set of proposals concerned the disposition of property at divorce. The existing rules permitted property division to be governed by fault. California was already a community property state in which both spouses had a claim to any property accumulated during their marriage. However, innocent parties in a divorce case were eligible for more than half of the community property. When the commission proposed banishing fault, a new rule had to be devised. Without much discussion of its potential consequences, the commission recommended establishing a presumption of equal distribution of community property, except in circumstances when some other division seemed appropriate. Alimony also was redefined. It too was set loose from a consideration of fault and was instead based on need "for such a period of time as the court may deem just and reasonable."

Finally, some questions of child custody were addressed. The commission took note of the fact that many mothers no longer provided full-time care even for very young children, but rather entrusted them to day care and pre-school nurseries. Consequently, the commission recommended ending the practice of automatically favoring mothers in deciding custody and establishing a new standard which required that the court consider the "best interests of the child" in determining which parent (or other person) should have custody of children of broken marriages. The report, however, gave little consideration to the precise meaning of that standard.

Despite the commission's elite membership and radical suggestions, its report produced scarcely a ripple of reaction. It was released in mid-December of 1966, during the last days of the Brown administration, as political reporters were speculating on the intentions of the incoming Reagan team and as the rest of world prepared for the Christmas holidays. Because the commission had operated without any publicity, few persons even knew that such recommendations had been made.

Backstage Negotiations and Legislative Maneuvering

Obscurity probably helped more than hurt the prospects of the commission's recommendations, because it shielded them from potential opponents. At the same time, it reflected the absence of organized opposition to its suggestions, because no lobbyist in Sacramento sounded an alarm.

The lack of hostility from the Catholic church was particularly notable. The Commission's report had tip-toed around the potential conflict between civil divorce and religious norms of family life. The report included a discussion of the matter in the following words:

> Our study has convinced us that . . . a "breakdown-of-marriage" standard in no way derogates ecclesiastical doctrines of the indissolubility of marriage. When a Civil Court orders the dissolution of a marriage, it does not reach the canonical bonds of the union; it acts rather on the complex of legal rights and duties that make up the legal status of marriage.

However, the commission did not simply rely on this argument. The absence of Catholic opposition was the result of careful cultivation of the Catholic hierarchy. That was facilitated by staffing decisions which substantially assisted communication with the northern California hierarchy. At the outset Governor Brown shrewdly appointed Richard Dinkelspiel as co-chair of the commission. Dinkelspiel was not only one of the core members of the Bay Area reform group, but more importantly, he was a very prominent Catholic layman with ties to the hierarchy. In addition, he was well known and widely respected in the San Francisco and California bars. Secondly, the governor appointed Aiden Gough to be the commission's executive director. Gough was a young law professor at Santa Clara University and perhaps the most available expert in matrimonial law. But he taught in a Jesuit institution, his university's president (who had encouraged him to take the position) was the brother of the Bishop of Stockton, and his family was friendly with the Archbishop of San Francisco. Those ties were helpful in keeping the bishops of northern California informed about the commission's work. The commission won their timely backing for its proposals in the form of a public statement of support for the commission's recommendations before Cardinal McIntyre of Los Angeles, who had more conservative leanings, discovered the outcome of the commission's work. Given the open support of the northern bishops, it was difficult for McIntyre to oppose them publicly, whatever his private thoughts.

Obscurity also permitted quiet cultivation of support for the commission's recommendations. California did not lack political controversies to occupy the attention of its legislature. Governor Reagan sought to reduce state expenditures; the campaign for abortion reform was nearing its climax; the state, like the remainder of the nation, was riveted on Vietnam and the growing domestic opposition to that war. During these distractions, proponents sought endorsement from the California Bar Association. Although the bar proposed numerous changes to the commission's proposal, it accepted its main thrust and told its lobbyist to support a bill which incorporated the bar's suggestions and the commission's proposals. Further, although the commission's proposals were introduced into the legislature in 1967, they lay fallow for two years. This interlude was used to familiarize legislators with the revolutionary concepts of the bill. When the legislature finally turned its attention to the bill, it seemed less radical and had garnered substantial support . . . .

[S]upporters of no-fault had quietly generated public support in the form of newspaper editorials and constituent letters. Even Catholic groups wrote to legislators in support of the no-fault bill. Thus, legislators like the Los Angeles assemblyman found divorce reform an attractive issue upon which to build their legislative reputations, even when their general policy stance was a conservative one. In the meantime, the liberals who had drafted the commission's proposals remained discreetly in the background. The coalition . . . led to legislative approval by June of 1969 with less public maneuvering and attention than had accompanied New York's much more modest legislation three years earlier.

Governor Reagan, himself once divorced, proved no obstacle to the bill and signed it into law with only a mild plea for future fine-tuning. It became effective in 1970 and came to be known as the nation's first no-fault divorce law.

The new law followed the general thrust of the governor's commission with respect to the grounds for divorce. It eliminated all fault grounds and permitted divorce only upon a showing of incurable insanity or "irreconcilable differences which have caused the irremediable breakdown of the marriage." The statute mandated the new style of divorce petitions which avoided the terminology of conventional litigation. It eliminated all consideration of fault with respect to property division. However, it went further than the governor's commission in mandating equal division of property by omitting the commission's recommendation by narrowing the exceptional circumstances justifying an unequal division. Finally, the new law altered alimony so that it would ordinarily be temporary support for the dependent spouse while he or she became self-sufficient.

The official legislative history of the law claimed that the new law was intended to facilitate gender equality. Kay argues that this was an entirely erroneous assertion. Indeed, the new law was not in any way a feminist product. The alimony provisions as enacted were less favorable to women than those that had been recommended by the commission. The principal change was that the legislature added the provision that the "ability of the supported spouse to engage in gainful employment" be considered in alimony decisions, thereby converting alimony to a transitional payment while the dependent spouse entered the labor market. In addition, the new law did not include the commission's recommendation to end the presumption in favor of mothers of young children in deciding custody. Instead, it reenacted the tender years doctrine. Finally, the new law reenacted several provisions which were soon to become anathema to feminists. One section stated: "The husband is the head of the family. He may choose any reasonable place or mode of living, and the wife must conform thereto." Another confirmed the husband's right to manage community property during the marriage. Gender equality was neither sought nor achieved by California's no-fault law. Indeed, there is no evidence that feminists were active supporters of the new law or held any expectation that women would be treated better under the new law than the old.

While the California no-fault statute was the product of many years of deliberation, the deliberative process attracted very little public attention. None of the principals claimed fame or fortune as the result of the law's enactment. While the leaders of the abortion struggle climbed to more prominent national office, the proponents of no-fault remained in relative obscurity. Perhaps the most telling evidence of the invisibility of the revision process is the complete absence of its mention in the oral history of the Brown and Reagan administrations. Interviews exist for activists over abortion proposals and many other legal initiatives, but none for those involved in the no-fault law.

However, the proponents of divorce reform almost made a fatal error. Carried by their enthusiasm for the therapeutic model, they advocated establishing a new tier of courts to handle family matters and facilitate conciliation. The expense of that proposal and its challenge to the authority of sitting judges threatened to arouse strong opposition. Those elements of the proposal were, however, dropped during its legislative consideration. Without that concession, it is likely that the issue of divorce reform would have become much more conjectural and would have faced Governor Reagan's fiscal veto. By eliminating the costly elements of their recommendations, no-fault advocates were able to utilize the routine policy process to achieve divorce reform.

NATIONALIZING NO-FAULT DIVORCE: THE NCCUSL

Policy making involves not only public but also private arenas. That is particularly true of policy changes which are defined as technical legal matters where specialized groups of legal experts play an exceptionally important role. Two such arenas exist in the United States. One is the American Law Institute, which periodically issues "Restatements of the Law of . . . " particular areas of the law, such as torts, that become influential accounts of black letter law in the United States. It was this group that issued the "Restatement of the Law of Torts" in 1965 articulating a rule of strict liability which came to play a prominent role in the litigation over asbestos damages. The second is the National Conference of Commissioners on Uniform State Laws (NCCUSL), which issues uniform state laws to guide state legislatures. The NCCUSL joined the American Law Institute in drafting the Uniform Commercial Code, a widely adopted body of commercial law in the United States. The NCCUSL was also a key actor in recommending no-fault divorce to the states.

The same process of routine policy making occurred in the NCCUSL as in California. The manner in which the divorce reformers in the NCCUSL managed to keep no-fault in the routine policy-making mode goes far in explaining how they succeeded in developing a uniform marriage and divorce act despite the organization's long record of failure in divorce law reform.

The NCCUSL is a unique quasi-public body. It was organized in 1892 to promote, among other reforms, a uniform marriage and divorce act for the states. However, after several unsuccessful attempts it abandoned that task and turned to the development of other uniform state laws on such subjects as wills, securities, and the determination of death. It is composed entirely of legal experts. State governors appoint its members from the ranks of law professors, prestigious attorneys, and well-placed legislators. Its budget comes from state appropriations as well as from such grants as it can procure. It works through drafting committees whose products are then debated at its annual conference and usually adopted with only minor changes. Its proposals then go to the American Bar Association (ABA), which generally endorses them. The double endorsement of the NCCUSL and ABA establishes the so-called "uniform act" as an influential model for state legislatures. Few uniform acts win approval from state legislatures without substantial alteration to suit local conditions, but the fundamental concepts underlying those model laws are given a powerful thrust by the endorsement of the NCCUSL and ABA.

However, unlike state legislatures, the NCCUSL avoids the limelight of publicity and the media seldom report its activities. It does not hold public hearings and is not subject to overt pressure group or partisan politics as are legislatures. Its committees often consult with representatives of diverse groups in order to increase the likelihood that its model statutes will win the approval of state legislatures, but such consultation occurs in a relatively unsystematic way through private rather than public channels. All of these characteristics made the NCCUSL an ideal vehicle for promoting no-fault divorce.

Unlike a legislature such as California's, the NCCUSL operates in the broad national arena rather than in the narrow confines of a single state and must reflect national conditions. It usually is more conservative than venturesome California, a fact that makes its adoption of no-fault particularly significant, for by its endorsement of this new standard, the conference placed the cachet of respectability upon no-fault. But it did not happen without considerable effort.

THE NATIONAL ENVIRONMENT FOR NO-FAULT DIVORCE

The Intellectual Environment

. . . [N]o-fault was an idea that was increasingly in vogue in several areas of the law. It had been most prominently discussed with respect to auto accident insurance, where reformers proposed that instead of attempting to assess blame for auto accidents, insurance companies should insure their own drivers, who would be reimbursed for damages and injuries regardless of who was at fault . . . .

Divorce had several parallels to traffic accidents. Like those mishaps, it was often difficult to assess blame in failed marriages. While a single event often precipitated the breakup, hundreds of trivial disputes generally precede it. Like personal injury suits, divorce cases often took long to conclude and the few which went to trial consumed much court time.

However, the link between no-fault in auto accident cases and divorce law remained a conceptual one; its advocacy in one field did not directly affect the other . . . . [W]hereas the application of no-fault to auto accident cases was hotly disputed by personal injury plaintiff lawyers, in part because it threatened to reduce their case-load by diverting claims to a purely administrative procedure, divorce lawyers were generally not hostile to no-fault because, among other reasons, divorces would still require court action and considerable litigation . . . .

Furthermore, the no-fault idea fit well with the therapeutic conceptions of divorce that had become widespread by the 1950s and 1960s. Family breakdown was seen less frequently as sinful and more often as evidence of social maladjustment that could be remedied through therapy. Some marriages could be saved through counseling; in other cases, men and women could be helped to start new marriages by permitted them to escape relationships that had become hopelessly entangled. Assessing blame, as traditional law required, interfered with this process. However, most of these ideas remained confined to a narrow elite of attorneys and therapists and were not widely diffused in the general legal literature on divorce before the 1970s, as witnessed by the fact that no-fault was scarcely mentioned in law review articles on divorce in the early 1960s.

The Social and Political Context

. . . [D]ivorce became increasingly common in the 1960s. Ordinary people began to notice that their neighbors, friends, and relatives were getting divorces, and the public careers of figures like governors Rockefeller and Reagan survived divorce. Making divorce less adversarial, therefore, was consonant with the increasingly accepted perception that divorce should not be made immensely difficult.

That perception also contributed to keeping divorce reform out of the political limelight. Maintaining the old legal order was not perceived to be an attractive issue among political entrepreneurs. Moreover, the feminist movement—which was reviving just when advocates of no-fault pressed their cause—was distracted by other matters. The dominant feminist organization, the National Organization for Women, was just being organized in 1966; it, and its predecessors, concentrated mostly on advocacy of legalized abortion, on equal legal rights for women, and on issues of direct economic significance to women, such as discrimination in the workplace. The potential consequences of no-fault divorce were scarcely visible to feminists, and they neither supported nor opposed them in their major public statements. The absence of feminist concern also kept anti-feminists away from the divorce issue. Anti-feminists mostly reacted to the agenda of the feminists: feminist advocacy of ERA provoked anti-ERA activity; feminist promotion of abortion aroused anti-abortion agitation. The lack of feminist support, therefore, also helps account for the absence of anti-feminist opposition and of political interest in the issue.

FORMULATING THE PROBLEM

As in California, a key element in channeling divorce reform into the routine policy-making mode was the formulation of the problem in such a manner that it would remain in the domain of technocrats rather than politicos. This was done in much the same manner as in California. A handful of little-known legal experts controlled the formulation of the problem.

The advocates of no-fault divorce were several unconnected groups of practicing lawyers and legal technocrats. Most prominent among the practicing lawyers were two matrimonial attorneys in Newark, New Jersey, Leonard Brown and Bernard Hellring, who had become disenchanted with the fault system of procuring divorces for their clients. They were members of the NCCUSL and thus represented the upper crust of the practicing bar, but they were unknown outside a small circle of elite divorce lawyers. As early as 1966, they prepared a report to the NCCUSL urging the formulation of a committee to draft a new divorce law; they did not use the term no-fault but spoke about it in terms of eliminating cumbersome and misleading "forms of action." They were joined eventually by three law professors who had few prior ties with one another or with the two practicing attorneys. One was NYU's Professor Henry H. Foster, who had built a wide reputation as one of the handful of leading matrimonial law specialists in the United States. Foster was well connected with the New York politicians who had produced the new divorce law in that state, was prominent in the ABA Family Law Section, and knew some of the leaders of the conference. The second law professor was Robert J. Levy of the University of Minnesota, a family law expert who was gaining a reputation for his knowledge of the social science literature on the family, but who had not established a wide reputation outside the scholarly world. The third law professor was Herma Hill Kay, who was a key player in the California reform but who did not know well any of the other core advocates of no-fault. All five were technocrats with no more than weak political affiliations. Moreover, until the conference mobilized to draft a new divorce law, they worked independently; indeed, Levy and Kay, who eventually played key roles in the formulation of the new law, were explicitly recruited into the effort by the conference.

The advocates perceived the problem which required a new divorce law in ways very similar to the California reformers. The problem, as they perceived it, was widespread dissatisfaction with divorce procedures that had become prevalent far beyond New York's and California's boundaries. The complaints had three common themes. First, attorneys throughout the country resented the extensive manufacturing or doctoring of evidence to fit the narrow provisions of existing divorce law. Divorce lawyers were under considerable pressure everywhere to put an acceptable gloss to the domestic discord that accompanied divorce petitions. In most states, the easiest way to do that was to base the divorce action on the mental cruelty provisions of the divorce law, which led attorneys to suggest to clients that they testify that their spouse had been disparaging and that they suffered many sleepless nights as a consequence; alternatively, a fictitious slap to the face evidenced physical cruelty. In truth, adultery may have been a cause for the divorce in some of these cases, while in others there was nothing more than a desire to end the marriage. Another cause for the manufacture of supporting evidence lay in state laws which did not allow as quick a divorce as the client demanded; in response, attorneys arranged phoney out-of-state residences so that the more lenient laws of another state could be used. These practices were no secret. Judges in every state quietly accommodated divorce lawyers by not probing into the truthfulness of the evidence they offered; the judiciary of those states with short residence periods like Nevada's openly participated in what became a substantial trade in divorce, which supported a sizable segment of the state's economy. Thus, perjury became a silent partner of divorce proceedings and cast a pall on the practice of family law.

The second widespread cause for dissatisfaction with divorce law was that it forced family disputes into the adversarial mode of court actions. Most divorce cases already had an uncomfortably high degree of emotional conflict. Many divorce attorneys felt that the requirements of the adversarial system heightened that conflict to unacceptable levels. Legal norms had several consequences. Clients could not share a common attorney but each had to have his or her own. Attorneys were bound by the ethical standards of the profession to seek the best settlement for their clients rather than a common compromise. The interests of children were poorly represented unless they too had a separate attorney. The system seemed designed to promote and exacerbate conflict, rather than to provide a way to find compromises and to get the divorce in as painless a fashion as possible.

A third common complaint about the nation's divorce laws was that they were a patchwork of provisions that differed for each state. This particularly bothered matrimonial lawyers handling high-status clients who had large property interests at stake and were more likely than others to live in different jurisdictions. Divorces in such cases seemed unnecessarily complicated . . . . Consequently, elite divorce lawyers advocated making divorce law uniform throughout the country.

This definition of the problem emphasized the legalistic concerns of the divorce lawyers and usually eschewed larger social issues. For instance, it avoided discussion of the effect of changing divorce rules on the roles of men and women. It implicitly denied any consequences of change for ongoing marriages by presuming that the proposed changes did little more than ratify existing but not legally sanctioned practices. It did not consider the possibility of reforming divorce rules as part of a more far reaching alteration of family policy in the United States, such as establishing family allowances (which might alter child support obligations) or the institutionalization of child care (which together with a parental leave policy might alter the distribution of child care responsibilities). Instead, the advocates of no-fault divorce framed their proposal in more limited, technical terms and thereby discouraged broader participation in the deliberations over the reforms.

FORMULATING AND ADOPTING THE NO-FAULT SOLUTION

The NCCUSL's embrace of no-fault divorce occurred in even greater obscurity and under more control of experts than had been the case in California. Motivated by their own disenchantment with divorce laws, Hellring and Brown rekindled the conference's interest in divorce reform in the early 1960s. Focusing their considerable energies on mobilizing the NCCUSL, they succeeded in placing marriage and divorce on its agenda in the mid-1960s . . . .

Two points seem clear from the available record. First, the drafting committee made little effort to obtain support from Catholics or to disarm potential Catholic opposition. Rather, it appeared to assume that the stance of the Catholic church was immaterial, a presumption that appeared well founded, given the lack of Catholic hostility in California toward no-fault divorce. Secondly, no evidence exists that the Catholic national hierarchy paid attention to the work of the drafting committee. In part that may be due to the fact that the Catholic church was oriented to represent its position in Washington and in state capitols but did not monitor the activity of organizations operating elsewhere. Whatever the cause, the consequence was that the church had no voice in the formulation of the UMDA.

Feminists had almost as little influence. No formal link existed between the drafting committee and the National Organization for Women nor with any other feminist organization. Some women who were also feminists were members of the advisory board, most notably Jessie Bernard and Alice Rossi. Neither, however, had been selected because of her feminist connections. The only two exceptions addressing feminist concerns recorded in available documents are to be found in Levy's 1968 monograph, which he wrote as a briefing paper for the drafting committee, and in positions taken by Alice Rossi. In the monograph, during a discussion of property distribution Levy quotes extensively from the 1963 report of the Committee on Civil and Political

Rights of the President's Commission on the Status of Women and from the 1968 Task Force on Family Law and Policy of the Citizen's Advisory Council on the Status of Women; his conclusion was that "the time is not yet ripe to insist upon a '50-50' formula," a change he labeled a "radical innovation." However, that was precisely what Rossi urged in her capacity as a member of the advisory group, together with equal consideration of both parents for custody and time-limited alimony. However, having proposed these provisions, she had no success in persuading the predominantly conservative members of the drafting committee to take her suggestions seriously. Thus feminists, like the Catholic church, had little input or influence in the formulation of UMDA . . . .

Adoption by the conference came after a long debate in which the commissioners examined each paragraph. As in the original formulation of the problem, the debate over the proposed solution used the language of legal technical terms rather than of social concepts and issues. The debate transcripts rarely display an articulated concern over such matters as the fate of divorced women or the differential impact of the law's provisions on minority groups or the poor. When commissioners had such concerns, they couched them in technical terms. That is well illustrated in the debate over whether judges should possess discretion over the granting of a divorce on the ground of matrimonial breakdown. Both in the drafting committee and during the debate by the conference as a whole, enormous attention was lavished on whether the statute should include the word "may" or "shall." At the manifest level it was an abstract, constitutional debate on judicial discretion and judicial power. However, the discussion reflected several, mostly unspoken, social issues. The debate over judicial discretion was also an argument over whether marital misbehavior should go unpunished; however, if judges retained discretion to deny divorces to persons who had acted badly in their marriage, fault would reenter through the back door. In addition, this discussion may have reflected disquiet over the possibility that judges might deny divorces to the poor, but it also betrayed a concern over the potential for increased welfare costs as well as a regard for equal treatment under the law. At the manifest level, the debate in the conference did not focus on social issues but rather concentrated on the judicial authority denoted by those two words and on the legal definition of irretrievable breakdown.

The technical character of the conference's debate reflected its structure and composition. It was not a representative body and its members did not have to answer to a constituency. Many were law professors who were comfortable in discussing legal technicalities. Neither interest groups nor reporters intervened to raise questions of social conflict. Furthermore, the technical cast of the debates also helped insulate the deliberations from the media. Media representatives were not routinely invited to conference sessions or to the meetings of the drafting committees. Thus the media were usually unaware of the conference's activities. However, even if they had been aware, conference debates would have provided poor copy and a pale television image because the commissioners did not speak the language of political conflict. Even the later dispute with the ABA produced only minimal coverage which failed to capture the essence of the differences between the two organizations.

By the time the NCCUSL debated its committee's proposal, California had already acted. When skeptics in the conference debate asked whether no-fault was practical or inquired about the opposition of the Catholic church, supporters were able to point to the California experience, where no-fault had been adopted under a conservative governor without active Catholic opposition.

None of the issues raised during the discussion seriously threatened the proposal, and it easily passed the NCCUSL to become the Uniform Marriage and Divorce Act in the terminology of the conference . . . .

With ABA approval achieved, the Uniform Marriage and Divorce Act became a model for state legislatures to emulate. Newspapers duly noted that no-fault divorce was now advocated by lawyers. The UMDA was published by the NCCUSL and distributed to each of its commissioners and sent to every state legislature. A handful of articles on the UMDA appeared in law journals. It was hardly a great event and . . . it had little immediate impact on the widespread adoption of no-fault divorce in the United States. Its most important effect was to legitimate no-fault in a way that California's adoption could not. Whereas California's adoption might be discounted because California often adopted avant-garde ideas belittled elsewhere, the NCCUSL and ABA's endorsement of no-fault divorce indicated that this was a reasonable idea that warranted serious consideration by state legislatures, for the NCCUSL and ABA were middle-of-the-road, conservative organizations little given to extravagant social experimentation.

CONCLUSION

The routine policy-making process within the NCCUSL and ABA was different from California's in one significant characteristic: their decisions had only the status of recommendations to the states rather than of laws with potentially irreversible effects. However, these groups undertook their tasks with great seriousness, believing that the reputations of their organizations were at stake in adopting model laws that could win the respect of the nation's lawmakers. Thus their actions were not without the risk and uncertainty that California legislators also faced.

What made divorce reform an attractive object for the routine policy process was the ability of its advocates to formulate the problem as a

matter which required special expertise more than broad public participation. As in California, the reformers did not portray no-fault as a dar-
ing experiment but rather as a logical extension of existing practices.
The NCCUSL's procedures guaranteed limited visibility among the
general public and confined decision making to inside experts until the
proposals were transmitted to the ABA. Ordinarily, the NCCUSL
would have coopted the relevant ABA experts as well and its proposals
would have been routinely adopted by the association. That did not
occur with the Uniform Marriage and Divorce Act . . . because of personal and institutional rivalries. Nevertheless, the proponents of reform
succeeded in confining conflict to the private arenas of the decision-
making processes of the two groups, where a compromise was reached
in typically technical terms. They did not allow the issue to become
transformed into a social conflict which would have invited other
groups and members of the general public to intervene . . . . □

NOTES AND QUESTIONS

1. Lawrence M. Friedman, in "Law Reform in Historical Perspective," 13
St. Louis University Law Journal 351, 363, 364 (1969), states that law reform
efforts often *ratify* what has already been done, reflecting rather than *causing
changes* in behavior or attitudes. He says:

> Even more commonly, perhaps, fresh law is a hybrid: half ratification,
> half real inducement to change. Formal legal change often comes at the
> middle point in a social process which requires a number of distinct
> steps already taken, but it forces or hurries society along with regard to
> the steps not yet taken. It is not easy to know whether or not "innova-
> tion" is only anticipation of a process bound to happen in any event . . . .
>   [A]n attempted legal change, in a non-revolutionary setting, will have
> most effect and be most meaningful when the change is relatively slight.
> Obviously, a fresh precept is in trouble if it goes against deep-seated
> interests or emotions . . . . A change that conforms to what most of the
> public already wishes to do or which calls for slight, familiar, acceptable
> change of behavior is far more palatable and far more likely to succeed.
> "Reform" that is half ratification and half real change is, therefore, not
> only typical of the work of Anglo-American courts; it is arguably the
> most vital and productive kind of change.

To what extent was Jacob's "Silent Revolution" the kind of hybrid Friedman
discusses? Was it "half ratification, half real inducement to change?" Should
we distinguish between legislation that *appears* to be only ratification but actually involves the opportunity for significant change as it is applied and that
which is truly only ratification?

2. Before "no-fault," as Jacob points out, divorce was *formally* hard to get,
but, *in fact*, it was very easy to get. Divorce proceedings often were a sham,
resting on perjured testimony. In theory, a collusive divorce was illegal. In
practice, many or most divorces *were* collusive.

What social forces brought about the situation before no-fault divorce—where those who could afford evading a state's legislation prevailed? If no-fault was a half-revolution, what brought about the *other* half, that is, the legal recognition of divorces obtained by perjury?

Grace Ganz Blumberg, in "Reworking the Past, Imagining the Future: On Jacob's *Silent Revolution*," 16 *Law & Social Inquiry* 115 (1991), points to such collusive practices in challenging Jacob's assertion that the movement to no-fault divorce was a revolution. Blumberg argued that Jacob is a political scientist who focused on statutory language rather than on what the courts were doing and what lawyers were doing in their practice. She argues: "Jacob's theory of routine policy making is meaningful only if *important* law reform is effected in routine, nonpublic ways. If . . . legal developments effect little substantive change, then the invisibility of their enactment is unexceptional" (p. 117).

She continues, saying that in New York divorce by contract was not novel:

> Most obviously, as long as there was any ground for divorce, the parties might always agree, after settling the terms, that one or the other, usually the husband, would be the nominal defendant but would not in fact defend against the plaintiff's claim. Those who found such a scenario distasteful because the sole ground was adultery might, also by agreement, send one spouse to Nevada for six weeks to falsely allege domicile in Nevada and to obtain an uncontested divorce on the pro forma ground of cruelty. (pp 120–21)

Jacob, in his "Reply to Blumberg," 16 *Law & Social Inquiry* 155 (1991), took exception to Blumberg's challenge. He said:

> [T]he changes in divorce law clearly legitimate a form of divorce that was previously only possible by committing perjury, and according to many they altered the expectations of those contemplating divorce. Divorce clients no longer can pursue the blaming game; they also have a different understanding of what belongs to each of them . . . .
>
> [T]o imply, as Blumberg does, that the law did not involve "any substantial change" is nonsense . . . . Blumberg's argument that consensual divorce was already available for those who were willing to go to Nevada, Mexico, the Virgin Islands, the Dominican Republic, or Haiti cavalierly takes an affluent person's approach to the law. For most New Yorkers, none of those alternatives were financially feasible in an era when airplanes had not yet become the functional equivalent of the Greyhound bus.

To what extent, if at all, does Blumberg's challenge qualify Jacob's description of a routine policy process? Were there groups of any importance in the United States likely to oppose a no-fault divorce reform? Why didn't these groups block the ideas of a group of academics and practitioners?

3. The various divorce reform bills were presented to American legislatures as the work of experts. Professors and practitioners of family law were involved in the drafting and advocacy of these statutes. Are they experts about the content of a divorce law? On what basis could they claim this status?

Blumberg thinks that legislators were led astray by the "obsessive focus of family law academics on what is fair *as between the parties* in view of the particulars of their marriage" [p. 149]. She argues: "When distribution according to the question, What is fair as between the parties? leaves a shortfall for the divorcing wife and children, the next question should be: What mix of private and public responses will appropriately address their needs?" (p. 150).

To what extent do legislators rely on such academic experts to resolve controversial social problems? Were the experts in the no-fault revolution telling the legislators only what they already believed? Carl E. Schneider reviewed Jacob's book in 86 *Michigan Law Review* 1121 (1988), and seems to accept this view. He argues:

> The revolution is, I think, sparked and sustained by a set of ideological assumptions which are widely shared among many elite segments of society, assumptions having to do with egalitarianism and with psychologically derived views of human nature. Professor Jacob tends to neglect such factors. While he is sensitive to the broad social changes that underlay the legislative reforms, he only hints at the process by which particular groups of people perceived those social changes, conceptualized them, brought them into social discourse, and proposed legislative responses to them.

How would you fashion a picture of the process by which the attitudes of legislators and their important constituents changed over time so that they would accept the experts' proposed no-fault reforms?

4. The no-fault movement was not just American; there was a strong trend in that direction in European countries as well. See Mary Ann Glendon, *Abortion and Divorce in Western Law* (Cambridge, Mass.: Harvard University Press, 1987). Particularly in the Scandinavian countries (and most especially in Sweden), a no-fault system now prevails. This is also true in Canada. Other European countries retain some shadow of the fault system, but "divorce is readily available when the spouses reach an agreement on all issues, as they eventually do everywhere in the great majority of cases" (p. 80). European countries, however, vest far less discretion in the judge on property and child support matters. Child support is usually calculated "according to formulas or tables in a relatively predictable fashion" (p. 82).

What accounts for the differences and similarities, as between American experience and European experience? Among other things, Glendon suggests that the United States is more decentralized, more individualistic, more rights-conscious than the countries of Western Europe, and has a less developed welfare state (pp. 112ff).

What light does a study like Glendon's shed on Jacob's thesis, and on the issues raised in this section? What kinds of information would we want about the dynamics of passage of the European or Canadian laws, in order to test Jacob's or Skocpol's hypotheses?

PLURALIST BARGAINING AND POWER: THE RETAIL PETROLEUM
DEALERS ATTEMPT TO CURB THE POWER OF THE MAJOR OIL
COMPANIES

25. Long-Term Continuing Relations: the American Experience Regulating Dealerships and Franchises[112]

Stewart Macaulay

IV. THE CAMPAIGN OF THE RETAIL GASOLINE DEALERS: LAW AND THE BALANCE OF POWER

☐ . . . The struggle over franchise laws teaches us much about the reality of regulation in the United States. The process involves battles in a never-ending war, moves in an endless game. Both franchisors and franchisees are well-armed with rhetorical symbols dear to Americans: "the free market" and "efficiency" battle "the virtues of small business," and the claims of expectations created by practice. While both sides bring experts into the contest, the manufacturers' economists more often are pitted against the dealers' victims of atrocities at the hands of franchisors. Dealers have advantages at the state level while franchisors usually are large corporations, well versed at playing in the national arena in Washington, D.C.

This is a story of the efforts of the retailers of branded gasoline to improve their position against the major oil companies. The tale of prolonged legal warfare will illustrate all the difficulties in such battles as well as the uncertain nature of the outcome. First, we will examine the nature of this "franchise" relationship—the norms and sanctions in this semi-autonomous social field, looking at the strains which prompted the dealers to seek outside help. We will then sketch the endless battles they won and lost, and we will try to indicate something of the impact of all these efforts.

Before the energy crisis in the early 1970s, the major oil refiners sought to maximize the amount of gasoline sold. Much of their profit came from products such as petrochemicals, and often gasoline was a by-product to be disposed at the best price available. It was uneconomic, because of the structure of the tax laws, to keep crude oil in the

112. In C. Joerges (ed.), *Franchising and the Law: Theoretical and Comparative Approaches in Europe and the United States* (Nomos Verlagsgesellschaft, 1991) pp. 179–237.

ground. Refining petrochemicals or heating oil also yielded gasoline which, as a practical matter, could not be stored for long. Even when a refinery run was planned to produce gasoline, the nature of the technology called for production in large quantities.

The major oil companies sold gasoline in many ways. Much, of course, was sold through service stations bearing the trade mark of a major oil company. The company usually owned some of these stations itself, hiring employees to manage them. Most companies, however, contracted with franchised dealers and leased service station premises to them. Until the 1970s, most oil companies worked to increase the number of stations offering their products, and many attempted to build national networks of distribution.

The major oil companies made the franchised dealer the focus of their retailing efforts in the 1930s. For a relatively small investment of capital, the companies told dealers that they could run "their own business." For example, a Shell Oil Company advertisement seeking new dealers said,

> Work for a good man—yourself. A Shell Dealership offers:
> —Paid training
> —Financing Assistance
> —High Income Potential

When it suited their purposes, the oil companies characterized the dealers as independent business people. However, the companies managed to retain almost the same degree of control over the dealers as they would have had over employees. The companies drafted standard form contracts and leases which guarded their interests. Dealers assumed many obligations under these contracts, including such things as the hours they stayed open, the products they would sell, and responsibility for handling credit card purchases. The franchise usually was for a relatively short term—sometimes as little as 30 days with an optional renewal feature—and franchises could be canceled at will with no need to show cause. Furthermore, some oil companies frequently refused to allow a dealer to have an attorney review their contracts and leases before they were signed because they would allow no changes.

Dealers were well aware that it was good policy to keep the companies' district managers pleased. Dealers knew that their franchise ran for a term, but most assumed that they would be renewed. This view was reinforced the longer they stayed in business and obtained renewals. District managers often told their dealers that there was nothing to worry about, as long as there were no problems. This both reassured dealers and served as a warning of what might happen if there were problems. If a dealer's performance were questionable, the company also could open another station across the street or a block or two away. Finally, the companies offered training for dealers in management skills and business systems. This not only helped dealers become profitable but also served to channel their operations into the companies' patterns.

The dealer was thus given a strong incentive to pour time and effort into managing the station, building good will in the immediate area, and investing in tools, tow trucks and the like. The companies benefited by characterizing their dealers as independent business people rather than as employees. Oil companies could not have devised a better incentive structure which would prompt most employees to work the long hours and take the responsibility assumed by dealers. Also, "independent" dealers were not subject to minimum wage and maximum hour regulations, and they would not unionize and ask to collectively bargain.

Sometimes everyone was happy. Often the oil company and the dealer shared interests. Successful dealers made money and had a degree of independence. Sometimes successful dealers even had some countervailing power. When major oil companies were expanding into new regions of the country, they might seek to entice experienced and capable dealers away from other companies. Companies probably threatened to cancel, both expressly and impliedly, far more than they actually terminated dealers. Oil companies usually renewed even slightly marginal dealers. There were costs in changing dealers by canceling franchises—the replacement, for example, might not do as well.

However, there often were strains in the relationship. These strains were provoked in part by the contradiction between the reality of the situation and the fiction that the dealer was an independent business person. Until the energy crisis of the 1970s, there were recurring price wars in many areas when one refiner wanted to get rid of surplus gasoline or wanted to establish itself. The oil company would order its dealers to cut prices to increase sales. The other major oil companies would respond by telling their dealers to meet the price cuts or to drop the price even lower in order to bring in new customers. The dealer usually had to bear part of the burden of lower prices. Dealers would be given allowances to enable them to survive a price war, but the major oil companies decided how great an allowance to offer and how long to keep it in effect. Truly independent dealers would have had the power to set their own prices based on their own judgment about long term benefits and their own particular situation. This independence was denied to most franchisees in gasoline price wars. Price competition was a tactic which might help a major oil company get rid of gasoline or bring in a few new people to a station once or twice. However, cuts were met quickly by cuts from the station across the street.

Also, dealers often could make more profit selling tires, batteries and accessories (TBA) and even motor oil which they bought from wholesalers than by offering only products supplied by the major oil companies. Refiners controlled the TBA offered by their dealers in many ways, ranging from requirements contracts to what the Federal Trade Commission and the courts later were to label as coercion.

In the late 1960s, many major oil companies decided to deemphasize neighborhood stations, and the servicing and repairing of automobiles and use marketing techniques which would sell more gasoline at fewer stations. Experts began to say that the United States had far too many gasoline stations for efficient distribution. Jordan described the tensions in the relationship as follows:

> The company sees the station as its means of selling petroleum products, with price competition and high volume as keys to profit. The dealer, in contrast, often sees the station primarily as *his* repair and maintenance operation. Since the bulk of his income tends to come from automotive services that he, not the oil company, provides, he is less concerned than the company about increasing sales of the relatively low-profit gasoline. Moreover, though some agreements do specify a maximum rent, rental rates are often based on a percentage of gasoline sales, in effect giving the dealer a *negative* incentive. This disparity between the interests of the company and the operator simply does not exist where both are exclusively interested in selling the same product and splitting the profits.[113]

Dealers were told to close service facilities which had been highly profitable to them and turn to self-service, trading stamps, contests, premiums, and extended hours of operation. Major companies began to withdraw from regions of the country where they did not have a large share of the market, leaving many canceled dealers in their wake. After the Arab Oil Embargo in 1973, many major oil companies worked even harder to close their less profitable stations. Gasoline no longer was merely something to be disposed of. This part of their operation had to maximize profit rather than volume.

The major oil companies rationalized their control of their dealership network by their property, trademark and contract rights. Often they owned the stations which were leased to dealers; they claimed ownership of trademarks such as "Standard," "Shell," and "Texaco" and thus controlled those who displayed them; and they drafted form contracts that gave them the right to cancel dealerships at their discretion. Often the oil companies justified their power and policies in terms of efficiency and benefits to consumers. They pictured canceled dealers as inefficient operators who survived by charging customers high prices and running dirty stations. They argued that consumers expected

---

113. Jordan, "Unconscionability at the Gas Station," 62 *Minnesota Law Review* 813, 817–818 (1978).

to find the same high quality of product and service at all stations displaying, for example, the "Shell" trademark. The oil companies also pointed out that they supplied most of the capital involved in the network of gasoline stations, and they said that as conditions changed, any particular dealer had few equities to offset required changes in the entire franchise system.

The dealers, of course, saw matters very differently. They said that they were independent business people who created the value of their service station by their labor and their efforts to build good will. They relied on having their franchise renewed because of representations made to them, expressly and impliedly, by the oil companies. They did not deal with the lawyers and top officials who fashioned the legal paper work. They talked to field representatives who led them to believe that they would keep their stations and their independence as long as they did a good job. The dealers' efforts, in partnership with the oil companies, had created the business at the local level. It was unfair for oil companies to pass back to the dealers a major part of the burdens of economic change brought about by OPEC—which was a response to the conduct of the major oil companies in third world countries. Finally, dealers made the classic argument of small business against competition: price competition in gasoline destroyed service and would end with a few near monopolists able to impose whatever prices they wanted, without offering service to customers.

The tensions in their relationship with the oil companies prompted gasoline dealers to organize. Gasoline dealers, both individually and through their organizations, tried to change the nature of their relationship with the major oil companies for more than thirty years. Trade associations proposed informal dispute resolution panels, but the oil companies were not interested. District managers of the oil companies would not allow a dealers' organization to represent dealers in meetings with the company. The managers said that they would only talk with dealers as individuals, and they pointed out a possible conflict of interest—the organizations represented dealers selling competitive products.

When these efforts at informal dispute resolution failed, the organized dealers turned to the legal system. Their basic strategy was to search for a new legal categorization of the relationship, and to collect atrocity stories to provoke a scandal. And dealers hired lobbyists and lawyers with enough experience and skill to counter the representatives of the major oil companies. They appealed to the Federal Trade Commission, state and federal courts, state legislatures, and the United States Congress with varying success over the years. Every legislative representative has retail gasoline dealers doing business in his or her district, and these retailers are "small business," a symbol dear to both major political parties.

From World War II through the 1960s, a number of antitrust actions attempted to protect the status of retail gasoline dealers as independent business people by lessening the oil companies' control. Victories were won by and for dealers; a notable line of cases in the Supreme Court of the United States developed. The Federal Trade Commission and private suits attacked the oil companies' control over the prices charged by their dealers and the response to price wars as well as various attempts to induce dealers to stock only the companies' TBA. The FTC won consent decrees limiting the use of short-term leases of service stations, which the Commission said made the dealers more vulnerable to the oil companies' coercion.

The FTC also attempted to solve many conflicts informally. President Nixon's Task Force on Productivity and Competition complained:

> The efforts of the Commission to protect small dealers from allegedly unfair and coercive business practices constitute a dark chapter in the Commission's history. Much of this enforcement activity does not eventuate in formal proceedings. What happens is that a dealer who is terminated, for whatever reason, is likely to complain to the Commission, knowing that the relevant Commission staff is well disposed toward "small business." The staff uses the threat of an FTC proceeding to get the supplier to reinstate the dealer, and if threats fail—usually they succeed—the FTC may file a complaint charging the supplier with having cut off the dealer because he was a price cutter, or for some other nefarious reason. Our impression, in sum, is that the Commission, especially at the informal level, has evolved an effective law of dealer protection that is unrelated and often contrary to the objectives of the anti-trust laws.[114]

While these victories undoubtedly changed day-to-day practices of major oil companies, some companies asserted that they always had honored the status of their dealers as independent business people . . . . Despite such policy statements, some dealers thought that too much pressure to take orders remained. The General Counsel of the National Congress of Petroleum Retailers appeared before a Congressional committee hearing on problems in gasoline retailing. He explained:

> The district manager comes in and sees that another TBA is in your station. That doesn't happen to be the brand they are selling, and he says, "Good heavens. What is this oil doing here?" And the dealer says, "You know, I thought I could sell it, and the *Texaco* case, and the *Simpson* case, and all the others say that I am entitled to sell anything I want to sell."
> The district manager says, "You certainly are, Joe Blow; you are a nice family man; you have six kids. Your lease will be over in 4 months, and I will tell you just a little ahead of time so you can be looking

114. BNA Antitrust and Trade Regulation Reporter, 1969: X–3.

around for a new job . . . ." When the pressure gets hard enough, you go
along with them.

The Executive Director of the National Congress thought that the
pressure often was more subtle. Dealers would be told that the company expected all aspects of the station to be highly profitable and certain targets would be set. Dealers could not achieve the goal for selling,
say, Standard's brand of oil if they sold too much Pennzoil or Quaker
State.

Since the 1950s, the retailers sought to limit the power of oil companies to cancel or refuse to renew franchises because this power is the
source of much of their leverage over dealers . . . . Throughout the
1950s and 1960s, both the House and Senate Small Business Committees held hearings where franchised dealers, including those who operated gasoline stations, made the populist appeal against big business
again and again . . . .

After the failure . . . at the federal level, the legislative battle moved
to New York. In 1969, the legislature there passed a statute which
would have required all franchisors to act in a fair, equitable and honest
manner and in accordance with reasonable standards of fair dealing
when granting, modifying, terminating or failing to renew a franchise.
However, Governor Rockefeller vetoed the bill because of the "unreasonable injunctive rights it would grant dealers."

Next, individual gasoline dealers who had been canceled or not
renewed, went to court. Their lawyers, backed by their trade associations, searched for legal concepts which would override the oil companies carefully fashioned positions based on property, trademark and
contract. Wall Street very successfully warded off Main Street, and the
dealers usually lost. For example, two lower New York courts refused
to apply the Uniform Commercial Code's provisions concerning "good
faith" and "unconscionability" to gasoline dealer franchises. The Code,
the courts explained, applies only to transactions in goods, and a franchise involves both goods and a lease of real estate. These courts also
refused to consider evidence of a custom to renew station leases absent
cause for cancellation. Any such custom would contradict the express
terms of the franchise document drafted by the oil company lawyers.
Yet even these defeats were to play a role in later developments as
indicating the need for legislation.

One of the judges emphasized the vetoed legislation and saw legal
change in this area as an appropriate legislative task. He remarked that
he was "not unsympathetic to the plaintiff's plight . . . " and said he
was sending copies of his opinion to the appropriate legislative committees. The other judge made the interesting statement that it is
"unconscionable, although legal at present, for the . . . [Mobil Oil
Company] . . . to be allowed, without cause, to terminate this lease
after 19 years of annual renewal." He thought Mobil's action "harks

back to the early days of our nation's industrial development when corporations were king and the workers were only to be used." He concluded that he "the Legislature and the Governor of this State will see fit to enact, again, legislation which will protect this vast number of our citizens."

Still a third New York lower court judge did not think he had to await legislation. He pointed to representations made by the Mobil Oil Company to a canceled dealer, noted that Mobil had not allowed the dealer to have an attorney present when the lease was signed since it "would not tolerate changes in any of the provisions of the printed agreements," and stressed that Mobil's refusal to renew because the dealer had not followed Mobil's price-setting directions violated the antitrust laws. He concluded that there was a "fiduciary relationship" which Mobil had violated. Thus, the court refused to grant Mobil's petition to recover possession of its station.[115] However, this innovative exercise was reversed on appeal.

In the early 1970s, state and local gasoline dealers organizations pressed for legislation in many states. After several failures, a bill offering all franchisees protection was passed in Wisconsin. Both Connecticut and New Jersey passed statutes providing that franchisors could not cancel or fail to renew franchises "without good cause." In addition, the Connecticut law provided that any franchisee could submit the question of "good cause" to arbitration in accordance with the rules of the American Arbitration Association.

In Connecticut, Mobil Oil Company led the attack on the new statute. It told twenty-six of its dealers who ran the most valuable stations in the state that it would not renew their franchises and would take over their stations. It could adopt this strategy because the statute did not apply retroactively to franchisees which had been created before the law became effective. At a legislative hearing, a representative of Mobil said that it could not leave $300,000 stations in the hands of dealers who had tenure granted by the law. Unless the statute were repealed, Mobil would have to take over all of its stations in the state.[116]

Members of the legislature reacted angrily to what they saw as coercion. Some legislators discovered that Mobil's representative was not

---

115. Fiduciary relationships exist when one purports to act for the benefit of another—lawyers are in such relationships with their clients, for example.

116. A member of Mobil's legal staff explained his firm's position in Connecticut:

> Our concern with the 1973 amendments to the Connecticut Franchise Act was that they had the effect of giving a dealer, who had invested approximately $10,000 in inventory and equipment, the same long-term property rights in a service station as an oil company supplier-landlord that had invested $300,000 in acquiring the property and constructing the service station improvements . . . .

Letter of November 14, 1974 to Professor Stewart Macaulay.

registered as a lobbyist, and they demanded prosecution. A story appeared in the *New York Times,*[117] which noted that if "Mobil was going to get in trouble for its efforts on behalf of all the oil companies, Mobil's brass would be embarrassed and many of the company's officers live in Connecticut—including the chairman of the board . . ." Mobil's officers may have recognized this. At any rate, they withdrew the heavy attack, apologized, and then joined with the Connecticut Gasoline Retailers Association to offer amendments to the statute. Under these changes, franchisors could cancel or refuse to renew a dealer's lease for failure to perform obligations under a contract or where the franchisor converted its property to a use not covered by the franchise agreement. In addition, the provision for arbitration was deleted as an interference with the franchisor's constitutional right of trial by jury.

In New Jersey, major oil companies canceled or refused to renew franchises in response to that state's franchise law. The Supreme Court of New Jersey, however, decided in *Shell Oil Co. v. Marinello*[118] that franchise agreements entered into before the state's law became effective were subject to an implied covenant that the franchisor would renew as long as dealers had substantially complied with their obligations. The New Jersey court was able to rely on the legislation as a declaration of the state's policy warranting the imposition of an term in the contract. Imposing an "implied term" is a well-known move in the contract doctrine game, but this was the first time that it was applied to franchises.

Once again action prompted reaction. At the request of oil companies, a federal district court found invalid the decision which implied a covenant to renew as well as the New Jersey statute because they conflicted with the federal Lanham Act governing trademarks.[119] This decision later was reversed on appeal,[120] but for a time it brought all efforts of gasoline dealers in the state legislatures into question.

Despite the dealers' difficulties in getting courts to protect existing franchises, the dealers' organizations did well before many state legislatures. By the mid-1970s, over thirty states had some kind of franchise protection law applicable to retail gasoline dealers whose franchises were created or renewed after the statutes went into effect. Some of these statutes applied only to gasoline dealers; others applied to all franchises including gasoline dealerships.

The dealers' lobbying organizations tried still another approach. They pressed for statutes that would restrict oil companies' operation

---

117. March 19, 1974, p. 47; March 20, 1974, p. 53.

118. 63 N.J. 402, 307 A.2d 598 (1973), *cert. denied,* 415 U.S. 920 (1974).

119. Mariniello *v.* Shell Oil Co., 368 F.Supp. 1401, 1407 (D.N.J. 1974).

120. Mariniello *v.* Shell Oil Co., 511 F.2d 853 (3d Cir. 1975).

of retail outlets. If these statutes were passed, oil companies no longer could threaten to take over stations before the effective date of franchise protection statutes as Mobil had done in Connecticut. They also could no longer open company stations to compete with franchised dealers or threaten to do so for leverage. By 1977, twenty eight states had given some consideration to such bills, and laws to this effect had passed in Maryland, Florida, Delaware, Virginia and the District of Columbia. Several bills to this end were introduced in Congress.

Exxon, Shell, Gulf, Phillips, Ashland, Continental and Commonwealth Oil Companies joined to challenge the constitutionality of the Maryland statute. However, the Supreme Court of the United States upheld it.[121] After this decision, the threat of passing these statutes was used to promote a federal legislative solution. The dealers' trade associations continued to struggle in the 1970s to gain federal legislation that would limit termination and nonrenewals and protect existing dealers . . . .

At the beginning of the decade, the large oil companies were supported by people in the Nixon and Ford administrations who opposed these bills as anticompetitive and promoting inefficiency. In 1974, President Nixon vetoed a comprehensive energy bill which included provisions prohibiting fuel sellers from terminating dealer franchises unless the dealer had failed to comply with reasonable requirements of the franchise. The Senate failed to override the veto, and the dealers suffered still another defeat . . . .

The dealers' lobbyists were undaunted after the veto of the energy bill in 1974, and they began still another major federal campaign. Individual dealers and groups of dealers met with their congressional representatives in district after district. They dramatized their plight by recounting atrocity stories and dwelling on the ideology of small business and traditional American hostility to large multinational corporations. International developments now made the dealers' story even more appealing. As the price of gasoline increased in the early 1970s, many Americans were angered by the major oil companies' extraordinary profits. Many thought that the large oil companies had manufactured the entire "oil crisis" to excuse price increases. Dealers claimed that these companies should not pass on the burdens of disruption in the oil business to their dealers and customers when the companies were making record profits.

During 1977, some of the major oil companies changed their position and supported federal dealer protection legislation. The dealers' lobbyists and the companies' lawyers worked out most of the technical objections to earlier legislative proposals, arriving at a compromise with the help of the staffs of the House and Senate committees considering legislation in this area . . . .

---

121. Exxon Corp. *v.* Governor of Maryland, 437 U.S. 117 (1978).

Perhaps a major reason for this change was that many companies now felt that they needed federal legislation to preempt the many varying state statutes and to ward off the threat of divestiture of all retail operations. The dealers' associations had produced enough state law that the companies valued uniformity itself. Furthermore, there was always a threat that the dealers could get states to pass laws less favorable to oil company interests than the compromise worked out at the federal level. Finally, the major oil companies were concerned about congressional reaction to proposals for such things as gasoline rationing and a windfall profits tax. Some officials of the large corporations thought it was time to withdraw from the public role as the villain who pushed around local small business.

Congress passed the Petroleum Marketing Practices Act (PMPA), which became effective in June of 1978. While this statute limits cancellation of a franchise to specified grounds, it also leaves the major oil companies relatively free to not renew dealer franchises. The franchisor need only negotiate in good faith for a renewal; it need not negotiate reasonably in light of the dealer's interests. The federal courts have read the PMPA's provisions on nonrenewal so that a dealer's threat of formal legal action is but a paper tiger. Moreover, the PMPA preempts all state legislation which might otherwise benefit gasoline dealers.

In 1984, The Service Station Dealers of America, Inc. returned to Congress seeking amendments to the PMPA, and it has lobbied for legislation at every session since then . . . .

The dealers and legislators championing their cause proposed a statute which would require changes and additions proposed by a franchisor in renewal negotiations to be "fair and reasonable" in addition to being in good faith . . . .

In 1988, the proposed statute amending the PMPA was passed by the House of Representatives but not by the Senate. It was reintroduced in 1989. The Director of Legislative and Political Affairs for the Petroleum Marketers Association of American stated that he thought there was a "50:50 chance that President Bush would veto" the PMPA Amendments if they were passed.

The retail gasoline dealers also returned to the state legislatures.[122] During the 1980s, they won victories in Massachusetts, Nevada and other states. However, their lawyers are now defending these statutes against constitutional challenges and charges that they attempt to regulate in an area taken from state power by the PMPA.

---

122. The International Franchise Association's treasurer discussed the success of this franchisor organization in blocking proposed state franchise protection legislation. The group works to kill these proposals in committee. This allows legislators to vote against these bills without publicity. He said in 1986, the IFA defeated 27 bills introduced in 18 states. See Bernstein, "IFA Faces Franchise Law Fracas," 21 *Nation's Restaurant News*, Feb. 9, 1987, p. 1.

Once again, move prompts countermove. The Federal Trade Commission began rule-making hearings on proposed franchising rules in 1986. This process continued through 1990 . . . .

What has been the impact of all this legal warfare? Certainly the organized gasoline dealers gained a federal law which gives them broad protection against cancellation during the term of a franchise . . . . However, the PMPA offers little protection against nonrenewal of a franchise. Moreover, . . . the PMPA preempts state legislation dealing with cancellation and nonrenewal.

The number of franchised dealers of gasoline has continued to decline even after the federal legislation went into effect.[123] The price of fuel remains high, and many motorists drive less and buy cars that get high mileage. This limits gasoline sales. Motorists are less willing to pay a few cents a gallon more at their neighborhood stations which do not discount their prices. Automobile manufacturers have decreased the frequency of needed maintenance, and dealers have lost oil change and lubrication business. Automobiles have become more difficult to repair, requiring specialized tools for each make and trained mechanics. This decreases the opportunity to repair cars at service stations. And the federal legislation came in 1978 rather than in 1968. Many of the dealers who might have benefited when the great wave of terminations and nonrenewals began, lost out long before the law was passed.

Thus, the long struggle to gain federal legislation may have produced a law with more symbolic significance than instrumental impact. Of course, it may have benefited those who managed to survive until it was passed. Some dealers may have won renewals before the oil companies established the judicial interpretations that are so favorable to them. There might have been even a greater decline in the number of service stations had there been no federal law.

As we noted, the gasoline dealers' efforts in some states produced statutes offering protection to most franchisees rather than just those who sold gasoline. These statutes are preempted by the federal Petroleum Marketing Practices Act only insofar as they apply to gasoline dealers. There is an ironic twist here. The gasoline dealers worked to pass these statutes, and they included other franchisees only to broaden the appeal of the proposed legislation. Those who just went along for the ride are the major beneficiaries of the retail gasoline dealers' lobbying efforts. □

---

123. "Although nobody knows the total number of retail gas outlets—estimates range from 150,000 to 300,000–Government figures show that the number of service stations is now 112,000, less than half the 1972 peak." From Hershey, "Fill'er Up and Check the Doughnuts," *New York Times*, July 1, 1989 p. 16, col. 1, 3.

NOTES AND QUESTIONS

1. How do you explain the passage of federal and state gasoline dealer franchise protection statutes? Does the situation fit the model put forward by Friedman and Ladinsky? What aspects of the story are explained by (a) elements of legal culture; (b) aspects of the *structure* of American law, for example, federalism; (c) power, class, and hegemony; (d) "outside" forces such as the Arab oil shock, technological change, and so on?

2. Can we generalize from Macaulay's story? Can you think of other attempts at reform that were gutted by the judicial and legal tactics of the powerful? To what extent have American civil rights statutes, regulations, and cases of the 1970s come to a fate in the 1980s and 1990s similar to that of gasoline dealer protective legislation?

3. Why didn't the judges implement the statutes more vigorously in favor of the dealers? Couldn't, for example, the federal statute have been read to require judges to examine negotiations about renewal of a service station for their fairness rather than leave a large loophole in the statute? Couldn't the Congress have responded quickly when the federal act was discovered to overturn all the state regulation while offering little protection to the dealers? How might we explain these failures to carry out the purposes of the reforms?

Consider Robert C. Ellickson, *Order Without Law: How Neighbors Settle Disputes* (Cambridge, Mass.: Harvard University Press, 1991), pp. 152–53. He points out that one form of sociological theory:

> holds that members of powerful interest groups manipulate the content of norms to serve their own selfish interests . . .
>
> Interest-group theorists would win more converts if they could identify the mechanisms through which well-placed interest groups might manipulate the norm-making process. One can readily understand how concentrated lobbies are able to influence the legal system. The informal-control system, by contrast, is much more diffuse. Florists undoubtedly have had some success in promoting the tradition of Mother's Day gifts, and diamond merchants, the custom of diamond engagement rings. Nevertheless, norms seem generally resistant to deliberate influence. Totalitarian Communist regimes were not able to produce a "new man," Madison Avenue cannot convince most motorists to buckle their seat belts, and the right-to-life movement has little success in stemming the incidence of abortion. One weakness of the various interest-group theories is that they say little about when and how an interest group can control the content of norms.
>
> A second shortcoming . . . is that [these theories] are seriously incomplete. Many fundamental social norms appear neutral in content. It is hard to see how common norms of honest, reciprocity, promise keeping, and respect for the bodily integrity of others serve the interests of the strong at the expense of the weak . . . . Interest-group analysis must amplify their theories so as to be able to explain norms that are distributively neutral or progressive.

To what extent can we explain the retail gasoline dealers' only partial success as a failure to control the content of informal norms? To what extent could changing the text in statute books affect the norms of those who represented the major oil companies in their everyday contacts with retail gasoline dealers? To what extent could changing the text in statute books change the informal norms held by judges and jurors who dealt with cases under the statute? Would such informal norms affect their reading of the formal ones found in statutory text?

4. Do the gasoline dealer statutes reflect law as the "will of the people?" Or are they special interest statutes likely to place the costs of changes in the petroleum industry on consumers who are not organized into a special interest group able to bargain before the legislatures? To what degree is this typical of American legislation?

5. Many groups—conservative as well as liberal, business as well as civil rights—use the courts as a tool for political action. See Susan M. Olson, "Interest Group Litigation in Federal District Courts: Beyond the Federal Disadvantage Theory," 52 *Journal of Politics* 854 (1990).

THE JUDICIAL SYSTEM FUNCTIONS IN A SOCIAL CONTEXT: STUDIES OF LITIGATION STATISTICS

26. The Routinization of Debt Collection: An Essay on Social Change and Conflict in Courts

Robert Kagan

18 *Law & Society Review* 323 (1984)

☐ In recent years, there have been a substantial number of historical studies of the dockets of American courts, stimulated in some cases by concerns that our society is becoming more litigious, in others by concerns that important kinds of grievances are left unadjudicated, and in still others by a sense that changes in the business of courts will provide insight into the dynamics of the legal system as a whole. There has been great interest in the apparent increase of certain types of court cases, such as product liability, malpractice, criminal procedure, and public law cases. These upsurges in litigation are sometimes taken as a sign that courts are at last dealing with injustices long neglected and sometimes as a sign that something is amiss in the social system if people and organizations more often resort to the courts to resolve their problems. Less attention has been given, however, to discovering precisely what kinds of social changes encourage or suppress particular kinds of litigation, and exactly how they do so. To stimulate further inquiry into those processes, this essay discusses the social, economic, political, and legal factors that have produced a recent decline in contested litigation in a significant sphere of court business—debt collection suits . . . .

In eighteenth- and nineteenth-century American courts, debt collection cases . . . seem to have dominated the judicial process. Bruce Mann reports that in a six-month period in 1754, a Windham, Connecticut, justice of the peace heard 47 actions on promissory notes, 4 debt actions on book accounts, and only 9 other kinds of cases. Wayne McIntosh tells us that debt collection cases accounted for over 80 percent of civil cases filed in the St. Louis, Missouri, Circuit Court in 1820 (a depression year), over 50 percent in the 1820–1850 period, and over one-third (still the largest single type of case) in 1865–1895. Debt collection cases were similarly prominent in California trial courts in 1890 and 1910, in Chippewa County, Wisconsin, between 1865 and 1894, and in the Boston Municipal Court and the Suffolk County Superior Court in 1880 and 1890.

While docketed cases usually reflect individual debtor creditor disputes, the role of the courts in forcible debt collection occasionally boiled up into political conflict. The history of the Constitutional Convention in 1787 and the document it produced reflect fears of populist democracy sown by agrarian debtors' attacks against the courts, as in Shays' Rebellion in Massachusetts, and occasionally successful attempts by debtors to obtain legislation staying the collection of debts or making payment easier by obliging creditors to accept hastily printed (and fast-depreciating) paper money. Similarly, the plight of agrarian debtors burdened by tight money and unyielding credit institutions was the fulcrum of widespread grass-roots political agitation and intense conflict over the gold standard during the Populist movement in the latter part of the nineteenth century. It should not be surprising, then, that even though most debt collection cases in the trial courts were settled or ended in uncontested default judgments, hard-fought debt cases also worked their way with considerable frequency up the judicial ladder to state supreme courts, which in the nineteenth century were often more active than legislatures as policy-making bodies. Debt cases accounted for almost 30 percent of the opinions of 16 representatively selected American state supreme courts in 1870 and about 26 percent of their opinions in the 1870–1900 period. Resolving conflicts and formulating rules of law concerning the debt collection process apparently absorbed more high court attention than any other type of legal or policy issue. In the twentieth century, however, there has been a dramatic decline, both proportionately and in absolute number, in debtor protection/creditors' rights opinions by state supreme courts, as indicated by Figure 1. The decline was gradual in the 1900–1935 period but has been dramatic since then. In the 1950–1970 period fewer than 7 percent of state supreme court (SSC) opinions involved debt collection matters; the 16 SSCs in the . . . sample decided an estimated 170 debt cases per year, on the average, as contrasted with an estimated 886 per year in 1880–1900 and 717 in 1905–1925.

The gradual disappearance of debt collection cases from state supreme court dockets gives rise to both an historical and a theoretical

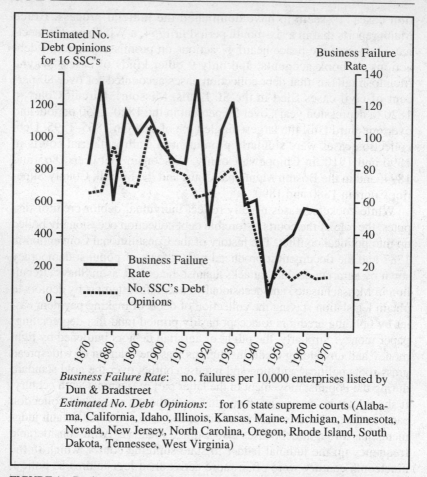

Business Failure Rate: no. failures per 10,000 enterprises listed by Dun & Bradstreet

Estimated No. Debt Opinions: for 16 state supreme courts (Alabama, California, Idaho, Illinois, Kansas, Maine, Michigan, Minnesota, Nevada, New Jersey, North Carolina, Oregon, Rhode Island, South Dakota, Tennessee, West Virginia)

FIGURE 1   Business Failure and Number of State Supreme Court Debt Case Opinions 1870-1970

puzzle. Why has a type of legal dispute so central to socioeconomic relations in a market economy and so often a focus of political conflict all but faded away as a subject for judicial policy-making? In an era in which, as the conventional wisdom has it, an "imperial judiciary" is intruding upon (or is being thrust into) ever-widening areas of economic and social life, why have high courts almost abandoned (or been permitted to neglect) debtor-creditor relations? These questions, in turn, relate to a persistent theoretical issue in the study of law and society: What determines the changing incidence of judicial involvement in a policy area? To address these questions, this essay will examine available data concerning the volume of contested and uncontested cases in trial courts and will discuss five factors or trends that seem likely to affect the incidence of debt litigation: (I) fluctuations in the number or rate of problem-generating events, i.e., debt repayment delinquencies and defaults; (2) litigation costs; (3) legal rationalization, i.e., trends toward the stabilization of legal rules and toward institutionalized contracting and collection processes designed to simplify or forestall litigation; (4) political conflict over existing legal rules and political demands for legal change and (5) trends toward systemic stabilization, i.e., development of regulatory programs, public and private insurance and loss-spreading arrangements, and diversified economic institutions that prevent or deflect debtor-creditor conflict. Examining the limited evidence relevant to each of these factors will lead to an inductively constructed model that suggests how the various factors interact and that helps us understand the changing incidence of litigation in other areas as well. Moreover, the overriding importance of the developments discussed under the heading "Systemic Stabilization" in limiting debt collection litigation emphasizes the powerful role of collective welfare state measures and economic development in shaping modern legal action.

DATA FOR FIGURE 1

Sample Year	Average No. Opinions per SSC	Percent Debt Collection	Average No. Debt Opinions per SSC	Estimated Total Debt Opinions, 16 SSC's	Rate of Business Failures @ 10,000 Businesses	Total Business Failures in U.S.
1870	131	32.1	42	672	83	3,546
1875	171	25.4	43	688	128	7,740
1880	208	28.2	59	944	63	4,735
1885	196	23.4	46	736	116	10,637
1890	233	19.4	45	720	99	10,907
1895	242	27.4	66	1056	112	13,197
1900	240	25.3	61	976	92	10,774
1905	213	23.6	50	800	85	11,520
1910	245	18.4	45	720	84	12,652
1915	292	13.2	39	624	133	22,156
1920	228	18.1	41	656	48	8,881
1925	254	19.4	49	784	100	21,214
1930	270	19.8	53	848	122	26,355
1935	215	18.8	40	640	62	12,244
1940	184	14.9	27	432	63	13,619
1945	119	5.9	7	112	4	809
1950	160	9.0	14	224	34	9,162
1955	158	5.6	9	144	42	10,969
1960	172	6.9	12	192	57	15,445
1965	182	4.9	9	144	53	13,514
1970	167	5.2	9	144	44	10,748

I. PROBLEM-GENERATING EVENTS

One obvious influence on the incidence of certain types of court cases might be the number of transactions or events in the surrounding society that can give rise to the kind of legal action in question. This "hypothesis" assumes that, over time, citizens and business organizations are inclined to take a relatively constant (even if small) proportion of their problems and disputes to court and to contest or appeal a relatively constant (even if small) proportion of those court cases. As potentially troublesome social and economic encounters or relationships take new forms or increase in number, one would expect the composition of court dockets to mirror, in a rough way, changes in the numbers of such conflict-producing transactions. In some legal areas, this relationship seems to exist. Thus, the proportion of domestic relations cases on state supreme court dockets has tended to rise and fall with changes in the national divorce rate. State supreme court tort cases involving railroads declined in the twentieth century along with the steady reduction in the number of railroad accidents, while motor vehicle tort appeals rose as deaths from auto accidents increased. From this perspective, fluctuations in the incidence of nonpayment of debts should produce corresponding changes in debt collection litigation. One available proxy for the incidence of debt delinquency is the recorded data on national business failures. As Figure I and its accompanying data show, between 1870 and 1930, some upswings and some declines in business failures were paralleled by less extreme trends in the number of debt cases in state supreme courts, while at other times the two curves moved in opposite directions. Strikingly, however, the most drastic phase of the decline in debt case appeals, in the mid-1930s and 1940s, matched an equally dramatic drop in the rate and number of business failures. The dockets of some trial courts for which longitudinal data exist also seemed to reflect the business cycle, especially in the 1930s and '40s:

–In Chippewa County, Wisconsin, debt cases which numbered 407 (40 percent of the civil docket) in 1915–1924, rose to 662 (55 percent of the civil docket) in the 1925–1934 period, which covered the depths of the Depression, only to decline to their earlier level after the holocaust of business failures and mortgage foreclosures of the early 1930s had run its course.

–In Alameda County, California, my estimates from Friedman and Percival's published data indicate that debt case filings climbed from 236 in 1890 to 929 in 1910 and 1329 in 1930, a path that parallels the rate and absolute number of business failures nationwide for those years, and then declined to 853 cases in 1950 as prosperity returned and the business failure rate went down (Friedman and Percival, 1976).[124]

124. [The reference is to Lawrence M. Friedman and Robert V. Percival, "A Tale of Two Courts: Litigation in Alameda and San Benito Counties," 10 *Law & Society Review* 267 (1976).]

But the post-World War II data tell a very different story. Between 1940 and 1970 (as Table I shows), farm loans, home mortgage loans, and corporate debt increased sixfold (far more than the rate of inflation), and consumer loans expanded by a factor of 16. Most of this mushrooming private debt, of course, is repaid on schedule and does not give rise to potential court cases. But defaulted and delinquent loans have undoubtedly increased in absolute numbers and amounts, probably in rough proportion to the increase in total debt. For example:

–If the delinquency rate for consumer debt held steady at its average level of 1.5 percent of outstanding loans (the bankers' rule of thumb, according to several consumer loan officers I interviewed), delinquencies would have increased in amount from a total of $322 million in 1950 to $2.4 billion in 1973. In fact, the delinquency rate for consumer loans increased by at least 50 percent beginning in the late 1960s, to 2.2 percent in 1973 and 2.6 percent in 1974. The gross dollar volume of new business reported by debt collection agencies to their trade association grew from $40 million in 1965 to $93 million in 1974.

–Home mortgage loans at least 30 days in arrears climbed from 2.08 percent of all loans at the end of 1955 to 3.06 percent in 1965 and 4.3 percent, twice the 1950 rate, in 1975. Nonfarm mortgage foreclosures numbering about 23,000 nationwide in 1950, grew to about 50,000 in 1960, 115,000 in 1965, 95,000 in 1970, and after the inflation and recession of recent years to about 175,000 in 1982.

–The national business failure rate climbed from 4 per 10,000 enterprises in 1945 to 34 in 1950 and to 64 in 1961, averaging 51.4 throughout the 1960s. Absolute numbers of business failures also grew (Table 1).

TABLE 1   Private Debt In Billions Of Dollars As Of End Of Year

	1929	1940	1950	1960	1970	1976–78
Corporate long term loans	$51.1	$43.7	$60.1	$139.1	$360.2	$568.8
Farm loans	$12.2	9.1	12.3	25.1	58.7	n.a.
Consumer loans	$7.1	8.3	21.5	56.1	127.2	292.7
Estimated amount delinquent*	$.1	.12	.32	.84	2.54	7.61
Mortgage loans (1–4 family res.)	$18.0	16.5	43.9	137.4	274.6	637.6
Estimated amount delinquent**	$n.a.	n.a.	.9	3.65	8.9	28.7

*Total amount delinquent estimated by using the following percentages: 1929, 1940, 1950, 1960—1.5 percent; 1970—2 percent; 1976–78—2.6 percent.
**Total amount delinquent estimated by using the following percentages: 1956—2.08%; 1960—2.66 percent; 1970—3.24 percent; 1977—4.5 percent.

In sum, in the 1950s, 1960s, and 1970s, the incidence of individual and business "crises" that one would expect to lead to litigation over debts all increased dramatically. Nevertheless, debt collection cases continued to decline in the 1950s and 1960s in absolute terms and as a proportion of state supreme court cases. Debt litigation in trial courts, too, does not seem to have increased proportionately, although the available data, shown in Table 2, are scattered and far from adequate:

–In rapidly growing Alameda County, California, my estimates, based on Friedman and Percival's published data, indicate that the number of debt cases did grow from 853 in 1950 to 1511 in 1970, but this growth barely exceeded population growth. In 1970, there were 1.4 debt cases per 1000 county residents, compared with 1.2 In 1950 and the much higher rates of 3.8 in 1910 and 2.8 in 1930 (Friedman and Percival, 1976).

–McIntosh's (1980–81)[125] published data on the St. Louis Circuit Court indicate that debt collection cases declined from their nineteenth-century highs to 15 percent of all civil cases filed in 1910, to less than 8 percent in 1940, and further to just under 5 percent in 1955 and 1970. Applying these percentages to the reported total cases yields an estimated 693 debt cases in 1940, 497 in 1955, and 477 in 1970. Thus, at least in this St. Louis court, the absolute number of debt cases filed throughout the 1940–1970 period actually declined.

Not only does the number of debt collection cases filed in trial courts in the post-World War II period seem to have fallen far short of the growth in business failures and loan delinquencies, but the number and rate of contested trial court debt cases declined, both absolutely and proportionately, in two of the three trial courts for which published data exist.

–Laurent's (1959)[126] data from the Chippewa County, Wisconsin, Circuit Court indicate that in contract cases (the overwhelming majority of which were debt collection matters) the proportion that apparently was contested fluctuated between 17 and 30 percent in the decades between 1865 and 1944, with no clear trend toward lower rates. Yet in 1945–1954, the last decade covered by the study, only 10 percent of debt cases were contested, the lowest rate in the century.

–Another measure of the incidence of strongly asserted legal defenses is the percentage of cases resulting in judgment for defendants. Here, too, the Chippewa County data show no clear trend between 1805 and 1944; defendants hit their peak victory rate in 1905–1914, winning contested judgments in 10.5 percent of contract cases, but then slipped

125. [The reference is to Wayne V. McIntosh, "150 Years of Litigation and Dispute Settlement: A Court Tale," 15 *Law & Society Review* 823 (1980–81).]

126. [The reference is to Francis W. Laurent, *The Business of a Trial Court: 100 Years of Cases* (Madison: University of Wisconsin Press, 1959).]

back in the 1915–1944 period to the historically average rate of 4.3 to 6.1 percent. Once again, however, in 1945–1954, at the outset of the post-World War II era, defendant victories in contested contract cases declined to an historical low, a mere 1.5 percent of the cases.

–McIntosh's (1980–81) St. Louis Circuit Court data indicate that the proportion of debt cases resulting in contested hearings and judgments was a steady 25 to 28 percent in 1820–1850, 1865–1895, and 1910–1925. Defendants won contested judgments in only about 5 or 6 percent of cases in each of those periods. In St. Louis, too, the post-World War II period reflects a sharp decline in contested cases, to about 10 percent of debt collection cases in the 1940–1970 period, and a decline in victories for defendants via contested judgments to 2.4 percent of cases.

–In Alameda County, California . . . the percentage of contract cases going to trial decreased from 30.3 percent in 1890 to 22.6 percent in 1912 but leapt upward to 57.1 percent in 1930. As in Chippewa County and St. Louis, the percent of cases tried in 1950 declined (to 19 percent) but jumped up to 27 percent in 1970 apparently counter to the trend in St. Louis.

One possibility . . . is that debt collection matters have been diverted to municipal and small claims courts. This suggestion is consistent with studies of contemporary municipal courts and small claims courts which show that their dockets are dominated by debt collection cases. While time series studies of small claims court dockets are lacking, my estimates based on data from California, presented in Table 4, indicate substantial growth in the number of debt collection cases in municipal and small claims courts. However, in the municipal courts, at least until 1980, debt cases did not increase more rapidly than the state's population. And in neither the municipal nor the small claims courts did collection cases grow as rapidly as the national debt delinquency totals shown in Table 1. Moreover, the ability of litigants to sue on small debts in small claims courts (the maximum jurisdictional amount in California was increased from $500 to $750 in 1977 and is now $1500) does not explain why debt collection cases arising from the mounting numbers of larger debts (mobile home loans, home mortgages, small business loans, corporate loans) have not increased in trial courts of general jurisdiction and have almost disappeared from state supreme courts. Thus, increased litigation in small claims courts accounts, at best, for only a small part of the decline in debt litigation in the general trial courts and courts of appeal.

II. LITIGATION COSTS

In discussing the linkage between problem-generating events (in this case, delinquencies in repayment) and litigation, I assumed that only "some proportion" of delinquencies would lead to declared defaults, and that only some (constant) proportion of defaults would end in collection suits. The "constant proportion" assumption is obviously too simplistic. Consider, for example, the likely impact on litigation volume of changes in the cost of litigation. Creditors are often deterred from bringing suit by the costs of hiring attorneys, enduring court delays, gaining the cooperation of sheriffs in serving process and executing judgments, and so on. Litigation costs, including opportunity costs such as taking time off work to appear in court, undoubtedly lead some debtors not to contest suits they think unfounded. Hence, court dockets might be expected to reflect only that subset of delinquencies or defaults in which the amount at issue exceeds the various costs of litigation, tangible and intangible. If so, court cases could be expected to decline, or to rise more sluggishly than problem-generating events, during periods in which the transaction costs associated with litigation are rising, either absolutely or in relation to the average amount at issue.

For example, one explanation for the post-World War II decline in debt cases in state supreme courts might be that during this period many states created a layer of intermediate appellate courts between trial courts and the supreme court, thus increasing the cost, in time, uncertainty, and attorneys' fees, of pursuing matters to the supreme court. This explanation would predict that the post-1945 fall-off in supreme court debt opinions would be sharper in states with intermediate appellate courts than in those without them. However, the prediction, and hence the explanation, does not hold, for the debt case decline was virtually as great in one group of states as in the others.

The impact of litigation costs on the incidence of debt cases, and especially of contested cases, may be more evident at the trial court level. Because a larger proportion of credit now involves small consumer loans (see Table 1), the average amount at stake in a loan default may be less financially significant to the parties than was the case in earlier eras when proportionately more loans were for the purchase of real estate, farm needs, and commercial goods and facilities, and lenders were less likely to be large financial institutions. In consequence, today's debtors and creditors faced with potential court cases may be more likely to absorb their losses rather than litigate or appeal.

Unfortunately, I have encountered no systematic evidence concerning the average amount of all debts, either in society at large or in the courts, today or in times past. And despite the general impression that court calendars today entail longer delays and that trials and pre-trial discovery proceedings are more expensive, I know of no studies that show that litigation expenses have in fact increased in relation to GNP per capita or some other meaningful baseline. It is undoubtedly true, of course, that credit cards and installment sales have generated vast numbers of smaller debts. In 1972 the average amount of the 1,210,000 "small loans" by California finance companies was $1069, indicating that most were under $1000; the average amount of the *defaulted* small loan, assuming some pay-back of principal, undoubtedly was even smaller. The average account handed over to debt collection agencies was only $55 in 1965, $90 in 1975, and $130 in 1980. Even given the existence of institutions like small claims courts that are expressly designed to reduce legal transaction costs when little money is at stake, many unpaid debts are probably not worth litigating. In California and other states that preclude debt collection agencies from using small claims courts, the point at which it pays to institute suit or to contest will reflect the fact that collection agencies must employ attorneys and use municipal courts, as must debtors inclined to resist. Hence, one would not expect small claims litigation to rise quite as rapidly as small debt delinquencies.

Nevertheless, the fact that litigation costs may deter lawsuits over small consumer debt delinquencies does not in itself explain the drop in debt collection cases in state supreme courts and in trial courts of general jurisdiction. As noted earlier, there has been a rapid increase in substantial loans—real estate mortgages, commercial and corporate loans—as well as increases in the annual numbers of mortgage defaults and business failures. The average amount of liabilities involved in business failures rose steadily, from $44,700 in 1948 to $175,000 in 1970. Many consumer loans, moreover, are for amounts seemingly worth litigating about. In 1972, the average loan on a new car was $3378. In 1980, debt consolidation loans by California's small loan finance companies (the most common type of finance company loan) averaged almost $2300. Hence, the post-World War II decline in debt litigation and appeals has occurred in the face of an increase in delinquent debts ostensibly large enough, in many cases, to exceed the direct litigation costs, such as attorneys' fees, that would be involved in collecting or contesting them.

It is impossible to reject the notion, however, that increased litigation costs, defined more broadly, have been an important factor in declining litigation rates. The issue is whether all the costs incurred by creditors and debtors in the litigation and appeal process—including the diversion of time and effort from other concerns, delay, the aggravation and anxiety associated with lawsuits and formal execution, damage to reputation—have made litigation over delinquent debts increasingly less attractive than alternative courses of action, such as extracting consensual repayment agreements, arranging refinancing, commercial arbitration, or in the case of the debtor simply conceding liability and in the case of the creditor giving in to debtors' excuses or legal defenses, and trying to recoup losses in other ways. Succeeding sections explore such influences on the relative costliness of litigation, first by examining legal changes that may have affected the availability of viable defenses and then by examining, under the head of "Systemic Stabilization," measures that may have made forbearance or "giving up" more feasible.

III. LEGAL RATIONALIZATION

According to one commonly held view of modern life, human and economic affairs are becoming increasingly subjected to rational legal rules and procedures designed to deal with recurrent kinds of problems. If so, the more complete and settled the law, the more one would expect "failed" transactions, accidents, and disputes to be perceived as having clear legal consequences, and the less the likelihood they would lead to contested court cases. Court dockets, then, would be expected to change in response to the social creation of new problems as the law attempts to "catch up." Thus, debt collection cases might well be prevalent in a rapidly growing and changing economy whose credit system was still struggling to achieve stability (as in the latter part of the nineteenth century). However, with the development of a mature commercial society, debt collection cases should become "old problems" covered by a comprehensive set of rules and precedents, and contested cases and appeals should fall from court dockets, except when radically new forms of credit and security arrangements arise.

Legal rationalization of this sort also implies the development of more efficient modes of adjudication. The institution and expansion of federal bankruptcy procedures, beginning with the Act of 1898, can be viewed as an example. At least one-third and probably more than half of the debt collection cases in state supreme courts in the late nineteenth and early twentieth centuries arose from situations in which a debtor's default visited loss or liability on a whole network of individuals or business firms that had dealt with him—creditors who had lent him money, sureties who had vouched for him and innocents who had purchased his property without knowing of liens upon it. As an example of the complexities that follow defaults, consider the not unusual situation of a company that is unable to pay for a new building. Immediately, the question arises of who should have priority in payment from the company's remaining assets—the construction company (pursuant to a mechanic's lien), suppliers of lumber and plumbing fixtures (pursuant to materialmen's liens), or the bank that had financed construction (secured by a mortgage on the real estate). State supreme courts were continually asked to resolve such conflicts among creditors.

Federal bankruptcy procedure, as first established in 1898 and expanded in 1910 to include voluntary filings by corporations, can be seen as an attempt to rationalize the problem of treating competing claimants fairly. State law created incentives for each creditor to rush to the courthouse to win a priority-establishing, winner-take-all judgment, even though such individualistic remedies might lead, as one legal scholar put it, "to a piecemeal dismantling of a debtor's business by the untimely removal of necessary operating assets." Federal bankruptcy sought to establish a collective system that marshals the debtor's assets, allocates them among all creditors according to a set schedule of entitlements and priorities, and thereby "provides a framework for implementing a consensual collective proceeding," either under the supervision of a trustee or outside the bankruptcy process.

The idea of legal rationalization also implies that in dealing with the complexities of modern legal systems, organizations and individuals increasingly will rely on lawyers and other specialists to handle problems and disputes. Legal specialists characteristically process and settle typical cases in law-regarding ways, but they do so informally, without judicial involvement. Thus, the growth of professional police departments, prosecutors' offices, and public defender offices should lower the proportion of criminal arrests that eventuate in trials. Claims adjustment offices in liability insurance companies should keep automobile tort litigation from increasing as rapidly as the number of accidents.

With respect to debt collection, one would expect contemporary sheriffs to be less prone to the legal errors and corruption that in the late nineteenth and early twentieth century often led to cases protesting the judgment collection and execution sale processes. One would also expect modern lending institutions to develop ways of forestalling expensive court contests over unpaid debts. As early as the eighteenth century, merchants began to insist that extensions of credit be memorialized in written promissory notes with clearly stated terms. This tended to foreclose court hearings in which equitable aspects of the underlying transaction would be contested. In his study of Boston courts in 1880 and 1900, Robert Silverman noted:

> The law of debt based on negotiable instruments and other commercial documents was better defined than was tort law in the late nineteenth century. Plaintiffs normally presented documents to substantiate their claims. A properly executed promissory note or other instrument of indebtedness made the calling of many witnesses unnecessary and also made it easier to determine the amount owed. Most debt actions were open and shut affairs in which defendants did not contest plaintiffs' demands.[127]

127. [The reference is to Robert A. Silverman, *Law and Urban Growth: Civil Litigation in the Boston Trial Courts, 1880–1900* (Princeton, N.J.: Princeton University Press, 1981).]

In the modern economy, as credit becomes dominated to an increasing extent by large, bureaucratized, legally sophisticated institutions such as banks, multi-state finance companies, and department stores, loan agreements contain standardized language designed to cover virtually every conceivable kind of contingency or dispute, thereby foreclosing possible legal defenses by debtors and competing creditors. Corporate loan agreements now run for pages, articulating the priority of liens to be imposed on the debtor's property or accounts receivable, clarifying the nature and valuation of collateral, and specifying the characteristics of financial reports that are to be submitted by the debtor at periodic intervals. Increasing recourse to bankruptcy by insolvent business firms has encouraged institutional lenders to insist on specific security arrangements that accord secured creditors priority under the law or entitle them to assert their rights before default. Today, a large proportion of loans by financial institutions to small businesses are secured. In consumer credit, as early as the mid-nineteenth century merchants developed conditional sales agreements that in the event of default entitled creditors to repossess and resell consumer durables without first going to court. It was also common to require borrowers to sign "confessions of judgment" or wage assignments that in the event of nonpayment enabled the creditor to obtain a judgment or garnish the debtor's wages without notice and without bringing suit, until this practice was banned about twenty years ago as a violation of due process. To forestall litigation, contracts among business firms for the supply of goods and services now almost routinely include provisions for binding arbitration of disputes concerning the justifiability of nonpayment.

More sophisticated credit information systems also help prevent legal problems and litigation over bad debts. By obtaining independent appraisals, title searches, and audited financial statements, banks evaluate their security interests before lending, thus minimizing the need to sue for deficiency judgments in the event of default and preventing disputes with other creditors. At the turn of the century, credit reference agencies were unreliable. Today, lenders subscribe to interstate services that compile and update credit histories on business and individual borrowers. Some banks now assign numerical credit ratings to individual loan applicants based on the borrower's particular "credit profile," which is calculated by comparing the applicant's financial characteristics with the bank's computerized analysis of the correlates of successful and unsuccessful loans. Consequently, a threat to impair a delinquent debtor's credit rating is often a more credible and effective collection tactic than is a lawsuit.

To the extent that these trends toward legal rationalization are strong and pervasive, one would expect a declining proportion of defaulted loans to result in court cases. A growing proportion of court fillings, moreover, would not signify real legal disputes, but would be filed to obtain an uncontested court order authorizing seizure and sale of the debtor's property, or to establish the creditor's legal priority over later-filing creditors. From this perspective, one might argue that appeals to state supreme courts in debt cases have become less frequent because the law has become settled, inter-creditor conflicts have been drawn into federal bankruptcy proceedings, precedents and carefully drafted agreements cover and resolve most disputes, and, in the growing number of state supreme courts with discretion to select cases on the basis of "importance," the judges are more concerned with new issues than with the complexities of old debtor-creditor law issues.

Some of the available evidence seems to support the legal rationalization hypothesis. In the federal courts, bankruptcy filings increased spectacularly from about 10,000 per year in 1946 to 250,000 in 1975. But the proportion (and perhaps the absolute number) of debt-related "contract" and "business organization" cases in federal Courts of Appeals declined, suggesting that the bankruptcy process was relatively successful in "settling" the claims of competing creditors in a consensual or routine way. Yet it seems unlikely that the marked decline in state supreme court debt cases after the mid-1930s can be explained by the sudden transformation of the law of debtors' and creditors' rights, which had figured in so many appellate cases between 1870 and 1930, into settled doctrine. In fact, as will be shown in the next section, this body of law has, if anything, become more turbulent in recent years.

At the trial court level, as I noted earlier, debt case filings had begun to decline in proportion to population growth by 1900, and this trend continued, with perhaps an interruption at the outset of the Great Depression, through 1970 (Table 2). This seems consistent with the idea that the legal process became increasingly rationalized as lenders became increasingly adept at devising loan agreements and security arrangements to forestall legal conflict and at routinizing nonjudicial debt collection procedures. On the other hand, from the mid-nineteenth century until after World War II, there was no consistent downward trend in the percentage or number of contested trial court cases or in the already small percentage of judgments for defendants (Table 3), which suggests that in those years the rationalization process was not increasingly effective in suppressing legal conflict. Why would declines in contested debt cases both at the trial court and state supreme court level show up only in the post-World War II period? One possibility, consistent with the legal rationalization hypothesis, is that federal bankruptcy, a primary device for "rationalizing" complex debt collection cases, reached its full jurisdictional and remedial range only after statutory amendments in 1938 and the post-World War II period. Not until the 1950s did annual numbers of business bankruptcy cases grow as rapidly as annual business failures, suggesting that only then did federal bankruptcy become a routine rather than an exceptional forum for resolving the claims of competing creditors. This explanation seems inadequate, however, because bankruptcy filings have not been sufficiently numerous to "absorb" more than a small proportion of state court debt cases and potential appeals. A second possibility, to be discussed in detail later, is that bureaucratized lending institutions did not really dominate a large proportion of the credit market until recent decades. This possibility suggests that the most fundamental causes of declining debt litigation lie not in the law but in fundamental changes in the economic and social system. Before discussing those systemic changes, however, another set of factors that seems to conflict, at least in part, with trends toward legal rationalization should be examined.

III. POLITICAL CONFLICT

The notion that the law will gradually become "rationalized" and "settled" as potential disputes are short circuited by carefully drafted legal documents and routinized procedures assumes that the losers in this process accept the existing law and contractual arrangements as the sole and legitimate measure of what they are entitled to complain about. It assumes, too, that the law will inevitably be shaped to reflect the "efficient" ways of doing business favored by large, impersonal, "economically rational" corporate enterprises.

Arguments for economic efficiency and the preferences of business elites certainly carry weight in the legal process. However, American politics has long had a populistic, antimoneyed-interests strain as well. Every legal rule has obvious distributive aspects as well as a relationship to economic efficiency, and every creditor's right may be experienced as a noose around the debtor's neck. Many debtors sense that they are being "ripped off" and some complain about it. Disputes between creditors and debtors are thus more than problems of commercial relations; they reflect politically important social cleavages. Politicians sometimes find it to their advantage to champion the interests of the many debtors in their constituencies against the impersonal practices of banks and merchants, and the well-organized interests that speak in the name of economic rationality or legal certainty do not necessarily prevail in the legislative arena. From this perspective, the law-on-the-books usually is no more than a temporary battle line in a never-ending political struggle between lenders and debtors, and one would expect debt litigation (and/or legislative activity on the subject) to increase whenever debtors or creditors as a politically organized "class" are actively seeking to change or reject the legal status quo.

A look at the numerous debt opinions written by state supreme courts in the late nineteenth century suggests that these courts were indeed being used as a political resource for escaping the strictures of

TABLE 2   DEBT COLLECTION CASES FILED IN THREE TRIAL COURTS

Alameda County Superior Court, California

	1890	1910	1930	1950	1970
Estimated number of debt cases	236	929	1,329	853	1,511
Percentage of all civil cases	33	28	26	12.1	12.8
Debt cases @ 1,000 population	2.5	3.8	2.8	1.2	1.4

Source: Friedman and Percival, 1976.

Chippewa County Circuit Court, Wisconsin

	1855–64	1865–74	1875–84	1885–94	1895–1904	1905–14	1915–24	1925–34	1935–44	1945–54
Estimated number of debt cases	225	635	1176	956	595	246	407	662	460	422
Percentage of all civil cases	77.3	64.8	59.4	62	52.3	32.8	40.6	54.5	41.4	35.9
Debt cases @ 1,000 population	366	76.4	75.9	38.0	18.0	7.7	11.2	17.8	11.3	9.9

Source: Laurent, 1959.

St. Louis Circuit Court

	1820	1835	1850	1865	1880	1895	1910	1925	1940	1955	1970
Estimated number of debt cases	600	234	976	461	800	1,016	897	764	693	497	477
Percentage of all civil cases	85.2	64.9	55.4	43.2	28.2	30	15	6.3	7.4	4.8	4.5
Debt cases @ 1,000 population	59.7	9.4	9.3	1.7	2.3	2.0	1.3	0.96	0.85	0.62	0.77

Source: McIntosh, 1980–81.

TABLE 3 CONTESTED DEBT COLLECTION CASES IN THREE TRIAL COURTS

Chippewa County Circuit Court, Wisconsin.

	1855–64	1865–74	1875–84	1885–94	1895–1904	1905–14	1915–24	1925–34	1935–44	1945–54
Percentage of contract cases contested	17	31	25	17	19	25	27	20	17	10
Percentage contested judgment for defendant	2.8	4.7	5.6	4.4	5.4	10.5	4.3	6.1	4.7	1.5
Percentage judgment for deft. in real estate cases*	2.9	3.0	2.5	0.7	3.4	5.8	2.0	1.4	1.4	1.7

Source: Laurent, 1959.
*at least half of which were mortgage foreclosures

St. Louis Circuit Court.

	1820–1850	1865–1895	1910–1925	1940–1970
Percentage of debt cases contested	28.1	25.5	26.8	9.5
Percentage contested judgment for defendant	5.3	6.1	5.4	2.4

Source: McIntosh, 1980–81.

Alameda County Superior Court, California.

	1890	1910	1930	1950	1970
Percentage of contract cases tried	30.3	22.6	57.1	19.0	27.0

Source: Friedman and Percival, 1976.

TABLE 4   ESTIMATED DEBT COLLECTION CASE FILINGS IN CALIFORNIA MUNICIPAL AND SMALL CLAIMS COURTS

Municipal Courts

	1955	1960	1965	1970	1975	1980
Total number of civil filings	191,591	213,311	285,217	275,450	302,250	48⁻,663
Estimated number of debt cases	95,796	106,656	142,609	137,725	151,125	240,832
Debt cases @ 1,000 population	7.4	6.7	7.7	6.9	7.0	10.1

Small Claims Courts

	1955	1960	1965	1970	1975	1980
Total number of filings	126,268	189,573	312,283	286,048	409,663	508 434
Estimated number of debt cases	82,074	123,222	202,984	185,931	266,281	330 482
Debt cases @ 1,000 population	6.3	7.8	11.0	9.3	12.4	13.9

Source: State of California, Administrative Office of the Courts

rationalized rules and procedures. Debt cases were often complex, involving conflicts between debtors and multiple creditors, guarantors, and innocent purchasers of lien-encumbered property. Precise "legal" answers, based on the detailed body of rules concerning priority of liens and execution procedures, were often available. These rules, however, frequently worked to the disadvantage of less sophisticated borrowers and lenders, who then appealed to the high courts, asking the judges, in effect, to reinterpret the language of contracts and precedent and render decisions that were equitable under the circumstances. Appellants argued that the creditor's document misstated the "true" agreement, or that property that the debtor had conveyed to relatives should be held subject to a "constructive" lien. Because appellate court judges were often willing, in Martin Shapiro's evocative phrase, to "keep clawing their way back toward the facts," to balance political and equitable considerations against efficency-enhancing impersonal legal rules, debt cases kept coming to the SSCs.

Debtors have periodically turned to legislatures, too, in their efforts to mitigate the legalistic enforcement of "settled" creditors' rights. Periods of deflation and recession (including the recent one) typically stimulate legislative action to restrict foreclosures, or to modify the process for the sale of repossessed property. Periodically, legislatures have expanded the amounts and kinds of debtor property that must be exempted from the execution of judgments. As a result of the "consumer movement" of recent years, the law of debtor-creditor relations, far from becoming more "settled," has changed rapidly. For example, the Uniform Commercial Code, adopted by most states in the 1960s, affirmed and enhanced the power of courts, increasingly suspicious of "contracts of adhesion," to refuse to enforce "unconscionable" provisions concerning sales of goods (UCC § 2-302), and to decline to compel payment on a contract when an "implied" warranty of merchantable quality is found to have been breached. State and federal courts and legislatures banned various agreements and procedures that had enabled creditors to seize or repossess consumer-debtors' property or to garnish their wages without first having to give notice and to go to court. In addition, the federal Consumer Credit Protection Act of 1968 restricted the proportion of debtors' wages that can be seized via garnishments and a number of state legislatures granted debtors protection from deficiency judgments after the sale of secured property. The federal Fair Debt Collection Practices Act (1977), following some state measures, banned harassment by collection agencies and expanded opportunities for debtors to raise questions and defenses.

To help debtors learn about and assert their expanding repertoire of legal rights creditors have been required to systematically notify consumers and borrowers of their rights in many situations. To prevent needy debtors from signing away statutory protections in return for further extensions of credit, legislation has expressly forbidden certain kinds of waivers. To counteract litigation expenses, laws such as the federal Truth in Lending Act (1968) have empowered successful debtors (and their lawyers) to recover attorneys' fees and punitive damages. Government has directly absorbed some of the costs of asserting debtors' rights through federally funded neighborhood-based lawyers for the poor and through state and local consumer fraud units that investigate complaints about lending and sales practices. Sometimes the notice and public assistance aspects have been combined, as in a California law that compels licensed debt collection agencies to include in each collection letter a prominent statement giving the debtor the telephone number of the state agency that enforces fair debt collection laws.

Creditors, of course, have not been wholly passive. In reaction to the increased litigation costs threatened by the elimination of pre-judgment remedies, lenders and merchants more often insist on credit agreements obligating debtors to pay the bank or finance company's attorneys' fees in the event of a default. Creditors, too, lobby the legislatures, seeking to carve out exceptions in recently enacted consumer protection statutes, adjust the categories of loans to which different maximum interest rates apply, and so on. To escape ceilings on interest, they invent new kinds of finance or service charges or base their calculations on a truncated 360-day year. Consumer advocates then return to lobby for amendments outlawing or restricting the creditor's adaptations. In recent decades, therefore, debtor and creditor law has constantly been in flux.

Reading this catalogue of legal changes, one might have expected a major explosion of contested debt cases in the courts during the last twenty years rather than the observed decline. A sample of state supreme court debt cases from 1965 and 1970, however, reflects an almost total absence of issues arising out of modern consumer protection law; the cases were hardly different in nature from those of 1900. From the standpoint of the hypothesis that political activism in a policy area will engender increased litigation, these results seem anomalous.

The anomaly can be partially resolved by recognizing that a major effect of new debtors' rights is to increase creditors' litigation costs, reducing the latter's incentive to sue (or to resist debtors' claims). If the law exempts larger amounts of debtors' property from execution, prevents creditors from collecting deficiency judgments, and so on, creditors are encouraged to resort to informal collection efforts rather than to use the courts. Greater debtor access to attorneys reduces creditors' inclinations to bring collection suits against feisty debtors or to pursue contested cases to trial or to higher courts.

The prominence of legislative and regulatory action in the elaboration of debtors' rights also suggests that the forum for political action has shifted, so that seekers of legal change no longer go to state supreme courts but to state and federal legislatures and regulatory rulemakers. Consumers with legal defenses, perhaps, now go to regulatory agencies for assistance, leaving only debtors with no defenses in the judicial process. Perhaps, with the rise of federal law, the federal courts are now where the action is. There is some weight to these arguments, but not enough to fully explain the decline in litigation. Although some legal changes may deter litigation, and major changes may now be sought more readily in legislatures, a rapidly changing body of law inevitably gives rise to enormous numbers of ambiguities of interpretation and application, any one of which provides thousands of creditors and debtors opportunities to seek some advantage in the courts. Losers in the legislature or regulatory agency still have every incentive to press cases in the courts, either on constitutional grounds or to settle a favorable statutory interpretation. Conflicts between the letter of the law and the equities of the situation, of the kind that filled state supreme court dockets decades ago, probably have become more rather than less numerous as the body of laws and regulations has grown. Finally, recent increases in contract-related cases in the federal courts are insufficient to make up for the decline of contested cases in state supreme and superior courts.

It might be argued that the expansion of debtor rights has not produced an explosion of hotly contested state court cases and appeals because debtors, by and large, remain ignorant of their rights or unwilling to assert them because of the direct and indirect costs of litigating. One study found that only 5 percent of a sample of consumer debtors who were sued in urban courts filed an answer, even though one-third believed that they had at least a partial defense. Stewart Macaulay[128] discovered that many Wisconsin attorneys knew little about recent federal laws affecting consumer rights and that they were unwilling to litigate consumer claims that did not involve large dollar amounts (Macaulay, 1979). Counsel for a large bank whom I interviewed also spoke of the ignorance of many debtors' lawyers about possible legal claims. Judges in small claims courts in fourteen states . . . said that federal and state consumer protection requirements are rarely raised, either affirmatively or as a defense. Finally, the president of California's association of collection agencies told me that members now encounter legal defenses in pre-litigation discussions in perhaps 5 percent of cases. This is an increase from the "almost never" of ten or fifteen years ago, but it is still a small proportion.

This research, however, relates entirely to the small claims debt collection process, which has remained a low-level, legally routinized process. Ignorance and litigation costs do not explain why contested cases involving larger debts, for which litigation costs are comparatively smaller, have not been stimulated by changes in the law. The Wisconsin Civil Litigation Project found little passivity among a sample of

---

128. [The reference is to Stewart Macaulay, "Lawyers and Consumer Law," 14 *Law & Society Review* 115 (1979).]

households with grievances growing out of debt or consumer problems amounting to $1000 or more. Households transformed such grievances into claims over 90 percent of the time. They persisted, usually successfully and not infrequently with lawyer's aid, when they met resistance (which was most of the time). Other studies of households with consumer grievances show a high propensity to protest and a high rate of success, which tends to counteract the image of the acquiescent debtor. A debt collection agency president, whom I asked to explain the significant decline in the average recovery rate achieved by collection companies—from about 33 cents on the dollar in 1965 to 24.7 cents in 1975–1980—emphasized changing attitudes: the bill collector's traditional asset—that debtors are afraid of him, plagued by guilt feelings, and embarrassed—has been eroded by an increasing proportion of debtors who seem unconcerned about their reputations and are willing to stall or be defiant.

In any case, there is no obvious reason to believe that debtors are in general more acquiescent when they have colorable claims than they were in earlier decades. Therefore, the apparent decline of legal disputes in recent decades might have occurred, as the legal rationalization concept suggests, because creditors quickly adapted to legal changes, so that many cases remain in which debtors quite accurately perceive that they have no legitimate defense. The trend toward legal rationalization may be complemented by a decline (for good economic reasons) in "toughness" on the part of creditors that is manifested in a tendency for lenders to acquiesce in new legal restrictions and to "give in" in the few cases in which debtors make some show of legal resistance. Political conflict over creditors' rights may not lead to more legal conflict if, despite legal change, creditors have become less disposed to enforce the law strictly against debtors and more attentive to other ways of cutting or recouping their losses. To these possibilities we now turn.

IV. SYSTEMIC STABILIZATION

The concept of legal stabilization discussed earlier refers to laws, contractual provisions, and procedures governing discrete transactions and disputes. The underlying hypothesis is that the gradual development of a more comprehensive body of laws and contractual arrangements, routinely applied by legal and bureaucratic specialists, has come to provide out-of-court legal "solutions" to an increasing proportion of individual conflicts. An even more significant litigation-suppressing factor, however, may be systemic stabilization. By this, I mean the development of large-scale economic and social institutions that ameliorate the conditions that cause individual conflicts or that provide collective, administrative remedies (as contrasted to case-by-case legal remedies).

The idea of systemic stabilization does not presume an ineluctable social evolution toward rational collective problem solving or toward stable and effective economic markets. But it does presume that in modern democratic and capitalist societies political demands will often reflect some version of those ideals. The political agenda of the debtor class over the last two centuries, for example, has been dominated less by the quest for specific legal rights, such as the better disclosure of finance charges in individual credit transactions, than by more fundamental (and controversial) demands for systemic solutions to common problems. Judging from Shays' Rebellion, the Populist movement, and New Deal era agitation, debtors' highest priorities have been (1) an "easy money" policy, (2) reliable and flexible sources of credit, and (3) some form of systemic relief—a moratorium, supplementary income, etc.—to help "honest debtors" over those "hard times" that make debt payments unmanageable because of events such as falling crop prices, economic depressions, illness, and lost jobs that are beyond the debtor's control. Modern democratic polities have often responded to demands for "easy money" and income support programs, and they have encouraged the stabilization of private markets through regulation and insurance schemes. To political and economic elites, the development of demand-enhancing, cushioning, and stabilizing measures has been perceived, at least up to a point, as more efficient as well as more politically popular than relying on a system based entirely on free market transactions, tempered and policed only by individually initiated lawsuits that punish individual delicts. Among the primary institutional vehicles for the favored type of systemic problem-solving are (1) governmental regulation and subsidization, designed to stabilize potentially problem-causing economic processes, and (2) loss spreading or absorption via large, diversified economic institutions and insurance systems.

The rise of effective regulatory and insurance mechanisms to deal with certain problems, or the domination of certain markets by large, diversified business units, can reduce the incidence or growth of private-law litigation by eliminating incentives to sue and by reducing the incidence of conflict. For example, the glut of litigation arising from motor vehicle accidents might be dampened both by the creation of comprehensive mandatory "no fault" self-insurance schemes and by governmentally enforced safety standards for highway design, trucking company practices, and the design of motor vehicles. The development of safer vehicles is also facilitated by the growth of large manufacturers with modern research and quality control capacities.

Similarly, the growth of large, diversified financial institutions and of private and governmental insurance against financial hardship may provide the most powerful explanation for the relative diminution, in recent decades, of intense debtor-creditor conflict in the courts. In relation to the factors discussed earlier, such systemic changes create a rich array of possibilities for recouping losses, and thereby: (1) reduce the incentives that creditors have to treat delinquencies as defaults that warrant immediate court action (2) make litigation and appeal for both debtors and creditors a relatively costly way of recouping or avoiding losses, and (3) encourage one aspect of legal rationalization, i.e., more rapid compliance by lending institutions with debtor protection legislation. To understand the impact of these systemic changes, however, we must first look back at the credit market as it was a century ago.

Sources of Instability

Reading the debt collection cases of late nineteenth century state supreme courts creates an overwhelming impression of a far less stable credit system than that which exists today. Many cases involved claims against failed banks or arose in the train of bank failures. In the 1890s, there were an average of more than 100 bank failures per year, out of a nationwide total of about 4000 state-chartered banks (There were also some 3500 federally chartered banks, which were more tightly regulated.) This suggests that there was a significant chance that the bank one trusted with one's money or borrowed from would shut down with little warning. It was even more likely that one's bank would close its doors for a time or suddenly call in or refuse to extend loans, because of the currency shortages that occurred almost every harvest season and periodically resulted in terrifying financial panics.

Late nineteenth-century state supreme court cases also suggest that lending then was far riskier and the security for loans far flimsier than is the case in today's credit markets. Competition for new sources of potential profit in a rapidly changing economy, . . . drove retailers, wholesalers, bankers, brokers, landlords or builders to extend credit unwisely. Reliable credit information about would-be borrowers was notably lacking. Many state supreme court cases grew out of situations in which con men (or desperate businessmen) mortgaged the same property to two creditors, or fraudulently acquired goods on credit and then skipped town. Most creditors whose cases reached state supreme courts in the late nineteenth and early twentieth centuries were not large companies or banks, but were individuals—such as small businessman who had extended credit on a sale of merchandise or a farmer who had bought extra land at an execution sale only to encounter the competing claim of an unknown lienholder. Often creditors' only security was that debtors had supplied individual sureties—friends or relatives—to back up their promises to pay. Viewed through the lens of [State Supreme Court] cases, credit transactions gave rise to an inordinate amount of litigation over how to distribute obligations among sureties or between sureties and the debtor or creditors.

If problems of insufficient information, inadequate security arrangements, and unstable financial institutions and markets were at the root of creditor-debtor (and inter-creditor) conflicts in the late nineteenth century, the most profound differences between the credit world of that era and the post-World War II period lie neither in changes in the law of creditors' rights nor in the changed incidence of delinquency or default. The crucial changes involve the various ways that today's creditors can insure against debtor delinquency and the greater access debtors now have to sources of emergency funds that can ensure, without recourse to litigation, that payment eventually will be made or that losses will be cushioned and spread. Some of these systemic developments are worth spelling out.

The Stabilization of Banking

In the 1890s, there were over 1300 bank failures in the United States; in the 1920s there were 2900. In 1930–1933, there were 9100 failures, a crisis exacerbated by the Federal Reserve Board's failure to distribute reserves and expand the money supply during 1930. In marked contrast, during the 1947–1960 period there were only 66 bank failures in the nation, and only 62 from 1961 through 1970. The few failures that occurred each year in recent decades were concentrated in banks with less than $100 million in deposits, and nearly three-fourths were among banks with less than $1 million in deposits. When large banks have failed, the Federal Deposit Insurance Corporation, established in 1933, has usually arranged for a merger; in cases of liquidation, depositors have been paid off immediately.

This stability has been encouraged by a number of factors including: (1) the establishment and comprehensive coverage of federal deposit insurance, which has helped forestall runs on banks, the sudden calling in of loans, and domino-type financial panics; (2) intensified federal regulation of bank reserves and lending practices, along with regulations that (until recently) limited inter-bank competition and prevented banks from engaging in risky nonbanking enterprises; (3) a Federal Reserve Board that has effectively made reserves available to member banks during general "credit crunches" or when particular institutions were suffering from illiquidity; and (4) a great reduction in the number and an increase in the average size of banks, with corresponding increases in the diversification of loan portfolios and sources of income and in the rationalization of banking practices.

Insurance for Individual Debtors

The consumer movement of the late 1960s and 1970s focused on providing new legal rights for individual buyers or debtors faced with unjust treatment or deception. But these victories have far less significance for debtor-creditor relations than the establishment of income security and welfare state protections during the New Deal and during the "Great Society" programs of the mid-1960s. A very large proportion of debtor delinquencies stems from serious illnesses or injuries, layoffs from work, and other sudden decreases in income or increases in expenses. In earlier eras, such events destroyed a debtor's capacity to keep up payments on loans. During the post-World War II period, however, unemployment insurance, disability insurance, more adequate workers' compensation payments, employer-provided health insurance, Medicare, Social Security, and private pension plans have all become widely available. For debtors, these programs guarantee some continuation of income in hard times and the possibility of maintaining some level of payments to creditors. For creditors, these income-support measures are a reason to prefer reduced payments or refinancing, backed by the debtor's continuing income stream, to a one-time attempt to attach the debtors assets.

In addition, virtually every homeowner, small business, and motor vehicle owner now carries liability insurance, which has transformed the collection of liability judgments, often a source of further dispute and litigation in times past, into the routine drafting and mailing of a check by the corporate treasurer of the judgment-debtor's insurance company.

Perhaps the most significant form of debtor insurance in the 1945–1975 period has been a relatively stable economy and an improving set of job opportunities. This is in part attributable to macro-economic policies—Keynesian fiscal policy and more enlightened monetary policy—that can be viewed as aspects of systemic stabilization, and in part attributable to the social insurance schemes mentioned above that limit the negative ripple effects of business failures and plant closings. In the 1940–1975 period, economic downturns were both shorter and shallower, on the average, than those in pre-World War II decades. The index of real average weekly earnings of production workers in manufacturing, using 1967 as 100, went from 66 in 1946 to 123 in 1977. Disposable income per capita, controlling for inflation, increased from $2200 to $4500 over that same period. As we have seen, rising income and job security have not prevented an increase in loan delinquencies. But delinquent debtors are likely to have better prospects for regaining solvency and more relatives with savings to bail them out, than did their counterparts in earlier decades. This may make creditors less inclined to sue defaulters immediately.

Insurance for Creditors

For creditors, a universe of debtors with more stable income has made a radical improvement in security. More and more, a creditor's real security lies not in pledges of individual sureties and cosigners, but in the debtor's job and job skills, which are more likely than in previous decades to generate a steady, and increasing, stream of income which, if default ensues, can be tapped via the garnishment process. Lending to a nation of civil servants, salaried managers, and unionized blue collar workers who work for substantial corporations is less risky than lending to a nation of farmers (before crop support payments), small proprietors, and workers in small firms. This enhanced security has been reflected in creditors' willingness to require smaller down-payments for consumer loans, and to extend average repayment periods from less than twelve months to more than two and a half years. The smaller monthly payments, in turn, mean that delinquencies can more easily be recouped, presumably reducing the incentive for creditors to rush to court.

Another important source of insurance for lending institutions are the loan guarantees provided by government units. Since the end of World War II, for example, the Federal Housing Authority and the Veterans' Administration have guaranteed millions of home mortgages. Although payments are not available to mortgagees until they foreclose and attempt to collect from their mortgagors, these guarantees should reduce the incentives for contested litigation and appeals. Why fight if the government will pick up the tab? The same would seem to be true of federal guarantees to banks that extend student loans for higher education.

Creditors have also incorporated insurance programs into lending agreements. For example, some lenders now offer purchasers of homes and consumer durables "credit life insurance," which guarantees payment of the unpaid balance of the loan to the creditor in the event of the debtor's demise, and "credit disability insurance" has also become common. Home mortgage lenders are also protected by fire insurance, which the borrower is obliged to provide and pay for in monthly installments. Thus, many adverse events, instead of creating litigation provoking zero-sum conflicts between debtors (or their estates) and their various creditors as to who will bear an entire loss, now result in charges to insurance companies or government welfare funds, which are in turn spread over millions of policy-holders or taxpayers.

Insurance for Business Debtors

Institutional arrangements designed to help precarious businesses maintain their debt payments are not as comprehensive as protections for individuals, but they are surely more significant than in the decades before the New Deal. Most striking is the rich array of federal income maintenance programs for farmers, including below-market rate loans, acreage restriction payments, crop insurance, and price guarantees through crop support payments or governmentally approved marketing agreements. These stabilization measures, together with the drastic decline in the number of smaller, economically less stable farms since the 1930s, have undoubtedly produced a huge reduction in the annual number of farm failures, a major source of debt repayment problems and litigation in the late nineteenth and early twentieth centuries.

Other specific kinds of business borrowers and their creditors benefit from loan guarantees offered by the federal Overseas Investors' Protection Corporation and the Security Investors' Protection Corporation, both loosely modeled on the FDIC. The Small Business Administration has guaranteed billions of dollars of low-interest private loans to small companies, a riskier-than-average set of debtors. When businesses are threatened with income losses or heavy expenses as a result of floods and earthquakes, the government refinances existing debts by offering below-market rate interest loans to firms in the "disaster area." Special federal loan guarantees have been given to creditors who extended existing loans to huge entities, such as Chrysler Corporation and New York City, that were on the verge of default and threatened to pull creditors down with them.

The result of these and similar programs is that, by some estimates, the federal government issues, guarantees, or stands as lender of last resort with respect to well over half of the total financial assets of the public. In addition, state governments stand as guarantors for many of the debt obligations of municipalities, housing authorities, irrigation districts, and the like, while federal and state grants enable financially hard-pressed public agencies to acquire money for special projects without having to commit themselves to repayment. These guarantees and direct grants are significant because repayment failures by local public bodies were an important source of litigation in the 1930s and in earlier depression periods.

Another indicator of systemic stabilization is the expectation that governments will take action to provide relief for debtors during hard times. The U.S. Constitution's "contract clause," promulgated in reaction to the "stay laws" and other state debtor relief laws of the 1780s, was used by the courts throughout the nineteenth century to block such measures. However, in 1934, in *Home Building and Loan v. Blaisdell*, the Supreme Court virtually removed the contract clause from the Constitution, upholding a Depression-inspired Minnesota law declaring a moratorium on mortgage foreclosure. Since then, there seems to be a widespread political expectation that governments will protect debtors and bail out their creditors in times of distress. During World War II, the federal Soldiers' and Sailors' Civil Relief Act granted servicemen a moratorium on foreclosures and debt actions, which may help explain the sharp drop in litigation in the 1940s. During the recent recession, Congress voted to appropriate several hundred millions of dollars to the Farmers Home Administration in order to provide farm mortgage relief, and $760 million to be used to maintain mortgage payments for unemployed homeowners (FHA and VA guaranteed loans had already obligated the lending institution to postpone foreclosure when the homeowner is unemployed).

Diversification in Credit Markets

Since 1950, a smaller proportion of loans has flowed directly between individuals, or between businesses and individuals. By 1970, loans to households and businesses were extended mostly by "financial intermediaries" to which households and businesses commit their funds—commercial banks, savings and loan associations, insurance companies, consumer finance companies, pension trusts, and governmental credit-granting agencies. Economists point out that financial intermediation increases the efficiency of the credit system because it makes for more professional and informed credit decisions and the diversification of risks. I discovered no indicators of how the growth of financial intermediation affects propensities to litigate over delinquent debts, but it is reasonable to suppose that the big bank or insurance company faced with mortgagors behind on payments can afford to be more lenient than a small landlord owed three months' rent by a tenant. Large lending institutions set aside reserves for bad debts and are prepared to live with delinquencies in amounts that don't threaten to exceed the planned reserves. Indeed, they write off bad debts *before* selling such accounts to collection agencies, which means that any that turn out to be recoverable are just "gravy." Unrecovered losses are treated as additional costs that can be reflected, at least in part, in next year's finance charges and spread over the pool of new borrowers. Losses can also be deducted from federal and state corporate tax obligations, which means not only that they are shared with millions of taxpayers but also that the "real" loss is smaller and more likely to exceed litigation costs. In economic theory, of course, a large lender operates under competitive pressure to limit losses and, like the small landlord or businessman, would litigate if necessary to collect any debt whenever the prospects for recovery exceed litigation costs. But because they have institutionalized mechanisms for routinely accounting for losses and attempting to recoup them, large lenders are, I suspect, less inclined to spend additional money to sue the debtor who fails to pay a judgment or to appeal the case that is lost in the lower courts. The government in its growing role as creditor seems even more inclined to absorb and spread losses rather than litigate to collect delinquent debts.

Diversification in financial markets goes beyond loss-spreading within the loan portfolios of large lenders. Borrowers have seen a remarkable diversification of sources of credit. The licensing of small loan companies to sell and the regulation of maximum interest rates have helped transform a turn-of-the-century industry of small and unscrupulous "loan sharks" into a more stable, lawful industry of consumer finance companies, many of which operate on a scale sufficient to spread their risks over thousands of borrowers and attract stable financing from banks and other lenders. The growth of nonbank lenders, such as pension funds, government agencies, and investment trusts, has also helped provide a more competitive and richer credit environment, thus multiplying opportunities for troubled debtors to forestall litigation by obtaining refinancing agreements, second mortgages on their homes, and additional credit. Under competitive pressure, banks have moved toward more flexible lending arrangements, including long-term loans to business firms and revolving credit.

Systemic stabilization has also been increased by the greater fluidity of credit brought about by the expansion of the proportion of loans that are "negotiable." Lenders hold transferable "commercial paper" and publicly traded corporate bonds instead of less marketable direct loans. In the 1960s, a secondary mortgage market made home mortgages, in effect, negotiable. Negotiability means greater liquidity; when lenders need funds, they can "sell" rather than call in loans. Liquidity is another form of insurance, in this instance for creditors, but one that would seem to reduce zero-sum conflicts with debtors.

Bankruptcy

I have noted that federal bankruptcy proceedings are a form of legal rationalization in that they provide an efficient forum for assembling and establishing priorities among competing creditors' claims. However, another feature of bankruptcy, the debtor's discharge from most existing debts, is empirically more important. Stanley and Girth[129] discovered that 70 to 75 percent of bankruptcy cases in the years 1965–68 were "no asset" cases in which creditors recovered nothing, and 10 to 15 percent were "nominal asset cases" in which creditors got little. In the remaining "asset cases," creditors asserted claims totaling $431 million but recovered only $70 million, or 16 cents on the dollar. The growing ratio of individual to business bankruptcy cases in the 1970s probably increased the proportion of no asset–no recovery cases. Therefore, in the vast preponderance of modern bankruptcy matters, competing creditors have little to litigate about. The prominence of the discharge function suggests that bankruptcy as it in fact operates is primarily a form of socially provided "insurance" for debtors, an escape hatch for victims of financial disaster, rather than a means of more efficient adjudication. Indeed, most of the justifications for bankruptcy suggest that it is a product of pressures for "systemic stabilization." Most legal commentators seem to view bankruptcy in wholly amoral terms as a system for inducing risk-taking and hence an engine for economic growth. The discharge of "failed" debtors in bankruptcy . . . "may be viewed as a cost of the existing credit system—a cost that is widely diffused . . . borne partly by borrowers as a whole through higher interest rates, but principally by customers of business through

---

129. [The reference is to David T. Stanley and Marjorie Girth, *Bankruptcy: Problem, Process, Reform* (Washington: Brookings Institute, 1971).]

higher prices." While voluntary bankruptcy at one time was morally suspect, the primary "moral" concerns of the 1970 Commission on the Bankruptcy Laws seemed to be only that individual debtors should be equally well-informed about the availability of discharge; that discharge should be made cheaper, less legalistic and lawyer-dominated, and more like a routine administrative proceeding and that debtors should be protected against creditors' attempts to secure the reaffirmation of debts discharged in bankruptcy in return for new extensions for credit.

This "non-stigmatizing" attitude toward bankruptcy, abetted by court rulings forbidding restrictions on lawyer advertising, has been reflected in steeply increasing individual bankruptcy filings—25,040 in 1950, 191,724 in 1967, and an estimated 450,000 in 1982, the equivalent of the population of a large city. Studies indicate that most non-business bankruptcy filings are preceded by a threat of legal action against the debtor (presumably in state court), but very few bankruptcy cases are preceded by an actual state court judgment in favor of creditors. This suggests that legally sophisticated debtors, those whom one might expect to raise possible legal defenses in state trial or appellate courts, are now more inclined to take the "escape hatch" route of bankruptcy. Compared to protracted litigation, the routinized "loss-spreading" bankruptcy mechanism becomes increasingly appealing.

V. CONCLUSION

In sum, despite the marked growth over the last thirty-five years in lending and in the volume of delinquent debts, the number of state supreme court debt cases has declined sharply, and there has been an apparent decrease in contested debt cases in trial courts of general jurisdiction. The decline in contested debt cases cannot be explained by a simple causal model that links the incidence of court cases in a policy area to the rate of problem-causing events. An intuitively obvious intervening factor is the variable cost of litigation, defined to include both direct costs (such as attorneys' fees) and opportunity costs (such as time lost from productive work, delays in attempting to collect judgments, etc.). Direct evidence is lacking, but it is reasonable to suppose that in the post-World War II era a smaller proportion of delinquencies led to collection cases and a smaller proportion of cases were contested because litigation costs rose, at least in relation to the cost of alternative courses of action—such as arbitration, bankruptcy, additional extensions of time, refinancing, "writing off" bad debts, or contesting liability. Although direct evidence is not available, it appears that three factors have contributed to the increased attractiveness of nonlitigation alternatives. One such factor has been legal rationalization, especially the development by lenders of legally "airtight" contractual provisions and security arrangements specifically designed to forestall litigation, and their increasing use of lawyers and other specialists in the routine settlement of debt cases. These measures presumably reduce the proportion of debt disputes involving viable defenses and make settlement correspondingly more attractive. The second factor is an increase in the political activity of debtors and their allies. Political action—primarily on behalf of homeowners, farmers, and small businesses in the 1930s and on behalf of consumers in the 1960s—has shifted the locus of demands for reformed debtor-creditor laws away from courts and toward legislatures and regulatory agencies, stimulated the enactment of a multitude of new defenses for consumer-debtors, and enhanced opportunities to learn about and assert these rights. Judging from the fact that the number of contested debt cases has not increased in recent decades, the primary effect of the expansion of debtors' rights and remedies has been to increase the cost of litigation for creditors in cases in which debtors show some inclination toward legal resistance.

The third factor forestalling debt collection litigation, and undoubtedly the most significant one, has been a trend toward systemic stabilization—the development of methods of loss spreading, diversification, insurance, and economic stabilization that prevent financial panics, blunt the edges of individual disputes, and encourage consensual refinancing or absorption of losses rather than protracted litigation. In the 1880s (and even in the 1920s, in the South) the farmer who could not pay off his crop mortgage was threatened simultaneously with the loss of his home and livelihood. The shopkeeper or small manufacturer who could not pay his debts faced similar ruin, as did many a creditor whose debtor could not pay. For them, it made sense to fight for survival in the courts if any plausible legal argument could be made. But this debtor class of small farmers, shopkeepers, and artisans has been replaced by a debtor class composed of incorporated businesses, whose owners and managers usually can find other jobs if their firms face insolvency, and of unionized workers and salaried government employees whose debts are backed by relatively reliable sources of income and various forms of social insurance. For both groups of debtors, bankruptcy has become an increasingly less stigmatizing and more frequently used way of escaping debt and obtaining a fresh start. In parallel fashion, from a creditor class of small banks, merchants and individual speculators, we have evolved a creditor class of large, diversified, insured lending institutions, department stores, and hospitals. Unpaid loans become tax write-offs and increased costs to be reflected in next month's prices or interest rates. The government and insurance companies back up mortgages. New lenders stand ready to refinance the failing and to relend money to the formerly bankrupt.

As a result of such systemic changes, in comparison to times past there are now fewer loans, proportionately and, perhaps absolutely, that debtors and creditors find worth "taking to the supreme court," or even worth contesting in the trial court. If debtors and creditors are better able as a class to absorb losses, or to pass them off on others, the opportunity costs of struggling toward legal victory in court have gone up and incentives to litigate have gone down. More merchants simply give in to the dissatisfied customer. Banks more often help arrange refinancing for a financially troubled corporation or entrepreneur rather than losing all by pushing the debtor into bankruptcy.

The rate of legal rationalization and the impact of political conflict have also been affected by systemic stabilization. Diversified and regulated credit markets have encouraged the growing dominance of large, bureaucratic credit institutions that are quick to learn about new legal rulings and quick to translate them into routine practices. Banks, finance companies, and department store chains treat new debtors' rights as another set of contingencies to be insured against, absorbed, and passed on as higher costs. Corporate lawyers devise new forms incorporating the prescribed warnings. Deprived of "holder in due course" defenses, banks and finance companies insert provisions for reimbursement in their contracts with merchants, or threaten not to deal with merchants whose customers often express dissatisfaction. An attorney for a major California bank told me that because the appellate courts are perceived as pro-consumer, adverse trial court decisions will not be appealed and novel debtors' rights claims will be settled. Complying with regulatory restrictions, a debt collection agency official told me, drives up collection costs, which renders it less feasible to pursue the substantial number of "skips," debtors who have left their home and the job they held at the time of the loan and hence are expensive to locate. The costs of compliance with regulations, and any additional losses in repayment that result, end up as costs of doing business, spread over the 95 percent of borrowers who repay their loans without incident.

Of course, as the last phrase suggests, there are costs, both economic and moral, associated with a system based on loss absorption and spreading, and hence there may be both political and economic limits on the toleration of unpunished delinquency. But even if systemic stabilization would in the long run counterpose some economic efficiency restraints against the political quest for security and harmony (and this is far from certain), it may not do so in the short run. The factors that drive systemic stabilization or disrupt it are undoubtedly both complex and poorly understood. Yet a full understanding of what has happened and is likely to occur with respect to the legal collection of debts requires further attention to the actions that constitute systemic stabilization and attention to the political and cultural forces that create and oppose it.

For example, the institutional stabilization of creditors and collective loss-spreading is not a monolithic, unidirectional trend. The most significant countertrend, perhaps, is the destabilization of households as reliable economic units through family disruption, as reflected in increased rates of divorce, unmarried parenthood, and female-headed homes. Governmental welfare programs represent a partial "collective," social-insurance approach to the resultant growth of financially hard-pressed households. But the splitting and diminution of household income stemming from family disintegration also increase the probability of loan defaults, and have given rise to what has probably been the most rapidly increasing form of debt-collection litigation in the last decade—suits both by abandoned mothers and by governmental units to recover unpaid child-support obligations.

Moreover, it is not clear that systemic stabilization, if it is viewed as a process that substitutes collective insurance and loss-spreading for particularistic legal conflict, applies as fully to other substantive areas of litigation or has the same impact. Whether the inefficiencies of personal injury litigation will be displaced by generous "no fault" systems of private or governmental insurance is, for example, far from clear. The private plaintiffs' bar and the cupidity engendered by occasional massive jury awards are not the only obstacles. Another is the strength of the cultural impulse to condemn, punish, and deter individuals and organizations whose carelessness causes human injury, illness, and death. Perhaps the strength of the movement toward insurance and loss spreading in the debt-collection field has gone as far as it has only because we are culturally willing to see the debtor who cannot pay as an unfortunate victim of circumstances rather than as a reprehensibly greedy or foolish individual. Perhaps we simply care more about economic expansion, upward mobility, and security, all fueled by credit and bolstered by insurance, than we care about the moral obligation to keep one's promise. It remains to be seen whether movement toward systemic stabilization will develop as fully and will affect other areas of litigation as deeply as it seems to have affected debtor-creditor relations.

Nevertheless, the importance of systemic stabilization in shaping the role of the courts with respect to debt litigation undoubtedly has broader significance for the study of law and society. Social scientists and legal scholars have focused primarily on the mobilization and operation of governmental institutions established specifically for the adjudication or settlement of particular legal disputes, on the patterns of individual-case decisions or outcomes produced by those legal institutions, and on the origins of and justifications for legal rules intended to guide official decisions. While these topics are surely important, study after study tells us that the use of formal decision-making and enforcement processes tends to be extraordinary rather than ordinary. The extent and quality of the justice people experience depends equally, if not primarily, on the operation of nonlegal social and economic institutions that prevent, suppress, or settle most problems and on the broader social, economic, and political factors that affect the incidence and seriousness of harmful acts, accidents, deprivations, and disputes. What matters most is the frequency and intensity of problems worth fighting about. As in the case of debt collection, the incidence and severity of problems and the modes in which people deal with them will be affected by systemic political measures that encourage economic growth, stabilize markets (without unduly impairing efficiency and diversification), cushion and spread losses, and otherwise restructure those social conditions that are underlying causes of disputes. Understanding the facets of systemic stabilization, the forces that encourage and impede it, and its effects, negative as well as positive, as those relate to various areas of the law is an important agenda for students of legal systems. □

NOTES AND QUESTIONS

1. Studies of the work of courts also show a decline in the number of disputes over title to real estate. In the 19th century, courts decided thousands of cases in which two, or more, parties argued over who owned what piece of land. These lawsuits have become more and more uncommon. Why do you think this is? Are the reasons the same as the reasons Kagan gives for the decline in debt collection litigation?

2. How would you categorize the reasons Kagan gives for the decline in debt litigation? Which of them are economic, which of them are social, which of them have to do with the structure and habits of legal institutions?

3. Modern bankruptcy seems to favor the debtor far more than the law of bankruptcy as it was in earlier times. Kagan's article discusses the impact of bankruptcy law on the law of debt collection. Bankruptcy is more than an economic matter—social norms about debts and obligations affect how people behave toward creditors. One hears stories about men and women who went bankrupt in the 1930s, during the Great Depression, and who spent much of the rest of their lives trying to pay their debts, even though these debts had been wiped off the books by the bankruptcy court. It is said that this feeling of obligation toward creditors is rare in modern American legal culture. For studies of wage-earner bankruptcy, see Herbert Jacob, *Debtors in Court: The Consumption of Government Services* (Chicago: Rand, McNally, 1969); Philip Shuchman, "New Jersey Debtors 1982–83: An Empirical Study," 15 *Seton Hall Law Review* 541 (1985). Teresa Sullivan, Elizabeth Warren, and Jay Westbrook, *As We Forgive Our Debtors—Bankruptcy and Consumer Credit in American* (New York: Oxford University Press, 1989) is a much discussed larger empirical study of individual bankruptcy. For consideration of this work, see, e.g., Marjorie L. Girth, "The Role of Empirical Data in Developing Bankruptcy Legislation for Individuals," 65 *Indiana Law Journal* 17 (1989); Lisa J. McIntyre, "A Sociological Perspective on Bankruptcy," 65 *Indiana Law Journal* 123 (1989); William C. Whitford, "Has the Time Come to Repeal Chapter 13?" 65 *Indiana Law Journal* 85 (1989).

Large corporations turned to bankruptcy to cope with drastic economic change in the 1980s. For an empirical study, see Lynn M. Lopucki and William C. Whitford, "Venue Choice and Forum Shopping in the Bankruptcy Reorganization of Large, Publicly Held Companies," 1991 *Wisconsin Law Review* 11.

4. In "Why the 'Haves' Come Out Ahead: Speculations on the Limits of Legal Change," 9 *Law & Society Review* 95 (1974), Marc Galanter distinguishes between "repeat players" and "one-shotters" in litigation. "Repeat players" can adapt their behavior to cope with the threat of litigation. They can

structure transactions so that they are likely to win any lawsuit that they bring or that is brought against them. They can take steps to make litigation unnecessary or less likely. To complete the picture which Kagan has painted, we might want to study the practices of firms such as Sears which sells on credit to consumers or, say, the Boeing Corporation which sells commercial jet aircraft to major airlines. Both are repeat players and both undoubtedly have taken steps to ward off and control litigation. What difference would you expect between the strategies of Sears and Boeing?

27. Trials and Tribulations: Crises, Litigation and Legal Change

John Stookey

24 *Law & Society Review* 497 (1990)

☐ The first half of the twentieth century was a time of unprecedented social and economic crisis. Within this brief period, two world wars and the Great Depression scarred the American social landscape, fundamentally and forever changing American politics and law. The Great Depression was the impetus for a set of legal accords known as the New Deal. The wars paved the way for increased government control and regulation of the private economy.

These crises provide an ideal perspective from which to compare two competing theories of trial court litigation in the American legal/political system. One of these theories emphasizes the role of litigation in the formation of social consensus, while the other focuses upon litigation as a means of economic and political competition and domination.

I. CONSENSUS VERSUS CONFLICT THEORIES OF LITIGATION

A. The Role of Litigation in Society

At the most simplistic level, trial court litigation is a means of dispute resolution. Thus, litigation rates presumably measure two characteristics of society—the frequency of particular types of disputes and the willingness and ability of individuals to convert those disputes into litigation. However, there are a variety of theoretical traditions from which these relationships between society and litigation may be examined. A "consensus"-oriented theoretical tradition emphasizes that litigation functions to achieve social integration when traditional forms of nonstate control weaken. Nonstate control includes customs, folkways, and regularized patterns of informal dispute resolution. A weakening of nonstate control is marked by more disputes and less reliance on informal and customary forms of dispute resolution (Kidder, 1983: 88).[130] An alternative theoretical tradition, which can be encompassed under the rubric of "conflict theory" argues that litigation does not merely provide an alternative to private social control, it also traces major changes in a society's political and economic balance of power (Turk, 1976).[131] From this perspective, changes in who uses the courts and who wins in that use serve as both a measure of power in society and a stimulus for political mobilization that may change the balance of power.

The differences between consensus theory and conflict theory stem from their different assumptions about the role of law. To the consensus theorist, law emerges in a passive evolutionary way to fill the vacuum created by the demise or weakening of informal private or customary means of social integration. The role of law is to maintain stability and harmony. Conversely, from a conflict perspective, law is a tool of group conflict and domination. It is not an invisible hand that ensures stability but is a device used by societal groups, most often economic or political elites, to advance their version of social control.

Conceptualizing court use as an aspect of political conflict prompts questions concerning the patterns of court use and who benefits or is disadvantaged by those patterns. A convenient way to address these questions is by characterizing the parties to disputes in terms of their status as individuals, on the one hand, or as organizations or businesses, on the other. Four types of disputes result from these characterizations. Type I cases occur between individuals and involve disputes such as divorces or disputes between neighbors concerning property boundaries. Type II cases involve a grieving business or organization (B/O) against an individual (I), as in debt collection or landlord/tenant disputes. Type III cases find an I initiating a complaint against a B/O. Many labor/management cases are of this type. Finally, Type IV cases pit B/O's against each other and may be as simple as a creditor/debtor dispute or as complicated as restraint of trade or merger disputes.

Conflict theory particularly focuses on disputes between individuals and businesses/organizations (Types II and III). Such "interstatus" disputes are important from the conflict perspective because they most clearly show how litigation is not merely a neutral form of dispute resolution, but a reflection of dominance patterns in society.

Conflict theory hypothesizes that businesses/organizations have a considerable advantage in suits with individuals. This hypothesis is based upon two underlying assumptions about the U.S. legal system. First, the use of the legal system requires resources, which are unevenly

130. [The reference is to Robert Kidder, *Connecting Law and Society* (Englewood Cliffs, N.J.: Prentice-Hall, 1983).]

131. [The reference is to Austin T. Turk, "Law as a Weapon in Social Conflict," 23 *Social Problems* 276 (1976).]

distributed in U.S. society. As a rule, B/O's have greater resources for litigation than typical individuals (Galanter, 1974b).[132] Second, the law that the courts apply is a result of the political process, which is also disproportionately influenced by those with resources and political skills.

In summary, the differences between consensus and conflict theories of litigation are best seen by identifying the issues to which each directs our attention. Consensus theory is particularly concerned with the long-term pattern of litigation as an indicator of social harmony. On the other hand, conflict theory directs our attention to who uses the courts and with what success. Consensus theory tells us that litigation measures the state's role in social integration. Conflict theory tells us that litigation measures the state role's in protecting or limiting economic and political domination.

B. Litigation and Political Change

Both consensus and conflict theories see litigation as an integral part of the policy process. While tracing litigation patterns is significant in and of itself, it is also significant for what it tells us about policy change. Whereas "the law" is not usually changed by trial court decisions, the pattern of trial court use and the success of such use may reflect and/or motivate policy change. From a consensus perspective, the litigation rate is an indicator of social instability. If the litigation rate increases, we might expect policy changes from the legislature or appellate courts to reestablish social integration. When such policy changes are made, the litigation rate is an indicator of the remedial action's success.

Conflict theory agrees that litigation both precipitates and measures policy change, but it views the linkages quite differently. The pressure for policy change is not merely motivated by a desire to restore social integration; it also reflects pressure from various groups to maintain or change policy in a way that is most beneficial to their interests. Therefore, an increase in litigation caused by social turmoil will not lead to a call for policy changes from all quarters. The litigants who are winning cases may not want a policy-induced return to "normality." In other words, while consensus theory posits social integration as the goal of policy, conflict theory believes that in some instances social disharmony and increased litigation may be advantageous to some sectors of society. Whether social disharmony and increased litigation lead to policy change depends upon the relative political power of those who wish to return to the status quo and those who do not.

From either a consensus or a conflict perspective, therefore, litiga-

---

132. [The reference is to Marc Galanter, "Afterword: Explaining Litigation," 9 *Law & Society Review* 347 (1974).]

tion (1) reveals the role of the state in dispute resolution; (2) is an impetus for policy change, and (3) shows the impact of policy change. However, as we have just seen, the characteristics of these linkages are different for each theory.

C. Linkages Between Crisis, Litigation, and Policy Change

Crises, such as war and depression, provide a unique opportunity to compare and contrast consensus and conflict theories of litigation. Both theories give center stage to destabilizing events. Consensus theory sees crises as times of increased litigation and pressure for policy to restore social harmony. Conflict theory sees them as periods of heightened group and class conflict, an ideal setting for understanding the court's role as an indicator of the political and economic balance of power.

Both theories agree generally on the relationships among crises, litigation, and policy change, as depicted in Figure 1. The model reveals four relationships. First, crises affect the rate and types of disputes in society. Second, the rate and types of disputes affect the litigation rate. Third, as the litigation rate and types change, there will be pressure for policy change. Fourth, policy changes will induce changes in the litigation rate. From the consensus perspective, crisis turmoil increases all types of disputes, raising the overall litigation rate.

The increased litigation is an indicator of social instability, which precipitates policy designed to restore social integration. The litigation rate also measures the effectiveness of such policy, with decreased litigation being an indicator of success. The conflict perspective accepts generally the significance of these four relationships but insists that we can only understand them by realizing that each is mediated by economic and political conflict. To help clarify this aspect of the conflict theory, I will consider each of the relationships individually.

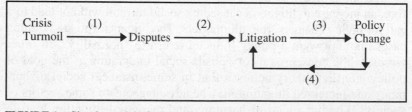

FIGURE 1 Simple model of crisis-related policy change

The Linkage Between Crises and Disputes. Both consensus and conflict theories predict a rise in disputes as a result of crises. However, consensus theories tend to emphasize the overall destabilizing effect of crises and thus their exacerbation of all disputes. Conflict theory, on the other hand, focuses on the particular effect of crises on interstatus disputants (Types II and III, i.e., B/O versus I and I versus B/O).

Consensus theories predict the rise of I versus I disputes, such as domestic relations conflicts, as well as the increase in interstatus disputes to demonstrate the overall destabilizing effect of crises. While not disagreeing with this point, conflict theory emphasizes the particularly large increase in crises-related interstatus disputes. A crisis will be a time of unusually high levels of such conflict. Rising levels of debt collection, foreclosures, shortages, and labor problems will inevitably increase interstatus disputes during crises. Conflict theorists believe that by focusing only on the aggregate level of disputes, consensus theorists miss the patterns of economic and political domination in crisis-related disputes.

The Linkage Between Disputes and Litigation. Following from its generally undifferentiated view of disputes, consensus theory is primarily concerned with measuring and explaining the aggregate increase in litigation that results from crisis-related increases in disputes. Conversely, the conflict theorist asks which individuals or groups are able and willing to convert their crisis-related disputes into litigation.

The answers predicted by each theory might well be the same if they had asked the same questions. However, the significant point is that they do not ask the same question. Unlike the consensus theorist, the conflict theorist would have us ask about the relative economic ability of various classes of disputants to use the courts. Similarly, conflict theory asks about the political origins of those advantages. In attempting to answer these questions, the conflict theorist looks to economic and political power as the bases of litigation success. While these patterns of domination are true at all times, the conflict theorist would predict that a crisis may even further enhance the ability of those with economic and political power to use the legal system successfully. Those with such power are disproportionately able to ride out a crisis and even further widen their advantage over individuals without such a reservoir of resources.

The Linkage Between Litigation and Policy Change. From a conflict perspective, the linkage between litigation and pressure for policy change is also shaped by economic and political group conflict. The goal of policy pressure is to achieve success, not social integration. Again this suggests that we focus our attention on interstatus disputes.

Consensus theorists see policy response as an almost automatic homeostatic device to remedy crises-caused social disruption and consequent increased litigation. Conflict theory directs us away from the automatic, toward the political. Who is advantaged by the current rise in litigation? Who is disadvantaged? What is the relative economic and political power of the disputants? Which litigants are likely to succeed in seeking policy relief from any hardship caused by increased litigation? Conflict theory suggests that those with economic and political power are likely to dominate the linkage between litigation and policy relief.

The Linkage Between Policy Change and Litigation. From a consensus perspective the impact of a particular policy change is evaluated by asking whether it has restored social harmony. Has it decreased the litigation rate? Conversely, from a conflict perspective policy impact is measured by assessing who was advantaged and who was disadvantaged by the change.

D. Some Tentative Propositions

Sole reliance on a consensus perspective limits the range of questions asked and hypotheses tested in research on litigation trends. Conflict theory may add to our understanding of litigation trends by raising different kinds of issues and by suggesting different hypotheses. However, it is not useful at this early stage in the development of a conflict theory of litigation to propose a critical test of the relative explanatory powers of consensus and conflict theories. Rather, the approach I take is to present several general propositions suggested by the foregoing discussion of conflict theory. If these propositions appear tenable in light of the data analysis that follows, further consideration of conflict theory to explain litigation would seem warranted.

Proposition 1: While all forms of litigation will increase during crises (as predicted by the social disruption assumptions of the consensus theories), crises will particularly increase interstatus litigation.

Proposition 2: Business and organization litigants may be expected to have more economic and political power than individual litigants and therefore will always be disproportionately successful in cases against individual litigants, but that advantage will become even greater during crises.

Proposition 3: The extent to which crisis litigation causes or reflects policy changes will depend upon the political and economic power of the proponents of those changes.

II. DATA COLLECTION AND CODING

In order to evaluate these propositions, I use docket data and other archival sources from the state of Arizona between 1912 (statehood) and 1951. While other forms of crises could be used, I focus upon major depressions and wars. In addition to the Great Depression of the 1930s, Arizona, like many midwestern and western states, experienced a severe post-World War I depression in 1921 and 1922. Thus, the study period encompasses alternating periods of good times (1912–20), depression (1921–22), good times (1923–29), depression (1929–37), good times (1938–51). The time frame also encompasses the two world wars and three periods of peace.

The data base consists of superior court cases[133] filed during the period 1912–51. A sampling of counties and of cases in those counties yielded a representative sample of 28,000. While the data certainly do not provide a perfect measure of the relative economic and political power of disputants, I coded the data in terms of the individual or business/organization character of the disputants, the assumption being that businesses/organizations will be both economically and politically superior to individuals. Therefore, for each year the rate of cases per 10,000 population was calculated for I versus I, I versus B/O, B/O versus I and B/O versus B/O.

Wars and depressions are characterized by significantly different economic and political manifestations. For example, while depression is a period of economic slowing and unemployment, war is a period of rapid mobilization, shortages, and overemployment. Therefore, it seems appropriate to evaluate each of the propositions with regard to these two types of crises separately.

Within the confines of these admittedly limited operational measures, proposition 1 suggests that crises will lead to disproportionate increases in interstatus litigation, particularly that initiated by B/O's against individuals. Proposition 2 in turn suggests that there will be a heightened degree of B/O victory during crisis periods. Finally, proposition 3 says that any linkage between these crisis-related litigation patterns and policy change will be weighted in favor of the interests of B/O's.

In order to evaluate proposition 1, I use an interrupted time series design, with the various litigation rates as dependent variables and war and depressions coded as interventions. Proposition 2 is evaluated by calculating the relative success of various types of litigants within each of the four litigant pairs (I versus I, I versus B/O, B/O versus I, and B/O versus B/O). Finally, proposition 3 is evaluated through an historical narrative of litigation-related policy changes during the crisis periods.[134]

133. The Superior Court of Arizona is the state's general jurisdiction trial court. Its jurisdiction extends to all cases in law and equity not specifically vested by the constitution in other courts, the latter consisting of those few cases reserved by the constitution for the supreme court and those civil cases under $500 reserved for the justice courts. Cases involving from $500 to $1,000 were under concurrent jurisdiction of both the justice and superior courts. The superior court also deals with all domestic relations cases but not probate matters. While the superior court does have criminal jurisdiction, such cases were not included in this analysis.

134. Data from the policy analysis came from Arizona Session Laws and from the state's leading newspaper. With two student coders I analyzed all volumes of the Arizona Session Laws. We sought to identify all pieces of legislation that concerned matters which either might influence litigation or reflected litigation. Obviously a subjective element was involved in this selection but resources precluded an analysis of all statutes and a purposive approach seems more appropriate for this study than some type of ran-

III. DATA ANALYSIS

A. Depressions

Proposition 1: Crises and Litigation. Figures 2–5 plot the rates of the four pairings of litigant types. Table 1 presents the time series analysis of the effects of the various crisis interventions of the four rates.

All four forms of litigation increased significantly during the 1921–22 depression. The actual impact of the depression was confounded somewhat, however, by its proximity to World War I. For example, the increase in I versus I cases resulted largely from increased divorce cases accompanying the end of the war. The remaining increase relates to the economic character of I versus I cases during the early years of Arizona history. In the teens and twenties most loans to individuals in Arizona were provided by other individuals rather than by banks (businesses or organizations). Therefore, with the onset of this early depression there were a considerable number of debt-collection cases involving I versus I. This was less so by the time of the Great Depression, when much of the loan activity had been taken over by banks and other commercial organizations, resulting in an increase in B/O versus I cases rather than I versus I.

This interpretation is supported by the data from the Great Depression. In that instance, I versus I litigation, including divorces, rather steeply decreases for the first few years of the depression, while the three other litigation types increase even more steeply. As the Great Depression continues, the slopes of the I versus B/O, B/O versus I, and B/O versus B/O litigation lines make a negative shift, reflecting the slowing of the economy and decreased debt-collection and labor-management litigation. On the other hand, the continuing social strain of the depression is manifested by a statistically significant increase in the slope of the line reflecting I versus I litigation.

The effect of depression is most pronounced with regard to B/O versus I cases. Between 1919 and 1921 the rate of such cases rose from 26.82 per 10,000 to over 67 per 10,000. Similarly, between 1929 and 1932 this same rate rose from 39.65 to 52.71. In terms of the mere number of people affected, these cases clearly experience the greatest increase.

Consensus theory has a role in explaining these patterns. All types of litigation do increase during depressions. In fact I versus I litigation shows the most lasting impact of depressions. However, these findings

---

dom sample. We carried out content coding of the Phoenix Gazette primarily for periods of crisis using random and purposive checks. Random checks were conducted for one day per month during depression and war years. Purposive checks were made for the entire week before and after an important piece of relevant legislation was passed such as the foreclosure moratorium of 1933.

also strongly support the underlying assumption of conflict theory. It would be a mistake simply to measure the aggregate impact of a depression on litigation. The relationship between a depression and litigation is a complex one that requires us to take into consideration the character of the disputes, and more importantly, the character of the parties.

An interesting aspect of that complexity is the rapid rise in interstatus litigation at the beginning of a depression and the equally rapid decline as the depression persists. This pattern suggests that both consensus and conflict theories of litigation must take into account that there comes a point in a depression when the social disruption is no longer converted into litigation. Conflict theory can be logically extended to include the proposition that an extended depression may lead to such great economic domination that litigation ceases to be a useful or necessary device for protecting the interests of the economically and politically powerful.

Proposition 2: Who Wins and Who Loses? We have already seen that individuals in cases initiated by B/O's experience the largest absolute increase in litigation during depressions. According to proposition 2 we should also expect B/O's to increase even further their normally high success rate in these cases.

Unfortunately, winners and losers are not as easily determined as one might first think. When either the defendant or plaintiff wins at the trial court level, the conclusion is simple. However, a large percentage of cases are terminated by dismissal with or without a settlement. The meaning of such dismissals is much more difficult to discern. Limiting discussion to the proportion of cases clearly won either by the defendant or plaintiff, I have determined the plaintiff and defendant pure victory rate (number of cases won by plaintiff or defendant divided by the total number of cases) for five-year intervals for each of the four major types of litigation (see Table 2).[135]

While the plaintiff has the advantage in all case types, the highest rate of success is achieved by the B/O plaintiff in actions against individuals. Similarly, the defendant in such cases has by far the lowest victory rate of any defendant type. The data in Table 2 show that while the rate of individual losses to B/O plaintiffs is always high, their loss rate increased even further during the Great Depression. Between 1932 and 1937, the B/O plaintiff won a full 63.1 percent of the cases it initiated against individual defendants. This is 17 percent higher than the victory rate for any other plaintiff type and 14 percent higher than the victory rate of B/O plaintiffs over individual defendants for any other time period.

---

135. Divorce cases were excluded from this analysis because the plaintiff is the victor in almost every such case. This fact, when combined with the large numbers of divorces, would totally mask the victory pattern for other I versus I cases.

TABLE 1 TIMES SERIES ANALYSIS OF THE RELATIONSHIP BETWEEN CRISES AND LITIGATION CHANGE

	Type of Case			
	I versus I	*I versus B/O*	*B/O versus I*	*B/O versus B/O*
Depression 1				
b	18.96	8.26	37.48	10.54
t	4.44	4.78	4.94	5.55
s	****	****	****	****
Great depression intercept				
b	−10.88	2.56	14.46	10.52
t	−2.38	2.01	2.71	5.99
s	***	**	***	****
Slope				
b	1.98	−.13	−2.80	−1.39
t	3.03	−.45	−3.44	−5.78
s	***		***	****
World War II intercept				
b	2.34	−4.05	−1.87	2.28
t	.31	−1.57	−.86	.67
s		*		
Slope				
b	11.54	−.12	.15	.33
t	4.40	−.19	.03	.28
s	****			
Post-World War II intercept				
b	−25.46	5.51	3.89	2.70
t	−3.39	2.03	.44	.90
s	****	**		
Slope				
b	−17.49	−.60	6.39	2.71
t	5.60	−.77	1.78	2.20
s	****		*	**
Trend				
b	0.87			
t	4.17	No significant trend present		
s	****			

NOTE: Types of Cases: I versus I = individual versus individual; I versus B/O = individual versus business/organization; B/O versus I = business/organization versus individual; B/O versus B/O = business/organization versus business/organization

* Significant at .10 level.

** Significant at .05 level.

*** Significant at .01 level.

**** Significant at .001 level.

TABLE 2   Plaintiff And Defendant Victory Rates By Type Of Case And Year (Divorce Cases Omitted)

	Type of Case							
	I versus I		I versus B/O		B/O versus I		B/O versus B/O	
Years	% Plaintiff won	% Defendant Won	% Plaintiff won	% Defendant won	% Plaintiff won	% Defendant won	% Plaintiff won	% Defendant won
1912–16	41.5	13.1	31.1	14.9	47.4	4.4	45.7	6.0
1917–21	31.0	7.8	25.7	14.3	39.8	3.9	31.3	6.6
1922–26	40.7	9.6	26.3	14.2	49.0	3.4	37.5	6.9
1927–31	35.4	14.0	32.7	6.4	46.4	1.8	42.2	7.3
1932–36	31.6	12.2	29.1	8.2	63.1	2.2	42.2	5.8
1937–41	29.1	7.5	26.8	12.3	47.4	2.6	39.4	7.9
1942–46	46.1	3.7	29.0	8.5	29.2	4.3	33.2	5.5
1947–51	27.3	7.0	24.5	12.6	39.5	1.5	31.7	5.0

Note: "% Plaintiff Won" and "% Defendant Won" do not sum to 100 percent because many cases were without resolution.

These data support the proposition that a depression is not merely a generalized destabilizing event. It works particular hardship upon individual disputants while strengthening the hand of business and organizational disputants. Charting and explaining these effects seem a necessary precondition of any successful theory of litigation and society.

Proposition 3: Policy Change and Losing Litigants. The preceding results suggest great motivation for political mobilization on the part of individuals during depressions. Not only are individuals taken to court much more often by B/O litigants during depressions, but the B/O victory rate increases substantially over and above an already impressive success record. However, conflict theory, as I have articulated it, predicts that such individuals would be unlikely to have the economic and political clout to push successfully for policy relief from B/O domination. Thus, we should expect little, if any successful pressure for such policy change.

My review of newspapers and *Session Laws* is consistent with that expectation. There was an almost total lack of political pressure and agitation for political change during the depressions. I found only one concerted and successful effort for policy change in response to the depression. Farmer organizing and mobilization in response to trial court eviction attempts received front-page headline attention in the *Phoenix Gazette* in February 1933: "Police Guard Statehouse at Mortgage Bill Hearing."

The mortgage bill provided that while foreclosure cases could be filed, they could not be terminated during a two-year moratorium. For the duration of the moratorium, the courts were to "manage" the properties for which foreclosure suits had been filed, balancing the rights and interests of the occupants as well as those of the financial institutions. The legislation rapidly passed both the House and Senate and was immediately signed into law by the governor. With the exception of several tax moratoriums, this was the only measure addressed to or passed for debt relief during the depression. There is no evidence of pressure for tenant relief or for relief from other types of debt.

Consensus theory explains the successful debt moratorium fight as a quintessential example of the homeostatic tendencies of the legal system. The farmers' success demonstrates the self-correcting nature of the system by showing the ability of disadvantaged groups to organize and to exert countervailing power against businesses and organizations.[136]

Conflict theory takes a different view. Creditor/debtor disputes dur-

---

136. That farmers were organized is indicated by the large number who attended the legislative session and by the groups represented at the hearings. The day of the vote on the legislation, the Senate gallery was filled to capacity with farmers and both the director of the American Farm Bureau Federation and the president of the American Farm Bureau were present (*Phoenix Gazette,* 22 February 1933, pp. 1–2).

ing a depression highlight the class character of crises. While the banks certainly would have preferred getting their money to acquiring "worthless" farms, the legal system is designed to allow the creditor to make the most of a bad situation. Why, then, were the farmers successful? There is a divergence of opinion among those who might support a conflict perspective. An instrumental Marxist, for example, who would likely predict that any policy change would be supportive of B/O's and the capitalist class, might be hard pressed to account for the success of the moratorium. A structural version of Marxist theory predicts some concessions to the working class and individual disputants as a way of rationalizing and protecting the system. The moratorium would thus be seen as a means of system maintenance.

A third version, best articulated by Fred Block (1977)[137] and Theda Skocpol (1980),[138] critiques the instrumental and structural approaches as failing to recognize that the state and state managers are not merely pawns of the economically and politically powerful but rather are independent self-interested actors. From this "state manager" view, we can only predict likely policy changes by considering the goals and motivations of state managers as well as the goals of disputants.

While accepting the general theoretical premise that state managers are normally more likely to respond to organization and business interests than individual interests, Block and Skocpol argue that crises are exceptions to this general rule. State managers are motivated by a desire to maintain their position. During good times this is most successfully accomplished by meeting the needs of elites and businesses, so as to ensure business confidence, private investment, and economic prosperity. However, crises simultaneously weaken the power of the usual power brokers, while increasing the extent to which government managers need the support, or at least acquiescence, of the general citizenry. Since state managers have

> a fundamental role in maintaining order and political peace, which crises jeopardize, state officials are apt to grant concessions, even though they may be at the expense of dominant groups. Such actions reflect the government's primary interest in extracting economic resources, recruiting military personnel, and diffusing potential violence during a difficult period of national management. (Rasler, 1986: 924)[139]

137. [The reference is to Fred Block, *Revising State Theory* (Philadelphia: Temple University Press, 1987).]

138. [The reference is to Theda Skocpol, "Political Response to Capital Crisis: Neo-Marxist Theories of the State and the Case of the New Deal," 10 *Politics and Society* 155 (1980).]

139. [The reference is to Karen Rasler, *War, Accommodation, and Violence in the United States,* 1890–1970 (1986).]

Unlike consensus theorists who see policy as a near-automatic means of maintaining social integration, or crude Marxist theorists who see policy as always a way of advantaging the elite, state manager theorists hypothesize that state manager self-interest leads to policy in favor of elites during good times but in favor of individual citizens during crisis times. This means that losing individual litigants who are able to organize have a better chance of achieving policy success during crises than during periods of normality.

Farmer policy success seems to provide some support for both consensus theory and the state manager version of conflict theory. As the consensus theorist tells us, the ability to organize is the key to successful political pressure and that ability is possessed by groups other than just the economic and political elite. However, the state manager version of conflict theory provides additional insight into the process by suggesting why policymakers would be particularly likely to respond to organized debtor interests during crises.

B. War

Proposition 1: Crises and Litigation. A preliminary analysis of the data revealed no relationship between World War I and any of the litigation rates. As a result, it has been dropped from the equations. Apparently the short duration of the war and its relative isolation from the Arizona economy restricted the war's direct pact on litigation. World War II, with its greater duration and impact on Arizona, significantly affected I versus I and I versus B/O litigation.

During World War II, as with the depressions, the large positive shift in the I versus I slope results primarily from divorce cases. If such cases are removed, I versus I litigation has a slight downward trend probably reflecting both decreases in disputes and willingness to convert disputes into litigation during wartime. Similarly, I versus B/O cases significantly decrease with the onset of World War II.

B/O-initiated litigation does not reveal significant change in the intercept or slope with the onset of World War II. If anything, there is a continuation of the decline in such litigation that had begun in the Great Depression. While the rapid economic mobilization and shortages associated with war ought to have increased disputes, all types of litigation (except divorce) show a decrease or continued downward trend. These patterns suggest that whether the theoretical framework is consensus or conflict, all crises cannot be treated as undifferentiated events.

Consensus theory sees war, as opposed to depression, as a force that facilitates rather than destroys informal means of dispute resolution. War draws people together and increases social harmony. Therefore, there is less demand for litigation. The downward trend in litigation is also strengthened by the absence of a large portion of the male population and the general unavailability of credit or other business/individual interactions that could lead to disputes.

Conflict theory must certainly accept the validity of these explanations. It adds two other operative factors, however. First, World War II came on the heels of the Great Depression. The legal system had already been used by the economic and political elite to the extent possible to protect its interests. All existing disputes had been exhausted. Second, as the war mobilization led to increased potential for such disputes, state manager theory expects the state to step in to limit and control the emergence of these new disputes. The role of state managers in controlling war-related interstatus conflict will be discussed below.

That B/O-initiated litigation was reduced by either government regulation or some type of war spirit is supported by post-World War II litigation patterns. While I versus I litigation returned dramatically to a lower level as war-related divorce decreased, both B/O-initiated litigation types significantly increased. This seems to suggest the possibility that such disputes were pent up because they had not been converted into litigation. As soon as the war was over, business-related disputes and interstatus disputes that had been building up during the war were released and converted into litigation.

Proposition 2: Who Wins and Who Loses? That the litigation consequences of war are different than those of depressions is further supported by the victory patterns In Table 2. While B/O plaintiffs in B/O versus I litigation had their greatest success during the Great Depression (63.1 percent), they had their lowest success rate during the war years of 1942 (29.2 percent). This may have resulted from a "war harmony" but more likely indicates that most of the debt-collection and foreclosure cases, which are almost sure wins for banks and other lenders and which had accounted for the great victory margin for B/O's during the depression, had dried up as a result of the long depression and war.

Proposition 3: Policy Change and Litigation. World War II presents an interesting relationship between litigation and crisis that again pits consensus theory against conflict theory. The relationship, however, seems to be different from the one we observed during the depression. World War II saw the passage of policy to facilitate litigation rather than limit it. The landlord/tenant issue is a good example of this.

As Figure 3 shows, the rate of I versus B/O cases doubled between 1945 and 1946 and then dropped back down to a more typical rate. Much of that increase is accounted for by suits initiated by tenants against landlords. The World War II rise to unprecedented levels of landlord/tenant cases is reflected in Figure 6. These cases increased so rapidly because of the housing shortage and policy changes that controlled rent level and allowed tenants to sue landlords for violations.

In January, 1942, the federal government passed the Price Control Act. In this act Congress granted legal authority to take violators of

these control to court. Most of the litigation that resulted from this legislation was taken to federal, not state, courts. However, at the encouragement of OPA officials, certain states passed legislation that stated,
in effect, that any OPA regulation violation would also be considered a
violation of state law. Arizona was one of only a handful of states to
pass such legislation.

While the war-related legislation had an obvious effect on the business of the Arizona trial courts, what was the source of this policy
change? As John Kenneth Galbraith, Director of OPA's Price Division,
wrote in 1942, "We hoped that the public would become aroused over
this bill. The public, by and large, [however] is unaware of the issues"
(U.S. Office of Price Administration, Office of Temporary Controls,
1947).

If individual citizens were not pushing for this legislation, who was?
The state manager version of conflict posits that the key to understanding this policy is to understand the motives of the policymakers themselves. Those motives are twofold. First, state managers desire to maintain social harmony to facilitate the war effort and protect their
positions. Second, the ideology of state managers that had developed in
the preceding years supported interventionist responses to crisis.

We get a picture of a set of state managers who came into office
with a reform-oriented administration, who then served their formative
years in attempts to develop state policy to ameliorate the depression.
When war approached, it was natural that such leaders would think in
similar terms and respond in a way consistent with their ideology (outlook), namely, by providing for state intervention in behalf of "have
not" interests (tenants and consumers).

Consensus theory, then, again responds that rent control is another
perfect example of the homeostatic tendency of the law. State manager
theory agrees that the state attempted to ameliorate the crisis, but
asserts that it offers a more explicitly theoretical explanation of how
and why such accommodation comes about. That explanation centers
on interstatus conflict, how that conflict changes during crisis, and the
role of state managers in mediating the conflict.

IV. IMPLICATIONS

The results presented here are obviously preliminary and tentative.
However, they are suggestive of the possible significance of a conflict
perspective on crises, litigation, and policy change. This does not
mean that the work of consensus theorists is wrong or should be abandoned. As we have seen, consensus theory provides important insights
into the role of litigation. However, what I have tried to show is that
the further questions suggested by conflict theory lead us to a more
complete and theoretically significant examination of litigation.

The keys to these theoretical developments are an understanding of

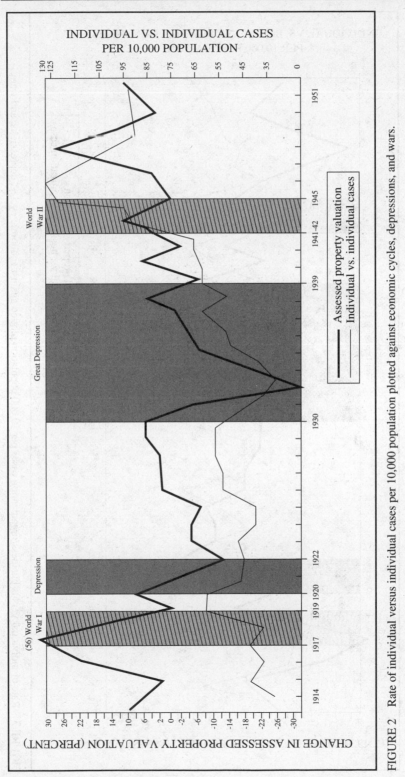

FIGURE 2   Rate of individual versus individual cases per 10,000 population plotted against economic cycles, depressions, and wars.

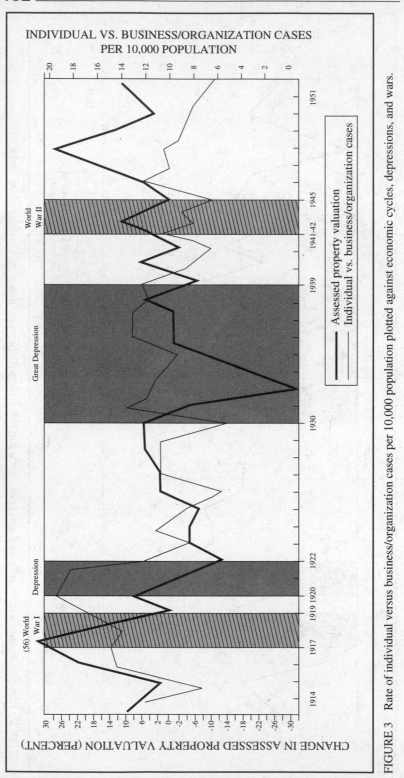

FIGURE 3   Rate of individual versus business/organization cases per 10,000 population plotted against economic cycles, depressions, and wars.

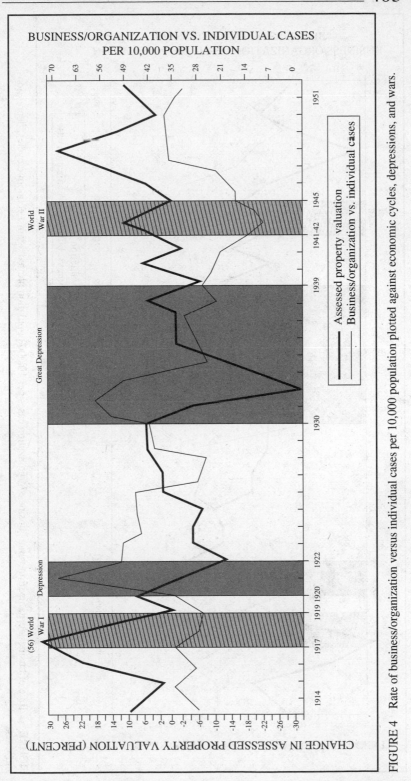

FIGURE 4   Rate of business/organization versus individual cases per 10,000 population plotted against economic cycles, depressions, and wars.

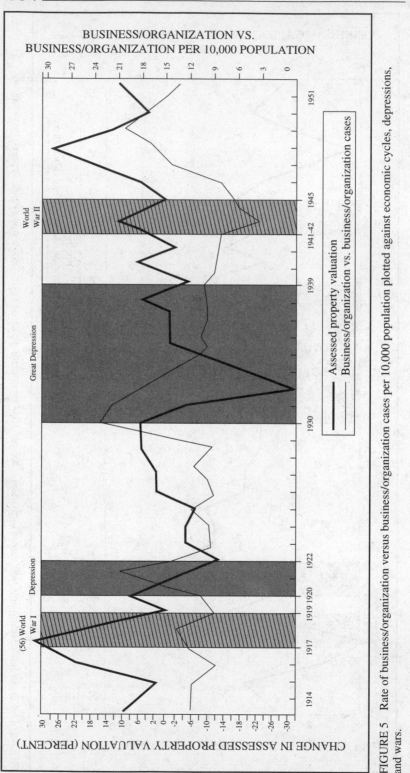

FIGURE 5   Rate of business/organization versus business/organization cases per 10,000 population plotted against economic cycles, depressions, and wars.

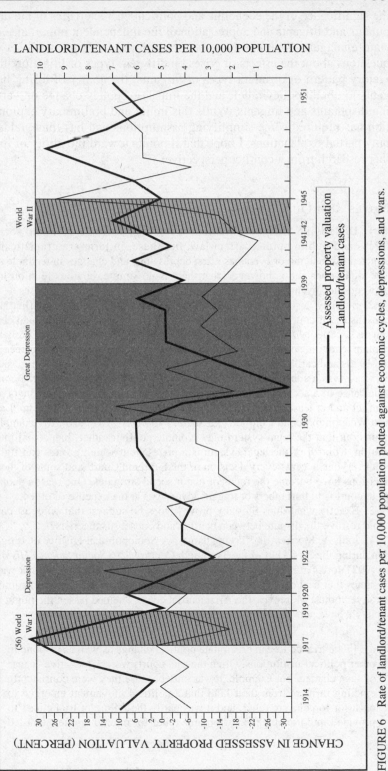

FIGURE 6   Rate of landlord/tenant cases per 10,000 population plotted against economic cycles, depressions, and wars.

the significance of the economic and political characteristics of the disputants and litigants and appreciation of the independent importance of
state managers. Keeping these factors in mind leads to a rich set of
questions about the effects of crises on different types of litigation; the
victory pattern of different types of litigants; the ability of losing litigants to obtain policy relief; and the impact of policy change on varying disputants and litigants. While this initial and preliminary exploration has required some simplifying assumptions and has thus yielded
only partial explanations, I hope that it points toward the utility of further research from a conflict perspective. □

NOTES AND QUESTIONS

1. Underlying Stookey's article is a common sense observation: social
forces and public opinion affect law, but these, in turn, are dramatically
affected by such major events as wars, depressions and changes in technology.
The study does show, however, that there is no simple, obvious relationship
between such events and *particular* legal phenomena, such as court cases.

2. Stookey describes two approaches to explaining litigation: conflict and
consensus. Of course, most if not all societies are a blend of conflict and consensus. A theory that stresses one while ignoring the other is unlikely to
explain legal phenomena very adequately. It is often said that social science in
the 1950s and early 1960s stressed consensus and downplayed conflict in society. Law was a substitute for violence; legal norms tended to reflect the common sense of a society. Nonetheless, we cannot forget that law itself involves
conflict and at least the threat of doing harm to people. Austin Turk, in "Law
as a Weapon in Social Conflict," 23 *Social Problems* 276 (1976), for example,
points out that the legal system may promote conflict rather than social integration. Control of the legal system is a prize about which groups can fight.
Not everyone accepts every decision of the Supreme Court, and some of these
decisions have become the focus of major social struggles. One reason people
go to court is to hurt others or to gain advantages at the expense of others.

3. Exactly what does Stookey prove? Does he suggest that *no* court data
could resolve the dispute between conflict and consensus theorists?

4. John A. Stookey, in "Trying Times: A Sociopolitical History of Litigation during the First Half of the Twentieth Century," 16 *Social Science History*
1 (1992), looks at his data on litigation in Arizona trial courts in another way.
He notes that trial courts have turned from general dispute resolvers to administrative bodies. Moreover, the Arizona trial courts "helped lessen the plight of
society's have nots" (p. 55). He concludes:

. . . [T]he trial court can precipitate political change as well as respond to
other political institutions. Often the trial courts were a "negative" cause
of such change. For example, it was only because they were consistently
evicting farmers from their land that a political movement emerged to
push for foreclosure relief, and it was partly the failure of trial courts to
provide rapid, reliable, and affordable relief for injured workers that led

to workers' compensation. Conversely, in the case of rent control, the courts were given new power to wield on behalf of the have-nots.

5. Stookey's article is an example of a longitudinal court study; a study of the work of a court over time. One of the first of these was Lawrence M. Friedman and Robert Percival, "A Tale of Two Courts: Litigation in Alameda and San Benito Counties," 10 *Law & Society Review* 267 (1976).

Friedman and Percival studied the work of two trial courts in California, one urban (Alameda) and one rural (San Benito) between 1890 and 1970. They tracked changes in the docket—for example, the percentage of family and tort cases filed rose dramatically in both counties, but property and contract cases fell just as drastically. Uncontested judgments—mostly judgments by default—rose in both counties, and the percentage of contested judgments dropped over time.

Friedman and Percival were also interested in the *volume* of litigation, especially in light of the furor over a so-called "litigation explosion." There was also a contrary hypothesis: A Spanish scholar, José Juan Toharia, in *Cambio Social y Vida Juridica en Espana, 1900–1970* (Madrid: Edicusa, 1974), found an inverse relationship between economic growth and the volume of formal litigation. That is, highly developed legal systems do not show growth in their litigation rates; on the contrary, rates tend to stabilize or decline in the face of rapid economic growth. A study of the volume of civil litigation at first instance in Sweden and Denmark, between 1930 and 1970, tended to confirm Toharia's findings. Britt-Mari P. Blegvad, P. O. Bolding, Ole Lando, *Arbitration as a Means of Solving Conflicts* (Copenhagen: Ronota, 1973), pp. 103–05.

Friedman and Percival continue as follows:

Why should this be so? The idea is that formal court processes are slow, expensive, technical. Court process is, from the economic standpoint, inefficient; and society will take no steps to encourage it for ordinary civil disputes. That formal court processes are inefficient and irrelevant to economic life, is quite consistent with our data. But it is not so clear that the two counties confirm the prediction that litigation declines as an economy develops. A number of interesting facts emerge . . . One is the convergence of the counties. In 1890, urban Alameda was more litigious than rural San Benito; differences today are very small.

Compared to 1890, both counties show an apparent rise in cases per 1,000 population. But the rate in Alameda in 1910 was higher than it is today; and San Benito's ratio declined slightly between 1950 and 1970. And the figures are too crude to be used as indicators of litigation rates. For one thing, they do not take into account either the federal courts or the inferior trial courts. For another thing, they do not take into account the nature of the cases litigated. Before we can speak of "litigation rates" we must define litigation: is an uncontested divorce "litigation?" . . . To test the hypothesis of declining litigation, we would really need some valid measure of dispute settlement, for all courts, in a community. "Litigation" would mean a proceeding containing elements of dispute, that were not resolved before one party filed a complaint, or perhaps not resolved without the intervention of a judge. Perhaps such a "true" rate would show a decline since 1890; but our figures do not permit us the luxury of a guess. . . .

Quantitative indicators of court performances in these two counties confirm one general hypothesis: the dispute settlement function in the courts is declining. In general, the trial courts today perform routine administration; dispute settlement has steadily shrunk as a proportion of their caseload. Most cases today are quite routine. In 1890, a higher percentage of cases involved genuine disputes, and the work of the courts was on the whole less stereotyped. The rate of uncontested judgments has multiplied while the incidence of contested judgments has fallen. A smaller percentage of cases are brought to trial today, and courts issue formal opinions or findings in far fewer cases. Court delays have significantly lengthened.

What factors account for the routinization of the work of modern courts? One possibility is that uncertainty—a prime breeder of litigation—has declined in the law; that rules are more "settled" than in 1890. Some kinds of dispute (over land titles for example) have been largely resolved, or reduced to order by new social arrangements, such as the use of title insurance, and improvement in county record-keeping. But there is no easy way to measure this factor in the aggregate. Our assumption is that some areas of law do become "settled;" but as they do, new uncertainties replace old ones. Land titles were less chaotic in 1930 than in 1890; but as this problem faded, the automobile accident more than replaced it, creating a new and complex field of law.

For another possible explanation, one may point to factors associated with urbanization and the particular brand of economic development that has occurred in the United States. The population in 1970 is mobile and rootless. Overwhelmingly, people live in metropolitan areas. They deal primarily with strangers. The ordered social relations of small towns and traditional courts—a world of face to face relations—has vanished.

In this light, we might expect the modern court in San Benito to resemble its 1890 ancestor, and traditional courts, more closely than we would expect of the Alameda court. Surprisingly, however, the data of 1970 do not show much difference between the counties. On the contrary, San Benito's courts play, if anything, a more routinized role than the courts in urban Alameda. In San Benito, more cases involve routine matters, a larger proportion are uncontested, fewer are brought to trial, and courts more rarely issue formal opinions or findings.

There is a general assumption in the literature that "modernization" brings about a general shift from social-harmony litigation to a more formal style of dispute-settlement. Our data suggests a rather different kind of evolution. To be sure, in 1890 it was already true that precious little of the work of the court conformed to the social harmony style. That had perhaps already virtually vanished in the United States, unless one were to find it in the justice courts, which is doubtful. Did it ever exist? The records of colonial courts suggest that at the very dawn of American history there were institutions that came closer to the anthropologists' model. But by 1890, the Superior Court of Alameda was already an urban court; and as for San Benito, while it was a small community, it was hardly a tightly-knit, traditional community. On the contrary, it was a raw and new community—a community of recent arrivals, transients, strangers. If anything, it is more of a face-to-face community today; and yet the social harmony style is even more absent.

The evolution, then, does not go from social harmony to legalistic style, and find a resting point. Rather, dispute settlement vanishes completely from the courts; it is replaced by routine administration. Whether the legalistic style was an intermediate phase, or whether the development was directly from social harmony style to routine, our data does not allow us to state with confidence.

Our evidence shows, then, that in the two California courts—one sitting in a bustling urban metropolis, the other not—the dispute settlement function has shriveled to almost nothing; the routine administrative function has become predominant.

This seems on the surface rather curious. Certainly, disputes still arise in society, and they probably must be settled. Yet for some reason, they are not settled in court. Of course, it is theoretically possible that fewer disputes go to court than in an earlier period because the number of disputes has fallen. We have no way to measure the number of disputes that might go to court, if court were costless and freely accessible. Nor do we have any information about the relative number of disputes in San Benito County, compared to Alameda, now or in any other period. It is barely possible that, when genuine disputes do occur in San Benito, a larger proportion of them may actually be taken to court than in Alameda. But there is no obvious reason why the number of actual "disputes" should be so low in the two counties; and the most likely assumption is that the court itself—its style, its mode of operation—discourages its use for dispute settlement, rather than that the number of issues or disputes has declined.

Apparently, litigation is not worthwhile, for the potential litigant; it is too costly, in other words; "Costs" may mean dollar costs. Delays and technicalities are also costly, because of the disruption and expense they may inflict, and the uncertainties they may introduce into outcomes. All of these costs in fact did rise during the 19th century, although the data are fragmentary. As costs rise, so does the threshold at which litigation becomes worthwhile.

But this pushes our inquiry back one step; it does not answer the basic question. If courts have become too "costly," why has society permitted this to happen? Why have there not been arrangements to keep the dispute settlement function of courts alive, and healthy and productive? Why has a situation been allowed to develop in which full scale court proceedings on the whole move slowly, cost a great deal, and proceed by rules that are a closed book to the average man—indeed, to the average businessman? Over the last two centuries, the use of courts for dispute settlement seems to have declined, while all other economic indicators in society have risen. Does this make sense?

A. Law and Development

Let us, for simplicity, assume economic growth as a goal widely shared in early nineteenth century American society. How could legal process contribute to this end? First of all, it was necessary to dismantle restrictions that restrained the free flow of commerce. Second, new legal arrangements might be instituted or encouraged that would stimulate trade and manufacture. A flourishing economy, a growing economy is an economy of increasing volume. The more of society's goods traded on the market, the better; the higher the turnover, the better.

The economy, then, was to be left as free as possible, not for its own sake, but because free trade would foster prosperity. Business, left to its own devices, would develop tools—forms and techniques—that permitted and encouraged rapid trade. Such forms would be highly standard; they would permit rapid, routine, trouble-free use, as much as was humanly possible. A vigorous market is one in which people absorb losses in the short run, and continue to trade. They do not break off commercial relationships in the midst of a competitive situation, nor do they funnel transactions through courts. Any legal agency which exercises discretion and is careful, slow and individuating, cannot help but interrupt the flow of trade. It is not healthy, then, for the economy, unless parties stay out of court except as a last resort.

Hence, costs are permitted to rise. No invisible cartel raises costs, but costs go up, and they are allowed to; there is little countervailing subsidy. Ordinary disputes, between members of the middle class, slowly drain out of the system. Business also tends to avoid the courts. Business can afford to litigate, but does not welcome the disruptiveness of litigation. For business, too, legal norms (especially procedural ones) disappoint legitimate expectations. This formalization is a cost which society has also allowed to rise, as lawyers professionalize, courts conceptualize, and the law becomes more "scientific."

Hence, too, the relative decline in litigation, although, as we have seen, this is not so easy to attest in our two courts. One must remember that the decline in disputed proceedings in court does not mean that "the law" (in a broader sense) is of declining importance in a developing country; quite the contrary. As the economy expands, so does the use of legal instruments: contracts, checks, deeds, articles of incorporation, wills, mortgages. The number of transactions which take legal form increases more rapidly than the population. But this does not mean more "trials" and more use of formal courts to "settle disputes." In modern society, most transactions are private, that is, they take place without the intervention of the state. Thousands of other transactions use the courts, but only in a routine way—to collect debts, legitimize status, and so on.

Routinization, then, accompanies a lowering of the public demand for settlement of disputes in formal courts. Much of the remaining docket hangs on from sheer necessity. One must go to court to win legal freedom to remarry, for example. It is a routine but necessary step. For the rest, ordinary people are deterred by the cost, the torpor, the technicality of court proceedings. Businessmen prefer to handle matters themselves, or go to arbitration, which is perhaps less disruptive, and where an arbitrator is more likely than a judge to understand the issues, as businessmen define them. Administrative bodies (zoning boards, workmen's compensation boards) settle many others of society's disputes.

In short, the dispute-settlement trial becomes rarer and rarer. The court system does not expand; the number of judges remains more or less static. The system is rationalized and "improved;" but it remains foreign to the average potential litigant. At the trial level, formal court systems gradually lose their share of dispute settlement cases. Their work becomes, in large part, routine administration.

B. City and Country

The most surprising result of the study, however, is the striking similarity between the two counties. San Benito is small, and the population is thin. In Oakland, one can talk about "crowded" city courts;" but certainly not in Hollister. There is less delay in San Benito, and the court is not rushed or overburdened. Yet little of consequence takes place in court. San Benito is still a small society; yet the main function of its Superior Court is to rubber stamp petitions for dissolution of marriage.

This fact allows us to reject the hypothesis that routinization is to be explained by "industrialization" or "urbanization." There is little industry in San Benito, and no real city. But San Benito is part of an urban, industrial society. It is not isolated from modern influence. It is an hour's drive from the Bay Area megalopolis. The mass media lace all communities together; people in Hollister watch the same programs, read much the same news, eat much the same food, as people elsewhere in the country. They are part of a common culture.

It is a culture in which there seem to be factors in the structure of courts—and, more fundamentally, in social attitudes—which have combined to make "going to court" obsolete, as part of the normal life-cycle of dispute settlement. We cannot identify these factors precisely. But their influence on the work of the courts is far more powerful than the gross demographic differences between "cities" and "small towns."

Whatever the causes, the figures for these two courts show a general movement from dispute settlement to routine administration over the past century. We believe this is a national phenomenon, too. It is a development which may pose problems for society. No doubt courts are still very useful, in a number of ways; but they are almost totally unused by ordinary individuals to resolve personal problems. The overwhelming majority of business disputes also avoid the courts. Citizen and businessmen alike either seek out some other agency, or make use of resources within the family, group, or trade association—or, as is frequently the case, handle the matter entirely on their own. The judicial system is often elaborately praised. The praise rings hollow if, as it appears, factors at work militate against the use of the system. We must ask, what are the institutions that have replaced the courts, and how do they operate? And, where no institutions have appeared to fill what may well be a gap, we must ask, what has society gained and lost, as an ancient structure of decision passes into history?

6. Friedman and Percival suggest a decline in the use of courts for resolving disputes. Does this mean the "litigation explosion" is mythical? See Hayden, *supra*, p. 181.

7. Can we assume a decline in litigation rates is necessarily a good thing? Why do people go to court? According to Niklas Luhmann, "Communication About Law," in Karin Knorr-Cetina and Aaron V. Cicourel (eds.), *Advances in Social Theory and Methodology* (Boston: Routledge & Kegan Paul, 1981), concrete situations must be "thematized" as legal questions before people will take disputes to court—that is, people must think of their problem as one which could be handled at law and transform it into legal concepts.

Luhmann thinks that there is a high cost if "thematization thresholds" to using law are too high:

> As a conflict-regulating system that is always belatedly set in motion, i.e., only when called upon, the legal system very seldom takes the initiative . . . . Excessive inhibition of the thematization of law may, therefore, lead to a kind of drying up of the legal system, and so leave the regulation of conflict to other mechanisms—e.g., morality, ignorance, class structure, or the use of force outside the law—whose social structural compatibility may be problematic. (p. 247)

Compare Albert W. Alschuler, "Mediation With a Mugger: The Shortage of Adjudicative Services and the Need for a Two-Tier Trial System in Civil Cases," 99 *Harvard Law Review* 1808 (1986). Alschuler argues that Americans settle too many cases for the wrong reasons. A person with a claim confronts too many pressures to compromise. He concludes:

> In a more civilized society, the extensive rationing of adjudication by price and queue would not assure wrongdoers that they always could "settle" and profit from their wrongs. In this society, a right would be something that one gets, not merely something that one has. People would know that they could take their disputes to the courts and that the courts would resolve them. With this assurance people might be less likely to take their disputes to the streets or to the subways. (p. 1859)

8. Many, if not most, of us assume that harmony is a good while conflict is always a bad. Laura Nader, in *Harmony Ideology: Justice and Control in a Zapotec Mountain Village* 321 (Stanford: Stanford University Press, 1990), reminds us:

> Conciliation, harmony and resolution have such different uses and consequences as to merit different labels . . . Harmony that leads to autonomy is different from harmony that leads to control or oppression or pacification; conciliation may lead to conflict as well as to peace; and resolution may lead to injustice as well as justice. Disputing processes cannot be explained solely as a reflection of some predetermined set of

social conditions. Rather, they reflect the processes of an evolving cultural construction, that may be a response to demand, a product of ruling interests, a result of class conflict or accommodation. Harmony as a general conception for life should be scrutinized in relation to the construction of law, much as conflict and controversy have been examined in relation to the development of law.

Recall the material, for example, on the impact of *mediation*, a form of conflict resolution, on divorced women, above, p. 127.

9. Richard Lempert, in "More Tales of Two Courts: Exploring Changes in the 'Dispute Settlement Function' of Trial Courts," 13 *Law & Society Review* 91 (1978), challenged Friedman and Percival's conclusions about the shift in function of trial courts. Lempert says that we cannot be sure from data about the kinds of cases filed that courts are playing a less important role in dispute settlement. Predictions of what judges might do can play a role in settling disputes without anyone filing a case. As the costs of litigation rise, this becomes a factor in dispute resolution by other means. All that Friedman and Percival can show from this data is that courts take on more and more administrative functions as a percentage of their total activity. They cannot show that their dispute resolution functions have become socially less important.

10. Lempert also stresses a problem which all scholars who study court records face. We do not, and perhaps cannot, know how many disputes in society could have been brought to court but were not. We do not, and perhaps cannot, know how perceptions of what a court might do affected what was done with those disputes. William L. F. Felstiner, Richard L. Abel, and Austin Sarat, in "The Emergence and Transformation of Disputes: Naming, Blaming, Claiming . . . ," 15 *Law & Society Review* 631 (1980–81), argue that experiences must be perceived as an injury, the victim must see someone else as to blame, and the victim must make a claim against that person. If the claim is rejected, then the victim may decide to see a lawyer. The victim and his or her lawyer then may decide to file a lawsuit.

Each step in this progression is problematic. They are not events that just happen. For example, some people will see particular action as offensive; others will not notice that it happened. Some people who suffer injury (at least minor injury) will turn the other cheek and go on with their lives. Some who blame others for their injury may make no claim. Many disputes are ended by "exit." An employee is fired or quits; a neighbor moves away; former friends avoid each other. Disputes get transformed as they move through this process—people remember some details and forget others, people inflate some claims and downgrade others, and so on. It is the unusual dispute that travels through the entire process and produces a complaint filed in court.

Clearly, Friedman and Percival were not studying the role of courts in the total process of disputing in their two counties. What happens in courts is far removed from most of this process of disputing, except where people need a judicial resolution of their problems—a divorce, for example.

11. Another longitudinal court study is Wayne McIntosh's, "150 Years of Litigation and Dispute Resolution," 15 *Law & Society Review* 823 (1981). This was a study of St. Louis, Missouri, between 1820 and 1970. A fuller account is in McIntosh's book, *The Appeal of Civil Law: A Political-Economic Analysis of Litigation* (Urbana, Ill.: University of Illinois Press, 1990). McIntosh, too, ques-

tions "the axiom that we have become a nation of pathological litigators. . . . From a historical perspective it is clearly evident that litigation . . . in the St. Louis community has alternately ebbed and flowed, exhibiting a legible pattern of cycles" (p. 191). See also the review essay by Stephen Daniels, "You Can't Interview the Dead: McIntosh's "The Appeal of the Civil Law and the Debate over Longitudinal Studies of Courts," 17 *Law & Social Inquiry* 291 (1992).

12. The article by John Stookey appeared in a special issue of the Law & Society Review, edited by Frank Munger, and devoted to longitudinal court studies. The issue contains many such studies, some of them cross-national, and critiques of the methods and aims of such studies. See also Frank Munger, "Afterward: Studying Litigation and Social Change," the final essay in the issue, 24 *Law & Society Review* 595 (1990).

4

The Impact of Law on Society

INTRODUCTION

In 1990, Congress enacted and the President signed into law two very different statutes, the Americans with Disabilities Act (ADA), 42 U.S.C. § 121 et seq., and the Crime Control Act of 1990. The ADA states as its purpose "to provide a clear and comprehensive national mandate for the elimination of discrimination against individuals with disabilities."[140] The Crime Control Act was a bundle of various anti-crime spending programs and changes in federal criminal law. One provision dealt with the new federal crime of "possession" of child pornography. Among other things, it required producers of pornography to keep a record of the age of people appearing in hard-core pornography (18 U.S.C. §§ 2252, 2275).

The two laws do have at least one thing in common: they seem to be trying to change human behavior. The ADA explicitly outlaws discriminatory behavior against people who have disabilities—the blind, the deaf, people in wheelchairs, and so on—whether this discrimination is on the job, or in hotels, motels, restaurants, or on trains, buses, and airplanes. The federal statute on child pornography clearly has as its goal stamping out child pornography—preventing people from making it, selling it, or possessing it.

A traditional legal scholar would undoubtedly be interested in the way these statutes changed the existing law. From the perspective of a

140. 1990 Congressional Quarterly Almanac, p. 452.

415

law-and-society scholar, the crucial questions might be different. Such a scholar would surely be interested in *impact*: what difference will these laws actually make in the real world? Will employers actually change their hiring and firing practices with regard to people with disabilities? Will theaters and restaurants become more accessible? Will people produce or use less child pornography? In short, will these laws change behavior?

The "law in action" perspective, discussed and used throughout this book, makes impact a natural concern. In an important sense, the new law of disability rights is not the words on the piece of paper that the president signed. Rather, it is the process which the law might set off: how employers, grocery store managers, bus companies, airlines, movie theaters, shopping malls—and the disabled themselves—react to it. Similarly, the new law of child pornography is not the formal language we read in the congressional record, but the behavior of producers and processors of this material.

Common sense and experience tell us that just because a law is passed, behavior does not necessarily change. For example, providing greater access for persons with disabilities requires employers and merchants to spend money. Doors have to be widened, restrooms remodeled, elevators added. We would expect that some businesspersons will do all they can to avoid these costs. In fact many business groups lobbied strongly against passage of the ADA for these very reasons. Similarly, child pornography is a multi-million dollar industry, and it caters to the tastes of a small but real segment of the population. This leads us to the first major question to be discussed in the chapters. What makes a law effective? How do we explain "compliance" with the law? Which people will disobey the law? Which ones will evade the law as much as possible? Who will simply ignore the law? And what will motivate these people to obey, disobey, evade, ignore or comply?

Law, of course, is more than statutes. In a broader sense of the word, "law" is any rule, command or order that carries with it authoritative force. In this sense, court decisions and administrative rulings, for example, are just as much types of law as are statutes. And a "law in action" perspective demands that we ask whether and to what extent such decisions and rulings will affect behavior.

While compliance is central to understanding how law affects society, the word does not fully capture the range of ways in which law might have an impact on society. For example, consider the following remark by an attorney, about the impact of the Supreme Court decision in *Bates v. State Bar of Arizona*[141] which struck down prohibitions against lawyer advertising as unconstitutional: "It is obvious to anyone who practices that lawyer advertising has done more than any single

---

141. 433 U.S. 450 (1977).

thing to lower the public's opinion of lawyers." The speaker is assuming some degree of compliance with *Bates* and is asking about further implications of that compliance—side-effects, ripple effects, broader and wider consequences. Questions about indirect impact can be asked about any law. Will the ADA drive some employers out of business? Will it make the disabled more or less militant? Will it add to their happiness or their prestige? What will the non-disabled think or do in response to attempts to enforce the statute?

If the police are forced to give criminal suspects constitutional rights, will "the guilty" go free? Will forbidding abortion simply drive it underground and increase the number of women who are injured or die? The impact of law on society includes any consequences which causally follow from a law. This chapter deals first with questions of compliance (direct impact), and then goes on to issues associated with more indirect, social consequences of law.

It is easy for amateurs to speculate about impact, and they do. For example, we hear from politicians that the crime rate is down because of more police work; or up because we need more police. However, they rarely marshal evidence to support the claim that police levels actually have the claimed impact on criminal behavior. Similarly, the lawyer who criticized the impact of *Bates* offers no evidence to support his conclusion that advertising "causes" lower opinions of lawyers. We can think of other explanations—if, in fact, people do hold lower opinions of lawyers. A secondary theme, throughout this chapter, will be how to differentiate between accurate and inaccurate assertions about the impact of law; how to measure impact; how to tell when impact occurs.

WHY DO PEOPLE OBEY THE LAW?

THE ROLE OF SANCTIONS

28. *Deterrence Theory and Research*

Jack Gibbs

In Gary Melton, *The Law as a Behavioral Instrument* (Lincoln: University of Nebraska Press, 1986)

☐ Deterrence occurs when a potential offender refrains from or curtails . . . activity because he or she perceives some threat of a legal punishment for contrary behavior and fears that punishment.

A legal punishment is a legal action by a legal official that is per-ceived by at least one potential offender as causing pain or discom-fort . . . . Note also that the definition goes beyond statutory penalties and even actual sentences to procedural steps in criminal justice, such as arrest or trial. Those actions presumably are perceived by potential offenders as painful.

TWO CONVENTIONAL TYPES OF DETERRENCE

With few exceptions, . . . writers on deterrence distinguish general deterrence and what is called specific, special, or individual deterrence. Full appreciation of the distinction's significance requires explicit defi-nitions.

General deterrence refers to the deterrence of potential offenders who have not been legally punished. To illustrate, suppose that a stu-dent *with no arrest history* reads of someone's receiving a six-month sentence for marijuana possession. Insofar as that experience deters the student, each time that he or she refrains from or curtails possession of marijuana constitutes general deterrence. The crucial consideration is not whether the student had possessed marijuana before reading about the punishment, nor is it the nature of that particular experience. All manner of experiences short of actually being punished, even coming to know of statutory penalties, could further general deterrence.

Specific deterrence refers to the deterrence of potential offenders who have been legally punished. The notion does not deny that vicari-ous experience of punishment can deter; rather, being punished suppos-edly furthers deterrence beyond any vicarious experience. Reconsider the individual who was sentenced to six months in jail for marijuana possession. If the incarceration prompts that individual to refrain from or curtail marijuana possession, each instance would be specific deter-rence. But contemplate this question: To what extent does punishment for one type of crime deter the offender from other types? Researchers have yet to treat the "generalization" question seriously and research is needed to realize a more defensible definition of specific deterrence.

Significance of the distinction

The importance of the general/specific distinction is most obvious when stipulating evidence of deterrence. Assume this finding: ex-con-victs commit more crimes per unit of time after incarceration than before. That finding would indicate no specific deterrence, but it would have little bearing on general deterrence.

To appreciate the policy relevance of the general/specific distinc-tion, consider the argument that legislators are preoccupied with general deterrence because it offers cheap crime prevention. What could be cheaper than simply threatening potential offenders? But if recidivists contribute substantially to the crime rate and can be deterred only by serving long prison terms, then crime prevention through deterrence becomes very expensive. Moreover, a strategy for promoting one type of deterrence may not be necessary for the other type. Thus, neither actual punishments nor statutory penalties need be publicized to promote specific deterrence.

A LESS CONVENTIONAL DISTINCTION

The difference between entirely refraining from a criminal act and curtailing commissions is so important that two additional types of deterrence should be distinguished. In the case of absolute deterrence, a potential offender has contemplated a crime at least once and has been deterred totally each instance. That an individual has never committed the crime is only a necessary condition for inferring absolute deterrence, because no individual can be deterred without contemplating a crime. To be sure, the term contemplating creates difficulties; but if social and behavioral scientists are unwilling to consider covert behavior, they should leave the deterrence doctrine alone.

The idea of partial crime prevention enters into the notion of *restrictive deterrence*. It occurs when, to diminish the risk or severity of a legal punishment, a potential offender engages in some action that has the effect of reducing his or her commissions of a crime. Briefly illustrating, suppose that a bad-check artist follows this rule: Never hang more than one piece of paper in any town. Such rules are indicative of restrictive deterrence because they have the effect of reducing the number of offenses. Driving behavior often illustrates restrictive deterrence, as when drivers exceed the speed limit by only five miles per hour to reduce the risk or severity of a legal punishment.

Significance of the distinction

Contemplate something improbable—evidence that every professional football player has snorted cocaine at least once. The evidence would fuel allegations that the legal control of narcotics is ineffectual, but it would reveal nothing about restrictive deterrence. Similarly, no crime rate is ever so great as to demonstrate negligible absolute deterrence. So although most writers and researchers ignore the distinction, evidence that bears on either type of deterrence—absolute or restrictive—has little bearing on the other type.

The distinction gives rise to a possible paradox; it may well be that so-called professional criminals are deterred the most. Given such an offender, the most commonly overlooked question is this: How many crimes would the offender have committed had there been no threat of legal punishment? Granted the question is unanswerable, it is relevant in debating penal policy. Critics who assert that legal punishments do not deter may never have thought of restrictive deterrence.

TOWARD A THEORY OF GENERAL DETERRENCE

Given the general/specific distinction and the absolute/restrictive distinction, there are four types of deterrence. That number alone precludes stating the deterrence doctrine as a simple proposition such as: Certain, swift, and severe punishments deter crime. Any such proposition would be a gross oversimplification even if types of deterrence could be ignored. It is not clear whether the proposition refers to statutory penalties, to actual punishments, or to both. Even if general deterrence requires some actual punishments, potential offenders may perceive statutory penalties as a threat.

Attempts to reduce the deterrence doctrine to a simple proposition conceal the doctrine's most significant feature; it is first and foremost a perceptual theory. Whether a punishment threat deters depends not on the certainty, celerity, or severity of punishment in any objective sense but on the potential offender's perception. Therefore, in stating the deterrence doctrine as a theory, a theorist should recognize two classes of punishment properties—the objective and the perceptual. The two can be distinguished roughly in terms of procedures for gathering data. The only systematic way to gather data on perceptual properties is to solicit answers from potential offenders to questions about punishments, but objective properties can be studied without such solicitation. □

NOTES AND QUESTIONS

1. While Gibbs and most other research on deterrence focus on criminal behavior, deterrence can relate to a wide range of legal attempts to control behavior through the threat of sanctions. For example, non-criminal fines and civil judgments are also sanctions that are designed to deter certain types of behavior. One of the societal justifications often heard for product liability suits is that they serve to deter the further production and distribution of dangerous products. To what extent does the law of contracts also assume a theory of deterrence?

As Gibbs' article suggests, there is an enormous amount of literature on deterrence—theoretical and empirical. Gibbs himself had earlier written a very thoughtful general account, *Crime, Punishment, and Deterrence* (New York: Elsevier, 1975). See, also, Franklin E. Zimring and Gordon J. Hawkins, *Deterrence: The Legal Threat in Crime Control* (Chicago: University of Chicago Press, 1973). An article by Isaac Ehrlich touched off an enormous methodological debate. The article is "The Deterrent Effect of Capital Punishment: A Question of Life and Death," 65 *American Economic Review* 397 (1975). A good critique and review of the debate is Richard O. Lempert, "Desert and Deterrence: An Assessment of the Moral Bases of the Case for Capital Punishment," 79 *Michigan Law Review* 1177 (1981).

2. Gibbs defines two types of studies of deterrence: those looking at objective sanctions and those looking at subjective sanctions. However, he also says that deterrence is "first and foremost a perceptual theory." What does he mean by this comment? What implications does his observation have on the way studies of deterrence should be designed and conducted?

3. A large body of work in the law and economics tradition ignores perception, and attempts to look at the "objective" deterrent effect of sanctions on the "rational" actor. For example, see: P. J. Cook, "Research in Criminal Deterrence," in M. Tonry and N. Morris (eds.), *Crime and Justice* Vol. 2 (Chicago: University of Chicago Press, 1980), pp. 211–268. Does this imply that economists disagree with Gibbs that deterrence is "perceptual"?

A rational actor, of course, balances the risks of getting caught and the likely penalties against the benefits from the criminal act. See Jan Palmer, "Economic Analysis of the Deterrent Effect of Punishment: A Review," 14 *Journal of Research in Crime and Delinquency* 4 (1977). Scott Decker, Richard Wright, and Robert Logie, in "Perceptual Deterrence Among Active Residential Burglars: A Research Note," 31 *Criminology* 135 (1993), compared responses of burglars with a control group. Almost all the members of the control group said that they were unwilling to commit burglary regardless of the risk, penalty, or reward. The active burglars, however, considered the anticipated gain, the perceived risk of being caught, and the likely penalties. Can these findings be explained within a rational actor theory of crime and deterrence?

The benefits of crime are not always economic in the narrow sense of that term. See Ralph A. Weisheit, "The Intangible Rewards From Crime: The Case of Domestic Marijuana Cultivation," 37 *Crime & Delinquency* 506 (1991). He interviewed growers and reports that many growers "cultivate marijuana as part of a larger lifestyle, of which marijuana use is often an important part" (p. 512). Patricia A. Adler, in *Wheeling and Dealing: An Ethnography of an Upper-Level Drug Dealing and Smuggling Community* (New York: Columbia University Press, 1985), finds dealers and smugglers engage in frantic hard work focused on short-term maximization of profit so that they can live a hedonistic lifestyle. See John J. Gibbs and Peggy L. Shelly, "Life in the Fast Lane: A Retrospective View by Commercial Thieves," 19 *Journal of Research in Crime and Delinquency* 299 (1982), stressing that commercial thieves enjoy the thrill of crime and the admiration of those who are impressed by their willingness to take chances. Thieves spend money without concern for the future because they expect to be caught and sent to jail sooner or later. They seek only to postpone what they accept as the inevitable. See, also, Jack Katz, *Seductions of Crime: Moral and Sensual Attractions in Doing Evil* (New York: Basic Books, 1988).

4. Recall the material on the development of no-fault divorce. Was the prior law a deterrent to divorce? Was it supposed to be? Does a no-fault system mean the legal system has abandoned any attempt to deter divorce?

29. Homicide and the Death Penalty: A Cross-National Test of a Deterrence Hypothesis

Dane Archer,
Rosemary Gartner,
and Marc Beittel

74 *Journal of Criminal Law & Criminology 991* (1983).

I. INTRODUCTION

☐ Debate over capital punishment has an extensive history. The debate is complex and confused, partly because support for the death penalty reflects no single theory but, instead, a conglomeration of several different theories. These include retribution, avoidance of economic costs associated with protracted imprisonment, a disbelief in rehabilitation, and, finally, a conception that has come to be called "deterrence theory." While each argument for the death penalty has its supporters, it is deterrence theory that has captured public imagination and scientific attention.

Briefly stated, deterrence theory holds that there is an effective relationship between specific qualities of punishment (for example, its certainty, celerity, or severity) and the likelihood that a punishable offense will be committed. A corollary of deterrence theory is that increasing the penalty for an offense will decrease its frequency while decreasing the penalty will cause infractions to multiply. Deterrence theory therefore envisions potential offenders as rational actors who weigh the qualities of potential punishment before acting.

Although capital punishment is ancient, the genealogy of deterrence theory is much more recent. Prior to the last few centuries, the death penalty was imposed often and for a variety of offenses, some of which seem trivial to the modern eye. For most of recorded history, the fate of the executed was regarded as deserved and morally unproblematic. Deterrence theory emerged in the last two or three centuries as societies have, for the first time, felt obliged to provide objective justifications for the death penalty. This need reflected a number of historical developments, including a growing distaste for torture, maiming, stoning, burning, and other forms of judicially-sanctioned violence.

Unique attributes of the death penalty contribute to abolitionist sentiment. The death penalty is both violent and irrevocable, and the discovery of judicial errors in capital cases emphasizes the fallibility of a finding of guilt. This recognition prompted Lafayette's famous remark,

"I shall continue to demand the abolition of the death penalty until I have the infallibility of human judgments demonstrated to me." Similarly, violent retribution has become less palatable than it once was. If, through executions, societies seek to exact horrible suffering, it is not clear that contemporary executions maximize this purpose, as Clarence Darrow observed:

> But why not do a good job of it . . . Why not boil them in oil as they used to do? Why not burn them at the stake? Why not sew them in a bag with serpents and throw them out to sea? . . . Why not break every bone in their body on the rack, as has often been done for such serious offenses as heresy and witchcraft?

At present, retribution, avoidance of economic costs and a lack of confidence in rehabilitation are not sufficiently acceptable justifications for punishment by death. Deterrence theory alone, therefore, occupies center stage in the debate over capital punishment. While deterrence theory may conceal elements of ancient themes (such as a desire for retribution), the theory's manifest doctrine is the saving of lives; the killing of convicted offenders is justified as a means of preserving the lives of future victims of potential or actual offenders. In this sense, somewhat ironically, deterrence theory is itself a manifestation of the increasing sanctity of life . . . .

The controversy has flourished in Western societies during the past two decades. In the United States, changes in crime rates and public opinion have fueled the debate. Support for the death penalty has shown a long-term decline, though more recently there has been a resurgence. In the 1930's, surveys showed that roughly two-thirds of the American people supported the death penalty, and as late as the 1950's there was an average of seventy executions per year in the United States. This number fell dramatically during the 1960's. Surveys showed that only a minority of Americans approved of the death penalty during the 1960's, and, from 1968 until January of 1977, there were no executions in the United States.

The recent resurgence of support for capital punishment has supplanted "abolitionist" sentiments with "restorationist" beliefs. The engine driving this reversal is almost certainly the soaring crime rate. After a steady decline since the 1930's, homicide rates and other crime rates began to increase sharply in the mid-1960's. As a single example, the rate for homicide and nonnegligent manslaughter in the United States doubled between 1963 and 1973. Concern over the rising crime rate presumably caused abolitionist sentiment to wane and support for the death penalty once again enjoys the support of a majority of the American people. While only a handful of executions have occurred since 1977, there has been an increase in the number of states restoring the death penalty. As a result, more than a thousand convicts are now under sentence of death in the United States, and the number grows with each passing week.

The crime rate's effect on the restorationist movement is an interesting *non sequitur*. A contemporary crime rate has no bearing on the validity of deterrence theory; executions do not become more of a deterrent merely because a nation's crime rate has increased. Crime rates and punishment have only a *political* relationship in that crime rates provide a context in which citizens and politicians may be willing to act *as if* the case for criminal deterrence was clear and proven. As a result, it should be stressed that scientific investigation into the deterrence hypothesis is only one of several actors in the dynamic process of abolition and restoration.

The history of this issue is cyclical. Although recent support for the death penalty has mounted rapidly, it could as easily subside. Apart from the seeming impermanence of these changes, the debate between abolitionists and restorationists concerning the deterrence question has centered upon a number of enduring questions, and it is to these more durable issues that this Article is devoted.

II. DIMENSIONS OF THE DETERRENCE HYPOTHESIS

The continuing debate over capital punishment is often muddied and convoluted because of fundamental confusion over the precise questions addressed. Therefore, any attempt to summarize this debate should begin with a brief description of some of the different issues and distinctions:

A. De Facto Versus De Jure

Research on the effect of the death penalty may center either upon the legal existence (*de jure*) of capital punishment, or its actual use (*de facto*). This distinction is important for two reasons. First, some have argued that the mere existence of the death penalty can have a deterrent effect, while others claim that only actual executions will deter. Second, even when two jurisdictions have the same *de jure* death penalty, there may be great variation between their *de facto* applications.

B. Severity, Certainty, and Celerity of Punishment

Various qualities of punishment might affect its deterrent effect. One of these is *severity*: Are severe punishments more of a deterrent than less severe penalties? Severity has been a classic focus of the deterrence debate since it concerns the relative deterrence value of executions on the one hand and long prison sentences on the other. A second quality of punishment is *certainty*: Is a punishment less of a deterrent if it is not regularly imposed? This distinction is similar to the *de jure* versus *de facto* distinction noted above. Still another quality of punishment is its *celerity*: Does the length of time between arrest and a punishment influence its deterrent value?

C. Extent of Public Knowledge of Legal Punishments?

Some researchers believe that the death penalty can be a deterrent even if its existence is only vaguely perceived. Others argue that the death penalty is a deterrent only if the public is vividly aware of its existence. This issue is of interest because convicted offenders tend not to know which offenses merit the death penalty, or whether the state in which they live has capital punishment. Since deterrence theory envisions that potential and actual offenders will weigh the consequences of their actions, offenders' knowledge of those consequences is of pivotal importance.

D. Rational Nature of the Criminal Act

There is disagreement about the degree to which the commission of a crime warranting the death penalty is a rational act. For example, while an assassination may be highly purposive, most homicides are unplanned, impulsive acts among intimates and acquaintances. Given the volatile nature of the offense, it is improbable that participants will consider the gravity of statutory punishments. Even if capital penalties are intellectually known, therefore, violent crimes are not compatible with the kind of dispassionate calculation envisioned by deterrence theory.

E. Rationales for Punishment

Societies can control or punish violent individuals by various means and for different purposes. *General deterrence* refers to the use of punishment to discourage criminal behavior of individuals other than the person convicted. *Specific deterrence* affects the future potential criminal activity of the convicted offender. *Incapacitation* makes offenders less of a threat through removal from society. *Retribution* uses punishment to satisfy the wronged party (narrowly defined as the victim or broadly defined as society) by making offenders suffer for their wrongdoing. The objective most often given for the death penalty is general deterrence. Both incapacitation or specific deterrence could be achieved by incarceration alone. The principle of retribution has adherents but, as already indicated, is less socially acceptable than the principle of deterrence.

F. Simultaneous Effects of Crime and Punishment

Any systematic test of deterrence theory must consider possible feedback effects between crime rates and punishments. For example, increased crime rates may overload the criminal justice system, reducing its efficiency. This could diminish the likelihood or speed of arrest, conviction, or execution of a capital offender. Any resulting decrease in deterrence would be due as much to the escalating crime rate as to the nature of statutory punishments. While specific qualities of a punishment may influence its effective deterrence, these qualities are not static but vary with the crime rate and other dynamic features of the criminal justice system.

G. Scientific Versus Philosophic Justifications

Much of the death penalty debate has centered upon *scientific* efforts to assess capital punishment's deterrent effects. Other approaches are, of course, moral and philosophical. These perspectives are influenced not by scientific data but by fundamental beliefs regarding the taking of human life as a form of punishment. For example, Gelles and Straus argue that support for the death penalty increasingly reflects a retributive orientation; that is, some people favor the death penalty not because they believe it deters crime but because they believe that offenders ought to suffer extreme punishment. The increasing significance of moral sentiments is also shown by a survey that found that seventy-five percent of those who oppose capital punishment would not change their position even in the face of conclusive proof that capital punishment deters homicide.

III. GENERAL APPROACHES TO THE DETERRENCE QUESTION

. . . Cross-sectional deterrence studies compare homicide rates at a single point in time. Such studies require a comparison of at least two jurisdictions. Both *de facto* and *de jure* questions have been studied using cross-sectional designs. The *de facto* issue could be studied by comparing either: (1) jurisdictions with a high execution risk (the probability of execution for a capital conviction) to those with a low execution risk, or (2) jurisdictions with many executions to jurisdictions with few executions within a specified period of time.

Cross-sectional studies of the *de jure* question compare jurisdictions that have abolished, or never had, the death penalty to those that have retained capital punishment. These *de jure* comparisons are typically made without regard to the *de facto* imposition of the death penalty. Cross-sectional studies look for linkages between higher execution risks, or retention of the death penalty, and differences in homicide rates.

Cross-sectional designs are inherently weak and subject to criticism on many grounds. For example, these studies assume that linkages between crime rates and penal structure result from the effect that the penal structure has on crime rates. However, high or low crime rates could have influenced the severity of punishment rather than the other way around. Limitations such as this have led most researchers to prefer longitudinal tests of the deterrence hypothesis. Longitudinal studies examine changes in homicide rates over time, making it feasible to disambiguate the causal relationship between crimes and punishments. Like cross-sectional studies, longitudinal studies can involve more than one jurisdiction, thus allowing increased control over unique factors in a single jurisdiction.

As with cross-sectional studies, longitudinal studies can examine either the *de facto* or the *de jure* question. *De facto* longitudinal studies compare changes in the homicide rate before and after executions or as the general risk of execution changes over time. Most longitudinal *de facto* research has studied only a single jurisdiction. *De jure* longitudinal studies compare homicide rates in one or more jurisdictions before and after the abolition or restoration of the death penalty.

Most tests of the deterrence hypothesis in this century have used one of the approaches just described. With the exceptions indicated below, very little research has extended beyond national boundaries. Most studies have examined only individual American states or aggregate United States statistics. With this limitation in mind, existing evidence on the deterrence hypothesis can be summarized briefly:

IV. SELECTED EVIDENCE ON THE EFFECTS OF CAPITAL PUNISHMENT

. . . Systematic deterrence research by social scientists began during a second "reform" era in the United States early in this century. Over a period of fifty years, social scientists conducted a number of analyses focused primarily on the *de jure* issue. The general conclusion drawn from these studies is captured by [T.] Sellin's much cited statement: "[T]he presence of the death penalty—in law or practice—does not influence homicide death rates." This body of *de jure* research has been criticized on several grounds, and, by the early 1970's, some social scientists seriously questioned the conclusion that the death penalty was not an effective deterrent. Critics of *de jure* research have pursued several different arguments:

> They have complained (1) that gross homicide rates are not sensitive enough to pick up deterrent effects, specifically, that the proportion of capital to noncapital homicides could be varying even when the overall homicide rate remains unaffected by abolition; (2) that the use of contiguous jurisdictions and before and after comparisons does not fully control for all factors which could conceivably be masking deterrent effects; and (3) that deterrent effects may not be "jurisdictionally specific" within a nation, that people may not be responsive to the presence of, or change in capital statutes in the particular state where they reside, as distinct from neighboring states.

These criticisms prompted new research designs using different methods. Relying chiefly on the statistical use of multiple regression, a number of studies have tried to control for differences across jurisdictions or over time that could influence homicide rates. In this way, researchers seek to determine how much of any observed change in homicide rate is due to the existence of capital punishment and actual executions or, alternately, to nonpunishment variables such as change in age structure and urbanization.

One of the first of these studies was conducted by [Isaac] Ehrlich. Using aggregate homicide data for the United States for the period 1933–70, Ehrlich analyzed the effect of the probability of execution upon homicide rates. Ehrlich also controlled for a variety of other factors, including unemployment, age distribution, and per capita income. Based upon this analysis, Ehrlich concluded that executions did have a deterrent effect and, specifically, that between seven and eight homicides were deterred by each execution.

Although Ehrlich's work found an eager audience among many policy makers, a number of researchers using similar and equally sophisticated methods have extensively criticized his work . . . . Because Ehrlich's work is one of very few studies to find any support for the deterrence hypothesis, it has garnered widespread scientific interest.

Attempted replications of Ehrlich's work using similar methods (multivariate analyses and econometric methods) have failed, however, to find a deterrence effect. For example, [Colin] Loftin did an elaborate ecological analysis of crime rates and social characteristics in the United States. When social and economic variables such as poverty, education, and family structure were controlled, Loftin's study found little or no evidence for the deterrence hypothesis. Similarly, [N.] Brier and [S.] Fienberg used econometric models to test for a deterrence effect, and they concluded that the claims made in Ehrlich's 1975 study were not supported by the evidence. Finally, some of the most interesting longitudinal evidence involves separate time-series analyses from five different states examining the relationship between execution risk and homicide rates. Here, again, the evidence runs counter to deterrence theory in three of the five states examined.

In recent research, there is even some evidence for what might be called an *"antideterrent"* effect. A fine-grained study by [William] Bowers and [Glen] Pierce examined monthly homicide rates in New York State between 1907 and 1963 and found an average *increase* of two homicides in the month after an execution. This finding led Bowers and Pierce to postulate, in direct opposition to the deterrence hypothesis, a "brutalizing" effect, that is, that executions might increase rather than deter homicides. In summary, recent studies of the *de facto* issue do not contradict the long-standing conclusion from *de jure* research that the death penalty has no consistent, demonstrable deterrent effect.

A number of specific issues continue to bear upon new research regarding deterrence theory. Two of these are of generic importance, and recent evidence on each can be summarized briefly . . . .

B. Does the Use of Contiguous Jurisdictions, Along with the Use of Before and After Comparisons Fail to Control for All Factors Which Could Mask Deterrent Effects?

Ernest van den Haag, a strong critic of much deterrence research, has argued that "[h]omicide rates do not depend exclusively on penalties any more than other crime rates. A number of conditions which influence the propensity to crime, demographic, economic, or social, . . . may influence the homicide rate." To control for these factors, some investigators have compared only presumably similar jurisdictions such as contiguous states.

Because of differences between even contiguous jurisdictions, critics have claimed that this procedure provides inadequate controls. In response, [William] Bailey compared states with and without the death penalty, while controlling for two socioeconomic and five demographic variables. As an additional control, retentionist and abolitionist states with similar rates of aggravated assault were compared to hold constant potentially significant etiological factors. Regardless of which control variables were included, Bailey found retentionist states had higher murder rates than abolitionist states. Again, the evidence runs contrary to the deterrence hypothesis. Therefore, while the inclusion of additional control variables would certainly have improved many studies, additional controls would not appear to have changed the conclusion that the death penalty does not deter crime.

V. GENERAL AND SPECIFIC DETERRENCE HYPOTHESES

According to the general deterrence hypothesis in its *de jure* form, *ceteris paribus*, abolition of capital punishment increases homicide rates.

The *de facto* form of the hypothesis is concerned with actual executions rather than changes in policy or law. While *de facto* research has incontestable importance, the *de jure* issue is inherently interesting since it is central to policy decisions. In addition to what is here called the general deterrence hypothesis, a number of more precise deterrence hypotheses can be derived.

A. Offense Deterrence

Criminal penalties, and therefore their hypothesized deterrent effects, are offense-specific. Where it exists, the death penalty is prescribed for a society's most grievous offenses. In terms of deterrence theory, the death penalty should have its most direct effects on the offenses for which the death penalty can be imposed.

This specific hypothesis, which might be called "offense deterrence," postulates that capital punishment will have its most perceptible effects on capital crimes, the offenses executions are imposed to deter. In terms of offense deterrence, the effect of capital punishment on lesser crimes is less predictable. If the hypothesis of offense deterrence has merit, abolition of the death penalty should be followed by increases in capital offenses. In addition, the increases in these capital offenses should be larger and more consistent than any other post-abolition crime rate changes.

B. Residual Deterrence

If the general deterrence hypothesis is correct, abolition should be followed by homicide rate increases. There is disagreement, however, about the temporal aspects of this relationship and, specifically, when the increases can be expected to occur. *De jure* case studies have uniformly found that the abolition of the death penalty does not produce any sudden or dramatic changes in homicide rates. While this result is frequently cited as evidence against the deterrence hypothesis, some have argued that it may reflect only public ignorance of changes in capital statutes. Individuals, ignorant of changes, may continue to be deterred as if capital punishment still existed.

Although research indicates that public ignorance of the law is widespread, it seems reasonable that people might be better informed about capital punishment because of the extremity of the punishment, extensive media attention, and frequent controversy. Some deterrence theorists still believe, however, that genuine deterrence effects are masked by public ignorance. [Accordomg to van den Haag] "A constant homicide rate, despite abolition, may occur because of unawareness and not because of lack of deterrence: people remain deterred for a lengthy interval by the severity of the penalty in the past, or by the severity of penalties used in similar circumstances nearby."

This hypothesis posits the existence of what might be called "residual deterrence," a deterrent effect that lingers after the death penalty is abolished. Residual deterrence may complicate studies of the death penalty, but it does not, as some have implied, make systematic evaluation impossible. For example, even if residual deterrence exists, it should weaken over time as more people become aware that the law has challenged; residual deterrence should be strong in the first year after abolition, weaker five years later, and weaker still as time goes on. As a result, if general deterrence theory is correct, one would expect to see progressive increases in homicide rates as residual deterrence erodes in the years following abolition.

C. Vicarious Deterrence

A parallel argument, that citizens are deterred by the existence of the death penalty in adjacent jurisdictions, might be called "vicarious deterrence." If deterrence is not jurisdiction-specific, people living in a state without the death penalty might be deterred by an incorrect belief in the possibility of capital punishment. If vicarious deterrence exists, the existence of any capital statute could affect citizens in retentionist and abolitionist states alike. As a result, the effects of abolition might be invisible in *de jure* studies conducted in contiguous states.

The possibility of vicarious deterrence lends increased importance to cross-national research. If vicarious deterrence has validity, one would expect to find invisible or "masked" deterrence in *de jure* studies local jurisdictions, but not in studies of independent societies. A cross-national study therefore provides a relatively pure test of the *de jure* hypothesis, unaffected by vicarious deterrence, because it seems extremely unlikely that legislation in one nation would have any vicarious deterrent effects in another nation.

Despite their obvious importance, cross-national studies of deterrence are relatively rare and large-sample comparisons are almost unknown. In the early 1930's, the (British) Royal Commission on Capital Punishment heard extensive testimony from expert witnesses representing European and Commonwealth nations. Based upon the available evidence, the Commission concluded: "Capital Punishment may be abolished in this country [Britain] without endangering life or property or impairing the security of society." Almost two decades later, the Commission was re-established for a more extensive, four-year examination of the question. The new Commission affirmed the earlier conclusion: "There is no clear evidence in any of the figures we have examined that the abolition of capital punishment has led to an increase in the homicide rate, or that its reintroduction has led to its fall." The 1962 European Committee on Crime Problems supported this conclusion.

The trend toward abolition increased during the 1960's but there have been no systematic efforts during this period to collect and evaluate data from a large sample of abolitionist nations. Individual case studies vary greatly in their procedures and use of controlled comparisons. As a result, existing cross-national evidence suffers from a confusing patchwork of results.

While a cross-national test of the deterrence hypothesis is not without complications, the principal obstacle has been the absence of longitudinal offense data from a large sample of societies. A cross-national archive of data on rates of homicide and four other offenses now exists. Called the Comparative Crime Data File (CCDF), this archive contains time series data beginning in 1900 for 110 nations and forty-four major international cities. With appropriate methodological caution, the CCDF makes possible a large number of comparative investigations, including research on deterrence theory. Data from the CCDF have been used to examine the effects of war on rates of violent crime, urban homicide rates, and a number of generic methodological issues. Because of the depth and breadth of its data, the CCDF offers considerable potential for systematic research on deterrence theory.

VI. CROSS-NATIONAL DATA ON FOURTEEN CASES OF ABOLITION

A first step in any cross-national test involves identifying sample abolition cases. This task is more complicated than one might imagine since the degree of abolition may vary from one society to another. Some may abolish capital punishment for mortal offenses generally but retain it for specific crimes, such as the murder of a prison guard by a prisoner serving a life term. Other nations may eliminate the death penalty but provide for its revival during civil emergencies or martial law. The de jure question is therefore complicated by the need for discrete classification when, in fact, shades of abolition may be present.

One solution to this classification problem is to roughly define a jurisdiction as "abolitionist" if capital punishment is generally prohibited, even if allowed for extraordinary crimes. It should be emphasized that this is a de jure classification; nations in which no executions have occurred for long periods of time cannot be considered abolitionist under this definition if capital punishment remains the law. A further problem in choosing abolition cases is determining the date of the abolition; it could be the date on which the penal code is changed or the date on which the change becomes effective.

After examining different lists of abolitionist nations and dates, we adopted a modified form of the classifications made by [W.] Bowers and [J.] Joyce. The list was compared to offense rate data from the Comparative Crime Data File. This process yielded a total of fourteen sets of time series data for twelve distinct cases of abolition. In two cases, Austria and Finland, separate records for Vienna and Helsinki provided the opportunity to "replicate" national cases with urban data.

Before presenting the results of these comparisons, it should be emphasized that most efforts to isolate the independent effects of abolition err on the side of simplification. Offense rates are driven by many factors, and single-variable evaluations understate this complexity by pretending that these other forces do not exist. For example, a number of abolitions occurred around war time, and recent research indicates that wars frequently elevate post-war rates of violent crime. Similarly, vast demographic changes—such as the coming of age of individuals from the post-World War II "baby boom" cohort—can greatly inflate offense rates or otherwise complicate efforts to assess the effects of legal change. In cross-national studies of deterrence, therefore, the effect of abolition is inevitably muddied by other changes . . . .

VII. CROSS-NATIONAL TESTS OF SPECIFIC DETERRENCE HYPOTHESES

Data from this sample of fourteen cases can be analyzed in a number of ways to provide a test of the *general deterrence* theory prediction that abolition of the death penalty causes a perceptible increase in homicide rates. More precise deterrence hypotheses can be examined as well. *Vicarious deterrence*, the alleged geographic spillover of deterrence from retentionist jurisdictions to abolitionist jurisdictions, is controlled by the examination of sovereign nations. *Residual deterrence*, the alleged temporal spillover of deterrence from retentionist years to abolitionist years, can be tested by examining post-abolition time intervals of progressively greater lengths. *Offense deterrence*, the prediction that post-abolition changes will be most conspicuous in rates of capital offenses, can be tested by contrasting homicide with several noncapital crimes.

A. General Deterrence

Table I depicts an initial comparison of the short-term effects of abolition. The percentages in this table indicate the increase or decrease in homicide rates between the year prior to abolition and the year after the abolition. The homicide rates upon which the percentages are based are included as a cautionary feature. In some cases, such as New Zealand, the homicide rate is so low in absolute terms that the addition of a single homicide can double the national offense rate. The precise indicators in this comparison—offenses known, convictions, etc.—are also shown since these differ for the fourteen cases.

With these cautions in mind, the picture in Table I is one of little change, and, in fact, eight of the fourteen cases (fifty-seven percent) show a homicide rate decrease in the year following abolition while only five (thirty-six percent) show an increase. In this crude short-term comparison, therefore, there is no evidence for the deterrence hypothesis. *De jure* abolition appears to have had little effect and, if anything, appears to slightly decrease homicide rates.

TABLE 1 HOMICIDE RATE LEVELS BEFORE AND AFTER ABOLITION: ONE YEAR COMPARISONS

Jurisdiction	Date of Abolition	Offense Indicator*	One Year Pre-Abolition Homicide Rate	One Year Post-Abolition Homicide Rate	% Change
Austria	1968	e	.72	.71	−1%
England and Wales	1965	a	.36	.35	−3
Finland	1949	a	1.05	.72	−31
Helsinki	1949	a	1.96	1.90	−3
Israel	1954	a	4.00	1.72	−57
Italy	1890	a	13.30	12.94	−3
Sweden	1921	b	.43	.15	−65
Switzerland	1942	d	45.25	35.65	−21
Vienna	1968	e	.93	.93	0
Canada	1967	a	1.10	1.52	38
Denmark	1930	c	33.89	35.68	5
Netherlands Antilles	1957	a	13.19	20.32	54
New Zealand	1961	b	.04	.08	100**
Norway	1905	b	.35	.39	11

*Key to Offense Indicators:
  a = homicide offenses known
  b = murder, manslaughter, or homicide convictions
  c = violent offenses known
  d = violent offenses convictions
  e = criminal statistics

**Because of an extremely low base rate, this 100% increase reflects a change from 1 to 2 cases.

B. Residual Deterrence

If one subscribes to the hypothesis of residual deterrence, however, the comparison in Table 1 is inconclusive. The effects on deterrence still could be present though masked by public ignorance of abolition, particularly in the first year following this change. For this reason, Table 2 compares longer intervals. It is unlikely that residual deterrence could continue to affect behavior five years after abolition, and the hypothesis becomes even less plausible over longer intervals. The five-year statistics in Table 2 compare the five years of homicide data before and after abolition. This comparison does not include all fourteen cases since some entries in the CCDF did not have data for all of these years. The "maximum possible" comparison in this table reflects the longest intervals before and after abolition for which homicide data were available.

Again, in this comparison there is little evidence for the deterrence hypothesis in general or residual deterrence in particular. In the five-year comparison, half of the ten cases for which the comparison can be made show homicide rate increases following abolition while half show decreases. There is even less support for the deterrence hypothesis when longer intervals are examined. When intervals of maximum possible length are compared, only five of the fourteen (thirty-six percent) cases show homicide rate increases after abolition, while eight

TABLE 2   HOMICIDE RATE CHANGES BEFORE AND AFTER ABOLITION: LONGER TRENDS

Jurisdiction	One Year	Five Year Means[a]	Maximum Possible Comparison[b]	Years Before Abolition/Years After
Austria	−1%	32%	9%	(15,5)
Canada	38	63	67	(5,6)
Denmark	5	—	4	(9,2)
England and Wales	−3	18	27	(14,7)
Finland	−31	−40	−59	(22,18)
Helsinki	−3	−27	−57	(22,18)
Israel	−57	−53	−65	(5,16)
Italy	−3	−5	−30	(10,24)
Netherlands Antilles	54	—	−4	(2,13)
New Zealand	100	117	0	(10,11)
Norway	11	—	−24	(2,35)
Sweden	−65	—	−63	(1,28)
Switzerland	−21	−36	−46	(13,28)
Vienna	0	94	85	(15,5)

[a] Comparison of mean offense levels for five-year periods before and after abolition.

[b] Comparison of mean offense levels for maximum length periods before and after abolition.

(fifty-seven percent) show decreases. This finding runs counter to the hypothesis of residual deterrence. Since homicide rate decreases are found most consistently when long intervals are compared, the idea that deterrence progressively erodes in the years following abolition seems untenable.

C. Offense Deterrence

A final comparison addresses the question of whether capital punishment has specific offense deterrence. The breadth of data in the CCDF makes it possible to contrast changes in capital offenses with changes in noncapital crimes. A deterrence theorist could conceivably argue that the patterns in Tables 1 and 2 conceal massive downward trends in crime generally and that capital offense rates might be falling more slowly than noncapital offense rates. The key test of offense deterrence, therefore, is whether homicide rate increases or decreases after abolition are greater, in absolute or relative terms, than increases or decreases for noncapital crimes.

Table 3 examines the offense deterrence hypothesis by comparing changes before and after abolition for three time periods—one year, five years, and the maximum interval possible—for homicide and five non-capital offenses. Median offense rate changes for all cases are shown at the bottom of Table 3. Missing percentages indicate that the comparison could not be made for this offense during this particular interval using the data in the CCDF.

In general, the data run strongly counter to the hypothesis of offense deterrence. No matter which time interval is examined, noncapital offense rates show increases larger than the changes observed for homicide rates. While noncapital crime rates increased following abolition—perhaps as a result of demographic or other changes—rates of homicide were stationary or declining. This difference between capital and noncapital rate changes is striking: it is difficult to imagine a result that more clearly contradicts the theory of deterrence. These cross-national findings fail to support the offense deterrence hypothesis and, in fact, provide strategic evidence that the death penalty has no discernible effect on homicide rates.

VIII. SUMMARY AND CONCLUSION

If punishment is a more effective deterrent than the alternative of life imprisonment, its abolition ought to be followed by homicide rate increases. The evidence examined here fails to support and, indeed, repeatedly contradicts this proposition. In this cross-national sample, abolition was followed more often than not by absolute decreases in

TABLE 3 COMPARISON OF HOMICIDE LEVELS BEFORE AND AFTER ABOLITION USING OTHER OFFENSES AS CONTROL VARIABLES

Jurisdiction	One Year						Five Years						Maximum Years Possible[a]					
	Homicide	M[b]	R	A	Ro	T	Homicide	M[b]	R	A	Ro	T	Homicide	M[b]	R	A	Ro	T
Austria[c]	−1%	+24	+12	−2	−9	+17	+32%	+57	+5	+8	+44	+55	+9%	+42	−3	+6	+72	+109
Canada	+38	+107	+32	+20	+42	—	+63	+11	+57	+76	+73	—	+67	+21	+68	+79	+78	—
Denmark	+5	—	0	+5	—	+8	—	—	—	—	—	—	+4	—	+25	—	—	+34
England	−3	+57	+23	+13	+44	+9	+18	+58	+56	+73	+102	+36	+27	+30	+86	+196	+248	—
Finland	−31	−27	+95	−10	−46	−43	−40	−44	+28	—	−80	−70	−59	−63	+102	—	−47	−9
Israel	−57	—	—	+40	−55	−6	−53	—	—	—	−75	+8	−65	—	—	—	−74	+60
Italy	−3	—	—	−10	+31	+4	−5	—	—	—	+32	—	−30	—	—	—	+35	—
Neth Antilles	+54	—	−50	—	+51	+13	—	—	—	—	—	—	−4	—	−20	—	+87	+18
New Zealand	+100	—	+11	+27	−43	−4	+117	—	+16	+46	−46	+7	0	—	—	—	−12	+46
Norway	+11	—	+36	−13	—	−10	—	—	—	—	—	—	−24	—	+100	−7	—	+10
Sweden	−65	—	−58	−33	−36	—	—	—	—	—	—	—	−63	—	+123	−3	+19	—
Switzerland	−21	—	+12	−21	+	+7	+36	—	—	−36	—	−3	−46	—	—	—	—	−15
Helsinki	−3	−35	+1	+3	−52	−42	−27	−42	+23	—	−86	+79	−57	−55	+73	—	−71	−43
Vienna	0	+30	+32	−2	−11	+22	+94	+100	+6	+20	+49	+53	+85	+138	−3	+33	+100	+145
Median	−2%	+27	+12	−2	−11	+6	+7%	+34	+23	+33	+32	+22	−14%	+26	+71	+20	+35	+26

[a] For the number of years included in this comparison, see Table 2.
[b] Crime types: M (Manslaughter), R (Rape), A (Assault), Ro (Robbery), T (Theft).
[c] Indicator Type and Year of Abolition are given in Table 1.

homicide rates. Further, the homicide rates of these nations also decreased relative to rates of noncapital offenses after abolition. Both of these findings hold true whether comparisons are made for short, medium, or the longest feasible time periods.

This cross-national research design controls for some possible defects in previous studies, including *vicarious deterrence*, the alleged jurisdictional nonspecificity of capital punishment. The results of this comparative analysis contradict general deterrence theory and also reject specific hypotheses derived from this theory, such as *residual deterrence* and *offense deterrence*. These findings lend new weight to the body of research running counter to deterrence theory:

> In the face of the mounting evidence against any deterrent advantage of the death penalty, proponents increasingly find themselves affirming more idiosyncratic explanations for the effects they presume the death penalty has, but which research has yet to reveal . . . . With each new set of findings their task becomes more arduous and their arguments become less plausible.

As indicated earlier, empirical evidence on deterrent effects is only one participant in the debate over capital punishment. Public attitudes toward crime and criminals, moral sentiments, and changing intellectual fashions also play major roles. The function of scientific inquiry in this debate, while limited, is also important. Research like that presented in this Article addresses deterrence, the most pervasive justification for capital punishment.

Combined with previous research, evidence from this comparative analysis consistently contradicts testable elements of deterrence theory. While there may be some persuasive reasons for capital punishment— such as retribution or economics—the deterrence of potential offenders is not among them. Other justifications for the death penalty can and presumably will be debated, but the deterrence hypothesis must be regarded at this time as scientifically insupportable.

Although this Article is grounded in empirical research, the evidence complements a very different argument, one grounded in logic and philosophy rather than science. Inquiry in this area addresses a question of literal life and death significance. In the United States the populations on death rows grow rapidly, and the debate over the death penalty is anything but abstract. In addition, the deterrence hypothesis is currently under discussion in many courts and state legislatures.

Clearly, the stakes in this debate are unusually high. Precisely for this reason, it seems fair to assume that the burden of proof is upon the restorationists to show that a deterrent effect does exist; unless, of course, our society is prepared to shift from deterrence to retribution or economic arguments as justifications for capital punishment. For the same reason, this burden of proof should require unusually exacting standards of evidence. Given the extreme and irrevocable nature of capital punishment, deterrence should be accepted as a justification for the death penalty only if this effect can be shown to be reliable, consistent, and strong. If the deterrent effect is anything less, executions cannot produce anything other than the deaths of the executed.

Empirical support for the deterrence hypothesis, including the evidence presented here, obviously cannot meet this exacting standard. The evidence runs contrary to deterrence theory, and, while more research can of course be done, the mere existence of this consistently contrary evidence demonstrates that the deterrent effect—if one exists at all—is not reliable, consistent, or strong. If the deterrent effect had these robust qualities, the effect surely would have surfaced vividly and repeatedly in these investigations . . . .

The issue of the exceptional burden of proof therefore provides common ground for logical and scientific arguments about the death penalty. A humane and rational society should consider taking human life only if there is overwhelming evidence that this act will save lives by deterring violence. As this comparative study and other research make abundantly clear, there is no overwhelming evidence for deterrence, and the contrary conclusions of existing research suggest that such evidence for deterrence will not be forthcoming. In the absence of thoroughly persuasive evidence, it seems inconceivable that our society would be willing to execute people in pursuit of what is almost certainly a hopeless objective. □

NOTES AND QUESTIONS

1. What are the strengths and weaknesses of the research method used in this study? Did you find the conclusions convincing? How would you go about studying the deterrent effect of the death penalty in the United States? Some states have the death penalty, some do not. You could compare the murder rates in the states that have the death penalty with the murder rates in states that don't have the death penalty. Or you could trace the murder rate in states as they have either adopted or done away with the death penalty. Methodologically, what are the strengths and weaknesses of such approaches? Some authors have argued that it is impossible to make a persuasive statistical case whether the death penalty does or does not have a deterrent effect. See, e.g., Ernest van den Haag, "On Deterrence and the Death Penalty," 60 *Journal of Criminal Law, Criminology & Police Science,* 141, 146 (1969). What are the special problems faced if we try to prove why someone did *not* do some particular act?

If we cannot prove that the death penalty deters, why do so many white Americans favor it? See M. Dwayne Smith and James Wright, "Capital Punishment and Public Opinion in the Post-*Furman* Era: Trends and Analysis," 12 *Sociological Spectrum* 127 (1992). Given the widespread support for the death penalty why have some state legislatures refused to impose it for major crimes? See Larry W. Koch and John F. Galliher, "Michigan's Continuing Abolition of the Death Penalty and the Conceptual Components of Symbolic Legislation," 2 *Social & Legal Studies* 323 (1993); Timony J. Flanagan, Debra

Cohen, and Pauline Gasdow Brennan, "Crime Control Ideology Among New York State Legislators," 18 *Legislative Studies Quarterly* 411 (1993); Herb Haines, "Flawed Executions, the Anti-Death Penalty Movement, and the Politics of Capital Punishment," 39 *Social Problems* 125 (1992).

2. Deterrence has a variety of dimensions, including severity, speed, and certainty of the punishment. The death penalty debate is primarily about the severity issue: Will the most severe punishment, the death penalty, deter more than a less severe punishment—life in prison, for example? The claim is often heard that the severity of the death penalty has no deterrent effect because there is such a long time between the crime and the punishment. The execution process, in the United States, is extremely slow. In 1992, Robert Alton Harris was executed in California, for a crime committed more than a decade before. Many of the men and women on death row have been there for ten, twelve, or even fifteen years.

The Supreme Court has shown signs of wanting to limit the number of appeals that can be filed by death row inmates, and in general of wanting to make the procedures faster and more efficient. See *McCleskey v. Zant*.[142] If the courts were successful in decreasing the average time between sentencing and execution to, say, five years, do you think the deterrent effect of capital punishment would be increased? Why? How would you go about testing your hypothesis?

3. Most people would agree that the death penalty is a worse penalty than imprisonment, even life imprisonment. It is no wonder, then, that economists (among others) insist that death must be at least something of a deterrent. Water can only flow down, not up, and they would argue that increased severity has to deter.

4. There is an enormous literature on the death penalty, and on the administration of the death penalty in the United States in particular. See, for example, Robert Weisberg, "Deregulating Death," 1983 *Supreme Court Review* 305.

30. *The Deterrence Curve*

Lawrence M. Friedman

Lawrence M. Friedman, *The Legal System: a Social Science Perspective*
(New York: Russell Sage Foundation, 1975)

☐ In any case, there is no simple, linear relationship between sanctions and sanctioned behavior. Suppose we plotted on a graph the rate of overtime parking at given levels of fine. As fines rose, we would expect the violation rate to fall, but we do *not* expect a perfect straight line on the graph. Doubling a $5 fine, in other words, will (enforcement staying constant) increase compliance, but compliance will not necessarily double. A threat of twenty years in jail will probably not be twice as effective as a threat of ten years. We expect some sort of curvilinear

142. 111 S. Ct. 1454 (1991).

relationship, a gradual flattening out. At some point, new inputs of fine will produce less and less new compliance, and one may or may not reach a zero effect. This is because, as compliance rises, there are fewer people to affect, and those few are the most difficult cases. One approaches a saturation point, a point of diminishing returns. This is another reason why capital punishment seems to have so little effect in the United States; murder is so heavily sanctioned by peers, conscience, and the state that the pool of potential murderers is small. Also, a person or group may become so saturated with punishment stimuli that nothing worse or more punishing is possible. A man about to be shot will risk anything; he has nothing to lose. His tormenters have lost the power to deter him with additional actions or threats. Totalitarian societies can reach this point. Gestapo tactics, concentration camps, and indiscriminate shooting may produce an atmosphere where many people feel life is intolerable, and nothing could be worse. Hence, more terror will have no effect; it merely drives people to join the resistance. If even the innocent face random, senseless terror, then revolution seems little more fearful than the risks of everyday life.

There are, alas, ample historical examples of such societies of terror. Gresham Sykes has made a similar point about prison life. He studied prisoners in the New Jersey State Prison and found that they misbehaved at what he thought a very high rate. The custodians, "far from being omnipotent rulers," were "engaged in a continuous struggle to maintain order"; in the struggle, they frequently failed. One reason was that officials were "dangerously close to the point where the stock of legitimate punishments has been exhausted and . . . the few punishments which are left have lost their potency." In this prison, Sykes felt, the curve had flattened out.[143]

Each legal act will have its own deterrence curve. Perhaps no two curves are exactly the same. That is, any intervention of the legal system—any rule or order communicated to one or more subjects and buttressed by a sanction, positive or negative—will affect behavior more or less, depending on the level of sanction threatened or promised. Many factors affect the slope and the shape of this deterrence curve. The following are some of the basic factors:

    I. Characteristics of the threat or promise
       A. The nature of the sanction. Is it a reward or a punishment? Is it light or severe?

143. Gresham Sykes, *The Society of Captives: A Study of a Maximum Security Prison* (Princeton, N.J.: Princeton University Press, 1958), pp. 42, 51. Sykes also felt that "the reward side of the picture has been largely stripped away." The prison gave away all its privileges at the outset—time off for good behavior, for example, was subtracted from the prisoner's sentence the day he entered prison. The prisoner therefore found himself "unable to win any significant gains by means of compliance."

B. The perceived risk of suffering a negative sanction or enjoying a positive one.

C. The speed at which the sanction is delivered. Is it immediate or far in the future?

II. Characteristics of the persons subject to the sanction

A. How many people are subject to the sanction? It is easier, for example, to achieve high enforcement of rules that apply only to a few prominent people or entities.

B. The personality type of the subjects, or the culture in which the subjects live.

III. Characteristics of the behavior to be controlled

A. How easy or difficult is it to detect and visit punishment on the behavior? For example, it is very hard to stamp out dangerous thoughts, much easier to burn dangerous books.

B. What is the nature of the demand for the behavior to be controlled? Some behavior is hard to control, because people find it so desirable that they will not readily give it up, or so unpleasant that the law cannot easily stimulate it. For some behavior, there is strong and relatively inelastic demand; sanctions have comparatively little effect; other behavior is quite elastic and responds very quickly to sanctions. □

NOTES AND QUESTIONS

1. Some studies, as we have seen, suggest that capital punishment does not in fact deter murder, compared to, for example, life imprisonment. Assuming this is true, does the concept of the deterrence curve help explain this finding?

2. The "deterrence curve" is presumably different for each particular crime or offense. Let us assume that one overtime parking violation out of five is caught. If we have a fine of $1, probably most people will simply park and take their chances. At higher levels, we will get more compliance. If we start towing away cars, we get still more. But at some point, it will be almost impossible to get more "bang" out of more severe punishments.

What would the deterrence curve look like for rape? armed robbery? embezzlement? shooting deer out of season? gambling in a state where gambling is against the law?

3. It should be clear by now that *all* studies of deterrence have their difficulties, and in particular all of them are bedeviled by problems of measurement and data. See, for example, James A. Inciardi, "The Uniform Crime Reports: Some Considerations on Their Shortcomings and Utility," 6 *Public Data Use* 3 (1978); Larry J. Cohen and Mark I. Lichbach, "Alternative Measures of Crime: A Statistical Evaluation," 23 *Sociological Quarterly* 253 (1982). On the special problems of measurement of crimes committed by juveniles (or by juveniles and adults), see Franklin E. Zimring, "Kids, Groups and Crime: Some Implications of a Well-Known Secret," 72 *Journal of Criminal Law & Criminology* 867 (1981).

4. Are studies of deterrence too mechanistic? Do they tend too much to treat criminals as rational calculators? Do they treat citizens as if they were constantly and rationally toting up the likelihood of getting caught and what

the punishment would be, and carefully measuring this against the amount of benefit or swag they would be likely to get from their crime?

The criticism—that this is too simple a picture or is just plain wrong—has been frequently leveled in particular against economists like Ehrlich who study deterrence. See Richard Lempert, "Desert and Deterrence: An Assessment of the Moral Bases of the Case for Capital Punishment," 79 *Michigan Law Review* 1177 (1981). Lempert quotes a famous passage from Sir James Fitzjames Stephen, a 19th century British legal historian. Stephen said:

> Some men probably abstain from murder because they fear that if they committed murder they would be hanged. Hundreds of thousands abstain from it because they regard it with horror. One great reason why they regard it with horror is that murderers are hanged.

Lempert remarks:

> The argument is reasonable. It may be that the main benefit of capital punishment is that it teaches people that it is wrong to kill. But the opposite position is also reasonable. It may be that capital punishment teaches people that life is not sacred and that killing is not always a moral wrong. (p. 1190)

Which view strikes you as more likely?

For another kind of attack on the general behavioral theories that underlie research on such subjects as sanctions, see the *Concluding Word* at the end of this Chapter.

5. What role does personality play in explaining why people commit crimes? At one time, many people, including scientists, believed there were "born criminals" and even that there were physical signs that gave the game away. The anthropologist E. A. Hooton, in a book published in 1939, noted that criminals seemed to have "low and sloping foreheads;" their noses tended to be "higher in the root and in the bridge, and more frequently undulating or concavo-convex" than normal people, and rapists had "narrow foreheads and elongated, pinched noses." E. A. Hooton, *Crime and the Man* 124, 367 (N.Y.: Greenwood Press, 1939). See Lawrence M. Friedman, *Crime and Punishment in American History* 335–39 (New York: Basic Books, 1993).

Serious scholars have largely given up the idea of physical signs of crime, but social and personality theories are another question. Many people have used social variables—unemployment rates, poverty, peer group cultures, and the like—to account for crime and deviance. Michael R. Gottfredson and Travis Hirschi, in *A General Theory of Crime* (Stanford: Stanford University Press, 1990), frame their theory in terms of "low self-control." Criminal acts, they argue, "provide *immediate* gratification of desires." Criminal acts are quick, exciting but require little skill or planning. However, they offer "few or meager long-term benefits." They appeal, then, to people with "low self-control," who tend to be "adventuresome, active, and physical. Those with high levels of self-control tend to be cautious, cognitive, and verbal" (p. 89).

How would you go about testing an idea like this? Does the theory strike you as plausible? Would you expect those who participate in various types of crime to be the same kinds of people?

6. The law has more tricks up its sleeves than sanctions (both rewards and punishments). One way of getting compliance is by structuring a situation so that compliance is easier than non-compliance. Karl Llewellyn, the famous legal theorist, who died in 1962, liked to talk about the highway "cloverleaf." This, of course, is a method of structuring entrance to and exit from a major highway or freeway. Legislatures could pass laws regulating or prohibiting left turns across busy lanes of oncoming traffic. However, these laws require police and traffic courts to enforce them. The cloverleaf is more effective. The roadway or ramp sharply turns off the main highway to the right, and then turns to cross over the road on a bridge, or under it through a tunnel. If the lanes of the main highway are separated by a fence or a ditch, it is almost impossible to make an illegal left turn. Also, highway engineers can force drivers to slow from superhighway speeds by the way they bank the cloverleaf. The socially desired behavior—slowing down—becomes far easier than deviance for the typical motorist.

The legal system is full of devices like the "cloverleaf." There are all sorts of structures, forms and arrangements that force "compliance" along certain lines or make non-compliance difficult. For example, federal income tax is withheld from wages. This makes it much harder to avoid paying what is owed. For a brief period automobiles would not start unless seat-belts were fastened. If anything, this "cloverleaf" was too effective and proved to be very unpopular. Some kinds of "cloverleaf" might make a dramatic difference to law enforcement: rather than crack down on drunk drivers, we could build cars that won't start if a driver's breath contains detectable amounts of alcohol. Instead of locking people up in jails, we might order them to be only in certain places and attach an electronic device to their bodies so that they may be monitored wherever they go.

What other kinds of "cloverleaf" can you think of in the criminal justice system? Can you think of examples on the civil side of the legal system?

31. Interrupted Time Series Studies of Deterrence of Drinking and Driving

H. Laurence Ross

in John Hagan (ed.) *Deterrence Reconsidered: Methodological Innovations* (Beverly Hills: Sage Publications, 1982).

☐ . . . Drinking and driving has been recognized as a cause of traffic crashes for many years, and punitive law has long been regarded as a promising tool in its control. Concern with the problem has increased over time as information has accumulated concerning the costs of crashes and the role of alcohol in their causation, and dissatisfaction has mounted with regard to the effectiveness of classical control efforts. This situation has led in recent years to a large number of efforts worldwide to redefine and reinforce the laws dealing with drinking and driving, per-

mitting the application of quasi-experimental designs, notably interrupted time series analysis, in evaluating the results obtained.

These efforts occur in a uniquely fortunate research setting for
investigating deterrence through law. An important characteristic of
drinking-and-driving law in this regard is its relative divorce from
other systems of social control. One is less likely to confuse legal
effects in this area with those due to custom and morality than in the
study of more traditional criminality. Paradoxically, the relative triviality of traffic law in general, which in the past led to its general disregard by criminology, makes its study more enlightening in understanding the effects of legal sanctions.

Another important advantage of drinking-and-driving studies is the
availability of relatively good-quality indexes of the target behavior
provided by series of fatal crashes, especially when refined according
to time of day and number of vehicles involved. Single-vehicle fatal
crashes at night overwhelmingly involve the presence of alcohol, and
changes in indexes like these reflect well the extent of alcohol-influenced driving. Because fatalities are involved, the "dark figure" problem frequently found in studies of traditional criminality is avoided.
Moreover, the gathering of those figures by hospitals and health
departments on a regular basis provides data series that are usually
insulated from political forces with interests in demonstrating results
one way or the other.

A particularly attractive advantage of drinking-and-driving law
studies is that innovations in this type of law very often meet the criteria for utilization in interrupted time series analysis. These criteria
include an independent variable that changes abruptly at a single point
in time, along with dependent variables that are expected to shift
sharply and simultaneously and that are reliably measured over an
extended time period. In the case at hand the independent variable is a
change in the drinking-and-driving law, which usually has its inception
at a particular date, and the dependent variables are the crash series
along with other series useful in interpreting the mechanism of
changes, such as traffic mileage data and sales of alcoholic beverages.
Deterrence theory usually predicts abrupt declines in the dependent
variables like those diagrammed schematically in the bottom line of
Figure 1. The left- hand diagram indicates a change expected to be lasting whereas the right-hand one indicates a temporary change that might
be expected if the deterrent stimulus were subsequently removed or
lost its effectiveness over time.

The interrupted time series analytical method is one of the best
quasi-experimental methods available for yielding conclusions immune
to the plausible rival explanations that frequently threaten conclusions
based on field research.

For example the observed change in a dependent variable can be compared with expectations of routine, normal or "chance" variation, by means of newly available tests of statistical significance to determine its likelihood of reflecting merely the "instability" of the curve. The plausibility of the change being explained as a "regression" artifact—a return to more normal levels following unusual and extreme ones—can be ascertained by tracing the course of the curve of the independent variable prior to the legal intervention. Likewise the possibility that the observed change at the time of the intervention formed part of some longer secular trend in the data can be investigated in the series, providing control for "maturation, "instrumentation," and "testing" effects among others. Finally although the interrupted time series does not control for "history"—the possibility that some simultaneous event rather than the legal intervention produced the change—it is often possible to control for this rival explanation through comparison of series in similar jurisdictions or under different theoretically relevant conditions (such as comparing nighttime with daytime fatalities).

In the following pages I will summarize the evaluative literature concerning three types of legal interventions related to drinking and driving (1) adoptions of "Scandinavian-type" laws in world jurisdictions, (2) enforcement campaigns based on these laws, and (3) formal and informal increments in threatened severity of sanctions for violating drinking-and-driving laws. The bulk of studies cited have used interrupted time series analytical methods, although there are considerable differences in the formality and sophistication of the designs. The more formal and elaborate studies have yielded the more informative and reliable results, but the cumulation of findings based as well on less formal and less adequate investigations supports the generalizability of the findings.

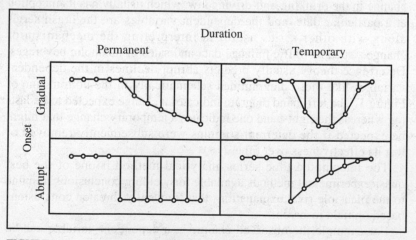

FIGURE 1   Impact Models of Deterrent Effects

ADOPTIONS OF "SCANDINAVIAN-TYPE" DRINKING-AND-DRIVING LAWS

In the early twentieth century, as the hazards posed by alcohol influenced driving in countries with mass automobile populations became evident, laws restricting this behavior were everywhere adopted. These typically took the form of prohibitions against "drunk driving" or "driving under the influence of alcohol." As further knowledge concerning the problem accumulated, these laws, which I term "classical," were perceived to be ineffective from the viewpoint of deterrence. Among the reasons for this conclusion were the fact that only a tiny fraction of drivers whose skills and abilities were importantly affected by alcohol were apprehended by traditional police patrol, and that the penalties received by those few who were convicted were regarded as trivial.

A new type of law addressing the problem was developed in Norway and Sweden in the years just prior to World War II. This Scandinavian-type law defined the prohibited conduct as driving with blood concentration (BAC) in excess of an arbitrary standard, to be ascertained with the aid of "scientific" tests of breath and blood, and provided for relatively severe punishments. In the Norwegian law of 1936 loss of license and a mandatory prison sentence were prescribed for driving with more than .05 percent BAC (a concentration obtainable by the average male consuming three drinks in one hour); in the Swedish law of 1941, the license was suspended at .08 percent and prison was mandatory at 15 percent BAC. Laws based on similar principles were adopted elsewhere following the war, most notably in Britain in 1967. Favorable reports of the British experience resulted in widespread adoptions of Scandinavian-type laws throughout the world during the following decades. Many of these adoptions have been subject to evaluation, although the quality of the research has not always been adequate . . . .

Great Britain

Great Britain adopted a Scandinavian-type drinking-and-driving law, The Road Safety Act of 1967, amid great publicity and great controversy, the latter centering on the originally proposed "random stops" permitted to the police to test drivers' breath for BAC levels. This provision was withdrawn in the final version of the law, but British police were empowered to test drivers involved in a traffic violation or an accident, regardless of fault, a provision authorities judged to retain significant elements of random testing. The Road Safety Act prohibited driving or attempting to drive with a BAC in excess of .08 percent. Its most feared penalty was a mandatory one-year license suspension, apparently far less severe than the prison sentences meted out in Scandinavia.

However, in contrast to the Scandinavian case, the deterrent effectiveness of the Road Safety Act was clearly demonstrable by interrupted time series analysis. Figure 2 shows the deseasonalized time series for crash-related fatalities in Britain from 1961 to 1970. The drop in October of 1967 can be seen; it is statistically significant. The most interesting comparison obtained is shown in Figure 3, presenting deseasonalized data on serious crashes during weekend nights, when alcohol-influenced driving is relatively common, and Figure 4, presenting similar data for the weekday commuting hours when alcohol-influenced driving is quite rare. The effect of the law is clearly seen in the former and, as expected, is absent from the latter. Figure 5 also reveals clearly the temporary nature of the Road Safety Act's deterrent effect. Its impact began to decline almost immediately. The existence of an important effect initially, disappearing over a period of several months, was further noted in independent studies of the proportion of casualties in drinking hours and of the proportion of fatally injured drivers with illegal BACs.

France

Nearly equally controversial in its setting was the French law of July 12, 1978, prohibiting driving with a BAC exceeding .08 percent and providing for mandatory license suspension under certain circumstances. The most remarkable feature of the French law was that,

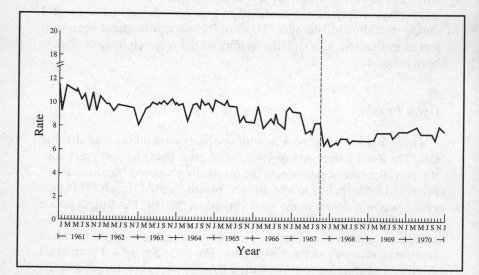

FIGURE 2   U.K. Fatality Rate, Corrected for Month with Seasonal Variations Removed

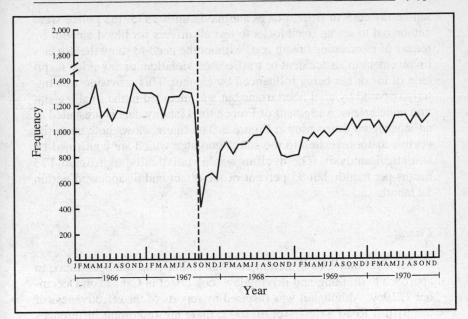

FIGURE 3   Fatalities and Serious Injuries in the U.K.*

*Combined for Friday 10 p.m.–midnight; Saturday midnight–4 a.m.; Saturday 10 p.m.–midnight; Sunday midnight–4 a.m.; corrected for weekend days per month and with seasonal variations removed.

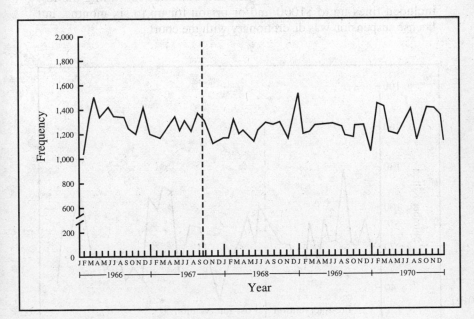

FIGURE 4   Fatalities and Serious Injuries in the U.K.*

*Combined for Monday–Friday 7 a.m.–10 a.m. and 4 p.m.–5 p.m.; corrected for weekdays per month and with seasonal variations removed.

unlike the case in Britain or Scandinavia until 1975, the police were authorized to set up roadblocks to test all drivers for blood alcohol by means of a screening breath test, without the need to show the driver's involvement in an accident or traffic code violation, or any prior suspicion of his or her being influenced by alcohol. This provision was bitterly opposed by civil libertarians but was included in the final legislation nonetheless. A segment of French total fatality data is presented as an interrupted time series in Figure 5. The figure shows both an initial decline and a reversion to the status quo ante which are confirmed by statistical analysis. The decline was a statistically significant 173 deaths per month, but 95 percent of the effect had disappeared within 12 months . . . .

Canada

The Criminal Law Amendment Act embodying the Scandinavian approach to drinking-and-driving law took effect in Canada on December 1, 1969. Although it was inspired by reports of the effectiveness of the British Road Safety Act of 1967, there are important differences between these laws. The Canadian police were empowered to require breath tests only on the basis of "reasonable and proper" grounds to believe a driver is impaired by alcohol. As in Britain, the Canadian legislation set a BAC limit of .08 percent. Penalties for failing the test included fines up to $1000 and/or prison for up to six months, but license suspension was discretionary with the court.

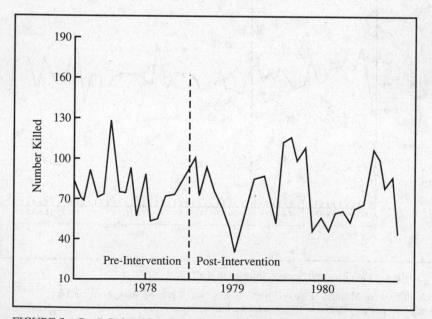

FIGURE 5   Crash-Related Deaths in France. Friday and Saturday, 9 p.m.–3 a.m.

The Canadian legislation has been subjected to two independent evaluations. The first analyzed data for injury involving crashes and fatal crashes for the Province of Ontario separately and for Canada as a whole. The fatality data for the entire country are presented here in Figure 6. Their form analysis follows the interrupted time series analytical model, although the statistical analysis is unorthodox. The analysts' conclusions were positive but guarded: fatalities in Canada following the inception of the law were nine percent below the trend, and the decline was considerably greater than that in the United States, offered as a control jurisdiction. They also noted dissipation of the effect within a year. Their principal reservations had to do with the fact that nighttime and weekend crashes did not show stronger variations.

The second evaluation by epidemiologists using the same data base but different methods was more positive and less guarded . . . . The writer concluded that the rate of incidence for crash related death and

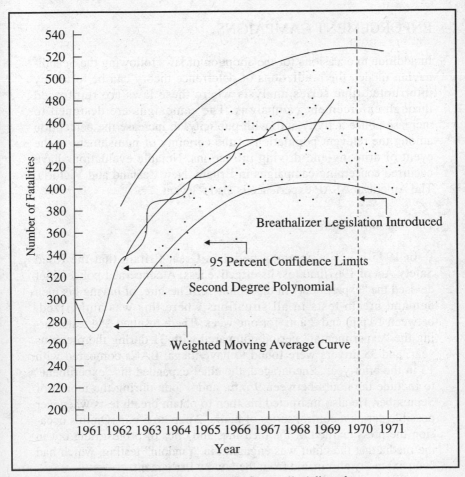

FIGURE 6   Crash-Related Fatalities in Canada, Seasonally Adjusted

injuries on the basis of population at risk declined by more than 9 deaths and injuries per 100,000 population per quarter, during the first five quarters of the new law and the bulk of the saving was during the nighttime hours.

Inasmuch as observers of the Canadian case concluded that the effect of their law was considerably less than that of the British law, the differences in the situations should be stressed. The level of threat posed by the Canadian law appears to have been lower. Police were not empowered to test a driver's breath without specific suspicion of alcohol influence, and because police cars did not carry testing devices in Canada the demand for a test was more difficult and therefore perhaps less likely to be made. License suspension was not mandatory but at the discretion of the court. Moreover the threat was not as widely publicized in Canada, perhaps because the apparent success of the British law and the more moderate provisions of the proposed Canadian legislation rendered the latter less controversial . . . .

ENFORCEMENT CAMPAIGNS

In addition to occasions for the adoption of laws following the Scandinavian model, the predictions of deterrence theory can be tested by interrupted time series analysis where these laws are reinforced through enforcement campaigns. The campaigns are designed to increase police activity and, with publicity, to increase the perception among the relevant population of the certainty of punishment in the event of drinking-and-driving infractions. Notable evaluations have occurred concerning campaigns in Britain, New Zealand and Victoria. The American ASAP experience is also relevant.

The Cheshire "Blitz"

In 1975 it was a common belief in Great Britain that the Road Safety Act of 1967 had lost its effectiveness. A concerned police chief devised the "experiment" in the County of Cheshire, of having his men demand breath tests in all situations where this was authorized, between 10 p.m and 2 a.m. for one week. There resulted 284 tests during the "experimental" period compared with 31 during the previous year, and 38 drivers were found to have illegal BACs compared with 13 in the prior year. Encouraged, the chief expanded his "experiment" to include the hours between 9 p.m. and 4 a.m. during the month of September. He also instructed his men to obtain breath tests whenever possible during a control series of hours, 2 p.m. to 5 p.m. On this occasion the press learned of the measure, and cries of protest rang out in the media that the chief was engaging in "random" testing, which had been expressly eliminated from the law by Parliament.

A result was the appearance of a deterrent effect, evident in monthly series of crash-linked serious injuries and fatalities for Cheshire in September of 1975. This is presented in Figure 7. The drop is statistically significant, even for the small data base on which the series rests.

The drop was also visible in casualties restricted to nighttime hours, though in that case, with a very small data base, the change did not quite reach statistical significance. No comparable change was found for low-alcohol-consumption hours of the day.

The New Zealand "Blitzes"

Although the 1969 New Zealand law was judged by its evaluator not to have produced important deterrent effects, intensified enforcement campaigns during the last part of July and in December of 1978 were found to be effective. Screening tests were quadrupled in the first blitz and doubled in the second, and both enforcement efforts were supported by official publicity campaigns. Evaluation included studies of liquor consumption in rental ballrooms, road injuries reported to a group of cooperating hospitals, claims filed with the Accident Compensation Commission and serious crashes. Figure 8 presents the ratio of nighttime to total crashes which seems particularly convincing evidence for the deterrent effectiveness of the blitzes.

Enforcement Campaigns in Melbourne, Australia

The state of Victoria adopted provisions for random breath testing of drivers in roadblocks in 1976, but use of this technique was initially very limited. However periods of intensified enforcement occurred in Melbourne in 1977 and 1978. The evaluation employed the criteria of reductions in crash fatalities, in serious casualty crashes, and in BACs among driver casualties at night. Changes in the patrolled areas of Melbourne were compared with those in selected control areas. The evaluation was flawed by various methodological deficiencies, but taken at face value the findings led to the conclusion of a substantial deterrent effect.

The American Alcohol Safety Action Projects (ASAPs)

In the early 1970s, 35 projects were funded in various locations throughout the United States embodying, among other things, increases in police patrol for drinking drivers and improvements in the processing of accused offenders in the courts. The typical project increased arrests by a factor of 2.5. Evaluations were planned for each site and for the projects taken together. The site-by-site evaluations were of

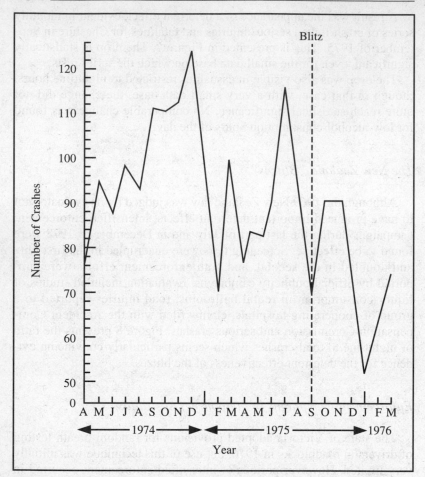

FIGURE 7   Crashes Producing Serious or Fatal Injuries in Cheshire, England

generally poor quality and are thus not considered dependable. However a formal evaluation by the U.S Department of Transportation (1979) compared changes in nighttime crashes in the ASAP communities with daytime crashes in the same communities, with experiences in matched control communities, and with national trends. Data from 12 of the 35 sites showed statistically significant diminutions in nighttime fatal crashes. Although this fraction is not impressive, the authors credibly argued that sites with low initial crash rates and those with growing populations would be less likely to show large reductions. Among those 13 sites with three or more nighttime fatal crashes per month and a growth rate of less than 10 percent, 8 showed significant reductions in nighttime fatal crashes, a more impressive fraction. It was also the case that a correlation between the level of enforcement and the reduction in nighttime fatalities was visible in these 13 selected sites.

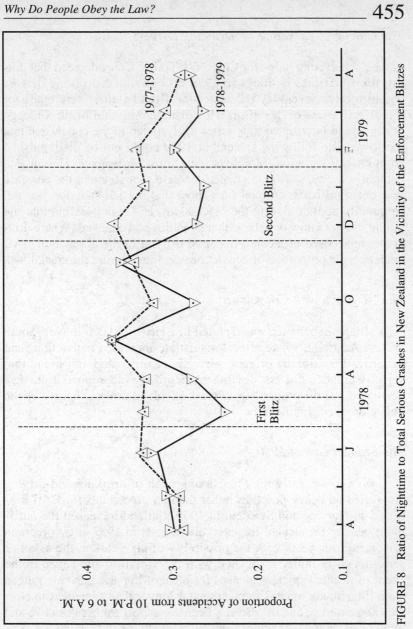

FIGURE 8   Ratio of Nighttime to Total Serious Crashes in New Zealand in the Vicinity of the Enforcement Blitzes

SEVERITY

A few evaluations were found of situations in which penalties for alcohol-impaired driving were substantially increased without accompanying increases in enforcement.

The Chicago Crackdown on Drinking Drivers

The supervising judge for Chicago's Traffic Court decreed that during the Christmas holidays in 1970 all convicted drinking drivers would receive seven-day jail sentences. Broad claims were made for the effectiveness of this effort. However, submission of the Chicago crash data to interrupted time series analysis led to the conclusion that the lower rate following December 1970 could not be distinguished from chance variation. Moreover, data from Milwaukee, chosen as a comparison city, showed a greater decrease though again the decrease was not significant. Official files show that the jail sanction was not frequently applied during the crackdown, and it is possible that the public did not know or believe that penalties had changed. Where drivers were accused of alcohol-impaired driving in the absence of BAC evidence, the proportion of convictions declined during the crackdown.

The "Traffictown" Crackdown

A similar experience was reported in a city of 30,000 in New South Wales, Australia, where a local magistrate increased convictions and penalties for drinking drivers. Analysis of this campaign found that serious crashes did not decline perceptibly, but reported crashes decreased and the proportions of crash-involved drivers charged by the police dropped significantly.

The Finnish Law of 1950

Until very recently the Finnish approach to drinking-and-driving law relied on heavy penalties rather than on procedures for BAC testing as in Norway and Sweden. In 1950, Finland increased the maximum penalty for alcohol-impaired driving, set in 1937 at two years in prison, to four years with the possibility of six years in the event of serious bodily injury associated with the violation and seven in the event of death. Typical sentences for alcohol-impaired driving ranged from three to six months in practice, far longer than sentences in Norway and Sweden, and the driver's license was lost for between two and three years on the first offense and permanently on the second.

Interrupted time series analysis was applied to the doubling of the maximum penalty for alcohol-impaired driving in 1950. Although there was a decline in crash-related fatalities in that year, which with certain assumptions could be considered significant, it is unreasonable to attribute it to the change in the drinking-and-driving law. This is because the drop was greater for less serious casualties (where alcohol is a smaller factor) than more serious, and no drop occurred in the series for single-vehicle crashes (in which alcohol is a major factor), whereas multiple-vehicle crashes declined considerably. The conclusion is that greatly increased severity of the drinking-and-driving law in Finland probably did not affect the target behavior.

CONCLUSION

The literature reviewed here finds that adoptions of Scandinavian type laws and campaigns to enforce these laws seem capable of producing important deterrent effects on drinking and driving. However, in all cases in which deterrent effectiveness was noted, it proved to be temporary, disappearing within months of its attainment. My interpretation of this phenomenon is that these legal innovations were successful because they raised drivers' perceptions of the certainty with which they were likely to be punished if they drank . . . . [T]he deterrence theoretical model is grounded in perception rather than actual levels of threat. Particularly where the new laws and campaigns were most strongly resisted, as in the case of the British Road Safety Act and the Cheshire blitz, public perception of the likelihood of punishment may very well have increased due to the publicity and newsworthiness of the legal changes.

However, in no reported case were the chances of apprehension and conviction raised to very important levels. In Britain, the chances of a driver encountering a breath test in the late 1960s were about one in every two million vehicle miles driven. A Canadian observer writes that according to official estimates there are 26,000 kilometers of impaired driving for every drinking-and-driving charge. In the United States, estimates of the proportion of alcohol-impaired drivers being apprehended run between 1 in 2000 and 1 in 200, the latter concerning driving on patrolled roads during the Kansas City ASAP. In Sweden, . . . [a writer] estimates that the real incidence of drinking-and-driving offenses is at least 200 times higher than the reported incidence. In short, it seems a reasonable speculation that notorious and publicized measures directed to drinking-and-driving offenses may increase the perceived probability of punishment, but that the actual level of enforcement has proven to be low. In these circumstances, learning occurs and drivers' perceptions of risk decline toward prior levels. There is not much literature directly reporting empirical data on this matter, but the occasional study dealing with the perceived risk of punishment . . . supports this speculation.

The matter is otherwise concerning severity. The three studies evaluating efforts to increase the severity of penalties provide little evidence supporting the effectiveness of these efforts. The doubling of very severe penalties in Finland apparently had no effect on alcohol-impaired driving. In Chicago and "Traffictown" the situation of drinking drivers did change, but in unexpected and undesired ways. The proportion of reported violations may have decreased, and the actual punishment of offenders may have diminished, due to efforts of violators and legal personnel to avoid the harsh punishments.

In short, the literature concerning drinking-and-driving law supports the theoretical model of deterrence in the specific hypothesis that the extent of the proscribed behavior is a positive function of the perceived certainty of punishment. It does not provide support for the hypothesis that proscribed behavior is reduced as a function of the severity of punishment. However, this finding has to be understood as obtained on the background of very low levels of actual and perceived certainly of punishment . . . . It is likely that the variables in the deterrence model are effective only on reaching a threshold level, and that certainty and severity interact. Thus, severity cannot be expected to have an effect on the background of subthreshold levels of certainly, nor can certainty have an effect on the background or subthreshold levels of severity. Research in the drinking-and-driving law area has not studied increments in marginal severity on the background of meaningful levels of certainty of punishment. It is possible that continued current interest in controlling drinking and driving by legal means may lead to situations in which this question can be studied . . . . □

NOTES AND QUESTIONS

1. Ross finds that severe drunk driving laws have a significant, but only temporary, deterrent effect. What accounts for the brevity of the impact? What, if anything, do these results tell us about the relative deterrent effects of punishment severity and certainty?

2. What policy recommendations follow from Ross's research? What would be the best way to deter drunk driving? Do the results he reports support the claim that it is useful to set up occasional roadblocks, and check drivers to see if they are sober?

3. Attempts to reduce drunk driving have received considerable attention in the 1980s and 90s. There have also been a number of efforts to evaluate these laws. Almost all studies reach conclusions similar to those presented in this article—stronger laws and enforcement only temporarily reduce drunk driving. See, e.g., H. Laurence Ross, *Deterring The Drinking Driver: Legal Policy and Social Control* 3rd ed. (Lexington, Mass.: D. C. Heath, 1984); H. Laurence Ross and Robert Voas, "The Philadelphia Story: The Effects of Severe Punishment for Drunk Driving," 12 *Law & Policy* 51 (1990). However, there are some researchers who claim that drunk driving laws actually have a more lasting deterrent effect. See, e.g., John R. Snortum, "Alcohol-Impaired Driving in Norway and Sweden: Another Look at 'The Scandinavian Myth'" 6 *Law & Policy* 5 (1984).

Can we say that the answer to effectiveness of the criminal law is high penalties and a real willingness to impose them? Maria Los, in *Communist Ideology, Law and Crime* (New York: St. Martin's Press, 1988), points out that the former Soviet Union used most of the available techniques of social control. By education, propaganda, and rewards it attempted to create good Soviet citizens. Its criminal statutes dealt with familiar crimes such as murder and stealing. It also criminalized much activity left unregulated in most capitalist societies. For example, there were "anti-parasite" laws enforcing the duty to work; there were crimes against the central plan; there were crimes against state property. "Hooliganism" was a catchall crime aimed at "intentional actions which grossly violate public order and express an obvious disrespect towards society."

The Soviet Union exerted great efforts to enforce its laws, at least against those who did not hold privileged positions. There were many different types of police who were not limited by American notions of due process. Citizens were watched by police and networks of informers. Police were aided by such things as laws restricting where people could live and work. People needed permits, authorizations, or registrations to engage in most spheres of everyday activity. People carried internal passports, and so it was much harder than in the West to avoid arrest by moving to another city or creating a new identity. Courts seldom acquitted those arrested. Criminal penalties were heavy, and large numbers of people were sent to prison. Prisons were terrible places. The state imposed capital punishment frequently.

Despite all this, Łos points out that the Soviet Union had a very high crime rate. "Conventional crime . . . appears to be not less wide-spread and diverse, and perhaps even more violent, than that in the countries of the West" (p. 304). Criminal statistics are notoriously hard to gather or to assess. Nonetheless, assuming that Łos's conclusion about the crime rate in the former Soviet Union is generally correct, can you explain why its legal system was not more successful? How would you fit her observations into the various theories of deterrence that have been set forth in this chapter?

4. The essential idea of deterrence, of course, is that people will try to avoid sanctions, that is, they do not want to be punished. But what is a punishment? We assume, no doubt correctly, that jail, fines, whipping, and hanging, are punishments. But we cannot assume that everybody reacts the same way to every threat of punishment. A $1,000 fine might mean very little to a rich person. A night in jail might be enormously humiliating to some people, routine to others, a badge of pride to others or a source of thrills to others. Also, there are acts which would not be half so attractive if they were not sanctioned—forbidden fruit, where the punishment (or danger of punishment) is part of the thrill, the pain. See Jack Katz, *Seductions of Crime: Moral and Sensual Attractions in Doing Evil* (New York: Basic Books, 1983).

All this seems true, but it makes it hard to measure the "severity" of a punishment. Also, in legal theory, if a person is arrested, kept in jail for a while, tried, and acquitted, she has not been "punished" at all. But we all know that is not the case; the defendant has been through a terrible ordeal, and may have suffered terribly in the process. Malcolm Feeley's study of the lower criminal courts of New Haven has the suggestive title: *The Process Is the Punishment* (New York: Russell Sage Foundation, 1979). For drunks, for example, a small fine or a brief stay in a cell is not the real punishment; the whole process, from arrest to release, is what delivers the sanction.

Sheldon Ekland-Olson, John Lieb, and Louis Zurcher, in "The Paradoxical Impact of Criminal Sanctions: Some Microstructural Findings," 18 *Law & Society Review* 159 (1984), give another example of this kind of "sanction." The article is based on extensive interviews with a group of drug dealers. The dealers were obviously not deterred by the threat of punishment—they were, after all, still carrying on their illegal business. But threat of punishment affected their behavior in many ways. As was true of the people Feeley studied, the process was often the punishment: "an arrest and the accompanying investigation were often perceived to be just as threatening as a prison sentence." Why should this be so? An arrest could ruin their business—it could destroy "a network of relations built over a period of years . . . ." Sources of drugs would dry up, customers would stay away, patterns of dealing with other people in the business could be disrupted, sometimes fatally.

Fear of sanctions also affected the way in which dealers carried on their business. It made them, for example, very careful in dealing with strangers (because of fear of selling to an underground detective, for example). Paradoxically, then, the fear of sanctions increased dealers' "involvement" in the drug business—the depth of their commitment, their "emotional attachment to dealing activities," and to other people in the drug business. The sanction process, in short, produced, or helped produce a distinctive sub-culture, with its own forms of solidarity.

The authors sum up their findings as follows:

1. The perceived severity of sanctions is in large measure tied to the degree of interpersonal disruption caused by the sanctioning process.
2. Criminal sanctions are socially complex. The degree of interpersonal disruption is determined in large measure by the organization of the sanctioning process and the tolerance or resilience of the affected network.
3. Network tolerance, the ability and willingness of a network of actors to withstand the impact of the sanction process, is in large measure a function of the strength of relationships among actors.
4. Sanctions become more disruptive as they reduce the degree of trust, affect, and normative agreement within the deviant target population and as they inhibit or throw out of balance exchange relationships among deviants. Thus, relational tolerance and the sanctioning process are often highly interdependent.
5. The sanctioning process has an important organizing influence on relationships among those engaged in criminal activities. This is revealed in many ways. For example:
   a. By increasing the constraining nature of activities, the fear of sanctions tends to increase network density and closure.
   b. Network closure and density reduce the chances that bridging ties to alternative networks will form. The structural influence of the hesitancy to form "weak ties" accounts for a substantial reduction in criminal activity not explained directly by the psychological processes of fear and avoidance.
6. The perceived certainty of punishment depends in large measure on what persons know about particular situations as well as on the degree to which they trust their coactors.
7. Persons engaged in criminal activities manipulate the perceived and actual certainty of punishment through choices of associates and the structuring of interaction.

What all these generalizations taken together imply is that perceptions of sanction severity and certainty are situational. Deterrence research, especially when restrictive deterrence is at issue, must move beyond official indicators of certainty and severity and beyond scaling procedures which assume stable attitudinal structures. Further understanding requires data that are sensitive to the dynamic relationship between the organization of the sanctioning process and the adaptive strategies of those who are the target of sanctions.

THE ROLE OF PEER GROUPS, CONSCIENCE, MORAL APPEAL, EMBARRASSMENT, AND SHAME

32. Conscience, Significant Others and Rational Choice: Extending the Deterrence Model

Harold G. Grasmick
and Robert J. Bursik, Jr.

24 *Law & Society Review* 837 (1990)

☐ In this reading, the authors argue that deterrence theory ought to be integrated with theories that "emphasize sources of compliance with the law other than the threat of legal sanctions," that is, "(1) moral beliefs about right and wrong," and "(2) attachments to peers, family and various significant others."

These variables, to be sure, are hard to measure and manipulate. But Grasmick and Bursik, quite plausibly, argue that they are very important variables in explaining why people obey or disobey laws; they also claim that these variables are not inconsistent with deterrence theory. After all, conscience and peer groups "function as potential sources of punishment which, like state-imposed legal sanctions, vary in both their certainty and their severity." It is, in short, a real punishment to be laughed at—or beaten up—by members of your gang or ostracized by your church. And a bad conscience, too can be very painful.

Hence conscience and peer group factors can fit easily into a "rational choice perspective" on behavior. Embarrassment, for example, can decrease "the expected utility of crime." It is a "physiological discomfort"; it also has or can have long-term consequences: "a loss of valued relationships and perhaps a restriction in opportunities to achieve other valued goals over which significant others have some control." The authors therefore propose to expand the whole notion of deterrence to include these non-state factors.

But how are we to measure potential embarrassment, guilt feelings, and the like? The authors collected data in 1985 from face-to-face interviews with a random sample of adults in an unidentified American city. They asked their subjects whether they were inclined to commit three offenses: tax cheating, petty theft (less than $20), and drunken driving. These offenses were chosen intentionally as offenses whose "consequences" tend to be "somewhat serious, in contrast to more minor offenses such as parking violations, littering, minor forms of illegal gambling, etc." Of the sample, 17% allowed that they would "fail to report certain income or claim an undeserved deduction" (tax cheating); 7.6% said they would "take something from someplace worth less than $20;" and 28% (!) said "they would drive an automobile while under the influence of a moderate amount of alcohol."

The authors report:

> One of our objectives is to develop comparable or parallel measures of perceived risks of shame, embarrassment, and legal sanction. At the same time, we need to assess both perceived certainty and perceived severity for each of the three kinds of costs. For certainty for each of the three offenses, respondents were asked:
>
> > SHAME: Would you feel guilty if you . . .
> > EMBARRASSMENT: Would most of the people whose opinion you value lose respect for you if you . . .
> > LEGAL SANCTIONS: Do you think you would get caught if you . . .
>
> Responses were given on a four-point scale ranging from "definitely would not" (coded 1) to "definitely would" (coded 4) . . .
> Our measure of perceived severity . . . captures the subjective severity of the punishment—the meaning the actor attaches to the punishment. Respondents were asked the following questions for each of the three offenses:
>
> > SHAME: If you did feel guilty for doing this, how big of a problem would it create for your life?
> > EMBARRASSMENT: If most of the people whose opinions you value did lose respect for you, how big a problem would it create for your life?
> > LEGAL SANCTIONS: If you were caught and the courts had decided what your punishment would be, how big a problem would it create for your life?

The respondent's options were "no problem at all" (1), "hardly any problem" (2), "little problem" (3), "a big problem" (4), and "a very big problem" (5). The means and standard deviations (in parentheses) are reported in Table 1 in the columns labeled "S."

With regard to "certainty," *shame* tended to score higher than the other types of threat; the "largest certainty" score was 3.67 for "certainty of shame for theft;" the lowest was 2.38 "for the certainty of embarrassment for tax cheating." As far as "severity" was concerned, the highest score was 4.31 for legal sanctions for drunk driving, followed by legal sanctions for theft (4.1) and tax cheating (3.97). The lowest score was severity of embarrassment for tax cheating (3.19).

The scores are set out in Table 1, which gives means and standard deviations. It also reports a figure in the third column of the table which consists of certainty and severity multiplied together. This figure represents the degree of "threat" which the sanction poses. So, for example, the threat score for shame as a sanction with regard to tax cheating is 10.626—lower than the effect of shame on theft (14.793), but higher than the threat of embarrassment on tax cheating (8.003).

Now comes the pay-off: some people admit they intend to cheat on their taxes, drive while drunk, or steal something. But do "present perceptions" of the threats influence "present inclinations to violate the law?" For all three offenses, the authors found "strong evidence of a deterrent effect of shame. For two of the three offenses (tax cheating, drunk driving) shame is the threat which has the greatest direct effect."

Embarrassment was a disappointment. Threat of embarrassment did not have a significant effect on any of the three offenses. The authors say that these findings are "problematic" because past research "suggests that significant others play an important role in generating conformity and nonconformity with legal norms."

TABLE 1   MEANS (AND STANDARD DEVIATIONS) OF
CERTAINTY (C), SEVERITY (S), AND THE PRODUCT OF C
AND S (C x S) OF SHAME, EMBARRASSMENT, AND
LEGAL SANCTIONS

	C	S	C x S
		Shame	
Tax cheat	3.025	3.307	10.626
	(0.96)	(1.16)	(5.79)
Theft	3.673	3.922	14.793
	(0.71)	(1.02)	(5.15)
Drunk Driving	3.242	3.538	12.165
	(0.92)	(1.21)	(6.12)
		Embarrassment	
Tax cheat	2.385	3.130	8.003
	(0.88)	(1.02)	(4.78)
Theft	3.171	3.709	12.209
	(0.81)	(0.99)	(5.26)
Drunk driving	2.891	3.525	10.824
	(0.94)	(1.08)	(5.71)
		Legal Sanctions	
Tax cheat	2.874	3.969	11.680
	(0.76)	(0.89)	(4.77)
Theft	2.894	4.103	12.171
	(0.79)	(0.88)	(4.86)
Drunk driving	2.749	4.313	12.050
	(0.81)	(0.79)	(4.70)

This study might not have measured the right thing: its measure "was designed to capture just one mechanism [embarrassment] through which significant others might influence illegal behavior." There might be other mechanisms not studied. Or respondents might feel that they would get away with the offense so that their significant others would not find out what they had done. Or perhaps Grasmick and Bursik's adult respondents were less amenable to peer pressure than the student subjects in most prior studies. In any event, the authors feel that their figures leave plenty of puzzles to be solved. They end with the usual plea for more research.[144]

NOTES AND QUESTIONS

1. Do you think that this study proved anything? One male colleague who read the article (and who wishes to remain anonymous) commented: "There is a whole line of research based on asking people if X, Y, and Z were so, would you commit a serious crime? It is a little like asking me if I were a woman and pregnant, would I have an abortion. How in hell do I know? Of course, I can try to project myself into the situation and guess. But when you know my guesses, what do you know?" Is this fair criticism?

2. There are some scholars who feel that shame is in fact a powerful weapon of deterrence; that some societies make effective use of shame as a mechanism for controlling deviant behavior; and that all societies might well invoke this tool as a means of social control. See John Braithwaite, *Crime, Shame, and Reintegration* (Cambridge: Cambridge University Press, 1989). Braithwaite asserts, however, that there is shame and shame. Social processes that result in shame followed by "reintegration" into society are effective while those that result in stigma and expulsion may be counterproductive.

3. Grasmick and Bursik talk about "extending" the rational-choice model of deterrence. Have they done so? If you include conscience, fear of disapproval from neighbors or others, embarrassment, and the like, do you have a rational-choice model any more? Is there anything that would *not* be consistent with a rational-choice model under their reasoning?

---

144. See Harold G. Grasmick, Robert J. Bursik, Jr., and Bruce J. Arneklev, "Reduction in Drunk Driving as a Response to Increased Threats of Shame, Embarrassment, and Legal Sanctions," 31 *Criminology* 41 (1993). Compare, however, Phillip B. Gonzales, "Shame, Peer, and Oscillating Frames in DWI Conviction: Extending Goffman's Sociological Landscape," 16 *Symbolic Interaction* 257 (1993), stressing that those convicted of driving while intoxicated, their friends, employers and others with whom they interact have ways of coping with the law's attempts to impose shame and embarrassment.

33. *Moral Appeal, Sanction Threat, and Deviance: An Experimental Test*[145]

Charles R. Tittle
and Alan R. Rowe

20 Social Problems 488 (1973)

RESEARCH PROCEDURES

☐ Three sociology classes were used in the experiment. One class was designated as the control group, while the other two were subjected to the experimental treatment. Each class was organized around a series of eight weekly quizzes worth ten points each. Quizzes were administered during the last 15 minutes of a class period and were collected as the students left. The quizzes were then graded and the scores recorded with no marks being made on the student's paper. At the beginning of the next class period they were returned, and the students were permitted to calculate their own grades.

The difference between the real score as previously determined by the instructor and the score which the student assigned to himself is taken as an indication of cheating. Since the amount that a student could cheat was limited by the maximum score of ten on a given quiz as well as by the actual real score he earned, the index of cheating to be analyzed is based on the proportion of cheating opportunities utilized. If a given student had a total of 21 real points on a series of three quizzes, he had the opportunity to cheat nine points. If he actually cheated three points, he is considered to have cheated 33 percent of the possible.

To minimize moral and ethical dilemmas associated with the research, the authors agreed in advance to keep secret the cheating activity of individual students, even from each other. They further agreed to calculate the course grade on the basis of the scores the students assigned to themselves, and to mark the midterm and final exams in so far as possible without reference to the student's quiz honesty.

In the control group no mention was made during the entire quarter of cheating, the necessity for honesty, or of the possibility of being caught or punished. It was simply explained that taking the quiz at the end of the period was less distracting to the lecture of that day and that

145. From Charles R. Tittle and Alan R. Rowe, "Moral Appeal, Sanction Threat and Deviance." *Social Problems* 20:4. Copyright Social Problems (Spring 1973). Reprinted by permission of *Social Problems,* The Society for the Study of Social Problems and the authors.

this procedure permitted students to leave early if finished or to stay later if more time was needed. Upon return of the quizzes, the instructor devoted about 45 minutes to class discussion of the topic covered on the quiz, during which the correct answers were made clear.

The treatment groups (which were taught in the quarter immediately following) were exposed to the same procedure for three quizzes. Upon return of the fourth quiz, but before self-grading, the class was reminded that they were being trusted to grade their quizzes honestly and that they had a moral obligation to be accurate. No other mention was made of cheating until the seventh quiz was returned. At that point the students were told that complaints about cheating had been lodged, so it was necessary for the instructor to spot check some of the quizzes for accuracy. When the eighth quiz was returned, the students were told that the spot check had revealed a case of cheating and that the person was to be penalized (in fact, nobody was penalized).

Hence, comparison of the patterns of cheating between the control group and the treatment groups should reveal the impact of a moral appeal and a sanction threat on the amount of cheating that occurs. First, if a moral appeal is effective, the level of cheating in the treatment groups after the moral appeal should be significantly less than before the moral appeal. Second, if a detection/sanction threat has any additional deterrent effect above and beyond that generated by the moral appeal, the level of cheating after such a threat should be significantly lower than before. Finally, variations from quiz to quiz in the treatment groups should be significantly different than variations in the control group.

Only those individuals who took and graded at least one quiz of the first six and of the last two were included in the analysis and only then if they had some opportunity to cheat on one of the two series. For instance, a student who made perfect scores on the last two quizzes would be excluded, since his inclusion would have contributed to a spurious decline in cheating after the threat. Although the pool of usable subjects was defined with reference to the comparison between quizzes 1–6 and 7–8, the same logic of exclusion was applied when other series of quizzes were compared. As a result, the N for a given series varies depending upon the comparisons being made.

For purposes of analysis, the mean percent of individuals' cheat opportunities utilized was calculated for given series of quizzes and the significance of the differences between series was assessed by a t-test for matched pair differences. Differences between groups were evaluated by a difference of means test. In all cases, tests were one-tailed.

Questionnaire data to enable compositional comparison of the classes and analysis of the differential impact of the threat on various categories of individuals were gathered at the beginning of each of the courses. Students were told that the information requested would make it possible for the instructor to tailor the level of presentation to the needs and capabilities of the students. There data were analyzed using

Goodman-Kruskal gamma (1963) and its associated test of significance. For calculation, major field of study was grouped into four categories; age was categorized into three groups—less than 21, 22–25, and 26 or over; motivation for earning a high grade was treated in three categories; expected grade was analyzed in three categories; reason for enrolling was treated in two categories—those indicating high motivation and those indicating low motivation; actual course grade was expressed in three categories; discrepancy between expected grade at the beginning of the quarter and actual grade earned was grouped into three categories—no discrepancy, one grade discrepancy, and two or more grades of discrepancy; and, of course, sex was in two categories.

In examining the impact of the sanction threat on various types of individuals, the percentage decrease in cheating following the sanction threat was used as an indicator. For each individual the difference between the amount of cheating on the two series, 1–6 and 7–8, was divided by the amount of cheating on the first series. The percentage decrease was used rather than the simple difference between the two series because the absolute decrease would have been influenced by the magnitude of cheating on the first series—those who cheated most on the first series would have artificially shown a greater decrease following the sanction threat.

RESULTS

The moral appeal apparently had no effect on the level of cheating (Table 1). In fact, cheating actually increased in both groups, but since there was a corresponding increase for the same series in the control group, it appears that the moral appeal was simply irrelevant to the amount of cheating. In test group A, students cheated an average of 31 percent of the opportunities prior to the moral appeal and an average of 41 percent of the opportunities after the moral appeal. In test group B, the pre-appeal cheat level was 41 percent and the post-appeal level was 43 percent. Among the control group, cheating on the quizzes corresponding to the pre-appeal condition of the test groups (quizzes 1–3) was 27 percent and in the series corresponding to the moral appeal condition (quizzes 4–6), the cheating level was 33 percent.

The data do seem to show that the threat of being caught and punished did have a significant effect in deterring cheating in both test groups. In test group A the pre-threat cheating average was 34 percent while the post-threat average was only 12 percent, a mean individual difference of −22.9 percent (p < .001). Test group B displayed a decline from 42 percent to 31 percent, a mean individual difference of −11.5 percent (p < .005). Although the mean cheating level of the control group also declined from 30 percent for the first six quizzes to 24 percent for the last two quizzes (a non-significant mean individual difference of −5.9 percent, p > .10), the difference between the pre- and

TABLE 1   MEAN PERCENT OF CHEATING OPPORTUNITIES UTILIZED

	Free (Quiz 1–3)	Moral Appeal (Quiz 4–6)	Spot-check Threat	Sanction Threat	X Individual Difference (1–6)–(7–8)
Test Group A (N = 30)	31% (N = 30)	41% (N = 29)	13% (N = 30)	11% (N = 26)	−.29
		34% (N = 30)		12% (N = 30)	
Test group B (N = 51)	41% (N = 47)	43% (N = 47)	32% (N = 46)	22% (N = 29)	−11.5
		42% (N = 51)		31% (N = 51)	
Control group (N = 26)	27% (N = 26)	33% (N = 24)	24% (N = 26)	28% (N = 12)	−5.9
		30% (N = 26)		24% (N = 26)	

Statistical Tests:

Q 1–6 group A vs. Q 7–8 group A (t = 7.50, df = 29, p < .0005)

Q 1–6 group B vs. Q 7–8 group B (t = 2.67, df = 50, p < .005)

Q 1–6 group C vs. Q 7–8 group C (t = 1:27, df = 25, p < .10)

Diff. [(Q 1–6)–(Q 7–8)] group A vs. Diff. [(Q 1–6)–(Q 7–8)] group C (t = 6.67, df = 54, p < .005)

Diff. [(Q 1–6)–(Q 7–8)] group B vs. Diff. [(Q 1–6)–(Q 7–8)] group C (t = 2.03, df = 79, p < .02)

post-threat conditions for each of the two test groups was significantly greater than the difference for the control group (test group A, p < .0005, test group B, p < .005).

The results appear to support the deterrent argument and to demonstrate that fear of sanction is a more important influence than moral appeal in generating conformity to the norm of class room honesty. However rival interpretations are possible. The findings could be spurious because of weaknesses in the method of data analysis. By using the percent of cheating opportunities utilized by each individual as the basic unit of analysis, we may have permitted considerable idiosyncratic variation because of the low base on which the percents were calculated. For example, a student who on the first four quizzes scored perfectly on four, and an eight and nine respectively on the other two would end up with only three possibilities of cheating on the first series. By "fudging" only two points, he would have a cheating score of 67 percent. This problem is particularly acute, since some of the series encompass only one or two quizzes. Consequently, no individual had more than 50 cheating opportunities on any series considered, and many had only one or two opportunities. Moreover, eliminating from the analysis all individuals who had no opportunity to cheat on either of the main series may have biased the results.

In order to assess the possible effect of these artifacts, the data were recalculated using the percent of all possible cheats utilized by the entire class during any given series of quizzes as the basic unit of analysis. For instance, in test group A, there was a total of 1090 cheating opportunities during the first six quizzes, of which 46 percent were utilized. This alternative type of analysis produced almost exactly the same result as did the analysis using individual data. The difference between the amount of cheating in the pre-threat series for test group A (35 percent) and that in the post-threat series (12 percent) was −23 percent, in comparison with the original figure of −22.9 percent. Similarly, the difference for test group B was −11 percent, a figure very close to the original −11.5 percent. Hence, the results do not seem to be distorted by the method of analysis.

A second possibility is that the test groups differed from control group in some way other than the sanction threat, which may have accounted for the greater decline in the level of cheating on the last two quizzes. After all, the students were not randomly assigned to the three classes, and there was evidence of some decline (although not statistically significant) in the control group. To evaluate this rival interpretation, the classes were compared in terms of the following compositional characteristics: age, sex, reason for enrolling, expected grade, motivation for earning a high grade, discrepancy between the expected grade at the beginning of the quarter and the actual grade earned, and major area of study. No significant differences were found between the control and test groups which could have accounted for the results. Test group B did differ significantly from the control group in motivation for earning a high grade and in discrepancy between the grade expected and the grade actually earned. But the direction of these differences works against the hypothesis. The higher motivation and greater grade discrepancy in the test group should have produced greater incentive to continue cheating during quizzes 7 and 8. The fact that cheating was reduced significantly more in the test group than in the control group therefore strengthens the conclusion that the sanction threat had a causative impact. Thus, it appears that the findings are not due to extraneous differences between the control group and the test groups. Of course, it is possible that other differences not measured could have accounted for the findings, but it seems unlikely since the design was a combination of time series and a control group. If the groups had differed in some way that might have influenced the level of cheating, this should have become evident in the cheating patterns prior to the sanction threat.

Not only did the groups not differ in crucial ways, but there is some "informal" indication that the decline in cheating among the control group was itself attributable to increased fear of sanction near the end of the quarter. A student in another class inquired of one of the authors, point blank, if he were going to check some of the quiz papers. She had heard rumors that students in that class were growing fearful that the "grade-your-own" policy had resulted in so much cheating that the instructor would surely do something before the end of the quarter.

It seems safe to conclude, therefore, that the findings support a deterrent argument. But further questions require some attention. First, the sanction threat had a much greater effect in group A than in group B. Why might this differential effect have occurred? Since the two groups did not differ significantly in the compositional characteristics previously mentioned, only two possibilities suggest themselves, both of which involve credibility. Group B was over twice as large as group A. Hence, a spot check in group A actually implied a greater probability of being caught than it did in group B. Since other research has found the certainty of punishment to be a key variable in predicting whether sanctions will deter, it seems reasonable to imagine that the greater effect of the threat in group A may have been due to the greater certainty of apprehension implied by the threat.

Further, the two instructors/experimenters may have been differentially feared so that the sanction threat was more credible in one case than in the other. In fact, the instructor for group B, which showed the lesser effect, had a reputation among students as lovable and understanding. It is, therefore, quite plausible to postulate that the spot check was a less menacing threat for the students in group B than for those in group A. This interpretation is consistent with the fact that the level of cheating prior to the threat was greater in group B than in group A (42 percent *v.* 34 percent) and with the apparent additional effect produced in group B by the declaration before quiz eight that a cheater had been discovered and penalized (average cheating declined from 32 percent on quiz seven to 22 percent on quiz eight). It could be that in group B, where credibility was relatively low, the sanction reinforcement made the spot check threat more believable, whereas in group A (a decline from 13 percent to 11 percent), the maximum credibility had already been achieved with the original threat. If this interpretation is correct, the findings lend support to the argument that the certainty of punishment is an essential dimension to be taken into account when dealing with deterrence theory. Moreover, it suggests the applicability to the college teacher (at least in his role as evaluator) of Machiavelli's cogent observation that since it is difficult to be both loved and feared, "it is much safer to be feared, than to be loved, if one must choose."

Second, it is important to determine the type of individual most affected by the sanction threat. Examination of the relationships between measured individual characteristics and the percentage decrease in cheating following the sanction threat reveals three important associations. First, there is a significant relationship between the sex of the person and the effect of the sanction threat ($.38$, $p < .01$), which remains when other variables are held constant. Females were influenced far more by the sanction threat than were males. Sixty-one percent of all the females registered a 100 percent decrease in cheating after the threat, while only 33 percent of the males responded so dramatically. Why this should have been true is not clear, although it is consistent with much research in social psychology showing females to be more conforming, more obedient to authorities, and less willing to take chances. Presumably socialization in the female role creates greater consciousness of status and sensitivity to reputation, both of which would intensify fear of exposure for dishonest behavior. At any rate, if this research is a fair indication, we can conclude that females are more likely to be deterred from deviance by fear of sanction than are males.

The data also show significant associations between the influence of the sanction threat and the actual grade the student received in the course ($-.42$, $p < .01$), as well as with the discrepancy between the grade he expected at the beginning of the course and the grade he actually received ($-.34$, $p < .05$). Those students who had the lowest grades and who were experiencing the greatest discrepancy between the grade they expected and the grade they were actually earning were least affected by the sanction threat. Sixty-seven percent of those who earned a B or higher registered a 100 percent decrease in cheating after being threatened, while only 24 percent of those who earned a D or F reduced their cheating by this much. Similarly, 70 percent of those who were experiencing no discrepancy between the grade they expected and the grade they were earning registered a 100 percent decline in cheating, while only 31 percent of those who were experiencing a two-grade discrepancy reduced cheating by that amount.

These figures are certainly consistent with deterrence theory. Classical criminologists, from whom formal deterrence theory stemmed, argued that the greater the utility of an act, the greater the potential punishment required to deter it. Apparently the students most in need of points were willing to take greater risks and were, therefore, less responsive to the sanction threat. Perhaps they too would have been deterred if the probability of detection had been greater; but it is also possible that increased certainty of detection would have had little additional influence on their behavior, since they were highly motivated and had little to lose anyway.

Interestingly enough, these data are also interpretable within the framework of anomie theory. Those students who lacked the means to achieve the culturally accepted goal of academic success (a goal which they also apparently accepted, if their expected grades are any indication) were most likely to continue cheating in the face of potential detection and punishment. Anomie theory may converge with deterrence theory in directing attention to behavior that is likely to have high utility.

DISCUSSION

Although the evidence does support the deterrent hypothesis, it is not overpowering. Not all cheating was deterred by the threat, and even before the sanction threat was issued many cheating opportunities were not utilized. The failure to deter, just as the differential impact of the threat in the two groups, could have been the result of low credibility. Some students may have believed they would escape detection since the instructor said he was only going to "spot check" the papers. Others may have believed that detection would not really have adverse consequences, since they could plead that it was an honest error or that they misunderstood the real answer. Moreover, a spot check did not pose a threat of detection at all for some types of cheating. A few students merely left questions blank and then filled in the correct answers when they were discussed in class, while others erased a previously wrong answer and put in the correct one. Spot checking such papers would reveal no cheating, although it had occurred in a blatant fashion. For all these reasons, then, it is logical to imagine that if the probability of being caught and punished had been greater, more of the cheating would have been deterred.

Still, it is possible that some of the cheating was simply not deterrable by a sanction threat. For some, fear of sanction may have been irrelevant because they were doing so poorly in the course that the maximum punishment they could imagine would have made no difference anyhow. Others may have been defiant or incapable of comprehending the fact that a threat had been made. And as indicated earlier, some may have been so highly motivated to increase their grade that they were willing to take whatever risk was necessary.

The fact that the moral appeal failed to reduce cheating suggests little commitment to the norm of classroom honesty. But given this apparent lack of commitment, how can we explain why there was not maximum cheating prior to the sanction threat? One reason may have been that the students experienced some fear of being caught and punished even without an actual threat. Being accustomed to instructor evaluation, students probably viewed with some suspicion a sudden reversal that permitted them to grade their own papers. They surely perceived that the instructor was in a position to check the perfect scores beforehand, since he kept them overnight. Moreover, they must have reasoned that perfect scores on all quizzes would create suspicion on the part of the instructor. Thus, although impossible to determine, it seems plausible that much cheating may have been deterred by fear of sanction even before a formal threat was made.

But it would probably be a mistake to attribute all of the conformity to fear of sanction. Moral commitment was no doubt operative to some extent. Some students cheated such a small amount, even when they needed the grade very badly, that one would have to entertain seriously the notion that they had internalized the norm of honesty. Furthermore, a few students actually graded themselves lower than they earned, both in response to a moral appeal and at other points throughout the course. These people may have been super cowards (or there may have been some clerical error); but it seems more likely that they were morally committed or that they were responding out of guilt from having cheated on earlier quizzes.

CONCLUSION

The findings support deterrence theory, and they converge with other recent studies in suggesting that sanctions may play an important role in the maintenance of conformity and social order. But it would be a mistake to draw sweeping conclusions from these results. We were testing the effect of a particular kind of sanction threat—one to be imposed formally by an authority figure. The experiment used a particular type of subject (young adults) and was concerned with obedience to a non-legal norm with little moral or normative support. In addition, the behavior under consideration was instrumental behavior (oriented toward long range goals) and probably episodic; that is, it did not involve deep personal commitments to the deviance as a style of behavior around which one could form an identity. At least three of these conditions are those theoretically most likely to permit formal sanctions to work as deterrents.

It has frequently been suggested that formal sanctions are likely to be effective primarily for those rules that lack general moral support. Presumably if we had been dealing with a norm resting on an internalized moral imperative, there would have been little deviance to deter, and that which was extant would have already resisted informal sanctions from peers, and hence would have been less responsive to formal sanction threats. It has also been argued that sanctions are relevant only to a certain proportion of any population—those who have not thoroughly internalized the norm and are therefore "potential" offenders. The lower the moral support for a norm, the larger is this "marginal" category, and the more likely it is sanction threats will have significant deterrent impact. □

NOTES AND QUESTIONS

1. What does this study prove? Look at the various statements in the last two paragraphs in which the authors express cautions about what they learned from their data and how far we can generalize what they found.

Tittle and Rowe are appropriately cautious about some of their variables. They point out, for example, that their subjects were young adults, but not everyone falls into this category. They were also Americans who were college students. Indeed, we might want to know more about the background and socio-economic status of their subjects.

The behavior studied, they say, "was instrumental . . . and probably episodic." It did not "involve deep personal commitments to the deviance as a style of behavior around which one could form an identity." Hence, presumably, the study tells us little or nothing about drug addition or rape or about the work and mind of career criminals.

2. Note the word "instrumental" in the passage from Tittle and Rowe just quoted. William Chambliss, in "Types of Deviance and the Effectiveness of Legal Sanctions," 1967 *Wisconsin Law Review* 703, draws a distinction between "instrumental" crimes and "expressive" crimes—that is, between, roughly, those that are a means to an end and those that come out of emotion, passion, or addiction. "Expressive" acts, Chambliss claims, resist deterrence; not so "instrumental" acts. Tittle and Rowe are referring to this kind of distinction in the passage to which we have just referred. Is this an important distinction? If so, why? Can we always distinguish an instrumental from an expressive act? How do we know whether many people experience an emotional urge to kill but do not because they are deterred by the threat of criminal punishment?

3. Moral appeal seemed to make little difference to the students who took part in this experiment. Contrast, in this regard, the findings in Richard D. Schwartz and Sonya Orleans, "On Legal Sanctions," 34 *University of Chicago Law Review* 274 (1967) who claim to find some impact of a moral appeal to pay taxes. For a critical analysis of the methods used and conclusions drawn in the Schwartz and Orleans study, see Lawrence M. Friedman and Stewart Macaulay, *Law and the Behavioral Sciences* 2d ed. (Indianapolis: Bobbs-Merrill, 1977), pp. 324–329.

It is hard to accept the idea that moral appeals have no effect on people's behavior. After all, most of us can think of times (can't we?) when we refrained from doing something because we thought that it was wrong. More objectively, people do respond to requests to recycle paper or save scrap metal during wartime or save water during droughts. Although there may be no external enforcement mechanism, people respond to a moral appeal and do such acts because they think they are right. Why do some moral appeals work while others do not?

THE ROLE OF LEGITIMACY AND GENERAL RESPECT FOR AUTHORITY

34. *Why People Obey the Law*

Tom Tyler

(Yale University Press, 1990)

NORMATIVE ISSUES AND COMPLIANCE

☐ Although the idea of exercising authority through social control is attractively simple, it has been widely suggested that in democratic societies the legal system cannot function if it can influence people only by manipulating rewards and costs. This type of leadership is impractical because government is obliged to produce benefits or exercise coercion every time it seeks to influence citizens' behavior. These strategies consume large amounts of public resources and such societies would be in constant peril of disequilibrium and instability . . . .

Given that the regulation of behavior through social control is inefficient and may not be effective enough to allow a complex democratic society to survive, it is encouraging that social theorists have recognized other potential bases for securing public compliance with the law. Two such bases are commonly noted: social relations (friends, family, and peers) and normative values. Concerns about social relations reflect the influence of other people's judgments: normative values reflects a person's own ethical views.

These two influences on behavior have been widely recognized by social scientists. They have emerged in studies by social psychologists on attitudes, and on the changing of attitudes, by sociologists on power, by political scientists on discontent, and by psychologists on moral development.

Influence by the social group can be instrumental. Like authorities, social groups reward and punish their members, either by withholding or conferring signs of group status and respect, or more directly by channeling material resources toward or away from particular members. Such variations in rewards and costs are not under the control of public authorities, but they function in the same manner as do public incentives and disincentives. In focusing on peer group pressures, the deterrence literature has recently documented that law breaking is strongly related to people's judgments about the sanctions or rewards their behavior elicits from members of their social group. People are reluctant to commit criminal acts for which their family and friends would sanction them.

Group influence may also exert normative pressure on people, because individuals look to their social groups for information about appropriate conduct. Such normative influences are similar to the influence of personal morality . . . People's behavior is strongly affected by the normative climate created by others.

The final influence on social behavior is the person's own set of normative values—the sense of what is right or appropriate. Normative influences respond to factors different from those affected by considerations of reward and punishment. People focus not on personal gain or loss within a given situation but on the relationship between various kinds of potential behavior and their assessments of what behavior is appropriate.

The key feature of normative factors that differentiates them from considerations of reward and punishment is that the citizen voluntarily complies with rules rather than respond to the external situation. Because of this, normative influences are often referred to by psychologists as "internalized obligations," that is, obligations for which the citizen has taken personal responsibility. This sense of the internalized quality of moral norms is captured by [M.] Hoffman: "The legacy of both Sigmund Freud and Emile Durkheim is the agreement among social scientists that most people do not go through life viewing society's moral norms as external, coercively imposed pressures to which they must submit. Though the norms are initially external to the individual and often in conflict with his desires, the norms eventually become part of his internal motive system and guide his behavior even in the absence of external authority" (1977, 85).

Voluntary compliance is of course important only to the extent that compliant behavior is different from behavior derived from self-interest. Moral influences would be substantially less important if people typically viewed the behavior that most benefited them as normatively appropriate. The suggestion that citizens will voluntarily act against their self-interest is the key to the social value of normative influences. Given this assumption, leaders can gain voluntary compliance with their actions if the actions are consistent with people's views about right and wrong, even if not personally beneficial.

If the effectiveness of legal authorities ultimately depends on voluntary acceptance of their actions, then authorities are placed in the position of balancing public support against the effective regulation of public behavior. Legal authorities of course recognize their partial dependence on public goodwill, and are concerned with making allocations and resolving conflicts in a way that will both maximize compliance with the decision at hand and minimize citizens' hostility toward the authorities making the decision.

The dilemma faced by legal authorities is not unique to law. All leaders need discretionary authority to function effectively in their roles. Industrial managers must direct and restrict those who work under them. They also require support and cooperation from those they manage. When managers lack the legitimacy they need to secure the cooperation of workers, inefficiencies such as those caused by slowdowns and sabotage occur. Similar problems of authority are encountered by teachers, political leaders, army sergeants, and any other authorities who need legitimacy to function.

The compliance literature has recognized two important types of internalized obligation. First, citizens may comply with the law because they view the legal authority they are dealing with as having a legitimate right to dictate their behavior; this represents an acceptance by people of the need to bring their behavior into line with the dictates of an external authority . . . .

A second type of internalized obligation is derived from a person's desire to behave in a way that accords with his or her own sense of personal morality. Like views that accord legitimacy to authorities, personal morality is an internalized sense of obligation characterized by voluntary compliance. It differs from legitimacy in content, however. Personal morality is not a feeling of obligation to an external political or legal authority. It is instead an internalized obligation to follow one's personal sense of what is morally right or wrong.

Consider a specific illegal activity such as using cocaine. What is a person's motivation for complying with the law prohibiting its use? If people refrain from using drugs because they think laws ought to be obeyed, then legitimate authority is influencing their behavior. If they do so because drug abuse violates their convictions, then personal morality is influencing their behavior. If they fear being caught and sent to prison, deterrence is influencing their behavior. And if they do not use drugs because they fear the disapproval of their friends, the social group is exerting its influence.

From the perspective of the authorities in a political or legal system, legitimacy is a far more subtle base on which to rest compliance than personal or group morality, for the scope of legitimate authority is much more flexible. It rests on a conception of obligation to obey any commands an authority issues so long as that authority is acting within appropriate limits. Leaders with legitimate authority have open-ended, discretionary authority within a particular range of behavior. They may act in ways that will most effectively advance their objectives, expecting to receive public support for their actions.

Unlike legitimacy, personal morality is double-edged. It may accord with the dictates of authorities and as a result help to promote compliance with the law, but on the other hand it may lead to resisting the law and legal authorities. The distinction between personal morality and legitimacy suggests that two dimensions underlie the different motivations that can influence compliance. The first is whether the motivation is instrumental or normative; the second is whether the normative motivation is linked to a political authority. (Legitimacy is linked to a political authority, but personal morality may or may not be.)

Because of its value as a normative base for authorities, legitimacy has been an important concern among social scientists. It has been prominent in treatments of law by sociologists . . . , and by psychologists, political scientists, and anthropologists. In each case citizens who accept the legitimacy of the legal system and its officials are expected to comply with their dictates even when the dictates conflict with their self-interest. Legitimacy is regarded as a reservoir of loyalty on which leaders can draw, giving them the discretionary authority they require to govern effectively . . . .

Efforts to explore public opinion about the police, the courts, and the law reflect the belief among judges and legal scholars that public confidence in the legal system and public support for it—the legitimacy accorded legal officials by members of the public—is an important precursor to public acceptance of legal rules and decisions. To the extent that the public fails to support the law, obedience is less likely.

This focus on public views of the law and legal authorities has heightened concerns about the extent of public support. A number of social scientists and social commentators have noted the low levels of public support in recent public opinion polls for legal and political authorities. Studies of the public's evaluation of political leadership, of such institutions as the Supreme Court and the presidency, suggest that large segments of the public have little confidence in their legal and political authorities. There is an implicit belief that these low levels of confidence in authority will lessen compliance with the law . . . .

LEGITIMACY AS AN EMPIRICAL ISSUE

Although the assumption that legitimacy enhances compliance has traditionally been accepted by lawyers and social scientists, it has been pointed out that the assumption is not supported by convincing data. Instead of testing the role of legitimacy in compliance, scholars have simply assumed that it is important, and as a result the value of the concept of legitimate authority has not been established . . . .

To examine whether legitimacy influences behavioral compliance with the law one must first develop indicators for each of the variables to be analyzed. The most direct way in which legitimacy has been measured is as the perceived obligation to comply with the directives of an authority, irrespective of the personal gains or losses associated with doing so . . . .

Typically, studies of perceived obligation pose such questions as the following: "If a policeman asks you to do something that you think is wrong, should you do it anyway?" These questions presume a conflict between self-interest or personal morality and the legitimacy of the authority making a request. The central question is whether people will allow their external obligations to authority to override their personal self-interest or their moral views. A second approach to assessing legitimacy is to measure the extent to which authorities enjoy the public's support, allegiance, and confidence (in political science often subsumed under the heading "trust in government"). Citizens are asked to indicate their affective orientation toward government leaders and institutions or to respond to general evaluations, such as "Government leaders can usually be trusted to do what is right," or "Most police officers are honest." . . .

Most empirical work examining legitimacy has focused on issues of allegiance or attachment to the political and legal systems, rather than studied directly the perceived obligation to obey the law . . . .

The fundamental difference between obligation and support lies in the clarity of the motivation underlying compliance. Theories that measure legitimacy by measuring support assume that support for the government leads to the type of discretionary authority directly tapped by measuring the perceived obligation to obey. Support is therefore a less direct means of examining the role of legitimacy. If a relationship between support and compliance is found, it must be inferred that citizens comply because they feel an obligation to obey.

In addition to the question of whether legitimacy matters is the question what legitimacy is. Three potential objects of legitimacy have been distinguished by political scientists: authorities, the regime, and the community. The legitimacy of authorities involves support for those in positions of power, such as judges and police officers, for elected representatives, and for the policies and actions of the authorities. The legitimacy of the regime involves support for the offices and institutions that officials occupy and for the procedural rules that guide their conduct. Finally, views about the social groups that make up the political community may also be important. This final type of influence represents the possible overlap of legal and political authorities with members of one's social groups. For example, if members of a society have a common ethnic or religious heritage, they may think of their leaders as members of their own social group as well as formal authorities.

The basic distinction for our purposes is between the legitimacy of particular authorities and the legitimacy of the institutions or procedures of government. [David] Easton refers to the latter type of legitimacy as diffuse support for the system, that is support accorded the procedures and institutions of government. He distinguishes it from support for particular incumbent authorities and their decisions and policies which he calls specific support.

Legitimacy can reside either in a person who occupies a position of authority or in an institution. Political and legal theories of legitimacy have emphasized that using legitimate institutions and rules when making decisions enhances the likelihood that members of the public will comply, even if they do not agree with the decisions or support those who have made them. . . .

Evidence for the role of normative concerns in securing compliance can be gathered by examining not only legitimacy but also the effects of personal morality. In studies of these effects, people are asked to what extent a law or rule accords with their own judgments of right and wrong, and these judgments are correlated to whether they obey the law. Five studies of this kind found that personal assessments of the morality of the law typically have a strong influence on whether citizens say that they break the law (see table 1). The average correlation across the studies is .45, suggesting that about 20 percent of variance in obedience to the law can be explained by differences in judgments about the morality of law.

The influence of moral assessment on behavior toward the law is also examined in the large literature on moral judgment and juvenile delinquency. Studies in this area are typically based on the assumption that children who are influenced by instrumental considerations of reward and punishment are more likely to break laws than are children who are influenced by issues of obligation to obey the law. This assumption has been generally supported. . . . [Of] fifteen studies . . . ten showed significant behavioral differences of the type predicted by developmental theory. As with legitimacy, studies of personal morality support the suggestion that normative concerns influence compliance.

Although the studies examined differ in many ways, such as in their topics, methods and subjects, they all reinforce the conclusion that nor-

TABLE 1   JUDGMENTS ABOUT MORALITY OF A LAW AND WILLINGNESS TO OBEY IT

Study	Sample	Results
Grasmick and Green (1980)	400 adults	Those who view a law as moral more likely to say that they have obeyed it ($r = .42$) and will do so in the future ($r = .55$)
Jacob (1980)	176 adults	Those who view a law as moral more likely to say they obey it ($r = .47$)
Meier and Johnson (1977)	632 adults	Those who view using marijuana as immoral less likely to report using it ($r = .21$)
Silberman (1976)	174 students	Those who view laws as immoral less likely to report that they obey them ($r = .56$)
Tittle (1980)	1,993 adults	Those who view laws as immoral significantly less likely to report obeying them

mative support for the system leads to compliant behavior. Whether legitimacy operates as obligation or as support, the studies reviewed suggest a moderately strong positive relationship between the legitimacy of legal and political authorities and behavioral compliance.

At the same time, there is merit to the concerns that research has failed to demonstrate compellingly the value of the concept of legitimacy. Given the important theoretical role that legitimacy plays in social science treatments of the law, the weaknesses of the evidence reviewed is disappointing. The lack of strong studies is especially striking with studies of the obligation to obey the law, the most direct measure of citizen's assessments of legitimacy. The evidence that does exist is positive, but it has clear limits . . . .

MEASURING LEGITIMACY AND COMPLIANCE

The Chicago study focuses on six laws chosen to represent the range of laws people deal with in their everyday lives. The laws examined differ in their severity. The forms of behavior they prohibit are as follows: making enough noise to disturb neighbors, driving faster than fifty-five miles an hour, taking inexpensive items from stores without paying, and parking illegally. In each case citizens were asked whether they had often, sometimes, seldom, or never violated the law during the year preceding the interview.

Like most earlier research on compliance, the Chicago study relies on self-reporting of compliant behavior. Its results must therefore be viewed with caution: citizens may not be reporting accurately how often they break the law . . . .

An additional potential problem in measuring compliance with the law is the time frame used. In the first wave of interviews respondents were asked about their behavior during the preceding year. Such a broad time frame was chosen so that respondents would be more likely to indicate that they had engaged in at least one illegal behavior. But even with an extended time frame self-reporting of some forms of behavior was low.

A consequence of the approach used to assess behavior in the Chicago study is that the behavior examined occurred before the interviews, whereas the attitudes reflected the views of people at the time of the interviews. This casts some doubt on the causal order assumed in this study—that attitudes cause behavior; it may in fact be behavior that causes attitudes. The extent to which this is a problem cannot be determined by using cross-sectional data; panel analysis is required.

Respondents' self-reporting on how often they broke the law is shown in table 2. People were most likely to say that they had committed less serious offenses, such as parking illegally (51 percent) and speeding (62 percent). Very few respondents said they had stolen items from a store (3 percent). For each of the other offenses, the proportion fell somewhere in between: for making noise, 27 percent; for littering, 25 percent; for drunk driving, 19 percent.

The various indices of law breaking were found to have a moderately strong positive relationship (mean r = .23). As would be expected

TABLE 2   FREQUENCY OF LAW BREAKING: FIRST WAVE (IN PERCENTAGES)

	Mean (standard deviation)	Often	Sometimes	Seldom	Never
Drove over 55 miles per hour on the highways	3.6 (.74)	16	28	18	38
Parked car in violation of the law	3.6 (.69)	6	22	23	49
Made enough noise to disturb neighbors	3.7 (.63)	2	8	17	73
Littered in violation of the law	2.8 (1.1)	2	8	15	75
Drove a car while intoxicated	4.0 (.27)	1	7	12	81
Took inexpensive items from stores without paying for them	3.1 (1.0)	0	1	2	97

n = 1,575

Because of rounding, percentages may not add to 100.

given the proportions shown in table 2, the overall scale of compliance with the law is skewed, with most respondents indicating little law breaking. In all, 22 percent of the respondents said they had never broken any of the six laws during the year preceding the interview.

Because many of the respondents in the first wave of interviews said they never broke the law, the questionnaire used in the second wave was designed to differentiate more finely among members of this law-abiding group, by using a more complex scale that included five frequencies of behavior: often, sometimes, seldom, almost never, and never. It was believed that the additional category, almost never, would be chosen by many respondents who had said in the first interview that they never broke the law.

A more differentiated scale was needed in the second wave especially because the period being asked about was shorter: instead of being asked whether they had broken the law "in the past year," respondents were asked about "the last several months." This abbreviated period was adopted because of concerns about the problem of casual order. Unfortunately, the use of this shorter period also increased the likelihood that respondents would say they never broke the law.

The results of the second wave of interviews suggest that the greater differentiation of the scale of behavior more than counteracted the effects of the shorter time period. Overall, there was slightly more variance in the second wave in self-reported law breaking. The proportions

TABLE 3   FREQUENCY OF LAW BREAKING: SECOND WAVE (IN PERCENT)

	Mean (standard deviation)	Often	Sometimes	Seldom	Almost Never	Never
Made enough noise to disturb neighbors	4.4 (.96)	1	6	10	18	65
Littered in violation of the law	4.4 (.98)	1	7	9	17	66
Drove a car while intoxicated	4.7 (.79)	0	4	6	9	81
Drove over 55 miles per hour on the highways	3.2 (1.5)	17	28	13	8	35
Took inexpensive items from stores without paying for them	5.0 (.27)	0	0	1	2	97
Parked car in violation of the law	3.7 (1.4)	5	22	15	11	47

n = 804.

Because of rounding, percentages may not add to 100.

of respondents who acknowledged having broken the law were as follows: for making excessive noise, 35 percent; for littering, 34 percent; for driving while intoxicated, 19 percent; for speeding, 65 percent; for shoplifting, 3 percent; for parking illegally, 53 percent (see table 3).

As in the first wave of the study, the six items studied were found to have a low but positive correlation (mean r = .20). The expanded set of categories produced greater variance in responses and as a result a less skewed scale of compliance.

Given differences in compliance among the people interviewed, the first question to be considered is who complies with the law. One way to address the question is by examining demographic correlates of compliance with the law. In this study demographic characteristics explain a substantial proportion of the variance in compliance (24 percent). Age and sex are the major influences: the old and women are more likely to say they comply with the law. Similar findings were obtained in the second wave of interviews.

INFLUENCES ON COMPLIANCE

The sociological framework focuses on three factors that influence compliance: deterrence, peer opinion and personal morality. Judgments based on deterrence involve assessments of the likelihood of being caught, the likelihood of being punished, the expected severity of punishment, or some combination of these factors. Because research suggests that certainty of apprehension and punishment most strongly influences behavior, this is the factor that was used in this study . . . . [T]he expected severity of punishment was not assessed.

To establish the strength of concerns about deterrence, citizens were asked how likely they thought it was that they would be "arrested or issued a citation by the police" if they committed each of the six offenses: very likely, somewhat likely, somewhat unlikely, or very unlikely.

Citizens generally thought that the likelihood of being arrested for law breaking was high. In the first wave of the survey 35 percent said this was very likely or somewhat likely for making too much noise; 31 percent said the same for littering; 83 percent said so for drunk driving; 72 percent said so for speeding; 78 percent said so for shoplifting; and 78 percent said so for violating parking rules.

A second factor considered was peer disapproval. Respondents were asked to what degree the "five adults they know best" would "disapprove or feel that [they] had done something wrong" if they were arrested for committing one of the six offenses. For four offenses about half of those interviewed said their peers would disapprove "a great deal" or "somewhat": for making too much noise, 53 percent; for littering, 51 percent; for speeding, 52 percent; for parking illegally, 44 percent. In two cases disapproval was higher: for drunk driving it was 86 percent and for shoplifting 89 percent.

Finally, citizens were asked whether breaking each law was morally "very wrong," "somewhat wrong," "not very wrong," or "not wrong at all." In each case breaking the law was considered very wrong or somewhat wrong by a large proportion of the respondents: 96 percent in the case of disturbing the neighbors (very wrong by 61 percent); 96 percent for littering (very wrong by 63 percent); 100 percent for drunk driving (very wrong by 95 percent); 84 percent for speeding (very wrong by 39 percent); 99 percent for shoplifting (very wrong by 92 percent); and 86 percent for parking illegally (very wrong by 37 percent).

Citizens seemed to view breaking laws as a violation of their personal morality. Almost all respondents felt it wrong to break any of the six laws studied. Most also thought that the likelihood of being caught for breaking the laws was high (70 percent to 80 percent felt this way, except for the minor offenses of littering and making too much noise, for which around 30 percent did). But respondents were not likely to feel that their friends or family would disapprove of their breaking the law (except for shoplifting and drunk driving). Peer disapproval therefore seems an unlikely source of pressure to obey the law.

One possibility is that people's views about each of the six laws studied are unrelated. But an examination of the correlations measuring reactions to the six laws suggests that this is not the case. Some viewed the likelihood of being arrested for breaking the laws as higher than did other citizens: the mean correlation between estimates during the first wave was .34. Similarly, the mean correlation of the peer items at the second wave was .39, suggesting a generalized view about peer feelings. Views about the immorality of breaking the various laws were also moderately related (mean r = .31 at the first wave).

An examination of the various sociological factors shows that they also are all related. Those who view law breaking as immoral are more likely to see it as being disapproved of by their peers (r = .46); they are also more likely to think that it will lead to arrest (r = .41), as are those who think that peers will disapprove (r = .41). Finally, all three factors are correlated with self-reported behavioral compliance with the law (for morality, r = .42; for peer disapproval, r = .34; for certainty of punishment, r = .28).

LEGITIMACY

Legitimacy was examined in two ways: as the perceived obligation to obey the law and as support for legal authorities. This parallels earlier studies. In examining obligation to obey the law, the researchers asked the respondents to what degree they felt they should comply with directives from police officers or judges, irrespective of their personal feelings (see table 4).

The extent to which respondents endorsed the obligation to obey is striking. For example, 82 percent agreed that "a person should obey the

TABLE 4   PERCEIVED OBLIGATION TO OBEY THE LAW

	Percentage agreeing
People should obey the law even if it goes against what they think is right.	82
I always try to follow the law even if I think that it is wrong.	82
Disobeying the law is seldom justified.	79
It is difficult to break the law and keep one's self-respect.	69
If a person is doing something and a police officer tells them to stop they should stop even if they feel that what they are doing is legal.	84
If a person goes to court because of a dispute with another person, and the judge orders them to pay the other person money, they should pay that person money even if they think that the judge is wrong.	71

n = 1,575.

law even if it goes against what they think is right." This uniformity of responses poses a problem, because without variance in responses it is not possible to identify the antecedents or consequences of views about obligation. To increase variance, the perceived obligation to obey was examined differently in the second wave: for each statement, respondents could agree strongly, agree, disagree, or disagree strongly.

The results of the first wave of interviews also suggest that some respondents had difficulty understanding the last two items of the obligation scale, which dealt with compliance in specific instances. To clarify the obligation scale in the second wave, the first four items of the original scale were combined with two new ones: "A person who refuses to obey the law is a menace to society," and "Obedience and respect for authority are the most important virtues children should learn." This elaborated scale seems to have been more effective in capturing variance in the perceived obligation to obey the law (table 5).

It is interesting to compare responses to the items on obligation with those to the items on personal morality. Just as respondents almost universally feel that breaking the law is immoral, they feel a strong obligation to obey the law: both personal morality and the legitimacy of legal authorities encourage citizens to be law-abiding. Although these two forces could be in conflict, in this study they support each other.

Legitimacy was also examined as a general affective orientation toward authorities, that is, as "allegiance" or "support" for the authorities involved. Support was measured separately for the police (table 6) and the courts (table 7). In each case the respondent was given a series

TABLE 5 PERCEIVED OBLIGATION TO OBEY THE LAW: SECOND WAVE (IN PERCENT)

	Agree Strongly	Agree	Disagree	Disagree Strongly
People should obey the law even if it goes against what they think is right.	33	52	13	2
I always try to follow the law even if I think that it is wrong.	27	58	15	1
Disobeying the law is seldom justified	25	57	16	2
It is difficult to break the law and keep one's self-respect.	22	49	25	3
A person who refuses to obey the law is a menace to society.	24	50	23	3
Obedience and respect for authority are the most important virtues children should learn.	31	51	15	3

n = 804.

TABLE 6 SUPPORT FOR THE POLICE (IN PERCENT)

	Agree strongly		Agree		Disagree		Disagree strongly	
	First wave	Second wave	First wave	Second wave	First wave	Second wave	First wave	Second wave
I have a great deal of respect for the Chicago police.	19	21	57	61	20	15	4	3
On the whole Chicago police officers are honest.	7	10	51	54	34	31	8	5
I feel proud of the Chicago police.	12	14	54	61	29	22	5	3
I feel that I should support the Chicago police.	20	25	68	66	10	7	3	2

First wave. n = 1,575.   Second wave n = 804.

Because of rounding, percentages may not add to 100.

TABLE 7 SUPPORT FOR THE COURTS IN PERCENT

	Agree strongly		*Agree*		*Disagree*		*Disagree strongly*	
	First wave	*Second wave*	*First wave*	*Second wave*	*First wave*	*Second wave*	*First wave*	*Second wave*
The courts in Chicago generally guarantee everyone a fair trial.	6	7	53	55	35	33	6	5
The basic rights of citizens are well protected in the Chicago courts.	4	5	53	57	37	34	6	5
On the whole Chicago judges are honest.	4	5	53	57	34	31	9	7
Court decisions in Chicago are almost always fair.	3	3	53	56	39	36	5	5

First wave: n = 1,575.   Second wave: n = 804.

Because of rounding, percentages may not add to 100.

of general statements about the authority with which to agree strongly, agree, disagree, or disagree strongly.

The respondents were much more evenly split on support than on obligation. Only a narrow majority of citizens agreed with positive statements about the police and the courts. For example, in the first wave 42 percent of the sample disagreed with the statement that police officers in Chicago are generally honest and 43 percent disagreed with the statement that judges are.

Although support and the perceived obligation to obey represent two aspects of the same underlying construct of legitimacy, the correlation between the two indices was only moderately strong (in the first wave r = .26, p < .001). This suggests that respondents differentiated between their generally positive affect toward the courts and police and their judgments about their personal obligation to obey the law. The revised obligation scale used in the second wave of the study had a higher inter-item correlation indicating that it is a stronger scale. It nevertheless continued to show only a moderately strong correlation to support (r = .25). Thus in the second wave, as in the first, the two ways of expressing legitimacy proved quite distinct . . .

Who feels obligated to obey the law and who indicates support? An analysis of demographic correlates suggests a weak relationship between the two groups. Demographic characteristics explain 24 percent of the variance in behavioral compliance with the law, but only 10 percent of the variance in legitimacy. As is true with compliance, the major demographic correlate of legitimacy is age. Older respondents view the law as more legitimate, according to each of the indicators of legitimacy. Education also is related to legitimacy, with highly educated respondents less likely to evince high levels of legitimacy . . . .

Correlations reveal that views about the personal morality of law breaking, judgments about peer disapproval, and judgments about deterrence are all related to support and to feelings of obligation to obey the law. These correlations are however small (mean r = .15); the two factors are largely distinct, although not totally so.

OTHER INFLUENCES ON COMPLIANCE

Another potentially important influence on compliance is the respondents' evaluation of the quality of service received from the authorities. Obviously, less feeling of obligation is required for one to support authorities viewed as solving problems well: if people feel that their interests are being furthered by the authorities, they will support the authorities for reasons of short-term gain. Evaluations of performance should therefore be distinguished from legitimacy, which is a perceived obligation to obey based on motivations other than short-term self-interest. In the Chicago study performance was evaluated separately for the police and the courts. In the case of the police the scale had fourteen items, assessing overall performance and the perceived likelihood of good performance in the future.

Satisfaction with performance was established by asking respondents how good a job the police (or courts) were doing, how well the police (or courts) solved problems and helped those who dealt with them, and how satisfied the respondents were with the fairness of outcomes when they dealt with the police (or courts). The results show general but far from universal satisfaction with legal authorities (table 8). In addition, they suggest that satisfaction is higher with the police than with the courts.

Satisfaction with the performance of legal authorities also involves assessing the quality of their work. Quality of performance was measured by asking respondents how frequently the police (or courts) provided satisfactory service, how often they handled problems satisfactorily, and whether they treated citizens fairly and dispensed fair outcomes. Similar questions were asked about those who went to court (table 9). The police and courts seem to be viewed as often failing to resolve problems satisfactorily and often as being unfair. Again the courts were viewed more negatively than the police.

Finally, respondents were asked whether they would receive satisfactory and fair outcomes and treatment if they called the police in the future. The answers were affirmative, even though citizens expressed the view that unsatisfactory and unfair treatment of citizens by the police and courts is widespread. They almost universally believe that their future dealings with these authorities will be satisfactory and fair.

A similar distinction between general judgments and feelings about

TABLE 8 SATISFACTION WITH LEGAL AUTHORITIES (IN PERCENT)

	First wave		Second wave	
	Police	Courts	Police	Courts
How good a job are they doing				
Very good	10	4	1	5
Good	44	22	48	25
Fair	38	47	36	45
Poor	6	18	5	21
Very Poor	2	9	1	4
How satisfied are you with the way they solve problems?				
Very satisfied	17	7	16	7
Somewhat satisfied	55	48	64	52
Neutral (volunteered)	2	1	1	1
Somewhat dissatisfied	21	32	16	32
Very dissatisfied	6	13	3	9
How satisfied are you with the fairness of the outcomes people receive?				
Very satisfied	13	7	12	8
Somewhat satisfied	52	49	65	57
Neutral (volunteered)	2	1	1	1
Somewhat dissatisfied	26	30	18	28
Very dissatisfied	8	12	4	7
How satisfied are you with the fairness of the way that people are treated				
Very satisfied	14	9	15	8
Somewhat satisfied	56	53	66	59
Neutral (volunteered)	0	0	0	0
Somewhat dissatisfied	24	30	17	28
Very dissatisfied	7	9	2	6

First wave: n = 1,575.　　Second wave: n = 804.

Because of rounding, percentage may not add to 100.

the self can be found in responses to questions about discrimination. When respondents were asked whether the police treated citizens equally or favored some citizens over others, 74 percent said there was favoritism; 72 percent made the same statement about the courts. When asked whether people like themselves were discriminated against, however, most respondents said no (75 percent for the police, 77 percent for the courts). People see widespread unfairness, yet do not see themselves as being discriminated against.

Because the various judgments about the police were found to be highly related, a single scale of performance was used. The ten items concerning the courts also were found to be highly correlated, so for these a single scale was used as well. These two scales for evaluating performance were found to be highly related, and performance evaluations were also related to assessments of legitimacy.

As with legitimacy, the correlation of evaluations of the police and

TABLE 9   PERCEIVED QUALITY OF LEGAL AUTHORITIES (IN PERCENT)

	First wave				Second wave			
	Police			Courts	Police			Courts
	Called police	Stopped by police	All police		Called police	Stopped by police	All police	
Handle the problem satisfactorily?								
Always	12	12		5	11	10		4
Usually	45	43		29	50	52		38
Sometimes	34	35		49	34	31		48
Seldom	10	10		18	5	7		11
Provide people with fair outcomes?								
Always			7	5			9	5
Usually			43	34			48	42
Sometimes			40	49			38	45
Seldom			10	13			5	8
Treat people fairly?								
Always			9	6			9	6
Usually			47	38			53	45
Sometimes			36	45			34	42
Seldom			8	11			4	8

First wave: n = 1,575.   Second wave: n = 804.
Because of rounding, percentages may not add to 100.

courts with demographic variables was low (mean r = .08). Police evaluations were influenced strongly by race (nonwhites gave more negative evaluations) and by age (older respondents gave more positive ones). Evaluations of the courts were influenced by sex (men gave more positive evaluations), by education (those with less education were more positive), and by income (those with high income were more negative).

The Chicago study's examination of legitimacy and compliance suggests several reasons why people obey the law. One is their instrumental concern with being caught and punished: people typically think it quite likely that this will happen if they commit serious crimes. Deterrence may be exerting an influence on their behavior. Obedience to the law is also strongly linked to people's personal morality. The data suggest a general feeling among respondents that law breaking is morally wrong. A similarly strong feeling emerges in the case of the perceived obligation to obey the law. Most of the respondents interviewed felt obliged to obey the law and the directives of legal authorities. In contrast to the strong normative commitment found in studying personal morality and perceived obligation to obey the law, support for the police and courts was not particularly high, and neither were evaluations of their performance. This does not mean, however, that dissatisfaction with the police or the courts is widespread.

The lack of a strong feeling of peer disapproval toward law breaking is also noteworthy. Although respondents thought that their friends and family would disapprove of some violations of the law, this perceived disapproval applied only to such serious crimes as drunk driving. In more mundane cases respondents thought their peers would not disapprove very strongly of illegal behavior.

DOES LEGITIMACY CONTRIBUTE INDEPENDENTLY TO COMPLIANCE?

Normative factors are widely held to have an important role in facilitating compliance with the law. Legitimacy is a particularly important normative factor for it is believed to be the key to the success of legal authorities. If authorities have legitimacy, they can function effectively; if they lack it it is difficult and perhaps impossible for them to regulate public behavior. As a result, those interested in understanding how to maintain the social system have been concerned with identifying the conditions that promote legitimacy; those seeking social change have sought to understand how to undermine it.

A review of the literature on legitimacy reveals no compelling evidence that legitimacy in practice has the important role given it in theory in facilitating compliance. The first concern of the Chicago study was to test whether legitimacy in fact makes an independent contribution to compliance. Does the extent to which people view legal authorities as having legitimate power influence their compliance with the law?

FIRST WAVE: CROSS-SECTIONAL ANALYSIS

The zero-order relationship between legitimacy and compliance is significant, suggesting that legitimacy is related to compliance. Those who regard legal authorities as having greater legitimacy are more likely to obey the law in their everyday lives. If legitimacy is used alone in a regression analysis to predict compliance, the analysis explains 5 percent of the variance in compliance. Respondents were divided into ten groups of about equal size based on their legitimacy scores, and the average level of compliance was then computed for each of the groups. The relationship between legitimacy and compliance was found to be linear: as legitimacy increases, so does compliance (fig. 1).

Although the significant correlation between legitimacy and compliance shows the two concepts to be related, it does not show causality: a correlational analysis ignores the possibility of spurious influences by

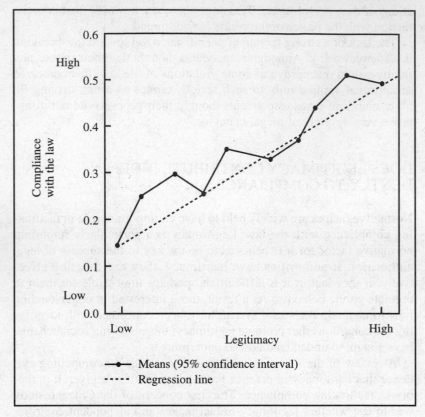

FIGURE 1   Legitimacy and compliance

third variables. Such influences occur when two measured variables are both related to a common, unmeasured one. The correlation between the two measured variables will therefore not represent the true relationship between the variables . . . .

THE USE OF PANEL RESPONDENTS

The finding that legitimacy influences compliance can also be replicated by analyzing the second wave of interviews. As before, legitimacy emerges as a significant predictor of compliance with or without adjustments for the reliability of measurement. Also as before, personal morality, sex, and age are important influences on compliance.

One potential problem with regression analysis based on cross-sectional data is that the dependent variable, behavioral compliance, measures behavioral compliance before the interview, whereas the independent variables measure judgments made at the time of the interview. It is therefore possible that the dependent variable of compliance causes the independent variables, not the other way around. Panel analysis can test whether legitimacy continues to contribute to behavioral compliance once this problem is corrected. In the panel analysis that was designed the independent variables were the attitudinal and demographic variables from the first wave of interviews and the dependent variable was compliance at the wave. When the measure of behavioral compliance from the second wave is substituted as the dependent variable in the regression equation and the independent variables from the first wave are kept, the level of the coefficients generally decreases, but a significant legitimacy effect remains. When panel data are used to ensure that the behavioral compliance follows the assessment of legitimacy, the significant influence of legitimacy on compliance remains as well . . . .

A key assumption of theories about legal authority is that legitimacy enhances the effectiveness of legal authorities by increasing public compliance with the law. The results of the Chicago study strongly support this assumption. People who regard legal authorities as legitimate are found to comply with the law more frequently. This relationship holds across a variety of types of analysis and is robust across changes in methodology.

IMPLICATIONS OF THE CHICAGO STUDY

Compliance is the basis for the effective operation of legal authorities. Widespread noncompliance leads to unstable system. Despite the value that authorities place on obtaining compliance with the law, they can never take it for granted. Legal authorities often find that they must tolerate occasional noncompliance with laws that are generally followed, and at some times they are faced with noncompliance so widespread that it threatens their ability to govern effectively. What determines the extent to which people will or will not follow the law in their daily lives? The Chicago study suggests that normative concerns are an important determinant of law-abiding behavior, in contrast to the instrumental concerns that have dominated the recent literature on compliance.

The most important normative influence on compliance with the law is the person's assessment that following the law accords with his or her sense of right and wrong; a second factor is the person's feeling of obligation to obey the law and allegiance to legal authorities. According to the Chicago study, those who feel that they "ought" to follow the dictates of authorities are more likely to do so. One important and striking finding of the study is the high level of normative commitment found among the public to abiding by the law. People generally feel that law breaking is morally wrong, and that they have a strong obligation to obey laws even if they disagree with them. Further, within the range of everyday laws studied, these two sources of commitment to law-abiding behavior reinforce each other. Law breaking is viewed both as morally wrong and as a violation of an obligation owed to authorities. This high level of normative commitment to obeying the law offers an important basis for the effective exercise of authority by legal officials. People clearly have a strong predisposition toward following the law. If authorities can tap into such feelings, their decisions will be more widely followed.

Although normative commitment is obviously desirable, if only for the money it saves, it may also be difficult to obtain. Unlike deterrence, the success of which depends primarily on the willingness of the authorities to spend money on enforcement, normative commitment requires intensive education and socialization, and these take time. Despite such problems authorities are not free to ignore the need for normative support. Democratic societies require normative commitment to function effectively. Authorities cannot induce through deterrence alone a level of compliance sufficient for effective social functioning. Society's resources are inadequate to such a task and some base of normative commitment to follow the law is needed.

Although the Chicago study found that people endorse the obligation to obey legal authorities, it did not disclose how people decide how much they ought to obey. It remains unclear why people endorse the obligation to obey so strongly. Their endorsement clearly reflects widely held views about the function of laws and authorities, but it is not known what people think would happen if they ignored legitimate authorities more often. What do people think would be the consequences, for example, if they behaved according to personal morality or the pressures of peer groups, and ignored legal authorities and the law? . . .

Personal morality is especially problematic for legal authorities in a pluralistic society such as the United States, which lacks a commonly accepted moral code. For example, the United States has no state church but instead accepts the idea that different moral values can coexist in a single society. In such a setting, authorities are likely to confront a wide range of moral values, none of which is the clearly appropriate standard for resolving policy issues or judging conduct. Against this pluralistic background the high levels of normative commitment to law-abiding behavior are striking.

Authorities draw on legitimacy because it is easier to influence behavior by so doing than through deterrence. Similarly, legitimacy is the main focus of the social critic, who seeks to promote a questioning of existing social rules that ultimately leads to disobedience. Because it is the key to discretionary authority, legitimacy is the natural focus of such efforts at reeducation. The social critic asks why the legitimacy was accorded in the first place and urges people to withhold it unless it is earned.

Several questions are left unanswered by the Chicago study. Although the study confirms the influence of legitimacy on compliance, it does not directly examine the nature of the perceived obligation to obey the law that brings about this influence. It does establish that the obligation to obey the law is a widely held value among those studied. It is also unclear what the boundaries of legitimacy are. To which authorities and to which of their actions is it granted? In the case of behavior that falls outside the range of what is appropriate, such as police brutality, the public becomes sharply divided about whether such behavior should be accorded legitimacy. Further, the basis of legitimacy is unexplored. What are the characteristics of authorities that lead them to be viewed as legitimate by those with whom they deal? To what extent is it the social position occupied by a third party (a police officer or judge), and to what extent is it an inference that the person being dealt with has particular characteristics, such as competence or trustworthiness? . . .

The findings of the Chicago study also support the suggestion that the influence of deterrence on compliance may be overrated. The Chicago study . . . found little evidence of deterrent effects. Although the study does not question the assumption that deterrence works, other studies may well.

Finally, personal views about the morality of law breaking are important in shaping compliance with the law. Although the Chicago study deals with legitimacy, personal morality is clearly a more important influence on compliance than legitimacy. This finding suggests a second type of normative support for the law, one not necessarily linked to views about the legal system. If the people interviewed in the study were to lose their sense that legal authorities are legitimate, many would still comply with the law, because of their moral belief that they should. The strength of this influence demonstrates that such moral influences on compliance are an important area for future research. □

NOTES AND QUESTIONS

1. What is Tyler's definition of legitimacy? How does he operationalize (measure) it? Are you convinced by that operationalization? Can you think of alternative ways to define and measure legitimacy? How is his concept related to the concept of "shame," as used by Grasmick and Bursik?

2. According to Tyler, what are the respective effects on compliance of morality, deterrence, and legitimacy? How are these results consistent or inconsistent with those found by Grasmick and Bursik, and Tittle and Rowe? What accounts for the differences?

3. Note the types of law-breaking which Tyler uses. How did he select these? Are they a fair sample of behavior that is against the law? What would you add to the list? Would "legitimacy" likely become more or less important as a predictor of compliance, if we were talking about serious offenses, such as burglary or robbery, instead of the crimes on his list?

4. Tyler contends that government can increase perceived legitimacy and therefore increase compliance. What steps would a government need to take to increase perceived legitimacy? Is there a problem, in a society that values free

speech and is suspicious of government propaganda, in suggesting such measures?

5. Tyler argues that "legitimacy" is a "far more stable base on which to rest compliance than personal or group morality." This is because it is more "open-ended" or flexible. To take an extreme case, Tyler seems to say that if a person is convinced that the authority of, say, an elder or chief in a certain society is "legitimate" (for whatever reason), the subject will obey no matter what the elder or chief orders. This, of course, makes the position of the elder or chief much more powerful than if he had to justify every order, or appeal to some sense of personal morality.

Is there anything in Tyler's findings, as reported here, that actually supports this argument? Do you think "legitimacy" in Tyler's sense is a powerful factor in making people obey the law in the United States? Is it getting weaker or stronger? It is widely believed that trust in government—surely a related concept—is getting weaker in the United States. Is this your impression as well? How do you account for this weakness?

What about legitimacy in other societies, for example, Mexico or Japan? What about authoritarian states like the People's Republic of China?

6. Tyler's conclusion is that "legitimacy influences compliance." Has he actually proved this? How far do his findings go? To what extent are they limited by the fact that he studied the population of Chicago, Illinois at one particular time? Does he have any reliable measure of behavior?

Tom R. Tyler and Gregory Mitchell, in "Legitimacy and the Empowerment of Discretionary Legal Authority: The United States Supreme Court and Abortion Rights," 43 *Duke Law Journal* 703 (1994), report a survey of a random sample in the San Francisco Bay Area. We have described some of its findings on p. 231. Unlike the subjects in Tyler's Chicago study, those in the Bay Area seemed more willing to reject laws with which they disagreed. Only 38% in this study felt that they should accept decisions made by government leaders in Washington even when they disagreed with those decisions. 48% said that there are times when it is all right to disobey the government, and 66% said that they could think of situations in which they would stop supporting government policies. Tyler and Mitchell say "local legal authorities are supported by much stronger presumptions of obligation to obey than are federal authorities" (p. 762). Does this explain the differences between the two Tyler studies?

7. Compliance based on a sense of legitimacy is considered a good thing by most people in this country. But of course not by everyone. The morality of compliance and legitimacy depends on whether this or any other society is good and just. Those who fought the apartheid regime of South Africa, or who fought against Hitler's Germany, are considered heroes, not criminals. Austin Sarat, in "Authority, Anxiety, and Procedural Justice: Moving from Scientific Detachment to Critical Engagement," 27 *Law & Society Review* 647 (1993), sees Tyler's book as studying a "thing"—legitimacy—that exists and is a basis for compliance with laws. Sarat advocates studying "legitimation," the process by which "law actively creates the shared sense that existing legal arrangements are as they ought to be" (p. 662).

Even in this society, compliance may be problematic. For one thing, there are those who admire rebels and outlaws—at least certain ones. Literature and the movies certainly suggest a certain amount of admiration of people outside the law. "Question authority" is a popular bumper sticker.

8. Refer back to Friedman's notion of the "deterrence curve", on p. 440. What would the curve look like for the offenses that Tyler used in his study?

9. Where does this sense of "legitimacy" come from? Why do people consider a regime, a rule, or an order legitimate or illegitimate? This subject has given rise to much speculation but not very much research. Here, of course, Tyler's work is certainly relevant. See also Craig A. McEwen and Richard J. Maiman, "In Search of Legitimacy: Toward an Empirical Analysis," 8 *Law & Policy* 257 (1986).

The most famous discussion of legitimate authority is that of Max Weber. Weber felt that there are three ultimate principles of legitimation in a society. The validity of a power or command could rest on personal authority. Personal authority falls into two categories. It may be based on *charisma*—the "surrender to the extraordinary," to "actual revelation or grace" which rests in the charismatic leader who is seen as a "savior, a prophet, or a hero." Or, personal authority could be based on the "sacredness of *tradition*." It could rest on what is "customary and has always been so and prescribes obedience to some particular person," for example, a king or a chief.

However, power or command may be valid for reasons that have nothing to do with personal authority. Power or command may be legitimate because it is expressed in a "system of consciously-made *rational* rules . . . which meet with obedience as generally binding norms." In a system based on "rational" legitimacy, obedience is "given to the norms rather than the person." This kind of legitimacy is thus sharply opposed to legitimacy based on tradition or charisma. See Max Rheinstein, ed., *Max Weber on Law in Economy and Society* (Cambridge, Mass.: Harvard University Press), 1954.

Modern law for the most part tends to fall into Weber's rational-legal category. Our laws are passed by legislatures which follow hopefully "rational" procedures. Some may be enunciated by judges who are trained in legal technique, a system which we hope is based on reason and policy. But are there elements of charismatic or traditional authority in modern law as well? What do Weberian forms of legitimacy mean for compliance with law? Does it seem likely that people comply with laws because they are based on rational procedures? Because the laws are the expression of a charismatic leader or one holding office because of tradition?

Suppose one of your professors drove to work this morning. She stopped at all stop signs and red lights. She obeyed all speed limits. She parked her car in a legal parking space no longer than the time allowed. She walked to her office without assaulting anyone. During the day she did not steal money from anyone. Her monthly paycheck will contain deductions that pay all applicable state and federal taxes. How much of this behavior can we explain by her sense that the state and federal government are legitimate or that the particular laws she obeyed were legitimate? Suppose on the way home the professor drove her car at a speed ten miles an hour faster than the speed limit. Can we explain her speeding in terms of her belief that the government or the speeding laws are illegitimate?

Suppose the professor worked on her computer with a word processing program which she had copied from a disk that a friend had purchased. Assume that this infringed the publisher's intellectual property rights in the word processing program. Can we explain the professor's use of "pirated" software in terms of her belief that the laws governing software are illegitimate? See G. Stephen Taylor and J. P. Shim, "A Comparative Examination of Attitudes

Toward Software Piracy Among Business Professors and Executives," 46 *Human Relations* 419 (1993). For an attack on the whole concept of legitimacy as a explanation of compliance, see Alan Hyde, "The Concept of Legitimation in the Sociology of Law," 1983 *Wisconsin Law Review* 379.

10. Niklas Luhmann, *Legitimation durch Verfahren* [Legitimation through Procedure] 2d ed. (Darmstadt: Luchterhand, 1975) presents an important treatment of legitimacy. Luhmann defines the sense of legitimacy as a person's general willingness or propensity to "accept decisions, whose content is yet unspecified, within certain limits of tolerance." In modern society legitimacy is essentially procedural. His definition fits, for example, two people who agree to accept the results of a coin toss or a person's willingness to accept the result of a majority vote in an election although his or her candidate might lose. We might not accept the results of an election if, say, an out-and-out Nazi were elected, but this is covered by Luhmann's phrase "within certain limits of tolerance." For a related treatment of legitimacy, see Lawrence M. Friedman, *The Legal System: A Social Science Perspective* 112 (New York: Russell Sage Foundation, 1975).

11. If legitimacy leads to compliance, does a feeling that law or the legal order is *illegitimate* lead to noncompliance? Or to worse? These propositions, of course, seem quite plausible. But under what conditions? And to what extent?

Questions of this type no doubt struck many scholars as particularly salient in the aftermath of the savage bombing of the federal building in Oklahoma City, Oklahoma, in late April 1995. Well over a hundred people died in the explosion, including many children in a day-care center. At this writing (summer 1995), the case has not been definitively solved; but the finger of blame points toward right-wing militants who believe fervently that the federal government is evil and illegitimate.

Consider, too, the following from a classic and controversial study:

35. *Obedience to Authority: An Experimental View*[146]

Stanley Milgram

☐ Obedience is as basic an element in the structure of social life as one can point to. Some system of authority is a requirement of all communal living, and it is only the man dwelling in isolation who is not forced to respond, through defiance or submission, to the commands of others. Obedience, as a determinant of behavior, is of particular relevance to our time. It has been reliably established that from 1933 to 1945 millions of innocent people were systematically slaughtered on command.

---

146. Abridged from pp. 1, 2–5, 7–8 in *Obedience to Authority: An Experimental View* by *Stanley Milgram*. Copyright © 1974 by Stanley Milgram. Reprinted by permission of the author and Harper & Row Publishers, Inc.

Gas chambers were built, death camps were guarded, daily quotas of corpses were produced with the same efficiency as the manufacture of appliances. These inhumane policies may have originated in the mind of a single person, but they could only have been carried out on a massive scale if a very large number of people obeyed orders.

Obedience is the psychological mechanism that links individual action to political purpose. It is the dispositional cement that binds men to systems of authority . . . .

The legal and philosophic aspects of obedience are of enormous import, but an empirically grounded scientist eventually comes to the point where he wishes to move from abstract discourse to the careful observation of concrete instances. In order to take a close look at the act of obeying, I set up a simple experiment at Yale University. Eventually, the experiment was to involve more than a thousand participants and would be repeated at several universities, but at the beginning, the conception was simple. A person comes to a psychological laboratory and is told to carry out a series of acts that come increasingly into conflict with conscience. The main question is how far the participant will comply with the experimenter's instructions before refusing to carry out the actions required of him.

But the reader needs to know a little more detail about the experiment. Two people come to a psychological laboratory to take part in a study of memory and learning. One of them is designated as "teacher" and the other a "learner." The experimenter explains that the study is concerned with the effects of punishment on learning. The learner is conducted into a room, seated in a chair, his arms strapped to prevent excessive movement, and an electrode attached to his wrist. He is told that he is to learn a list of word pairs; whenever he makes an error, he will receive electric shocks of increasing intensity.

The real focus of the experiment is the teacher. After watching the learner being strapped into place, he is taken into the main experimental room and seated before an impressive shock generator. Its main, feature is a horizontal line of thirty switches, ranging from 15 volts to 450 volts, in 15-volt increments. There are also verbal designations which range from SLIGHT SHOCK to DANGER—SEVERE SHOCK. The teacher is told that he is to administer the learning test to the man in the other room. When the learner responds correctly, the teacher moves on to the next item; when the other man gives an incorrect answer, the teacher is to give him an electric shock. He is to start at the lowest shock level (15 volts) and to increase the level each time the man makes an error, going through 30 volts, 45 volts, and so on.

The "teacher" is a genuinely naive subject who has come to the laboratory to participate in an experiment. The learner, or victim, is an actor who actually receives no shock at all. The point of the experiment is to see how far a person will proceed in a concrete and measurable situation in which he is ordered to inflict increasing pain on a protesting victim. At what point will the subject refuse to obey the experimenter?

Conflict arises when the man receiving the shock begins to indicate that he is experiencing discomfort. At 75 volts, the "learner" grunts. At 120 volts he complains verbally; at 150 he demands to be released from the experiment. His protests continue as the shocks escalate, growing increasingly vehement and emotional. At 285 volts his response can only be described as an agonized scream.

Observers of the experiment agree that its gripping quality is somewhat obscured in print. For the subject, the situation is not a game; conflict is intense and obvious. On one hand, the manifest suffering of the learning presses him to quit. On the other, the experimenter, a legitimate authority to whom the subject feels some commitment, enjoins him to continue. The aim of this investigation was to find when and how people would defy authority in the face of a clear moral imperative.

There are, of course, enormous differences between carrying out the orders of a commanding officer during times of war and carrying out the orders of an experimenter. Yet the essence of certain relationships remain, for one may ask in a general way: How does a man behave when he is told by a legitimate authority to act against a third individual? If anything, we may expect the experimenter's power to be considerably less than that of the general, since he has no power to enforce his imperatives, and participation in a psychological experiment scarcely evokes the sense of urgency and dedication engendered by participation in war. Despite these limitations, I thought it worthwhile to start careful observation of obedience even in this modest situation, in the hope that it would stimulate insights and yield general propositions applicable to a variety of circumstances.

A reader's initial reaction to the experiment may be to wonder why anyone in his right mind would administer even the first shocks. Would he not simply refuse and walk out of the laboratory? But the fact is that no one ever does. Since the subject has come to the laboratory to aid the experimenter, he is quite willing to start off with the procedure. There is nothing very extraordinary in this, particularly since the person who is to receive the shocks seems initially cooperative, if somewhat apprehensive. What is surprising is how far ordinary individuals go in complying with the experimenter's instructions. Indeed, the results of the experiment are both surprising and dismaying. Despite the fact that many subjects experience stress, despite the fact that many protest to the experimenter, a substantial proportion continue to the last shock on the generator.

Many subjects will obey the experimenter no matter how vehement the pleading of the person being shocked, no matter how painful the shocks seem to be, and no matter how much the victim pleads to be let out. This was seen time and again in our studies and has been observed in several universities where the experiment was repeated. It is the extreme willingness of adults to go to almost any lengths on the command of authority that constitutes the chief finding of the study and a fact most urgently demanding explanation.

A commonly offered explanation is that those who shocked the victim at the most severe level were monsters, the sadistic fringe of society. But if one considers that almost two-thirds of the participants fall into the category of "obedient" subjects, and that they represent ordinary people drawn from working, managerial, and professional classes, the argument becomes very shaky . . . .

[T]he most common adjustment of thought in the obedient subject is for him to see himself as not responsible for his own actions. He divests himself of responsibility by attributing all initiative to the experimenter, a legitimate authority. He sees himself not as a person acting in a morally accountable way but as the agent of external authority. In the post-experimental interview, when subjects were asked why they had gone on, a typical reply was "I wouldn't have done it by myself. I was just doing what I was told." Unable to defy the authority of the experimenter, they attribute all responsibility to him. It is the old story of "just doing one's duty" that was heard time and time again in the defense statements of those accused at Nuremberg. But it would be wrong to think of it as a thin alibi concocted for the occasion. Rather, it is a fundamental mode of thinking for a great many people once they are locked into a subordinate position in a structure of authority. The disappearance of a sense of responsibility is the most far-reaching consequence of submission to authority.

Although a person acting under authority performs actions that seem to violate standards of conscience, it would not be true to say that he loses his moral sense. Instead, it acquires a radically different focus. He does not respond with a moral sentiment to the actions he performs. Rather, his moral concern now shifts to a consideration of how well he is living up to the expectations that the authority has of him. In wartime, a soldier does not ask whether it is good or bad to bomb a hamlet; he does not experience shame or guilt in the destruction of a village; rather he feels pride or shame depending on how well he has performed the mission assigned to him . . . .

[Milgram varied the content of this famous experiment in a number of ways. Further refinements seemed to suggest strongly that what people obeyed was authority; they hated the situation they were in, but they felt they must obey. For example, in one experiment, a "rigged telephone call takes the experimenter away from the laboratory;" before he leaves he asks an accomplice, whom the subject thinks is merely another subject like himself, to conduct the experiment. Here there was a sharp drop in compliance; 16 of 20 subjects refused to go on to the bitter end. Milgram, op. cit. pp. 95–97.

Group effects were also interesting. When the subject was placed between two peers, who defied the experimenter (verbally), only 4 of 40 subjects went on to the bitter end (pp. 116–122)].[147] ☐

NOTES AND QUESTIONS

1. Tyler contends that a society cannot rely solely on deterrence and must find ways to make people comply because they think the authorities are "legitimate." Milgram demonstrates the dangers of uncritical obedience to authority. Are their positions consistent or inconsistent? What advice does each study have for a democratic society? Is their advice consistent or inconsistent?

2. Why did Milgram's subjects obey him or his researchers? As M. D. A. Freeman notes, in "Milgram's Obedience to Authority—Some Lessons for Legal Theory," 1 *Liverpool Law Review* 45, 49–50 (1979), the experimenter "had no power to enforce his imperatives. Disobedience to his commands could lead to no loss, no punishment . . . Subjects often believed they were doing wrong . . . . yet they could not bring themselves to break with authority." The basis for obedience was internalized inside so many of us—we obey the instructions of those we see holding positions of authority. Freeman asserts: "The lessons for legal theory are clear—the importance of sanctions has been overrated." The important question, he argues, is how do norms get "socialized" into people so that the response becomes more or less automatic. Does your experience support this view?

3. In the background of Milgram's experiments is the terrible, bloody history of the 20th century—and in particular the murder of 6,000,000 Jews and millions of Poles and Gypsies, among others, by the Nazi regime under Adolf Hitler during the Second World War. The Nazi leaders who planned the Holocaust were undoubtedly monstrously evil men. But what about some of the underlings, people like Adolf Eichmann, the faceless bureaucrat who played such a key role in the process of organized murder but who claimed that he was only following orders? It was an attempt to understand what made an Eichmann tick that drew Milgram to study obedience.

Eichmann, of course, did not *personally* commit the murders of Jews—the so-called "final solution." These callous murders of men, women, and children were carried out by vast legions of "ordinary" Germans as well as citizens of other countries. What made these actions possible? For a discussion of this question, making explicit reference to the Milgram experiments, see Christopher R. Browning, *Ordinary Men: Reserve Police Battalion 101 and the Final Solution in Poland* (New York: Harper Collins, 1992). This remarkable book discusses the men of German Reserve Police Battalion 101, a unit which in

---

147. [Milgram's studies, when they were originally reported, evoked a good deal of criticism on ethical grounds. The subjects were all under much tension; three underwent "full-blown uncontrollable seizures" during the experiment. Is this infliction of anxiety in the name of science justifiable? Is this kind of experimentation on human beings acceptable? See Herbert Kelman, "Deception in Social Research," 3 *Transaction* 20 (1966). For Milgram's defense, see *Obedience to Authority,* pp. 193–202. For a criticism of Milgram on methodological grounds, see Wrightman, "The Most Important Social Psychological Research in this Generation," 19 *Contemporary Psychology* 803 (1974). See also, Arthur G. Miller, Barry Gillen, Charles Schenker, and Shirley Radlove, "The Prediction and Perception of Obedience to Authority," 42 *Journal of Personality* 23 (1974).]

1942 carried out orders to kill approximately 1,500 Jewish women, children, and elderly men who lived in the Polish village of Jozefow.

Browning explains why the men of Battalion 101 carried out their orders on pages 184–85:

Along with ideological indoctrination, a vital factor touched upon but not fully explored in Milgram's experiments was conformity to the group. The battalion had orders to kill Jews, but each individual did not. Yet 80 to 90 percent of the men proceeded to kill, though almost all of them—at least initially—were horrified and disgusted by what they were doing. To break ranks and step out, to adopt overtly nonconformist behavior, was simply beyond most of the men. It was easier for them to shoot.

Why? First of all, by breaking ranks, nonshooters were leaving the "dirty work" to their comrades. Since the battalion had to shoot even if individuals did not, refusing to shoot constituted refusing one's share of an unpleasant collective obligation. It was in effect an asocial act vis-a-vis one's comrades. Those who did not shoot risked isolation, rejection, and ostracism—a very uncomfortable prospect within the framework of a tight-knit unit stationed abroad among a hostile population, so that the individual had virtually nowhere else to turn for support and social contact.

This threat of isolation was intensified by the fact that stepping out could also have been seen as a form of moral reproach of one's comrades: the nonshooter was potentially indicating that he was "too good" to do such things. Most, though not all, nonshooters intuitively tried to diffuse the criticism of their comrades that was inherent in their actions. They pleaded not that they were "too good" but rather that they were "too weak" to kill.

Such a stance presented no challenge to the esteem of one's comrades; on the contrary, it legitimized and upheld "toughness" as a superior quality. For the anxious individual, it had the added advantage of posing no moral challenge to the murderous policies of the regime, though it did pose another problem, since the difference between being "weak" and being a "coward" was not great. Hence the distinction made by one policeman who did not dare step out at Jozefow for fear of being considered a coward, but who subsequently dropped out of his firing squad. It was one thing to be too cowardly even to try to kill; it was another, after resolutely trying to do one's share, to be too weak to continue.

Albert Breton and Ronald Wintrobe, in "The Bureaucracy of Murder Revisited," 94 *Journal of Political Economy* 905 (1986), challenge Eichmann's claim to have only followed orders. They say:

[I]t may not be necessary to introduce such concepts as brainwashing, the manipulation of human personality, and others like them that are so often employed to deal with human behavior in totalitarian societies: the unusual amount of loyalty that appears to exist in such regimes could be an entirely rational response to the unusual structure of incentives facing people . . . .

Eichmann did not obey orders any more than a self-employed entrepreneur does when he or she responds to the *demands* of the marketplace in order to make money. His rewards took the form of promotions, per-quisites, and power rather than negotiated contractual sums, but that makes no difference to the question of his guilt or innocence . . . . Eichmann . . . would in all likelihood not even have been sanctioned, let alone executed, if he had pursued the Nazi solution to the Jewish ques-tion with less zeal. He would simply have participated less in the infor-mal rewards that would then have gone to the more ardent entrepreneurs . . . [S]ubordinates in large organizations . . . are placed in a competitive framework in which they are rewarded for entrepreneurial initiatives that promote the interests and objectives of their superiors. The more useful they are to their superiors, the larger the rewards.

To what extent, if at all, is Breton and Wintrobe's explanation of Eich-mann's actions inconsistent with that of Milgram?

4. The articles in this section have suggested a variety of factors that may influence a person's decision to obey the law. These factors have included: legal sanctions, social groups, moral conceptions, and perceived legitimacy. After having read these studies, how would you put these factors together into a theory of compliance? Which factors are most important? Which are least important? How does the importance of various factors vary across different types of crimes, different times, and different people?

Theories of compliance are important not only for criminal justice; they also are essential to the study of how any agency or bureaucracy works (or doesn't work). Any complex system of law will try to use a mix of devices to get people to go along: carrots, sticks, and sermons. Often this is done in an ad hoc, seat-of-the-pants way. For a thoughtful discussion of how regulation can be made "responsive" by deliberately putting together a package of "soft" and "hard" incentives, forming a regulatory pyramid in which the toughest mea-sures are reserved for the toughest cases, see Ian Ayres and John Braithwaite, *Responsive Regulation: Transcending the Deregulation Debate* (New York: Oxford University Press, 1992).

It is easy to talk about the people at the other end of a legal rule or order as "subjects," but, of course, they are in fact human beings. Human beings come in a bewildering variety of shapes and sizes, not to mention a bewildering vari-ety of psychological make-ups. A propensity to obey or disobey will depend on *who* the person is, culturally and psychologically. There is, for example, an enormous literature on what it is that makes a criminal a criminal. There is also a literature on legal socialization—the way in which people are educated or trained into a particular legal culture. See, for example, the essays collected in June L. Tapp and Felice J. Levine (eds.), *Law, Justice, and the Individual in Society* (New York: Holt, Rinehart & Winston, 1977); Ellen S. Cohn and Susan O. White, *Legal Socialization: A Study of Norms and Rules* (New York: Springer-Verlag, 1990).

5. Refer back to the discussion of "legitimacy" and Weber's famous classi-fication of principles of legitimate authority. See p. 498. How would you describe the authority of the experimenter in the Milgram study? To what extent, if at all, is that authority analogous to the authority commanded by any government official?

36. *Images of Law in Everyday Life: The Lessons of School, Entertainment, and Spectator Sports*

Stewart Macaulay

21 *Law & Society Review* 185, 188, 189–92 (1987)

☐ Our national attitudes about complying with law are complex and sometimes contradictory . . . . Whatever our attitudes, how compliant are we? Despite our resistance to surveillance and coerced compliance, Americans are relatively law-abiding. Our modern concern with law breaking suggests that while there may be less compliance than we like, we expect a high degree of it. For the most part, our lives and fortunes are not at serious risk in day-to-day living unless we are poor. We do not live under an occupying army enforcing rules at gunpoint. However, most of us do not murder, rape, or rob others. We get licenses, fill out forms, and pay taxes by what we call a voluntary self-assessment system.

Having said this, we could easily compile a long catalogue of American's breaking the law. Civil disobedience is as American as apple pie. We need mention only the Boston Tea Party, the resistance to the fugitive slave acts, draft riots, and today [1987] the selling of Nicaraguan postage stamps to defy the embargo . . . .

Americans also break the law for less lofty goals. We can laugh when we remember that they call the University of Oklahoma football team the Sooners. Those who reached Oklahoma Territory sooner violated the rules for homesteading on public land and defended what they took by force . . . . We also made treaties with the Native American nations as a ploy that served to trick these people into parting with their land.

There is the whole Prohibition experience as well. American folklore romanticized bootlegging, speakeasies, and the Roaring Twenties. Instead of feeling morally bound to honor the law, many Americans found violating Prohibition a game . . . .

Our inventory of American evasion and shading of the law is long. Probably most of us drive automobiles at speeds greater than those posted. Inflight magazines and catalogues carry advertisements for police radar detectors so we can speed without getting caught. Many drive while intoxicated. Large numbers of Americans also participate in the second, or underground, economy. The IRS estimates that only 35 percent of those who are self-employed report their true income. Noncompliance is greatest for independent professionals such as management consultants, CPAs, lawyers, and doctors. Cleaning ladies, handymen, and all kinds of small businesses work to keep income off the books and invisible to tax collectors . . . .

Americans smuggle items across the border and buy stolen goods.

There is a large and successful industry importing and distributing illegal drugs that depends on the willingness of many to use controlled substances . . . .

Individuals acting alone are not the only ones who evade the law. Major corporations also break antitrust laws and violate environmental protection and industrial safety regulations. Illegal kickbacks are standard operating procedure in some industries. Other corporate representatives bribe public officials here and abroad. Some of the Fortune 500 also evade the tax laws despite constant audit.

Where do these contradictory attitudes and actions come from? We are socialized to obey authority but also to disobey it on some occasions and in certain ways. Perhaps the message is that we should not "really" violate the law, but the definition of "really" is very vague. For example, [British] mystery writer Dick Francis wrote of one of his character's employees at a wine shop,

> She was honest in all major ways and unscrupulous in minor. She would never cheat me through the till, but . . . spare light bulbs and half-full jars of Nescafe tended to go home with Mrs. P. if she was short. Mrs. Palissey considered such things "perks" but would have regarded taking a bottle of sherry as stealing. I respected the distinction and was grateful for it, and paid her a little over the norm. ☐

NOTES AND QUESTIONS

1. Why do so many Americans violate at least some laws? Why don't their attitudes, sanctions of conscience, and threats of criminal penalties deter them? Stewart Macaulay, in "Popular Legal Culture: An Introduction," 98 *Yale Law Journal* 1545, 1554–56 (1989), asserts that school children learn to cheat on exams as part of learning to cope with authority. He continues,

> Americans also learn from sports about breaking rules or honoring them in form but not in substance. Part of the lesson is taught in school and part by sports programs on television. Professional baseball, for example, honors tricking and intimidating umpires. A cynic might speculate that American intercollegiate athletics shows that many universities act as if they honored only the amoral principle: "Don't get caught!" Gambling on professional sports is illegal in almost all states. Nonetheless, newspapers regularly publish the current odds, and CBS Television long offered Jimmy the Greek, a former gambler giving up the inside dope about professional football . . . .
> We can draw an analogy to classic jazz. Composers such as Gershwin, Porter, and Berlin wrote songs which jazz musicians reinvented in many ways . . . . [L]awyers, trial judges, court commissioners, political candidates, office holders, clients, and even people standing at a working class bar are all jazz performers. They play variations on legal themes, and sometimes attempt to put new melodies to the chords . . . .
> Individuals in their everyday activities have an amazing variety of ways of bending the seemingly inflexible rules governing these activities . . . .

At least some Americans reason that although a sign announces 65 miles per hour speed limit, almost everyone drives faster, the police are aware of this as are the legislators, and so there is a conventional interpretation of 65 mph to mean "a reasonable speed in excess of 65 mph." Insofar as people engage in a rationalization somewhat like this, does it indicate the weakness of the obligation to obey the law or, on the contrary, the power of that obligation?

Can you think of examples of justifications for breaking the law? For example, how do students who cheat on examinations explain doing this? How do those who are below the legal drinking age explain buying alcohol? How do those who use marijuana explain breaking the laws prohibiting its sale? How do those who buy Cuban cigars in Canada and then bring them into the United States explain breaking the laws against doing this? See M. B. Scott and S. M. Lyman, "Accounts, Deviance, and Social Order," in Jack Douglas (ed.) *Deviance and Respectability: The Social Construction of Moral Meanings* 89 (1970), a classic work on excuses.

2. One way to avoid the need to justify breaking the law is not to concede that you are breaking it, whatever others might think. Marvin Harris, in *Cultural Materialism: The Struggle for a Science of Culture* 275 (New York: Random House, 1979), argues:

> Rules facilitate, motivate, and organize our behavior; they do not govern or cause it. The causes of behavior are to be found in the material conditions of social life. The conclusion to be drawn from the abundance of "unless" and "except" clauses is not that people behave in order to conform to rules, but they select or create rules appropriate for their behavior.

Do you agree?

Doreen McBarnet has investigated what she calls "whiter than white collar crime," where those with resources can manage the threat of legal sanctions and stigma as they straddle the line between tax evasion and tax avoidance. Those who can afford to hire accountants and lawyers can label their activities as legitimate. She discusses "non-disclosing disclosure" which involves disclosing the relevant facts to taxing authorities but doing so in a way which makes it difficult or impossible for the reader to recognize the presence or extent of a taxable transaction. For example, "[o]ne may bury the salient point on p. 195 of a 300 page document and leave tax inspectors to spot it and its significance if they can . . . . One may spread salient points which only take on avoidance significance when read together, between pages 12, 119 and 164, or hide crucial facts in a welter of irrelevancies . . ." She concludes:

> Non-disclosing disclosure plays on the problems of policing complex financial areas, the low risk of being caught, the scope for settlement if one is challenged, and the protection from stigma involved in *having* disclosed however obscurely. Non-disclosing disclosure minimises the chances of being caught while providing "fraud insurance" if one is.

See McBarnet, "Whiter Than White Collar Crime: Tax, Fraud Insurance and the Management of Stigma," 42 *British Journal of Sociology* 323 (1991). See also McBarnet, "Law, Policy and Legal Avoidance: Can Law Effectively Implement Egalitarian Policies?" 15 *Journal of Law and Society* 113 (1988).

What does McBarnet's description suggest about deterrence and an obligation to comply with the law? To what extent is formal and technical compliance enough? To what extent is a plausible argument that one has formally and technically complied enough? Or does whiter-than-white-collar-crime suggest that people feel little obligation to comply; only a desire to avoid legal and social penalties for not complying?

3. We might be tempted to dismiss American's views about obeying the law as "Don't *really* break the law" or "Don't get caught." However, occasionally we are reminded about the power of the norm of law-abidingness. In January of 1993, President Clinton nominated Zoe Baird to serve as Attorney General of the United States. Baird at the time was the General Counsel of Aetna Life & Casualty Co. Her husband was a Yale law professor. They had a combined income of $660,345 and a net worth of $2.3 million. Ralph Nader and other liberals were not pleased with the nomination. Among other things, Ms Baird had endorsed Vice President Dan Quayle's proposals on tort reform to curb the alleged litigation explosion.

The New York Times found another problem with the nomination: In 1990, as Ms Baird began work for Aetna, the couple had difficulty finding someone to care for their three year old son. They hired two Peruvians who were living illegally in the United States. They did not pay Social Security taxes. Both hiring the couple and failing to pay the taxes are illegal. After she was nominated, the couple paid the taxes plus penalty and interest as well as a civil fine for violating the immigration law.

The IRS estimates that about two million families employ domestic workers but only one-quarter of them file the required taxes. Many hire illegal aliens because citizens willing to work as live-in help are hard to find in many parts of the country.

Baird testified "I was forced into this dilemma to care for my child." She said that she had been told that the law against hiring illegal aliens was one that the Immigration and Naturalization Service did not enforce. However, she apologized and said, "People are fairly questioning if there are classes of individuals who hold themselves above the law. I do not."

Senator Orrin G. Hatch, the ranking Republican on the Senate Judiciary Committee, dismissed Baird's action as "an honest mistake." *The Wall Street Journal* editorialized in her favor:

What was found was a violation of the immigration laws on domestic help, an area of law so complicated, so unrealistic and so morally ambiguous that in the normal course of business the government doesn't dare to enforce it. The IRS and immigration service pour impossible paperwork on millions of middle-class parents who try to comply, and millions of others avoid this burden by committing Ms. Baird's offense. If identified they are pressed for back taxes, but never prosecuted. Ms. Baird has now not only paid up the taxes to the IRS, but also a fine to the immigration service.

Of course someone can protest, "but it's the law." If this kind of offense bars an otherwise qualified nominee, speeding tickets cannot be far behind. And if it does defeat her, we'd like to know the immigration status of all household help employed by the members of the Senate

Committee, its staff, the editorial boards of the Times . . . and Mr. Nader and his plaintiff-lawyer buddies.[148]

The Senators on the Judiciary Committee heard from the public. People who communicated with the Senators were overwhelmingly opposed to the nomination, and many who participated in call-in or talk television and radio programs found Ms. Baird's conduct offensive. They did not view this as a technical violation. A majority of the committee members decided that they could not vote for the nomination. Senator Herbert Kohl, a Democrat from Wisconsin, said: "There was just too much concern over her having broken the law and knowingly having broken the law." Ms. Baird withdrew before the Committee completed its hearings or voted on her nomination.

Why did the public react so negatively? Why didn't ordinary people accept the position taken by Senator Hatch and *The Wall Street Journal*? Was it the office Ms Baird was seeking? Was it the fact that both she and her husband were lawyers, and, as such, were held to a higher standard than most people? Was it that she was a professional woman and, as such, was held to a higher standard of conduct than a man? Was it her wealth? Aetna announced that it welcomed Ms. Baird back as its General Counsel. Yale Law School took no action against her husband. Why didn't the couple's action affect their qualifications to hold these positions? Does this suggest that there is something special about the position of Attorney General that is not true of the roles of corporate lawyer or law professor?

THE SOCIAL IMPACT OF LAW

WHAT IMPACT IS LAW SUPPOSED TO HAVE IN SOCIETY?

37. *Moral Passage: The Symbolic Process in Public Designations of Deviance*[149]

Joseph R. Gusfield

15 *Social Problems* 175 (1967)

☐ Recent perspectives on deviant behavior have focused attention away from the actor and his acts and placed it on the analysis of public reactions in labeling deviants as "outsiders." This perspective forms the background for the present paper. In it I will analyze the implications

---

148. *Wall Street Journal,* Jan. 18, 1993, A10, cols. 1–2.

which defining behavior as deviant has for the public designators. Several forms of deviance will be distinguished, each of which has a different kind of significance for the designators. The symbolic import of each type, I argue, leads to different public responses toward the deviant and helps account for the historical changes often found in treatment of such delinquents as alcoholics, drug addicts, and other "criminals," changes which involve a passage from one moral status to another.

INSTRUMENTAL AND SYMBOLIC FUNCTIONS OF LAW

Agents of government are the only persons in modern societies who can legitimately claim to represent the total society. In support of their acts, limited and specific group interests are denied while a public and societal interest is claimed. Acts of government "commit the group to action or to perform coordinated acts for general welfare." This representational character of governmental officials and their acts makes it possible for them not only to influence the allocation of resources but also to define the public norms of morality and to designate which acts violate them. In a pluralistic society these defining and designating acts can become matters of political issue because they support or reject one or another of the competing and conflicting cultural groups in the society.

Let us begin with a distinction between *instrumental* and *symbolic* functions of legal and governmental acts. We readily perceive that acts of officials, legislative enactments, and court decisions often affect behavior in an instrumental manner through a direct influence on the actions of people. The Wagner Labor Relations Act and the Taft-Hartley Act have had considerable impact on the conditions of collective bargaining in the United States. Tariff legislation directly affects the prices of import commodities. The instrumental function of such laws lies in their enforcement; unenforced they have little effect.

Symbolic aspects of law and government do not depend on enforcement for their effect. They are symbolic in a sense close to that used in literary analysis. The symbolic act "invites consideration rather than overt reaction." There is a dimension of meaning in symbolic behavior which is not given in its immediate and manifest significance but in what the action connotes for the audience that views it. The symbol "has acquired a meaning which is added to its immediate intrinsic significance." . . . The use of the wine and wafer in the Mass or the importance of the national flag cannot be appreciated without knowing their symbolic meaning for the users. In analyzing law as symbolic, we are oriented less to behavioral consequences as a means to a fixed end; more to meaning as an act, a decision, a gesture important in itself.

An action of a governmental agent takes on symbolic import as it affects the designation of public norms. A courtroom decision or a legislative act is a gesture which often glorifies the values of one group and demeans those of another. In their representational character, governmental actions can be seen as ceremonial and ritual performances, designating the content of public morality. They are the statement of what is acceptable in the public interest. Law can thus be seen as symbolizing the public affirmation of social ideals and norms as well as a means of direct social control. This symbolic dimension is given in the statement, promulgation, or announcement of law unrelated to its function in influencing behavior through enforcement.

It has long been evident to students of government and law that these two functions, instrumental and symbolic, may often be separated in more than an analytical sense. Many laws are honored as much in the breach as in performance. Robin Williams has labeled such institutionalized yet illegal and deviant behavior the patterned evasion of norms. Such evasion occurs when law proscribes behavior which nevertheless occurs in a recurrent socially organized manner and is seldom punished. The kinds of crimes we are concerned with here quite clearly fall into to this category. Gambling, prostitution, abortion, and public drunkenness are all common modes of behavior although laws exist designating them as prohibited. It is possible to see such systematic evasion as functioning to minimize conflicts between cultures by utilizing law to proclaim one set of norms as public morality and to use another set of norms in actually controlling that behavior.

While patterned evasion may perform such harmonizing functions, the passage of legislation, the acts of officials and decisions of judges nevertheless have a significance as gestures of public affirmation. First, the act of public affirmation of a norm often persuades listeners that behavior and norm are consistent. The existence of law quiets and comforts those whose interests and sentiments are embodied in it. Second, public affirmation of a moral norm directs the major institutions or the society to its support. Despite patterned practices of abortion in the United States, obtaining abortions does require access to a subterranean social structure and is much more difficult than obtaining an appendectomy. There are instrumental functions to law even where there is patterned evasion.

A third impact of public affirmation is the one that most interests us here. The fact of affirmation through acts of law and government expresses the public worth of one set of norms, of one sub-culture vis-a-vis those of others. It demonstrates which cultures have legitimacy and public domination and which do not. Accordingly it enhances the social status of groups carrying the affirmed culture and degrades groups carrying that which is condemned as deviant. We have argued elsewhere that the significance of Prohibition in the United States lay less in its enforcement than in the fact that it occurred. Analysis of the enforcement of Prohibition law indicates that it was often limited by the unwillingness of Dry forces to utilize all their political strength for fear of stirring intensive opposition. Great satisfaction was gained from the passage and maintenance of the legislation itself.

Irrespective of its instrumental effects, public designation of morality is itself an issue generative of deep conflict. The designating gestures are dramatistic events, "since it invites one to consider the matter of motives in a perspective that, developed in the analysis of drama, treats language and thought primarily as modes of action." For this reason the designation of a way of behavior as violating public norms confers status and honor on those groups whose cultures are followed as the standard of conventionality and derogates those whose cultures are considered deviant. My analysis of the American Temperance movement has shown how the issue of drinking and abstinence became a politically significant focus for the conflicts between Protestant and Catholic, rural and urban, native and immigrant, middle class and lower class in American society. The political conflict lay in the efforts of an abstinent Protestant middle class to control the public affirmation of morality in drinking. Victory or defeat were consequently symbolic of the status and power of the cultures opposing each other. Legal affirmation or rejection is thus important in what it symbolizes as well or instead of what it controls. Even if the law was broken, it was clear whose law it was.

DEVIANT NONCONFORMITY AND DESIGNATOR REACTION

In [Emile] Durkheim's analysis of the indignant and hostile response to norm-violation, all proscribed actions are threats to the existence of the norm. Once we separate the instrumental from the symbolic functions of legal and governmental designation of deviants, however, we can question this assumption. We can look at norm-violation from the standpoint of its effects on the symbolic rather that the instrumental character of the norm. Our analysis of patterned evasion of norms has suggested that a law weak in its instrumental functions may nevertheless perform significant symbolic functions. Unlike human limbs, norms do not necessarily atrophy through disuse. Standards of charity, mercy, and justice may be dishonored every day yet remain important statements of what is publicly approved as virtue. The sexual behavior of the human male and the human female need not be a copy of the socially sanctioned rules. Those rules remain as important affirmations of an acceptable code even though they are regularly breached. Their roles as ideals are not threatened by daily behavior. In analyzing the violation of norms we will look at the implications of different forms of deviance on the symbolic character of the norm itself. *The point here is that the designators of deviant behavior react differently to different norm-sustaining implications of an act.* We can classify deviant behavior from this standpoint.

The Repentant Deviant

The reckless motorist often admits the legitimacy of traffic laws even though he has broken them. The chronic alcoholic may well agree that both he and his society would be better off if he could stay sober. In both cases the norm they have violated is itself unquestioned. Their deviation is a moral lapse, a fall from a grace to which they aspire . . . . There is a consensus between the designator and the deviant; his repentance confirms the norm.

Repentance and redemption seem to go hand in hand in court and church. [Gresham] Sykes and [David] Matza have described techniques of neutralization which juvenile delinquents often use with enforcement agencies.

> The juvenile delinquent would appear to be at least partially committed to the dominant social order in that he frequently exhibits guilt or shame when he violates its proscriptions, accords approval to certain conforming figures and distinguishes between appropriate and inappropriate targets for his deviance.

A show of repentance is also used . . . to soften the indignation of law enforcement agents. A recent study of police behavior lends support to this. Juveniles apprehended by the police received more lenient treatment, including dismissal, if they appeared contrite and remorseful about their violations than if they did not. This difference in the posture of the deviant accounted for much of the differential treatment favoring middle-class "youngsters" as against lower class "delinquents."

The Sick Deviant

Acts which represent an attack upon a norm are neutralized by repentance. The open admission of repentance confirms the sinner's belief in the sin. His threat to the norm is removed and his violation has left the norm intact. Acts which we can perceive as those of sick and diseased people are irrelevant to the norm; they neither attack nor defend it. The use of morphine by hospital patients in severe pain is not designated as deviant behavior. Sentiments of public hostility and the apparatus of enforcement agencies are not mobilized toward the morphine user. His use is not perceived as a violation of the norm against drug use, but as an uncontrolled act not likely to be recurrent.

While designations of action resulting from sickness do not threaten the norm, significant consequences flow from such definitions. Talcott Parsons has pointed out that the designation of a person as ill changes the obligations which others have toward the person and his obligations toward them. Parsons' description sensitizes us to the way in which the sick person is a different social object than the healthy one. He has now become an object of welfare, a person to be helped rather than punished. Hostile sentiments toward sick people are not legitimate. The sick person is not responsible for his acts. He is excused from the consequences which attend the healthy who act the same way.

Deviance designations . . . are not fixed. They may shift from one form to another over time. Defining a behavior pattern as one caused by illness makes a hostile response toward the actor illegitimate and inappropriate. "Illness" is a social designation, by no means given in the nature of medical fact. Even left-handedness is still seen as morally deviant in many countries. Hence the effort to define a practice as a consequence of illness is itself a matter of conflict and a political issue.

The Enemy Deviant

Writing about a Boston slum in the 1930's, William F. Whyte remarks:

> The policeman is subject to sharply conflicting pressures. On one side are the "good people" of Eastern City, who have written their moral judgments into law and demand through their newspapers that the law be enforced. On the other side are the people of Cornerville, who have different standards and have built up an organization whose perpetuation depends upon the freedom to violate the law.

Whyte's is one of several studies that have pointed out the discrepancies between middle-class moralities embodied in law and lower class moralities which differ sharply from them. In Cornerville, gambling was seen as a "respectable" crime, just as antitrust behavior may be in other levels of the social structure. In American society, conflicts between social classes are often also cultural conflicts reflecting moral differences. Coincidence of ethnic and religious distinctions with class differences accentuates such conflicts between group values.

In these cases, the validity of the public designation is itself at issue. The publicly-defined deviant is neither repentant nor sick, but is instead an upholder of an opposite norm. He accepts his behavior as proper and derogates the public norm as illegitimate. He refuses to internalize the public norm into his self-definition. This is especially likely to occur in instances of "business crimes." The buyer sees his action as legitimate economic behavior and resists a definition of it as immoral and thus prohibitable. The issue of "off-track" betting illustrates one area in which clashes of culture have been salient.

The designation of culturally legitimate behavior as deviant depends upon the superior power and organization of the designators. The concept of convention in this area, as Thrasymachus defined justice for Socrates, is the will of the stronger. If the deviant is the politically weaker group, then the designation is open to the changes and contingencies of political fortunes. It becomes an issue of political conflict, ranging group against group and culture against culture, in the effort to determine whose morals are to be designated as deserving of public affirmation.

It is when the deviant is also an enemy and his deviance is an aspect of group culture that the conventional norm is most explicitly and energetically attacked. When those once designated as deviant have achieved enough political power they may shift from disobedience to an effort to change the designation itself. This has certainly happened in the civil rights movement. Behavior viewed as deviant in the segregationist society has in many instances been moved into the realm of the problematic, now subject to political processes of conflict and compromise.

When the deviant and the designator perceive each other as enemies, and the designator's power is superior to that of the deviant, we have domination without a corresponding legitimacy. Anything which increases the power of the deviant to organize and attack the norm is thus a threat to the social dominance symbolized in the affirmation of the norm. Under such conditions the need of the designators to strengthen and enforce the norms is great. The struggle over the symbol of social power and status is focused on the question of the maintenance or change of the legal norm. The threat to the middle class in the increased political power of Cornerville is not that the Cornerville resident will gamble more; he already does gamble with great frequency. The threat is that the law will come to accept the morality of gambling and treat it as a legitimate business. If this happens, Boston is no longer a city dominated by middle-class Yankees but becomes one dominated by lower-class immigrants, as many think has actually happened in Boston. The maintenance of a norm which defines gambling as deviant behavior thus symbolizes the maintenance of Yankee social and political superiority. Its disappearance as a public commitment would symbolize the loss of that superiority.

The Cynical Deviant

The professional criminal commits acts whose designation as deviant is supported by wide social consensus. The burglar, the hired murderer, the arsonist, the kidnapper all prey on victims. While they may use repentance or illness as strategies to manage the impressions of enforcers, their basic orientation is self-serving, to get around the rules. It is for this reason that their behavior is not a great threat to the norms although it calls for social management and repression. It does not threaten the legitimacy of the normative order.

DRINKING AS A CHANGING FORM OF DEVIANCE

Analysis of efforts to define drinking as deviant in the United States will demonstrate the process by which designations shift. The legal embodiment of attitudes toward drinking shows how cultural conflicts find their expression in the symbolic functions of law. In the 160 years since 1800, we see all our suggested types of non-conforming behavior and all the forms of reaction among the conventional segments of the society . . . .

The Repentant Drinker

The definition of the drinker as an object of social shame begins in the early nineteenth century and reaches full development in the late 1820's and early 1830's. A wave of growth in Temperance organizations in this period was sparked by the conversion of drinking men to abstinence under the stimulus of evangelical revivalism. Through drinking men joining together to take the pledge, a norm of abstinence and sobriety emerged as a definition of conventional respectability. They sought to control themselves and their neighbors.

The norm of abstinence and sobriety replaced the accepted patterns of heavy drinking countenanced in the late eighteenth and early nineteenth century. By the 1870's rural and small-town America had defined middle class morals to include the Dry attitude. This definition had little need for legal embodiment. It could be enunciated in attacks on the drunkard which assumed that he shared the normative pattern of those who exhorted him to be better and to do better. He was a repentant deviant, someone to be brought back into the fold by moral persuasion and the techniques of religious revivalism. His error was the sin of lapse from a shared standard of virtue. "The Holy Spirit will not visit much less will He dwell within he who is under the polluting, debasing effects of intoxicating drink. The state of heart and mind which this occasions to him is loathsome and an abomination."

Moral persuasion thus rests on the conviction of a consensus between the deviant and the designators. As long as the object of attack and conversion is isolated in individual terms, rather than perceived as a group, there is no sense of his deviant act as part of a shared culture. What is shared is the norm of conventionality; the appeal to the drinker and the chronic alcoholic is to repent. When the Woman's Anti-Whiskey Crusade of 1874 broke out in Ohio, church women placed their attention on the taverns. In many Ohio towns these respectable ladies set up vigils in front of the tavern and attempted to prevent men from entering just by the fear that they would be observed. In keeping with the evangelical motif in the Temperance Movement, the Washingtonians, founded in 1884, appealed to drinkers and chronic alcoholics with the emotional trappings and oratory of religious meetings, even though devoid of pastors.

Moral persuasion, rather than legislation, has been one persistent theme in the designation of the drinker as deviant and the alcoholic as depraved. Even in the depictions of the miseries and poverty of the chronic alcoholic, there is a decided moral condemnation which has been the hallmark of the American Temperance movement. Moral persuasion was ineffective as a device to wipe out drinking and drunkenness. Heavy drinking persisted through the nineteenth century and the organized attempts to convert the drunkard experienced much backsliding. Nevertheless, defections from the standard did not threaten the standard. The public definition of respectability matched the ideals of the sober and abstaining people who dominated those parts of the society where moral suasion was effective. In the late nineteenth century those areas in which temperance sentiment was strongest were also those in which legislation was most easily enforceable.

The Enemy Drinker

The demand for laws to limit alcoholic consumption appears to arise from situations in which the drinkers possess power as a definitive social and political group and, in their customary habits and beliefs, deny the validity of abstinence norms. The persistence of areas in which Temperance norms were least controlling led to the emergence of attempts to embody control in legal measures. The drinker as enemy seems to be the greatest stimulus to efforts to designate his act as publicly defined deviance.

In its early phase the American Temperance movement was committed chiefly to moral persuasion. Efforts to achieve legislation governing the sale and use of alcohol do not appear until the 1840's. This legislative movement has a close relationship to the immigration of Irish Catholics and German Lutherans into the United States in this period. These non-evangelical and/or non-Protestant peoples made up a large proportion of the urban poor in the 1840's and 1850's. They brought with them a far more accepting evaluation of drinking than had yet existed in the United States. The tavern and the beer parlor had a distinct place in the leisure of the Germans and the Irish. The prominence of this place was intensified by the stark character of the developing American slum. These immigrant cultures did not contain a strong tradition of Temperance norms which might have made an effective appeal to a sense of sin. To be sure, excessive drunkenness was scorned, but neither abstinence nor constant sobriety were supported by the cultural codes.

Between these two groups—the native American middle-class evangelical Protestant and the immigrant European Catholic or Lutheran occupying the urban lower class—there was little room for repentance. By the 1850's the issue of drinking reflected a general clash over cultural values. The Temperance movement found allies in its political efforts among the nativist movements. The force and power of the anti-alcohol movements, however, were limited greatly by the political composition of the urban electorate, with its high proportion of immigrants. Thus the movement to develop legislation emerged in reaction to the appearance of cultural groups least responsive to the norms of abstinence and sobriety. The very effort to turn such informal norms into legal standards polarized the opposing forces and accentuated the symbolic import of the movement. Now that the issue had been joined, defeat or victory was a clear-cut statement of public dominance.

It is a paradox that the most successful move to eradicate alcohol emerged in a period when America was shifting away from a heavy-drinking society, in which whiskey was the leading form of alcohol, to a moderate one, in which beer was replacing whiskey. Prohibition came as the culmination of the movement to reform the immigrant cultures and at the height of the immigrant influx into the United States.

Following the Civil War, moral persuasion and legislative goals were both parts of the movement against alcohol. By the 1880's an appeal was made to the urban, immigrant lower classes to repent and to imitate the habits of the American middle class as a route to economic and social mobility. Norms of abstinence were presented to the non-abstainer both as virtue and as expedience. This effort failed. The new and larger immigration of 1890–1915 increased still further the threat of the urban lower class to the native American.

The symbolic effect of Prohibition legislation must be kept analytically separate from its instrumental, enforcement side. While the urban middle class did provide much of the organizational leadership to the Temperance and Prohibition movements, the political strength of the movement in its legislative drives was in the rural areas of the United States. Here, where the problems of drinking were most under control, where the norm was relatively intact, the appeal to a struggle against foreign invasion was the most potent. In these areas, passage of legislation was likely to make small difference in behavior. The continuing polarization of political forces into those of cultural opposition and cultural acceptance during the Prohibition campaigns (1906–1919), and during the drive for Repeal (1926–1933), greatly intensified the symbolic significance of victory and defeat. Even if the Prohibition measures were limited in their enforceability in the metropolis there was no doubt about whose law was public and what way of life was being labeled as opprobrious.

After Repeal, as Dry power in American politics subsided, the designation of the drinker as deviant also receded. Public affirmation of the temperance norm had changed and with it the definition of the deviant had changed. Abstinence was itself less acceptable. In the 1950's the Temperance movement, faced with this change in public norms, even introduced a series of placards with the slogan, "It's smart *Not* to Drink."

Despite this normative change in the public designation of drinking deviance there has not been much change in American drinking patterns. Following the Prohibition period the consumption of alcohol has not returned to its pre-1915 high. Beer has continued to occupy a more important place as a source of alcohol consumption. Hard drinkers are not as common in America today as they were in the nineteenth century. While there has been some increase in moderate drinking, the percentage of adults who are abstainers has remained approximately the same (one-third) for the past 30 years. Similarly Dry sentiment has remained stable. . . . In short, the argument over deviance designation has been largely one of normative dominance, not of instrumental social control. The process of deviance designation in drinking needs to be understood in terms of symbols of cultural dominance rather than in the activities of social control.

The Sick Drinker

For most of the nineteenth century the chronic alcoholic as well as the less compulsive drinker was viewed as a sinner. It was not until after Repeal (1933) that chronic alcoholism became defined as illness in the United States. Earlier actions taken toward promotion of the welfare of drinkers and alcoholics through Temperance measures rested on the moral supremacy of abstinence and the demand for repentance. The user of alcohol could be an object of sympathy, but his social salvation depended on a willingness to embrace the norm of his exhorters. The designation of alcoholism as sickness has a different bearing on the question of normative superiority. It renders the behavior of the deviant indifferent to the status of norms enforcing abstinence.

This realization appears to have made supporters of Temperance and Prohibition hostile to efforts to redefine the deviant character of alcoholism. They deeply opposed the reports of the Committee of Fifty in the late nineteenth century. These volumes of reports by scholars and prominent men took a less moralistic and a more sociological and functional view of the saloon and drinking than did the Temperance movement.

The soundness of these fears is shown by what did happen to the Temperance movement with the rise of the view that alcoholism is illness. It led to new agencies concerned with drinking problems. These excluded Temperance people from the circle of those who now define what is deviant in drinking habits. The National Commission on Alcohol Studies was formed in 1941 and the Yale School of Alcohol Studies formed in 1940. They were manned by medical personnel, social workers, and social scientists, people now alien to the spirit of the abstainer. Problems of drinking were removed from the church and placed in the hands of universities and the medical clinics. The tendency to handle drinkers through protective and welfare agencies rather than through police or clergy has become more frequent.

"The bare statement that 'alcoholism is a disease' is most misleading since . . . it conceals what is essential—that a step in public policy is being recommended, not a scientific discovery announced." John Seeley's remark is an apt one. Replacement of the norm of sin and repentance by that of illness and therapy removes the onus of guilt and immorality from the act of drinking and the state of chronic alcoholism. It replaces the image of the sinner with that of the patient, a person to be helped rather than to be exhorted. No wonder that the Temperance movement has found the work of the Yale School, and often even the work of Alcoholics Anonymous, a threat to its own movement. It has been most limited in its cooperation with these organizations and has attempted to set up other organizations which might provide the face of Science in league with the tone of the movement.

The redefinition of the alcoholic as sick thus brought into power both ideas and organizations antithetical to the Temperance movement. The norm protected by law and government was no longer the one held by the people who had supported Temperance and Prohibition. The hostility of Temperance people is readily understandable; their relative political unimportance is crucial to their present inability to make that hostility effective.

MOVEMENTS OF MORAL PASSAGE

In this paper we have called attention to the fact that deviance designations have histories; the public definition of behavior as deviant is itself changeable. It is open to reversals of public opinion and the development of social movements and moral crusades. What is attacked as criminal today may be seen as sick next year and fought over as possibly legitimate by the next generation.

Movements to redefine behavior may eventuate in a moral passage, a transition of the behavior from one moral status to another. In analyzing movements toward the redefinition of alcohol use, we have dealt with moral crusades which were restrictive and others which were permissive toward drinking and toward "drunkards." (We might have also used the word "alcoholics," suggesting a less disapproving and more medical perspective.) In both cases, however, the movements sought to change the public designation. While we are familiar with the restrictive or enforcing movements, the permissive or legitimizing movement must also be seen as a prevalent way in which deviants throw off the onus of their actions and avoid the sanctions associated with immoral activities.

Even where the deviants are a small and politically powerless group they may nevertheless attempt to protect themselves by influence over the process of designation. The effort to define themselves as ill is one plausible means to this end. Drug addiction as well as drunkenness is partially undergoing a change toward such redefinition. This occurs in league with powerful groups in society such as social workers, medical professionals, and university professors. The moral passage achieved here reduces the sanctions imposed by criminal law and the public acceptance of the deviant designation.

The "lifting" of a deviant activity to the level of a political public issue is thus a sign that its moral status is at stake, that legitimacy is a possibility. Today the moral acceptance of drinking, marijuana and LSD use, homosexuality, abortion, and other "vices" is being publicly discussed and movements championing them have emerged. Such movements draw into them far more than the deviants themselves. Because they become symbols of general cultural attitudes they call out partisans for both repression and permission. The present debate over drug addiction laws in the United States, for example, is carried out between defenders and opposers of the norm rather than between users and non-users of the drugs involved.

As the movement for redefinition of the addict as sick has grown, the movement to strengthen the definition of addiction as criminal has responded with increased legal severity. To classify drug users as sick and the victims or clients as suffering from "disease" would mean a change in the agencies responsible for reaction from police enforcement to medical authorities. Further, it might diminish the moral disapproval with which drug use, and the reputed euphoric effects connected with it, are viewed by supporters of present legislation. Commenting on the clinic plan to permit medical dispensing of narcotics to licensed addicts, U.S. Commissioner of Narcotics [Harry] Anslinger wrote:

> This plan would elevate a most despicable trade to the avowed status of an honorable business, nay, to the status of practice of a time-honored profession; and drug addicts would multiply unrestrained, to the irrevocable impairment of the moral fiber and physical welfare of the American people.

In this paper we have seen that redefining moral crusades tends to generate strong counter-movements. The deviant as a cultural opponent is a more potent threat to the norm than is the repentent, or even the sick deviant. The threat to the legitimacy of the norm is a spur to the need for symbolic restatement in legal terms. In these instances of "crimes without victims" the legal norm is *not* the enunciator of a consensus within the community. On the contrary, it is when consensus is least attainable that the pressure to establish the legal norms appears to be the greatest. □

NOTES AND QUESTIONS

1. Does Gusfield convince you that an unenforced law may still be important because of its symbolic functions? Remember his position: "Legal affirmation or rejection is thus important in what it symbolizes as well or instead of what it controls. Even if the law was broken, it was clear whose law it was." See also, Murray Edelman, *The Symbolic Uses of Politics* (Urbana, Ill.: University of Illinois Press, 1964). What exactly is the symbolic function of law? How does it perform that function? Who is the audience? How do messages about the content of law get to members of that audience?

2. Many states have laws which prohibit various kinds of sexual behavior—sodomy, oral and anal sex—even among consenting adults, and even

between married couples. These laws are rarely enforced. From the perspective of Gusfield, what explanation can be offered for the persistence of these unenforced laws? Are they "symbolic"? If so, of what? Are there other possible explanations why these laws have been kept on the books?

3. Gusfield has treated the temperance movement in more detail in his book, *Symbolic Crusade: Status Politics and the American Temperance Movement* (Urbana, Ill.: University of Illinois Press, 1963). He has also written about the symbolic meaning of drunk driving in *The Culture of Public Problems: Drinking, Driving and the Symbolic Order* (Chicago: University of Chicago Press, 1981).

4. A law can be symbolic because the people who proposed it want it to be symbolic only, because a symbolic law is the best they can get under the circumstances or because the proponents are mistaken about what is needed to make the law instrumental. Which one of these explanations fits the history of Prohibition? The history of the sodomy laws?

5. Gusfield describes a pattern in the designation of deviants—from repentant to enemy to sick. He thinks this pattern fits the history of narcotics laws and liquor laws. Can you think of other cases that fit this pattern? Can you think of any situations in which the designation of deviants has gone the other way—from sick to enemy or to repentant? How would you describe the pattern in the way society has treated drunk drivers? People who smoke cigarettes in public places? Companies that dump toxic wastes into rivers?

SOCIAL IMPACT—THE ROLE OF
IMPLEMENTING ORGANIZATIONS

38. Rape Law Reform and Instrumental Change in Six Urban Jurisdictions

Julie Horney and Cassia Spohn

25 *Law & Society Review* 117 (1991)

☐ . . . During the past twenty years there has been a sweeping effort to reform rape laws in this country. Reformers questioned the special status of rape as an offense for which the victim, as well as the defendant, was put on trial. They suggested that the laws and rules of evidence unique to rape were at least partially responsible for the unwillingness of victims to report rapes and for the low rates of arrest, prosecution, and conviction. They cited evidence that these laws and rules of evidence resulted in pervasive skepticism of the victim's claims and allowed criminal justice officials to use legally irrelevant assessments of the victim's status, character, and relationship with the defendant in making decisions regarding the processing and disposition of rape cases . . . .

Concerns such as these sparked a nationwide, grass-roots movement in which women's groups lobbied for rape law reforms. Their efforts resulted in changes in the rape laws of all fifty states. The overall purpose of the reforms was to treat rape like other crimes by focusing not on the behavior or reputation of the victim but on the unlawful acts of the offender. Advocates of the new laws anticipated that by improving the treatment of rape victims the reforms would ultimately lead to an increase in the number of reports of rape. They also expected that the reforms would remove legal barriers to effective prosecution and would make arrest, prosecution, and conviction for rape more likely.

In this study we address these expectations. Using time-series data on more than twenty thousand rape cases in six major urban jurisdictions, we examine the impact of rape reform legislation on reports of rape and the outcome of rape cases.

RAPE LAW REFORM

States enacted reform statutes that vary in comprehensiveness and encompass a broad range of reforms. The most common changes were (1) changes in the definition of rape; (2) elimination of the resistance requirement; (3) elimination of the corroboration requirement; and (4) enactment of a rape shield law. We briefly describe each of these reforms below.

1. Many states replaced the single crime of rape with a series of offenses graded by seriousness and with commensurate penalties. Historically, rape was defined as "carnal knowledge of a woman, not one's wife, by force and against her will." Thus, traditional rape laws did not include attacks on male victims, acts other than sexual intercourse, sexual assaults with an object, or sexual assaults by a spouse. The new crimes typically are gender neutral and include a range of sexual assaults.

2. A number of jurisdictions changed the consent standard by modifying or eliminating the requirement that the victim resist her attacker. Under traditional rape statutes, the victim, to demonstrate her lack of consent, was required to "resist to the utmost" or, at the very least, exhibit "such earnest resistance as might reasonably be expected under the circumstance," (Tex. Penal Code 1980). Reformers challenged these standards, arguing not only that resistance could lead to serious injury but also that the law should focus on the behavior of the offender rather than on that of the victim. In response, states either eliminated resistance of the victim as an element of the crime to be proved by the prosecutor or attempted to lessen the state's burden of proving nonconsent by specifying the circumstances that constitute force—using or displaying a weapon, committing another crime at the same time, injuring the victim, and so on.

3. The third type of statutory reform was elimination of the corroboration requirement—the rule prohibiting conviction for forcible rape on the uncorroborated testimony of the victim. Critics cited the difficulty in obtaining evidence concerning an act that typically takes place in a

private place without witnesses. They also objected to rape being singled out as the only crime with such a requirement.

4. Most states enacted rape shield laws that placed restrictions on the introduction of evidence of the victim's prior sexual conduct. Under common law, evidence of the victim's sexual history was admissible to prove she had consented to intercourse and to impeach her credibility. Reformers were particularly critical of this two-pronged evidentiary rule and insisted that it be eliminated or modified. Critics argued that the rule was archaic in light of changes in attitudes toward sexual relations and women's role in society. They stressed that evidence of the victim's prior sexual behavior was of little, if any, probative worth. Confronted with arguments such as these, state legislatures enacted rape shield laws designed to limit the admissibility of evidence of the victim's past sexual conduct. The laws range from the less restrictive, which permit sexual conduct evidence to be admitted following a showing of relevance, to the more restrictive, which prohibit such evidence except in a few narrowly defined situations. The laws also usually specify procedures for determining the relevance of the evidence; most states require an *in camera* hearing to determine whether the proffered evidence is admissible.

THE IMPACT OF RAPE LAW REFORM

Proponents of rape law reform predicted that the various statutory changes would produce a number of instrumental results. They expected the reforms, particularly the rape shield laws, to improve the treatment of rape victims and thus to prompt more victims to report the crime to the police. They believed that elimination of resistance and corroboration requirements would remove major barriers to conviction; as a result, prosecutors would be more likely to indict and fully prosecute rape cases, and juries and judges would be more likely to convict in rape trials. They expected that conviction would also be facilitated by the enactment of rape shield laws that restricted admission of evidence of the complainant's sexual history. Finally, reformers believed that definitional changes would make it easier to prosecute cases that did not fit traditional definitions of rape, would prevent jury nullification by having penalties commensurate with the seriousness of the offense, and would lead to more convictions through plea bargaining because appropriate lesser offenses would be available to prosecutors in their negotiations.

Reformers clearly had high hopes for the rape law reforms, but their expectations may have been unrealistic. In fact, the literature on legal impact, which abounds with examples of the remarkable capacity of criminal courts to adjust to and effectively thwart reforms, should lead us to predict that the rape law reforms would have only limited effects on reports of rape and the outcome of rape cases.

The chronic failure of reforms aimed at the court system suggests that reformers have misperceptions about the nature of the judicial process. Most reform proposals assume that we have a hierarchic, centralized, obedient system of courts that will automatically and faithfully adhere to new rules. These misperceptions cause reformers to overestimate the role of legal rules in controlling the behavior of decisionmakers and to underestimate the role of discretion in modifying the legal rules. Statutory changes like the rape law reform must be interpreted and applied by decisionmakers who may not share the goals of those who championed their enactment and who therefore may not be committed to their implementation. Numerous studies have demonstrated limited impact of reforms when officials' attitudes were at odds with reformers' goals.

Even if criminal justice officials agree with the legal change in principle, they may resist if it impinges on interests protected by the courtroom workgroup. Officials may modify or ignore reforms that threaten the status quo by impeding the smooth and efficient flow of cases or that require changes in deeply entrenched and familiar routines. Studies have shown that reforms that interfere with plea bargaining and the production of large numbers of guilty pleas, or that attempt to alter the going rates established by the workgroup are especially at risk of being undermined . . . .

Other reforms may have limited impact because their passage was primarily symbolic. Faced with a vocal constituency demanding action, decisionmakers might adopt a policy with little bite to provide symbolic reassurance that needs are being attended to, problems are being solved, help is on the way. Policymakers might, for example, placate constituents by enacting a very weak version of the legal change being sought, by adopting a law that differs very little from other laws on the books or from case law, or by adopting a reform that they know full well will not be enforced.

All the foregoing suggest that the advocates of rape law reform may have been overly optimistic about the effects of the reforms. It also suggests that we should approach the task of interpreting the outcomes of the reforms with great care. It obviously is important to consider not only the specific provisions of the laws themselves but also the comprehensiveness of the reforms, the contexts in which the reforms are to be implemented, and the consequences for decisionmakers charged with enforcing the reforms . . . .

THE CURRENT STUDY

In this study we assess the impact of rape law reform in six urban jurisdictions. The jurisdictions—Detroit, Michigan; Cook County (Chicago), Illinois; Philadelphia County (Philadelphia), Pennsylvania; Harris County (Houston), Texas; Fulton County (Atlanta), Georgia; and Washington, D.C.—represent states that enacted different kinds of rape law reforms . . . . [W]e selected Detroit, Chicago, and Philadelphia to represent jurisdictions with relatively strong reforms and Atlanta, Washington, D.C., and Houston to represent jurisdictions with weaker reforms. The reforms enacted in the six jurisdictions are summarized below . . .

The Michigan law, considered by many to be the model rape law reform, included all the changes described above. The Michigan statute redefines rape and other forms of sexual assault by establishing four degrees of gender-neutral criminal sexual conduct based on the seriousness of the offense, the amount of force or coercion used, the degree of injury inflicted, and the age and incapacitation of the victim. The law states that the victim need not resist the accused and that the victim's testimony need not be corroborated.

Michigan also enacted a very restrictive rape shield law. Evidence of prior sexual activity with persons other than the defendant is admissible only to show the source of semen, pregnancy, or disease. Evidence of the victim's past sexual conduct with the defendant can be admitted only if a judge determines that it is material to a fact at issue (generally consent) and that its inflammatory or prejudicial nature does not outweigh its probative value.

Although we categorized the reforms adopted in Illinois and Pennsylvania as "strong" reforms, they are neither as broad nor comprehensive as those enacted in Michigan. The Illinois reforms were incremental; in 1978 the state implemented a strong rape shield law very similar to the law enacted in Michigan, but it was six years later before definitional changes were adopted and the resistance requirement was repealed. In 1976 Pennsylvania passed a strong rape shield law and repealed the corroboration and resistance requirements. Although there are significant changes, Pennsylvania retains Model Penal Code definitions of rape and involuntary deviate sexual intercourse, which many reformers believe still place undue focus on the circumstances that define nonconsent.

The reforms adopted in Washington, D.C., Georgia, and Texas are much weaker. Although corroboration requirements have been eliminated or weakened in each jurisdiction, all three jurisdictions continue to require resistance by the victim. Georgia and Texas passed very weak rape shield laws that give judges considerable discretion to admit sexual conduct evidence. Washington, D.C., has not amended its rape statutes since 1901, but case law restricts the introduction of evidence of the victim's prior sexual conduct. Washington, D.C., and Georgia have traditional carnal knowledge definitions of rape, as did Texas until relatively minor definitional changes were made in 1983 . . . .

Case Selection

We gathered court records data on rape cases processed from 1970 through 1984 in the six jurisdictions. We collected data on rapes reported to the police during the same time period from the FBI's Uniform Crime Reports (UCR). In each jurisdiction we collected data on forcible rape cases and on other sexual assaults that were not specifically assaults on children. We performed all analyses for both forcible rape and total sexual assaults. Because the pattern of results did not differ with the inclusion of other sexual assaults (and because the types of offenses included varied from jurisdiction to jurisdiction), we present here only the results for forcible rape cases since they are the most comparable. In Michigan, where the reforms included definitional changes, we selected the closest equivalent crimes for the forcible rape analysis (details described below).

Dependent Variables

The dependent variables include the number of reports of forcible rape; the indictment ratio (indictments divided by reports); the percentage convicted (convictions divided by indictments); the percentage convicted on the original charge (convictions for rape divided by indictments); the percentage incarcerated (incarcerations divided by convictions); and the average sentence (average maximum sentence—in months—for defendants incarcerated after a conviction for rape).

Our unit of analysis was the indictment (the term indictment will be used broadly to include informations filed in those jurisdictions in which the grand jury is not used). When we calculate the indictment ratio, we use data from two sources—the UCR and our population of cases from the court files. Thus we do not have the perfect correspondence that we would have if we had been able to follow individual cases from report through court filing. Because most indictments seem to follow the reports fairly closely in time and because there is no good model for making other assumptions, we divided the number of indictments filed in a given month by the number of rapes reported in that same month. In all other analyses the data are based on the indicted cases, and month of indictment is used for the time variable. Thus when we calculate convictions as a percentage of indictments, we are looking at the percentage of cases indicted in a particular month that resulted in conviction.

Time-Series Analysis

We used interrupted time-series analysis to evaluate the impact of the rape law reforms on the dependent variables. We analyzed monthly data over the fifteen-year period to see whether changes in the rape laws produced increases or decreases in the level of the series. In each time-series analysis the interruption was the change in the rape law of the particular jurisdiction. The number of years before and after the reform varied somewhat, depending on when the law was reformed in each state.

Controls

The major weakness of the time-series design is that it does not control for the "history" threat to internal validity. Even when a discontinuity in the series occurs at the time of the intervention, other events occurring at about the same time actually may be responsible for the effects noted. In the case of rape law reforms, increased national attention to the problems surrounding the prosecution of rape cases might have sensitized criminal justice officials and led to any observed changes in processing. We were able to control for history in this research by using a multiple time-series design because the reformed jurisdictions made their legal changes at different times. If national attention to rape issues led to changes in the processing of rape cases, these changes should appear at approximately the same time for all jurisdictions. If, on the other hand, these changes coincided with the legal reforms in each jurisdiction, we have strong evidence that the legal reforms caused the changes.

Interviews with Criminal Justice Officials

To more fully evaluate the rape law reforms, in 1985 and 1986 we interviewed criminal justice officials in the six jurisdictions. We conducted lengthy, structured, face-to-face interviews with a sample of 162 judges, prosecutors, and defense attorneys. We selected officials who had experience with rape cases before and after the legal reforms went into effect or who had handled a substantial number of rape cases in the postreform period. We also interviewed police officers and rape crisis center personnel in each jurisdiction.

RESULTS

The results of the time-series analyses are summarized in Table 2. The results of our analyses indicate that, contrary to reformers' expectations, the reforms had little effect on reports of rape or the processing of rape cases. The only clear impact of the laws was in Detroit, and even there the effects were limited. Below we discuss the results for Detroit in detail and then briefly summarize the results for the other five jurisdictions.

The statutory changes adopted by Michigan in 1975 produced some of the results anticipated by reformers. There was an increase in the number of reports of rape and in the ratio of indicted to reported cases. Additionally, the maximum sentence for those incarcerated increased. On the other hand, there was no change in the percentages of indictments resulting in conviction or in conviction on the original charge or in the percentage of convictions resulting in incarceration.

TABLE 2   SUMMARY OF THE RESULTS OF THE TIME-SERIES ANALYSIS

Jurisdiction	Reports	Indictment Ratio	% Convicted	% Convicted— Orig. Charge	% Incarcerated	Average Sentence
Detroit	26.53**	.18***	−2.26	0.07	−.15	62.54***
Chicago[a]	0.95	−.42	−0.16	1.03	NA[b]	47.67***
Intervention moved back one year						49.20***
Philadelphia[c]	1.65	.04	−0.01	0.19	.07*	10.35**
Intervention moved back one year					.09***	13.46**
Washington, D.C.						
Shield law	−0.80	.002	0.02	0.01	.06	35.33
Corroboration	−5.07**	−.003	0.04	0.06	.08	70.86
Atlanta[a]						
Shield law	−3.94	−.09	0.01***	−0.05	−.003	29.17
Corroboration	0.02	−.05	0.01	−0.07**	.01	42.74*
Intervention moved back one year			0.01***	−0.07**		42.86*
Houston Num =	1.30***	−.14***	0.12***	0.09***	.06*	73.63***
Den =	0.99***					
First two years after reform	17.25***	−.08*	0.06	0.02	.07	84.94**

NOTE: For each jurisdiction we present the intervention coefficient. Detailed results are available from the authors.

[a] In Chicago the percentage indicted variable was logged.

[b] We did not analyze the percentage incarcerated in Chicago because almost all values were 100 percent.

[c] In Philadelphia the percentage convicted on the original charge variable was logged.

[d] In Atlanta the percentage indicted and the percentage convicted variables were logged.

$^*p < .05$ $^{**}p < .01$ $^{***}p < .001$

Our analysis of monthly reports of rape revealed that the new law produced a significant increase of about twenty-six reports per mouth (see Fig. 1). Because our measure of reports did not allow us to separate changes in reporting from changes in crime rates, we compared reports of rape with reports of robbery and felony assault for the period 1970 through 1980. If the increase in reported rapes reflected a general trend in violent crimes, we should have seen similar increases for these other crimes. Such increases were not evident. The pattern for felony assault reports was much like that for reported rapes, but the time-series analysis indicated no significant change coincident with changes in the rape laws. The pattern for reported robberies was quite different, and there was no significant change at the time when reporting of rapes increased.

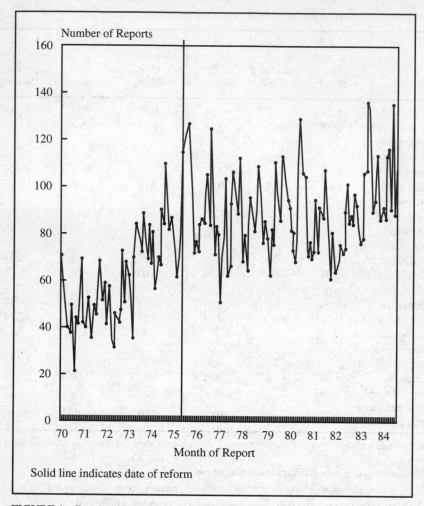

FIGURE 1   Reports of rape, Detroit, Michigan, 1970–1984

Our results also indicate that the reforms had some effects on case processing in Detroit. The case processing variables are measured for the offenses of rape, sodomy, and gross indecency before the 1975 legal changes and for the offenses of first- and third-degree sexual conduct after the changes. Figure 2 presents the plot of the ratio of indictments to reported rapes. The time-series analysis of these data indicated that the indictment ratio increased by .18. Thus, not only were there more indictments simply because of an increase in the number of cases reported, but prosecution of these cases was more likely following the legislative changes.

The likelihood of conviction, on the other hand, did not change as a result of the reforms (Fig. 3). With the increase in reports and indictments, however, the steady conviction rate indicates that prosecutors were obtaining more total convictions in the postreform period. This

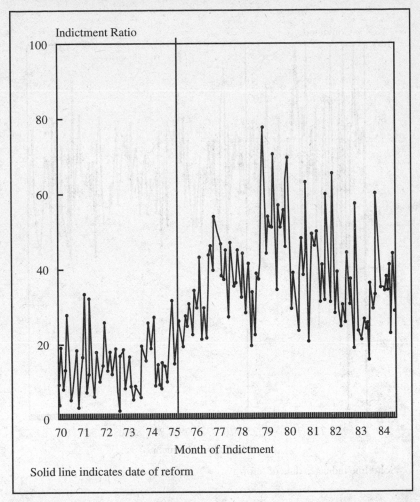

FIGURE 2   Indictment ratio for rape, Detroit, Michigan, 1970–1984

was confirmed by a statistical analysis of the absolute number of convictions. We also found that the reforms did not change the likelihood of incarceration but that the average sentence received by those incarcerated increased by about sixty-three months.

Some reformers predicted that the definitional reforms would lead to an increase in plea bargaining, since the graded criminal sexual conduct offenses would make it possible to reduce original charges to charges still within the sexual offense category. When we examined the percentage of cases convicted on original charges, we found no evidence of a decrease that would correspond to a greater reliance on plea bargaining. In fact, the percentage of cases convicted on the original charge increased after the new laws went into effect, although the increase was not statistically significant.

Michigan's strong and comprehensive reforms produced some, but

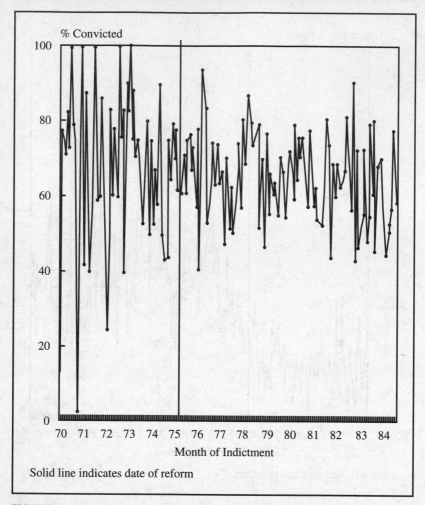

FIGURE 3   Percentage convicted for rape, Detroit, Michigan, 1970–1984

not all, of the effects anticipated by reformers. The strong evidentiary changes enacted in Illinois (1978) and Pennsylvania (1976), in contrast, had no effect on reports of rape or the processing of rape cases in Chicago or Philadelphia. Figures 4–7 present the plots for reports and indictment ratio for those two cities.

The three cities with weaker reforms also showed almost no evidence of impact for the changes in rape laws. The only significant effect found for Washington, D.C., was a decrease in reported rapes after the elimination of the corroboration requirement. We have no theoretical rationale to explain such a decrease; we suspect that it was merely coincidental with the new law. In Atlanta there were some changes in the processing of rape cases but none that could be attributed to the legal reforms.

We found a number of changes in Houston, but most occurred years

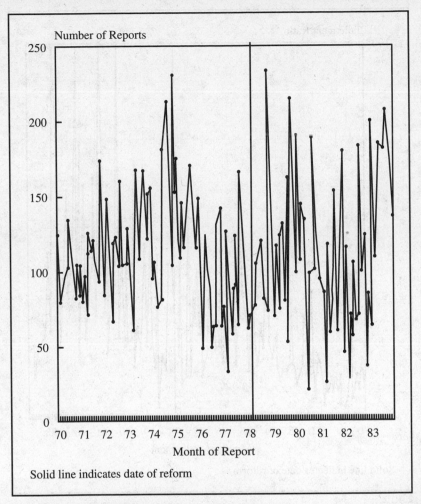

FIGURE 4   Reports of rape, Chicago, Illinois, 1970–1983

after implementation of the new laws, suggesting that they were due to other causes. Still, some charges occurred at the time of the rape law reform. The number of reported rapes increased by an average of 17.25 reports per month, and the indictment ratio *decreased* by .08. The average sentence for those incarcerated for rape increased by almost eighty-five months.

The graph of reported rapes (Fig. 8) shows a long-term increasing trend, and the statistical model that best fit the data was one representing a very gradual increase. Such an effect is quite unlikely to be produced by a legal reform. To test whether the trend might simply be part of a general increase in crime in Houston during those years, we looked at the monthly data for reported robberies and reported assaults for the same period. The plots show long-term trends similar to the trend for reported rapes, but without the increase in level apparent for reported

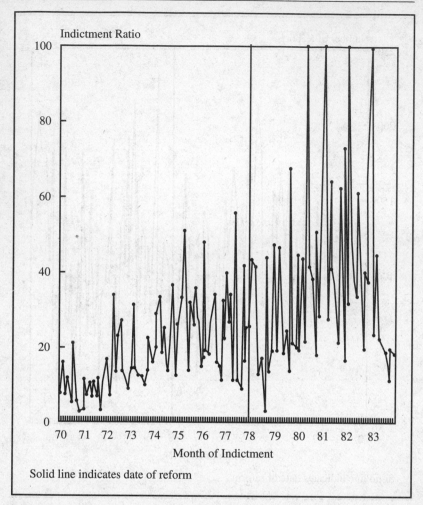

FIGURE 5   Indictment ratio for rape, Chicago, Illinois, 1970–1983

rapes immediately after the law reforms. That slight increase in reported rapes thus might have been produced by the publicity surrounding the reforms.

The significant decrease in the indictment ratio was not what reformers predicted. We suspect that it was a result of the increase in the number of rape reports; as reports of rapes increased in Houston, the number of indictments did not keep pace (Fig. 9). Similarly, the impact on sentences probably follows from the decrease in the indictment ratio. As more cases came into the system and as prosecutors became more selective, it is quite likely that the average case being prosecuted was more serious, producing an increase in average sentence length.

DISCUSSION

Our analysis of the impact of rape law reforms in six major urban jurisdictions revealed that legal changes did not produce the dramatic results anticipated by reformers. The reforms had no impact in most of the jurisdictions. While the greatest, albeit limited, impact was found in Detroit, where a single reform dramatically changed all the rape laws, a simple strong reform-weak reform distinction cannot explain the pattern of results. We found no greater impact in two jurisdictions with relatively strong reforms—Chicago and Philadelphia—than in the three jurisdictions with relatively weak reforms.

As noted earlier, many reforms have failed because reformers assumed that the behavior of decision makers in the criminal justice system is controlled by legal rules. A failure to appreciate the role of

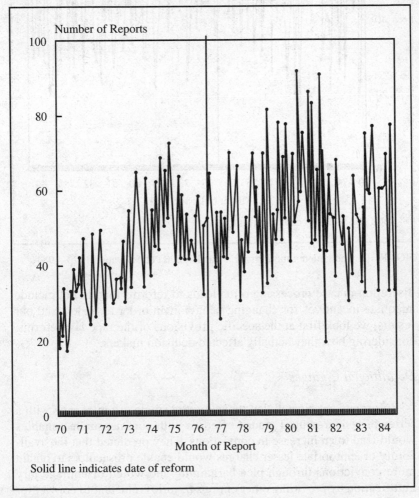

FIGURE 6   Reports of rape, Philadelphia, Pennsylvania, 1970–1984

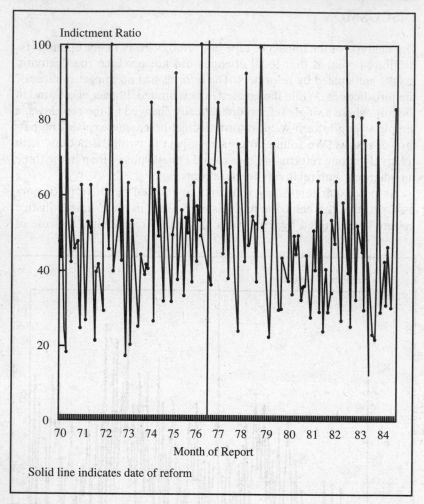

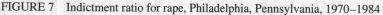

FIGURE 7   Indictment ratio for rape, Philadelphia, Pennsylvania, 1970–1984

discretion in case processing often leads to reforms that do not include adequate incentives for changing behavior. In order to understand our results, we look first at the specific provisions of the rape law reforms, considering how they actually affected decision makers.

Definitional Changes

Reformers anticipated that replacing the single crime of rape with a series of gender-neutral graded offenses with commensurate penalties would lead to an increase in convictions. They predicted that the availability of appropriate lesser charges would enable prosecutors to obtain more convictions through plea bargaining and would discourage jury nullification by providing other options to juries reluctant to convict for forcible rape.

We found no evidence of an increased likelihood of convictions in Detroit, where definitional changes took effect, or in any of the other jurisdictions. The fact that we found no decrease in the proportion of cases resulting in convictions on the original charge indicates that there was no increase in plea bargaining. Our interviews led us to believe that the reforms' implicit focus on the seriousness of the crime of rape may have created an unwillingness to plea bargain that counteracted the facilitative effects of the definitional changes. In Detroit, in fact, the Wayne County Prosecutor's office has an explicit policy restricting plea bargaining. The policy requires the complainant's approval prior to reducing charges. In addition, the policy provides that charges of criminal sexual conduct in the first degree may only, except in unusual circumstances, be negotiated down to criminal sexual conduct in the third degree (CSC3) and that CSC3 charges may not be reduced.

Reformers also expected that the new laws would encourage juries

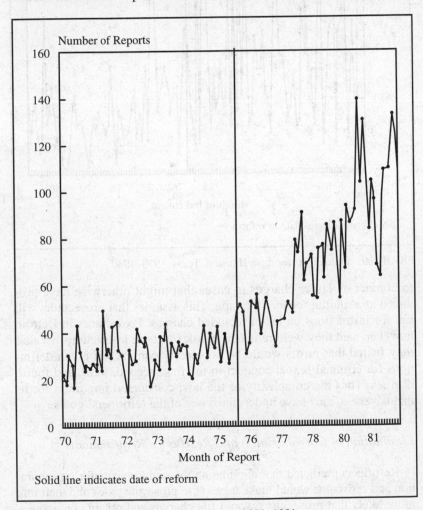

FIGURE 8   Reports of rape, Houston, Texas, 1970–1981

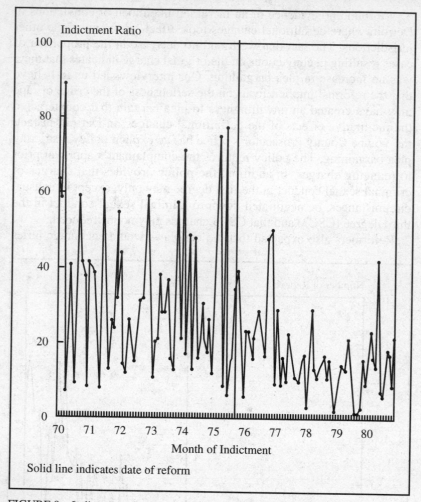

FIGURE 9   Indictments for rape, Houston, Texas, 1970–1980

to convict on lesser charges in cases that might otherwise have produced an acquittal for forcible rape. This assumes that prosecutors will ask for instructions on lesser included charges. Prosecutors in Detroit, however, said they were reluctant to ask for these instructions because they feared that jurors would be hopelessly confused if given definitions for criminal sexual conduct in the first, second, third, and fourth degrees. Thus the complexity of the law, considered important for its inclusiveness, may have undermined one of the reformers' goals.

Elimination of Corroboration and Resistance Requirements

Reformers predicted that eliminating the requirements for corroboration and resistance would make it easier to prosecute cases and therefore more likely that prosecutors would file charges and obtain convictions.

We believe that reformers were overly optimistic about the effects of these largely symbolic changes. For one thing, court decisions over the years had already considerably loosened both requirements. Officials in every jurisdiction reported that a prompt report or physical evidence of intercourse could corroborate the victim's testimony; thus, it was almost always possible to get past a motion for a judgment of acquittal. As one judge stated, "the case law was so broadly interpreted that a scintilla of corroboration was satisfying." Similarly, courts had ruled that a victim was not required to put her life in jeopardy by resisting an attack, and that evidence of force on the part of the offender was tantamount to proof of nonconsent by the victim. By the mid-1970s the corroboration and resistance requirements could be viewed as minor hurdles if prosecutors wanted to proceed with a case, and formal elimination of the statutory requirements was therefore irrelevant in practice.

More important, elimination of the requirements does nothing to constrain the discretion of decision makers . . . . [R]eformers often assume that removing alleged legal obstacles will allow decision makers to behave in the "correct" way, when in fact problems are typically not the product of artificial barriers or constraints but of conscious behavioral choices made both individually and as a group by professionals within the system. As one of our respondents explained, the law may no longer require corroboration, but that does not mean that the prosecutor will file charges when the complainant's story is totally uncorroborated.

Prosecutors often make charging decisions based on their estimates of whether cases could be won before a jury; if they believe a jury will look for corroboration and resistance, they will continue to require them for charging. Many prosecutors we interviewed believed, in fact, that jurors are unlikely to convict in the absence of these factors. As one prosecutor noted, "Juries still expect some resistance or some explanation as to why there was none. This is especially true if it was a date gone sour; if we can't show some resistance in this case we're in a lot of trouble." Concerning corroboration, another stated, "If you're talking about consent defenses, jurors are still looking for corroborating evidence—physical injury, a weapon, a hysterical call to the police; old habits and old attitudes die hard, and we can change the law but we can't necessarily change attitudes."

Juries might be influenced if instructed that the victim need not resist her attacker and that her testimony need not be corroborated. Many officials we interviewed believed, in fact, that it could be very important for jurors to hear this, not from the prosecutor, but from the judge. Even when a statute explicitly states the lack of a need for resistance or corroboration, however, such instructions are given at the discretion of the judge and the prosecutor. Some judges routinely give the instruction; others instruct only if requested to do so by the prosecutor. Some judges reported that the prosecutor always asks for the instruction; some said that prosecutors never do. Thus, the potential for impact of the reforms is again diminished by the discretionary nature of the criminal justice system.

Analysis of elimination of corroboration and resistance requirements, then, suggests that reformers had unrealistic expectations concerning their impact. Although these reforms may have sent an important symbolic message, they did not significantly alter the decision-making context. Neither requirement was an insurmountable hurdle before the reforms, and the reforms themselves did not constrain the discretion of prosecutors or jurors. In the post-reform period, as in the pre-reform period, corroboration and resistance evidence may still be important to the successful prosecution of at least some kinds of rape cases.

Rape Shield Laws

Reformers predicted the rape shield laws would have a greater impact on the processing and disposition of sexual assault cases than would the other reforms. They anticipated that the restrictions on evidence damaging to the complainant would prompt more victims to report rapes to the police and would lead directly to an increase in convictions and indirectly to an increase in arrests and prosecutions.

Effects of Weak Shield Laws

We did not expect the weak shield laws of Washington, D.C., Georgia, and Texas to have a significant impact on case processing. The laws adopted in each of these states continue to allow judges considerable discretion in deciding whether to admit sexual history evidence. Case law in Washington, D.C., for example, excludes evidence of the victim's prior sexual conduct with parties other than the defendant but allows evidence of the victim's reputation for chastity if the judge determines that its probative value outweighs its prejudicial effect. The Georgia law allows evidence of the victim's sexual reputation or sexual conduct with third parties if the judge finds it supports an inference that the accused reasonably could have believed the victim consented. And . . . Texas does not categorically exclude any sexual conduct evidence; rather, such evidence can be admitted if the judge finds that the evidence is relevant.

By leaving so much to the judge's discretion, the shield laws enacted in these jurisdictions did little to alter the "rules" for handling rape cases . . . . [T]he Texas shield law in essence made no change. The motion *in limine* had always been available to prosecutors to exclude irrelevant evidence, and the judge always determined relevance. Prosecutors in Atlanta suggested that Georgia's rape shield law was actually weaker than the case law in effect prior to the law's passage. In both states, much stronger reforms had been presented to legislators. The weak shield laws that were passed can be viewed as symbolic policies designed to placate the interest groups lobbying for change.

Effect of Strong Shield Laws

The rape shield laws enacted in Michigan, Illinois, and Pennsylvania are much stronger. The laws in all three states generally prohibit the introduction of evidence of the victim's past sexual conduct. The prohibition includes evidence of specific instances of sexual activity, reputation evidence, and opinion evidence. There are only very narrow exceptions to the shield. All three jurisdictions permit introduction of the victim's past sexual conduct with the defendant, but only if the judge determines that the evidence is relevant. The shield laws enacted in these states, then, sent a strong message to defense attorneys, prosecutors, and judges. They clearly stated that certain types of sexual history evidence are inadmissible. Unlike the laws adopted in Texas, Georgia, and the District of Columbia, they also attempted to place meaningful limits on judges' discretion to admit certain kinds of evidence.

One important procedural aspect of the rape shield laws is the requirement of an *in camera* hearing for determining admissibility of evidence relating to the victim's sexual history. Our interviews with judges, prosecutors and defense attorneys, however, revealed that *in camera* hearings are rarely if ever held, especially if the evidence concerns sexual conduct between the victim and the defendant. Prosecutors reported that they generally concede the relevance of evidence of a prior sexual relationship between the victim and the defendant and do not challenge defense attorneys who attempt to introduce the evidence without requesting a hearing. Similarly, judges use their discretion to overlook the *in camera* requirement or to overrule prosecutors' objections to the introduction of the evidence.

It is not surprising that criminal justice officials have found ways to circumvent the formal procedural requirements of the shield laws . . . . *In camera* hearings are time consuming and would be a waste of time if judges routinely rule that evidence of a prior relationship between the victim and the defendant is relevant. Rather than going through the motions of challenging the evidence and perhaps alienating other members of the courtroom workgroup, prosecutors concede the point.

Noncompliance might also be attributed to agreement among prosecutors and judges that evidence of a prior sexual relationship between the victim and the defendant is always relevant to the issue of consent. Reformers believed that the relevance of this kind of evidence would depend on factors such as the nature and duration of the sexual relationship or the separation in time from the alleged rape. We believe decision makers have developed a much simpler rule based on shared norms of relevance and fairness in evidentiary issues. Their "admissibility rule" states that if the sexual conduct was with the defendant, it is relevant. Like "going rates" in sentencing . . . or "normal crime" categories in charging . . . the rule routinizes and simplifies the decision-making process.

The disregard of the requirement for hearings contradicts . . . [one writer's] assertion that legal rules are most effective when they specify procedural steps in case processing. The *in camera* hearings required by rape shield laws, however, differ from other procedural requirements in one important way. While the laws mandate hearings in certain situations and clearly specify the procedures to be followed, they do not provide for review or sanction of judges who fail to follow the law. Moreover, if a defendant is acquitted because the judge violated the law and either admitted potentially relevant evidence without a hearing or allowed the defense attorney to use legally inadmissible evidence, the victim cannot appeal the acquittal or the judge's decisions. If, on the other hand, the judge followed the law and refused to admit seemingly irrelevant sexual history evidence, the defendant can appeal his conviction. All the consequences, in other words, would lead judges to err in favor of the defendant.

The avoidance of *in camera* hearings clearly undermines the reforms to the extent that issues of relevance are not debated if the sexual conduct was between the victim and the defendant. Their absence does not mean legally prohibited evidence of sexual conduct between the victim and third parties is being admitted. To the contrary, it appears that hearings are avoided on these issues because the members of the workgroup agree that such evidence cannot be admitted. The other side of the admissibility rule, in other words, is that sexual conduct between the victim and parties other than the defendant is not relevant. Judges in every jurisdiction stated that defense attorneys don't even attempt to introduce the more questionable kinds of sexual history evidence. As one judge in Chicago explained, "Attorneys are warned that I will interpret the law strictly and they don't even try to bring it up unless it concerns the victim and the defendant."

If evidence clearly proscribed by the law is effectively excluded, we must consider other explanations for the lack of impact of the strong rape shield laws. Why is it that even these strong laws did not produce the types of changes envisioned by reformers? For one thing, the shield laws primarily affect cases that go to trial and, particularly, the small percentage of cases tried before a jury. Moreover, sexual history evidence is only relevant in cases where the defense is consent. Since it is unlikely that consent will be the defense when a woman is raped by a total stranger, this means that sexual history evidence will be relevant only when the victim and the defendant are acquainted. The shield laws, then, have the potential to affect directly only the relatively few rape cases in which the victim and the defendant are acquainted, the defendant claims the victim consented, and the defendant insists on a trial.

Unfortunately, no data are available on how often a complainant's sexual history entered into cases before the rape shield laws were enacted. Although reformers cited horror stories regarding harassment of victims in court, most respondents in jurisdictions we studied could recall few, if any, pre-reform cases in which defense attorneys used this tactic. If testimony regarding the victim's sexual history with third parties was rarely introduced, then restricting the use of such evidence would produce little change. Respondents in several jurisdictions reported, in fact, that previous case rulings had accomplished much of what the rape shield laws were designed to do.

We have discussed the weaknesses of the individual reforms and have explained why the reforms did not produce the instrumental results anticipated by reformers. These results might also be due to the fact that the reforms had the potential to affect only certain types of cases . . . . [There is an important] distinction between aggravated rape and "simple" rape. Aggravated rapes are those that involve strangers, multiple assailants, or armed force; simple rapes are committed by unarmed acquaintances, acting alone . . . . [M]ost of the rape law reforms have been directed at simple rape cases, and thus the greatest impact should have been seen in these cases. If, as we argue above, the laws fail to place meaningful constraint on the discretion of decision-maker, then impact could only be achieved by modifying decisionmakers' basic distrust of victims of simple rape. Further research should address this issue.

Evidence of Impact

Two sites did show some evidence of impact. In Detroit we found increases in reports of rape, in the ratio of indictments to reports, and in the length of the maximum sentence. In Houston also we found some evidence of increases in reporting and sentence length, but they were accompanied by a decrease in the indictment ratio.

Reports

We were surprised to find increased reports of rape in the jurisdiction with the weakest reforms (Houston) as well as in the jurisdiction with the strongest reforms (Detroit). The appearance of the increase just as the new laws went into effect suggests that the increases may have resulted from the publicity surrounding the reforms. If an increase in reporting resulted from actual improved treatment of victims due to the legal changes, we would expect a more gradual impact on reporting as knowledge of the improved treatment spreads through the community. Unfortunately, the scope of our study limits our ability to interpret these results. Because the legal reforms in Houston and Detroit were among the earliest in the country and because they coincided with extensive national media attention to the crime of rape, we suspect that their implementation may have occasioned more publicity than resulted in the other jurisdictions. However, we have no data to support this speculative explanation.

It is also possible that the increases in reporting we detected actually reflect changes in police behavior rather than in the behavior of victims. We had to rely on Uniform Crime Reports to measure reporting by victims, and these data are a product not only of victim complaints, but also of police decisions on whether to count complaints as valid reports of criminal incidents. Again, however, we do not have data on police department operations that would allow us to test this possibility.

Indictments

The most interesting results are our findings on the impact of reforms on the likelihood of indictment. Our analysis revealed a significant increase in the ratio of indictments to reports in Detroit, but a significant decrease in the likelihood of indictment in Houston. As we noted earlier, it seems very likely that the decrease in Houston represents a failure to keep up with the increase in reported rapes. If prosecutors simply continued to prosecute about the same number of cases, an increase in cases entering the system would result in a decrease in the indictment ratio. In Texas, indictment is by grand jury; the additional burden of taking a case to the grand jury may have affected judgments about how many cases could be prosecuted.

In Detroit we found an increase in the indictment ratio even as the number of reported cases increased. The results could have been produced by changes in police or prosecutor decisions or by both. It seems more likely that prosecutors would be most affected, because the legal changes generally involved evidentiary rules affecting the likelihood of obtaining convictions at trial. Our interviews tended to confirm this. Detroit police reported that prosecutors were refusing fewer warrants in rape cases since passage of the laws, and a victim-witness unit respondent said that more "date rape" cases were getting into the court system.

This increase in the indictment ratio suggests that prosecutors are more willing to file charges in borderline cases. We can speculate that some of the additional cases being reported in the post-reform period were the kinds of cases victims were reluctant to report prior to the passage of reform legislation: cases involving acquaintances, cases involving sexually promiscuous men or women, cases with little or no corroborating evidence, and so on. Presumably, some of these additional cases were the simple rape cases that . . . were so difficult to prove in the pre-reform era. Given this assumption, we might have expected the indictment rate to decline. The fact that it increased even as reports increased is thus an important finding.

The greater willingness to prosecute might be due in part to the fact that the definitions of the various degrees of criminal sexual conduct are much clearer than the old definition of rape. The current Michigan law provides clear guidelines for prosecutors to follow in screening rape cases. It carefully defines the elements of each offense, specifies the circumstances that constitute coercion, and lists the situations in which no showing of force is required. Although the judges, prosecutors, and defense attorneys we interviewed in Detroit thought the new laws might be confusing to jurors, they nevertheless spoke approvingly of the clarity and precision of the new statute. One prosecutor commented that "the elements of force and coercion are clearly spelled out." Another explained that the law "sets out with greater particularity what the elements of the offense are." By spelling out the acts that constitute sexual assault, the circumstances that imply consent and nonconsent, and the types of evidence that are unnecessary or irrelevant, the Michigan laws may have made it easier to recognize acceptable cases.

Although our finding of no increase in the conviction ratio in Detroit represents a failure of reformers' expectations, the stability of that ratio is important. If, as we suggested, the increase in indictments that occurred resulted from more borderline cases entering the system, we might have expected a decline in the overall likelihood of conviction. The fact that the total number of convictions kept pace with the increase in indictments suggests that defendants in these borderline cases are being convicted.

Sentencing

We found an increase in average sentence coinciding with the change in law in Houston and Detroit and increases in sentence length over the time period studied but not attributable specifically to the law reforms in other jurisdictions. We suspect that these widespread increases reflect changes in attitudes toward the crime of rape rather than changes in the laws of rape. The enactment of rape law reforms, while not aimed directly at increasing sentences for rape, reflected public demands that rape be treated as a very serious offense. Judges may have responded by imposing more severe sentences on those convicted for rape. These changes in attitudes toward the crime of rape might also have fostered a reluctance to plea bargain—and a consequent increase in sentence severity—in rape cases.

The Effect of Comprehensive Changes

Although we found some evidence in Houston of increases in reporting and in sentence length, the impact we found in Detroit, although limited, stands out as the only example of the reforms affecting official decisionmaking in the manner predicted by reformers. One interpretation of the finding is that the criminal justice system can only be affected by the kind of dramatic, comprehensive changes enacted in

Michigan. Clearly, the Michigan reform was broader than those adopted in the other five jurisdictions we studied. It also was accomplished in one major revision of state codes. Although we have explored the weaknesses of the individual legal changes, it may be that only a comprehensive reform package, by sending a strong and unambiguous message to decisionmakers, can overcome the resistance to change inherent in the system.

Our findings clearly contradict [Raymond] Nimmer's prediction that "the probability of system change is inversely related to the degree of change sought by a reform." . . . [He argues] that a reform involving drastic change will encounter greater resistance within the system, especially when the behavior affected is perceived as important . . . . [He] cited as an example the impact of required plea bargaining conferences in Detroit and Denver. The reform in Detroit, which required relatively minor changes in behavior, was successful, while the Denver reform, which sought to drastically shift the time to disposition, had no impact on timing of guilty pleas. The kinds of reforms involving speedy dispositions are very different from the rape law reforms, which attempted to effect major changes . . . . We suspect that if attitudes are to be changed, dramatic, comprehensive changes that demand attention may be required . . . .

We do not have measures of officials' attitudes before and after the law reforms, but we did conduct interviews across our six jurisdictions following the reforms. Although respondents in all jurisdictions expressed attitudes generally favorable toward the legal reforms, Detroit officials took the strongest positions on excluding complainant's sexual history when they were questioned about a series of hypothetical cases. We cannot be sure, of course, that those attitudes were the product of the comprehensive reforms and not a causal factor that led to their enactment . . . .

CONCLUSION

We have shown that the ability of rape reform legislation to produce instrumental change is limited. In most of the jurisdictions we studied, the reforms had no impact. Our results are not surprising in light of the large body of literature detailing the failure of legal reforms. We found, like many others who have studied reforms aimed at the court system, that the rape law reforms placed few constraints on the tremendous discretion exercised by decision makers in the criminal justice system.

The results of our study suggest that instrumental change will be especially difficult to achieve when reforms are designed to remove legal barriers to prosecution and conviction. If, for example, workgroup norms support prosecution and conviction of rape cases in which the victim did not resist or her allegations cannot be corroborated, then officials find ways to circumvent the legal barriers, and as a result the official removal of these barriers will have little effect in practice. If, on the other hand, informal norms oppose prosecution and conviction of these kinds of cases, simply removing the legal barriers will be ineffective unless the discretion that allows informal norms to guide decision making is constrained or meaningful incentives to change the norms are created.

Reforms aimed at improving the treatment of victims may be less likely than other reforms to provide even minimal constraints on discretion or incentives to change. Victim-oriented reforms are unlikely to facilitate the smooth and efficient flow of cases through the system, and they may conflict with values concerning the rights of defendants. In our legal system, the defendant has considerably more "power" than the victim. Not only are the rights of the defendant constitutionally protected, but in defending those rights the defendant has, at least in theory, an advocate in the defense attorney. The prosecutor does not play the same role for the victim, but is instead an advocate for the state, and the interests of the state may often conflict with those of the victim. The protections afforded the defendant are further guaranteed by the process of appellate review. Judicial decisions that negatively affect the defendant can be appealed to a higher court; decisions that impinge on a victim by decreasing the likelihood of conviction are legally unreviewable.

This suggests that the advocates of rape law reform may need to create incentives for change by monitoring implementation of the reforms and by applying public pressure on criminal justice officials who fail to comply. In some jurisdictions the officials we interviewed said that there was intense monitoring at the time of the law reforms but that the public and the media lost interest shortly thereafter. These officials perceived very little continuing attention to their handling of rape cases. Such attention may be necessary to produce and preserve change.

The fact that the rape law reforms did not produce the broad effects anticipated by reformers does not mean, of course, that the reforms had no impact. Most respondents in the six jurisdictions expressed strong support for the reforms, which they felt had resulted in more sensitive treatment of victims of rape. Officials believed that passage of the reforms sent an important symbolic message regarding the treatment of rape cases and rape victims.

In the long run, this symbolic message may be more important than the instrumental change that was anticipated but generally not accomplished. Under the old laws it was assumed that chastity is relevant to consent and credibility; that corroboration is required because women tend to lie about being raped; and that resistance is required to demonstrate nonconsent. These assumptions clearly were archaic in light of changes in attitudes toward sexual relations and toward the role of women in society. Those who lobbied for rape law reform sought to refute these common law principles and to shift the focus in a rape case from the reputation and behavior of the victim to the unlawful acts of the offender. In doing so, the reforms may have produced long-term attitude change that is difficult to measure in a legal impact study.

We did find more than symbolic impact in Detroit. We speculated that the increase in the indictment ratio there represented a greater willingness to prosecute in "borderline" cases. Because we were not able to examine the impact of the reforms on different kinds of cases, we could not test this hypothesis directly. We also could not test for more subtle kinds of impact that might have been masked when we analyzed case outcomes overall. We have discussed . . . the distinction between "aggravated" rape and "simple" rape and . . . [the] assertion that these cases have always been dealt with in very different ways. If the proportion of real and simple rapes entering the courts has changed, some effects of the rape law reform could have been masked. Further research should address this issue. □

NOTES AND QUESTIONS

1. Horney and Spohn suggest that the rape law reforms did not produce much in the way of real (instrumental) change in the way rapes were handled, the number of incidents reported, and so on. They claim, however, that there were important symbolic changes. What did these consist of? What was important about them? How would Gusfield have characterized the results of the rape reform laws?

2. This chapter is about the impact of law. In earlier readings, we asked who obeys the law, and why. One part of the answer (not the whole answer, of course) is that people are afraid of punishment, and are deterred. Are the reforms that Horney and Spohn discuss likely to increase the deterrent effect of rape laws? If so, how? Recall the material on the "deterrence curve."

3. Enforcement of a criminal law is never automatic; it depends on police, prosecutors, judges, juries, and others. The rape laws are no exception. What aspects of the institutions and personnel charged with enforcing the rape laws had an impact on whether or not the reforms made much of a difference? What suggestions do the authors make for ways to overcome barriers to implementation of the rape reform laws?

4. Horney and Spohn argue that big changes, dramatic reforms, may sometimes produce more impact than smaller or incremental changes. Can you think of good examples of big changes that had big effects—and of big changes that were failures? Prohibition itself was of course a big change in the law; and it is usually considered a failure.

5. The effect or impact of law is in almost every case problematic. Legal change almost never follows smoothly and automatically from passage of a law. There are many studies of institutional barriers that stand in the way of reforms. See, for example, Malcolm Feeley, *Court Reform on Trial: Why Simple Solutions Fail* (New York: Basic Books, 1983). For an overview of the various ways in which intended effects or impacts fail, see Shari Seidman Diamond, "Detecting Legal Change and its Impact," in Leonard Bickman (ed.), 2 *Applied Social Psychology Annual* 139 (Beverly Hills: Sage Publications, 1981).

Diamond gives many examples of "noneffects" of legal interventions. She points out that legal reform "rarely involves a system-wide intervention." Typically, it simply changes one aspect or step in a complicated system. What happens then is that the rest of the system makes adjustments "so that ultimate outcomes remain unaffected." In Illinois, a law imposed strict and mandatory sentences on very serious crimes—murder, rape, and so on. But prosecutors and other actors in the system changed their charging practices when they did not see these mandatory sentences as appropriate, and the system was thus "able to absorb legal reform with an apparent minimum of reverberation" (p. 151).

6. Another empirical study of the impact of rape reform law is Wallace D. Loh, "The Impact of Common Law and Reform Rape Statutes on Prosecution: An Empirical Study," 55 *Washington Law Review* 543 (1980). This study of rape prosecutions in the Seattle area found only modest changes in prosecutions for rape after enactment of reform law. But Loh, at the end of the study, expresses the opinion that rape reform may have a greater impact than its "immediate" results in the criminal justice system might indicate. This is because the reform may act as a "catalyst" for changes in "official and lay attitudes" toward the crime. "The new rape law symbolizes and reinforces newly emerging conceptions about the status of women and the right of self-determination in sexual conduct . . . [T]he criminal law complements and enhances the moral learning initially acquired through non-legal processes."

Still another study, this time of California, was reported in Kenneth Polk, "Rape Reform and Criminal Justice Processing," 31 *Crime and Delinquency* 191 (1985). This study found meager results in one sense—the probability that a man arrested for rape would be convicted was about the same before and after the reform laws. On the other hand, after the reforms, men convicted of rape were more likely than before to "receive an institutional sentence."

Rape reform has not been confined to the United States. On British reform of rape law and what followed, see Zsuzsanna Adler, *Rape on Trial* (New York: Routledge, Kegan, and Paul, 1987).

7. Are some laws *too* effective? We hear constant complaints about the baleful effect of new doctrines and practices in the law of torts, especially medical malpractice and products liability. They have reached, it is said, a point where they are driving insurance rates sky-high, stifling business innovation, and hurting American competitiveness. These charges, of course, are exceedingly difficult to prove or disprove.

There have been, however, a few attempts to measure the impact of particular changes in tort doctrine. See, for example, Gregory A. Caldeira, "Changing the Common Law: Effects of the Decline of Charitable Immunity," 16 *Law & Society Review* 669 (1982), and the study of the impact of the *Tarasoff* case dealing with the liability of mental health workers, reported on p. 626.

8. It is very hard to measure legal impact experimentally. Life does not allow us to put the actual functioning legal system in a laboratory and test the consequences of changes in laws or procedures. Social scientists can attempt to simulate aspects of the legal system in a laboratory where they can control all the independent variables. However, while such studies may be suggestive, we cannot be sure that we can take findings produced this way and generalize them to the functioning legal system. The simulation may not capture enough of what makes the functioning system tick. Perhaps the best we can hope for are "quasi-experiments" or "natural experiments." The most promising type is "interrupted time-series analysis," a sophisticated form of before-and-after studies.

In other words, if a law is passed that mandates or forbids certain conduct, and if we can measure the conduct before and after the law became effective, we can make a good guess as to whether the law made a difference. However, we have to be very careful because there are many threats to the validity of such a conclusion. It is unlikely that the law is the only thing that changed in the society. For example, rape law changed *along with* changes in men and women's attitudes, and it is hard to be sure how much change was caused by the law and how much by the changes in attitudes. A law increasing the penalties for speeding might appear to reduce accidents, but the reduction of accidents following passage of the law actually might be caused by redesign and reconstruction of unsafe highways in the state. Similarly, if we find little or no change after a law formally takes effect, there might be a good explanation somewhere in the social context or background. For a discussion of this subject in detail, see Donald T. Campbell and H. Laurence Ross, "The Connecticut Crackdown on Speeding: Time Series Data in Quasi-Experimental Analysis," 3 *Law & Society Review* 33 (1968).

39. *Miranda In Pittsburgh—A Statistical Study*

Richard H. Seeburger

and R. Stanton Wettick, Jr.

29 *University of Pittsburgh Law Review* 1 (1967)

[In 1966, the Supreme Court decided the famous case of *Miranda v. Arizona*, 384 U.S. 436 (1966). The Court ruled that police and other law enforcement officials must tell those they arrest about their rights, including the right to remain silent. This became known as the "Miranda warning."]

II. STATISTICAL STUDY

☐ The purpose of this statistical study is to determine the extent to which the *Miranda* decision has impaired the ability of Pittsburgh's law enforcement agencies to apprehend and convict the criminal and has created a backlog in the Allegheny County criminal courts. We have collected data showing, *inter alia*, the change in the confession rate following *Miranda*; the percentage of cases in which a confession probably was or would have been necessary in order to obtain a conviction; the change in Pittsburgh's clearance rate following *Miranda*; and the percentage of criminal cases in Allegheny County disposed of through a guilty plea before and after *Miranda*.

Source of Data

Most of the data for this study was obtained from the files of the Detective Branch of the Pittsburgh Police Bureau. This Branch is the investigative arm of the Pittsburgh Police Bureau. It conducts investigations of every homicide committed within the city and most serious felonies other than those immediately solved by the uniformed policemen from the precincts for which no investigative assistance is needed to build the case.

The Detective Branch makes a file for each case which it clears. Such files contain all the written information which the Branch has on the case. Such information usually includes a description of the crime, the suspects, the case against the suspects and any statements (oral or written) made by the suspects.

For this study we examined the entire contents of each file of the Detective Branch for each case, starting in 1964, which has been tried or dropped and involves the following types of crime: homicide, forceful sex, robbery, burglary (including receiving stolen goods) and auto larceny. We understandably were not permitted to examine the cases which had not yet come to trial . . . .

This study does not include any cases which were not investigated by the Detective Branch. Therefore its data is based solely upon the more difficult cases for which investigation was deemed necessary by the police. According to Assistant Superintendent Coon, these are the cases in which confessions play a more important role because they are generally the police's weaker cases.

Police Procedure

For almost every file which we examined, the Detective Branch attempted to obtain a confession from all the suspects involved. It is standard practice for the Branch to question every suspect in all cases in which it makes an arrest.

The questioning occurs at the time the suspect is taken into custody. As of January 1, 1965, the Pennsylvania Rules of Criminal Procedure (Rule 116) require that a defendant who has been arrested be taken without unnecessary delay before the proper issuing authority for preliminary arraignment. This requirement, as construed by the Detective Branch, prohibits holding a suspect in custody for questioning for long periods of time, but it does not prevent holding a suspect for questioning for a period of time sufficient to give the police a fair opportunity to obtain a confession.

In almost all cases this is the only time at which a suspect (held for preliminary arraignment) is questioned. There is no further questioning of such suspects regardless of whether they are released on bond or placed in jail to await trial.

Even before the *Miranda* decision, the Detective Branch met many of the requirements imposed by *Miranda*. For at least 10 and probably 25 years before the *Miranda* decision, it has been the procedure of the Detective Branch to advise suspects of their right to remain silent, and shortly after the *Escobedo* decision, the Detective Branch began to advise suspects of their right to counsel. This advice, however, did not include an offer to provide counsel free of charge to those who could not afford counsel. Moreover, this advice was not given clearly and unequivocally at the beginning of the interrogation, but rather was woven into the conversation between the suspect and the detective. Furthermore, the detectives would attempt to persuade the suspect who indicated that he wanted to remain silent or to be assisted by counsel to change his mind and make a statement.

Within one week after the *Miranda* decision the Detective Branch began complying with the additional requirements imposed by *Miranda* that the indigent suspect be offered counsel at no cost, that the suspect be advised of his right to remain silent and to the assistance of council in clear and unequivocal terms at the beginning of the questioning, and that all questioning cease if the suspect indicates that he wishes to remain silent or to be assisted by counsel.

Assistant Superintendent Coon believes that within a short time after the *Miranda* decision there was almost total compliance with the above requirements by the Detective Branch. As he pointed out, the members of the Detective Branch are professional investigators. They usually have no emotional tie to the cases; they are aware of the legal penalties for failure to comply with the law's requirements; and they are trained to obey procedures and regulations.

It is the policy of the Detective Branch to require compliance with *Miranda* only for the interrogation of a suspect in custody. It considers a suspect to be in custody when he is no longer free to walk away from the detective at any time he wishes. As long as a suspect is not in custody, the *Miranda* regulations of the Detective Branch permit questioning without the giving of any warnings.

It is also the policy of the Detective Branch to interrogate any suspect who indicates a willingness to talk after being advised of his rights to remain silent and to be assisted counsel. If a suspect who has been advised of these rights indicates a willingness to talk, this is deemed to be sufficient evidence of an intelligent and understanding waiver of his constitutional rights in most situations. No further attempt is made to determine whether the waiver is intelligent and understanding.

Miranda has not been accompanied by any significant changes in Pittsburgh's other investigative procedures. There has been no significant increase in expenditures for additional investigators. In fact since June, 1966 there has been approximately a 10% reduction in the manpower of the Detective Branch, as a result of the transfer of the vice and narcotics enforcement functions from the Branch.

The Pittsburgh police picture is probably representative of most of the larger cities. In 1966 Pittsburgh's crime rate per 1000 population was 29.2 (13/18) as compared to the median rate of 28.1–27.4 for the 18 cities in this country, with populations between 500,000 and 700,000; its per capita budget required an expenditure of $18.60 per resident (5/18) as compared to the median figure for the 18 cities of $15.53–$15.34; and its number of police officers per 1000 population was 2.67 (4/18) as compared to the median figure for the 18 cities of 1.76.

On the investigative side, Pittsburgh had 157 criminal investigators, which ranked it 10th among the 18 cities. About half of these investigators were paid between $574–$620 per month. This would place Pittsburgh at the middle to lower end of the pay scale for the 18 cities.

Number of Confessions

To determine the impact of *Miranda* on the police's ability to obtain confessions, we compared the percentage of cases involving confessions in which the arrest was made prior to the Detective Branch's compliance with the *Miranda* requirements with the percentage of cases involving confessions in which the arrest was made after the Detective Branch's compliance with the *Miranda* requirements.

Our criteria for classifying statements made to the police were to include as confessions all admissions (oral or written) to police officers which were self-incriminating and contained no self-serving declarations which would substantially lessen the offense and all admissions which were helpful to the police's case even if they contained such self-serving declarations. On the other hand, we did not include as confessions any statements which contained certain self-incriminating statements but were primarily self-serving in nature and of little value to the police and any statements which did not directly incriminate the suspect even though they could be helpful to the police (for example an alibi which the police found to be a lie).

For purposes of this comparison we chose June 21, 1966 as the time at which the Detective Branch began complying with the *Miranda* requirements.

Even though the Detective Branch, as we have mentioned, advised suspects of their rights to remain silent and to be assisted by counsel prior to the *Miranda* decision, the giving of such advice, according to Assistant Superintendent Coon, did not impair the police's opportunity for effective interrogation. The significant requirements imposed by *Miranda*, according to Assistant Superintendent Coon, are that a suspect in custody be *clearly* advised of his rights to be assisted by counsel and to remain silent *before* any questioning and that all questioning cease once the suspect advises the police that he wishes to remain silent or wants the assistance of counsel. These are the requirements that prevent effective interrogation. Accordingly, for purposes of our comparison we used the time at which the Detective Branch began complying with these requirements.

The comparison of the percentage of cases involving confessions before and after compliance with the *Miranda* requirements is contained in Table 1. For purposes of these figures one case consists of the commission of one or a series of crimes by the same suspects. Figures relating to cases instead of suspects probably give a more accurate picture of the extent to which *Miranda* has hampered the police because frequently crimes are committed by more than one person and one confession is sufficient to solve the case and to provide evidence for the conviction of all participants in the crime. A second or third confession is of limited benefit to the police.

These figures show that before compliance with the *Miranda* requirements the Detective Branch obtained confessions in 54.4% of the cases and after compliance in only 37.5% of the cases. If the comparison is limited to robbery and burglary—the crimes with which most of the post-Miranda cases are involved—the decline in the confession rate is even greater. Before *Miranda* the Detective Branch obtained confessions in 59.9% of the burglary and robbery cases and after *Miranda* this percentage dropped to 40.3% of the cases. The most significant decline was in robbery—more than 25%. Burglary, on the other hand, fell only 14%.

TABLE 1 CONFESSION RATE

Type of Crime	No. of Cases with Confessions	No. of Cases without Confessions	% of Cases with Confessions
Homicide			
Pre-Miranda	51	36	58.6
Post-Miranda	5	11	31.3
Robbery			
Pre-Miranda	108	65	62.4
Post-Miranda	22	38	36.7
Burglary (including RSG)			
Pre-Miranda	123	92	57.2
Post-Miranda	30	39	43.5
Auto Larceny			
Pre-Miranda	55	46	54.5
Post-Miranda	3	6	33.3
Sex (forceable)			
Pre-Miranda	16	57	21.9
Post-Miranda	3	11	21.4
Total			
Pre-Miranda	353	296	54.4
Post-Miranda	63	105	37.5

TABLE 2   CONFESSION RATE—SUSPECTS

Type of Crime	No. of Suspects who Confessed	No. of Suspects who did not Confess	% of Suspects who Confessed
Homicide			
Pre-Miranda	54	37	59.3
Post-Miranda	6	13	31.6
Robbery			
Pre-Miranda	167	106	61.2
Post-Miranda	26	64	28.9
Burglary (including RSG)			
Pre-Miranda	185	217	46.0
Post-Miranda	37	62	37.4
Auto Larceny			
Pre-Miranda	62	81	43.4
Post-Miranda	3	7	30.0
Sex (forceable)			
Pre-Miranda	20	78	20.4
Post-Miranda	3	11	21.4
Total			
Pre-Miranda	488	519	48.5
Post-Miranda	75	157	32.3

In Table 2 we have made the same comparison using figures relating to the number of suspects rather than the number of cases. The figures show that before compliance with the *Miranda* requirements the Detective Branch obtained confessions from 48.5% of the suspects and after compliance from only 32.3% of the suspects. This decline (16.2%) in the percentage of suspects making statements is almost identical to the decline (16.9%) in the percentage of cases with confessions.

Another comparison can be made through the use of Table 2's pre-*Miranda* figures and post-*Miranda* figures collected from forms prepared by the Detective Branch.

As of June 20, 1967, all detectives in the Detective Branch were instructed to fill out a form for each suspect taken into custody which would show whether the suspect had relied on his constitutional right to remain silent or whether he was willing to answer any of the detective's questions, whether the suspect requested the assistance of counsel, whether the suspect made a self-incriminating statement and whether the suspect was arrested or released. The figures for the period from June 20 through September 5, 1967 are tabulated in Table 3.

Using the post-*Miranda* figures from Table 3, the percentage of suspects making statements has dropped since *Miranda* from 48.5% to 27.1% for the types of crimes covered by our study. These statistics also show that in more than 40% of the cases the suspect relied on his

TABLE 3   POST-MIRANDA CONFESSION RATE—SUSPECTS—POLICE FIGURES

	Homicide	Robbery	Burglary (including RSG)	Auto Larceny	Sex (forceable)	Others	Totals
Number of							
Suspects	5	47	38	13	5	65	173
Refused to Talk	1	19	15	3	3	33	74
Requested							
Counsel	1	8	10	2	1	24	46
Held for							
Magistrate	1	18	15	3	3	33	73
Released	0	1	0	0	0	0	1
Willing to Talk	4	28	23	10	2	32	99
Held for							
Magistrate	4	22	21	10	2	30	88
Released	0	6	2	0	1	2	11
Confessed	2	12	11	5	1	15	46
% of Suspects							
who Confessed	40.0	25.5	28.9	38.5	20.0	23.1	26.6

constitutional right to remain silent, thus depriving the Detective Branch of all opportunities for interrogation because of the *Miranda* prohibition against any further interrogation once the suspect has elected to remain silent. That 11 out of 99 suspects who talked were released suggests that the innocent are more willing to talk. That 73 out of 74 suspects who did not talk were held over suggests the police do not need confessions to justify arrests.

Necessity of Confessions for Conviction Purposes

To evaluate the importance of confessions for obtaining convictions, we have compiled figures showing the percentage of cases that we examined in which a confession was necessary to obtain a conviction, figures showing the major reason leading to the arrest of the suspect in each case, figures showing the percentage of convictions in cases in which the suspect did and did not confess and figures comparing the percentage of convictions before and after *Miranda*.

The figures showing the number of cases in which a confession was or would have been necessary to obtain a conviction are contained in Tables 4 and 5. Table 4 refers to all cases and Table 5 only to those cases in which a confession was obtained.

In preparing these Tables a confession was deemed necessary if we believed that a conviction would not have been likely without the use of a confession and any additional evidence obtained as a result of the confession. In making this determination we assumed the competent

TABLE 4   CONFESSIONS—NECESSITY—TOTAL CASES

Type of Case	Total Cases	No. where Confession is or would be Necessary	% of Total Cases where Confession is or would be Necessary
Homicide	99	20	20.2
Robbery	221	44	19.9
Burglary (including RSG)	271	57	21.0
Auto Larceny	102	17	16.7
Sex (forceable)	78	18	23.1
Total	771	156	20.2

TABLE 5   CONFESSIONS—NECESSITY—CASES WITH CONFESSIONS

Type of Case	No. of Cases with Confessions	No. where Confession is Necessary	% where Confession is Necessary
Homicide			
Pre-Miranda	49	13	26.5
Post-Miranda	5	2	40.0
Robbery			
Pre-Miranda	102	24	23.5
Post-Miranda	20	7	35.0
Burglary (including RSG)			
Pre-Miranda	117	29	24.8
Post-Miranda	27	9	33.3
Auto Larceny			
Pre-Miranda	50	11	22.0
Post-Miranda	3	0	0
Sex (forceable)			
Pre-Miranda	14	5	35.7
Post-Miranda	3	1	33.3
Total			
Pre-Miranda	332	82	24.7
Post-Miranda	58	19	32.8

gathering of available evidence, average presentation of the case by counsel for both sides, decisions based on the merits of the case at the arraignment and trial levels and cooperation by witnesses (other than the defendant and his family) who supplied evidence to the police during their investigation.

We recognize the guess work involved in basing such a determination solely on information in police files, many of which are quite sketchy. This is particularly true when the case rests on eye witnesses.

In such cases we relied on any comments in the file concerning the witness' opportunity to observe and remember the suspect, the certainty with which he made the description and his demeanor.

In preparing Tables 4 and 5, we frequently ran into the situation in which a confession was or would have been necessary for conviction on certain but not all charges. This was particularly true with burglary cases. Frequently a confession would be necessary to convict the defendant of burglary but not receiving stolen goods or to convict him of other burglaries in addition to those which could be established without the use of a confession. We considered the confession necessary only if the file gave some indication that the suspect had committed some other crime and if the conviction which would have been obtained for these other charges probably would have resulted in a substantially more severe punishment.

The figures from Table 4 show that in approximately 20% of all cases a confession is probably necessary to obtain a conviction. The figures in Table 5 show that in approximately 25% of the cases with confessions, the confession was probably necessary to obtain a conviction and that this percentage has not declined for post-*Miranda* cases . . . .

The . . . figures [in Table 6], which were gathered by the District Attorney's Office of Allegheny County, cover all crimes committed in Allegheny County which were prosecuted in the criminal courts of Allegheny County . . . . These figures show that the conviction rate has remained steady. For the first six months after *Miranda* the conviction rate dropped slightly but it then bounced back in the first half of 1967.

Other figures with which to measure the value of a confession for conviction purposes are the percentages of convictions in situations in which the defendant has confessed as compared to the percentage of convictions in situations in which the defendant has not confessed.

TABLE 6   CONVICTION RATE—ALLEGHENY COUNTY—ALL INDICTMENTS

	Guilty	Not Guilty	Nolle Pros. or Dismissed	% of Cases in which Def. was Found Guilty
1964	5,288	2,374	286	66.5
1965	5,470	2,096	579	67.2
1966 (through June 30)	3,396	1,364	321	66.8
1966 (July 1–Dec. 30)	2,094	847	354	63.6
1967 (through June 30)	2,691	895	330	68.7
Pre-Miranda Totals (7/1/64–6/30/66)	14,154	5,834	1,186	66.8
Post-Miranda Totals (7/1/66–6/30/67)	4,785	1,742	684	66.4

Figures compiled from those burglary and robbery files which we examined which indicated the outcome of the case show that defendants who had confessed were convicted 78.7% of the time (138/189 defendants), while defendants who had not confessed were convicted 54.5% of the time (174/319 defendants). These figures include cases dismissed at the arraignment and grand jury levels and cases nolle prossed and dismissed at the trial level.

Importance of Confessions for Solving Crimes

To this point we have been concerned only with the significance of confessions for conviction purposes. It is frequently contended that confessions are also necessary for solving crime.

This is obvious in those situations in which a crime is committed by more than one person or in which one or more persons have committed more than one crime. Often a confession is necessary here to learn the identity of the other participants to the crime and to link the suspect to crimes in addition to those for which he was apprehended. It is quite possible, however that confessions in these situations—particularly the former—will not be reduced by *Miranda* because it is frequently to the defendant's advantage to make the confession in such situations.

Figures on the clearance rate are relevant to ascertain the impact of *Miranda* on the ability of the police to solve cases. As we have mentioned, a case is considered cleared once the police have apprehended the persons they believed to be responsible for the crime regardless of whether the persons eventually are convicted.

The clearance rate for the city of Pittsburgh for the types of crime with which this study is concerned is contained in Table 7.

These figures show that the clearance rate for the first half of 1966 was 3 1/2% higher than the post-*Miranda* clearance rate. But when the 1965 figures are included in the pre-Miranda clearance rate, the *post-Miranda* clearance rate exceeds the pre-*Miranda* rate by 1.4%.

Court Backlog

To determine whether *Miranda* has reduced the percentage of cases disposed of by guilty pleas, Tables 8 and 9 compare the percentage of dispositions by guilty pleas before and after the *Miranda* decision. Table 10 contains figures showing the number of indictments presented before the Criminal Courts of Allegheny County and the number of guilty pleas to these indictments for . . . major crimes . . .

These figures show that the percentage of cases disposed of by guilty pleas has risen since the *Miranda* decision by 5.5% for the more serious crimes and by 2.9% for all crimes.

TABLE 7 CLEARANCE RATE—CRIMES—PITTSBURGH BUREAU OF POLICE

	Murder			Rape (Forceable)			Robbery			Burglary			Auto			Totals		
	No. of Crimes	Crimes Cleared	% of Crimes Cleared	No. of Crimes	Crimes Cleared	% of Crimes Cleared	No. of Crimes	Crimes Cleared	% of Crimes Cleared	No. of Crimes	Crimes Cleared	% of Crimes Cleared	No. of Crimes	Crimes Cleared	% of Crimes Cleared	No. of Crimes	Crimes Cleared	% of Crimes Cleared
1965	40	37	92.5	139	100	71.9	1,373	608	44.3	6,001	735	12.2	5,988	564	9.4	13,541	2,044	15.1
1966 (First Half)	13	13	100.0	92	57	62.0	779	362	46.5	2,938	625	21.3	2,689	396	14.7	6,511	1,453	22.3
1966 (Second Half)	16	14	87.5	104	82	78.8	792	200	25.3	2,859	603	21.1	2,647	365	13.8	6,418	1,264	19.7
1967 (First 7 Mos.)	20	20	100.0	105	74	70.5	1,013	356	35.1	3,549	569	16.0	3,373	434	12.9	8,060	1,453	18.0
Pre-Miranda Total (1/1/65–6/30/66)	53	50	94.3	231	157	68.0	2,152	970	45.1	8,939	1,360	15.2	8,677	960	11.1	20,052	3,497	17.4
Post-Miranda Total (7/1/66–7/31/67)	36	34	94.4	209	156	74.6	1,805	556	30.8	6,408	1,172	18.3	6,020	799	13.3	14,478	2,717	18.8

TABLE 8   GUILTY PLEAS—ALLEGHENY COUNTY—MAJOR CRIMES

	No. of Indictments	No. of Pleas	Percentage of Guilty Pleas to Indictments
Pre-Miranda			
7/1/65–6/30/66	1,224	274	22.4
Post-Miranda			
7/1/66–6/30/67	1,217	340	27.9

TABLE 9   GUILTY PLEAS—ALLEGHENY COUNTY—ALL CRIMES

	No. of Indictments	No. of Pleas	Percentage of Guilty Pleas to Indictments
1964	7,948	1,730	21.8
1965	8,145	1,850	22.7
1966 (through June 30)	5,081	1,093	21.5
1966 (July 1–Dec. 30)	3,295	807	24.5
1967 (through June 30)	3,916	996	25.4
Pre-Miranda Totals			
(1/1/64–6/30/67)	21,174	4,673	22.1
Post-Miranda Totals			
(7/1/66–6/30/67)	7,211	1,803	25.0

III. OBSERVATIONS

The figures which we have collected appear to support the following observations:

(1) Confession rate—

Following *Miranda*, there has been a significant decline (almost 20%) in the percentage of cases in which confessions are obtained (Tables 1 and 2). The decline has occurred for each type of crime which we examined other than forceable sex, the only crime for which confessions played no significant role prior to *Miranda*. But contrary to certain criticisms of the *Miranda* decision, confessions are still being obtained in a substantial number of instances—in more than one-third of the cases and from more than one-quarter of the suspects.

The decline in the confession rate would appear to be attributable largely to the new requirements imposed by the *Miranda* decision. The Detective Branch continues to attempt to obtain a confession from every suspect. The only new factor is the restrictions imposed by *Miranda*.

It would not be reasonable to attribute the decline in the confession rate solely to an abnormal sample of cases. Excluding the forceable sex cases, the confession rate for post-*Miranda* cases fell at least 14% for every type of crime. In contrast, in comparing the confession rate for various types of crimes (other than forceable sex) between 1964, 1965 and the first half of 1966, figures obtained from our study showed that the largest variation was an 11% decrease in the confession rate for burglary between 1965 and the first half of 1966.

(2) Conviction rate—

In at least 20% of the cases which we examined, a confession was probably necessary to obtain a conviction (Table 4). The *Miranda* decision has not resulted in a more significant decline in the confession rate in these cases in which a confession is necessary (Table 5). Therefore assuming that the use of a confession would have resulted in a conviction, that the same percentage of cases are being processed to trial and that the confession rate has declined by 20% on account of *Miranda*, the conviction rate should have declined approximately 4% as a result of *Miranda*.

Almost the same result is reached when the difference in the percentage of convictions between suspects who confess and suspects who did not confess is considered. There is approximately a 25% higher conviction rate for suspects who confess. Consequently a 20% decline in the number of suspects from whom confessions are obtained should result in a 5% decline in the conviction rate.

The conviction rate figures do not bear out the above conclusions; the conviction rate has not declined since the *Miranda* decision.

An explanation which would reconcile the above conclusions with the fact that the conviction rate has not declined is that a larger percentage of cases—those cases weakened by *Miranda*—are being thrown out at the arraignment and grand jury levels.

Figures showing the disposition of cases at the arraignment level are not available, so we do not have sufficient statistics to verify or refute this explanation. Figures for Allegheny County showing the disposition of cases at the grand jury level, however, offer some support to this explanation. In the first half of 1966 the Grand Jury refused to indict in 13.6% of the presentments (504/3209); in the second half of 1966 the Grand Jury refused to indict in 15.9% of the presentments (336/1778); and in the first three quarters of 1967 the Grand Jury refused to indict in 16.3% of the presentments (326/4243).

Another explanation is that only about 30% of the cases . . . were cases of the Detective Branch. The remainder were cases of the Pittsburgh uniformed police and of the law enforcement agencies of other jurisdictions in Allegheny County. These two groups may not have been as vigorous with *Miranda*, in which case the conviction figures . . .

would not reflect the full impact of *Miranda* on the ability of police to obtain confessions.

(3) Clearance rate

While the figures covering Pittsburgh's clearance rate between January 1, 1965 and July 31, 1967 (Table 9) do not require the conclusion that Miranda has had an impact on the ability of the Pittsburgh police to solve crime, there has been a decline in the clearance rate from the first half of 1966. One of several possible explanations for this is the imposition of the *Miranda* requirements on the Pittsburgh police.

Table 3's arrest and release figures for the suspects taken into custody by the Detective Branch who refused to make any statement to the police, however, would tend to negate the validity of this explanation. In 73 out of 74 instances the suspect who refused to talk was nevertheless held for arraignment . . . .

V. CONCLUSION

Information from other jurisdictions is so limited that it is difficult to make any generalizations concerning the effect of *Miranda* on law enforcement throughout the country. This is so because significant differences in police and prosecution procedures between the various jurisdictions frequently introduce additional factors which weaken any generalizations based on the experiences of one jurisdiction. Nevertheless, until further statistics and further knowledge of the police and prosecution procedures of other jurisdictions are available, the Pittsburgh figures collected through this study support the generalization that *Miranda* has not impaired significantly the ability of the law enforcement agencies to apprehend and convict the criminal. □

NOTES AND QUESTIONS

1. This is one of several studies conducted soon after *Miranda* to determine its impact on criminal justice. Two other studies have been particularly important. Michael Wald, R. Ayers, D. W. Hess, M. Schantz, and C. W. Whitebread II, "Interrogations in New Haven: The Impact of Miranda," 76 *Yale Law Journal* 1519 (1967); Richard Medalie, Leonard Zeitz, and Paul Alexander, "Custodial Interrogation in Our Nation's Capital: The Attempt to Implement Miranda," 66 *Michigan Law Review* 1347 (1968).

2. The Pittsburgh study got prominent mention in a United States Justice Department report, issued in 1986, which called for getting rid of *Miranda*. (Report to the Attorney General: The Law of Pre-Trial Interrogation. U.S. Department of Justice, Office of Legal Policy, February 12, 1986). This report

was issued during the administration of President Ronald Reagan, and reflected a conservative, "law and order" point of view.

The Report claims that the Pittsburgh study "observed a substantial reduction in the number of confessions. Police detectives in Pittsburgh had for many years advised suspects of a right to remain silent, and shortly after the *Escobedo* decision they also began to advise suspects of a right to counsel. Notwithstanding this partial compliance with [*Miranda*] . . . the proportion of suspects confessing in the crime categories studied fell from 48.5 percent . . . to 32.3 percent" after *Miranda*. "Particularly great decreases occurred in the categories of homicide and robbery, in each of which the number of confessions was roughly cut in half."

The Report also mentioned a few blatant cases in which "killers, rapists, and other serious offenders were freed." For example, one case of this sort involved a Brooklyn resident, Jose Suarez, who had slaughtered his wife and five small children with a knife, but had to be let go because his confession was inadmissible."

Is this fair use of the Pittsburgh study? Does that study suggest that *Miranda* damaged law enforcement?

In later years, there were further reports on the results of *Miranda*. Some of these suggested that while confession rates declined at first, the conviction rate bounced back to "normal" levels within a year or two. For a review of studies of the impact of *Miranda*, see Stephen J. Schulhofer, "Reconsidering *Miranda*," 54 *University of Chicago Law Review* 435 (1987).

3. The point of *Miranda*, of course, was not to hamstring law enforcement, but to improve it; and to make sure the police and other law enforcement officers treat people accused of crime fairly and decently. Did the case accomplish this purpose?

Consider the following excerpt from an account by a journalist of a year observing Baltimore homicide detectives.

40. Homicide: A Year on the Killing Streets

David Simon

(Boston: Houghton Mifflin, 1991)

☐ You are a citizen of a free nation, having lived your adult life in a land of guaranteed civil liberties, and you commit a crime of violence, whereupon you are jacked up, hauled down to a police station and deposited in a claustrophobic anteroom with three chairs, a table and no windows. There you sit for a half hour or so until a police detective—a man you have never met before, a man who can in no way be mistaken for a friend—enters the room with a thin stack of lined notepaper and a ball-point pen.

The detective offers a cigarette, not your brand, and begins an uninterrupted monologue that wanders back and forth for a half hour more, eventually coming to rest in a familiar place: *"You have the absolute right to remain silent."*

Of course you do. You're a criminal. Criminals always have the right to remain silent. At least once in your miserable life, you spent an hour in front of a television set, listening to this book-'em-Danno routine. You think Joe Friday was lying to you? You think Kojak was making this horseshit up? No way, bunk, we're talking sacred freedoms here, notably your Fifth Fucking Amendment protection against self-incrimination, and hey, it was good enough for Ollie North, so who are you to go incriminating yourself at the first opportunity? Get it straight: A police detective, a man who gets paid government money to put you in prison, is explaining your absolute right to shut up before you say something stupid.

"Anything you say or write may be used against you in a court of law."

Yo, bunky, wake the fuck up. You're now being told that talking to a police detective in an interrogation room can only hurt you. If it could help you, they would probably be pretty quick to say that, wouldn't they? They'd stand up and say you have the right not to worry because what you say or write in this godforsaken cubicle is gonna be used to your benefit in a court of law. No, your best bet is to shut up. Shut up now.

"You have the right to talk with a lawyer at any time—-before any questioning, before answering any questions, or during any questions."

Talk about helpful. Now the man who wants to arrest you for violating the peace and dignity of the state is saying you can talk to a trained professional, an attorney who has read the relevant portions of the Maryland Annotated Code or can at least get his hands on some Cliffs Notes. And let's face it, pal, you just carved up a drunk in a Dundalk Avenue bar, but that don't make you a neurosurgeon. Take whatever help you can get.

"If you want a lawyer and cannot afford to hire one, you will not be asked any questions, and the court will be requested to appoint a lawyer for you."

Translation: You're a derelict. No charge for derelicts.

At this point, if all lobes are working, you ought to have seen enough of this Double Jeopardy category to know that it ain't where you want to be. How about a little something from Criminal Lawyers and Their Clients for $50, Alex?

Whoa, bunk, not so fast.

"Before we get started, lemme just get through the paperwork," says the detective, who now produces an Explanation of Rights sheet, BPD Form 69, and passes it across the table.

"EXPLANATION OF RIGHTS," declares the top line in bold block letters. The detective asks you to fill in your name, address, age, and education, then the date and time. That much accomplished, he asks you to read the next section. It begins, "YOU ARE HEREBY ADVISED THAT:

"Read number one," the detective says. "Do you understand number one?"

"You have the absolute right to remain silent."

Yeah, you understand. We did this already.

"Then write your initials next to number one. Now read number two."

And so forth, until you have initialed each component of the *Miranda* warning. That done, the detective tells you to write your signature on the next line, the one just below the sentence that says, "I HAVE READ THE ABOVE EXPLANATION OF MY RIGHTS AND FULLY UNDERSTAND IT."

You sign your name and the monologue resumes. The detective assures you that he has informed you of these rights because he wants you to be protected, because there is nothing that concerns him more than giving you every possible assistance in this very confusing and stressful moment in your life. If you don't want to talk, he tells you, that's fine. And if you want a lawyer, that's fine; too, because first of all, he's no relation to the guy you cut up, and second, he's gonna get six hours overtime no matter what you do. But he wants you to know—and he's been doing this a lot longer than you, so take his word for it—that your rights to remain silent and obtain qualified counsel aren't all they're cracked up to be.

Look at it this way, he says, leaning back in his chair. Once you up and call for that lawyer, son, we can't do a damn thing for you. No sir, your friends in the city homicide unit are going to have to leave you locked in this room all alone and the next authority figure to scan your case will be a tie-wearing, three-piece bloodsucker—a no-nonsense prosecutor from the Violent Crimes Unit with the official title of assistant state's attorney for the city of Baltimore. And God help you then, son, because a ruthless fucker like that will have an O'Donnell Heights motorhead like yourself halfway to the gas chamber before you get three words out. Now's the time to speak up, right now when I got my pen and paper here on the table, because once I walk out of this room any chance you have of telling your side of the story is gone and I gotta write it up the way it looks. And the way it looks right now is first-fucking-degree murder. Felony murder, mister, which when shoved up a man's asshole is a helluva lot more painful than second-degree or maybe even manslaughter. What you say right here and now could make the difference, bunk. Did I mention that Maryland has a gas chamber? Big, ugly sumbitch at the penitentiary on Eager Street, not twenty blocks from here. You don't wanna get too close to that bad boy, lemme tell you.

A small, wavering sound of protest passes your lips and the detective leans back in his chair, shaking his head sadly.

What the hell is wrong with you, son? You think I'm fucking with you? Hey, I don't even need to bother with your weak shit. I got three witnesses in three other rooms who say you're my man. I got a knife from the scene that's going downstairs to the lab for latent prints. I got blood spatter on them Air Jordans we took off you ten minutes ago. Why the fuck do you think we took 'em? Do I look like I wear high-top tennis? Fuck no. You got spatter all over 'em, and I think we both know whose blood type it's gonna be. Hey, bunk, I'm only in here to make sure that there ain't nothing you can say for yourself before I write it all up.

You hesitate.

Oh, says the detective. You want to think about it. Hey, you think about it all you want, pal. My captain's right outside in the hallway, and he already told me to charge your ass in the first fuckin' degree. For once in your beshitted little life someone is giving you a chance and you're too fucking dumb to take it. What the fuck, you go ahead and think about it and I'll tell my captain to cool his heels for ten minutes. I can do that much for you. How 'bout some coffee? Another cigarette?

The detective leaves you alone in that cramped, windowless room. Just you and the blank notepaper and the Form 69 and . . . first-degree murder. First-degree murder with witnesses and fingerprints and blood on your Air Jordans. Christ, you didn't even notice the blood on your own fucking shoes. Felony murder, mister. First-fucking-degree. How many years, you begin to wonder, how many years do I get for involuntary manslaughter?

Whereupon the man who wants to put you in prison, the man who is not your friend, comes back in the room, asking if the coffee's okay.

Yeah, you say, the coffee's fine, but what happens if I want a lawyer?

The detective shrugs. Then we get you a lawyer, he says. And I walk out of the room and type up the charging documents for first-degree murder and you can't say a fucking thing about it. Look, bunk, I'm giving you a chance. He came at you, right? You were scared. It was self-defense.

Your mouth opens to speak.

He came at you, didn't he?

"Yeah," you venture cautiously, "he came at me."

Whoa, says the detective, holding up his hands. Wait a minute. If we're gonna do this, I gotta find your rights form. Where's the fucking form? Damn things are like cops, never around when you need 'em. Here it is, he says, pushing the explanation-of-rights sheet across the table and pointing to the bottom. Read that, he says.

"I am willing to answer questions and I do not want any attorney at this time. My decision to answer questions without having an attorney present is free and voluntary on my part."

As you read, he leaves the room and returns a moment later with a second detective as a witness. You sign the bottom of the form, as do both detectives.

The first detective looks up from the form, his eyes soaked with innocence. "He came at you, huh?"

"Yeah, he came at me."

Get used to small rooms, bunk, because you are about to be drop-kicked into the lost land of pretrial detention. Because it's one thing to be a murdering little asshole from Southeast Baltimore, and it's another to be stupid about it, and with five little words you have just elevated yourself to the ranks of the truly witless.

End of the road, pal. It's over. It's history. And if that police detective wasn't so busy committing your weak bullshit to paper, he'd probably look you in the eye and tell you so. He'd give you another cigarette and say, son, you are ignorance personified and you just put yourself in for the fatal stabbing of a human being. He might even tell you that the other witnesses in the other rooms are too drunk to identify their own reflections, much less the kid who had the knife, or that it's always a long shot for the lab to pull a latent off a knife hilt, or that your $95 sneakers are as clean as the day you bought them. If he was feeling particularly expansive, he might tell you that everyone who leaves the homicide unit in handcuffs does so charged with first-degree murder, that it's for the lawyers to decide what kind of deal will be cut. He might go on to say that even after all these years working homicides, there is still a small part of him that finds it completely mystifying that anyone ever utters a single word in a police interrogation. To illustrate the point, he could hold up your Form 69, on which you waived away every last one of your rights, and say, "Lookit here, pistonhead, I told you twice that you were deep in the shit and that whatever you said could put you in deeper." And if his message was still somehow beyond your understanding, he could drag your carcass back down the sixth-floor hallway, back toward the sign that says Homicide Unit in white block letters, the sign you saw when you walked off the elevator.

Now think hard: Who lives in a homicide unit? Yeah, right. And what do homicide detectives do for a living? Yeah, you got it, bunk. And what did you do tonight? You murdered someone.

So when you opened that mouth of yours, what the fuck were you thinking?

Homicide detectives in Baltimore like to imagine a small, open window at the top of the long wall in the large interrogation room. More to the point, they like to imagine their suspects imagining a small, open window at the top of the long wall. The open window is the escape hatch, the Out. It is the perfect representation of what every suspect believes when he opens his mouth during an interrogation. Every last one envisions himself parrying questions with the right combination of alibi and excuse; every last one sees himself coming up with the right words, then crawling out the window to go home and sleep in his own bed. More often than not, a guilty man is looking for the Out from his first moments in the interrogation room; in that sense, the window is as much the suspect's fantasy as the detective's mirage.

The effect of the illusion is profound, distorting as it does the natural hostility between hunter and hunted, transforming it until it resembles a relationship more symbiotic than adversarial. That is the lie, and when the roles are perfectly performed, deceit surpasses itself, becoming manipulation on a grand scale and ultimately an act of betrayal. Because what occurs in an interrogation room is indeed little more than a carefully staged drama, a choreographed performance that allows a detective and his suspect to find common ground where none exists. There, in a carefully controlled purgatory, the guilty proclaim their malefactions, though rarely in any form that allows for contrition or resembles an unequivocal admission.

In truth, catharsis in the interrogation room occurs for only a few rare suspects, usually those in domestic murders or child abuse cases wherein the leaden mass of genuine remorse can crush anyone who is not hardened to his crime. But the greater share of men and women brought downtown take no interest in absolution. Ralph Waldo Emerson rightly noted that for those responsible, the act of murder "is no such ruinous thought as poets and romancers will have it; it does not unsettle him, or frighten him from his ordinary notice of trifles." And while West Baltimore is a universe or two from Emerson's nineteenth-century Massachusetts hamlet, the observation is still useful. Murder often doesn't unsettle a man. In Baltimore, it usually doesn't even ruin his day.

As a result, the majority of those who acknowledge their complicity in a killing must be baited by detectives with something more tempting than penitence. They must be made to believe that their crime is not really murder, that their excuse is both accepted and unique, that they will, with the help of the detective, be judged less evil than they truly are.

Some are brought to that unreasoned conclusion by the suggestion that they acted in self-defense or were provoked to violence. Others fall prey to the notion that they are less culpable than their colleagues—I only drove the car or backed up the robbery, I wasn't the triggerman; or yeah, I raped her, but I stayed out of it when them other guys started strangling her—unaware that Maryland law allows every member of the conspiracy to be charged as a principal. Still others succumb to the belief that they will get a better shake by cooperating with detectives and acknowledging a limited amount of guilt. And many of those who cannot be lured over the precipice of self-incrimination can still be manipulated into providing alibis, denials and explanations—statements that can be checked and rechecked until a suspect's lies are the greatest evidentiary threat to his freedom.

For that reason, the professionals say nothing. No alibis. No explanations. No expressions of polite dismay or blanket denials. In the late 1970s, when men by the names of Dennis Wise and Vernon Collins were matching each other body for body as Baltimore's premier contract killers and no witness could be found to testify against either, things got to the point where both the detectives and their suspects knew the drill:

> Enter room.
> Miranda.
> Anything to say this time, Dennis?
> No, sir. Just want to call my lawyer.
> Fine, Dennis.
> Exit room.

For anyone with experience in the criminal justice machine, the point is driven home by every lawyer worth his fee. Repetition and familiarity with the process soon place the professionals beyond the reach of a police interrogation. Yet more than two decades after the landmark Escobedo and Miranda decisions, the rest of the world remains strangely willing to place itself at risk. As a result, the same law enforcement community that once regarded the 1966 Miranda decision as a death blow to criminal investigation has now come to see the explanation of rights as a routine part of the process—simply a piece of station house furniture, if not a civilizing influence on police work itself.

In an era when beatings and physical intimidation were common tools of an interrogation, the Escobedo and Miranda decisions were sent down by the nation's highest court to ensure that criminal confessions and statements were purely voluntary. The resulting Miranda warning was "a protective device to dispel the compelling atmosphere of the interrogation," as Chief Justice Earl Warren wrote in the majority opinion. Investigators would be required to assure citizens of their rights to silence and counsel, not only at the moment of arrest, but at the moment that they could reasonably be considered suspects under interrogation.

In answer to Miranda, the nation's police officials responded with a veritable jeremiad, wailing in unison that the required warnings would virtually assure that confessions would be impossible to obtain and conviction rates would plummet. Yet the prediction was soon proved false for the simple reason that those law enforcement leaders—and, for that matter, the Supreme Court itself—underestimated a police detective's ingenuity.

Miranda is, on paper, a noble gesture which declares that constitutional rights extend not only to the public forum of the courts, but to the private confines of the police station as well. Miranda and its accompanying decisions established a uniform concept of a criminal defendant's rights and effectively ended the use of violence and the most blatant kind of physical intimidation in interrogations. That, of course, was a blessing. But if the further intent of the Miranda decision was, in fact, an attempt to "dispel the compelling atmosphere" of an interrogation, then it failed miserably.

And thank God. Because by any standards of human discourse, a criminal confession can never truly be called voluntary. With rare exception, a confession is compelled, provoked and manipulated from a suspect by a detective who has been trained in a genuinely deceitful art. That is the essence of interrogation, and those who believe that a straightforward conversation between a cop and a criminal—devoid of any treachery—is going to solve a crime are somewhere beyond naive. If the interrogation process is, from a moral standpoint, contemptible, it is nonetheless essential. Deprived of the ability to question and confront suspects and witnesses, a detective is left with physical evidence and in many cases, precious little of that. Without a chance for a detective to manipulate a suspect's mind, a lot of bad people would simply go free.

Yet every defense attorney knows that there can be no good reason for a guilty man to say anything whatsoever to a police officer, and any suspect who calls an attorney will be told as much, bringing the interrogation to an end. A court opinion that therefore requires a detective—the same detective working hard to dupe a suspect—to stop abruptly and guarantee the man his right to end the process can only be called an act of institutional schizophrenia. The Miranda warning is a little like a referee introducing a barroom brawl. The stern warnings to hit above the waist and take no cheap shots have nothing to do with the mayhem that follows.

Yet how could it be otherwise? It would be easy enough for our judiciary to ensure that no criminal suspect relinquished his rights inside a police station: The courts could simply require the presence of a lawyer at all times. But such a blanket guarantee of individual rights would effectively end the use of interrogation as an investigative weapon, leaving many more crimes unsolved and many more guilty men and women unpunished. Instead, the ideals have been carefully compromised at little cost other than to the integrity of the police investigator.

After all, it's the lawyers, the Great Compromisers of our age, who have struck this bargain, who still manage to keep cuffs clean in the public courts, where rights and process are worshiped faithfully. It is left for the detective to fire this warning shot across a suspect's bow, granting rights to a man who will then be tricked into relinquishing them. In that sense, Miranda is a symbol and little more, a salve for a collective conscience that cannot reconcile libertarian ideals with what must necessarily occur in a police interrogation room. Our judges, our courts, our society as a whole, demand in the same breath that rights be maintained even as crimes are punished. And all of us are bent and determined to preserve the illusion that both can be achieved in the same, small room. It's mournful to think that this hypocrisy is the necessary creation of our best legal minds, who seem to view the interrogation process as the rest of us look upon breakfast sausage: We want it on a plate with eggs and toast; we don't want to know too much about how it comes to be.

Trapped in that contradiction, a detective does his job in the only possible way. He follows the requirements of the law to the letter—or close enough so as not to jeopardize his case. Just as carefully, he ignores that law's spirit and intent. He becomes a salesman, a huckster as thieving and silver-tongued as any man who ever moved used cars or aluminum siding—more so, in fact, when you consider that he's selling long prison terms to customers who have no genuine need for the product.

The fraud that claims it is somehow in a suspect's interest to talk with police will forever be the catalyst in any criminal interrogation. It is a fiction propped up against the greater weight of logic itself, sustained for hours on end through nothing more or less than a detective's ability to control the interrogation room. □

NOTES AND QUESTIONS

1. Richard A. Leo, in "Police Interrogation and Social Control," 3 *Social & Legal Studies* 93 (1994), studied police interrogations at a large urban American police department. He found that "[i]nterrogators self-consciously and strategically employ influence techniques to control the attitudes and actions of suspects during custodial questioning" (p. 100). They attempt to create a relationship where the suspect feels compelled to cooperate. They attempt to play the role of a suspect's friend, confidant or counselor. They attempt to deceive the suspect, particularly about how much evidence of guilt the police have. They help the suspect neutralize the crime and its seriousness. They "appeal to a suspect's belief in certain moral norms, his capacity for shame and redemption, or his desire to be normal" (p.113).

Leo argues that cases such as the *Miranda* decision, have:

> instructed police that they can no longer use physically coercive or psychologically overbearing techniques to elicit confessions. However, the law has also signalled to police that they can lie, they can cajole and they can manipulate in the process of obtaining confessions . . . . The law has, in effect, given police license to act as confidence men and develop their skills in human manipulation.

He concludes that interrogation, unlike practices sixty years ago, "no longer assaults and brutalizes criminal suspects, but instead explicitly respects their dignity." Moreover, "police interrogators have become progressively more oriented to the rule of law" (p. 117). How can the practices described by Simon and Leo be characterized as a respect for dignity and oriented to the rule of law? If you object to the manipulation of suspects, how would you have the police enforce the law?

2. Setsuo Miyazawa, in *Policing in Japan: A Study on Making Crime* (Albany: State University of New York Press, 1992), studied Japanese police practices. Japanese police, because of their numbers and the crime rate, have more time to devote to each case than police in most other countries. Most cases result in confessions. "In 1987, trial courts in Japan passed judgment on 76,483 defendants . . . . Among them, 69,851 completely admitted their guilt" (p. 236).

Some have explained the high rate of confessions in terms of Japanese culture. Miyazawa, however, explains this in terms of the legal rules surrounding police investigations and arrests. Japanese police generally receive more or less voluntary cooperation from suspects. They interrogate suspects before arrest at police stations. He notes that "police tactics have to be very 'compelling' indeed in order to be judged illegally 'coercive'" (p. 17). "Once arrested, a suspect can be confined by police for forty-eight hours before appearing before a prosecutor, and then the prosecutor may confine the suspect for another twenty-four hours before applying to the judge for detention" (p. 19). When suspects are arrested, they are told of their right to counsel. However, lawyers are few and expensive. The government provides counsel to defendants when they are indicted, but they generally meet their lawyer just before their first court appearance.

Japanese detectives talk about gaining confessions after establishing a human relationship with the suspect. They talk about parents and families. However, supervisors advocate letting a suspect talk freely and then challenging the suspect with contradictions and inconsistencies. Although the Japanese do not have plea bargaining in the American sense, Miyazawa reports:

[S]ometimes a lighter sentence is held out as an instrument of persuasion. In an embezzlement case, the detective describes how he persuaded the suspect. He urged, "Why don't you admit it, and later ask for leniency? Isn't that better? What do you think?" (p. 160)

From one point of view, the Japanese system works because the crime rate is acceptably low and most cases are solved. However, Miyazawa points out: "Forced confessions to false charges repeatedly appear both in the courts and in the news" (p. 3).

In view of Simon's account of Baltimore police practices and Leo's account of the American urban police department that he studied, how different in substance are the American and Japanese systems? Many Japanese reformers want to alter their system to be more like that of the United States. For example, they want to limit police detention and provide legal advice earlier in the process. What do Simon's and Leo's accounts suggest about the likely impact of such proposals?

3. The thrust of a number of studies of the *Miranda* case and the like is pessimistic. They show that the system absorbs and neutralizes the attempted reform (see also the excerpt from Diamond, above, p. 551). But this is by no means what happens to all attempts to reform criminal justice or expand the rights of defendants.

Consider, for example, Myron W. Orfield, Jr., "The Exclusionary Rule and Deterrence: an Empirical Study of Chicago Narcotics Officers," 54 *University of Chicago Law Review* 1016 (1987). The exclusionary rule, enunciated in *Mapp v. Ohio*, 367 U.S. 643 (1961), does not allow the courts to use evidence that was gathered improperly—for example, in a search without a warrant. Orfield conducted intensive interviews with narcotics officers in Chicago. He found, to begin with, that officers were not opposed to the rule. One officer stated flatly, "I believe in the principle of the exclusionary rule." Another said, "Of course there has to be an exclusionary rule. I don't want this to be a police state" (pp. 1052–53). Orfield's conclusion was that, in the Narcotics Section of the Chicago Police Department, the rule "has created a system of incentives for individual officers, reinforced by institutional practices also prompted by the rule, that deters unlawful police searches" (p. 1054). Problems such as abuse and perjury remain—and the officers would like to see certain modifications. Nonetheless, by and large, the rule has had a pervasive and beneficial effect.

SOCIAL IMPACT—DOES THE INSTITUTION THAT MAKES THE LAW INFLUENCE THE IMPACT?

In *The Hollow Hope*, Professor Gerald Rosenberg explores the impact of the decisions of the United States Supreme Court in various fields. One of these is racial segregation. In *Brown v. Board of Education*, decided in 1954, the Supreme Court outlawed such segregation in elementary and secondary schools. At the time, there was mandatory segregation in 17 southern and border states, plus the District of Columbia; and in four more states, local segregation was allowed. The *Brown* decision was unanimous.

41. *The Hollow Hope*

Gerald Rosenberg

(Chicago: The University of Chicago Press, 1991)

☐ . . . The National Association for the Advancement of Colored People (NAACP) was euphoric over the unanimous decision. Thurgood Marshall, the chief litigator for the black plaintiffs, told reporters that the Supreme Court's interpretation of the law was "very clear." If the decision were violated anywhere "on one morning" Marshall said, "we'll have the responsible authorities in court by the next morning, if not the same afternoon." When asked how long he thought it would take for segregation to be eliminated from public schools, Marshall replied that "it might be 'up to five years' for the entire country." Finally, "he predicted that by the time the 100th anniversary of the Emancipation Proclamation was observed in 1963, segregation in all its forms would have been eliminated from the nation."

The decision, however, did not include any announcement as to the appropriate relief for the plaintiffs. This was postponed for reargument due to the "considerable complexity" of the matter. Reargument lasted for four days in April 1955, and the parties to the case, including the United States, were joined by the attorneys general of Arkansas, Florida, Maryland, North Carolina, Oklahoma, and Texas, as *amici curiae* pursuant to the Court's invitation in *Brown*.

The remedy was announced on May 31, 1955, slightly more than a year after the initial decision and two and one-half years after the initial argument. The Court in *Brown II* (1955) held that, because local school problems varied, federal courts were in the best position to assure compliance with *Brown I*, an end to legally enforced public-school segregation. The cases were reversed and remanded to the lower courts which were ordered to "take such proceedings and enter such orders and decrees consistent with this opinion as are necessary and proper to admit to public schools on a racially nondiscriminatory basis with all deliberate speed the parties to these cases." The phrase "with all deliberate speed" was picked up by commentators, lawyers, and judges as the applicable standard. Thus the end result of the Brown litigation was a unanimous Supreme Court clearly and unequivocally holding that state-enforced segregation of public schools was unconstitutional and ordering that it be ended "with all deliberate speed."

During the years from 1955 through the passage of the 1964 Civil Rights the Court issued only three full opinions in the area of segregation of elementary and secondary schools. It routinely refused to hear cases or curtly affirmed or reversed lower-court decisions . . . However, in *Cooper v. Aaron* (1958) the first case after *Brown*, the Court spoke strongly.

Cooper v. Aaron involved the attempt of Governor Faubus and the Arkansas legislature to block the desegregation of Central High School in Little Rock, Arkansas. The Court convened in a special session for only the fifth time in thirty-eight years to hear the case. After reviewing the history of attempts to desegregate the public schools in Little Rock, the Court faced the question of whether violence or threat of violence in response to desegregation and resulting in turmoil in the school disruptive of the educational process justified the suspension of desegregation efforts for two and one-half years. In answering in the negative, rejecting the school board's claim and reversing the federal district court, the Supreme Court held that the "constitutional rights of respondents [black students] are not to be sacrificed or yielded to the violence and disorder" which was occurring. This was, as the opinion stated, "enough to dispose of the case," but the Court continued for several pages to underline its determination that *Brown* be followed. It reminded the parties that Article VI of the Constitution makes the Constitution the "supreme law of the land." Further, the Court unearthed *Marbury v. Madison* (1803) and Chief Justice Marshall's words that "[i]t is emphatically the province and duty of the judicial department to say what the law is." The opinion also pointed out that the decision in "*Brown* was unanimously reached by this Court only after the case had been briefed and twice argued and the issues had been given the most serious consideration." Not stopping here, the justices stressed that twelve justices had considered and approved the Brown doctrine (the nine who originally agreed to it and the three who had joined the Court since then). Finally, in an unprecedented move, all nine justices individually signed the opinion. *Cooper v. Aaron* was a massive and unswerving affirmation that desegregation was the law and must be implemented.

The next full opinion in the elementary and secondary education field came in *Goss v. Board of Education of Knoxville* (1963). At issue was a desegregation plan that included a provision allowing students to transfer from a school where their race was a minority to one where it predominated. This provision was challenged on the ground that since race was the sole criterion of the plan it would perpetuate rather than alleviate racial segregation, denying plaintiffs the right to attend desegregated schools. The Court agreed, unanimously holding the one-way transfer plan to be violative of the Fourteenth Amendment and contrary to *Brown.*

The third decision, *Griffin v. Prince Edward County* was handed down in 1964. The case involved the constitutionality of the closing of Prince Edward County public schools to avoid desegregation and the use of state tuition grants and tax credits to support private segregated education for white children. The Court unanimously found both acts unconstitutional, being essentially devices to avoid the constitutional mandate of desegregation, and denying plaintiffs the equal protection of the law.

Brown I and *II* stated the law and stated clearly that steps had to be taken to end state-enforced segregation. *Cooper v. Aaron* emphatically reiterated it. And *Goss* and *Griffin* unanimously held that patent attempts to avoid desegregation were unconstitutional. The Court had spoken clearly and forcefully.

In the first four years after the passage of the 1964 Civil Rights Act, the Supreme Court remained quiet in the education area. However, the lower federal courts, particularly in the Fourth and Fifth Circuits, became increasingly involved in litigation . . . .

The Supreme Court re-entered the field in 1968 and issued, for the first time since Brown, a detailed opinion on remedies. *Green v. County School Board of New Kent County, Va.* (1968), involved a freedom-of-choice plan under which no white child had transferred to the "formerly black school" and only about 15 percent of the black children had transferred to the "formerly white school." In a unanimous opinion, written by Justice Brennan, the Court threw out the freedom-of-choice plan and suggested that such plans would be unlikely to meet constitutional standards. Showing a good deal of impatience, the opinion stated that "the burden on a school board today is to come forward with a plan that promises realistically to work, and promises realistically to work now." In the fall of 1969, in *Alexander v. Holmes County*, the Court continued with its impatience, reinstating a July 1969 Fifth Circuit order requiring thirty Mississippi school districts to desegregate by the start of school in September in accordance with *Green*. In a terse, two-page *per curiam* ruling in October, the Court rejected a delay until December, holding that "continued operation of segregated schools under a standard of allowing 'all deliberate speed' for desegregation is no longer constitutionally permissible." Further, the Court held that school districts were required to "terminate dual school systems at once and to operate now and hereafter only unitary schools."

Finally, in *Swann v. Charlotte-Mecklenburg Board of Education* (1971), the Court upheld the power of district judges to include busing as part of a remedial decree. Writing for a unanimous Court, Chief Justice Burger held that "once a right and a violation have been shown, the scope of a district court's equitable powers to remedy past wrongs is broad." This included, Burger noted, busing, because "desegregation plans cannot be limited to the walk-in school."

From 1954 through 1971, the Court remained steadfast in its commitment to end public-school segregation. Repeatedly, it reminded parties before it, and the nation, that segregation violated the Constitution. And, as shall soon be shown, for many of those years it was the only branch of the federal government that acted.

CONGRESSIONAL AND EXECUTIVE BRANCH ACTION

Congressional and executive branch action in the area of public-school desegregation was virtually non-existent until the passage of the 1964 Civil Rights Act. In stark contrast to the actions of the Supreme Court in *Brown*, the other two branches of the federal government remained essentially passive.

In 1957 Congress passed the first civil rights act since 1875. In the education field the act was most notable for its lack of provisions. While an attempt was made to give the Department of Justice the authority to file suits on behalf of individuals alleging segregation in education, it was unsuccessful. The Eisenhower administration opposed the provision because, in the words of Attorney General William P. Rogers, it "might do more harm than good."

Congress passed a second civil rights act in 1960. Unlike the 1957 act, this one gave a fair amount of attention to segregation in education, but as with the earlier act, little of substance was enacted. In particular, the Department of Justice was not given the authority to file desegregation suits on behalf of individuals nor was the federal government given the power to cut off funds to school districts refusing to desegregate. The bill's educational provisions were aimed at violent interference with court-ordered school desegregation and at providing education for children of military personnel stationed in places where the public schools had been closed to avoid desegregation.

The 1964 act was a major departure from its predecessors. The most sweeping civil rights legislation since the Civil War and Reconstruction era, the act touched many fields. In education, Congress finally empowered the attorney general to bring desegregation suits on behalf of individuals. Also, Title VI of the act gave the federal government the power to cut off federal funds to school districts that discriminated on the basis of race. Its key language held:

> No person in the United States shall, on the ground of race, color, or national origin, be excluded from participation in, be denied the benefits of, or be subjected to discrimination under any program or activity receiving Federal financial assistance.

The 1964 act, as I will demonstrate shortly, had a major impact on school desegregation.

Until 1964, executive action was little better. Although the president and the administration can be a "particularly powerful agenda setter," the power and prestige of the presidency was not employed in support of civil rights until the mid-1960s. Little was done by President Eisenhower in the 1950s and only slowly did Presidents Kennedy and Johnson bring their administrations into the civil rights battle. . . .

In the spring of 1965 Congress enacted the Elementary and Secondary Education Act (ESEA), providing federal aid to school districts with large percentages of low-income children. The act was heavily directed at the South, and nearly $1 billion was expended in the first year of operation. A total of $1.3 billion was authorized for 1966 and in fiscal year 1968 alone, $1.5 billion of federal money was sent to the states.

Title VI required some kind of government response. The task of formulating procedures fell to HEW and, specifically, to the Office of Education. Action became imperative with the enactment of ESEA in the spring of 1965, because there was now a large pot of federal money available to Southern school districts. While the details of government actions are both fascinating and complicated, brief summary is possible.

HEW acted slowly to implement Title VI. At first, it asked school districts for assurances of non-discrimination. The first regulations, adopted on December 3, 1964, allowed federal aid to school districts that either submitted assurances that their schools were totally desegregated, that were under court orders to desegregate and agreed to abide by such orders, or that submitted voluntary desegregation plans. Further, state agencies were instructed not to renew programs or to authorize new ones until the commissioner of education certified that local districts were in compliance with Title VI. These regulations, however, were vague on what was an acceptable voluntary desegregation plan. In April 1965, guidelines were issued that required the opening of all grades to freedom of choice by the start of the 1967 school year. These guidelines were upheld by the Fifth Circuit in *Singleton*, discussed above. The guidelines were again revised and tightened in March 1966, setting standards for acceptable freedom-of-choice plans. The March 1966 guidelines established standards based on the percentage increase in students transferring from segregated schools. In most cases, the guidelines required a doubling or tripling of the percentage of blacks in "formerly white schools" for the 1966–67 school year. It was these guidelines that the Fifth Circuit upheld in the *Jefferson County* case discussed above. Regulations were further tightened in March 1968 when school districts were ordered to submit plans for complete desegregation by the fall of 1968, or, in some cases, the fall of 1969. The Supreme Court, in *Green*, essentially seconded these result-oriented standards that went past freedom of choice. Thus, by the end of the Johnson administration, HEW had come to officially require complete desegregation as a requirement for receiving federal funds under Title VI.

The Nixon administration appeared to back off from this strict requirement. In a July, 1969, statement, HEW Secretary Finch and Attorney General Mitchell announced modifications of the guidelines in several important ways. Chief among them was rejection of the 1969–70 terminal date for all districts as "arbitrary" and "too rigid to be either workable or equitable." In terms of freedom of choice, a plan that "genuinely promises to achieve a complete end to racial discrimination at the earliest possible date" would be acceptable. In addition, the statement pledged the administration to rely more heavily on "stepped-up enforcement activities of the Department of Justice" and to "minimize" the number of HEW fund cut-off proceedings. However, the statement did not purport to change the guidelines. "In general," the administration announced, the "terminal date" for acceptable plans "must be the 1969–70 school year." Also, the statement pointed to the courts, holding that "policy in this area will be as defined in the latest Supreme Court and Circuit Court decisions." Finally, the statement quoted approvingly the language from *Green*, quoted above that desegregation plans must work *now*.

Enforcement proceedings and fund terminations under Title VI were uncommon but not unheard-of. Although by the early 1970s the federal government had "investigated, negotiated with, and arm-twisted over 3,000 districts," only a small percentage of these districts ended up in enforcement proceedings or had their eligibility for federal funds terminated. Of the approximately 2,800 school districts in the eleven Southern states, 320 were involved in enforcement proceedings from September 15, 1965, through June 30, 1967. While few districts suffered from fund terminations, the period from the passage of Title VI to the end of the Johnson administration saw over 200 such terminations, slightly more than 7 percent of all Southern districts. While terminations were unlikely, the threat was real.

RESULTS AND COMPARISON

The decade from 1954 to 1964 provides close to an ideal setting for measuring the contribution of the courts vis-a-vis Congress and the executive branch in desegregating public schools. For ten years the

Court spoke forcefully while Congress and the executive did little. Then, in 1964, Congress and the executive branch entered the battle with the most significant piece of civil rights legislation in nearly ninety years. In 1965, the enactment of ESEA made a billion dollars in federal funds available to school districts that, in accord with Title VI, did not discriminate. This history allows one to isolate the contribution of the courts. If the courts were effective in desegregating public schools, the results should show up before 1964. However, if it was Congress and the executive branch, through the 1964 Civil Rights Act and 1965 ESEA, that made the real difference, then change would occur only in the years after 1964 or 1965 . . . .

. . . [F]airly good statistics on the progress of school desegregation are available. A summary is presented in table 1 and figure 1 . . . The table and graph present the number of black children attending public school with whites as well as their percentages out of all black school children in the seventeen states (and the District of Columbia) which required segregation in public schools at the time of Brown. While this way of presenting the numbers does not discriminate between token and substantial integration, and thus suggests more desegregation than actually occurred, it does allow for a time-series comparison.

TABLE 1   BLACK CHILDREN IN ELEMENTARY AND SECONDARY SCHOOL WITH WHITES, 1954–1972, SELECTED YEARS

Year	South %	South #	South without Texas and Tennessee %	South without Texas and Tennessee #	Border %	Border #	Border without D.C. %	Border without D.C. #
1954–55	.001	23	.001	20	NA	NA	NA	NA
1955–56	.12	2,782	.002	47	NA	NA	NA	NA
1956–57	.14	3,514	.002	34	39.6	106,878	18.1	35,378
1957–58	.15	3,829	.005	109	41.4	127,677	25.2	57,677
1958–59	.13	3,456	.006	124	44.4	142,352	31.1	73,345
1959–60	.16	4,216	.03	747	45.4	191,114	35.5	117,824
1960–61	.16	4,308	.02	432	49.0	212,895	38.7	131,503
1961–62	.24	6,725	.07	1,558	52.5	240,226	42.8	151,345
1962–63	.45	12,868	.17	4,058	51.8	251,797	43.7	164,048
1963–64	1.2	34,105	.48	11,619	54.8	281,731	46.2	182,918
1964–65	2.3	66,135	1.2	29,846	58.3	313,919	50.1	207,341
1965–66	6.1	184,308	3.8	95,507	68.9	384,992	64.1	275,722
1966–67	16.9	489,900			71.4	456,258		
1968–69	32.0	942,600			74.7	475,700		
1970–71	85.9	2,707,000			76.8	512,000		
1972–73	91.3	2,886,300			77.3	524,800		

NOTE: Numbers in the column marked "%" are the percentages of black students, out of all black schoolchildren, attending school with whites.

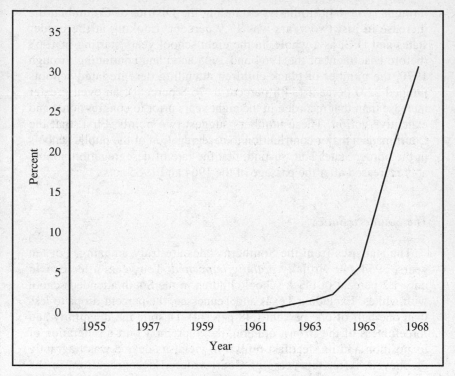

FIGURE 1   Percentage of All Southern Black Schoolchildren Attending
School with Whites

The Border States and the District of Columbia

The Supreme Court appears to have had an important impact on
school desegregation in the six border states and the District of Columbia. Unfortunately, reliable figures are not available until the 1956
school year. However, during the eight school years from the fall of
1956 until the passage of the 1964 act, the number of black children in
school with whites rose 15.2 percent (39.6 percent to 54.8 percent) in
the region as a whole and 28.1 percent (18.1 percent to 46.2 percent)
excluding the District of Columbia. However, the lack of data for the
two years immediately following Brown may understate the change.
That is, the change may have been even greater than these numbers
suggest, for substantial change may have taken place in the years
1954–56. Thus, the Supreme Court's actions appear to have had an
effect.

The passage of the 1964 Civil Rights Act increased the rate of
desegregation. During the two school years after enactment of the 1964
act, there was an increase of 14.1 percent (54.8 percent to 68.9 percent)
in the number of black children in desegregated schools in the region
as a whole, nearly equal to the eight-year increase from 1956–57

through 1963–64. Similarly, excluding the District of Columbia, the increase in just two years was 17.9 percent. Looking at the border states and D.C. as a whole, in the eight school years starting in 1963 (before enactment of the 1964 and 1965 acts) and continuing through 1970, the number of black children attending desegregated schools jumped 22.0 percent (54.8 percent to 76.8 percent), an even greater increase than that recorded in the eight years prior to congressional and executive action. These numbers suggest two points. First, that the Court made a major contribution to desegregation of the public schools in the border states and, second, that the rate of desegregation noticeably increased after the passage of the 1964 and 1965 acts . . . .

The Southern States

The statistics from the Southern states are truly amazing. For ten years, 1954–64, virtually *nothing happened.* Ten years after Brown only 1.2 percent of black school children in the South attended school with whites. Excluding Texas and Tennessee, the percent drops to less than one-half of one percent (.48 percent). Despite the unanimity and forcefulness of the *Brown* opinion, the Supreme Court's reiteration of its position and its steadfast refusal to yield, its decree was flagrantly disobeyed. After ten years of Court-ordered desegregation, in the eleven Southern states barely 1 out of every 100 black children attended school with whites. The Court ordered an end to segregation and segregation was not ended. As Judge Wisdom put it, writing in the *Jefferson County* case, *"the courts acting alone have failed."* The numbers show that the Supreme Court contributed virtually nothing to ending segregation of the public schools in the Southern states in the decade following *Brown.*

The entrance of Congress and the executive branch into the battle changed this. As figure 1 graphically demonstrates, desegregation took off after 1964, reaching 91.3 percent in 1972 (not shown). In the first year of the act, 1964–65, nearly as much desegregation was achieved as during all the preceding years of Supreme Court action. In just the few months between the end of the 1964–65 school year and the start of the 1965–66 year, nearly three times as many black students entered desegregated schools as had in the preceding decade of Court action. And the years following showed significant increases. While much segregation still existed, and still exists, the change after 1964 is as extraordinary as is the utter lack of impact of the Supreme Court prior to 1964. The actions of the Supreme Court appear irrelevant to desegregation from *Brown* to the enactment of the 1964 Civil Rights Act and 1965 ESEA. Only after the passage of these acts was there any desegregation of public schools in the South.

What accounts for the phenomenal increase in desegregation in the post-1964 years, particularly the 1968–72 period? Was it the action of

HEW? The courts? Local school officials? All three? Part of the answer may be found in the responses of nearly 1,000 school superintendents to a U.S. Commission on Civil Rights survey of school districts containing at least some minorities. When superintendents reported that "substantial steps to desegregate" had been taken, the survey asked, among other questions, "which was the single most important source of pressure for initiation of desegregation?" Table 2 presents the results. While the survey's coding rules underestimate the effect of HEW, it can be seen that, overall, state-local pressures were mentioned most often, followed by courts and HEW. It can also be seen that while courts were mentioned in only 20 of 154 districts in the years 1954–67, in the 1968–71 period 160 of 343 districts that initiated desegregation pointed to the courts. Those years also recorded 103 mentions of HEW, suggesting that it was quite active too. The survey suggests that while HEW was active, the courts played an important role in desegregation in the 1968–72 period.

In terms of success, the survey found extremely large decreases in segregation between 1968 and 1972 from both court and HEW action and more moderate decreases with local action. It also found that districts desegregating under HEW pressure were less segregated in 1972 than were districts desegregating under court orders. However districts desegregating under court orders were more segregated to start with, had, on average, higher percentages of minority students, and achieved a somewhat greater decline in segregation than those desegregating under HEW pressure. Yet perhaps because courts faced a tougher task,

TABLE 2   DESEGREGATED SCHOOL DISTRICTS, BY PRIMARY SOURCE OF INTERVENTION, AND BY YEAR OF GREATEST DESEGREGATION, 1901–1974

| | *Source of Intervention* | | | | | | | |
| | *Courts* | | *HEW* | | *State-Local* | | *Total* | |
Years	#	%	#	%	#	%	#	%
1901–53	—	—	—	—	6	2	6	1
1954–65	12	6	18	12	52	21	82	13
1966–67	8	4	19	13	45	18	72	12
1968–69	53	26	42	28	34	13	129	21
1970–71	107	52	61	40	46	18	214	35
1972–73	12	6	5	3	38	15	55	9
1974–75	15	7	7	5	31	12	53	9
Total	207	101	152	101	252	99	611	100
Percent of total number of districts		34		25		41		

NOTE: Percentages do not equal 100 because of rounding.

desegregation in districts under court orders proceeded less smoothly: "school districts that reported school desegregation by court intervention were far more likely to experience disruptions than those that desegregated under HEW or local pressures."

[If we compare] actual levels of segregation in [1,362 Southern] school districts under HEW and court enforcement in 1968 and 1970, . . . [we find that] districts under H.E.W. enforcement were significantly less segregated than court-ordered districts in both 1968 and 1970. [There was also] greater decline in desegregation in court-ordered districts than in those under HEW enforcement.

VOTING

Court Action

The right to vote has long been denied American minorities. Although the Fifteenth Amendment guaranteed blacks the right to vote, the failure of Reconstruction and its replacement by Jim Crow laws and practices put an effective end to black voting in the South. By 1903, every Southern state had passed legislation limiting the vote. Throughout the twentieth century the Supreme Court heard and decided a number of cases in which it held unconstitutional various state attempts to prevent blacks from voting. As early as 1915, the so-called "Grandfather Clause," limiting voters to those who could prove that their ancestors had the right to vote (i.e., whites), was held unconstitutional (*Guinn & Beal v. U.S.* 1915). This, of course, was but one of many different ways states attempted (and succeeded) to disenfranchise blacks.

The best-known Supreme Court cases dealing with voting are the Texas Primary Cases. In Texas, as in the rest of the South, the Democratic primary was the real election, with the general election being merely a required procedural formality. The Democratic parties of all eleven Southern states, aware of the realities of political life, banned blacks from voting in Democratic primaries. This exclusion was challenged as violative of the Fourteenth Amendment in *Nixon v. Herndon* in 1927, and the Supreme Court struck it down. Texas responded by enacting legislation giving the state executive committee of each party the power to prescribe voting qualifications for its own members. The Democratic Party Executive Committee then required that its members be white. Mr. Nixon again brought suit, challenging this new bar to his ability to vote. In *Nixon v. Condon* (1932), the Supreme Court, citing *Nixon v. Herndon*, struck down the law, holding that the power to determine membership qualifications resides in the party in convention assembled. Thus, executive committee action was state action violative of the Fourteenth Amendment. Undaunted, and relying on the loophole in the *Condon* opinion, the Texas Democratic party in its convention voted to exclude blacks. This exclusion was upheld by the Supreme Court in *Grovey v. Townsend* (1935), where the Court held that since the action had been taken by the "representatives of the party in convention assembled," it was "not state action" (1935, 48) and therefore was constitutional. This position was reversed nine years later in *Smith v. Allwright* (1944), where the Court essentially held that primary and general elections are one process and that denying blacks the right to vote in primaries could be held to be state action. The final Texas Primary Case, *Terry v. Adams* (1953), involved the Jaybird Democratic Association, purportedly a self-governing voluntary private club whose nominees, it just so happened, "nearly always" ran unopposed in the Democratic primaries. The Jaybirds, of course, denied membership to blacks. The Court, realizing that the Jaybird election was the real election in Texas, accordingly struck down the exclusion.

The Court also acted to invalidate other blatant attempts to disenfranchise black voters. One case came from Tuskegee, Alabama, where the Alabama legislature had redrawn the city boundaries to exclude nearly all black residents. The local newspapers made much of the "joke" that Tuskegee's blacks had suddenly "moved out of town." In *Gomillion v. Lightfoot* (1960), the Court saw past the facially neutral character of the statute and threw out the redistricting plan.

The Court, then, with one exception subsequently reversed, consistently upheld the right of blacks to take part in the electoral process. It continually struck down attempts by state legislatures to prohibit blacks from participating in a meaningful way in the electoral process.

CONGRESSIONAL AND EXECUTIVE BRANCH ACTION

Until 1957, congressional and executive branch action in voting discrimination was, as in other civil rights areas, virtually non-existent. As with education, the Supreme Court was left to speak alone.

. . . Congress passed the Voting Rights Act [in 1965] making a major break with the past. The 1965 act . . . provided for direct federal action to enable blacks to vote. Federal examiners could be sent to election districts to list eligible voters where tests or devices were required as a precondition for voting or registering and where less than 50 percent of the total voting-age population was registered. The act also suspended all literacy tests in the jurisdictions it covered and directed the attorney general to file suit challenging the constitutionality of the poll tax. The 1965 Voting Rights Act, as will be seen shortly, had a major impact on black registration . . . .

RESULTS AND COMPARISON

Voting rights provide a good comparison of the relative contribution of the courts and the other two branches of the government to civil rights. Until 1957, the Court acted alone. It was joined half-heartedly by the other branches in 1957 and strongly in 1965. Figure 2 shows the change in the estimated number of black registered voters over the years and table 2.4 contains the raw data. Striking is the large jump in the number and the percentage of blacks registered to vote from just prior to the passage of the 1965 act to just after it. As table 3 records, the number of registered blacks in the eleven Southern states in this period jumped from approximately 2 million to 2.9 million, an increase of nearly 900,000, or 45 percent. In the first few months after the passage of the act more than 300,000 blacks were registered. No other time period shows such an increase. Prior to 1957, when only the Court acted, only 1 out of every 4 blacks was registered to vote in the South where nearly 3 out of every 4 whites were. Nearly three-quarters as many blacks registered to vote merely in the two years after passage of the act as had been registered in all the years prior to 1957. The gains in some states

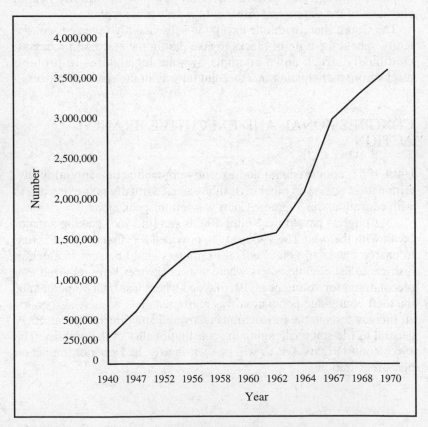

FIGURE 2   Black Voter Registration in the Southern States

TABLE 3   BLACK VOTER REGISTRATION IN THE SOUTHERN
STATES, 1940–1970, SELECTED YEARS

Year	Estimated # of Black Registered Voters	% of Voting-Age Blacks Registered
1940	250,000	5
1947	595,000	2
1952	1,008,614	20
1956	1,238,038	25
1958	1,266,488	25
1960	1,414,052	28
1962	1,480,720	29.4
1964	2,005,971	40.0
1967	2,903,284	57.6
1968	3,112,000	58.7
1970	3,506,000	66.9

NOTE: As the U.S. Commission on Civil Rights states: "Registration figures themselves vary widely in their accuracy."

were enormous. Mississippi, for example, showed a nine-fold increase in three years. There can be no doubt that the major increase in the registration of blacks came from the action of Congress and the executive branch through the 1965 Voting Rights Act.

The best case that can be made for Court influence is that the increases from 1940 to 1956 were due to the holdings of the Texas Primary Cases, particularly *Smith v. Allwright* in 1944 and *Terry v. Adams* in 1953. However, as the U.S. Civil Rights Commission pointed out, the end of World War II brought home many black servicemen who, having risked their lives for America, were determined to exercise the right to vote. Also, the black literacy rate had been continually growing, from 33 percent in 1898 to 82 percent by 1960. And . . . blacks had been moving in large numbers from the rural South to the urban South, where registration was sometimes possible, and to the North, where there were few, if any, registration barriers. Although the issue of what accounted for the increase in the percentage of blacks registered to vote between 1940 and 1956 is by no means clear, what is clear is that important societal changes were taking place, independently of the Court, that surely affected registration.

The lack of impact of governmental action prior to the 1965 act can also be seen by the lack of direct results of proceedings initiated with the courts under the 1957 and 1960 acts. In 1963, for example, the U.S. Civil Rights Commission concluded that five years of litigation under the acts had "not provided a prompt or adequate remedy for wide-spread discriminatory denials of the right to vote." It cited the efforts in 100 counties in eight states where, despite the filing of thirty-six voting rights suits by the Department of Justice, registration increased a measly 3.3 percent between 1956 and 1963, from approximately 5 percent to 8.3 percent. Another study found that eight years of litigation under the two acts in the forty-six most heavily segregated Southern counties resulted in the registration of only 37,146 blacks out of 548,358 eligibles, a mere 6.8 percent. Even administration officials came to the conclusion that litigation was fruitless. For example, Deputy Attorney General Katzenbach concluded that the weakness of litigation to produce change "meant essentially that you had to bring a separate lawsuit for each person who was discriminated against, and there were thousands, It would take years to get them registered to vote." And Attorney General Robert F. Kennedy, testifying before Congress in 1962, noted that the "problem is deep rooted and of long standing. It demands a solution which cannot be provided by lengthy litigation on a piecemeal, county-by-county basis." These figures and statements provide further evidence that Court action was ineffective in combating discrimination in voting rights.

On the other hand, there is evidence in addition to the figures that suggests the important direct effect of the 1965 act. In July 1966, about one year after the passage of the 1965 act, the Voter Education Project of the Southern Regional Council studied the effects on registration of sending federal examiners to Southern counties. The findings show substantially higher levels of black registration in counties where federal examiners were working than in those where they were not. For example, comparing counties where federal examiners were present to those where they were not, the study found increases in the percentage of blacks registered of 22.6 percent in South Carolina (71.4 percent versus 48.8 percent), 18.3 percent in Alabama (63.7 percent versus 45.4 percent), and 17 percent in Mississippi (41.2 percent versus 24.2 percent). Coupled with the huge increase in black registration immediately after the 1965 act, these figures buttress the attribution of those changes to the 1965 Act.

In sum, the bottom line in voting is that the actions of the Court contributed little to the increase in black registration. When major change did occur, it was clearly attributable to the actions of Congress and the executive . . . .

CONCLUSION

The use of the courts in the civil rights movement is considered the paradigm of a successful strategy for social change . . . . Yet, a closer examination reveals that before Congress and the executive branch acted, courts had virtually no direct effect on ending discrimination in the key fields of education [and] voting . . . . Courageous and praiseworthy decisions were rendered, and nothing changed. Only when Congress and the executive branch acted in tandem with the courts did change occur in these fields. In terms of judicial effects, then, *Brown* and its progeny stand for the proposition that courts are impotent to produce significant social reform. *Brown* is a paradigm, but for precisely the opposite view. □

NOTES AND QUESTIONS

1. Rosenberg goes on to discuss segregation in other areas. One of these is transportation. Here too a series of court cases, some as early as the 1940s, clearly outlawed racial segregation in transportation facilities—trains, for example. Yet segregation continued in the South. In 1961, blacks tried to desegregate interstate buses in the South, during the so-called "Freedom Rides;" riots and bloodshed followed. The Interstate Commerce Commission issued "new and stronger regulations." After 1961, and "particularly after the passage of the Civil Rights Act of 1964," segregation finally came to an end in transportation. This, says Rosenberg, was the result "not of court action but of the action of the other branches of the federal government."

Rosenberg makes a similar argument about public accommodations (hotels, motels, restaurants). It was the Civil Rights Act, not the courts, which put an end to segregation.

Race discrimination in housing "is one of the most virulent and intractable forms of discrimination." The Court, in *Shelley v. Kraemer* (1948), outlawed racially restrictive covenants. In 1968, the Court also decided *Jones v. Mayer Co.*, which relied on an old law (passed in 1866!) to hold that "all racial discrimination, private as well as public, in the sale or rental of property" was illegal. Housing is covered by the Civil Rights Act. Yet "racial segregation in housing has not been eliminated by government action. In fact, by the 1970s it appeared to be getting worse as whites fled to the suburbs where blacks could not afford houses or were not allowed to buy in." Court action has done little or nothing to alleviate the situation. Since other government action has been similarly ineffective, the vast majority of blacks continue to live in all-black neighborhoods.

2. Rosenberg's conclusion is that "courts are impotent to produce significant social reform." Do his data really demonstrate that this is true? What is his (implicit) definition of "impact"? How does he go about measuring it? Does he leave out any evidence that you would like to have presented?

3. On the other hand, Rosenberg argues that actions by the executive and legislative branches were more effective in ending certain forms of segregation. What is his evidence for this? Why should this be the case? Can one argue that Congress and the executive were, in some measure, nudged ahead by *Brown*? After all, Congress and the executive did nothing before the case was decided. Does Rosenberg pay too little attention to the civil rights movement? What was the impact of *Brown* on blacks and their leaders?

Court decisions, legislative rules, and administrative regulations are not self-enforcing. There are enormous problems measuring the impact of new laws and regulations. What was the actual impact of the Voting Rights Act of 1965? One way of measuring this impact is by looking at actual voter registration, as Rosenberg does. The actual story was, in fact, exceedingly complex. See Howard Ball, Dale Krane, and Thomas P. Lauth, *Compromised Compliance: Implementation of the 1965 Voting Rights Act* (Westport, Ct.: Greenwood Press, 1982).

Whatever zigs and zags occurred along the way, it does seem clear that the Voting Rights Act set in process an extremely important social change in the South. When blacks began to vote in substantial numbers, they could no longer be ignored by white candidates. At least at the local level, they could also elect black candidates. Unquestionably, black votes and black voters have revolutionized Southern politics, and, indirectly, national politics as well.

4. In another section of the chapter from Rosenberg's book, he discusses higher education (colleges and universities) and comes to the same general conclusion that he does with regard to elementary schools. However, today, although most black children still attend elementary schools that are all black or almost all black, colleges and universities are much more integrated. A small number of historically-black colleges remain overwhelmingly black; but elsewhere the degree of integration is fairly high at the college level. Can you think of reasons? Why should court decisions and governmental actions be more effective in colleges than in elementary schools? For that matter, why is housing harder to integrate than hotels and restaurants?

5. Nobody would deny the enormous *symbolic* meaning of the *Brown* case. Hence one way to read Rosenberg is as an argument that symbolic changes do not bring about much in the way of attitude or behavior changes. Is this a fair reading of Rosenberg? If it is, do you agree or disagree?

6. How does civil rights legislation change behavior? It can have direct instrumental impact—the law may command and people may obey. However, the process may be more complicated. Frank Dobbin, John R. Sutton, John W. Meyer, and W. Richard Scott, in "Equal Opportunity Law and the Construction of Internal Labor Markets," 99 *American Journal of Sociology* 396 (1993), point out: "Federal law typically establishes broad guidelines for behavior, and corporate actors respond by designing practical compliance strategies that are in turn reviewed by courts and administrative agencies. Once approved, organizationally devised solutions act as prescriptions for legal compliance" (p. 401). Lauren Edelman, in "Legal Ambiguity and Symbolic Structures: Organizational Mediation of Civil Rights Law," 97 *American Journal of Sociology* 1531 (1992), has studied the operation of equal employment opportunity law and affirmative action in operation. The law itself focuses more on procedures than on outcomes, and enforcement mechanisms are weak. Still, studies of the work force have shown that the status of minorities and women has improved significantly between 1964 and 1980. She says that this has come about because businesses and other organizations "do not simply ignore or circumvent weak law, but rather construct compliance in a way that, at least in part, fits their interests" [1541].

Organizations have created new offices, positions, rules, and procedures to deal with equal employment opportunity law and the requirements of affirmative action. These mechanisms look good to outsiders and seem not to interfere too much with managerial power. But what managers may see as largely symbolic and fairly toothless may come in time to act as a real constraint on management. The people hired to monitor and deal with affirmative action and equal opportunity tend to be more committed to these programs than the executives and administrators who hired them. Record-keeping requirements—and the vague threat of legal trouble—reinforce the position of personnel departments charged with handling EEO/AA matters. A certain amount of internal bargaining takes place. Managers at least know they are accountable to inside and outside constituencies when they deal with women and members of minority groups. Action takes place in the somewhat uncertain shadow of the law. Edelman notes, in conclusion:

> [O]ver time, pressure shifts from the legal realm to the societal and organizational realms. As EEO/AA structures become institutionalized responses to law, personnel and affirmative action professionals are likely to institute these structures because of their apparent rationality; thus the waning political support [during the Reagan and Bush administrations] has little immediate effect. And as attention to EEO/AA becomes more widespread, local minority and female communities may become more likely to demand change; in some cases, a new affirmative action officer may help to mobilize community or employee demands for change. [p. 1568]

In an earlier article, "Legal Environments and Organizational Governance: The Expansion of Due Process in the American Workplace," 95 *American Journal of Sociology* 1401 (1990), Edelman asked why "a growing number of employers have implemented due process protections for their nonunion employees in the absence of any direct [legal] mandates to do so" (p. 1402). Many large firms changed their procedures and limited managerial discretion so that employees could not be discharged without hearings, warnings and the like. She explained this in terms of "legal environment theory." Law creates important indirect effects, influencing "the normative environment." She argues that the civil rights movement and the legal requirements of the 1960s "created a normative environment in which legitimacy was conditioned on fair governance. Pressure from that normative environment led employers to create formal protections of due process rights" (p. 1402). The civil rights laws opened organizations to public scrutiny, and many managers and employees generalized these laws to a right of all employees to fair treatment. The personnel profession was the engine that drove the process. Personnel offices became an internal constituency for formal protection of employee rights because personnel department officials sought to ensure the survival and increased importance of their own positions and functions. She cautions, however, "[i]t is important to recognize that the formalization of due process rights does not guarantee substantive justice in the workplace . . . [D]ue process protections may reinforce employers' control over labor by giving the appearance of fair governance while channeling conflict into a forum that, especially in the nonunion context, is unlikely to produce significant reform" (p. 1436).

How does Edelman's story fit with Rosenberg's argument in *The Hollow Hope*? How is a normative environment created or changed?

7. Among the most controversial Supreme Court decisions were those cases of the 1960s that outlawed prayer and Bible reading in the public schools. On the impact of these cases, see Kenneth M. Dolbeare and Phillip E. Hammond, *The School Prayer Decisions, from Court Policy to Local Practice* (Chicago: University of Chicago Press, 1971); William K. Muir, *Prayer in the Public Schools: Law and Attitude Change* (1968). Muir argues that a major function of Supreme Court opinions in areas such as school prayers or the relationships of racial groups in America is to put questions on the social agenda. A successful Supreme Court opinion is one that contributes to long-term attitude change or clarification of the meaning of American values.

8. The last several readings have discussed the importance of *implementa-*

tion of court decisions and statutes. What factors seem to be crucial in determining whether and how implementation will be successful? Can you draw any general conclusions from the readings in this section?

Bradley C. Cannon, "Courts and Policy: Compliance, Implementation and Impact," in Charles Johnson and John Gates (eds.), *American Courts* (Washington, D.C.: CQ Press, 1991), makes a number of interesting distinctions that may be helpful in analyzing problems of impact and implementation of, for example, a judicial decision. He distinguishes between a person's "psychological reaction" to a decision, which he calls an "acceptance decision," and the person's "behavioral response," what the person actually does in response to a decision.

Cannon also divides the consequences of a decision into three broad categories which he calls "compliance," "implementation," and "broad impact." "Compliance" refers to "whether lower courts or implementors such as the police abide by the decision." "Implementation" refers to the "degrees to which agencies such as the police and school systems are taking the necessary steps to meet the decision's real goals." In other words, "compliance is carrying out the letter of the decision and implementation is fostering its spirit."

"Impact" is a broader concept. For Cannon, it can mean "every event that can be traced to a judicial decision or policy." But he uses the term primarily to mean "second-order consequences of a decision." Impact, in other words, includes all the ripple effects of a decision. It is obviously the most difficult aspect of a decision to measure.

SOCIAL IMPACT—HOW CAN WE DIFFERENTIATE IMPACT FROM RATIFICATIONS OF THE EXISTING PATTERN?

42. State Implementation of Supreme Court Decisions: Abortion Rates Since Roe v. Wade

Susan B. Hansen

42 *The Journal of Politics* 372 (1980)

☐ In Nineteen Seventy-Three, the United States Supreme Court ruled in *Roe v. Wade* (410 U.S. 113) that access to abortion during the first three months of pregnancy was guaranteed by Constitutional provisions concerning privacy . . .

Three competing views have been advanced concerning the impact of the Supreme Court's *Roe* decision. The first two anticipate considerable social change, but dispute its direction. Conservatives and "Right to Life" proponents anticipate unwelcome changes in family and child-rearing patterns: increased promiscuity, population decline, a loss of respect for human life, and the use of abortion as a means of birth control. Supporters of the Court's decision, groups such as Planned Parenthood, the National Organization for Women, and the National Abortion Rights Action League, expect different social consequences:

superior life chances available, planned and wanted children, freedom of choice for women, lack of business for "back-alley butchers," and a resulting decline in death from illegal abortions. The availability of abortion, they argue, should also lead to fewer illegitimate births, with their attendant social and economic costs.

A third view is that Supreme Court decisions simply reflect ongoing social and political change, and have only a minor and gradual impact on society . . . .

This view would predict essentially no change in the reproductive behavior of American women which could be attributed to the *Roe* decision or its implementation.

NUMBER OF ABORTIONS

The number of American women receiving abortions has certainly increased, from 193,000 in 1970 to almost 1.3 million in 1977 (Figure 1). What is striking is the apparent lack of any sharp bend in the curve after *Roe*. Almost no legal abortions were performed in the United States before 1965; middle- and upper-class women could go to Mexico or Sweden, while poor women did without or suffered from self-induced or black-market abortions. After the thalidomide scare, the Sherri Finkbine case, and an epidemic of German measles, 15 states revised their nineteenth-century laws on abortion. Thousands of women took advantage of the easy availability of abortion in states such as New York, Washington and Colorado. Consequently, the largest increase in abortion occurred *before* the *Roe* decision, not after it.

Abortion rates may be viewed as a product of economic and demo-

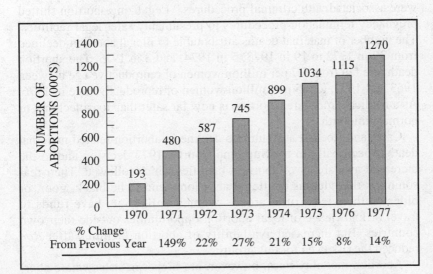

	1970	1971	1972	1973	1974	1975	1976	1977
NUMBER OF ABORTIONS (000'S)	193	480	587	745	899	1034	1115	1270
% Change From Previous Year		149%	22%	27%	21%	15%	8%	14%

FIGURE 1   Number of Abortions and Change from previous year, 1970–77

graphic changes as well as legal and technological innovations. As of 1975, the U.S. abortion rate was in the middle range for industrial countries—below rates in Japan or Eastern Europe, but above France, England or Italy. In view of these data, the Court appears to be reflecting social change rather than legislating it as its conservative opponents have claimed.

Fertility and Illegitimate Births

Birth rates have undergone a long-term decline in most industrialized countries as a product of economic development, movement from farm to city, increase in the number of working women, preference for smaller families, and the increased probability of infants surviving into adulthood. The U.S., despite the "baby boom" of the 1940s and 1950s, is no exception to this overall trend . . . . [B]irth rates per 1000 women age 15 to 44 have continued to decline since 1960. But for both blacks and whites, more rapid change occurred *before* rather than after 1973. More trend data would of course be desirable to explore this pattern more fully, but no precipitous decline of birth rates appears to have followed the *Roe* decision. The business recession of 1974–75, rather than the increased availability of abortion, may have produced the marginal decline which did take place . . . .

Abortion Mortality

One dramatic result of the legalization of abortion has been decrease in abortion-related maternal deaths. Cates and Roehart report that between 1940 and 1972, "More than 75 percent of abortion deaths were associated with criminal procedures." Legalizing abortion shifted pregnancy termination procedures to presumably safer legal facilities. The number of maternal deaths attributable to illegal abortion declined from 39 in 1972 to 19 in 1973, 5 in 1974, and 3 in 1975. The abortion death rate fell from 5.7 per million women of reproductive age between 1963 and 1973, to 0.5 per million women of reproductive age in 1976. As a medical procedure, abortion is now far safer than tonsillectomy or normal childbirth.

Cates and Roehart attribute the decline in abortion-related maternal deaths specifically to the Supreme Court's 1973 decision and to the increased availability of abortion facilities which followed. Their reasoning is that victims of illegal abortions tend to be black, poor, or older mothers from rural areas—women unlikely to have funds to travel or knowledge of legal abortion opportunities outside their own countries. But increased availability of abortion facilities after *Roe* reduced the risk even for this group.

Abortion mortality rates, however, are higher in states where abortion is easily obtainable, and are highest of all in Washington D.C. The explanation is that in states with liberal laws, more abortions are performed late in pregnancy when the risk is greater.

Overall, a decline in abortion mortality has resulted from *Roe*. Legalization has also encouraged medical experimentation, better techniques, and safer procedures.

Despite the concerns of anti-abortion groups, abortion rates and illegitimacy have not shown an appreciable increase since 1973. Nor have fertility rates declined. Greater social changes were associated with the legalization of abortion in a few states around 1970 than with the Supreme Court's actions in *Roe*.

Equalization of State Abortion Rates

Conservatives since Calhoun have argued for a geographic solution to intense political preferences. In theory, if certain policies are available in some political units but not in others, people can move to find policies which suit their preferences. Nevertheless, freedom to move varies with socioeconomic status; inner-city residents cannot easily escape the vicious cycle of high taxes and bad public services. Similarly, poor women in need of abortion are unlikely to have the means to travel to other areas for medical attention, and may not even know about the availability of such services. This pattern holds between states as well as within a state. A primary result of *Roe*, therefore, should have been equalization of abortion rates across states.

This equalization has indeed been the case. Table 1 compares abortion rates from 1972 through 1976 for states grouped according to their pre-*Roe* abortion policies. The percentage of total abortions per-

TABLE 1   PERCENT OF TOTAL ABORTIONS IN MOST AND LEAST RESTRICTIVE STATES 1972–1976

	Pre-Roe State Laws		
	Abortion[a] on Demand	Reformed[b] Laws	Restrictive Laws
1972	84%	16%	.1%
1973	57	24	19
1974	42	29	29
1975	38	30	32
1976	35	30	35
Total *N* of states	4	22	24

[a]Includes District of Columbia, New York, Alaska, Hawaii, and Washington State.

[b]Includes Arizona, California, Colorado, Delaware, Georgia, Kansas, Maryland, New Mexico, North Carolina, Oregon, South Carolina, and Virginia.

formed by the least restrictive states (Alaska, District of Columbia, New York, Hawaii and Washington) fell from 84 percent in 1972 to 35 percent in 1976. But abortions performed by the most restrictive states rose from 0.1 percent in 1972 to 35 percent in 1976. Three years after *Roe*, three states (Louisiana, North Dakota, and South Dakota) had no hospitals, public or private, which performed abortions. By 1976, however, all states reported at least some abortions (the lowest number being 600 in Wyoming). Further, the proportion of abortions performed outside women's home states fell from 45 percent in 1972 to only 10 percent in 1966. While the mean abortion rate across states rose from 10.2 to 18.4 from 1973 to 1976, the standard deviation declined from 9.66 to 8.8.

Despite this trend toward reduced variance, abortion rates for women of child-bearing age still differ considerably. In 1976, abortion rates ranged from lows of six or less per 1000 women of childbearing age in West Virginia and Mississippi, to highs of 42.6 in New York, 39.0 in California, and 192.0 in Washington D.C. (Table 2) Some of this variation is no doubt the result of differing needs or demand for different areas of the country; urban areas with large proportions of

TABLE 2   ABORTION RATES PER 1000 WOMEN AGE 15–45 BY STATE, 1976

State	Rate	State	Rate
New York	42.6	Delaware	18.8
California	39.0	Alaska	17.2
Hawaii	31.0	Minnesota	17.1
Florida	30.3	Arizona	15.9
Massachusetts	29.2	Wisconsin	13.8
Illinois	29.0	New Hampshire	13.6
Nevada	27.7	Nebraska	13.5
Washington	27.7	Kentucky	13.4
Kansas	25.6	Missouri	12.8
Vermont	25.0	Oklahoma	12.5
New Jersey	24.9	North Dakota	11.9
Colorado	24.2	Maine	11.5
Oregon	24.2	South Dakota	11.0
Maryland	24.2	Iowa	10.8
Tennessee	24.0	Alabama	10.2
Michigan	23.6	Montana	10.0
Georgia	22.4	Louisiana	9.9
Connecticut	22.3	Arkansas	9.4
Pennsylvania	22.0	Utah	9.1
Virginia	22.0	South Carolina	9.0
Ohio	21.9	Indiana	7.2
New Mexico	21.6	Idaho	7.2
Texas	21.4	Wyoming	6.5
Rhode Island	19.6	Mississippi	3.3
North Carolina	19.1	West Virginia	2.5

poor or black residents and high rates of illegitimacy tend to have higher abortion rates. Catholic Louisiana and Mormon Utah have very low rates, since religious opposition has resulted in few abortion facilities and lack of public funding.

Explanations for State Differences

In addition to population factors, abortion rates should also vary with the availability of services, public funding, and political support for liberalized abortion policies. If a state's election officials are opposed to *Roe*, numerous institutional roadblocks (funding limitations, legal challenges withholding of licenses for medical facilities or personnel) can be devised to delay implementation, forcing pregnant women to travel to other states or to forgo the procedure altogether. But abortion rates should be higher in states which had permitted abortions before *Roe*. This could reflect more supportive attitudes by the public and elected officials, as well as greater availability of abortion services in previously established facilities . . . .

State population characteristics proved to be generally poor predictors of abortion rates; correlations are weak, and the signs are the reverse of those hypothesized. Thus abortion rates tend to be low in states where a high proportion of poor families, who are less able to support children and whose family life is more likely to be unstable, should indicate greater need for abortion facilities.

Neither does the racial composition of a state affect abortion rates. Although most women who obtain abortions are white, . . . abortion rates for black women were over twice as high as those for whites, because of the poverty, unemployment, and high rates of illegitimacy which so often afflict young black women. But this individual-level relationship does not hold when we compare states with different proportions of black residents. A closer look at the state data indicates considerable variability, Mississippi, with a large, poor, black population, has a very low rate, while many other rural southern states have high rates. Washington D.C., over 80 percent black, has the highest rates in the country (although many of the city's abortions are not performed on local residents). The weak correlation between percent black and 1976 abortion rates may also result because many Southern states spend relatively little on welfare or Medicaid for their large black populations.

A third indicator of abortion need is the estimated unwanted fertility rate for women age 15-19 in each state. But the higher the unwanted fertility rate, the *lower* the abortion rate. The young women most in need of abortions seem least able to obtain them . . . .

Differences in public preferences might well account for inter-state differences in abortion rates. Harris Poll data from 1976 suggest some variation in opinions by region, with support for liberal abortion policies lowest in the South (39 percent in favor) and highest in the West (64 percent in favor). Unfortunately, survey data on abortion are not available for every state, and cannot be predicted on the basis of demographic factors such as church membership; opinions of Catholics and Mormons do not differ greatly from those of Protestants. Supportive public opinion, however, is not sufficient to insure abortion availability; in Massachusetts and Michigan only the governor's veto has prevented state legislatures from cutting off Medicaid funds, despite popular majorities in favor of liberal abortion.

Predictions based on "supply" factors performed considerably better than population characteristics in predicting abortion rates. The proportion of a state's hospitals performing abortions, Medicaid funds for family planning, and the population of a state residing in SMSA's all showed strong correlations with state abortion rates from 1973 to 1976.

To index the effect of pre-*Roe* abortion legalization on current abortion rates, states where abortion was illegal before 1973 were coded 0; states with limited access to abortion, 1; and states with abortion on demand, 2. Positive correlations with the index show higher abortion rates in states which had liberalized their abortion laws before Roe. The impact of this early liberalization has declined between 1973 and 1976, however, as other states have taken steps to implement services

On the basis of these correlations, one might reasonably conclude that abortion rates are functions of the greater availability of abortion services in metropolitan states; political support and demographic factors have very little effect. But we are then faced with a more fundamental question: what factors affect the availability of medical services? And do these services have an impact independent of population demand or political support for abortion? To answer such questions, causal and interactive patterns in these data must be considered.

CONCLUSION

The redistributive implications of abortion policy have merited almost as much attention as the moral dilemma raised by this highly salient issue. The most vocal groups supporting liberalized abortion laws have been middle- and upper-class white women, but primary beneficiaries of such laws have been poor and black women. Women with economic means have always been able to obtain abortions, illegally in the U.S. or legally abroad. But medically safe, legal abortions were denied to disadvantaged American women in most states until after *Roe*.

Five years after *Roe*, changes in access to abortion have been apparent throughout the United States. The trend over time has been toward greater equalization of access with the largest increases in abortion rates in the most restrictive states. But rates in New York and Washington, D.C. remain many times as high as those in Louisiana, Mississippi, or the Dakotas. This analysis has accounted for some of these differences in terms of interstate variations in funding, hospital services, metropolitan population, religion, and political support for liberal abortion laws.

One additional factor affecting access to abortion is the availability of abortion services in neighboring states. This analysis has been based only on abortions performed within particular states, and has not considered flows across state boundaries. Overall, only ten percent of abortions are performed on nonresidents. But many states' abortion rates are substantially higher or lower than one might predict on the basis of population factors or religious preference. Several northern industrialized states (Connecticut, Delaware, Pennsylvania, and Indiana) had abortion rates lower than predicted. Proximity to New York or Chicago might explain why these states have been slow to develop abortion services.

In an open political system, variability in access to abortion may in fact offer advantages. When much of a state's population opposes abortion, policy outcomes can be congruent with popular preferences without seriously disadvantaging women in need of abortion. Women from poor, rural states may receive better medical care in better trained, better equipped clinics in metropolitan areas. Many women may also prefer the anonymity of a large city away from their home communities. Such considerations notwithstanding, abortion remains a highly redistributive issue. Middle-class women have the funds and knowledge to seek abortion opportunities outside their home states. But poor women will continue to be denied access to the abortion services many of them want and need unless and until all states provide adequate services.

The Supreme Court decided in June 1977 that states are not obliged to provide funding for abortions under Medicaid programs. Congress in 1976, 1977, and 1978 adopted restrictive amendments to the HEW appropriations bill, limiting most federal funds for abortions except under conditions threatening the life or health of the mother. Poorer states cannot easily pick up the 90 percent federal portion of Medicaid funding for abortions. Poor women will no doubt have difficulty paying for their abortions, since their average cost in 1976 was more than the entire average monthly welfare payment per family; and medical costs have increased faster than other prices.

Limits on public financing appear likely to accentuate the redistributive implications of abortion policies. But the overall impact of these new limits on abortion availability remains unknown. The current debate over legal issues, funding formulas, and administrative discretion has resulted in such frequent policy changes that policy outcomes are difficult to determine . . . [There was] a share decline in some states, but in others such as Missouri, abortions actually increased between 1976 and 1978 despite a cutoff in public financing. The analysis reported above indicated that abortion rates were indeed higher in states with large amounts of Medicaid funding, but this association could be explained by size of population and the extreme case of California, which spends the most public moneys on abortions and also has a high abortion rate. Fifteen states and the District of Columbia still provide full or partial coverage for abortions for women on welfare; these states accounted for almost sixty percent of all abortions in 1976. Private sources such as Planned Parenthood offer direct aid or loans, and have continued to fund legal challenges to attempts at cutoffs in state aid. Even without public financing, the availability of safe, legal abortion services provides women with a far greater range of options than were available before *Roe*, even if travel to another state is necessary. Certainly no surge in abortion-related maternal deaths has been observed, indicating that few women have been forced to find illegal means of terminating their pregnancies . . . . □

NOTES AND QUESTIONS

1. According to Hansen, what is the impact of *Roe* on the abortion rate? Consider what is meant by "impact." What would have happened to the abortion rate if *Roe* had never been decided? The table on p. 601 is of interest. From: Lawrence Baum, *The Supreme Court* 4th ed. (Washington, D.C.: CQ Press, 1992), p. 247.

2. The Supreme Court has held that federal and state governments do not have to fund abortions. See *Webster v. Reproductive Health,* 492 U.S. 490 (1989).

3. In 1992 the Supreme Court reaffirmed that a woman has a constitutional right to an abortion in *Planned Parenthood v. Casey,* 112 S. Ct. 2791 (1992), by a narrow, 5 to 4 vote. Suppose the Court had gone the other way, and declared *Roe* unconstitutional. What would have been the likely impact? Consider as wide a range of impacts as you can. For example, consider not only abortion rates, but also women's health and the political activity that would result at the federal and state levels. Formulate your expectations into a series of hypotheses. How would you construct a study to test these hypotheses?

4. Can you analyze the impact of *Roe v. Wade* in terms of Canon's categories? What sorts of consequences would make up the total *impact* of the case?

The *Roe* decision is very controversial. There has been an enormous literature on the subject. See, for example, Gilbert Y. Steiner (ed.) *The Abortion Dispute and the American System* (Washington, D.C.: Brookings Institution, 1983); Kristin Luker, *Abortion and the Politics of Motherhood* (Berkeley: University of California Press, 1984). People have taken sides who probably have no immediate personal interest in the issue. Is *Roe v. Wade* a good example of a decision whose main effect is *symbolic*? What does it symbolize, and to whom?

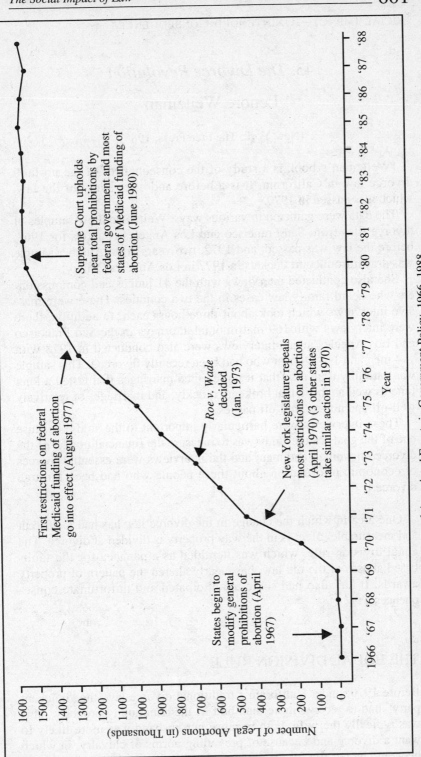

FIGURE 2   Estimated Legal Abortion Rates and Associated Events in Government Policy, 1966–1988

43. *The Divorce Revolution*

Lenore Weitzman

(New York: The Free Press, 1985)

☐ [Weitzman's book is a study of the consequences of the no-fault divorce law in California. It is a before and after study of the law, which was passed in 1970.

The data were gathered in various ways. Weitzman drew samples of divorce files from San Francisco and Los Angeles counties for 1968, before the law was passed, and 1972, two years after. Another sample was drawn from court dockets in 1977 in Los Angeles County.

She also conducted interviews with the 41 judges and commissioners who heard family law cases in the two counties. These were massive interviews which took about three hours each. In addition, there were interviews with 169 matrimonial attorneys in the San Francisco and Los Angeles areas. Interviews were also conducted in 1978 with 114 men and 114 women who had been recently divorced. This sample was carefully drawn so that it represented marriages that lasted a long time as well as those that broke up quickly, and marriages of relatively well-off and not-so-well-off parties.

These interviews were particularly important to the study, because one of the goals of the study was to measure the financial impact of the divorce on women and men; and the interviews were essential sources of economic information about these people who had been through divorce.]

One area in which the change in the divorce law has had a clearcut and measurable effect is in the way property is divided at divorce. The equal division rule, which was heralded as a panacea for the fault-based abuses of the old law, has clearly altered the pattern of property awards. It has also had some unanticipated and unfortunate consequences.

THE EQUAL DIVISION RULE

Before 1970, under California's traditional divorce law, the "innocent party" had to receive more than half of the community property. This was typically the wife, both because her husband was more likely to want a divorce and because of prevailing norms of chivalry, in which he would let her file for the divorce.

The no-fault law, in contrast, instructs the court to divide the community assets and liabilities *equally*. A husband and wife may agree to a nonequal division, either in writing or orally in court, but a judge is bound to award each spouse half of the total community assets. The court may make an unequal division only if the total of the community property is under $5,000 and one spouse's whereabouts are unknown, or if the debts exceed the assets . . . .

The drafters of the 1970 California legislation had three justifications for the equal division rule. First, the target of their reform was the fault-based divorce law, and one major aim was to rid the legal process of the "economic blackmail" of property awards based on fault:

If we eliminate fault as a major basis for divorce action, then we would also eliminate finances as a major weapon either for "bargaining" or for the punishment of the apparently "guilty" party. Instead, alimony and property settlement would be based on equitable judgment as to what is available and how it can be divided.

Professor Herma Hill Kay, an influential member of the Governor's Commission that proposed the no-fault legislation, reports that because the division of property was specifically tied to fault under the old law, the reformers were eager to ensure the separation of the two under the new law. To do this they needed a strict rule, such as the equal division requirement. They were so convinced of the benefits to be gained from the elimination of fault that they wanted an absolute standard that could not be swayed by a party's behavior—even if it meant allowing a hypothetical "rat-fink" to retain his full half share of the property:

. . . the separation of the property award from marital fault was a sensitive policy issue for the Commission. Ultimately, however, it was decided that even where the divorce was awarded at the behest of a "rat-fink" (in a spontaneous hypothetical case, the Commission's rat-fink was seen to be a male medical student who allowed his nurse-wife to support him through his expensive training, only to divorce her and marry the Dean's daughter after his residency was completed), division of property would remain equal. Punishment as well as fault was to be abolished; the Commission's minutes propose that inequities in the rat-fink hypothetical case should be resolved by the alimony award.

Thus consistent with their general effort to abolish the influence of both real and fabricated marital fault, the reformers proposed a hard and fast rule for marital property: that it always be divided equally upon divorce.

A second reason for the equal division rule was the reformers' belief that the community property system adequately protected wives . . . .

The fact that California already had a community property system, and already regarded the wife as an equal economic partner, played a part in "reassuring those scrutinizing the proposed change" that dependent wives were adequately protected in California. Both the community property system, and the equal division rule, were seen as an affirmation of the presumption that marriage was an equal partnership in which the financial and nonfinancial contributions of the two spouses were of equal worth. Each therefore deserved, and would receive, half of the couple's jointly accumulated property.

The third rationale for the equal division requirement was to limit judicial discretion. When the equal division rule was first proposed, the State Bar opposed it. Instead they recommended that judges be allowed to divide the property unequally (but not punitively) "where the court finds an exception (to equal division) is warranted . . . in such proportions as it deems just." When the members of the State Bar realized, however, that their language would unduly broaden judges' discretion—and might reintroduce the very same fault-based considerations that the new law sought to abolish—they withdrew their proposal.

In summary, the drafters of the California legislation believed that an equal division standard, by limiting judicial discretion and assuring each partner an equal share of their jointly accumulated property, was more fair than the vague standard of an "equitable" division of property. The equitable standard, which is now used in most of the separate property states, not only gives judges the power "to do justice" by dividing the marital property according to need, it also allows judges to use their own subjective standards of equity (and therefore results in a greater diversity of awards).

Equal vs. Equitable Distribution

The debate over "equal" versus "equitable" rules for the division of marital property is a continuing one. In both New York and Wisconsin, for example, the standards for property division were hotly contested in recent years. In Wisconsin feminists successfully pressed for the California rule, arguing that without a guarantee of one-half of the property most wives in separate property states received no more than a third of the family property.

In New York the organized bar won the day and passed an equitable distribution law. They asserted that women would be better off under an *equitable* standard that allowed judges to "do justice" according to the circumstances of the parties and, where appropriate, to award women more than half of the property by allowing them to keep the family home.

Which set of assertions is correct? How do the two sexes fare under equal versus equitable rules? Although the state bar convinced the New York legislature to adopt an equitable division law in 1980, and the feminists convinced the Wisconsin legislature to adopt an equal division law in 1977, neither decision was based on empirical data . . .

OVERALL DIVISION OF COMMUNITY PROPERTY

Table 1 shows dramatic changes in the distribution of marital property in California since the no-fault law was instituted. In 1968, under the old law, the wife, as the "innocent" plaintiff, was typically awarded the lion's share of the property. She received more than half (i.e., 60 percent or more) in four out of five divorce cases in San Francisco, and in three out of five cases in Los Angeles. Many of these unequal awards involved the family home and furnishings. In 1968 the property was divided equally in only 12 percent of the cases in San Francisco and 26 percent of the cases in Los Angeles.

Under the no-fault law, the percentage of cases in which the property was divided equally increased from 12 to 59 percent in San Francisco between 1968 and 1972, and from 26 to 64 percent in Los Angeles. By 1977 equal division was the norm.

The new law brought a corresponding drop in the percentage of wives who were awarded most of the community property, as Table 1 shows. In addition, the wife's share of the property dropped under no-fault. For example, in Los Angeles county, wives who were awarded close to 80 percent of the property under the old fault law were awarded closer to half (54 percent) under no-fault.

Thus the adverse economic effects of the changing pattern of property awards has fallen on women. Under the old law, women were typically awarded most of the marital property, and this tended to cushion the economic impact of the divorce. Today, under the equal division rule, they receive much less. The clearest result of this change is the increase in court orders for the matrimonial home to be sold upon

TABLE 1   DIVISION OF PROPERTY UNDER FAULT AND NO-FAULT LAWS

	San Francisco		Los Angeles		
	Fault (1968)	No-fault (1972)	Fault (1968)	No-fault (1972)	No-fault (1977)
Majority to husband*	2%	7%	6%	21%	10%
Approximately equal division**	12	59	26	44	64
Majority to wife*	86	34	58	35	26
Mean percentage to wife	91%	62%	78%	54%	—***

*Majority = over 60%.

**Approximately equal = between 40 and 60%.

***1977 information not specified in detail sufficient for precise percentage.

This table is based on random samples of court dockets. San Francisco County and Los Angeles County, California divorce so that the property can be divided equally. The disruptive effects of this pattern are discussed below . . .

One of the justifications for the equal division rule was the reformers' belief that property was usually divided in roughly equal proportions under the old law. (A 51/49 percent division of the property was in technical compliance with the rule that "more than one-half" of the assets be awarded to the injured party.) An equal division rule, the reformers asserted, would merely codify the common practice of roughly equal property splits.

The data strongly contradict those assertions. They indicate that property was not being divided equally under the old law, and certainly not in 51/49 percent ratios. Rather, three-quarters of the 1968 cases involved a substantially unequal division. Thus, these findings challenge the widespread misbelief that the no-fault divorce law merely codified existing practice. They indicate instead that the new law has dramatically altered the way property is divided upon divorce.

One might ask how it is possible, under a strict equal division rule, to still have a minority of cases in which property is not divided equally. Since property may be divided unequally only if both parties agree, the question is why one party would agree to accept less than half of the property. The answer probably lies in a property-support tradeoff in which, for example, a wife receives more than 60 percent of the tangible property in exchange for a lower support award. Because property settlements are nonmodifiable, whereas spousal support awards are vulnerable to later modification and to enforcement difficulties, attorneys may advise their female clients to settle for an advantageous property settlement, knowing it to be a "sure thing," instead of seeking a high spousal support award. The low percentage of spousal support orders . . . makes this interpretation appear likely.

In fact, a small proportion of the cases contained a specific reference to a nonmodifiable integrated settlement of property and support. That is, the property award was explicitly linked to spousal support, indicating that the wife or husband received more of one in exchange for less of the other. These were found in 7 percent of the files in the 1968 sample, 9 percent in 1972, and 19 percent in 1977.

It is important to keep in mind the average value of the community property when thinking about the practical implications of the trend toward an equal division of marital property. Since close to 60 percent of the divorcing couples in the 1978 interview sample have less than $20,000 in net worth, . . . most spouses could expect to be awarded about $10,000 worth of property—assuming the property was divided equally. Or, to put it another way, only two out of five divorced spouses could expect a property award of more than $10,000.

THE ABSENCE OF FAULT

The reformers were, in fact, successful in removing fault as a basis for awarding property. As one attorney said:

> I've seen men get away with the most outrageous conduct and they still get half of the property . . . . I've seen instances where women have literally been driven to psychiatrists and psychologists; they are extremely emotionally upset and disturbed by their husbands' wrongful conduct. He flaunts it to her, knowing that it will have no effect upon the required equal division of the community property.

Under the old law, when fault affected the division of property, the identity of the petitioner, or "innocent party," made considerable difference in the property distribution. In the 1968 cases in which the wife was the plaintiff, wives received an average of 89 percent of the community property. When the husband was the plaintiff, wives received only 60 percent of the property. Corresponding awards to wives were 60 and 56 percent under the new law (in 1972), an insignificant difference that suggests fault has become irrelevant . . . . [U]nder the old law, . . . [a] wife who would successfully accuse her husband of adultery or mental cruelty would be granted the divorce and most of the property. But the property consequences were equally predictable if the wife had been at fault. If she was found guilty of adultery or mental cruelty she too would be punished and lose her home.

Under the no-fault law both of these scenarios would have the same outcome. For example, when they responded to hypothetical cases, even though the judges and attorneys we interviewed knew that one of the parties was responsible for the dissolution, they were unlikely to be influenced by that fact in predicting the case outcome under the no-fault law. Rather, they were likely to predict that the family home would be sold under the present law, and that the equity would be divided equally between the two spouses . . . .

THE FAMILY HOME

The home is typically the family's major asset. The legal tradition was to award the family home to the wife upon divorce, both because it was assumed to be hers—in the sense that she organized, decorated, and maintained it—and because she was usually the "innocent" party and therefore entitled to a larger share of the community property. In addition, if she had custody of the children, she needed the home to maintain a stable environment for them.

With the absence of fault and the trend toward equal division, it is not surprising to find an increase in the number of homes being divided equally: from less than a quarter (23 percent) of the homes in 1968 to

TABLE 2 DISPOSITION OF FAMILY HOME UNDER FAULT AND NO-FAULT LAWS

	Fault Law	No-Fault Law	
Division of Home (Or Equity)	1968	1972	1977
Majority to husband*	16%	24%	19%
Approximately equal division**	23	25	35
Majority to wife	61	51	46

*Majority = over 60%.

**Approximately equal = between 40 and 59%.

This table is based on random samples of court dockets, Los Angeles County, California.

more than a third (35 percent) in 1977. There has been a corresponding decline in cases where the majority of equity in the home is awarded to the wife, from 61 percent in 1968 to 46 percent in 1977. These data are shown in Table 2.

"Equal division" of a house can mean either that the two parties maintain joint ownership after the divorce, or that the house is sold and the proceeds divided equally. The number of cases in which there was an explicit order to sell the home rose about from one in ten in 1968, to about one in three in 1977. By that year, an equal division of the home typically meant that the house was ordered sold.

In her review of divorce cases in San Diego County, Dr. Karen Seal found a similar trend. In 1968 wives in San Diego were awarded the house in 66 percent of the cases. By 1977 that percentage dropped to 42 percent. As Seal notes, the minority of women who were able to keep the family home under no-fault "paid" for their husbands' share: either the wife agreed to buy out her husband's half of the equity, or she relinquished her claim to some other comparable asset, such as his pension plan.

Surprisingly, the presence of minor children did not increase the likelihood that the wife would be awarded the family home. Our data reveal that 66 percent of the couples who were forced to sell their homes had minor children.

Although the overwhelming majority of the attorneys and judges we interviewed said they thought the equal division rule was basically fair (and preferable to the fault-based standards of the old law), many expressed concern about a forced sale of the family home, especially in families with minor children. Close to 40 percent of the attorneys thought judges should be allowed more discretion in dividing property so that they would not be bound by an equal division rule for families with minor children. As one attorney stated:

So often the only asset of any consequence is the family residence. When the couple divorces, it is ordered sold and the children are deprived of their home . . . . There should be a way to keep the home intact for the children.

One way of maintaining the family home for the children is to award the home to the custodial spouse, and to award an asset of equal value, such as the husband's retirement pension or a vacation home, to him. Indeed this solution has been approved by several courts and was often the way the women we interviewed managed to keep the home. But such tradeoffs are possibly only for the minority of families that have other assets to offset the award of the home, and as we already know, most families cannot utilize this "solution." Less than a quarter of the divorcing couples have a pension, and only one in nine has a business or other real estate . . . .

Another possibility for the custodial mother who is determined to maintain the home for her children is to "trade" whatever she has for the option, and the only thing she may have left to trade is a support award. Several attorneys said they recommended this solution to women whose husbands were "difficult" because of the problems they anticipated in collecting support. While bemoaning the situation—"It's tough," said one attorney, "because she has to forgo her support to pay him off"—the attorneys saw no other solution than to change the legal rules.

Since a large number of divorcing women do not have either of these options—that is, there is no pension or other property to "trade" for the home, and they cannot afford to "trade" their support because they cannot live without it—they are forced to sell the home. Consider, for example, the story of one thirty-eight-year-old woman we interviewed. She pleaded with her attorney, and then the court, to work out some arrangement to allow her to stay in the family home. She had lived there for 15 years. Her fourteen-year-old son was living with her and was experiencing "a lot of emotional turmoil" as a result of the divorce. He needed the security of a stable home. The mortgage payments were $280 a month, which she could manage on her $600 a month alimony and child support award. But alternative housing in her neighborhood was much more expensive and vastly inferior: a minimum one- bedroom apartment would cost $500 a month.

This woman had tried to negotiate with her husband. She offered to forgo her interest in his pension plan, valued at approximately $85,000, which would have covered the equity in the house. But her husband would agree to this only if she also agreed to a) forgo alimony and b) accept $100 a month in child support (for less than three years until her son reached age eighteen), a proposal that seemed both unfair and unmanageable to a woman who had been a full-time homemaker with no recent job experience.

Nor was she able to refinance the house to pay off her husband. She thought she would be able to use the $600 in support she was promised to pay the mortgage. However in her words:

No bank would give me a loan and no one was willing to accept my spousal support as "income." One loan officer said to me, "Spousal support and child support don't count. Most men stop paying them and we have to repossess the house." Another bank officer said he had seen "hundreds of women like me." He was "sympathetic," but said I was too poor a risk to get through the loan committee.

Since the woman could not buy out her husband's share of the house, and since the parties were unable to "agree" on a division of property, the judged ordered the house sold and gave the woman three months to vacate it. As the woman said,

> I begged the judge . . . All I wanted was enough time for Brian [her son] to adjust to the divorce . . . . I broke down and cried on the stand . . . but the judge refused. He gave me three months to move—three months to move 15 years—right in the middle of the school semester . . . my husband's attorney threatened me with contempt if I wasn't out on time . . . he also warned me to not to interfere with the real estate people—in *my* house—he said if I wasn't cooperative in letting them show the house when they wanted to, he'd "haul me into court for contempt." . . . It was a nightmare . . . . The most degrading and unjust experience of my life.

Similar threats were recounted by a fifty-four-year-old woman who was "ordered" to vacate her house so that it could be sold.

> I had lived in that home for 26 years and my three children still considered it their home. But the judge ordered it sold . . . . He said he had to follow the letter of the law . . . . I married at 'a time when a woman who spent 30 years of her life raising a family was worth something . . . but in the eyes of the court I was merely "unemployed." No one would rent me an apartment because my only income was $700 a month spousal support and landlords said that was "unstable" and "inadequate." Two months later my husband's attorney took me into court for contempt because I hadn't moved . . . . He said I was interfering with the sale of the house . . . . The judge gave me ten days to get out . . . . I am still outraged. It is a total perversion of justice. I was thrown out of my own house.

. . . Significantly, the California legislature did not intend that the family home be sold in order to meet the equal division requirement. Indeed, a 1970 Assembly Committee report specifically states that a temporary award of the home to the spouse who has custody of minor children should be seen as a valid reason to delay the division of property:

> Where an interest in a residence which serves as the home of the family is the major community asset, an order for the immediate sale of the residence in order to comply with the equal division mandate of the law would, certainly, be unnecessarily destructive of the economic and social circumstances of the parties and their children.

Most of the justification for maintaining the family home for the children has focused on the social and psychological disruption they experience in forced moves and changed schools and neighborhoods. There are, however, also sound economic reasons for allowing the wife to retain the family home. As Karen Seal suggests, the home provides the wife with leverage to insure the husband's payment of support:

> When a husband receives his half of the assets immediately upon divorce, it is much easier for him to overlook his responsibilities. If he stood to lose his interest in the family home for nonsupport, however, perhaps he would be more likely to comply. Or at least if he did not comply, the wife should be able to claim a larger share of the ownership of the home as a result of his default. At a minimum, a property interest of this nature should be held as security for compliance with support orders.

Fran Leonard, attorney for The Older Women's League, echoes some of these thoughts in asserting the importance of a similar delay to allow older homemakers to retain their homes:

> Unlike her spouse, she may have no credit history, no income aside from alimony, and almost no prospects of recovering her lost earning capacity. The chances of her ever buying another home are almost nil. Yet all too commonly the court orders the home sold, in order to divide its value. Attorneys frequently favor this, because their fees can be paid out of escrow . . . . Instead, older women should try to keep the family home and, if necessary, leave their husband's name on the deed as a tenant in common: This will give the husband an investment that is growing, and she effectively has a lien on his spousal support and child support.

Leonard also stressed the critical psychological importance of the home for a woman who has built her world there:

> For the older woman, especially a homemaker [the sale of the family home] is a major cruelty. Upon divorce, she loses her husband and her occupation—then all too often, her home. This nearly comprises her universe.

The California appellate courts have upheld the rationale for maintaining the family home for minor children when a sale would have an adverse economic, emotional, or social impact on them. Consider, for example, the 1973 case of *In re Marriage of Boseman*. The family home was the only asset the parties had. The wife was awarded custody of the three minor children, ages thirteen, eleven, and three. The trial court issued an order for the house to remain in joint ownership, but gave the wife possession of the house for the "use and benefit" of the minor children until the youngest child reached majority. Thereupon, the house was to be sold and the proceeds divided. The award of the home to the wife was upheld on appeal.

But despite the legislative and judicial authority for exempting the house from the immediate and equal division of community property, the judges we interviewed in 1974–1975, 1981, and 1983 attested to the prevailing pattern of ordering the home sold and the proceeds divided upon divorce. While some judges were willing to leave the homes in joint ownership for "a few years," very few were willing to let it remain unsold until small children attained majority. Even fewer were willing to make an exception for an older woman who, they asserted, didn't "need" the home anymore (even if her college age children considered it their home as well) . . . .

DISPOSITION OF OTHER MARITAL ASSETS

There is a clear trend between 1968 (under the old law) and 1972 and 1977 (under the new law) toward an equal division of community assets and debts. This is shown in Table 3.

Although the pattern is evident for each of the assets listed, some sex typing of awards still persists. For example, wives continued to be awarded more homes and household furnishings than were husbands (when there were sufficient assets to offset these awards with items of comparable value for the husband). Similarly, husbands continued to be more likely to be awarded the family business and the single family car. (In families with two or more cars (not shown), an equal division was more common with each spouse keeping one car.)

The pattern of dividing each of the major family assets—the family business, pensions, money, and debts—is discussed below.

Disposition of a Business

It has traditionally been assumed that a business belongs to the husband, even in cases where it is legally part of a couple's community property. In the past, the easy property settlement in this regard was one in which the divorcing parties owned both a home and a business: the wife could be awarded the home, the husband could be awarded the business, and the two assets were assumed to balance each other out. Since an equal division was not required under the old law, identifying the exact values of the two assets was not considered necessary.

Table 3 reveals that husbands were almost always awarded the business (91 percent of all cases) in 1968 under the old law. This pattern remained strong under the new law in both 1972 and 1977, with businesses awarded to the husband about 80 percent of the time. (These awards were typically offset by notes, with interest, payable over time or by awards of comparable value to the wife.)

These data reveal an interesting paradox; while the courts are anxious to sell the matrimonial home to effect an equal division of property, they do not seem to feel any similar pressure when it comes to a

TABLE 3   DIVISION OF ASSETS AND DEBTS UNDER FAULT AND NO-FAULT LAWS

	Fault Law	No Fault Law	
Division of Assets	*[1968]*	*[1972]*	*[1977]*
Family Home			
Majority to husband*	16%	24%	19%
Approximately equal division**	23	25	35
Majority to wife	61	51	46
Household furnishings			
Majority to husband*	6	8	7
Approximately equal division**	3	5	42
Majority to wife	91	87	51
Single family car			
Majority to husband*	62%	59%	54%
Approximately equal division**	—	—	—
Majority to wife	39	42	44
Money, stocks, and bonds			
Majority to husband*	27%	38%	24%
Approximately equal division**	29	27	50
Majority to wife	44	35	26
Family business			
Majority to husband*	91%	78%	81%
Approximately equal division**	0	13	14
Majority to wife	10	9	6
Community-property debts			
Majority to husband*	88%	85%	58%
Approximately equal division**	6	7	29
Majority to wife	7	8	13

*Majority = over 60%.

**Approximately equal = between 40 and 59%.

This table is based on random samples of court dockets, Los Angeles County, California, 1968, 1972, and 1977.

business. Instead, the courts go to great length to keep the business intact (and typically in the name of the husband) and utilize the same procedures that they find unworkable when discussing the delayed sale of the home.

The courts face three questions in dealing with community-property business at divorce: How much is it worth? How should the equity be divided? And, who should retain possession and control?

The task of determining the worth of a business has become much more critical since the equal division rule was instituted. Attorneys report that they now have to be more careful and thorough in establishing its value. In fact, in response to the question, "What has been the main impact of the new law on the way you prepare a case?" the most common reply was that there is more time spent on the financial aspects of the case and the valuation of property and businesses.

Similarly, when asked, "Is there any change in the skills you need as a lawyer?" 69 percent of the attorneys mentioned an increased emphasis on finance-related skills such as projecting the tax consequences of awards, reading financial statements, evaluating appraisals of businesses and pensions, and working with accountants and other expert witnesses. As one lawyer put it, "You spend less time investigating dirt and more time on business ledgers."

We were surprised to discover that, despite the need for more precise valuation spurred by the new equal division requirement, the old-law practice of valuing a business as equal to the price of the house was still fairly common. As one attorney said:

> I think since property does have to be divided equally, the courts are much more inclined, assuming that the husband is running the family business, to find a substantial value [to the business] that offsets the house. I tried a case last week and surprise, surprise, the court found a $40,000 value for the business and by an amazing coincidence the equity in the family home was $40,000.

Many attorneys pointed out that this method of division tends to favor the husband. For example, one attorney said:

> I think there's a tendency on the part of the judges to give the wife less than one-half of the business, even under the new law, and it works this way: You take a going business which the husband is usually awarded. In evaluating that business, the judge has wide discretion. The wife will put on the stand an expert who will value the business at, let us say, $300,000, and the husband will put on an expert who values the business at $100,000. If the judge wants to lean in the direction of the husband, and many of the judges are obviously husband-oriented, he'll take the lesser value and award [the business] to the husband. This is especially easy for him to do if the house is worth $100,000 or $150,000. He sets the business as equal to the house, and the husband picks up an extra $75,000 or $100,000. I find that happening all the time.

Another attorney pointed out that the husband generally has the advantage of controlling business profits and losses and can manipulate its balance sheet to a certain extent. In addition, since he controls expenditures, he can charge both living expenses and luxuries to the business. As one attorney suggested, the possibilities are endless:

> The husbands always get the break. They have the business acumen, so they get the biggest piece. The skill of the wife's lawyer determines how close to one-half she gets. In a family business, if she takes her share in stock, she never gets a dividend. He keeps the profits for himself by buying cars, a boat, etc., for the business. Even if the wife gets one-half

of the business, the husband still has control. He can threaten not to work and he can appoint a receiver and put the business up for sale. Meanwhile, he can start a new corporation. No one will buy the old business, as the husband probably won't sign a covenant not to open a competitive business. The wife always has the uphill battle.

Other attorneys, while agreeing that granting control of the business to the husband may give him more than half the property, argue that this measure is necessary:

> In an ongoing business, the owner always gets the biggest piece because much of the value cannot be proven. The wife usually gets less than half of the true value. But you've got to be realistic. You don't want to kill the entrepreneur goose.
>
> Under the old law, if the judge really felt strongly about giving the husband the business, they'd find enough fault on her side to give it to him without very much offset. Now they have to give her what they regard as a fair value. While the values are generally low, nevertheless they are better than they used to be, because the courts are forced to place a value on the business.
>
> But the reason they're low is not because the judges are necessarily sympathetic to businessmen, but because the question is, "Where's the money going to come from to buy her out?" Then you've got to look at the kind of cash flow he's got. You deduct his taxes, because he's going to have to pay his federal income taxes and so on, and look at the net dollars he has available to him. Then you've got to pay for the asset, child support, and the alimony from the same net dollars. And you've got to leave him enough so that he has an incentive to go on, which has to be more than half.

While many judges echoed these sentiments and asserted that *the husband needed the business*, or that the husband could not afford to buy out his wife's share of the business, few of them used the same logic to argue that *the wife (or the children) needed the family home*. The results of these attitudes are reflected in Table 3 above, as the husband is awarded most of the family business in 81 percent of the cases. In addition, if a business remains in joint ownership, possession and control is invariably awarded to the husband (88 percent of the time according to the attorneys), because judges say it is unfair and unrealistic to expect him to share control with his wife. As one judge said, "you can't run a business by majority rule." . . .

Disposition of pensions

In California 24% of the husbands acquired pension rights during marriage, compared to only 11% of the wives. This striking difference in pension ownership results from the structure of female work patterns—which accommodate family responsibilities and are less likely to include continuous full-time employment—and the structure of the labor market where women are concentrated in jobs with less pension coverage.

In 1976 the California Supreme Court held that both non-vested and vested pensions acquired during marriage were community property and were subject to equal division. By 1977 (not shown in Table 3) our data show that pensions were included in the community property and divided at divorce. For younger couples most of the California attorneys we interviewed favored "cashing-out" the pension at the time of the divorce, with an offsetting award of other assets to the non-worker spouse.

For older couples however, a "future-share" approach was preferred. When a couple divorces in their fifties, and if one spouse faces limited prospects for employment after divorce, both spouses will need the income from the primary wage earner's pension. (In many of these cases the husband's pension was the most valuable asset appraised at divorce.) In these cases the "division" of the pension was likely to be delayed until the pension benefits were paid, with a "future share" awarded to each spouse. (Once again this seemingly fair solution may have unanticipated inequities: Because the working spouse, who is typically the husband, retains control over the timing and the structure of the pension, the non-employee spouse, who is typically the wife, can find herself seriously restricted or barred from receiving her full share of the pension benefits.)

Disposition of Savings, Stocks, and Bonds

Money stocks and bonds are most amenable to an equal division and their disposition reflects the equalization trend observed for all community assets. It is not surprising, however, to find only about a quarter of these assets awarded to one or the other spouse because these assets are commonly used to offset other awards and to equalize the overall division of property.

Disposition of Community Property Debts

The court records reveal a rising percentage of divorcing couples with debts, from 15 percent in 1968, to 26 percent in 1977 . . . .

Under the old law, the husband was typically ordered to pay the community debts because it was assumed that he was the wage earner with the income to pay them. Eighty percent of the Los Angeles judges said they generally "awarded" the debts to the husband under the old law. Only 8 percent said they typically split the debts, while another 8 percent said they tried to "award" the debts to the spouse who kept the property.

Here again, the data from court records show a steady increase in the percentage of debts that are divided equally. Nevertheless, the husband continues to be ordered to pay the community debts in more than half of the cases—58 percent in 1977, compared to 80 percent in 1972 and 88 percent in 1968. The share of debts to be paid by wives has increased under the new law. Yet even in 1977, only 29 percent of the debts were divided equally (see Table 3 above).

The attorneys in our study reported that the major difference in the way debts are handled under no-fault is that while the husband is still required to pay them off, he now is given a "credit" for the obligation by being awarded an asset of equivalent value.

In recent years case law developments have clarified the rule for the disposition of community debts. In general, debts are to be considered along with assets, and the total net worth is to be divided equally between the two spouses. If, however, there are only debts at the time of divorce, or if the debts exceed the assets so that the community has a negative net worth, the judge has the discretion to dispose of the debts in an equitable manner depending on the earning capacities of the two spouses and other relevant factors. In addition, there is a statutory exception for debts incurred for educational purposes: they may be awarded to the student spouse who benefited from the educational loan . . . .

CONCLUSION: IS EQUAL MORE EQUITABLE?

Is marital property being divided "equally" upon divorce? Has the equal division rule brought more equitable results?

On the one hand, the data presented in this chapter show that the divorce law reforms have brought a dramatic change in the way property is divided. On the whole, property (as the term is presently defined) is being divided more equally in accord with the explicit directives of the new law.

On the other hand, the word "equality" suggests fairness and equity for all parties involved. In this light, the results of the legal reform are less clear. The required equal division of property has brought more forced sales of family assets, especially the family home, so that the proceeds can be divided between the two spouses. The result is increased dislocation and disruption in the lives of minor children (in contrast to the old law pattern in which the wife with custody of minor children was typically awarded the family home). This does not seem fair, in that the needs and interests of the children are not considered. It is as if the family consisted of two people—a husband and a wife—rather than the average four people. Under the equal division rule, "equality" means that three people (the wife and, on average, two children) share one-half of the marital assets while one person (the husband) is awarded the other half for himself.

One obvious solution to this inequity is to allow an exception to—or delay of—the equal division rule to accommodate the interests of minor children. This would recognize that the parent who cares for children both needs and is entitled to a larger share of the family's resources.

In a sense, it is ironic to label this an exception, since most divorcing couples have children. It might be wiser to begin to formulate policy for this average case and then worry about the exceptions when there are no children . . . .

A second problem of "equality" emerges from these data: a 50/50 division of family property may not produce equality of results—or equality of standards of living after divorce—if the two spouses are unequally situated at the point of the divorce. This is most evident in the situation of the older housewife under the new law. In contrast to the traditional pattern of awarding a larger share of the community assets to the wife, ostensibly because she was "innocent" but in practice because her greater need was recognized, the new rules require that she be treated "equally." Yet after a marital life devoted to homemaking, she is typically without substantial skills and experience in the labor force and typically needs a greater share of the property to cushion the income loss she suffers at divorce. She is, simply put, not in an equal economic position at divorce. The traditional law took her special needs into consideration and gave her more than half of the family property because she needed more than half. Today, with only half of the tangible assets and with a lesser capacity to earn a reasonable income after divorce, she is severely disadvantaged by the so-called "equal" division of property.

One solution to this inequity is to allow a second exception to—or to require a delay in applying—the equal division rule for women who have been housewives and mothers in marriages of long duration. If these women are at a clear disadvantage in their ability to earn a comparable income after divorce, and if the detriment is a result of their family responsibilities during marriage—both of which are likely conditions in such cases—then they should be awarded a larger share of the property to achieve the goal of "equality of results," i.e., quality in the post-divorce standards of living of the two spouses. Here again, it seems ironic to label the remedy for this common situation an exception. In fact, a substantial majority of divorced women have either raised children or are currently raising children, and these responsibilities are directly related to their disadvantaged earning capacity at divorce. These "average" divorced women ought to be awarded more property in recognition of their greater need.

A third issue is suggested by the question of whether the equal division rule has brought more equitable results: what is the basis for comparison? In California, the implicit comparison is with the traditional law, under which wives typically received more than half of the property (especially if the family's major asset was the home). But this does not mean all wives benefited under the old rules, or that awards based on fault produced more equitable results. As we have seen, a woman who was labeled guilty under the old law was barred from a larger share of property even if she had minor children. This was so even if she had been a homemaker for 30 years. Thus the fault system created its own inequities, and there are few incentives to return to it in order to provide the average "innocent" wife with the property award she needs. Rather, the time has come to fashion rules that overcome the inequities of both systems. What we need is a new standard based on equality of results for the two spouses . . . .

The question of whether the equal division rule produces more equitable results invites another comparison: How fair are the results of this rule when compared with the results of the "equitable distribution" standard used in most other states? While there has been no comparable empirical research on property awards in common law states, two recent studies, which rely on testimonies at hearings and reported cases, are suggestive.

The first is a 1983 report by a judicial task force in New Jersey on women in the courts. After conducting hearings throughout the state, the task force concluded that their state's equitable distributions standard typically resulted in awards to wives that were significantly *less than half* (i.e., 35 to 40 percent of the family property. As the judicial report states:

> Attorneys from all parts of the State observed that there appears to be an unofficial standard that the wife will receive no more than 35 percent to 40 percent of the net marital assets in equitable distribution, . . . even when there are small children in the custody of the wife.

They concluded that "women suffer inequitable long range outcomes with respect to property division."

A second review of property awards in an equitable distribution state, New York, similarly concludes that wives are awarded less than half of the marital property in the vast majority of cases. Attorneys Harriet Cohen and Adria Hillman analyzed the 70 reported decisions during the first four years of New York's Equitable Distribution Law and concluded that "the courts are not treating the wife as an equal partner in the marriage." As they summarize their findings:

> . . . judicial dispositions of marital property upon the dissolution of a marriage reflect that property is not being distributed equally to the marital partners. Except in rare instances, such as where a husband attempted to murder a wife and was in prison, where a wife was dying of cancer, or where a wife had had sufficient foresight to take back promissory notes for the invaluable medical school education she had afforded her physician husband during the marriage, . . . dependent wives whether they worked in the home or in the paid market place . . . were relegated to less than a 50 percent overall share of marital property; . . . de minimis share of business and professional practices

which, in addition, the courts undervalued; . . . and inadequate or no
counsel fee awards. These findings demonstrate that the marriage partners' contributions to each other and to the marriage itself are not
being viewed as of equal value . . . .

These conclusions are supported by attorney Lester Wallman, who
chaired the Legislative Committee of the Family Law Section of the
New York State Bar Association. Although Wallman originally supported the "equitable" division law in New York, by 1982 he called for
its revision and chastised the courts for failing to carry out the law's
goal of treating wives as full economic equals:

> It was the intention of this bill that women were to share on an equitable
> basis in the distribution of the marital assets. But recent court decisions
> have held that medical and legal practices and certain family businesses
> were to be excluded from distribution to wives. More discouraging is
> that the yardstick for distribution of assets is being disregarded by the
> courts, inasmuch as women are not getting equitable distribution but
> seem to be averaging only twenty-five to thirty-five percent of the total
> marital estate.

These studies indicate that wives are likely to be awarded less than
half of the tangible property in equitable distribution states. Although
some legal scholars, and some practicing attorneys, continue to assert
the contrary—and to claim that wives are better off under these discretionary rules because judges can award them *more than half* of the
property in case of obvious need—there is simply *no empirical evidence* to suggest that this is what typically happens. Perhaps in cases in
which the sole family asset is a home, the judge may be favorably disposed to award it to a young mother or older housewife. But the data
reveal that this occurs in a minority of the cases: it is the exception, not
the rule.

What, then, of our question about whether "equal" or "equitable"
rules are preferable? Clearly, equitable distribution standards are not
more favorable to wives. Wives are, in fact, likely to fare better under
rules that guarantee them an equal share of the marital property. Thus,
rather than abandon the equal division rule, the best route to reform
seems to be to delay its application in cases in which the family home
is the only significant asset . . . .

THE NEW PROPERTY OF CAREER ASSETS

The word "property" evokes an image of substantial assets. When we
think of dividing property most people assume that there will be
enough property to cushion the financial hardships of divorce. However, our research indicates that most divorcing couples have very little

property; most have cars and furniture and television sets, but only half own or are purchasing a home at the time of the divorce, and even fewer own a business or pension.

Even more surprising is the low monetary value of the property they do own. About half of the divorcing couples in California had less than $20,000 net worth (in 1984 dollars). If that property is divided equally, each spouse will receive less than $10,000 worth of assets. That is hardly a security blanket; it is not likely to be enough for even the down payment on a home.

These data are open to two interpretations. One is that most divorcing couples do not have much property to divide upon divorce. The alternative is that most divorcing couples have invested in something else—something the courts do not yet label as property—and that their real wealth lies in this other type of investment.

In fact, *most couples do have another form of wealth: they have what I call "career assets"—their earning capacities and the benefits and entitlements of their employment.* These assets are at least as valuable, and are often much more valuable, than the tangible assets they have acquired in the course of their marriage. Our data show that in less than one year the average couple will earn more money than all of their tangible assets are worth together. This fact underscores the value of earning capacity, which is only one of the many forms of the "new property."

A major theme in my analysis of property awards is that the nature of property itself is changing. We no longer invest in family farms—today we invest in ourselves and in our ability to earn future income—that is, in our human capital and our careers. The new property that results from these investments includes enhanced earning capacities, pensions, and job-related benefits. Since these new forms of property are often the major assets acquired during marriage, I argue that the law must recognize them as part of the marital property that is divided at divorce.

For example, although California requires an equal division of property, I believe the courts are actually violating this mandate because they allow one spouse, typically the husband, to keep the couple's "career assets" for himself. If one partner builds his or her earning capacity during marriage, while the other stays out of the labor force to be a homemaker and parent, the earning partner has acquired the major asset of the marriage. If that person's earning power—or the income it produces—is not divided upon divorce, the two spouses are left with very unequal shares of their family assets. Thus, the courts cannot divide marital property "equally" if they do not recognize and divide these career assets as marital property.

"Career assets" are the tangible and intangible assets that are acquired as part of either spouse's career or career potential (Weitzman, 1974, 1985). The term includes a large array of specific assets such as pensions and retirement benefits, a professional education and license, enhanced earning capacity, medical and hospital insurance, the goodwill value of a business, entitlement to company goods and services, and government benefits such as social security.

The first rationale for recognizing career assets as marital property is that most married couples acquire them in much the same manner as they acquire tangible assets. A career developed in the course of a marriage is just like the income that is earned or the real property that is accumulated as a product of the couple's joint efforts and resources. As a result of the couple's united efforts, one spouse may obtain a network of professional contacts, a valuable education or training, a license to practice a trade or profession, job experience and seniority, a track record and reputation, and professional or business good will.

While this may seem self-evident in families in which the husband is the sole wage earner, it is also evident in two-income families. Even though both spouses work, it is common for them to give priority to one spouse's career in the expectation that both will share the benefits of that decision, and even dual-career professional couples seem to follow this pattern.

If a spouse enters a marriage with a preestablished career, that person's career assets should be regarded as his or her separate property. But if a career is partially or wholly built during marriage, it seems reasonable to view that career (and the assets that are attached to it) as a product of the marital partnership. If only part of a career is developed during marriage, courts should recognize both the separate and joint interests in it, just as they do with tangible property. And if both spouses' careers have been developed during marriage, the assets of both careers should be calculated and the difference adjusted.

The second rationale for recognizing career assets as marital property is that many of them are a form of deferred compensation for work performed during marriage. Many career assets are benefits that employees earn, even though they may not be paid directly to the worker and may not be used immediately. For example, compensation packages include such career assets as life, health, hospital, and disability insurance; the right to unemployment and social security benefits; entitlement to discounted or free goods and services; the right to paid sick leave and vacation benefits; and the right to a pension and other retirement benefits.

The third, and one of the most persuasive arguments for recognizing career assets as marital property, comes from the conception of a marital partnership as it is expressed by the divorcing couples themselves. Consider, for example, the following quotation from a 51-year-old woman who was married to a college professor for 30 years:

We married at 21, with no money. . . . When he was a graduate student I worked as a secretary, then typed other papers at night to make extra money. When he became an assistant professor I "retired" to raise our children but I never stopped working for him—typing, editing, working on his books. . . . My college English degree was very useful for translating his brilliant ideas into comprehensible sentences. . . . My name never appeared on the title page as his co-author, where it belonged, only in the dedication or thank you's. . . . There's more, lots more—the hours mothering his graduate students, hosting departmental parties, finding homes for visiting professors. . . . I was always available to help . . .

I got $700 a month for three years. The judge said, I was "smart and healthy enough to get a job." I am to "report back like a school girl" in 3 years. Never mind that I am 51. . . . Never mind that I *had* a job and did it well and am old enough to be entitled to a pension. . . . It's not that I regret my life or didn't enjoy what I did. *But it was supposed to be a partnership*—a 50:50 split. It isn't fair that he gets to keep it. It isn't fair for the court to treat it as his. . . . I earned it just as much as he did.

Sharing and supporting one's spouse's career may be equally important to younger couples. For example, in a parallel case, a young woman explained that instead of taking a job, she "invested in her husband because they were partners in his career."

Although I focus on three types of career assets here—pensions, professional education, and medical insurance—the concept of new forms of property in employment-related benefits extends far beyond the scope of this discussion. . . .

How does this discussion of career assets affect our conclusions about the extent to which property is being divided equally or equitably upon divorce?

We have seen that career assets, along with the family home, are often the most valuable assets a couple owns at the time of the divorce. If courts do not recognize some or all of these assets as marital property, they are excluding a major portion of a couple's property from the pool of property to be divided upon divorce. In addition, if the courts treat these assets as the sole property of the major wage earner, they are in most cases allowing the husband to keep the family's most valuable assets. It is like saying we are going to divide the family jewels, but will set aside the diamonds for the husband. Because career assets are the "diamonds" of marital property, it is impossible to have either an equal or an equitable division of marital property without them. ☐

NOTES AND QUESTIONS

1. In a later article, "Marital Property: Its Transformation and Division in the United States," in Lenore Weitzman and Mavis Maclean, eds. *The Economic Consequences of Divorce: The International Perspective,* Oxford University Press, 1992, pp. 85–142, Weitzman discusses the tension between two of the aims of the law in dividing marital property at divorce: recognizing the marital "partnership" by recognizing each spouse's contribution to the acquisition of marital property; and providing a remedy for marriage-based dependency and need. (For example, the needs of minor children or an older homemaker who does not have the earning capacity to support herself.)

It is easy to see how these two goals may conflict. If the only tangible asset is the family home, the partnership-theory standard would lead to an equal award to each partner, while the need-based standard would lead to an award to the custodial parent or older homemaker.

2. In another section of this chapter in her book, Weitzman compares English law and practice with that of California. In England, under the Matrimonial Causes Act of 1973, "a fault-based divorce is still permitted if one party is guilty of marital misconduct." The "innocent" spouse, too, can prevent a divorce until the parties have lived apart for five years. This gives an "innocent" spouse some leverage—she can delay a divorce for five years, and this is an important bargaining chip.

England is not a community property jurisdiction. Before 1970, each spouse simply "owned the property he or she held title to or earned in marriage." This meant, in most cases, that husbands held title to far more property than wives. Under English divorce law reforms of 1970 and 1973, courts gained the power to divide up the property in "reasonable" ways, so as to do "justice." The rule of thumb has been to give the wife one-third of the assets. There is considerable variation, however; and wives can get anything all the way from zero to the bulk of their husband's property.

English practice puts heavy emphasis on the welfare of the children. It is more likely that the wife and children will be permitted to stay in the family home, than in California. It is common in England to award the house to the wife until the children are grown.

Another major difference is the much greater amount of discretion English law allows the judge. But the most important difference, according to Weitzman, is that the two systems "rely on different *conceptions of justice and equity*. In England, justice is typically seen as requiring provisions that assure the future security of a dependent housewife (and any minor children in her custody) after divorce." This means a division of family resources "so as to provide roughly equal standards of living for husbands and wives after divorce." In California, on the other hand, the "underlying assumption is that justice is best assured by severing the financial ties of the marriage, awarding both the husband and wife one-half of the family assets," and giving each one the "freedom" to start over again. The California woman "is . . . expected to bear the economic consequences of the divorce without help from her former husband." The California vision of justice "relies heavily on the assumption of a new equality between the sexes." But that equality simply does not exist in the real world. "Equal" treatment in California thus means that "divorced women . . . will be left alone to shoulder the economic disadvantages they face."

Since the English *rule* is not that different from the "equitable" division rule in New York, why do women do better in England than New York (if this is in fact the case)?

3. Weitzman argues that under the prior law, wives had greater bargaining power. Often a husband wanted a divorce so that he could remarry. A wife would only supply the needed cooperation if the husband agreed to a favorable property settlement and award of alimony. After no-fault divorce, a husband no longer needed to buy his wife's cooperation at such a high price.

Marygold S. Melli, in "Constructing a Social Problem: The Post-Divorce Plight of Women and Children," 1987 *American Bar Foundation Research*

Journal 759, suggests that "the promise of post-divorce support under traditional law was never fulfilled . . . . Alimony has never been a source of post-divorce support for a majority of women . . . . [H]ad she [Weitzman] made the same investigation in 1960 when fault divorce was still in its prime, she would have found those women in the same straits." Melli concludes:

[B]y assuming that the disastrous economic consequences of divorce were caused by a change in the law, *The Divorce Revolution* makes the problem appear to be a simple one: a few more changes in the law and the problems will be rectified . . . . But the consequences of divorce for women who devote their major energies to homemaking and the children for whom they care is a problem that has long preceded the current controversies. It defies easy solution and has survived any number of divorce reforms . . . .

Weitzman, in "Bringing the Law Back In," 1987 *American Bar Foundation Research Journal* 791, 797, responded: "[I]t seems clear to me that we can . . . greatly improve the lot of many divorced women and children in the immediate future, by providing them with more property, alimony, and child support. *And we can do that by changing the law.*" What does "changing the law" mean in this context? Would it be as easy in the 1990s as during the 1960s and early 1970s to make the kinds of changes that might provide "more property, alimony, and child support?"

4. Martha Fineman, in "Implementing Equality: Ideology, Contradiction and Social Change—A Study of Rhetoric and Results in the Regulation of the Consequences of Divorce," 1983 *Wisconsin Law Review* 789, studied the passage of no-fault divorce in Wisconsin. The reformers who pushed the new law, Fineman says:

appeared to have shared some significant socioeconomic characteristics, and these may have influenced the ways they approached the issue of divorce reform. All expressed strong identification with women's issues and the women's movement, and most identified themselves as feminists . . . . They were all well-educated women and most were working in professional capacities; several were attorneys. At the same time, they had established stable, traditional family relationships; most were married and had children . . . [M]ost of these women had no direct experience with divorce either in their personal lives or in their professional capacities as attorneys . . . .

The reformers were committed to gender neutrality. They believed housewives were being victimized by the existing law which typically awarded them one-third or less of the assets at divorce. They did not consider nonprofessional working mothers, women who supported their husbands and children during marriage or women who were in their second marriage and had obligations and assets from their first. Fineman argues that the reformers failed to look at need rather than an equal division of assets because this might have characterized women as less capable of looking out for themselves. Nonetheless, some women, she argues, are hurt by laws that appear to be gender neutral but that fail to take into account the actual social position and economic circumstances of women who are not part of the social and economic elite. As a result, there were "many women whose circumstances have not been addressed by the legislation and who will not benefit from the reform."

Would a better law have come out had there been more conflict and controversy before the legislature? Are nonprofessional working mothers a likely lobbying group? If not, who might have represented them? Would feminist activists have championed their cause? Even if such feminists had tried such advocacy, would they have seen what nonprofessional working mothers wanted and needed?

5. Is there a way that a study could have been designed and implemented *before* the enactment of no-fault laws that would have allowed us to anticipate the results observed by Weitzman? Why do legislatures so rarely carry out such studies of potential impact?

6. In the light of Weitzman's findings, what should be done? What kinds of policy would make the divorce process fairer to women? Weitzman does not think we ought to return to a fault-based system. Would a system of mandatory mediation, letting each side to the divorce put forth its wants and needs, end up in a more equitable distribution of property? There is some reason to be skeptical; see Penelope E. Bryan, "Killing Us Softly: Divorce Mediation and the Politics of Power," 40 *Buffalo Law Review* 441 (1992), and the discussion of this issue following Mnookin and Kornhauser, Reading #9, on p. 111.

7. In 1986 the California legislature responded to Weitzman's book, and the public debate it stimulated, by establishing a blue ribbon "Task Force on Family Equity." The Task Force was charged with reviewing the findings of *The Divorce Revolution,* Weitzman's book, and developing specific proposals for new legislation "to equalize the effects of divorce."

In its final report the Task Force recommended 23 pieces of legislation (on child support, custody, alimony, and judicial education as well as those on property) largely following the policy recommendations in Weitzman's book. As of 1990, 18 of these recommendations were introduced as bills in the California legislature and, to date, 14 have become law.

One of these bills, passed in 1988, returned some discretion to judges to defer the sale of the family home when a couple does not have enough assets to award the family home to a custodial spouse and still provide for an equal division of property. This was to be done when it would be in the best interests of the children. See California Family Code, Sections 3800–10 (1994). What is the likely impact of such a provision?

8. What is the source of the problem? Is it the way the law was drafted, and the structures it set up? You could argue that the answer is yes: after all, the before-after differences Weitzman found are quite striking. But you could also argue that it is wrong to blame the law itself and its structures. The New York law, which is quite different, turns out also to disadvantage women. If so, the villain must be American society itself, which is dominated by men and systematically disadvantages women. Yet surely this situation did not suddenly get worse when California passed its no-fault law. How then do you explain Weitzman's findings?

SOCIAL IMPACT—THE IMPORTANCE OF COMMUNICATION
NETWORKS

44. *Tarasoff, Myth and Reality: An Empirical Study of Private Law in Action*

Daniel J. Givelber,
William J. Bowers
and Carolyn L. Blitch

1984 *Wisconsin Law Review* 443

☐ When the California Supreme Court ruled in *Tarasoff v. Regents of the University of California*[150] that psychotherapists owe a duty of care to third parties threatened by their patients, it did so in the face of claims from professional organizations that this new duty would interfere seriously with the practice of psychotherapy. The court announced that "[i]n this risk-infested society we can hardly tolerate the further exposure to danger that would result from a concealed knowledge of the therapist that his patient was lethal." The court appeared confident that its ruling would not interfere with psychotherapy, particularly with respect to the potentially violent, but the source of that confidence was not readily apparent. In *Tarasoff,* as in other well known tort decisions, a court announced a rule designed to change private behavior without reliable data regarding the practices it was intending to change, the extent of the problem it was trying to remedy, or the costs which the proposed cure would impose. Moreover, like other appellate courts, the California Supreme Court had insufficient means of securing this information before it ruled, and no mechanism for monitoring the impact of its decision.

Courts often create tort rules in the context of a dispute between a seriously injured party and the putative injurer, and thus are subject to the pressures created by sympathy for the plight of the plaintiff. There may be vivid evidence of the plaintiff's suffering, and possibly testimony dealing with industry practice and the feasibility of precautions and safety measures. Rarely, however, will there be reliable data concerning what is, to a trial court, a legally irrelevant issue—the costs and benefits generated by a new rule applicable to all future conduct. In place of reliable data, the court will be confronted with the exaggerated and conflicting arguments of counsel. Lawyers, those in academia as well as those in practice, are among the most skilled practitioners of

150. 17 Cal.3d 425, 551 P.2d 334 (1976).

"worst case" analysis. Judges, in turn, are among our most practiced skeptics. This combination of circumstances may often lead appellate courts to discount a defendant's prediction of disaster. Whether for this reason or others, the California Supreme Court in *Tarasoff* dismissed as "speculative" the professional claims that the new duty would hamper psychotherapy while embracing the equally speculative conclusion that the new rule would enhance public safety.

The court, like other appellate courts, also lacked the means by which to communicate its new rule to the group whose behavior it was designed to govern—California psychotherapists. Once copies of the opinion were mailed to the parties and made available to the public, the court's role was at an end. The court had no control over who learned about the case or what they learned. Nor did the court have any role in initiating enforcement of its rule; that remains the prerogative of the injured. Yet, if the court's ruling was to enhance public safety, someone had to tell the therapists about their new obligation and how to meet it.

Who filled this role? It seems doubtful that psychotherapists, or any other group of dispersed individuals, retain lawyers to advise them of changes in their tort obligations. If so, then other groups such as the media or professional organizations (including the very ones opposed to the duty in the first instance), may have had the primary role in educating therapists as to what they were now supposed to do. The information about *Tarasoff* disseminated by these professional organizations and publications may well have skewed the court's message to reflect the concerns and perspectives of mental health professionals. The message may also have travelled further than anticipated. While *Tarasoff* is a California opinion, it deals with a question which concerns therapists everywhere. Professional discussions may understandably concentrate on the substance of *Tarasoff,* without emphasizing its limited jurisdictional reach.

This Article presents data relevant to the issues before the California Supreme Court in *Tarasoff,* as well as to the broader debate of how tort rules influence behavior. We have investigated a number of the claims concerning psychotherapist understanding of and response to *Tarasoff.* We have two goals in mind with regard to the findings we present. First we propose to substitute data for rhetoric with respect to the *Tarasoff* debate itself. Given the publicity surrounding the *Tarasoff* case and the amount of commentary it has spawned, it is important to evaluate how much the *Tarasoff* duty has in fact contradicted and influenced psychotherapeutic practice. Our second goal is to present empirical data regarding how an appellate decision becomes translated into a rule of conduct. All agree that *Tarasoff* was an important decision—that it would have an impact on psychotherapeutic practice. But how are court decisions disseminated and presented? Our findings raise questions about the accepted wisdom that courts should not attempt to articulate specific rules of conduct . . . .

II. THE *TARASOFF* CONTROVERSY

The *Tarasoff* decision of the California Supreme Court held that a therapist has an obligation to exercise reasonable care to protect those whose physical well-being is threatened by the therapist's patient. To trigger this duty, a mythical, if familiar, figure called the "reasonable therapist" must believe that the patient actually might harm some identified or identifiable person. Once this belief exists, the therapist must exercise care to protect the potential victim. Warning the likely victim of the potential danger, the California Supreme Court has suggested, likely would be a response under many circumstances, but the specification of what care is reasonable "depends upon the circumstances of each case, and should not be governed by any hard and fast rule."

The version of *Tarasoff* requiring therapists to exercise "reasonable care" to protect potential victims is the second, and now official, *Tarasoff* decision. In the first, and subsequently withdrawn, opinion *(Tarasoff I)*, the California court imposed an explicit duty on therapists to warn potential victims threatened by their patients.

When *Tarasoff I* was originally published, the Northern California Psychiatric Society spearheaded a drive to persuade the court to reconsider its ruling. In a petition seeking reconsideration, the Society, the American Psychiatric Association, and state and local organizations of psychologists and social workers, all of whom joined together as *amici curiae,* successfully urged the California Supreme Court to rehear the case.

The brief seeking review of *Tarasoff I* argued that the decision severely and negatively impinged upon the work of psychotherapists and upon those in need of psychotherapy. This argument rested on a number of points. First, the duty to warn was ill-advised since it compromised the confidentiality necessary for effective psychotherapy, particularly with regard to potentially violent patients. Furthermore, it contradicted professional ethical standards which both emphasize the need for privacy in therapeutic communications and command therapists to concern themselves solely with the welfare of their patients. Second, the duty to warn would ultimately decrease the public safety as well as the liberty of potentially violent patients, rather than increase both as the court hoped, because awareness of the legal obligation would either complicate the treatment of potentially violent patients or deter therapists altogether. Those therapists who did treat such patients would be left with few realistic options other than involuntary commitment and treatment. Third, since therapists tend to overpredict future violence and share no legitimate criteria for evaluating the likelihood of violence, requiring therapists to warn whenever a "reasonable therapist" would evaluate the patient as imminently dangerous was both ill advised and unfair since it required therapists to act according to a professional standard which did not exist.

In July 1976, eighteen months after the original decision, the Cali-

fornia Supreme Court issued a new opinion which modified the therapist's obligation from warning the potential victim to exercising reasonable care to protect potential victims. Warning the threatened third
party was still prominently mentioned as an example of reasonable care
but was no longer considered the exclusive means by which a therapist
could meet his or her legal obligations . . . .

III. STUDY METHODOLOGY

We surveyed a sample of 2875 psychiatrists, psychologists and social
workers located in Boston, Chicago, Detroit, Los Angeles, New York,
Philadelphia, San Francisco and Washington, D.C.–the eight largest
standard metropolitan statistical units as of the 1970 census. The sample was drawn from the biographical directories of the American Psychiatric Association, the American Psychological Association, and the
National Association of Social Workers. For each professional group in
each location, the sample was first stratified by location, profession,
experience and apparent setting of practice (private, institutional, or
both). Respondents were then randomly selected from within each cell.
The survey was mailed early in 1980, and 59.5% of the sample
returned questionnaires—48% of the psychiatrists, 62% of the psychologists and 68% of the social workers. The respondents were well distributed in terms of the sample criteria—profession, location, experience, and type.

Since our survey was designed in part to measure legal impact and
since the first *Tarasoff* decision was promulgated five years prior to the
date of our investigation, we faced the twin difficulties of asking our
respondents to recall their behavior, and changes in that behavior, over
a five-year period and of relying on our respondents to describe accurately what motivated any behavioral changes which they did report.
Moreover, knowing that *Tarasoff* was a highly publicized and politicized case, we were afraid that our respondents might follow a "party
line" propagated within their professions in answering the questionnaire.

To deal with the "party line" problem we decided to separate our
questions about behavior from our specific questions concerning the
Tarasoff case and not to mention the decision until the very end of the
questionnaire. We originally went even further and prepared two versions of the questionnaire. One version contained all questions, including those about *Tarasoff*. The other version was divided into two parts:
the first contained all questions except those dealing with *Tarasoff;* the
second contained questions about *Tarasoff* alone and was to be sent to
respondents only after they had returned the first part of the questionnaire. We pre-tested both versions on equal samples of 100 therapists
in Boston and San Francisco and found no meaningful differences in
responses, whether *Tarasoff* was mentioned only at the end of the ques-

tionnaire, or not at all. Since there was a lower response rate from the therapists who received the bifurcated questionnaire, we decided to proceed with the single questionnaire with the *Tarasoff* questions placed at the end . . . .

A. KNOWLEDGE OF *TARASOFF*

1. Do Therapists Know about Tarasoff?

The answer to this question, as Table 1 demonstrates, is overwhelmingly yes. The figures pertaining to California therapists are truly striking—virtually every psychiatrist, and nine out of ten psychologists and social workers had heard of the decision by name or had heard of a case "like it" but did not recognize the name. Knowledge of the case among 96% of the California psychiatrists is remarkable; it is a fair guess that there is no other legal decision, with the possible exception of controversial cases such as *Brown v. Board of Education,* which could command this level of recognition among a subgroup of laypersons. Yet psychiatrists from places other than California are not far behind—87% know the case by name and another 7% have heard of a case like it. Indeed, psychiatrists outside California have as great or greater knowledge of the case than California based psychologists and social workers. The strong showing by psychiatrists should not obscure two other facts: nine out of ten California psychologists and social workers also know about the case, while almost three out of four out-of-state psychologists know about it, as do more than half of the non-California social workers. These data demonstrate that the court and its

TABLE 1   Knowledge Of The Tarasoff Case By Profession And Location

| Knowledge of the Tarasoff Case | Percent each profession/location | | | | | |
| | Psychiatrist | | Psychologist | | Social Worker | |
	California	Other States	California	Other States	California	Other States
Heard of *Tarasoff* Case	96	87	86	56	76	32
Heard of case like it	1	7	8	18	13	24
Never heard of *Tarasoff* or a case like it	3	6	6	26	11	44
Total Percent	100%	100%	100%	100%	100%	100%
Total Respondents	(113)	(341)	(146)	(432)	(163)	(472)

critics were justified in believing that the *Tarasoff* decision would be well known and therefore might have a substantial influence on therapeutic practice.

2. From Which Sources Did Therapists Learn the Most about Tarasoff

Since therapists, particularly those who practice outside of California, are unlikely readers of California court decisions, it seems safe to assume that information about the case comes from professional rather than legal sources. This is what Table 2 shows.

Professional organizations and literature provided our respondents with their primary source of information about *Tarasoff*. The professional contrasts are striking: psychiatrists were more likely to identify professional organizations and literature as their primary source than were psychologists, who in turn were considerably more likely to name these sources than social workers. These figures reflect both *Tarasoff*'s controversial history and the extent to which the case was addressed in the literature of the respective professions. If we combine professional sources, i.e., professional organizations and literature, colleagues and administrators, we see that more than eight out of ten psychiatrists and psychologists and more than seven out of ten social workers learned most about *Tarasoff* from professional sources. Very few people, one out of ten or less for every group, learned about the case from lawyers.

Two facts emerge. The first is that the case is extremely well known. The second is that mental health professionals learned about the case from professional organizations and each other, not from lawyers or

TABLE 2   AMONG RESPONDENTS KNOWLEDGEABLE ABOUT TARASOFF, PRIMARY SOURCE OF KNOWLEDGE OF THE CASE BY PROFESSION AND LOCATION

| | Percent each profession/location | | | | | |
| | Psychiatrist | | Psychologist | | Social Worker | |
Source of Knowledge	California	Other States	California	Other States	California	Other States
Attorney	10	6	8	6	7	9
Administrator/Supervisor	6	1	9	4	15	17
Colleague	14	8	18	17	21	25
Professional Organization/ Literature	65	77	53	62	37	31
Newspaper	4	4	6	7	10	12
Other	1	4	6	4	10	6
Total Percent	100%	100%	100%	100%	100%	100%
Total Respondents	(104)	(287)	(124)	(276)	(123)	(222)

general circulation newspapers. Given that the message has been delivered by groups which actively intervened in the case and by publications likely to be critical of the decision, we can speculate that our respondents may not have a favorable view, or even an accurate understanding, of the decision. To that question, among others, we now turn.

DO THERAPISTS UNDERSTAND WHEN *TARASOFF* APPLIES?

The *Tarasoff* duty arises whenever a therapist determines, or pursuant to the standards of the profession, should determine, that his or her patient presents a serious danger of violence to another. The court's approach thus shifts the inquiry from what an individual therapist actually believed to what a competent therapist ought to have believed. Courts typically evaluate conduct in this manner, making social judgments about the appropriateness of questioned behavior. Do therapists appreciate the distinction between a subjective and objective test? Table 3 presents our respondents' answers to the trifurcated question of when *Tarasoff* imposes the duty to protect another: whenever the patient makes a threat, whenever a reasonable therapist would assess the patient as dangerous towards another, or whenever the therapist actually makes such an assessment. Nine out of ten thought that the *Tarasoff* obligation applies both when a therapist actually believes someone is dangerous and also when a reasonable therapist would believe this. They understand correctly the court's statement in this regard.

Only about one out of four (slightly more for social workers) believed it applied whenever there was a threat. There are two ways of viewing this figure: with satisfaction that three out of four understand that *Tarasoff* is concerned with danger, not threats, or with distress that one out of four does not. The appropriate view the *Tarasoff* critics might suggest is probably the latter—it is somewhat unsettling to find a substantial number of therapists who believe that threats per se should trigger a warning.

DO THERAPISTS BELIEVE THAT THEY CAN MAKE MEANINGFUL ASSESSMENTS OF FUTURE VIOLENCE?

The *amicus* brief asserted that therapists cannot predict future violence, citing studies tending to show that therapists overpredict violence and are more often wrong than correct in such predictions. The studies cited were studies of people who had been committed because of alleged violent tendencies and later released. There are, however, no comparable studies demonstrating the same level of unreliability regarding predictions made about people who are in the community or have ready access to it. Without taking a position in this debate, we investigated how therapists viewed their own ability. The results are contained in Table 4.

Our respondents proved to be rather more confident about their ability to predict future violence than the arguments of the *Tarasoff* critics suggested. When asked to indicate the firmest prediction they would be willing to make about the possibility that an outpatient of theirs might physically harm another, only 5% of our respondents felt that there was "no way to predict" such behavior, and over three-quarters felt that they could make a prediction ranging from "probable" to "certain."

TABLE 3   AMONG RESPONDENTS KNOWLEDGEABLE ABOUT TARASOFF, BELIEF THAT THE CASE APPLIES UNDER SELECTED CIRCUMSTANCES BY PROFESSION AND LOCATION

| | Percent each profession/location | | | | | |
| | Psychiatrist | | Psychologist | | Social Worker | |
Circumstance	California	Other States	California	Other States	California	Other States
Whenever a patient/ client threatens to harm another person	29	20	22	25	29	35
Whenever a patient/ client threatens to harm another person, and the therapist believes there is a serious possibility he might do so	94	89	96	86	93	92
Whenever a patient/ client threatens to harm another person and a reasonable therapist would believe that there is a serious possibility that he would do so	89	89	93	90	94	91
Total Number of Respondents*	(107–110)	(293–315)	(123–135)	(299–306)	(136–140)	(225–242)

*Due to non-response, number of respondents may vary within the range shown.

TABLE 4   POSSIBILITY OF PREDICTING DANGEROUSNESS FOR OUTPATIENTS BY PROFESSION AND LOCATION

	Percent each profession/location					
	Psychiatrist		Psychologist		Social Worker	
Possibility of Prediction:	California	Other States	California	Other States	California	Other States
Impossible to predict	3	5	7	4	6	6
Patient possibly violent	14	15	16	18	19	24
Patient probably violent	35	28	27	25	20	19
Patient almost certainly violent	35	31	33	33	33	34
Patient certainly violent	13	21	17	20	22	17
Total Percent	100%	100%	100%	100%	100%	100%
Total Respondents	(112)	(333)	(139)	(409)	(146)	(438)

WHAT DO THERAPISTS BELIEVE THAT *TARASOFF* REQUIRES: WARNING, REASONABLE CARE, BOTH OR NEITHER?

We present our findings in Table 5, which has two parts. Table 5A indicates the percentage of our respondents who believed that *Tarasoff* requires particular interventions. Table 5B has a narrower focus; it presents data on two formulations, warning and reasonable care, and shows the percentage who believe the case requires one of these interventions but not the other, the percentage who believe it requires both, and the percentage who believe it requires neither.

Table 5A shows that more than three out of four respondents believe *Tarasoff* requires warning the victim, while only slightly more than one-third believe that it mandates the exercise of reasonable care. Californians—again over 90% for each group—are more likely than non-Californians to believe it requires warning, and less likely than non-Californians to believe it requires reasonable care. Perhaps even more striking are the relative percentages of therapists who believe that it requires only warning as against those who believe that it demands only reasonable care. As Table 5B indicates, Californians tend to believe the decision requires warning but not reasonable care, with psychiatrists (68%) leading the parade. In contrast, only about 5% believe the case requires reasonable care but not warning. The remainder tend to believe that it requires both reasonable care and warning. The majority of California respondents misstate the formal holding of *Tarasoff*.

The figures are somewhat better for non-Californians. Yet this dif-

TABLE 5A   AMONG RESPONDENTS KNOWLEDGEABLE ABOUT TARASOFF, BELIEF THAT CASE
REQUIRES CERTAIN INTERVENTIONS BY PROFESSION AND LOCATION

| | Percent each profession/location | | | | | |
| | Psychiatrist | | Psychologist | | Social Worker | |
Belief Tarasoff Requires	California	Other States	California	Other States	California	Other States
Warn potential victim	92	84	91	76	94	72
Notify superiors or administrators if in an institutional setting	17	37	36	44	50	53
Warn guardian, family, friends	21	33	42	41	39	38
Use reasonable care to protect victim	30	33	31	43	38	40
Inform police	25	33	41	26	43	29
Deal with potential violence in therapy	13	20	21	30	30	33
Seek professional consultation	6	14	11	17	22	24
Seek emergency involuntary commitment	10	20	8	11	13	15
Total Number of Respondents	(112)	(326)	(140)	(321)	(146)	(257)

ference is slight; by and large, the case appears to be misunderstood as involving and requiring the warning of potential victims.

Again, therapists may be reacting very practically to a genuine uncertainty when they conclude that the decision requires warning. Warning, after all, is an intervention specifically identified by the California Supreme Court as a sometimes appropriate means of satisfying the *Tarasoff* duty. Faced with possible legal liability and the anxiety of dealing with a potentially violent patient, therapists may take refuge in the certainty of concrete rules. Warning a victim is very specific behavior, readily explainable to the patient as being legally required. Moreover, it may seem to the therapist to be the one sure way of avoiding liability. Unfortunately, this perception may not be entirely accurate; it will depend on what a "reasonable" therapist would do under the circumstances.

Other misinterpretations of the case by our respondents demonstrate their desire for concrete rules to guide behavior. Thus, as Table 5A

TABLE 5B AMONG RESPONDENTS KNOWLEDGEABLE ABOUT TARASOFF BELIEF THAT CASE
REQUIRES WARNING POTENTIAL VICTIM, REASONABLE CARE, NEITHER OR BOTH, BY PROFESSION
AND LOCATION

Belief Tarasoff Requires	*Percent each profession/location*					
	Psychiatrist		*Psychologist*		*Social Worker*	
	California	*Other States*	*California*	*Other States*	*California*	*Other States*
Warning the victim only	68	57	66	46	59	46
Using reasonable care to protect the victim only	5	6	5	13	3	14
Warning the victim and using reasonable care	24	27	25	30	34	26
Neither warning the victim nor using reasonable care	3	10	4	11	4	14
Total Percent	100%	100%	100%	100%	100%	100%
Total Respondents	(112)	(326)	(140)	(321)	(146)	(257)

shows, "notifying superiors" rather than exercising reasonable care is the second most frequently identified behavior thought to be required by *Tarasoff*. This is extremely specific behavior which is not required by the *Tarasoff* decision, but it may represent exactly what administrative personnel in a mental health setting would want a therapist to do. We see that social workers who are less likely than psychiatrists to have ultimate administrative responsibility are much more likely than psychiatrists to identify this as being required by *Tarasoff*. Therapists who are troubled by how to respond to a particular violent patient may also find notifying a superior to be a congenial response; it transfers, or at least shares, the responsibility for what may be a very difficult decision. Here again, our respondents may be grasping for certainty to minimize the risk of liability rather than responding to the actual requisites of the *Tarasoff* ruling.

Given that therapists believe *Tarasoff* requires warning, how does this requirement change clinical behavior? The amicus brief characterized the duty to warn as a breach of confidentiality, and argued that confidentiality is central to the therapeutic process and zealously guarded by therapists. To determine whether this is so we asked the next question.

WHAT ARE THE PRACTICES OF PSYCHOTHERA-PISTS REGARDING COMMUNICATING INFORMA-TION CONCERNING A PATIENT TO THIRD PAR-TIES?

Table 6 presents data showing the percentage of our respondents who have made various extratherapeutic communications within the twelve months prior to responding to the survey. The pattern is remarkably consistent. The overwhelming majority have communicated about patients to other health professionals and insurers, and a substantial majority have done so to family, friends and public authorities. Very few have communicated to potential victims. Psychiatrists are most likely to have made extratherapeutic communications, social workers the next most likely, and psychologists the least likely. For four of the five forms of communication, California psychiatrists lead the other five groups in percentage making the communication. Thus, while confidentiality may well represent an important ethical and therapeutic value, it is apparently a value which therapists, in their work, will frequently be forced to compromise.

The infrequency of warnings deserves comment. It is hardly surpris-

TABLE 6   COMMUNICATION OF INFORMATION ABOUT A PATIENT/CLIENT TO THIRD PARTIES DURING LAST TWELVE MONTHS BY LOCATION AND PROFESSION

	Percent each profession/location					
	Psychiatrist		Psychologist		Social Worker	
Communication To:	California	Other States	California	Other States	California	Other States
Governmental or private health insurers	90	91	76	77	82	69
Patient's/client's family or friends	74	69	62	65	69	70
Other health professionals	96	93	81	86	89	90
Persons threatened by patient/client	17	14	5	5	9	14
Public authorities (e.g., police, child welfare, correctional personnel)	70	66	55	61	67	67
Total Number Of Respondents*	(106–116)	(303–342)	(122–135)	(362–408)	(149–151)	(400–465)

*Due to non-response, number of respondents may vary within the range shown.

ing that fewer therapists warned than communicated with other health professionals, or insurance companies, or family and friends, but it is striking that so many more therapists communicated with public authorities than with potential victims. These differences may reflect either the relative difficulty of locating warnable victims, or a therapist's preference to discharge his or her obligation for the welfare of others by dealing with public authorities.

Some of the communications noted in Table 6 may require greater breaches of confidentiality than others. Patient and therapist may agree, for example, about the need for the therapist to communicate with third party insurers and little may be lost from the relationship as a result. Communications to other health professionals may stand on the same footing. Indeed, so may any communication if it is sensitively handled within the therapeutic relationship. Nonetheless, there may be communications which the therapist feels constrained to make even though making them contradicts the therapist's best clinical judgment. To determine whether warnings have this quality, we investigated the next question.

TO THE EXTENT THAT THERAPISTS DO WARN THIRD PARTIES, ARE SUCH WARNINGS MADE CONTRARY TO THE THERAPIST'S CLINICAL JUDGMENT?

Table 7 shows the percentage of our respondents who have made a given type of extratherapeutic communication and who have, at some time in their careers, done so contrary to their best clinical judgment. We see that 45% of those who have communicated with potential victims feel that they have had to violate their own clinical judgment in making an extratherapeutic communication, as against between 30% and 32% of those who have made other communications. This Table suggests that the therapists who warn victims are those most likely to feel that they have at one time acted contrary to their best clinical judgment.

The tension between warning and sound clinical judgment may simply be inherent in the *Tarasoff* requirement that therapists protect victims. The California Supreme Court, after all, never suggested that it was adopting the *Tarasoff* duty because it made clinical sense. Rather, it adopted the duty out of a view that the increase in public safety compensated for whatever was being taken from professional autonomy. Whatever the public safety gains, our data suggest that therapists feel they pay a higher clinical price by warning than by making other forms of third party disclosures . . . .

TABLE 7   DISCLOSURE OF INFORMATION TO THIRD PARTIES IN LAST YEAR BY BELIEF THAT RESPONDENT HAS COMPROMISED CLINICAL JUDGMENT AT SOME POINT IN HIS OR HER CAREER

Disclosure To	Percent Compromised Clinical Judgment	Total Number of Respondents
Governmental or private health insurers	32	(1245)
Patient's/client's family or friends	31	(1081)
Other health professionals	30	(1406)
Persons threatened by patient/ client	45	(144)
Public authorities (e.g., police, child welfare, correctional personnel)	32	(982)

HAS *TARASOFF* INFLUENCED THERAPIST ATTITUDES REGARDING APPROPRIATE INTERVENTIONS IN THE TREATMENT OF POTENTIALLY VIOLENT PATIENTS?

To answer this question, we asked therapists to indicate changes between 1975 and 1980 in their willingness to employ certain interventions in the treatment of potentially violent patients. This period runs from the date of the first *Tarasoff* opinion (December 1974) to the date of the survey and should reflect *Tarasoff*'s influence. To further insure that we are measuring *Tarasoff*'s impact, we divided our respondents into three groups: those who believed themselves legally bound by the *Tarasoff* principle, (2) those who believed themselves ethically, but not legally, bound, and (3) those who either had not heard of the decision or did not believe themselves legally or ethically bound by it. We reasoned that if *Tarasoff* has influenced psychotherapeutic practice, it would be most evident among those respondents who have heard of the case and believe that they are legally bound by it.

Table 8 presents the data. The most dramatic effect of *Tarasoff* can be seen exactly where one would expect it: in increased willingness to notify potential victims (line 5), public authorities (line 4), and police (line 6). Those who feel legally bound have become more willing since *Tarasoff* to employ warning interventions than those who believe themselves only ethically bound, and clearly more willing than those who don't consider themselves bound by *Tarasoff* at all.

Tarasoff appears to have influenced willingness to take notes (line 3), and to initiate involuntary hospitalization (line 9). Here, however, the ethically bound psychiatrists prove slightly more willing than those legally bound, although the differences are neither great nor entirely

TABLE 8 PERCENT OF RESPONDENTS IN EACH PROFESSION WITH VARYING BELIEFS ABOUT TARASOFF WHOSE WILLINGNESS TO EMPLOY CERTAIN INTERVENTIONS WITH DANGEROUS PATIENTS CHANGED BETWEEN 1975–1980

Change in Willingness to Employ: Intervention	Psychiatrist			Psychologist			Social Worker		
	Legal	Ethical	Neither	Legal	Ethical	Neither	Legal	Ethical	Neither
1) Less willing to treat	32	42	45	32	31	32	28	28	26
2) More willing to terminate	30	29	34	24	24	27	27	23	24
3) More willing to take notes	36	43	23	45	34	25	42	41	30
4) More willing to notify public authorities	59	54	36	51	36	25	47	49	42
5) More willing to notify victims	75	60	35	70	52	31	56	57	28
6) More willing to notify police	48	33	25	50	34	23	39	28	25
7) More willing to consult lawyers	37	48	31	30	30	28	30	24	28
8) More willing to consult administrator	39	35	37	33	23	23	36	30	36
9) More willing to initiate involuntary hospitalization	32	30	20	39	23	28	37	38	30
10) More willing to initiate voluntary hospitalization	34	32	31	50	39	41	43	39	46
Total Number of Respondents*	(217–224)	(89–91)	(59–61)	(246–254)	(94–99)	(109–115)	(226–236)	(68–71)	(195–207)

*Due to non-response, numbers of respondents may vary within the range shown.

consistent. These findings provide support for the view that *Tarasoff* may encourage efforts to document patient treatment and some slight support for the claim that *Tarasoff* will lead to an increased use of involuntary commitment. Such conclusions must be viewed with caution: these findings could reflect general changes in views over time regarding the treatment of the potentially dangerous patient. It is also possible that changes in therapeutic practice reflect differences in the patient populations seen by our respondents. We return to this issue below.

Interestingly, those who view themselves as bound by *Tarasoff* do not indicate either less willingness to treat dangerous patients than the others (line 1) or more willingness to terminate treatment (line 2). To explore this issue further, we asked the following question:

HAS *TARASOFF* DISCOURAGED THERAPISTS FROM TREATING POTENTIALLY DANGEROUS PATIENTS?

Table 9 presents data regarding whether and when our respondents treated patients they assessed as likely to be harmful to others. The amicus position suggests that awareness of the decision will discourage therapists from treating dangerous patients. Furthermore, traditional notions of deterrence suggest that the aversion should be greatest among those who believe themselves legally obligated. As the Table indicates, this is clearly not the case. If the proposition were valid, people believing themselves legally bound would be more likely than others to have stopped treating such patients. Therefore, those legally bound by *Tarasoff* would be more likely than others to have treated such patients in the past, but not currently, or less likely to have treated such patients in both the current year and in prior years. The data (lines 2 and 4) show the opposite. Therapists bound by *Tarasoff* are more likely, not less, to have treated such patients during the current year and earlier and are less likely, not more, to have last treated such a patient prior to the current year. These data on professional practices are consistent with our findings regarding changes in willingness to treat.

The clear majority of all therapists have treated a dangerous patient, and a reasonably high percentage have treated them in the past and were continuing to do so in 1980, when the survey was conducted. Among those who do treat such patients, has *Tarasoff* actually influenced interventions?

TABLE 9 PERCENT OF RESPONDENTS IN EACH PROFESSION WITH VARYING BELIEFS ABOUT TARASOFF PRINCIPLE WHO HAVE OR HAVE NOT TREATED DANGEROUS PATIENTS DURING VARIOUS TIME PERIODS

	Psychiatrist			Psychologist			Social Worker		
	Legal	Ethical	Neither	Legal	Ethical	Neither	Legal	Ethical	Neither
1) Never treated a dangerous patient	15	14	27	25	27	39	23	25	29
2) Treated dangerous patient before 1979–80	16	20	19	20	17	26	14	19	25
3) Treated dangerous patient only during 1979–80	9	6	8	6	9	6	9	11	8
4) Treated dangerous patients both prior to and during 1979–80	60	60	46	49	47	29	53	45	39
Total Percent	100%	100%	100%	100%	100%	100%	100%	100%	100%
Total Respondents	(271)	(111)	(67)	(310)	(115)	(141)	(28)	(89)	(246)

HAS *TARASOFF* INFLUENCED THERAPISTS TO WARN POTENTIAL VICTIMS, INVOLUNTARILY HOSPITALIZE POTENTIALLY VIOLENT PATIENTS, OR OTHERWISE ATTEMPT TO RESPOND TO THE LEGAL OBLIGATION TO PROTECT POTENTIAL VICTIMS?

We examined this question by asking our respondents to provide details concerning their interventions in the most recent case in which they treated a patient they assessed as dangerous. We also asked for information about another situation: the most recent case in which the patient uttered an explicit threat. The results are presented in Tables 10 and 11.

Turning first to the data on the last dangerous case presented in Table 10, we see that awareness of *Tarasoff* and the belief that it is legally or ethically binding has a consistent and noticeable influence across professions in one situation: warning the potential victim. Beliefs also seem to have a positive influence in two other areas: including notes about the patient and recommending voluntary hospitalization. There is a very small difference with regard to initiating involuntary hospitalization.

There are two points about these differences in hospitalization and note taking practices. First, the hospitalization and note interventions are not uniform: with regard to hospitalizations, ethically bound social workers and psychologists are more likely than legally bound ones to have initiated involuntary hospitalization, and ethically bound therapists in each profession were at least as likely as legally bound ones to recommend voluntary hospitalization. With regard to making notes, social workers show no patterns of influence. Second, and most importantly, most of the differences that do exist are quite small. The largest difference is in terms of warning practices between legally bound psychiatrists and those who reject or are ignorant of *Tarasoff*: a difference of sixteen percentage points. However, comparable differences for psychologists and social workers are seven points in each case.

To understand more clearly how *Tarasoff* has influenced actual behavior, however, we must examine the final Table (11) dealing with interventions in cases involving threats. The *Tarasoff* case involved a patient who threatened an identified person. Therapists may therefore view *Tarasoff* as dealing with threatening patients specifically rather than dangerous patients generally. Indeed, this view is the emerging judicial interpretation: therapists have not been liable to victims of their patients when the victim could not have been identified beforehand. When we look to cases involving threats, beliefs about *Tarasoff* do have consistent patterns of influence with respect to warning and, more importantly, the differences between the groups are greater. With regard to warning, there is a twenty-eight point difference among psychiatrists, a fourteen point difference among psychologists, and a nine-

TABLE 10 Percent Of Respondents In Each Profession With Varying Beliefs About Tarasoff Who Employed Certain Interventions In Most Recent Case (1975–1980) Involving Dangerous Patient

Intervention Employed:	Psychiatrist			Psychologist			Social Worker		
	Legal	Ethical	Neither	Legal	Ethical	Neither	Legal	Ethical	Neither
1) Declined or terminated treatment	5	4	5	2	8	3	11	6	8
2) Included note	67	61	51	50	42	47	59	58	50
3) Notified public authorities	11	9	14	10	9	5	15	20	17
4) Notified potential victim	21	16	5	19	18	9	19	15	11
5) Notified police	10	12	11	6	12	7	9	2	3
6) Consulted lawyer	10	7	5	6	10	3	6	9	6
7) Consulted administrator	12	7	11	9	12	10	12	20	17
8) Initiated involuntary hospitalization	32	29	27	12	12	7	21	18	15
9) Recommended voluntary hospitalization	26	32	22	27	25	19	30	36	26
Total Number of Respondents	(197)	(75)	(37)	(188)	(67)	(58)	(188)	(55)	(145)

TABLE 11 PERCENT OF RESPONDENTS IN EACH PROFESSION WITH VARYING BELIEFS ABOUT TARASOFF WHO EMPLOYED CERTAIN INTERVENTIONS IN MOST RECENT CASE (1975–1980) INVOLVING A THREAT

Intervention Employed	Psychiatrist			Psychologist			Social Worker		
	Legal	Ethical	Neither	Legal	Ethical	Neither	Legal	Ethical	Neither
1) Declined or terminated treatment	5	5	16	3	12	0	8	14	6
2) Included note	61	51	47	56	62	25	58	57	57
3) Notified public authorities	11	13	5	3	12	0	15	21	12
4) Notified potential victim	33	23	5	37	31	25	31	21	14
5) Notified police	24	10	11	7	15	6	18	21	8
6) Initiated involuntary hospitalization	30	36	0	13	19	0	25	14	8
7) Initiated voluntary hospitalization	22	26	16	22	39	19	16	7	26
Total Number Of Respondents	(110)	(39)	(19)	(76)	(26)	(16)	(87)	(14)	(51)

teen point difference among social workers, between those believing themselves legally bound by *Tarasoff* and those who reject or have not heard of it. Differences in note taking and involuntary hospitalization also exists between polar groups.

These data suggest that *Tarasoff* has influenced therapists' behavior most markedly in situations which gave rise to the case in the first instance, threatening behavior. This conforms to our earlier findings that therapists believed that the case required warning. It also suggests that our respondents tend to read the case narrowly; that is, that *Tarasoff* requires particular interventions with regard to the threatening patient specifically, rather than the dangerous patient generally.

V. CONCLUSION

. . . As we have shown, many therapists misstate the [*Tarasoff*] case in two major respects: they believe that it demands warning rather than reasonable care, and they believe that it is legally binding upon them when technically this may not be true. Yet, given the sources of information upon which the therapists relied, these views are readily understandable. In their rush to condemn the *Tarasoff* decision, the professional critics may have disseminated information leading to the very misperceptions which they sought to avoid.

Ultimately, however, the decisions themselves, rather than the criticisms, have been the likely source of confusion among therapists concerning their legal obligations. Rules designed to facilitate ad hoc and post hoc resolutions of disputes between an injured and his injurer do not provide very much guidance to those who attempt to behave in a way that avoids liability. The "reasonableness" standard may give courts and juries the discretion necessary to achieve situational justice; what it clearly does not do, however, is tell psychotherapists, any more than it tells police, "public servants" or insurance adjusters, how to behave in a concrete situation. "Warn the victim," on the other hand, does provide a clear, if rather simplistic, guide for the risk averse.

Moreover, therapists may be entirely reasonable in viewing *Tarasoff* as requiring warning. First, the court told them that they had to warn. The court then took eighteen months to reconsider and shift to a reasonable care standard. Having been alerted to their new obligation, therapists may not have felt free to suspend action with potentially violent patients while awaiting word from the court. Rather, they may have moved to incorporate the new rule into their practice.

Whatever their source, these legal misapprehensions have had consequences. The belief that the case requires warning influences therapists to do just that, particularly when the patient utters a threat, even though therapists are most likely to identify warning as the kind of third party communication which compromises their clinical judgment. Clearer understanding of the final ruling in the case would not eliminate all, or even a large percentage, of warnings, but it might encourage at least some therapists to respond with more clinically appropriate interventions in at least some cases . . . .

Our findings also suggest a somewhat heretical point about tort doctrine and its influence on behavior. They suggest that if an appellate court desires to change behavior, it should use judicially established standards of behavior, not jury determined standards. The judicially determined rule of *Tarasoff I,* protect through warning, appears to have affected therapist attitudes, knowledge and behavior to a far greater degree than *Tarasoff II* . . . .

. . . [T]he prevailing view that courts should not attempt to set specific standards of conduct needs reexamination. To the extent that it is based on the notion that courts are impotent when it comes to changing behavior, the anti-court argument does not comport with reality. To the extent that it is based on the proposition that compensation should be the primary goal of tort law, it is unnecessary. It may be justified on the grounds that courts cannot develop sound behavioral rules, but that case has yet to be made. ☐

NOTES AND QUESTIONS

1. Another impact study of a tort decision is Jerry Wiley, "The Impact of Judicial Decisions on Professional Conduct," 55 *Southern California Law Review* 345 (1981). In *Helling v. Carey,* 83 Wash.2d 514, 519 P.2d 981 (1974), the defendant was an eye doctor. The plaintiff sued the doctor because the doctor had not detected the plaintiff's glaucoma; other eye doctors testified that routine glaucoma tests were not given to young patients. The jury found for defendant, but the appellate court reversed, and opened the way to liability. Eye doctors were required to give tests for glaucoma, or face tort suits if a patient contracted this condition.

Wiley's study of the impact of the case came up with a surprising result: there was little impact, because most eye doctors were already testing for glaucoma. The expert testimony, in other words, was simply wrong.

What factual assumptions were at issue in the debate over the *Tarasoff* case? One, which was prominently mentioned, was whether psychiatrists could in fact predict if a patient was liable to become violent or dangerous. There is considerable dispute on this point. See Alexander D. Brooks, "The Constitutionality and Morality of Civilly Committing Violent Sexual Predators," 15 *University of Puget Sound Law Review* 709 (1992).

2. There are many other situations in which a rule or doctrine is communicated through professional channels. For example, officials at state departments of education tell school teachers whether they can hold prayers in classes or decorate Christmas trees in their classrooms. Officials in the state attorney generals' offices and local district attorneys' offices tell police officers about the latest interpretations of Supreme Court decisions concerning the proper procedures for arrest. Obviously, there is room for differences of opinion if not distortion in the process.

Someone must tell officials of large corporations about legal requirements and help them comply. Lauren B. Edelman, Steven E. Abraham, and Howard

S. Erlanger, "Professional Construction of Law: The Inflated Threat of Wrongful Discharge," 26 *Law & Society Review* 47, 77–78 (1992), studied how corporate lawyers and officials in personnel departments interpreted legal rules fashioned in the 1970s and 1980s that seemed to limit the rights of employers to fire employees when the employers did not have a legally recognized reason to do so. Courts in many states, particularly California, seemed to grant new rights to employees, and limits on the rights of employers to fire at will became news in the business press. Enterprising entrepreneurs sold elaborate programs designed to train employers about how to deal with these new cases. However, Edelman, Abraham, and Erlanger point out that many of these people exaggerated the real threat posed by the new rules. They argue:

[P]ersonnel professionals and practicing lawyers have a shared interest in constructing the threat of wrongful discharge in such a way that employers perceive the law as a threat and rely upon those professions to curb the threat. That threat—and the proffered solution—would help both professions to gain a symbiotic jurisdiction over corporate response to the legal environment.

The limitation of the professional power perspective is that it has a somewhat conspiratorial tone, implying that professions (or individual professionals) pay conscious attention to issues of power and jurisdiction. Of course, motivations and interests are extremely difficult to measure. But even without empirical verification of the argument we have set out, the perspective may be useful in pointing to the effect of professions' activities, regardless of their motivations.

See also Lauren B. Edelman, "Legal Environments and Organizational Governance: The Expansion of Due Process in the American Workplace," 95 *American Journal of Sociology* 1401 (1990).

How do ordinary people learn about rules and doctrines? Since a rule that nobody knows obviously can have no impact whatsoever, what institutions and roles in the legal system are designed to teach or tell people about rules and doctrines? How do people learn that murder, rape, and robbery are against the law? How do people learn the requirements of the federal and state laws imposing income taxes? How do people learn about the traffic laws and changes in those laws? How do people learn about laws that their dogs and cats must be licensed, and cannot roam about uncontrolled (the so-called "leash laws")? To whom was the *Miranda* case communicated, and how?

3. In a classic study, the late Norwegian sociologist of law, Vilhelm Aubert, investigated the impact of a Norwegian law about the work conditions of housemaids. The maids were poor women, mostly uneducated; they were not unionized, and they worked in people's homes. The message embodied in the law never got through to them. See Vilhelm Aubert, "Some Social Functions of Legislation," 10 *Acta Sociologica* 98 (1967). How big a role does wealth and class play in the communication process? Might the poor have a more accurate perception of the law in action, at least in some areas, than the middle class and the wealthy?

4. The psychologists and psychiatrists who knew (or thought they know) about *Tarasoff* were (technically) incorrect in their understanding of the case. What exactly was their misunderstanding? How did it come about? Compare their understanding with the way the police understand *Miranda*.

Roe v. Wade and *Brown v. Board of Education* are two of the most famous Supreme Court decisions of this century. Very many if not most people have heard of them. How accurately do you think they are understood by most people? Through what channels did they learn about these cases? Are these channels likely to be different for whites and blacks, men and women, people in different regions of the country, or those with different levels of formal education?

5. Lawyers play an important role in the legal system as middlemen, or information brokers. They know the law, and they convey that knowledge to clients, when the clients need it. A couple that plans to get a divorce probably knows only a little about the divorce laws (some of it no doubt wrong); but they rely on the lawyer for more precise information. On the role of lawyers in the communication network, see also Chapter 5, p. 837–98.

6. There have been a number of other studies of the impact of the *Tarasoff* case. D. L. Rosenhan, Terri Wolff Teitelbaum, Kathi Weiss Teitelbaum, and Martin Davidson, in "Warning Third Parties: The Ripple Effects of *Tarasoff*," 24 *Pacific Law Journal* 1165 (1993), report on a survey conducted in 1987. A questionnaire about *Tarasoff* was filled out by 872 psychiatrists and clinical psychologists in California. The overwhelming majority of the respondents had heard of the case.

The results of the survey suggested to the authors that the case "seems to have changed the nature of clinical practice." Some 37% of the respondents said that the case "has led them to focus more frequently on dangerousness with their patients. In addition, 32% of therapists reported that they concentrate more often on patients' less serious threats" (p. 1210). The survey results also suggest that the case has altered therapists views of confidentiality. They are more willing than before at least to *consider* disclosing confidences because of the case. The therapists are also more likely to consult other professionals if they feel a patient is potentially dangerous.

See also Peter C. Carstensen, "The Evolving Duty of Mental Health Professionals to Third Parties: A Doctrinal and Institutional Examination," 17 *International Journal of Law and Psychiatry* 1 (1994). Carstensen notes another impact of the *Tarasoff* decision far beyond the borders of California. The mental health professions in many states have lobbied successfully for statutes that limit the potential liability of therapists in the *Tarasoff* situation. Often the statutes narrowly limit the kind of threat by a patient that can give rise to liability. Some statutes also define responses to a threat that the therapist may make that will discharge the duty to rescue the threatened third party. Is it likely that these statutes will undercut the ripple effects of the *Tarasoff* decision that Rosenhan and his colleagues discovered?

7. The *Tarasoff* case was disseminated through professional groups. A decision that applies to the public at large gets whatever communication it gets through newspapers, radio, and TV. The following article raises the issue of the way in which the media, especially television, affect the impact of court decisions; indeed, of law in general.

45. *Media Coverage of Supreme Court Decision-Making: Problems and Prospects*

Elliot E. Slotnick

75 *Judicature* 128 (1991)

☐ The importance of journalistic coverage of governmental activities in the policy-making arena is difficult to overestimate since the media serve as the primary link between the government and the governed . . . .

Clearly, the media are more than passive conduits for information. They serve as filters and funnels for the universe of events that could appear before the public's eye. Events are interpreted, placed into context, speculated about, and shaped by the media for . . . facts do not speak for themselves. Indeed, in a world in which the press decides what not to report, the press becomes almost as important as the events themselves in the formulation of perceived reality. The obverse also applies: what the press considers worthy of emphasizing becomes quite obviously a major part of reality.

More broadly the media can be a vehicle for "normation" in American society, serving as "attitude and behavior models." While creating news images, the media can indicate which views and behavior are acceptable and which are unacceptable or outside the mainstream. Similarly, the media may indicate what conforms to prevailing standards of justice and morality.

The centrality of the media link between governmental institutions, their policy making, and the polity may be most telling for the judiciary, the branch of government about which most Americans are decidedly uninformed. Indeed, for most Americans, the press may be the sole source of information about the Supreme Court. As noted by Caldeira,[151]"Research on the attitudes of adults reveals that there is only a relatively shallow reservoir of knowledge about . . . the Court in the mass public . . . . Few . . . fulfill the most minimal prerequisites of the role of a knowledgeable and competent citizen vis-a-vis the Court." It is in this context of the importance of media coverage for public information and opinion about the Court that this essay focuses on the inherent problems in and future prospects for media coverage of Supreme Court decision making.

The reasons for the Court's relative invisibility and the fact the public must rely virtually exclusively on the news media for information about the Court lay partly at the doorstep of the institution itself and its

---

151. [The reference is to Gregory Caldeira, "Neither the Purse Nor the Sword: Dynamics of Public Confidence in the Supreme Court," 89 *American Political Science Review* 1209, 1211 (1986).]

members. As noted by [Paul] Duke, "The justices themselves are among the most anonymous public figures, preferring to stay out of the spotlight . . . . In the face of trends toward more openness in government, the Court still clings to its Delphic ways, perpetuating the remoteness that is part of its character." . . .

The Court's shunning of the public eye, low general levels of knowledge about the Court and its work, and the primacy of media coverage for whatever understanding of the Court that does exist all serve to strengthen the media's role in determining the public consequences of judicial decisions . . . .

THE IMPORTANCE OF TV

The media are not monolithic, and, increasingly, an understanding of the role of television news for explicating public policy has taken primacy. Studies have documented for over two decades that television is perceived by the majority of the public as its "main source" of information and the advantage enjoyed by television has, if anything grown as an increasing proportion of the citizenry has been "raised" in a television-dominated environment. The majority of the public admit to receiving all of their news from television, while a plurality cite television as the "most thorough" national news source. Indeed, as Ron Nessen, a former network news correspondent and presidential press secretary has noted, "if it didn't happen on network television, then it didn't happen."

On a daily basis, over 100 million Americans view the news on TV and millions more are likely to gain their familiarity with public issues secondhand through their interaction with television news viewers. The advantage of "telenews" is, of course the visual medium's ability to portray events with a sense of realism and emotional drama. The commercial and time constraints of the television news format, however, as well as the difficulties faced by a TV audience that cannot, like its print counterpart, dwell on stories, review them, and digest them in a setting relatively free of distractions, raises significant questions about television's ability to portray accurately and in sufficient complexity the substance of events . . . .

The problems associated with television news take on added significance with reference to coverage of the judiciary because of the Court's isolation and relative public invisibility. [Larry] Berkson has characterized two publics that receive Supreme Court messages: a "continuous public" (composed of attorneys, judges, law enforcement officers, and lawmakers) and a less attentive "intermittent public." Continuous publics have, in most instances, the greatest need for accurate information and, arguably, they generally "utilize the most reliable channels." It is the unknowledgeable intermittent publics who are most likely to depend on the media for the information they possess. When they look to television, they are met by a medium that has been portrayed as having a "lack of interest in what the Court does. Even if a citizen desired to learn more about the operation and output of the Court, this information could not be obtained by relying on the coverage in the mass media." . . .

THE MEDIA-COURT LINK

. . . [T]he media-Court link generates concern from many sources and has important implications. For one, the media help to shape the judiciary's views of the public its decisions affect. Perhaps more importantly the centrality of television news in the public's information network suggests that much of what we know and our attitudes about our perceptions are derived from the media's message . . . . If the press "gets it wrong," important consequences can follow. Thus, for example, public misperception of a ruling can have a direct effect on compliance with the ruling as well as on its broader impact. Public perceptions may have importance for the development of further litigation, and its broadest implications may be felt in the distorted role a misinformed democratic polity may play in ongoing policy formulation and debate.

Commentary has been frequent in criticism of the press for its coverage of the judiciary . . . . Justice William O. Douglas . . . characterized coverage of the Court as producing "news stories which the author of the court opinion would hardly recognize as descriptive of what he had written." . . .

While press coverage of the Court has historically presented an easy target, it is critical to view such coverage in the context of the special problems reporting on the Court entails, the nature of the Supreme Court press corps, and the unique considerations characterizing television reporting of the Court, subjects to which we now turn . . . .

THE COURT AND THE PRESS

Analyses of the media-Court relationship have always been premised, and justifiably so, in the unique circumstances that coverage of the Court entails for the reporter . . . .

Supreme Court decisional processes are not open to the reporter's view as they are, at least in part, in other governmental settings. Yet, as Anthony Lewis has noted, "The process of decision is often more newsworthy than the end result. And it can certainly be more instructive in the ways of our government . . . . Judges make accommodations just as their political brothers do, but we can only guess at what they were. While critical judicial decisions are made in private, what reporters see inside the Courtroom—all they see—is designed more to elevate than to display the judicial process."

An inherent danger for those reporting on the Court is the "intimidation factor" and acquiescence that the elevation of process can lead to. Shaw has noted that, "The formal panoply of the courtroom and the stilted language of the lawyers and judges cow some reporters into silence." . . .

Clearly, a large part of the problem for the Court reporter stems from the dearth of traditional news sources. The Court's members and functionaries all place a premium on secrecy and, to the extent that the relationship between journalists and their sources are generally based on mutually beneficial exchanges, journalists are perceived to have little to offer to the Court in this regard. Veteran journalist Fred Graham who covered the Court for many years for the New York Times and CBS News notes that Supreme Court justices could hardly be considered "news sources" in the journalists' lexicon . . . .

Covering the Supreme Court was like being assigned to report on the Pope. Both the Justices and the Pope issue infallible statements, draw their authority from a mystical higher source, conceal their humanity in flowing robes, and because they seek to present a saintly face to the world are inherently boring. They also both have life tenure which implies a license to thumb their noses at the news media . . . [T]he justices were so withdrawn that covering the Court for any news medium was in a journalistic class by itself.

REPORTING DECISIONS

Any consideration of the problems that exist in media coverage of the Court must take full account of the inherent difficulties associated with understanding complex litigation and technical legal arguments and then filing stories on them with a few minutes or a few hours. Case decisions often include numerous concurring and dissenting opinions that may obfuscate the issues even further.

Supreme Court opinions are not written for a lay or journalistic audience and justices rarely do anything to make them more accessible to such publics. Indeed, some justices seem to go to great lengths to trump complex legal questions with complexities in their own prose . . . .

LITTLE ASSISTANCE

For its part, the Court appears to be relatively unconcerned about journalistic difficulties. Indeed in the words of Anthony Lewis, "All of official Washington except the Supreme Court is acutely conscious of public relations. The Supreme Court is about as oblivious as it is conceivable to be." There is much truth in Lewis' comment. The Court does have a clerk of the court as well as a press officer, but neither sees their job as a vehicle for fostering the Court's public image. Indeed the press officer's role is very different than that of a public information officer or press secretary in other institutional settings . . . .

In an institutional setting where the press officer serves almost exclusively as a conduit for information, Supreme Court reporters find themselves more isolated than journalists acting in other governmental arenas. Interviews with justices remain rare, despite their relative increase during the past decade, and they remain inadequate and inappropriate mechanisms for in-depth coverage of actual cases and controversies. Press briefings and press conferences are not held by justices or other Court personnel . . . .

THE COURT PRESS CORPS

The Supreme Court beat is a relatively uncluttered one when compared with the number of reporters who routinely cover the White House or the halls of Congress. Except, perhaps, for landmark decision days and crowded oral arguments in prominent, dramatic, and often emotionally laden cases, approximately 50 reporters cover the Court on a routine basis . . . . Among the regulars at the Court are wire service reporters for UPI, AP and Dow Jones, reporters for major "national" newspapers such as *The New York Times, Washington Post,* and *Wall Street Journal,* and broadcast journalists from the three major networks, CNN and NPR . . . .

Clearly, Supreme Court reporters are less "participatory" in the processes that they cover than are their colleagues in other governmental settings and it would be difficult to sustain the argument that journalists have any impact on what the Court actually decides. It is in this sense that the Court's press corps probably has less power and influence than any other major news group in Washington. Nevertheless, as we have seen, the media have a potentially great role in developing public perceptions of the Court and in providing a baseline of information about what the Court has done.

Because of the unique institutional setting in which the Court reporters operate, the skills that are required of them may be somewhat different than those that would best lead to success among their colleagues. Indeed, the prototypical model of the aggressive investigative reporter with all of its connotations may give way in this domain to the primacy of one's analytical skills. Supreme Court reporters often spend more time reading than they do on their feet or on the telephone . . . .

[T]he posture the Court reporter takes towards the institution tends to be more laden with respect and deference than one finds on other governmental beats . . . .

One of the major problems confronting the Supreme Court reporter is the greater tension that often exists between making a story both understandable to a lay audience as well as accurate . . . .

Perhaps the most common inaccuracy to appear in print or over the airwaves is the assertion that the Court "affirmed," "upheld," or "let stand" a lower court ruling when, in fact, its only "decision" may have been an allegedly neutral denial of certiorari. While certiorari denials, of course, may have critical implications for the party denied review, their policy implications are less clear and they are certainly different actions in kind from holdings and affirmations . . . .

TV NEWS AND THE COURT

The primary differences between television and the newspaper coverage of the Supreme Court stem from the fundamental differences of the broadcast and print media themselves as well as from the different commercial environments in which they operate. Clearly, both newspapers and television networks are business enterprises yet ostensibly the "product" through which newspapers attract the public is the news. Network television news, however, is much less central to the network's operation . . . .

Entertainment is, in some senses, as important to television news as it is to the remainder of the broadcast day. This has important implications for the reporting of governmental affairs and, in particular, the relatively "invisible" Supreme Court . . . .

Commercial and audience concerns place far more constraints on television producers than they do on newspaper editors. Such constraints allow newspapers far more leeway in including stories with relatively narrow readership appeal. According to Reuven Frank, former president of NBC News,

> A television news program must be put together with the assumption that each item will be of some interest to everyone that watches. Every time a newspaper includes a feature which will attract a specialized group it can assume it is adding at least a little bit to its circulation. To the degree a television news program includes an item of this sort . . . it must assume its audience will diminish.

The relative lack of attention to the Court by television could have particularly significant consequences for a public that knows little about the institution and what it does and, further, relies mostly on television news for what it does know. The tendency to focus on the Court's activities only when important decisions "come down" could prove particularly unfortunate. [According to Fred Graham]

> Its decisions are controversial . . . and misunderstood . . . so there is every reason to publicize what is under consideration. It unsettling enough in a democratic society to have unpopular edicts come thundering down from an unelected priesthood, but to have them burst upon the scene with little advance warning and inadequate explanation compounds the damage. Yet that happens regularly at the Supreme Court, because . . . the public . . . has been deprived [of] a full view of the pro-

cess. Stories about Court arguments can't compete for television time because TV executives hate to leaden their screens with color-pencil sketches and secondhand recitations of what happened inside. The result is that there has been inadequate coverage of the Supreme Court because television reporters have been restricted to the video equivalent of communicating with a quill pen. □

NOTES AND QUESTIONS

1. The result, Slotnick goes on to say, is that many important stories about the work of the Supreme Court never make it on network television at all. There is a tendency, moreover, to report news about reactions to the Court's decisions, rather than what the Court actually did or said.

Why should this be the case? The answer is that these reactions are more dramatic, more entertaining. The Court itself is not very photogenic, even if the Court allowed television to cover its deliberations, which it doesn't. But if, say, the Court hands down a striking abortion decision, the television cameras can race about and record the dramatic reactions of people who are for or against the decision; it can get their views, and record their actions. This is what television does best. But by focusing on "impact" rather than the decision itself, the media blur the message, and may actually influence the impact of the case.

2. See also Ethan Katsh, "The Supreme Court Beat: How Television Covers the U.S. Supreme Court," 67 *Judicature* 8 (1983). Katsh analyzed a five year period (1976–1981) of coverage of the Court on national network news. He found that the networks reported only about one case out of five of the Court's rulings. Business and economic decisions were the least likely to gain television time; abortion and civil liberties cases were much more likely to be covered. This should come as no surprise. But, again, the public gets a distorted picture of the actual work of the Court.

3. The Supreme Court is, of course, only one court of many in the country. The media neglect state courts and lower federal courts even more. How much coverage is there of other bodies that make law, that is, legislatures, administrative agencies, and the Executive?

4. It is not only through news that the media communicate information (and misinformation) about the legal system. There have been programs like *L.A. Law* on TV, and countless stories about crime, trials, police and detective work, not to mention straight dramatic stories that include some message about law or the legal system. There is very little research on the way such messages influence public attitudes and behaviors.

A CONCLUDING WORD

The materials in this chapter make one thing very clear: the impact or effectiveness of law is not to be taken for granted. Even deciding *whether* a law is effective is often debatable. How, for example, should we label a law that achieves about 60% of its goals? Measurement typically is difficult. Every scholar who works in this area would agree that the question of impact is important but that scholarship has just scratched the surface. It is troubling that there is no general agreement about some basic theoretical issues.

A more fundamental criticism of the whole area of scholarship has been launched by Gunther Teubner, in "Regulatory Law: *Chronicle of a Death Foretold,*" 1 *Social and Legal Studies* 451 (1992). Teubner's title refers to *Chronicle of a Death Foretold,* by the great Latin American novelist, Gabriel Garcia Marquez. As Teubner describes the story, a beautiful girl, Angela Vicario, is married in a Colombian village. But her husband discovers that she is not a virgin. In this culture, the "culprit" would have to die. Everyone in the village realizes that her brothers will kill the "culprit," Santiago Nasar. Nothing can save the victim because he has violated the village code of honor. The crime follows inevitably.

Teubner uses this story rather boldly as a launching pad for his criticism of what he considers the orthodox way of looking at impact and effectiveness. The Marquez story can be read as a case-study of ineffectivenss: the murder of Nasar with the knowledge of the whole village is an instance where the law against murder has no impact. That is nothing startling—we have seen many instances of laws that fail to reach their target. But Teubner argues that to look at the "case" in terms of effectiveness or ineffectiveness misses the point. The murder was not "arrived at after a careful weighing of positive and negative sanctions;" nor was it a case where there was "a kind of inner conflict between law and honour." Rather, the law-realm and the honor-realm operated in two entirely different, self-contained spheres. Each was a mode of "discourse" of its own.

Teubner's essay is subtle and difficult. However, the central point seems to be that the orthodox view of impact fails because it is too wooden, too narrow, and it ignores the way social systems are actually structured. Social life is made up of a whole series of codes or realms ("discourses"), which are little worlds in themselves. "Impact" studies should really be studies of how such little worlds are coupled or fail to couple. The law is one such little world; the honor code another. Each little world may be "immune" to the other, may ignore the others totally, or may be "structurally coupled." The study of effectiveness should really be dissolved into a study of how various "discourses" collide, harmonize, or interfere with each other. This approach to the study of law, Teubner thinks, would make research on, for example, regulatory success or failure much richer and yield better insights.

Teubner's article is a response to Hubert Rottleutner, "The Limits of Law: The Myth of a Regulatory Crisis," 17 *International Journal of the Sociology of Law* 273 (1989), a very thoughtful critique of Teubner's approach. Do you find Teubner's approach, as you understand it, fruitful? Suppose that Teubner were to analyze the various readings in this section on the impact of law or laws. How different would his analysis be from the way the authors of the readings approached the subject?

5

The Legal System
as a Social System:
Structure, Rules,
and Roles

INTRODUCTION

Though we have used the term "legal system" many times, we have not yet defined it. Basically, what we mean when we speak of the legal system is a set of sub-systems which, for one reason or another, people choose to call "legal." There is room for dispute about which sub-systems fit most comfortably within the definition of law. But it is clear that some of them fit very well—for example, the judicial system, made up of courts and their supporting personnel. By common consent, this is a sub-system which is part of the legal system.

When we call the judicial system a system, we mean nothing more than that it is a network of people, institutions, and relationships, which has a recognizable boundary; that is, we can either see where it begins and ends, or define it in such a way as to make that point clear. We can, in other words, talk about the judicial system, and define it so that no one could reasonably confuse the judicial system with the army, the educational system, the Bureau of Standards, or a circus.

A system, then, is some bounded part of that gigantic reality we call society. Unless it is wholly insulated from society—which is impossible—a system must adapt to its social environment and to its externally generated needs. In other words, it must coordinate the activity of those people who are part of the system, so that they work together (more or less) to attain its goals.

In much of the material considered up to this point, we have ignored or postponed considering the legal system as a system. We have assumed a simple arrangement in which "the law" gives out orders to the public, that is, people outside in society. In Chapter 3, we considered how the legal system gets its orders from society. Mostly, we treated the legal system as if it were a single person or entity, or a kind of undifferentiated mass. We know, however, that the legal system is quite complex. Even the court system is complicated. There are high courts and low courts. Lines of force and communication move up and down. Appeals go up; orders come down. In an administrative agency, the top must get feedback from the bottom, the bottom must get and obey orders from the top. These processes, however, never work perfectly—any more than in the outside world.

What we have learned so far applies to the internal workings of the legal system too. If level A of a system promulgates rules to be obeyed by level B, when will there be compliance? What was considered in Chapter 4 is relevant to this question also. That is, we must think about sanctions, about the value system at level B, about the pressure of peers.

Nevertheless, it is useful to focus, as this chapter does, on the special problems that arise within the legal system. The chapter is divided into two major parts. The first part deals with the consequences of the way legal systems are structured. Some legal systems, particularly those in continental Europe and Latin America, rely more on action by legal officials while others, particularly Anglo-American ones, rely on the parties' lawyers to gather and present evidence. Then there are problems of coordination and control; here we look at many of the devices legal systems use to coordinate activity—rules and surveillance as well as much more. Second, certain specialized roles—notably the lawyer, and the judge—are peculiar to legal systems; in the second part of the chapter we deal with these roles.

THE STRUCTURE OF THE LEGAL SYSTEM

ADVERSARY VS. INQUISITORIAL STRUCTURES: ANGLO-AMERICAN CONTRASTED WITH CONTINENTAL EUROPEAN APPROACHES

The Anglo-American "adversary" system of conducting trials is often contrasted with the approach taken in continental Europe that is sometimes called "inquisitorial." How do these legal processes affect the outcome of trials? Which approach is better? John H. Langbein, in "The German Advantage in Civil Procedure," 52 *University of Chicago Law Review* 823 (1985), as his title suggests, comes out strongly in favor of the continental system.

Under German practice, the court, not the lawyers, bears the "main responsibility for gathering and sifting evidence." Also, the system, unlike the American approach, does not draw a sharp distinction between "pretrial and trial, between discovering evidence and presenting it. Trial is not a single continuous event. Rather, the court gathers and evaluates evidence over a series of hearings, as many as the circumstances require."

In Germany, a case begins with a complaint. However, the plaintiff's lawyer in his complaint will talk not only about the facts of his case but also about the kind of proofs to be presented. He may append actual documents or records. The judge will read the pleadings and start work on an "official dossier, the court file." The judge, when she is ready, may schedule a hearing. At the hearing, she "serves as the examiner-in-chief." Lawyers, according to Langbein, do not coach witnesses, and the elaborate rhythm of examination and cross-examination familiar in an American court is largely absent. At the end of a witness' testimony, the judge prepares a summary. Compared to the "long-winded narrative of American pretrial depositions and trial transcripts," the German system is concise and economical. Also, there are virtually no rules of evidence, mainly because there is no jury in civil cases. If experts are needed to deal with an "issue of technical difficulty," the court will choose the experts and define their role. The battle of experts that is so common in American courts—the partisan nature of expert testimony—is largely, if not entirely, avoided.

The German system also "lessens tensions and theatrics" and "encourages settlement." German proceedings "have the tone not of the theatre, but of a routine business meeting—serious rather than tense." Most of the advantages that Langbein sees in the German system depend on the centrality of the judge, who does not have to share power with a jury and who is stronger vis-a-vis the lawyers than an American judge.

But doesn't this position of strength pose a danger to efficiency or fairness? The Anglo-American system "of partisan fact-gathering has the virtue of its vices: It aligns responsibility with incentive. Each side gathers and presents proofs according to its own calculation of self-interest." What is the system of incentives in Germany? It rests, according to Langbein, on the professionalism of the judges. Judging is a separate career line. Unlike in America, experienced lawyers are not named by political officials to be judges. And judging is, Langbein claims, a career "that creates incentives for diligence and excellence." Thus, one does not find the party hacks—lawyers rewarded with judgeships by political leaders—who so disfigure local justice in the United States.

NOTES AND QUESTIONS

1. Samuel R. Gross, in "The American Advantage: The Value of Inefficient Litigation," 85 *Michigan Law Review* 734, 740–41, 753, 756 (1987), responds to Langbein's article. Gross argues: "efficiency is a poor measure of the quality of a procedural system . . ." He contends:

The main measure of the social value of a judgment [from a court], however, is not speed but accuracy . . . . Langbein believes that the German system is more likely than ours to reach factually correct results. While this is a plausible consequence of his description of the superior rationality of German procedure, I am unconvinced. I do not think that there is enough evidence for a useful comparison, for two reasons: *First,* while the cost and duration of a legal proceeding are (at least in principle) directly observable, its accuracy is almost always unknown since we rarely have any external evidence by which to judge it . . . .

Second, the important question is not how these two fact-finding systems might perform in the abstract, but how many errors they produce in practice. In practice, however, most cases are not litigated. As a result the answer to the question depends in part on the composition of the set of cases that are presented for adjudication, and in part on the resolution of those that are not. This makes cross-national comparisons extraordinarily difficult. In the civil context it would be necessary to consider: (1) the effect of each system of adjudication on the composition of that small subset of disputes that are channeled to litigation in each country, and (2) the "accuracy" of the dispositions of those disputes that are not pursued at all, or settled short of litigation . . . . The data for these comparisons do not exist and would be exceedingly difficult (perhaps impossible) to gather, and the systems involved are so complex that I am skeptical of arguments on either side made without data, especially arguments based solely on the nature of the processes of formal adjudication . . . .

The more substantial benefits of procedural inefficiency have to do with its effects on conduct *outside* of court. Every legal system leaves some "zone of immunity" around individuals, a sphere of actions that become of their nature or magnitude are not as a practice matter subject to governmental control . . . . In other words, inefficiency limits the effectiveness, the "penetration" of formal legal rules, and creates room for divergent results and for patterns of behavior based on nonlegal norms . . . . Often, however, [we cannot bring] formal rules into line with developing operational norms. Informal norms of behavior suffer from the limitations of their advantages: their relative flexibility, and their responsiveness to interests that legal systems are hard pressed to regulate—trust, reputation, civility, etc. Because of these features, such norms may operate very well in practice, and yet be too vague, too complex, too changeable, or too personal to enact as laws, or even fully to articulate.

2. Marc Galanter, in "Adjudication, Litigation, and Related Phenomena" in L. Lipson and S. Wheeler (eds.) *Law and the Social Sciences* (New York: Russell Sage Foundation, 1986), pp. 151, 177, makes the following comment:

One durable stereotype depicts the common-law judge as a passive umpire, in contrast to the civil-law judge who actively manages the case before him . . . . The contrast is a serviceable one, although contemporary common law and civil law courts hardly represent polar opposites. The spectrum of forum passivity and activity runs from the sort of complete disputant control found in many mediative processes to the total control by the forum familiar in commissions of inquiry . . . .

Common-law judging lies at some distance from the passive end of the spectrum . . . . What is more striking about the common-law judges than their purported passivity is their tendency to delegate and supervise rather than to engage in continuous and detailed work on the case . . . . This tendency for common-law judges to be management rather than production workers is connected with the lower ratio of judges to lawyers [in common law compared to civil law systems]. . . ., the higher status enjoyed by common-law judges, and their relative freedom from hierarchic control.

On the actual, as contrasted with the ideal, role of the civil law judge, Galanter refers to John Henry Merryman, *The Civil Law Tradition: an Introduction to the Legal Systems of Western Europe and Latin America* 2d ed. (Stanford, Ca.: Stanford University Press, 1985). Merryman recognizes the differences between judges in the two systems, but he cautions us not to put undue stress on these differences. He writes:

People talk about an "inquisitorial" system of proof-taking as contrasted with the "adversary" system of the common law. The characterization is quite misleading. In fact, the prevailing system in both the civil law and the common law world is the "dispositive" system, according to which the determination of what issues to raise, what evidence to introduce, and what arguments to make is left almost entirely to the parties. Judges in both traditions have some power to undertake inquiries on their own, and in Germany the law and the judicial tradition encourage the judge to play an active role in the proceedings. Elsewhere, however, civil law judges are more passive. (pp. 114–15)

3. There are fewer studies of the law-in-action in the civil law systems of Europe, Latin America or Asia than studies of American or British police, lawyers and courts—at least fewer studies available in English. This is understandable. Something of the flavor of these systems in action can be gleaned from popular literature. For example, Nicholas Freeling's Inspector Henri Castang novels or George Simenon's mysteries which feature Inspector Maigret show us the French criminal justice system in action.

Of course, in the United States too there are thousands of books, plays, movies, and television shows that pivot their action about police, trials, and other aspects of criminal justice. Such literature is a lot more fun than reading scholarly studies. However, we can question these stories' accuracy and whether the world they portray is typical.

4. Professor Langbein has also written about the merits of German criminal procedure. See Langbein, "Land Without Plea Bargaining: How the Germans Do It," 78 *Michigan Law Review* 204 (1979). Mirjan Damaska's, *The Faces of Justice and State Authority: A Comparative Approach to the Legal Process*

(New Haven: Yale University Press, 1986), pp. 186–200, is a thoughtful discussion of the difference between the two types of systems.

5. Is there some way to *test* differences between procedural systems? One possibility is to mount mock trials, differing only in one or another aspect of procedure that corresponds to differences between civil and common law. See John W. Thibaut and Laurens Walker, *Procedural Justice* (Hillsdale, N.J.: Lawrence Erlbaum Associates, 1975).

6. In *A Sociological Theory of Law* (Milan, Italy: Dott A. Giuffrè Editore, 1991), pp. 150–51. Adam Podgorecki draws a distinction between "legal systems based mainly on statute law and legal systems based mainly on precedent." The "statute" systems tend to be "hierarchical" and to stress legal logic. A "statute" system "provides specific directives on how to create new norms and how to incorporate them, into the already existing normative body." The system "alienates both the state officials and average citizens from the real social problems and from each other." Still, this "gap" may be "functional in the long run for officialdom since it gains more authority over the population." But "access of the average member of the society to the law" is limited.

Legal systems based on "precedent" have a different character. They "correspond to the more pluralistically structured societies. Their binding messages come from many scattered sources which are often contradictory." They tend to be flexible, adaptive. The legal profession has a sort of "inductive ability" to find relevant cases. In these systems, professionals build a highly technical world, but they are less "servile" than the lawyers in statute systems. "Statute law systems" may flourish in totalitarian societies "due to their manageability." Precedent-based systems "invite and utilize the participation of heterogeneous social groups while being in this way vulnerable to potential disruptions. Statute legal systems, on the contrary, when they are challenged become even more closed."

Obviously, Podgorecki is thinking of differences between the legal systems of, for example, his native Poland particularly in the period before the end of Communist rule, and that of Canada, where he was living when his book appeared. Do the differences he points to between the two systems really flow from the *form* of the systems? Are there other reasons that account for these differences? Even if we suspect that there is more to it than the *form* of the legal systems involved, does such a conclusion suggest that the form plays no part in explaining these differences?

See, further, on the contrast between "adversary procedure" and "non-adversary or inquisitorial procedure," Blair H. Sheppard and Neil Vidmar, "Adversary Pretrial Procedures and Testimonial Evidence: Effects of Lawyer's Role and Machiavellianism," 39 *Journal of Personality and Social Psychology* 320 (1980).

THE ARRANGEMENT OF LEGAL INSTITUTIONS

The following article reports some of the findings of a study of 16 state Supreme Courts, in the period 1870 to 1970. The states included large states and small ones from every part of the country. The data consisted of a sample of roughly 6,000 cases, drawn from the opinions of the various state supreme courts, from which coders extracted data on the type of case, the procedural history, who won and who lost, what authorities were cited, who the litigants were, and so on.

46. *The Evolution of State Supreme Courts*

Robert A. Kagan,

Bliss Cartwright,

Lawrence M. Friedman,

and Stanton Wheeler

76 *Michigan Law Review* 961 (1978)

I. THE CHANGING CASELOADS OF STATE SUPREME COURTS

☐ The population of the sixteen states in our sample increased steadily over time, from fewer than eleven million in 1870 to over seventy-three million in 1970. The sixteen supreme courts issued an average of 131 opinions in 1870, or 170.8 opinions per million persons. From 1870 to 1880, both the average number of supreme court opinions per state and the total opinions per million persons rose with the population. But soon after 1880, these numbers began to diverge. After reaching a peak of 201 in 1880, the number of opinions per million persons per year has shown a consistent downward trend, averaging a fairly level forty-two since the end of World War II. The average number of opinions per state, however, continued to rise, although at an irregular rate, and reached its high point in 1915, when the sixteen courts issued an average of 291 opinions. It then began a generally downward move, bottoming at 119 opinions per year at the end of World War II. Thereafter, the average number of opinions rose roughly in relation to population growth. In 1970, the sixteen courts wrote an average of 167 opinions per year.

The main trend . . . seems clear: from the latter part of the nineteenth century through the middle of the twentieth state supreme court caseloads (as measured by published opinions) have been brought under greater control, first by breaking the relationship between population and per capita caseload, then by an absolute decline in opinions even as population continued to grow . . . .

II. THE STRUGGLE FOR CASELOAD CONTROL

Notwithstanding the distinctive developments in each state, supreme courts in very different states, confronted with rising caseloads, changed in rather similar and predictable ways, although some states were much quicker than others to make those changes. The crucial developments have been in court structure and jurisdiction. Two changes are especially important: grants of power to supreme courts to select their own cases from petitions for review, and the establishment of intermediate appellate courts between the trial courts and supreme courts.

We can distinguish three rough phases in this evolution and three corresponding "types" of state supreme courts. In the first phase, courts had light caseloads and little or no discretion in selecting cases. In the second phase, courts in states with growing populations were burdened by heavy caseloads, but still had little case-selecting discretion. The courts of the third phase had light caseloads (as measured by opinions issued) and great case-selecting discretion; this phase tended to emerge only after extended political struggle. This part will discuss the three phases in turn, pausing to examine the patterns of transition between the second and third phases.

A. The Low Caseload-Low Discretion State Supreme Court

The United States in 1870 was still predominantly a country of small towns, small farms, and small businesses, run by small government. The national population was about 40,000,000, less than one-fifth of what it is today. Illinois, the fourth most populous state (after New York, Pennsylvania, and Ohio) and the largest in our sixteen-state sample, had about 2,500,000 citizens. Oregon's population was 90,000; Nevada's just over 42,000. The absolute volume of litigation was certainly far smaller than it is today, though almost no research exists on this question.

Most states in 1870 had only one level of appeal from their trial courts. Of the sixteen states in our sample, only New Jersey had an appellate court between its trial court of general jurisdiction and its highest court. In none of our sixteen states could the supreme court select cases from those appealed or screen out frivolous or unimportant appeals—the courts were obligated to hear and decide whatever cases litigants chose to appeal. In constructing their dockets of business, supreme courts in the main were *reactive* rather than *proactive;* the volume and content of their caseloads were "litigant-controlled."

This system worked decently enough, especially for states with small populations. Caseloads were not impossibly large; few supreme courts in 1870 decided more than 200 cases with full opinions each year. Seven states in our sample never rose above one million in population in the nineteenth century: Maine, Rhode Island, West Virginia, South Dakota, Idaho, Oregon and Nevada. From 1870 to 1900, their supreme courts averaged fewer than 100 opinions per year. Five of these states remained smaller than one million through 1970: Maine,

Rhode Island, South Dakota, Idaho and Nevada. Their annual supreme court caseloads in the twentieth century generally remained below 150 cases, and often below 100.

B. The High Caseload-Low Discretion State Supreme Court

Other states, however, had larger populations, and some grew quite rapidly. Increases in population generally meant more cases in the trial courts. If the proportion of lower-court litigants who appeal stayed constant (or fell at a rate slower than the rate of increase in the number of lower-court cases), and if appeal remained available as of right, then we would expect population growth to bring more and more appeals. Our data confirm this guess. Supreme court opinions in some of the more populous and faster-growing states reached averages of 400 or 500 a year.

In California and Michigan, population doubled between 1870 and 1895; the number of opinions issued each year jumped from 200 or less in 1870 to over 550 in 1890 and 1895. North Carolina's population took longer to double (its population was 1.1 million in 1870, and 2.2 million in 1910), but its supreme court also doubled its output, from 208 opinions in 1870 to an average of 440 in 1910 and 1915. In Illinois, where the population had reached three million, the supreme court issued 624 opinions in 1875. When population topped one million in Alabama and Minnesota, the supreme court caseloads quickly grew to over 350 per year.

A court whose caseload jumps in a short time to 300, 400, or 500 cases a year cannot be quite the same kind of court as one which decides 50, 75, or 100 cases. Courts, of course, have a certain capacity to accommodate increases in business. Judges can do less research on their own and lean more on the research of lawyers. Judges can spend less time on each case, restrict oral argument, or eliminate it entirely. They can limit the length of briefs and produce shorter or even brief "per curiam" opinions. Still, supreme court judges must read at least some briefs, consider competing arguments, decide cases, and write opinions. If their caseload doubles, the judges are harder pressed to keep up, unless they can devise some drastic shortcuts or divisions of labor.

In any event, judges on busy courts had less time to invest in each case than their predecessors who heard fewer cases. At the least, the flood of cases *threatened* the quality of decision-making, and some supreme courts clearly saw it that way. Lawyers and legal scholars in the early twentieth century often complained of intolerable delays in the state supreme courts. They also complained that there was not enough time for oral argument or for judges to discuss cases among themselves, and that high courts wasted time on trivial cases. Moreover, some critics contended that the hard-pressed judges relied mechanically on precedent and wrote excessively formalistic opinions which offered only feeble guidance for lower courts and the bar. Of course, our data cannot measure directly the effect of the bursting caseloads on the thoughtfulness and craftsmanship of decisions in the late nineteenth century. But between 1870 and 1900, courts with heavy caseloads did differ from their less burdened counterparts in several distinct ways. Table 1 presents evidence of the possible effects of caseload on three variables that may bear on the quality of opinions in supreme courts: their length, density of citations, and tendency to cite authorities other than cases.

As Table 1 shows, the relationships vary a good deal in strength, but on the average, courts with larger caseloads wrote opinions which were shorter, which used fewer citations, and which referred less often to treatises, legal encyclopedias, and law reviews. Although by no means overwhelming, the evidence is fairly consistent.

It would be rash to conclude from these findings that the decisions of heavy-caseload supreme courts were slap-dash or ill-considered; conciseness can be a virtue and long strings of citations can be a vice. These findings are consistent, however, with the idea that courts with massive caseloads were forced to limit the time, effort, and research devoted to each case. This may have increased the risk of routine, poorly crafted opinions.

C. Patterns of Adaptation to High Caseload

How do organizations in general react to an increasing volume of business? A common way is to hire more staff. More staff means more people to supervise and coordinate, and it leads to functional specialization and more layers of authority. The organizations grow and take on the familiar bureaucratic form.

But growth also makes possible economies of scale. The organization works out routines and rules to cover recurring problems. Nonroutine problems are shifted to top officials, who have experts on their staff. A complex organization also tries to stabilize its relationship with the outside world. It attempts to "smooth out" fluctuations in demands that flow in, sometimes by rationing its services. Sometimes it feels it will be better off by taking on some jobs too important to leave to outsiders. A steel mill, for example, might want to control the sources of iron or coal; a police department might patrol aggressively instead of relying entirely on citizens' complaints.

A supreme court faced with growing demands on its time, and worried about the quality of its work, might want to use these classic adaptations. That would mean more staff, new levels of courts, perhaps more specialized appellate bodies, and more efficient ways to allocate judicial work. Such a court would want to limit the number and kinds

TABLE 1   THE POSSIBLE EFFECT OF CASELOAD ON THREE MEASURES OF THE QUALITY
OF STATE SUPREME COURT OPINIONS, 1870–1900

Average Number of State Supreme Court Opinions	AVERAGE STATE SUPREME COURT OPINION LENGTH, IN PAGES		
	Longer than Median	Shorter than Median	Mean
Over 200*	Ill. (4.2)	N.C. (3.9)	3.6 pages
		Kan. (3.8)	
		Mich. (3.5)	
		Cal. (3.3)	
		Minn. (3.2)	
		Ala. (3.0)	
Under 200**	W. Va. (8.6)	Me. (3.5)	4.7 pages
	Nev. (5.0)	R.I. (3.2)	
	S.D. (4.7)		
	N.J. (4.5)		
	Ida. (4.4)		
	Ore. (4.2)		
	Tenn. (4.1)		

Average Number of State Supreme Court Opinions	PERCENT OF STATE SUPREME COURT OPINIONS CONTAINING CITATIONS TO MORE THAN EIGHT PRECEDENTS		
Over 200*	More than Median	Fewer than Median	Mean
	Ala. (42.1)	N.C. (26.9)	24.3%
	Kan. (30.1)	Ill. (23.8)	
		Mich. (19.9)	
		Cal. (15.9)	
		Minn. (11.1)	
Under 200**	W. Va. (45.6)	Ore. (28.0)	32.8%
	S.D. (41.5)	Tenn. (25.4)	
	R.I. (39.7)	Ida. (17.0)	
	Me. (35.2)		
	N.J. (32.5)		
	Nev. (30.1)		

Average Number of State Supreme Court Opinions	PERCENT OF STATE SUPREME COURT CASES WITH CITATIONS TO LEGAL WRITING (TREATISES, ENCYCLOPEDIAS, LAW REVIEWS)		
Over 200*	More than Median	Fewer than Median	Mean
	Ala. (61.8)	Kan. (34.3)	37.0%
	N.C. (42.6)	Ill. (38.0)	
		Minn. (35.6)	
		Cal. (22.0)	
		Mich. (19.7)	
Under 200**	Ore. (56.9)	S.D. (37.5)	44.4%
	W. Va (55.9)	Me. (22.3)	
	Tenn. (49.0)	Ida. (19.0)	
	Nev. (47.8)		
	N.J. (44.5)		
	R.I. (39.8)		

*Except for Kansas, the average was over 300.
**Except for Tennessee, the average was 136 or less.

of appeals that it received. Ideally, it would enunciate general rules or principles that lower courts could apply routinely and accurately, so that it need hear only the most serious and important cases.

How could a supreme court ensure that it heard those cases, and only those? It would have to develop a system for identifying significant legal problems and screening out the trivial ones; it would not leave the selection process to the whims and pocketbooks of litigants. A professional staff to help research and write might be more reliable than litigants' lawyers, who differ widely in ability, integrity, and energy. The state's highest court, wrote [Benjamin] Cardozo in 1927, exists not for the "individual litigant, but for the indefinite body of litigants . . . . The wrongs of aggrieved suitors are only the algebraic symbols from which the court is to work out the formula of justice." In short, busy state supreme courts would strive to become less reactive, less controlled by litigants, more self-directed and bureaucratically organized.

Reform-minded jurists, like those who founded the American Judicature Society, shared these notions . . . . Reformers pressed for integrated, rational court structures, supported by administrative staffs, to monitor the flow of business and assure that judicial manpower was sensibly allocated. They called in particular for intermediate appellate courts and they felt a supreme court should be able to choose its cases and write its own rules of procedure.

Some of these steps toward reorganization were taken, but some were not. Not until the 1960s did most large and medium-sized states establish intermediate appellate courts and allow supreme courts substantial discretion over caseloads. Through much of the past century, many state supreme courts struggled along year after year, writing 400 or more opinions, using techniques and procedures that had hardly changed in generations. Nonetheless, several different adaptations to the caseload problem can be distinguished.

1. Early Intermediate Appellate Courts and Discretion

Among our sixteen sample states, New Jersey, Tennessee, and West Virginia were unusually successful in controlling the volume of their supreme courts' caseloads, and they began this process remarkably early. New Jersey . . . had established an intermediate appellate court for cases "at law" (as opposed to equity) in 1844. This court, called the Supreme Court, was later divided into several three-judge panels, each of which heard appeals from different trial courts. Although New Jersey's highest court, the Court of Errors and Appeals, could not reject appeals from the lower appellate courts, its volume remained extraordinarily small, averaging 145 opinions per year between 1900 and 1935, even though the state's population grew from 1.8 million to 4 million.

Tennessee established an intermediate appellate court for equity cases in 1895 and for all civil cases in 1907. The state expanded this Court of Civil Appeals in 1925. The supreme court's caseload remained at 150 opinions or fewer throughout the century. West Virginia, a smaller state, controlled its supreme court's caseload without intermediate appellate courts. Rather, from 1872 on, it allowed the supreme court to screen appeals and to reject those clearly without merit.

2. Functional Equivalents for Intermediate Appellate Courts

California's experience exemplifies the full battery of methods used to control heavy caseloads. In the late nineteenth century, California responded to rapid growth by increasing the size of its supreme court—from three to five judges in the 1860s. In 1879, when the court was hearing over 500 cases a year and writing 350 opinions, the number of justices was increased to seven. The court was also authorized in 1879 to divide into three-judge panels or departments to hear cases separately. The full court gathered en banc only for extraordinarily important cases. Other states, too, adopted this innovation. The department system was also important because it recognized differences among appeals. Some appeals were more "significant" than others; the less important were treated in one way, more important cases in another. In effect, the division into panels created two intermediate appellate courts—or at least alternative supreme courts—for most appeals.

The California Supreme Court judges issued 402 opinions in 1885, 122 en banc and 280 in departments. At this point, the legislature authorized the court to delegate to three "commissioners" power to hear cases and make preliminary decisions. Commissioners, in effect, were auxiliary judges (or, perhaps, highly trained and experienced staff members). The court could review and modify the commissioners' opinions, but in practice it simply issued them as its own. This innovation, too, gave the Supreme Court some choice of cases it wished to concentrate on. The California Supreme Court continued to produce a prodigious number of opinions (well over 500 in 1895 and 1900), but the judges themselves wrote only 300 per year, 100 en banc, 200 in departments; commissioners handled another 200.

The use of commissioners was discontinued in 1904, when California set up a system of intermediate appellate courts, called courts of appeals. In some types of cases, litigants could appeal only to a court of appeals; in others, they could go directly from the trial court to the supreme court. The California Supreme Court could, however, transfer some of its cases to the court of appeals. It also had discretion to review decisions of the lower appellate courts. Although the supreme court gradually transferred more and more of its cases to the court of appeals, it still averaged over 250 opinions a year from 1910 to 1935, most of them decided en banc.

3. The Weak Intermediate Appellate Court System

Illinois wove a different pattern. It created an intermediate appellate court in 1877 (when its supreme court heard over 600 cases) but allowed these courts only a limited role. Appellants could still proceed directly from trial courts to supreme court as of right unless the amount at issue was less than $1,000. Moreover, appeals from the lower appellate court to the supreme court were available as of right.

The Illinois Supreme Court caseload fell to an average of 240 opinions in 1880 and 1885, but by 1900 and 1905, as population and litigation grew, the volume had climbed back to an average of 475 opinions per year. Statutory amendments in 1909 further limited appeals to the supreme court; however, litigants could still appeal directly in felony, tax, real estate, and most constitutional cases. The Supreme Court's caseload remained high. The court seemed reluctant to use its discretionary power to deny appeals from the appellate courts; hence, double appeals were common. As late as 1958, court reformers in Illinois complained that the supreme court was "hamstrung," that it heard "a wide variety of cases with little legal significance."

4. States Without Intermediate Appellate Courts

Other states dragged their feet even more than Illinois. Minnesota never established an intermediate appellate court, and its supreme court caseload averaged a staggering 425 cases per year from 1890 through 1935. The load declined during the 1940s and 1950s without any notable change in supreme court jurisdiction, but it climbed again in the 1960s, and reached 332 in 1970. Kansas, after brief experiments in the 1890s with commissioners and intermediate appellate courts, abandoned both. Its supreme court averaged 407 opinions a year from 1910 to 1935. Yet here too, without any major structural change, the caseload dropped off; it averaged a high but not unbearable 225 opinions a year from 1950 to 1970. North Carolina had no lower appellate court until the 1960s. Its supreme court had averaged well over 300, and sometimes over 400, opinions per year since the 1890s.

Surprisingly, Michigan, one of the big industrial states, had no intermediate appellate court until 1965. The Supreme Court issued 438 opinions in 1880 and 413 in 1885. The legislature increased the court from four judges to five, and then in 1903 to eight. But this seemed only to invite more appeals. The caseload topped 500 cases from 1905 to 1915. In 1917, the Michigan legislature freed the Supreme Court of its duty to hear appeals from civil cases where the amount in dispute was less than $500, but this had no significant effect on caseload, for the court continued to write over 400 opinions a year in the 1920s. In 1927, Michigan's Supreme Court gained the discretion to accept or reject criminal appeals, which had comprised an average of 22% of its caseload in 1920 and 1925. That percentage was considerably reduced after 1927, but the court still wrote more than 400 opinions a year in the 1930s. As was true of almost every supreme court, the Michigan court's caseload declined sharply in the 1940s. Still, the court averaged 256 opinions a year from 1945 to 1960. Caseload was controlled partly by holding criminal cases to an unusually low 12% of the docket.

5. Some Speculations on the Politics of State Supreme Court Reorganization

We are not sure why supreme court caseloads remained so high so long in so many states, and why structural reform did not come sooner. One crucial factor, it would seem, is that in many states the structure of the judicial system was embedded—one might say frozen—in the state constitution. For many reasons, too, legislators and political leaders were uninterested in reform, or opposed to it outright. Politicians certainly did not see backlogs and overloads in the supreme court as the most pressing problem of the day. Spending money on salaries for new intermediate appellate judges was never politically inviting. The work of some state courts was controversial. Judges were sometimes perceived as reactionaries and as enemies of social legislation; to give such judges more power and discretion would only encourage "government by judiciary." Supreme court reform was often part of a general reform package that included reshaping the lower courts, and thus local magistrates, justices of the peace, court clerks, and others who felt they might suffer in a reorganization outshouted the few reformers. Political and party officials threatened with loss of patronage were also part of the opposition.

Indeed, supreme court judges themselves did not always strongly advocate reorganization. Their self-interest called for caseload control, of course; in modern court systems, more cases do not bring more fees or higher salaries, but simply more work. A court that decides 200 or fewer cases a year and concentrates on difficult and important problems tends to be more prestigious than one struggling through 400 mostly routine cases. But judges also have a tradition of reticence. It is thought unseemly for them to lobby, to seek more power, or to press for reforms that encourage the use of courts.

In addition, in some states, there seem to have been strong feelings about a *right* to appeal. It was argued that every litigant, big or small, should have a chance to take his case, big or small, to the state supreme court. Finally, some jurists feared that reforms would impair the law's uniformity and certainty. A single supreme court was better, the argument ran, than a multitude of commissioners, divisions, or lower appellate courts, all issuing their own pronouncements on "the law."

But ideologies have been shifting over the years. Gradually, judges have espoused a somewhat different view of themselves and their roles. "Sociological jurisprudence" and legal realism have made their mark. At least *some* state supreme court judges now feel that making policy is an inevitable part of their work, and they wonder whether they should not approach it more systematically. To do so, they must be able to winnow out the trivial cases and concentrate on the important. That cannot be done without structural reform, intermediate appellate courts, control over dockets, and larger staffs.

Meanwhile, reform has become better organized. Since 1917, the American Judicature Society has published a journal which stresses judicial reform. Since the 1920s, state judicial councils, staffed by judges and legislators, have gathered statistics on court business, issued reports and recommendations, and lobbied for reform.

Nevertheless, state supreme courts have not acquired caseload control easily; it has been a long, complicated process, heavily dependent on the political skill of judicial reformers and on the local political climate. Apparent victories have often been subverted. Kansas established an intermediate appellate court in 1895 and abolished it six years later. Illinois set up a lower appellate court, but still allowed direct appeals to the supreme court for cases involving certain politically important interests. Not until the 1960s did the reformers gain real momentum. Only eleven states had intermediate courts in 1948; by 1970, twenty-three did . . . .

D. The Low Caseload-High Discretion State Supreme Court

By the end of the 1960s, most of the medium-sized and larger states in our sample of sixteen had created intermediate appellate courts and given their supreme courts substantial discretion to select cases from petitions for review. (Kansas and Minnesota were the only exceptions.) Consequently, supreme court caseloads, as measured by opinions issued, were sharply reduced . . . .

This increasing discretion and diminishing caseload implied corresponding changes in the function of the supreme courts. It suggested an emerging societal consensus that state supreme courts should not be passive, reactive bodies, which simply applied "the law" to correct "errors" or miscarriages of justice in individual cases, but that these courts should be policy-makers and, at least in some cases, legal innovators. After the 1967 reform in North Carolina, the Supreme Court, it was said, could now concentrate on "truly significant questions of law." Even in smaller states, the ideal was a low-volume, well-staffed supreme court which "delegated" routine appeals and supervision of trial courts to lower appellate courts and concentrated on important, far-reaching cases. Rhode Island's supreme court had no case-selecting discretion; one justice complained in 1974 that half of the court's cases "don't belong in the highest court of a state." Moreover, requiring appellants to petition the court for a share of its precious time encouraged a new, more policy-oriented judicial role. Appellants could not merely argue that the trial court had committed "errors." They had to demonstrate that they deserved to be heard for special reasons. When addressing the modern high-discretion supreme court, therefore, appellants often emphasized the case's legal significance and social consequences, for which the court was urged to assume responsibility.

E. A Typology of State Supreme Courts

Table 2, which shows the population and caseload for each state in seven time periods, summarizes the movement toward caseload control. We grouped the states by the "type" into which they fell during most of the 1870–1970 period. Because of their dramatic shifts, we placed Oregon and California in the type that best characterized them in the last two decades. The three types, which represent different combinations of population, supreme court caseload, and discretion, are as follows:

Type I: Low population states (under one million) with no supreme court case-selecting discretion, no lower appellate court, and relatively light caseloads. Rhode Island, Maine, South Dakota, Idaho, and Nevada were in this category throughout the century. Their supreme courts averaged fewer than 100 opinions per year.

Type II: Medium-sized (over one million) and large states with little or no supreme court case-selecting discretion, and heavy caseloads. Illinois, Michigan, Minnesota, Kansas, North Carolina and Alabama were in this category for most of the century. Oregon joined it in population terms in the 1930s and in caseload terms (over 220 opinions) in the 1915–1930 and 1960–1970 years. These supreme courts averaged well over 200 opinions a year in most time periods, and often 350 or more.

Type III: Medium-sized or large states with substantial controls over supreme court caseloads (lower appellate courts handled most appeals or supreme courts had wide discretion to choose cases) and relatively light caseloads, measured by published opinions. New Jersey, Tennessee and West Virginia were in this category for most of the century. California's Supreme Court joined it about 1940, when it began exercising its discretion to assign most appeals to the court of appeals. These supreme courts averaged under 200 opinions a year, and often fewer than 150 . . . .

III. THE CONSEQUENCES OF CASELOAD CONTROL

We have suggested that state supreme courts fall into three different types in terms of caseload and discretion to select cases. There has been a pronounced evolution toward a structure that grants high discre-

TABLE 2 Average Population And Opinion Caseloads For State Supreme Courts, 1870–1970

States	1870–1880		1885–1895		1900–1910		1915–1925		1930–1940		1945–1955		1960–1970		Growth Ratio[a]
	Population Mean	Opinion Mean	Population Mean	Opinion Mean	Population Mean	Opinion Mean	Population Mean	Opinion Mean	Population Mean	Opinion Mean	Population Mean	Opinion Mean	Population Mean	Opinion Mean	Opinions to Population 1945–1970
R.I.	0.3	39	0.4	81	0.5	106	0.6	76	0.7	89	0.8	88	0.9	162	5.95
Nev.	0.1	45	0.1	20	0.1	23	0.1	43	0.1	39	0.2	36	0.4	131	2.11
Ida.	—	—	0.1	48	0.2	101	0.4	131	0.5	110	0.6	81	0.7	105	1.70
Me.	0.6	83	0.7	122	0.7	105	0.8	119	0.8	80	0.9	55	1.0	71	3.79
S.D.	—	—	0.4	106	0.5	196	0.6	153	0.7	111	0.7	61	0.7	68	4.10
mean	0.3	56	0.3	77	0.4	106	0.5	104	0.6	87	0.6	64	0.7	107	3.55
N.C.	1.2	257	1.6	336	2.1	351	2.6	397	3.4	421	4.1	275	4.8	308	0.65
Ore.	0.1	37	0.3	115	0.5	152	0.8	267	1.0	168	1.5	115	2.0	274	4.84
Ill.	2.8	448	3.9	309	5.2	435	6.5	399	7.8	302	8.7	232	10.6	261	0.57
Ala.	1.1	263	1.5	358	2.0	356	2.4	415	2.7	392	3.1	268	3.4	243	-0.96
Kan.	0.7	170	1.3	256	1.6	277	1.8	457	1.8	324	1.9	190	2.2	236	1.69
Minn.	0.6	140	1.3	408	1.9	375	2.4	423	2.7	352	3.0	162	3.6	234	2.28
Mich.	1.4	267	2.1	523	2.6	499	3.7	458	5.1	454	6.4	253	8.3	194	-0.91
mean	1.1	226	1.7	329	2.3	349	2.9	402	3.5	345	4.1	214	5.0	248	1.16
Cal.	0.7	314	1.2	506	1.9	360	3.6	270	6.3	260	10.9	165	17.9	153	-0.11
N.J.	1.0	38	1.5	57	2.2	120	3.2	138	4.1	146	4.9	132	6.6	129	-0.07
Tenn.	1.4	229	1.8	125	2.1	119	2.4	124	2.8	136	3.3	132	3.8	128	-0.21
W. Va.	0.5	50	0.8	121	1.1	147	1.5	256	1.8	175	2.0	87	1.8	93	0.69
mean	0.9	158	1.3	202	1.8	187	2.7	197	3.8	179	5.3	129	7.5	126	0.08
Grand Mean	0.9	170	1.2	25	1.6	233	2.1	258	2.6	223	3.3	146	4.3	174	F = 5.29 Sig = .021

[a]Growth ratio is the ratio of growth in volume of state supreme court opinions to growth of population in the state. The overall figures remain about the same, but the mean-differences among the three state groups are less significant. Growth ratios have also been calculated for the average opinions per judge to population. The mean-differences among the three state groups are 3.72 for the low-discretion states, 0.72 for the mixed-discretion states and 0.16 for the high-discretion states. The F value for mean differences are 2.71 (a borderline significance level of .10).

tion and permits lighter caseloads. One might expect supreme courts even in smaller states to take this form if caseloads continue to grow. In this part, we inquire whether differences in court type produced measurable changes in the types of cases that came before the court, in opinion style, and in case results. We concentrated on the 1940–1970 period, during which our courts fell rather neatly into three types.

A. Type of Cases

If we take the last century as a whole, we find a marked decline in percentage of state supreme court cases that stemmed from private business or property transactions (contract, debt collection, real property), the categories that dominated court dockets in the late nineteenth century. Conversely, the number of tort, criminal, and public-law cases grew considerably. In the most recent third of our survey period—1940–1970— criminal and constitutional cases increased the most sharply.

To a large extent, these trends are independent of the structure of state supreme courts. They reflect nationwide changes in society, economy, and law. The automobile produced more tort cases in almost every state from the 1920s on. Beginning in the late 1930s, as the rate of business failures declined, debt-collection cases declined in every court, regardless of caseload or the level of a state's economic development. That trend probably reflected a stronger, more rational banking and credit system; deposit insurance; and perhaps the long boom that followed World War II. Criminal cases increased dramatically in almost all state supreme courts in the 1960s, again regardless of structure, partly because of a rising crime rate and perhaps also because the Warren Court imposed on the state courts new due process rights for criminal defendants.

These trends were general but by no means uniform. In theory, state supreme courts with discretion to select their cases could more easily resist the kinds of cases litigated in great number in the lower courts. Had they chosen, they could have concentrated on statistically less frequent, and presumably more significant, types of cases, and they could have stimulated new areas of litigation. We hypothesized that courts with high discretion and low caseload would tend, on the average, to *lead* the shift away from private-law cases toward criminal- and public-law cases and that they would also lead the shift toward cases raising constitutional issues. We assumed that high-discretion courts would be less likely to consider private-law cases worth their scarce time.

The basic data appear in Table 3. The relationships between type of court and type of case are not powerful, but they do point in the predicted direction. From 1840 to 1970, the percentage of property, contract, collection, and corporate cases declined in every state (compared to 1905– 1935), but courts with greater power over case selection tended to have lower percentages of these cases. Criminal and public-law cases increased in all states, but the courts with most case-selecting discretion

TABLE 3 CONSEQUENCE VARIABLES: TYPE OF CASE, 1940–1970

State	Property, Contract, Collection, & Corporate-Law Cases			Criminal- & Public-Law Cases			Private Torts (Without Workmen's Compensation)			Constitutional Cases		
	Percent State Supreme Court cases 1940–1970	Rank order	Percent change from 1905–1935	Percent State Supreme Court cases 1940–1970	Rank order	Percent change from 1905–1935	Percent State Supreme Court cases 1940–1970	Rank order	Percent change from 1905–1935	Percent State Supreme Court cases 1940–1970	Rank order	Percent change from 1905–1935
Rhode Island	26.2	11	−9.5	31.0	11	14.3	21.4	3	−3.2	5.6	15	0.8
Nevada	32.5	3	−11.1	40.5	5	7.2	10.3	14	7.1	15.9	5	3.2
Idaho	31.7	4	−32.6	30.2	12	6.4	16.7	7	10.4	13.5	10	1.6
Maine	28.6	7	−20.6	41.3	4	25.5	15.9	8	0.1	14.3	8	9.5
South Dakota	26.9	10	−31.8	37.4	8	19.2	15.8	10	8.7	14.3	8	11.9
mean	29.2	7	−21.1	36.1	8	14.5	16.0	8.4	4.6	12.7	9.2	5.4
North Carolina	28.6	7	−20.5	38.1	6	15.9	12.8	12	−5.4	7.9	12	−5.4
Oregon	33.3	2	−22.2	22.2	16	2.3	28.5	1	16.6	7.1	13	3.2
Illinois	17.5	15	−13.5	68.3	1	18.3	3.1	16	−2.4	33.3	1	26.2
Alabama	41.2	1	−14.4	26.2	15	8.8	15.1	11	2.4	5.6	15	−1.6
Kansas	29.3	6	−16.0	30.2	12	4.8	18.3	6	0.1	7.1	13	2.4
Minnesota	25.4	13	−17.5	28.6	14	2.4	25.4	2	9.5	10.3	11	4.8
Michigan	26.2	11	−25.3	35.7	10	19.8	19.9	4	0.1	15.1	7	7.1
mean	28.8	7.9	−18.5	35.6	10.6	10.3	17.6	7.4	3.0	12.4	10.3	5.2
California	22.2	14.9	−19.9	48.4	3	16.7	10.4	13	0.9	31.8	2	12.7
New Jersey	27.8	9	−23.8	36.5	9	22.3	19.0	5	−3.2	15.9	5	9.5
Tennessee	14.3	16	−16.7	50.0	2	9.5	7.9	15	−2.4	16.7	4	0.8
West Virginia	29.9	5	−20.0	38.1	6	14.3	15.9	8	−0.7	19.8	3	7.1
mean	23.6	11	−20.1	43.3	5	15.7	13.3	10.3	−1.4	21.0	3.5	7.5
Grand Mean	27.6	—	−19.7	37.7	—	13.0	16.0	—	2.4	14.6	—	5.9
F Value	1.15	—	0.22	0.65	—	0.85	0.54	—	1.1	1.78	—	0.13
F Sig.	.347	—	.805	.540	—	.449	.596	—	.362	.208	—	.884

had more of these, on the average. Tort cases (resulting primarily from automobile accidents) increased somewhat in the supreme court dockets of most Type I and II states, but they declined in higher-discretion courts, except in California, where they stayed steady at an already low level.

However, the differences are by no means great, and marked individual variations exist within each type of court. Illinois, for example, had more criminal cases and fewer private-law cases than most states with greater caseload discretion. Differences within types of states tended to be larger than differences among types. We have, then, definite but quite modest evidence that the states with greater caseload discretion tended to lead the generally shifting emphasis from "private law" to "public law" cases.

Table 3 also shows that in the 1940–1970 years, Type III supreme courts more frequently decided constitutional issues. Cases with constitutional issues made up more than a fifth of the supreme court docket in high-discretion states, compared to about an eighth of the cases in other states. Caseload control does, therefore, seem to provide the courts with the ability to concentrate on frontier regions of law and on cases of constitutional significance. Still, despite their more "primitive" structure, other states participated in these trends. Court structure influences, but does not alone determine, the types of cases state supreme courts hear . . . .

C. Case Results

Are the actual results of cases affected when supreme courts control their caseload? We looked at three measures of case results: the percentage of reversals by a supreme court; the percentage of non-unanimous supreme court decisions (the dissent rate); and the percentage of cases declaring laws, decisions, or practices unconstitutional, among cases that raise such issues. Table 5 displays the results of these three measures.

The three measures, especially the reversal rates, indicate that caseload control does make a difference. From the first third to the second third of the twentieth century, the reversal rate for Type I courts declined, while the reversal rate for Type III courts increased. From 1940 to 1970, Type I courts reversed only one-third of all the cases they reviewed. Type III courts reversed nearly half. Individual states ranged from the low reversal rate of 24.6% in Kansas to the high 59.5% of West Virginia. Except for North Carolina, however, the reversal rate was higher in each of the Type III jurisdictions than in any of the courts that had less discretion to winnow out unmeritorious appeals. Of course, case-selecting discretion does not necessarily mean that supreme courts only take cases they intend to reverse. After all, most Type III courts reversed fewer than half of their cases.

The dissent rates were not so uniform. Dissent has always been

TABLE 4   CONSEQUENCE VARIABLES: OPINION STYLE

State	Page Length of Majority Opinion			Law Review Citations			Citations of Prior Court Cases			Citations to the Case by Out-of-State Courts		
	Average opinion length	Rank order	Percent change from 1905–1935	Average opinion length	Rank order	Percent change from 1905–1935	Average opinion length	Rank order	Percent change from 1905–1935	Average opinion length	Rank order	Percent change from 1905–1935
Rhode Island	4.8	13	0.3	2.9	14	2.9	24.4	16	-5.2	0.7	13	-1.6
Nevada	6.8	3	1.0	5.7	6	3.2	51.6	10	10.1	1.8	4	0.0
Idaho	6.1	8	1.3	3.2	12	3.2	69.8	2	33.0	1.2	11	-0.8
Maine	5.8	11	1.4	4.3	9	4.3	50.8	11	7.6	1.3	7	-0.9
South Dakota	4.5	14	0.5	6.9	5	4.4	41.1	13	19.7	1.3	7	-0.4
mean	5.6	9.8	0.9	4.6	9.2	3.6	47.5	10.4	13.0	1.2	8.4	-0.7
North Carolina	5.1	12	0.8	4.2	10	4.2	61.0	6	9.0	0.7	13	-0.7
Oregon	6.8	3	1.6	14.9	3	14.9	54.0	9	14.8	1.8	4	-0.1
Illinois	6.0	9	0.6	4.7	8	3.7	58.0	8	13.6	2.2	3	-0.7
Alabama	6.0	9	1.9	2.1	15	2.1	65.0	5	8.0	0.6	16	-1.1
Kansas	6.3	7	2.4	2.0	16	2.0	48.0	12	18.6	1.3	7	-1.3
Minnesota	6.5	6	2.3	14.0	4	10.6	59.5	7	28.3	1.7	6	-1.0
Michigan	4.5	14	0.3	5.6	7	5.6	38.4	15	14.6	1.3	7	-0.6
mean	5.9	8.6	1.4	6.8	9.0	6.2	54.8	8.9	15.3	1.4	8	-0.8
California	7.5	1	1.4	17.5	2	17.5	73.0	1	22.8	4.0	1	1.3
New Jersey	6.8	3	2.6	19.6	1	18.6	66.6	3	42.0	3.0	2	0.6
Tennessee	4.5	14	-0.7	3.4	11	3.4	39.7	14	-15.9	1.2	11	-1.7
West Virginia	7.1	2	2.1	3.0	13	3.0	65.1	4	18.9	0.7	13	-1.0
mean	6.5	5	1.4	10.9	6.75	10.6	61.1	5.5	17.0	2.2	6.75	-0.2
Grand Mean	5.9	—	1.2	7.1	—	6.5	54.1	—	15.0	1.5	—	-0.6
F Value	0.87	—	0.47	1.36	—	1.99	1.2	—	0.08	1.66	—	0.68
F Sig.	.441	—	.635	.291	—	.177	.331	—	.924	.229	—	.522

uncommon in Tennessee, but the other three Type III courts, West Virginia, California and New Jersey (all of which indeed had greater discretion than Tennessee), had higher dissent rates than the averages for Type I and Type II courts. This suggests either that these courts chose controversial issues or that they had the time and inclination to emphasize the controversial issues in their cases. Yet here too, differences among states are more striking than differences among categories. Idaho, for example, had an unexpectedly high rate of dissent (22%), although Nevada, a neighbor with a rapidly increasing caseload, was becoming increasingly unanimous. The Michigan Supreme Court, noted for its contentiousness, produced many dissents (28.6%) despite its heavy caseload for most of the 1940–1970 period. In California and New Jersey, which perhaps represent the wave of the future, fully a third of the cases generated dissents.

We noted that the Type III courts more often heard cases that raised constitutional issues. Table 5 shows that they were also more likely to declare a law or practice unconstitutional. Holding the number of constitutional issues constant, the small population states of Type I became on the whole less likely in the 1940–1970 period to declare an act or practice unconstitutional; on the average, they did so in only 13.5% of their cases. In Type III states, allegations of unconstitutionality were sustained about three times out of ten (30.1%), compared to an average of 17.4% for the busier, low-discretion courts of Type II (although Michigan and Minnesota also scored high in this measure).

Finally, the Type III courts were more likely, on the average, to decide in favor of defendants in criminal appeals, the most rapidly increasing and changing area of law during the last two decades of our research period. The Type III courts may or may not have been more sympathetic to the underdog; the results may simply reflect their greater capacity to screen claims of defendants that were legally more tenuous . . . . Clearly, however, the courts with case-selecting discretion had a greater opportunity to use their time and energy to articulate new law at the frontiers of criminal procedure, rather than dealing with routine criminal matters routinely . . . .

On balance, our rough indicators suggest that measurable changes in the subject and style of judicial opinions [on this point, see Table 4], and in results of decisions, coincide with increased discretion to select cases, with court reorganization, and with the changes in judges' sense of their own function that are likely to accompany reorganization . . . . [F]rom 1940 to 1970, the high-discretion courts tended to move more rapidly into new areas of law and to accept more constitutional cases. Their higher rate of dissenting and separate concurring opinions suggests that their cases were more often controversial or that the judges were more likely to treat them as such. They reversed lower-court decisions more often, and they wrote longer opinions which cited cases and law reviews more often.

TABLE 5   CONSEQUENCE VARIABLES: OUTCOMES, 1940–1970

State	Cases Reversed			Non-unanimous Decisions			Declarations of Unconstitutionality in Cases with Constitutional Issues			Criminal Cases Decisions for Defendant		
	Percent	Rank order	Percent change from 1905–1935	Percent	Rank order	Percent change from 1905–1935	Percent	Rank order	Percent change from 1905–1935	Percent	Rank order	Percent change from 1905–1935
Rhode Island	35.2	9	0.2	5.6	13	4.0	14.3	11	14.3	61.2	2	11.2
Nevada	28.2	15	−9.4	6.4	11	−9.5	20.0	7	−17.5	19.3	14	−5.7
Idaho	32.8	11	−5.6	22.3	4	6.3	0.0	15	−6.7	26.6	13	−15.2
Maine	30.3	14	−10.4	4.8	14	3.2	16.7	9	−33.3	26.7	12	6.7
South Dakota	40.3	6	−2.9	16.8	8	−3.0	16.7	9	16.7	36.3	7	−20.8
mean	33.4	11.0	−5.6	11.2	10.0	0.2	13.5	12.2	−5.3	34.4	9.6	−4.8
North Carolina	47.2	2	12.0	17.7	7	5.7	10.0	14	10.0	27.5	11	6.1
Oregon	39.2	8	9.6	18.2	6	10.2	0.0	15	−20.0	33.3	9	−4.2
Illinois	33.1	10	−13.3	6.4	11	−6.3	19.1	8	−14.3	15.8	15	−39.8
Alabama	32.0	12	−6.9	2.4	15	−4.0	14.3	11	3.2	35.7	8	19.0
Kansas	24.6	16	−8.7	15.1	9	7.2	11.1	13	11.1	4.5	16	−16.9
Minnesota	39.3	7	15.5	9.5	10	0.0	30.8	3	2.2	30.8	10	16.5
Michigan	31.5	13	−10.1	28.6	3	20.7	36.8	1	26.8	64.3	1	28.6
mean	35.3	9.3	−0.3	14.0	8.7	4.8	17.4	9.3	2.7	30.3	10.0	1.3
California	46.1	3	10.1	32.6	2	23.9	30.0	4	9.2	56.7	3	36.7
New Jersey	40.5	5	4.8	35.4	1	10.4	30.0	4	5.0	36.8	6	3.5
Tennessee	40.8	4	−1.9	2.4	15	0.0	28.6	6	13.6	41.4	5	−13.6
West Virginia	59.5	1	6.2	20.8	5	7.3	32.0	2	19.5	56.3	4	25.0
mean	46.7	3.25	4.8	22.8	5.75	10.4	30.1	4.0	11.8	47.8	4.6	12.9
Grand Mean	35.5	—	−0.7	15.3	—	4.8	19.4	—	2.5	33.8	—	2.3
F Value	4.66	—	1.53	1.51	—	1.54	3.53	—	1.24	1.51	—	0.82
F Sig.	.030	—	.252	.257	—	.252	.060	—	.323	.251	—	.464

These rough measures do not necessarily mean that Type III courts write better opinions, of course. Nor can we say that the courts with low discretion do not invest substantial effort and debate in those cases they regard as important. At most we can say, rather timidly, that the reduction of caseload in courts with high-discretion may increase our *chances* of getting better judicial opinions. It would be bold to carry the matter much further. A century ago, the United States Supreme Court heard many quite ordinary cases—appeals from will contests or contract cases in the District of Columbia and diversity cases of all sorts—along with more dramatic fare. Those ordinary cases rarely reach the Supreme Court today, but can we confidently say that the Court's workmanship has therefore drastically improved? We think not. But we can say that today's Court cuts farther into the fabric of society and that its power and reach have grown tremendously. So, too, of state supreme courts with discretion, in the smaller realms of their states.

In sum, the findings set out in the tables, taken together, suggest that discretion to select cases affects the behavior of state supreme courts . . . .

IV. CONCLUSION

In the late nineteenth century, American state supreme courts were mainly reactive bodies. By and large, litigants chose the cases and determined the issues. The judicial system was democratic in theory; the states' highest courts were open to everyone, regardless of wealth or political influence, whether the claim represented a widespread issue, or was peculiar to a single suitor. As state populations grew, accessibility produced enormous caseloads for the high courts. Supreme courts in the larger states sometimes issued over 400 or even 500 opinions a year. Compared to courts with smaller caseloads, their opinions were shorter and (perhaps) more perfunctory. The courts were criticized for delays and backlogs, for the technical quality of their opinions, and for their inattention to a changing society. Some of these complaints were unfair or were unrelated to judicial structure, but they helped spur a movement for structural reform.

By 1970, all the large and most of the not-so-large states had achieved some measure of reform, though changes had generally occurred slowly and painfully. Political opposition and traditional notions of the judicial function impeded reform. Finally, most of the medium-sized and large states created intermediate appellate courts to absorb much of the supreme court caseload; these states also gave their courts discretion to choose the appeals they wanted to hear. The courts could therefore concentrate on appeals that they thought meritorious or that raised important issues of policy or principle. Their job was no longer defined primarily as one of correcting lower court errors. They had larger professional staffs and, in many instances, considerable power to issue rules of procedure.

These changes affected the daily work of the courts. Between 1940 and 1970, the supreme courts with high discretion wrote fewer opinions than the other courts. Their opinions tended to be longer and to cite more cases. They also reversed lower court decisions more often. Their opinions contained more dissents and concurrences. These courts tended to decide more constitutional issues and they invalidated statutes or procedures more often, on the average, than the low-discretion courts. They spent somewhat less time with commercial and real estate cases (the traditional staples of state supreme court business), and more time on criminal- and public-law cases. And in criminal cases, they more frequently reversed the lower courts. Some of these differences were surprisingly slight, and not all high-discretion courts behaved alike. Nevertheless, our rough indicators point in the same direction: changes in court organization tended to make some difference in the agendas, opinion styles, and decisions of the state supreme courts.

Intermediate appellate courts and case-selecting discretion do, to be sure, solve the *workload* problem for state supreme courts. The number of cases decided with full opinions seems manageable, but supreme court judges and their clerks must somehow find time to screen the petitions for review that flood the courts. In California, example, petitions to the supreme court for review of lower appellate court decisions climbed from 803 in the 1961–1962 term to 2,417 in 1971–1972; total case filings including original actions, were 3,238. Some observers think that the job of screening petitions and the methods used to speed up that job have hurt the quality of the court's work. In a way, then, the largest states may have reached a fourth stage of high discretion, low caseload, but high workload. In those states, the court must devise more efficient case-selection techniques. The question is no longer whether this screening should be done, but how and by whom. By the judges themselves? By a professional staff? Or by some combination? And with what procedures?

Most states have accepted the idea that a supreme court should concentrate primarily on the most important cases, on articulating and elaborating principles of law. Some observers applaud this development and call it progress. Our society benefits, they say, when the states' highest courts are aware of issues, policies, and consequences and are responsive to changing circumstances and values. Others find the trend disturbing. The courts, they say, are ill-equipped to act as "roving commissions" in solving social problems. Because there are inevitable limits on the information available to supreme courts, and because of the piecemeal, case-by-case manner in which they act, it is dangerous, the critics charge, to let courts select out big issues and change the law in big steps. Thus, there are those who fear grave miscalculation and social disruption if a handful of judges, unrestrained by the ordinary electoral process, or the need to balance a budget, are encouraged to concentrate on important cases with incredible social impact.

The debate goes on, perhaps endlessly. Are judges capable of policy-making and innovation? Should they take the initiative in problems of policy and justice, when legislatures, police departments, and bureaucracies are deadlocked or inert? No amount of data will resolve that question. Our study has revealed patterns of supreme court evolution toward smaller numbers of opinions and greater case-selecting discretion. State supreme courts indeed are now designed to concentrate on "key" cases. This has weakened some traditional institutional restraints on activism. For these, as well as other reasons, the courts are unlikely to turn back to a less activist role.

NOTES AND QUESTIONS

1. Kagan and his associates present evidence that suggests the *structure* of a court system seems to affect how the system works. They also describe a process of trying to control an expanding workload. As a result, high courts have a lighter case-load than they did at many points in the past. What effect does this have on the kinds of cases the courts hear, and the actual *results* of the cases? Do Kagan and his associates have any evidence of an effect on the results of cases?

For a comparative study of three American state supreme courts (Alabama, Ohio, and New Jersey), see G. Allan Tarr and Mary Cornelia Aldis Porter, *State Supreme Courts in State and Nation* (New Haven, Yale University Press, 1988).

2. W. T. Austin, in "Portrait of a Courtroom: Social and Ecological Impressions of the Adversary Process," 9 *Criminal Justice and Behavior* 286 (1982), looked at the layout of a North Carolina courtroom where criminal cases were tried. The judge sat on a raised bench placed against the back wall of the courtroom. The jurors sat in seats along a side wall to the judge's left. The witness, court reporter and prosecutor all were located *within* an area—a triangle—bounded by the judge's bench and the jury box. The defense sat to the judge's right *outside* of this area. Bailiffs sat behind the defense table, close enough to control a defendant if necessary. Information flowed from the witnesses and the judge to the jury. The prosecutor could face the jurors while the defense looked on from behind the prosecutor. The prosecutor could look directly at witnesses and stare, smile, frown, and otherwise communicate by body language to the jurors. Austin concedes that this study cannot tell us about the impact of this arrangement on the outcome of cases. Is it possible that furniture arrangements might affect the outcome of cases? How could you find out?

3. There is a theatrical element to judicial process. Judges wear costumes (robes) and we can see law books, depositions, and official documents as stage props. Moreover, the stage setting—courtrooms, legislative chambers, and the like—may affect what happens there. Consider Murray Edelman, "Space and the Social Order," 32 *Journal of Architectural Education* 2 (1978):

The scale of the structure reminds the mass of political spectators that they enter the precincts of power as clients or as suppliants, susceptible to arbitrary rebuffs and favors, and that they are subject to remote authorities they only dimly know or understand. And the same monumentality carries a reciprocal meaning for the functionaries who enter these buildings regularly to exercise power. For them, the grand scale of the setting in which they make decisions emphasizes their authority and their distinction as a class from those who are subject to their decisions. Such spaces legitimize the power of elites and of officials in exactly the same way that they highlight the vulnerability of nonelites . . . . Spaces affirm the established social roles by encouraging those who act and those who look on to respond to socially sanctioned cues and to ignore incompatible empirical ones.

What message is given out by the theatrical aspects of court room behavior? By the use of the term, "Your Honor," and the requirement that everybody rise when the judge enters? Would justice be better served in a more relaxed and less formal setting?

4. Stewart Macaulay, in "Access to the Legal Systems of the Americas: Informal Processes," unpublished paper (1974), notes:

The structure of the legal system itself tends to discourage these citizens from using it. Factors of distance and convenience are important. Some agencies are found only in the large towns in a region, and others are located in the capital of the country. The time and cost of transportation becomes a barrier because the citizen must go to the agency in most instances; few agencies come to the citizen. Even office hours are important. High status people can leave their employment at a relatively low cost, but lower status people may lose a day's wages or even their job if they go to a government office or courtroom [during working hours] . . . .

The citizen seeking some government service faces delay and what appears to be an utterly unreasonable and irrational process. He or she must get in line and wait, only to be sent to yet another line where he or she is told to come back next week. Any transaction seems to require multiple copies of several documents, and each must bear the documentary tax stamps. One must produce documentary evidence of birth, payment of taxes and entitlement to the service. In Chile, at least, these were part of what was called *"trámites,"* a term that often struck an English speaker as far too close to "trauma" in his or her language . . . .

Those without influence can wait, rebel, or just give up and not seek the service supposedly offered to all by the legal system . . . . Many just stay away, making a calculation, the economists tell us, that the value of the service does not outweigh the cost of waiting to get it. Part of those costs may be frustration and a sense of powerlessness in the face of such a process. Others wait, fill out forms (if they are literate), buy tax stamps, go from office to office and finally emerge with the desired documents entitling them to the service. Sometimes it's worth the trouble, sometimes not.

Macaulay points out that those with influence do not stand in lines. In many countries they can hire people who are experts at coping with the bureaucracies. On the functions of lines and delay, see Barry Schwartz, "Waiting, Exchange and Power: The Distribution of Time in Social Systems," 79 *Ameri-*

can Journal of Sociology 841 (1974); Yoram Barzel, "A Theory of Rationing by Waiting," 17 *Journal of Law and Economics* 73 (1974).

Do factors such as the location of courts and administrative agencies, the cost of transportation, problems involved in missing work, lines, forms, and delays affect American and European legal systems or is this only a Third World problem?

5. One of the most widely cited articles in the law and society field is Marc Galanter, "Why the Haves Come Out Ahead: Speculations on the Limits of Legal Change," 9 *Law & Society Review* 95 (1974). In this piece, Galanter tries to explain the outcomes of cases in trial courts in essentially structural terms. He discusses "the way in which the basic architecture of the legal system creates and limits the possibilities of using the system as a means of redistributive (that is, systematically equalizing) change."

Galanter divides parties into "one-shotters" and "repeat players." A *one-shotter* is a person or business that seldom deals with the legal system. Their claims are too large (relative to their size) or too small (relative to the cost of remedies) to be managed routinely and rationally. A *repeat player* has had, and anticipates having, repeated litigation; it has low stakes in the outcome of any one case, and it has the resources to pursue its long-run interests.

Repeat players, such as large corporations, cope with litigation: they have advance intelligence, and so they are able to structure the next transaction and build a record to justify their actions. They develop expertise and have access to specialists, both lawyers and expert witnesses skilled in dealing with particular types of transactions. They enjoy economies of scale and have low start-up costs for any particular case. For example, an auto manufacturer may be challenged by many buyers about the safety of the gas tanks on its vehicles. It can afford to plan a basic legal strategy and to invest in the needed engineering studies to defend itself. Repeat players can develop informal relations with institutional incumbents such as judges, hearing examiners, and clerks of court. These officials may learn, for example, that they can trust the repeat player's assertions and claims.

Repeat players may not settle a particular case when a one-shotter would do this. Repeat players must establish and maintain credibility as a combatant. If they give in too easily in one case, it may affect the demands made in the next one. They can play the odds and maximize gain over a series of cases, even suffering maximum loss in some cases. Seldom will they find any one case critically important. As a result, they can play for rules as well as immediate gains. They are interested in anything that will favorably influence the outcomes of future cases. Repeat players may settle cases where they expect unfavorable rule outcomes. They are likely to discern which rules may "penetrate" and which are merely symbolic, and they can trade off symbolic defeats for tangible gains. Finally, repeat players can invest the resources necessary to secure the "penetration" of rules favorable to them.

Galanter discusses four litigation patterns. *One-shotters may sue one-shotters.* Often such cases are between parties who have some intimate tie, who are fighting over some unsharable good. Such disputes may have overtones of spite and irrationality. Cost barriers ration access to the legal system for many of these cases. *Repeat players may sue repeat players.* However, the sanctions of long-term continuing relations minimize such cases; disputes here usually are settled without going to court. A few of these cases occur frequently: For example, an organization such as the American Civil Liberties Union may push a case to trial and appeal to vindicate what it sees as a fundamental right. Governmental units may find it hard to settle cases because of the unfavorable publicity likely to be generated. Occasionally, both parties are repeat players but they do not deal with each other often or they lack mutually advantageous long-term continuing relations. For example, two computer software firms may battle over intellectual property rights to features of competing computer programs.

Perhaps the remaining two litigation patterns are more interesting. *Repeat players may sue one-shotters.* Often cases here take the form of stereotyped mass processing with little of the individuated attention of full-dress adjudication. Lenders seek default judgments, attachments of wages, confirmation of their title to property sold under conditional sales, and so on. The court serves almost as an administrative agency rather than a place where bargaining takes place in the shadow of the law. The great bulk of litigation falls in this category. No particular case raises major policy concerns; taken together all of these cases reflect the conditions of a mass society in the face of an ideology of individualism.

Finally, *one-shotters may sue repeat players.* The one-shotter seeks outside help to create leverage against an organization with which he or she has been having dealings. Now the one-shotter is at the point of divorce. For example, a consumer is unhappy with the failure of repairs to his or her car; an employee wants to dispute his or her firing by an employer; a tenant wants to force a landlord to make repairs to an apartment. Here all of the advantages of repeat players play out in full. While some one-shotters do win such suits, the configuration of the parties suggests that we should expect repeat players to defeat their claims in most of such cases.

Galanter also talks about how the nature of American legal institutions increases the advantages of repeat players. Our claim handling facilities are largely *passive* and *reactive;* the client must mobilize them and so faces cost barriers to access. However, parties are treated as if they were *equally endowed* with economic resources, investigative opportunities, and legal skills. Most American legal institutions are characterized by *overload* which also affects the balance of advantages and protects the possessor of money or goods against a claimant. For example, overload means that decisions will be delayed. Delay discounts the value of recovery. Overload requires that a litigant raise money to pay the costs of keeping a case alive. Overload induces institutional incumbents to place a high value on clearing dockets, discouraging full-dress adjudication in favor of bargaining, stereotyping situations and routine processing. Moreover, it serves to induce judges and administrators to adopt restrictive rules to discourage litigation.

Galanter looks at the implications of the system that he has described:

> Structurally, (by cost and institutional overload) and culturally (by ambiguity and normative overload) the [American legal] system effects a massive covert delegation from the most authoritative rule-makers to field level officials (and their constituencies) responsive to other norms and priorities than are contained in the "higher law." . . . It permits unification and universalism at the symbolic level and diversity and particularism at the operating level. (pp. 147–48)

SYSTEMS FOR CONTROLLING BEHAVIOR WITHIN LEGAL INSTITUTIONS

RULES AND THEIR RIVALS

47. *Legal Rules and the Process of Social Change*[152]

Lawrence M. Friedman

19 *Stanford Law Review* 786 (1967)

I. RULES OF LAW

A. General Introduction

☐ The common word "rule" has a variety of meanings. We speak of rules of law and also of rules of the game of checkers and rules of personal behavior (as when a person says, "I go to bed at midnight as a rule" or "I make it a rule to avoid fried foods"). In general, the word "rule" is used in law to describe a proposition containing two parts: first, a statement of fact (often in conditional form) and, second, a statement of the consequences that will or may follow upon the existence of that fact, within some normative order or system of governmental control. Or, as Roscoe Pound has put it, a rule is a "legal precept attaching a definite detailed legal consequence to a definite detailed statement of fact." Pound's definition is accurate enough for present purposes. It is broad enough to include statements of common-law doctrine as well as statutory provisions, administrative regulations, ordinances, decrees of dictators, and other general propositions promulgated by legitimate authorities which are intended to govern or guide some aspect of social or individual conduct. All of these propositions may be called legal "rules" in that they all append legal consequences to given facts.

It is very clear that some of the propositions enunciated in appellate cases are (or purport to be) rules . . . . Statutory phrases or sentences are also rules. The heart of the federal patent law—"[w]hoever invents

---

or discovers any new and useful process . . . may obtain a patent"—is a rule. The consequences of a rule may sometimes be omitted from the verbal formulation but if the rule is to be operational, the consequences must be there, even if not expressed. "Thou shalt not kill" is a rule of law under the definition used here if (and only if) there is an implication that he who kills will or may be visited with consequences imposed upon him by some authority sanctioned by law. Most of the consequences mentioned so far have been punishments, but they just as easily may be rewards, as in the case of the patent rule quoted . . . . All rules are directed toward conduct, and the kind of conduct they are concerned with can be called the *substantive* aspect of the rule.

In addition, however, rules have what might be called a *formal* aspect. Rules differ from each other in more than their subject matter. There are certain highly abstract categories into which rules can be sorted and classified. These correspond to the most basic and abstract categories of legal relationships. Thus, some rules grant rights, some grant privileges, some permit, some forbid, and some give positive commands. Some rules say "may" and some say "shall." Some rules of evidence set up (in legal jargon) rebuttable presumptions; others, conclusive presumptions. Differences among rules in regard to these dimensions are differences in *form.*

In addition, all rules have a *jurisdictional* aspect, or an aspect of *distribution of power.* This is an aspect of legal rules that is sometimes overlooked. A legal rule, as we use the term here, attaches consequences to facts. But consequences do not attach to conduct by themselves; someone must manipulate the strings. Each rule, to be a meaningful rule, must carry with it a ticket to some person, agency, or institution, authorizing, permitting, forbidding, or allowing some action to take place. Each rule has its institutional and distributive side as well as its formal and substantive side. It distributes, or redistributes, power within the legal system or within the social order. Without this aspect, a rule would be a mere exhortation, essentially empty or rhetorical, like the preamble to a statute.

The distributive aspect of a rule is often implicit. An ordinary criminal statute, for example, contains no explicit jurisdictional statement; it merely defines certain conduct as criminal and assesses punishment for commission of that crime. The jurisdictional aspects of the ordinary criminal law rule are implicit and, in actuality, quite complex. They can be understood only by understanding the institutional context and the history of the common-law system. This tells us that appellate courts will have some responsibility for administration of the law—for example, by deciding its outer limits of applicability. Primarily, however, the law will be carried out by policemen, district attorneys, trial judges, and other operational arms of the criminal process. Other statutes or rules are addressed in the first instance to lawyers, or to judges, or to administrative officials. In many, but by no means all, cases the rule explicitly grants power or authority. Still other rules may be addressed to doctors, plumbers, or private citizens generally, authorizing, preferring, or forbidding certain behavior. Here too, however, there is ultimately in the background an explicit or implicit grant of jurisdiction to some governmental authority to take the steps necessary to implement the provisions of the rule.

The three aspects of a rule just discussed are interrelated. Substantive, formal, and distributive aspects of a rule cannot really be understood in isolation and cannot be sharply distinguished from each other. Nonetheless, it is useful to analyze rules according to these aspects in order to see more clearly the way aspects of rules respond to specific social and institutional conditions.

B. A Note on Rule Skepticism

One reason why more jurisprudential and sociological attention in the last generation has not been paid to rules is because rules no longer enjoy quite the favor they once did. Indeed, it is fashionable in the academic world to decry them. Many legal realists described themselves as "rule skeptics," and legal education is heavily influenced by rule skepticism. Many students begin, naively, with the notion that rules of law are always precise and that these rules can be easily and mechanically applied to clear-cut situations. Much professional energy is directed toward dispelling these notions and toward demonstrating that certainty in the law is an illusion, since life is far too complex to be summed up in little maxims. As a result, legal scholarship is strongly influenced by the attitudes of rule skepticism, and the bulk of scholarly writing today is rule skeptical, in one way or another.

Rule skepticism, reduced to the extreme, means either (1) that some pretended rules are not the true operating rules; or (2) that some rules are unreal in the sense that they are varied, misused, or ignored as they are applied and that those who apply rules actually govern in their discretion, using the rules as mere handles or shams. The first of these two possible meanings is not an objection to the study of rules, but only a call for more sophistication in the study. Indeed, many of the realists were rule skeptics only in a limited sense; they recognized that their job was not to destroy rules, but to gain more precision in understanding the true operational rules . . . .

The second meaning of rule skepticism is a more fundamental objection to the reality of legal rules, because it goes to the heart of the problem of government. Laws on paper are meaningless; they must be enforced or applied. At the cutting edge of law, rules devolve upon human operators, not machines. In their hands rules may become a mockery. Thus, for example, a criminal statute may say that he who commits assault suffers such-and-such a penalty. No exceptions or mitigations are mentioned. But the policeman who finds two men brawling in a bar may close his eyes and ignore the fight, break up the fight and say nothing further, or arrest the two men and throw them in jail. The district attorney may decide to let both of them go or book them for trial. At trial the judge may dismiss the case if he wishes. Therefore, the statutory rule is (so the argument goes) in part or in whole unreal. The policeman, the district attorney, the judge—these govern, not the rule.

To examine the problem more closely let us go back to a consideration of the nature of a rule. A rule is a direction; it is a tool for carrying out some task of government. Government can be effectuated either through personal surveillance or through formal directives to other persons (rules). Control exclusively through personal surveillance would be possible only for very simple societies. As society and government become more complicated, specific functions are allocated to this agency or that person, and bureaucratic organization necessarily replaces personal rule. At this point, rules enter into the structure of government. There is always, however, an operating level—a level at which laws are personally administered—by a policeman, for example. Yet, if it is true that administration at this level is never governed by rules, then government is not merely difficult, it is impossible—and no country, state, city, hospital, army, or large corporation can be run with any semblance of plan.

What is meant, then, is not that the policeman and other operating units of a system disregard formal rules altogether, but that they sometimes completely disregard them, and other times displace them a little. They may in some cases not disregard them at all. One of the major accomplishments of behavioral scientists—and of the legal realists—has been to highlight the gap between living law and book law. But this gap is not constant; it varies from region to region, from field of law to field of law, from time to time. However, the extent to which discretion is allowed and the extent to which it is actually exercised are social facts which, if we knew enough, could be explained by general laws of behavior.

Moreover, as an empirical proposition, it is probably not true that most legal rules are "unreal" in the sense that they are not or cannot be translated into behavior or enforcement. Most legal rules are in fact obeyed by those to whom they are addressed. Violations of the rules are promptly and efficiently punished. The general meaning of rules is in many—probably most—cases clear enough to form the basis of behavior. Nevertheless, there is a view among some students of the legal process that most rules are inherently uncertain and that most legal concepts are flexible and variable in meaning . . . . In fact, however, if one views impartially the whole of the legal system, it can be differentiated into three major areas. Some of the substantive content of the legal system consists of rules which are dormant—that is, there is no attempt at conscious, consistent enforcement. Other parts raise classic problems of uncertainty. These are the unsettled, but living, problems of law—such as the question of what constitutes due process of law. A third—and vital—part of the legal system consists of rules which are well settled in the special sense that they are acted upon by many persons in a particular manner and their applicability to given situations is not challenged. "Well settled" may mean, then, not that a dubious situation cannot be imagined or that the application of a rule is inherently free of doubt, but that it is actually free of doubt as a matter of ordinary, patterned human behavior. If most of the operating (as opposed to the dormant) rules of the legal system were not well settled in this sense, many of the normal processes and activities of life that people carry on with reference to legal rules would be profoundly altered. In a complex social and economic system, a legal system on the model of law school appellate cases would be insupportable. There are strong needs to know what is lawful and unlawful in our common, everyday actions. We need to know, for example, whether we are validly married if we go through certain forms (valid in the sense that our claim to validity will be either unchallenged or highly likely to survive any possible challenge). We need to know the permissible ranges of speed. Moreover, in business affairs, we need to know that a deed in a certain form executed in a standard manner truly passes title to a piece of land. If every such transaction had to be channeled through a discretionary agency, the economic system could not survive in its present form. A market economy and a free society both impose upon the legal system a high demand for operational certainty in parts of the law which regulate important aspects of the conduct of everyday life and everyday business.

The legal system must therefore limit operating rules which do not govern—that is, which do not in themselves provide a clearcut guide to action on the part of those persons to whom the rule is addressed. Some rules do provide the possibility of a clear-cut mandate; others do not. There is a significant difference between a rule which provides that no will is valid unless it is signed by two witnesses and a rule which provides that wills need or do not need witnesses, depending upon the circumstances and the demands of equity and good faith. Rules of the latter sort (discretionary rules) are tolerable as operational realities only in those areas of law where the social order or the economy can afford the luxury of slow, individuated justice. If there is a social interest in mass handling of transactions, a clear-cut framework of nondiscretionary rules is vital.

Of course, it has to be emphasized once more that when one speaks of the needs of the social order and the economy, one is speaking of operational realities, rather than of the way rules look on paper . . . . Some rules which appear discretionary on paper may not be truly discretionary in their manner of application, and vice versa. Some formally discretionary rules do not imply discretionary practice because the discretionary feature of those rules is jurisdictional only; it is a delegation to some lower agency, which in turn may adopt nondiscretionary rules. Suppose, for example, a rule of law purports to impose a punishment upon any person who sells "unwholesome" and "diseased" food. "Unwholesome" and "diseased" are critical items in this rule, but they obviously have no single objective meaning. Who shall decide what they mean? If the rule is statutory and if it is silent as to mode of enforcement, we may assume that the usual processes of criminal justice will provide whatever enforcement is needed or wanted. If policemen, district attorneys, and private citizens feel the law is being violated, they may invoke the criminal process. Ultimately, an appellate judge may put some additional meaning into the terms, though it is not likely that the problem will be litigated often enough for him to do so in a very precise way or that he will have the means at his command to frame intelligent regulations. He might, however, hold that some specific practice is a purveying of "unwholesome" food as a matter of law. On the other hand, the task of enforcing these provisions may be handed over to an officer of the executive branch and his staff or to an administrative agency. In Wisconsin, for example, at the end of the nineteenth century it became the "duty" of the dairy and food commissioner "to enforce the laws regarding . . . the adulteration of any article of food or drink." The statutes defined "adulteration" in broad language. For example, food was adulterated if "any substance or substances have been mixed with it, so as to lower or depreciate or injuriously affect its strength, quality or purity." Under these statutes the commissioner and his staff might assume the task of laying down further rules capable of clear obedience; or they might delegate rulemaking power further down the administrative hierarchy . . . .

As a general proposition, we may guess that there is a strong tendency within the legal system toward the framing of nondiscretionary rules at some level and that it is strongest where it is socially important to have mass, routine handling of transactions, which are channeled through some agency of the legal system, or where relative certainty of legal expectation is important. A rule can be nondiscretionary in operation so long as it is formally nondiscretionary at any one rulemaking level of the legal system (which has many, many such levels) or if it is nondiscretionary at the point of application. Consequently, the legal system may have many more discretionary rules formally speaking than operationally speaking . . . .

III. JUDICIAL RULEMAKING

Courts, as we have stressed, are equipped to handle a normal flow of trouble cases (which for them are routine). They must also be equipped to assimilate and bring about change, at least in a gradual manner. Finally, they must be able to deal with "crises." A "crisis" in the non-quantitative sense is a sudden demand upon the court, different from past demands, which puts the smooth, normal functioning of the court in jeopardy. A crisis is not simply a difficult case in the usual sense—that is, a case which lies within a gray area of law and evokes sharply different responses . . . . In a "crisis case," sharp, widespread impact can be foreseen as the result of decision. In such a case, demands are made on the court, which, however met, might so alienate or disappoint one important segment of society that social support of the court might be endangered. This kind of crisis case is never common, and is particularly rare on the trial court level.

The response of high courts to what they sense as a potential source of crisis has been a frequent subject of study. Most of the study concerns, quite naturally, the United States Supreme Court. The arts by means of which the Supreme Court delays, equivocates, and avoids some extraordinary issues are therefore well known and have been frequently catalogued. The Court has at its disposal an enormous arsenal of tools of defense. It can temporize and compromise. It can split a case down the middle. It can balance results against ideology by deciding a case on grounds so narrow that those grounds evade some burning issue. The Court also can simply refuse to hear certain cases. Others it can accept but delay from term to term. Some matters, if delayed long enough, will vanish or be diverted into another forum. Finally, some issues can be decided in such a way as to limit the notoriety of the result. The Court cannot hide the precise outcome of its cases, but it may issue brief, unsigned, per curiam decisions. Newspapers and trade journals are unlikely to note or notice these low-key opinions . . . .

[A]ctivism contains potentially grave dangers for the Court. Any highly charged issue is likely to be costly. In most of its work, the Court is protected from harm by the general support it enjoys in the country (and as to which it does not essentially differ from other legitimate institutions—the Presidency, the Congress, officers of state) . . . . [T]he legitimacy of the Court is an outstanding bulwark of protection against harmful criticism.

. . . Since the Court itself has no instruments for measuring public reaction, and certainly no mode of predicting impact other than common sense, it must rely on its own judgment as to the best course to follow, and, in appropriate cases, fall back upon a firm body of principle. Strictly as a matter of political expediency, the Court can be dangerously wrong . . . .

[However,] . . . most crisis-like crises are not crisis producing for the Court *as an institution*. Though the underlying issues are highly controversial, they can be efficiently decided by the Court since society welcomes a once-and-for-all resolution by a legitimate, impartial tribunal. When the precise *event* or the *person* at issue is the source of the crisis, then the crisis is nonrecurring in the sense used here, and it poses (in our society) few or no long-term difficulties for the Court.

Institutionally more serious is a crisis which is made up of recurrent cases and which does not vanish with a single resolution, but which heralds a new situation for the courts. Either a new social problem emerges out of the social background (as in the segregation cases) or a demand on the courts is met by a judicial response which in turn creates additional demand for fresh definitions of the rights and duties of the parties and the forces that they represent (as in the obscenity cases).

A rational court will attempt to reduce such a situation to institutionally manageable proportions. In the face of recurrent events, the court is therefore likely to develop a rule that can be delegated to other authorities for administration. From the standpoint of the court, this is an important element of a solution to the problem. Of course, the solution must be substantively "correct" as well; it must be in accordance with principle as the Court defines principle. But the form of resolution of such problems (as distinct from substance) is likely to be dictated by institutional needs. The kind of rule which emerges from a recurrent crisis of substance will be a rule which serves the formal requirements of the system and answers the substantive social demands.

What sort of solution will meet this requirement? From the formal standpoint, it is likely to be a rule which perhaps can end the constant probing by litigants for definition and the constant search for the boundaries of the rule. Such a rule will be as objective, as quantitative as possible. An objective, quantitative rule minimizes the risk of further litigation and maximizes the extent to which other private or public agencies can apply the rule, thus taking pressure for decision away from the courts. Such a rule, in form, will be either a rule of refusal or a rule expressed or expressible in quantitative form. A rule of refusal is not usually a rule which accepts and satisfies a fresh demand for social reform, but on occasion it can serve this function. For example, a court might conceivably rule that no power existed in any branch of government to censor any book on the grounds of obscenity. This would be a rule which refused to litigate the question of obscenity at all, not for jurisdictional reasons, but by obliterating the concept of obscenity as a basis for judicial exercise of discretion. Notice that such a rule is hard-and-fast and therefore expressible in quantitative terms—rules of refusal are rules whose quantitative term is zero. In essence, then, crisis situations will tend to generate in a court a movement of doctrine toward quantitative expression . . . .

[As an example of this process, the author uses the so-called reapportionment cases. The Supreme Court of the United States had long refused to hear cases in which citizens complained that electoral districts, in state legislatures for example, were unfairly apportioned.

Colegrove v. Green[153] adhered to this rule, though by a weak 4-3 majority. A later case overturned a racially motivated gerrymander of a town in Alabama. All this encouraged fresh attacks on the rule of refusal.

In *Baker v. Carr*,[154] the Supreme Court reversed itself, and held that a complaint about the apportionment of the General Assembly of Tennessee did "present a justiciable constitutional cause of action." But the court said nothing about the standards that would or should govern apportionment; they merely sent the case back for trial. The court, in other words, made only a minimum decision—conceivably the problem would then go away; or the legislatures would rouse themselves and do the work of reapportionment themselves.

When this did not happen, the court was faced with a continuing problem; within a year, a flock of lawsuits had been filed on the strength of *Baker v. Carr,* and the legality of virtually every legislature was under a cloud. Finally, in 1964, the court decided a group of six cases, headed by *Reynolds v. Sims,*[155] which reached a more quantitative solution.]

In essence, these cases enunciated a rule that both houses of a bicameral legislature must be apportioned substantially on a population basis. Anything short of this offends the Constitution . . . . [T]he rule laid down by the Court was as logical, as quantitative, and hence as workable as the situation permitted. A more discretionary rule would have invited constant litigation; it would have lacked even the bare formal prerequisites of stable solution. The actual formulation—"one man, one vote"—met these formal prerequisites. It contained in itself, by virtue of its relatively clear-cut contours, at least the possibility of a stable solution—a relatively permanent and operational delegation of authority to the lower courts and, hopefully, to the state legislatures.

Of course, a hard-and-fast rule is only an attempt to provide a solution; it was yet possible for the Court to be submerged in a storm of protest. To serve as a stable solution, the new rule must be generally accepted, or the costs of challenge, measured against the likelihood of change, must successfully deter challenges. If the new rule is unacceptable, it will be followed by more and more challenges, and the Court may either have to retreat from its rule or (even more serious) suffer losses in power or prestige. There is often, then, a period of anxious waiting. In the case of the reapportionment rule, there now seems little doubt that the rule will prevail . . . .

153. 328 U.S. 549 (1946).
154. 369 U.S. 186 (1962).
155. 377 U.S. 533 (1964).

When a rule can be stated in "yes-no" terms, it satisfies the conditions of quantitative certainty, and it is formally capable of stable delegation. Not all rules, however, are susceptible of statement in such terms. The . . . doctrine [before *Baker v. Carr*] was a rule of refusal, capable of statement as a simple "no"; once it was abandoned, no simple "yes" rule was possible. It was necessary, then, for the Court to work its way toward a rule capable of quantitative statement in a more literal sense. As we have seen, the Court did so. But it is not always easy for appellate courts to work out quantitative rules, even when, sociologically speaking, circumstances impel the Court toward such rules and when societal patterns or the Court's great reservoir of prestige would allow any solution to be stable . . . .

[T]he ultimate application of a rule to a fact situation must be concrete or precise, or it is not an application at all. Similarly, appellate decisions take a simple "yes–no" form, they reverse or affirm. But in formulating general rules to govern whole classes of cases, courts do not find it easy to lay down obviously precise, quantitative rules. In Anglo-American law it would be completely unthinkable that a court could decree or even evolve a workmen's compensation system or a social security law. Those programs rest on statutes with elaborate quantitative tables, schedules of rates, dollars, and ages. They require a taxing system and a large administrative staff. They presuppose some means of gathering information, of evaluating it, and of devising technical instruments for carrying policy into effect. All this is beyond the customary power, as well as the customary role, of the courts. Laws of this form in our legal system are promulgated only by legislative bodies.

. . . There is nothing inherent in a "court" to prevent it from devising new programs and, specifically, from promulgating rules in precise, quantitative terms. There is nothing inherent in a "legislature" that prevents it from deciding concrete cases. Historically, the institutional ancestors of American courts and legislatures performed many tasks which, to the modern eye, seem curious reversals of their roles. Legislatures long exercised appellate jurisdiction; the name of the highest English court (the House of Lords) preserves the memory of this period. In the United States, too, appellate decision-making in state legislative bodies persisted well into the nineteenth century, and county courts in the American colonies were important administrative agencies—levying taxes and overseeing construction of roads, for example . . . .

The legitimacy of an institution is not unchanging, and, with respect to the courts, does not rest on a single ideal core of meaning. Legitimacy is culturally defined; its effect on the power and style of courts is specific to a given time and place. In the recent history of the common-law system, it was conventionally stated that judges could not legitimately "make law." . . .

In the main, courts still deny their power to make new law. This denial is itself no small limitation on their power. It helps ensure that judge-made law results in only small, incremental changes in the existing fabric of doctrine. A great leap forward is rare. Even constitutional law—where a major change can be legitimated through appeal to the higher mandate of the Constitution—shuns sudden advances. The reapportionment cases, for instance, exemplify a cautious, step-by-step movement. In general, judge-made law inches forward in a glacial kind of creep. When a court overrules a past decision, it often claims to be redressing an error rather than changing the law. Cases make small changes in law and call them no change; big changes are called small changes . . . .

In the twentieth century, partly because of the effect of legal realism upon the style of judicial opinions, judicial creativity is somewhat less verbally restrained than it was in the late nineteenth century . . . . New theories legitimate particular kinds of bold creativity—the duty of courts to expound the Bill of Rights to protect the individual against government or the duty of courts to keep law in touch with what is deemed to be the temper of the times. Yet changes in judicial behavior, all in all, are not deep; they are style rather than substance. Change in the law, through the medium of courts, remains incremental and gradual, rather than sudden or revolutionary. There is still a commitment to the common-law approach, to evolutionary movement, and to constant recourse to grand principles of law, established precedent, or constitutional phrases as the major premises of judicial reasoning. Legal realism has not freed the courts from an obligation to society, only from an obligation to a certain style of legal logic; the pull of social responsibility, coupled with an awareness of the limits of judicial knowledge and the limits of judicial capacity to effect social change, may lead to greater, not lesser, caution in action and to greater, not lesser, accountability in principle and reasoning.

But past and present disabilities on the kind of rules that can be legitimately enunciated are an embarrassment to courts when problem situations call for rules of stable delegation, since these, as we have seen, will tend to be quantitative rules. The evolutionary, incremental character of judicial behavior in rulemaking implies (on the contrary) slow, inductive movement along a continuum, and clandestine changes in law—qualitative rules, rules expressed in terms of reasonableness, rules empty of content except as courts fill them with content, rules capable of expansion by small degrees, discretionary rules concealing the reality of change. Thus, the history of judicial systems harbors a considerable dilemma: How can the legitimate limits of judicial rulemaking be reconciled with the institutional need for quantitative rules?

One solution, frequently adopted, is to enunciate rules of a flat "yes–no" nature—rules of refusal, for example. But such rules are not always appropriate. Still another technique is to ratify or absorb into judge-made law quantitative measures whose legitimacy derives from other branches of the legal system or from elsewhere in society. One example of this technique can be seen in the course of the evolution of the Rule Against Perpetuities. The rule, in essence, puts a limit on the length of time property can be "tied up" in a family or held in a family trust. Originally phrased in terms of "reasonableness," the rule could not in the long run remain in that form, just as the rule in *Baker v. Carr* had to move in the direction of more certainty. In sharp contrast to the swiftness of *Baker v. Carr,* the evolution of the Rule Against Perpetuities from a rule of reason to a stable quantitative rule took more than a century. The process was much the same, however. A rule of "reasonableness" in perpetuities law would have precluded any stable delegation to conveyancers, lower courts, and the general public. Rational calculations in the dynastic planning of estates would have been much more difficult without a hard-and-fast rule to ensure safe predictability. Perhaps the simplest solution might have been a flat quantitative limit on the duration of trusts containing contingent interests—perhaps fifty or one hundred years; or fifty years following the duration of a life estate. A legislature might choose such a method, but it is not the style of a court. Hence the evolutionary character of the rule. The original formulation was characteristically vague; the final formulation, "lives in being plus twenty-one years," for all its irrationalities, is in theory capable of "mathematical" accuracy in application. The twenty-one-year period is not measured by anybody's minority, although the choice was not entirely accidental. It has some rational relationship to the period of minority, but it was powerfully influenced by the fact that twenty-one years was an available number with preexisting legal significance, so that it could be adopted and embodied within a rule of law without transgressing the bounds of judicial legitimacy. The history of the Rule Against Perpetuities, then, illustrates not only the tendency of courts to evolve rules that are mathematical in the broadest sense, but also one technique for solving the dilemma of how to achieve quantitative results without the legitimate means available to a legislative body . . . .[156]

For courts the most embarrassing area of conflict is one lacking the possibility of quantitative rulemaking, stable delegation, agreement upon policy, or any signs of a nonjudicial solution. In such areas of law

---

156. The evolution of a formally stable rule does not ensure its survival for any period. No sooner had the Rule Against Perpetuities reached its "mathematical" form than it began to decay—that is, it began to lose some of its mathematical properties . . . . A formally stable rule may indeed be all the more vulnerable to pressure in that its results are "harsh"—that is, universalistic. As we have noted, *Baker v. Carr* began a process of evolution by overturning a formally stable rule of refusal . . . . At any given time, of course, some changes in the law will be in the direction of bringing substantive ends into conformity with formal prerequisites, while other changes will, temporarily at least, be in the other direction by virtue of social or judicial dissatisfaction with the substantive aspect of some prior, formally stable rule.

the courts are continually plagued by pressure from litigation for constant redefinition and refinement. In these areas, public awareness of the problem is high, but no consensus is visible, and no solution to the substantive problem seems feasible. In such an area, the law will show a considerable degree of uncertainty and flux, prediction will be difficult, and "trends" will be ambiguous. Indeed, the very term "trend" implies a high degree of policy agreement on the part of the courts. A trend means substantive movement in one policy line toward some absolute limit. As we have seen, courts prefer making changes by degrees when they can. Many areas of law have characteristics which rule out any current formal solution. How far the Constitution permits suppression or control of "obscene" literature and art is one such question . . . . The law is now in a period of constant testing of boundaries. The courts are the forum for dispute between those who wish to push literature further toward graphic sexuality (out of conviction or, in the case of some publishers, for gain) and those who see grave social dangers in unbridled literary sexuality. There is no obvious solution. Rules that might satisfy the formal requirements of stability are unacceptable—that is, either a rule allowing all censorship or all censorship of such-and-such a type, or a rule so formulated as to bar once and for all any control by the state over the limits of sexual frankness in literature and art . . . .

Ultimately, if the Court cannot solve the problem and if the problem does not vanish of its own accord (through a radical change in popular tastes or levels of toleration), some extrajudicial solution will have to be reached. This is so because the very definition of a problem implies a social impulse toward solving it. No "issue" or "problem" lasts more than two or three generations. There are, to be sure, eternal issues or problems, but these are not problems in the sense used here; rather they are formulations of human dilemmas on so high a level of abstraction that they cannot ever really be resolved. Problems such as poverty, crime, or the ugliness of cities can exist through all time, but such specific issues as whether slavery shall exist in Missouri Territory, whether fair-housing ordinances can constitutionally be enacted, whether fetishistic literature can be sold in drug stores, and whether hospitals shall be immune from tort actions must be resolved; they cannot drag on forever. If an issue is sharply enough defined to be perceived as a "problem" by the public or some significant segment of the public, there is a strong movement toward resolution, by definition. Society has a whole battery of institutions and mechanisms for resolving current problems. Otherwise society could not survive. If the first agency to which the issue is referred cannot resolve it, those raising the issue will seek a more authoritative agency (or a more efficient one). If worst comes to worst, the issue will not find its agency, and society might even be destroyed by the ensuing struggle.

NOTES AND QUESTIONS

1. Friedman makes the point that you need *quantitative* rules to mass process transactions. It is easy to register voters who can show that they are 18 years old, but it would be very hard to make the right to vote depend on whether the voter "is mature enough reasonably to understand the American system and able to cast an informed vote." Who would make the determination? On what basis? How could we keep bias from affecting the decision? Even if we could solve these problems, could we afford the cost of making such a determination in every case?

Formalism, however, has many uses (and abuses). A hard and fast rule, as enunciated, is not necessarily carried out in a hard-and-fast way. Keith Hawkins, "The Use of Legal Discretion: Perspectives from Law and Social Science," in Keith Hawkins (ed.) *The Uses of Discretion* (New York: Oxford University Press, 1992), pp. 13, 36–37, pointed out:

> where the form of a rule or set of rules is devised to circumscribe or channel discretion, the objective may not actually be achieved. Sometimes the opposite effect will happen. ["Discretion" is slippery and "adaptive." Rules] may serve to displace discretion to other sites for decision-making within a legal system, and thereby possibly to enlarge it, or create the conditions for its exercise in more private, less accountable settings . . . . Rules are valuable to legal actors, not simply because they can offer secure guidance, but because any ambiguity, factual or normative, surrounding them gives leeway for the exercise of discretion, which grants flexibility in their application.

Doreen McBarnet and Christopher Whelan, in "The Elusive Spirit of the Law: Formalism and the Struggle for Legal Control," 54 *The Modern Law Review* 848, 871 (1991), discuss what they call "creative compliance"—that is, "using the law to escape legal control without actually violating the law." People who are supposed to be subject to legal rules manipulate these rules legalistically and literally, to rationalize their own purposes. The authors comment:

> The irony is that if the rule of law may be used as a weapon to limit rulers and further the interests of underdogs, it is much more readily available for use by those who already have the resources, expertise and power to use the rhetoric, and the mechanisms of law, effectively.
>
> This is not, however, to say that formalism is inevitable in law. The drift to form we describe here in the context of law and finance is the product of a complex and dynamic interplay of structures, situations, ideologies and motivations. The repertoire of formalist mechanisms and ideologies is available but only brought into play when there is motivation to do so, and when those with such motivations have adequate resources, organisation or political muscle to use the system in this way. Rules are not always "privileged" in practice. Broad standards may be tolerated, even by sophisticated subjects, in other situations with other motivations in play. There need not always be a perceived interest in clear rules. There may also be countervailing interests in vague open regulation. Creative compliance is just one of several strategies in deal-

ing with law. Negotiation may be preferred by regulatees and may be seen to be enhanced by vague laws. Negotiation may also be preferred by regulators. Parties may settle out of court to *avoid* establishing rules. Law may be perceived as symbolic and ineffective anyway so that there is a preference for simply keeping quiet and letting policies of anti-avoidance and anti-formalism prevail, but only as empty words. In short, demand for formalism is not inevitable. Nevertheless, where formalism *is* wanted and pressed for, it may be hard to resist within the current structures and ideologies of law.

2. During the war in Vietnam, courts in the United States refused to consider whether or not this was an aggressive war under the Treaty of London, signed by the United States in 1945, which declares that "waging a war of aggression" is a "crime against peace." Suppose the Supreme Court had decided, in 1967, that the war was in fact a "war of aggression." What impact would such a decision have had on:

(1) those who opposed the war and were subject to the draft?
(2) the conduct of the war?
(3) the position of those who directed the war?
(4) the Supreme Court of the United States?
(5) the course of American politics?

Was this issue "recurring" or "non-recurring"? Why do you think the courts refused to consider the issue?

3. Can you think of other examples of the movement of vague, open-ended rules toward a more objective or numerical form? How about examples of the opposite movement?

In the abortion decision, *Roe v. Wade,* 410 U.S. 113, 35 L.Ed. 2d 147, 93 S.Ct. 705 (1973), the United States Supreme Court decided that states could not regulate abortion at all, except to require that it be performed by a doctor, during the first three months of pregnancy; until viability (roughly three more months), the states could regulate only to protect the health of the mother; after the fetus becomes viable—the last three months of pregnancy—states may prohibit abortion altogether, and take any other steps it deems proper to protect the interests of the unborn child.

Does this case illustrate the movement of rules toward the quantitative? How would Friedman analyze the rule enunciated in this decision? Do you agree with Friedman's position? To what extent, if at all, can we say that the attempt at a quantitative rule worked to solve the abortion problem? The problem certainly has not gone away. Indeed, there has been persistent attack on the "trimester" rule. How would Friedman explain these attacks?

COMMUNICATION AND CONTROL

This section will consider some of the general problems in designing a system for controlling the behavior of persons within a large organization. Our main focus in the chapter is on legal and governmental institutions, but in this section we will be dealing with the problem more generally.

There are many ways to set up a system of control. In some sense every company, hospital, or organization of any sort devises its own particular method. Nevertheless, the methods reduce to a few basic types. In *Politics, Economics and Welfare,* by Robert A. Dahl and Charles E. Lindblom (New York: Harper & Row, 1953),[157] four "central socio-political processes" are mentioned; that is, four means of "control and calculation." The first is the price system or, in other words, the market. The other three they call hierarchy, polyarchy, and bargaining. Hierarchy is a "process in which leaders control nonleaders. One of its most familiar forms is bureaucracy." Polyarchy is a "process, sometimes called democracy, in which nonleaders control leaders." Bargaining is a "process in which leaders control each other. The American system of checks and balances is a bargaining process; so also is political control through the great pressure groups—business, labor, and agriculture" (p. 23).

The process of control which we discuss in this chapter is mostly hierarchy, at least in theory. That is, it is a process in which there is a clearly defined top and bottom—leaders and followers, superiors and inferiors—and in which orders are given from the top. Within an organization, there is only limited scope for democracy, and the marketing system hardly operates at all. Bargaining, however, is another matter. Dahl and Lindblom define it as a process in which leaders control each other; but within an organization it is the process whereby rulers and the ruled interact with each other and control each other. We have seen bargaining at work at many points in this volume.

We start, then, with a simple idea. Most organizations are supposed to be organized on a hierarchical basis. In fact, however, hierarchy is much modified by bargaining. How does the top control the bottom? How does it see to it that policy is carried out? Any reader can, off the top of his/her head, state some of the techniques that are used: rules, inspections, reports, and so on. The readings will examine these techniques in more detail.

One of the basic requirements for a legal system is that rules, directives, doctrines, or standards must be *communicated* to those people who are supposed to act on the basis of the rules. It is possible that some laws are intended only to be symbolic and that these are an exception. But usually, a rule is useless unless it reaches its audience.

Many legal rules and practices control or facilitate communication from *outside to inside.* Law students become familiar with the need to file papers, give notices, enter formal complaints in court, make petitions to the legislature, and so on. Other rules and practices concern communication *within the system.* Modern legal systems are so large and so complex that they must constantly face and meet problems of

---

157. Excerpts reprinted by permission of Harper & Row, Publishers, Inc. Copyright © 1953, by Harper & Row.

information and control within the system. When a system is large and complex surveillance and spot checks alone will not do. These must be supplemented with formal rules. How are these rules to be articulated? How are they to be communicated to other people within the system, and to the public?

The methods are enormously varied. Forms of communication range all the way from direct personal contact, to formal, published regulations. There is a great difference, too, between a huge sign on an interstate highway which states simply that the speed limit is 65 miles per hour, and the complicated regulations of the Internal Revenue Service, which fill volume upon volume upon volume, and which basically only lawyers and tax accountants can read.

The problem of highly formal rule systems is one which becomes more acute in large societies, and particularly in areas where there is an attempt to control complicated activities in detail. Victor A. Thompson has described such a process in his book, *The Regulatory Process in OPA Rationing* (New York: King's Crown Press, 1950).[158] The Office of Price Administration (OPA), was the agency which, during the Second World War, fixed prices on all commodities, and administered the rationing of scarce commodities. Naturally, this required an enormous body of rules and regulations. Everything from shoes to sealing wax to cabbages, had to have a ceiling price, and the volume of regulations was immense.

By law, regulations of "general applicability and legal effect" must be filed and published in the Federal Register. The Federal Register is the official collection of federal regulations. It is not very interesting reading. Even most attorneys do not regularly read the Register. Publication in the Register is "obviously communication with intermediaries or interpreters" rather than with people supposed to follow the rules. Publication is, however, also a "means of communicating instructions to judges"—a way of making a regulation valid and official.

Not all regulations are legally required to be published in the Federal Register, only those which are to be enforced with sanctions. Yet officials of OPA regularly published great quantities of other material in the Federal Register. For instance, applicants were "told where to pick up application forms, how to fill them out, where to mail them. They were told the form number of the forms they were to use . . . . They were told what kind of pencils to use . . . in filling out the form." What was the source of this peculiar behavior? Thompson thinks that attorneys who drafted regulations thought the public had a "right" to be informed; that this right was satisfied by publication in the Federal Register; and hence they published much material beyond what was strictly required.

158. Excerpts reprinted by permission.

Yet, at the same time, some important items were excluded from the regulations published in the Federal Register. For example, official interpretations and field instructions were materials of great importance, but they were not put in the Federal Register. (Some were reproduced in mimeographed form and distributed to field attorneys). For example, if people could not get along with the amount of fuel oil that they were allocated, it was possible to get a "hardship" ration. The regulations did not say how one could tell if his situation amounted to a hardship. A field instruction, however, laid down a rather precise standard. A person who had less than half the fuel oil he should have, at a given point in the year, faced a "hardship." The public was never told about this rule of thumb.

It is no wonder that legal documents and nonlegal instructions became so scrambled that members of the public and local officials had trouble telling them apart. In 1943, OPA adopted a loose-leaf system. They distributed the loose-leaf binders and pages which could be replaced to local boards. Legal documents, together with annotations which explained the legal documents, were kept in the loose-leafs. The annotations were not found anywhere except in the loose-leafs that were sent to the board, and they were not printed in the Federal Register. Also important statements of enforcement policy were not communicated to the public.

Rationing legal documents were drafted by attorneys. They made heavy use of cross-references. There were few sections of the regulations which could be read, without many references to other sections of the regulations; these referred to still other sections; meanwhile the reader no doubt became completely lost.

Why was this elaborate system of cross-references used? In part, Thompson thinks it was simple laziness. Drafting attorneys did not want to repeat what they said. But another reason was a "strong reluctance . . . to rephrase something already in the regulations. The attorney learns that the best way to get a consistent reaction from a court is to use words which a court has already interpreted. Synonyms for those words will not do." The attorneys carried this attitude over into their drafting of regulations, even though no court would ever interpret the vast majority of these. There were other strange drafting practices: Sometimes drafting attorneys would make a major change by changing a key word or two in some part of the regulations. Unfortunately, changes of this sort "were completely uninformative to anyone but the legal researcher." For example, in 1942 OPA decided to change the rules about eligibility to buy recapped and second grade tires. At first, only the driver of an automobile which regularly carried passengers to work had been eligible. OPA decided to make all members of the car club who had cars eligible. The original provision stated that the driver had to present to the board a certificate "that other practicable means of transportation are not available." The amendment changed this to read "that other practicable means of transportation, exclusive of the automobiles of other workers, are not available." This does the trick, but in a devious and uninformative way. In fact, the real message about the change was carried by newspapers, instructions, meetings, and so on. Thompson also recounts how the drafting attorneys sometimes terminated provisions, not by repealing them, but by inserting a date after which the regulation was ineffective. If the date was the same as the date of the amendment, this got rid of the provision without saying so.

One fuel-oil hardship provision was amended by changing the phrase "may apply" to read "may before September 13, 1943 apply." The amendment was issued September 10, effective September 13. Thus, "after September 13, a person would be informed by the legal document that he could apply for a hardship ration if he did so before September 13, a date already passed. He would be instructed fully how to apply, etc. Such a person must have thought Washington was full of practical jokers."

Another drafting tool was the attorney's use of the amendment as a kind of printer's instructions. Attorneys drafted amendments which were simply instructions to someone "to make certain changes in words and phrases in various pages of a mythical document called the regulations." Thompson gives an example of a rather simple change in the fuel-oil rationing system which took the form of the following amendment, a printer's instruction of one sentence:

> Subparagraph (1) of paragraph (a) of 1394.5001 is amended, a new subparagraph (16a) is added to such paragraph (a) and in subparagraph (23) of such paragraph (a), the phrase "structure, including a house trailer," is substituted for the word "structure"; in subdivision (iii) of subparagraph (1) of paragraph (a) 1394.5151, the word "or" is added after the phrase "its use"; and a new subdivision (iv) is added to subparagraph (1) of such paragraph (a); in paragraph (a) of 1394.5253 the phrase "other than a house trailer," is inserted between the phrase "in any premises," and the phrase "or for hot water;" in paragraph (a) 1394.5256 the phrase "other than a house trailer" is inserted between the words "private dwelling premises" and the words "during the heating year"; in paragraph (b) of such section, the phrase "private dwelling premises other than a house trailer" is substituted for the phrase "the premises"; in paragraph (c) of such section the phrase "other than a house trailer," is inserted between the words "private dwelling premises" and the words "and the amount"; a new paragraph (d) is added to such section; in 1394.5259, the phrase "paragraphs (c) and (d)" is substituted for the phrase "paragraph (c)"; in paragraph (a) of 1394.5403, the phrase "(other than those which are house trailers)" is inserted between the word "cars" and the word "may"; and a new paragraph (k) is added to 1394.5902; as set forth below.

The attorneys were the "defenders of complete accuracy in all documents. Every written document was 'cleared' by the attorneys for accuracy. They insisted upon completely refined and qualified statements, both in the legal document they drafted and in non-legal documents which they cleared. The result was often a document or statement so qualified as to be almost unreadable. The attorneys appeared not to be concerned at all with ease in reading, but only with the accuracy of the statement." They were therefore tremendously preoccupied with definitions. Every ration order contained a long list of words, all of them carefully defined. The result was great complication—and poor communication.

Thompson describes a system which operated at three quite distinct levels. Attorneys wrote documents to satisfy what they imagined to be the needs of "the law," not to mention their own professional urge. The loose-leaf system, among others, was devised to do the real job of communicating with the local boards and other officials. And still other techniques had to be used to take care of the general public. These included news stories, industry letters or bulletins mailed out to all interested members of a particular industry, and so on. OPA had a whole information department, charged with the duty of keeping the public informed about OPA programs.

The loose-leaf system did not work perfectly by any means. It was hard to follow changes in the regulations and instructions. Changes appeared in the form of page replacements. To make the amendment process more communicative, the practice arose of sending along a newsletter which would explain what it was that the amendments were all about. But the newsletter itself tended to become rather uninformative.

The loose-leafs had other disadvantages. It was hard to keep them up-to-date and accurate. Once a loose-leaf became inaccurate because of some mistake in insertion of pages, it was almost impossible to correct it. Spot checks of loose-leafs in 1945 indicated that most of them were not accurate or up-to-date. The only way to solve this problem was to educate carefully the people who had the job of making the page replacements. But apparently very little of this was done; hence, "probably few of the Board loose leafs were accurate." In short, OPA, with a task of great complexity, seemed at times almost deliberately anxious to complicate its own life and the life of the public.

There is obviously a tremendous difference between the simplicity and directness of a posted speed limit, and the highly involute documents of OPA. Some of the problems obviously stemmed from the fact that the legal documents were designed for so mixed an audience: actual users of OPA rulings, that is, merchants and the public, the field offices of the OPA, and the audience of lawyers. This last audience, whether or not it made actual use of legal documents, was thought to judge them for accuracy and craftsmanship, and would presumably think worse of the draftsmen if they fell short. You might think that it was foolish to consider this audience at all, but Thompson brings in considerable evidence of its invisible presence.

How do you explain the conduct of the OPA lawyers, who were, one imagines, reasonably competent people, anxious to help OPA do its job, aware of the country's wartime needs, and probably aware too of the complexities of the problems they faced? Why did they act in the fashion that Thompson describes? Why were they so neglectful of the need to communicate with the public part of their audience?

Was all the lawyering in OPA dysfunctional? Consider the general performance of the agency as described by John Kenneth Galbraith, in a book review (*New York Times,* May 18, 1975, Section VII, p. 4, col. 1):[159]

> The Office of Price Administration, with which I was associated in World War II, had a heavy complement of lawyers . . . by some it was said to be overlawyered. It was an excellent fault. Few agencies have ever had a higher potential for corruption. A minor decision on the price of oil could mean millions which sundry predators would gladly have shared. The agency went through the war without a scandal. The lawyers, combining professional suspicion with a high sense of rectitude, were a principal reason. (We also ensured that enough people participated in every decision so that any predation would have to be a conspiracy).

Consider the standard American appellate decision as a communication device. It too has multiple audiences. For example, the Supreme Court decisions on the admissibility of confessions in criminal cases could have the following audiences: (a) the immediate parties; (b) the lower court whose ruling has been affirmed, reversed, or to which the case is remanded; (c) other lower courts which will have cases in the future; (d) police officials, prosecutors, and other enforcement officers; (e) lawyers, especially criminal lawyers, who serve as "brokers" of information for the general public; (f) actual and potential criminals and their families; (g) the general public which does not commit crime, but which grants or withholds prestige to the Court, and which assesses the political meaning of acts of government; and (h) the academic community, mostly in law schools or political science departments, which will judge the merits of the case from the standpoint of policy, craftsmanship, and soundness as law. Obviously the appellate opinion will not reach all of these audiences with equal force and effect, and it will affect behavior in each sphere rather differently. Which audiences will best understand the message? Which ones will be most likely to alter their behavior? To which audiences is the court really addressing itself? Which audience does it most try to please? Are there still other audiences?

What audiences were the lawyers in Thompson's study trying to

---

159. Copyright © 1975 by The New York Times Company. Reprinted by permission.

reach? Which ones did they reach? Considering the nature of the regulations, and the communication flowing from OPA offices in Washington to the local rationing boards, how much discretion did the local boards have? What can we assume were the limits on that discretion?

How does the bureaucratic organization of an agency affect its success in operating? During World War II, there were very many violations of OPA rules and orders. See Marshall B. Clinard, *The Black Market: A Study of White Collar Crime* (Montclair, N.J.: Patterson, Smith, 1952).

The following excerpt from Herbert Kaufman's book is from a study of the way in which the national forests are administered. Like a number of other agencies, the Forest Service has jurisdiction over a big domain, geographically scattered. There is need for some control from the center; field officers need guidance. Some of their decisions, in other words, have to be specified in advance, or, as Kaufman puts it, "preformed."

There are various degrees of "preforming." The central administration may "spell out several series of steps among which the employee shall choose. It may allow the option of acting or not acting, but define the steps . . . to be followed if the decision is to act." This Kaufman calls an "authorization." An authorization says, in effect, that if you do such and such in such and such a way, you will not be punished. Indeed, you will in fact be backed or supported; hence an authorization is, in a way, a grant of power. It is, of course, also a limit on behavior.

A *direction* ordinarily leaves no options; directions "constitute notice that if cases of a given class arise, failure to take the prescribed steps will result in the imposition of penalties. They are descriptions of what must be done in particular circumstances." Still more restrictive is the *prohibition,* "promulgated to prevent designated actions by establishing penalties for those who commit them."

48. The Forest Ranger: A Study in Administrative Behavior[160]

Herbert Kaufman

☐ Although authorizations, directions, and prohibitions (and, indeed, goals) may accurately be described in the formal sense in terms of penalties and immunities from punishment, it is quite clear that they do not depend for their effect entirely, or even mostly, on fear of organiza-

160. Copyright © 1960 John Hopkins Press, Baltimore, published for Resources For the Future, Inc. Reprinted from pp. 91–99, 101–07, 126–40, 142–45, 149–53, by permission.

tional sanctions. Far more importantly, their effectiveness turns on the desire of organization members to observe official requirements, on the feelings of guilt—the pangs of conscience, or, in a manner of speaking, the intrapsychic sanctions—aroused in members who violate official requirements, established by the leaders of the organization. In every conversation with field men in the Forest Service, it quickly becomes evident that anxieties about sanctions are by no means absent; it also becomes apparent, however, that other factors play a major part in producing adherence to requirements.

By issuing authorizations, directions, and prohibitions, it is therefore possible to influence the behavior of the members of organizations. An extensive, elaborate network of such issuances envelopes every district Ranger. The network is anchored in more than eighty Federal statutes providing explicitly for the establishment, protection, and management of the national forests; in scores of Presidential proclamations and executive orders on the same subject; in hundreds of rules, regulations, and orders of the Secretary of Agriculture; in many court decisions. It is also rooted in uncounted statutes, Presidential orders, departmental rulings, and regulations of staff agencies (the Civil Service Commission, the Bureau of the Budget, the General Services Administration, and others) governing the federal service over-all. But it is not to them directly that the Rangers look to find out what they are authorized, directed, and forbidden to do; for the Rangers, the "bible" is the *Forest Service Manual* put out by the Washington office of the Forest Service, which incorporates, explicates, and interprets the relevant legal documents applicable to the agency, and which contains also additional provisions promulgated by the Washington office under the authorizations in those documents.

The *Manual* currently in force consists of seven volumes. Three more were projected to complete the series, but, before the job could be finished, complaints about its unwieldiness led to a revision and simplification now in progress. Until this is done, however, these volumes remain in effect, serving as the agency Baedeker . . . .

The volumes of the Manual are loose-leaf binders. Additions are inserted at appropriate points; rescinded portions are removed; amended portions are inserted after the changes in the original sections have been posted. In the course of a year, hundreds of additions, rescissions, and modifications are issued from Washington; just getting them filed and posted takes many hours every month. But, in this fashion, the categories of authorization, direction, and prohibition, are constantly defined, made more precise, and kept up to date as errors, omissions, uncertainties, and conflicts are corrected . . . .

Each region, in addition, puts out its own authorizations, directions, and prohibitions controlling field personnel. They take the form of supplements to the Service-wide Manual, interpreting and clarifying and rendering more specific the materials emanating from Washington so as to fit them to the needs of each Region. Printed on paper of a different color, but using the same system of classification, they are inserted in the volumes of the Manual beside the sections to which they refer; like the Washington office, the regional offices issue additions, changes, and rescissions, and scarcely a day goes by without at least one arriving in each Ranger's mail . . . .

Over and above these administrative manuals are technical handbooks describing minutely the conduct of technical operations. Some are published by the Washington office, most by the regional offices. They set forth in detail the standards and procedures for timber surveys and valuation; construction and maintenance of recreation areas; location and construction and maintenance of roads; automotive and equipment maintenance; design and procurement and erection of signs; siting and building permanent improvements (warehouses, lookout towers, etc.); planting trees; fire reporting and damage appraisal. In different regions, depending on the character of their workloads, one finds different books, but none of the Ranger districts visited in the course of this study had fewer than a half dozen on hand. They add hundreds of pages of instruction for field personnel.

Some regions issue "Guides" for field personnel. These pull together the essence of existing regulations and assemble them, with explanations and additional requirements, in handbooks that are somewhat easier to read and follow and consult than the formal rules . . . .

Finally, when most of the functions that make up resource management attain a level of activity higher than can be handled by cursory, rule-of-thumb methods, formal district plans for them are drawn up. Indeed, for two functions, the Washington office requires every Ranger district to have a plan; there is none without a fire plan and a timber plan. For the others, Regional offices establish requirements . . . .

Plans, at least as they are treated in the Forest Service, are preformed decisions. They set long-range (eighty to a hundred or more years for a function like timber management; five, ten, or twenty years for others) quantitative and qualitative goals, break these down into shorter-range objectives, and sometimes reduce these to annual targets. They spell out the steps and stages by which the goals are to be achieved, including methods of operation, and priorities by geographical area, in each district. Out of these functional plans grow the substantive targets and quotas of the Service as a whole. At the same time, once adopted, the field plans govern the actions of the field officers and their work crews; if they depart from the procedures, or fail to fulfill their quotas, and the departures are detected, they may be called to account just as if they had violated authorizations or directions or prohibitions in the *Forest Service Manual* . . . .

All functional plans of this formal kind, combined with the guides and handbooks and the *Manual* with all its supplements, constitute an impressive network of standing orders influencing Ranger behavior.

They are not the whole network, though. For there is a steady flow of *ad hoc* instructions from higher headquarters to the Ranger districts—memoranda, letters, circulars. And there are inspectors (described later) and visitors from above who issue informal, oral directives in the course of their sojourns in the field. Intermittent, irregular, unpredictable, these are usually directed to very limited aspects of district management, and are of temporary duration. All the same, in the aggregate, added to the other types of preformed decisions, they provide the finishing touches to a remarkably complete means of administrative control touching every facet of official Ranger activity.

Clearance and Dispute Settlement

Yet authorization, direction, and prohibition are only one category of preformed decisions. Equally important in the day-to-day functioning of a district is the process of channeling decisions proposed by Rangers through higher headquarters before permitting them to take effect—that is to say, before investing them with the immunities and guarantees implicit in formal authorizations. This enables supervisors and regional foresters and their respective staffs to reshape such proposed decisions, and thereby to determine in advance what will actually take place on the Ranger districts.

The formal mechanism for ensuring review is limitation of authorization. Much of the business on a Ranger district involves transactions that can be legally completed only by higher headquarters; a sale of timber worth more than two thousand dollars, for example, can legitimately be consummated only by a forest supervisor (or by a regional forester if the volume exceeds 10 million board feet, or by the Chief if it is 50 million board feet or more), and only very small sales are below these limits . . . . While the Rangers and their subordinates do most of the physical and paper work of preparing items for higher action, the actions are not binding until the approval is obtained. Sometimes it comes almost automatically; sometimes proposals are radically modified or even rejected. The decision rests with the higher officers.

Clearance is complemented by dispute settlement as a means of bringing policy questions to the attention of higher officials for resolution. From time to time, a supervisor's staff assistant specializing in a particular function (or group of functions on the smaller forests) takes issue with the way a given Ranger manages the function that is the staff man's specialty. Staff assistants concentrating on recreation, for example, are wont to complain that this function is not given due attention, or that some activities charged to recreation management accounts would be more appropriately charged to the control of something else . . . . In fact, each staff officer at every level, since his energies and attention are concentrated on one segment of the total spectrum of Forest Service policy, displays an inclination to feel more can be done in his function than is actually done by the men in the field. Some of them gradually, and probably inadvertently, edge over from exerting pressure to see that their work is adequately done to commanding line officers as to precisely what ought to be done . . . .

If a Ranger gives in to a staff officer, or if a staff officer does nothing about a Ranger's resistance to his actions or recommendations, such clashes subside. If a staff man attempts to pressure a Ranger into compliance, the Ranger will ordinarily protest to the forest supervisor. If a Ranger objects to staff interference or ignores staff suggestions, the staff officer may carry his case to the forest supervisor. In either event, the supervisor convenes the disputants, hears their arguments, and adjudicates the conflict. Almost without exception, this settles the matter.

The net effect of this procedure is to call to the attention of the forest supervisors (and higher line officers) policy alternatives in the management of Ranger districts that might otherwise go unnoticed. It thus gives them additional opportunities to clear the air of uncertainty, to eliminate ambiguities in standing orders, to say what will be done in particular instances. It suspends the force of decisions until they have been reviewed and approved, modified, or rejected at higher levels. It is a method of preforming decisions in the field that would otherwise not rise for clearance. It employs conflict for purposes of organizational integration.

That is not to say the Forest Service is constantly beset by internal wrangling. Indeed, it is a classic illustration of the process of multiple oversight of administration; although the Rangers, like all line officers below the Chief, are at the focal point of many converging lines of communication from many sources in the administrative levels above them, they find reason to object to only a fraction of the suggestions of the staff men, frequently call upon them for advice and assistance, and manage to work out many differences of opinion without resort to formal adjudicatory proceedings. But the lines of appeal are clear and available to administrative officials, and they are not unused.

The consequences of clearance and dispute settlement, however, cannot be measured by the actual frequency of their employment alone. For almost every Ranger, knowing that works he undertakes and agreements he negotiates and plans he proposes (particularly if these are offensive to one of the agency's clientele) are subject to review and possible change or veto, screens out projects and requests to which the reactions of the reviewers are difficult to anticipate or likely to be negative, and concentrates instead on those more apt to win approval. If a project seems particularly desirable or necessary, or an applicant for the purchase of timber or the use or exchange of national forest property is especially insistent, and a Ranger therefore feels under pressure to proceed along a doubtful line, he normally queries his supervisor or his supervisor's staff assistants before acting. Sometimes, unwilling to risk the embarrassment of having an applicant go over his head and possibly win approval for what he denied, or of commencing negotiations only to be overruled, a Ranger refers the applicants to higher headquarters in the first instance. Thus, over and above what is required by explicit regulations, there is considerable informal clearance. This avoids some clashes with staff assistants that might otherwise arise, and eliminates some rejections and vetoes and criticisms by higher headquarters. But it also gives officers at higher levels additional opportunities to preform decisions about what goes on in Ranger districts.

Of course, the absence of disputes may just as well be evidence that staff officers are failing to influence the Rangers as that the Rangers are fully compliant. So the anticipation of reactions cut both ways—but more toward Ranger compliance with staff officers' recommendations than toward staff officers' hesitation to offer advice and suggestions. For staff officers and staff assistants are ordinarily in closer and more continual touch with supervisors, than are the Rangers, and they share the supervisors' broader territorial perspectives. While the Rangers will not brook what they regard as interference in their administration of their districts, they also recognize that the shared contact and vantage points of the line and staff officers at the higher level mean those officers are likely to see many things the same way—and for valid reasons. So the Rangers are not apt to protest vigorously unless the provocation seems to them particularly great.

Then, too, if no disputes arise a supervisor cannot be sure that excessively compliant Rangers or unduly timid staff officers are not permitting the work in the field to proceed further and further from the objectives proclaimed by Forest Service leaders. Anticipation of reactions simplifies the influence of dispute settlement as an influence on Ranger behavior because there *are* occasional reactions, they are resolved at higher levels, and more often than not are resolved in favor of the staff officers.

Clearance and dispute settlement, as a result, reach far beyond what the formal mechanisms *per se* imply. They are for this reason among the major techniques by which Ranger behavior in the field is molded by the organization.

DETECTING AND DISCOURAGING DEVIATION

Reporting

To determine whether behavior of men in the field conforms to the requirements of preformed decisions promulgated by organization leaders, the leaders must obviously keep themselves informed about what actually goes on in the field. The easiest way for them to do so is to ask the field men what they are doing. Hence, reporting is a common characteristic of all large-scale organizations . . . .

Data on individual actions are primarily for financial and bookkeeping purposes rather than for program and policy control; they permit administrators in the forest and regional offices to maintain surveillance of receipts and expenditures. But they also keep the higher administrative echelons informed about what their subordinates are doing. The payrolls, requisitions, and vouchers sent from the field to be charged against the functional accounts and sub-accounts established for a district constitute a running record of what goes on in the district. By consulting the record from time to time, the Rangers' superiors can keep abreast of the Rangers' activities, and they are able to assemble from such reports the statistics embodied in their own summaries.

Moreover, as noted earlier, many transactions—large timber sales, for example, and special-use permits—must be signed by supervisors and regional foresters before they take effect. As a result, these officers do not have to ask for special reports on many functions in order to compile their own reports; the information is readily at hand . . . .

Over and above regular, periodic reports of both the tabular and individual-action types, there are frequent calls for special reports on an *ad hoc* basis. In addition, the written documents are supplemented by uncounted informal reports; every time the Rangers get in touch with higher headquarters for guidance or advice or preliminary clearance of a proposed field action or to settle a dispute with a staff man, and every time a visitor from a higher level appears on a district, the Rangers' superiors get new insights into what is happening in the field.

All in all, then, the flow of information from the districts to the forests, the regions, and to Washington is steady, massive, detailed, and comprehensive. In one way or another, the Rangers themselves furnish facts revealing how closely they are adhering to the preformed decisions of the Service leaders, facts that disclose any deviations from the promulgated standards. It is doubtless true, as members of the Forest Service at every level aver, that the system of reporting has not been set up to expose deviations so much as to provide the leaders with the knowledge they need realistically to plan and guide the destinies of the agency. Distrust is not the driving force behind the system. Just the same, whatever the intentions of those who established and maintain the upward flow of reports, one result is to bring to their attention any continued departures from announced behavioral norms.

Theoretically, a field officer who does depart from announced policies, as a result of the tendencies toward fragmentation that pull at all Rangers, could falsify his reports to conceal his digression. In practice, this is seldom feasible, for misrepresentation in one report would soon produce contradictions with so many others that it would require almost all a man's time and energy as well as the most extraordinary ingenuity to tamper with all of them so as to make them consistent. What is more, many people—employees, users of national forest products and facilities—would eventually have to be drawn into the conspiracy. And even if all the reports were successfully altered, the information in the reports would then conflict with that obtained by higher levels through the other channels described in this chapter. It is almost inconceivable that manipulations of the records could long escape detection.

In any case, the incentives to falsify reports are not very strong. In the first place, the penalties for occasionally inadequate performance are far less severe than those for misrepresentation: the risks of dishonesty are infinitely greater than those of honesty. Secondly, . . . the whole ethos of the Service discourages falsification. The observer of the organization quickly gets the feeling such behavior would be regarded as not only immoral, but cowardly, unmanly, degrading to the individual and to the Service (whose members have a fierce pride in it), and that any man who practices it must end with contempt for himself for not having the courage to fight for those departures from policy that he believes right or to admit his errors when he is wrong.

Official Diaries

Rangers, assistant Rangers, and their principal aides are required to keep official diaries throughout the year. The diaries show to the nearest half-hour how each workday is spent. On standard Service-wide forms, the field officers and employees record each thing they do, describing the activity in enough detail for any inspector to identify it, the functions to which the activity is chargeable, the time at which it began and was completed, and the amount of office, travel, and field time it entailed. They thus compile a full running record of the way they employ their time . . . .

Forest Service officials do not designate disclosure of deviation as the chief function of the diaries. Rather, they contend the information in the diaries is needed to enable the leaders to formulate and adjust policies and objectives to what the record shows is practicable on the ground; it puts the leaders in touch with reality, and tells them as much about the shortcomings of their own programs and goals as it does about the men in the field. The diaries, they say, are designed for the guidance of the top echelons rather than to force field officers to testify against themselves. And there is no denying the diaries are used for this purpose.

But the fact remains that the diaries also expose deviations from decisions issued at higher levels to regulate the behavior of men in the field. The practice of keeping diaries may have been instituted for other reasons, and it may be employed in other connections. Nevertheless, exposure of deviation is one of the consequences, and few members of the organization are unaware of this.

The diaries are kept accurately for the same reasons that reports are not "doctored." In the first place, falsifying them is far too difficult. If inconsistencies between the diaries and work reports were not quickly discovered, then contradictions between what the diaries recorded and what was actually accomplished in the woods would soon come to light. Furthermore, discrepancies between the entries in the diary of one forest officer and those of his colleagues, subordinates, and superiors could not be long concealed. In any event, the entries are made throughout the year, so manipulating them for purposes of hiding the truth would take elaborate, long-range planning, and great investments of effort . . . .

Secondly, there is apparently a feeling of ethical, professional, and organizational obligation to keep the records straight. Members of the Service speak with obvious repugnance of tampering; it is regarded as petty and contemptible conduct, contrary to the traditions and the welfare of the agency. To be sure, few diaries are actually current, as regulations require; except for what one Ranger called "streaks of religion," during which he enters his activities faithfully at the end of each day, most men rely on their memories, aided by brief notes and consultations with co-workers, to fill out the forms for days—or even weeks—during which more urgent business was given precedence. And there is by no means unanimous enthusiasm for the diaries; some men argue that other reports supply all the information that can be gleaned from them. Still, even one Ranger who objected strongly to keeping one admitted that he is conscientious about its accuracy and completeness even though it has disclosed occasional failings for which he was reprimanded. Unquestionably, they are not precise to the minute, but they do reflect fairly closely what actually happens in the field.

The diaries are collected by higher headquarters and analyzed periodically. Current pages, kept in the field for the use of field administrators, are available to visiting inspectors. And they are studied by representatives of higher levels.

Along with diaries of their own activities, officers in the field are also required to maintain equipment-use records that are in effect diaries of their equipment. Each piece of apparatus and each vehicle is covered by a log in which an entry must be made every time it is employed. The ostensible objectives are to furnish cost data, and to provide information from which it can be determined whether the equipment is used enough to justify it; in the language of the Forest Service, equipment must "earn" its purchase. But discrepancies between reported use of equipment and technical and financial plans, travel allowances, travel entries in personnel diaries, and work accomplished in the woods are occasionally discovered by comparing equipment records with other documents and inspection reports. Within limits, property records and other reports must tally. They send up warning flags when what happens in the field diverges from what is enunciated as policy at the center.

District Rangers and their subordinates thus leave behind them in time a wake of paper that is a highly visible chronicle of their operations. If they stray from the designated channels, they do not ordinarily get very far before their divagations are disclosed . . . .

Inspection

In the end, however, regardless of how much of their field behavior is described in what the field men tell about their achievements, and in their inadvertent disclosures when they employ staff services, the only sure way to find out what goes on at the level where the physical work of the organization is done is to visit the field and see. This practice has been highly developed and carefully systematized in the Forest Service . . . .

TYPES OF INSPECTION

The broadest type of inspection—that is, the type that covers the broadest range of activities—is the General Integrating Inspection . . . . [A] General Integrating Inspection is designed to find out how good a job a line officer is doing when his total responsibilities are considered. Taking the whole gamut of national forest administration tasks as its subject, it reveals whether an organizational unit is administered in accord with policy, and whether everything that could be done is done.

Functional Inspections are narrower in scope but greater in depth than General Integrating Inspections. They normally concentrate on individual functions—timber management, wildlife management, recreation management, information and education, engineering, etc.—and explore in detail the way they are administered. A General Integrating Inspection takes up the balance among functions; a Functional Inspection turns to the balance among tasks within a function. A General Integrating Inspection relies on samples and general impressions; a Functional Inspection rests on minute examination and analysis of figures and methods. General Integrating Inspectors strive for "horizontal" sweep; Functional Inspectors aim at "vertical" comprehensiveness . . . .

Fiscal-Administrative Inspections—essentially, audits of fiscal operations and administrative housekeeping functions—do for office management, including accounting and record-keeping and reporting, what General Functional Inspections do for field operations. Books, files, and records are examined for maintenance according to standard. Manuals and work plans are reviewed to see if they are up-to-date and accessible. Procedures for handling paper work are studied. Diaries are checked for currency and completeness. Reporting promptness and accuracy are evaluated. Thus, not only is behavior compared with pre-formed decisions by means of reports and records; in addition, reports and records are themselves inspected to ensure the reliability of the data they provide, and to make sure field officers are familiar with the decisions to which they are expected to conform.

Two additional types of inspection are *ad hoc* in character rather than recurrent. They are substantially hearings on major failures of one kind or another, although they are sometimes employed to see what can be learned from unusual accomplishments as well. Boards of review look into the causes and consequences of large-scale, unexpected reverses, such as huge fires; investigations are inspections of alleged misconduct on the part of forest officers. Unlike the other kinds of inspection, these occur only when something extraordinary happens; they focus on the exceedingly unusual . . . .

When a region is inspected by Washington, or a national forest by a regional office, the inspectors ordinarily visit randomly chosen Ranger districts, for every inspection involves study of field work. Every Ranger interviewed has had the experience of being visited by people from Washington and region offices as well as being checked by their own respective supervisors. Since the number of inspections of one kind or another by supervisors' offices average three or more a year over and above the reviews by higher levels, every Ranger can count on at least several inspections every year; inspectors and functional specialists thus come through with high frequency, and the chances of defections from preformed decisions going undetected are correspond-ingly reduced . . . .

[Yet] the more experienced Rangers are quite casual about inspec-tion, for they know that only the most grievous mismanagement is likely to get them into serious trouble. The atmosphere of inspection is not one of a trial or even a competitive examination. In the evenings, when the work is done and notes written up, the inspectors and the inspected gather socially to discuss personal and organizational affairs—such things as shifts of personnel, promotions, retirements, additions to staff, organization policies and strategies and problems—meeting as professional equals rather than as superiors and subordi-nates, inquisitors and defendants. The practice of rotation and transfer of foresters, combined with the travels of inspectors, acquaints mem-bers of the Service in each region with their workers; inspection is a mode of communication and of face-to-face contact that helps bind the agency into a unity. Men in the field, rather than fearing inspection, tend to welcome the opportunities it affords them to keep abreast of developments in the organization, to learn the latest rumors and gossip, and to give their own ideas to their superiors at first hand.

The fact remains, however, that the written reports following every inspection are blunt and hard-hitting; criticisms are not softened, punches are not pulled . . . .

Inspectors summarize their principal findings for the officers they investigate, and the inspected officers are thus both forewarned of what is to be reported and given a chance to answer the criticisms and thus possibly to have some of them explained or eliminated. If a report nevertheless contains material to which they object, they may submit a written protest; several of the Rangers interviewed have done so on occasion. One Ranger expressed mild annoyance at the appearance in reports of findings not actually discussed with him in advance, and another was somewhat irritated by intimations that he was unaware of deficiencies that any good forester would recognize—deficiencies, in some instances, that he himself called to the attention of the visitors. On the whole, however, the Rangers indicate they believe inspection reports are accurate and fair despite their sometimes painful candor.

But inspections are not only a mode of detection. They are also a method of communicating preformed decisions to the men in the field, of reducing the ambiguities of previously issued policy statements, and of finding out whether such policy statements require revision in the light of field experience. That is, they are an additional technique of preforming Ranger decisions; they help determine the contents of such decisions.

For inspectors do not merely note violations of policy pronouncements and suggest in general terms that the field men look up the appropriate provisions and figure out how to conform. Rather, they indicate quite precisely what is to be done—what neglected projects should be undertaken, what activities should be reduced or halted or expanded or intensified, what procedures should be improved or corrected. They direct and prohibit action. They interpret authorizations and plans and budgets. They clarify ambiguous statements. In so doing, they claim merely to explain what policy statements and rules and regulations mean; this, in fact, is why they are said to be engaged primarily in training. Yet it is clear that they fill in whatever interstices may remain in the fabric of preformed decisions; they tighten the weave.

Not every such elaboration of the body of administrative issuances is initiated by the inspectors. To be sure, in the written documents, in the conversations during tours of the physical facilities, in the discussions of tentative findings and recommendations, and even in the informal social evenings, the visitors volunteer their ideas on a great many matters even in the course of a couple of days. But some of their advice and suggestions are requested by field men unable to interpret an instruction, or uncertain about how to resolve apparent contradictions between various provisions, or anxious to find impressive support for an interpretation on which they have been overruled by someone else. The inspectors do not simply impose themselves on the field officers; the field officers take whatever advantage they can of the presence of representatives of higher levels by inviting interpretations and elaborations of the rules. In a sense, this is a form of clearance. In any event, the Rangers elicit by their queries some of what is told them by their superiors.

At the same time that inspections increase the volume and specificity of decisions flowing *to* the field, they afford the Rangers opportunities to influence the formation of some of the decisions they will be expected to abide by. For the Rangers take advantage of the personal contacts with the inspectors to voice their complaints, their needs, their preferences, and their aspirations. If objectives are unattainable with the funds available, they point this out. If a prescribed procedure is excessively burdensome, they let the inspectors know. If they see potentialities in the management of their districts that call for amendments or additions to existing orders, they do not hesitate to urge them . . . . There is a flow of communication upwards as well as downwards within the inspection process, and it may be presumed to guide and limit to a small degree the contents of the rules and orders Rangers are called upon to observe.

Yet while inspections generate elaborations of authorizations, directions, prohibitions, and other preformed decisions, and contribute to the substance of those decisions, their distinctive function is to uncover deviation by field men from the behavior prescribed by the organization. Even if there were no inspectors, orders would flow out to the field, and reports and reactions would flow back to the center. But leaders would then be dependent entirely on evaluations of field accomplishments by the very men who did the physical work, men with heavy stakes in making their performance look as good as possible. Inspectors from higher levels, checking the field work, furnish more disinterested judgments as to whether or not the work conforms to policy pronouncements. In the last analysis, this is the rationale of inspection. □

NOTES AND QUESTIONS

1. Kaufman describes a system of communication and control that is, in some ways, quite complicated. Yet it does not seem to be as dysfunctional as the system described by Thompson. Are there important differences between the two situations?

2. Kaufman mentions the strong esprit de corps of the Rangers. It is possible, of course, that this spirit—and the devotion to duty that flows from it—exists in spite of, rather than because of, the elaborate rules and regulations that hedge about the work environment of the Rangers. Is there any evidence in the piece which enables one to judge one way or the other? How could we test the impact of the network of regulation on the performance of the Rangers?

Connie A. Bullis and Phillip K. Tompkins, in "The Forest Ranger Revisited: a Study of Control Practices and Identification," 56 *Communication Monographs* 287 (1989), studied the Forest Service some twenty years after Kaufman's research. They approached the Forest Service as an example of what they call "concertive control" of large organizations. They tell us:

Concertive control operates through the process of identification . . . . As contributors cooperate and communicate in a natural effort to overcome division, an overlap between the individual and group develops. As members identify more strongly with the organization and its values, the organization becomes as much a part of the member as the member is a part of the organization. Members then allow organizational decision premises to be inculcated into them. When the identity of the contributor is merged with the perceived corporate interest, this process is easier and more effective. Members think in organizational terms and act as agents of these juristic persons, experiencing autonomy while making organizationally preferred decisions. Beliefs, values, and symbols direct behavior indirectly.

This concertive form of control is simultaneously unobtrusive and a source of high morale. Rather than focusing on more obvious compliance with commands or rules, the focus is on less obvious compliance in decision making. The theory posits that this process of identification results in a profound internalization of the preferred decisional premises of two kinds: First, the factual and value premises valued by the organization are internalized. Second, consideration of the organization's interests above other parties' interests becomes a natural and preferred premise . . . .

[R]esearch has not addressed the core claims of the theory: (1) the relationship posited between organizations' use of concertive control and members' identification and (2) the claim that members who identify more highly with the organization (a) place organizational value premises as most important in their decision making and (b) consider the organization's interests first in making decisions.

The exception is Kaufman's (1960) descriptive study of the U.S. Forest Service . . . [However] [s]ince 1970, several environmental factors have had strong impacts on the [Forest Service] organization. The most relevant of these was that the relationship between the organization and the public was clearly redefined. During the 1970s, two prominent court decisions brought about this change. The Forest Service was indicted for clearcutting; clearcutting is the practice of harvesting all the trees on a tract before replanting and stands in contrast with methods which leave some trees while others are harvested. While clearcutting is still held by many to be an ecologically sound method, a public political movement made a "sustained and intense" effort to stop the practice. Not only did the Forest Service lose on this issue, it also saw the end of the era in which the agency could act as if it alone knew what was best for the public. The court decisions contributed to a series of environmentalist laws, most notably the Renewable Resource Planning Act of 1974 and the National Forest Management Act of 1976 which required integrated, continuous, long-term planning for the management of resources and for public participation in that planning. The diverse relevant publics have become consistently active in establishing national forest management priorities. Expert management (based on values) gave way to managing based on the (political) public will.

In other words, the relationship between this organization and its relevant environment changed. Previously, decisions were made based on shared values, or decision premises, among members. Currently, diverse, powerful, and active outside audiences constantly participate in decisions. Rather than accepting Forest Service decisions as expert decisions, public groups and individuals regularly work to have them reversed. The shared values which provide the basis for concertive control are no longer able to operate in relative isolation from the multiple, competing external values and external laws. Scholarship has questioned whether centralization is workable or desirable in more complex environments such as this. Yet, culture control has been offered as an alternative in some cases. The Forest Service example represents an opportunity to examine this relationship . . . .

[W]e conducted fifty-five interviews with key professional employees such as personnel and training officers, staff officers, line officers, and resource specialists [of the Forest Service] . . . . The results indicate that there have been several changes in the system of control since Kaufman wrote. We present our findings as they compare with Kaufman's.

Bureaucratic Control

In the first loop of the double-interact system, the Manual continues to hold a primary position. It explains "what to do, who is to do it, how, when, where and why to do it" (Kaufman, 1960, p. 96) as it did in the past. At the time of this study, it had tripled in size since Kaufman wrote. The agency continues to devote considerable human resources to the maintenance and updating of the Manual. A regional officer in charge of public appeals reported that there is now a more rigid criterion for judging whether the lower officer made the "right" decision. The appeals officers first determine whether the Manual was followed. In the past, this determination was far less rigid and formal than it is today. Sixty-five percent of the decisions discussed were reportedly based partially on the Manual. Fifty percent echoed the regional officer's report that the Manual had increased in importance while the others reported that it had always been consulted.

Kaufman identified planning as another method of preforming decisions in situations which were less routine than those covered in the Manual. Due to laws enacted during the 1970s, planning has increased since Kaufman wrote. Plans are comprehensive, detailed, and take a long-range view. Some rangers believe that planning has cost fifty cents per acre, an investment that takes the place of "getting things done on the ground." Plans are now generated for larger areas of land and involve more balancing of multiple resources and uses. Rather than relying on individual functional plans at the district level, the Forest Service relies on fully integrated plans at the forest level. Moreover, according to three planners (a full-time position which was new since Kaufman's time), national practices, and the Washington office, a computer system functions to integrate these comprehensive plans fully with the budgets. Interviewees referred to plans in their accounts of fifteen percent of decisions. One hundred percent reported that planning had increased in importance.

Kaufman identified ad hoc instructions, letters, memos, and oral communication as useful in situations which are not covered through standing orders. The ongoing written and verbal communication further directs those implementing policy. Seventy-eight percent of decision accounts included this type of communication. Eighty-eight percent reported that this ongoing communication is more strongly emphasized now due to better communication technology and more people concentrated together in larger offices. In Kaufman's time, many offices relied on radio contact because telephones were not universally available. Many ranger district offices were more remote, making physical contact difficult. In contrast, over 100 ranger districts had been eliminated during the interim; most of these were combined into adjacent district offices, making contact far more routine.

Clearances and dispute resolutions also are more important today. As Kaufman noted, authority is limited such that higher officers must clear lower officers decisions. Forest supervisors and regional specialists reported that they are now required to review and approve lower officers' "problem formulation" statements. In other words, rather than "rubber stamping" decisions post hoc as was done in the past, higher officers are now involved in the formulation of the decisions. One forest supervisor, in reprimanding a ranger who acted without approval, admonished, "you're not running your own private ranch anymore. I WILL be involved earlier in the process." The "onslaught of the public" as well as the better communication technology changed decision making so that the regional office and the public have more decision power than the ranger. Forty-five percent of interviewees reported early clearance or concern with warding off later disputes as part of their decision making process. One hundred percent reported that this is more prevalent than in the past.

Kaufman pointed out the value of financial and work-load planning in preforming decisions. The detailed records of budget allocations and expenditures are now integrated with the forest-level planning discussed earlier. Previously, rangers could occasionally make small adaptations by using funds from one account to complete a project supposedly funded from another account. With the current integration, the monitoring of funding as integrated with the work actually carried out on the ground is very thorough, allowing for little deviation. Twenty-eight percent of the discussed decisions involved financial considerations. One hundred percent reported this channel to be stronger than in the past.

Overall, this system by which decisions are preformed by higher officers has become stronger since Kaufman wrote. There is even less leeway for deviance in the 1980s than in 1960.

Like the practices functioning to preform decisions, the deviation detection loop is multi-channeled. Should organizationally incorrect decisions be made, the deviation would most likely be detected by the channels of this loop. How have feedback practices changed?

First, many reports are demanded. All of our interviewees agreed that reports are more frequent and more comprehensive than they were. Together, they provide a running record of all that happens on the ground. In one staff officer's words, "We know what's going on as well as they do." With more complexity in the reports, a more aware and involved public, and more communication between administrative units, there is a stronger disincentive to falsify reports now than in the past. Twenty-three percent of decisions involved direct considerations of reports to be made to higher offices. One hundred percent reported that there are more reports and more lengthy or complex reports now than in the past.

One channel in the feedback loop, the daily diaries maintained by rangers, has been discontinued. Rangers found them to be cumbersome to maintain.

As in the past, overhead services are provided from the higher offices in the interest of helping those on the ground and relieving them of paper work. More diverse resource expertise is available now than in the past. For example, archaeologists and economists are employed. However, with a strong focus on efficiency, one policy reported by the Washington office, and practiced in several cases we observed, is to concentrate this expertise at higher offices rather than lower offices. For example, bridge designing specialists had been frequently assigned to forest level offices. There were not enough bridge needs at the forest level to occupy them full-time so they spent a portion of their time in less specialized work. By moving such employees to the regional level, they could serve a number of forests and work in their specialty area full-time. Similarly, forests are encouraged by higher offices to concentrate specialists in the forest office for use on a number of districts. Some specialists such as a historian, are available only at the national office. Higher office staff, then, are more likely to be directly involved "on the ground" in providing recommendations and decisions. Ten percent of decisions involved considerations of such available resources. Thirty-eight percent reported that this practice is more prevalent than in the past.

Inspections were used as higher officers regularly visited ranger districts with the goal of detecting and correcting any problems or deviations. These visits are no longer termed "inspections" but rather, "reviews." Reviews carry a more positive connotation. Official policy dictates that reviews occur in specified time periods. However, some of officers conduct more reviews than required, depending on problems and preferences. Three regional officers reported conducting surprise reviews. Thus Kaufman's comment could be made today just as well as in the past: "Whether going along quietly and routinely or beset by catastrophe, members of the Forest Service can be as certain of inspections (or reviews) as they are of death and taxes" (p. 140). Eighteen percent reported decisions involved considerations of reviews. Forty percent reported them to be more prevalent than in the past. Sixty percent reported them to be as prevalent as in the past.

Every interviewee reported that appeals by the public have increased due to the public's increased involvement. An information office reported that the number of appeals increased more than five times between 1960 and 1980. The public has changed from a primarily friendly or neutral one (with the exception of those who abused the resources) to a multifaceted, often hostile one. Rangers are concerned about maintaining superiors' support when the appeals occur rather than if the appeals occur. Thirty percent of decisions included considerations of possible appeals.

Frequent transfer of employees also discouraged deviation. If an employee moved, the replacement would likely discover and report any deviations which were evident. Although no one indicated an official change in policy, the regional and forest level officers we interviewed indicated that in practice, moves are less frequent now than in the past. Both regional personnel officers estimated that rather than moving every two to three years, employees may stay in one place for more than five years. However, transfers do occur and do continue to provide an impetus to keep one's house in order, so that one's successor will find no dirty laundry. Five percent reported decisions involved considerations of leaving appropriate records for one's successor. Ten percent reported that transfers had increased while sixty percent reported that they had decreased. The remainder did not perceive a change.

Sanctions continue to serve as a threat to potential deviations. Demotions, suspensions, and reprimands are all clearly delineated in policy. The regional personnel officers and appeals officer indicated that they are used, and are potent in an organization which prides itself on its scandal-free history. The appeals officer reported needing to use official sanctions more than in the past although use continues to be rare. Subtle sanctions are used as well. In reporting on difficult decisions, fourteen interviewees reported that those who disagree with the organization eventually must leave. Eighteen percent reported directly considering sanctions in their decision examples. Sixty percent reported that this practice is more prevalent than in the past. Twenty-five percent reported that it was similar to the past. Sanctions were mentioned as threats on four occasions during meetings.

Overall, the network of communication practices which discourages and detects deviations has become stronger since Kaufman wrote. While the tone of the field visits has changed and the diary has been deleted, the increase in reports and public appeals as well as generally closer communication ties between hierarchical levels have created a far more powerful deviation-detection system . . . .

The use of symbols noted by Kaufman has also declined. Offices are more frequently located in federal buildings with other federal offices, rather than the distinctive log cabins they once were. Policy has changed so that fewer employees are given uniform allowances, and consequently cannot be formally expected to wear uniforms. Forest Service employees might never be identified by community members as such; this was once unavoidable. One employee wished uniforms were required because "if you run into people in the woods, you don't know if they are or are not Forest Service people anymore." Eighty-five percent reported this decrease.

The overwhelming trend has been a decline in these unobtrusive control practices which encourage the strong identification of members with the organization.

The single exception is in the practice of participation in policy setting from the field officers. Their "input" into policy changes is solicited as it has been through the years; field officers continue to feel as though they do in fact exercise some power in this process by providing valuable knowledge about specific situations. Washington officers agree that they could not/would not revise policies without this consultation. This practice continues to provide a participative climate. Participation in policy setting, is, however, consultative rather than delegative.

Conclusions

Unlike the networks which serve to communicate preformed decisions and detect and discourage deviations, concertive control practices have weakened dramatically. *Control, while continuing to be strong, has been transformed by placing more emphasis on external, bureaucratic control and less emphasis on internal, concertive control through identification* . . . .

[T]his research has supported the theory's crucial connection between identification and implementation. It answers the question: How, at the concrete level, does organizational identification serve the organization? The answer: It is associated with more than a feeling of good will among members. It is associated with the premises perceived as most important by members in day-to-day decision making, the point most important to organizational activity.

These results have supported the theorized connection between concertive control practices and member identification . . . . [I]n this organization, identification was stronger when concertive control practices were stronger. These results emphasize the distinction between bureaucratic and concertive control. The bureaucratic control practices serve to communicate decision premises explicitly. The organization must exert more communicative "energy" in controlling employees. Concertive control engenders identification more implicitly. Adapting the individual so that s/he actively seeks to internalize the premises is a less obvious practice.

. . . [I]nterviewees led us to a serendipitous finding. They consistently expressed a yearning for the past when employees made "correct" decisions "autonomously." They continue to feel a strong *urge to identify* with the organization. Employees seem less satisfied with bureaucratic than concertive control. This active desire should not be ignored in future research. It is part of the identification process.

Finally, concertive control, or strong culture, should be approached with caution. While we are sympathetic to the nostalgia expressed by employees for the identities and identification of the past, the homogeneity of that "strong" culture made the organization less flexible and adaptive to the changes in its environment. During the 1970 legal cases . . . , some of the people on the ground recognized the organizational threat at early stages of the Monongahela and Bitterroot controversies. They were unable to communicate their concerns up the line successfully in the face of the strong homogeneous culture which emphasized concertive action. Opposition was not "heard." The heterogeneity of the current "weak" culture is no doubt more flexible, more adaptive in relation to its environment—including the political climate and its inevitable fluctuations. Strong culture, then, may create inflexibility as members think in concert.

3. Lief H. Carter's *The Limits of Order* (Lexington, Mass.: Lexington Books, 1974),[161] is a study of a prosecuting attorney's office in a California

---

161. Excerpts reprinted by permission of Lexington Books, a Division of D. C. Health & Co., Lexington, Mass.

county with a population of about 600,000. It is modeled on studies such as Kaufman's investigation of the forest ranger, but Carter found a different pattern of operation. Great discretion was given to the deputy prosecutors. Almost all important decisions relating to the prosecution of a particular case were made by those at the bottom of the chain of command with little effective guidance from the supervisors. Attempts to use rules and surveillance as means of supervisory control tended to fail.

Carter explains the tendency toward a case specific approach in terms of organizational technology and environment. The techniques for deciding whether a deputy prosecutor had done a good or a proper job were underdeveloped. The superior officials disagreed among themselves about the goals of the prosecutor's office, the weight to give each goal, and the appropriateness of the means that might be used to achieve these differing goals. Moreover, deputy prosecutors had no career commitment to the office—most of them served for a few years to gain experience and contacts and then left for the greater financial rewards of private practice. The young lawyers recruited to be deputies saw themselves as independent professionals and not as subordinates carrying out orders. The job itself was one in which prosecutors deal with situations of uncertainty and unpredictability. Information comes both from the arresting officer and from defense attorneys. One never knows the whole truth. The deputies must accommodate conflicting requests and expectations from the police, the judges, and the defense attorneys. The police want the person they arrested punished; the judges want efficient processing of cases; the defense attorneys want all mitigating factors to be given weight. Because the prosecutors have continuing relationships with court personnel and defense attorneys, they must reach some sort of accommodation.

Other sources of uncertainty and diversity also undercut efforts by supervisors to exercise control. Cases are infinitely various. Sometimes the law is unclear; sometimes the evidence is shaky; sometimes it is hard to tell how the judge will react on procedural matters or in sentencing. Carter remarks that the situation is something like an assembly line, where those in charge cannot agree whether they are producing Cadillacs or Chevettes, and where the supervisors cannot predict what materials will be at the plant at any given time (p. 42).

Carter does not condemn this discretionary system. He comments:

> When we assess the performance of the criminal justice system, we should not limit ourselves to using only the criteria of order and regularity . . . . Bureaucratic controls can interfere with the alternative conception of justice as learning. This alternative conception requires that those who do justice maintain the capacity to learn new information about the cases they handle, about social preferences concerning crime, and about the consequences of punishment. . . . Such a strategy does, of course, increase the degree of idiosyncratic behavior—people in similar organizational positions will operate differently—but in conditions of technological and informational ambiguity and uncertainty, diverse behavior is rational, not only because it avoids wasteful segmentation and duplication of effort but because diverse behavior is a wise strategy for seeking ways of improving technology itself. (p. 162)

There are other studies of prosecutors' offices and other aspects of the criminal justice system that contain information about systems of control or lack of control. See, for example, Roy B. Fleming, Peter F. Nardulli, and James Eisenstein, *The Craft of Justice: Politics and Work in Criminal Court Communities* (Philadelphia: University of Pennsylvania Press, 1992). An earlier and quite important study of the criminal courts as organizations is James Eisenstein and Herbert Jacob, *Felony Justice: An Organizational Analysis of Criminal Courts* (Boston: Little, Brown & Co., 1977).

4. An organization exercises control the same way a state exercises control: it can use force and incentives, but it can also try to get compliance through other means. If there is solidarity inside the organization, then peer pressure may do the trick. Also there may be internalized norms: just as some people, as Tyler suggested, are disposed to obey the law, so some employees are disposed to follow company or agency rules, do their best for the organization, and so on.

A special kind of "peer group" orientation is professionalism. A company doctor will presumably follow medical ethics and medical norms—will act as a "professional"—whether or not there are company rules that say she must. The same may be true of a company lawyer. But these are not the only examples. *Every* occupation has its "professional" norms, and these exert a more or less powerful effect on job-holders. But, as Carter noted, "professionalism" is not always a factor that pushes toward compliance with organizational goals. It may well pull in the opposite direction.

What mix of the various factors mentioned best accounts for behavior within the Forest Service?

5. The word "bureaucracy" sometimes conjures up an image of a system where top-level people make decisions and give orders which bottom level people follow mindlessly. Jeffrey M. Prottas, in *People Processing: The Street-Level Bureaucrat in Public Service Bureaucracies* (Lexington, Mass.: Lexington Books, 1979), points out, however, that the lowest ranking nonclerical workers often have a great deal of power. This power rests on their complex relationship with clients and supervisors. A bureaucracy often has the job of categorizing and processing people, as a condition of their receiving benefits, treatment or services. Superiors control the rules and the procedures. The targets of regulation—the clients—control information about themselves, subject to what has been stored in the computer. Street-level bureaucrats create "the file." They can exercise discretion and rationalize it by what they put in the file. They can highlight some facts and ignore others. The way in which decisions get made, and power is exercised, in bureaucratic systems, is extremely variable and complex.

A classic article, David Mechanic, "Sources of Power of Lower Participants in Complex Organizations," 7 *Administrative Science Quarterly* 349 (1962), stresses the power of clerks, secretaries, those who run duplication rooms, and the like. They have access to information. They learn how to circumvent rules and directions that they see as illegitimate. Those who have held their jobs for a long time often know how to go around ordinary procedures and get things done. (They may, for example, know other secretaries and clerks who owe them favors). They have many ways to reward supervisors they like and punish those they dislike. Young lawyers in law firms learn to cultivate the secretaries in their office and the people they deal with in the office of the Clerk of Court. Often, they find to their surprise, that such people know more about the law in certain areas and how things are done than experienced lawyers and judges.

Perhaps the most important street-level bureaucrats who play a role in the legal system are the police, although we do not usually think of them this way. Their role in the operation of criminal justice is crucial. There is a rich and growing literature on the police, their functions and dysfunctions. Two classic studies are James Q. Wilson, *Varieties of Police Behavior* (Cambridge, Mass.: Harvard University Press, 1968) and Jerome H. Skolnick, *Justice Without Trial: Law Enforcement in Democratic Society* (New York: John Wiley & Sons, 1966). Another important article is Donald Black, "The Social Organization of Arrest," 28 *Stanford Law Review* 1087 (1971).

More recent works include Herman Goldstein, *Policing a Free Society* (Cambridge, Mass.: Ballinger Publishing Co., 1977); Jerome H. Skolnick, *The New Blue Line: Police Innovation in Six American Cities* (New York: Free Press, 1986); and Samuel Walker, *The Police in America: An Introduction*, 2d ed. (New York: McGraw-Hill, 1992). On the history of the police, see Samuel Walker, *A Critical History of Police Reform: The Emergence of Professionalism* (1977); and Erik Monkkonen, *Police in Urban America* (New York: Cambridge University Press, 1981).

Lawrence M. Friedman, in *Crime and Punishment in American History* (New York: Basic Books, 1994), p. 461, comments on the structure of criminal justice in America:

Indeed, the criminal justice "system" is not a system at all. This particular mirror of society is a jigsaw puzzle with a thousand tiny pieces. No one is really in charge. Legislatures make rules; police and detectives carry them out (more or less). Prosecutors prosecute; defense attorneys defend; judges and juries go their own way. So do prison officials. Everybody seems to have veto power over everybody else. Juries can frustrate judges and the police; the police can make nonsense out of the legislature; prison officials can undo the work of judges; prosecutors can ignore the police and the judges. The system is like a leaky garden hose: you can try to turn up the pressure at one end, but more water does not come out at the other. All you get is more water squirting out of the holes.

It is illuminating, of course, to compare policing in the United States with policing in other countries. For a fascinating comparison with Japan, see Setsuo Miyazawa, *Policing in Japan: A Study on Making Crime* (Albany, N.Y.: State University of New York Press, 1992). See the material in Chapter 4, on the police. There is a growing literature on the Japanese police. See Patricia G. Steinhoff, "Pursuing the Japanese Police," 27 *Law & Society Review* 827 (1993).

6. Every bureaucracy and every administrative agency has an organizational structure that can be analyzed in two ways: first, as an internal skeleton, a way of controlling itself, of managing its staff, workers and the like; and second, as an external force—a way of doing (or trying to do) what it has been mandated to do in the outside world.

There are innumerable studies of administrative agencies and each one can be analyzed in these terms. The task of the agency determines, in part, its structure. An agency that the public goes to voluntarily probably will behave differently than an agency which "regulates" in some hostile way or that tries to control behavior. Contrast the Forest Service, for example, with the activities of the Securities and Exchange Commission that regulates the stock markets and which tries to ferret out and punish stock fraud. On this agency, see Susan P. Shapiro, *Wayward Capitalists: Target of the Securities and Exchange Commission* (New Haven, Ct.: Yale University Press, 1984). Nancy Reichman, in "Regulating Risky Business: Dilemmas in Security Regulation," 13 *Law & Policy* 263 (1991), argues that to understand the activities of agencies that regulate such matters as the market in corporate securities we must consider both the structure of the federal and state agencies involved as well as the structure of the targets of regulation. Privileged players with knowledge, skill and resources can play the regulatory system in ways that undercut its protections for those lacking these resources.

THE ROLES OF ACTORS IN THE LEGAL SYSTEM: JOB DESCRIPTIONS, WHO GETS THE JOBS, AND REWARDS AND PUNISHMENTS

JUDGES

The judge is a more ubiquitous figure in legal history than the lawyer or any other legal professional. There are many societies that do not have lawyers but few that do not have courts and judges. A judge is a third person who has authority to resolve disputes between two or more disputants. A judge can make his or her decisions "stick," that is, judges have power to implement their decisions, unlike a *mediator* who can only persuade and facilitate.

Societies do not grant the power to apply their laws to just anyone. How does society make sure that judges will do their job in a satisfactory manner? In part, society relies on formal rules and sanctions. Judges who take bribes can be prosecuted as criminals. There are judicial codes of ethics. Statutes may state formal qualifications for the position. In extreme situations, judges can be impeached and thrown out of office.

However, formal rules and sanctions concerning judging probably are not very important to the day-to-day functioning of the judiciary. Less formal practices, rules and sanctions probably do most of the work most of the time in most societies. A society is likely to exercise care in selecting people for this position. Whether by appointment or election, the process should keep the wrong people from gaining positions as judges. The legal culture has norms about judges and judging. Political officials, leaders of the legal profession, and those who watch television programs about lawyers and trials hold more or less well formed ideas about what a good judge should do. In the United States, judicial appointments interest few people, apart from those seeking the position and their relatives, and a few politicians and members of the bar. Occasionally judicial confirmation hearings can be national news and provoke intense feelings. This was true, for example, of the hearings on President Bush's nomination of Clarence Thomas for a seat on the Supreme Court in 1991.

The work of most judges in this society goes on without a great deal of publicity. The Supreme Court gets massive media coverage of some of its work, but much of its work never reaches the general public. Other judges, for the most part, operate in the shadows. Occasionally, what a judge does may be controversial and get some play in the newspapers, but most judges, most of the time, work far below the threshold of public notice. Other judges and lawyers, of course, pay more attention. They may applaud good judging or criticize bad judging. Judges naturally wish to satisfy their peers. This has an impact on behavior. Moreover, men and women with unconventional views are not likely to be nominated, appointed, or elected to the bench in the first place.

In other societies, the work of judges is even more obscure and anonymous than in our society. High court judges in France, for example, do not sign their opinions, which are dull, dry, and didactic. These opinions convey a message that decision making is a purely technical task. The personality of a judge writing an opinion in an American high court is more likely to shine through. On the other hand, lower-level investigative judges in civil law countries play a role that American judges do not. For example, the Mafia in 1992 assassinated two Italian judges whose investigations threatened its power. In South Africa, a judge, Richard Goldstone, uncovered police scandals in the same year.

Does it matter who gets appointed to the bench in the United States? Should we care whether judges are Republicans or Democrats, men or women, white or African- or Asian-American, young or old, rich or poor? Do judges who are former prosecutors treat defendants differently than judges who were former defense lawyers? Have we reason to think that decisions differ systematically from category to category? How important is it to have "diversity" on the bench? How important is it to have judges who are really expert in the law? Exactly how much creativity does a judge have?

These are difficult questions. We must remember, too, that there are judges and judges. In this society, "judges" include justices of the Supreme Court, local justices of the peace, traffic and police court judges, administrative law judges and so on. There are also "arbitrators" who decide labor and commercial disputes, and they, like judges, have the authority to impose a solution on the parties. We do not usually call arbitrators judges because they do not sit in a court. "Mediators" are something less than judges because they do not have authority to impose their will on the parties. They can only try to guide parties to a settlement.

What type of decision-maker is best suited to resolve a particular type of conflict or deal with a particular type of problem? As noted, business people and labor unions often use arbitrators. Mediators are common in family disputes. See Vilhelm Aubert, "Competition and Dissensus: Two Types of Conflict and of Conflict Resolution," 7 *Journal of Conflict Resolution* 26 (1963), which draws a distinction between conflicts over "values" and those over "interests." Aubert argues that the type of conflict affects the appropriate type of person or body to resolve it. It is, for example, very difficult to mediate a conflict of value because most people do not think it proper to sell out their values. Something is either right or wrong. Of course, conflicts of value can be transformed into conflicts of interest which can be compromised, but this is not easy to do. Volkmar Gessner draws a somewhat similar distinction. He says that there are "people" conflicts, "role" conflicts, and "norms" conflicts. These are best resolved, respectively, by "advisers" (or mediators), "arbitrators," and "judges." See his *Recht und Konflikt* [Law and Conflict] 179 (1976). On the "ideology" of mediation and its disadvantages, see Karla Fischer, Neil Vidmar, and Rene Ellis, "The Culture of Battering and the Role of Mediation in Domestic Violence Cases," 46 *Southern Methodist University Law Review* 2117 (1993), and see also the material on the use of mediation in family law matters discussed in note and question 6 to Weitzman's article.

49. The Bush Imprint on the Judiciary: Carrying on a Tradition

Sheldon Goldman

74 *Judicature* 294 (1991)

☐ On March 25, 1969, just about two months after the start of the Nixon presidency, White House aide Tom Charles Huston wrote a memorandum for the President in which he argued:

> Through his judicial appointments, a President has the opportunity to influence the course of national affairs for a quarter of a century after he leaves office . . . . He [the President] may insist that some evidence exists as to the attitude of the prospective judge toward the role of the court. He may insist upon a man who has a passion for judicial restraint . . . . The criteria he can establish are as varied as the views held in different political, social, and legal circles today. But if he establishes *his* criteria and establishes his machinery for insuring that the criteria are met, the appointments he makes will be his, in fact, as in theory.

. . . [I]t was left to the Reagan administration to implement what Huston and Nixon envisioned. The Bush administration, by continuing the screening process, has institutionalized it and in this sense can be seen as carrying on a tradition . . . .

JUDICIAL SELECTION OVERVIEW

George Bush was elected to the presidency on November 8, 1988, by an electoral college landslide and by a comfortable but not overwhelming popular vote majority. At the same time the nation elected a Republican president for the fifth of the last six presidential elections, it also elected a Democratic Party controlled House and Senate . . . .

[One] highlight of judicial selection activity during the first two years of the Bush administration was, of course, the selection of David H. Souter to replace retiring Justice William J. Brennan. Filling the vacancy was a potential minefield because of the abortion issue, but the administration avoided a contentious confrontation battle by choosing a low-profile, non-doctrinaire, conservative judge with no public position on abortion rights. After a tour-de-force performance before the Senate Judiciary Committee, Souter was confirmed on October 2, 1990, by a vote of 90 to 9.

Another general point of note concerning the selection process is the increasing activity of interest groups in the selection process. The Alliance for Justice along with People for the American Way, both civil liberties oriented groups, began issuing annual reports on lower court nominations and distributing them to the media. Other liberal as well as conservative groups paid close attention to who was nominated. These groups communicated their views to the Justice Department and to senators, particularly those on the Senate Judiciary Committee.

At the start of the Bush administration there were a number of questions about how judicial selection would proceed and what would be the Bush imprint on the judiciary. After two years of the Bush administration the answers to those questions are taking shape. We will next examine in greater detail the judicial selection process under Bush. This will be followed by the professional, demographic, and attribute profiles of the Bush appointees compared to those of previous Republic Presidents Reagan, Ford, and Nixon and Democratic Presidents Carter and Johnson. The final portions of this article will consider whether there is already a Bush imprint on the judiciary . . . and what the likely shape of the judiciary will be after the administration has filled the 85 newly created judgeships along with current and expected vacancies.

Principal data sources for Tables 1 and 2 included the questionnaires completed by the judicial nominees and submitted to the Senate Judiciary Committee, transcripts of confirmation hearings, personal interviews, certain biographical directories, and answers by nominees to queries from this author. Occasionally, newspaper stories from the appointee's home state contained relevant data. The data appearing in the tables are for those confirmed by the 101st Congress to lifetime appointments on courts of general jurisdiction.

TABLE 1   HOW BUSH'S APPOINTEES TO THE DISTRICT COURTS COMPARE TO THE APPOINTEES OF REAGAN, CARTER, FORD, NIXON, AND JOHNSON

	Bush % N	Reagan % N	Carter % N	Ford % N	Johnson % N	Nixon % N
Occupation						
Politics/gov't	10.4%	12.8%	4.4%	21.2%	10.6%	21.3%
	5	37	9	11	19	26
Judiciary	47.9%	37.2%	44.6%	34.6%	28.5%	31.1%
	23	108	90	18	51	38
Large law firm						
100+ members	6.2%	5.9%	2.0%	1.9%	0.6%	0.8%
	3	17	4	1	1	1
50–99	4.2%	5.2%	6.0%	3.9%	0.6%	1.6%
	2	15	12	2	1	2
25–49	6.2%	6.6%	6.0%	3.9%	10.1%	—
	3	19	12	2	18	—
Moderate size firm						
10–24 members	10.4%	10.3%	9.4%	7.7%	8.9%	12.3%
	5	30	19	4	16	15
5–9	8.3%	9.0%	10.4%	17.3%	19.0%	6.6%
	4	26	21	9	34	8
Small firm						
2–4	4.2%	7.6%	11.4%	7.7%	14.5%	11.5%
	2	22	23	4	26	14
Solo	—	2.8%	2.5%	1.9%	4.5%	11.5%
	—	8	5	1	8	14
Professor of law	2.1%	2.1%	3.0%	—	2.8%	3.3%
	1	6	6	—	5	4
Other	—	0.7%	0.5%	—	—	—
	—	2	1	—	—	—
Experience						
Judicial	50.0%	46.6%	54.5%	42.3%	35.2%	34.4%
	24	135	110	22	63	42
Prosecutorial	37.5%	44.1%	38.6%	50.0%	41.9%	45.9%
	18	128	78	26	75	56
Neither one	27.1%	28.3%	28.2%	30.8%	36.3%	33.6%
	13	82	57	16	65	41
Undergraduate education						
Public	41.7%	35.5%	57.4%	48.1%	41.3%	38.5%
	20	103	116	25	74	47
Private	50.0%	50.3%	32.7%	34.6%	38.5%	31.1%
	24	146	66	18	69	38
Ivy League	8.3%	14.1%	9.9%	17.3%	19.6%	16.4%
	4	41	20	9	35	20
None indicated	—	—	—	—	0.6%	13.9%
	—	—	—	—	1	17
Law school education						
Public	47.9%	42.4%	50.5%	44.2%	41.9%	40.2%*
	23	123	102	23	75	49
Private	39.6%	45.5%	32.2%	38.5%	36.9%	36.9%
	19	132	65	20	66	45
Ivy League	12.5%	12.1%	17.3%	17.3%	21.2%	21.3%
	6	35	35	9	38	26
Gender						
Male	89.6%	91.7%	85.6%	98.1%	99.4%	98.4%
	43	266	173	51	178	120

TABLE 1 (CONTINUED)

	Bush % N	Reagan % N	Carter % N	Ford % N	Johnson % N	Nixon % N
Female	10.4% 5	8.3% 24	14.4% 29	1.9% 1	0.6% 1	1.6% 2
Ethnicity or race						
White	95.8% 46	92.4% 268	78.7% 159	88.5% 46	95.5% 171	93.4% 114
Black	2.1% 1	2.1% 6	13.9% 28	5.8% 3	3.4% 6	4.1% 5
Hispanic	2.1% 1	4.8% 14	6.9% 14	1.9% 1	1.1% 2	2.5% 3
Asian	— —	0.7% 2	0.5% 1	3.9% 2	— —	— —
A.B.A. Ratings						
EWQ/WQ	58.3% 28	54.1% 157	50.9% 103	46.1% 24	45.3% 81	48.4% 59
Qualified	41.7% 20	45.9% 133	47.5% 96	53.8% 28	54.8% 98	49.2% 60
Not Qualified	— —	— —	1.5% 3	— —	— —	2.5% 3
Party						
Democratic	4.2% 2	4.8% 14	92.6% 187	21.2% 11	7.3% 13	94.3% 115
Republican	93.8% 45	93.1% 270	4.4% 9	78.8% 41	92.7% 166	5.7% 7
Independent	2.1% 1	2.1% 6	2.9% 6	—	—	—
Past Party Activism	62.5% 30	58.6% 170	60.9% 123	50.0% 26	48.6% 87	49.2% 60
Religious origin or affiliation						
Protestant	64.6% 31	60.3%** 175	60.4% 122	73.1% 38	73.2% 131	58.2% 71
Catholic	22.9% 11	30.0% 87	27.7% 56	17.3% 9	18.4% 33	31.1% 38
Jewish	12.5% 6	9.3% 27	11.9% 24	9.6% 5	8.4% 15	10.7% 13
Net Worth						
Under $200,000	6.2% 3	17.6% 51	35.8%*** 53	NA	NA	
200–499,999	29.2% 14	37.6% 109	41.2% 61	NA	NA	NA
500–999,999	31.2% 15	21.7% 63	18.9% 28	NA	NA	NA
1+ million	33.3% 16	23.1% 67	4.0% 6	NA	NA	NA
Total number of appointees	48	290	202	52	179	122
Average age at nomination	49.6	48.7	49.7	49.2	49.1	51.4

*Two Johnson appointees (1.6%) did not attend law school.

**There was one Reagan district court appointee self-classified as non-denominational.

***These figures are for appointees confirmed by the 96th Congress. Professor Elliot Slotnick of Ohio State University generously provided the net worth figures for all but six Carter district court appointees for whom no data were available.

TABLE 2   How Bush's Appointees To The Appeals Courts Compare To The Appointees Of Reagan, Carter, Ford, Nixon, And Johnson

	Bush % N	Reagan % N	Carter % N	Ford % N	Johnson % N	Nixon % N
Occupation						
Politics/gov't	11.1%	6.4%	5.4%	8.3%	4.4%	10.0%
	2	5	3	1	2	4
Judiciary	55.6%	55.1%	46.4%	75.0%	53.3%	57.5%
	10	43	26	9	24	23
Large law firm						
100+ members	5.6%	3.9%	1.8%	—	—	—
	1	3	1	—	—	—
50–99	11.1%	2.6%	5.4%	8.3%	2.2%	2.5%
	2	2	3	1	1	1
25–49	—	6.4%	3.6%	—	2.2%	2.5%
	—	5	2	—	1	1
Moderate size firm						
10–24 members	16.7%	3.9%	14.3%	—	11.1%	7.5%
	3	3	8	—	5	3
5–9	—	6.4%	1.8%	8.3%	11.1%	10.0%
	—	5	1	1	5	4
Small firm						
2–4 members	—	1.3%	3.6%	—	6.7%	2.5%
	—	1	2	—	3	1
Solo	—	—	1.8%	—	—	5.0%
	—	—	1	—	—	2
Professor of law	—	12.8%	14.3%	—	2.2%	2.5%
	—	10	8	—	1	1
Other	—	1.3%	1.8%	—	6.7%	—
	—	1	1	—	3	—
Experience						
Judicial	55.6%	60.3%	53.6%	75.0%	57.8%	65.0%
	10	47	30	9	26	26
Prosecutorial	33.3%	28.2%	32.1%	25.0%	46.7%	47.5%
	6	22	18	3	21	19
Neither one	38.9%	34.6%	37.5%	25.0%	17.8%	20.0%
	7	27	21	3	8	8
Undergraduate education						
Public	33.3%	24.4%	30.4%	50.0%	40.0%	32.5%
	6	19	17	6	18	13
Private	50.0%	51.3%	50.0%	41.7%	35.6%	40.0%
	9	40	28	5	16	16
Ivy League	16.7%	24.4%	19.6%	8.3%	20.0%	17.5%
	3	19	11	1	9	7
None indicated	—	—	—	—	4.4%	10.0%
	—	—	—	—	2	4
Law school education						
Public	22.2%	39.7%	39.3%	50.0%	37.8%	40.0%
	4	31	22	6	17	16
Private	44.4%	37.2%	19.6%	25.0%	26.7%	32.5%
	8	29	11	3	12	13
Ivy League	33.3%	23.1%	41.1%	25.0%	35.6%	27.5%
	6	18	23	3	16	11
Gender						
Male	88.9%	94.9%	80.4%	100.0%	100.0%	97.5%
	16	74	45	12	45	39

TABLE 2 (CONTINUED)

	Bush % N	Reagan % N	Carter % N	Ford % N	Johnson % N	Nixon % N
Female	11.1% 2	5.1% 4	19.6% 11	— —	— —	2.5% 1
Ethnicity or race						
White	88.9% 16	97.4% 76	78.6% 44	100.0% 12	97.8% 44	95.0% 38
Black	5.6% 1	1.3% 1	16.1% 9	— —	— —	5.0% 2
Hispanic	5.6% 1	1.3% 1	3.6% 2	— —	— —	— —
Asian	— —	— —	1.8% 1	— —	2.2% 1	— —
A.B.A. Ratings						
EWQ/WQ	77.8% 14	59.0% 46	75.0% 42	58.3% 7	73.3% 33	75.0%* 30
Qualified	22.2% 4	41.0% 32	25.0% 14	33.3% 4	26.7% 12	20.0% 8
Not Qualified	— —	— —	— —	8.3% 1	— —	2.5% 1
Party						
Democratic	— —	— —	82.1% 46	8.3% 1	6.7% 3	95.0% 38
Republican	94.4% 17	97.4% 76	7.1% 4	91.7% 11	93.3% 42	5.0% 2
Independent	5.6% 1	1.3% 1	10.7% 6	— —	— —	— —
Other	— —	1.3% 1	— —	— —	— —	— —
Past Party Activism	66.7% 12	69.2% 54	73.2% 41	58.3% 7	60.0% 27	57.5% 23
Religious origin or affiliation						
Protestant	55.6% 10	55.1% 43	60.7% 34	58.3% 7	75.6% 34	60.0% 24
Catholic	38.9% 7	30.8% 24	23.2% 13	33.3% 4	15.6% 7	25.0% 10
Jewish	5.6% 1	14.1% 11	16.1% 9	8.3% 1	8.9% 4	15.0% 6
Net Worth						
Under $200,000	5.6% 1	15.6%** 12	33.3%*** 13	NA	NA	NA
200–499,999	33.3% 6	32.5% 25	38.5% 15	NA	NA	NA
500–999,999	22.2% 4	33.8% 26	17.9% 7	NA	NA	NA
1+ million	38.9% 7	18.2% 14	10.3% 4	NA	NA	NA
Total number of appointees	18	78	56	12	45	40
Average age at nomination	48.5	50.0	51.9	52.1	53.8	52.2

*There was one Johnson appointee for whom no ABA rating was requested.

**Net worth was unavailable for one appointee.

***Net worth only for Carter appointees confirmed by the 96th Congress with the exception of five appointees for whom net worth was unavailable.

SELECTION UNDER BUSH

Two major judicial selection innovations of the Reagan administration—the systematic screening process emphasizing judicial philosophy and including extensive personal interviews of the major candidates, and the creation of the President's Committee on Federal Judicial Selection—were continued by the Bush administration. The interviewing of prospective nominees is done essentially within the Justice Department. The leading candidates for appeals court and district court judgeships are invited to Washington . . . and are interviewed by various Justice Department officials, including the deputy attorney general and the solicitor general. The interviews are for the purpose of allowing Justice officials to gain a firsthand understanding of the candidate's judicial philosophy as well as his/her intellectual ability. Candidates are *not* asked, just as they were not asked in the Reagan administration, how they would decide particular cases or whether they favor overturning such Supreme Court precedents as *Roe v. Wade.*

As part of the screening process, Justice officials analyze a candidate's judicial record if the candidate has one. Analysis of the judicial record is also undertaken in the White House Counsel's office . . . .

The President's Committee on Federal Judicial Selection meets weekly at the White House, usually for two to three hours. The agenda is distributed in advance and the committee is chaired by White House Counsel C. Boyden Gray. The meetings themselves are run informally . . . . Like the committee during the Reagan administration, the committee during the Bush administration also consists of the attorney general, the deputy attorney general, the assistant to the president for personnel, and the assistant to the president for legislative affairs. The White House Chief of Staff, just as during the Reagan administration, is a member of the committee and also just as during the Reagan administration is usually too preoccupied with other matters and attends meetings infrequently.

For district court appointments, the Justice Department asks Republican senators to submit three names for Department consideration. There has been some resistance on the part of some senators, but the administration is not sympathetic to senators who submit one name and insist that person be named. However, the Justice Department will consider one candidate at a time provided that if the person proposed is not satisfactory to Justice, the senator will submit another name until a suitable candidate is found.

Bush has told those in the administration handling judicial nominations to keep in mind four points: (1) that he wants to name highly qualified persons who are philosophically conservative; (2) that he is looking for persons sensitive to the separation of powers under the Constitution; (3) that recruitment of judges should be opened up to provide greater access for qualified people than achieved under old-boy networks; and (4) that recruitment should be expanded to search out appropriately qualified women and minorities . . . . It is difficult to determine just how successful the Bush administration has been in opening the process beyond what appears to be the willingness of Justice officials to consider highly qualified persons without strong party connections. As for the Bush record of women and minority appointments, Tables 1 and 2 . . . reveal the extent of their success.

Another feature of the Bush selection process is what appears to be an even more subtle shift to the White House in terms of the process of determining who is to be nominated . . . . The Reagan administration effectuated a formal White House role with the establishment of the President's Committee on Federal Judicial Selection that met regularly at the White House and which produced shared control of the nomination process. Now the Bush administration has not only continued the committee and maintained shared control, but appears to have expanded the role of the White House counsel's office in the nomination process . . . .

White House Counsel C. Boyden Gray ordinarily consults with and briefs the president on judicial nomination matters. When the president has thoughts concerning judicial selection, the chain of communication is typically from the president to the White House counsel to the attorney general. This, of course, does not suggest any strain in relationship between the Justice Department and the White House. Indeed, all the evidence suggests a close day-to-day working relationship between the attorney general's office and the White House counsel's office . . . . But the stage may be set for some future administration employing the same institutional arrangement to assert the supremacy of the Office of the White House Counsel over the Justice Department in deciding whom to nominate. If in some future administration the White House is more concerned with patronage considerations than professional merit and the reverse is true for the Justice Department, the end result could have a considerable impact on the judiciary.

After the initial strain in relations with the ABA [American Bar Association] Committee was resolved, the Justice Department resumed submitting names of likely nominees to the committee. One name, and not several, is given for each vacancy. Thus far, no one with a majority rating of *Not Qualified* has been nominated. However, seven nominees received a split majority *Qualified*/minority *Not Qualified* rating. No doubt, this was as unwelcome for the Bush administration as similar split ratings were for the Reagan administration, despite the ABA's assurance that a majority *Qualified* rating means that the individual receiving it is fully qualified for judicial office. The ABA Committee continues its policy of not explaining individual ratings and not revealing the raw vote totals. Its meetings continue to be closed to the public . . .

DISTRICT COURT APPOINTMENTS

In Table 1 we find selected backgrounds and attributes of the 48 Bush appointees to the federal district courts confirmed by the 101st Congress in 1989 and 1990 as compared to the federal district court appointees of Bush's five predecessors.

Occupation

The figures for occupation at the time of appointment suggest that the proportion of appointees recruited from the largest law firms was approximately the same as that of the Reagan appointees, which in turn was higher than that of previous administrations. This is particularly true for the proportion recruited from the superfirms (100 or more partners/associates). Overall, however, the proportion of Bush appointees drawn from private practice was lower than that for the Reagan administration.

Close to half of the Bush appointees were recruited directly from the judiciary, and this was the highest proportion of all six administrations. These figures lend support to the suggestion that the administration was more concerned with recruiting highly qualified, philosophically compatible persons (with judicial records that could be scrutinized) than with recruiting those whose most prominent qualifications were their political activism.

Unlike the Reagan administration that drew in excess of 10 per cent of its appointees from the U.S. attorney's office, the Bush administration proportion was about 6 per cent. Of the six administrations, the only one with a lower proportion was the Carter administration. Like the Reagan administration, however, the proportion of law professors appointed to the district courts was lower than that of the Carter, Nixon, and Johnson administrations. Because Republican senators play an important role in judicial selection and also because the number of Bush appointees is relatively low, these findings should be kept in perspective.

Experience

Half the Bush appointees had previous judicial experience with all but one of them a sitting judge at the time of appointment. In terms of judicial experience, only the Carter appointees exceeded Bush's. As for prosecutorial experience, the Bush proportion was lower than that for the Reagan appointees and the lower of all six administrations. Similarly, the proportion of Bush appointees with neither judicial nor prosecutorial experience was also the lowest of all six administrations.

Starting with the Carter administration, there was a tendency for the appointees to have more judicial than prosecutorial experience. Previously, it was the other way around. A judicial record, of course, can be evaluated to determine the judge's philosophical orientation, judicial temperament, and dispositional tendencies. We know that these were concerns of the Bush administration. Additionally, by promoting state judges or federal magistrates or bankruptcy judges to the federal district bench, the concept of a professionalized career judiciary was reinforced

Education

If socioeconomic differences between the Republican and Democratic parties are reflected in the backgrounds of judicial appointees, they are likely to show up in the type of education of the appointees. The findings in Table 1 for undergraduate education do seem to hint at such differences. Only a minority of the appointees of Democratic presidents Johnson and Carter had a private undergraduate school experience, whereas the majority of the appointees of Republicans Nixon, Ford, Reagan, and Bush received a private school education. When law school education is examined, the proportion of Bush appointees with a prestigious Ivy League law school education is about the same as that of the Reagan appointees, and the proportions of both sets of appointees were lower than that of the Carter, Ford, Nixon, and Johnson appointees. Including such prestigious non-Ivy League law schools as Berkeley, Duke, Georgetown, Northwestern, Stanford, Texas, and Virginia raises the proportion of Bush appointees with a prestige legal education to about 42 per cent.

Affirmative Action

The record of the Bush administration of selecting qualified women to the district courts is better proportionately than the Reagan administration's record. Indeed, it surpasses all previous administrations with the exception of Carter's. The record of black-American appointments, however, matches the low proportion of appointments by Reagan, which was the worst record since Eisenhower. The proportion of Hispanic-American appointments is also low and is less than half the Reagan proportion. No Asian-Americans received appointments for the first time since the Nixon administration.

ABA Ratings

As recounted earlier, the Bush administration's dispute with the ABA Committee on Federal Judiciary was resolved, in part, by the committee's agreement to eliminate the *Exceptionally Well Qualified* rating. Now the highest rating is *Well Qualified*. Table 1 merges the *Exceptionally Well Qualified* and the *Well Qualified* ratings for the Reagan, Carter, Ford, Nixon, and Johnson appointees so as to enable a comparison to the Bush appointees. When that comparison is made, it appears that the Bush appointees have the highest ABA ratings of all six administrations. If the ABA ratings are taken as fair representations of legal ability, the Bush appointees as a group have the largest proportion of appointees with the highest ABA ratings since the Kennedy administration.

Despite the unprecedented proportion of those with the highest ABA ratings, 30 per cent of those with the *Qualified* rating received a split *Qualified/Not Qualified* rating which meant that an unspecified number of members of the ABA committee, although not in the majority, perhaps even only one member, rated the appointee to be *Not Qualified*. This was a higher proportion than that of the Reagan second-term appointees (about 25 per cent). This lack of consensus within the committee may suggest that some less-than-first-class lawyers are coming to the bench. Without a majority and minority report justifying the basis for each rating, it is difficult to know precisely why some appointees met with a less than unanimous seal of committee approval. However, it should be stressed that the official committee position is that any appointee receiving a *Qualified* rating is considered to be fully qualified for judicial office whether or not the committee is unanimous.

Other Considerations

As expected, President Bush appointed an overwhelming proportion of Republicans to the district courts, a proportion about the same as that of Reagan's. Table 1 also presents figures for party activism which show over 62 per cent of the Bush appointees with a history of party activism. This is an even higher proportion than that of the Reagan administration and proportionally is the highest of all six administrations. These figures, however, seem to undermine the observation made earlier that the Bush administration may be placing *less* emphasis on party activity than previous administrations. The explanation for this contradiction lies simply in the fact that an appointee was classified as being a party activist if at any time (including college and law school years) the appointee was politically active. Much of the Bush appointees' party activism was not recent involvement in national politics or even necessarily close political ties with Republican senators . . . . Thus the high proportion for the Bush appointees does not signal that party activism was an unusually important criterion in the selection process.

The religious origins or religious affiliations of the appointees is shown in Table 1. Before the Reagan administration, Democratic administrations appointed larger proportions of Catholics than Republican administrations, reflecting the large proportion of Catholics affiliated with the Democratic party and represented in the pool from which the judiciary is drawn. But Catholic political allegiances shifted significantly towards the Republican party particularly in the 1980s. Indeed, the proportion of Catholics appointed by Reagan exceeded Carter's and about equaled Johnson's. The proportion of Catholics appointed by Bush, however, appears to have declined somewhat although it is higher than Nixon's and Ford's. The proportion of Jewish appointees by Bush was the highest of all six administrations, but the relatively small numbers involved requires us to treat this finding as no more than highly tentative. It appears that religion is not a factor in the selection process.

Table 1 also presents the net worth of the Bush, Reagan, and Carter appointees. In 1989, the previous analysis of judicial appointments contained the observation that: "Without a more competitive pay scale, we can expect an increase in the number of wealthy individuals who become judges as some non-wealthy highly qualified lawyers will not be able to afford a pay cut to go on the bench." That expectation was borne out as the proportion of millionaires appointed by Bush reached one-third, an increase over the proportion for the Reagan appointees, which, in turn, had been a dramatic increase over the Carter proportion of millionaires. However, effective January 1, 1991, judicial salaries increased by 28.6 percent . . . Although the new judicial salaries still are not at the level recommended by the Commission on Executive, Legislative and Judicial Salaries in 1988, they come close. It will be of interest to see two years from now whether proportionately more people of more modest means are becoming judges now that the salaries are somewhat more attractive.

If the Bush administration is seeking to recruit younger judges, much like it appeared during Reagan's second term, that is not necessarily reflected in the findings reported in Table 1. The average age at the time of nomination of the Bush appointees was higher than that for the Nixon, Ford, and Reagan appointees. During the Reagan administration the proportion of those appointed under the age of 40 was about 7 per cent for the first term and about 12 per cent for the second term. The proportion for the Bush appointees was about 8 per cent. For the Reagan appointees the proportion *under* the age of 45 was 26 per cent in the first term and 37 per cent in the second term. For the Bush appointees the proportion was about 31 per cent.

APPEALS COURT APPOINTMENTS

Table 2 reveals the findings regarding the Bush administration's 18 appointees to the courts of appeals. The relatively low number of Bush appointees as well as the low number of Ford appointees requires that percentage differences be treated cautiously.

Occupation and Experience

When examining Table 2, we note that the proportion of appeals court appointees drawn by Bush from the sitting judiciary was about the same as that of the Reagan, Nixon and Johnson administrations. But whereas about one in four Reagan appointees came from private law practice and one in eight from law schools, about one in three Bush appointees came from private practice and none from the law schools. About one in eight Bush and Reagan appointees came from large law firms. It is possible that the Reagan administration exhausted the supply of prominent conservative law professors and that no obvious academic bright light was there to be chosen by Bush in the geographic area in which there were appeals court vacancies. It is also possible that the lack of appointing law professors was more a matter of finding the right academic for the right vacancy. If the latter reflects the reality, we can expect law professors to be selected; but it is uncertain whether Bush will match the relatively high proportions of law professors appointed by Reagan and Carter.

The proportion of Bush appointed appeals judges with neither previous judicial nor prosecutorial experience was similar to that for the Reagan and Carter administrations. For these administrations, lack of such experience apparently posed no serious obstacles to appointment.

Education and Affirmative Action

Like the Reagan and Carter appointees, the large majority of Bush appointees were educated as undergraduates and law school students in non-public schools. The Bush appointees had the lowest proportion of all six administrations of those educated at a publicly supported law school. The proportion of Bush appointees with an Ivy League law school education was higher than that of the Reagan appointees. However, when prestige non-Ivy League law schools such as those mentioned in the discussion of district court appointees are included, the proportion of both the Bush and Reagan appointees is approximately the same—about 45 per cent.

The Bush record of appointment of women is proportionately the second best in our history, exceeding that of the Reagan administration.

Because the total number of Bush appeals court appointees is low, it cannot be said with certainty that this reflects either a trend or an appointment priority. However, taken in conjunction with the larger proportion (than achieved by the Reagan administration) of women district court appointees, it is plausible to argue that this proportion can be seen as demonstrating a Bush administration commitment to the recruitment of qualified women.

Only one African-American and one Hispanic-American received appointments by the Bush administration. No Asian-American received an appointment . . . .

ABA Ratings

About three out of four Bush appointees received the highest ABA ratings compared to the Reagan record of three out of five. Only one Bush appointee received a split *Qualified/Not Qualified* rating, but that split rating went for the first time to a sitting federal district judge. Because the ABA committee does not offer reasons for its ratings there is no basis for knowing what moved the minority of the committee to a rating of *Not Qualified*. Before the Bush administration, the ABA ratings of U.S. district judges nominated for elevation were typically *Well Qualified* or *Exceptionally Well Qualified*. It is possible that political-ideological considerations were behind the elevation of this judge. It is also possible that political-ideological considerations motivated the minority *Not Qualified* rating. Alternatively, this appointee may in fact be only marginally qualified. Nevertheless, on balance, if the ABA ratings are considered a measure of professional quality, none of the previous five administrations exceeded the Bush record in appointing qualified people. In general, then, the Bush appointees can be considered to be among the best qualified judges to assume the appellate bench.

Other Considerations

Like the Reagan administration before it, the Bush administration failed to name even one Democrat to the appeals courts. Before the Reagan administration, it was the Kennedy administration that provided an instance of a president failing to find even one member of the opposition party worthy of a position on an appeals court. Also like the Reagan appointees, about two out of three appointees had some background of party activism . . . Only the Carter appointees had a higher proportion of appointees with a background of prior partisan activism. The relatively small number of Bush appointees means that comparisons of proportions of the Bush appointees to those of previous administrations must not place too much emphasis on somewhat small percentage differences. Nevertheless, it appears from Table 2 that the Bush administration exceeded the Reagan administration in the proportion of Catholics appointed to the appeals courts, a proportion that appears to be the highest of all six administrations. Once again, this may be a manifestation of the changing composition of the Republican party, and also it may be indicative of the total eradication of religious discrimination of the most subtle kind in judicial recruitment.

The net worth of the Bush appointees is presented in Table 2 and reveals that just as with Bush's district court appointees about one out of three appeals court appointees were millionaires. There was a lower proportion of Reagan appointees who were millionaires and a much lower proportion for the Carter appointees . . . . It will be of interest to see whether the new salary scale of the federal judiciary will broaden the socio-economic backgrounds of the appointees. Of course, the Republican party tends to attract larger proportions of the upper-income electorate than does the Democratic party, thus the relationship between salary scale and net worth may not be able to be tested until there is a Democratic administration in the White House appointing federal judges.

In contrast to the findings concerning average age at time of nomination for Bush's district court judges, the findings for the Bush appeals court appointees show them to have the youngest average age of all six administrations. The average age was 1.5 years younger than that for the Reagan appointees, almost 3.5 years younger than the Carter appointees, and over 5 years younger than the Nixon appointees. Administrations, of course, have more leeway over appeals court appointments than district court appointments, and these findings for age may indeed reflect a deliberate attempt on the part of the administration to select younger rather than older people so as to extend the Bush legacy.

THE BUSH IMPRINT?

Has there been a Bush imprint on the judiciary? The answer, of course, is how can there not be? More to the point, however, is the nature of that imprint. It is obvious that the full portrait of the Bush judiciary can only be drawn when the Bush administration has appointed its final judge. But the sketch we can see (and have seen) has lines extending back to the Reagan and also to previous administrations . . . .

There has been some evidence suggesting that there has been a decisional impact of the Reagan appointees that has moved the federal courts and federal law decidedly to the right of the philosophical spectrum. It is too soon to be able to gauge the decisional impact of the Bush appointees, but it is likely to be similar. It is not insignificant to note that of the 10 Bush appointments of sitting judges to the courts of appeals, nine were elevations of federal district court judges, *all* of whom had been Reagan district court appointees.

. . . [B]y 1993 George Bush will likely have named over 200 lower federal court judges, itself a major accomplishment. Added to the over 325 Reagan appointees remaining on the bench, about two-thirds of the judiciary will have been appointed by Reagan and Bush alone. By 1993, Democrats will account for only about 25 per cent of the federal bench, an imbalance exceeded only after the 20 years of appointments by Roosevelt and Truman. Just as the Roosevelt and Truman appointees carried through the constitutionalization of the New Deal, which meant institutionalizing judicial restraint in matters of governmental economic policymaking, so too the Reagan and Bush appointees will be likely to constitutionalize the Reagan-Bush social agenda, which means institutionalizing judicial restraint in matters of governmental civil liberties and civil rights policymaking. Rights and liberties may be subjected to majority rule in each state and in the nation to an extent not seen in almost 60 years. Whether this bodes well or ill for the nation will be a subject for continuing and vigorous debate. □

Notes and Questions

1. In November, 1992, President George Bush was defeated for reelection, and Bill Clinton, a Democrat, took his place. Thus, the Republican "imbalance" in the federal courts will be at least partially reversed in President Clinton's term of office. As this is written, it remains to be seen what impact the Clinton administration will have on judicial selection and behavior in the courts. President Clinton, during his first year in office, had the opportunity to fill one vacancy on the Supreme Court of the United States. He appointed Judge Ruth Bader Ginsburg, a federal judge who had been active in the battle against sex discrimination before she was appointed to the federal bench. During his first year, President Clinton also nominated 47 people to the federal courts of appeal and the district courts. More than a third of the nominees were women and 28% were black or Hispanic. More than half of President Clinton's nominees during his first year in office were state judges or federal magistrates, appointed by federal courts to assist judges. (Later, Clinton appointed a second Supreme Court justice, Stephen Breyer, another sitting Federal judge).

The end of the Bush administration gave Professor Goldman the opportunity to bring his study of the Bush appointments up to date. See Sheldon Goldman, "Bush's Judicial Legacy: The Final Imprint," 76 *Judicature* 282 (1993). In this article, he compared the judges appointed in 1989–1990 ("Bush I") with the judges appointed in 1991–1992 ("Bush II"). Goldman compiled the follow table of data about the Bush federal district judges (who preside at the trial level):

TABLE 1   U.S. DISTRICT COURT APPOINTEES CONFIRMED IN 1989–1990 (BUSH I) COMPARED WITH APPOINTEES CONFIRMED IN 1991–1992 (BUSH II)

	Bush I Appointees % (N)	Bush II Appointees % (N)		Bush I Appointees % (N)	Bush II Appointees % (N)
Occupation			*Gender*		
Politics/government	10.4%(5)	11.0%(11)	Male	89.6%(43)	76.0% (76)
Judiciary	47.9%(23)	39.0%(39)	Female	10.4%(5)	24.0% (24)
Large law firm			*Ethnicity/race*		
100+ members	6.2%(3)	13.0%(13)	White	95.8%(46)	86.0% (86)
50–99	4.2%(2)	9.0%(9)	African American	2.1%(1)	9.0% (9)
25–49	6.2%(3)	8.0%(8)	Hispanic	2.1%(1)	5.0% (5)
Medium size firm			Asian	—	—
10–24 members	10.4%(5)	8.0%(8)	*Percent white male*	85.4%(41)	67.0% (67)
5–9	8.3%(4)	5.0%(5)	*ABA rating*		
Small firm			Well qualified	58.3%(28)	57.0% (57)
2–4 members	4.2%(2)	3.0%(3)	Qualified	41.7%(20)	43.0% (43)
solo	—	2.0%(2)	*Political Identification*		
Professor of law	2.1%(1)	—	Democrat	4.2%(2)	6.0% (6)
Other	—	2.0%(2)	Republican	93.8%(45)	86.0% (86)
Experience			Independent	2.1%(1)	8.0% (8)
Judicial	50.0%(24)	45.0%(45)	*Past party activism*	62.5%(30)	60.0% (60)
Prosecutorial	37.5%(18)	40.0%(40)	*Religious origin/affiliation*		
Neither one	27.1%(13)	34.0%(34)	Protestant	64.6%(31)	64.0% (64)
Undergraduate education			Catholic	22.9%(11)	31.0% (31)
Public	41.7%(20)	46.0%(46)	Jewish	12.5%(6)	5.0% (5)
Private	50.0%(24)	37.0%(37)	*Net worth*		
Ivy League	8.3%(4)	17.0%(17)	Under $200,000	6.2%(3)	12.0% (12)
Law school education			$200,000–499,999	29.2%(14)	32.0% (32)
Public	47.9%(23)	55.0%(55)	$500,000–999,999	31.2%(15)	24.0% (24)
Private	37.5%(18)	31.0%(31)	$1+ million	33.3%(16)	32.0% (32)
Ivy League	14.6%(7)	14.0%(14)			
Average age at nomination				49.6	47.4
Total number of appointees				48	100

Goldman notes a number of interesting aspects of Bush II appointments. About 3 out of 10 Bush II appointees came from large law firms—this was about double the proportion of Bush I appointees. The increase in the number of women appointed was very striking. This was, apparently, the result of an explicit policy decision. Goldman also suggests that Republicans "were under some pressure . . . to demonstrate . . . sensitivity to women's rights," because of the battle over Clarence Thomas' confirmation as a Supreme Court Justice. Anita Hill accused Judge Thomas of sexual harassment, and the nationally televised hearings provoked intense reactions, particularly among women. Goldman's table also shows a sharp increase in minority appointments.

Goldman also notes that the "figures appear to show a continuation of the trend toward a career judiciary, although the American judiciary is far from approximating the European career judiciary" (p. 288). All six of the most recent appointments to the Supreme Court have come from the lower courts.

Table 2 of Goldman's article shows the figures for court of appeals appointments during the Bush I and Bush II periods. These numbers, naturally, are much smaller than those for the district courts, but here too there was a marked increase in the appointment of women.

Goldman continues to follow federal judicial appointments. See Sheldon Goldman and Matthew D. Saronson, "Clinton's Nontraditional Judges: Creating a more Representative Bench," 718 *Judicature* 68 (1994).

BLE 2   U.S. APPEALS COURT APPOINTEES CONFIRMED IN 1989–1990 (BUSH I) COMPARED WITH
OINTEES CONFIRMED IN 1991–1992 (BUSH II)

	Bush I Appointees % (N)	Bush II Appointees % (N)		Bush I Appointees % (N)	Bush II Appointees % (N)
upation			*Gender*		
itics/government	11.1% (2)	10.5% (2)	Male	88.9% (16)	73.7% (14)
iciary	55.6% (10)	63.2% (12)	Female	11.1% (2)	26.3% (5)
ge law firm			*Ethnicity/race*		
00+ members	5.6% (1)	10.5% (2)	White	88.9% (16)	89.5% (17)
0–99	11.1% (2)	5.3% (1)	African American	5.6% (1)	5.3% (1)
25–49	—	—	Hispanic	5.6% (1)	5.3% (1)
dium size firm			Asian	—	—
0–24 members	16.7% (3)	—	*Percent white male*	77.8% (14)	63.2% (12)
5–9	—	5.3% (1)	*ABA rating*		
all firm			Well qualified	77.8% (14)	52.6% (10)
2–4 members	—	—	Qualified	22.2% (4)	47.4% (9)
solo	—	—	*Political identification*		
fessor of law	—	5.3% (1)	Democrat	—	10.5% (2)
perience			Republican	94.4% (17)	84.2% (16)
icial	55.6% (10)	68.4% (13)	Independent	5.6% (1)	5.3% (1)
secutorial	33.3% (6)	26.3% (5)	Past party activism	66.7% (12)	73.7% (14)
ither one	38.9% (7)	26.3% (5)	*Religious origin/affiliation*		
dergraduate education			Protestant	55.6% (10)	63.2% (12)
blic	33.3% (6)	26.3% (5)	Catholic	38.9% (7)	10.5% (2)
vate	50.0% (9)	68.4% (13)	Jewish	5.6% (1)	26.3% (5)
League	16.7% (3)	5.3% (1)	*Net worth*		
w school education			Under $200,000	5.6% (1)	5.3% (1)
blic	22.2% (4)	36.8% (7)	$200,000–499,999	33.3% (6)	26.3% (5)
vate	44.4% (8)	36.8% (7)	$500,000–999,999	22.2% (4)	21.0% (4)
League	33.3% (6)	26.3% (5)	$1+ million	38.9% (7)	47.4% (9)
erage age at nomination				48.5	48.8
tal number of appointees				18	19

How long does a President's "legacy" of appointments last? How long do his judges stay on the bench after his administration comes to an end? Twelve years after Jimmy Carter left the White House, about 9 out of 10 of his appointees were still sitting on the bench. Some of these judges had "senior" status (retired judges who still decide cases and have workloads ranging from "the equivalent of full time to occasional presiding"), but almost two-thirds of the Carter judges were still on "active service." Goldman concludes that a "judicial legacy is felt for at least two decades after [a President] leaves office" (p. 295).

We can ask, how real is this legacy? Some Supreme Court justices have been a severe disappointment to the Presidents who put them on the bench. Federal judges have life tenure, and they can change their (political) minds if they feel like it. To be sure, most conservative judges stay conservative, and most liberals stay liberal. On the actual performance of the Bush judges, see Robert A. Carp, Donald Songer, C.K. Rowland, Ronald Stidham, and Lisa Richey-Tracy, "The Voting Behavior of Judges Appointed by President Bush," 76 *Judicature* 298 (1993).

2. Federal judicial selection obviously is a political process. Technical legal skill is but one factor considered by the President and the Senate Judiciary Committee. Political leaders have long considered religious and ethnic background, race and gender important. Why? In part, their concern is *symbolic*. Appointing Jews, African-Americans, or women says something positive about their place in American society. In part, the reasons are political: these appointments satisfy groups from which they come, or repay the activism of the branch of the group which supported the Administration.

Is there an *instrumental* significance as well? Did the Supreme Court of the United States decide cases differently than it otherwise would have decided them because Thurgood Marshall, an African-American, or Sandra Day O'Connor, a woman, were Associate Justices, participating in the deliberations and voting? Of course, it would be difficult to prove the influence of any one Justice on the outcome of particular cases. It would be even more difficult to prove what part of their influence turned on their race or gender as opposed to, say, their experience as a civil rights lawyer or as a state political leader.

Elaine Martin, in "Men and Women on the Bench: Vive la Difference?," 73 *Judicature* 204, 208 (1990), surveyed men and women federal judges appointed by President Carter. She says:

This study examined the sex role conflicts, sex role attitudes and personality characteristics of men and women federal judges appointed by President Carter in an effort to determine if women brought a perspective to the federal bench not otherwise represented. In all respects, the findings suggest that women have certain expectations and attitudes that are not the same as men's.

Despite their high status as judicial elites, women federal judges continue to carry a heavier burden at home and experience more conflict between their parental and career roles than their men colleagues. The majority of women had to overcome sex discrimination, as well as sex-role conflict, in order to purse their legal careers. Women judges remain attuned to the difficulties that other women face in combining family and career as evidenced by their advice to young women lawyers.

Women judges in this study, perhaps as a consequence of these personal experiences, evidence greater attitudinal feminism than men. Women are also stronger in their support of increased political, judicial and social roles for women than men judges.

There are a variety of ways in which the different perspectives represented by the women studied here could have an impact on their behavior as judges. Their differences might influence such things as decisional output, especially in cases involving sex discrimination; conduct of courtroom business, especially as regards sexist behavior by litigators; influence on sex-role attitudes held by their male colleagues, especially on appellate courts where decisions are collegial; administrative behavior, for example, in hiring women law clerks; and . . . collective actions, through formal organizations, undertaken to heighten the judicial system's response to gender bias problems in both law and process . . . .

[A]ny gender differences among judges in voting and sentencing behavior may be limited to a narrow category of cases. . . . All women are not alike any more than all men are alike. As the numbers of women judges increase, more sophisticated analysis can include such variables as judicial role orientations, feminist ideology and political partisanship . . .

See also Peter McCormick and Twyla Job, "Do Women Judges Make a Difference? An Analysis by Appeal Court Data," 8 *Canadian Journal of Law and Society* 135 (1993). The authors found no evidence from a large sample of cases that women judges responded to legal issues in ways that distinguished them from men judges. The authors felt that "the class and character preferences built into the triple hurdles of university entrance, law school admission, and judicial recruitment," combined with the traditions and prejudices of the profession, "may seriously limit the immediate impact of women on the bench" (p. 147). For a critique of this article, suggesting that the differences are too subtle to be captured by the kind of research employed, see Joan Brockman, "A Difference without a Distinction," id at 149.

In an interesting (but as yet unpublished) study, Joyce Sterling in 1990–1991 surveyed the attitudes of practicing lawyers in Colorado toward women judges. In "Women on the Bench: How are their Voices Heard?," presented at the Annual Meeting of the Law and Society Association, May 1992, she found that women judges ranked significantly *lower* than male judges, as appraised by lawyers. The lawyers also, somewhat surprisingly, ranked women judges much lower than men on items that dealt with courtesy, compassion, and satisfactory performance in settling cases. Were these rankings just gender bias? Perhaps, but women lawyers were just as negative, or more so, with regard to these attributes. Were women judges too tough? If so, was it because they were trying not to appear "feminine" and weak? At this point, it is not possible to explain Sterling's results.

It is fair to say that questions about the impact of race, ethnicity, and gender on the judging process are still open. Certainly, the existing small amount of research does not give definitive answers. What would you *expect* to be the result if the bench came to "look like America?" Suppose the proportion of women and minority judges was about what it was in the general population.

What changes, if any, might come about in style or substance? Why? What is there in the experiences of women and minority group members that might affect their behavior? What factors in the ideology and structures of the legal system might, to some extent, offset the gender or race of the judges? See Donald R. Songer, Sue Davis, and Susan Haire, "A Reappraisal of Diversification in the Federal Courts: Gender Effects in the Courts of Appeals," 56 *Journal of Politics* 425 (1994). In this study of obscenity, search and seizure, and employment discrimination cases, female judges differed from their male colleagues only in employment discrimination decisions. See, also, Elaine Martin, "Differences in Men and Women Judges: Perspectives on Gender," 27 *Journal of Political Science* 74 (1989); John Gruhl, Cassia Spohn, and Susan Welch, "Women as Policy Makers: The Case of Trial Judges," 25 *American Journal of Political Science* 308 (1981).

3. Unlike federal judges, most American *state* judges are elected. The systems differ: sometimes the voters choose between two or more candidates; sometimes they vote only to approve or disapprove a candidate nominated by the governor. Many people wonder whether voters know enough about the judges and about the requirements of the position to make an intelligent choice. A distinguished Justice of the Supreme Court of Wisconsin, for example, was defeated in his race for reelection after he wrote an unremarkable opinion affirming a decision allowing the Milwaukee Braves baseball team to move and become the Atlanta Braves.

Nicholas P. Lovrich, Jr., John C. Pierce, and Charles H. Sheldon, in "Citizen Knowledge and Voting in Judicial Elections," 73 *Judicature* 28 (1989), studied "what kind of person votes in the low-salience [judicial] elections." Their study was part of a survey in the Spokane, Washington metropolitan area. They determined that people who *think* that they are well informed about the courts are likely to *be* well informed. Moreover, those who are well informed are more likely to vote than those who are unsure of their knowledge. Knowledge is an important element in deciding whether or not to vote. Those who actually voted do not differ markedly in their socio-economic or neighborhood status. See, also, Nicholas P. Lovrich, Jr. and Charles H. Sheldon, "Voters in Contested, Nonpartisan Judicial Elections: A Responsible Electorate or a Problematic Public?" 36 *Western Political Quarterly* 241 (1983). Lovrich and Sheldon also remarked in "Is Voting for State Judges a Flight of Fancy or a Reflection of Policy and Value Preferences?" 16 *Justice System Journal* 57 (1994) "[P]erhaps the much maligned judicial voters deserve more credit than heretofore granted."

Joel Goldstein, in "The Impact of the Louisville Courier-Journal's Editorial Endorsements on the Outcome of Local Judicial Elections," 73 *Judicature* 108, 112 (1989), found that voters who used the newspaper's endorsements in voting for candidates for the local district court were better educated, more ideological, and had a greater sense of political efficacy. However, the study "found that the newspaper endorsements had a large gross impact upon the vote, but that its influence on electoral outcomes was muted by the fact that about half of the voters used it as a positive referent, while the other half used it as a negative referent."

4. Do elections influence the way judges behave? In theory, they do, and should. A judge facing election, we would think, would be sensitive to what

the electorate wants. Of course, this sensitivity would apply only to a few relatively controversial or highly publicized cases. On this subject, see Melinda Gann Hall, "Electoral Politics and Strategic Voting in State Supreme Courts," 54 *Journal of Politics* 427 (1992). Hall looked at the behavior of elected state judges in death penalty cases. Liberal judges dislike the death penalty, but white Americans across sociodemographic categories seem to favor capital punishment. See M. Dwayne Smith and James Wright, "Capital Punishment and Public Opinion in the Post-*Furman* Era: Trends and Analysis," 12 *Sociological Spectrum* 127 (1992). Hall found evidence that liberal state judges, facing reelection campaigns, had some tendency to "join conservative majorities in death penalty cases" in the four states that she studied. These results, though limited to this one situation, suggested to Hall that it "may well be the case that justices behave much more strategically than originally believed. Instead of public policy goals driving judicial decisions, basic self-interest may also be an important consideration to the state supreme court justice when rendering decisions" (p. 443).

Hall notes, quite properly, that her results do not in any way suggest "a general model of judicial decision making." In many states, judicial elections are not contested in any meaningful sense. And, as we pointed out, only a few cases are likely to have much meaning for the constituency.

Judges who run for re-election have to raise money for their campaigns, just as candidates for Congress do. Judges probably have less leeway to make explicit promises than candidates for Congress. Presumably, however, big contributors expect *something* from a judge they support, even if that something is left fairly implicit. See Anthony Champagne, "Campaign Contributions in Texas Supreme Court Races," 17 *Crime, Law and Social Change* 91 (1992). Champagne points out that judicial campaign finance can be an aspect of interest group politics. For example, physicians, outraged over "what they perceived as the pro-plaintiff tone of the Supreme Court's malpractice decisions" in Texas, mounted "a major funding effort for their slate of Supreme Court candidates in the 1988 election" (p. 104).

50. *Law and Life in the United States*[162]

Carol Greenhouse

□ . . . In some respects, the common law reflects perfectly a logic of linear time in its reliance on precedent, its commitment to reform, and its acknowledgment of individual persons and rights. But the common law also involves larger claims beyond linear time. Reasoning by analogy to precedent creates a *false* historicity in that it perpetually reclaims the past for the present: in theory, a current dispute can be settled by reference to cases from the beginning of the legal record almost a millennium ago. "The law" thus accumulates, but it never passes; at any

---

162. Chapter 5 of an unpublished book.

instant, it represents a totality. It is by definition complete, yet its completeness does not preclude change. It is a human achievement, yet, by its reversible and lateral excursions, and by its collective voice, it is not identifiably the product of any particular individual or group . . . .

. . . My general argument is that, given American commitments to particular democratic forms and meanings of representation, the American judiciary faces specific difficulties in mobilizing its symbols of succession and continuity. In particular, while the United States shares with Europe and other places a rich legacy of temporal concepts, the ambiguities of Western temporality are particularly problematic with regard to the judicial branch . . . [L]inear time is the time of national histories and political events in the United States, but . . . judicial institutions are charged with the stewardship of another aspect of western temporality in the American context. In the judicial context, time is not only a line, but is also selectively opened toward principles that are symbolically represented as timeless . . .—these are principles of justice, culturally conceived . . . . [I]n the general area of judicial succession . . . multiple temporalities—of the law, personal lifetimes, public lives and larger structures of significance—as well as their indeterminacies, must be worked out . . . .

The case studies I develop here involve these . . . symbolic claims and distinctions. In particular, they highlight the tensions between cultural understandings of biography and justice, interests and renunciation, profession and representation, and politics and law—all juxtaposed here as involving irreconcilable constructions of time. The cases are the confirmation hearings for Judge Robert Bork (whose nomination failed in Congress), and Judge (now Justice) Clarence Thomas. My evidence derives almost exclusively from the published transcripts of the Senate Judiciary Committee hearings in 1987 and 1991, respectively. Though their outcomes were different, the cases are related in that they involve explicit reference both to partisan contest over the nomination within the committee and among the public, as well as over control of the nomination process between the White House and the Congress. In that context, the Bork hearings defined a certain implicit relevance of the candidate's biography that was insistent and explicit in the Thomas hearings. Overall, my argument is that the increasing display of judicial candidates' biographies shifts the traditional meanings of justice from those of transcendent neutrality . . . to those of representation. Indeed, by the end of the Thomas hearings, it appeared that the symbolization of justice had not only shifted, but had been proffered in exchange, as the president himself appropriated the symbols of the transcendent "everyman" who could by his nature respond to all interests . . .

JUDGE BORK AND THE POLITICS OF TIME

[In the hearings on the confirmation of Robert Bork, the candidate was quizzed about two articles he wrote. One, in the *New Republic,* 1963, expressed doubts about the proposed Civil Rights Act. In 1971, Bork wrote an article on his views of the First Amendment, which appeared in the *Indiana Law Journal.* Both of these articles contained controversial statements.]

Let us begin with Judge Bork's own words. In 1982, in his testimony at the Senate Judiciary Committee's hearings on his nomination to the Circuit Court of Appeals, Bork responded to an invitation to discuss the Indiana article. In his response, he distanced himself from that article by alluding to the nature of "theoretical argument", and emphasizing his view of the nature of an academic's writings generally:

> . . . [The] first amendment protects the free exercise of religion and the freedom of the press as well as speech. Within the speech area, I was dealing with an application of Prof. Herbert Wechsler's concept of neutral principles, which is quite a famous concept in academic debate. *I was engaged in an academic exercise in the application of those principles, a theoretical argument, which I think is what professors are expected to do . . . . It seems to me in my putative function as a judge that what is relevant is what the Supreme Court has said, and not my theoretical writings in 1971.* (Emphasis added)

In 1973, he answered a similar question on the same article in a similar vein:

> . . . It was speculative writing which professors are expected to engage in, without meaning that that is what they believed for all time or that is what they think would be appropriate for some other organ of Government to pick up at that time and it is explicitly stated to be speculative in that sense.

Senator Tunney (this is 1973) went on to ask Bork to comment on an excerpt from Bork's 1969 article in *Fortune,* assessing the Nixon administration's plan "to wage war on conglomerate mergers . . . as one of the bleakest, most disappointing developments in antitrust history."

> Q. Do you continue to hold this true of the Nixon administration's antitrust policy?
> MR. BORK. Senator, in my opinion, which is my opinion as an academic in this field, the conglomerate merger campaign was an antitrust mistake. However, it should be said that this administration, and this Justice Department, continues to enforce the antitrust laws vigorously.

They have guidelines about conglomerate mergers. Those will be enforced, and *should such a case come up to me that case will be dealt with in line with that policy and not in line with my academic opinion I expressed in that article.* (Emphasis added)

. . . Tunney continued by asking Bork if his actions as Solicitor General would be guided by his personal views:

MR. BORK. I think that whether I think the Supreme Court is likely to do it, whether to come down more in line with my views, or perhaps less in line with my views, if I have reason to believe that the Supreme Court wants to consider this subject, it seems to me, as an officer of the court, I ought to bring that case up and explain the varying positions that are available.

Bork's responses to such questions about his past views and his future predictability were entirely consistent from 1973 through the opening days of his Supreme Court interviews. Throughout that period, he responded to questions by detailing his understanding of the structural accountabilities and limits of the office he aspired to, and the customary canons of ethics and etiquette each position involved. For example, in 1982, in response to the question of whether he would "feel [himself] obliged to follow Supreme Court precedent even though [he might] greatly disagree with its application in a particular case." Bork responded:

Mr. Chairman, it seems to me that a lower court judge owes a duty of absolute obedience to Supreme Court precedent. If that were not true, the legal system would fall into chaos, so that my personal views certainly cannot affect my duty to apply the law as the Supreme Court has framed it.

In 1973, Bork responded to a similar question by Senator Hart:

Q. What if the Government takes a position in the field of antitrust or civil rights that you think is wrong, and have said in the past is wrong, what do you do?
MR. BORK. What will I do? I will enforce the policy of the Government in antitrust as the Government defines it. I do not define it, Senator.
I might say that in practice both for defendants in antitrust cases and for plaintiffs in antitrust cases I frequently urged positions that as an academic I would criticize. (Emphasis added)

. . . Well into the 1987 hearings, Bork continued to invoke the separate offices he had held and might hold as more or less distinct professional and normative contexts. He distinguished among what "academics," Solicitor Generals, and judges and Special Masters *do* and *are expected to do,* by way of accounting for the different positions he had brought to legal issues over time. In particular, Bork consistently relied on the sociological concept of the profession—particularly the academic profession—to rhetorically subordinate questions of his personhood (e.g., his personal opinions) to issues of office.

THE 1987 HEARINGS

. . . Bork's responses changed significantly (from the cultural point of view that we are pursuing here) midway through the 1987 hearings. He not only stopped resisting the attempts of committee members to place him on the "line" between his past and his future; he ultimately used that temporal idiom himself . . . .

There were essentially three different positions in the controversy, each invoking a different temporal idiom. Bork's critics, who characterized Bork's retractions as "confirmation conversions", made their case by placing all of Bork's writings, utterances and opportunities on a single time line, emphasizing their sequence and—by definition of a time line—their consequences . . . . [L]inear time is the time of personal (and political) interests. Linear time has provided the canonical form for personal investment and redemption ever since the theologians and industrialists of the middle ages merged both their metaphors and institutions of salvation and economy. Indeed, the mocking reference to "conversion" is a play on this canonical temporal form and its root metaphors.

Bork's advocates, on the other hand, worked with a dual temporality. Where Bork's critics combined the personal and the professional on the single time line of the political careerist, his supporters divided that line into two strands. One strand represented Bork the *person,* vital, growing, pruning, thriving: the metaphors were distinctly *natural,* even *evolutionary* ones. The other strand, coextensive with but neither explaining nor to be explained by the first, represented his *career.* The doubling of the time line gave Bork's supporters a rhetorical vantage point form which to respond to the critics' charges of cynical conversion on the retraction question.

Bork himself employed neither of these temporal idioms in the hearings in 1973 and 1982. Through the opening questions in 1987, too, he resisted *both* the critics' single-stranded linear time idiom, with which they portrayed his self-interest, *and* his supporters' double-stranded time line, with which they portrayed his independence . . . . Bork initially voiced a third possibility, emphasizing his plural professional engagements and their separate normative requirements. For example, particularly in reference to his writings while an academic, which were the focus of the retraction controversy, he insisted on a meaning of "theory" that set it at some indeterminate remove from "personal opinion."

The first sign that Bork's rhetorical resistance to both his critics' and supporters' constructions of "interest" and "independence" had begun to soften came on the first day of the 1987 hearings. In response to Senator Kennedy's question as to when he first "publicly" changed his position on the Civil Rights Act, Bork began his response with a reference to the classroom. Kennedy interrupted him, repeating the one word, "publicly", apparently rejecting the idea of the classroom as a public space. Bork then said:

> Well, I think it is *implicit in some of the things that I wrote earlier,* but I first said it, I think, where it was written down at least, in a confirmation hearing in 1973. *But, one has to know the evolution of my thinking* about political matters to understand where that article came from and why I no longer agree with it and have not agreed with it for a long time. (Emphasis added.)

Bork's reference to evolution is crucial here, since it is the first time that he invoked the temporal metaphors of the double-stranded time line, the one which braids together the evolving inner man and the committed public man, an author of "fixed texts." . . .

[T]he full conversion to the double-linear time idiom seems to have come in an exchange with Senator DeConcini, who asked him when he had ceased "being a libertarian." Bork responded by narrating the circumstances of his authorship of the *Fortune Magazine* article while on sabbatical, only to discover in the classroom—through a colleague's chance observation—that he was no longer voicing the positions the article defined . . . .

Eventually, even Bork's two-stranded temporal idiom flattened into a single-stranded time line. Where in the earlier hearings he had used the first person singular pronoun only to situate himself as a professional, his usage of the first person singular mid-way through the 1987 hearings was, by comparison, crowded and personal . . . .

[H]e draws . . . [an] image connecting Bork as self, Bork as judge, the committee, and—via television and the print media—the American public:

> . . . [This] is a hearing which you gentlemen refer to [as] historic, you refer to it as one of the most complete and so forth. I have expressed my views here, and those views are widely known, more widely known than any views of mine before have been.
>
> It really would be preposterous for me to sit here and say the things I have said to you and then get confirmed and get on the Supreme Court

and do the opposite. I would be disgraced in history. Aside from everything else, I am not going to do that . . .

This statement completes the rhetorical fusion of Bork as self and Bork the professional into a single time line . . . .

The relevance of Bork's initial invocation of the multitemporality of his professional engagements is that it involved a temporal idiom that—from a cultural point of view—approached but ultimately subverted the idealized model of justice . . . It approached it in its implications of independence, renunciation and responsibility; it subverted it in that it made "justice" a profession, like teaching, like other forms of work. In the public symbols of the United States, however, justice is not a profession, but a distinct modality of being. Culturally speaking, justices are not supposed to have autobiographies. Their public lives are supposed to be entirely textualized in the law itself; there is—can be—no other story . . .

Until the mid-point of his 1987 testimony, Bork's self-representation, against convention, featured a series of professional engagements. Each of these engagements—as all professions do—required its characteristic renunciation, and it was the series of *renunciations* that structured Bork's initial, unconventional autobiographical narrative on the retraction issue. In successfully translating his self-presentation into conventional male autobiographical form, the committee reinterpreted his life story as one of successive *engagements;* his supporters and critics differed only as to their characterization of these engagements and his effectiveness in representing the interests they involved. In the collaborative effort to transform his life into a *representative* life, the senators succeeded in improvising a vocabulary with which the hearings could become an arena in which the contest between the conservative executive branch and the relatively liberal legislative branch could be addressed as (barely) a subtext.

In the Thomas hearings four years later, that subtext became explicit as the framework for the hearings altogether. Certainly, in those hearings, the Senators themselves stressed the partisan political contest between the President and Congress, and within the Congress, in relation to the nomination and conformation process . . . .

THE THOMAS HEARINGS

Before [Clarence] Thomas took the stand for the first time on September 10, 1991, his life story had been told—in condensed or extended form—eight times that same day by different Senators, most of whom spoke for his confirmation. Early on, [Senator] Simpson drew the contrast between the Bork and the Thomas candidacies, expressing the view that Thomas' prior confirmations would preclude challenges on his record . . . . But it was [Senator] Nunn, on that first afternoon, who made explicit the connection between Thomas' biographical litany as a preemptive rhetorical strike against interest groups arrayed against him.

> Our duty is not to create or deny another vote on abortion or sex discrimination or affirmation action or any other particular issue. Our duty, as I see it, is to confirm a Supreme Court Justice who, subject to good behavior under the Constitution, may serve for many years on the Court, indeed, may serve for life. I doubt seriously, Mr. Chairman, that many of today's—maybe most of today's—burning issues will still be raising the blood pressure of our nation seven years from now when Judge Thomas is 50, much less when he reaches the still relatively young judicial age of 60.

The relevance of Thomas' life story—the "climb" from poverty and discrimination in Pinpoint [the small town in Georgia where Thomas was born] to success and power in Washington, D.C.—was well established in the hearings even before Thomas told it himself. Narrators stressed the comprehensive aspect of Thomas' life story, in repeatedly juxtaposing his unpromising origins and his present success. This aspect of his story was then leveraged rhetorically against the narrow interests of any particular interest group. His success story was also invoked as an inspiration to others. But, primarily, Thomas' life story was offered as the promise of his future memories as a justice, memories that would inspire him to fight for "fairness and equal justice." Significantly, the life story as the principal idiom of qualification was the work of Thomas' supporters; in Bork's case, it was the work of his critics. Bork resisted the single-stranded autobiographical time line because of its implication that the future justice could be "read" by past professional commitments. Thomas, on the other hand, was a full participant in the collaborative narrative of his autobiography . . . .

In context, the . . . evocations and recitations of Thomas' life story by himself and others repeatedly made reference to Thomas' physical presence as an African American, though in highly selective and patterned ways. His racial identity as such as repeatedly dissociated from his candidacy and the confirmation process, though both supporters and critics referred to their belief that his race had symbolic value—though in very different ways. The prevalent direct racial references were to the *past* and *future* relevance of Thomas' identity as an African American—in the past, as a target of racist discrimination during his childhood in the South; in the future, anticipating his service as associate justice as the fruit of Justice Marshall's harvest from his years on the Supreme Court . . . . Otherwise, Thomas' racial identity tended to frame the story of his upward mobility, the fact of his success contrasting with what were repeatedly said to be the stronger possibilities against it; for example, Thomas recalled watching a group of criminal defendants board a bus from the window of his EEOC [Thomas was the Chair of the Equal Employment Opportunity Commission] office and thinking, "But for the grace of God, there go I . . . "

Critics tended to narrow the issues . . . . [They] reiterated themes of the balance of powers, the current state of the Supreme Court, and the criteria of judicial qualification. Supporters, on the other hand, tended to broaden the issues, referring to the quality of Judge and Mrs. Thomas as people . . . and the unanimity of Thomas' support from people who had known him at the EEOC . . . Thomas supporters closed ranks around the premise of a moral hierarchy, in which Thomas was asserted to be "quality"; his critics closed ranks around the issue of legal expertise, by which Thomas was deemed to lack quality. These references to quality are of very different kinds—the former refers to moral superiority in a world of limited good; the latter refers to intellectual and technical superiority in a world of unlimited good.

. . . Both dimensions of this frame—the life story and the professional performance—were tightened around him [Thomas] considerably when the committee resolved to settle in public the ambiguities raised by the sexual harassment charges. These intensified the scrutiny he and his supporters initially deliberately focused on his personal life and professional conduct as the text of his record; however, they also substantially shifted that scrutiny to the life itself. When race dominated the life story narrative, Thomas' performance could be rhetorically distanced from his "self" . . . When the second hearings took the same life story and reexamined it for its gendered and sexual content, such distancing appears to have been foreclosed. In this sense, the second hearings both extended and overturned the first.

It is worth noting that while the second hearings aimed at tightening the seams in Thomas' adult life story (Thomas' own metaphor was to a lynching), Thomas appears to have felt constrained by the single-stranded approach to his life during the earlier hearings, as well. Bork had essentially been forced to adopt the linear autobiography as a device to account for (and to be held accountable) for his "paper trail"; Thomas sought to disaggregate his professional autobiography to account for his silences. While Thomas readily accepted (and offered) a narrative version of his life that stressed the sequence of his commitments, he quickly expressed reluctance to permit his written and spoken record from one professional context to "speak for" another. Anticipating confirmation, he declined to express his views on numerous legal issues on the grounds that they might compromise his impartiality later. In the context of questions on the constitutional guarantees of abortion, for example, [Senator] Metzenbaum distinguished an individual's belief from that individual's future vote on a case; Thomas consistently equated the expression of opinion with a compromised vote.

These rhetorical efforts to create some space *within* his autobiography culminated in Thomas' references to the need to "strip down" (that is, refrain from expressing personal views) in accepting a judicial position. The autobiographical frame within which Thomas and his supporters presented his career paradoxically highlighted Thomas' commitment to silence on these and other matters, and provided the rhetorical basis for his critics' challenges on substantive policy (and other) questions. . . .

THE SECOND THOMAS HEARINGS

. . . The moral hierarchy implicit in Thomas' presentation (by himself and others) is clearer in relation to the contest over the sexual harassment report by Anita Hill. Her report did not, in fact, involve an appeal for redress, though the committee defined its role as one of investigating charges, and *of necessity* deciding which of Thomas and Hill was lying. This definition of the committee's role is consistent with a moral hierarchy, in which status is held to reflect virtue in finite supply. Thomas' self-presentation in effect rhetorically controlled the second hearings, both in demanding a single-stranded life story from Hill, and in defining the question of those hearings, too, around the truth-value of autobiographical narrative.

CONCLUSION

In the American context, . . . the indeterminacy of the constructed distinction between linear time and some larger field of permanent value around it appear to be essential elements of American cultural understandings of the idea of justice. I believe that it was the collapse of that distinction that became problematic in the Bork candidacy, as it is in contexts where judicial acts are perceived by the public to be in the service of some particular agenda . . .

. . . [J]ustice implies both a progress for the world and a critique, that is, an imagined vantage point from which history itself might be judged. While legal actors' claims to legitimacy might be conventionally or historically cast in terms of the connection between reason and fixed, timeless truths, the cultural interpretation developed here situates the cultural force of law in its engagement with multiple, mutually contesting temporalities which potentially impose rival claims on social actors. To say that the law is cultural does not by itself dismantle the force of the idea of justice. Just at the point where cultural and political inquiry would intersect, justice and justices return to the separate temporal domains which, in cultural terms, give them life. □

NOTES AND QUESTIONS

1. Greenhouse points to one part of our cultural portrait of Supreme Court Justices: they are men and women who find and follow the law, a timeless neutral body of principles. They are not people who *create* law. Of course, this is not the only strand in American legal culture that relates to court appointments. People on both sides of the abortion controversy, for example, were convinced that it made a big difference to their cause if A rather than B were appointed to the Supreme Court. They did not expect a neutral, open-minded justice, who would carefully sift the law they expected and wanted a partisan for their side. They were, of course, right in thinking that who was appointed made a big difference.

How do people reconcile these two views of what a judge is and does? Do they reconcile them at all?

Compare with Greenhouse's analysis, Michael H. Gottesman and Michael R. Seidl, "A Tale of Two Discourses: William Gould's Journey from the Academy to the World of Politics," 47 *Stanford Law Review* 749 (1995).

2. As we noted, most state court judges are elected. They are, thus, part of the political process, although in many states these elections are supposed to be non-partisan. In some states, the judge may not run *against* anybody. The public simply votes "yes" or "no" on his or her candidacy. As you can imagine, a "no" vote is not very common. Do these various ways of appointing and electing judges affect Greenhouse's argument in any way?

3. As Greenhouse shows, the confirmation process can be highly political, the recent history of Supreme Court confirmations makes this abundantly clear. For an interesting account of the appointment in the 1920s of Justice Pierce Butler, see David J. Danelski, *A Supreme Court Justice is Appointed* (New York: Random House,1964).

51. Role Perceptions and Behavior in Three U.S. Courts of Appeals

J. Woodford Howard, Jr.

39 *Journal of Politics* 916 (1977)

☐ The concept of "Judicial Role" refers to normative expectations shared by judges and related actors regarding how a given judicial office should be performed. Scholars have long debated whether judges' perceptions of these norms influence judicial decisions . . . . Since the Supreme Court grants certiorari in less than 2% of federal appeals, internalized professional values have traditionally been regarded as essential controls binding federal courts into a system. Yet, the appropriate roles and functions of federal appellate judges have never been fixed nor universally accepted . . . . Outside the Supreme Court empirical proofs are inconclusive that judges' prescriptions guide their decisions rather than rationalize personal preferences.

... [T]his paper ... explore[s] the relationships among judicial role perceptions and voting behavior in three leading intermediate tribunals—United States Courts of Appeals for the Second, Fifth, and District of Columbia Circuits—against a backdrop of the political orientations of their members. We shall consider (1) how Circuit judges on the three courts view a central issue of judicial role—the permissible range of discretion to make law; (2) the relation of their role conceptions to their professed political orientations before becoming federal judges; and (3) the extent to which both political orientations and role perceptions associate with the judges' voting behavior in selected areas of public policy.

The data concerning political values and role perceptions are all derived from off-the-record interviews conducted by the author together with 35 active and senior circuit judges of the three tribunals during 1969–71. The voting data are derived from analysis of all decisions by the three tribunals after hearing or submission during FY 1965–67 (N = 4,941), roughly 40 percent of total cases so decided by U.S. circuit courts in this period. Thirty judges, slightly less than a third of total federal circuit judges, participated in both the interviews and decisions . . . .

ROLE PERCEPTIONS

These judges shared a strong consensus, heavily influenced by official and professional prescriptions, that their central mission is to adjudicate appeals as agents of the national government. Little disagreement also existed about their duty to enforce the laws of Congress, Supreme Court, and their circuits. Considerable tension emerged, nonetheless, over the proper scope of judicial lawmaking in an estimated tenth of their cases having innovative potential . . . .

... [S]tudies of judges suggest that the sharpest role conflicts in American appellate courts concern judges' functions as legislators. However, it is important to note that these federal circuit judges, unlike some members of state supreme courts, differed over issues of degree rather than of kind. Virtually all of them agreed that, while bold policy ventures such as *Brown v. Board of Education* should be left to the high court or Congress, *stare decisis* is "not an unbreakable rule." Within these extremes, their responses to questions concerning the propriety of judicial innovation fell into three broad groupings along a continuum which for convenience will be summarized in Table 1 as ideal types.

Innovator

Five judges left the impression that they felt obliged to make law "whenever the opportunity occurs." Creative opportunities were usually described as legal vacuums created by unclear precedents, unanticipated situations, and political stalemates. In aiding the Supreme Court, Innovators also emphasized their filtering or "gatekeeping" functions less than their lawmaking . . . . The most unqualified expression of this view came from a jurist who considered the best part of the job to be "launching new ideas." Did this mean that circuit courts participate in policy formation? "Certainly," he said. "And the greatest abuse of power is failure to exercise it."

Interpreter

At the opposite pole were nine judges who emphasized that judicial lawmaking should be held to a minimum. Two judges, harboring a "phobia" against "the modern trend of judicial legislation," bitterly denounced jurists who "can't wait for the people's representatives; they must seize power for themselves." . . . Only one judge, a Southern newcomer, unqualifiedly endorsed the view that judges should merely interpret the law, a traditional conception of judicial duty still prominent on several state supreme courts and trial courts. Recognizing that lacunae inevitably occur in statutes and case law, these judges objected most to courts reaching out "beyond the case" to legislate . . . .

Realist

Almost two-thirds of these circuit judges, including the majority of the Fifth Circuit and all but one member of the Second Circuit, took middle positions, recognizing more demands for judicial creativity than Interpreters and more restraints than Innovators. Like Innovators, Realists saw no conflict with *stare decisis* when precedent is ambiguous or

TABLE 1　ATTITUDES TOWARD JUDICIAL LAWMAKING

	Innovator	*Realist*	*Interpreter*	*Other*	*Total*
Circuit	N	N	N	N	N
Second	0	8	1	1	10
Fifth	2	9	6	0	17
D.C.	3	3	2	0	8
Sums	5	20	9	1	35

"when Congress abdicates." Like Interpreters, Realists cautioned against anticipating the Justices and emphasized "the professional way" of initiating legal change. What distinguished Realists from the other judges was their common tendency, when acknowledging legislative responsibilities, to differentiate carefully among various types of judicial lawmaking and appropriate occasions for innovation. For example, several judges saw more room for creativity in civil rights than in commercial law, which requires planning and stable rules, and attributed the conservatism of the Second Circuit to its heavy commercial docket. A few judges . . . stressed the innovative potential of "shaping the rules to the facts." . . .

This summary scarcely captures the subtlety with which these jurists pondered the dilemmas of lawmaking by intermediate courts in a federal republic. But it helps to delimit the problems of relating roles and behavior in circuit courts . . . . Despite robust commitment to rendering justice in individual cases, and recognition that Supreme Court reversal is rare in practice, nearly all of them manifested strong precedent orientations. Most agreed further that, lacking docket control, their opportunity to fashion new legal rules seldom exceeds a tenth of their cases. Though they may disagree as to what cases properly constitute the fertile tenth, these judges felt obliged to lead as well as to follow. Hence, their conflicts over judicial lawmaking are inadequately caught by such popular dichotomies as "activism" versus "restraint," or the so-called "objective" role of adherence to precedent versus subjective preference. For them . . . the question is perhaps more one of pace and timing, not essentially one of function . . . . The real issue is how they combine in an estimated tenth of the cases in which circuit judges confront "gaps in the law."

Because circuit judges are called upon to reconcile values of continuity and change in adjudication, usually in advance of the Justices and with little assurance that their mistakes will be corrected, tension is inherent in their positions. Strain among expectations *within* a role perhaps characterizes their situation better than does the concept of conflict *between* roles. In any event, ambiguity of appropriate limits on lawmaking by intermediate courts softens the control of received interpretations and elevates the significance of situational factors in decision-making. *Stare decisis* is thus an open norm, . . . which cannot specify precise forms of action in all cases. When norms are open to further specification, individuals or groups can establish socially approved rules of conduct of greater particularity . . . . When judges are free to choose, personalities, predilections, and group relations perforce fill the void. Open or ambiguous roles inevitably enlarge the personal discretion of judges.

POLITICAL ORIENTATIONS

What then guides a circuit judge's conception of judicial duty when rules and roles are unclear? Of the welter of factors that may bear on this issue—psychological, social, institutional—we shall focus on political and professional values. Both are central to popular theories of the judicial process. According to political interpretations, judicial decisions are heavily influenced by the political philosophies that judges bring to the bench. In legal theory, contrarily, professional norms control political and other personal preferences. The trouble with these formulations is that political orientations and role conceptions are not mutually exclusive. In plumbing the sources of role conceptions among these circuit judges, for instance, we find intriguing associations among the judges' political orientations before ascending the bench and their attitudes toward judicial lawmaking . . . . [R]ole conceptions, unlike party or participation variables, ran in the same direction as self-estimated political orientations. Four of the five Innovators identified themselves as having been political liberals before becoming federal judges; only one of nine Interpreters did so. A single Innovator called himself a former political conservative, perhaps as a joke. Otherwise, the large majority were men in the middle, self-styled moderates before becoming jurists, who likewise straddled the conflict over lawmaking.

The fuzziness of both political and role categories, not to mention the small number of judges involved, warns against pushing attitudinal associations very far. The data do not prove that philosophies of the judicial function are berobed political ideologies. Yet, on the whole, these jurists tended to favor conceptions of judicial role in accord with their prior political convictions. Hardly surprising given the realities of their recruitment, this connection is an important link among personal values and the judicial process. Because the socialization of American judges is largely informal and anticipatory, in contrast to jurists in France, federal circuit judges are expected to learn their roles largely via experience prior to appointment. Their perceptions of judicial duty are likely to interact with their prior political beliefs, because both sets of values develop from the same antecedent experiences.

Political values thus pervade the world of circuit judges as well as other political elites. Their philosophies of politics and the judicial function, notwithstanding official efforts to separate the two, *are* entwined in resolving and rationalizing the normative ambiguities of their work.

TABLE 2   POLITICAL BACKGROUNDS OF CIRCUIT JUDGES AND ATTITUDES TOWARD
JUDICIAL LAWMAKING

	Attitudes Toward Judicial Lawmaking			
	Innovator	Realist	Interpreter	Realist
	N	N	N	N
Political Background Characteristic:	(5)	(20)	(9)	(35)*
Political Party Affiliation:				
Democrat	4	13	4	22*
Republican	1	6	4	11
other	0	1	1	2
Political Participation:				
voter only	0	3	2	5
party worker	0	2	3	5
party official	3	6	1	10
candidate**	2	9	3	15*
Political Values Before Appointment:				
conservative	1	0	3	4
moderate	0	11	4	16*
moderate-liberal	1	0	1	2
liberal	3	5	0	8
other	0	4	1	5

*Includes one unscorable response.
**Includes 1 Innovator and 2 Realists who were candidates for party posts only.

VALUES AND VOTES

The proof of the pudding is whether political values and role conceptions affect adjudication . . . . [I]s judging "political behavior" or "judicial role behavior"? . . . [There are] many pitfalls confronting efforts to
answer this question. Theoretically, a person's political self-images
and role perceptions are but single aspects of a vast cognitive network,
which may be rooted in the irrational. Even discounting disparities
between what people say and think, a direct relationship is seldom to
be expected among an individual's social roles, role perceptions, and
conduct.

Methodological problems compound the difficulty of establishing
links. The most formidable are subjectivity in classifications, a multiplicity of competing variables (e.g., collegial decision-making or personality) intervening between general attitudes and specific choices,
and the lack of transitivity among aggregated votes. Panel techniques

were used to reduce the subjectivity of inferred role perceptions, but disagreement among the author and two assistants regarding 6 of 35 judges on both margins of the Realist category indicate that standardization of terms remains a serious problem in judicial role analysis. Similarly, self-estimates of political orientations eliminated neither regional differences nor the vagaries of recall. Equally problematic is the assumption that votes accurately mirror individual attitudes on collegial courts, where "give and take" is also expected. More troublesome is violating the assumption of transitivity (i.e., that all judges participated in the same cases) for purposes of aggregation in rotating courts. Even though this study rests on a sample of over 5,000 votes, relaxation of transitivity standards proved necessary because panel rotation and low dissent rates on these courts yielded frequencies too small for conventional analysis of variance of different subjects and individuals. Finally, the difficulty of isolating the cases that comprise the creative opportunities of circuit judges precluded testing of judicial role perceptions in exclusively lawmaking situations.

Political orientations and role perceptions, like most analytical constructs, are riddled with oversimplification. Still, for exploratory purposes it is useful to establish whether general political and professional predispositions are related to aggregate voting behavior. If we cannot test judicial role perceptions in lawmaking situations, we can invert the hypothesis and test whether judges' role conceptions related to their voting behavior defined politically. Presumably different role perceptions which are consistent with different political results did not screen out policy values from these decisions, as legal theory suggests. For this purpose the judges' political orientations and attitudes toward judicial lawmaking will be compared with the policy outcomes of their votes in selected subjects.

Few concepts in the American political lexicon are more elusive than "liberal" and "conservative." While these jurists readily classified their prior political values on a liberal-conservative continuum, they often affirmed common observations that neither label describes a unitary ideology but rather a cluster of attitudes toward different policy referents. To capture some of this complexity, broad policy subjects are differentiated . . . which compare the political orientations and role perceptions of these jurists with the outcome of their votes during FY 1965–67. The political hypotheses . . . are that self-styled former liberals, more than other political animals who became circuit judges, would tend to favor workers in employee-injury cases and claimants in other personal injury cases while opposing claimants in patent and copyright suits. Similarly, self-styled former liberals would tend to defer to the NLRB and the government in income tax litigation while supporting individuals in civil rights controversies, prisoner petitions, and criminal cases. Conversely, self-styled conservatives would resolve doubts in opposite directions.

The distribution of votes . . . lends little support to these hypotheses. Different political orientations were not statistically significant when correlated with mean percentages of liberal voting per judge, a procedure which preserves differences among individuals. Using a one-sample chi square test for policy fields, the political categories were statistically significant only in other personal injuries and civil rights. While the direction of voting conformed to expectations in three fields—employee injuries, income tax, and civil rights—only the civil rights correlations (y = .194) were noteworthy. In civil rights self-styled former liberals favored individuals against governments more than did self-styled conservatives by almost a three-to-one margin.

The data may be too weak to prove the absence of a relationship among political ideologies and voting behavior, but they are strong enough to cast doubt on a common interpretation that circuit decisions are dominated by the past political predispositions of the judges. For all the concern over their political outlooks during the selection process, broad political differences were not reflected significantly in the judges' votes, except possibly in civil rights.

Analysis of individual voting patterns in separate fields, though too small to rule out chance variations, suggests the presence of other variables, especially circuit influences and discrete preferences. Civil rights are the best illustration of the pull of the group. The Fifth Circuit dominated the cases, only two of its seventeen judges voting against civil rights more often than not. If we use . . . [a] definition of activism as favoring individuals against governments, almost the whole court was activist. By contrast, only one judge outside the Fifth Circuit voted in favor of civil rights claims more than half the time. Another judge, described by a colleague as "inclined to be activist," in fact voted against civil rights claims in all recorded instances. At the same time, the circuit variable appears weaker in other subjects except patents.

. . . The fact that the political Moderate category contained both the highest and second-lowest extremes of so-called liberal voting (64.1 percent and 30.8 percent) also underscores regional variations in political labels. Consequently, these associations of political values and votes no more rule out the effects of region and group than they refute the Cardozo-Ehrlich caveat that "In the long run 'there is no guaranty of justice . . . except the personality of the judge.'" The appellate process is too complex to be cabined by a simple cognitive dimension.

The relation of judicial role perceptions to voting behavior, albeit stronger, points to similar conclusions. Assuming that role conceptions were in fact related to political values evident in circuit decisions . . . as . . . implied by the overlapping attitudes in Table 2, Innovators should have been more likely than Interpreters to favor workers and claimants in injuries cases, public rights in patent and copyright cases, and the government in NLRB and tax cases. Innovators more than other judges also would be expected to favor individuals in civil rights, prisoner petitions, and criminal cases.

The distribution of votes . . . offers moderate support for the proposition that Innovators generally were more libertarian in voting behavior than were Realists and Interpreters. The evidence bolsters confidence especially in the distinction between Innovators and Interpreters and in the association of Innovators on the Courts of Appeals with "libertarian activism." For one thing, unlike prior political orientations, differences among Innovators and the other judges were statistically significant when role perceptions were compared with mean percentages of liberal voting per judge. For another, though prisoner petitions and criminal appeals were the only fields to withstand the null hypothesis, the direction of voting between the two groups of judges followed the liberal-conservative continuum in every field save the ideologically elusive subject of income tax. Furthermore, the strongest overlap among role conceptions and voting behavior occurred precisely in subjects, e.g., civil rights ($y=.200$) and criminal justice ($y=.282$), with which the judges illustrated their disputes over lawmaking. In criminal appeals Innovators favored defendants more than did Interpreters by a 2-to-1 margin. The odds that this occurred by chance were less than 1-in-1,000.

Granted, judges and cases are not fungible. Given the size of the voting universe and the low levels of dissensus in these courts, even these modest relationships are among the most positive associations yet uncovered between judicial role perceptions and aggregate voting behavior.

The biggest surprise, in view of the overlapping professional and political attitudes in Table 2, is that role conceptions were more consistent with liberal-conservative voting than were past political orientations. If the two sets of values were related, we would expect votes to be, too. Yet civil rights is the only significant field in which the direction of votes was mutually reinforcing. Further, if a relationship existed between only one set of values and votes, the expected link would surely be with political rather than with role orientations. After all, voting behavior is defined politically in terms of who wins or loses. Turning professional theories on their heads, do contrary findings mean that role conceptions are rationalizations of political behavior? What accounts for the weak association of values and votes in these decisions? Do the anomalies in aggregate behavior contradict the conclusion drawn earlier that political values and role conceptions interact?

One obvious explanation is that the data reflect well-known vagaries of establishing general categories of political ideology. This problem is accentuated by the tendency of these judges to flock toward the middle. In addition, the two orientations refer to distinguishable values, one to past and more remote political convictions, the other to the permissible scope of judicial lawmaking without reference to specific policies. The voting patterns also aggregate outcomes on a crude liberalism scale, not the degrees or direction of innovation. Lawmaking . . . can travel several ideological paths.

Closely related is the generality of both evaluative dimensions. Because political orientations and role conceptions are seldom so specific as to command particular decisions, a judge may be an "activist" or a "liberal" in one field and not another. Some judges in this study confessed to being conservative toward property rights and liberal toward human rights—and voted accordingly. The lack of overlapping associations in particular fields buttresses an impression . . . that the effects of ideology may be issue-specific.

Simple correlations, to be sure, cannot distinguish cause from coincidence, let alone interactions or the direction of any influence between attitudes and behavior. This fact raises the possibility that methodological flaws, already noted, distorted the results. Since the variables as defined hardly exhaust the possible relationships among attitudes and behavior in these circuits, role conceptions perhaps were related to different or more contemporary political values, implicit in the decisions, than the past political orientations examined here. Ultimately, however, both professional and political ideologies should offset the discreteness of cases and individuals if they have the causal power attributed to them in standard theories of judicial decision. The slippage between general values and specific votes in these circuits thus raises a final possibility of some theoretical import.

That is, we may overestimate the impact of general professional and political attitudes on voting behavior in circuit courts and underestimate the impact of personal, group, and situational factors. Even simple cross-tabulations reveal more at work in these circuit decisions than general political or professional ideologies. For individuals the evidence may be sufficient to sustain the old notion that judges' predilections affect their decisions, but for circuit judges generally that is doubtful of the broad social values under consideration. The data lend little support to ideological theories of judicial decision, either political or professional, that are not further refined according to personality, group, and issue. The methods used here offer inconclusive proof of this episodic view of the appellate process. But the conception avoids the trap of single-factor causation, accords with the fractured nature of political ideology among American political elites, and squares with every sophisticated account on record of deciding appeals in collegial courts. As Justice Holmes concluded, "No general proposition is worth a damn." Within broad limits choice is personal and judges know it. Just as concepts of law are ideological constructs vying for allegiance, so circuit judges are obliged to choose among competing conceptions of judicial duty in the very cases at the edges of legal change. □

52. The Role Concept in Judicial Research

James L. Gibson

3 *Law & Policy Quarterly* 291 (1981)

☐ Over the last two decades substantial research effort has been directed to applying role theory to the process of decision-making within judicial institutions . . . . Few other theories have generated as much empirical research, nor have made as sweeping claims of applicability and generalizability.

Yet role theory to date has generated few empirical payoffs; the potential of the approach has not been realized. Most seriously, very little research has been successful in linking role concepts to actual decisional behavior. In part this stems from the preoccupation with typology building, although few of the efforts to test role-behavior hypotheses have been successful. As a heuristic device, role theory may have some utility: As a theory of decision-making, its utility has only rarely been demonstrated.

Why have role variables been such weak predictors? First, the dominant conceptualization of the manner in which role orientations influence behavior is inadequate. A direct, covariation relationship between role attributes and behavior is usually hypothesized. For instance, a typical hypothesis is that "activism" (a role orientation) is related to "liberal" decisions. Yet there is no theoretical structure supporting such a hypothesis—activism may be in favor of conservative values (e.g., the Hughes Court) or liberal values (e.g., the Warren Court). Thus, the relationship needs to be reconceptualized, and more appropriate statistical models need to be developed.

The second reason why role attributes have not been good predictors of behavior stems from the inadequate conceptualization and measurement of the role orientation construct . . . . [T]his area of research is rich in measurement problems, with inadequate consideration of the problems of validity, reliability, measurement error, and dimensionality. Without proper conceptualization and valid measurement, prediction and explanation of role behavior is nearly impossible.

. . . [T]his article focuses on the second issue, that of measurement . . . . A new measure of role orientations, one relying on a somewhat different conceptual approach, is . . . presented and results from two empirical applications of the scale are evaluated. As a more general and theoretical measure of role orientations this scale should aid in future research employing role concepts.

MAJOR ROLE CONCEPTS

To role theorists the most salient characteristic of decision-making within institutions is the constraint imposed on decision makers by the institutional context. These constraints on choices limit, but do not eliminate, discretion in the interest of advancing organizational objectives. Few institutions exist that do not attempt to circumscribe the alternatives available to the decision maker. Thus, role theory posits that individuals acting within institutions act differently than they act in noninstitutional settings; the context of their behavior influences how they behave. But precisely what elements of the context constrain behavior and how do the constraints operate?

Institutions can be defined in part by positions. That is, within every institution a number of formally defined positions exist. Within a judicial system the positions include those of "judge," "prosecutor," "defense attorney," and the like. Each of these is assigned particular responsibilities, and prescriptions and proscriptions (e.g., Code of Judicial Ethics) are attached to the position. Within role theory the position is known as a "role" and the particular person occupying the role is known as the "role incumbent" or "role occupant." Thus, the first set of constraints on behavior stems from the formal definition of the role itself.

Beyond this, however, the individuals with whom the role incumbents interact (known as "role alters") develop expectations of how the role incumbent should behave. Judges, for instance, are expected by others to act impartially; in the views of the role alters, a necessary component of the role of judge is impartial behavior. These expectations, which are normative, are referred to as "role expectations," and emanate from those who interact with the role occupant. By supplementing the formal requirements of the position, role expectations also constrain institutional behavior.

Individuals occupying institutional positions also develop beliefs about what constitutes proper behavior on their part. This belief is a "role orientation" and may stem from role expectations. More likely, role orientations represent a synthesis of perceptions of expectations and the occupants' own values. Role behavior is constrained by these role orientations.

According to role theory, role behavior is to some extent a function of the role orientation of the role occupant. Most research therefore focuses upon role orientations as the key determinant of behavior . . . . [R]esearchers define role orientations as varying in the degree to which the judge feels bound to adhere to precedents, constitutions, and statutes in making decisions. "Adherence" includes "following" precedents, "strict construction" of constitutions, and deference to "legislative intent." In essence, the role orientation construct represents a unidimensional continuum of legitimate discretion in decision making, the degree to which legitimate opportunities for decisional creativity exist.

MEASURES OF ROLE ORIENTATIONS

Four approaches to measuring role orientations characterize this research: (1) inferences from the decisional behavior of judges; (2) typologies based on open ended questions; (3) self-reports of the influence of certain stimuli on decisions; and (4) multi-item scales. Each of these approaches has several liabilities which severely limit its utility.

Inferential Approaches

The inferential approach is a direct extension of attitudinal research on appellate courts. Because interviews with judges were thought to be difficult to secure, the researchers had to make inferences from the observed decisional behavior of judges to their role orientations . . . . Thus, statistical examination of the process by which judges make decisions is used to infer the existence of particular role orientations.

In the absence of interview data this approach is necessary, and indeed, a conceptual approach that emphasizes how decisions are made is extremely useful. However, several limitations are imposed on the analysis when independent measures of role orientations and behavior are not available. In particular, the degree to which role orientations are related to behavior cannot be specified. Indeed, the hypothesis that role attributes and behavior are unrelated cannot be tested. Nor can the relative impact of role orientations and other possible determinants of behavior be estimated. Finally, it is not possible to test sophisticated models . . . of the process through which role orientations influence behavior. This approach, though necessary under some conditions, is suboptimal—a much more direct measurement strategy is needed.

Open-Ended Typologies

Research in the 1960s demonstrated that some judges can indeed be interviewed. The earliest interview measures of role orientations adopted open-ended measures that essentially asked judges to characterize the nature of their decisional process . . . .

Perhaps the most enduring set of categories of judges', role orientations emerging from this research, is the "law making" versus "law interpretation" distinction. As opposite ends of a continuum measuring decisional role orientations, these categories purport to identify "activist" and "restraintist" judges. However, a number of conceptual and methodological problems exist, making it unclear just what the lawmaker-law interpreter typology measures. Consider statements by a judge Vines considers to be prototypic of law interpreters:

> I think that it is terrible that judges interpret the laws or the Constitution in accordance with what they think it should be instead of interpreting the language of the Constitution or the statute . . . . The United States Supreme Court and other state courts, too, have set themselves up as some sort of super-Congress, and they interpret the Constitution to mean what they think it should say. That's a violation of the separation of powers.

It is clear that this judge believes that interpreting the "language of the Constitution or the statute" is not only desirable but possible. In this respect he is at odds with legal realists who believe that precedents and statutes and even constitutions are ambiguous, conflicting and generally capable of providing only post hoc rationalization and legitimation of decisions. On the other hand, the lawmaker [judge] asserts:

> Inevitably, a judge makes law as does a legislative body. No matter how you decide a case, you're making law . . . . That whole idea about whether a judge makes law or whether he found what the law always was by looking somewhere up in the blue is not true. Judges always made law and always will . . . . In interpretation you're trying to give answers to problems that were not considered by the legislature, and you try to guess what the legislature would have thought had they thought about this problem. But you get away from this quickly. What do you do when you get a question like this? You can't send it back to the legislature for a decision . . . . The question comes up, and you decide it.[163]

This judge is *not* necessarily making a normative statement about the desirability of law interpretation but instead is arguing, as a realist would, the empirical position that judges *cannot* make decisions on the basis of precedents, statutes and constitutions. In fact, it is possible that disagreement between "lawmakers" and "law interpreters" is largely over the *empirical* question of the degree to which precedents, statutes and constitutions allow logically deducible decisions, rather than over the normative question of what a judge ought to do. Because role orientations represent normative positions it is imperative that the analyst maintain the distinction between "is" and "ought."

In addition to the conceptual problem, measurement deficiencies exist. First, the question generates little variance among judges . . . . Most studies have revealed that a majority of judges are "law interpreters," but it is extremely unlikely that judges are as homogeneous as the

---

163. [The quotations are from K. N. Vines, "The Judicial Role in the American States: an Exploration," in J. Grossman and J. Tanenhaus (eds.) *Frontiers of Judicial Research* (New York: John Wiley & Sons, 1969), pp. 461, 475.]

responses to this question make them appear. Instead there is probably substantial variation in the beliefs of "interpreters" about what constitutes the proper bounds of "interpretation," variation which is critically important to understanding the decisions of the judges.

Because the format of this question is open-ended, serious threats to reliability also exist. Even though coding open-ended responses is a perilous task, intercoder reliability coefficients are rarely reported . . . . This approach also makes comparison across studies difficult, especially since there is no evidence that different researchers use a standardized set of coding instructions. Finally, the question results only in a trichotomy . . . , ignoring gradations within each category. While there are some advantages to open-ended questions at exploratory stages of research, the potential for judges to give self-serving, traditional and largely symbolic responses is quite high.

Self-Reports Decision-Making

A second major interview-based approach to judges' role orientations comes out of Becker's (1966)[164] research on Hawaiian judges. Becker's measure reads: "How influential do you believe the following factors to be in your deciding a case?" and includes in the list of factors: "highly respected advocate (as a lawyer)," "my view of justice in the case," "what the public needs, as the times may demand," "precedent, when clear and directly relevant," "common sense," "highly respected advocate (as a member of the community)," "what the public demands" and "other." It is similar to the lawmaker-law interpreter typology in that its main concern is with the role of precedent in judges' decisions. Becker reports that 43% of the judges who rated "precedent, when clear and directly relevant" at the highest point on the scale ("extremely influential") decided a simulated case "objectively" (i.e., consistent with a "clear and directly relevant precedent"). Presumably, the objective decision was contrary to the preferences of the judges. Of the judges rating "precedent" as less than extremely influential, only 13% decided "objectively". There is also some relationship between the judges' responses to "my view of justice" and "common sense" and a propensity to decide objectively.

This question suffers from the same shortcomings of the open-ended measure of role orientations, but also has unique difficulties. First, there is very little variance in the responses to the question. Over 90% of the judges in Becker's study rated "precedent" as "extremely" or "very" influential, and the remaining two judges rated it as "influen-

164. [The reference is to T. L. Becker, "A Survey Study of Hawaiian Judges: The Effect on Decisions of Judicial Role Variations," 60 *American Political Science Review* 677 (1966).]

tial." The variance of the responses to this item is smaller than the variance for any of the other items. Becker's analysis is based in part on dichotomizing the judges into two groups: those who rated precedent as "extremely influential" and those who rated precedent as "very influential" or as just "influential." This seems a rather artificial division point, one which is dictated by the lack of variance in the responses rather than by a theoretical concern. Again, it seems possible that a great amount of within-group variance still exists.

Perhaps a more significant problem with the measure lies in its lack of conceptualization. What does it mean to say that a judge is strongly oriented toward precedent? Is this a measure of activism-restraintism? If strong precedent orientation is one end of the continuum, what is the other end? Does a weak precedent orientation necessarily mean that judges rely on their own values in making decisions? What about the numerous instances of judicial decision-making in which precedent has little if any relevance (e.g., sentencing, bail, questions of fact, certiorari decisions, and so on)? Indeed, further examination of the responses of the Hawaiian judges indicates that responses to "precedent" are most strongly correlated with responses to what the public demands ($r = -.38$; computed from the data presented in Becker, 1966: 679). However, Becker essentially argues a "subjective-objective" dimension to this role orientation, with the dimension presumably bounded by precedent and subjective criteria such as common sense and the judge's own view of justice. But the correlations of the precedent responses with these two criteria are .12 and $-.04$, respectively . . . .

One further problem arises with the Becker measure of role orientations. The question requires judges to determine how influential several decisional criteria actually are in their decision calculus. As such the question is empirical and nonnormative. The proper form of the question, if it is to be used as a measure of role orientations, should express valuation of each of the criteria; the question should ask how influential the criteria should be. Much, however, of what is known about judges' role orientations is based on this question.

Scales

The last of the approaches to measuring judges' role orientations is that of multi-item inventories. Scales of this type have a number of advantages: the response sets are closed-ended; the use of multiple indicators reduces the impact of measurement error; and continuous ordinal or interval level scale scores can be generated. However, just as with the other approaches, the conceptualization of the orientation idea is crucial. Operationalization and scaling techniques are also somewhat more complex . . . .

It appears . . . that a new conceptualization and a new operationalization of role orientations is in order. There is no doubt that precedent is a quite important element of judicial role orientations and any new measure must be sensitive to this. However, researchers must be very careful in measuring role orientations with precedent questions: the highly abstract notion of "following precedent" may have virtually no impact on how judges feel about making decisions. Few judges, even activists, are likely to publicly disavow precedent; as legal realists have asserted for years, the abstract commitment to precedent may be compatible with any of the variety of styles of dealing with precedents in making decisions. The more important question is the degree to which judges believe it legitimate to manipulate precedent to achieve the decision results they prefer. Any reconceptualization should be sensitive to this fact.

A RECONCEPTUALIZATION OF ROLE ORIENTATIONS

The position of judge is incredibly complex. Consequently, judges' beliefs about the limits of proper behavior are also complex. Simplistic typologies of role orientations, such as the lawmaker-law interpreter distinction and orientation toward precedent, are unlikely to be of much utility for understanding judges' role orientations or behavior . . . .

Judges' role orientations are their beliefs about the kind of behavior that is proper for a judge. In the case of decisional role orientations, the beliefs concern proper decision behavior. "Proper" does not, however, refer as much to the policy content of the behavior as it does to the *process* of decision-making and, in particular, to the kinds of stimuli that influence decisions. A decisional role orientation identifies for the judge the criteria that are legitimate for proper decision-making. Some judges may believe it proper to be influenced by a particular stimulus while other judges regard it as improper. More generally, judges vary in the breadth of stimuli they deem legitimate.

Such a conceptualization of role orientations is compatible with the traditional norms for judging. A central expectation of judicial and legal traditions concerns the decision-making criteria employed by judges. For instance, equality before the law is not an empirical statement; it does not assert that individual litigants are in fact equal. Rather, the phrase is an exhortation to ignore the variables (stimuli), such as power, on which litigants are unequal and render decisions only on variables that provide for equality. For instance, it is generally regarded as illegitimate to discriminate on the basis of social class in sentencing decisions. This means that it is illegitimate to allow the social class of the defendant to influence the decision: class should be weighted at zero. Similarly, such concepts as the presumption of innocence in criminal cases are expectations that court officials will not allow empirical stimuli relating to the factual guilt of the defendant to influence their pretrial decisions (e.g., bail) . . . .

Thus, the basic function of decisional role orientations is to specify which variables can legitimately be allowed to influence decision-making, and in the case of conflict, what priorities to assign to different decision-making criteria. Role orientations are conceptualized as normative weights attached by each judge to different decisional stimuli. A stimulus viewed as illegitimate therefore would receive a weight of zero . . . . [D]ecision-making is viewed as a process of combining bits of information to form a choice . . . . [R]ole theory posits that the primary basis for assigning weights is normative.

While this conceptualization is more general and theoretical, it is not entirely incompatible with the lawmaking, law interpretation and precedent approaches. Lawmakers, it might be hypothesized, rely on more and different criteria for decision making than law interpreters. They might consider social injustice as a legitimate criterion upon which decision can be based. Law interpreters probably view social injustice as a less legitimate, and possibly as even an illegitimate, basis for decision-making. The law interpreter would surely assign greater weight to precedents, statutes and constitutions. Generally, lawmakers would rely on extralegal decisional criteria while law interpreters would rely on strictly legal criteria as much as possible. But although this notion of role orientations is compatible with the lawmaking, interpreting and precedent approaches, it has the advantage of being more general (incorporating all criteria, not just precedents, statutes and constitutions), and also provides a more theoretical basis for expecting role orientations to influence role behavior . . . .

OPERATIONALIZING ROLE ORIENTATIONS

One approach to measuring role orientations might be to ask judges to rate a large number of decisional stimuli in terms of the degree of legitimate influence on decisions. In some contexts this approach may be useful. However, less lengthy scales can be developed by taking advantage of the highly salient and symbolic positions of precedent and ideology in the American legal system. Because these decisional criteria are so fundamental to the legal process, beliefs about their proper role in decision-making can serve as a useful summary measure of role orientations. The data in Table 1 report the responses of a group of California and Iowa judges to a set of items designed to measure role orientations from this perspective.

Several aspects of these data are worthy of discussion. First, the responses of the two groups of judges are generally similar. Only the last item generated substantially different response patterns, overall the statements seem to be tapping the same dimension . . . .

TABLE 1   SCALE FOR MEASURING PRECEDENT ROLE ORIENTATIONS—IOWA AND CALIFORNIA TRIAL JUDGES

| | Response (in percentages)[a] | | | |
Item	Strongly Agree	Agree	Disagree	Strongly Disagree
1. A good judge is one who sticks as closely to precedents as possible.				
California	10.5	37.8	16.2	2.7
Iowa	23.1	65.4	7.7	0
2. Judges should be allowed great discretion in decision making to insure that their decisions are "just."				
California	18.9	48.6	27.0	5.4
Iowa	34.6	46.2	15.4	0
3. It is wrong for a judge to allow his personal philosophy to influence his decisions				
California	21.6	29.7	40.5	8.1
Iowa	23.1	46.2	23.1	3.8
4. Precedents are rarely conclusive: usually a judge can find a precedent which supports his own point of view.				
California	13.5	43.2	37.8	5.4
Iowa	3.8	34.6	43.3	11.5
5. Precedents and statutes are only a few of the factors which should influence judges' decisions.				
California	5.4	35.1	40.5	18.9
Iowa	11.5	69.2	19.2	0
6. It is just as legitimate to make a decision and then find the precedent as it is to find the precedent and then make the decision.				
California	5.4	35.1	43.2	16.2
Iowa	7.7	15.4	50.0	15.4

[a]The Ns are: California, 37; Iowa, 26.

Very considerable variation across items also exists. The "easiest" item to accept is number 1: Significant majorities of both groups agree that good judges follow precedents. Yet what does the response to this item mean? A quite significant proportion of these judges believe that "precedents" should not and do not limit the degree to which a judge's own views influence their decisions. One half of the total group believes it possible to find a precedent compatible with the judges' own view of justice, while one-third openly assert the legitimacy of such a decisional strategy. Thus, questions that reference "precedent" in a very general way tend to produce a "restraintist" consensus. This consensus, however, is illusory and therefore it is essential to use multiple indicators.

The concept measured by these six items is a general orientation toward a style of decision-making. Judges at one end of the scale perceive it legitimate to use considerable discretion in making decisions whereas judges at the opposite end of the dimension reject discretion in

TABLE 2   CORRELATIONS OF GENERAL ROLE
ORIENTATION SCALE AND NORMATIVE EVALUATIONS OF
SPECIFIC DECISIONAL CUES

Cue	Iowa	California
Judge's sense of justice	.49	.13
Common sense	.32	.25
Precedent	.10	−.15
What the public needs	.37	.12
What the public demands	.55	.21
Judge's own values	.30	.37
Social Consequences	—	.16

favor of deference to precedents, constitutions, and so on. The first group of judges are probably more "results" oriented than the "process" oriented group and therefore may be termed "lawmakers" or "activists." This general, normative orientation toward discretion is an extremely important part of the judicial role.

In that these judges were asked to evaluate the decisional cues constructed by Becker, the relationship between the general scale and the specific cues can be evaluated. The results are shown in Table 2. While the correlations are not in all cases particularly strong, in every instance except "precedent," the "activists" on the general scale are more likely to view the cue as legitimate. Moreover, the correlations between the mean response to the cues (for each judge) and the general role orientation scale are .53 and .31 for the Iowa and California judges respectively. These correlations suggest that while the scale is designed to be a measure of general decisional role orientations, it also has some utility for evaluations of particular decisional cues.

In summary, this scale has several advantages over previous instruments: (1) its format is closed-ended; (2) it is a multiple item measure, with considerable variation on the items; (3) it is unidimensional; and (4) the measure has generated reasonably stable response patterns across two different groups of judges . . . .

NOTES AND QUESTIONS

1. Why are scholars interested in the concept of "role?" Basically, the issue is, how do judges decide cases? What motivates them? Scholars, it is fair to say, reject the naive position that judges merely "find" the law. Every student of law and political science knows that at least sometimes judges make decisions in a creative, open-ended, discretionary way.

How do judges reach *this* kind of decision? Is it political prejudice? class bias? Do they toss a coin? Do they honestly and scrupulously *try* to reach the right "legal" decision, assuming that they can find such a thing? Are they conscious or unconscious of their true motivations?

The value of "role theory" is that it allows us to take seriously what judges say about their behavior, and what certain kinds of legal theory suggest judges *ought* to do, without falling into a naive mechanical view of the matter. It allows us to say that judging is a *role*, a patterned set of social expectations. Most judges, most of the time, earnestly try to behave the way the role says they should. An actor playing the role of Hamlet has some leeway in deciding how to recite the lines, but the lines are pretty much fixed. The judicial role is not as constraining as the role of Hamlet—most people accept that—but the question is, exactly how far-fetched is the analogy between judging and acting? How much *does* "role" constrain the average judge? How does a patterned set of social expectations affect what a judge does in general or in a particular case? Recall the material on the function of judges and courts in Chapter 2.

There has been a great deal of research on the role perceptions of judges. John T. Wold, in "Going Through the Motions: The Monotony of Appellate Court Decisionmaking," 62 *Judicature* 59, 62, 64, 65 (1978), suggests that we may be placing too much emphasis on judicial creativity. He interviewed 34 justices on the intermediate courts of appeal in California. He reports:

> They [the judges] perceive their job as primarily one of "processing" a largely repetitious caseload. Specifically, the judges felt their basic mission to be the tasks of *reviewing* for correctness the records of trial courts and *applying* the law as enunciated by the state supreme court.
>
> "We have chances for creativity a couple of times a year, maybe," asserted one justice. "But we're too busy to think that much. We give each case full consideration, but this is essentially an assembly line." . . . [M]any jurists stressed that they also had had to develop methods for coping in psychological terms with the less intriguing aspects of their job . . . .
>
> "Liberal" and "conservative" political ideologies, as well as notions of judicial "activism" and "restraint," appear to have very limited relevance to the work of the California intermediate courts. Any attempts to base judicial appointments to the courts of appeal on ideological considerations may thus fail to accomplish their intended purpose. Apparently, whatever the ideological stripe of newly-appointed justices, they quickly become cogs in a system of case processing and routine dispositions.

Lenore Alpert, Burton M. Atkins, and Robert C. Ziller, in "Becoming a Judge: the Transition from Advocate to Arbiter," 62 *Judicature* 325 (1979), suggest that many judges leave the bench because the job is not what they expected. Judges find that they are isolated socially and politically by the demands of their role. They find that they do not make as much money as they made as lawyers because judicial salaries do not keep up with inflation. Those who remain judges tend to conform to organizational expectations and rewards.

2. Is the role of the American—or British—judge radically different from the role of the civil law judge? In theory, yes. The common-law judge has a more "active" role in law-making than is conceded to the civil-law judge. See the discussion of Professor Langbein's views and our notes and questions, on pp. 660–61. But there may not be so great a difference in practice. José Juan Toharia, in a study of Spain's judiciary, divided judges into "active" and "pas-

sive" ones, depending on how they conceived their function. An "active" judge stresses the judge's creativity, and his or her role as a defender of rights and liberties. Such a judge values flexibility and is concerned with the social consequences of decisions. The "passive" judge is more attuned to formalism and judicial autonomy. See José Juan Toharia's *El Juez Español: un Análisis Sociológico* [The Spanish Judge: A Sociological Analysis] (Madrid: Editorial Tecnos, 1975). See, also, Martin Shapiro, *Courts: A Comparative and Political Analysis* (Chicago: University of Chicago Press, 1981). Shapiro offers a chapter on "judging and mediating in Imperial China" and a chapter on Islamic courts.

3. American judges, and judges in the Western world in general, have a great deal of independence. Even elected judges do not fear reprisals if they decide, say, against the government. But in many totalitarian countries that may not be the case. How much freedom did judges have in Nazi Germany or in the Soviet Union under Stalin? How much freedom did judges have in China or Cuba in the early 1990s? Compare Raymond J. Michalowski, "Between Citizens and the Socialist State: The Negotiation of Legal Practice in Socialist Cuba," 29 *Law & Society Review* 65 (1995).

There is a particularly rich and interesting literature on the German judiciary under Adolf Hitler between 1933 and 1945. See, for example, Ingo Mueller, *Hitler's Justice: The Courts of the Third Reich,* Deborah L. Schneider, trans. (Cambridge, Mass.: Harvard University Press, 1991). For a thoughtful essay on cultural differences in the reaction to this book, see Walter Weyrauch, "Limits of Perception: Reader Response to *Hitler's Justice,*" 40 *American Journal of Comparative Law* 237 (1992). On the behavior of the judges in the former German Democratic Republic (East Germany) under the Communist regime and their fate when German reunification did away with their jobs and their station in life, see Inga Markovits, "Law's Last Days," 80 *California Law Review* 55 (1992). Contrast the post-World War II largely favorable treatment of the Nazi judges, as Mueller describes it, with the treatment of the Communist judges, as Markovits recounts.

In the Philippines, a period of martial law ended when an authoritarian leader lost power, and a more democratic period followed. How did all of this affect the work of the Supreme Court of this country? For an attempt to answer this question rigorously, see C. Neal Tate and Stacia L. Haynie, "Authoritarianism and the Functions of Courts: A Time Series Analysis of the Philippine Supreme Court, 1961–1987," 27 *Law & Society Review* 707 (1993).

4. The role of the trial judge differs from that of the appellate judge. In the lower criminal courts, for example, due process is at a minimum and large numbers of people are processed for relatively minor crimes. Here "the process itself is the primary punishment," that is, the stigma, detention, and the whole cluster of the costs of pretrial process, may loom larger than the actual sentence that the judge hands out. See Malcolm M. Feeley, *The Process Is the Punishment: Handling Cases in a Lower Criminal Court* (New York: Russell Sage Foundations,1979).

In an important study, *Felony Justice: An Organizational Analysis of Criminal Courts* (Boston: Little, Brown & Co., 1977), James Eisenstein and Herbert Jacob argue that court studies have focused too much attention on judges. Eisenstein and Jacob argue that courts are "organizations"; that what goes on in a courtroom is most profitably analyzed "as a group activity." Their book is a study of courtroom "workgroups," made up of all the personnel in the courtroom—prosecutors, defense counsel, clerks, bailiffs, as well as the judge. It is the interaction between the members of the workgroups that "determines the outcome of criminal cases" (p. 10). See also Jeffery T. Ulmer, "Trial Judges in a Rural Court Community: Contexts, Organizational Relations, and Interaction Strategies," 23 *Journal of Contemporary Ethnography* 79 (1994).

Austin Sarat, in "Judging in Trial Courts: An Exploratory Study," 39 *Journal of Politics* 291 (1977), suggests that trial judges can be divided into four types: (1) The *game type* enjoys the activities of judging and likes the rituals and rules of the court; (2) the *status type* is motivated to prove that they are in charge, and this type of judge often demeans others to elevate him or herself; (3) the *obligation type* sees being a judge a chance to do good and a duty; (4) the *program type* enjoys working on problems and pushes compromises or acceptable solutions rather than trying cases and letting the chips fall where they may. While these categories point to particular behaviors, Sarat's research failed to find that the *type* of judge made significant differences in the sentences given those convicted of crimes.

Marc Galanter, Frank S. Palen, and John M. Thomas, in "The Crusading Judge: Judicial Activism in Trial Courts," 52 *Southern California Law Review* 699 (1979), offer a slightly different set of categories: (1) The *legalist judge* who is oriented to the application of general rules in individual cases; (2) the *mission-oriented judge* who perceives his or her responsibility as using the law and judicial power to advance substantive goals such as cracking down on drunken driving; (3) the *programmatic judge* who responds to patterns of cases coming to the court; and (4) the *entrepreneurial judge* who steps outside the court and uses the press and politics to get results. The authors claim that local legal culture establishes the roles of trial judges. Active judges can move up to higher courts if their activity pleases those who influence judicial selection. Lawyers have many ways informally to sanction judges who step out of appropriate roles. For example, lawyers gossip about judges among themselves and with newspaper reporters. This may create a reputation which becomes more widely known. This reputation, in turn, may affect other rewards and punishments from the larger community.

5. Marc Galanter, in "Judicial Mediation in the United States," 12 *Journal of Law and Society* 1 (1985), discusses a new emphasis and openness about one aspect of the role of trial judges in civil (noncriminal) cases. Trial judges more and more accept promoting settlements as part of their task and exchange information about how to succeed in getting parties to settle. Judges, for example, call conferences for reasons related to preparation for trial, but they use the opportunity to push for settlement. Galanter reports:

Judges will often attempt to define "the present value of this case" or otherwise suggest the terms of settlement. A number of judges proudly sketch what some call the "Lloyds of London method": lawyers are asked to estimate what they think the case is worth and the probability that they will prevail; by combining these calculations the judges produce a figure that is "the synthesis of the probabilities of liability and the possibilities of damages." This is, of course, a fancy version of splitting the difference—a prospect which some find undisturbing since "All [that equally competent lawyers] . . . need from the court is an indication that a figure somewhere between their two figures is fair." Other judges pursue the search for agreement by asking the parties to reveal their best offer: each hands the judge a slip of paper and the judge, comparing them, can tell whether there is a possibility of agreement . . . .

Judges are advised to give the lawyer something to "take back" to his client—often a calculation or estimate that has the judge's imprimatur on it. Some judges warn against attempts to influence litigants, but others include clients in settlement conferences and even hold private discussions with parties . . . .

Why have trial judges turned into settling judges? Galanter offers a strategic explanation:

There is more law—more legislation, more administrative regulation, more published judicial decisions. This proliferation of legal controls responds to and stimulates higher expectations of protection and redress among wider sections of the public. As the body of authoritative material becomes more massive, more complex and more refined, decision-makers (and other actors) are both constrained and supplied with resources and opportunities for legal innovation.

Adjudication has become more complex, more expensive, more protracted, more rational—and more indeterminate. It is freer of arbitrary formalities, more open to evidence of complicated states of fact, and responsive to a wider range of argument. As the cost and complexity of litigation increases, both the potential inputs as well as the possible outcome of the trial became a source of bargaining counters that can be used at other phases of the process . . . . As the process became more costly and complex, it creates new strategic options for litigants while subjecting them to new contingencies . . . .

Demand for brokers who can help secure this information at low cost and risk converges with changes in judicial ideology. Judges share the widespread elevated expectations of a beneficient result at the same time that they have less faith that legal doctrine provides a single right answer; or that full-blown adjudication will produce the most appropriate outcome. Concern with outcomes is juxtaposed with the realization that outcomes are affected by the contingencies of the process—by cost, delay, uncertainty, bargaining power and so forth . . . . Judicial promotion of settlements, along with interest in arbitration, mediation, and various alternatives, is a response to these concerns.

See, also, Ronald Bacigal, "An Empirical Case Study of Informal Alternative Dispute Resolution," 4 *Ohio State Journal on Dispute Resolution* 1 (1988). This a study of Federal District Judge Robert R. Merhige's handling of the Westinghouse uranium cases of the 1970s: "Addressing the merits of the case, Merhige offered a qualified ruling which he used to maneuver the parties toward a settlement on damages. His settlement efforts varied from hosting negotiation cocktail parties in his own home to requiring counsel to work on 'Saturdays, Sundays, and some days that aren't even on the calendar.'" See, further, Peter Schuck, "The Role of Judges in Settling Complex Cases: The Agent Orange Example," 53 *University of Chicago Law Review* 337 (1986).

6. There are many studies of sentencing by trial judges in criminal cases. The key question in most of this research concerns the degree to which factors

other than the law and evidence affects sentences imposed on those convicted of crime. See Lawrence E. Cohen and James R. Kluegel, "Determinants of Juvenile Court Dispositions: Ascriptive and Achieved Factors in Two Metropolitan Courts," 43 *American Sociological Review* 162 (1978). Several studies suggest that girls and women are given harsher punishment than boys and men, particularly when sexual delinquency is involved. See Meda Chesney-Lind, "Judicial Enforcement of the Female Sex Roles: The Family Court and the Female Delinquent," 8 *Issues in Criminology* 51 (No. 2, 1973); Steven Schlossman and Stephanie Wallach, "The Crime of Precocious Sexuality: Female Juvenile Delinquency in the Progressive Era," 48 *Harvard Educational Review* 65 (1978).

What kind of judge would be more likely to be severe toward juvenile delinquents—a well-read young judge who kept up with professional literature, did not wear robes to court, and was knowledgeable about delinquency; or a judge with the opposite traits? Somewhat surprisingly, a team of social scientists studying juvenile justice in the Boston area found that the more "professional" judge was the more severe; that is, he more often recommended procedures that ended up with commitment of the juvenile. They were the judges who were most concerned with delinquency as a social problem, who were most trusting of the institutions to which juveniles were sent and most open to a "social welfare ideology." See Stanton Wheeler, Edna Bonacich, M. Richard Cramer, and Irving K. Zola, "Agents of Delinquency Control: A Comparative Analysis," in *Controlling Delinquents*, Stanton Wheeler, ed. (New York: John Wiley, 1968), pp. 31, 54.

An intriguing article, which can be compared with the Wheeler study, is Martin A. Levin's, "Urban Politics and Judicial Behavior," 1 *Journal of Legal Studies* 193 (1972). Levin compared criminal court judges in two cities, Pittsburgh and Minneapolis. In Pittsburgh, old-time machine politics was still vigorous at the time of the study. Judges, nominated by the political parties and elected in partisan elections, tended to be lawyer-politicians. In Minneapolis, city elections were nonpartisan, political parties were weak, and judges were selected through a process heavily influenced by the organized bar. Judges tended to be men without a history of political activity.

The Minneapolis judges were much harsher toward people accused of crime. They were "more oriented toward 'society' and its needs and protection, and towards the goals of their professional peers." Pittsburgh judges were "oriented towards the defendant rather than towards punishment or deterrence." They were "particularistic and pragmatic." Proceedings in Pittsburgh were more informal than in Minneapolis; judges seemed to understand and sympathize more with young ethnics who got in trouble; they were ethnics themselves. The style of the Minneapolis judges (typically white Protestants) was formal, the outcomes considerably more severe.

What is particularly interesting is that no one *intended* these differences in outcome, as such. Certainly, the political bosses in Pittsburgh, who made up slates of judges, were not interested in lighter sentences for those who stole cars or held up gas stations. The difference in output would seem to come from the structural difference in the process of selection and recruitment of judges in the two cities. The structural difference was reflected in a cultural difference— a difference in the attitudes and work habits of the judges. The attitudes of the judges were, in turn, reflected in how they handled their cases.

7. One of the most important developments in criminal cases affecting judges in recent years is the movement to reduce their discretion in sentencing. To many observers, sentencing policy often appeared to be completely irrational or arbitrary. Within broad limits, judges did whatever they pleased. Thus, some asserted that two people charged with, for example, burglary or even two burglars who worked together could and would suffer quite different penalties.

One proposed solution was to adopt sentencing guidelines. The pioneer was Minnesota. It established a special sentencing commission in 1978, which was charged with producing guidelines. When these appeared, the state approved them. The Minnesota system was a complicated arrangement. Judges were supposed to weigh certain factors such as seriousness of the crime, whether the defendant was a repeat offender and so on, and the judges were to come up with a numerical score. This produced a "presumptive sentence," which the judge had to impose or explain why he or she did not do this.

The federal government also adopted guidelines which went into effect in 1987. The federal sentencing system is very complicated. Perhaps it had to be because it must take so many factors into account. It, too, has a complicated formula for producing a score which then gets translated into a convicted criminal's sentence. So, for instance, robbery has a basic score of 20; bank robbery gets a criminal two extra points, add seven if you shoot a gun, but only five if you brandish it.

The guidelines have been and continue to be controversial. Opponents have pointed out that the use of guidelines forces judges to ignore the individual and the circumstances of the particular case. A guideline that seems to make sense in one case, may not make sense in another that only appears to be the same. On the guidelines in action, see Stephen J. Schulhofer and Ilene H. Nagel, "Negotiated Pleas under the Federal Sentencing Guidelines: The First Fifteen Months," 27 *American Criminal Law Review* 231 (1989).

Some federal judges have been highly critical of the guidelines. It has been reported that "at least two senior judges now refuse to hear drug cases," and one federal judge quit the bench in 1991 "in disgust" over the sentencing laws. See *New York Times,* Nov. 8, 1993, A8. The *Times* also recounts the story of a young man, who, to raise money to fix his van, accepted an offer from a fellow groupie of the Grateful Dead to find somebody who would sell LSD. The "fan" turned out to be a federal narcotics agent. The young man, a first offender, is serving a ten year sentence. The judge who sentenced him "criticized the mandatory penalty," but felt that his hands were tied.

Stanton Wheeler and associates studied the sentencing behavior of federal judges in cases involving white collar crime. The data were gathered before the federal guidelines went into effect. Interview with judges indicated that the sentencing process in these cases was hardly "lawless;" indeed, there was "substantial consensus" about the things that were important in arriving at sentencing decisions: seriousness of the crime and so on. See Stanton Wheeler, Kenneth Mann, and Austin Sarat, *Sitting in Judgment: The Sentencing of White-Collar Criminals* (1989), p. 166. For a comparison of "common law" sentencing and "guideline" sentencing, see pp. 186–87 of Wheeler, Mann, and Sarat.

8. Do judges discriminate in sentencing between blacks and whites, men and women, rich and poor? Do they treat white collar criminals differently than "ordinary" criminals? On all of these subjects there is a large amount of

literature, but in no case is there a clear answer. For a review of the literature on race, see Chapter 9, "Crime and the Administration of Criminal Justice" in Gerald David Jaynes and Robin M. Williams, eds., *A Common Destiny: Blacks and American Society* (Washington, D.C.: National Academy Press, 1989), pp. 451, 483–89. Professor Joel Handler of the UCLA Law School was the chair of a panel of experts that prepared this chapter.

9. Will black judges sentence black defendants differently than white judges? Most judges on the bench in the early 1990s were white males, and until not long before then *all* judges were white males. See Professor Goldman's articles reprinted and summarized on pp. 734–49. For this and other reasons, there are few studies of the sentencing behavior of minority group judges. But see, on the behavior of Hispanic judges in El Paso County, Malcolm D. Holmes, Harmon M. Hosch, Howard C. Daudistel, Dolores A. Perez, and Joseph B. Graves, "Judges' Ethnicity and Minority Sentencing: Evidence Concerning Hispanics," 74 *Social Science Quarterly* 496 (1993).

LAWYERS

53. Six Score Years and Ten: Demographic Transitions in the American Legal Profession, 1850–1980

Terence C. Halliday

20 *Law & Society Review* 53 (1986)

☐ . . . This article . . . places the detailed descriptions of lawyer changes over the last 5 and 30 years in a . . . circumscribed demographic context. I shall draw upon . . . data sources neglected by sociologists of professions, namely the United States *Census* for each decade point from 1850 through 1980 . . . .

. . . I shall place the experience of the past thirty years in the context of changes in lawyer population between 1850 and 1980. The paper treats in turn (1) national lawyer population trends, [and] (2) regional lawyer population trends . . . .

I. NATIONAL LAWYER POPULATION TRENDS, 1850–1980

The most startling demographic transitions . . . for 1950 to 1980 are the massive increase in the number of lawyers and the rapidly rising lawyer to population ratio. How do these changes relate to the long-term development of the American legal profession?

Three alternative profiles of this long-term growth (over a period of more than 100 years) might be expected. First, the profession and the population might steadily expand and thus the lawyer to population ratio would remain relatively constant—a straight-line, or steady-state, model. Second, the profession's growth might follow a rather more dynamic step profile, with expansion succeeded by a plateau of consolidation, which in turn yields to further expansion as population and demands for legal services increase. A third hypothesis posits even more fluctuation—a cyclical, or wave, model in which the institutions of the profession press for expansion, followed by contraction as economic circumstances reduce demand, and then return to expansion as demand outstrips supply. Each of these models, of course, is based upon an implicit theory of lawyer labor force dynamics . . .

A. National Population Trends

. . . [T]he United States population expanded in a relatively straight line from 1850 to 1980, but . . . the expansion of the legal profession did not correspond exactly. Indeed, the growth in the profession better approximates a somewhat smoothed-step function. From 1850 to 1870, the lawyer population tracked the general population in a slight expansion; but, whereas the number of lawyers almost doubled from 1850 to 1870, it tripled from approximately 40,000 in 1870 to about 115,000 in 1900. The next twenty years represent another plateau, when the profession increased only marginally. Expansion occurred again rather more rapidly through 1930, followed by a plateau until 1950, when the profession began . . . pronounced growth . . . . Therefore, until 1960— or even 1970—the absolute growth in the number of lawyers followed a reasonably discernible pattern. It was only the last decade that witnessed growth in the lawyer population at a rate without precedent in the previous 140 years.

B. National Lawyer to Population Ratios

The comparison of general and lawyer population expansion . . . makes it clear that, although the latter has more or less kept pace with the former, the relationship has not been invariant . . . . If the profession's growth were determined entirely by population, the lawyer to population ratio would be constant. In fact, if the absolute size of the profession follows a step profile . . . , the relative size of the profession . . . more closely approximates a wave profile, with long-term alternations between expansion and contraction. Between 1850 and 1870, the ratio was fairly steady: 1.03 lawyers to every 1,000 population at the beginning and 1.07 at the end. It then rose steeply to 1.5

in 1900, but then contracted to 1.16 in 1920. A smaller wave occurred between 1920 and 1960: In the first two decades the ratio rose from 1.16 to 1.35, but in the last two decades it fell back to 1.21 as the increase in the general population caught up with the earlier growth among lawyers. Since 1970 the ratio has increased rapidly to historically unparalleled levels. Finally, for most of the past 140 years the ratio has averaged around 1.25 lawyers to 1,000 population.

. . . Although the absolute number of lawyers has been increasing in steps, the 1920 ratio of lawyers to general population resembled that of 1870, the 1940 ratio resembled that of 1885, and the 1960 figure resembled that of the late 1870s. Hence, it is a salutary reminder that the lawyer to population ratio in 1960 was very similar to what it had been eighty-five years earlier. Moreover, the twentieth-century profession regained its 1900 ratio of lawyers to population only in the early 1970s. In the long-term historical perspective, therefore, until the late 1970s the expansion of lawyer population that began in 1960 appeared only slightly more dramatic than that which had begun in 1870. Consequently, there is a suggestion from the data that the ratio of lawyers to population may be following half-century cycles from peak to peak, or trough to trough, in successive waves.

II. REGIONAL LAWYER POPULATION TRENDS, 1850–1980

National population transitions mask regional variations. Surprisingly, little or no work has been done on the migration of lawyers, a gap in research especially unfortunate because information on interstate mobility would make it possible to test economic and population theories of lawyer distribution.

A. Regional Distribution of Lawyers

. . . The country [can be] divided into seven regions. "Greater D.C." includes Washington, D.C., Virginia, Maryland, and West Virginia because so many lawyers resident in those states actually work in the District . . . . The decline in the concentration of lawyers in New England occurred most strikingly between 1850 and 1890; thereafter the proportion of lawyers in that area remained fairly constant. The mid-Atlantic states also experienced a decline, from 31 percent in 1850 to 24 percent in 1908, followed by a return to the 1850 level in 1940, and then a sharp contraction to the 1890 level by 1980—that is, a double wave of contraction and expansion relative to the rest of the country. Rather surprisingly, the Greater D.C. area maintained a fairly stable proportion of the national lawyer population for 130 years. Although there was a modest decline from 1850 through 1910 and then a slight incline more recently, the figures for the region fluctuated only between 5.9 percent and 9 percent for the entire period.

The distribution of lawyers in the South declined by about one-third between 1850 and 1940, when this region included 16 percent of the national lawyer population, but there was a modest recovery subsequently. Although the Midwest, like the South, contained one-fifth of the profession in 1980, it reached that proportion by a different pattern: Its proportion expanded rapidly from one-quarter to one-third of the profession between 1850 and 1870 and thereafter steadily declined to its present level.

The Pacific states display the most noticeable proportional gain: Their share of the national profession grew steadily from 1 percent in 1850 through 6 percent in 1900 to 9 percent in 1950 and 16 percent in 1980. The West followed a similar course from 1850 to 1890, then held steady for three decades, but declined to about 8 percent in 1930 and fluctuated near that proportion thereafter.

Several general regional trends are worthy of recognition. First, the percentage of the lawyer population in the Northeast—namely, the New England, Mid-Atlantic, and Greater D.C. areas—contracted from 50 percent of the profession in 1850 to 35 percent in 1980. Second, the proportion in the West and Pacific states expanded at the partial expense of the Northeast, from 1 percent in 1850 to 24 percent in 1980, with most of this expansion occurring in the Pacific states. Hence the two monotonic changes in regional distribution of lawyers can be found in the Northeast, where there was a steady decline, and in the West, where there was a steady expansion. Viewed a little differently, most variability over time in the regional distribution of lawyers occurred in the West and Pacific states, whereas most constancy occurred in New England and the Washington, D.C., area . . . .

III. GENDER AND LAWYER POPULATION TRENDS, 1850–1980

. . . [P]erhaps the single most radical transformation in the modern legal profession . . . [is] the massive influence of women. That few women were members of the profession before the 1970s seems indisputable. To what degree, however, has the entry of women into legal practice been a linear development? Or, has it been the case in law, as in some other professions, that in an earlier period women composed a rather large proportion of the profession? Table 1 demonstrates that there were no female lawyers until 1870, that it took another thirty years for their number to reach 1,000, and that they did not exceed

10,000 until 1970. The ratio of women to men expresses the gender differences even more forcefully. Women did not comprise .01 of the legal profession until 1920, and another half-century transpired before that proportion reached .05. Then, in just one decade, the ratio of women to men trebled—from .051 in 1970 to .16 in 1980. In short, for most of the last century, women have comprised between 1 percent and 5 percent of all lawyers.

IV. THEORETICAL ISSUES AND EXPLANATORY MODELS

The data . . . raise two sets of issues: the attribution of meaning to particular findings and the absorption of individual explanations into general theories . . . .

For example, how should we interpret the fact . . . that the legal profession expanded at a rate faster than the general population? The step function of changes in absolute numbers of lawyers is represented as waves of varying lawyer to population ratios. Here again particular historical explanations can be suggested. For instance, the declines in the ratio of lawyers to population coincided with wars in the 1860s and

TABLE 1 GROWTH OF THE LEGAL PROFESSION BY GENDER, UNITED STATES, 1850–1980*

Year	Male Lawyers	Female Lawyers	Ratio of Female to Male Lawyers
1850	23,939	0	—
1860	33,980	0	—
1870	41,786	5	.0001
1880	64,062	75	.001
1890	89,422	208	.002
1900	113,450	1,010	.009
1910	120,806	1,343	.011
1910	114,146	558	.005
1920	120,781	1,738	.014
1930	157,220	3,385	.022
1940	173,456	4,187	.024
1950	174,205	6,256	.036
1960	210,089	7,434	.035
1970	273,044	13,964	.051
1980	452,494	72,312	.160

*1850 to 1910 includes semiprofessionals; 1910 to 1980 excludes semiprofessionals.

1940s, as substantial numbers of young men deferred legal education or entrance into the work force, and with the rise in professional self-regulatory powers in the first two decades of the twentieth century. Even these interpretations, however, provide little insight into regional changes in the lawyer population. Is the contraction of the profession in the Northeast a function of that area's declining population and industry? Has the West expanded both its lawyer population and ratio of lawyers to population because of economic changes? And, given the very substantial growth in federal government, how are we to make sense of the fairly constant proportion of lawyers in the greater Washington, D.C., area over the last hundred years? Furthermore, the very high ratio of lawyers to population in the Pacific states in the last half of the nineteenth century seems quite unexpected. And how are we to account for the steep decline after 1900 in the lawyer to population ratio in the West and Pacific states? Finally, what explanations can be advanced for the exclusion and inclusion of female lawyers since 1870?

The dearth of answers to these specific questions highlights not only the lack of empirical investigation but also the paucity of more comprehensive, empirically sustained theories of professional growth and migration . . . . [W]e are left without any real understanding of the conditions that produce the expansion, contraction, or distribution of the legal profession. Given both the practical and theoretical ramifications of these trends, this is a most fundamental absence indeed.

The demography of the legal profession will be better understood when the gap is narrowed between the descriptive data . . . and [two] bodies of theory: (1) demand theories of lawyer population dynamics; [and] (2) monopoly theories of lawyer population dynamics . . .

A. Demand Theories of Lawyer Population Dynamics

The central question in the study of the demography of the legal profession is as simple to pose as it is complex to resolve: What are the determinants of the rise, fall, and movement of lawyer populations? There are at least two approaches to this problem, the one concerning forces within the profession, or forces over which it can exert control, and the other concerning determinants outside, and causally prior to, the profession.

Taking the latter approach first, the most obvious point of explanatory departure is the variation in general population . . . . [T]here is face validity to a *population theory* of lawyer population growth and decline. For the first two decades (1850 to 1870), and in some later decades, the rate of increase in lawyers paralleled that of the general population. Nevertheless, a gross correlation between the absolute size of both populations fails to solve two problems: First, what determines the baseline ratio of lawyers in 1850? And second, what explains the fluctuating pace of lawyer expansion in growth spurts and at a rate faster than that of the population at large? An answer to the first question rests on a theory of lawyer use. An answer to the second question implies increments or changes of use and users. Changes in use may be a result of new statutes, increased government regulation, shifts in legal culture, the enlargement of rights, and economic changes and growth. Changes in users may signify a wider pool of individual users as well as the rise of new fictive persons—corporations, municipalities, and the like.

Of these changes in demand for and demanders of legal services, those dealing with shifts in the economy are most readily amenable to empirical analysis. Yet an *economic theory* of lawyer population dynamics is notably absent from the law and society field . . .

What sorts of economies do increase the demand for lawyers? . . . To obtain a proxy of different economies, without going outside the census and without covering the entire period of 1850 to 1970, labor force data have been coded for each state from the censuses of 1940, 1950, 1960, 1970, and 1980. The data break down employment into twelve categories: (1) agriculture, (2) mining, (3) manufacturing, (4) transportation, (5) trade, (6) finance, (7) business and repair services, (8) personal services, (9) entertainment and recreation, (10) professional services, (11) public administration, and (12) construction. The configuration of these sectors provides an approximation of a state's economic profile.

The results of this exploratory—and illustrative—analysis may be seen in Table 2. The census of 1980 asked workers for both their job title and the industry sectors in which they were employed. The second column from the left on Table 2 crossclassifies these responses for lawyers. The vast majority of lawyers practice within the professional services sector, that is, the private practice of law in firms and law teaching. Ranked second in absolute numbers are lawyers employed in public administration in all three branches of federal, state, and local government. Only two other sectors have sizable lawyer populations: finance, which includes banking, insurance, investments, and real estate; and manufacturing, where it is likely that lawyers are house counsel or in management but still identify themselves as lawyers. Smaller numbers of practitioners, counted in the thousands, may be found in mining, trade, business and repair services, and construction.

The ratio of lawyers per 1,000 employed in each sector is also shown in the table, and the differences between absolute and proportional representation in industrial sectors makes for interesting speculation about demand conditions for lawyer use. Not surprisingly, the ratio of lawyers to total employed is very high in those two sectors where the absolute number of lawyers is greatest—professional services and public administration. However, when one compares the three largest sectors of the economy, professional services, manufacturing, and trade, the ratio of lawyers varies dramatically. Whereas it is very high in professional services (19.478), it differs considerably in manufacturing (.536) and trade (.162). By contrast, although the absolute number of lawyers in mining is small, the ratio is comparatively large (1.957).

If ratio of lawyers to size of industrial sectors varies so considerably, then it must be assumed that there are factors within each sector which determine the likelihood that legal services generated by the sector will be satisfied within it. In other words, the demand for lawyers in a sector may be expressed in two ways: The demand may be direct and the legal needs satisfied within the sector, as, for example, by house counsel in manufacturing; or the demand may be equally strong but need to be satisfied outside the sector, as, for instance, by law firms within the professional services category. Hence it appears that even if the

TABLE 2   LAWYERS AND EMPLOYMENT BY LABOR FORCE SECTOR, 1980, AND REGRESSION OF LAWYERS ON LABOR FORCE SECTORS, UNITED STATES, 1940–80 (N = 257)

| Labor Force Sectors | 1980 | | | 1940–80 |
	Lawyers	Total Employed	Lawyers per 1,000 Employed	Unstandardized Weighted Least-Squares Regression Coefficient (× 1000)
Agriculture	165	2,913,589	.057	.89
Mining	2,012	1,028,178	1.957	2.74
Manufacturing	11,756	21,914,754	.536	1.61
Transportation	5,648	7,087,455	.797	32.09*
Trade	3,242	19,933,926	.162	−25.15*
Finance	16,159	5,898,059	2.740	19.84
Business and repair services	2,807	4,081,677	.688	133.61*
Personal services	276	3,075,764	.090	33.20*
Entertainment and recreation	554	1,007,070	.550	*52.56*
Professional services	385,898	19,811,819	19.478	12.10*
Public administration	95,075	5,147,466	18.470	39.87*
Construction	1,214	5,739.598	*.212	−63.65*

R^2 .917

F 227.89

*p < .001

demands for legal services in manufacturing and trade were similar—and that is only an assumption—manufacturing firms may be better able to satisfy their legal needs internally. How can this be explained? One determining factor might well be organization. If it is assumed that the larger a firm, the greater its capacity to employ its own legal staff, and if we further assume that this is more likely to occur in manufacturing, where average firm size is greater than in trade, then it may be concluded that the reason for the ratio difference between trade and manufacturing lies in the fact that the former must find legal services outside the sector whereas the latter can structure their services within. This difference is attributable to the size of the firm, not of demand. But again it must be emphasized that these hypotheses are intended only as a stimulus to further study: Levels of demand and the ways they are satisfied must be established empirically.

The fifth column in Table 2 takes the economic analysis a step further by seeking to develop a model that indicates which configurations of state economies best predict the size of the legal profession. Fifty observations, plus those for the District of Columbia and Puerto Rico, for five decade points provide 257 cases for analyzing the relationship between economic composition of the labor force and lawyer population.[165] Great care must be taken in interpreting this very tentative and quite exploratory equation . . . . Nonetheless, the model is useful if only to indicate that economies that are dominated by certain industry sectors may have an important effect on the population of lawyers.

Keeping these caveats in mind, it appears that economic factors are indeed important in determining the size of the legal profession, for several industry sectors are strongly associated with increased lawyer populations. For example, a difference of 1,000 employed in public administration will change the number of lawyers employed in the sector by 39.87, other things being equal. Strong positive effects, in order of size, are also to be found in business and repair services (133.61), personal services (33.20), transportation (32.09) and finance (19.84), although the number of lawyers employed in personal services is so small that this category should be excluded. For statistical reasons, more caution is needed with the negative coefficients, except perhaps in the case of trade.

Excluding nonsignificant coefficients, or those based on industries with small numbers of lawyers, this model suggests that in the last fifty years the size of the profession will increase in an economy with a higher percent of the work force in business and repair service, public administration, transportation, and finance, and the size will decrease with a higher percent of the work force in trade.

If these findings are more than statistical artifacts, they suggest that

165. Data on Hawaii, Alaska, and Puerto Rico are not included for 1940.

the configuration of a state's economy has a highly significant effect on the size of its legal profession. But of course, while a useful step forward, this analysis still does not answer the critical question of what within each economic sector positively or negatively affects the number of lawyers. While public administration and professional services seem obvious in their effects, business and repair services and transportation are much less so. Two alternative, or possibly complementary, interpretations may be posited. Business and repair services include, for example, advertising, management and consulting, computer and data processing services, automotive repair services, and electrical repair. The simpler explanation for the high ratio of lawyers is that vast amounts of legal work are generated by advertising, consulting, and legal matters arising out of automobiles. More compelling, perhaps, is the explanation that the size of the legal profession is not a direct effect of increased legal work arising from these services, but their size is an indirect indicator of economic activity in other industry sectors that do generate a great deal of demand for lawyers' services. The business and repair services example, however, suffices to show that we are far from a coherent theory of lawyer demand, although this model may provide hints as to where to look and distinctions about the means by which demands are articulated.

Nonetheless, the exploration will have to go much farther than the illustration offered here. Changes over time must be built into the models since it is entirely plausible to expect that a given economy will generate more or less legal work in one period than in another. Better indicators, with less measurement error, will produce more accurate predictions and more reliable theories. Most basically, the explication of why a given economic sector demands more legal services than others is a critical element missing in current thinking.

In addition to population and economic factors, a third element in a theory of lawyer population dynamics must concern developments in the *state*. The expansion of legal entitlements, the growth of regulation, the more rigorous prosecution of crime, the expansion of the welfare apparatus—all will influence the demand for lawyers, although the episodic character of changing demands, coupled with the general growth in the size of government, may help explain both the general upward trend in the size of the profession as well as fluctuations around the mean.

The specific questions raised at the outset of this section lead to a fourth set of factors—the influence of rare but catastrophic events. Do international conflicts such as the two World Wars, internal convulsions such as the Civil War, or severe economic changes such as the Great Depression have consistent effects on the demand for lawyers? Although our data suggest such associations, the post-factum attribution of historical meaning to downturns in graphs is coarse at best.

Finally, the demand for lawyers may be a function of broad movements in American *culture*. For example, the gathering impetus for the emancipation of slaves, the impulses toward the formation of a welfare state during the New Deal, the rise of the civil rights movement for blacks in the 1950s and 1960s, and the women's movement in the 1970s have all had repercussions for legal services, whether by increasing the demand for lawyers or intensifying the pressure on the profession to admit previously excluded groups.

B. MONOPOLY THEORIES OF LAWYER POPULATION DYNAMICS

If lawyer population dynamics may be partially explained by factors external to the profession, the explanation must also rest on internal institutional factors that shape, mold, or mitigate the effects of economic, political, cultural, and other forces.

. . . [W]idening circles of scholarship locate economic control at the center of their interpretations of professional collective action. In [Professor Richard] Abel's terms, control over production by lawyers occurs through legal education, state licensure of lawyers, and the regulation of legal practice by means of boundaries against unauthorized practitioners, limits on competition and advertising, and the like. A strong version of the monopoly thesis effectively conceives of the profession as a faucet that attempts to turn the flow of lawyers into the labor force on and off as it suits the economic purposes of the profession.

I have numerous doubts about the validity and empirical evidence for these assumptions . . . . Nevertheless, it is impossible to view lawyer to population dynamics without reflecting on their significance for monopoly or the regulation of supply. Both Curran's (1986) data[166] and my own suggest that even if the profession did once regulate supply, in the last 15 years it has lost control almost completely. The recent explosion in the number of lawyers, without precedent in the last 130 years, suggests that the professional monopoly has buckled under the onslaught of more powerful economic, cultural, and political impulses. Therefore, if the theory of market control is to be retained, it is necessary to specify the external conditions—social, political, economic—under which monopoly will be attainable. That is, a supply-side interpretation of population dynamics must become a more *contingent theory*, and the contingencies must relate to both the capacities of the profession to mobilize as well as the strength of wider social forces.

---

166. [The reference is to Barbara A. Curran, "American Lawyers in the 1980s: A Profession in Transition," 20 *Law & Society Review* 19 (1986).]

Of course, if a contingent notion were adopted, both Curran's and my data might provide some face validity to a supplyside theory. The long-term decline in lawyer to population ratio throughout the United States from 1900 to 1920 coincided with the rise of the organized bar in many metropolitan centers and the more populous states. However, if other factors remained constant and bar associations steadily increased their influence over admission to the profession from their founding decade of the 1870s, then the decline might well have begun a decade or two earlier. Here, as elsewhere, it is difficult to differentiate among competing theories or even counterforces. In either case, it is simply too easy and too implausible to attribute minor perturbations to any particular cause when the determining complex of factors seems so intricate.

It is true that a counterinterpretation could be offered by the pundits of monopoly theory. Their argument might go as follows: Lawyers have *not* lost control of their market. The spurt in the number of lawyers in the 1970s and 1980s represents a volitional adjustment of supply that had become too restricted; the population and economic demands had outstripped the capacity of lawyers to cope. Since it was imperative for the profession not to lose its market through undersupply, control had to be loosened radically—and was. But as this counterthesis suggests, without institutional evidence to complement demographic data, the supply-control theory is virtually unfalsifiable . . . . [T]he monopoly thesis can deal with an apparent reversal by reinterpreting the profession's loss in terms of strategic demonopolization. Yet even this qualification hardly seems consistent with a doubling of the profession in twenty years.

These conflicting interpretations raise two other questions. First, in his discussion of changes in lawyer supply, Pashigian (1978)[167] observes that it may take from fifteen to twenty years for a profession to respond institutionally to the need to increase the supply of lawyers by 50 percent—a time period that should caution those who confer on the profession rather more flexibility in market control than they could possibly have. Second, even if the "profession" had lost control, such control could have been maintained by the law schools, although with different mechanisms and quite possibly different ends. (But here again, the continued opening of new law schools seems to imply that their entrepreneurial vigor outweighed notions of control.) There is value in this argument, but it still begs the question of when a profession qua profession can be considered to be acting collectively in its economic interests . . . . [T]here is still considerable need for careful

---

167. [The reference is to Peter B. Pashigian, "The Number and Earnings of Lawyers: Some Recent Findings," 1978 *American Bar Foundation Research Journal* 51.]

empirical and conceptual analysis of how closely the institutional sub-components of a profession, such as educational institutions, should be considered parts of the profession. To the extent that law schools are autonomous from the principal collective bodies of the practicing profession, especially in areas concerning supply of new lawyers, the force of monopoly theory begins to dissipate.

The demographic transitions have another consequence for control theories. The long-standing research tradition in professional socialization was based on the premise that professional self-regulation and normative consensus as an internal ethical control of practice were defining characteristics of professional communities. The professional school experience was thought to socialize future practitioners in a manner that would obviate the need for external, extraprofessional controls. Hence the autonomy of a professional community was justified, especially if coupled with the supposed incapacity of nonprofessionals to judge professional performance.

The extraordinary size and rate of lawyer population expansion in the last two decades pose significant issues for both sets of control theories—monopoly and professional socialization—that bear careful analysis. For instance, if it is accepted that professional socialization is crucial for the integrity of legal practice and the adherence to intraprofessional normative and ethical codes, then such expansion weakens socialization processes both in the institutions where inculcation of values is intended to be accomplished, and in the profession, where it is expected to be efficacious. With respect to the former, a great increase in the size of law school populations without compensating structural adaptations probably lessens the corporate impact of values that are purported to be taught. The expansion of private law schools may similarly add to value eclecticism at best and value dissensus at worst.

Even more pronounced is the effect of the lawyer population increase on cohorts in the profession. If, in times of more placid expansion, the socialization efforts of law schools were reinforced by the expectations of more experienced practitioners, the radically altered ratio of new to experienced practitioners, reflected in the falling mean age of the legal profession, suggests that control exercised by senior lawyers must surely be attenuated. Regulation of practice poses a double conundrum—for work organizations and for bar associations—each of which is charged, in different ways, with the responsibility for control.

Rapid expansion of the profession, especially in tandem with more diverse cohorts of new lawyers, has undoubtedly eroded much of whatever normative integration and community cohesion formerly existed in the American legal profession. This erosion can strike, therefore, at the likely efficacy of either theory of professional control. Socialization is accordingly a less effective means of control, but then professional

monopoly is less easily attained by the strict enforcement of professional ethics. Thus, if the thesis is correct that the rapid expansion in
the number of lawyers represents a blow to monopoly and monopoly
theorists, the changing experience ratio and the increase in the raw size
of the profession compound both strikes against the theory or practice
of monopoly .... ☐

NOTES AND QUESTIONS

1. Richard L. Abel has written a great deal about the legal profession. He is
prominent among those who emphasize the monopoly aspects of the profession: The profession tries to maintain a strong grip on the supply of lawyers by
lobbying lawmakers to require three years of law school, to prohibit practice
by those without a license, to defend ethical rules against competition, and the
like. See Richard L. Abel, "The Rise of Professionalism," 6 *British Journal of
Law and Society* 83 (1979); "Toward a Political Economy of Lawyers," 1981
Wisconsin Law Review 1117. Halliday is skeptical about monopoly arguments.
Consider Halliday's case against the monopoly view carefully. If you were
asked to respond to Halliday and defend Abel's position, what would you say?

Professor Abel also has been a pioneer in the comparative study of the legal
profession. He has published a book on the legal profession in the United
Kingdom, *The Legal Profession in England and Wales* (Oxford: Basil Blackwell, 1988). Perhaps the most notable comparative work on lawyers is the
three volume collection edited by Abel and Philip S. C. Lewis, *Lawyers in
Society* (Berkeley: University of California Press, 1988 and 1989). The genesis
of this book was the formation of a Working Group for the Comparative Study
of Legal Professions, created by the Research Committee on Sociology of Law
of the International Sociological Association. Under the leadership of Abel and
Lewis, national reporters collected information about the legal profession in 19
nations. The first volume of *Lawyers in Society, The Common Law World,*
contained essays on the United States, Canada, Great Britain, Australia, New
Zealand and India. Volume 2, on the *Civil Law World,* contained essays on
Norway, Germany, Japan, the Netherlands, Belgium, France, Geneva (Switzerland), Italy, Spain, Venezuela, and Brazil. The third volume contained more
general and interpretive essays.

A valuable overview, in the third volume, is Philip S. C. Lewis, "Comparison and Change in the Study of Legal Professions," p. 27. For a critical review
of the entire three-volume effort, see Miek Berends, "An Elusive Profession?
Lawyers in Society," 26 *Law & Society Review* 161, 177 (1992).

There are, of course, many other books and articles in English on the comparative study of legal professions. See, for example, John Morison and Philip
Leith, *The Barrister's World and the Nature of Law* (Philadelphia: Open University Press, 1992) (on English barristers); Dietrich Rueschemeyer, *Lawyers
and their Society: A Comparative Study of the Legal Professions in Germany
and the United States* (Cambridge, Mass.: Harvard University Press, 1973).

It often is said that the American legal profession is the largest in the world,
in terms of lawyers per 100,000 population. However, the legal professions of
many other countries are also growing quite rapidly. The Japanese legal pro-

fession, on the other hand, is notoriously small. As of 1980, there were some 11,466 "registered practicing attorneys" in Japan. One reason is the severe difficulty of passing the Japanese Legal Examination. Less than 2% of those who take this exam actually pass! See Kahei Rokumoto, "The Present State of Japanese Practicing Attorneys: On the Way to Full Professionalization?," in Volume 2 of Abel and Lewis, pp. 160, 163, 165. We must be careful when we compare lawyers in various countries. Nations differ as to which people they will allow to call themselves lawyers. Nonetheless, if we look closely, we may find members of various occupations doing the same work in different countries.

2. There is a very large literature on the sociology, history, and economics of the American legal profession. Many of the most important of these studies are cited in notes and questions in this chapter. For a general overview, see Richard L. Abel, *American Lawyers* (New York: Oxford University Press, 1989).

3. Does it matter who becomes a lawyer any more than it matters who becomes a dry cleaner, television repair-person, or accountant? A classic statement that it does is: David Riesman, "Law and Sociology: Recruitment, Training, and Colleagueship" in William Evan (ed.), *Law and Sociology* (New York: Free Press, 1962).[168] Reisman argues:

> Precisely because the commitment of going to law school and the socialization that ensues for those who do go is less thorough-going than medical education imposes, and because, moreover, no . . . [official policy] has limited the numbers who can get a legal education, the law remains par excellence the career open to talent. Librarian of Congress, President of Chrysler, Secretary of State, and at less exalted levels insurance executive, realtor, publisher—almost any managerial, commercial, or nonspecialized intellectual job you can think of—are within the reach of the law-trained . . . [person]. It is arguable that this escalator that the law provides is at least as important as a function of legal training as the functions more frequently discussed; arguable that the criminal law, or the sanctioning, legitimation, and interpreting functions, which Talcott Parsons among others has discussed, have no greater impact on the social order than this function of keeping open the channels of mobility for the boy [or girl] who can talk, who is not too narrowly self-defined— who is a kind of roving fullback of American society and can and does go anywhere.
>
> I have . . . described the so-called legal mind, as selected and turned out by the best national law schools, as the nonlegalistic mind: the mind that has learned skepticism of abstractions and yet at-homeness with them. (pp. 17–18)

4. Admission to law schools has increased over the last twenty-five years. The numbers peaked in the early 1970s and then declined until 1985. Since then the number of law students has grown steadily. Despite a downturn in

---

168. A version of the essay also appears in 9 *Stanford Law Review* 643 (1957).

employment opportunities, there were more than 94,000 law school applicants nationally in 1991. The total number of law students in the nation's law schools was 127,261 in the fall of 1990. The percentage of first-year women dropped from 42.7 percent in 1989 to 42.1 percent in 1990. African-Americans, Hispanics, Asian-Americans, and Native Americans constituted 13.6 percent of all law students in 1990, up from 12.3 percent in 1989. See Ken Myers, "Like Lemmings, Law Students Ignore Any Danger Signs Ahead," *The National Law Journal,* March 18, 1991, p. 4; Ken Myers, "Students Flock to Law Schools Despite Sagging Opportunities," October 29, 1990, *The National Law Journal,* p. 4.

In the spring of 1992, several law schools in the Northeast noted a decline in applicants. The University of Connecticut saw an 8 percent decrease in applications while applications to the Yale Law School declined about 6 percent. The economy in this region was poor, and undergraduates from the region were applying to schools elsewhere. Southern schools reported an increase in applications. Schools such as Harvard, Cornell, and Stanford all saw applications drop. See Rosemary P. McNicholas, "Law School Applications Drop Sharply in Northeast," *The Connecticut Lawyer,* May 4, 1992, p. 3. By 1994, there had been an 11% drop in applications over the 1991 peak. See Junda Woo, "Law-School Applications Decline, But Institutions Aren't Worried," *Wall Street Journal,* March 8, 1994, B12, col. 1. However, this decline will not provoke a decline in the number of new lawyers. There are still far more applicants than places in law schools.

Minority attorneys constitute only 2 percent of the 2,538 partners at the 25 largest firms based in New York, according to a September 1989 survey. Black, Hispanic, Asian-American, and Native American associates were only 6 percent of the 7,335 associates at these large firms. There were 219 women partners, 9 percent of the total. The 2,313 women associates were 32 percent of the associate ranks at these large firms. Nationally, the partnership ranks of 69 of the largest 250 firms are all white. On average, the 250 largest firms each have less than one black, Hispanic, Asian American, or Native American partner. In 1981, 2.9 percent of associates at the nation's 151 largest firms were minorities while 9.2 of all law students that year were minority group members. As of 1989, 12.4 percent of law students were minorities, while members of these groups constituted only 5.4 percent of associates at large firms. See Edward A. Adams, "Survey Shows Few Minorities Making Partner: Women Also Fare Poorly at Largest Firms in City," *New York Law Journal,* February 13, 1990, p. 1. The large firms have the highest prestige within the profession. See, for example, Howard S. Erlanger, "The Allocation of Status Within Occupations: The Case of the Legal Profession," 58 *Social Forces* 882 (1980). Presumably, unless women and minority lawyers "make partner" at major firms, their prestige, status, income—and influence—will be less than it might otherwise be.

5. Many people are alarmed at the sheer size of the American legal profession. They have worried aloud about the impact of this horde of lawyers on the economy and the polity. There is a lively debate over the question of whether lawyers are a drag on the economy. See Charles R. Epp, "Do Lawyers Impair Economic Growth?" 17 *Law & Social Inquiry* 585 (1992); Frank B. Cross, "The First Thing We Do, Let's Kill All the Economists: An Empirical Evaluation of the Effect of Lawyers on the United States Economy and Political Sys-

tem," 70 *Texas Law Review* 645 (1992). Derek C. Bok, then President of Harvard University (and a lawyer himself), thought that lawyers might be a drag on the economy. In his "A Flawed System of Law Practice and Training," 33 *Journal of Legal Education* 571, 573 (1983), he wrote:

> Not only does the law absorb many more young people in America than in any other industrialized nation; it attracts an unusually large proportion of the exceptionally gifted. The average College Board scores of the top 2,000 or 3,000 law students easily exceed those of their counterparts entering other graduate schools and occupations, with the possible exception of medicine. The share of all Rhodes scholars who go on to law school has approximated 40 percent in recent years, dwarfing the figures for any other occupational group. Some readers may dismiss these statistics on the ground that lawyers often move to careers in business or public life. But the facts fail to support this rationalization, for roughly three-quarters of all law school graduates are currently practicing their profession . . . .
>
> The net result of these trends is a massive diversion of exceptional talent into pursuits that often add little to the growth of the economy, the pursuit of culture, or the enhancement of the human spirit. I cannot press this point too strongly. As I travel around the country looking at different professions and institutions, I am constantly struck by how complicated many jobs have become, how difficult many institutions are to administer, how pressing are the demands for more creativity and intelligence. However aggressive our schools and colleges are in searching out able young people and giving them a good education, the supply of exceptional people is limited. Yet far too many of these rare individuals are becoming lawyers at a time when the country cries out for more talented business executives, more enlightened public servants, more inventive engineers, more able high school principals and teachers.

For a response, see Robert McKay, "Too Many Bright Law Students?" Id. pp. 596, 599. (Rather than limiting the number of law students, "a better approach would be to make other professions more attractive than they now appear to be, in terms of educational challenge and long-range career attractions.")

Is Bok correct? What sorts of evidence would you need in order to check if he is right or wrong? Does his statement assume that lawyers are essentially parasites? What is the counter-argument?

6. Many writers have argued that law students are socialized in unfortunate ways by their experiences in law school. See, for example, Robert Granfield and Thomas Koenig, "The Fate of Elite Idealism: Accommodation and Ideological Work at Harvard Law School," 39 *Social Problems* 5 (1992); Robert Granfield and Thomas Koenig, "Learning Collective Eminence: Harvard Law School and the Social Production of Elite Lawyers," 33 *The Sociological Quarterly* 503 (1992). Any socialization in law school away from public interest concerns, of course, is powerfully reinforced by the reward and sanction system of practice.

54. *Cultural Capital, Gender, and the Structural Transformation of Legal Practice*

John Hagan,

Marjorie Zatz,

Bruce Arnold,

and Fiona Kay

25 *Law & Society Review* 239 (1991)

☐ . . . This article . . . [based on data about lawyers in Toronto, Canada] is concerned with major changes that have occurred in the legal profession over the past several decades and with what these changes can tell us about the places of cultural capital and gender in contemporary class relations. Because the legal profession has grown so fast, because women have joined this profession in such large numbers, because this profession depends so heavily on cultural symbols and the centralization and concentration of cultural capital, and because law is such a prominent profession, what we can learn about the transformation of legal practice is likely to have great significance.

Marxian and postindustrial theories provide insights into the structural transformation of legal practice. Both theories suggest that a centralization and concentration of ownership positions in the legal sector, as elsewhere, will result in a smaller proportion of lawyers holding ownership positions (partnerships) in the large firms that will increasingly dominate the profession. However, while Marxian theory as well predicts an expansion in a nonautonomous professional proletariat at the base of the profession, postindustrial theory predicts the expansion of a more autonomous class that occupies a contradictory position between the nonautonomous and managerial levels of the profession, with the former nonautonomous class expected to decline. We have suggested that a focus on the role of cultural capital in legal practice makes a further possibility even more likely: namely, that *all* classes of employed lawyers are growing, while the employer classes are declining through a centralization and concentration of partnerships. This focus emphasizes the sensitivity of firms to the perceived need to *both* grow *and* provide some mobility to new recruits, since this process involves, after all, not the simple accumulation of physical capital, but rather the coordination and control of professionally trained manipulators of cultural symbols, and a resulting centralization and concentration of cultural capital. Ironically, the logic of the growth process in large firms seems to require that the ratio of partners to associates remain low so that new associates will perceive room for expansion in the ownership class . . . . [I]n the last decade young women lawyers have come to be seen as compliant and controllable participants in the growth process and that they may therefore have been even more affected than men by the processes we have described.

Macro and micro-level analyses . . . are consistent with these expectations. At the macro level, . . . the broad contours of structural change that are occurring in the legal profession have, as the cultural capital perspective predicts, involved a centralization and concentration of partnerships which combines a proportionate shrinking of the employer classes and an expansion of all the employee classes, not just a nonautonomous class of employed lawyers. These changes are also, as expected, especially pronounced for women . . . . [W]hile women are more affected than men by their declining partnership shares in larger firms, this is especially true in smaller firms. Aggregate adjustments for changing experience distributions and employment in the government and industrial sectors do not change this picture. Finally, the same general picture of men prevailing over women in partnership decisions, especially in smaller firms, emerged in a separate micro-level analysis of the individual careers of men and women lawyers.

If the picture we have presented is accurate, it depicts a changing legal profession in which both men and women are losing their proportionate shares of partnership positions but with women losing more than men. The tremendous growth in the legal profession has taken the form of larger firms dominated by proportionately fewer lawyers. The greatest growth has been in the managerial, semiautonomous, and nonautonomous levels of firms, with women especially likely to be represented at these levels. Alternatively, the greatest contraction is in the low representation of women as partners in smaller firms. This may either result from the failure to grant partnerships to women in smaller firms, or from the movement of women away from employment in these firms, or most likely from a combination of both of these trends. In any event, the large-scale movement of women into larger firms marks a major change in the gender stratification of the profession, in that while women once were shunned by and avoided large firm practice, these firms are now destinations of choice, at least as points of entry. Yet the culture of these firms, which is still dominated by men, does not yet treat women as equal to men, and the findings of this study are consistent with the thesis that lower levels of compensation and mobility for women are providing a hedge against spiraling demands for rewards that are accompanying the centralization and concentration of cultural capital in larger firms. The earnings differentials of women and men in this Toronto sample are quite striking. A new gender stratification is emerging in conjunction with the structural transformation of this prominent profession.

Several decades ago there were so few women practicing law that it would have made little sense to engage in the kind of analysis presented here. However, monitoring the emerging contours of this rapid change is only a beginning. Observation of these changes provokes new and different questions, for example, about how the changing place of women in the profession is influencing their everyday work as well as that of men, and as to how all of this might be altering the more general social organization of law firms. We know even less about such questions than we do about the changing demographic profile of lawyers.

However, . . . [we can] suggest some hypotheses. For example, . . . the movement of women away from smaller and toward larger firms and other bureaucratic settings suggest that the male-dominated smaller firms may be especially resistant to modifying the work roles assumed by men and women in the profession.

. . . [T]he largest proportion of women who began practice in small firms but who were not made partners remained in these firms as associates seven and more years later. So it seems doubtful that much change is occurring in these firms. It is also, of course, important to learn more about the kinds of gender-linked accommodations and compromises that are being reached in larger firms. Many of the women made partners in larger firms may be in restricted types of partnership arrangements, sometimes referred to by special designations such as tax partners, "non-equity" partners, junior partners, and the like. Some women who did not make partner in these firms also seem to have stayed on as associates in these firms. We are currently undertaking a five-year follow-up survey to examine in greater detail the kinds of work and family arrangements women and men lawyers in our sample are pursuing as their careers unfold.

Meanwhile, there is no certainty that the legal profession will continue to grow as it has over the past several decades, that shifts in the economic cycle will continue to operate on this profession as they have in the past, or that the results of this research can be generalized to other settings. In short, there is much that remains to be learned about the structural transformation of legal practice. □

Notes and Questions

1. The authors refer to Marc Galanter and Thomas Palay, *Tournament of Lawyers: The Transformation of the Big Law Firm* (Chicago: University of Chicago Press, 1991). Galanter and Palay trace the history of the very large law firm and offer an explanation for major changes now taking place.

During the Golden Age of the large firm—1950 through the early 1960s—major law firms that served corporate clients grew, particularly in New York City. They were built by promotion to partnership. The most prestigious firms hired recent graduates of elite law schools with the best credentials. These young associates tended to be white Christian males. They competed for promotion to partnership. Only a small minority of those hired as associates achieved this status. The chance of "making partner" ranged from one in seven to one in fifteen. Those who did not make partner had to leave the firm. Often they found positions in one of the firm's client's legal departments or in smaller firms. Partners were selected by proficiency, hard work, and ability to relate to clients. The firm might also consider a person's ability to bring business to the firm. Once a person became a partner, he could expect to hold that position for the rest of his working career. Generally, firms did not hire senior people laterally.

The situation of big-firm practice in the 1980s was sharply different. Major firms had grown in numbers and locations. One estimate is that in 1988 there were 35,000 lawyers at 115 firms with more than 200 lawyers and a total of 105,000 lawyers in 2000 firms larger than 20 lawyers. These large firms grew rapidly. Moreover, the practice of law became more specialized. Routine work went increasingly to the law departments of corporations—"in-house" counsel. The major law firms more and more dealt with the large contest and/or risk prone one-of-a-kind, "bet your company" transaction—litigation, takeovers, bankruptcies. Conditions in big-firm practice became much more competitive. Firms engaged in aggressive marketing. Furthermore, firms began merging or hiring laterally to get the people they needed to compete. Firms dissolved as well. The ratio of associates to partners increased sharply. This meant that a smaller percentage of associates would be promoted to partner. Firms began retaining senior associates as employees who would not be promoted to partner. The situation of a junior lawyer became more precarious and more pressured.

Firms have always made money by billing clients for the work that associates do at a higher rate than they paid the associates. As former associates are promoted to partner, firms need more associates to keep the stream of income flowing. New partners needed their own new associates to produce firm income. Moreover, firms had to promote at least some of their associates so that they could keep young lawyers working under high pressure at long hours—there had to be a chance at the reward of partnership as an incentive. As long as business increased, the system worked. However, like a house of cards, the system might collapse when business failed to increase to support more and more lawyers in a firm. Firms would then have to look to permanent associates or an even greater turn-over of associates to contain growth which could not be supported by increased business.

Hagan and his colleagues suggest that the increasing number of women in the profession helped firms cope with the new economic situation. Talented women were hired, worked very hard, but then would leave without being promoted to partner. They would be replaced by another wave rolling in from the law schools, ready to start the process again. Why might it be easier to exploit young women lawyers than young men—that is, in Hagan and his colleagues' words, why "in the last decade [have] young women lawyers . . . come to be seen as compliant and controllable participants in the growth process"? What are the likely consequences of this use of women's services? Are those women who do make partner likely to advocate changes in their firms' promotion practices to better the lot of women associates? How might women partners rationalize *not* advocating such changes? See also Sharyn L. Roach-Anleu, "Recruitment Practice and Women Lawyers' Employment: an Examination of In-House Legal Departments in the United States," 26 *Sociology* 651 (1992);

Hilary Sommerlad, "The Myth of Feminisation: Women and Cultural Change in the Legal Profession," 1 *International Journal of the Legal Profession* 31 (1994).

2. No development in the legal profession in recent years has been quite so important, perhaps, as the entry of women in substantial numbers. There were no women lawyers in the United States before the 1870s, and there were insignificant numbers until the 1960s. Most law firms before the 1950s would not hire women and those that did hire them were unlikely to promote them. Today, as we have seen, over 40% of American law students are women, and this means that a steadily rising percentage of the profession itself is made up of women. See, in general, Cynthia Fuchs Epstein, *Women in Law* 2d ed. (New York: Basic Books, 1993); Carrie Menkel-Meadow, "Feminization of the Legal Profession: The Comparative Sociology of Women Lawyers," in Volume 3 of Abel and Lewis (eds.), *Lawyers in Society,* (Berkeley: University of California Press,) p. 196.

3. Law students often go deeply in debt to pay for training so that they can play in the tournament of lawyers. In an uncertain job market, how do students gain the information needed to judge whether attending a particular law school—or law school in general—is a good investment? *U.S. News and World Report* annually rates law schools and publishes information about what it sees as the top twenty-five. It lists the average starting salary of graduates of these schools. How useful is this information for prospective law students? How do graduating law students gain the information needed to judge whether taking a position with a particular law firm is a good risk? For example, how would a woman law student discover the actual attitudes and practices of a particular firm concerning women associates? What would she likely learn from the partners who interview her when she applied for a position as an associate?

55. *Losing Its Allure: Lawyer/Legislators Are a Dying Breed. It Just Doesn't Pay*

Andrew Blum

National Law Journal, September 7, 1992, p. 1

☐ . . . Nowadays, many lawyer/legislators are finding it increasingly difficult to hold down both jobs. With law much more competitive and legislating more time-consuming and complicated, many lawyer/legislators have left public service. Though some observers say this is affecting legislation, many say the public—and lawyers' clients—aren't concerned about the departure and see no difference in their handiwork.

There is "less interest on the part of lawyers in standing for legislative office," says Joel F. Henning, senior vice president of Somerville, N.J.'s Hildebrandt, Inc., a legal consulting firm. "There is not the sense of public service that used to suffice the Jeffersonian ideal, [and] being in a state legislature no longer necessarily correlates with maximizing your legal business."

Clients don't care if a lawyer is in the legislature, Mr. Henning asserts, adding, "There are no benefits. No state legislator makes enough money to justify the investment of his or her time."

He notes that with the passage of strict ethics laws and reduced government spending for contracts, the advantage for business contacts of being a lawyer/legislator has dropped.

In Virginia, legislators make $18,000 a year plus $6,000 in expenses. The House of Delegates meets for 60 days in even-numbered years and 45 days in odd-numbered years. And New York's high-salaried Legislature meets from January through June/July, with annual pay of $57,000 plus stipends for committee and leadership positions: hardly a lot of money if you're used to raking in the contingency fees or partnership draws . . .

It seems as if many lawyers are making the salary calculations: A study of all 50 states shows a trend away from lawyers serving in state legislatures. The study, conducted by the National Conference of State Legislatures in 1986, is the most current nationwide survey. Keeping track of the number of lawyer/legislators is not as easy as it might seem. Observers say surveys can be skewed because some lawyers list their sole occupation as legislator.

Sixteen percent, or 1,200, of the nation's 7,500 state legislators are attorneys, the study showed. That's down from 20 percent in 1979 and 22 percent in 1976. The study also found that in 43 state legislatures the percentage of lawyers had dropped since 1976, while in five states the percentage had increased and in two state legislatures there was no change . . . .

The only survey of lawyer/legislators since the 1986 NCSL survey was released this year by Mark C. Miller, an assistant professor of government at Clark University. He delivered his findings to the Law and Society Association in Philadelphia in May . . . .

"There was an overall sharp decline of lawyer/legislators in the 1970s, but then it leveled off in 1980s," he says. Professor Miller's survey was less definitive: He focused only on nine states—Texas, California, Massachusetts, Ohio, North Carolina, Colorado, New Hampshire, Delaware and Virginia—comparing the years 1979, 1986 and 1991.

In Virginia, for example, Professor Miller's study found that lawyers comprised 67 percent of the state Senate in 1979, 40 of the 1986 and 43 percent in 1991. In Texas, meanwhile, the numbers went from 58 percent in 1979 to 55 percent in 1986 to 45 percent last year . . . .

[T]he jury is still out on whether the departure of lawyer/legislators makes a difference . . . .

New York's Mr. Hannon says having fewer lawyers hurts the daily

ATTORNEYS IN STATE LEGISLATURES

State	Number of Legislators	Attorneys
Virginia	Senate: 40 members	43% (17)
	Lower house: 100 members	43% (43)
Texas	Senate: 31 members	45% (14)
	Lower house: 149 members	33% (49)
California	Senate: 39 members	25% (10)
	Lower house: 80 members	20% (16)
Massachusetts	Senate: 39 members	48% (19)
	Lower house: 158 members	23% (36)
Ohio	Senate: 33 members	27% (9)
	Lower house: 99 members	18% (18)
North Carolina	Senate: 50 members	34% (17)
	Lower house: 120 members	17% (20)
Colorado	Senate: 35 members	22% (8)
	Lower house: 65 members	18% (12)
New Hampshire	Senate: 24 members	8% (2)
	Lower house: 391 members	8% (8)
Delaware	Senate: 21 members	5% (1)
	Lower house: 41 members	2% (1)

Source: Mark C. Miller, assistant professor of government, Clark University, 1992 presentations to the Law and Society Association and the American Political Science Association.

process. With fewer lawyers, he says, "you have . . . many decision-makers who come to rely on their own counsels or some other staff counsels and therefore go through the diffusing effect of understanding . . . a proposed statute."

Clark's Professor Miller disagrees, noting that most academic research has found little substantive effect from fewer lawyers. "The only effect there is, is when court reform comes up and there are a lot of lawyers in the legislature, it is supported by trial lawyers," he says.

Otherwise, Professor Miller says, when there are a lot of lawyers in the legislature, they are more concerned with process and procedure. And with fewer lawyers, legislators are better able to reach a consensus faster—though the laws passed are not necessarily different.

Allan Rosenthal, director of the Eagleton Institute of Politics at Rutgers University in New Brunswick, N.J., says fewer lawyers have an effect in that you "don't get the legal perspective as much." And, he adds, it is useful for them to be in the process.

"Legislation is more dependent on staff than before," Mr. Rosenthal says. "If lawyers are members, it provides a good counterbalance to the reliance on staff." Nonetheless, he believes that legislation is essentially the same with fewer lawyers, the only difference being marginal and subtle . . . □

NOTES AND QUESTIONS

1. Our stereotype of the lawyer is of a man or woman trying a case before a court. But presidents, governors, legislators, and directors of administrative agencies, or members of the ever-growing staffs of these people also are often lawyers. The number of lawyer-legislators may be declining, but it is still substantial. Does it make a difference to legislatures whether they have many or few lawyers? Dick Dahl, "A Natural Marriage," *Massachusetts Lawyers Weekly*, September 28, 1992, p. 29, says:

> In 'Democracy in America,' which was written more than 150 years ago, Alexis de Tocqueville commented at length about the remarkable preponderance of lawyers in American legislative life, and he did so in a manner that would not please those who say there are too many lawyers. To de Toqueville, lawyers were a critically necessary component of democracy, comprising a class "of the people," yet with aristocratic inclinations.
>
> "Lawyers, forming the only enlightened class not distrusted by the people, are naturally called on to fill most public functions," he wrote . . . . [L]awyers tended to serve the status quo, operating as "an almost invisible brake" when "the American people let themselves get intoxicated by their passions." . . .
>
> [Benjamin Fierro III, General Counsel of the Massachusetts Bar Association, says:] if one has the personal characteristics which the practice of law rewards, one is drawn to elective office almost by definition.
>
> "Lawyers deal with people all the time," he says. "If you run for office, you have to like people."
>
> Lawyers are accustomed to the role of being advocates for their clients. In the legislature, or other elective body, they take readily to the role of advocates for their constituents, Fierro says . . . .
>
> [Another lawyer/legislator said:] "I think there's a tendency [by lawyers] to go down there [to the legislature] and try to get along with everybody . . . ."

In 1992, is it likely that lawyers are "a class of the people, yet with aristocratic inclinations?" Are they likely to serve as "an almost invisible brake?" If they represent their constituents, will they fail to consider the general interest beyond their district? Are lawyers likely to fight for principle or, as suggested, are they likely to get along by going along and negotiating compromises? How might we answer any or all of these questions?

2. Mark C. Miller, in "Lawyers in Congress: What Difference Does It Make?," 20 *Congress & The Presidency* 1 (1993), interviewed over 75 members and staff of the U.S. House of Representatives in 1989. His informants said that lawyer-members understood the process better and respected such things as following procedures and the techniques of legislative drafting. A major difference between lawyers and non-lawyers was their attitudes toward the federal courts. "Because lawyer members seem extremely hesitant to make rash decisions concerning decisions from the courts, the lawyers in Congress feel that congressional reactions to court decisions should be much slower than

reactions to [administrative] agency decisions, which are perceived to be much more politically motivated" (p. 16). In this way, the lawyer-members and staff protect the courts.

3. Lawyers often serve in high level positions in executive agencies in both state and federal governments as well. For example, both President Clinton and his wife, Hillary Rodham Clinton are graduates of the Yale Law School. Over 75% of the Clinton cabinet members and over 35% of the key sub-cabinet appointments were lawyers.

Does a background as a lawyer make any difference? Some have speculated that lawyers would be more legalistic, less willing to compromise, more insistent on following procedures and the like than those trained in other fields who run agencies. Kenneth E. Boulding, an economist, in 190 *Science* 423 (1975) asserts:

> The lawyer's "problem" is not to produce testable propositions, but to win the case. For politicians, likewise, the problem is to win elections and to please the majority of their constituents. The "scientific" problem-solving which is involved in getting the best legislation or the best decisions is incidental to the larger problem of political survival. We should not necessarily blame lawyers and politicians for behaving like lawyers and politicians. It is, in fact, what we hire them and elect them to do. The legal and political subculture is not the result of pure chicanery and foolishness. It has evolved over many generations for some very good reasons. The main reason is that where decisions involve distributional changes, that is, where they make some people better off and some people worse off, problem-solving in the scientific sense would not come up with any answers. Legal and political procedures, such as trials and elections, are essentially social rituals designed to minimize the costs of conflict. The price of cheap conflict, however, may be bad problem-solving in terms of the actual consequences of decisions. So far, the social invention that will resolve this dilemma does not yet seem to have been made.[169]

John P. Plumlee, "Lawyers as Bureaucrats: The Impact of Legal Training in the Higher Civil Service," 41 *Public Administration Review* 220 (1981), found that government executives who had legal training tended to be more liberal and less cynical than those without such training. However, the differences were not great enough to be statistically significant. Generally, he found, those who rise to the top of administrative agencies tend to act in a similar fashion whatever their education or professional credentials. There is little published material on the work of lawyers *inside* government, but see Donald L. Horowitz, *The Jurocracy* (Lexington, Mass.: Lexington Books, 1977). An interesting historical account of an important period in which lawyers played a crucial role in government is Peter H. Irons, *The New Deal Lawyers* (Princeton, N.J.: Princeton University Press, 1982).

4. Lawyers also are lobbyists, pressing client interests before Congress and

---

169. Copyright © 1975 by the American Association for the Advancement of Science. Reprinted by permission.

state legislatures. Robert L. Nelson, John P. Heinz, Edward O. Laumann, and Robert H. Salisbury, in "Private Representation in Washington: Surveying the Structure of Influence," 1987 *American Bar Foundation Research Journal* 141, interviewed 776 people who represented private interests. They found that lawyers are a significant group among such representatives, but they are not as numerous nor as active in policy making as generally assumed. Representatives, lawyers, and others, are not likely to exercise influence in the policy-making process beyond that exerted by their client organizations. Laumann and Heinz, in "Washington Lawyers and Others: The Structure of Washington Representation," 37 *Stanford Law Review* 465, 501 (1985), conclude:

> [E]ven the formal occupational distinctions between lawyer and nonlawyer representatives may be breaking down. If it is true not only that lawyer and nonlawyer representatives do similar work, serve much the same clients, are recruited from similar social backgrounds, and maintain relationships with substantially overlapping networks of government officials and industry contacts, but also that they work side-by-side in the same firms and are hired in common by clients, then one would be hard pressed to identify the functional distinctions between lawyers and nonlawyers. As we noted . . . the distance between the lawyer and client may also be narrowing. That some Washington lawyers are creating, housing, and maintaining trade association clients is an example of how tenuous the distinction between lawyer and client has become.

The authors end their article by asserting: "for many purposes we might safely ignore the fact that the Washington lawyer is a lawyer" (p. 502). The work of this research team has been published as a book, John P. Heinz, Edward O. Laumann, Robert L. Nelson, and Robert H. Salisbury, *The Hollow Core: Private Interests in National Policy-Making* (Cambridge, Mass.: Harvard University Press, 1993).

56. What Have Lawyers Done for American Business? The Case of Baker & Botts of Houston

Kenneth Lipartito

64 *Business History Review* 490 (1990)

☐ From its earliest years, big business has needed lawyers. Beginning in the 1860s, corporations sought out top New York attorneys for their skills in drafting increasingly complex charters, indentures, and business contracts, as well as for their advice in economic matters. Within a few years, these new demands were reshaping the legal profession in the nation and bringing forth a new breed of corporate lawyers who earned their livelihood not through florid courtroom speeches, but by giving opinions on the law concerning specific issues that affected business firms. Attorneys entered the behind-the-scenes world of conferences and negotiations, representing business especially before government and regulatory bodies. They became administrators and managers of large volumes of legal work for corporate clients, with whom they established ongoing relationships. And they became organizers and managers of their own growing law firms . . . .

LAWYERS IN LEGAL AND BUSINESS HISTORY

. . . The services that legal specialists provided to business can be broken down into three categories. First, they solved the many legal problems surrounding corporate organization that arose as business grew and expanded. Second, they oversaw relations between their clients and the state. Third, they served as a link between entrepreneurs and investors. Some also wrote influential treatises on matters of obvious interest to corporations, such as freedom of contract, regulation of interstate commerce, and the implications of the Fourteenth Amendment. Most of their work, however, involved neither precedent-setting decisions nor the articulation of abstract legal theories. Rather, attorneys focused on mundane, instrumental questions of what was legal and acceptable in a certain place at a certain time and how to accomplish their clients' wishes. In all areas, moreover, doctrinal expertise was only one of the things that they provided to corporations. Business firms also needed their counselors' social connections and political influence, especially in the years before the New Deal. For a variety of reasons, lawyers in America have been called on to fulfill roles and to execute functions for which other social groups have been responsible in other societies.

LAWYERS AND CORPORATE REORGANIZATIONS

Partners in great eastern firms such as Cravath, Swaine and Moore, Sullivan & Cromwell, and Shearman & Sterling undertook much of the legal work surrounding corporate organizations and reorganizations. Beginning in the 1870s and 1880s, they served as tacticians in the struggles of the "robber barons," developing a wide array of legal ploys in the process. By the 1890s, a fraternity of corporate counselors, mainly located in New York, had established themselves as the premier experts in the emerging practice of business reorganization. In these endeavors, they were much more than technicians, . . . [because they] advise[d] clients both as to the practical and legal aspects of questions.

The numerous panics and downturns of the late nineteenth and early twentieth centuries provided lawyers with plentiful experience with reorganizations. During this period nearly every major railroad went into receivership and had to be restructured. Bankrupt railroads had little value. Like most large enterprises, they were worth far more as going concerns than as inert collections of tangible assets. Investors—and indeed society as a whole—therefore had much to gain by keeping the property intact. In this work, lawyers proved invaluable. They persuaded the courts to appoint receivers acceptable to investment bankers, fended off threats of foreclosure by jittery creditors, and simplified the corporate structure of the roads when reorganizations were completed. Of these tasks, the first two were the most important. Most of the railroads were a hodge-podge of lines financed by a wide array of instruments, including first and second mortgage bonds, income bonds, and common and preferred stock. The diversity of interests among lienholders and creditors was extremely wide and their behavior highly unpredictable. Each creditor of each line in each state could file suit and block reorganization plans. Groups of bondholders, many of them foreign, were also prone to panic and to start foreclosure proceedings, which could result in liquidation of property at fire sale prices.

Lawyers found the route through these entanglements. Before the passage of the federal Bankruptcy Act of 1898, judges provided an opening in the famous—and, to some, infamous—equity receivership. This extremely flexible device protected property from immediate foreclosure while cutting off many smaller creditors' claims. Under its umbrella, New York lawyers and investment bankers were able to form reorganization committees, which assumed control of the property by getting bondholders to exchange their securities for new trust certificates. By handing over their bonds, the creditors gave consent to the protective committee to manage the property. Lawyers drew up the contracts and supervised the negotiations that decided who would receive what when the reorganization was completed. Generally, all creditors brought into the reorganization were expected to give up something of value and then to contribute more capital, so the atmosphere cold be rife with suspicion and acrimony. Handling this situation required both a cool head at the negotiating table and fine legal draftsmanship to write contracts that secured multiple types of financial instruments and comported with common law doctrine.

Lawyers also oversaw a final step—dealing with unsecured creditors and others left out of the reorganization. Dangerous legal brushfires could break out if this group took the corporation to court to secure its claim on assets. The law generally specified the order of priority for payment, but in some reorganizations, stockholders—legally the last entitled to payment—were brought in ahead of general creditors. This arrangement had practical value; stockholders, it was hoped, would advance more money. But general creditors, many of them small contractors and workers, had the law on their side. They were able to make themselves heard as legal doctrine shifted in their favor in the early twentieth century. Lawyers thus had to remain abreast of the law to gain for receivers the broad discretionary powers that they sought in order to effect reorganization.

Through the law, corporate attorneys helped to bring into a consolidated plan large numbers of diverse investors with conflicting interests. Of course, the law was far from a perfect device for these purposes. Sometimes judges insisted on recognizing minority shareholders and small creditors with whom the larger investors would have happily dispensed. In these cases, the courts refused to sanction plans that, though economically efficient, violated deeply embedded notions of equity. Skillful attorneys steered their clients around these shoals. They used the law to bring contentious parties to the bargaining table and to enforce contracts that secured needed capital. Although attorneys . . . dreamed of a simpler system in which the courts merely oversaw and enforced agreements forged by the majority of investors, in fact the complex instruments worked out by corporate counselors provided a method of consolidating and reorganizing properties where no other existed.

Much of this work touched on sensitive legal questions at the state and local levels. Western and southern states, already hostile to railroads, resented the legal fictions that apparently allowed outside capitalists to escape scrutiny by state courts and to emerge with their control of properties intact. Investors who felt cheated by the terms of reorganization or shippers who feared the monopoly power of the railroads influenced the state legislatures that wrote corporation laws. Wary of the power that corporations exerted, Texas, for example, added restrictions on railroad consolidations, excess capital, trust arrangements, subsidiary investments, and mergers to its laws between 1875 and 1900 . . . . There was still enough flexibility in the federal system to allow state governments, representing local producers and competitors of corporations, to affect the process of reorganization.

Facing hostile state governments, lawyers often had to carve out legal sanction for corporate activities where none yet existed. In the agrarian South and West, the situation was particularly unstable. The legality of any particular action was often unclear, and many steps, though legal, could lead to a backlash, as often happened with railroad reorganizations . . . .

Regional and local lawyers, rather than prominent metropolitan attorneys, spearheaded the effort against this legal localism. Establishing connections with major national corporations active in their areas, these lawyers formed modern corporate law firms in second-tier cities such as Kansas City, Houston, and St. Louis. Big business clients provided sufficient income to allow them to organize their firms like top-level partnerships in New York and Chicago. Unlike their peers who were still wedded to the local economy, these regional firms gradually deemphasized land conveyancing, debt collection, and title investigations and oriented their practices around major corporate clients. They represented national-scale organizations before state courts, regulatory agencies, and municipal councils. Borrowing doctrine and precedents established earlier in more industrial states, they helped to break down legal limits and to reverse suspicion of corporations across the country.

The Houston law firm of Baker & Botts was typical of these regional corporate firms. Beginning in the 1870s and 1880s, this partnership represented the railroad barons Jay Gould and Collis P. Huntington, who were fighting for control of Texas's transportation network. Over time, the firm deliberately identified itself with other examples of "alien," or northern, capital in Texas: interstate railroad combines, major oil companies, insurance underwriters, and utility holding companies. By the early twentieth century, Baker & Botts was an outpost of Wall Street values in what was still largely a rural, agrarian society. When corporations operating in the state wanted to rearrange their enterprises, acquire subsidiaries, or issue new securities, they relied on Baker & Botts to steer them through the thicket of laws reflecting suspicion of large, outside corporations.

One of the firm's most important early cases involved the effort of Southern Pacific president E. H. Harriman to consolidate and refinance some of his Texas lines in 1905. The first roadblock Harriman encountered was a state constitutional prohibition against railroad mergers. That barrier fell when Baker & Botts attorney Hiram Garwood secured a special dispensation from the state legislature. Legislative approval was only the first step in a long and winding trail, however. Effecting reorganization raised a host of legal issues: what rights did minority stockholders have? How would bondholders and others with liens on railroad property be treated? Who would be paid dividends and on what earnings? Texas law provided little guidance on these matters. Where statutory and state common law spoke, it was generally in favor of local and minority investors. This proved a dangerous combination when one group of bondholders filed a "strike" suit against the consolidation, forcing a costly settlement on the Southern Pacific.[170]

Before the consolidation was completed, the railroad also had to face the Texas Railroad Commission, a regulatory body charged with overseeing corporate finance to prevent stock watering. Since the reorganized Southern Pacific lines planned to issue new long-term debt, the question of their value was crucial. Under Texas law, total capitalization could not exceed assessed value of property. But there was no clear method by which to establish value. Important accounting categories such as net earnings, good will, and depreciation were open to interpretation. In the end, the key decisions on these matters were made through negotiation between the railroad's lawyers and the members of

---

170. These suits were a common nuisance and were filed by "professional obstructors" to extort payment from reorganizing corporations . . .

the railroad commission. The commission eventually "corrected" its figures, permitting the railroad to issue the obligations it wanted.

Throughout the early decades of the twentieth century, lawyers assisted in corporate reorganizations for other industries in a similar manner. New York attorneys with close ties to major investment houses such as J. P. Morgan and Kuhn, Loeb handled the legal affairs surrounding horizontal and vertical integration. This elite group wrote the agreements that merged companies, and exchanged old capital for new. Progressive Era reforms aimed at sniffing out monopoly, managerial malfeasance, and financial impropriety sometimes raised challenging problems for corporate attorneys, but in most other aspects this work became fairly routine.[171]

At the regional level, matters were less easily settled, and suspicion of high finance and corporate power provided a steady stream of work for lawyers. In Texas in the 1920s and 1930s, for example, utility holding companies hired Baker & Botts attorneys to represent them before the state attorney general's office to gain approval of financial innovations such as open-ended mortgages and no-par value stock. Consolidations also presented special problems in a state wary of trusts and monopolies. In one instance, the lawyers had to find an organizational form that would allow their client to sidestep legal restrictions, negotiate settlements with old investors, and serve as the incorporators and officers of a subsidiary enterprise. This sort of day-to-day work required people on the spot, which explains why even giant interstate combines engaged regional firms in each state in which they operated.

LAWYERS AND THE POLITICS OF BUSINESS

. . . Lawyers were well positioned to handle corporations' relations with government for a variety of reasons. First, they have always occupied key positions on the "fringes of the state," as officers of the courts and frequently as elected lawmakers. Also, since American society lacked the well-developed civil service bureaucracy of other nations, lawyers were often called on to serve in key administrative posts, and this expertise became available to corporate clients as lawyers went in and out of the revolving door between the private and public sectors. America's own ambivalence over strong central administration also contributed to the presence of lawyers in public policy. When federal judges struck down laws and regulations on constitutional grounds, their rulings gave lawyers ammunition with which to snipe at government policies. To defend themselves, regulators had to pay strict atten-

---

171. Beyond handling the technical issues of consolidation, lawyers also carried on the negotiations that created cartels and trusts, though their work in formal matters was perhaps more significant, given the importance of this form of combination in American business history.

tion to due process and to give equal representation to all parties. The outcome was an intensely "legalistic" type of regulation. In this environment, lawyers representing private parties became crucial policymakers. They did not, however, act as independent experts searching for efficient and equitable solutions to social and economic problems. Rather, they doggedly pursued the interests of their clients, which often made them among the strongest foes of the new regulatory state . . . .

Although federal law in the late nineteenth and early twentieth centuries set policy in many areas, before the New Deal much of the politics of business still consisted of day-to-day relations between state governments and their corporate citizens. In this period, the Supreme Court was still determining the balance between state and federal regulation. Gradually the Court moved to strengthen federal power, but throughout the Progressive Era it also abandoned earlier doctrines that had been used to strike down state and local laws. Southern states' rights advocates, joined surprisingly at times by national corporations, also made sure that the boundary between federal and state power was not set too far inside federal territory. But most important, social and economic conditions made business-government relations below the national level an important and hotly contested arena.

The economy of early twentieth century America was still marked by strong conflicts between national corporations and small-scale, local producers, farmers, and merchants. Numerous, vocal, and organized, these local interests pressed their state legislatures to pass laws and regulations that protected them against interstate combines . . . . Clashes between local and corporate interests . . . remained a feature of the American political economy.

Although it has commonly been assumed that corporations had little to fear from state regulation, the record shows that states possessed substantial common law and statutory powers and that they were prepared to use them. At the state level, *quo warranto* proceedings, unlike the narrower Sherman Act, could be employed against virtually any perceived corporate abuse. Even interstate companies were subject to such proceedings, and at various times Standard Oil, American Tobacco, Armour Packing, and American Sugar Refining found themselves brought before state courts. The Texas legislature wrote its antitrust laws with the "intent to terrify" and for a time enforced them effectively against the Standard Oil combine. Until 1917, Texas state law even prohibited vertical integration, reflecting the fears of small oil products that they would be "swallowed up" by the giants of the industry. This highly charged political environment forced executives of Texas oil companies to consult closely with their attorneys in nearly everything they did.

There is good reason to suspect that lawyers were largely responsible for overcoming the roadblocks thrown up by state governments against corporations . . . . [W]hen state regulatory endeavors failed, it was more from a want of effective, day-to-day implementation of existing laws than from a lack of will or legal authority . . . . [S]tate labor laws designed to protect workers suffered from poor administration. This was a weakness that lawyers were likely to have exploited. In antitrust as well, states were ill-equipped to combat corporations and their attorneys. Small, underfunded offices of attorneys general were no match for corporate law firms, with their access to the resources of huge interstate corporations. Moving from courtroom to boardroom to legislative hall, lawyers found ways around restrictive state laws, negotiated compromises that benefited their clients, and lobbied for changes and amendments to regulatory statutes.

Regional corporate law firms handled most of this sort of work. Tied to the national economy through their clients, they possessed the necessary familiarity with state law and local customs to counter the activities of aggressive state governments. In Texas, for example, Baker & Botts helped to free interstate railroads from some of the regulations enacted by the Texas Railroad Commission. In an important series of cases, the Texas attorneys joined forces with New York-based counsel to circumscribe the commission's powers. Robert Scott Lovett, then a partner in Baker & Botts, and well-known corporation lawyer John Dillon teamed up in the important *Reagan v. Farmer's Loan and Trust* case of 1894 to challenge the commission's rate-making authority. There the United States Supreme Court ruled that rate regulation, though legal, had to guarantee railroads a fair return on their property. With the high court ready to review any rate decision that it felt unduly confiscated private property, lawyers possessed a powerful club to use against commissions. In Texas, they wielded this club effectively in 1898 by securing an injunction against the railroad commission's tariffs, eventually forcing negotiations. Thereafter the regulators knew that corporation attorneys were carefully monitoring their decisions and were prepared to carry out protracted challenges to those that adversely affected their clients' welfare. Pressure of this sort no doubt intimidated regulators and made them more tractable to corporations.

It was not always necessary for lawyers to undermine regulatory authority to frustrate the aims of state laws. Texas continued to ban consolidations of competing rail lines, but roads such as the Southern Pacific were able to operate their properties in the state under subsidiaries that appeared to be independent. Baker & Botts attorneys worked out the legal fictions necessary for such arrangements. They incorporated each subsidiary separately, wrote leasing agreements and negotiated asset purchases that allowed the parent company to gain control of properties, and argued before the public and the attorney general for a narrow construction of the state's anti-consolidation laws. If nominal from a managerial point of view, these arrangements were very important politically. They permitted the railroad to maneuver around regulations that reflected a deep ambivalence in the society toward modern business enterprise. In this way, Texas gained an integrated transportation system without having to reopen highly charged and divisive issues.

Often successful at overturning or circumventing restrictive state laws, lawyers also found points of compromise between their clients and local interests. As the representatives of what were perceived to be "foreign" corporations, attorneys in firms like Baker & Botts operated at a pivotal position between the local economy and the emerging national one. The tensions in this position were apparent. Identified as the advance guard of corporate penetration, regional corporate attorneys were attacked as "the capitalist's caddie" and as lawyers "as soulless as the corporations [they] serve" by rural critics and small-town business people. These interests also employed their own attorneys, who did battle with the corporate representatives in the courts, the legislatures, and eventually the bar associations over hotly disputed issues such as monopoly and antitrust. Under these conditions, corporate attorneys sought compromises where they could. By doing so, they ultimately made it possible for localists to accept the presence of large-scale corporations.

By combining the roles of big business advocates and pro-business community boosters, prominent regional attorneys were able to forge accords between contentious parties. In early twentieth-century Houston, Baker & Botts lawyers performed frequently in this dual role to settle fights between the city and its utility service companies. Exhibiting more finesse than iron fist, they wrote settlements that mildly regulated the utilities while keeping the city on a growth-first path. These accords secured extended franchises for the city's gas, transit, and electric companies in exchange for modest rate reductions or promises of rapid service expansion. In one particularly creative example, Baker & Botts lawyers designed a profit-sharing plan between Houston Lighting & Power Company (HL&P) and the city. Under the plan, the utility paid no taxes and was free to earn up to an 8 percent return on capital; HL&P split any further profits equally with the city. This arrangement gave Houston consumers protection against monopoly exploitation and the company an incentive to expand service rapidly in a growing market . . . .

Although negotiation and litigation often surmounted adverse regulations, sometimes it was necessary for lawyers to intervene directly in the legislative process. Lobbying went beyond the formalities of law, but lawyers often made good lobbyists; they were familiar with legal doctrine and had useful rhetorical and oratorical skills. Perhaps even more important, their wide range of clients allowed them special insight into the political concerns and ideological leanings of their communities.[172]

Hiram Garwood of Baker & Botts exploited such insight before the Texas legislature during a protracted debate over a bill to form a state

---

172. . . . [L]awyers were successful when they could use their professional status to appear objective.

utilities commission. The former state representative understood which arguments to deploy against the proposed legislation. Focusing on a provision that exempted "all cities and towns with regulatory powers" from oversight by the new regulatory administration, he effectively played on the jealousies between incorporated municipalities, which had already written regulatory powers into their charters, and unincorporated places, which could not. Thus, Garwood used a provision originally intended to gain support for the bill by recognizing Texas's strong tradition of home rule to provoke a controversy that prevented a solid majority from forming behind the bill. Only a skillful and knowledgeable local attorney could have known how to exploit these issues.

Although state and local regulatory laws gradually grew more permissive, through the 1920s there were sufficient business-government conflicts to keep lawyers busy. In Texas railroad consolidations remained illegal, and on occasion an ambitious attorney general would enforce state antitrust laws against companies suspected of price fixing. Before the creation of the Securities and Exchange Commission (SEC), Texas and several other states also passed "blue-sky laws" to regulate securities trading. None of these regulatory ventures had quite the impact of the Populist-inspired anti-corporation campaigns of the late nineteenth century, but they required attorneys to go behind the scenes in negotiations with regulators to chart permissible courses. This labor was often fruitful. In 1927 Baker & Botts lawyers gained permission from a tolerant attorney general to fold all of the Southern Pacific's Texas lines into a single subsidiary.

While state-level business regulation was declining in significance, new challenges to corporate autonomy were arising from other quarters, such as labor, consumer, and liability laws. Railroads, for example, confronted numerous tort cases as definitions of liability widened at the end of the nineteenth century. Farmers took railroads to court for damages caused by fires started from sparks given off by wheels and engines; passengers demanded compensation for injuries sustained during travel; disabled workers sued their employers. Though individually such suits involved small settlements, collectively they added up to a significant sum.

Legal doctrines of the day could have protected businesses from such claims, but, for a variety of reasons corporations suffered breaches in their legal lines of defense. Many states modified probusiness rules, through legislation. Often the judges and juries who heard liability cases let their own feeling about railroads and corporations spill over into their decisions. In remote counties of the South and West in particular, citizens were not disposed to look favorably on an enterprise that they regarded as a grinding monopoly.

Antipathy toward big business turned Texas into a hot-bed for anti-railroad personal injury litigation. In the early twentieth century, railroads there were paying out six to ten times the amount of damages per mile as in neighboring states. Edwin Parker of Baker & Botts believed that part of the problem stemmed from long-held resentments against railroads, particularly during the years in which they had been in receivership and thus not liable for such claims. Part of the cause was also the "damage-suit fraternity," which was drumming up business against deep-pocketed defendants by employing "strikers" and "runners" to induce injured parties into contingency-fee suits rather than taking the settlements offered by the railroads. In West Texas plaintiffs were virtually assured of jury trials by sympathetic peers, and few judges were willing to risk their chances for reelection by overturning on error the resulting large awards. In Parker's view, the entire court system had become politicized, from the top judges down to the county commissioners who provided courts with advice on prospective jurors.

For Parker and the lawyers who represented business clients, the cure for this plague of litigation was bar reform. It was up to the leaders of the profession to use the state bar association against the "corruption of public morals" caused by the practices of money-grubbing lawyers . . . . Although the reformers enjoyed a brief flourish of success, their efforts eventually collapsed . . . .

While some attorneys tried to help their clients by reforming the profession, others developed legal strategies for combating litigants. In Texas the Southern Pacific called on the many lawyers it engaged in towns along its extensive right-of-way to try damage suits. These so-called division and local attorneys were far better equipped for this sort of work than lawyers from New York or even from Houston, for success often turned on a lawyer's close connections to the community. The railroad needed attorneys with "local influence" and "familiarity and influence with the jurors as well as standing with the local judges." Railroad attorneys were expected to get to know members of jury panels and to bring every legitimate influence to bear to overcome any local prejudice which may exist against the railroad. They were also to promote good feeling between the Company and the people, and to mold public opinion and create a sentiment favorable to railroad companies.

Railroads provided the resources needed to carry out these tasks. They authorized negotiation and settlement in place of litigation; they struck secret bargains that paid off claimants and rewarded attorneys who agreed not to take cases against railroads. Perhaps most effective and controversial were free passes, handed out to lawyers as well as to state representatives, sheriffs, commissioners, bailiffs, and others of local influence. Attorneys who took the passes had to promise not to represent clients against railroads. In an age of high transportation costs and in a state of long distances, such inducements were hard for struggling lawyers to turn down.

Railroads also began to rationalize and routinize their litigation. The Southern Pacific relied on its chief Texas counsel, Baker & Botts, to oversee and coordinate the activities of the scattered division and local attorneys. The law firm passed on directives and guidelines set by Southern Pacific executives concerning standards for settlements, range of payments, and remuneration for railroad lawyers. The Houston attorneys also distributed the highly desirable free passes and exhorted all attorneys working for the railroad to take a broad personal interest in the well-being of their client. Management such as this cut across lawyers' traditional prerogatives of independence, and some attorneys resented what they felt was treatment more befitting an employee than a professional. Work for modern corporate enterprise, however, demanded subordinating some professional independence and judgment to the corporate hierarchy, even taking orders from "peers" in Houston. Those who accepted the new managerial order accepted as well some intrusions into their professional lives in exchange for the rewards of regular pay and referrals to other clients . . . .

LAWYERS AND FINANCE

No aspect of lawyers' work demonstrates their wide range of functions beyond the law better than finance, where they served as intermediaries to forge a national capital market. Lawyers became active in this realm because they possessed needed technical expertise in securities law, because their opinions on credit-worthiness and legality provided needed assurances to investors, and, perhaps most important, because they had a wide array of personal and professional contacts that put them at the nexus of many financial relationships.[173] Involvement in their clients' business affairs gave lawyers exposure to a variety of investment opportunities into which they could direct their own funds or those of others who came to them for advice. Legal work also furnished them with the political connections, knowledge of local economic conditions, and personal acquaintance with business leaders that were a necessary part of financial deals. Others were also capable of bringing together capital and capitalist, but lawyers—with their cosmopolitan education and experience and their carefully cultivated investment in reputation—were especially well prepared for this work. By the nature of their profession, lawyers were paid to render advice and opinions, and successful attorneys prospered in good part because their opinions commanded trust. This same asset—trust—could be exploited in nonlegal advice to structure deals involving distant lenders and borrowers. Lenders could be assured that someone was on hand to repair contractual breakdowns or to fight adverse government regulations.

173. Lawyers also tended to be articulate, educated and persistent of place, qualities that would have helped make them well entrenched in elite networks . . . .

Borrowers in turn depended on the connections of corporate attorneys within and outside the community to find sources of funds. And both were willing to trust a professional with substantial experience in handling other people's money.

For these reasons, lawyers at the local and regional levels had long been important mobilizers of capital for the communities in which they lived . . . . If lawyers personally commanded only a small percentage of the capital needed for investment, they nonetheless had access to other sources. Many were appointed trustees for estates, which often gave them control over substantial accumulations of funds. The $9.8 million Rice Trust in Houston, for example, was overseen by Baker & Botts partner James A. Baker, who guided its funds into the first generation of downtown office buildings in the city.

Lawyers' professional and client connections outside their communities also gave them access to important sources of investment capital. Frequently selected for their trustworthy reputations to sit on bank boards, they had opportunities to draw on interregional capital flows through correspondent banking relationships. Those regional and local attorneys who served large national corporations forged still other external contacts that helped to build a national capital market. When urban utilities came under the control of holding companies, the lawyers serving them gained access to New York and Chicago banking houses. Such financial ties could be exploited in favor of other clients . . . .

THE CORPORATE LAW FIRM

Corporate lawyers were able to perform successfully the functions described in large part because they pioneered a new type of organization—the corporate law firm. This organization followed closely behind the emergence of modern corporate legal practice. Between 1870, when the first were founded, and 1915, they were the fastest growing segment of the profession. Usually "office lawyers" started them, people like Thomas Shearman and John Sterling, who broke with the famous jurist David Dudley Field to go to work for Jay Gould. These attorneys had a pragmatic and instrumental view of the law. Paying little attention to the line between law and business, they saw their legal training as a set of practical skills that could be applied to business needs. The organizational embodiment of this entrepreneurial spirit was the large law firm, which allowed lawyers to capture remunerative opportunities for legal services to corporations while retaining a measure of control over their work.[174] By 1904 a hundred of these

---

174. Lawyers were also motivated to change by the loss of traditional work in land conveyances, title investigations, and debt collections to title, mortgage, insurance and estate management companies . . . .

firms were in existence in New York and other cities across the nation. Gradually they evolved from two- to four-person partnerships into semibureaucratic organizations tailored specifically to the needs of big business clients.

The large law firm provided corporations with the same sort of ongoing, loyal, exclusive representation they could have expected from inside counsel. In general, American lawyers have conceived of their representational role in narrow terms: to obtain for clients what they want. The lawyers who developed large law practices were no exception to this rule. They also specialized at an early stage in corporate representation, separating themselves from other practitioners who served individuals and small businesses. Through specialization they gained an intimate inside knowledge of their clients' affairs, extremely useful in the many complex matters they handled. Specialization also helped breed strong loyalties, which assured that even the most "independent" corporate law firm would be closely tied both to its specific clients and to the corporate sector of the economy generally.

As closely as corporate attorneys identified with their clients, however, they still maintained some distance through their firms. Particularly before the New Deal, this line of division offered several important advantages. In matters involving trust, such as finance or bankruptcy proceedings, lawyers' professional status and organizational independence were reassuring to all parties involved. Labor representatives, stockholders, and creditors probably considered lawyers from law firms somewhat more trustworthy in negotiations than house counsel for corporations. In cases with strong political overtones, lawyers from outside firms could also present a more credible defense than could corporate employees . . . .

Professionals in law firms were also better equipped than inside counsel to provide corporations with the wide range of services that they needed. Corporate clients wanted ongoing, day-to-day representation in a variety of forums—before regulatory bodies, with financiers, in front of judges, in legislatures. Since, as noted, much of this work involved not simply technical skill, but connections, contacts, and local influence and knowledge, lawyers in strong, ongoing organizations well entrenched in the local environment were better able to develop these resources than lawyers who were corporate employees. Wall Street attorneys drew on their contacts in the financial community, Washington advocates on their influence with the federal government, Houston lawyers on their close connections with state and local authorities.

Before the New Deal explosion of national administrative bodies, the political and legal systems remained so decentralized that corporations had to contract for their legal needs from the outside in this fashion . . . . [O]utside firms enjoyed both economies of scale and, more important, economies of scope. Because they served a variety of clients, such organizations could develop a range of expertise, even in esoteric matters, far exceeding that of the lawyer working for just one company. They could also cultivate a web of contacts to draw on in representing corporations before local populations. In addition, such firms enjoyed efficiencies in the use of fixed capital—law libraries in the nineteenth century, sophisticated information processing equipment in recent years. Corporations would have needed to maintain huge legal staffs to have provided a comparable level of service by themselves. And unless they had been able to decentralize these staffs some how, they could never have linked them to the many places and environments in which their businesses operated.[175]

LAWYERS, LAW FIRMS, AND THE RATIONAL-IZATION OF THE LAW

. . . [C]hanges in the legal profession and in the practice of law have helped to spawn a new national market for legal services, one in which technical expertise rather than strong local influence or personal contacts matters most. In finance, for example, lawyers must now craft prospectuses that simultaneously meet SEC disclosure requirements, convince investors to invest their money, and do not jeopardize the client's competitive position. The explosion of federal regulations since the New Deal has also given lawyers new responsibilities. Securities laws, for example, make it incumbent on lawyers to use their expertise not just to serve their clients, but to assist in the smooth functioning of financial markets.

In a competitive market supplying universally available expertise, the old hierarchy of law firms has broken down. Partnerships in San Francisco, Los Angeles, Houston, and Atlanta now compete with traditional top firms in New York, Chicago, Boston, and Philadelphia. Many firms have opened branch offices around the country. Most have diversified their partnerships and eliminated nepotism; in a world governed by the supply and demand of expertise, local influence and contacts, social and ethnic background, and familial relations are no longer necessary to serve clients. Similarly, in-house legal staffs now handle

---

175. Depending heavily on demand for this sort of custom work to survive, law firms have watched over their client lists carefully. Only those customers requiring this sort of special attention provided the fees and challenging work needed to attract top-flight new lawyers and hold on to mature ones. As early as 1927, the Houston firm of Baker & Botts made it quite clear in its professional listings that "small claims [were] not desired." Similar considerations in recent years have induced big Wall Street law firms to send much routine lending work for commercial banks in-house. With multimillion-dollar loans for construction and bond indentures fairly routine and safe in the post-SEC financial world, aggressive law firms have sought other, more exotic areas of practice, such as mergers and acquisitions.

more work, since corporations are no longer quite so dependent on the local knowledge and connections enjoyed by independent law firms.

These recent trends suggest that to some degree corporate lawyers have helped to promote the rationalization of law in America. Building strong firms, they were able to specialize in the areas of law that affected their corporate clients. Operating at the national, state, and local levels, they fought the many variations in laws that hemmed in corporate development. Organizing themselves into professional bodies, they worked through the legislatures to remove inefficient roadblocks to corporate growth and to promote legal uniformity and standardization. Lawyers have apparently been so successful in this regard that most of the functions they formerly carried out are now becoming obsolete.

Rationalization, however, has its limits. Even today standardization of the law remains incomplete. Local law continues to hold sway in many areas, since states retain exclusive control of the police power. Conflicts and jealousies between regions still exist, and few communities remain unmoved when powerful national or international corporations treat them callously. In short, federalism in America is alive and well, maybe even on the upswing again. As a result, the market for legal services remains "textured" and segmented. Not all law practice has been reduced to technical problems that can be solved with an application of universally available expertise. In-house counsel can now carry out more functions, but there remain significant branches of cutting-edge law amenable only to the skills of lawyers in outside firms. These lawyers must still draw on local business contacts, understanding of the culture of their region, and carefully acquired knowledge of the politics of business to serve their clients . . . .

Although national-scale businesses often supported efforts to purge localisms from the law and to make it more uniform, conflicting aspirations sometimes made it impossible for them to agree on a reform proposal. Business leaders called repeatedly for a federal incorporation statute to override the variations of state law, but they stopped short of uniting behind a concrete measure because of differences over specifics. In other instances, corporations have actually called on their attorneys to fight legal reforms designed to promote uniformity. Bemoaning their state's limitations on consolidations, Texas railroads had throughout the early twentieth century supported the passage of comprehensive national railroad laws to cut through the idiosyncracies of individual state regulations. But in 1913 they reversed course and argued against extension of ICC oversight into matters that had been the responsibility of the state railroad commission, in part because divided jurisdiction gave them more leverage to use against both regulatory bodies . . . .

These problems arose because the law, though open-ended, malleable, and responsive to numerous groups, could not be controlled by any one party or interest. Instead, it underwent a continual process of interpretation, as different groups strove to make it the fulfillment of what they believed it should be. Legal interpretation involved respect for ideas, arguments, and traditions; it required that the implications of a line of reasoning be followed consistently. To achieve of the law the things they wanted, business people had to enter into this process. Corporate lawyers provided the services that their clients demanded, but, as members of the community of professionals responsible for interpreting the law, they did so by addressing existing legal ideas and interpretations. Sometimes achieving the ends that their clients desired, they also contributed to a legal discourse that furthered the process of interpretation. New interpretations invariably opened up new strategic opportunities for both business interests and their opponents. Sometimes the results were a deadlock, or a reading of the law that no one had foreseen. The law as applied by corporate attorneys was thus a device for business expansion and rationalization, but a limited one that reflected divisions within the business community, conflicts in society at large, and traditions of legal reasoning . . . . □

NOTES AND QUESTIONS

1. Much of the literature on the legal profession focuses on things *other* than what lawyers *actually do:* we learn about their background, training, ethics, the structure of the profession, status within the profession, and so on. This is because, for one thing, it is not easy to study what large-firm lawyers do. All lawyers are elusive creatures. They are concerned about the attorney-client privilege. High-prestige lawyers may be particularly difficult to study. Their time is very valuable, and they may be unwilling to give it to a researcher. They go to great lengths to avoid offending clients that pay huge retainers. Hence, it is not easy to know exactly what tasks corporate lawyers accomplish. John Flood, in "Doing Business: The Management of Uncertainty in Lawyers' Work," 25 *Law & Society Review* 41 (1991), did his research as an associate in a large law firm. He tells us that corporate lawyers put together business deals in ways that limit their clients' concerns about uncertainty. Sometimes they give formal opinions about legal aspects of transactions; often they offer informal reassurance.

Consider, in addition, the following:

A former corporate lawyer argued in the *Wall Street Journal,* February 23, 1984, 26, col. 3, that large-firm lawyers engage in "public-interest work" in their everyday practice by suggesting ways for major businesses to accomplish what they desire safely within legal restraints:

Because . . . [business lawyers] advise powerful public and private entities, these lawyers have a more consistent impact on the lives of American citizens than other types of counsel. The typical company seeks their advice to avoid future costly legal battles. Yet, by advising a company of the legal parameters within which it must operate, the business attorney necessarily serves as guardian of the public interest. He has the daily responsibility of ferreting out and making certain that his client honors the myriad of pollution, pension, occupational safety, securities and other laws that protect the public . . . .

Tediously stitching and restitching boundaries and spaces, decade after decade, hoping the design someday will show itself, does not, of course, make for exciting copy . . . . But most of the real progress toward evolving a system of laws that will allow more people to act as they choose takes place largely through day-to-day wrangling of attorneys daily confirming laws that protect others, while protecting the aspirations of their client.

Professor Robert Gordon, in "Bargaining with the Devil," 105 *Harvard Law Review* 2041 (1992), discusses "the ideology of the corporate lawyer as the responsible counsellor who does not simply tell clients what they can get away with, but rather tries to persuade them to adopt corporate policies that will comply with the general norms and purposes of the legal system and that will benefit society as a whole" (p. 2052). He notes, however:

It is quite unclear whether corporate lawyers have ever lived up to this ideal of the counsellor-in-legal-and-social responsibility. It is clear, however, that this ideal was, until recently, a standard part of the self-image and general belief system of the corporate bar, and therefore probably had some effect on practice . . . . It is also clear, unfortunately, that in the last decade most traces of this admirable ideology have vanished, except among retiring lawyers. (pp. 2052–53)

Assume that the counsellor-in-legal-and-social responsibility ideology has all but died. Does this undercut the point of the corporate lawyer quoted above in the first example?

Robert S. Strauss played several key roles in the Carter administration, such as Chairman of the Democratic National Committee, and he returned to government from private practice to serve as President Bush's Ambassador to Russia. In an article describing what happened to lawyers who held top positions in the Carter Administration, Ruth Marcus, "What Price Fame—and Who Pays It?" *National Law Journal,* August 12, 1981, p. 1, col. 2, p. 54, cols 2–3, writes:

He doesn't pretend to be the typical lawyer, buried in the minutiae of cases and versed in arcane points of tax or securities law. It's been years since he was in the firm library . . . .

But . . . Mr. Strauss knows people across the country and abroad, so that when a client in Chicago wants to open a factory in Canada, say, Mr. Strauss can pick up his phone, talk to the Canadian businessman who might be interested in sharing such a venture, and arrange a meeting—all in five minutes of work and five of small talk.

"If you're around people and make a good impression, they think of you favorably and look you up when they need somebody . . . ."

It's not so much a matter of knowing the law as of having common-sense knowledge of people. "I've never been a great intellectual, never a great academic, but I've been a great performer," Mr. Strauss explains, "And clients come to people who get things done."

Mr. Strauss can put together the ingredients for the factory deal and leave it to the contract lawyers to work out the details. He can negotiate takeover tactics for a corporate client; [his firm's] antitrust, securities and contract lawyers worry about the technicalities . . . .

"I just had a man here in my office this morning talking about his estate," Mr. Strauss says in explanation of his sort of practice. "He didn't want my legal advice. He wanted my judgment."

2. In his classic work, *The Growth of American Law: The Law Makers* (Boston: Little, Brown & Co., 1950), J. Willard Hurst discussed the role of lawyers as "social inventors." Lawyers "contrived or adapted institutions (the corporation), tools (the railroad equipment trust certificate), and patterns of action (the reorganization of corporate financial structure or the fashioning of a price structure for a national market)" (p. 337). Lawyers, in other words, made a contribution to the growth of the economy and to the development of the American polity by inventing legal devices and putting them to use—presumably in ways that facilitated business or economic growth or (more neutrally) in ways that had an impact on society.

What type of law firm is more likely to be the source of innovation and develop new business practices or legal devices? Will this role be played by general corporate firms or those that specialize in some line of practice such as mergers and acquisitions? On this point, see Michael J. Powell, "Professional Innovation: Corporate Lawyers and Private Lawmaking," 18 *Law and Social Inquiry* 423 (1993), an account of a modern instance of social invention by lawyers to cope with unwanted corporate take-overs during the merger-mania of the 1980s. See also Ronald Gilson, "Value Creation by Business Lawyers: Legal Skills and Asset Pricing," 94 *Yale Law Journal* 239 (1984); Ian M. Ramsay, "What Do Lawyers Do? Reflections on the Market for Lawyers," 21 *International Journal of the Sociology of Law* 355 (1993).

3. James Gould Cozzens, in *Guard of Honor* (New York: Harcourt, Brace and Co., 1948), a controversial novel, dramatizes what some lawyers in positions of power do. The action in the book takes place at a World War II United States Army Air Force base in the Deep South. The United States Army had always been heavily segregated. African-Americans were given only menial jobs, and officers were always white. As a result of various pressures, the Army ordered desegregation. The Air Force formed a squadron of "Negro" pilots who later went into battle over Germany.

In the novel, Bus, the General in charge of an air base in Florida, was a great leader of fighter pilots but ill suited to running a large training base. Several of the officers who served under him were old Army and Army Air Force types who also had little experience coping with the demands of running a large base. Colonel Ross had served in the Air Force in World War I and then held a Reserve Officer's Commission. He was a lawyer and judge in civilian life. He serves as the General's chief adviser and trouble shooter. The novel tells how Ross handled several crises in such a way as to protect the General. All of these crises involved the problems of race in American society in the early 1940s.

The General's best friend, Benny, an Air Force colonel, pilots the General's plane. Benny approaches the airfield for a night landing, and discovers a B-26 bomber landing immediately in front of him. Benny narrowly avoids a crash by outstanding flying. After landing, Benny confronts the B-26 pilot, hits him in the face, and this sends him to the hospital. The B-26 pilot is black—part of a newly formed squadron of black bomber pilots from Tuskegee Institute. A radical young white lieutenant brings a black newspaperman and the injured pilot's father to the base, thus threatening publicity about the incident. The General does not want his friend Benny charged in a disciplinary proceeding. In such a proceeding, Benny would be subject to strong sanctions. The Judge manipulates the situation. Benny is not charged but apologizes. The injured pilot is awarded a medal as a result of his actions before coming to the base, and the Judge uses the award ceremony to defuse the conflict.

One of the General's administrative officers created a segregated Officers' Club at the base for the black pilots, and they are quartered in segregated barracks. This violates explicit Air Force regulations. Some of the black pilots attempt to enter the white officers' club, and one takes a Military Policeman's gun from him. Two black leaders are arrested by the MPs. The Judge also manipulates this situation to keep the blacks from being formally charged, but the Air Force General Staff learns what happened. It writes an order for the General's signature requiring the black squadron to stay together during their training "in order to promote the close integration essential in a self-sustaining combat unit." The Judge modifies the order to make it less burdensome on the black pilots and crew. He then explains it at a meeting with the black officers, and their resentment is directed at him rather than at the General. He persuades them that it is more important for them to show that black pilots can be successful in combat than to desegregate this base's officers' club.

Colonel Ross is sympathetic to the black squadron, and he does not believe in segregation. He thinks that the black pilots have been treated badly. However, he knows that the General's skills are needed in the war effort. An officer from the Air Staff in Washington tells Colonel Ross that the General "was the best man we had to command large scale fighter operations." Colonel Ross knows that if there are formal legal proceedings, the General would be in serious trouble. He would be disciplined, and he probably would not be given a command when Allied forces invade Europe and Japan.

Cozzens' story involves the Colonel's use of evasion, legalism, cover-up, and compromises, all in the service of *what the Colonel sees* as the priorities of the situation. As a result of the Colonel's efforts, the black pilots are treated much better than the career Army officers at the base would have treated them. Nonetheless, their rights are not vindicated. It is the Colonel who decides that the General is essential to defeating Germany and Japan, and that this goal outweighs desegregation, civil rights, and following the letter of Air Force directives. Cozzens portrays the Colonel as a wise lawyer making difficult but important judgments. He portrays the radical white lieutenant who championed the black pilots' rights as young and foolish.

Colonel Ross, of course, is a fictional character. But there are probably many "Colonel Rosses" in the legal profession managing affairs in large organizations. On balance, do you think they do more harm than good? Why? Should they be disbarred as lawyers who help their clients break the law? Can you defend those who play such roles?

4. The literature on large law firms is surprisingly small. The pioneering work was Erwin O. Smigel, *The Wall Street Lawyer* (Bloomington, Ind.: University of Indiana Press, 1964). An important recent study is Robert L. Nelson,

Partners with Power: The Social Transformation of the Large Law Firm (Berkeley: University of California Press, 1988).

Most lawyers, of course, do not work for big law firms representing major corporations. On "solo" practitioners, see Jerome Carlin, *Lawyers on their Own: A Study of Individual Practitioners in Chicago* (New Brunswick, N.J.: Rutgers University Press, 1962). For a similar study of lawyers outside a big city, see Joel Handler, *The Lawyer and His Community: The Practicing Bar in a Middle- Sized City* (Madison, Wis.: University of Wisconsin Press, 1967).

57. Lawyers and Consumer Protection Laws

Stewart Macaulay

14 *Law & Society Review* 115 (1979)

☐ The conventional model of the practice of law views lawyers as those who apply legal rules in the service of client interests, checked only by the constraints of the adversary system. A study of the impact of consumer protection laws on the practice of Wisconsin lawyers shows this to be an oversimplification. Lawyers for individuals tend to know little of the precise contours of consumer protection law. They most often serve as mediators between buyer and seller, relying on general norms of fairness and good faith. Lawyers for businesses are more likely to make use of the law, but they are seldom called on to deal with particular disputes. Lawyers' own values and interests are reflected in the way in which they represent clients. As a result, reform laws which create individual rights are likely to have only symbolic effect unless incentives are devised to make their vindication in the long-range interest of members of the bar. Moreover, an understanding of the many roles played by lawyers also requires a more expanded picture of practice. The picture of the lawyer as litigator in the adversary system may itself serve largely symbolic functions.

I. INTRODUCTION

Towards a New Model of the Practice of Law

In Western culture the lawyer has been regarded with both admiration and suspicion for centuries. Both judgments seem to rest on a widely held image of what it is that lawyers do or ought to do. On one hand, the profession paints a picture of itself defending individual liberties by advocacy and facilitating progress by creative social engineering. Novels, plays, motion pictures, and television programs have reinforced this view. On the other hand, a debunking tradition . . . shows lawyers as people who profit from the misfortunes of others, as manipulators who produce results for a price without regard to justice, and as word magicians who mislead people into accepting what is wrong. Fiction supports this view too. Yet much of this writing may cost us understanding because the debunkers accept the classic stereotype of good lawyering as a yardstick, measured against which actual practice falls short.

In this classical model of practice, *lawyers apply the law.* They try cases and argue appeals guided by their command of legal norms. They negotiate settlements and advise clients largely in light of what they believe would happen if matters were brought before legal agencies. Of course, it is this mastery of a special body of knowledge, certified by success in law school and passing a bar examination, which gives one the status of being a lawyer and justifies the privileges which come with being a member of the profession. In the common law version of the model, *lawyers represent clients in an adversary system.* They take stock of a client's situation and desires and seek to further the client's interests as far as is possible legally. The lawyer is a "hired gun" who does not judge the client but vigorously asserts all of the client's claims of right, limited only by legal ethics. Lawyers place the interests of clients ahead of their own. A high place in the legends of the profession, for example, is awarded to the heroic and lonely advocate for an unpopular client, who battles for justice in the face of threats to person and pocketbook. However, even these aggressive lawyers cannot go too far because of the operation of the adversary system. An aggressive lawyer on one side will be matched on the other, and from this kind of advocacy a proper outcome will emerge. As a result, lawyers need not, and should not, be influenced by their own ethical judgment of the client's cause.

Only the most innocent could think that this classical model describes professional practice. The model may reflect some of what goes on, but it is, at best, a distortion. Both Wall Street and Main Street lawyers often operate in situations where they do not know much about the relevant legal norms or where those norms play an insignificant part in influencing what is done. Lawyers regularly engage in the politics of bargaining, seeking to work out solutions to problems which are acceptable to the various interests. Rather than playing hired gun for one side, lawyers often mediate between their client and those not represented by lawyers. They seek to educate, persuade and coerce *both* sides to adopt the best available compromise rather than to engage in legal warfare. Moreover, in playing all of their roles, ranging from arguing a case before the Supreme Court of the United States to listening to an angry client, lawyers are influenced by their own values and self interest. They will be more eager to do things which they find satisfying and not distasteful and which will contribute to their income both today and in the future.

The legal profession may find the classical model valuable in justifying its activities and status. The public may benefit too insofar as this conventional view of practice is a normative indicator of what a lawyer ought to do and what influences behavior. Nonetheless, the classical model has costs: it may serve to mislead clients about what lawyers can, should, or will do. It may obstruct serious thought about the techniques and ethics of counseling, mediation and negotiation. And it may undermine effective efforts at reforms through law. Over the past twenty years when reformers have won victories in such areas as civil rights, sex and racial discrimination, and consumer protection, their successes have come in the form of cases, statutes, and regulations which, along with other things, have granted rights to individuals or groups. But the actual nature of law practice may leave these rights as little more than symbolic words on paper with only marginal life as resources in the process of negotiation.

This case study will develop some ideas about an expanded picture of the practice of law. I will consider the roles played by lawyers in connection with a number of consumer protection laws which create individual rights . . . .

A. Description of the Research

The research on which this article is based began as a study of the impact of the Magnuson-Moss Warranty Act, 15 U.S.C. 2301-12 (Supp. V 1975) in Wisconsin. This statute, which became effective on July 4, 1975, was heralded as an important victory for the consumer protection movement, and was given national news coverage and prompted an outpouring of law review articles.

As our research developed, it quickly became apparent that the focus of the study was too narrow. We found that most lawyers in Wisconsin knew next to nothing about the Magnuson-Moss Warranty Act; many had never heard of it. When asked about the statute, they tended to respond with comments on consumer protection in general. It was extremely difficult to find lawyers who knew much about any specific consumer protection law other than the Wisconsin Consumer Act [WCA], Wis. Stat. 421-427 (1975), a law largely concerned with procedures for financing consumer transactions and collecting debts. A few lawyers were well informed about the WCA, but most knew only of "atrocity stories" about debtors who had used the statute to evade honest debts. However, we also found that, in spite of this ignorance of the specific contours of consumer protection regulation, most lawyers had techniques for dealing with complaints voiced by clients, or potential clients, who were dissatisfied with the quality of products or services or could not pay for what they had bought. These techniques will be the major focus of this article.

What follows is based on in-person and telephone interviews conducted by a research assistant and me during the summer of 1977. We talked with about 100 lawyers in five Wisconsin counties and with representatives from each of the state's ten largest law firms, from the legal services programs in Milwaukee and Madison, from Wisconsin Judicare, a program for paying private lawyers to handle cases for the poor in the northern and western parts of the state and from all the group legal service plans registered with the State Bar of Wisconsin. In addition, a questionnaire concerning experiences with the Magnuson-Moss Warranty Act was sent to all lawyers who had attended an Advanced Training Seminar dealing with that statute, sponsored by the State Bar of Wisconsin. While in no sense is this study based on a representative sample of all lawyers in Wisconsin, there was an attempt to seek out lawyers whose experiences might differ. The great consistency in the stories that this very diverse group of lawyers had to tell suggests that almost any sample would have served for the study. Even at points where very divergent interpretations were offered by the lawyers interviewed, their description of practice was consistent. Moreover, the information I gathered was consistent with, and helps explain, the findings about lawyers and consumer problems of the American Bar Association American Bar Foundation study of the legal needs of the public. This ABA-ABF study was based on a random sample of the adult population of the United States, excluding Alaska and Hawaii.

However, my study has some obvious limitations. I cannot offer percentages of the lawyers who have had certain experiences or who hold particular opinions. Often the lawyers themselves could say no more than they get a certain kind of case "all of the time," or that they "almost never" litigate. Since lawyers have no reason to compile statistics, usually they offered only general estimates of their caseload. Many informal contacts and telephone calls never appear in lawyers' records, and lawyers are unlikely to have a very precise memory of them. Moreover, many of the attorneys interviewed were former students of mine, and others seemed glad to aid a University of Wisconsin law professor's research. This effort to be helpful, while appreciated, may have introduced some distortion. On one hand, these lawyers may have been willing to go along with the interviewer's definition of the situation, which was implicit in the questions asked, rather than challenge the entire basis of the inquiry. On the other hand, a few may have modified a fact here and there to present a good story to entertain their old professor or to make themselves look good. While I cannot be sure that this did not happen, again the consistency of the stories across 100 lawyers suggests that this was not a major problem.

Finally, it should be noted that this article reports the author's interpretations of what he was told. Not all of the attorneys were asked exactly the same questions since, as the study progressed, the responses dictated a change in the focus from the Magnuson-Moss Warranty Act to consumer protection laws and then finally to the practice of law itself. This article, then, is an empirical description of a corner of the legal world that my assistant and I explored in some depth rather than a report of quantifiable data from a survey of a random sample of the bar. It should be read as a report from a preliminary study, offering suggestions the author thinks are true enough to warrant reliance until someone is willing to invest enough to produce better data and lucky enough to find a way to get them.

II. THE IMPACT OF CONSUMER PROTECTION STATUTES ON THE PRACTICE OF LAW

Heinz and Laumann (1978:1114)[176] tell us that "the tendency of lawyers' work to address congeries of problems associated with particular types of clients organizes the profession into types of lawyers: those serving corporations, and those serving individuals and individuals' small businesses." They point out that corporate work is likely to involve "symbol manipulation," while work for individuals will carry a heavy component of "people persuasion." My study offers additional confirmation of these observations. Certain members of the Wisconsin bar were much more likely to see an individual with a consumer complaint, while others were much more likely to be asked to lobby against consumer protection legislation, to draft contracts to cope with such laws, and to plan defensive strategies for dealing with consumer complaints. We will deal with these two types of lawyers separately.

Lawyers for Consumers

Lawyers see but a small percentage of all of the situations where someone might assert a claim under the many consumer protection laws. Some claims are never asserted because consumers fail to recognize that the product they receive is defective, that the forms used in financing the transaction fail to make the required disclosures, or that the debt collection tactics used by a creditor are prohibited. Other claims are recognized but resolved in ways not involving lawyers. Some consumers see the cost of any attempt to resolve a minor consumer problem as not worth the effort. Resolving never to buy from the offending merchant or manufacturer again, they just "lump it." Some fix a defective item themselves, while others complain to the seller or the creditor and receive an adjustment which satisfies them. It is likely

176. The reference is to John P. Heinz and Edward O. Laumann, "The Legal Profession: Client Interests, Professional Roles, and Social Hierarchies," 76 *Michigan Law Review* 1111 (1978).

that most potential claims under consumer protection statutes are resolved in one of these ways.

Some consumers go directly to remedy agents without consulting lawyers. For example, they may turn to the Better Business Bureau in Milwaukee or to one or more of several state agencies which mediate consumer complaints. A few may go directly to a small claims court. Others contact the local district attorney who, at least in the smaller counties in Wisconsin, often offers a great deal of legal advice or even a rather coercive mediation service to consumers who are potential supporters in the next election.

Many lawyers in private practice reported to us that they never saw a case involving an individual consumer. Those who represented businesses and practice in the larger firms were likely to say this, but some business lawyers reported that they answered questions about consumer matters from clients and friends. Other lawyers talked about encountering consumer cases only now and then. Lawyers did see what they called "products liability" cases where a defective item had caused personal injury. However, these cases typically do not fall under consumer protection statutes, and the fact of personal injury opens the door to the chance of a substantial recovery. A specialized group of attorneys is expert in the techniques of asserting or defending products liability cases. Most lawyers knew these specialists and many referred cases to them. No similar network of access to specialists in consumer protection law seemed to exist. Several attorneys mentioned one lawyer whom they thought was an expert in consumer protection, but when I interviewed him, he said that he now tried to avoid such cases.

Those few dissatisfied consumers who survive the screening process and come to lawyers may have special characteristics or kinds of problems. First, some people will bring cases to lawyers that others would see as trivial but which they see as a matter of principle. Second, when regular clients appear with minor consumer problems, a lawyer may attempt to handle them in order to keep a client's good will; one lawyer called this a kind of "loss-leader" service. For example, a lawyer in a small county had drafted a wealthy farmer's estate plan and set up a corporation to handle some of his dealings in land development. The farmer, dissatisfied with a Chevrolet dealer's attempts to make a new car run satisfactorily, called his lawyer and told him to straighten out matters. The lawyer successfully negotiated with the dealer and sent the farmer a bill for only a nominal amount. Third, debtors who cannot pay are sometimes pushed into a lawyer's office by the actions of a creditor. The debtor or the lawyer may see consumer protection law as offering a way to lift some or all of the burden of indebtedness for an expensive item such as a car, a recreational vehicle, or a mobile home. Problems which the consumer might have been willing to overlook may now become the basis for a legal attempt to rescind the sale.

Consumer cases also are brought to the attention of lawyers through informal social channels . . . . Many lawyers pointed out that they had friends, relatives, and neighbors who asked for advice informally. People who might not make a visit to a lawyer's office about a consumer matter will raise their problem with a lawyer they see at a church supper, a PTA meeting, or a cocktail party. One lawyer noted that it was hard to have a drink at a bar in Madison on a football weekend without being called on for free legal advice . . . .

Decisions about whether or not to contact a lawyer are affected by personal factors. One lawyer remarked that many people seem to need reassurance that it is legitimate to complain and make trouble for others. Many people are hesitant about admitting that they were cheated by a retailer or manufacturer when they think they should have known better. Some lawyers said that most of their clients, both those who come to their office and those who ask for advice during informal contacts, come to them through friendship networks. A former client may talk with a friend at work or at a bar and end up sending the friend to see the lawyer. Some people seem to need the encouragement of friends before they can take the plunge. There seems to be a "folk culture" that defines, among other things, which kinds of cases one should take to a lawyer, which call for solutions not involving lawyers, and which should be just forgotten. Those facing aggressive debt collection procedures are likely to be told to see lawyers; those with complaints about the quality of products are usually advised just to forget it.

Many lawyers seek to avoid taking clients with consumer protection problems. Firms that specialize in representing businesses discourage individuals from bringing their personal problems to the firm by the expensive elegance of their offices and often by the location of those offices. Everything about these firms tends to tell potential clients that these are expensive professionals who deal only with important people on important matters. One who is not to the manor born would hesitate to waste the time of this professional establishment with a mere personal matter.

Even lawyers who look more approachable have techniques for avoiding cases they do not want to take. Receptionists try to screen cases so that minor personal matters will not waste their bosses' time. Lawyers engage in techniques of conversion or transformation of attitudes. Some try to brush off individuals by talking to them briefly on the telephone in order to keep them from coming to the office. Some listen to people who come to the office for only a few minutes and then interrupt to spell out the cost of legal services. These attorneys see their role as that of educating would-be clients to see that they cannot afford to pursue the matter. The lawyer serves as a gatekeeper, keeping people from burdening the legal system.

If the potential client with a consumer matter is not rejected out of hand, lawyers may still limit their response to nonadversary roles. One part played fairly often might be that of the therapist or knowledgeable friend. The client is allowed to blow off steam and vent anger to a competent-seeming professional sitting in an office surrounded by law books and the other stage props of the profession. By body language and discussion, the lawyer can lead the client to redefine the situation so that he or she can accept it. What appeared to the client to be a clear case of fraud or bad faith comes on close examination to be seen as no more than a misunderstanding.

The lawyer may then "help" the client consider the practical options open in the situation. It may be against the client's interests to pursue the matter; legal action may cost more than it is worth, either directly or indirectly in terms of the client's long-run interests. The client may also have adopted too narrow—perhaps too legalistic—a view of the case. The client's grievance may be one which the lawyer could translate into a perfectly legitimate—indeed compelling—legal argument, but the "law" may not be the only standard by which the merits of each party will be judged. Such arguments, needless to say, may anger the potential client; or they may make the client feel foolish for being upset and bothering a lawyer. On the other hand, by helping the client see the case in a new light, the lawyer may be indulging in a kind of therapy.

Perhaps the lawyer will take a further step and combine the therapist role with that of an information broker or a coach, hearing the complaint and then referring the client elsewhere for a remedy. This gets the would-be client out of the office less unhappy than had the lawyer just rejected the case and offered nothing. People can be sent to state agencies which mediate consumer claims or to private organizations such as the Better Business Bureau. Some lawyers go further and try to coach clients on how to complain effectively to a seller or creditor or how to handle a case in a small claims court without a lawyer. Sometimes this information and coaching may be of more help than formal legal advice. Consumers may need to be reassured that they have a legitimate complaint, to be given the courage to complain, to learn where to go and whom to see, and to be given a few good rhetorical ploys to use in the process of solving their problems. Sometimes the coaching does not help the client. The referral only prompts the client to give up. Few lawyers know what happens when they tell a client to complain to the seller or go to a state agency. Clients rarely report back to the lawyer unless they are friends or neighbors. On the other hand, such referrals may serve to help lawyers see themselves as helpful people.

Attorneys who become more involved in a case may find themselves playing the part of go-between or informal mediator. They may telephone or write the seller or creditor to state the consumer's complaint. The very restatement of that complaint by a professional is likely to make it a complex communication. On one level, the attorney is reporting a version of the situation which may be unknown to the seller or creditor even in cases where consumers have complained before seeing a lawyer. The lawyer may be able to organize a presentation so that the basis of the complaint is more understandable, and transform it so that it is more persuasive. The fact that the report comes from a lawyer is likely to give the complaint at least some minimal legitimacy. The lawyer is saying that he or she has reviewed the buyer or debtor's story, that the assertions of fact are at least plausible, and that the buyer or debtor has reason to complain if these are the facts.

The lawyer is more likely than the consumer to get to talk to someone who has authority to do something about a problem. For example, the consumer may have gotten no farther than the sales person, while the lawyer may gain access to the manager or owner of the business. The lawyer is likely to speak as a social equal of the representative of the seller or debtor, though such may not be the case for the consumer. This may be important. A retailer, for example, may care little about the opinions of a factory worker complainant, but wish to avoid having a professional judge him or her as foolish or unreasonable. Finally, the attorney's professional identification conveys a tacit threat that an unsatisfactory response could be followed by something the seller or creditor might find unpleasant. Indeed the unstated and vague threat of further action may be coercive precisely because it is vague. If sellers and creditors were aware of the cost barriers to litigation, and if they knew, or appreciated, just how much of a paper tiger most attorneys are in consumer matters, they would be less easily intimidated.

At this point, a seller or creditor may assert that the client has just misunderstood the situation or has told the lawyer only part of the story. At this stage lawyers often discover that a client's case is not as clear-cut as the client claimed. However, sellers and creditors still are more likely to make conciliatory responses to lawyers than to buyers or debtors, as long as the lawyers do not ask for too much. And it is part of a lawyer's stock in trade to know how much is too much. One lawyer told us:

> I enjoy negotiation. Of course, what happens is not determined by the merits . . . One has a discussion about what is best for everyone. You do not make an adversary matter out of it. It is a game, and it is funny or sad, depending on how you look at it. You call the other side and tell him that you understand that he has a problem satisfying customers but that you have a client who is really hot and wants to sue for the principle of the thing. Then you say, "Maybe I can help you and talk my client into accepting something that is reasonable." The other side knows what you are doing. It is a game. You never want to get to the merits of the case.

The seller or creditor is likely to make some kind of gesture so that the lawyer will not have to return to the client empty-handed. The simplest gesture the seller or creditor can make is a letter of apology, explaining how the problem occurred and accepting some or all of the blame. A supervisor may attempt to blame an employee with whom the consumer dealt, perhaps remarking that it is difficult to find good sales people or mechanics. Manufacturers often blame dealers, and dealers, in turn, seem eager to pass the blame on to manufacturers. In addition to an apology, the merchant may also offer token reparations such as minor repairs or free samples of its products.

More rarely, the lawyer may be able to persuade a seller or manufacturer to offer the consumer a refund or replacement for a defective product. Sometimes a lawyer can gain a refund or replacement even where the flaw in the thing purchased was not so material as to warrant "revocation of acceptance" under Section 2-608 of the Uniform Commercial Code. New car dealers or fly-by-night merchants are unlikely to do this; new car dealers are tightly controlled by manufacturers, who seem to value cost control more than consumer goodwill; fly-by-night operators seldom worry about repeat business. But Sears, Montgomery Ward, J.C. Penney, and many other large department stores, have an announced policy of consumer satisfaction. One can get his or her money back without having to establish that there is something materially wrong with the product. Other retailers and manufacturers do not announce this as their policy, but will grant refunds or replacements selectively when their officials think that the customer has reason to complain or if repeat business is valued. In such cases, a telephone call from a lawyer may be enough to swing the balance in favor of the complainant—it probably seems easier to make a refund than to argue with a lawyer. Occasionally, a lawyer may be able to persuade a new car dealer who has sold a client a used car to pay some percentage of the cost of repairs of a major item such as a transmission, provided the work is done in the dealer's shop. A lawyer may be able to persuade a creditor to give a client more time in which to pay rather than repossessing the item in dispute. But lawyers are seldom able to persuade a seller or creditor to pay a large sum as damages to an aggrieved buyer or debtor.

The lawyer's view of the adequacy of the remedy offered by the merchant or lender will necessarily turn on a reappraisal of the client's case in light of the other side's story, the ease of taking further action, the likelihood of success of such action, and the client's probable reaction to what has been offered. The lawyer may have to persuade the client to see the situation in a new light. The response of the merchant or lender must also be considered. The axiom that "there are two sides to every story" now becomes a reality for the client. An important part of the lawyer's task now is to persuade the client to see the problem as an adjustment between competing claims and interests, rather than as one warranting a fight for principle. From the lawyer's perspective, the client must now be guided to the view that what the merchant or lender has offered is probably the best that could be expected. Anything more may require legal services more costly than the client can afford or is prepared to pay.

In this context, lawyers are often pushed into a role Justice Brandeis described as "counsel for the situation." . . . [S]uch a lawyer must be advocate, mediator, entrepreneur, and judge all rolled into one. He or she is called on to be expert in problem solving and asked to produce a solution which will be acceptable over time rather than only an immediate victory for the client. This often means persuading or coercing both the other party and the client to reach what the lawyer sees as a proper solution, often "translating inarticulate or exaggerated claims . . . into temperate and mutually intelligible terms of communication." At all levels of law practice, this is a difficult task. The client tends to want vindication, while the lawyer is talking about costs balanced against benefits. It is an especially difficult task when the client is angry but has what the lawyer sees as a questionable case that involves too little money to warrant even drafting a complaint—let alone litigating. Clients in consumer protection cases often find it hard to believe that they cannot do better than the lawyer says they can . . . .

Only in rare instances will lawyers go further than conciliatory negotiation in a consumer matter. If the antagonist fails to offer a satisfactory settlement, the lawyer may counter with more explicit threats of unpleasant consequences. But some lawyers report that once overt threats are made, one is likely to have to draft and file a complaint before any offer of settlement will be made by the other side. One reason is that serious threats from a lawyer are likely to prompt sellers or creditors to send the matter to their lawyers. But even at this point, the lawyers for both sides have every reason to settle rather than litigate . . . .

There are a number of reasons why lawyers either refuse to take consumer protection cases or tend to play only nonadversarial roles when they try to help a client with such a complaint. The most obvious explanation is that the costs of handling these cases in a more adversarial style would be more than most clients would be willing to pay. Few consumers can afford many hours of lawyers' time billed at from $35 to $75 an hour just to argue about a $400 repair to their car or even a repossession of a $5,000 used car. Few lawyers can afford to spend time on cases that will not pay . . . .

Consumer product quality cases are very similar to products liability litigation except for the factor of personal injury. But this factor in products liability offers the chance for recovering very large damages and prompts lawyers to work for contingent fees.

Not only are consumer protection cases unlikely to warrant substantial fees, but they usually require a major investment of professional time if litigation is to be considered seriously. Those most expert about consumer laws tend to be the lawyers who counsel businesses and draft documents in light of these laws. Yet these are the lawyers least likely to see an individual consumer's case—except, perhaps, as a favor to a friend. Most other lawyers in Wisconsin know very little about any of the many consumer protection laws, and it is difficult for most attorneys to master all of the relevant statutes, regulations, and cases in this area. Most of them did not study consumer law in law school. Either they graduated before most of it was passed or they did not take elective courses in this area when they were in law school. Moreover, since consumer protection cases worth an investment of time come up so infrequently, a lawyer is not even likely to know whom to call for help. Most lawyers in Wisconsin lack easy access to the text of consumer protection law. Most are unlikely to own the necessary law books themselves. The folk wisdom of private practice dictates that one should buy only those law books that are likely to pay for themselves. Most lawyers have access to the Wisconsin statutes, the decisions of the state courts, and at least some of the state administrative regulations. Fewer have access to federal materials dealing with statutes such as Truth in Lending (15 U.S.C. 1601, et seq. [1970]) or the Magnuson-Moss Warranty Act; and only a very few have ready access to loose-leaf services dealing with trade regulation. Many lawyers rely heavily on practice manuals and on continuing legal education handbooks for most of their legal research. However, there are not many of these in the area of consumer protection. Lawyers in Milwaukee and Madison have access to relatively complete law libraries. Lawyers in other areas could travel to these cities to do research or hire a lawyer who practices there to do the work. But this is not practical if the potential recovery in a case is small. Even those in Milwaukee or Madison would have to leave their offices to use the libraries located there, and the time invested in doing this might be too much for a client who can pay only a modest fee.

Furthermore, consumer protection law is complex and involves many qualitative concepts, such as "reasonable" or "unconscionable." This uncertainty makes the law hard to apply; even an expert cannot be sure how a court would decide a particular case . . . .

Apart from the nature of the law itself, consumers often face difficult burdens of proof under these laws. The buyer who wants to return the car, in our example, would have to establish that the car was defective when it was delivered or that the seller or manufacturer was in some way responsible for a defect that appeared later. This kind of evidentiary problem is faced often in products liability litigation where personal injury puts several hundred thousand dollars at issue, and there the matter usually is established by expert testimony . . . . However, experts are expensive, and one cannot afford to use them in the typical action arising under a consumer protection statute or regulation. One office offering legal services to the poor was able to use expert testimony in cases involving complaints about automobiles because it could call on a program which trained poor people to be automobile mechanics, but this kind of access to experts is rare.

We were told about a case where all of these difficulties were surmounted, and it can serve as an example of how rarely one might expect a consumer case to be taken as far as the complaint stage on the way toward litigation. A wealthy doctor ordered a $500,000 custom-made yacht from a boat yard. He refused to accept delivery, asserting that the boat was defective in many respects. He sued to recover his down payment, and also asked for a large sum as damages. His complaint reflected a high degree of creativity in the blending of traditional and newly developing contract and consumer protection theories. Only the wealthy can afford to pay for such creativity as well as the expert testimony that was called for. The example suggests that consumer protection law may most benefit an unintended population—the wealthy who can afford to pursue individual rights in dealing with the purchase of yachts and other luxury goods. The reformers may have aimed an inadequate weapon at the wrong target.

Problems of cost and difficulty in litigation have not gone completely unnoticed by those who draft consumer protection legislation. Some of these statutes seem based on the assumption that the individual rights they create will be reinforced by provisions for lawyers at low or no cost either as part of an antipoverty program or as a benefit of membership in a particular group. Other statutes award attorneys' fees to consumers who win, and many of these newly created rights open the way for class action suits. Magnuson-Moss even makes a bow toward encouraging suppliers of consumer goods to set up informal arbitration schemes. All of these approaches may have had some effect, but neither singly or all together do they offer an adequate solution to the problems of cost and difficulty in consumer litigation. There are a number of reasons why this is so.

Low-cost or free legal service plans employ lawyers who are willing to deal with consumer problems. Legal Action for Wisconsin (LAW), a program to supply legal services to people with low incomes in Milwaukee and Madison, probably sees as many consumers as any group of nongovernmental lawyers in the state. However, LAW's services are limited and must be rationed carefully. LAW's attorneys may make a telephone call or write a letter seeking relief if either strategy looks appropriate but most often its lawyers refer clients to the consumer mediation service of the Department of Justice or to the Concerned Consumers' League, a private organization which trains low-income consumers to complain effectively or to use the Small Claims Court. Occasionally, LAW lawyers will make an appearance in the Small Claims Court on a consumer matter, but they try to avoid this so that they can devote their time to what they see as more important matters. Sometimes, the LAW lawyers will attempt to work out a complicated consumer financing problem that looms large in the life of a poor client, and they frequently attempt to use the federal Truth-in-Lending law or the Wisconsin Consumer Act to strike down a transaction. Sometimes they assert a highly technical defense based on these statutes as a surrogate for bankruptcy or to fight a breach-of-warranty claim. For example, it may be easier to find a clause in a form contract which violates statutory requirements than to prove that the goods were defective and that the seller is responsible for the defects . . . .

Members of a number of labor unions, condominiums, cooperatives, and student organizations are entitled to the benefit of legal services under various plans. However, under almost all plans the amount of service is limited and carefully defined. Usually a member is entitled to a specified number of telephone calls or office visits. If a legal problem warranting more service is discovered, the member can retain a plan lawyer at a reduced rate. The use of these plans by members with consumer disputes varies, but few lawyers working for plans see many of these matters.

Members of cooperatives and of primary and secondary school teachers' unions almost never bring consumer matters to the lawyers who serve those plans. Lawyers employed by these plans believe that members face few consumer disputes which they cannot resolve by their own actions. One lawyer reports that members of his plan tend to read Consumer Reports, to shop carefully both for price and the cost of financing, to be able to borrow from a credit union rather than paying high rates to a loan company or an automobile dealer, and to buy goods that would need servicing only from businesses likely to be able to provide it. In short, they are model consumers who need little legal advice. Another lawyer suggests that they are the type of people who are unwilling to admit it when they do make a bad purchase or allow themselves to be fooled or cheated. Those who deny they have problems also have little need for legal advice.

The members of the condominium group plans also bring few consumer protection problems directly to their lawyers. However, these lawyers attend condominium association meetings and often make presentations on how to avoid common consumer frauds and what to look for in consumer contracts. Before or after these meetings, individual members often ask for informal advice about consumer matters, and this may be the extent of the legal service needed by these condominium owners.

When we turn to student plans we see a very different picture. Students at several campuses of the University of Wisconsin are entitled to legal service, and many of them use these benefits. Typically, plan employees train the students to handle their own case before a small claims court or tell them how to invoke the complaint procedure of the state agency that mediates consumer complaints in the area in question. Students often prefer to assert their rights rather than compromise. Some students seem to delight in battling local landlords and merchants in whatever forum they can find. But students tend to have the time to devote to such battles, and landlords and retailers tend not to value student patronage enough to remedy complaints voluntarily. When a pattern of unfair practice by a particular retailer or landlord is discovered, the plan's lawyers attempt to find a general remedy for the students to prevent future abuses.

Members of plans that benefit industrial unions fall somewhere between cooperative members and the students in terms of using their services in the consumer area. Industrial union plans usually are framed so that the lawyers cannot get rich off them, and often have problems of overload. As a result, their services are strictly rationed. One firm which provides legal services to many union locals' plans will write letters to merchants or refer members with consumer complaints to a small claims court or the mediation service of a state agency, but little more. One of their attorneys says that he only writes letters and will not telephone sellers, because if he telephoned, he would have to listen to the seller's side of the story and there is never time to do this. This lawyer sees consumer matters as less important than the many other kinds of cases that plan members regularly bring to him . . . .

Some consumer protection statutes have followed the pattern set by civil rights acts and allowed successful consumers to recover reasonable attorneys' fees. One might expect this to be an incentive for lawyers to handle these matters. However, few lawyers know about the attorney's fee provisions in consumer protection statutes, and those who do know about them point out that these really are contingent fees because one must win the case in order to benefit. As a result, these statutes are unlikely to be very attractive in close cases, since they do not give lawyers the opportunity to win very large fees in some cases to offset the cases they lose, where they will have invested their time for no return. Furthermore, most statutes leave the amount of recovery to the discretion of the trial judge. Many trial judges do not like awarding bounties to lawyers who bring certain types of cases. These judges often will award fees at a rate far below that usually paid in the community for attorney's services . . . .

The economic barriers to claims made under consumer statutes might be overcome to some extent if many small claims could be aggregated into a class action . . . . However, this is not a technique suited to most consumer problems, which turn on the facts of individual cases and present no common problem to aggregate. Moreover, class actions are hard to manage successfully . . . .

There may be other important factors besides the economic ones we have discussed that make Wisconsin lawyers reluctant to take consumer cases, and that affect the way they handle the ones they do take. Some of the information gained in our interviews suggests that problems with an individual rights strategy in the consumer area would not be solved if these cases were made only a little more attractive economically. Many of the attorneys interviewed represent banks, lenders, local car dealers, or even the major automobile manufacturers when they are sued in local courts. These lawyers would face a pure conflict of interest if they were to take a consumer protection case against one of their regular clients.[177] Other lawyers have less direct but nonetheless important ties to the business community. Although these ties to a segment of that community may enable a lawyer to be more effective in working out reasonable settlements or at least gaining a gesture, an over-aggressive pursuit of a consumer claim might risk the goodwill of existing and potential clients or endanger a whole network of contacts. Even lawyers who would face no direct conflict of interest think it important to avoid offending business people unnecessarily. One lawyer in northern Wisconsin stressed that, "you can always get a merchant's name in the newspaper just by filing a complaint. However, this will make him bitter, and you will pay for it in the future." Lawyers' contacts are part of their stock in trade. They know, for example, where to get financing or who might want to invest in a business deal their client is interested in. Lawyers also often get clients through referrals and recommendations, and bankers and retailers frequently serve as experts who can tell others where to find a good lawyer. In short, most lawyers in private practice must work hard to become and stay members in good standing of the local business and political community if they are to prosper.

We cannot expect lawyers concerned with the reaction of business people to take a tough approach to solving consumer problems; they have too much to lose and little to gain. It is safer to refuse these cases or refer them to a governmental agency which mediates consumer complaints against business. It is safer to call an influential business person to try to work out matters in a low-key conciliatory manner than to file complaints. If the lawyer handles the situation skillfully, a conciliatory approach can even gain the appreciation of the business person against whom the consumer is complaining. A dissatisfied customer can be transformed into a person with much less sense of grievance. Whether or not the consumer is persuaded that a conciliatory approach is the best one, considering the whole picture, the consumer's lawyer serves at least the short-run interest of the business complained against if the client is persuaded to drop the matter and go away.

The local legal community recognizes legitimate and not so legitimate ways of resolving problems. For example, most lawyers feel strongly that one should not escalate a simple dispute into full-scale warfare which will benefit neither the parties nor the lawyers. Lawyers interested in the good opinion of other members of the bar and bench

177. A conflict of interest problem does not always stop a lawyer from acting as a mediator. One lawyer told us that "in one case a customer came to the office, and he had a complaint against a store we represent. Clearly, the store should have made good on the matter, and so I called the store and told them to fix things up. They did without question, and the man left my office happy."

will follow accepted, routine, and simple ways of dealing with consumer problems. Only when one is doing a public service by going after a fly-by-night company or some other disreputable firm is a tough adversary stance seen as appropriate. There is also a segment of the legal community that is hostile to consumer protection law and to those who assert their rights under them. They view business people—at least local business people—as honest and reasonable. While misunderstandings are always possible, these lawyers doubt that serious wrongs are ever committed by the local bank, automobile dealer, or appliance store. Consumers who complain often are seen as deadbeats trying to escape honest debts or as cranks who are unwilling to accept a business' honest efforts to make things right. For example, one lawyer who practices in a large city states:

> Most of the fraud now is against the lenders. Debtors, especially the young kids, are wise to the tricks. They know that it costs money and takes time to get the wheels in motion, and it isn't worth the trouble if there isn't too much money involved. Recently a young woman bought a brand new car and financed it through a bank. She got a job delivering photographic film and put over 100,000 miles on that car within a year. Then when she was tired of making payments, she just left the car in the bank's parking lot and put the keys and all the papers into the night deposit slot with a note saying, "Here's your car back." What can the bank do realistically? They may be entitled to a deficiency judgment, but it is not worth the trouble to get it under the new laws . . . .
>
> The hallways outside small claims courts are crowded with little old people, crying because of the way young kids have screwed them out of several month's rent . . . . A judgment is just a piece of paper and the Wisconsin Consumer Act has made collection procedures so difficult that a judgment is almost worthless.

. . . [M]ost lawyers serve business interests or relatively well-off individuals who run businesses. Undoubtedly the quotations are accurate descriptions of some consumers whom lawyers encounter. On the other hand, some lawyers view the average consumer-client more positively. Another lawyer in the same small town as the two interviewed together says, "local people are being ripped off by local merchants every day . . . . Attorneys in town can't believe that these guys whose fathers went to the country club with their fathers could be dishonest. They consider these ripoffs just 'tough dealing.' But the local merchants have absolute power—people have to deal with them, and merchants just can't resist the temptation to use this power for all they're worth."

Many lawyers also have personal reasons for hostility to consumers and consumer protection laws. Lawyers are engaged in small businesses themselves. They may face problems when they try to collect fees from clients. They see and read about dissatisfied clients who have been bringing enough malpractice suits to drive up the malpractice insurance rates for all lawyers. Moreover, they themselves are unlikely to face serious consumer problems. Attorneys tend to be affluent enough and sufficiently well connected that the businesses they have personal dealings with will make efforts to keep them happy. Some lawyers make many major purchases from or through clients. Lawyers generally understand the consumer contracts that they sign . . . .

As I have suggested, a lawyer who holds such a negative view of consumer laws and consumers who complain is likely to find wholly inappropriate an aggressive pursuit of the remedies granted by these laws. A number of attorneys suggested that a lawyer has an obligation to judge the true merit of a client's case and to use only reasonable means to solve problems. These lawyers seemed to be saying that an attorney should not aggressively assert good cases under ill-advised or unjust statutes, but no one went so far as to say this explicitly. A reasonable approach in the consumer area was seen as a compromise. For example, several attorneys were very critical of other members of the bar who had used the Wisconsin Consumer Act so that a lender who had violated what they saw as a "technical" requirement of the statute would not be paid for a car which the consumer would keep. While this might be the letter of the law, apparently a responsible lawyer would negotiate a settlement whereby the consumer would pay for the car but would pay less as a result of the lender's error. Several lawyers said that if a lawyer for a consumer offered an honest complaint about the quality of a product or service, it would be resolved in a manner that ought to satisfy anyone who was reasonable. A lawyer who sued in such a matter would be only trying to help a client illegitimately wiggle out of a contract after he or she had a change of heart about a purchase, particularly if the case was one a manufacturer or retailer could not afford to defend on the merits. A lawyer who represents Ford in actions brought in certain areas of Wisconsin commented, "The economics are not only a problem for consumers. How many $200 transmission cases can Ford defend in Small Claims Court? Lots of suits are bought out only because it is easier to buy them off than defend them. A lot of people forget that there are cost barriers to defending cases too. Ford cannot bring an expert from Detroit and pay me to defend product quality cases, and a lot of lawyers for plaintiffs know this and count on it when they file a complaint."

Those attorneys who often press consumer rights are called such things as members of the "rag-tag bar" who have no rating in Martindale-Hubbel and who ignore the economic realities of practice. An older lawyer comments that many younger lawyers are very consumer minded and seem to be "involved emotionally with clients when the word consumer comes up." One attorney who characterizes himself as an "establishment lawyer" explains that in Madison and Milwaukee there now are many lawyers who do not depend on practice for their total income or who live life styles in which they need far less than most people. He is particularly concerned about women lawyers who, he believes, live off their husbands' income and thus are freed to play games and crusade without recognizing the economic realities of practice. Still another attorney points out that consumer cases are often brought by young lawyers just beginning practice. Since they have few cases and want to gain experience, these beginners often refuse to accept reasonable settlements and file complaints. Similar objections are made to some legal services program lawyers who fail to go along with the customs of the bar about the range of reasonable settlements, and who are seen as far too aggressive in asserting questionable claims against established businesses. Some older "establishment" lawyers are annoyed by the mavericks, while others view the younger lawyers with amusement, predicting that they would learn what to do with such cases as they grew up.

Not all lawyers are tied to the local business and legal establishments. Yet even those lawyers who are not in the club face disincentives to using consumer lawyers. Of course, these lawyers are not free to treat every potential client who walks in from the street as the bearer of a major cause. They must ration their time among the worthwhile cases that come to them and balance their good works with enough paying clients so that they can meet payrolls and pay the rent and utility bills. Many who call themselves "movement" lawyers and who are engaged in representing various causes do not honor consumerism any more than do establishment lawyers. Consumer protection is viewed by many of these "progressive" lawyers as only a middle-class concern. It just is not as important as criminal defense of unpopular clients or battling local government authorities on behalf of migrant laborers. Even some who see themselves as radicals seem to have internalized many of the norms of capitalist society about paying debts and avoiding trouble by being careful at the outset of transactions. This attitude is reflected in the following comments of a person who regards himself as a progressive lawyer and who has represented a number of unpopular clients:

> You want to avoid filing complaints and trying consumer law suits. Partly this is economic, but we cannot overlook another important reason. What have you done when you win one of these cases? You have saved a guy a couple of bucks in a minor rip-off. It just isn't fun. It would be a boring hassle. If you win, the client gets only a marginal benefit, and he won't be grateful. So this kind of case will fall to the bottom of the pile of things to do. There are many cases that are far more satisfying. We take consumer cases sometimes, but they are not the things we really enjoy.
>
> You may feel funny about even negotiating consumer cases. A lawyer often can get his client something he is not really entitled to. For example, one client had a contract with a health club. There was nothing

really wrong with it. The client was just tired of the club. We wrote a letter on our letterhead, and the club folded and let him out of the deal. This isn't the way the case should have come out, but it is the way it works. You do not get a great deal of satisfaction out of such a case, and you will try to avoid doing this sort of thing when you can.

. . . A number of lawyers report that many Wisconsin-judges and their clerks are not sympathetic to an adversary handling of consumer protection laws. One lawyer explained that the local judges are all experienced lawyers who understand how such cases should be handled, and so he could end consumer cases without much difficulty by simple motions; the judges just were not going to let these cases go to juries or even to trial. Judges and clerks will see that their time is not wasted by cases which they think never should have been brought to them. Many judges will help consumers handling their own cases in a small claims court reach some kind of settlement, but if a consumer wants to try the case, some judges respond by applying the rules of procedure and evidence very technically so that they will not have to reach the merits. These lawyers tell stories about trial judges who refuse to enforce individual claims based on Wisconsin administrative regulations designed to protect consumers. The judges, it is said, seem to view these regulations as illegitimate enactments by liberal reformers in Madison who are out of touch with conditions in the rest of the state.

Judges are also likely to be unfamiliar with these regulations and with federal materials, and they may lack ready access to copies of these laws or to articles in law reviews explaining various provisions. A lawyer for a local retailer, it was reported, successfully defended a consumer case, in which his client had violated a state regulation, on the ground that the Wisconsin Administrative Code lacked a good index; the lawyer for the consumer had not played fairly when he raised a law with which lawyers in the community and the judge were not familiar. Another lawyer remarked that he would not use the Magnuson-Moss Warranty Act in a case brought in a state court, although this is just what the drafters of that act planned, because "as soon as you throw federal law at a state judge, they freak out since they have no familiarity with federal law. You would have to spend an hour and half convincing them that they had jurisdiction." Still another attorney commented "judges hate consumer cases because they simply do not understand the new law. The courts are just now getting used to the Uniform Commercial Code [the UCC became effective in Wisconsin in 1965]. If you try to use consumer laws, you are letting yourself in for a lot of briefing to educate the judges." One trial judge gained some measure of local fame among the bar by threatening to declare the Uniform Commercial Code's provisions on unconscionable contracts void for vagueness. Other trial judges, or their clerks, flatly tell lawyers that consumer cases just will not be tried in their courts. Of course, a lawyer who wanted the formal state or federal law to penetrate into a county in which such a judge sat would always be free to appeal, but the cost barriers placed before this route assure trial judges a large degree of freedom to do what they see as justice in the teeth of consumer protection laws which displease them.

Perhaps "atrocity stories" about judges are exaggerated, but insofar as they are repeated among lawyers, they are likely to affect the strategy any attorney will pursue. For example, few lawyers would look forward to arguing that a contract was "unconscionable" under Section 2-302 of the Uniform Commercial Code before the trial judge who was so unhappy about the open texture of this provision of the UCC. Young lawyers who have mastered the administrative regulations designed to protect consumers will learn to hesitate to display their wisdom before a trial judge who has never heard of such laws and who is unlikely to sympathize with their goals. Reformers and law professors often assume that laws published in the state capital automatically go into effect in all the county courthouses in the state. Experienced lawyers know better.

Lawyers for Business

In contrast to lawyers for individuals, attorneys for business play fairly traditional lawyer's roles when they deal with consumer law: they lobby, draft documents, plan procedures, and respond to particular disputes by negotiating and litigating. Indeed, our idea of what is a traditional lawyer's job may flow largely from what this part of the bar does for clients who can afford to pay for these services . . . . But even when we turn to business practice, the classical model of lawyering is only a rough approximation of what happens. This suggests that the amount of the potential fee is not the only factor prompting problems with the classical view. I will consider each of these traditional kinds of lawyer's work in the business setting, looking at what is done for clients, which lawyers do what kinds of work, and the degree of independent control exercised by lawyers in each instance.

Lawyers working for manufacturers, distributors, retailers and financial institutions are likely to be present at the creation of any law that purports to aid the consumer . . . .

Not surprisingly, the role of the lobbyist for business is a specialized one, usually played by a small number of lawyers from the larger firms in Milwaukee or Madison, or by lawyers employed by industry trade associations. Smaller businesses seldom hire lobbyists. They rely on being represented by larger businesses or trade associations, or they contact their representatives in the legislature directly. Often legislators who are lawyers find themselves representing home-town businesses before state agencies as a matter of constituent service . . . .

In order to gain concessions from those pushing consumer protection, business has to give something. These lawyer-lobbyists make judgments about which regulations are reasonable, acceptable or inevitable, and then try to sell this view to their clients. Only a few lawyer-lobbyists have the power to make decisions without consulting their clients, and some clients will not accept their lawyers' opinions about what is reasonable and what is not. Nonetheless, the lawyers generally have great influence on the decisions about which laws must be accepted and which ones can be fought. One reason for this is that often they control much of the information necessary for making such judgments. For example, to a great extent they are the experts both about the political situation facing the agencies and legislators and about the intensity of commitment to a particular proposal of those who speak for consumers.

After consumer laws and regulations are passed, business lawyers help their clients cope with them. Much of the work involves drafting documents and setting up procedures for using these forms. For example, both the federal Truth-in-Lending Law and the Wisconsin Consumer Act required a complete reworking of most of the form contracts used to lend money and sell on credit. The Magnuson-Moss Warranty Act demanded that almost every manufacturer, distributor and retailer selling consumer products rewrite any warranty given with the product and create new procedures to make information about these warranties available to consumers. This is traditional lawyers' work, requiring a command of the needs of the business, a detailed understanding of the law, and drafting skills. Moreover, the uncertainties and complexities of many consumer protection laws call for talented lawyering if the job is to be done right.

Counseling business clients about consumer protection laws and drafting the required contracts and forms is the stock-in-trade of the largest firms in the state and a small group of lawyers with a predominantly business practice; some of this work is also done by the inside legal staff of some large corporations. Some of this work can be mass-produced by lawyers for trade associations. Many lenders, retailers, and suppliers of services in smaller cities rely on standard forms supplied by these trade associations. Small manufacturers and financial institutions may send problems concerning consumer protection laws to lawyers in Milwaukee or Madison, either directly or through a referral by their local attorney. There is also a "trickle-down" effect: lawyers who are not expert in consumer law often collect copies of the work product of the more expert, receiving them from clients who get them from trade associations or through friends who work for the larger law firms. They may simply copy these forms or they may produce variations on them but with little or no independent research.

Several lawyers commented that the flood of regulation of the past ten years has made it hard for a smaller law firm or a solo lawyer to keep up with all the new law and to maintain the resources needed to advise business. Some do very well for their business clients, but it is difficult for younger lawyers to gain all the needed knowledge quickly. Lawyers who represent business must be ready to alert their clients to changes in the law which require review of the way business is done. These lawyers usually have their own copies of the federal and state administrative regulations as well as the expensive loose-leaf services necessary to keep up to date. Large law firms and corporations with house counsel can afford to have someone in their office specialize in the various consumer laws. They can send them to continuing legal education programs put on at the state or national level. Indeed, many of these law firms face the problem of coordinating their large staff so that all of their lawyers will recognize a problem of, say, the Truth-in-Lending Act and then call on the resident expert in the area. A consumer law specialist in a large law firm often can call on people working for the various agencies for informal advice about how the agency is likely to respond to particular procedures or provisions in form contracts. Of course, any lawyer can call on the agency, but often these specialists from the large firms will know the administrative officials from previous contacts or from participating in continuing legal education programs.

Some of the lawyers who have been involved in this redrafting of forms and fashioning of new procedures saw the task as one of making the least real change possible in traditional practices while complying with the new laws or regulations. They designed new forms to ward off both what they saw as the unreasonable governmental official and the unreasonable consumer in the unlikely event that the matter ever came close to going to formal proceedings before agencies or courts. Other business lawyers, however, used the redrafting exercise as a means to press their clients to review procedures and teach their employees about dispute avoidance and its importance. In some cases the lawyer's views significantly influenced the client's response to a new law. For example, many business people are proud of their product and service and want to give broad warranties, but their lawyers usually convince them that this is too risky. The Magnuson-Moss Warranty Act attempts to induce manufacturers of consumer products to create informal private processes for mediating disputes. At least some business people have expressed interest in taking such steps to avoid litigation and in experimenting with new procedures for dealing with complaints by consumers. However, lawyers, in at least two of the largest firms in Wisconsin strongly advise their clients to avoid creating private dispute resolution processes. These lawyers see the benefits as unlikely to be worth the risks, and they are in the position to have the final word with many clients about such matters. This is an area about which lawyers are supposed to be expert; a business person who has paid for an expert opinion is likely to listen to it.

Finally, business lawyers do become directly involved in the process of settling particular disputes when attempts to avoid or otherwise deal with them have failed; lawyers in the largest firms seldom have to help ward off individual consumers, but some lawyers for business regularly are involved in particular cases. For example, lawyers represent banks and other creditors in collections work. At one time this was a routine procedure that yielded a default judgment and made clear the creditor's right to any property involved. However, many of the traditional tactics of debt collection have been ruled out of bounds or are now closely regulated by state and federal laws. Lawyers who do collections work describe what seems to them to be a new legal ritual to be followed whenever a debtor who is armed with legal advice resists a collection effort. The lender first attempts to collect by its own efforts, and then it files suit, often in a small claims court. The debtor responds, asserting that something was wrong with the credit transaction under the Truth-in-Lending Act or the Wisconsin Consumer Act, or by asserting that the creditor engaged in "conduct which can reasonably be expected to threaten or harass the customer . . ." or used "threatening language in communication with the customer . . ." as is prohibited and sanctioned by the Wisconsin Consumer Act (Wis. Stat. 427.104 [g], [h] [1975]). The lender then has to respond, either by offering to settle or by claiming to be ready to litigate the legal issues. Then the lawyers on both sides negotiate and, occasionally, battle before a judge.

Large retailers who sell relatively expensive products or services face a regular flow of consumer complaints. Almost all of them are resolved without the participation of lawyers, but an attorney may have to enter the picture occasionally. This may not happen until the consumer files a complaint in court. Often the business lawyer will be facing an unrepresented consumer in a small claims court. Several of these lawyers commented that the consumer was only formally unrepresented since the judge often seemed to serve both as judge and attorney for the plaintiff, particularly in pre-trial settlement negotiations. These are expensive cases for a business to defend if the consumer gets a chance to present the merits of the claim to the court. One law firm in Madison represents one of the largest automobile manufacturers in such matters, but it sees only three of four such cases a year. Interestingly, these cases almost never involve an application of the many consumer protection laws or even the Uniform Commercial Code; the real issue is almost always one of fact concerning whether the product or service was defective. The law firm's recommendation about whether to settle is almost always final. Their recommendation will be rejected only where the manufacturer wants to defend a particular model of its automobiles against a series of charges that the model has a particular defect; the manufacturer may be far more worried about a government order to recall that model than a particular buyer's claim.

Another situation that brings out lawyers is the consumer complaint that prompts a state agency to begin a regulatory enforcement action. Typically, a business lawyer will try to settle rather than litigate this kind of case, but, of course, the possibility of formal action affects the bargaining by both sides. Here, too, the lawyer has great influence on the client's decision about whether to settle or fight. The lawyer's advice is likely to involve a mixture of predictions about the practical consequences of the proposed settlement, the outcome of a formal enforcement proceeding, and the risks of adverse publicity if the matter goes to a public forum.

It should be stressed that most of these lawyers for business do not see themselves as hired guns doing only their clients' bidding. However, most of our sample viewed their clients as responsible people trying to do the right thing. Members of the elite of the bar seldom see any "but the most reasonable business people," at least when it comes to consumer problems. Of course, it is not surprising that these lawyers tend to see their clients as reasonable people, since the lawyers are likely to hold the same values as the clients. Business lawyers concede that consumer protection laws make more work for them, and thus increase their billings, but they also see their clients as being swamped by governmental regulation and paper work which serves little purpose. They are unhappy because they cannot explain these laws to their clients in common-sense terms. Some business lawyers are concerned about easy credit practices and how simple it is for consumers to evade debts when they become burdensome. They worry that the importance of keeping promises and paying one's debts is being undermined by reforms directed at problems which politicians invented. Several remarked that when they left law school, they were strongly in favor of consumer protection, but after a few years in practice, they see matters differently. In short, as we might expect, Wisconsin business lawyers are not radicals and are comfortable representing business interests.

At the same time, some business lawyers concede that occasionally they must persuade their clients to change practices or to respond to a particular dispute in what the lawyers see as a reasonable manner. For example, these lawyers may tell their clients that they must appear to be fair when they are before an agency in order to have any chance of winning in this era of consumer protection. In this way, they may be able to legitimate sitting in judgment on the behavior of their clients and occasionally manipulating the situation to influence clients' choices.

A few of the lawyers we interviewed reported having to act to protect their own self-interest when dealing with a business client. One prominent lawyer, for example, described a case where he represented an out-of-state book club in a proceeding before one of the state regulatory agencies; he took the case only as a favor to a friend who had some indirect connection with the club's officers. As the case unfolded, the lawyer discovered that the book club had failed to send books to many people who had paid for them. It was not clear whether the situation involved fraud or merely bad business practices. The lawyer insisted that the book club immediately get books or refunds to all of its Wisconsin customers and sign a settlement agreement with the agency which bound the club to strict requirements for future behavior. The attorney explained that the business had been trading on his reputation as a lawyer when it got him to enter the case on its behalf. Once it became clear that the administrative agency had a good case against the client involving conduct at least on the borders of fraud, the lawyer felt that the client was obligated to help him maintain his reputation as an attorney who represented only the most ethical businesses.

III. DISCUSSION

In this section I will try to integrate the findings of this study into a broader picture of the practice of law, with some special attention to a question central to other recent research on the legal profession: are lawyers agents of social control or are they so tied to their clients as to lack the professional autonomy so often ascribed to them?

A descriptive model of practice would accept much of the classical view as a starting point. Traditionally, we have emphasized lawyers being involved in certain transformations: clients bring problems to lawyers who, in Cain's terms (1979: 343),[178] "translate [issues] into a meta-language in terms of which a binding solution can be found." For example, lawyers translate client desires to transfer property to others into such legal forms as declarations of trust, deeds, and wills. Lawyers try to convert some of the many factors involved in an automobile accident into a winning cause of action for negligence. Indeed, . . . it is the lawyer's authority over this meta-language which gives the profession much of its status and market control; one goes to law school to master it in order to enter the profession, and entry usually is gained by passing a bar examination where that mastery can be displayed.

However, even when clients come to lawyers for relatively defined services such as drafting a will or a contract, the lawyers' work may involve often overlooked interactions whereby lawyers influence the outcome, and these interactions also must be part of our sketch of practice. For example, some may hesitate to ask for certain provisions in their will if they fear even implicit disapproval by a lawyer who, with his gray hair, three-piece suit, and symbols of membership in the legal profession, may be seen to represent conventional morality. The lawyer, also, may ask questions necessary for counseling or drafting which

---

178. [The reference is to Maureen Cain, "The General Practice Lawyer and the Client: Towards a Radical Conception," 7 *International Journal of the Sociology of Law* 331 (1979).]

force the client to consider possible consequences and make choices that he or she has not foreseen or has avoided thinking about. The lawyer may tell a client that the law blocks taking certain action, but sometimes an attorney can suggest other ways of achieving at least some of the client's purposes. Just by explaining the requirement for a cause of action in negligence, the lawyer can affect the client's memory, or willingness to lie, and thus affect the outcome.

If our model is to have a wider focus, we will have to recognize other translations and transformations which only indirectly involve legal rules but which often take place in interactions between attorneys, clients, opponents, and legal officials. As I have pointed out in this article, lawyers play many roles in these interactions, including the gatekeeper who teaches clients about the costs of using the legal system, the knowledgeable friend or therapist, the broker of information or coach, the go-between or informal mediator, the legal technician, and the adversary bargainer-litigator. In playing these roles, lawyers often have to transform their clients' perception of the problem and their goals. Sometimes clients do come to lawyers seeking fairly specific services—a client may want to make a will, to convey property, or gain a license to run a television station. However, the lawyer is often involved in transforming both the client's perception of the problem and the goals. Sometimes the lawyer will turn away a client, saying that (1) the client has no case legally, (2) it is against the client's best interest to pursue the matter as the costs will exceed the likely benefits, (3) the client is unreasonable to complain or seek certain ends as judged by standards other than the law, or (4) some mixture of these arguments. On the other hand, the lawyer may seek . . . to redefine a conflict of value into a conflict of interest which can be settled by payment of a reasonable amount of money rather than by a public declaration of right and wrong.

And the lawyer may be involved in transforming the views of the opponent about both the client and the situation so that an acceptable settlement will be forthcoming. Sometimes lawyers use their status as experts in the law, legal arguments, and express or implied threats of legal action in this process of persuasion. Often, however, a legal style of argument fades into the background. The attorney may not be too sure about the precise legal situation or may worry about seeming to coerce the other party. In such situations lawyers are likely to appeal to some mixture of the interest of the opponent and to standards of reasonableness apart from claims of legal right. Then, as I have stressed, if there is a settlement offer, the lawyer must sell it to the client, and here again appeals are likely to be made primarily in terms of reasonableness or interest rather than right.

The research reported here shows lawyers for individuals playing these nonadversary roles without great knowledge of the contours of consumer law, while the lawyers for corporations act more traditional parts—lobbying, counseling, drafting documents, and defending cases after complaints are filed. However, lawyers for corporations are at least occasionally pushed out of the character of legal technician. For example, a lawyer for one of the nation's largest law firms, who has an extensive corporate practice, sees himself as engaged in "the lay practice of psychiatry." He explains that a manager of a large corporation often is worried about making a decision, but he or she has few people with whom to talk openly. Others in the corporation tend to be rivals; psychiatric help is unthinkable as it would indicate weakness. However, it is legitimate to see an attorney seeking legal advice. Often this lawyer finds himself asking questions which lead the manager to see the options and their likely costs and benefits. The questions are justified as necessary in the process of giving legal advice; their actual function, the lawyer says, is a very directive short-term therapy. Sometimes he does not need to ask many questions, because it is enough to serve as an audience while the manager thinks aloud. Another lawyer engaged in corporate commercial litigation sees lawyers as curbing the influence of ego and pride on the part of business executives in dispute resolution . . . .

An evaluation of what I have discovered about lawyers in the consumer protection area suggests a number of things about the strategy of creating individual rights to bring about social change. On the positive side, one might view the practices of the lawyers I studied as yielding a kind of rough justice. Lawyers for business, prompted by federal and state statutes and regulations, work hard to help their clients comply with the disclosure requirements that have been demanded . . . .

Lawyers for individuals have guarded an expensive social institution—the legal system—from overload by relatively minor complaints. Consumers who are dissatisfied with such things as warped phonograph records, defective hair dryers, or inoperative instant cameras can return them to the seller. Almost always, the seller will replace them or offer a refund if they cannot be fixed. If the seller refuses, the buyer can shop elsewhere next time, and the buyer has an "atrocity story" with which to entertain friends which, in turn, may affect the seller's reputation. In short, many problems can be left to the market. At the other extreme, consumers who have suffered serious personal injuries as the result of defective products usually can find a lawyer to pursue their case aggressively, since the growing law of products liability offers generous remedies which will support contingent fees. Moreover, products liability and government-ordered product recalls together give manufacturers a great incentive to pay attention to quality control and avoid problems.

It is necessary to sort out claims falling between these poles. Defects in new automobiles and mobile homes, for example, often warrant buying at least a little of a lawyer's time, especially when manufacturers and sellers fail to remedy the problem after a customer makes a complaint. But a full-scale war using elaborate legal research and expert testimony usually would be a waste of resources. A telephone call or a letter from a lawyer may be all the effort the claim is worth. If all clients with cases supporting substantial fees had to subsidize cases involving only small sums, then lawyers might buy all of the necessary law books and learn all the details of consumer law, but this might price legal services out of the reach of some who now can afford them. Alternatively, lawyers could be subsidized by governments to master consumer laws and litigate, but many citizens would see better uses for tax revenues.

Also on the positive side, those lawyers who are willing to do something for clients with a consumer case may be defending the values of social integration and harmony. In Laura Nader's (1969)[179] phrase, they are seeking "to make the balance" by restoring personal relations to equilibrium through compromise. They do this by clearing up misunderstandings and promoting reasonableness on both sides, avoiding vendettas aimed at hurting the opponent. They offer their clients their status and contacts—but rarely an expensive-to-acquire legal knowledge—which allow them to reach the person who has power to apologize, to offer a token gesture, or to make a real offer of settlement. The fact that a manager or owner accepts the blame and apologizes may be as effective in placating the client as a recovery of money. The real grievance may rest on a sense of being taken, insulted, or treated impersonally. Lawyers can help their clients see themselves not as victims but as people with minor complaints; they can help them get on with the business of living rather than allowing a $200 to $300 problem to become the focus of their lives . . . .

Rather than pour gasoline on the fire of indignation in members of a "self-centered, demanding, dissatisfied population which has grudges," almost all of the lawyers interviewed in this study seem far more likely to use some type of fire extinguisher. Even lawyers who see themselves as progressive and those who work for group legal service plans try to push aside potential clients whom they judge to be "crazy," to want something for nothing, or to be acting in bad faith.

It would be difficult deliberately to plan and create a system such as the one I have described. Perhaps it could only have arisen in response to laws that created a number of individual rights which could not be fully exercised. By relying on lawyers as gatekeepers, we get enough threat of trouble to prompt apologies, gestures, and settlements which are acceptable, but not enough litigation to burden legal or commercial institutions. We avoid having to reach complete agreement on the precise boundaries of the appropriate norms governing a manufacturer's and

179. [The reference is to Laura Nader, "Styles of Court Procedure: To Make the Balance," in L. Nader (ed.), *Law in Culture and Society* (Chicago: Aldine Publishing Co., 1969).]

seller's responsibility for quality defects and for misleading buyers short of absolute deliberate fraud. We avoid having to live with inappropriate norms which might result from the confrontation of interest groups in the legislative and administrative processes. We avoid having to resolve difficult questions of fact concerning the seller's responsibility for the buyer's expectations and for the condition of the goods—questions which often cannot be resolved in a satisfactory manner. Finally, we offer some deterrence to consumers who want to defraud sellers or creditors or to those who are eager to get something for nothing.

On the negative side, one could highlight the unequal access consumers have to remedies, despite the merits of their cases. Some do not see lawyers at all, but we cannot be sure that their complaints lack merit or are trivial or that they are resolved in some other manner. Those few who do seek legal services will get only what the lawyer sees as appropriate, some will get turned away with little more than token gestures, while a very few will recover their full statutory remedies through legal action . . . .

Arguably, whether or not a claim is trivial or significant does not turn on whether there is enough at stake to support a substantial legal fee. For example, in this era of inflation, perhaps, the $400 many spent to replace four defective "Firestone 500" steel-belted radial tires would have seemed trivial to successful lawyers, or many consumers would have thought that to be the case. Nonetheless, the amount was not trivial to many of those faced with this problem . . . .

Conciliatory settlements may subvert the purposes of consumer protection law because they can shield socially harmful practices from effective scrutiny by the public or some legal agency . . . . The conciliatory tactics favored by lawyers may block the market correction called for by consumer protection legislation and prevent public awareness that the markets are not being corrected.

We can ask whether we should be satisfied to delegate the power of deciding which claims will be asserted, and to what extent, to individual lawyers who are typically white, middle-class males well integrated into their communities . . . .

Lawyers who play "counsel for the situation" may leave the rest of us a little uneasy. What qualifies these lawyers as experts in problem solving? Certainly this was not the approach of their law school training, and we can wonder if their professional experiences have produced wisdom in finding good solutions to such problems as are involved in women's rights, consumer protection, racial discrimination, or environmental protection. In short, there is a problem of legitimacy. As is true in the case of so many empirical studies related to law, once again we have stumbled on the problem of discretion and the expert whose skill rests on experience rather than on training and science. And a counsel for the situation has little accountability to much beyond his or her own conscience.

The mystification involved in the gap between the classical picture of the lawyer's role and the portrait painted here also may be objectionable. Clients may find themselves manipulated and fooled. Few clients probably go to lawyers seeking to have their situations redefined or their problems solved by apologies and token gestures. At least some clients do not want a "counsel for the situation" but a lawyer who will take their side. The settlement worked out after a five-minute telephone call may be the best possible in light of the lawyer's and the business' interest, and an objective observer might be able to defend it as serving some social interest. But do clients know how their interests regularly are offset by all of the others involved? If they knew, would they accept the situation?

Conciliatory strategies require little investment of professional time as compared to more adversarial ones. Mediation does not require much knowledge of consumer law, and a lawyer can negotiate a settlement based on rules of thumb rather than hard legal research. However, lawyers get an exclusive license to practice because they are supposed to be expert in the law . . . . Many who have never seen the inside of a law school might be better conciliators than lawyers, since legal education does little to train students for this part of practice, but non-lawyers are not given the privilege of representing clients. In theory, lawyers are qualified to negotiate and mediate because they assess the legal position and work from this as a baseline. Lawyers who know almost nothing about consumer law are operating from a different baseline . . . . [A]n official of the Federal Trade Commission who was concerned about the failure of the Magnuson-Moss Warranty Act condemned Wisconsin lawyers who were not fully acquainted with that statute two years after it had become effective as being guilty of serious malpractice. He thought that perhaps a malpractice action or two might wake up the Wisconsin bar. Several lawyers interviewed in this study commented that many lawyers do not know enough consumer law to recognize that it offers a good legal theory and that if they did see this, it might change the course of their negotiations.

But it seems unfair to blame lawyers who almost never see a consumer case involving more than a few hundred dollars for not mastering a complicated and extensive body of law and for not purchasing expensive loose-leaf services to keep up to date. While, perhaps, we can ask lawyers to do some charity work, they cannot provide reasonably priced services for every case that comes in the door. There is no way that any lawyer can know much about all branches of the law; lawyers naturally become expert in the areas they see regularly.

The lawyers studied seem to be responding predictably to the social and economic structures in which the practice of law is embedded. Liberal reforms such as consumer protection laws create individual rights without providing the means to carry them out. Grand declarations of rights may be personally rewarding to those who struggle for legislative and appellate victories, but, in practice, justice is rationed by cost barriers and the lawyer's long-range interests. Even lawyers working for lower-income clients must pick and choose how much of their time and stock of goodwill to risk investing in a particular case.

We could see most of the individual rights created by consumer protection laws, as well as many other reforms of recent times, as primarily exercises in symbolism. The reformers gained the pretty words in the statute books and some indirect impact, but the practice of those to be regulated was affected only marginally . . . . Of course, it is possible that as time passes, lawyers will become more and more aware of at least some reform laws. It may take a generation or two for some of them to penetrate into day-to-day practice. Perhaps as new forms of delivering legal services develop and old areas of practice are reformed out of existence, lawyers will turn to some of these new reforms as an unmined resource and find ways to make exploitation commercially feasible. Nonetheless, if awareness of a more empirically accurate view of legal practice is not developed, reformers are likely to go on creating individual rights which have little chance of being vindicated, and, as a result, they may fail to achieve their ends repeatedly. And a gap between the promise of the law and its implementation may have consequences for the society.

A kind of classic response to the empirical picture of professional practice that I have drawn is to call for a return to the adversary model with, perhaps, some additional legal services supported as a government or group benefit and with new institutions for dispute resolution, such as neighborhood justice centers. Whatever the merit of any of these new measures and the philosophically comforting virtues of such proposals, the issues raised by the empirical sketch I have drawn are not likely to go away so easily . . . .

Apart from mediating and acting as counsel for the situation, this study seeks to add to the classical model of practice the idea that the lawyer's own interests and values play an important role whatever the ideal of service asserted in professional theory . . . .

It is probably the case that if a new reform law can be seen as likely to yield substantial fees, some lawyers will gear their practice toward clients who want to bring such cases . . . . [P]ersonal injury practice has relatively low prestige among the attorneys . . . . Nonetheless, the development of the doctrines of products liability during the 1960s prompted many lawyers to become specialists in the area—contingent fees, a good chance to win high verdicts and settlements, and real advantages from specialization have produced a recognizable segment of the bar. Moreover, causes such as civil rights may draw the attention of organizations such as the NAACP which will provide the lawyers. But if one has neither an organized cause nor the chance of a real monetary payoff, reforms resting on individual rights are likely to produce no more than the conciliatory gestures reported by this study. In such situations, the inability to mobilize needed legal services may be a form of social control blunting the impact of efforts at reform through law . . . .

Undercutting the conventional picture of practice may have costs. Law, as is the case with many professions, justifies its position by the mastery of a special body of knowledge, and this mastery is produced by training and certified by examinations. Law school and bar examinations deal with the rule of law and not deals reflecting cost-benefit calculations and the emotions of clients. This view may help give or defend a measure of status and wealth for those who learn the law so that some will be induced to try to master it. And it may be useful in our kind of society to have a group of people capable of calling governmental, corporate and private power to account by legal standards. The theory of the adversary system may offer unpopular or powerless people some degree of protection from bias or a politically expedient solution to the problem they present to the powerful. This theory is a major part of the reason why our government provides some amount of legal service to those accused of a crime when they cannot afford their own lawyer. It is a major part of the rationalization that a lawyer for an unpopular client can offer in an attempt to ward off pressures against causing difficulties by vigorous advocacy. The ideal of disinterested service to clients may draw some people into the profession and offer nonpecuniary rewards to lawyers so that more of this kind of service exists than it would in a system where the single-minded pursuit of self-interest was recognized as fully legitimate.

Of course, this argument rests on untested empirical assumptions. We do not know whether these normative ideals have enough influence on behavior to be worthy of concern. It may be that the classical view has had little importance beyond making lawyers who do little public service feel bad on occasion. However, the empirical assumptions are only untested. They have not been disproved, and the argument is plausible enough for attention. Nonetheless, many of the nonadversary roles played by lawyers also seem to have some social value—experts in coping with the claims of other individuals, corporations or the government by using all available tools including, but not limited to, legal rules can offer useful help to citizens. Perhaps the classical position does serve as a golden lie (Plato, The Republic, Book III), misleading both lawyers and the public for a good purpose. Yet it has costs, particularly as more and more people discover that lawyers' behavior so often fails to conform to the model. There seems, moreover, no reason to assume without even making an attempt that we cannot rationalize when a lawyer can be expected to refuse a case, to mediate and play counsel for the situation and when to vindicate rights. Perhaps no ideological statement ever can be without flaw, but the classical picture of the practice seems to fit the legal profession of the 1980s so poorly as to be embarrassing. □

NOTES AND QUESTIONS

1. Macaulay describes several strategies a lawyer might follow when faced with a consumer protection case. How far can you generalize his findings? Are there analogies in family law practice? torts practice? criminal practice? Would many corporate lawyers serve as gatekeepers or coaches to their clients, as Macaulay uses these terms? If not, why not? When would what kinds of lawyers be most free to reject a potential client or refuse to carry out the wishes of an existing client?

Herbert M. Kritzer, William L.F. Felstiner, Austin Sarat, and David M. Trubek, in "The Impact of Fee Arrangement on Lawyer Effort," 19 *Law & Society Review* 251 (1985), report that lawyers working on a contingent fee spend less time than hourly fee lawyers on cases with stakes of $6,000 or less. However, contingent fee lawyers may spend more time than hourly fee lawyers on larger cases where the potential payoff to them is very large. Herbert M. Kritzer, *The Justice Broker* (New York: Oxford University Press, 1990), pp. 90, 168–76. argues that rather than acting as a professional, lawyers in ordinary civil matters typically act more as brokers. A professional uses the kind of knowledge associated with a formal academic program; a broker uses insider knowledge associated with working in a setting day-in and day-out. He says:

> Some kinds of cases, particularly in the federal courts, draw very heavily on the formal legal skills (e.g., legal research and analysis) around which legal education is centered, and it is clear that for those areas the lawyer as portrayed by the professional image makes the most sense. However, in the most typical areas of ordinary litigation, torts and contracts, the lawyer must draw much more heavily on the informal, insider kinds of legal skills than on the formal skills.

Kritzer argues that people other than lawyers could handle many of the ordinary disputes. There is little in a lawyer's training that gives her an advantage in developing contacts with insiders, bargaining and convincing clients to accept solutions to their problems which their broker has worked out with the other party. Would you expect most lawyers in small towns and medium-sized cities to agree? What might they say in response to Kritzer? Recall the discussion of bargaining in the shadow of the law in Chapter 2.

2. Macaulay stresses that we must avoid the assumption that the interests of lawyer and client are identical. Lawyers are not simply agents. To what extent, if at all, would you expect lawyer self-interest to play a part in transactions involving lawyers and major corporate clients? That is, to what extent would you expect a major corporate client to be able to bend a large law firm to its will? How about in-house counsel?

Roman Tomasic, an Australian sociologist of law, considers similar issues in his "Defining Acceptable Tax Conduct: The Role of Professional Advisers in Tax Compliance," Centre for National Corporate Law Research, Discussion Paper No 2, 1990. Tax practitioners—both lawyers and accountants—in Australia protect their firms. They note that they are in business for the long-run. When clients appear with unrealistic expectations about avoiding taxes, the practitioner must teach the client to be realistic. Advisers talk about being unpaid agents for the Australian Tax Office (ATO).

However, Tomasic notes:

In the hard light of practice reality the temptation and pressure to cut corners can be very great for the smaller practitioner. Many small to medium firms have little desire to come to the attention of the ATO even though they are probably less able to resist client pressure than are the larger firms. The smaller firms tend to deal directly with the owners of small businesses and they are likely to be placed under greater pressure than are the larger firms. The corporate clients of larger firms tend to be represented by an employee who, inevitably, has less financial stake in the result of the tax advice given by the larger firm than will the owner of the smaller business. (p. 18)

3. Macaulay's essay reminds us that the problem of communicating the law is one which the legal system constantly faces. See above pages 649–50. Often communication, as we noted, is a function of the work of lawyers. However, lawyers tend to have a repertoire of problems which they deal with regularly. Once they are pushed beyond that repertoire, they may lack practical access to the necessary legal materials, and they may fail to serve as efficient channels of communication about the law.

4. Austin Sarat and Susan Silbey, in "The Pull of the Policy Audience," 10 *Law & Policy* 97 (1988), criticize Macaulay's article. Their article attacks much of the work of the law and society movement (see p. 85, supra, for their critique of Blumberg). They consider most work in the field too respectful of the status quo, too geared to the audience of policy-makers, and too meekly reformist. They use Macaulay's article as an example of an essay animated by ideas of "liberal reform," which does not go far enough to penetrate to the roots of problems in American society.

They concede that the article does expose the ways in which law practice maintains a "facade of responsiveness despite the systematic denial of remedy." But they say that, for Macaulay, the essential problem is "[a]wareness, or lack of awareness," rather than "the fundamental contradictions" of the social situation. Law reform failed, according to their reading of Macaulay, because of a "problem of perception not intention . . . . Consumer protection is no longer seen as a rationalization of fundamentally inequitable market relations . . . ; the problem is not the ends but the means chosen to achieve consumer protection."

Do you agree with Sarat and Silbey? How might you defend Macaulay's work against Sarat and Silbey's attack? Or is their criticism well taken? Could we explain the conflicting positions by seeing Macaulay as far more pessimistic about the possibilities of major social change while Sarat and Silbey are more romantic and utopian? Consider, particularly, the last two paragraphs of Macaulay's article.

5. One important change in the work and structure of the legal profession is the increasing trend toward a more "globalized" practice. Business is transnational, and thus there is an increasing amount of transnational legal practice. Many American firms, for example, have branches in foreign countries.

Most transnational lawyers probably do not think of their practice as "ideological" or as based on an "ideology." However, Bryant G. Garth has pointed out that there is an international ideology of "free trade, minimal governmental regulation, and a common understanding of how conflicts ought to be normally resolved."

Transnational legal practice rests on this ideology and presupposes it. On this and other aspects of the practice, see the thoughtful article by Garth, "Transnational Legal Practice and Professional Ideology, in *Issues of Transnational Legal Practice* (Vol VII, Michigan Yearbook of International Studies, 1985), p. 3.

58. *Law and Strategy in the Divorce Lawyer's Office*

Austin Sarat and

William L. F. Felstiner

20 *Law & Society Review* 93 (1986)

I. INTRODUCTION

☐ Traditionally, the sociology of the legal profession has portrayed lawyers as important intermediaries between clients and the legal system, many more people see lawyers than have direct contact with formal legal institutions. Lawyers serve clients as important sources of information about legal rights, help clients relate legal rules to individual problems, and introduce clients to the way the legal process works. The information provided by lawyers shapes in large measure citizens' views of the legal order and their understanding of the relevance, responsiveness, and reliability of legal institutions. What lawyers say to their clients is not necessarily derived from statutes, rules, and cases and does not involve a literal translation of legal doctrine, nor could the legal system as it is presented in the lawyer's office be understood by clients from untutored observation.

More is at stake, however, in the interaction between lawyers and clients than a unidirectional movement of information and advice from lawyer to client. In addition, this interaction provides one important setting where law and society meet and where legal norms and folk norms come together to shape responses to grievances, injuries, and problems. In some instances those worlds may be complementary; in others there may be little fit between them.

Despite the importance of the discourse between lawyers and their clients, we know very little about what actually goes on in the lawyer's office. Our understanding of lawyer-client interaction has a very shallow basis in systematic empirical research. Legal sociologists are, in this respect, far behind sociologists of medicine, who have over many years conducted numerous studies of doctors and patients. Researchers have been frustrated by norms of confidentiality, the routines of busy professionals, and an inability to convince lawyers of the need for research on lawyer-client communications. Yet without direct knowledge of such communications, it is difficult to pose or answer major questions about the content, form, and effects of legal services, the nature of dispute transformation, and the transmission of legal ideology. Indeed it may be that we have ignored an important means of understanding the law itself . . .

II. THE RESEARCH, THE CASE, AND THE CONFERENCE

In the research from which this paper is derived, we developed an ethnographic account of lawyer-client interaction in divorce cases. We chose to examine divorce because it is a serious and growing social problem in which the involvement of lawyers is particularly salient and controversial. Concern among many divorce lawyers about their role suggested that field research on lawyer-client interaction in this area would encounter less resistance than in other areas of legal practice.

We observed cases over a period of thirty-three months in two sites, one in Massachusetts and one in California. This effort consisted in following one side of forty divorce cases, ideally from the first lawyer-client interview until the divorce was final. We followed these cases by observing and tape-recording lawyer-client sessions, attending court and mediation hearings and trials, and interviewing both lawyers and clients about those events. Approximately 115 lawyer-client conferences were tape-recorded.[180]

180. Neither the lawyers nor the clients that we studied were randomly selected . . . We began the process of securing lawyer participation by asking judges, mediators, and lawyers to name the lawyers in each community who did a substantial amount of divorce work. In each instance, the list eventually contained about 40 names. We stopped trying to add names to the list when additional inquiries were not providing new names. We asked all lawyers on each list to cooperate in the research. Most agreed, but only slightly more than one-quarter in each site actually produced one or more clients willing to participate in the research. We left the choice of clients to the lawyers, except that we did ask them to focus on cases that promised to involve several lawyer-client meetings.

The lawyer samples have two obvious biases. In both sites they involve a higher proportion of women than exists either in the bar or among divorce lawyers generally. Nevertheless, the samples contain more men than women lawyers. More importantly, the samples appear not to include many lawyers high in income, experience, and status. We have come to this conclusion first because of the general clientele of our lawyers; very few doctors, lawyers, businessmen, and others with substantial income and assets are represented. Second, our lawyers are not generally talked about in these communities as the most prominent divorce practitioners. And third, the lawyers in our samples generally attended less prestigious law schools than did those usually considered to be at the top of local divorce practice. As a result, the findings of this project should not be considered representative of all divorce lawyers. However, other than their relative status within the local bar, we know of no other relevant trait on which these lawyers differ from the rest of the divorce bar and consider it fair to say that the findings are based on samples that are characteristic of the lawyers that most people with ordinary financial resources are likely to consult . . . .

Our major objectives were to describe the ways in which lawyers present the legal system and legal process to their clients, to identify the roles that lawyers adopt in divorce cases, to describe the actual context of legal work, to analyze the language and communication patterns through which lawyers carry out these functions, and to examine the ways that lawyer-client interaction affects the development and transformation of divorce disputes. In this paper we describe the interaction between one lawyer and one client in one conference. Not all of the themes of our research are represented here; rather, the paper is devoted to exploring the ways in which lawyers and clients negotiate their differing views of law and the legal process and how that negotiation influences decisions about preferred paths to disposition.

We have observed several patterns through which such decisions are made. Some result in a contested hearing on the main issues. Most, however, do not. In this paper we describe the most common pattern that we observed, namely an exchange in which the lawyer persuades a somewhat reluctant client to try to reach a negotiated settlement. This pattern involves three steps. First, the legal process itself is discussed and interpreted. Here we ask the following questions: What do lawyer and client say about the process? What information does the client seek? What kind of explanations does the lawyer provide? The description of the legal process prepares the way for a decision about settlement by providing the client with a sense of the values and operations inherent in formal adjudication. Second, there is a discussion of how best to dispose of the case. What issues should be settled? What issues, if any, should be fully litigated? What allocation of work does the client prefer? How does the lawyer respond to this preference? Third, there is a discussion of what the client will have to do and how she will have to behave if a settlement is to be reached. Here we examine what the legal process values in human character and what it wishes to ignore, what the process validates and what it leaves for others to reinforce. This discourse we call the "legal construction of the client."

In this lawyer-client conference these themes are interwoven so that an understanding of each is necessary to the full comprehension of the others. The discussion of the nature of the legal process serves to introduce and then justify the lawyer's argument about the best method of disposing of the case. Having reached agreement on method, he must decide how to produce satisfactory outcomes and encourage the client to think and act in a way appropriate to achieving them. Because each of these elements is developed as part of a dialogue that is shaped by client questions, expectations, and demands, discussions of these themes are neither linear nor free of contradiction.

In this paper we focus on one lawyer-client conference to provide the reader with the maximum opportunity to follow these themes and see them at work "on location." Only through such concentration are we able to convey the level of detail that we believe is necessary to convey the full social significance of the interplay between the lawyer and client.

This conference is typical of our sample of conferences . . . .

The lawyer involved in this case graduated from one of the country's top-ranked law schools. He was forty years old at the time of the conference and had practiced for fourteen years. His father was a prominent physician in a neighboring city. The lawyer had spent four years as a public defender after law school and had been in private practice for ten years. He considers himself a trial lawyer and states that he was drawn to divorce work because of the opportunity it provides for trial work. He is married and has never been divorced.

The client and her husband were in their late thirties and had no children. Their marriage had been stormy, involving both substantial separations and infidelity by the husband. Both had graduate degrees and worked full-time; financial support was not an issue. They owned a house, bank stocks, several limited partnerships in real estate, his retirement benefits, and personal property. The house was their major asset. It was an unconventional building to which the husband was especially attached. Housing in the area is very expensive. This divorce was the client's second; there were no children in the first marriage either. She had received extensive psychological counseling prior to and during the case which we observed.

The parties in this divorce initially tried to dissolve their marriage by engaging a mediator and did not at that time individually consult lawyers. The mediator was an established divorce lawyer with substantial experience in divorce mediation. At the first substantive session, the mediator stated that he did not think that further progress could be made if both the spouses continued to live in the house. Although she considered it to be a major sacrifice, the wife said that she had moved out of the house to facilitate mediation after her husband absolutely refused to leave. Thereafter, she visited the house occasionally, primarily to check on plants and pets. The client reported that she was careful to warn her husband when she intended to visit.

Over time, however, this arrangement upset her husband. Rather than raise the problem at a mediation session, he hired a lawyer and secured an *ex parte* order restraining the client from entering the property at any time for any reason. The husband had previously characterized the lawyer that he hired as "the meanest son-of-a-bitch in town." The restraining order ended any prospects for mediation and the client, on the advice of the mediator and another lawyer, hired the lawyer involved in this conference.

Subsequently, a hearing about the propriety of the *ex parte* order was held by a second judge. The issues at this hearing were whether the order should be governed by a general or a divorce-specific injunction statute, what status quo the order was intended to maintain, and whether the husband's attempt to secure the order violated a moral obligation undertaken when the client agreed to move out of the house. The second judge decided against the client on the first two issues, but left consideration of the bad faith question open to further argument. The client's therapist attended the hearing and the lawyer-client conference that immediately followed. At that conference the therapist stressed that contesting the restraining order further might not be in the client's long-term interest even if it corrected the legal wrong.

The conference analyzed in this paper followed the meeting attended by the therapist and was the seventh of twelve that occurred during the course of the case. It took place in the lawyer's office five weeks after the first meeting between lawyer and client. Its two phases, interrupted for several hours at midday, lasted a total of about two hours.

The people referred to in this conference are:[181]

Lawyer	Peter Edmunds
Client	Jane Carroll
Spouse	Norb
Spouse's lawyer	Paul Foster
First judge	John Hancock
Second judge	Mike Cohen
Therapist	Irene
Financial consultant	Bob Archer

III. THE LEGAL PROCESS OF DIVORCE

Clients look to lawyers to explain how the legal system works and to interpret the actions and decisions of legal officials. Despite their lack of knowledge about and contact with the law, clients are likely to have some general notions that the law works as a formally rational legal order, one that is rule governed, impersonal, impartial, predictable, and relatively error free. How do lawyers respond to this picture? In this conference we are interested in the image of the legal process that the lawyer presents. Does he subscribe to the formalist image or does he present the kind of picture that would be drawn by a legal realist, one in which rules are of limited relevance, impersonality gives way to communities of interest shaped by the needs of ongoing relationships, routinization provides the only predictability, and errors are frequently made but seldom acknowledged? Or does he present some mix of the two images or a set of messages different from both?

In this conference the lawyer presents the legal process of divorce

---

181. Fictional names have been assigned to all the participants and places.

largely in response to questions or remarks by the client. In many conferences clients ask for an explanation of some aspect of the legal system's procedures or rules. In this conference the client repeatedly inquires about both. While most of her questions concern the details of her own case, several are general. Thus, she invites her lawyer to explain the way that the legal process operates as well as to justify its operation in her case. At no point does the lawyer deliver a monologue on how it works. Instead his comments are interspersed in the discussion of major substantive issues, particularly concerning what to do about the restraining order and how to proceed with settlement negotiations. Throughout the conference the client persists in focusing on the restraining order until finally she asks:

> *Client:* How often does a case like this come along—a restraining order of this nature?
> *Lawyer:* Very common.
> *Client:* It's a very common thing. So how many other people are getting the same kind of treatment I am? With what, I presume, is very sloppily handled orders that are passed out.
> *Lawyer:* Yeah, you know, I talked, I did talk to someone in the know—I won't go any further than that—who said that this one could have been signed purely by accident. I mean, that the judge could have if he looked at it now—said, I would not sign that, knowing what it was, and it could have been signed by accident, and I said, well, then how does that happen? And he said, well, you've got all this stuff going; you come back to your office, and there's a stack of documents that need signatures. He says, you can do one of two things: you can postpone signing them until you have time, but then it may be the end of the day; the clerk's office is closing, and people who really need this stuff aren't going to get the orders, because there's someone else that needs your attention, so you go through them, and one of the main things you look for is the law firm or lawyer who is proposing them. And you tend to rely on them.

The lawyer thus states that a legal order of immense consequence to this woman may have been handled in a way that in several respects is inconsistent with the formalist image of a rational system: It may have been signed by accident. Moreover, the lawyer claims that he has received this information from "someone in the know," someone he refuses to identify. By this refusal, he implies that the information was given improperly, in breach of confidence. Furthermore, the lawyer's description of how judges handle court orders suggests a high level of inattention and routinization. Judges sign orders without reading them to satisfy "people who really need this stuff." While the judge is said to ignore the substance of the order, he does pay attention to the lawyer or law firm who requests it. The legal process is thereby portrayed as responding more to reputation than to substantive merit. Thus, the client is introduced to a system that is hurried, routinized, personalistic, and accident prone.

Throughout this conference, the theme of the importance of insider status and access within the local legal system is reinforced by references to the lawyer's personal situation . . . .

The lawyer later claims that he knows one of the judges involved in this client's case well enough to tell him off in private ("I'll tell you when this is over, I'm going to take it to John Hancock and I don't think he'll ever do it again") and that he supported the other's campaign for office. These references suggest that a lawyer's capacity to protect his client's interests depends in part on his special access to the system's functionaries who will react to who he is rather than what he represents. We found this emphasis on insider status, reputation, and local connections repeatedly in the cases that we observed. The lawyer in this case and the other lawyers we studied generally presented themselves as well-connected insiders, valuable because they are known and respected rather than because they are expert legal technicians.

The kind of familiarity with the way the system works that insiders possess is all the more important in divorce cases because the divorce process is extremely difficult to explain even to acute outsiders.

> *Client:* Tell me just the mechanics of this, Peter. What exactly is an interlocutory?
> *Lawyer:* You should know. It's your right to know. But whether or not I'm going to be able to explain this to you is questionable . . . . It's a very . . . It's sort of simple in practice, but it's very confusing to explain. I've got an awful lot of really smart people who've—who I haven't represented—who've asked me after the divorce is over, now what the hell was the interlocutory judgment?

The communications that we have been discussing are, for the most part, explicit. The message is in the message. But there is also a way in which the language forms that the lawyer employs to describe the legal process communicate something about that process itself. Although this lawyer is articulate and knowledgeable, his reactions to many of the client's questions are nevertheless circuitous and confusing. Interviews with clients, as well as our observations, suggest that this failing is common. Instead of direct description, lawyers frequently use analogies that seem to obscure more than they reveal. This practice, of course, may be seen as a simple problem of communication. Yet it also suggests that law and legal process are themselves so dense and erratic that they pose a formidable barrier even to well educated and intelligent laypeople . . . .

Moving from the restraining order to the question of how a settlement could be reached, the client asks why her lawyer did not acknowledge to the other side what he had shared with her, namely that a court battle might end in defeat. In response the lawyer might simply have said that it is poor strategy in a negotiation to tell the other side that you recognize that you may lose. Instead he says:

> *Lawyer:* Okay. I'll do it in my usual convoluted way, using lots of analogies and examples. When you write to . . . when a lawyer writes to an insurance company, representing a person who's been injured in an automobile accident, usually the first demand is somewhat higher than what we actually expect to get out of the case. I always explain that to clients. I explain it very, very carefully. I don't like to write letters of any substance without my client getting a copy of it, and inevitably, I will send a copy of it to my client with another letter explaining, "This is for settlement purposes. Please do not think that your case, which I evaluate at $10,000, is really worth $35,000." And then months later when I finally get the offer to settle for $10,000, I will convey it to my client, and they'll say, well, I've been thinking about this, and I think that you're right; it really was worth $35,000. I then am in a terrible position of having to talk my own client down from a number that I created in the first place and that I tried to support and convince them—of course, they wanted to be convinced, so it was easy—that's the difference between a letter that you send to your adversary and a letter that you, or than what you communicate to your client. They're two different kinds of communications. I truly, I mean, where I am is that I . . . The way I evaluate the case is the way I did when Irene was here. This is an objective evaluation for your use, and there is this tension and conflict in every representation. You have hired me to represent your interests. I do that in two fashions. One, I tell you the way I truly see the picture, and then I try to advance your cause as aggressively as I can. Sometimes almost always—those are inconsistent. I mean, the actions, the words, and so forth are inconsistent.

. . . This example is . . . drawn from an area of law unrelated to divorce. The lawyer's point is the hypocrisy of orthodox settlement negotiations. Even if warned, he claims, clients are likely to confuse demands and values. That is their error. In the legal process words and goals, expressed objectives and real objectives, are usually "inconsistent." . . .

To the client, "justice" demands that the error of the restraining order be righted. For the lawyer that kind of justice simply gets in the way of what for him is the real business of divorce: to reach a property settlement, not to right wrongs or vindicate justice. There is, if you will, a particular kind of justice that the law provides, but it is not broad enough to include the kind that the client seeks. For her justice requires some compensation, or at least an acknowledgment that she has "been treated unjustly." When she finally gets the lawyer to speak in terms of justice, he admits that it cannot be secured through the legal process.

Client: But as you say, if you want justice in this society, you look somewhere other than the court. I believe that's what you were saying to Bob.

  Lawyer: Yeah, that's what I said. Ultimate justice, that is.

Legal justice is thus juxtaposed to ultimate justice. The person seeking such a final accounting is clearly out of place in a system that focuses much more narrowly. To fit into the system the client must reduce her conception of justice to what the law can provide. But perhaps the language of justice serves, for this client, a purpose that is neither as abstract nor as disinterested as her language suggests. This client identifies justice solely with the vindication of her own position. She never refers to a more general standard. Thus the failure of law to provide justice is, for her, a failure to validate her position. The language of justice also serves to bolster her image of herself as an innocent, rather gracious, victim of an evil husband and his untrustworthy lawyer. Tendencies toward self-exculpation and blaming are quite common in the divorces in our sample, although the use of the language of justice toward such ends is not. This language also serves to exert moral pressure on this lawyer to validate the client's sense of herself even as he attempts to explain the limits of the legal process.

In total, the lawyer's description of the legal process involves an open acknowledgment of human frailties, contradictions between appearance and reality, carelessness, incoherence, accident, and built-in limitations. The picture presented is both cynical and probably considered by the lawyer to be realistic. Whereas others claim that legal actors, particularly appellate judges, present the law in highly formalistic terms and work to curtail inconsistencies and contradictions in legal doctrine, many of the lawyers that we observed engage in no such mystification. If critical scholars are right in arguing that mystification and the presentation of a formalist front are necessary to legitimate the legal order, then what we and others have seen in the legal process as it is experienced at the street level suggests that one tier of the legal system, in this case divorce lawyers, may work to unwind the bases of legitimation that other levels work to create. Of course, it is possible, although unlikely, that the legal order derives its legitimacy from its most remote and least accessible elements or that the legitimacy of law is not much affected by how it is presented by lawyers and perceived by clients in the lawyer's office.

IV. TO FIGHT OR TO SETTLE?

Given such a legal process, how should divorce disputes be managed? This concern is central in most of the cases that we observed, and it is an issue that may recur as lawyer and client discuss each of the major controversies in a divorce case. Generally the question is whether the client should attempt to negotiate a settlement or insist on resolution before a judge. This question is sometimes posed issue by issue and sometimes across many issues.

While many clients think of the legal process as an arena for a full adversarial contest, most divorce disputes are not resolved in this manner. Although not all lawyers are equally dedicated to reaching negotiated agreements, most of those we observed advised their clients to try to settle the full range of issues in the case. This is not to say that these divorces were free of conflict, for the negotiations themselves were often quite contentious. Although some of our lawyers occasionally advised clients to ask for more than the client had originally contemplated or to refuse to concede on a major issue when the client was inclined to do so, most seemed to believe that it is generally better to settle than contest divorce disputes. Thus, we are interested in the ways in which lawyers get their clients to see settlement as the preferred alternative.

The conference we are examining revolves around two major issues: (1) whether to ignore or contest the restraining order; and (2) what position to take concerning disposition of the family residence. Much of the conference is devoted to discussing the restraining order—its origins, morality, and legality; the prospects for dissolving it; the lawyer's stake in contesting it; and the client's emotional reaction to it. Substantively the order is not as important as the house itself, which received much less attention and generated much less controversy. Both issues, however, force the lawyer and client to decide whether they will retain control of the case by engaging in negotiations or cede control to the court for hearing and decision. The lawyer definitely favors negotiations.

> *Lawyer:* Okay. What I would like your permission to do then is to meet with Foster, see if I can come up with or negotiate a settlement with him that, before he leaves . . . I leave his office or he leaves my office, he says, we've got something here that I can recommend to my client, and I can say, I've got something here that I can recommend to my client. My feeling is, Jane, that if we reach that point, both lawyers are prepared to make a recommendation on settlement to their respective clients, if either of the clients, either you or Norb, find something terribly disagreeable with the proposal that we have, the lawyers have come to between themselves, then the case just either can't be settled or it's not ripe for settlement. But we would have given it the best shot. But I wouldn't . . . as you know, I'm very concerned about wasting a lot of time and energy trying to settle a case where two previous attempts have been dismally unsuccessful.

The major ingredient of this settlement system is the primacy of the lawyers. They produce the deals while the clients are limited to initial instructions and after-the-fact ratification. The phrase "we would have given it the best shot" is crucial. The "we" seems to refer to the lawyers. Indeed, their efforts could come to nothing if either client backs out at the last minute. The settlement process as described thus has two dimensions—a lawyer to lawyer phase, in which an arrangement is worked out, and a lawyers versus clients phase, in which the opposing lawyers join together to sell the deal to their clients. If the clients do not accept the settlement as a package, the only alternative is to go to trial. Furthermore, if the professionals are content with the agreement they have devised, dissatisfied clients not only have nothing to contribute but also had perhaps better seek psychotherapy:

> *Lawyer:* And if we have to come down a little bit off the 10 percent to something that is obviously a real good loan—9 percent—a percentage point on a one-year, eighteen-month, $25,000 loan does not make that much difference to you. And that's worth settling the case, and I'll say, Jane, *if we're going to court over what turns out to be one percentage point, go talk to Irene some more.* So that's the kind of a package that I see putting together.

The client in this case is reluctant to begin settlement negotiations until some attention is paid to the restraining order. While she acknowledges that she wants a reasonable property settlement, she reminds her lawyer that that is not her exclusive concern:

> *Client:* Yes, there's no question in my mind that that [a property settlement] is my first goal. However, that doesn't mean it's my only goal. It's just my first one. And I have done a lot of thinking about this and so it's all this kind of running around in my head at this point. I've been looking very carefully at the parts of me that want to fight and the parts of me that don't want to fight. And I'm not sure that any of that ought to get messed up in the property settlement.

The lawyer responds by acknowledging that he considers the restraining order to be legally wrong and that he believes it could be litigated. Thus, he confirms his client's position and inclination on legal grounds. Yet he dissents from her position and opposes her inclination to fight on other grounds. First, he states that the restraining order, although legally wrong, is "not necessarily . . . completely wrong" because it might prevent violence between spouses. This complicated position is a clear example of a tactic frequently used by lawyers in divorce cases—the rhetorical "yes . . . but." The lawyers we observed often appeared to be endorsing the adversarial pursuit of one of the client's objectives only to remind the client of a variety of negative consequences associated with it. In this way lawyers present themselves as both an ally and an adviser embracing the wisdom of a long-term perspective.

Second, the lawyer is worried that an effort to fight the restraining order would interfere with the resolution of the case, that is, of the outstanding property issues. Although the lawyer considers the restraining order to be a legal mistake, its effect would end upon final disposition of the house. In the meantime, the client can either live with the order or pay for additional hearings. He believes that it would be unwise for her to fight further not only because the contest would be costly but also because it would postpone or derail entirely negotiations about the house and other tangible assets. Thus when the client asks whether the issue of the restraining order has been raised with her husband's lawyer, her lawyer says:

> *Lawyer:* Well, we've talked to him. My feelings are still the same. They're very strong feelings that what has been done is illegal, that I want to take it to the Supreme Court. I told Foster off. I basically told him the contents of the letter. I said that I think that Judge Cohen is dead wrong, and I would very much like to litigate the thing. On the other hand, I have to be mindful of what Irene said, which is absolutely correct, does that move us toward or away from the ultimate goal, which is the resolution of the case and what you told me when we started off now in very certain terms.

The lawyer's position in this case can be interpreted as a preference for negotiations over litigation based on his determination that this client has more to lose than gain by fighting the restraining order and for the house. In this view the lawyer is neutral about settlement in general and is swayed by the cost-benefit calculation of specific cases. Thus there is a conflict between the client's desire for vindication on what the lawyer perceives to be a peripheral issue and the lawyer's interest in reaching a satisfactory disposition on what for him is a much more important issue. Time and again in our study we observed lawyers attempting to focus their client's attention on the issues the lawyers thought to be major while the clients often concentrated on matters that the lawyers considered secondary. While the disposition of the house in this case will have long-term consequences for the client, the restraining order, as unjust as the lawyer understands it to be, is in his view a temporary nuisance. His sense of justice and of the long-term best interests of his client lead him to try to transform this dispute from a battle over the legality and morality of the restraining order to a negotiation over the more narrow and tangible issue of the ultimate disposition of the house and other assets, which he believes can and should be settled.

In attempting this transformation, the lawyer allies himself with the therapist:

> *Lawyer:* I agree with Irene that that [fighting the restraining order] is not the best way . . . . It's probably the worst way. This [negotiating] hopefully is the best way.

This reliance on the therapist is noteworthy because it is often assumed that a therapeutic orientation is antithetical to the adversarial inclination of law and the legal profession. Yet in this case the lawyer uses the therapist to validate his own position. The legal ideology and the therapeutic ideology seem to him to be compatible; both stress settlement and disvalue legal struggles . . . . However we interpret this observation, it is clear that this lawyer, and most of those we observed, construct an image of the appropriate mode of disposition of a case that is at odds with the conventional view in which lawyers are alleged to induce competition and hostility, transform noncontentious clients into combatants, and promulgate a "fight theory of justice."

The client's own ambivalence toward settlement continues throughout the conference . . . .

> *Client:* Are you familiar with Chief Joseph?
> *Lawyer:* No.
> *Client:* He was a Nez Perce Indian, and he fought the troops of the U.S. government for years and finally he saw that his whole tribe would be killed off and the land devastated so he put down his weapons. And I think the full quote is something like: "From the time the moon sets, I will fight no more forever." I went away that day, that Monday, feeling that this fight had to end, and that's still what I feel . . . .
> One of the thoughts I had that afternoon was that—probably it came a lot from what Irene had to say—that I've been arguing with this man for a good many years of my life. You know, first in the living room, then involving family and friends, then involving therapists, and now involving attorneys. How many forums am I going to spend arguing with this person? And I really want the war to end. So that's my basic conflict. I feel I've been treated unjustly. I feel there's a very good case here, but I don't want to fight any more. And that's what this really is about—a continuing war. So a part of me is still very much with Chief Joseph—I don't want to fight any more. There are other and better things to do with this life.

However, as they move further into the discussion of whether to fight or settle, the client begins to interpret settlement as a capitulation and to reiterate her own ambivalence about how to proceed.

> *Client:* And I think I feel some level of fear about this process of negotiation and how much more I'm going to have to give up. I don't feel tremen—, you know, there's a part of me that does not feel very satisfied with having capitulated repeatedly, and now we're simply doing it with a property settlement.
> *Lawyer:* That's, yea, that's a . . .
> *Client:* I mean, I don't want to fight and I do want to fight, right? That's exactly what it comes down to.
> *Lawyer:* Yes, you're ambiguous.
> *Client:* Oh, boy, am I ever. And I have to live with it.

She may have to live with her ambivalence, but her lawyer needs a resolution of this issue. The lawyer seeks this resolution by allying himself with the "don't fight" side of the struggle. Her advocate, her "knight," has thus become the enemy of adversariness. Through him the legal system becomes the champion of settlement. Ironically, the client's ambivalence serves to validate the lawyer's earlier suggestion that he might be wasting his time and her money trying to settle this case because she might refuse at the last minute to agree to a deal. The conference reaches closure on the fight/settle issue when the lawyer again asks whether he has her authority to negotiate on the terms they had discussed and repeats his earlier warning that this is their last chance for a settlement:

> *Lawyer:* Well, then I will make a . . . my best effort—we are now coming full circle to where we were this morning, which is fine, which is where we should be. I will make my best effort to effect a settlement with Foster along the lines that you and I have discussed and the specific terms of which I can say to you, Jane, I recommend that you sign this. The decision, of course, is yours. If you don't want to sign it, we're going to go ahead with the litigation on the restraining order and probably a trial. Things can change. We can effect a settlement before the restraining order, which is highly unlikely, or between the time the restraining order issue is resolved and the actual time of trial, maybe there will be another settlement. I'm not going to suggest or advise, after this attempt, that either one of us put any substantial energy in another try at settlement. I just think it's a waste of time and money.

The lawyer's reference to "coming full circle" reflects both the centrality of the dispositional question and the amount of time spent talking about issues the lawyer considers to be peripheral. Having invested that time the lawyer secures what he wanted, both an authorization to negotiate and an agreement on the goals that he will pursue. The client, on the other hand, has aired her ambivalence and resolved to try to end this dispute without a legal contest. Both her ambivalence and her eventual acceptance of settlement are typical of the clients we observed.

V. THE LEGAL CONSTRUCTION OF THE CLIENT

To get clients in divorce cases to move toward accepting settlement as well as to carry out the terms of such agreements, lawyers may have to try to cool them out when they are at least partially inclined toward contest. In divorce as in criminal cases, the lawyer must help redefine the client's orientation toward the legal process. In the criminal case this means that lawyers must help the client come to terms with dropping the pretense of innocence; in divorce work this means that lawyers must help their clients view the emotional process of dissolving an intimate relationship in instrumental terms. In both instances, lawyers and clients struggle, although rarely explicitly, with the issue of what part of the client's personality is relevant to the legal process. Thus, the discussion of whether to fight or settle is more than a conversation about the most appropriate way to dispose of the case. Contained within the discourse about negotiation is the construction of a legal picture of the client, a picture through which a self acceptable to the legal process is negotiated and validated. This construction is necessary because the legal process will not or cannot deal with many aspects of the disputes that are brought to it. Legal professionals behave as if it were natural and inevitable that a litigant's problems be divided up in the manner that the legal process prescribes. Lawyers thus legitimate some parts of human experience and deny the relevance of others, but they do not explicitly state what is required of the client. Rather, the approved form of the legal self is built up from a set of oppositions and priorities among these oppositions.

The negotiation of the legal self in this case begins by focusing on the relative importance of emotions engaged by the legal process and the symbolic aspects of the divorce as opposed to its financial and material dimensions. Throughout this conference the lawyer warns his client not to confuse the realms of emotion and finance and instructs her that she can expect the legal process to work well only if emotional material is excluded from her deliberations.

This emotional material is rather complex and difficult for both lawyer and client to sort out. The client is, in the first instance, eager to let her lawyer know that she feels both anger and mistrust toward many participants in the legal process. This combination of feelings is clearly expressed as she talks about the restraining order and the manner in which it was issued:

> *Client:* So I was a total ass. I moved out of the house and left myself vulnerable to that, which I was certainly not informed of by any attorney in the process of mediation. And I was setting myself up for that.
> *Lawyer:* In my view, it would have been a rather extraordinary attorney that could have advised you of that, because, in my view, that's not the law. So I'm hard-pressed to see how a lawyer could have said, don't move out of the house or you may prejudice your situation by moving out of the house.
> *Client:* But obviously, some attorney did, right? We have the case of Paul Foster, who interprets the law in that fashion. Well, I'm angry about all that. However . . .

While her lawyer once again validates her sense of the legal error involved in issuing the restraining order, her anger is fueled by the failure of her husband's lawyer to accept this interpretation of the law.

The client continues to express her anger throughout the conference, especially when the conversation turns directly to her husband's lawyer:

> *Client:* The other option I see could have been that Norb would have gotten different legal advice from the beginning. So the thing, I suppose, that I'm concerned about, I'm concerned about Foster. I'm concerned about the kind of person he is. I distrust him as thoroughly as I do Norb, and I think you have been very measured in your statements about him. I think he's a son-of-a-bitch, and there's nothing I've seen that he's done that changed my mind about that. And I think that he has a client that can be manipulated.

The client's mistrust is not reserved exclusively for the opposition. She is, to an extent, wary of her own lawyer as well:

> *Client:* But when I think of myself—you know, this is a very vulnerable time in my life, and one of the things that has happened is a major trust relationship has ended. And then suddenly in the space of what—six weeks or something—I'm supposed to entrust somebody else, not only with the intimate details of my life, but with the responsibility for representing me. And that's not easy for me under any circumstances. I really like to speak for myself.

The predicament in which the client finds herself—needing to trust a stranger when trust has just been betrayed by an intimate is one that faces and perplexes divorce clients generally . . . .

Because she feels betrayed by her husband, the client wants "some gesture from him" as a means of establishing the basis for negotiations. Moreover, she feels that she is already two points down vis-a-vis her husband. First, he has the house and has denied her any access to it, although her departure was an act of generosity done for the good of the marital community. Second, she "knows" that he is going to get the house and that she will at best get half its market value. She repeatedly asks the lawyer about gestures or concessions to even this score:

> *Client:* So I wrote this as a draft to send to Norb . . . . And obviously I'm still waffling . . . . I mean, I don't know exactly how to give up this hearing. Part of me says, it's real clear and I ought to. But I want some gesture from him . . . .
>
> *Client:* Okay. That's not going to be a problem for me, all right? I don't think that one percentage point is going to be a problem for me. This is the problem for me. I feel that, even to get to this point, I have given up a substantial amount. One thing that I've given up is the home in Pacificola . . . . I want some attention to be paid to what I have already conceded to even get to this point . . . .
>
> *Client:* I just think that's a very, very big concession, and I think if

I'm to take another kind of settlement, then that is the first thing that ought to be seen. Now, that's a very good faith negotiation thing for me to do, say, okay, Norb has this tremendous emotional investment in the house; I'm willing to let go of mine . . . .

How does the lawyer respond to the client's emotional agenda, to her efforts to define those parts of herself that are legally relevant? With respect to the problem of trust and the need for a gesture, the lawyer once says, "Ouch," once, "I don't blame you," and once he changes the subject. He does tell the client that her husband is unlikely to reestablish trust by giving up the restraining order. In addition, there is a brief exploration of whether she could buy the husband's share of the house, an alternative doomed by earlier recognition that it would involve an expensive and probably fruitless court battle. There is a joke about taking $25,000 to forget the restraining order. Otherwise nothing is said.

Why? Lawyer and client could have discussed the kind of gestures short of unconditional surrender that might have satisfied her and been tolerable to her husband. The lawyer could have explored the possibility that the husband might agree to his client's occasional, scheduled visits to the property or to $5,000 more than a 50/50 split in recognition of giving up the house. Perhaps he feared that further exploration might complicate his efforts to have his client focus on reaching an acceptable division of property. There can be little doubt that this objective governed his thinking.

Lawyer: Okay, Now, that disagreement—or, it wasn't even a disagreement—that—where we weren't on the same wave-length-was really a matter of style than of end result. Right?

Client: You mean, what part?

Lawyer: Where you said was that you wanted me to start these negotiations by making it clear that major concession was being made at the outset and it was being made by you.

Client: Yes.

Lawyer: Okay, I understand that now. Let's come back to the end of it . . . . What am I shooting for? Okay, I agree. That's the way it ought to be begun, and that point ought to—during my conversations, I ought to keep coming back to that, if I have to use it. Just make that strongly. But what am I shooting for? What's the end result? Is it what I was talking about initially?

Client: Sure. I mean, that's as much as can be expected, I believe. Am I right in that?

The lawyer proposes to turn the client's demand for concessions into an opening statement and implies that an equal division of assets is the only possible legal settlement. The client, on the other hand, appears to believe that it is dangerous to trade values with someone that you do not trust for both the chance that they will take advantage of you in making the deal and the probability that they will fail to do what they promise are increased. The lawyer is, and can afford to be, disinterested in trust. Protection of his client does not lie in fostering good will and mutual respect between the spouses but rather in the terms of the bargain and in its enforcement powers. His duty is to see that the settlement agreement is fair to his client, whatever the motives or morals of the other side may be, and that the structure of the agreement guarantees that his client gets what she bargained for or its substitute, or at least the best approximation available.

By playing down the question of trust the lawyer is telling the client that the emotional self must be separated from the legal self. Gestures and symbolic acknowledgment of wrongs suffered belong to some realm other than law. He is, in addition, defending himself against a kind of emotional transference. Much of the emotion talk in this conference involves the lawyer himself, directly or indirectly. In the discussion of trust the client makes the lawyer into a kind of husband substitute ("a major trust relationship has ended. And then . . . I'm supposed to entrust somebody else . . ."). The client described him as her "knight in shining armor," an image of protection and romance; she acknowledges having sexual fantasies about him and she speaks of her expectation that he would protect her from "judicial abuse." These demands on her lawyer typify the kind of environment in which divorce lawyers work. Moreover, the discussion of trust and its betrayal signals to her lawyer the need for an elevated watchfulness. He may, like her earlier source of protection and romance, not be fully trusted. The gesture implicitly demanded of him is an embrace of her sense of justice and of what that implies in practical terms.

By downplaying emotions and signaling the limited relevance of gestures, the lawyer defends himself against both the transference and the test. He must find a way to be on his client's side (e.g., repeatedly acknowledging the legal error of the restraining order) and, at the same time, to keep some distance from her . . . Achieving this precarious balance is a peculiar, although not unique, difficulty of divorce practice . . . . To maintain this balance the lawyer acknowledges the difficulty of separating emotional and property issues, but continually reminds the client of its necessity if they are going to reach what he calls a "satisfactory disposition" of the case:

> *Lawyer:* I mean, people have a very, very hard time of separating whatever it is—so I think for shorthand, we call it the emotional aspect of the case from the financial aspect of the case. But if there is going to be a settlement, that's kind of what has to happen, or the emotional aspect of the case gets resolved and then the financial thing becomes a matter of dollars and cents and the client decides, I'm tired and I don't want to fight over the last $500 or the last $100.

The need to exclude emotional issues is thus linked to a warning that emotions can jeopardize satisfactory settlements. The notion of satisfactory disposition, however, is itself problematic. The lawyer's definition of "satisfactory" tends to exclude the part of the client's personality that is angry or frustrated. Satisfactory dispositions are financial. The question of who is satisfied is left unasked. For the client, no definition of the case that ignores her emotions seems right; to the lawyer, this is the only definition that seems acceptable. Moreover, the responsibility for finding ways to keep emotions under control is assigned to the client. The lawyer offers no help in this task even as he acknowledges its relevance for this client and for the practice of divorce law. If no settlement is reached it will, at least as far as their side is concerned, be because of a failure on the part of the client.

Throughout this conference the lawyer stresses the need for two parallel separations: the separation of the emotional issues from the legal and the separation of the client and her husband.

> *Lawyer:* . . . I'd say the ambiguity goes even deeper than the issue of fighting and not fighting. It's how . . . The ambiguity is what Irene talked about and that is—it's the real hard one; it's terminating the entire relationship. You do and you don't, and the termination . . . I mean, you're angry; you're pissed off. You've said that. And are you ready to call a halt to the anger and I'm not so sure that that's humanly possible. Can your rational mind say, okay, Jane, there has been enough anger expended on this; it is time to get on with your life. If you are able to do that, great. But I don't know.

As the lawyer sees it, the client will only be able to make an adequate arrangement with her husband when she can contemplate their relationship unemotionally. As the client sees it, the second separation seems impossible if the first is carried out. She cannot become free of her husband if she thinks about legal problems in material terms only— if she fails to take her feelings into account she will continue to be affected by them. Thus, the program the lawyer presents to the client appropriates her marriage to the realm of property and defines her connection to her husband exclusively in those terms. She, on the other hand, sees property issues embedded in a broader context. The client speaks about the separation of the emotional and financial issues as being difficult to effect because it is unnatural. The market does not exhaust her realm of values, and she has difficulty assigning governing priority to it. Yet this is what the lawyer indicates the law requires.

Nevertheless, the separation of emotional and economic matters may benefit the client. While it does exact an emotional toll, concentrating on the instrumental, tangible aspects of the divorce may produce a more satisfactory disposition than focusing on the emotional concerns. The lawyer may be trying to explain to his client that in the long run she is going to be more interested in the economics of the settlement than in the vindication of her immediate emotional needs. In his view, legal justice, although narrow, is justice nonetheless, and his job is to secure for her the best that can be achieved given the legal process as he knows it.

Putting emotional matters aside may also serve the interests of lawyers untrained in dealing with emotional problems and unwilling to find ways to cope with them. It allows lawyers to sidestep what is clearly one of the most difficult and least rewarding aspects of divorce practice. In so doing they are able to avoid assuming a sense of responsibility for the human consequences of being unresponsive to emotion. In this conference, for example, the lawyer suggests that the legal process works best for those who can control their emotions and concentrate on the instrumental, the calculating, the pecuniary . . . .

VI. CONCLUSION

Lawyer-client interaction involves attempts to negotiate acceptable resolutions of problems in which lawyers and clients usually have different agendas, expectations, and senses of justice. As in any negotiation, the parties possess different information and have different needs to fulfill. Clients know their histories and goals, lawyers must learn about them. Lawyers know the law and the legal process, clients must find out about them. Every conference is thus to some extent competitive: Each of the participants sets out to fulfill their own agenda and generally only provides what the other wants on demand.

Competition and accommodation between lawyer and client shape the course of divorce litigation—when negotiations are initiated, how they are conducted, what is asked for and offered, and whether a case is settled. Moreover, the manner in which the contest over agendas and expectations is resolved may also have a powerful effect on the way clients feel at the end of the process, on their levels of satisfaction, and on their views of the legitimacy of law. Interactions between lawyers and clients also provide one occasion for the construction and transmission of legal ideology. The dialogue between lawyers and clients reveals the sense of rights, actionable injuries, and justice that people bring to the legal process and that the process, through the words and actions of lawyers, is willing to recognize and act upon.

A. *Lawyer-Client Interaction: The Lawyer's Perspective*

Clients bring to their encounters with lawyers an expectation that the justice system will impartially sort the facts in dispute to provide a deductive reading of the "truth." They expect the legal process to take their problems seriously, and they usually seek vindication of the positions that they have adopted. They expect the legal process to follow its own rules, to proceed in an orderly manner, and to be fair and error free . . . .

To some extent, it is the job of lawyers to bring these expectations and images of law and legal justice closer to the reality that they have experienced. For them legal justice is situational and outcomes are often unpredictable. The legal process provides an arena where compromises are explored, settlements are reached, and, if money is at issue, assets are divided. Lawyers are intimately familiar with the human dimensions of the legal process. They know that in most instances the process is not rule governed, that there is widespread use of discretion, and that decisions are influenced by matters extraneous to legal doctrine. Moreover, they believe that most clients cannot afford or would not want to pay the cost of a full adversarial contest. They may conclude, therefore, based on experience, that the client who demands vindication today will want both a larger financial settlement and a smaller lawyer's bill tomorrow.

Because lawyers' experience is so much more extensive than that of clients, lawyers attempt to "teach" their clients about the requirements of the legal process and to socialize them into the role of the client. Some of the client's problems and needs will be translated into legal categories and many more will have legal labels attached to them. The client in contact with a lawyer and the legal process must frequently be talked into a frame of mind appropriate to the needs of legal business . . . . In the lawyer's office the client is likely to be introduced to a system of negotiations in which formal hearings are rare, rights are no guarantee of remedies, unfamiliar rules of relevance are asserted, and the nature of their own disputes and objectives are transformed . . . .

In fact, the range of client expectations with which lawyers must come to terms covers almost everything that is involved in a divorce— the distribution of property, the level of support, the rights to custody, the speed with which things are done, the wisdom of the rules and the judges, the roles that lawyers are willing to play, the times at which they are available, and the fees that they charge. Moreover, the clients that we studied expect their lawyers to tell them about their rights and obligations and to predict how they will fare in contests over houses, retirement benefits, visitation rights, support payments, and the like. Whatever their reservations about lawyers as a group and litigation as a means of resolving disputes, they expect their lawyers to navigate them through troubled waters. They want to believe that charts exist, that shoals are marked, and that channels to safe harbors are defined. But lawyers present a different picture: Where clients want predictions and certainty, lawyers introduce them to the frequently unpredictable reality of divorce. While not every client is mistaken about all of these matters, many divorce lawyers understandably feel that they must constantly be on their guard against clients who seek what cannot be delivered. A major professional function therefore is to attempt to limit clients' expectations to realistic levels.

A heavy dose of cynicism helps lawyers accomplish this goal. The cynic chips away at the legal facade until the client realizes that she is enmeshed in a system ridden with hazards, surprises, and people who are out to get her. By focusing on the mistakes, irrationality, or intransigence of the other side, the lawyer creates an inventory of explanations that puts some distance between himself and responsibility for any eventual disappointment. Yet at the same time that he creates doubts about the legal process, the lawyer must give the client some reason to rely on him. The lawyer's emphasis on his insider status is one means of doing this. Nothing is guaranteed, the lawyer acknowledges, but the best chance for success rests with those who are familiar with local practice and who have a working relationship with officials who wield local power. This formula is repeatedly presented to clients by the lawyers in our sample. By stressing the importance of being an insider, the lawyer is not necessarily suggesting that the system is corrupt. He is not promising that he has an illegal way to deal with an illegal system but rather creating an atmosphere in which the client will feel that she is being helped to attain a reachable goal despite being trapped in a system laced with uncertainties. The interests of the legal professional in this instance depart from the interests of the legal system. This lawyer constructs a picture of the legal process that fixes the client's dependency on him as it jeopardizes her trust in any other part of the system. The consequences of this for the client's view of law in general or participation in its legitimation rituals seems quite remote from his concerns. His talk, the image of the legal process that he constructs, is the talk of a cynical realist. The legal process he presents inspires neither respect nor allegiance . . . .

The conference discussed in this paper . . . first consists of an effort by the lawyer to talk about the details of a settlement proposal, an effort that is frequently derailed by the client's attempts to discuss the origins and effects of the restraining order, her need to regain trust in her husband, her desire to secure some recognition of the sacrifices that she has already made, and her feelings about her husband's lawyer. Given this situation, much of the conference may be seen as an effort by the lawyer to determine whether his client really wants to settle, to identify the ingredients of a legitimate proposal, to put the issue of the restraining order in the background, and to regain control of the settlement process. If either the client was not committed to settlement or the behavior of the other side reflected anything other than an intention to settle, the lawyer wanted to close down negotiations to avoid useless expenditures and then to proceed to trial on the main issue.

From the lawyer's point of view, this case should have been easy to settle, except that the client's anger threatened to become a stumbling block to a reasonable property arrangement. The case was objectively easy because it involved no children, no support issues, and no assets that were unusually difficult to value, and the couple's debts were small in comparison to their assets. Moreover, except for the husband's desire to keep the house, neither party seemed inextricably wedded to any particular property, the couple were living separately, and neither was suffering from acute emotional distress. However, the failure of mediation and the client's strong and persistent anger about the restraining order suggested the likelihood of emotional barriers to settlement.

The lawyer hoped that once the client understood the legal process she would be willing to adopt the strategic posture that he believed was appropriate for the case. He saw a settlement of property issues as the primary goal, hence his emphasis on the unpredictability of contested procedures. To this end he needed to get the client to agree to postpone any decision about contesting the restraining order, thus his emphasis on the need to keep her emotions under control. He also needed her to agree to a format for negotiations that excluded her direct participation, hence his focus on both the dangers posed by her emotions and the importance of his insider status. The lawyer's arguments thus stress the need to maintain control over the disposition of assets by preferring negotiations over hearings and emphasize that the client's repression of emotions and distance from the actual proceedings are to be preferred over expression and participation . . . .

B. Lawyer-Client Interaction: The Client's Perspective

Because divorce clients may not direct their litigation does not mean that they play no part in it. Because clients may acquiesce in the end to the lawyer's agenda does not mean that they do not make demands on their lawyer during the process. Clients may insist that lawyers attend to issues beyond those that are technically relevant and with which lawyers do not feel particularly comfortable; they may persist in bringing these matters into the conversation even after lawyers think that they have been settled. Clients may, in addition, resist recommendations that a lawyer believes are obviously in the client's interest. They may press lawyers to explain and justify advice given, actions taken, and results produced. Finally, clients may insist that lawyers interpret and account for the actions of others, particularly their spouse, their spouse's lawyer, and judges, and that lawyers justify these actions in light of the client's sense of what is appropriate and fair. In these ways, clients transform the agendas of lawyers as well as their preferred professional style.

This conference allowed the client to express her frustrations with a legal process that refused to protect her "rights." . . .

In addition, the conference provided the client with an opportunity to work through conflicting goals: She did not want to capitulate to her husband but she did want to put an end to the fighting between them. Like many of the clients we have observed, she is uncertain about what she really wants. The wisdom of a negotiated settlement is clear to the lawyer, but for her it is fraught with ambiguity and difficulty. She insists that her lawyer concede, at least to her, that her need for a symbolic "gesture" is comprehensible and legitimate. In so doing she secures some acknowledgment of her self-conceived victimization and some limited vindication. This drama, in which clients insist that their lawyers validate their partial and biased understandings, is a routine part of the divorce process. Lawyers, especially experienced divorce lawyers, understand this and provide such validation even when, as in this case, they attempt to discourage their clients from seeking it in the courtroom.

C. The Consequences of the Two Perspectives

The competing perspectives of lawyer and client and the manner in which they are articulated establish the boundaries within which the strategy and tactics of divorce litigation develop. When the client feels betrayed and victimized, the lawyer may have to spend a significant amount of time and energy in selling negotiation as the means of resolving the case. This effort may affect the timing as well as the style and success of settlement efforts. Most of the lawyers we observed invest considerable effort in these client management activities. In our sample it is the exceptional lawyer who fans the flames of the client's anger or accepts uncritically the client's version of events without reminding the client of the difficulties and costs of acting out of emotion.

Moreover, when divorce clients demand to know about the legal rules that will be applied, the probabilities of achieving various results, the costs they will incur, the pace at which various things will happen, and the roles that different actors will play, there are no standard answers that lawyers can give. What the client is asking for is a distillation of the lawyer's experience as it is relevant to cases like hers. What the lawyer can provide is not a *corpus juris* learned in law school or available in any texts but rather a personal view of how the legal system actually works in the community in which he is practicing.

The lawyer's emphasis on the uncertain and personalistic nature of that process may have three effects. First, the extent to which the lawyer's picture of the legal system is at variance with the image that the client brings to her contact with the law may help to explain the common finding that experience with the legal process often results in dissatisfaction and a lower level of respect for law, regardless of substantive outcome. Clients are brought face-to-face with the law's shortcomings by the testimony of their own lawyers as well as by the results that they experience.

Second, this characterization of the legal process may increase the client's dependence on the lawyer. People in the midst of divorce frequently feel a reduced sense of control over their lives. Their former lover and friend has become an enemy. They cannot live where and as they did, they must relate to their children in new ways, they may face new jobs and major economic threats, and their relations with family and friends may be strained, sometimes to the breaking point. When lawyers then introduce clients to an uncontrollable and unpredictable legal system, their sense of reduced control over their lives may become even stronger. They are, in essence, further threatened by a system that they had expected would reintroduce structure and predictability into their lives. In this situation, the lawyer's services become more essential and the lawyer himself more indispensable.

Finally, the lawyer's emphasis on the client's need to separate emotional and instrumental issues may help to construct or reflect a vision of law in which particular parts of the self are valued while others are denied or left for others to validate. In the legal realm, lawyers insist that the rational and instrumental are to govern. While this lawyer clearly recognizes the human consequence of this opposition and hierarchy, he never questions it but instead treats it as both necessary and inevitable. Throughout this conference the lawyer encourages the client to be clear headed and to grant priority to monetary issues. By defining the ultimate goal as the resolution of the case and resolution in terms of the division of property, and by seeking to exclude the emotional focus that the client continues to provide, he expresses the indifference of the law to those parts of the self that might be most salient at the time of the divorce. The legal process of divorce becomes at best a distraction, at worst an additional trauma. By the end of the conference both lawyer and client speak in terms of a divided self, she, if only briefly, to fight against it or at least to express her ambivalence, he to do its bidding in the name of a system that is unchanging and unchangeable . . . . □

NOTES AND QUESTIONS

1. In *Lawyer and Client: Who's in Charge?* (New York: Russell Sage Foundation, 1974), Douglas E. Rosenthal studied personal injury claim cases. He was interested in the relationship between lawyers and clients, and the exercise of authority and control over problems that the clients see as important. According to the traditional view of the relationship, the client is "passive, follows instruction, and trusts the professional without criticism, with few questions or requests"; lawyers believe that such clients "will do better than the difficult client who is critical and questioning" (pp. 13–14). Opposed to this is the "participatory" ideal, where the client is active, informed, and shares

in responsibility and devices. The "participatory theory" asserts "that it is primarily the client's own responsibility to grapple with the problem. Instead of delegating responsibility to the professional and leaving the decisions to him, while being kept only minimally informed, the participating client seeks information to help him define his problem and what he wants to accomplish, rather than waiting to be told how to proceed." The client reviews and assesses what has been done, and how the professional did it; he questions and appraises the consistency and accuracy of the professional's answers. The client is "aware that there are open choices to be made in solving his problem and expects to have his concerns reflected in the choices made."

Contrary to expectations, Rosenthal found that participating clients not only "do not get worse results, they actually get better recoveries from their legal claims." He says: "The single form of client participation which appears to have the greatest influence on successful case outcome is making follow-up demands for attention . . . . Even the most experienced and skillful [lawyers] make errors of fact as well as judgment. If a client is active in following the details of his case and resourceful in informing himself about the elements of a claim, he may be able to catch something pertinent that the lawyer misses . . . . [T]he more . . . activities the client employs and the more persistently he employs them, the better his chances of protecting his emotional and economic interests in the case outcome. The client who is most likely to suffer is the one who has strongly motivated interests but fails to express or safeguard them . . . . The participatory model does not diminish the importance of the lawyer's role in problem solving. The benefits of client activity appear to derive only from greater collaboration with the attorney, not from the client's exclusively performing the attorney's functions."

Was the client in Sarat and Felstiner's study an "active" or a "passive" client? Would Rosenthal's conclusions hold up in a study of divorce practice as well as in personal injury?

2. Sarat and Felstiner point out that lawyers must educate their clients about the way the legal system works. Clients may want justice. However, the legal system may offer only a negotiated settlement or judgments based on discretion, caprice, and bias. Lawyers may demystify the legal system, but this often doesn't empower divorce clients. The reality of the divorce system makes an aware client more dependent on his or her lawyer's skill at navigating past the reefs of discretion, bias, and caprice, and at negotiating with an unreasonable lawyer on the other side. See also William L.F. Felstiner and Austin Sarat, "Enactments of Power: Negotiating Reality and Responsibility in Lawyer-Client Interactions," 77 *Cornell Law Review* 1447 (1992); Austin Sarat and William Felstiner, "Lawyers and Legal Consciousness: Law Talk in the Divorce Lawyer's Office," 98 *Yale Law Journal* 1663 (1989).

Under certain circumstances, lawyers may become the great champions of mediation in a divorce setting. Craig A. McEwen, Richard J. Maiman, and Lynn Mather, in "Lawyers, Mediation, and the Management of Divorce Practice," 28 *Law & Society Review* 149 (1994), describe a Maine procedure under the control of the court and lawyers. "By providing an official settlement event, mediation can sharpen the focus on and make more efficient the process of divorce negotiation. By putting all the parties and lawyers together in one place at one time, it can increase party participation in, and knowledge about, the negotiation process" (p. 183). Suppose, in Sarat and Felstiner's story, Jane and Norb as well as their two lawyers had to appear before a mediator who was not a lawyer. How, if at all, might the story have changed?

3. We've looked at many of the roles played by lawyers in American society. John Heinz and Edward Laumann, in *Chicago Lawyers: The Social Structure of the Bar* (New York: Basic Books, 1982), suggest that the legal profession is made up of distinct strata. Stewart Macaulay, in "Law Schools and the World Outside Their Doors II: Some Notes on Two Recent Studies of the Chicago Bar," 32 *Journal of Legal Education* 506, 508–10 (1982), has described their study:

> Heinz and Laumann tell us that different kinds of lawyers do very different things and that there is a clear hierarchy in the legal profession. They say that one could posit a great many legal professions, but much of the variation within the profession can be accounted for by one fundamental difference—that between lawyers who represent large organizations and those who represent individuals or the small businesses controlled by those individuals. Corporate work is likely to involve "symbol manipulation," while work for individuals will carry a heavy component of "people persuasion." Corporate lawyers tend to have far fewer clients a year than those who represent individuals, and corporate lawyers are paid to discover unique legal issues and cope with them rather than mass process routine work for many clients.
>
> How do they arrive at these conclusions? They tell us that lawyers tend to specialize and represent limited, identifiable groups or types of clients and to perform as broad or narrow a range of tasks as the clientele demands. There is virtually no likelihood of co-practice across five distinct clusters of legal work: (1) large corporate business work, (2) specialty corporate business practice such as patent law or admiralty, (3) labor affairs, (4) municipal government work, and (5) service to individuals and their businesses. In brief, a patent lawyer is unlikely to be competent to try a first-degree murder case; corporate lawyers know little about divorce practice; and if you want to get something from City Hall in Chicago, you need a lawyer who knows the right people.
>
> The work some lawyers do is likely to be far more highly regarded by the profession than the work done by others. A subsample of the lawyers interviewed by Heinz and Laumann were asked to rate the "general prestige with the legal profession at large" of each of thirty fields. A panel of law professors from Northwestern University and researchers from the American Bar Foundation was asked to rank these same fields as to intellectual challenge, rapidity of change, degree of work done for altruistic motives, ethical conduct, and freedom from client demands. Heinz and Laumann tell us that the general pattern of prestige ranking is unambiguous: fields serving "big business" clients such as securities, corporate tax, antitrust, and banking are at the top of the prestige ranking while those serving individual clients such as divorce, landlord and tenant, debt collection, and criminal defense are at the bottom. That is, the more a legal specialty serves the core economic values of the society, the higher its prestige within the profession. Moreover, the higher the score of a field on service-based, altruistic, or reformist motives, the

lower its prestige. The fields with the highest prestige were seen as having the highest intellectual challenge by the law professors and researchers who rated them. Many attorneys do not consider "people persuasion" to be real lawyer's work. However, the income lawyers received from various types of practice was not significantly associated with the prestige of particular fields.

Heinz and Laumann give us a picture of lawyers and clients in various fields by using a type of correlational analysis. A striking U-shaped pattern emerged from the association of nine variables across the thirty fields of practice examined. The variables were (1) the extent to which a field had business rather than individual clients, (2) the percentage of clients represented by the lawyer for three years or more, (3) the degree to which clients were referred by other lawyers, (4) the freedom lawyers had to select their cases, (5) the degree to which a field involved negotiating and advising clients rather than "highly technical procedures," (6) the amount of governmental employment in a field, (7) the presence of lawyers in a field who attended local rather than national elite law schools, (8) the number of high-status Protestant lawyers in a field, and (9) the number of lawyers of Jewish origin in a field.

One can describe the associations Heinz and Laumann find by imagining a circle which represents the legal profession in Chicago. First, the circle could be divided horizontally. The top half would represent lawyers who primarily go to court; the bottom, lawyers who primarily counsel clients in their offices. Second, the circle could be divided vertically. The side to the left would be occupied by lawyers whose clients were primarily individuals and their businesses; the side to the right would contain lawyers who represent larger corporations. Lawyers in each quarter of the circle are more alike than those in the other quarters, at least when measured on the nine variables used in the research. However, to reflect the profession more accurately, the circle would have to be pushed apart at the top since lawyers who litigate for individuals are very unlike those who litigate for large corporations. On the other hand, those who counsel wealthy individuals are likely to be somewhat similar to those who counsel corporations. Thus, when they look at the thirty fields of practice, Heinz and Laumann get a U-shaped pattern of association.

Fields closer together in the U-shaped pattern tend to be more similar, as measured by Heinz and Laumann's nine variables, than those further apart. Divorce, representing plaintiffs in personal injury work, and criminal defense involve appearances in court for individuals and are clustered together. Other clusters include: probate and personal tax work, which involve a great deal of office practice for individuals; general corporate and banking practice, which tend to involve office work for corporate clients; and business litigation and antitrust defense, which involve court appearances for corporations. If we start in the upper left corner of the U, we find lawyers who specialize in divorce, personal injury work for plaintiffs, and criminal defense. These fields also have the lowest prestige within the profession; those who specialize in them tend to practice alone or in small firms; and these attorneys almost always attended local law schools. As we go around the U, prestige increases, the law firms become larger, and the lawyers tend to have gone to national law schools.

Interestingly, there is substantial support from all lawyers for normative statements asserting the rights of individuals against concentrations of power in large corporations, labor unions, or the state. Also surprising, perhaps, is the finding that lawyers whose fields had the highest prestige ratings tended to support such civil liberties as free speech far more than nonlawyers or lawyers whose fields are in the personal business cluster. General corporate lawyers, not surprisingly, tend to score fairly low on a scale of economic liberalism used by the researchers.

What difference, if any, does the status and prestige of various legal specialties make? There are clearly behavioral differences. Wall Street firms do not, for example, advertise, and they do not make use of grubby ways of getting business such as paying ambulance drivers for referrals. However, many elite law firms publish newsletters on slick paper that purport to keep their clients up to date on the latest legal developments that might affect them. See Carroll Seron, "New Strategies for Getting Clients: Urban and Suburban Lawyers' Views," 27 *Law & Society Review* 399 (1993).

Can we say, for example, that better lawyers tend to work for richer people? See Jack Ladinsky, "Careers of Lawyers, Law Practice, and Legal Institutions," 28 *American Sociological Review* 47 (1963). Would that depend on what we meant by "better"? Heinz and Laumann find that the *higher* the score of a field with regard to service-based, altruistic, or reformist motives, the *lower* its prestige. What does that tell us, if anything, about the profession? For a thoughtful discussion of some of the issues raised by Heinz and Laumann, see Howard Erlanger, "The Allocation of Status Within Occupations: The Case of the Legal Profession," 58 *Social Forces* 882 (1980).

4. Roman Tomasic, in "Social Organisation Amongst Australian Lawyers," 19 *Australia and New Zealand Journal of Sociology* 445 (1983), reports on a study of the legal profession in Australia. Tomasic asked his sample of lawyers how much time they spent on various activities. He ended up with four "clusters" of activities, corresponding to four types of lawyers: property lawyers, litigation lawyers, commercial lawyers, and generalists. Like Heinz and Laumann, he concluded that the legal profession "is far from being a homogeneous occupational group." It would be "more realistic to speak of a number of legal professions," with a "multiplicity of roles and functions."

THE JURY

The roles we have discussed so far have been, basically, roles of professionals within the legal system. But one peculiarity of the American trial system—especially criminal trials—is the extraordinary power given to lay people, chosen more or less randomly, acting as a jury. Most systems of law, outside of common law countries, have nothing exactly like the jury. In England, the civil (noncriminal) jury is almost dead.

Even in the United States, the use of juries is rather limited. Many American proceedings do not take place before juries. Most "cases" settle out of court, and most criminal defendants are convicted by means of a plea bargain. Nonetheless, the jury is by no means an unimportant institution. The biggest and showiest criminal cases go to the jury. Many of the biggest and showiest civil cases go there as well.

There is an enormous literature on the workings of the jury system. A classic study is Harry Kalven, Jr. and Hans Zeisel, *The American Jury* (Chicago: University of Chicago Press, 1966). This was a study of criminal trials. The central question asked was this: what difference does the jury system make to the outcome of cases? Suppose the identical case were tried by a judge, sitting alone, instead of by a jury. How would the case come out?

This is not an easy question to answer if we want to study real cases. Each trial is a unique event, and it is either decided by a judge or by a jury, not by both. The authors of *The American Jury* tried to get at the issue through an indirect route. They drew a sample of criminal trials, and they sent a questionnaire to the judges who presided at these trials. The judges were asked to record what the case was about, how it was decided by the jury, and how *they* would have decided it in the absence of a jury. If they disagreed with the jury verdict, they were also asked why they thought the jury decided as it did.

The basic finding was that judge and jury agreed in 75.4% of the cases. In 13.4% of the cases, judge and jury agreed on acquittal, and in 62% of the cases, both thought that the defendant should be convicted. The disagreements—roughly one out of four cases—ran in one direction. Only rarely did a judge think that a jury should have acquitted when it had convicted. Most of the disagreements were over jury acquittals. The judge would have convicted in a large percentage of these cases. Juries, in other words, are more lenient than judges.

What are some of the problems with Kalven and Zeisel's methods? How can they be sure that the judges *would* have decided the way they said they would? Assuming for sake of argument that the data are correct, what do Kalven and Zeisel's figures show about the workings of the jury system? Is there a lot of disagreement or only a little?

Of course, if judge and jury almost always behaved identically, we could ask, why bother with a jury at all? The jury is supposed to represent the "perspectives, experiences, and values of ordinary people in the community," and because traditionally there are twelve members of a jury, they can represent a "range of viewpoints."

The quotations are from Phoebe C. Ellsworth, "Are Twelve Heads Better Than One? 52 *Law and Contemporary Problems* 205 (1990). Ellsworth's article reports a study that she conducted, using randomly selected adults in northern California. The subjects watched a videotape of a simulated homicide trial. They were then divided into mock juries (groups of twelve) to deliberate. The study found "the process of deliberation seems to work quite well" in bringing out the facts. But jurors tended not to understand the law. After all, how could they, when the judge gives them instructions in "convoluted, technical" language presented in a "dry and abstract" form, divorced from the realities of the particular case?

If Ellsworth correctly reports that juries do not understand the law, how does this bear on the question, whether "twelve heads" are better than "one," especially if the one head belongs to a trained judge? What are the real, as opposed to the ideal, functions of a jury? Juries are not supposed to be "lawless," or to decide according to whim, passion, or prejudice. How does Ellsworth's work bear on the question whether they are, in fact, lawless? Would the type of case considered make a difference? To what extent, if at all, does our society want juries to be lawless? Can we argue that we must *want* "lawlessness," or we would not allow judges to give almost impossible-to-understand jury instructions? See, also, Larry Heuer and Steven Penrod, "Juror Notetaking and Question Asking During Trials: A National Field Experiment," 18 *Law and Human Behavior* 121 (1994).

In any event, psychologists of law, as well as other scholars, continue to be fascinated by the American jury. New studies appear in the journals every year. Are there problems in studying jury behavior through mock juries in simulated trials? People in these experiments are playing the role of "subject" rather than making decisions that count. While they may become involved in their experimental task, they never confront someone who may be hurt by their decisions and at some level they know that they are playing a game. They are not socialized into the role of juror as they would be in an actual trial. See Wallace Loh, "Perspectives on Psychology and Law," 11 *Journal of Applied Social Psychology* 314 (1981). For an overview of the voluminous research on the jury, see Valerie P. Hans and Neil Vidmar, *Judging the Jury* (New York: Plenum Publishing, 1986); Robert E. Litan (ed.) *Verdict: Assessing the Civil Jury System* (Washington, D.C.: Brookings Institution. 1993); Reid Hastie, *Inside the Juror: The Psychology of Juror Decision Making*. (New York: Cambridge University Press, 1993).

Social scientists have attempted to help lawyers select a fair or a favorable jury. In most jurisdictions a pool of potential jurors is created by drawing names from information such as lists of voters. Lawyers can challenge jurors who might be biased, but in many jurisdictions they also can challenge a limited number of jurors without offering a reason. Shari Seidman Diamond, in "Scientific Jury Selection: What Social Scientists Know and Do Not Know," 73 *Judicature* 178 (1990), is very skeptical about "scientific jury selection." However, lawyers' folklore about trial practice and jury behavior is also of questionable accuracy.

Article and Book Credits

Law, Lawyers, and Popular Culture is reprinted by permission of the Yale Law Journal Company and Fred B. Rothman & Company from The Yale Law Journal, Vol. 98, pp. 1578–1606; The Question of Jury Competency and the Politics of Civil Justice Reform: Symbols, Rhetoric, and Agenda Setting is copyright © 1989 by Law and Contemporary Problems. Reprinted with permission; Notes on the Future of Social Research in Law is reprinted by permission of Marc Galanter, unpublished paper, February 1974; "Handling" Family Violence: Situational Determinants of Police Arrest in Domestic Disturbances is reprinted from Law & Society Review. Copyright © 1981 by the Law and Society Association. Reprinted with permission; Police Discretion Not to Invoke the Criminal Process: Low-Visibility Decisions in the Administration of Justice is reprinted by permission of the Yale Law Journal Company and Fred B. Rothman & Company from The Yale Law Journal, Vol. 69, pp. 543–594; The Practice of Law as a Confidence Game: Organizational Cooptation of a Profession is reprinted from Law & Society Review. Copyright © 1967 by the Law and Society Association. Reprinted with permission; Non-Contractual Relations in Business: A Preliminary Study is reprinted by permission of Gtewan Macaulay; Settled Out of Court: The Social Process of Insurance Claims Adjustment is copyright © 1980 by and reprinted with the permission of Aldine de Gruyter; Bargaining in the Shadow of the Law: The Case of Divorce is reprinted by permission of the Yale Law Journal Company and Fred B. Rothman & Company from The Yale Law Journal, Vol. 88, pp. 950–997; Participation and Flexibility in Informal Processes: Cautions from the Divorce Context is reprinted from Law & Society Review. Copyright © 1987 by the Law and Society Association. Reprinted with permission; The Calculus of Consent is copyright © 1962 by the University of Michigan Press, Ann Arbor. Reprinted with permission; Going by the Book: The Problem of Regulatory Unreasonableness is copyright © 1982 and reprinted with the permission of Temple University Press; Social Factors in the Development of Legal Control: A Case Study of Two Israeli Settlements is reprinted by permission of the Yale Law Journal Company and Fred B. Rothman & Company from The Yale Law Journal, Vol. 63, pp. 471–491; Max Weber on Law in Economy and Society is excerpted by permission of the publisher from pp. 63–64, 303–308, 351–352, 355 of Max Weber on Law in Economy and Society, Max Rheinstein, ed., and translator with Edward Shils, Cambridge: Mass, Harvard University Press. Copyright © 1954 by the President and Fellows of Harvard University; Social Change and the Law of Industrial Accidents is reprinted with permission. Copyright © 1967 Columbia Law Review; The Cultural Logic of a Political Crisis: Common Sense, Hegemony and the Great American Liability Insurance Famine of 1986 is copyright © 1991 by and reprinted with permission of JAI Press, Inc.; Parental Authority: The Community and the Law is copyright © 1958 Rutgers University Press. Reprinted from pp. 76–78, 193–95 by permission; Review of Cohen, Robson & Bates is copyright © 1959 Michigan Law Review. Reprinted by permission; Legal Culture and the Welfare State is excerpted by permission of the publisher from Gunter Teubner (ed.), Dilemmas of Law in the Welfare State, 1985; American Legal Culture: The Last Thirty-five Years is copyright © 1991 Saint Louis University Law Journal. Reprinted with permission; Worker Insurgency, Radical Organization and New Deal Labor Legislation is reprinted by permission from the American Political Science Review. Copyright © 1989 by the American Political Science Association; Explaining New Deal Labor Policy is reprinted by permission from the American Political Science Review. Copyright © 1989 by the American Political Science Association; Silent Revolution is excerpted by permission of the publisher Silent Revolution. Copyright © 1988 University of Chicago Press; Long-Term Continuing Relations: the American Experience Regulating Dealerships and Franchises is copyright © 1991 Nomos Verlagsgesellschaft. Reprinted with permission; The Routinization of Debt Collection: An Essay on Social Change and Conflict in Courts is reprinted from Law & Society Review. Copyright © 1984 by the Law and Society Association. Reprinted with permission; Trials and Tribulations: Crises, Litigation and Legal Change is reprinted from Law & Society Review. Copyright © 1990 by the Law and Society Association. Reprinted with permission; Deterrence Theory and Research is reprinted from the 1985 Nebraska Symposium on Motivation by permission of the University of Nebraska Press. Copyright © 1986 by the University of Nebraska Press; Homicide and the Death Penalty: A Cross-National Test of a Deterrence Hypothesis is reprinted by permission of the author, originally published by Northwestern University School of Law in the Journal of Criminal Law and Criminology; The Deterrence Curve is reprinted by permission of the author; Interrupted Time Series Studies of Deterrence of Drinking and Driving is excerpted from H. Lawrence Ross, "Interrupted Time Series Studies of Deterrence of Drinking and Driving" in John Hagan (ed.), Deterrence Reconsidered: Methodological Innovations (Beverly Hills, California: Sage Publications, 1982). Reprinted by permission of the publisher; Conscience, Significant Others and Rational Choice: Extending the Deterrence Model is reprinted from Law & Society Review. Copyright © 1990 by the Law and Society Association. Reprinted with permission; Moral Appeal, Sanction Threat, and Deviance: An Experimental Test is copyright © 1973 by the Society for the Study of Social Problems. Reprinted from Social Problems, Vol. 20, p. 488, by permission; Why People Obey the Law is copyright © 1990 Yale University Press. Reprinted by permission; Obedience to Authority: An Experimental View is selected excerpts from pp. 1, 2–5, 7–8 from Obedience to Authority by Stanley Milgram. Copyright © 1974 by Stanley Milgram. Reprinted by permission of HarperCollins Publishers, Inc.; Images of Law in Everyday Life: The Lessons of School, Entertainment, and Spectator Sports is reprinted from Law & Society Review. Copyright © 1987 by the Law and Society Association. Reprinted with permission; Moral Passage: The Symbolic Process in Public Designations of Deviance is copyright © 1967 by the Society for the Study of Social Problems. Reprinted from Social Problems, Vol. 15, p. 175, by permission; Rape Law Reform and Instrumental Change in Six Urban Jurisdictions is reprinted from Law & Society Review. Copyright © 1991 by the Law and Society Association. Reprinted with permission; Miranda in Pittsburgh—A Statistical Study is copyright © 1967 University of Pittsburgh Law Review. Reprinted with permission; Homicide: A Year on the Killing Streets is copyright © 1991 Houghton Mifflin. Reprinted with permission; The Hollow Hope is copyright © 1991 University of Chicago Press. Reprinted with permission; State Implementation of Supreme Court Decisions: Abortion Rates Since Roe v. Wade is reprinted from The Journal of Politics. Copyright © 1980 by the University of Texas Press. Reprinted with permission; The Divorce Revolution is excerpted from The Divorce Revolution by Lenore Weitzman. Copyright © 1985 by the Free Press. Reprinted with permission; Tarasoff, Myth and Reality: An Empirical Study of Private Law in Action is copyright © 1984 Wisconsin Law Review. Reprinted with permission; Media Coverage of Supreme Court Decision-Making: Problems and Prospects was originally published in 75 Judicature 128 (1991). Reprinted by permission of Elliot E. Slotnick; The Evolution of State Supreme Courts is copyright © 1978 Michigan Law Review. Reprinted with permission; Legal Rules and the Process of Social Change is copyright © 1985 by the Board of Trustees of the Leland Stanford Junior University and Fred B. Rothman & Co. Reprinted with permission; The Forest Ranger: A Study in Administrative Behavior is copyright © 1960 Johns Hopkins Press, Baltimore, published for Resources for the Future, Inc. Reprinted from pp. 91–99, 101–107, 126–140, 142–145, 149–153, by permission; The Bush Imprint on the Judiciary: Carrying on a Tradition was originally published in 74 Judicature 294 (1991). Reprinted by permission of Sheldon Goldman; Law and Life in the United States is reprinted by permission of Carol Greenhouse; Role Perceptions and Behavior in Three U.S. Courts of Appeals is reprinted from The Journal of Politics. Copyright © 1977 by the University of Texas Press. Reprinted with permission; The Role Concept in Judicial Research is reprinted from Law & Policy Quarterly. Copyright © 1981 by Blackwell Publishers. Reprinted with permission; Six Score Years and Ten: Demographic Transitions in the American Legal Profession, 1850–1980 is reprinted from Law & Society Review. Copyright © 1986 by the Law and Society Asso-

Excerpt Credits

Index of Articles and Books Cited

905